INSURANCE FOR REAL ESTATE-RELATED ENTITIES

INSURANCE FOR REAL ESTATE-RELATED ENTITIES

Robert E. Frankel

2019

fastcase FULL COURT PRESS

Cover Design: Sharon D. Ray

Printed in the United States of America.

1 2 3 4 5 6 7 8 9 0

ISBN 978-1-949884-00-5

Dedication

This treatise is dedicated to my wife, Aimee, and our four children, Jake, Lynne, Nicholas, and Jaimee, for their consistent, unconditional, and unwavering support and for the sacrifice they endured throughout the entire process of my writing this work.

Summary of Contents

Table of Contents

CHAPTER 1

Introduction

This book focuses on legal issues concerning insurance recovery and bad faith for real estate and real estate-related entities. The following entities are, among others, the target audience because they have an interest in understanding the insurance needed in their businesses:

1. those who own, operate, and use real property;
2. landlords and tenants;
3. real estate developers, builders, construction contractors and subcontractors;
4. real estate lenders;
5. real estate investment trusts;
6. professionals involved in real estate, such as brokers, realtors, agents, engineers, architects, and appraisers; and
7. Bankruptcy professionals handling bankrupt estates of these businesses.

If a lawyer represents clients, or if someone is himself or herself employed by or otherwise involved, in any of these lines of businesses, it behooves that person to understand the insurance coverages discussed in this treatise. Likewise, if a plaintiff's attorney may envision suing one of the enumerated businesses, it would behoove the lawyer to understand the insurance funds that may be available to fund settlements and judgments being sought on behalf of the tort plaintiff.

Why would this book be that important? Those involved in these and other businesses face innumerable liabilities, costs, and losses that impact balance sheets, income statements, and cash-flow reports. These liabilities and losses cost money to resolve or repair. Insurance is one of the few ways to use someone else's money to pay for losses or damages, which has a positive impact on the business's financial performance. Understanding situations where insurance can be used to reimburse a business is therefore an element essential to success. The same is true for plaintiffs' attorneys because insurance often is the only source of funding to reimburse the plaintiffs for their losses.

This work has been divided into three principal parts. The first, comprised of Chapters 2 and 3, sets forth the fundamentals related to insurance. Chapter 2 discusses the key "terms of art" and the types and kinds of insurance available to real estate and related businesses. Chapter 3 deals with insurance contract interpretation and construction, including regulatory approval and lost-policy issues. An insurance policy is nothing more than a contract, albeit technical and specialized, and its interpretation and construction is governed by the same principles that govern contracts in general.

Chapters 4 through 12, which comprise the second principal part, deal with various types of coverages and recoveries thereunder. Chapter 4 discusses the central issues in connection with first-party property and business interruption insurance, which is needed by owners and occupiers of real property to protect against direct damage to (and loss of income from) improvements to real property. Chapters 5 through 9 analyze the important issues faced by real estate-related businesses under their comprehensive general liability insurance policies, including issues under Coverage A for "bodily injury" and "property damage" liability (Chapter 5), duty to defend (Chapter 6), exclusions to Coverage A (Chapter 7), the special standards applicable to pollution exclusions (Chapter 8), and Coverage B for "personal and advertising injury" liabilities (Chapter 9).

Chapter 10 explains the principles of directors and officers liability insurance, which affects publicly traded entities and those in which the operators and managers are answerable to third parties for their management of the business. Chapter 10 also covers professional liability insurance, which affects those entities providing professional services. Chapter 11 focuses on surety bonds, which help ensure a party's performance under a contract with a third party. Chapter 12 discusses title insurance, which involves coverage for issues relating to certain defects in the title of owned and acquired property.

Finally, the last section, Chapters 13 and 14, deals with other sources of insurance recoveries for real estate-related businesses, which includes accessing other persons' insurance and using loss control offensively. Specifically, Chapter 13 deals with the use of other persons' insurance policies, while Chapter 14 delves into loss control services for commercial policies, with coverage of claims for improper provision of those services and estoppel arising from those services.

CHAPTER 2

Types, Lines, and Categories of Applicable Insurance

Chapter Contents

❖

§ 2.01 Overview

There are two general categories of insurance policies available for purchase by those who want or need insurance, no matter how they are legally structured or whether they are for profit businesses, nonprofits, or other entities and/or persons: (1) first-party insurance and (2) third-party insurance. Within each of these categories, there are two lines—personal lines and commercial lines—applicable to individuals and commercial enterprises, respectively. Within each category and line, there are a number of different types and kinds of insurance policies.

People and businesses involved in real estate, construction, and related industries can purchase a myriad of first-party and third-party insurance policies to protect against risks they encounter on a daily basis. This chapter first sets forth relevant definitions for the "terms of art" that appear extensively in this treatise. It then discusses the meaning of first-party and third-party insurance, gives relevant examples of each, and explains the distinction between them.

§ 2.02 Terms of Art

In insurance parlance, there are certain "terms of art," which are used throughout this treatise and defined below.

"*CGL*" refers to comprehensive general liability insurance or commercial general liability insurance, a type of third-party insurance widely sold to cover a large group of liabilities faced by the policyholder.[1]

"*Commercial Lines*" refers to a line of insurance that is available for use by and sold to businesses or commercial enterprises, public entities, and nonprofits.[2]

"*Coverage Form*" refers to the main body of the insurance policy contract, including many of the essential terms, agreements, conditions, definitions, and exclusions.[3]

"*D&O*" refers to directors and officers liability insurance, a type of insurance covering the policyholder for liabilities attributable to third-party liabilities related to actions of directors or officers of an entity and sometimes of the entity itself.[4]

"*Declarations*" or "*Declarations Page*" refers to a form attached to the insurance policy, usually at the beginning or front, setting forth a summary of the terms, including, without limitation, the insurance company's identity, the named insured's identity, the limits of indemnity available, the deductible or self-insured retention, the coverages provided, the premium charged, and the forms applicable.[5]

"*Deductible*"[6] or "*Self-Insured Retention*" ("*SIR*")[7] refers to an amount of money, usually set forth in the declaration pages, that the policyholder is responsible to pay out of its own pocket and as a condition precedent to the receipt of insurance coverage under the insurance policy. The deductible or *SIR* may be on a per occurrence or aggregate basis, meaning the initial liability of the policyholder may be an initial exposure for each claim or loss that is made for coverage or for the total of all claims made during the policy period.

"*Duty to Defend*" in the third-party loss category refers to the duty of a liability insurance company to provide, or pay for the provision of, a defense for its policyholder in an underlying action.[8]

"*Duty to Indemnify*" in the third-party loss category means the duty of a liability insurance company to pay any judgment, jury verdict, settlement, or other legal obligation of its policyholder.[9]

"*E&O*" refers to errors and omissions insurance, which is also known as professional liability insurance, a type of third-party insurance covering the policyholder for damages to others caused by the policyholder's or its employees' professional negligence.[10]

"*Endorsements*" refer to forms attached to the policy form that are intended to change, amend or otherwise modify the terms of the contract as contained in the coverage form.[11]

"*First Party*" in an insurance contract refers to the policyholder. The other party to an insurance contract (namely, the insurance company) is considered the second party. First-party insurance is insurance covering losses sustained by the first party—namely the policyholder.[12]

"*Indemnity Limits*" or "*Limits*" refers to the amount of coverage available to pay for: (1) settlements, judgments, or damages assessed as a legal liability of the policyholder under a third-party liability insurance policy or (2) repair, replacement, or damage caused as a result of a covered event under a first-party policy.[13] These limits may include other items such as defense costs, depending upon the specific policy at issue.[14]

"*Insurance Policy*" or "*Policy*" refers to the contract under which insurance coverage is sought or purchased.[15]

"*Insurance Company*" means the insurer, underwriter, or company that sold the insurance policy to the policyholder for which insurance coverage is sought.[16]

"*Loss*" refers to a claim or event for which the policyholder seeks insurance coverage. Losses can be in the form of either first-party losses or third-party losses, depending upon the identity of who actually suffers the loss or damages.[17]

"*Personal Lines*" refers to a whole line of insurance that is available for individuals and families for personal or non-business uses.[18]

"*Policyholder*" means the purchaser of the insurance policy, the insured, and/or the person or entity claiming a right to insurance coverage under the policy.[19]

"*Primary Layer Insurance*" refers to insurance that provides either first dollar coverage or coverage after satisfaction of a deductible or self-insured retention.[20]

"*Third Party*" in an insurance contract refers to a person or entity that is neither a policyholder nor the insurance company but who indirectly seeks benefits under the insurance policy as a result of liability of the policyholder to that third party.[21]

"*Trigger*" or "*Triggering Event*" means, as its name implies, the act or event that has taken place to cause an insurance company to owe duties to its policyholder under the terms of its insurance policy.[22]

"*Umbrella Policy*"[23] or "*Excess Policy*"[24] refer to a type of insurance policy that provides coverage only after exhaustion of coverage of all underlying insurance, including the primary layer. The level of umbrella or excess insurance sitting on top of the primary layer is referred to as "*First Layer Excess*" or "*Umbrella,*"[25] and each layer on top of each succeeding layer is referred to as subsequently numbered layer excess or umbrella.

"*Underlying Action*" or "*Underlying Suit*" in the third-party loss category means the claim, lawsuit, or other action brought by a claimant against the policyholder and for which insurance coverage may be sought by the policyholder (and indirectly by the third party).[26]

§ 2.03 Third-Party Insurance

Third-party insurance is commonly known as "litigation insurance" because it protects the policyholder from the liabilities and costs associated with litigation brought by third parties.[27] Hence, third-party insurance is insurance that provides insurance coverage that, in part, benefits persons who have suffered a loss but who are not parties to the insurance contract (i.e., a third party), as distinct from the parties to the insurance contract—namely, the policyholder (the first party) and the insurance company (the second party).[28] That third person who has suffered a loss seeks compensation from the policyholder by way of the assertion of a claim, a civil action, or lawsuit against the policyholders. Third-party insurance provides coverage to the policyholder in the form of both: (1) a duty to defend the policyholder in the third-party suit (or a duty to reimburse the policyholder for defense costs incurred in the third-party suit); and (2) a duty to indemnify or pay any judgments or settlements rendered against the policyholder in such third-party litigation.[29]

Examples of third-party insurance[30] include, among other things: CGL (known as commercial or comprehensive general liability insurance)[31] employment practices liability insurance, environmental impairment liability insurance, workers' compensation liability insurance, employers liability insurance, automobile liability insurance,[32] D&O or directors and officers liability insurance,[33] E&O or errors and omissions or professional liability insurance,[34] and excess or umbrella liability insurance.[35]

§ 2.04 First-Party Insurance

First-party insurance policies provide insurance coverage that compensates the policyholder for losses that are suffered by the policyholder himself, herself, or itself.[36] For example, life insurance pays benefits as a result of the death of the policyholder.[37] Likewise, health insurance pays for medical expenses incurred as a result of an illness or injury to the policyholder.[38] Disability insurance pays for the loss of earnings as a result of a disabling injury or illness suffered by the policyholder.[39] Fidelity bonds or commercial crime insurance provide coverage for theft of the policyholder's property as a result of employee theft.[40]

Similarly, homeowners or renters insurance compensates the policyholder for damages to the policyholder's real and personal property at premises occupied by the policyholder.[41] Commercial property and business interruption insurance compensate a business for both damages to its real and personal property and the consequential loss of income during a period of restoration as a result of a covered accident.[42]

Additionally, builders risk insurance provides coverage for developers and contractors for losses that take place to the property they are developing or building until the project is completed.[43] Of course, once operations are completed, the property should be covered by first-party property insurance—either residential or commercial property insurance.

§ 2.05 Hybrid Policies

Some insurance policies are hybrid in the sense they provide both first-party and third-party benefits. In particular, some policies that are commonly thought of as third-party insurance policies have first-party benefits available.

For instance, automobile liability insurance policies provide third-party liability coverage for liability associated with the use of one's automobile. They also typically can contain some first-party benefits in the form of: (a) no-fault medical coverage; and (b) uninsured motorists (UM) and underinsured motorists (UIM) benefits.

As for no-fault coverage, the automobile liability policy may provide first-party personal injury protection coverage (PIP) or first-party property damage, which provides for the policyholder's insurance company's payment of the policyholder's medical expenses or property damage, respectively, regardless of fault.[44] With respect to UM and UIM benefits, they can provide compensation to the policyholder if the policyholder is involved in an accident with another driver who either does not have automobile liability insurance (UM benefits) or who does not have sufficient limits to cover the other driver's liability in the accident (UIM benefits). Under such circumstances, the policyholder may be able to collect the amount of tort liability, up to the UM/UIM limits of the policyholder's policy, that the uninsured/underinsured driver owes to the policyholder as a result of the accident. With regard to UM coverage, the measure of recovery will be the lesser of the UM limits of his/her/its own policy and the actual tort liability of the uninsured driver in the accident. On the other hand, the amount of recovery in a UIM claim will be the lesser of: (1) the UIM limits of his/her/its own policy and (2) the amount of underinsurance involved. The amount of underinsurance is calculated by subtracting the limits of the underinsured driver's automobile liability policy from the actual tort liability of the underinsured driver in the accident.[45]

Likewise, some policies commonly thought of as first-party insurance policies also are hybrid in the sense that they provide some third-party coverage to the policyholder. For instance, first-party property policies, such as homeowners or renters property insurance policies, often contain some form of general liability coverage for the policyholder, usually for liabilities arising out of the policyholder's personal, as opposed to business, activities.[46]

§ 2.06 Distinction between First- and Third-Party Insurance

As previously discussed, first-party insurance is distinguishable from third-party insurance by the policyholder's relationship to or with the loss.[47] In particular, unlike first-party insurance, where the policyholder seeks reimbursement for losses suffered by the policyholder himself, herself, or itself,[48] third-party insurance provides insurance coverage to the policyholder for litigation risks or liability related to losses suffered by third parties.[49] As explained in one instance:

> "In many insurance contexts . . . , the courts recognize the conceptual and practical difference between—
>
> - 'First party' insurance, which is a contract between the insurer and insured protecting the insured's own actual losses and expenses, such as property insurance, fidelity insurance, and medical/health insurance.
> - 'Third party' insurance, which is a contract to protect the insured from actual or potential monetary liability to a third party, such as liability insurance."[50]

Notes

1 *Black's Law Dictionary* at 723 (5th ed. 1979). See also Chapter 5 *infra*.

2 *Black's Law Dictionary* at 721 (5th ed. 1979).

3 The policy form refers to the body of the insurance contract. Insurance can be written in manuscript form or standard form. See, e.g.:

Second Circuit: Newmont Mines Ltd. v. Hanover Insurance Co., 784 F.2d 127 (2d Cir. 1986); *In re* September 11th Liability Insurance Coverage Cases, 243 F.R.D. 114 (S.D.N.Y. 2007).

Fifth Circuit: In re Consolidated Cos., 106 F.3d 396 (5th Cir. 1996).

Ninth Circuit: Westlands Water District v. Zurich American Insurance Co., 2006 WL 279310 (E.D. Cal. Feb. 6, 2006).

State Courts:

California: County of San Diego v. Ace Property & Casualty Insurance Co., 37 Cal.4th 406, 118 P.3d 607, 33 Cal. Rptr.3d 583 (2005); Lockheed Corp. v. Continental Insurance Co., 134 Cal. App.4th 187, 35 Cal. Rptr.3d 799 (2005).

Connecticut: Northeast Utilities v. Century Indemnity Co., 1999 WL 476274 Conn. Super. June 21, 1999).

Illinois: Sears, Roebuck and Co. v. Seneca Insurance Co., 254 Ill. App.3d 686, 627 N.E.2d 173, 194 Ill. Dec. 57 (1993).

Indiana: PSI Energy, Inc. v. Home Insurance Co., 801 N.E.2d 705 (Ind. App. 2004).

Louisiana: Doerr v. Mobil Oil Corp., 774 So.2d 119 (La. 2000).

Massachusetts: Eastern Partnerships v. Hanover Insurance Co., 1995 WL 499386 (Mass. Super. Aug. 18, 1995).

New Jersey: Diamond Shamrock Chemicals Co. v. Aetna Casualty & Surety Co., 258 N.J. Super. 167, 609 A.2d 440 (1992).

Ohio: Western Reserve Mutual Casualty Co. v. Williams, 2005 WL 1953062 (Ohio App. Aug. 16, 2005).

Under the manuscript form policies, each provision can be drafted from scratch or pre-approved language can be cut and pasted together to form an unique policy particular to the policyholder or risk at issue. *Id.* The majority of insurance policies are standard-form agreements in the sense that the agreements are contained in pre-printed forms that contain the same or substantially similar provisions. *Id.*

The Insurance Services Office, Inc. (ISO) is an association of approximately 1400 domestic property and casualty insurers and operates as the "almost exclusive source of support services in this country for CGL [comprehensive general liability] insurance." See Hartford Fire Insurance Co. v. California, 509 U.S. 764, 772, 113 S.Ct. 2891, 125 L.Ed.2d 612 (1993) ("ISO develops standard policy forms and files or lodges them with each State's insurance regulators; most CGL insurance written in the United States is written on these forms.").

See also:

New York: In re Hoechst Celanese Corp., 184 A.D.2d 223, 584 N.Y.S.2d 805, 806 (1992) (ISO is the "principal rating, statistical and drafting organization for the general liability insurance industry in the United States, whose primary function is to draft standard-form comprehensive general liability ('CGL') insurance policy language for the industry. . . .").

Washington: American Star Insurance Co. v. Grice, 121 Wash.2d 869, 854 P.2d 622, 627 n.19 (Wash. 1993) (ISO "is an insurance industry trade association which develops standard form insurance policies and often secures regulatory approval for their insurance").

4 See Chapter 10 *infra.*

5 See http://www.irmi.com/online/insurance-glossary/terms/d/declarations.aspx (last visited Jan. 23, 2013).

6 See http://www.irmi.com/online/insurance-glossary/terms/d/deductible.aspx (last visited Jan. 23, 2013).

7 See http://www.irmi.com/online/insurance-glossary/terms/s/self-insured-retention-sir.aspx (last visited Jan. 23, 2013).

8 See Chapter 6 *infra.*

9 See §§ 2.03, 2.04, 2.06, 6.02 *infra.*

10 *Black's Law Dictionary* at 722 (5th ed. 1979). See also Chapter 10 *infra.*

11 See http://www.investorwords.com/1706/endorsement.html (last visited Jan. 23, 2013).

12 See §§ 2.04, 2.06 *infra.*

13 See http://www.riskheads.org/insurance-indemnity-limits-types-examples (last visited Feb. 6, 2013).

14 See §§ 6.02, 9.03[2][b] *infra.*

15 *Black's Law Dictionary* at 721, 725, 1041–1042 (5th ed. 1979).

16 *Black's Law Dictionary* at 721, 725 (5th ed. 1979).

17 See §§ 2.03, 2.04, 2.06 *infra*.

18 See http://www.irmi.com/online/insurance-glossary/terms/p/personal-lines.aspx (last visited Jan. 23, 2013).

19 *Black's Law Dictionary* at 1041 (5th ed. 1979).

20 See http://www.patrons.com/html/body_glossary.html (last visited Jan. 23, 2013).

21 See §§ 2.03, 2.06 *infra*.

22 See http://www.ahtins.com/glossary/ccc/c184.htm (last visited Jan. 23, 2013).

23 See http://info.insure.com/auto/umbrella.html (last visited Jan 23, 2013). See also, http://www.1stsource.com/business_banking/business_insurance-c.cfm (last visited Jan. 23, 2013).

24 See *Black's Law Dictionary* at 722 (5th ed. 1979).

25 See Wollner, "Self-Insurance, Primary Insurance, and Excess Insurance: Adventures in Contract Interpretation," IRMI.com (Feb. 2002), available at http://www.irmi.com/Expert/Articles/2002/Wollner02.aspx (last visited Jan. 23, 2013).

26 See Kvaerner Metals v. Commercial Union Insurance Co., 908 A.2d 888 (Pa. 2006).

27 See, e.g.:

First Circuit: Ryan v. Royal Insurance Co., 916 F.2d 731 (1st Cir. 1990); Barletta Heavy Division, Inc. v. Travelers Insurance Co., 2013 U.S. Dist. LEXIS 153555 (D. Mass. Oct. 25, 2013); New England Environmental Technologies Corp. v. American Safety Risk Retention Group, Inc., 810 F. Supp.2d 390 (D. Mass. 2011); Liberty Mutual Insurance Co. v. Black & Decker Corp., 383 F. Supp.2d 200, 219 (D. Mass. 2005); American Employers' Insurance Co. v. DeLorme Publishing Co., 39 F. Supp.2d 64 (D. Me. 1999).

Second Circuit: Barney Greengrass, Inc. v. Lumbermens Mutual Casualty Co., 445 Fed. Appx. 411 (2d Cir. 2011); Allianz Insurance Co. v. Lerner, 416 F.3d 109, 116 (2d Cir. 2005); Continental Casualty Co. v. JBS Construction Management, Inc., 2010 U.S. Dist. LEXIS 85467 (S.D.N.Y. July 1, 2010); Specialty National Insurance Co. v. English Brothers Funeral Home, 606 F. Supp.2d 466 (S.D.N.Y. 2009); City of West Haven v. Liberty Mutual Insurance Co., 639 F. Supp. 1012 (D. Conn. 1986).

Third Circuit: NL Industries, Inc. v. Commercial Union Insurance Co., 926 F. Supp. 446 (D.N.J. 1996); Harristown Development Corp. v. International Insurance Co., 1988 WL 123149, at *12 (M.D. Pa. Nov. 15, 1988).

Fourth Circuit: Perdue Farms, Inc. v. Travelers Casualty & Surety Co., 448 F.3d 252, (4th Cir. 2006) ("'Although the type of policy here considered is most often referred to as liability insurance, it is "litigation insurance" as well, protecting the insured from the expense of defending suits brought against him.'"); Provident Bank of Maryland v. Travelers Property Casualty Corp., 236 F.3d 138 (4th Cir. 2000); Stewart Title Guaranty Co. v. Sanford Title Services, LLC, 2013 U.S. Dist. LEXIS 145302 (D. Md. Oct. 8, 2013); Baker's Express, L.L.C. v. Arrowpoint Capital Corp., 2012 WL 4370265 (D. Md. Sept. 20, 2012); Lott v. Scottsdale Insurance Co., 827 F. Supp.2d 626 (E.D. Va. 2011); Capital Environmental Services, Inc. v. North River Insurance Co., 536 F. Supp.2d 633 (E.D. Va. 2008); Zurich American Insurance Co. v. Fieldstone Mortgage Co., 2007 WL 3268460 (D. Md. Oct. 26, 2007).

Sixth Circuit: Ndabishuriye v. Albert Schweitzer Society, USA, Inc., 136 Fed. Appx. 795, 796 (6th Cir. 2005); Keely v. Fire Insurance Exchange, 833 F. Supp.2d 722 (E.D. Mich. 2011); Taylor v. Temple & Cutler, 192 F.R.D. 552, 558 (E.D. Mich. 1999) ("'In a sense, liability insurance is nothing more than litigation insurance.'").

Seventh Circuit: Sampson v. Western Sierra Acceptance Corp., 2004 WL 1588280 (N.D. Ill. July 1, 2004).

Eighth Circuit: Pekin Insurance Co. v. Tysa, Inc., 2006 WL 3827232 (S.D. Iowa Dec. 27, 2006); Schipp v. General Motors Corp., 457 F. Supp.2d 917 (E.D. Ark. Oct. 5, 2006).

Ninth Circuit: Newmont USA Ltd. v. American Home Assurance Co., 676 F. Supp.2d 1146 (E.D. Wash. 2009); Intel Corp. v. Insurance Company of Pennsylvania, 2009 WL 81393 (N.D. Cal. Jan. 9, 2009); Kla-Tencor Corp. v. National Union Fire Insurance Co., 2006 WL 2479106 (N.D. Cal. Aug. 28, 2006).

Tenth Circuit: Hurtado v. Passmore & Sons, L.L.C., 2011 WL 2533698 (D. Colo. June 27, 2011); Westport Insurance Corp. v. Ong, 2008 WL 892941 (D. Utah Mar. 28, 2008); American States Insurance Co. v. Ridco, Inc., 1996 WL 33401184, at *3 (D. Wyo. Feb. 8, 1996); Weitzman v. Blazing Pedals, Inc., 151 F.R.D. 125 (D. Colo. 1993).

Eleventh Circuit: Illinois Union Insurance Co. v. NRI Construction, Inc., 846 F. Supp.2d 1366 (N.D. Ga. 2012); Smith v. Williams, 819 F. Supp.2d 1264 (M.D. Fla. 2011); Colonial Oil Industries, Inc. v. Underwriters, 1995 WL 692691, at *10–11 (S.D. Ga. Nov. 6, 1995).

District of Columbia Circuit: Pierce Associates, Inc. v. St. Paul Mercury Insurance Co., 421 F. Supp.2d 11, 17 (D.D.C.), *vacated on other grounds* 437 F. Supp.2d 16 (D.D.C. 2006).

State Courts:

Alaska: Langdon v. Champion, 752 P.2d 999 (Alaska 1988).

Connecticut: Ferri v. Powell-Ferri, 2014 Conn. Super. LEXIS 1377 (Conn. Super. June 5, 2014); Community Healthcare Credit Union, Inc. v. Cuna Mutual Group, 2007 WL 1827837 (Conn. Super. June 1, 2007).

Delaware: Liggett Group, Inc. v. Ace Property & Casualty Insurance Co., 798 A.2d 1024, 1031 (Del. 2002); Deutsche Bank Trust Company v. Royal Surplus Lines Insurance Co., 2012 WL 2898478 (Del. Super. Ct., New Castle Cnty., Sept. 12, 2012).

Florida: Contreras v. 21st Century Insurance Co., 53 So.2d 1194 (Fla. App. 2011).

Illinois: General Agents Insurance Co. of America, Inc. v. Midwest Sporting Goods Co., 215 Ill.2d 146, 828 N.E.2d 1092, 293 Ill. Dec. 594 (2005); Illinois Tool Works Inc. v. Travelers Casualty and Surety Co., 2015 IL App (1st) 132350, 26 N.E.3d 421, 389 Ill. Dec. 331 (2015).

Indiana: Transamerica Insurance Services v. Kopko, 559 N.E.2d 322 (Ind. App. 1990).

Kansas: Miller v. Westport Insurance Corp., 288 Kan. 27, 200 P.3d 419 (2009).

Maryland: BGE Home Products & Services, Inc. v. Owens, 833 A.2d 8, 14 (Md. 2003); Sherwood Brands, Inc. v. Hartford Accident & Indemnity Co., 698 A.2d 1078, 1083 (Md. 1997); Brohawn v. Transamerica Insurance Co., 347 A.2d 842, 851 (Md. 1975); Back Creek Partners, L.L.C. v. First American Title Insurance. Co., 213 Md. App. 703, 75 A.3d 394 (2013).

Massachusetts: Hanover Insurance Co. v. Golden, 436 Mass. 584, 766 N.E.2d 838, 841 (2002); Hingham Mutual Fire Insurance Co. v. DeWolfe, 72 Mass. App. Ct. 1117 (2008); Celanese Corp. v. OneBeacon America Insurance Co., 2008 WL 5784444 (Mass. Super. Dec. 29, 2008).

Michigan: Allstate Insurance Co. v. Freeman, 443 N.W.2d 734 (Mich. 1989).

New York: K2 Investment Group, L.L.C. v. American Guarantee & Liability Insurance Co., 22 N.Y.3d 578, 6 N.E.3d 1117, 983 N.Y.S.2d 761 (2014); Bovis Lend Lease LMB Inc. v. Garito Contracting, Inc., 65 A.D.3d 872, 885 N.Y.S.2d 59 (N.Y. App. Div. 2009); BP Air Conditioning Corp. v. One Beacon Insurance Group, 33 A.D.3d 116, 821 N.Y.S.2d 1 (N.Y. App. Div. 2006), *modified on other grounds* 871 N.E.2d 1128 (N.Y. 2007) ("For this reason, when a policy represents that it will provide the insured with a defense, we have said that it actually constitutes 'litigation insurance' in addition to liability coverage."); Automobile Insurance Company of Hartford v. Cook, 850 N.E.2d 1152, 1155 (N.Y. 2006) ("For this reason, when a policy represents that it will provide the insured with a defense, we have said that it actually constitutes 'litigation insurance' in addition to liability coverage."); City of New York v. Certain Underwriters of Lloyd's of London, 2005 WL 319709, at *2 (N.Y. App. Div. Feb. 10, 2005).

North Carolina: SPX Corp. v. Liberty Mutual Insurance Co., 709 S.E.2d 441 (N.C. App. 2011); Brown v. Lumbermens Mutual Insurance Co., 369 S.E.2d 367 (N.C. App. 1988), *review denied* 373 S.E.2d 541 (N.C. 1988).

Texas: Lamar Homes, Inc. v. Mid-Continent Casualty Co., 242 S.W.3d 1 (Tex. 2007).

Virginia: Veney v. Duke, 2005 WL 3476760, at *2 (Va. Cir. Oct. 26, 2005) ("'liability insurance' essentially constitutes 'litigation insurance'").

Washington: National Surety Corp. v. Immunex Corp., 176 Wash.2d 872, 297 P.3d 688 (2013) (*en banc*).

Wyoming: Shoshone First Bank v. Pacific Employers Insurance Co., 2 P.3d 510, 516 (Wyo. 2000); First Wyoming Bank, N.A. v. Continental Insurance Co., 860 P.2d 1064 (Wyo.), *vacated in part* 860 P.2d 1094 (Wyo. 1993).

28 As stated in White v. Insurance Company of State of Pennsylvania, 282 F. Supp.2d 618, 625 (N.D. Ohio 2003), *vacated on other grounds* 405 F.3d 455 (6th Cir. 2005):

> "'Liability' insurance constitutes 'an agreement to cover a loss resulting from one's liability to a third party, such as a loss incurred by a driver who injures a pedestrian.'... The claim under the policy 'arises once the insured's liability to a third party has been asserted...."
>
> "In contrast to this 'third-party insurance,' there is also 'indemnity' insurance which is characterized as 'first-party insurance' and defined as '[a] policy that applies to oneself or one's own property, such as life insurance, health insurance, disability insurance, and fire insurance.'"

See also:

Third Circuit: Port Authority of New York and New Jersey v. Affiliated FM Insurance Co., 311 F.3d 226 (3d Cir. 2002).

Fourth Circuit: ABT Building Products Corp. v. National Union Fire Insurance Co. of Pittsburgh, Inc., 472 F.3d 99 (4th Cir. 2006).

Eighth Circuit: R.D. Offutt Co. v. Lexington Insurance Co., 494 F.3d 668 (8th Cir. 2007).

Ninth Circuit: Anthem Electronics, Inc. v. Pacific Employers Insurance Co., 302 F.3d 1049 (9th Cir. 2002).

State Courts:

California: Black Diamond Asphalt Co. v. Superior Court, 7 Cal. Rptr.3d 466, 470 n.2 (Cal. App. 2003) ("In first party insurance, a person insures himself or his property against loss. In third party insurance, a person insures himself against liability he may incur to others."); Century Indemnity Co. v. Hearrean, 120 Cal. Rptr.2d 66, 69 (Cal. App. 2002) ("'third party liability insurance policies... obligate insurers to pay money to third parties to whom their insureds are liable'").

Colorado: Brodeur v. American Home Assurance Co., 169 P.3d 139 (Colo. 2007).

Hawaii: Ferrer v. Ngo, 73 P.3d 73, 76 (Haw. App. 2003) ("A 'third-party' policy... provides coverage for the insured's *liability to another* (e.g., CGL [comprehensive general liability], directors' and officers' liability, and errors and omissions insurance) wherein the carrier generally assumes a contractual duty to pay judgments recovered against the insured arising from the insured's negligence.") (emphasis in original).

Indiana: Sanyo Laser Products, Inc. v. Royal Insurance Company of America, 2003 WL 23101793, at *3 n.2 (S.D. Ind. Nov. 7, 2003) ("'third party' insurance protects the insured from potential liability to a third party").

Kentucky: Aetna Casualty & Surety Co. v. Kentucky, 179 S.W.3d 830, 845 (Ky. 2005) ("Third party insurance involves protection for the policyholder for liability it incurs to someone else.").

Louisiana: Felham Enterprises, Ltd. v. Certain Underwriters of Lloyds, London, 2004 WL 2984296, at *4 (E.D. La. Dec. 6, 2004) ("'third party insurance' covers liability of the insured to another person").

Pennsylvania: Toy v. Metropolitan Life Insurance Co., 928 A.2d 186 (Pa. 2007).

Texas: Allstate Insurance Co. v. Hunter, 2007 WL 4126055 (Tex. App. Nov. 21, 2007).

Washington: State Farm Fire & Casualty Co. v. English Cove Association, Inc., 88 P.3d 986, 992 (Wash. App. 2004) ("Third party insurance provides protection for the policyholder for liability it incurs to someone else.").

29 *Id.* See also:

Third Circuit: In re Asousa Partnership, 2004 WL 1043149, at *8 (Bankr. E.D. Pa. Apr. 26, 2004).

Sixth Circuit: White v. Insurance Company of State of Pennsylvania, 282 F. Supp.2d 618, 625 (N.D. Ohio 2003), ***vacated on other grounds*** 405 F.3d 455 (6th Cir. 2005).

State Courts:

Alaska: United States *ex. rel.* North Star Terminal & Stevedore Co. v. Nuggett Construction Co., 2006 WL 2251122, at *2 n.3 (D. Alaska July 28, 2006).

California: Montrose Chemical Corp. v. Admiral Insurance Co., 42 Cal. Rptr.2d 324, 332 (Cal. 1995); Garvey v. State Farm Fire & Casualty Co., 770 P.2d 704 (Cal. 1989); Black Diamond Asphalt Co. v. Superior Court, 7 Cal. Rptr.3d 466, 470 n.2 (Cal. App. 2003); Century Indemnity Co. v. Hearrean, 120 Cal. Rptr.2d 66, 69 (Cal. App. 2002).

Hawaii: Sentinel Insurance Co. v. First Insurance Company of Hawaii, Ltd., 875 P.2d 894, 906 (Haw. 1994); Ferrer v. Ngo, 73 P.3d 73, 76 n.3 (Haw. App. 2003).

Illinois: Emerson Electric Co. v. Aetna Casualty & Surety Co., 815 N.E.2d 924, 950 (Ill. App. 2004).

Indiana: Sanyo Laser Products, Inc. v. Royal Insurance Company of America, 2003 WL 23101793, at *3 n.2 (S.D. Ind. Nov. 7, 2003).

Kansas: Allstate Insurance Co. v. Johnston, 339 F. Supp.2d 1191, 1195 (D. Kan. 2004).

Kentucky: Aetna Casualty & Surety Co. v. Kentucky, 179 S.W.3d 830, 845 (Ky. 2005).

Louisiana: Felham Enterprises, Ltd. v. Certain Underwriters of Lloyds, London, 2004 WL 2984296, at *4 (E.D. La. Dec. 6, 2004).

Mississippi: Watson Quality Ford, Inc. v. Great River Insurance Co., 909 So.2d 1196, 1199 (Miss. App. 2005).

Washington: State Farm Fire & Casualty Co. v. English Cove Association, Inc., 88 P.3d 986, 992 (Wash. App. 2004).

30 See Standard Fire Insurance Co. v. Spectrum Community Ass'n, 46 Cal. Rptr.3d 804, 818–819 (Cal. App. 2006) (setting forth examples of third-party insurance including "a CGL policy, a directors and officers liability policy, or an errors and omissions policy").

31 See Chapter 5 *infra*.

32 See, e.g., Pepper v. State Farm Mutual Automobile Insurance Co., 813 N.W.2d 921 (Minn. 2012).

33 See Chapter 10 *infra*.

34 See Chapter 10 *infra*.

35 See *Black's Law Dictionary* at 722 (5th ed. 1979). See also: http://info.insure.com/auto/umbrella.html (last visited June 26, 2007); http://www.fnbv.com/site/insuring/business/umbrella.html (last visited June 26, 2007).

36 See, e.g.:

First Circuit: deVries v. St. Paul Fire and Marine Insurance Co., 716 F.2d 939 (1st Cir. 1983); Utica Mutual Insurance Co. v. Hall Equipment, Inc., 73 F. Supp.2d 83 (D. Mass. Oct. 28, 1999), *aff'd* 292 F.3d 77 (1st Cir. 2002).

Second Circuit: Travelers Insurance Co. v. Henry, 470 F.3d 56 (2d Cir. 2006); Riordan v. Nationwide Mutual Fire Insurance Co., 756 F. Supp. 732 (S.D.N.Y. 1990), *aff'd in part, question certified,* 977 F.2d 47 (2d Cir. 1992), *certified question withdrawn* 984 F.2d 69 (2d Cir. 1993).

Third Circuit: Port Authority of New York and New Jersey v. Affiliated FM Insurance Co., 311 F.3d 226, 233 (3d Cir. 2002); Daniel P. Fuss Builders-Contractors, Inc. v. Assurance Company of America, 2006 WL 2372226, at *4 n.2 (E.D. Pa. Aug. 11, 2006); *In re* Asousa Partnership, 2004 WL1043149, at *8 (Bankr. E.D. Pa. Apr. 26, 2004).

Fourth Circuit: A & E Supply Co. v. Nationwide Mutual Fire Insurance Co., 798 F.2d 669 (4th Cir. 1986), *cert. denied* 479 U.S. 1091 (1987); 17th Street Associates, LLP v. Markel International Insurance Co. Ltd., 373 F. Supp.2d 584 (E.D. Va. 2005); Provident Life and Accident Insurance Co. v. Cohen, 137 F. Supp.2d 631 (D. Md. 2001), *reconsideration granted* 2002 WL 500673 (D. Md. Mar. 28, 2002).

Fifth Circuit: Ross v. Citifinancial, Inc., 344 F.3d 458 (5th Cir. 2003), *cert. denied* 546 U.S. 813 (2005); Rx.Com Inc. v. Hartford Fire Insurance Co., 364 F. Supp.2d 609 (S.D. Tex. 2005); Felham Enterprises (Cayman) Ltd. v. Certain Underwriters at Lloyds, London Companies, 2004 WL 2984296 (E.D. La. Dec. 6, 2004), *reconsideration denied* 2005 WL 167585 (E.D. La. Jan. 24, 2005).

Sixth Circuit: Rawe v. Liberty Mutual Fire Insurance Co., 462 F.3d 521 (6th Cir. 2006); Barrow v. Amica Mutual Insurance Co., 2007 WL 3038031 (E.D. Mich. Oct. 17, 2007).

Seventh Circuit: Metropolitan Chicago Healthcare Council v. UNUM Life Insurance Co. of America, 149 F.3d 744 (7th Cir. 1998); CitiMortgage, Inc. v. Absolute Title Services, Inc., 2012 WL 1108249 (N.D. Ill. Apr. 2, 2012); Spearman Industries, Inc. v. St. Paul Fire and Marine Insurance Co., 128 F. Supp.2d 1148 (N.D. Ill. Jan. 23, 2001).

Eighth Circuit: Siegfried v. B.I.A., 2007 WL 512876 (D.N.D. Feb. 12, 2007); Dairy Farmers of America, Inc. v. Ace American Insurance Co., 2006 WL 2850563 (W.D. Mo. Sept. 29, 2006); Metro Renovation, Inc. v. Allied Group, Inc., 389 F. Supp.2d 1131(D. Neb. Sept. 29, 2005).

Ninth Circuit: TIG Insurance Co. v. ACE American Insurance Co., 236 Fed. Appx. 336 (9th Cir. 2007); United States *ex rel.* North Star Terminal & Stevedore Co. v. Nugget Construction, Inc., 2006 WL 2251122 (D. Alaska July 28, 2006); Bernstein v. Travelers Insurance Co., 2006 WL 2567875 (N.D. Cal. Sept. 5, 2006).

Tenth Circuit: Seabron v. American Family Mutual Insurance Co., 862 F. Supp.2d 1149 (D. Colo. 2012); Garcia v. Berkshire Life Insurance Co. of America, 2007 WL 4578333 (D. Colo. Dec. 27, 2007); Crabb v. State Farm Fire and Casualty Co., 2006 WL 1214998 (D. Utah May 4, 2006).

Eleventh Circuit: Mid-Continent Casualty Co. v. Royal Palm Estate Builders, Inc., 2007 WL 4225801 (S.D. Fla. Oct. 2, 2007).

District of Columbia Circuit: Athridge v. Aetna Casualty and Surety Co., 474 F. Supp.2d 102 (D.D.C. 2007), *reconsideration denied* 2007 WL 509224 (D.D.C. Feb. 13, 2007).

State Courts:

California: Standard Fire Insurance Co. v. Spectrum Community Association, 46 Cal. Rptr.3d 804, 818–819 (Cal. App. 2006); Black Diamond Asphalt Co. v. Superior Court, 7 Cal. Rptr.3d 466, 470 n.2 (Cal. App. 2003) ("In first party insurance, a person insures himself or his property against loss."); Century Indemnity Co. v. Hearrean, 120 Cal. Rptr.2d 66, 69 (Cal. App. 2002) (stating that first-party insurance policies obligate an insurer to pay money directly to an insured for a loss sustained by the insured as a result of a particular covered peril).

Florida: North Pointe Insurance Co. v. Tomas, 999 So.2d 728 (Fla. App. 2008).

Georgia: White v. State Farm Fire and Casualty Co., 291 Ga. 306, 728 S.E.2d 685 (2012).

Hawaii: Ferrer v. Ngo, 73 P.3d 73, 76 n.3 (Haw. App. 2003) ("A 'first-party' policy provides coverage for *loss or damage* sustained by the *insured* (e.g., life, disability, health, fire, theft, and casualty insurance) whereby the insurer usually promises to pay money to the insured upon the happening of the risk insured against.") (emphasis in original).

Illinois: Aurelius v. State Farm Fire and Casualty Co., 384 Ill. App.3d 969, 894 N.E.2d 765, 323 Ill. Dec. 739 (2008); Emerson Electric Co. v. Aetna Casualty & Surety Co., 352 Ill. App.3d 399, 815 N.E.2d 924, 287 Ill. Dec. 280 (2004).

Indiana: Wagner v. Yates, 912 N.E.2d 805 (Ind. 2009); Sanyo Laser Products, Inc. v. Royal Insurance Company of America, 2003 WL 23101793, at *3 n.2 (S.D. Ind. Nov. 7, 2003) ("'first party' insurance is a contract between the insurer and insured protecting the insured's own actual losses and expenses").

Kansas: Lytle v. Pepsi Cola General Bottlers, Inc., 656 P.2d 786 (Kan. App. 1983).

Kentucky: Aetna Casualty & Surety Co. v. Kentucky, 179 S.W.3d 830, 845 (Ky. 2005) ("first party insurance involves protection for losses to the policyholder's own property").

Louisiana: Niemann v. Crosby Development Co., 92 So.3d 1039 (La. App. 2012); Mangerchine v. Reaves, 63 So.3d 1049 (La. App. 2011).

Massachusetts: Quincy Mutual Fire Insurance Co. v. Crispo, 80 Mass. App. Ct. 484, 954 N.E.2d 27 (2011).

Minnesota: Western World Insurance Co. v. Hall, 353 N.W.2d 221, 223 (Minn. App. 1984).

Mississippi: Hankins v. Maryland Casualty Co./Zurich American Insurance Co., 101 So.3d 645 (Miss. 2012); Watson Quality Ford, Inc. v. Great River Insurance Co., 909 So.2d 1196, 1199 (Miss. App. 2005) ("First party coverage is a promise by an insurer to pay its own insured.").

New Jersey: Universal Underwriters Group v. Heibel, 901 A.2d 398, 404 (N.J. Super. 2006).

New Mexico: Salas v. Mountain States Mutual Casualty Co., 145 N.M. 542, 202 P.3d 801 (2009).

North Dakota: Grinnell Mutual Reinsurance Co. v. Thies, 755 N.W.2d 852 (N.D. 2008).

Pennsylvania: Zimmerman v. Harleysville Mutual Insurance Co., 860 A.2d 167, 178 (Pa. Super. 2004), *alloc. denied* 881 A.2d 820 (Pa. 2005).

Tennessee: Holt v. Pyles, 2007 WL 1217264 (Tenn. App. Apr. 24, 2007).

Texas: Lamar Homes, Inc. v. Mid-Continent Casualty Co., 242 S.W.3d 1 (Tex. 2007).

Utah: Tucker v. State Farm Mutual Automobile Insurance Co., 53 P.3d 947 (Utah 2002); Billings v. Union Bankers Insurance Co., 918 P.2d 461 (Utah 1996).

Virginia: McCullough v. Standard Pressing Machines. Co., 1996 WL 1065525, at *3 (Va. Cir. Apr. 18, 1996).

Washington: Aluminum Company of America v. Aetna Casualty & Surety Co., 998 P.2d 856 (Wash. 2000); State Farm Fire & Casualty Co. v. English Cove Ass'n, Inc., 88 P.3d 986, 992 (Wash. App. 2004) ("first party insurance provides protection for losses to the policyholder's own property").

West Virginia: Loudin v. National Liability and Fire Insurance Co., 228 W. Va. 34, 716 S.E.2d 696 (2011); Miller v. Fluharty, 500 S.E.2d 310 (W. Va. 1997); Marshall v. Saseen, 450 S.E.2d 791, 797 (W. Va. 1994).

[37] See, e.g.:

Fourth Circuit: Goff v. Penn Mutual Life Insurance Co., 729 S.E.2d 890 (W. Va. 2012).

Ninth Circuit: Ferrer v. Ngo, 73 P.3d 73, 76 n.3 (Haw. App. 2003).

[38] See, e.g.:

Fourth Circuit: Loudin v. National Liability and Fire Insurance Co., 228 W. Va. 34, 716 S.E.2d 696 (2011).

Ninth Circuit: Ferrer v. Ngo, 102 Haw. 119, 73 P.3d 73, 76 n.3 (Haw. App. 2003).

[39] See, e.g.:

Ninth Circuit: Ferrer v. Ngo, 102 Haw. 119, 73 P.3d 73, 76 n.3 (Haw. App. 2003).

Tenth Circuit: Morgan v. Unum Life Insurance Company of America, 2012 WL 3156569 (D. Utah Aug. 3, 2012).

[40] See Standard Fire Insurance Co. v. Spectrum Community Association, 141 Cal. App.4th 1117, 46 Cal. Rptr.3d 804, 819 (2006) (examples of first-party insurance include "life, disability, health, fire, theft and casualty insurance"). See also, Loudin v. National Liability and Fire Insurance Co., 228 W. Va. 34, 716 S.E.2d 696 (W. Va. 2011).

[41] See, e.g., Missouri State Government, Renters Insurance Guide, http://insurance.mo.gov/consumers/documents/RentersInsuranceGuide.pdf (last visited Jan. 23, 2013). See also:

First Circuit: Utica Mutual Insurance Co. v. Hall Equipment, Inc., 73 F. Supp.2d 83 (D. Mass. Oct. 28, 1999), *aff'd* 292 F.3d 77 (1st Cir. 2002).

Fifth Circuit: Hankins v. Maryland Casualty Co./Zurich American Insurance Co., 101 So.3d 645 (Miss. 2012).

[42] See ISO Form CP 00 30 04 02. See § 4.05 *infra.*

[43] See § 4.03 *infra.*

[44] States' no-fault statutes have different provisions and sometimes provide medical benefits to others, such as passengers, bystanders, and pedestrians. The following cases discuss some of the aspects of the PIP coverage. See, e.g.:

Eighth Circuit: Babinski v. American Family Insurance Group, 569 F.3d 349 (8th Cir. 2009).

Tenth Circuit: Breaux v. American Family Mutual Insurance Co., 554 F.3d 854 (10th Cir. 2009).

State Courts:

Colorado: American National General Insurance Co. v. Rivera, 217 P.3d 1257 (Colo. App. 2007).

Florida: Vasques v. Mercury Casualty Co., 947 So.2d 1265 (Fla. App. 2007).

Kentucky: Coleman v. Bee Line Courier Service, Inc., 284 S.W.3d 123 (Ky. 2009).

Massachusetts: Metropolitan Property and Casualty Insurance Co. v. Blue Cross and Blue Shield of Massachusetts, Inc., 451 Mass. 389, 885 N.E.2d 825 (2008).

Michigan: Johnson v. Recca, 492 Mich. 169, 821 N.W.2d 520 (2012); Amerisure Insurance Co. v. Plumb, 282 Mich. App. 417, 766 N.W.2d 878 (2009).

Minnesota: Auto Owners Insurance Co. v. Perry, 749 N.W.2d 324 (Minn. 2008).

New Jersey: Livsey v. Mercury Insurance Group, 197 N.J. 522, 964 A.2d 312 (2009).

New York: LMK Psychological Services, P.C. v. State Farm Mutual Automobile Insurance Co., 12 N.Y.3d 217, 906 N.E.2d 1046, 879 N.Y.S.2d 14 (2009).

Pennsylvania: Schappell v. Motorists Mutual Insurance Co., 594 Pa. 94, 934 A.2d 1184 (2007).

Rhode Island: Shepard v. Harleysville Worcester Insurance Co., 944 A.2d 167 (R.I. 2008).

Texas: Texas Farm Bureau Mutual Insurance Co. v. Sturrock, 146 S.W.3d 123 (Tex. 2004).

But see:

California: 21st Century Insurance Co. v. Superior Court, 47 Cal.4th 511, 213 P.3d 972, 98 Cal. Rptr.3d 516 (2009) (there is no statutory obligation in California to provide no-fault coverage).

As for first-party property damage, see, e.g., Foveon, Inc. v. Advanced Semiconductor, Inc., 2012 WL 4458647 (Cal. App. Sept. 27, 2012).

45 See, e.g.:

First Circuit: Lamontagne v. North American Specialty Insurance Co., 353 F. Supp.2d 129 (D. Me. 2005).

Second Circuit: Wittik v. State Farm Insurance Co., 142 Fed. Appx. 523 (2d Cir. 2005).

Third Circuit: Nationwide Mutual Insurance Co. v. Schmidt, 307 F. Supp.2d 674 (W.D. Pa. 2004).

Fourth Circuit: Moody v. Federated Mutual Insurance Co., 886 F. Supp. 5 (W.D. Va. 1994), *aff'd* 48 F.3d 1216 (4th Cir. 1995).

Fifth Circuit: Accardo v. America First Lloyds Insurance Co., 2012 WL 1576022 (S.D. Tex. May 3, 2012); Owen v. Universal Underwriters Insurance Co., 252 F. Supp.2d 324 (S.D. Miss. 2003).

Sixth Circuit: Hindall v. Winterthur International, 337 F.3d 680 (6th Cir. 2003).

Seventh Circuit: Allstate Insurance Co. v. Keca, 368 F.3d 793 (7th Cir. 2004).

Eighth Circuit: State Farm Mutual Automobile Insurance Co. v. Shahan, 141 F.3d 819 (8th Cir. 1998).

Ninth Circuit: Osborn v. Leader Insurance Co., 129 Fed. Appx. 379 (9th Cir. 2005); Bass v. Farm Bureau Financial Services, 2012 WL 3585206 (D. Ariz. Aug. 20, 2012).

Tenth Circuit: State Auto Insurance Co. v. Clifford, 195 Fed. Appx. 786 (10th Cir. 2006).

Eleventh Circuit: State Farm Mutual Automobile Insurance Co. v. Causey, 509 F. Supp.2d 1026 (M.D. Ala. 2007).

State Courts:

Alabama: Pontius v. State Farm Mutual Automobile Insurance Co., 915 So.2d 557, 563 (Ala. 2005).

Arizona: Ballesteros v. American Standard Insurance Company of Wisconsin, 223 Ariz. 269, 222 P.3d 292 (Ariz. App. 2009).

California: Weston Reid, L.L.C. v. American Insurance Group, Inc., 174 Cal. App.4th 940, 94 Cal. Rptr.3d 748 (2009).

Connecticut: Enviro Express, Inc. v. AIU Insurance Co., 901 A.2d 666, 671 (Conn. 2006).

Illinois: Pajic v. Old Republic Insurance Co., 394 Ill. App.3d 1040, 917 N.E.2d 564, 334 Ill. Dec. 738 (2009).

Indiana: Balagtas v. Bishop, 910 N.E.2d 789 (Ind. App. 2009).

Louisiana: McElroy v. Continental Casualty Co., 15 So.3d 377 (La. App. 2009).

Maryland: Maryland Automobile Insurance Fund v. Baxter, 186 Md. App. 147, 973 A.2d 243 (2009).

Minnesota: Schwickert, Inc. v. Winnebago Seniors, Ltd., 680 N.W.2d 79, 85 n.2 (Minn. 2004).

Missouri: Ritchie v. Allied Property and Casualty Insurance Co., 307 S.W.3d 132 (Mo. 2009).

Nebraska: Kline v. Farmers Insurance Exchange, 277 Neb. 874, 766 N.W.2d 118 (2009).

New Jersey: One Beacon Insurance Group v. Brownlee, 2006 WL 2129055 (N.J. Super. App. Div. Aug. 1, 2006).

New Mexico: Arias v. Phoenix Indemnity Insurance Co., 147 N.M. 14, 216 P.3d 264 (N.M. App. 2009).

New York: State Farm Mutual Automobile Insurance Co. v. Gray, 68 A.D.3d 1002, 891 N.Y.S.2d 151 (2009).

Oklahoma: Broadway Clinic v. Liberty Mutual Insurance Co., 139 P.3d 873, 883–884 (Okla. 2006).

Oregon: Vogelin v. American Family Mutual Insurance Co., 346 Or. 490, 213 P.3d 1216 (2009).

Pennsylvania: Bonenberger v. Nationwide Mutual Insurance Co., 791 A.2d 378, 381 (Pa. Super. 2002); Newkirk v. United States Automobile Association, 50 Pa. D. & C.3d 328, 331–332 (Pa. C.P. Lehigh Cnty. 1988), *aff'd* 564 A.2d 1263 (Pa. Super. Ct.), *alloc. denied* 597 A.2d 1153 (Pa. 1990).

Texas: In re American National County Mutual Insurance Co., 2012 WL 4477371 (Tex. App. Sept. 25, 2012).

Wisconsin: Danner v. Auto-Owners Insurance Co., 629 N.W.2d 159, 170 & n.4 (Wis. 2001).

46 See, e.g.:

First Circuit: Sentry Insurance a Mutual Co. v. McWhinnie, 510 F. Supp.2d 165 (D. Mass. 2007).

Second Circuit: Royal Indemnity Co. v. King, 512 F. Supp.2d 117 (D. Conn. 2007).

Third Circuit: State Farm Fire & Casualty Co. v. Platt, 4 F. Supp.2d 399 (E.D. Pa. 1998).

Fifth Circuit: United Fire and Casualty Co. v. Reeder, 9 F.3d 15 (5th Cir. 1993).

Sixth Circuit: Kentucky National Insurance Co. v. Lawrence, 187 Fed. Appx. 423 (6th Cir. 2006); Nationwide Mutual Fire Insurance Co. v. Creech, 431 F. Supp.2d 710 (E.D. Ky. 2006).

Seventh Circuit: Harper v. Vigilant Insurance Co., 433 F.3d 521 (7th Cir. 2005); Damore v. Winnebago Park Association, 876 F.2d 572 (7th Cir. 1989).

Eighth Circuit: Emcasco Insurance Co. v. Diedrich, 394 F.3d 1091 (8th Cir. 2005); State Farm Fire and Casualty Co. v. Ewing, 269 F.3d 888 (8th Cir. 2001).

Ninth Circuit: Farmer v. Allstate Insurance Co., 171 Fed. Appx. 111 (9th Cir. 2006); Allstate Insurance Co. v. Harris, 445 F. Supp. 847 (N.D. Cal. 1978).

Tenth Circuit: Safeco Insurance Co. of America v. Mares, 71 Fed. Appx. 808 (10th Cir. 2003).

State Courts:

Alabama: Rice v. State Farm Fire and Casualty Co., 628 So.2d 582 (Ala. 1993).

Alaska: Allstate Insurance Co. v. Falgoust, 160 P.3d 134 (Alaska 2007).

Colorado: Colorado Farm Bureau Mutual Insurance Co. v. Snowbarger, 934 P.2d 909 (Colo. App. 1997).

Delaware: Engerbretsen v. Engerbretsen, 675 A.2d 13 (Del. Super. 1995).

Florida: Garcia v. Federal Insurance Co., 969 So.2d 288 (Fla. 2007).

Georgia: McCullough v. Reyes, 651 S.E.2d 810 (Ga. App. 2007); Nalley v. Nationwide Mutual Fire Insurance Co., 472 S.E.2d 82 (Ga. App. 1996).

Illinois: Country Casualty Insurance Co. v. Fisher, 676 N.E.2d 1379 (Ill. App. 1997).

Iowa: Shelter Mutual Insurance Co. v. Davis, 715 N.W.2d 769 (Iowa. App. 2006).

Louisiana: Parkview Baptist Church and School v. White, 2007 WL 2713324 (La. App. Sept. 19, 2007).

Maine: Dechert v. Maine Insurance Guarantee Association, 711 A.2d 1290 (Me. 1998).

Massachusetts: Utica Mutual Insurance Co. v. Fontneau, 875 N.E.2d 508 (Mass. App. 2007).

Minnesota: Metropolitan Property Casualty Insurance Co. v. Armada, 2006 WL 696462 (Minn. App. Mar. 21, 2006).

Nebraska: Amco Insurance Co. v. Norton, 500 N.W.2d 542 (Neb. 1993).

Pennsylvania: Wall Rose Mutual Insurance Co. v. Manross, 2007 WL 4465070 (Pa. Super. Dec. 21, 2007).

West Virginia: Aluise v. Nationwide Mutual Fire Insurance Co., 625 S.E.2d 260 (W. Va. 2005).

[47] See §§ 2.03–2.05 *supra.*

[48] See § 2.04 *supra.*

[49] See § 2.03 *supra.*

[50] See the dissenting opinion in Zimmerman v. Harleysville Mutual Insurance Co., 860 A.2d 167, 178 (Pa. Super. 2004), *alloc. denied* 881 A.2d 820 (Pa. 2005). See also:

First Circuit: David v. Hingham Mutual Fire Insurance Co., 2007 WL 4322792 (D. Mass. Dec. 7, 2007).

Second Circuit: Travelers Insurance Co. v. Henry, 470 F.3d 56, 58 n.2 (2d Cir. 2006) ("'First-party coverage' refers to an insurer's direct promise to pay the insured, as compared to 'third-party coverage' where the insurer pays the claim of a third party such as the victim of the insured's negligent operation of a motor vehicle.").

Third Circuit: Bukofsky v. USAA Casualty Insurance Co., 2009 WL 1609402 (M.D. Pa. June 9, 2009) ("Insurance claims can be broken down into the following two categories: first-party benefit claims, where an insurance company promises to pay an insured an amount for a loss for such things as property damage, death or illness and third-party claims where the insurance protects the insured from actions brought by persons who are third parties to the insurance contract, covering the cost of defense and indemnity."); Port Authority of New York and New Jersey v. Affiliated FM Insurance Co., 311 F.3d 226, 233 (3d Cir. 2002) ("The primary aim of third party insurance is to defend and indemnify insureds against liability for claims made against them as a result of their own conduct. First party coverage, on the other hand, protects against loss caused by injury to the insured's own property."); *In re* Asousa Partnership, 2004 WL 1043149, at *8 (Bankr. E.D. Pa. Apr. 26, 2004).

Fourth Circuit: Rhodes, Inc. v. Morrow, 937 F. Supp. 1202, 1213 n.1 (M.D.N.C. 1996) ("'An insurer's first-party insurance obligation is its duty to compensate the insured for direct losses with the policy coverage. An insurer's third-party insurance obligation is its duty to defend the insured against claims by another, injured party and to indemnify the insured for losses sustained through such claims.'").

Fifth Circuit: In re Katrina Canal Breaches Consolidated Litigation, 263 F.R.D. 340, 2009 WL 2922305 (E.D. La. Sept. 8, 2009); Felham Enterprises, Ltd. v. Certain Underwriters of Lloyds, 2004 WL 2984296, at *4 (E.D. La. Dec. 6, 2004) ("'[F]irst party insurance' generally is understood to provide coverage for the insured against loss or damage sustained by it, whereas 'third party insurance' covers liability of the insured to another person.").

Sixth Circuit: White v. Insurance Company of the State of Pennsylvania, 282 F. Supp.2d 618, 625 (N.D. Ohio 2003), *vacated on other grounds* 405 F.3d 455 (6th Cir. 2005) ("'Liability' insurance constitutes 'an agreement to cover a loss resulting from one's liability to a third party, such as a loss incurred by a driver who injures a pedestrian.' The claim under the policy 'arises once the insured's liability to a third party has been asserted.' In contrast to this 'third party insurance,' there is also 'indemnity' insurance which is characterized as 'first party insurance' and defined as '[a] policy that applies to oneself or one's own property, such as life insurance, health insurance, disability insurance, and fire insurance.'") (citations omitted).

Seventh Circuit: CitiMortgage, Inc. v. Absolute Title Services, Inc., 2012 WL 1108249 (N.D. Ill. Apr. 2, 2012) ("Each of the cited decisions involved third-party insurance, purchased by an insured from an insurer for protection against the claims of another party. This case deals with first-party insurance. The insured is to be paid by the insurer in the event of a loss."); Hall v. Travelers Property Casualty Co. of America, 2009 WL 1148231 (S.D. Ind. Apr. 27, 2009) (same); Sanyo Laser Products, Inc. v. Royal Insurance Company of America, 2003 WL 23101793, at *3 n.2 (S.D. Ind. Nov. 7, 2003) ("'first party' insurance is a contract between the insurer and insured protecting the insured's own actual losses and expenses, while 'third party' insurance protects the insured from potential liability to a third party").

Eighth Circuit: Vincent Soybean & Grain Co. v. Lloyd's Underwriters of London, 246 F.3d 1129 (8th Cir. 2001); Mesaba Holdings, Inc. v. Federal Insurance Co., 2002 WL 1378221 (D. Minn. June 25, 2002).

Ninth Circuit: National Union Fire Insurance Co. v. Greenwich Insurance Co., 2009 WL 1794041 (W.D. Wash. June 22, 2009) ("The instant dispute involves third-party insurance coverage, which indemnifies an insured for covered claims that other third-party claimants file against her. By contrast, first-party coverage pays specified benefits directly to the insured when a determinable contingency occurs, allowing an insured to make her own personal claim for payment against her insurer.") (citations omitted); United States *ex. rel.* North Star Terminal & Stevedore Co. v. Nuggett Insurance Co., 2006 WL 2251122, at *2 n.3 (D. Alaska July 28, 2006).

Tenth Circuit: Allstate Insurance Co. v. Johnston, 339 F. Supp.2d 1191, 1195 (D. Kan. 2004).

State Courts:

Alabama: Titan Indemnity Co. v. Riley, 679 So.2d 701, 706 (Ala. 1996).

California: Griffin Dewatering Corp. v. Northern Insurance Co. of New York, 176 Cal. App.4th 172, 97 Cal. Rptr.3d 568 (2009) (In "a 'first party' case, . . . the policyholder's loss was directly compensable by the insurance company—the relationship is direct between insurance company and policyholder. . . . [In] a 'third party' case, . . . the insurance company is to defend and if necessary indemnify a 'third party's' claim against the policyholder, so the compensation is indirect."); Montrose Chemical Co. v. Admiral Insurance Co., 10 Cal.4th 645, 913 P.2d 878, 42 Cal. Rptr.2d 324, 332 (1995); Garvey v. State Farm Fire & Casualty Co., 48 Cal.3d 395, 770 P.2d 704, 257 Cal. Rptr. 292 (1989); California Insurance Guarantee Association v. Workers' Compensation Appeals Board, 203 Cal. App.4th 1328, 138 Cal. Rptr.3d 24, 30–31 (2012) ("In the context of first party insurance, original claimant has been construed to mean the original insured. In the context of third party insurance, original claimant has been construed to mean a person who institutes a claim against an insured for liability.") (citations omitted); Pacific Civil Constructors, Inc. v. Western Heritage Insurance Co., 2011 WL 2112676, at *11 (Cal. App. May 27, 2011) ("The terms are defined as follows: 'First party' insurance policies provide coverage for loss or damage sustained by the insured (e.g., life, disability, health, fire, theft and casualty insurance). 'Third party' insurance policies provide coverage for liability of the insured to another (e.g., comprehensive general liability, directors and officers liability and errors and omissions insurance)."); Black Diamond Asphalt Co. v. Superior Court, 114 Cal. App.4th 109, 7 Cal. Rptr.3d 466, 470 n.2 (2003) ("In first party insurance, a person insures himself or his property against loss. In third party insurance, a person insures himself against liability he may incur to others."); Century Indemnity Co. v. Hearrean, 98 Cal. App.4th 734, 120 Cal. Rptr.2d 66 (2002) ("'CGL policies are third party liability insurance policies which obligate insurers to pay money to third parties to whom their insureds are liable. In contrast to first party insurance policies which obligate an insurer to pay money directly to an insured for a loss sustained by the insured. . . .'").

Florida: Progressive Express Insurance Co. v. Scoma, 2007 WL 1296007 (Fla. App. May 4, 2007).

Hawaii: Ferrer v. Ngo, 73 P.3d 73, 81 (Haw. App. 2003); Sentinel Insurance Co. v. First Insurance Company of Hawaii, Ltd., 875 P.2d 894, 906 (Haw. 1994).

Illinois: Emerson Electric Co. v. Aetna Casualty & Surety Co., 815 N.E.2d 924, 950 (Ill. App. 2004).

Indiana: Wagner v. Yates, 912 N.E.2d 805 (Ind. 2009) ("First-party insurance is insurance which applies to the insured's *own property or person.* In contrast, liability insurance indemnifies against liability on account of injuries to the person or property of another.") (quotations and citations omitted; emphasis in original).

Kentucky: Aetna Casualty & Surety Co. v. Commonwealth of Kentucky, 179 S.W.3d 830, 845 (Ky. 2005) ("Third party insurance involves protection for the policyholder for liability it incurs to someone else, while first party insurance involves protection for losses to the policyholder's own property.").

Louisiana: Niemann v. Crosby Development Co., 92 So.3d 1039, 1043 n.3 (La. App. 2012) ("'First-party' insurance covers a loss sustained by the insured, the first party to the insurance contract, as opposed to liability or 'third-party' insurance, which covers the insured's liability to a third party (a non-party to the insurance contract) for that party's loss."); Mangerchine v. Reaves, 63 So.3d 1049 (La. App. 2011) (similar).

Maryland: Maryland Automobile Insurance Fund v. Baxter, 186 Md. App. 147, 973 A.2d 243 (2009) ("[U]ninsured motorist coverage is first-party coverage, i.e., a promise by an insurer 'to pay its own insured, rather than a promise to pay some third party.'").

Mississippi: Watson Quality Ford, Inc. v. Great River Insurance Co., 909 So.2d 1196, 1199 (Miss. App. 2005) ("'First party coverage is a promise by an insurer to pay its own insured, rather than a promise to its insured to pay a third party.'").

Missouri: Billings Mutual Insurance Co. v. Cameron Mutual Insurance Co., 229 S.W.3d 138 (Mo. App. 2007).

New Jersey: Edward Leske Co. v. Crum & Forster Insurance Co., 2006 WL 3391236 (N.J. Super. App. Div. Nov. 27, 2006).

Ohio: Ponser v. St. Paul Fire & Marine Insurance Co., 821 N.E.2d 173 (Ohio 2004).

Oklahoma: Broadway Clinic v. Liberty Mutual Insurance Co., 139 P.3d 873 (Okla. 2006).

Pennsylvania: Pantelis v. Erie Insurance Exchange, 890 A.2d 1063 (Pa. Super. 2006).

Texas: Lamar Homes, Inc. v. Mid-Continent Casualty Co., 239 S.W.3d 236 (Tex. 2007); Tellepsen Builders, L.P. v. Kendall/Heaton Associates, Inc., 325 S.W.3d 692 (Tex. App. 2010).

Vermont: Travelers Insurance Co. v. Henry, 882 A.2d 1133, 1138 (Vt. 2005).

Washington: State Farm Fire & Casualty Co. v. English Cove Ass'n, Inc., 88 P.3d 986, 992 (Wash. App. 2004) ("Third party insurance provides protection for the policyholder for liability it incurs to someone else, while first party insurance provides protection for losses to the policyholder's own property.").

West Virginia: Loudin v. National Liability and Fire Insurance Co., 228 W. Va. 34, 716 S.E.2d 696 (2011).

CHAPTER 3

The Insurance Contract

Chapter Contents

❖

§ 3.01 Overview

An insurance policy is nothing more than a commercial agreement, albeit extremely specialized, between two parties: (1) an insurance company and (2) its policyholder. The essential feature of the insurance policy is the transfer of certain risks by the policyholder to the insurance company in exchange for the policyholder's payment of a sum of money or premium to the insurance company. That risk transfer is limited in scope and subject to the terms and conditions set forth in the insurance contract.

As discussed previously, there are generally two categories of insurance policies—first-party and third-party. For and within each of these categories, there are two lines—personal and commercial, applicable to individuals and commercial enterprises, respectively. Within each category and line, there are a number of different types and kinds of insurance policies.[1]

Remarkably, despite this great variety of insurance available and in use in the market, many of the principles uniformly apply across all categories, lines, and types of insurance policies. This chapter is intended to discuss many of these common elements, aspects, and provisions applicable to all categories, lines, and types of insurance policies.

First, the chapter discusses rules of construction that are generally used by courts when interpreting insurance policies, irrespective of the kind of insurance at issue.[2] The chapter then covers the regulatory landscape in the sense of the approvals generally necessary to authorize the use of certain insurance policy language for many of the types of policies.[3] A further discussion addresses the mechanism for establishing the terms of coverage where the actual policies, regardless of the type, are misplaced, stolen, destroyed, or lost.[4] Finally, there is coverage of miscellaneous provisions generally seen in all types of policies, including provisions dealing with arbitration,[5] choice of law and choice of forum,[6] contractual limitations,[7] and subrogation.[8]

§ 3.02 Insurance Policies as Ordinary Contracts

The most important rule in the interpretation and construction of an insurance policy is that an insurance policy is no different than any other commercial contract, although it is a specialized contract. Accordingly, the same rules for interpretation and construction for contracts in general apply to insurance policies.[9]

[1]—Freedom to Contract

To arrive at the proper construction of contracts in general and of insurance policies in particular, the plain meaning of the document controls unless there is some law, statute, regulation, constitutional provision, or public policy preventing application or enforcement of such construction.[10] In other words, parties generally enjoy the freedom to contract. They are free to contract about anything, and whatever they contract and how they draft the contract are generally enforceable as written unless a constitution, statute, law, regulation, or public policy would prevent such an interpretation, application, or enforcement.[11]

This freedom to contract rule has significance in two material respects. First, the language used generally will ultimately control. Second, the language itself can be used to override common-law interpretations.

As stated above, one significant impact of the freedom to contract is that insurance policies are governed by the language contained in the policies themselves.[12] Dictionaries can help explain the plain meaning of the language used in the policies.[13] Other sources that are useful in arriving at the plain meaning of words in an insurance policy include, among other things: (a) the definitions set forth in the insurance policy (which should be consulted first);[14] and (b) common everyday usage and understanding of the words utilized.[15] Additionally, case law may be relevant, helpful, and potentially precedential or persuasive where identical or substantially similar language has been construed or interpreted by other courts in similar factual circumstances. However, cases construing the same provisions under materially different facts and/or provisions that differ in material respects should have no influence on the meaning of the particular language at issue. Accordingly, when interpreting and applying an insurance policy to a given set of facts, the language contained in the policy is generally the best starting point. This principle is reflected throughout this treatise.

Of equal or greater significance is the second material effect of contractual freedom. The freedom to contract permits insurance companies to change language in their policies in an attempt to mitigate or alleviate themselves from precedential decisions regarding construction of particular terms or phrases, which they view as harmful or otherwise detrimental to their business.[16] This theme is also often repeated in this treatise.

Of course, the freedom to contract is not without its limitations. For instance, any language change might need to be pre-approved for use by state insurance regulators.[17] However, such regulatory hurdles do not negate the ultimate freedom to contract.

In addition, even after regulatory approval is obtained, changes to the terms of current insurance policies can usually not be made until the renewal of those policies. And with respect to such changes in terms at renewal, an insurance company may be required to do more than send a policy with the revised terms included. Often, at the time of renewal, the insurance company is required to notify its policyholder of the changes in coverage and the significance of the changes, and in the absence of its strict compliance with these rules, may be unable to rely upon the revised terms as part of the renewed policy.[18]

[2]—Interpretation and Construction of Insurance Policies

Interpretation of insurance policies is a question of law within the province of the court.[19] In construing or interpreting insurance policies, courts should first determine whether the policy is ambiguous.[20] If it is not ambiguous, courts should construe the unambiguous policy in accordance with its plain meaning.[21] On the other hand, courts will find a policy to be ambiguous where its meaning is unclear or where there is more than one reasonable interpretation as to its meaning.[22] Ambiguous policies are generally construed in favor of coverage and the policyholder, and they are generally construed against the insurance company as the drafter of the incomprehensible or ambiguous contract.[23]

[a]—Parties' Mutual Intentions

The paramount goal, and indeed the governing rule, in insurance policy construction is to ascertain and enforce the mutual intentions of the parties based on the policy's terms and conditions.[24] In interpreting an insurance policy in accordance with the parties' mutual intentions, the court first looks to the insurance policy itself, including review of the entire policy as a whole, the language used, any definitions set forth, and the attendant circumstances surrounding the contract formation, such as the type of insurance, the nature of risks involved, and the purpose of the transaction.[25] If the policy does not define a significant term, the court will apply the term's plain meaning taken from the viewpoint of the ordinary purchaser of insurance, often, but not always, with resort to the policy's definitions and/or a dictionary.[26]

[b]—Rules of Construction

In attempting to arrive at the meaning of a policy, where the language of the policy is not otherwise clear,[27] courts may, and often do, utilize various rules of construction, such as:

1. Construing a policy as a whole to harmonize its provisions and avoid an interpretation that creates an internal conflict.[28]
2. Construing a policy as a whole to effectuate each provision and to avoid redundancy, superfluousness, and surplusage.[29]
3. Construing the policy as a whole to ensure that the interpretation of it comports with the purposes the parties had contemplated in entering into the transaction.[30]
4. Construing a policy to comport with the policyholder's reasonable expectations.[31]
5. Construing policies to avoid a construction providing what appears to be illusory coverage—namely, the payment of premiums for effectively no insurance coverage.[32]
6. When two parts of a policy appear to conflict irreconcilably and the conflict cannot be harmonized, construing the policy such that the irreconcilably conflicting specific provisions control over the general ones.[33]

7. Utilizing the doctrine of ***expression unius est exclusion alterius***, meaning interpreting policies in such a way that the expression of one thing implies the exclusion of anything not mentioned.[34]

8. Construing a policy in a fair, reasonable, practical, sensible, just, logical, and unstrained manner to avoid absurd results.[35]

9. Construing an ambiguous insurance policy against ambiguities and/or against the drafter.[36]

§ 3.03 State Insurance Regulation

The insurance industry has traditionally been regulated by states, with the relevant statutory and regulatory law administered by the insurance departments of the various states.[37] Among other things, states often require that the insurance departments approve new policy language forms and/or changes in premium rates before they may be employed or applied in insurance sold in the state.[38]

[1]—Regulatory Filings

[a]—Required Regulatory Approval

Except with respect to surplus lines insurance,[39] and often with respect to self-insurers and uninsured entities or persons,[40] most jurisdictions make it unlawful to issue or sell any kind of insurance policy, including endorsements, until the language in the policy has been submitted and formally approved by the state's Insurance Commissioner. For example, in Pennsylvania, a statute provides:

> "It shall be unlawful for any insurance company, association or exchange . . . doing business in this Commonwealth, to issue, sell, or dispose of any policy, contract, or certificate, covering life, health, accident, personal liability, fire, marine, title, and all forms of casualty insurance, or contracts pertaining to pure endowments or annuities, or any other contracts of insurance, or use applications, riders, or endorsements in connection therewith, until the forms of the same have been submitted to and formally approved by the Insurance Commissioner, and copies filed in the Insurance Department. . . ."[41]

[b]—Surplus Lines Insurance Exception

As stated above, surplus lines insurance is often exempted or partially exempted from many of the regulatory requirements in order to induce these surplus lines insurance companies to fill a void and transact business in the state by providing insurance that under normal market conditions would not be available.[42] For instance, in heavy hurricane or storm areas, such as Florida, Louisiana, and Texas, surplus lines insurance might be necessary because of the inability or unwillingness of registered or approved insurers to provide all of the insurance needed in the state.[43]

[c]—Non-Compliance

Issues arise with respect to the effect of non-compliance with these regulatory requirements. With regard to surplus lines insurers, failure to use a licensed surplus lines agent or an eligible surplus lines insurer may prevent enforceability of the policy by the non-compliant surplus lines insurer.[44]

With regard to insurance companies other than surplus lines insurers, issues arise when considering the effect of such regulatory or statutory non-compliance. First, how do courts interpret or enforce policy language when the language at issue has been rejected by regulators after being formally submitted? Similarly, what if the language at issue was never formally submitted but would have been rejected if it had been submitted? Furthermore, how do courts interpret or enforce policy language when the language was never submitted for approval? Alternatively, what happens where the language was submitted but not approved until after the policy became effective?

[i]—Express Rejection

Cases construing statutes similar to the Pennsylvania statute quoted above[45] hold that insurance policy language is void and unenforceable, when the language is used in the face of either: (1) evidence that the insurance company did not seek approval and the insurance department would have rejected such language had approval been sought;[46] or (2) express rejection of the policy language by the insurance department.[47]

[ii]—Lack of Submission and Approval

A line of cases involves policy forms that were issued and sold despite never having been formally submitted and approved. There are some decisions invalidating never-before-submitted and unapproved language, as distinguished from disapproved and expressly rejected, policy forms.[48] However, the majority of decisions dealing with never submitted and unapproved language in policy forms hold that such a statutory violation is a mere technicality, and refuse to invalidate the contested provision.[49] Many of these cases recognize the distinction between forms that are unapproved, on the one hand, and forms that are expressly disapproved and rejected, on the other hand.[50]

[2]—Language at Variance with Approved Forms

With respect to insurers other than surplus line insurers, a related issue arises where the policy at issue is at variance with the approved form or otherwise in conflict with the state rules, regulations, and laws governing insurance. Under such circumstances, courts may hold the policy language at issue to be valid,[51] voidable,[52] void,[53] or otherwise reform the policy to be in compliance with the applicable law or regulation.[54]

§ 3.04 Lost Policies

Sometimes, original insurance policies cannot be located because they are lost, misplaced, stolen, destroyed, or otherwise missing. Lost policies are potentially damaging to a policyholder if a coverage dispute arises. To wit, in a coverage dispute, the burden of proof usually rests with the policyholder. That burden of proof is the same as with other breach of contract cases. The party asserting the breach is required to prove the existence of a valid contract, the essential terms thereof, and the other party's breach. Lost policies obviously create a huge impediment to proof of the existence of a valid contract and its terms.

When the writing is unavailable, issues arise under the statutes of fraud and the parol and best evidence rules. In particular, as a prerequisite to validity and enforceability, statutes of fraud exist that may apply to require a signed written and/or executed contract.[55] In addition, even if the statute of frauds were inapplicable, the parol evidence rule might prevent proof of the existence and terms of a contract via oral testimony or other documents outside the four corners of the contract itself, especially where there might have been a no oral modification or complete integration clause in the original, lost insurance policy.[56] Furthermore, where a policy is lost, the best evidence rule might prevent admissibility of anything other than the original contract itself.[57]

[1]—Absence of Bad Faith

In order to offer secondary evidence of the terms of a missing contract, the offering party often must show that he or she or it made a diligent search for the contract, and the contract is unavailable due to something other than the offering party's bad faith.[58]

[2]—Secondary Proof of Existence and Terms of Coverage

Thus, as long as the document is not missing as a result of policyholder bad faith, the policyholder may be able to prevail in a coverage dispute if a policyholder can demonstrate the existence of coverage and the likely terms thereof.[59] Generally, issues arise as to proof of the terms of coverage of such lost policies.[60] With respect to a lost policy, extrinsic evidence of the existence of the coverage, the terms of another policy, and evidence that such other policy is similar in form to the lost policy, is admissible to prove the terms of coverage.[61] Indeed, in proving terms of lost insurance policies, the "evidence is usually comprised of business records, expert testimony, and standard forms made by and found in the possession of the party against whom they were being offered."[62] Courts may differ on the appropriate standard of proof. For example, some courts follow a preponderance of the evidence standard,[63] while others follow a clear and convincing evidence standard.[64]

§ 3.05 Miscellaneous Policy Provisions

[1]—Arbitration

Insurance statutes, such as state no-fault automobile statutes, often require arbitration of disputes.[65] Insurance policies also sometimes include provisions mandating or requiring arbitration of any dispute arising under, or in connection with, the insurance policy.[66] Arbitration is viewed by some as a forum that favors the insurance company,[67] although that is not always accurate. What is accurate, however, is that arbitration results are less predictable and more flawed than the judicial process. Although many insurance policy forms, particularly Directors and Officers forms and Errors or Omissions forms, contain arbitration provisions, these provisions have been enforced with mixed success.[68]

At least two important considerations arise with arbitration clauses. First, insurance companies sometimes are willing to, and do delete the arbitration provision as part of the negotiations at the time of sale. Second, there is the possibility that the inability to bring an action in a court of law may reduce the policyholder's ability to contest effectively unreasonable positions in a subsequent dispute with the insurance company over claims. Of course, the opposite is likely true as well. In particular, arbitration provisions might reduce an insurance company's ability to obtain the interpretation it views as applicable to the policy language in question.

Accordingly, if the policyholder truly believes arbitration venues favor the insurance company and wants to preserve his/her/its right to redress through the judicial process, it behooves him/her/it to negotiate the arbitration provision out of the policy at the time of renewal. In addition, if the insurance company believes that the arbitration process truly is less predictable and more subject to flawed interpretations, it is imperative that the insurer remove the arbitration clause from the policy in the first instance.

[2]—Choice of Forum and Choice of Law

Choice of venue and/or governing law are also important issues, which, like arbitration,[69] can be compelled by either contract or law. Unlike arbitration, which, if not provided for by contract or statute, will not become an issue in the case, choice of law and venue issues must be resolved in a coverage dispute. This is because the case cannot be resolved without first ascertaining which state's laws to apply and whether the venue has appropriate jurisdiction over the subject matter and the parties. As discussed below, choice of law and venue issues are often outcome determinative in insurance coverage disputes, and they can be handled either through a contract provision[70] or common-law[71] methodology to arrive at the governing state's law.

[a]—Provisions Selecting the Governing Law and Venue in the Event of a Dispute

Policies sometimes contain and/or choice of forum provisions. Such provisions are triggered only in the event of a dispute between the policyholder and its insurance company, and in such a dispute, they require either the application of a particular law to the dispute or the institution of dispute resolution, through litigation in a particular forum. Sometimes, there is also a consent to jurisdiction clause. These provisions are generally enforced,[72] although there are some notable exceptions.[73]

[b]—Absence of Choice of Law and Choice of Venue Provisions

In the absence of a choice of venue and/or consent to jurisdiction provision in an insurance policy, the jurisdiction and venue rules of the chosen forum will apply. Thus, without a contractually agreed upon venue and/or consent to jurisdiction clause, the parties are generally free to sue each other in any venue, subject, of course, to general rules on in personam jurisdiction, subject matter jurisdiction, and venue.[74]

In addition, in the absence of a choice of law provision in the policy, the governing law is determined by detailed choice of law rules of the jurisdiction where the lawsuit is initiated.[75] Some states follow a choice of law rule applying the law of the state where the policy is issued and delivered.[76] However, the majority of states follow the modern approach to choice of law questions, and in property and casualty insurance policies, these states usually apply the law of the state where the principal location of the insured risk is located.[77] Where the policy has insured risks located in several states, the courts may view the transaction as involving separate policies, each insuring an individual risk, and apply the law of the site of the principal location of the particular risk at issue.[78]

The foregoing discussion demonstrates why forum shopping is prevalent in insurance coverage disputes. In fact, forum selection is a mandatory part of every coverage analysis because it is often case determinative. For instance, many times, application of one interested state's substantive law would result in a different conclusion than application of other interested states' substantive laws.[79] Under those circumstances—namely, where a true conflict of laws among all interested states exists—different fora might come to different conclusions as to which state's law is the governing law because they may have different choice of law rules or because they differ as to the most significant factor. Where different fora could come to different conclusions as to the governing law at issue, potential litigants will need to consider filing in the forum where the most favorable governing law would be applied.

In considering where to file suit, the party initiating the suit will want to consult coverage counsel to analyze the various possible options where it would want to consider filing suit and how each such option will impact the applicable governing law. These considerations can often be case dispositive, meaning the wrong choice would be fatal to the case whereas the correct choice could enhance the prospects of the case. Use of a trained coverage attorney will help the party select an appropriate forum.

[3]—Contractual Limitations Clauses

Many insurance policies contain contractual limitations clauses, which set forth a maximum period of time within which a lawsuit must be brought by the policyholder to resolve a dispute as to coverage.[80] In the absence of such a provision, various jurisdictions have different time limits for bringing suits, set forth in statutes of limitations.[81]

Irrespective of whether a contractual or statutory limitations period applies, issues arise as to accrual of a claim, computation of when the claim becomes barred, and tolling of the period, among other things.[82] In addition, a question may arise as to whether a bad-faith claim is governed by the same limitations period as the claim under the policy.[83]

Contractual limitations provisions have been generally upheld, although issues may arise if the period for initiating suit is unreasonably brief, such as less than twelve months, and there may be issues as to prejudice suffered by the policyholder where the limitation clause is less than that contained in the relevant statute of limitations.[84]

Depending on the circumstances, an insurance company may not even owe a duty to its policyholder to apprise the policyholder of the existence of the suit limitation clause in the policy, even when state insurance regulations provide for such notice.[85] Moreover, the doctrines of waiver and estoppel could operate to negate operation of the contractual limitations clause, particularly where the insurance company waived the provision or otherwise did something that induced the policyholder to sit on its rights and not file a lawsuit.[86]

[4]—Subrogation

[a]—Right to Subrogation

Subrogation refers to the rights of an insurance company, after providing insurance coverage to its policyholder for a loss, to recover funds, up to the amount of its payment to or on behalf of its policyholder, from parties who are primarily responsible for the loss, such as parties who committed tortious or other actions that caused the loss.[87] Apart from the receipt of contribution or indemnification from other insurance companies that insured the policyholder for the same risk,[88] insurance policies generally permit the insurance company to assert subrogation claims against any responsible party except the policyholder or any other person or entity insured under the policy because the liability and/or fault of the policyholder or other insured person or entity is one of the risks insured under the policy through which the payment was made.[89]

Frequently, policies explicitly provide for the right to subrogation. For example, a widely used liability policy form provides:

> "If the insured has rights to recover all or part of any payment we have made under this coverage part, those rights are transferred to us. The insured must do nothing after loss to impair them. At our request, the insured will bring 'suit' or transfer those rights to us and help us enforce them."[90]

Similarly, a widely used property policy form provides:

> "If any insured or organization to or for whom we make payment under this Coverage Part has rights to recover damages from another, those rights are transferred to us to the extent of our payment. That person or organization must do everything necessary to secure our rights and must do nothing after loss to impair them. But you may waive your rights against another party in writing:
>
> 1. Prior to a loss to your Covered Property or Covered Income.
> 2. After a loss to your Covered Property or Covered Income only if, at time of loss, that party is one of the following:
>   a. Someone insured by this insurance;
>   b. A business firm:
>   (1) Owned or controlled by you; or
>   (2) That owns or controls you; or
>   c. Your tenant.
>
> "This will not restrict your insurance."[91]

Irrespective of whether the insurance policy expressly provides for subrogation, the common law recognizes subrogation by operation of law,[92] and some statutes explicitly grant the right of subrogation when the insurance company pays the policyholder's claim.[93] Such common-law or statutory rights are often recognized, exercised, and/or enforced even when the policyholder waives its rights against third parties who know or should know of the insurance company's subrogation rights.[94]

If a conflict arises between terms of the policy and common law, the contract would control.[95]

[b]—Recoveries Limited to Tort Damages

Interesting issues arise in subrogation. One such issue involves the measure of recovery by the subrogated insurance company. It is universally true that an insurance company cannot recover greater than it paid, because such excess recoveries generally belong to the policyholder or other insurance companies.[96] A subrogated insurance company will try to recover everything it paid to its policyholder, which was paid under the terms of a contract, namely, the insurance policy through which the subrogation right is derived explicitly or in equity by operation of law. That recovery may or may not be equivalent to what it can recover in subrogation. Subrogation itself means that the subrogated insurance company generally stands in the shoes of its policyholder, and its claims are those that its policyholder would have against others.[97] Usually, the insurance company has paid an insurance claim under a first-party policy and the claim it had paid arose from an act or event that may have been caused in part by another's actions. The subrogated insurer would then succeed to its policyholder's rights vis-à-vis that third-party wrongdoer and have claims against that third-party wrongdoer usually sounding in tort. When all the smoke clears, the subrogated insurer may have a recovery in the subrogation action that is limited to tort recovery, which may or may not be the same as what it paid its policyholder under the insurance policy at issue.[98]

[c]—Against Parties with Whom Policyholder Does Business

Frequently, subrogation claims will be brought or threatened against third parties closely aligned with the policyholder, such as its accountants, attorneys, or entities with which it transacts business.[99] For example, in the construction liability context, a general contractor's insurance company will often need to institute suit against an architect, engineer, component part manufacturer and supplier, and various subcontractors with whom the policyholder regularly transacts business.[100] Likewise, a property owner who is paid for a loss may potentially inadvertently hand its insurance company a subrogation claim against its tenant if that tenant is the cause of the loss.[101] Such actions might be limited by the terms of the contract between the policyholder and the tortfeasor with whom it regularly conducts business.[102] Such actions against people or entities with whom the policyholder regularly transacts business can seriously disrupt the policyholder's business. At the point at which the insurance company is asked to reimburse for an underlying covered claim, the insurance company may offer to forego its subrogation rights, but, often, only if the policyholder accepts less than what is due under the policy.[103]

[d]—Division of Proceeds

[i]—Mechanism and Timing

As previously stated, subrogation involves the recovery of funds from tortfeasors and/or others who are primarily responsible for the loss.[104] It is axiomatic that this third-party recovery can occur in any of three ways: (1) by the policyholder, directly or through counsel, before coverage, including a defense, has been provided; (2) by counsel hired on behalf of the policyholder while an insurance company paid defense is being provided but before any indemnity is paid; or (3) by the insurance company, directly or through counsel, after indemnity coverage is afforded.

Regardless of how the recovery occurs, if subrogation proceeds are recovered before the payment of insurance proceeds (other than payment of defense), the subrogation proceeds are more appropriately called reimbursement proceeds, and are used as a setoff from any recovery under the policy.[105] If, on the other hand, subrogation proceeds are recovered after payment of insurance proceeds (other than the payment for defense), direct apportionment of such proceeds becomes necessary.[106] In either event, the economic results are the same.[107]

[ii]—Principle against Double Indemnity

When analyzing recoveries from multiple sources, the universal principle against double indemnity is important to remember. The principle against double indemnity provides that a policyholder, unlike a tort plaintiff who is permitted double recovery under the collateral source rule as discussed below,[108] is generally prohibited from collecting more than its overall loss, taking into account recoveries from all sources, be it insurance or otherwise.[109]

Of course, the principle against double indemnity for insurance coverage litigation runs counter to the collateral source rule available in tort litigation, which holds that a tortfeasor is liable for all damages it causes, irrespective of whether health, workers' compensation, or other insurance and/or sources of funds paid for the damages claimed.[110]

[iii]—Priority

When a policyholder pays a large deductible or self-insured retention, issues often arise as to how the proceeds from subrogation are shared between paying insurance companies and the policyholder and the priority of recovery. Three possibilities exist.[111]

First, there is policyholder priority, whereby the policyholder is entitled to be made whole for all amounts up to its loss, with the remainder inuring to the insurance company.[112] Second, at the opposite extreme, there is insurance company priority, whereby the insurance company obtains all funds up to its payment first, with the remainder going to the policyholder.[113] Third, there is no priority and allocation scheme dividing the proceeds on a *pro rata* basis between the policyholder and the insurance company.[114]

[A]—"Made-Whole" Rule

At one extreme, the policyholder will argue for the "made-whole" rule, asserting first priority to the recovery to the extent of its loss. Under the made-whole rule, the policyholder should be made whole for its loss first before any setoff for recoveries from third parties.[115] One case described the "made-whole" rule as follows:

> "It is a general equitable principle of insurance law that, absent an agreement to the contrary, an insurance company may not enforce a right to subrogation until

> the insured has been fully compensated for [his or] her injuries, that is, has been made whole."[116]

The made-whole rule includes the policyholder's full recoupment for its loss, including its payment of insurance deductibles, uninsured or excluded losses, and some or all of the litigation expenses incurred in the recovering funds from the third party.[117]

Courts adopting the made-whole rule do not believe that it provides "the policyholder with a windfall" because the policyholder is simply put "back in the situation [it] would have been had [its] loss not occurred."[118] These courts likewise reason that the made-whole result is not "unfair to the insurance company" because "if either the policyholder or the carrier must to some extent go unpaid because the policyholder has recovered less than her total loss, 'the loss should be borne by the insurer for that is the risk the insured has paid it to assume.'"[119]

Although "[t]here is authority that language in an insurance policy that grants the insurance company 'all rights of recovery to the extent of its payment' overrides the common law made whole rule . . . [t]he more recent cases, however, require that the contractual provision that intends to vitiate this rule must 'clearly and specifically [give] the insurer a priority out of proceeds from the tortfeasor regardless whether the insured was first made whole.'"[120] Thus, as previously stated,[121] insurance companies are free to draft around the made-whole rule to give themselves priority.

One court[122] refused to ignore the made-whole rule when faced with a policy provision more favorable to the insurance company than the commonly used Insurance Services Offices, Inc., forms previously quoted.[123] The policy stated that insurer "is entitled to all the rights of recovery that the insured person to whom payment was made has against another," and "when an insured person has been paid by [the insurer] under this policy and also recovers from another person, entity, or organization, the amount recovered will be held by the insured person in trust for [the insurer] and reimbursed to [the insurer] to the extent of [the insurer's] payment."[124] Likewise, a provision similar to the one in the standard form previously quoted,[125] which read "If any person or organization to or for whom we make payment under this Coverage Form has rights to recover damages from another, those rights are transferred to us," was held insufficient to change the made-whole doctrine.[126]

An example of a provision that was held to abrogate the made-whole doctrine is:

> "[We] shall be entitled to the payment, reimbursement, and subrogation as provided in this Section C(1) regardless of whether the total amount of the recovery of the [policyholder] on account of the injury or illness is less than the actual loss suffered by the [policyholder]."[127]

Courts that permit parties to contract around the made-whole doctrine have deemed this language as adequate to override the made-whole rule because it states that the insurance company has the first right to any amounts the policyholder recovers, even where the policyholder is not made whole.[128]

[B]—Insurance Company Priority

Insurance companies have been known to argue that they are entitled to priority to the subrogation proceeds first or as an initial "setoff" if the policyholder collects from the other responsible parties before the insurance company makes payment under the policy.[129] The companies seek priority for all amounts recovered by the policyholder up to the amount it paid before the policyholder is entitled to a share in the proceeds from third-party recoveries.[130] Insurance company priority is often based on express contractual language meant to override the made-whole rule.[131]

Insurance company priority purportedly can also be based on equitable principles, providing recovery to the party with, according to the insurance company, a greater right to reimbursement from the payment.[132] The insurance company's position is that the deductible only has meaning if the policyholder is fully on the risk for that deductible first before the insurance company is on the risk, and to the extent third-party recoveries change this risk transfer, such a result alters the agreement negotiated between the parties. There is very little authority for this result, likely because the litigation centers around whether the made-whole rule applies in the first instance, and factual circumstances, such as whether the policyholder has any non-reimbursed out-of-pocket losses, generally determine whether the insurance company is entitled to the entirety of the proceeds or whether there is a need for some sort of equitable allocation, as discussed in the next section.[133]

[C]—Allocation

As a third, intermediate alternative, the parties can share equitably in the subrogation proceeds.[134] The allocation scheme provides that:

> "If an insurer paying a claim for a loss caused through the negligence of a third person requests that the insured prosecute his claim against the tortfeasor, assists in the prosecution of the claim, and bears its share of the burden of preparing the case for trial, it is entitled, out of the judgment recovered, to the amount which it has paid on account of the loss, notwithstanding the judgment recovered is not, according to the insured's claim, equal to the full value of the property destroyed."[135]

If a policyholder must incur a deductible per occurrence, any recoveries from third parties would result in partial subrogation rights to both the insurance company and the policyholder. In these circumstances, where the policyholder has a separate right to sue the responsible parties, an insurance company with an interest in recovering a setoff or contribution from the third-party tortfeasors has two options: "(1) a separate lawsuit against the responsible third party [or intervention in the policyholder's lawsuit against the third party], or (2) recoupment of payments directly out of the insured's recovery from the responsible third party."[136] However, the second option places the insurance company at the mercy of the policyholders' "efforts and success in recovering from the responsible third party."[137] This is because the policyholder has little incentive to seek a recovery from the third party greater than the amount needed to make himself whole.[138]

The insurance companies, could, arguably, require a *pro rata* share of a subcontractor recovery if they were to participate with the policyholder and share the policyholder's expenses in gaining that recovery.[139]

[D]—Common Fund Doctrine

The common fund doctrine applies when a plaintiff incurs attorneys' fees to protect a common fund for administration or distribution under the direction of the court, or where such fund has been raised for like purpose.[140] In this situation, the court will order plaintiff to be reimbursed for costs and expenses, including counsel fees, from the property of the fund, or order those benefited to contribute proportionately toward that expense.[141] The common fund doctrine applies in the insurance contexts of subrogation and reimbursement.

Notes

[1] See Chapter 2 *supra*.

[2] See § 3.02 *infra*.

[3] See § 3.03 *infra*.

[4] See § 3.04 *infra*.

[5] See § 3.05[1] *infra*.

[6] See § 3.05[2] *infra*.

[7] See § 3.05[3] *infra*.

[8] See § 3.05[4] *infra*.

[9] See:

First Circuit: Peterborough Oil Co. v. Great American Insurance Co., 397 F. Supp.2d 230 (D. Mass. 2005).

Second Circuit: In re Cosmetics Plus Group, Ltd., 379 B.R. 464 (Bankr. S.D.N.Y. 2007); Acadia Insurance Co. v. American Crushing & Recycling, LLC, 475 F. Supp.2d 168 (D. Conn. 2007).

Third Circuit: Travelers Personal Insurance Co. v. Estate of Parzych, 675 F. Supp.2d 505 (E.D. Pa. 2009); Transamerican Office Furniture v. Travelers Property & Casualty Insurance Co., 222 F. Supp.2d 689 (E.D. Pa. 2002).

Fourth Circuit: Factory Mutual Insurance Co. v. Liberty Mutual Insurance Co., 518 F. Supp.2d 803 (W.D. Va. 2007).

Fifth Circuit: Little v. USAA Casualty Insurance Co., 655 F. Supp.2d 625 (W.D. La. 2009); Buente v. Allstate Insurance Co., 422 F. Supp.2d 690 (S.D. Miss. 2006).

Sixth Circuit: Tooling, Manufacturing and Technologies Association v. Hartford Fire Insurance Co., 2012 WL 3931802 (6th Cir. Sep. 11, 2012); Southeast Mental Health Center, Inc. v. Pacific Insurance Co., 439 F. Supp.2d 831 (W.D. Tenn. 2006).

Seventh Circuit: St. Paul Travelers Companies, Inc. v. Corn Island Shipyard, Inc., 495 F.3d 376 (7th Cir. 2007); Nichols v. National Union Fire Insurance Co. of Pittsburgh, Pennsylvania, 509 F. Supp.2d 752 (W.D. Wis. 2007).

Eighth Circuit: Missouri Bank and Trust Company of Kansas City v. OneBeacon Insurance Co., 688 F.3d 943 (8th Cir. 2012); Tinucci v. Allstate Insurance Co., 487 F. Supp.2d 1058 (D. Minn. 2007); Carlson Marketing Group, Inc. v. Royal Indemnity Co., 517 F. Supp.2d 1089 (D. Minn. 2007).

Ninth Circuit: United Guaranty Mortgage Indemnity Co. v. Countrywide Financial Corp., 660 F. Supp.2d 1163 (C.D. Cal. 2009); Executive Risk Indemnity, Inc. v. Pacific Educational Services, Inc., 451 F. Supp.2d 1147 (D. Haw. 2006).

Tenth Circuit: Zurich North America v. Matrix Service, Inc., 426 F.3d 1281 (10th Cir. 2005); Farmers Alliance Mutual Insurance Co. v. Cutrone, 448 F. Supp.2d 1226 (D. Colo. 2006).

Eleventh Circuit: Rolyn Companies, Inc. v. R & J Sales of Texas, Inc., 671 F. Supp.2d 1314 (S.D. Fla. 2009); Fabricant v. Kemper Independence Insurance Co., 474 F. Supp.2d 1328 (S.D. Fla. 2007); Essex Insurance Co. v. H & H Land Development Corp., 2007 WL 4225665 (M.D. Ga. Nov. 14, 2007).

District of Columbia Circuit: Ross v. Continental Casualty Co., 420 B.R. 43 (D.D.C. 2009).

State Courts:

Alabama: Lambert v. Coregis Insurance Co., 2006 WL 2089921 (Ala. July 28, 2006).

Arkansas: Parker v. Southern Farm Bureau Casualty Insurance Co., 104 Ark. App. 301, 292 S.W.3d 311 (2009).

California: Federal Insurance Co. v. Steadfast Insurance Co., 2012 WL 4336237 (Cal. App. Sep. 24, 2012); American International Underwriters Insurance Co. v. American Guarantee and Liability Insurance Co., 181 Cal. App.4th 616, 105 Cal. Rptr.3d 64 (2010); London Market Insurers v. Superior Court, 146 Cal. App.4th 648, 53 Cal. Rptr.3d 154 (2007); O'Hanesian v. State Farm Mutual Automobile Insurance Co., 52 Cal. Rptr.3d 463 (Cal. App. 2006).

Colorado: Hoang v. Assurance Company of America, 149 P.3d 798 (Colo. 2007).

Connecticut: Enviro Express, Inc. v. AIU Insurance Co., 901 A.2d 666 (Conn. 2006).

Delaware: Intel Corp. v. American Guarantee and Liability Insurance Co., 2012 WL 3889138 (Del. Sept. 7, 2012).

Florida: American Strategic Insurance Co. v. Lucas-Solomon, 927 So.2d 184 (Fla. Dist. App.), *review denied* 940 So.2d 1125 (Fla. 2006).

Georgia: Trinity Outdoor, L.L.C. v. Central Mutual Insurance Co., 285 Ga. 583, 679 S.E.2d 10 (2009); Murphy v. Ticor Title Insurance Co., 316 Ga. App. 97, 729 S.E.2d 21 (2012); Those Certain Underwriters at Lloyds London v. DTI Logistics, Inc., 300 Ga. App. 715, 686 S.E.2d 333 (2009); RLI Insurance Co. v. Highlands on Ponce, LLC, 635 S.E.2d 168 (Ga. App. 2006).

Hawaii: Tri-S Corp. v. Western World Insurance Co., 135 P.3d 82 (Haw. 2006).

Illinois: Baxter International, Inc. v. American Guarantee & Liability Insurance Co., 369 Ill. App.3d 700, 308 Ill. Dec. 198, 861 N.E.2d 263 (2006).

Indiana: P.R. Mallory & Co., Inc. v. American Cas. Co. of Reading, PA., 920 N.E.2d 736 (Ind. App. 2010); Citizens Insurance Co. v. Ganschow, 859 N.E.2d 786 (Ind. App. 2007).

Iowa: Jones v. State Farm Mutual Automobile Insurance Co., 760 N.W.2d 186 (Iowa 2008).

Kansas: Ochs v. Federated Mutual Insurance Co., 43 Kan. App.2d 127, 221 P.3d 622 (2010).

Louisiana: Samuels v. State Farm Mutual Automobile Insurance Co., 939 So.2d 1235 (La. 2006).

Maryland: Harleysville Mutual Insurance Co. v. Zelinski, 899 A.2d 835 (Md. 2006).

Massachusetts: Boston Gas Co. v. Century Indemnity Co., 454 Mass. 337, 910 N.E.2d 290 (2009); Commerce Insurance Co. v. Blackburn, 81 Mass. App. Ct. 519, 964 N.E.2d 1005 (2012).

Michigan: Rory v. Continental Insurance Co., 703 N.W.2d 23 (Mich. 2005).

Minnesota: Farmers Insurance Exchange v. Letellier, 820 N.W.2d 597 (Minn. App. 2012); Metropolitan Property & Casualty Insurance Co. v. Jablonske, 722 N.W.2d 319 (Minn. App. 2006).

Missouri: Penn-America Insurance Co. v. The Bar, Inc., 201 S.W.3d 91 (Mo. App. 2006).

Nebraska: Rickerl v. Farmers Insurance Exchange, 277 Neb. 446, 763 N.W.2d 86 (2009).

New Hampshire: Brown v. Concord Group Insurance Co., 163 N.H. 522, 44 A.3d 586 (2012); Tech-Built 153, Inc. v. Virginia Surety Co., 898 A.2d 1007 (N.H. 2006).

New Jersey: Wakefern Food Corp. v. Liberty Mutual Fire Insurance Co., 406 N.J. Super. 524, 968 A.2d 724 (2009).

New York: Nautilus Insurance Co. v. Matthew David Events, Ltd., 69 A.D.3d 457, 893 N.Y.S.2d 529 (N.Y. App. Div. 2010); Jahier v. Liberty Mutual Group, 64 A.D.3d 683, 883 N.Y.S.2d 283 (N.Y. App. Div. 2009).

North Carolina: Builders Mutual Insurance Co. v. Glascarr Properties, Inc., 688 S.E.2d 508 (N.C. App. 2010); Trophy Tracks, Inc. v. Massachusetts Bay Insurance Co., 195 N.C. App. 734, 673 S.E.2d 787 (2009).

Ohio: Auto-Owners Insurance Co. v. Merillat, 854 N.E.2d 513 (Ohio App. 2006).

Oklahoma: May v. Mid-Century Insurance Co., 151 P.3d 132 (Okla. 2006).

Oregon: Rhiner v. Red Shield Insurance Co., 208 P.3d 1043 (Or. App. 2009).

Pennsylvania: Bishops, Inc. v. Penn National Insurance Co., 984 A.2d 982 (Pa. Super. 2009).

Rhode Island: Progressive Northern Insurance Co. v. Lyden, 981 A.2d 231 (R.I. 2010); Children's Friend & Service v. St. Paul Fire & Marine Insurance Co., 893 A.2d 222 (R.I. 2006).

South Carolina: South Carolina Farm Bureau Mutual Insurance Co. v. Dawsey, 638 S.E.2d 103 (S.C. App. 2006).

South Dakota: Cole v. Wellmark of South Dakota, Inc., 776 N.W.2d 240 (S.D. 2009).

Texas: Progressive County Mutual Insurance Co. v. Kelley, 284 S.W.3d 805 (Tex. 2009); Johnson v. State Farm Lloyds, 204 S.W.3d 897 (Tex. App. 2006).

Utah: Bear River Mutual Insurance Co. v. Williams, 153 P.3d 798 (Utah App. 2006).

Washington: Ki Sin Kim v. Allstate Insurance Co., 153 Wash. App. 339, 223 P.3d 1180 (2009); State Farm Fire & Casualty Co. v. Parrella, 141 P.3d 643 (Wash. App. 2006).

West Virginia: Wrenn v. West Virginia Department of Transportation, Division of Highways, 224 W.Va. 424,686 S.E.2d 75 (2009); Blake v. State Farm Mutual Automobile Insurance Co., 224 W.Va. 317, 685 S.E.2d 895 (2009).

Wisconsin: Froedtert Memorial Lutheran Hospital v. National States Insurance Co., 317 Wis.2d 54, 765 N.W.2d 251 (2009); Marnholtz v. Church Mutual Insurance Co., 341 Wis.2d 478, 815 N.W.2d 708 (2012); *In re* Estate of Anderson, 720 N.W.2d 124 (Wis. App. 2006).

[10] See:

First Circuit: First Specialty Insurance Corp. v. Maine Coast Marine Construction, Inc., 2008 WL 176157 (D. Me. Jan. 18, 2008); Emhart Industries, Inc. v. Home Insurance Co., 515 F. Supp.2d 228 (D.R.I. 2007).

Second Circuit: Alamia v. Nationwide Mutual Fire Insurance Co., 495 F. Supp.2d 362 (S.D.N.Y. 2007).

Third Circuit: Liberty Mutual Insurance Co. v. Sweeney, 689 F.3d 288 (3d Cir. 2012); Post v. St. Paul Travelers Insurance Co., 691 F.3d 500 (3d Cir. 2012); Canal Insurance Co. v. Underwriters at Lloyd's, London, 435 F.3d 431 (3d Cir. 2006); Travelers Personal Insurance Co. v. Estate of Parzych, 675 F. Supp.2d 505 (E.D. Pa. 2009); Schneider v. UNUM Life Insurance Co., 149 F. Supp.2d 169 (E.D. Pa. 2001); Quinney v. American Modern Home Insurance Co., 145 F. Supp.2d 603 (M.D. Pa. 2001).

Fourth Circuit: Studio Frames Ltd. v. Standard Fire Insurance Co., 483 F.3d 239 (4th Cir. 2007); Factory Mutual Insurance Co. v. Liberty Mutual Insurance Co., 518 F. Supp.2d 803 (W.D. Va. 2007).

Fifth Circuit: Federal Insurance Co. v. CompUSA, Inc., 319 F.3d 746 (5th Cir. 2003); Little v. USAA Casualty Insurance Co., 655 F. Supp.2d 625 (W.D. La. 2009).

Sixth Circuit: Continental Casualty Co. v. Law Offices of Melbourne Mills, Jr., P.L.L.C., 676 F.3d 534 (6th Cir. 2012); Florists' Mutual Insurance Co. v. Ludy Greenhouse Manufacturing Corp., 521 F. Supp.2d 661 (S.D. Ohio. 2007).

Seventh Circuit: First National Bank of Manitowoc v. Cincinnati Insurance Co., 485 F.3d 971 (7th Cir. 2007); Nichols v. National Union Fire Insurance Co. of Pittsburgh, Pennsylvania, 509 F. Supp.2d 752 (W.D. Wis. 2007); St. Paul Fire & Marine Insurance Co. v. CSX Transportation, Inc., 502 F. Supp.2d 792 (C.D. Ill. 2007).

Eighth Circuit: Missouri Bank and Trust Company of Kansas City v. OneBeacon Insurance Co., 688 F.3d 943 (8th Cir. 2012).

Ninth Circuit: Tamarack Capital, LLC v. Access Healthsource, Inc., 91 Fed. Appx. 551 (9th Cir. 2004); United Guaranty Mortgage Indemnity Co. v. Countrywide Financial Corp., 660 F. Supp.2d 1163 (C.D. Cal. 2009); Clarendon National Insurance Co. v. Insurance Company of the West, 442 F. Supp.2d 914 (E.D. Cal. 2006); Hanson v. Employers Mutual Casualty Co., 336 F. Supp.2d 1070 (D. Mont. 2004).

Tenth Circuit: Western World Insurance Co. v. Markel American Insurance Co., 677 F.3d 1266 (10th Cir. 2012); Bonham v. Indemnity Insurance Co. of North America, 507 F. Supp.2d 1196 (D.N.M. 2007); Farmers Alliance Mutual Insurance Co. v. Cutrone, 448 F. Supp.2d 1226 (D. Colo. 2006).

Eleventh Circuit: Rolyn Companies, Inc. v. R & J Sales of Texas, Inc., 671 F. Supp.2d 1314, (S.D. Fla. 2009); *In re* Health South Corp., 308 F. Supp.2d 1252 (N.D. Ala. 2004); Neiman v. Provident Life & Accident Insurance Co., 217 F. Supp.2d 1281 (S.D. Fla. 2002).

District of Columbia Circuit: Hartford Accident & Indemnity Co. v. Pro-Football, Inc., 127 F.3d 1111 (D.C. Cir. 1997), *cert. denied* 523 U.S. 1077 (1998); Ross v. Continental Casualty Co., 420 B.R. 43 (D.D.C. 2009).

State Courts:

Arkansas: Lewis v. Mid-Century Insurance Co., 210 S.W.3d 113 (Ark. 2005); Parker v. Southern Farm Bureau Casualty Insurance Co., 104 Ark. App. 301, 292 S.W.3d 311 (2009); Anderson Gas & Propane, Inc. v. Westport Insurance Corp., 140 S.W.3d 504 (Ark. App. 2004).

California: American International Underwriters Insurance Co. v. American Guarantee and Liability Insurance Co., 181 Cal. App.4th 616, 105 Cal. Rptr.3d 64 (2010).

Colorado: Thompson v. Maryland Casualty Co., 84 P.3d 496 (Colo. 2004).

Connecticut: Peerless Insurance Co. v. Gonzalez, 697 A.2d 680 (Conn. 1997); New London County Mutual Insurance Co. v. Bialobrodec, 137 Conn. App. 474, 48 A.3d 742 (2012).

Delaware: State Farm Mutual Automobile Insurance Co. v. Clarendon National Insurance Co., 604 A.2d 384 (Del. 1992).

Florida: Griffin v. American General Life & Accident Insurance Co., 752 So.2d 621 (Fla. Dist. App. 1999), *review denied* 770 So.2d 156 (Fla. 2000).

Georgia: Trinity Outdoor, L.L.C. v. Central Mutual Insurance Co., 285 Ga. 583, 679 S.E.2d 10 (2009); Murphy v. Ticor Title Insurance Co., 316 Ga. App. 97, 729 S.E.2d 21 (2012); Those Certain Underwriters at Lloyds London v. DTI Logistics, Inc., 300 Ga. App. 715, 686 S.E.2d 333 (2009); Fidelity National Title Insurance Co. v. OHIC Insurance Co., 619 S.E.2d 704 (Ga. App. 2005).

Hawaii: Enoka v. AIG Hawaii Insurance Co., 128 P.3d 850 (Haw. 2006).

Idaho: Treasure Valley Transit v. Philadelphia Indemnity Insurance Co., 88 P.3d 744 (Idaho 2004).

Illinois: Golden Rule Insurance Co. v. Schwartz, 786 N.E.2d 1010 (Ill. 2003); Norris v. National Union Fire Insurance Co., 368 Ill.App.3d 576, 306 Ill. Dec. 460, 857 N.E.2d 859 (Ill. 2006), *appeal denied* 862 N.E.2d 235 (Ill. 2007).

Indiana: Peabody Energy Corp. v. Roark, 973 N.E.2d 636 (Ind. App. 2012); P.R. Mallory & Co., Inc. v. American Cas. Co. of Reading, PA., 920 N.E.2d 736 (Ind. App. 2010); Gheae v. Founders Insurance Co., 854 N.E.2d 419 (Ind. App. 2006).

Iowa: Jones v. State Farm Mutual Automobile Insurance Co., 760 N.W.2d 186 (Iowa 2008); Lee v. Grinnell Mutual Reinsurance Co., 646 N.W.2d 403 (Iowa 2002).

Kansas: Ochs v. Federated Mutual Insurance Co., 43 Kan. App.2d 127, 221 P.3d 622 (2010); Richert v. McHone, 135 P.3d 767 (Kan. App. 2006).

Kentucky: Kentucky Association of Counties All Lines Fund Trust v. McClendon, 157 S.W.3d 626 (Ky. 2005); York v. Kentucky Farm Bureau Mutual Insurance Co., 156 S.W.3d 291 (Ky. 2005).

Louisiana: Bonin v. Westport Insurance Co., 930 So.2d 906 (La. 2006); Guidry v. Lee Consulting Engineering, Inc., 945 So.2d 785 (La. App. 2006).

Maryland: Harleysville Mutual Insurance Co. v. Zelinski, 899 A.2d 835 (Md. 2006); Kurtz v. Erie Insurance Exchange, 849 A.2d 1050 (Md. Spec. App. 2004).

Massachusetts: Boston Gas Co. v. Century Indemnity Co., 454 Mass. 337, 910 N.E.2d 290 (2009); Santos v. Lumbermens Mutual Casualty Co., 556 N.E.2d 983 (Mass. 1990).

Michigan: Cruz v. State Farm Mutual Automobile Insurance Co., 648 N.W.2d 591 (Mich. 2002); Amerisure Insurance Co. v. Graff Chevrolet, Inc., 669 N.W.2d 304 (Mich. App. 2003), *rev'd on other grounds* 674 N.W.2d 379 (Mich. 2004).

Minnesota: Travelers Indemnity Co. v. Bloomington Steel & Supply Co., 718 N.W.2d 888 (Minn. 2006); Kelly v. State Farm Mutual Automobile Insurance Co., 666 N.W.2d 328 (Minn. 2003); Farmers Insurance Exchange v. Letellier, 820 N.W.2d 597 (Minn. App. 2012).

Mississippi: Hankins v. Maryland Casualty Co./Zurich American Insurance Co., 2012 WL 4711437 (Miss. Oct. 4, 2012); Titan Indemnity Co. v. American Justice Insurance Reciprocal, 758 So.2d 1037 (Miss. App. 2000).

Missouri: Williams v. National Casualty Co., 132 S.W.3d 244 (Mo. 2004); Grissom v. First National Insurance Agency, 371 S.W.3d 869 (Mo. App. 2012).

Montana: Hardy v. Progressive Specialty Insurance Co., 67 P.3d 892 (Mont. 2003).

Nebraska: Rickerl v. Farmers Insurance Exchange, 277 Neb. 446, 763 N.W.2d 86 (2009); Poulton v. State Farm Fire & Casualty Cos., 675 N.W.2d 665 (Neb. 2004); Mefferd v. Sieler & Co., 676 N.W.2d 22 (Neb. 2004).

New Hampshire: Bertolami v. Merchants Mutual Insurance Co., 414 A.2d 1281 (N.H. 1980).

New Jersey: Gibson v. Callaghan, 730 A.2d 1278 (N.J. 1999); Wakefern Food Corp. v. Liberty Mutual Fire Insurance Co., 406 N.J. Super. 524, 968 A.2d 724 (2009); Hampton Medical Group, P.A. v. Princeton Insurance Co., 840 A.2d 915 (N.J. Super. App. Div. 2004); MetLife Automobile & Home Insurance Co. v. Palmer, 839 A.2d 83 (N.J. Super. App. Div. 2004).

New Mexico: United Nuclear Corp. v. Allstate Insurance Co., 285 P.3d 644 (N.M. 2012); State Farm Mutual Automobile Insurance Co. v. Luebbers, 119 P.3d 169 (N.M. App. 2005).

New York: Nautilus Insurance Co. v. Matthew David Events, Ltd., 69 A.D.3d 457, 893 N.Y.S.2d 529 (N.Y. App. Div. 2010); Jahier v. Liberty Mutual Group, 64 A.D.3d 683, 883 N.Y.S.2d 283 (N.Y. App. Div. 2009); Steven S. v. GHI, 787 N.Y.S.2d 828 (N.Y. Civ. 2004).

North Carolina: Builders Mutual Insurance Co. v. Glascarr Properties, Inc., 688 S.E.2d 508 (N.C. App. 2010); Trophy Tracks, Inc. v. Massachusetts Bay Insurance Co., 673 S.E.2d 787 (N.C. App. 2009).

Ohio: Scott-Pontzer v. Liberty Mutual Fire Insurance Co., 710 N.E.2d 1116 (Ohio 1999); Grange Mutual Casualty Co. v. Rosko, 767 N.E.2d 1225 (Ohio App. 2001).

Oklahoma: Hoar v. Aetna Casualty & Surety Co., 968 P.2d 1219 (Okla. 1998); Baldridge v. Kirkpatrick, 63 P.3d 568 (Okla. Civ. App. 2002).

Oregon: Fleming v. United Services Automobile Ass'n, 996 P.2d 501 (Or. 2000); Rhiner v. Red Shield Insurance Co., 228 Or. App. 588, 208 P.3d 1043 (2009).

Pennsylvania: Central Dauphin School District v. American Casualty Co., 426 A.2d 94 (Pa. 1981); Bishops, Inc. v. Penn National Insurance Co., 984 A.2d 982 (Pa. Super. 2009).

Rhode Island: New London County Mutual Insurance Co. v. Fontaine, 45 A.3d 551 (R.I. 2012); Progressive Northern Insurance Co. v. Lyden, 981 A.2d 231 (R.I. 2010); Mendez v. Brites, 849 A.2d 329 (R.I. 2004).

South Carolina: B.L.G. Enterprises, Inc. v. First Financial Insurance Co., 514 S.E.2d 327 (S.C. 1999); United Services Automobile Ass'n v. Markosky, 530 S.E.2d 660 (S.C. App. 2000); South Carolina Farm Bureau Mutual Insurance Co. v. Dawsey, 638 S.E.2d 103 (S.C. App. 2006).

South Dakota: Cole v. Wellmark of South Dakota, Inc., 776 N.W.2d 240 (S.D. 2009); Phen v. Progressive Northern Insurance Co., 672 N.W.2d 52 (S.D. 2003).

Tennessee: Merrimack Mutual & Fire Insurance Co. v. Batts, 59 S.W.3d 142 (Tenn. App. 2001).

Texas: Progressive County Mutual Insurance Co. v. Kelley, 284 S.W.3d 805 (Tex. 2009); SA-OMAX 2007, L.P. v. Certain Underwriters at Lloyd's, London, 374 S.W.3d 594 (Tex. App. 2012); Tankersley v. Durish, 855 S.W.2d 241 (Tex. App. 1993).

Utah: Surety Underwriters v. E & C Trucking, Inc., 10 P.3d 338 (Utah 2000).

Vermont: State Farm Mutual Automobile Insurance Co. v. Powers, 732 A.2d 730 (Vt. 1999).

Virginia: National Housing Building Corp. v. Acordia of Virginia Insurance Agency, Inc., 591 S.E.2d 88 (Va. 2004); Dairyland Insurance Co. v. Douthat, 449 S.E.2d 799 (Va. 1994).

Washington: New Hampshire Indemnity Co. v. Budget Rent-A-Car Systems, Inc., 64 P.3d 1239 (Wash. 2003); Ki Sin Kim v. Allstate Insurance Co., 153 Wash. App. 339, 223 P.3d 1180 (2009).

West Virginia: Wrenn v. West Virginia Department of Transportation, Division of Highways, 224 W.Va. 424, 686 S.E.2d 75 (2009); Blake v. State Farm Mutual Automobile Insurance Co., 224 W.Va. 317, 685 S.E.2d 895 (2009); Bender v. Glendenning, 632 S.E.2d 330 (W. Va. 2006).

Wisconsin: Froedtert Memorial Lutheran Hospital v. National States Insurance Co., 317 Wis.2d 54, 765 N.W.2d 251 (2009); Mullenberg v. Kilgust Mechanical, Inc., 612 N.W.2d 327 (Wis. 2000); Blazekovic v. City of Milwaukee, 610 N.W.2d 467 (Wis. 2000).

Wyoming: Cathcart v. State Farm Mutual Automobile Insurance Co., 123 P.3d 579 (Wyo. 2005).

11 *Id.*

12 See:

First Circuit: Specialty National Insurance Co. v. OneBeacon Insurance Co., 486 F.3d 727 (1st Cir. 2007); Demers Brothers Trucking, Inc. v. Certain Underwriters at Lloyd's, London, Subscribing to Certificate Number SRS IM MA 04-124, 600 F. Supp.2d 265 (D. Mass. 2009); GE HFS Holdings, Inc. v. National Union Fire Insurance Co. of Pittsburgh, Pennsylvania, 520 F. Supp.2d 213 (D. Mass. 2007); Padilla v. Triple-S, Inc., 500 F. Supp.2d 43 (D.P.R. 2007).

Second Circuit: Macey v. Carolina Casualty Insurance Co., 674 F.3d 125 (2d Cir. 2012); SR International Business Insurance Co., Ltd. v. World Trade Center Properties, LLC, 467 F.3d 107 (2d Cir. 2006); RSUI Indemnity Co. v. RCG Group (USA), 2012 WL 3100636 (S.D.N.Y. July 31, 2012); SCW West L.L.C. v. Westport Insurance Corp., 856 F. Supp.2d 514 (E.D.N.Y. 2012); Empire Fire and Marine Insurance Co. v. Lang, 655 F. Supp.2d 150 (D. Conn. 2009); Drake v. Town of Mansfield, 652 F. Supp.2d 236 (D. Conn. 2009).

Third Circuit: Liberty Mutual Insurance Co. v. Sweeney, 689 F.3d 288 (3d Cir. 2012); Regents of Mercersburg College v. Republic Franklin Insurance Co., 458 F.3d 159 (3d Cir. 2006); Federal Insurance Co. v. KDW Restructuring and Liquidation Services, L.L.C., 2012 WL 3579840 (M.D. Pa. Aug. 17, 2012); New Hampshire Insurance Co. v. Diller, 678 F. Supp.2d 288 (D.N.J. 2009); Baughman v. United States Liability Insurance Co., 662 F. Supp.2d 386 (D.N.J. 2009); Continental Insurance Co. v. Davis, 56 F. Supp.2d 513, 516 (E.D. Pa. 1999), *aff'd* 216 F.3d 1075 (3d Cir. 2000).

Fourth Circuit: Dooley v. Hartford Accident and Indemnity Co., 2012 WL 2370115 (W.D. Va. June 22, 2012); White v. American General Life Insurance Co., 651 F. Supp.2d 530 (S.D. W. Va. 2009); Bohreer v. Erie Insurance Group, 475 F. Supp.2d 578 (E.D. Va. 2007).

Fifth Circuit: Looney Ricks Kiss Architects, Inc. v. State Farm Fire and Casualty Co., 677 F.3d 250 (5th Cir. 2012); *In re* TransTexas Gas Corp., 597 F.3d 298 (5th Cir. 2010); *In re* Katrina Canal Breaches Consolidated Litigation, 466 F. Supp.2d 729 (E.D. La. 2006).

Sixth Circuit: Continental Casualty Co. v. Law Offices of Melbourne Mills, Jr., P.L.L.C., 676 F.3d 534 (6th Cir. 2012); Florists' Mutual Insurance Co. v. Ludy Greenhouse Manufacturing Corp., 521 F. Supp.2d 661 (S.D. Ohio. 2007); Comerica Inc. v. Zurich American Insurance Co., 498 F. Supp.2d 1019 (E.D. Mich. 2007).

Seventh Circuit: Grinnell Mutual Reinsurance Co. v. Haight, 2012 WL 4372520 (7th Cir. Sept. 26, 2012); Jonathan Pepper Co. v. Hartford Casualty Insurance Co., 520 F. Supp.2d 977 (N.D. Ill. 2007).

Eighth Circuit: Heacker v. Safeco Insurance Company of America, 676 F.3d 724 (8th Cir. 2012); J.E. Jones Construction Co. v. Chubb & Sons, Inc., 486 F.3d 337 (8th Cir. 2007); Westchester Fire Insurance Co. v. Wallerich, 2007 WL 2821656 (D. Minn. Sept. 25, 2007).

Ninth Circuit: Caliber One Indemnity Co. v. Wade Cook Financial Corp., 491 F.3d 1079 (9th Cir. 2007); Tri-Star Theme Builders, Inc./PCL Construction Services, Inc. v. Hawkeye-Security Insurance Co., 653 F. Supp.2d 973 (D. Ariz. 2009); Apana v. TIG Insurance Co., 504 F. Supp.2d 998 (D. Haw. 2007); Sciranko v. Fidelity & Guaranty Life Insurance Co., 503 F. Supp.2d 1293 (D. Ariz. 2007).

Tenth Circuit: Western World Insurance Co. v. Markel American Insurance Co., 677 F.3d 1266 (10th Cir. 2012); Boggs v. Great Northern Insurance Co., 659 F. Supp.2d 1199 (N.D. Okla. 2009); Bonham v. Indemnity Insurance Co. of North America, 507 F. Supp.2d 1196 (D.N.M. 2007).

Eleventh Circuit: Lubin v. Cincinnati Insurance Co., 677 F.3d 1039 (11th Cir. 2012); St. Paul Fire and Marine Insurance Co. v. ERA Oxford Realty Company Greystone, L.L.C., 572 F.3d 893 (11th Cir. 2009); Penzer v. Transportation Insurance Co., 509 F. Supp.2d 1278 (S.D. Fla. 2007).

District of Columbia Circuit: Essex Insurance Co. v. Cafe Dupont, L.L.C., 674 F. Supp.2d 166 (D.D.C. 2009); Ross v. Continental Casualty Co., 420 B.R. 43 (Bankr. D.D.C. 2009); MDB Communications, Inc. v. Hartford Casualty Insurance Co., 479 F. Supp.2d 136 (D.D.C. 2007).

State Courts:

California: Bosetti v. United States Life Insurance Company in City of New York, 175 Cal. App.4th 120, 96 Cal. Rptr.3d 744 (2009); ACS Systems, Inc. v. St. Paul Fire & Marine Insurance Co., 53 Cal. Rptr.3d 786 (Cal. App. 2007).

Colorado: Fire Insurance Exchange v. Sullivan, 224 P.3d 348 (Colo. App. 2009).

Connecticut: Enviro Express, Inc. v. AIU Insurance Co., 901 A.2d 666 (Conn. 2006).

Florida: Allstate Insurance Co. v. Suarez, 833 So.2d 762, 765 (Fla. 2002); Penzer v. Transportation Insurance Co., 29 So.3d 1000 (Fla. 2010).

Georgia: Murphy v. Ticor Title Insurance Co., 316 Ga. App. 97, 729 S.E.2d 21 (2012); Banks v. Brotherhood Mutual Insurance Co., 301 Ga. App. 101, 686 S.E.2d 872 (2009).

Idaho: Armstrong v. Farmers Insurance Company of Idaho, 147 Idaho 67, 205 P.3d 1203 (2009).

Illinois: American Family Mutual Insurance Co. v. Niebuhr, 860 N.E.2d 436 (Ill. App. 2006).

Indiana: Peabody Energy Corp. v. Roark, 973 N.E.2d 636 (Ind. App. 2012).

Iowa: Bituminous Casualty Corp. v. Sand Livestock Systems, Inc., 728 N.W.2d 216 (Iowa 2007).

Kansas: Ochs v. Federated Mutual Insurance Co., 43 Kan. App.2d 127, 221 P.3d 622 (2010).

Louisiana: Robinson Brothers, Inc. v. Carter, 2007 WL 466586 (La. App. Feb. 14, 2007).

Massachusetts: Boston Gas Co. v. Century Indemnity Co., 454 Mass. 337, 910 N.E.2d 290 (2009).

Minnesota: Farmers Insurance Exchange v. Letellier, 820 N.W.2d 597 (Minn. App. 2012); Jarvis and Sons, Inc. v. International Marine Underwriters, 768 N.W.2d 365 (Minn. App. 2009).

Mississippi: Corban v. United Services Automobile Association, 20 So.3d 601 (Miss. 2009).

Missouri: Derousse v. State Farm Mutual Automobile Insurance Co., 298 S.W.3d 891 (Mo. 2009); Rice v. Shelter Mutual Insurance Co., 301 S.W.3d 43 (Mo. 2009); Grissom v. First National Insurance Agency, 371 S.W.3d 869 (Mo. App. 2012); Penn Star Insurance Co. v. Griffey, 306 S.W.3d 591 (Mo. App. 2010).

Montana: United National Insurance Co. v. St. Paul Fire and Marine Insurance Co., 352 Mont. 105, 214 P.3d 1260 (2009).

Nebraska: Peterson v. Ohio Casualty Group, 724 N.W.2d 765 (Neb. 2006).

New Jersey: S.T. Hudson Engineers, Inc. v. Pennsylvania National Mutual Casualty Co., 909 A.2d 1156 (N.J. Super. App. Div. 2006).

New Mexico: Truck Insurance Exchange v. Gagnon, 33 P.3d 901, 903 (N.M. App.), *cert. denied* 36 P.3d 953 (N.M. 2001).

New York: Catucci v. Greenwich Insurance Co., 830 NY.S.2d 281 (N.Y. App. Div. 2007).

North Carolina: Builders Mutual Insurance Co. v. Glascarr Properties, Inc., 688 S.E.2d 508 (N.C. App. 2010).

Oregon: Totten v. New York Life Insurance Co., 696 P.2d 1082 (Or. 1985); Gonzales v. Farmers Insurance Company of Oregon, 150 P.3d 20 (Or. App. 2006); Smith v. State Farm Insurance Co., 927 P.2d 111 (Or. App. 1996).

Pennsylvania: Bishops, Inc. v. Penn National Insurance Co., 984 A.2d 982 (Pa. Super. 2009); Burton v. Republic Insurance Co., 845 A.2d 889, 893 (Pa. Super. 2004).

Rhode Island: Derderian v. Essex Insurance Co., 44 A.3d 122 (R.I. 2012); Lynch v. Spirit Rent-A Car, Inc., 965 A.2d 417 (R.I. 2009).

South Carolina: Stringer v. State Farm Mutual Automobile Insurance Co., 386 S.C. 188, 687 S.E.2d 58 (S.C. App. 2009).

Tennessee: Spears v. Tennessee Farmers Mutual Insurance Co., 300 S.W.3d 671 (Tenn. App. 2009).

Texas: SA-OMAX 2007, L.P. v. Certain Underwriters at Lloyd's, London, 374 S.W.3d 594 (Tex. App. 2012); Safeco Lloyds Insurance Co. v. Allstate Insurance Co., 308 S.W.3d 49 (Tex. App. 2009); Hartrick v. Great American Lloyds Insurance Co., 62 S.W.3d 270, 274 (Tex. App. 2001).

Vermont: Mann v. Adventure Quest, Inc., 186 Vt. 14, 974 A.2d 607 (2009).

Virginia: Virginia Farm Bureau Mutual Insurance Co. v. Williams, 278 Va. 75, 677 S.E.2d 299 (2009).

Washington: Ki Sin Kim v. Allstate Insurance Co., 153 Wash. App. 339 (Wash. App. 2009).

West Virginia: Blake v. State Farm Mutual Automobile Insurance Co., 224 W.Va. 317, 685 S.E.2d 895 (2009).

Wisconsin: Bormann v. Sohns, 727 N.W.2d 341 (Wis. App. 2006).

[13] See, e.g.:

Third Circuit: Liberty Mutual Insurance Co. v. Sweeney, 689 F.3d 288 (3d Cir. 2012); American Automobile Insurance Co. v. Murray, 658 F.3d 311 (3d Cir. 2011); Toffler Associates, Inc. v. Hartford Fire Insurance Co., 651 F. Supp.2d 332 (E.D. Pa. 2009); Whole Enchilada, Inc. v. Travelers Property Casualty Company of America, 581 F. Supp.2d 677 (W.D. Pa. 2008); Colony National Insurance Co. v. Hing Wah Chinese Restaurant, 546 F. Supp.2d 202 (E.D. Pa. 2008).

Fourth Circuit: Zurich American Insurance Co. v. Public Storage, 743 F. Supp.2d 525 (E.D. Va. 2010); Sunex International, Inc. v. Travelers Indemnity Company of Illinois, 185 F. Supp.2d 614 (D.S.C. 2001).

Sixth Circuit: Tooling, Manufacturing and Technologies Association v. Hartford Fire Insurance Co., 2012 WL 3931802 (6th Cir. Sept. 11, 2012); Minges Creek, L.L.C. v. Royal Insurance Company of America, 442 F.3d 953 (6th Cir. 2006).

Seventh Circuit: OmniSource Corp. v. NCM Americas, Inc., 313 F. Supp.2d 880 (N.D. Ind. 2004).

Eighth Circuit: Design Professionals Insurance Co. v. Chicago Insurance Co., 454 F.3d 906 (8th Cir. 2006); Mitzan v. Western Heritage Insurance Co., 623 F. Supp.2d 993 (E.D. Mo. 2009).

Ninth Circuit: California Dairies Inc. v. RSUI Indemnity Co., 617 F. Supp.2d 1023 (E.D. Cal. 2009).

Tenth Circuit: Cyprus Plateau Mining Corp. v. Commonwealth Insurance Co., 972 F. Supp. 1379 (D. Utah 1997); Metro Wastewater Reclamation District v. Continental Casualty Co., 834 F. Supp. 1254 (D. Colo. 1993).

Eleventh Circuit: York Insurance Co. v. Williams Seafood of Albany, Inc., 223 F.3d 1253 (11th Cir. 2000); General Fidelity Insurance Co. v. Foster, 808 F. Supp.2d 1315 (S.D. Fla. 2011); Essex Insurance Co. v. Zota, 607 F. Supp.2d 1340 (S.D. Fla. 2009).

State Courts:

Alabama: Carpet Installation and Supplies of Glenco v. Alfa Mutual Insurance Co., 628 So.2d 560 (Ala. 1993).

California: Baker v. National Interstate Insurance Co., 180 Cal. App.4th 1319, 103 Cal. Rptr.3d 565 (2009). But see, MacKinnon v. Truck Insurance Exchange, 31 Cal.4th 635, 73 P.3d 1205, 3 Cal. Rptr.3d 228 (2003) (noting that although various dictionary definitions are useful, they do not necessarily define the ordinary and popular sense of the word if they disregard the policy's context).

Colorado: Compass Insurance Co. v. City of Littleton, 984 P.2d 606 (Colo. 1999); Miller v. Hartford Casualty Insurance Co., 160 P.3d 408 (Colo. App. 2007).

Delaware: Liggett Group, Inc. v. Ace Property and Casualty Insurance Co., 798 A.2d 1024 (Del. 2002).

Florida: Penzer v. Transportation Insurance Co., 29 So.3d 1000 (Fla. 2010); Garcia v. Federal Insurance Co., 969 So.2d 288 (Fla. 2007); Barcelona Hotel, L.L.C. v. Nova Casualty Co., 57 So.3d 228 (Fla. App. 2011).

Georgia: State Farm Fire and Casualty Co. v. Bauman, 313 Ga. App. 771, 723 S.E.2d 1 (2012); Banks v. Brotherhood Mutual Insurance Co., 301 Ga. App. 101, 686 S.E.2d 872 (2009).

Illinois: Valley Forge Insurance Co. v. Swiderski Electronics, Inc., 223 Ill.2d 352, 860 N.E.2d 307, 307 Ill. Dec. 653 (2006).

Iowa: LeMars Mutual Insurance Co. v. Joffer, 574 N.W.2d 303 (Iowa 1998).

Maryland: Fister *ex rel.* Estate of Fister v. Allstate Life Insurance Co., 366 Md. 201, 783 A.2d 194 (Md. 2001).

Massachusetts: Citation Insurance Co. v. Gomez, 426 Mass. 379, 688 N.E.2d 951 (1998).

Michigan: Citizens Insurance Co. v. Pro-Seal Service Group, Inc., 477 Mich. 75, 730 N.W.2d 682 (2007); Pugh v. Zefi, 294 Mich. App. 393, 812 N.W.2d 789 (2011); Vushaj v. Farm Bureau General Insurance Company of Michigan, 284 Mich. App. 513, 773 N.W.2d 758 (2009).

Missouri: Foremost Signature Insurance Co. v. Montgomery, 266 S.W.3d 868 (Mo. App. 2008).

New Hampshire: Progressive Northern Insurance Co. v. Concord General Mutual Insurance Co., 151 N.H. 649, 864 A.2d 368 (2005).

New Jersey: Boddy v. Cigna Property and Casualty Companies, 334 N.J. Super. 649, 760 A.2d 823 (N.J. Super. App. Div. 2000).

New Mexico: United Nuclear Corp. v. Allstate Insurance Co., 285 P.3d 644 (N.M. 2012); Davis v. Farmers Insurance Company of Arizona, 140 N.M. 249, 142 P.3d 17 (N.M. App. 2006).

North Carolina: Herring v. Liner, 163 N.C. App. 534, 594 S.E.2d 117 (2004).

North Dakota: Center Mutual Insurance Co. v. Thompson, 618 N.W.2d 505 (N.D. 2000).

Ohio: Stiriz v. Motorists Mutual Insurance Co., 2002 WL 479826 (Ohio App. Mar. 29, 2002).

Oregon: Ortiz v. State Farm Fire and Casualty Co., 244 Or. App. 355, 260 P.3d 678 (2011).

Pennsylvania: Kvaerner Metals Division of Kvaerner U.S., Inc. v. Commercial Union Insurance Co., 589 Pa. 317, 908 A.2d 888 (2006); Wolfson v. Medical Care Availability and Reduction of Error Fund, 39 A.3d 551 (Pa. Commw. 2012); Allstate Fire and Casualty Insurance Co. v. Hymes, 29 A.3d 1169 (Pa. Super. 2011); Erie Insurance Exchange v. E.L. *ex rel.* Lowry, 941 A.2d 1270 (Pa. Super. 2008); Wall Rose Mutual Insurance Co. v. Manross, 939 A.2d 958 (Pa. Super. 2007).

South Carolina: Hutchinson v. Liberty Life Insurance Co., 393 S.C. 19, 709 S.E.2d 130 (S.C. App. 2011).

Texas: Certain Underwriters at Lloyd's Subscribing to Policy No. WDO-10000 v. KKM Inc., 215 S.W.3d 486 (Tex. App. 2006).

Washington: No Boundaries, Ltd. v. Pacific Indemnity Co., 160 Wash. App. 951, 249 P.3d 689 (2011); State Farm Fire and Casualty Co. v. Ham & Rye, L.L.C., 142 Wash. App. 6, 174 P.3d 1175 (2007).

Wisconsin: Stuart v. Weisflog's Showroom Gallery, Inc., 311 Wis.2d 492, 753 N.W.2d 448 (2008); Marnholtz v. Church Mutual Insurance Co., 341 Wis.2d 478, 815 N.W.2d 708 (2012); Zarder v. Humana Insurance Co., 316 Wis.2d 573, 765 N.W.2d 839 (Wis. App. 2009).

[14] See, e.g.:

First Circuit: Wright-Ryan Construction, Inc. v. AIG Insurance Company of Canada, 647 F.3d 411 (1st Cir. 2011); Medical Mutual Insurance Company of Maine v. Indian Harbor Insurance Co., 583 F.3d 57 (1st Cir. 2009).

Second Circuit: Champion International. Corp. v. Continental Casualty Co., 546 F.2d 502 (2d Cir. 1976).

Third Circuit: J.C. Penney Life Insurance Co. v. Pilosi, 393 F.3d 356 (3d Cir. 2004).

Fourth Circuit: Zurich American Insurance Co. v. Public Storage, 743 F. Supp.2d 525 (E.D. Va. 2010); Geico Insurance Co. v. Larson, 542 F. Supp.2d 441 (E.D.N.C. 2008).

Fifth Circuit: Great American Insurance Co. v. AFS/IBEX Financial Services, Inc., 612 F.3d 800 (5th Cir. 2010); Roland v. Transamerica Life Insurance Co., 570 F. Supp.2d 871 (N.D. Tex. 2008).

Sixth Circuit: Bondex International, Inc. v. Hartford Accident and Indemnity Co., 667 F.3d 669 (6th Cir. 2011); Keely v. Fire Insurance Exchange, 833 F. Supp.2d 722 (E.D. Mich. 2011); Amerisure Mutual Insurance Co. v. Carey Transportation, Inc., 578 F. Supp.2d 888 (W.D. Mich. 2008).

Seventh Circuit: Archer-Daniels-Midland Co. v. Phoenix Assurance Company of New York, 975 F. Supp. 1129 (S.D. Ill. 1997).

Eighth Circuit: Owners Insurance Co. v. European Auto Works, Inc., 2012 WL 4052406 (8th Cir. Sept. 17, 2012); Graybar Electric Co., Inc. v. Federal Insurance Co., 567 F. Supp.2d 1116 (E.D. Mo. 2008).

Ninth Circuit: Alexander Manufacturing, Inc. Employee Stock Ownership Plan and Trust v. Illinois Union Insurance Co., 560 F.3d 984 (9th Cir. 2009); Chartis Specialty Insurance Co. v. Queen Anne HS, L.L.C., 867 F. Supp.2d 1111 (W.D. Wash. 2012); Newmont U.S.A. Ltd. and Dawn Mining Co. v. American Home Assurance Co., 787 F. Supp.2d 1208 (E.D. Wash. 2011); Malbco Holdings, L.L.C. v. AMCO Insurance Co., 629 F. Supp.2d 1185 (D. Or. 2009).

State Courts:

Alabama: St. Paul Fire and Marine Insurance Co. v. Christiansen Marine, Inc., 893 So.2d 1124 (Ala. 2004).

California: Baker v. National Interstate Insurance Co., 180 Cal. App.4th 1319, 103 Cal. Rptr.3d 565 (2009).

Colorado: Continental Western Insurance Co. v. Heritage Estates Mutual Housing Association, 77 P.3d 911 (Colo. App. 2003).

Florida: State Farm Mutual Automobile Insurance Co. v. Menendez, 70 So.3d 566 (Fla. 2011).

Idaho: State Farm Fire and Casualty Co. v. Doe, 130 Idaho 693, 946 P.2d 1333 (*Id.* 1997).

Illinois: American National Fire Insurance Co. v. National Union Fire Insurance Company of Pittsburgh, PA, 343 Ill. App.3d 93, 796 N.E.2d 1133, 277 Ill. Dec. 767 (2003).

Kansas: Ochs v. Federated Mutual Insurance Co., 43 Kan. App.2d 127, 221 P.3d 622 (2010).

Louisiana: McDonald v. American Family Life Assurance Company of Columbus, 70 So.3d 1086 (La. App. 2011); Smith v. Reliance Insurance Company of Illinois, 807 So.2d 1010 (La. App. 2002).

Mississippi: Corban v. United Services Automobile Association, 20 So.3d 601 (Miss. 2009).

Missouri: Wasson v. Shelter Mutual Insurance Co., 358 S.W.3d 113 (Mo. App. 2011); Ulsas v. Progressive Northwestern Insurance Co., 275 S.W.3d 366 (Mo. App. 2009).

Nebraska: Mortgage Express, Inc. v. Tudor Insurance Co., 278 Neb. 449, 771 N.W.2d 137 (2009).

North Carolina: Patel v. Scottsdale Insurance Co., 728 S.E.2d 394 (N.C. App. 2012); Production Systems, Inc. v. Amerisure Insurance Co., 167 N.C. App. 601, 605 S.E.2d 663 (2004).

Oregon: Gonzales v. Farmers Insurance Company of Oregon, 345 Or. 382, 196 P.3d 1 (Or. 2008); Capitol Specialty Insurance Corp. v. Chan & Lui, Inc., 248 Or. App. 674, 274 P.3d 238 (2012); Laird v. Allstate Insurance Co., 232 Or. App. 162, 221 P.3d 780 (2009).

Texas: Evanston Insurance Co. v. Legacy of Life, Inc., 370 S.W.3d 377 (Tex. 2012); Lancer Insurance Co. v. Perez, 308 S.W.3d 35 (Tex. App. 2009); Certain Underwriters at Lloyd's, London Subscribing to Policy Number 509/QF037603 v. LM Ericsson Telefon, AB, 272 S.W.3d 691 (Tex. App. 2008).

Washington: Sauter *ex rel.* Sauter v. Houston Casualty Co., 168 Wash. App. 348, 276 P.3d 358 (2012); S & K Motors, Inc. v. Harco National Insurance Co., 151 Wash. App. 633, 213 P.3d 630 (2009).

[15] See, e.g.:

First Circuit: Medical Mutual Insurance Company of Maine v. Indian Harbor Insurance Co., 583 F.3d 57 (1st Cir. 2009); Fire Insurance Exchange v. Pring-Wilson, 831 F. Supp.2d 493 (D. Mass. 2011); Panagora Asset Management, Inc. v. St. Paul Mercury Insurance, 674 F. Supp.2d 315, (D. Mass. 2009).

Second Circuit: American Automobile Insurance Co. v. Security Income Planners and Co., 847 F. Supp.2d 454 (E.D.N.Y. 2012); U.S. Specialty Insurance Co. v. LeBeau, Inc., 847 F. Supp.2d 500 (W.D.N.Y. 2012); HSB Group, Inc. v. SVB Underwriting, Ltd., 664 F. Supp.2d 158 (D. Conn. 2009).

Third Circuit: New Hampshire Insurance Co. v. Diller, 678 F. Supp.2d 288 (D.N.J. 2009); Allstate Insurance Co. v. Hopfer, 672 F. Supp.2d 682 (E.D. Pa. 2009).

Fourth Circuit: Schwartz & Schwartz of Virginia, L.L.C. v. Certain Underwriters at Lloyd's, London who Subscribed to Policy Number NC959, 677 F. Supp.2d 890 (W.D. Va. 2009).

Fifth Circuit: Martco Limited Partnership v. Wellons, Inc., 588 F.3d 864 (5th Cir. 2009).

Sixth Circuit: United Financial Casualty Co. v. Youth Alive, Inc., 846 F. Supp.2d 760 (W.D. Ky. 2012); Continental Casualty Co. v. Auto Plus Insurance Agency, L.L.C., 676 F. Supp.2d 657 (N.D. Ohio 2009).

Seventh Circuit: Ohio Casualty Insurance Co. v. Herring-Jenkins, 830 F. Supp.2d 566 (N.D. Ind. 2011); Kimmel v. Western Reserve Life Assurance Company of Ohio, 678 F. Supp.2d 783 (N.D. Ind. 2010).

Eighth Circuit: TAMKO Building Products, Inc. v. Factual Mutual Insurance Co., 2012 WL 3596155 (E.D. Mo. Aug. 21, 2012).

Ninth Circuit: Fier v. Unum Life Insurance Co., 629 F.3d 1095 (9th Cir. 2011); Chartis Specialty Insurance Co. v. Queen Anne HS, L.L.C., 867 F. Supp.2d 1111 (W.D. Wash. 2012); Align Technology, Inc. v. Federal Insurance Co., 673 F. Supp.2d 957 (N.D. Cal. 2009).

Tenth Circuit: DISH Network Corp. v. Arch Specialty Insurance Co., 659 F.3d 1010 (10th Cir. 2011).

Eleventh Circuit: Great American Fidelity Insurance Co. v. JWR Construction Services, Inc., 2012 WL 1193848 (S.D. Fla. Apr. 9, 2012).

State Courts:

California: Baker v. National Interstate Insurance Co., 180 Cal. App.4th 1319, 103 Cal. Rptr.3d 565 (2009); American International Underwriters Insurance Co. v. American Guarantee and Liability Insurance Co., 181 Cal. App.4th 616, 105 Cal. Rptr.3d 64 (2010).

Colorado: Bailey v. Lincoln General Insurance Co., 255 P.3d 1039 (Colo. 2011) (*en banc*).

Connecticut: Merrimack Mutual Fire Insurance Co. v. Ramsey, 117 Conn. App. 769, 982 A.2d 195 (2009).

Florida: Penzer v. Transportation Insurance Co., 29 So.3d 1000 (Fla. Jan. 28, 2010); Pompano Motor Co. v. Chrysler Insurance Co., 875 So.2d 754 (Fla. App. 2004).

Illinois: American National Fire Insurance Co. v. National Union Fire Insurance Company of Pittsburgh, PA, 343 Ill. App.3d 93, 796 N.E.2d 1133, 277 Ill. Dec. 767 (2003).

Indiana: State Automobile Mutual Insurance Co. v. Flexdar, Inc., 964 N.E.2d 845 (Ind. 2012); Gasser v. Downing, 967 N.E.2d 1085 (Ind. App. 2012); P.R. Mallory & Co., Inc. v. American Casualty Co. of Reading, PA, 920 N.E.2d 736 (Ind. App. 2010).

Kentucky: Hoskins v. Kentucky Farm Bureau Mutual Insurance Co., 2012 WL 4841094 (Ky. App. Oct. 12, 2012).

Minnesota: West Bend Mutual Insurance Co. v. Allstate Insurance Co., 776 N.W.2d 693 (Minn. 2009).

Mississippi: Corban v. United Services Automobile Association, 20 So.3d 601 (Miss. 2009).

Missouri: Mendenhall v. Property and Casualty Insurance Company of Hartford, 375 S.W.3d 90 (Mo. 2012) (*en banc*).

New York: Federal Insurance Co. v. International Business Machines Corp., 18 N.Y.3d 642, 965 N.E.2d 934, 942 N.Y.S.2d 432 (2012); Christodoulides v. First Unum Life Insurance Co., 96 A.D.3d 1603, 946 N.Y.S.2d 773 (2012); Nautilus Insurance Co. v. Matthew David Events, Ltd., 69 A.D.3d 457, 893 N.Y.S.2d 529 (N.Y. App. Div. 2010).

Oregon: Capitol Specialty Insurance Corp. v. Chan & Lui, Inc., 248 Or. App. 674, 274 P.3d 238 (2012); Laird v. Allstate Insurance Co., 232 Or. App. 162, 221 P.3d 780 (Or. App. 2009).

Rhode Island: New London County Mutual Insurance Co. v. Fontaine, 45 A.3d 551 (R.I. 2012).

South Carolina: Hutchinson v. Liberty Life Insurance Co., 709 S.E.2d 130 (S.C. App. 2011).

South Dakota: Cole v. Wellmark of South Dakota, Inc., 776 N.W.2d 240 (S.D. 2009)

Texas: Lancer Insurance Co. v. Perez, 308 S.W.3d 35 (Tex. App. 2009).

Utah: Lopez v. United Automobile Insurance Co., 274 P.3d 897 (Utah 2012); Doctors' Co. v. Drezga, 218 P.3d 598 (Utah 2009).

Washington: Vision One, L.L.C. v. Philadelphia Indemnity Insurance Co., 174 Wash.2d 501, 276 P.3d 300 (2012) (*en banc*); Sauter *ex rel.* Sauter v. Houston Casualty Co., 168 Wash. App. 348, 276 P.3d 358 (2012).

West Virginia: Wrenn v. West Virginia Department of Transportation, Division of Highways, 224 W.Va. 424, 686 S.E.2d 75 (2009); Blake v. State Farm Mutual Automobile Insurance Co., 224 W.Va. 317, 685 S.E.2d 895 (2009).

16 One such example is the anti-efficient proximate causation clause, which attempted to draft around precedential decisions. A number of mudslide or earth movement decisions in California found coverage existed even though there was an earth movement exclusion. The California decisions rested upon the finding that the efficient proximate cause of the losses was negligence of the builder, architect, or engineer rather than the earth movement itself. Accordingly, the exclusion for earth movement was determined to be inapplicable. Faced with these decisions, insurance companies created an anti-efficient proximate causation clause, which attempted to avoid the negative impact of application of the efficient proximate causation doctrine by excluding the loss if it were caused in part by an excluded cause of loss and irrespective of the efficient proximate cause doctrine. The enforcement of such anti-efficient proximate causation clauses has had mixed results in the courts. See §§ 4.03[4][b][ii] and [iii] *infra*.

17 See § 3.03 *infra*.

18 See, e.g., §§ 6.10[2][a]–[d] *infra*.

19 See:

First Circuit: OneBeacon America Insurance Co. v. Commercial Union Assurance Company of Canada, 684 F.3d 237 (1st Cir. 2012); Bristol West Insurance Co. v. Wawanesa Mutual Insurance Co., 570 F.3d 461 (1st Cir. 2009); Panagora Asset Management, Inc. v. St. Paul

Mercury Insurance Co., 674 F. Supp.2d 315 (D. Mass. 2009); Whittaker Corp. v. American Nuclear Insurers, 671 F. Supp.2d 242 (D. Mass. 2009).

Second Circuit: SR International Business Insurance Co., Ltd. v. World Trade Center Properties, LLC, 467 F.3d 107 (2d Cir. 2006); HSB Group, Inc. v. SVB Underwriting, Ltd., 664 F. Supp.2d 158 (D. Conn. 2009).

Third Circuit: Liberty Mutual Insurance Co. v. Sweeney, 689 F.3d 288 (3d Cir. 2012); Regents of Mercersburg College v. Republic Franklin Insurance Co., 458 F.3d 159 (3d Cir. 2006); American Legacy Foundation v. National Union Fire Insurance Company of Pittsburgh, PA, 640 F. Supp.2d 524 (D. Del. 2009); Somerset Industries, Inc. v. Lexington Insurance Co., 639 F. Supp.2d 532 (E.D. Pa. 2009).

Fourth Circuit: Republic Franklin Insurance Co. v. Albemarle County School Board, 670 F.3d 563 (4th Cir. 2012); Bohreer v. Erie Insurance Group, 2007 WL 569901 (E.D. Va. Feb. 16, 2007).

Fifth Circuit: Philadelphia Indemnity Insurance Co. v. Creative Young Minds, Ltd., 679 F. Supp.2d 739 (N.D. Tex. 2009); *In re* Katrina Canal Breaches Consolidated Litigation, 466 F. Supp.2d 729 (E.D. La. 2006).

Sixth Circuit: Pedicini v. Life Insurance Company of Alabama, 682 F.3d 522 (6th Cir. 2012); Gooch v. Life Investors Insurance Company of America, 264 F.R.D. 340 (M.D. Tenn. 2009).

Seventh Circuit: Home Federal Savings Bank v. Ticor Title Insurance Co., 695 F.3d 725 (7th Cir. 2012); Johnson v. State Farm Mutual Automobile Insurance Co., 641 F. Supp.2d 748 (C.D. Ill. 2009).

Eighth Circuit: Grinnell Mutual Reinsurance Co. v. Schwieger, 685 F.3d 697 (8th Cir. 2012); Merriam v. National Union Fire Insurance Company of Pittsburgh, PA, 572 F.3d 579 (8th Cir. 2009).

Ninth Circuit: Chartis Specialty Insurance Co. v. Queen Anne HS, L.L.C., 867 F. Supp.2d 1111 (W.D. Wash. 2012); Align Technology, Inc. v. Federal Insurance. Co., 673 F. Supp.2d 957 (N.D. Cal. 2009).

Tenth Circuit: Maldonado v. Allstate Fire and Casualty Insurance Co., 849 F. Supp.2d 1080 (D. Colo. 2012); Boggs v. Great Northern Insurance Co., 659 F. Supp.2d 1199 (N.D. Okla. 2009).

Eleventh Circuit: United Rentals, Inc. v. Mid-Continent Casualty Co., 843 F. Supp.2d 1309 (S.D. Fla. 2012); St. Paul Fire and Marine Insurance Co. v. Sea Quest International, Inc., 676 F. Supp.2d 1306 (M.D. Fla. 2009).

District of Columbia Circuit: Essex Insurance Co. v. Cafe Dupont, L.L.C., 674 F. Supp.2d 166 (D.D.C. 2009).

State Courts:

California: State v. Continental Insurance Co., 55 Cal.4th 186, 281 P.3d 1000, 145 Cal. Rptr.3d 1 (2012); TRB Investments, Inc. v. Fireman's Fund Insurance Co., 145 P.3d 472 (Cal. 2006); American International Underwriters Insurance Co. v. American Guarantee and Liability Insurance Co., 181 Cal. App.4th 616, 105 Cal. Rptr.3d 64 (Cal. App. 2010); Arce *ex rel.* Arce v. Kaiser Foundation Health Plan, Inc., 181 Cal. App.4th 471, 104 Cal. Rptr.3d 545 (Cal. App. 2010); ACS Systems, Inc. v. St. Paul Fire & Marine Insurance Co., 53 Cal. Rptr.3d 786 (Cal. App. 2007).

Connecticut: Enviro Express, Inc. v. AIU Insurance Co., 901 A.2d 666 (Conn. 2006); Fiallo v. Allstate Insurance Co., 138 Conn. App. 325, 51 A.3d 1193 (2012).

Delaware: Intel Corp. v. American Guarantee and Liability Insurance Co., 51 A.3d 442 (Del. 2012).

Florida: Liebel v. Nationwide Insurance Company of Florida, 22 So.3d 111 (Fla. App. 2009).

Georgia: Murphy v. Ticor Title Insurance Co., 316 Ga. App. 97, 729 S.E.2d 21 (2012); Banks v. Brotherhood Mutual Insurance Co., 301 Ga. App. 101, 686 S.E.2d 872 (2009).

Idaho: Farm Bureau Mutual Insurance Company of Idaho v. Eisenman, 286 P.3d 185 (Idaho 2012).

Illinois: American States Insurance Co. v. CFM Construction Co., 398 Ill. App.3d 994, 923 N.E.2d 299, 337 Ill. Dec. 740 (2010); American Family Mutual Insurance Company v. Niebuhr, 860 N.E.2d 436 (Ill. App. 2006).

Indiana: Peabody Energy Corp. v. Roark, 973 N.E.2d 636 (Ind. App. 2012); Wurster Construction Co., Inc. v. Essex Insurance Co., 918 N.E.2d 666 (Ind. App. 2009).

Iowa: Bituminous Casualty Corp. v. Sand Livestock Systems, Inc., 728 N.W.2d 216 (Iowa 2007).

Kentucky: Coleman v. Bee Line Courier Service, Inc., 284 S.W.3d 123 (Ky. 2009); Hoskins v. Kentucky Farm Bureau Mutual Insurance Co., 2012 WL 4841094 (Ky. App. Oct. 12, 2012).

Louisiana: Robinson Brothers, Inc. v. Carter, 2007 WL 466586 (La. App. Feb. 14, 2007).

Massachusetts: Surabian Realty Co. v. NGM Insurance Co., 462 Mass. 715, 971 N.E.2d 268 (2012); Boston Gas Co. v. Century Indemnity Co., 454 Mass. 337, 910 N.E.2d 290 (Mass. 2009); Massachusetts Property Insurance Underwriting Association v. Gallagher, 75 Mass. App. Ct. 58,911 N.E.2d 808 (2009).

Minnesota: Quade v. Secura Insurance Co., 814 N.W.2d 703 (Minn. 2012); Kasid v. Country Mutual Insurance Co., 776 N.W.2d 181 (Minn. App. 2009).

Mississippi: Hankins v. Maryland Casualty Co./Zurich American Insurance Co., 2012 WL 4711437 (Miss. Oct. 4, 2012); Corban v. United Services Automobile Association, 20 So.3d 601 (Miss. 2009).

Montana: Giacomelli v. Scottsdale Insurance Co., 354 Mont. 15, 221 P.3d 666 (2009).

Nebraska: Peterson v. Ohio Casualty Group, 724 N.W.2d 765 (Neb. 2006); Dutton-Lainson Co. v. Continental Insurance Co., 279 Neb. 365, 778 N.W.2d 433 (2010).

New Mexico: United Nuclear Corp. v. Allstate Insurance Co., 285 P.3d 644 (N.M. 2012).

New York: Christodoulides v. First Unum Life Insurance Co., 96 A.D.3d 1603, 946 N.Y.S.2d 77 (2012); Park Country Club of Buffalo, Inc. v. Tower Insurance Company of New York, 68 A.D.3d 1772, 893 N.Y.S.2d 408 (N.Y. App. Div. 2009).

North Dakota: Schleuter v. Northern Plains Insurance Co., 772 N.W.2d 879 (N.D. 2009).

Ohio: Blake v. Thornton, 182 Ohio App.3d 716, 914 N.E.2d 1102 (2009).

Oregon: Totten v. New York Life Insurance Co., 696 P.2d 1082 (Or. 1985); Gonzales v. Farmers Insurance Company of Oregon, 150 P.3d 20 (Or. App. 2006); Farmers Insurance Co. v. Munson, 930 P.2d 878 (Or. App. 1996), *appeal denied* 939 P.2d 45 (Or. 1997).

Pennsylvania: Berg v. Nationwide Mutual Insurance Co., 44 A.3d 1164 (Pa. Super. 2012); Kropa v. Gateway Ford, 974 A.2d 502 (Pa. Super. 2009).

Tennessee: Naifeh v. Valley Forge Life Insurance Co., 204 S.W.3d 758 (Tenn. 2006).

Texas: Burlington Northern and Santa Fe Railway Co. v. National Union Fire Insurance Company of Pittsburgh, PA, 2009 WL 4653406 (Tex. App. Dec. 9, 2009).

Washington: Reliable Credit Association v. Progressive Direct Insurance Co., 2012 WL 5332477 (Wash. App. Oct. 30, 2012).

Wisconsin: Bormann v. Sohns, 727 N.W.2d 341 (Wis. App. 2006).

[20] See, e.g.:

First Circuit: Certain Interested Underwriters at Lloyd's, London v. Stolberg, 680 F.3d 61 (1st Cir. 2012); Zurich American Insurance Co. v. Watts Regulator Co., 860 F. Supp.2d 78 (D. Mass. 2012).

Second Circuit: In re The Brunswick Hospital Center, Inc., 399 B.R. 582 (Bankr. E.D.N.Y. 2009).

Third Circuit: Travelers Property Casualty Company of America v. Chubb Custom Insurance Co., 864 F. Supp.2d 301 (E.D. Pa. 2012); Rothschild v. Foremost Insurance Co., 653 F. Supp.2d 526 (D.N.J. 2009).

Fourth Circuit: State Farm Fire and Casualty Co. v. Nationwide Mutual Insurance Co., 596 F. Supp.2d 940 (E.D. Va. 2009); Geico Insurance Co. v. Larson, 542 F. Supp.2d 441 (E.D.N.C. 2008).

Fifth Circuit: ACE American Insurance Co. v. Freeport Welding and Fabricating, Inc., 2012 WL 5077688 (5th Cir. Oct. 19, 2012); First American Bank v. First American Transportation Title Insurance Co., 585 F.3d 833 (5th Cir. 2009).

Sixth Circuit: Pedicini v. Life Insurance Company of Alabama, 682 F.3d 522 (6th Cir. 2012); Isner v. Minnesota Life Insurance Co., 677 F. Supp.2d 950 (E.D. Mich. 2009).

Seventh Circuit: St. Paul Fire and Marine Insurance Co. v. Schilli Transportation Services, Inc., 672 F.3d 451 (7th Cir. 2012).

Eighth Circuit: Owners Insurance Co. v. European Auto Works, Inc., 2012 WL 4052406 (8th Cir. Sept. 17, 2012); TAMKO Building Products, Inc. v. Factual Mutual Insurance Co., 2012 WL 3596155 (E.D. Mo. Aug. 21, 2012); *In re* Acceptance Insurance Companies, 383 B.R. 128 (Bankr. App. Pan. 8th Cir. 2008).

Ninth Circuit: Century Surety Co. v. Casino West, Inc., 677 F.3d 903 (9th Cir. 2012); Chartis Specialty Insurance Co. v. Queen Anne HS, L.L.C., 867 F. Supp.2d 1111 (W.D. Wash. 2012); Scanlon v. Life Insurance Company of North America, 670 F. Supp.2d 1181 (W.D. Wash. 2009); Tri-Star Theme Builders, Inc./PCL Construction Services, Inc. v. Hawkeye-Security Insurance Co., 653 F. Supp.2d 973 (D. Arz. 2009).

Tenth Circuit: Apartment Investment and Management Co. (AIMCO) v. Nutmeg Insurance Co., 593 F.3d 1188 (10th Cir. 2010).

Eleventh Circuit: James River Insurance Co. v. Oscar I. Garcia, Architect, P.A., 856 F. Supp.2d 1284 (S.D. Fla. 2012); Essex Insurance Co. v. Zota, 607 F. Supp.2d 1340 (S.D. Fla. 2009).

District of Columbia Circuit: Essex Insurance Co. v. Cafe Dupont, L.L.C., 674 F. Supp.2d 166 (D.D.C. 2009).

State Courts:

California: State v. Continental Insurance Co., 55 Cal.4th 186, 281 P.3d 1000, 145 Cal. Rptr.3d 1 (2012); American International Underwriters Insurance Co. v. American Guarantee and Liability Insurance Co., 181 Cal. App.4th 616, 105 Cal. Rptr.3d 64 (Cal. App. 2010); Baker v. National Interstate Insurance Co., 180 Cal. App.4th 1319, 103 Cal. Rptr.3d 565 (Cal. App. 2009).

Connecticut: Fiallo v. Allstate Insurance Co., 138 Conn. App. 325, 51 A.3d 1193 (2012).

Delaware: Intel Corp. v. American Guarantee and Liability Insurance Co., 51 A.3d 442 (Del. 2012).

Florida: Allstate Insurance Co. v. Suarez, 833 So.2d 762, 765 (Fla. 2002).

Georgia: Rentrite, Inc. v. Sentry Select Insurance Co., 293 Ga. App. 643, 667 S.E.2d 888 (2008).

Hawaii: Allstate Insurance Co. v. Pruett, 118 Haw. 174, 186 P.3d 609 (2008).

Idaho: Farm Bureau Mutual Insurance Company of Idaho v. Eisenman, 286 P.3d 185 (Idaho 2012); Armstrong v. Farmers Insurance Company of Idaho, 147 Idaho 67, 205 P.3d 1203 (2009).

Illinois: Ismic Mutual Insurance Co. v. Michaelis Jackson & Associates, L.L.C., 397 Ill. App.3d 964, 921 N.E.2d 1156, 337 Ill. Dec. 18 (2009).

Indiana: FLM, L.L.C. v. Cincinnati Insurance Co., 973 N.E.2d 1167 (Ind. App. 2012).

Iowa: Thomas v. Progressive Casualty Insurance Co., 749 N.W.2d 678 (Iowa 2008).

Kansas: Ochs v. Federated Mutual Insurance Co., 43 Kan. App.2d 127, 221 P.3d 622 (Kan. App. 2010).

Louisiana: R.L. Lucien Tile Company *ex rel.* Cage v. American Security Insurance Co., 8 So.3d 753 (La. App. 2009).

Massachusetts: Surabian Realty Co. v. NGM Insurance Co., 462 Mass. 715, 971 N.E.2d 268 (2012); Kanamaru v. Holyoke Mutual Insurance Co., 72 Mass. App.Ct. 396, 892 N.E.2d 759 (2008).

Minnesota: Kasid v. Country Mutual Insurance Co., 776 N.W.2d 181 (Minn. App. 2009).

Mississippi: Hankins v. Maryland Casualty Co./Zurich American Insurance Co., 2012 WL 4711437 (Miss. Oct. 4, 2012); Architex Association, Inc. v. Scottsdale Insurance Co., 27 So.3d 1148 (Miss. 2010).

Missouri: Mendenhall v. Property and Casualty Insurance Company of Hartford, 375 S.W.3d 90 (Mo. 2012) (*en banc*); Foremost Signature Insurance Co. v. Montgomery, 266 S.W.3d 868 (Mo. App. 2008); Nautilus Insurance Co. v. Jesse James Festival, Inc., 269 S.W.3d 442 (Mo. App. 2008).

Nebraska: Rickerl v. Farmers Insurance Exchange, 277 Neb. 446, 763 N.W.2d 86 (2009).

New Jersey: Hardy *ex rel.* Dowdell v. Abdul-Matin, 198 N.J. 95, 965 A.2d 1165 (2009).

New Mexico: United Nuclear Corp. v. Allstate Insurance Co., 285 P.3d 644 (N.M. 2012); Truck Insurance Exchange v. Gagnon, 33 P.3d 901, 903 (N.M. App.), *cert. denied* 36 P.3d 953 (N.M. 2001).

New York: Catucci v. Greenwich Insurance Co., 830 N.Y.S.2d 281 (N.Y. App. Div. 2007); Encompass Indemnity Co. v. USAA Casualty Insurance Co., 61 A.D.3d 974, 878 N.Y.S.2d 132 (N.Y. App. Div. 2009); Italian Designer Import Outlet, Inc. v. New York Central Mutual Fire Insurance Co., 26 Misc.3d 631, 891 N.Y.S.2d 260 (N.Y. Sup. Ct., King's Cnty. 2009).

North Carolina: Builders Mutual Insurance Co. v. Glascarr Properties, Inc., 688 S.E.2d 508 (N.C. App. 2010).

North Dakota: Grinnell Mutual Reinsurance Co. v. Thies, 755 N.W.2d 852 (N.D. 2008).

Ohio: Nationwide Insurance Co. v. Alli, 178 Ohio App.3d 17, 896 N.E.2d 742 (2008).

Oregon: Smith v. State Farm Insurance Co., 927 P.2d 111 (Or. App. 1996).

Pennsylvania: Miller v. Poole, 45 A.3d 1143 (Pa. Super. 2012).

Rhode Island: Riel v. Harleysville Worcester Insurance Co., 45 A.3d 561 (R.I. 2012).

South Carolina: Southern Glass & Plastics Co. v. Kemper, 732 S.E.2d 205 (S.C. App. 2012).

South Dakota: Cole v. Wellmark of South Dakota, Inc., 776 N.W.2d 240 (S.D. 2009).

Texas: Farmers Insurance Exchange v. Greene, 376 S.W.3d 278 (Tex. App. 2012); SA-OMAX 2007, L.P. v. Certain Underwriters at Lloyd's, London, 374 S.W.3d 594 (Tex. App. 2012); Hartrick v. Great American Lloyds Insurance Co., 62 S.W.3d 270, 274 (Tex. App. 2001).

Washington: Reliable Credit Association v. Progressive Direct Insurance Co., 2012 WL 5332477 (Wash. App. Oct. 30, 2012); Ki Sin Kim v. Allstate Insurance Co., 153 Wash. App. 339 (2009).

West Virginia: Wrenn v. West Virginia Department of Transportation, Division of Highways, 224 W.Va. 424, 686 S.E.2d 75 (2009); Blake v. State Farm Mutual Automobile Insurance Co., 224 W.Va. 317, 685 S.E.2d 895 (2009).

21 *Id.*

[22] See:

First Circuit: Certain Interested Underwriters at Lloyd's, London v. Stolberg, 680 F.3d 61 (1st Cir. 2012); Zurich American Insurance Co. v. Watts Regulator Co., 860 F. Supp.2d 78 (D. Mass. 2012).

Second Circuit: Acadia Insurance Co. v. American Crushing & Recycling, LLC, 2007 WL 610164 (D. Conn. Feb. 28, 2007).

Third Circuit: Travelers Property Casualty Company of America v. Chubb Custom Insurance Co., 864 F. Supp.2d 301 (E.D. Pa. 2012); Employers Mutual Casualty Co. v. Loos, 2007 WL 665841 (W.D. Pa. Feb. 28, 2007).

Fourth Circuit: Firemen's Insurance Company of Washington, D.C. v. Kline & Son Cement Repair, Inc., 2007 WL 519230 (E.D. Va. Feb. 13, 2007).

Fifth Circuit: ACE American Insurance Co. v. Freeport Welding and Fabricating, Inc., 2012 WL 5077688 (5th Cir. Oct. 19, 2012); First American Bank v. First American Transportation Title Insurance Co., 585 F.3d 833 (5th Cir. 2009).

Sixth Circuit: Pedicini v. Life Insurance Company of Alabama, 682 F.3d 522 (6th Cir. 2012); Smith v. Stonebridge Life Insurance Co., 2007 WL 466742 (W.D. Wis. Feb. 12, 2007).

Seventh Circuit: St. Paul Fire and Marine Insurance Co. v. Schilli Transportation Services, Inc., 672 F.3d 451 (7th Cir. 2012).

Eighth Circuit: Owners Insurance Co. v. European Auto Works, Inc., 2012 WL 4052406 (8th Cir. Sep. 17, 2012); TAMKO Building Products, Inc. v. Factual Mutual Insurance Co., 2012 WL 3596155 (E.D. Mo. Aug. 21, 2012); *In re* Acceptance Insurance Companies, 383 B.R. 128 (Bankr. 8th Cir. 2008).

Ninth Circuit: Century Surety Co. v. Casino West, Inc., 677 F.3d 903 (9th Cir. 2012); Chartis Specialty Insurance Co. v. Queen Anne HS, L.L.C., 867 F. Supp.2d 1111 (W.D. Wash. 2012); Scanlon v. Life Insurance Company of North America, 670 F. Supp.2d 1181 (W.D. Wash. 2009); Tri-Star Theme Builders, Inc./PCL Construction Services, Inc. v. Hawkeye-Security Insurance Co., 653 F. Supp.2d 973 (D. Ariz. 2009).

Tenth Circuit: Apartment Investment and Management Co. (AIMCO) v. Nutmeg Insurance Co., 593 F.3d 1188 (10th Cir. 2010).

Eleventh Circuit: James River Insurance Co. v. Oscar I. Garcia, Architect, P.A., 856 F. Supp.2d 1284 (S.D. Fla. 2012); Fabricant v. Kemper Independence Insurance Co., 2007 WL 458023 (S.D. Fla. Feb. 9, 2007).

District of Columbia Circuit: Essex Insurance Co. v. Cafe Dupont, L.L.C., 674 F. Supp.2d 166 (D.D.C. 2009).

State Courts:

California: State v. Continental Insurance Co., 55 Cal.4th 186, 281 P.3d 1000, 145 Cal. Rptr.3d 1 (2012); E.M.M.I Inc. v. Zurich American Insurance Co., 84 P.3d 385 (Cal. 2004); MacKinnon v. Truck Insurance Exchange, 73 P.3d 1205 (Cal. 2003); Pacific Gas & Electric. Co. v. G. W. Thomas Drayage & Rigging Co., 442 P.2d 641 (Cal. 1968); ACS Systems, Inc. v. St. Paul Fire & Marine Insurance Co., 53 Cal. Rptr.3d 786 (Cal. App. 2007); Benedek v. PLC Santa Monica, LLC, 129 Cal. Rptr.2d 197, 202 (Cal. App. 2002); Solis v. Kirkwood Resort Co., 114 Cal. Rptr.2d 265, 269 (Cal. App. 2001).

Colorado: Hecla Mining Co. v. New Hampshire Insurance Co., 811 P.2d 1083, 1090 (Colo. 1991); City of Englewood v. Commercial Union Assurance Co., 940 P.2d 948 (Colo. App. 1996).

Connecticut: Fiallo v. Allstate Insurance Co., 138 Conn. App. 325, 51 A.3d 1193 (2012).

Delaware: Intel Corp. v. American Guarantee and Liability Insurance Co., 51 A.3d 442 (Del. 2012); AT&T Corp. v. Faraday Capital Ltd., 2007 WL 329218 (Del. Super. Feb. 5, 2007).

Florida: Lenhart v. Federated National Insurance Co., 2007 WL 461335 (Fla. Dist. App. Feb. 14, 2007); Ward v. Nationwide Mutual Fire Insurance Co., 364 So.2d 73, 77 (Fla. Dist.

App. 1978); Effort Enterprises of Florida v. Lexington Insurance Co., 666 So.2d 930, 931 (Fla. Dist. App. 1995); Airmanship, Inc. v. United States Aviation Underwriters, Inc., 559 So.2d 89, 91–92 (Fla. Dist. App.), *review denied* 576 So.2d 294 (Fla. 1990).

Idaho: Farm Bureau Mutual Insurance Company of Idaho v. Eisenman, 286 P.3d 185 (Idaho 2012).

Indiana: FLM, L.L.C. v. Cincinnati Insurance Co., 973 N.E.2d 1167 (Ind. App. 2012); McGuire v. Century Surety Co., 861 N.E.2d 357 (Ind. App. 2007).

Iowa: Bituminous Casualty Corp. v. Sand Livestock Systems, Inc., 728 N.W.2d 216 (Iowa 2007).

Louisiana: Robinson Brothers, Inc. v. Carter, 2007 WL 466586 (La. App. Feb. 14, 2007).

Massachusetts: Surabian Realty Co. v. NGM Insurance Co., 462 Mass. 715, 971 N.E.2d 268 (2012).

Michigan: Nickerson v. Citizens Mutual Insurance Co., 224 N.W.2d 896 (Mich. 1975).

Mississippi: Hankins v. Maryland Casualty Co./Zurich American Insurance Co., 2012 WL 4711437 (Miss. Oct. 4, 2012).

Missouri: Mendenhall v. Property and Casualty Insurance Company of Hartford, 375 S.W.3d 90 (Mo. 2012) (*en banc*); Seeck v. Geico General Insurance Co., 212 S.W.3d 129 (Mo. 2007).

Montana: Swank Enterprises, Inc. v. All Purpose Services, Ltd., 154 P.3d 52, (Mont. 2007).

New Mexico: United Nuclear Corp. v. Allstate Insurance Co., 285 P.3d 644 (N.M. 2012).

New York: Continental Casualty Co. v. Rapid-American Corp., 609 N.E.2d 506, 512 (N.Y. 1993).

Ohio: Professional Rental, Inc. v. Shelby Insurance Co., 599 N.E.2d 423, 427 (Ohio App. 1991).

Pennsylvania: Miller v. Poole, 45 A.3d 1143 (Pa. Super. 2012); Continental Casualty Co. v. Pro Machine, 916 A.2d 1111 (Pa. Super. 2007); Erie Insurance Exchange v. Transamerica Insurance Co., 533 A.2d 1363, 1368 (Pa. 1987).

Rhode Island: Riel v. Harleysville Worcester Insurance Co., 45 A.3d 561 (R.I. 2012).

South Carolina: Southern Glass & Plastics Co. v. Kemper, 732 S.E.2d 205 (S.C. App. 2012).

Texas: Farmers Insurance Exchange v. Greene, 376 S.W.3d 278 (Tex. App. 2012); SA-OMAX 2007, L.P. v. Certain Underwriters at Lloyd's, London, 374 S.W.3d 594 (Tex. App. 2012).

Washington: Greer v. Northwestern National Insurance Co., 743 P.2d 1244, 1249 (Wash. 1987); Reliable Credit Association v. Progressive Direct Insurance Co., 2012 WL 5332477 (Wash. App. Oct. 30, 2012).

23 *Id.*

24 See:

First Circuit: Bristol West Insurance Co. v. Wawanesa Mutual Insurance Co., 570 F.3d 461 (1st Cir. 2009).

Second Circuit: SR International Business Insurance Co., Ltd. v. World Trade Center Properties, LLC, 467 F.3d 107 (2d Cir. 2006); SCW West L.L.C. v. Westport Insurance Corp., 856 F. Supp.2d 514 (E.D.N.Y. 2012).

Third Circuit: Post v. St. Paul Travelers Insurance Co., 691 F.3d 500 (3d Cir. 2012); Regents of Mercersburg College v. Republic Franklin Insurance Co., 458 F.3d 159 (3d Cir. 2006); Continental Insurance Co. v. Davis, 56 F. Supp.2d 513, 516 (E.D. Pa. 1999), *aff'd* 216 F.3d 1075 (3d Cir. 2000).

Fourth Circuit: State Auto Property and Casualty Insurance Co. v. Wohlfeil, 2012 WL 3687490 (N.D. W. Va. Aug. 27, 2012); Hartford Fire Insurance Co. v. St. Paul Fire and Marine Insurance Co., 606 F. Supp.2d 602 (E.D.N.C. 2009); Bohreer v. Erie Insurance Group, 475 F. Supp.2d 578 (E.D. Va. 2007).

Fifth Circuit: Looney Ricks Kiss Architects, Inc. v. State Farm Fire and Casualty Co., 677 F.3d 250 (5th Cir. 2012); Little v. USAA Casualty Insurance Co., 655 F. Supp.2d 625 (W.D. La. 2009); *In re* Katrina Canal Breaches Consolidated Litigation, 466 F. Supp.2d 729 (E.D. La. 2006).

Sixth Circuit: Bondex International, Inc. v. Hartford Accident and Indemnity Co., 667 F.3d 669 (6th Cir. 2011); Whitt Machine, Inc. v. Essex Insurance Co., 631 F. Supp.2d 927 (S.D. Ohio. 2009).

Seventh Circuit: North Shore Bank, FSB v. Progressive Casualty Insurance Co., 674 F.3d 884 (7th Cir. 2012); Krueger International, Inc. v. Federal Insurance Co., 647 F. Supp.2d 1024 (E.D. Wis. 2009).

Eighth Circuit: Interstate Bakeries Corp. v. OneBeacon Insurance Co., 686 F.3d 539 (8th Cir. 2012); *In re* Acceptance Insurance Companies, 567 F.3d 369 (8th Cir. 2009); Orthopedic Resources, Inc. v. Nautilus Insurance Co., 654 F. Supp.2d 1307 (N.D. Okla. 2009).

Ninth Circuit: Zurich Specialties London Ltd. v. Bickerstaff, Whatley, Ryan & Burkhalter, Inc., 650 F. Supp.2d 1064 (C.D. Cal. 2009).

Tenth Circuit: Long v. St. Paul Fire and Marine Insurance Co., 589 F.3d 1075 (10th Cir. 2009); EMC Insurance Cos. v. Mid-Continent Casualty Co., 2012 WL 3150528 (D. Colo. Aug. 2, 2012).

Eleventh Circuit: HR Acquisition I Corp. v. Twin City Fire Insurance Co., 547 F.3d 1309 (11th Cir. 2008); Essex Insurance Co. v. Zota, 607 F. Supp.2d 1340 (S.D. Fla. 2009).

State Courts:

Arkansas: Parker v. Southern Farm Bureau Casualty Insurance Co., 104 Ark. App. 301, 292 S.W.3d 311 (2009).

California: State v. Allstate Insurance Co., 45 Cal.4th 1008, 201 P.3d 1147, 90 Cal. Rptr.3d 1 (2009); American International Underwriters Insurance Co. v. American Guarantee and Liability Insurance Co., 181 Cal. App.4th 616, 105 Cal. Rptr.3d 64 (2010); ACS Systems, Inc. v. St. Paul Fire & Marine Insurance Co., 53 Cal. Rptr.3d 786 (Cal. App. 2007).

Colorado: DeHerrera v. American Family Mutual Insurance Co., 219 P.3d 346 (Colo. App. 2009).

Connecticut: Enviro Express, Inc. v. AIU Insurance Co., 901 A.2d 666 (Conn. 2006); New London County Mutual Insurance Co. v. Bialobrodec, 137 Conn. App. 474, 48 A.3d 742 (2012).

Idaho: Armstrong v. Farmers Insurance Company of Idaho, 147 Idaho 67, 205 P.3d 1203 (2009).

Illinois: DeSaga v. West Bend Mutual Insurance Co., 391 Ill. App.3d 1062, 910 N.E.2d 159, 331 Ill. Dec. 86 (2009); American Family Mutual Insurance Co. v. Niebuhr, 860 N.E.2d 436 (Ill. App. 2006).

Indiana: Grinnell Mutual Reinsurance Co. v. Ault, 918 N.E.2d 619 (Ind. App. 2009).

Iowa: Swainston v. American Family Mutual Insurance Co., 774 N.W.2d 478 (Iowa 2009); Bituminous Casualty Corp. v. Sand Livestock Systems, Inc., 728 N.W.2d 216 (Iowa 2007).

Louisiana: George S. May International Co. v. Arrowpoint Capital Corp., 97 So.3d 1167 (La. App. 2012); Parekh v. Mittadar, 97 So.3d 433 (La. App. 2012); Robinson Brothers, Inc. v. Carter, 962 So.2d 446 (La. App. 2007).

Michigan: Tenneco Inc. v. Amerisure Mutual Insurance Co., 281 Mich. App. 429, 761 N.W.2d 846 (2008).

Missouri: Haulers Insurance Co. v. Pounds, 272 S.W.3d 902 (Mo. App. 2008).

Montana: United National Insurance Co. v. St. Paul Fire & Marine Insurance Co., 352 Mont. 105, 214 P.3d 1260 (2009).

Nebraska: Peterson v. Ohio Casualty Group, 724 N.W.2d 765 (Neb. 2006).

Nevada: Physicians Insurance Company of Wisconsin, Inc. v. Williams, 279 P.3d 174 (Nev. 2012).

New Jersey: S.T. Hudson Engineers, Inc. v. Pennsylvania National Mutual Casualty Co., 909 A.2d 1156 (N.J. Super. App. Div. 2006).

New York: J.P. Morgan Chase & Co. v. Indian Harbor Insurance Co., 98 A.D.3d 18, 947 N.Y.S.2d 17 (2012).

North Carolina: Fulford v. Jenkins, 195 N.C. App. 402, 672 S.E.2d 759 (2009).

North Dakota: Schleuter v. Northern Plains Insurance Co., 772 N.W.2d 879 (N.D. 2009).

Ohio: Blake v. Thornton, 182 Ohio App.3d 716, 914 N.E.2d 1102 (2009).

Oklahoma: Andres v. Oklahoma Farm Bureau Mutual Insurance Co., 227 P.3d 1102 (Okla. App. 2009).

Oregon: Totten v. New York Life Insurance Co., 696 P.2d 1082 (Or. 1985); Laird v. Allstate Insurance Co., 232 Or. App. 162, 221 P.3d 780 (2009); Ruede v. City of Florence, 231 Or. App. 435, 220 P.3d 113 (2009); Gonzales v. Farmers Insurance Company of Oregon, 150 P.3d 20 (Or. App. 2006).

Pennsylvania: Adamitis v. Erie Insurance Exchange, 2012 WL 4355527 (Pa. Sept. 25, 2012); Burton v. Republic Insurance Co., 845 A.2d 889, 893 (Pa. Super. 2004).

Tennessee: Garrison v. Bickford, 377 S.W.3d 659 (Tenn. 2012); Spears v. Tennessee Farmers Mutual Insurance Co., 300 S.W.3d 671 (Tenn. App. 2009).

Texas: Chrysler Insurance Co. v. Greenspoint Dodge of Houston, Inc., 297 S.W.3d 248 (Tex. 2009); SA-OMAX 2007, L.P. v. Certain Underwriters at Lloyd's, London, 374 S.W.3d 594 (Tex. App. 2012).

Washington: Campbell v. Ticor Title Insurance Co., 166 Wash.2d 466, 209 P.3d 859 (2009).

Wisconsin: Wadzinski v. Auto-Owners Insurance Co., 342 Wis.2d 311, 818 N.W.2d 819 (2012); Bormann v. Sohns, 727 N.W.2d 341 (Wis. App. 2006).

Wyoming: State *ex rel.* Arnold v. Ommen, 201 P.3d 1127 (Wyo. 2009).

[25] *Id.*

[26] See § 3.02[1] *supra*. See also:

First Circuit: Wright-Ryan Construction, Inc. v. AIG Insurance Company of Canada, 647 F.3d 411 (1st Cir. 2011); New Hampshire Insurance Co. v. Dagnone, 475 F.3d 35 (1st Cir. 2007); Fire Insurance Exchange v. Pring-Wilson, 831 F. Supp.2d 493 (D. Mass. 2011).

Second Circuit: Champion International. Corp. v. Continental Casualty Co., 546 F.2d 502 (2d Cir. 1976); Macey v. Carolina Casualty Insurance Co., 674 F.3d 125 (2d Cir. 2012); RSUI Indemnity Co. v. RCG Group (USA), 2012 WL 3100636 (S.D.N.Y. July 31, 2012); SCW West L.L.C. v. Westport Insurance Corp., 856 F. Supp.2d 514 (E.D.N.Y. 2012); American Automobile Insurance Co. v. Security Income Planners and Co., 847 F. Supp.2d 454 (E.D.N.Y. 2012); U.S. Specialty Insurance Co. v. LeBeau, Inc., 847 F. Supp.2d 500 (W.D.N.Y. 2012); Chicago Title Insurance Co. v. Kent School Corp., 361 F. Supp.2d 4 (D. Conn. 2005).

Third Circuit: Liberty Mutual Insurance Co. v. Sweeney, 689 F.3d 288 (3d Cir. 2012); American Automobile Insurance Co. v. Murray, 658 F.3d 311 (3d Cir. 2011); Federal Insurance Co. v. KDW Restructuring and Liquidation Services, L.L.C., 2012 WL 3579840 (M.D. Pa. Aug. 17, 2012).

Fourth Circuit: Dooley v. Hartford Accident and Indemnity Co., 2012 WL 2370115 (W.D. Va. June 22, 2012); Zurich American Insurance Co. v. Public Storage, 743 F. Supp.2d 525 (E.D. Va. 2010); Bohreer v. Erie Insurance Group, 2007 WL 569901 (E.D. Va. Feb. 16, 2007).

Fifth Circuit: Looney Ricks Kiss Architects, Inc. v. State Farm Fire and Casualty Co., 677 F.3d 250 (5th Cir. 2012); Great American Insurance Co. v. AFS/IBEX Financial Services, Inc., 612 F.3d 800 (5th Cir. 2010).

Sixth Circuit: Continental Casualty Co. v. Law Offices of Melbourne Mills, Jr., P.L.L.C., 676 F.3d 534 (6th Cir. 2012); Tooling, Manufacturing and Technologies Association v. Hartford Fire Insurance Co., 2012 WL 3931802 (6th Cir. Sep. 11, 2012); Bondex International, Inc. v. Hartford Accident and Indemnity Co., 667 F.3d 669 (6th Cir. 2011); Keely v. Fire Insurance Exchange, 833 F. Supp.2d 722 (E.D. Mich. 2011); United Financial Casualty Co. v. Youth Alive, Inc., 846 F. Supp.2d 760 (W.D. Ky. 2012); Southeast Mental Health Center, Inc. v. Pacific Insurance Co., 439 F. Supp.2d 831 (W.D. Tenn. 2006).

Seventh Circuit: Grinnell Mutual Reinsurance Co. v. Haight, 2012 WL 4372520 (7th Cir. Sept. 26, 2012); Archer-Daniels-Midland Co. v. Phoenix Assurance Company of New York, 975 F. Supp. 1129 (S.D. Ill. 1997); Ohio Casualty Insurance Co. v. Herring-Jenkins, 830 F. Supp.2d 566 (N.D. Ind. 2011).

Eighth Circuit: Heacker v. Safeco Insurance Company of America, 676 F.3d 724 (8th Cir. 2012); Owners Insurance Co. v. European Auto Works, Inc., 2012 WL 4052406 (8th Cir. Sep. 17, 2012); American Economy Insurance Co. v. Jackson, 476 F.3d 620 (8th Cir. 2007); TAMKO Building Products, Inc. v. Factual Mutual Insurance Co., 2012 WL 3596155 (E.D. Mo. Aug. 21, 2012).

Ninth Circuit: Fier v. Unum Life Insurance Co., 629 F.3d 1095 (9th Cir. 2011); Chartis Specialty Insurance Co. v. Queen Anne HS, L.L.C., 867 F. Supp.2d 1111 (W.D. Wash. 2012); Newmont U.S.A. Ltd. and Dawn Mining Co. v. American Home Assurance Co., 787 F. Supp.2d 1208 (E.D. Wash. 2011); Gary G. Day Construction Co. v. Clarendon America Insurance Co., 459 F. Supp.2d 1039 (D. Nev. 2006).

Tenth Circuit: Western World Insurance Co. v. Markel American Insurance Co., 677 F.3d 1266 (10th Cir. 2012); DISH Network Corp. v. Arch Specialty Insurance Co., 659 F.3d 1010 (10th Cir. 2011).

Eleventh Circuit: Lubin v. Cincinnati Insurance Co., 677 F.3d 1039 (11th Cir. 2012); Great American Fidelity Insurance Co. v. JWR Construction Services, Inc., 2012 WL 1193848 (S.D. Fla. Apr. 9, 2012); General Fidelity Insurance Co. v. Foster, 808 F. Supp.2d 1315 (S.D. Fla. 2011); Fabricant v. Kemper Independence Insurance Co., 2007 WL 458023 (S.D. Fla. Feb. 9, 2007).

State Courts:

Alabama: Lambert v. Coregis Insurance Co., 2006 WL 2089921 (Ala. July 28, 2006).

Arizona: Lennar Corp. v. Auto-Owners Insurance Co., 151 P.3d 538 (Ariz. App. 2007).

California: American International Specialty Lines Insurance Co. v. Continental Casualty Insurance Co., 49 Cal. Rptr.3d 1 (Cal. App. 2006).

Colorado: Bailey v. Lincoln General Insurance Co., 255 P.3d 1039 (Colo. 2011) (*en banc*); Progressive Specialty Insurance Co. v. Hartford Underwriters Insurance Co., 148 P.3d 470 (Colo. App. 2006).

Connecticut: R.T. Vanderbilt Co. v. Continental Casualty Co., 870 A.2d 1048 (Conn. 2005).

Delaware: AT&T Corp. v. Faraday Capital Ltd., 2007 WL 329218 (Del. Super. Feb. 5, 2007).

Florida: State Farm Mutual Automobile Insurance Co. v. Menendez, 70 So.3d 566 (Fla. 2011); Barcelona Hotel, L.L.C. v. Nova Casualty Co., 57 So.3d 228 (Fla. App. 2011); Lenhart v. Federated National Insurance Co., 2007 WL 461335 (Fla. Dist. App. Feb. 14, 2007).

Georgia: Murphy v. Ticor Title Insurance Co., 316 Ga. App. 97, 729 S.E.2d 21 (2012); State Farm Fire and Casualty Co. v. Bauman, 313 Ga. App. 771, 723 S.E.2d 1 (Ga. App. 2012).

Indiana: State Automobile Mutual Insurance Co. v. Flexdar, Inc., 964 N.E.2d 845 (Ind. 2012); Gasser v. Downing, 967 N.E.2d 1085 (Ind. App. 2012); Peabody Energy Corp. v. Roark, 973 N.E.2d 636 (Ind. App. 2012).

Iowa: Bituminous Casualty Corp. v. Sand Livestock Systems, Inc., 728 N.W.2d 216 (Iowa 2007).

Kentucky: Hoskins v. Kentucky Farm Bureau Mutual Insurance Co., 2012 WL 4841094 (Ky. App. Oct. 12, 2012).

Louisiana: McDonald v. American Family Life Assurance Company of Columbus, 70 So.3d 1086 (La. App. 2011); Robinson Brothers, Inc. v. Carter, 2007 WL 466586 (La. App. Feb. 14, 2007).

Maryland: State Farm Mutual Automobile Insurance Co. v. DeHaan, 900 A.2d 208 (Md. 2006).

Michigan: Pugh v. Zefi, 294 Mich. App. 393, 812 N.W.2d 789 (2011).

Minnesota: Farmers Insurance Exchange v. Letellier, 820 N.W.2d 597 (Minn. App. 2012).

Mississippi: Caldwell Freight Lines, Inc. v. Lumbermens Mutual Casualty Co., 947 So.2d 948 (Miss. 2007).

Missouri: Mendenhall v. Property and Casualty Insurance Company of Hartford, 375 S.W.3d 90 (Mo. 2012) (*en banc*); Seeck v. GEICO General Insurance Co., 212 S.W.3d 129 (Mo. 2007); Grissom v. First National Insurance Agency, 371 S.W.3d 869 (Mo. App. 2012); Wasson v. Shelter Mutual Insurance Co., 358 S.W.3d 113 (Mo. App. 2011).

Nebraska: Lovette v. Stonebridge Life Insurance Co., 716 N.W.2d 743 (Neb. 2006).

Nevada: Griffin v. Old Republic Insurance Co., 133 P.3d 251 (Nev. 2006).

New Mexico: United Nuclear Corp. v. Allstate Insurance Co., 285 P.3d 644 (N.M. 2012); Rehders v. Allstate Insurance Co., 135 P.3d 237 (N.M. App.), *cert. denied* 136 P.3d 569 (N.M. 2006).

New York: Federal Insurance Co. v. International Business Machines Corp., 18 N.Y.3d 642, 965 N.E.2d 934, 942 N.Y.S.2d 432 (2012); Christodoulides v. First Unum Life Insurance Co., 96 A.D.3d 1603, 946 N.Y.S.2d 77 (2012); Catucci v. Greenwich Insurance Co., 830 NY.S.2d 281 (App. Div. 2007).

North Carolina: Patel v. Scottsdale Insurance Co., 728 S.E.2d 394 (N.C. App. 2012); Vogler v. Branch Erections Co., 640 S.E.2d 419 (N.C. App. 2007).

Oregon: Holloway v. Republic Indemnity Company of America, 147 P.3d 329 (Or. 2006); Capitol Specialty Insurance Corp. v. Chan & Lui, Inc., 248 Or. App. 674, 274 P.3d 238 (2012); Ortiz v. State Farm Fire and Casualty Co., 244 Or. App. 355, 260 P.3d 678 (2011).

Pennsylvania: Sunbeam Corp. v. Liberty Mutual Insurance Co., 781 A.2d 1189, 1193 (Pa. 2001) (adopting *Restatement (Second) of Contracts* § 202 as applicable to insurance policy construction); Wolfson v. Medical Care Availability and Reduction of Error Fund, 39 A.3d 551 (Pa. Commw. 2012); Allstate Fire and Casualty Insurance Co. v. Hymes, 29 A.3d 1169 (Pa. Super. 2011); Continental Casualty Co. v. Pro Machine, 916 A.2d 1111 (Pa. Super. 2007).

Rhode Island: New London County Mutual Insurance Co. v. Fontaine, 45 A.3d 551 (R.I. 2012); Derderian v. Essex Insurance Co., 44 A.3d 122 (R.I. 2012).

South Carolina: Hutchinson v. Liberty Life Insurance Co., 709 S.E.2d 130 (S.C. App. 2011).

Texas: Evanston Insurance Co. v. Legacy of Life, Inc., 370 S.W.3d 377 (Tex. 2012); SA-OMAX 2007, L.P. v. Certain Underwriters at Lloyd's, London, 374 S.W.3d 594 (Tex. App. 2012); Global Aerospace v. Pinson, 208 S.W.3d 687 (Tex. App. 2006).

Utah: Lopez v. United Automobile Insurance Co., 274 P.3d 897 (Utah 2012); State Farm Mutual Automobile Insurance Co. v. DeHerrera, 145 P.3d 1172 (Utah App. 2006).

Washington: Vision One, L.L.C. v. Philadelphia Indemnity Insurance Co., 174 Wash.2d 501, 276 P.3d 300 (2012) (*en banc*); Sauter *ex rel.* Sauter v. Houston Casualty Co., 168 Wash. App. 348, 276 P.3d 358 (2012); No Boundaries, Ltd. v. Pacific Indemnity Co., 160 Wash. App.

951, 249 P.3d 689 (2011); Nationwide Mutual Insurance Co. v. Hayles, Inc., 150 P.3d 589 (Wash. App. 2007).

See *Restatement (Second) of Contracts* § 202(5).

"Wherever reasonable, the manifestations of intention of the parties to a promise or agreement are interpreted as consistent with each other and with any relevant course of performance, course of dealing, or usage of trade."

Wisconsin: Marnholtz v. Church Mutual Insurance Co., 341 Wis.2d 478, 815 N.W.2d 708 (Wis. App. 2012).

[27] See:

Second Circuit: Citigroup, Inc. v. Industrial Risk Insurers, 336 F. Supp.2d 282 (S.D.N.Y. 2004).

Fifth Circuit: Little v. USAA Casualty Insurance Co., 655 F. Supp.2d 625 (W.D. La. 2009).

Seventh Circuit: Kimmel v. Western Reserve Life Assurance Company of Ohio, 678 F. Supp.2d 783 (N.D. Ind. 2010).

Eighth Circuit: American Home Assurance Co. v. Pope, 591 F.3d 992 (8th Cir. 1010); Mitzan v. Western Heritage Insurance Co., 623 F. Supp.2d 993 (E.D. Mo. 2009).

Ninth Circuit: Church Mutual Insurance Co. v. United States Liability Insurance Co., 347 F. Supp.2d 880 (S.D. Cal. 2004).

Tenth Circuit: Park University Enterprises, Inc. v. American Casualty Company of Reading, PA, 442 F.3d 1239 (10th Cir. 2006); Riordan v. Lawyers Title Insurance Corp., 393 F. Supp.2d 1100 (D.N.M. 2005).

Eleventh Circuit: Mega Life and Health Insurance Co. v. Pieniozek, 585 F.3d 1399 (11th Cir. 2009); Penzer v. Transportation Insurance Co., 509 F. Supp.2d 1278 (S.D. Fla. 2007); PowerSports, Inc. v. Royal and Sunalliance Insurance Co., 307 F. Supp.2d 1355 (S.D. Fla. 2004).

District of Columbia Circuit: Sigmund v. Progressive Northern Insurance Co., 374 F. Supp.2d 33 (D.D.C. 2005).

State Courts:

Arizona: Lennar Corp. v. Auto-Owners Insurance Co., 214 Ariz. 255, 151 P.3d 538 (Ariz. App. 2007).

Arkansas: Anderson Gas and Propane, Inc. v. Westport Insurance Corp., 84 Ark. App. 310, 140 S.W.3d 504 (Ark. App. 2004).

California: Everett v. State Farm General Insurance Co., 162 Cal. App.4th 649, 75 Cal. Rptr.3d 812 (2008).

Georgia: Georgia Farm Bureau Mutual Insurance Co. v. Harper, 272 Ga. App. 536, 612 S.E.2d 861 (Ga. App. 2005).

Kansas: Travelers Indemnity Company of Illinois v. Challenger Fence Co., 34 Kan. App.2d 276, 119 P.3d 666 (2005).

Louisiana: Andrews v. Columbia Casualty Insurance Co., 960 So.2d 134 (La. App. 2007).

Maryland: Medical Mutual Liability Insurance Society of Maryland v. Goldstein, 388 Md. 299, 879 A.2d 1025 (Md. 2005).

Missouri: Shelter Mutual Insurance Co. v. Ballew, 203 S.W.3d 789 (Mo. App. 2006).

Nebraska: Peterson v. Ohio Casualty Group, 272 Neb. 700, 724 N.W.2d 765 (Neb. 2006).

New Hampshire: Webster v. Acadia Insurance Co., 156 N.H. 317, 934 A.2d 567 (2007).

New Mexico: Krieger v. Wilson Corp., 139 N.M. 274, 131 P.3d 661 (N.M. App. 2005).

New York: Jahier v. Liberty Mutual Group, 64 A.D.3d 683, 883 N.Y.S.2d 283 (N.Y. App. Div. 2009); Travelers Indemnity Co. v. Commerce and Industry Insurance Company of Canada, 36 A.D.3d 1121, 828 N.Y.S.2d 658 (N.Y. App. Div. 2007).

North Carolina: North Carolina Farm Bureau Mutual Insurance Co. v. Fowler *ex rel.* Rudisill, 162 N.C. App. 100, 589 S.E.2d 911 (2004).

North Dakota: Grinnell Mutual Reinsurance Co. v. Thies, 755 N.W.2d 852 (N.D. 2008).

Pennsylvania: Estate of Higgins *ex rel.* Higgins v. Washington Mutual Fire Insurance Company of Lawrence County, PA, 838 A.2d 778 (Pa. Super. 2003).

Rhode Island: Progressive Northern Insurance Co. v. Lyden, 981 A.2d 231 (R.I. 2010).

Texas: Verhoev v. Progressive County Mutual Insurance Co., 300 S.W.3d 803 (Tex. App. 2009).

But see:

First Circuit: MIB Group, Inc. v. Federal Insurance Co., 473 F. Supp.2d 142 (D. Mass. 2006) (rules of construction apply to ascertain plain meaning).

Fourth Circuit: Reel v. Selective Insurance Co. 407 F. Supp.2d 737 (E.D.N.C. 2005) (same).

District of Columbia Circuit: National Railroad Passenger Corp. v. Lexington Insurance Co., 445 F. Supp.2d 37 (D.D.C. 2006) (same).

State Courts:

Idaho: Arreguin v. Farmers Insurance Company of Idaho, 145 Idaho 459, 180 P.3d 498 (2008) (same).

North Carolina: Trophy Tracks, Inc. v. Massachusetts Bay Insurance Co., 195 N.C. App. 734, 673 S.E.2d 787 (N.C. App. 2009) (same).

[28] See:

First Circuit: Ferrara & DiMercurio, Inc. v. St. Paul Mercury Insurance Co., 169 F.3d 43 (1st Cir. 1999).

Second Circuit: HSB Group, Inc. v. SVB Underwriting, Ltd., 664 F. Supp.2d 158 (D. Conn. 2009); United States Underwriters Insurance Co. v. Affordable Housing Foundation, Inc., 256 F. Supp.2d 176 (S.D.N.Y. 2003).

Third Circuit: Northern Shipping Co. v. Arkwright Boston Manufacturers Mutual Insurance Co., 617 F. Supp. 136 (E.D. Pa. 1985).

Fourth Circuit: Resource Bankshares Corp. v. St. Paul Mercury Insurance Co., 407 F.3d 631 (4th Cir. 2005); Schwartz & Schwartz of Virginia, L.L.C. v. Certain Underwriters at Lloyd's, London who Subscribed to Policy Number NC959, 677 F. Supp.2d 890 (W.D. Va. 2009).

Fifth Circuit: Leonard v. Nationwide Mutual Insurance Co., 499 F.3d 419 (5th Cir. 2007); Graphia v. Balboa Insurance Co., 517 F. Supp.2d 854 (E.D. La. 2007).

Sixth Circuit: Comerica Inc. v. Zurich American Insurance Co., 498 F. Supp.2d 1019 (E.D. Mich. 2007).

Seventh Circuit: Hartford Accident and Indemnity Co. v. Neff, 594 F. Supp. 317 (N.D. Ill. 1984).

Eighth Circuit: Ohio Casualty Insurance Co. v. Union Pacific Railroad Co., 469 F.3d 1158 (8th Cir. 2006).

Ninth Circuit: Great Divide Insurance Co. v. AOAO Maluna Kai Estates, 492 F. Supp.2d 1216 (D. Haw. 2007).

Tenth Circuit: Riordan v. Lawyers Title Insurance Corp., 393 F. Supp.2d 1100 (D.N.M. 2005).

Eleventh Circuit: Penzer v. Transportation Insurance Co., 509 F. Supp.2d 1278 (S.D. Fla. 2007); Preis v. Lexington Insurance Co., 508 F. Supp.2d 1061 (S.D. Ala. 2007).

State Courts:

Arizona: Aztar Corp. v. United States Fire Insurance Co., 223 Ariz. 463, 224 P.3d 960, (Ariz. App. 2010); Tritschler v. Allstate Insurance Co., 144 P.3d 519 (Ariz. App. 2006).

Colorado: Progressive Specialty Insurance Co. v. Hartford Underwriters Insurance Co., 148 P.3d 470 (Colo. App. 2006).

Connecticut: Heyse v. Case, 114 Conn. App. 640, 971 A.2d 699 (2009).

Georgia: ALEA London Ltd. v. Woodcock, 286 Ga. App. 572, 649 S.E.2d 740 (2007); Coregis Insurance Co. v. Nelson, 639 S.E.2d 365 (Ga. App. 2006).

Illinois: Abram v. United Services Automobile Association, 395 Ill. App.3d 700, 916 N.E.2d 1175, 334 Ill. Dec. 287 (2009).

Indiana: Bradshaw v. Chandler, 916 N.E.2d 163 (Ind. 2009); State Farm Mutual Automobile Insurance Co. v. D.L.B., 862 N.E.2d 678 (Ind. App. 2007); Elliott v. Allstate Insurance Co., 859 N.E.2d 696 (Ind. App. 2007).

Louisiana: Fontenot v. Diamond B Marine Services, Inc., 937 So.2d 425 (La. App. 2006).

Massachusetts: Surabian Realty Co. v. NGM Insurance Co., 462 Mass. 715, 971 N.E.2d 268 (2012).

Michigan: Tenneco Inc. v. Amerisure Mutual Insurance Co., 281 Mich. App. 429, 761 N.W.2d 846 (2008).

Minnesota: Farmers Insurance Exchange v. Letellier, 820 N.W.2d 597 (Minn. App. 2012).

Missouri: Ritchie v. Allied Property and Casualty Insurance Co., 307 S.W.3d 132 (Mo. 2009); Jones v. Mid-Century Insurance Co., 287 S.W.3d 687 (Mo. 2009); Golden Rule Insurance Co. v. R.S., 368 S.W.3d 327 (Mo. App. 2012); Gateway Hotel Holdings, Inc. v. Lexington Insurance Co., 275 S.W.3d 268 (Mo. App. 2008); Stone v. Farm Bureau Town & Country Insurance Company of Missouri, 203 S.W.3d 736 (Mo. App. 2006).

New Hampshire: Great American Insurance Co. v. Christy, 164 N.H. 196, 53 A.3d 538 (2012).

North Carolina: Patel v. Scottsdale Insurance Co., 728 S.E.2d 394 (N.C. App. 2012).

Oregon: Marsh v. American Family Mutual Insurance Co., 231 Or. App. 332, 218 P.3d 573 (2009).

South Carolina: Southern Glass & Plastics Co. v. Kemper, 732 S.E.2d 205 (S.C. App. 2012).

Tennessee: Garrison v. Bickford, 377 S.W.3d 659 (Tenn. 2012); Travelers Indemnity Company of America v. Moore & Associates, Inc., 216 S.W.3d 302 (Tenn. 2007).

Texas: SA-OMAX 2007, L.P. v. Certain Underwriters at Lloyd's, London, 374 S.W.3d 594 (Tex. App. 2012).

Utah: Bear River Mutual Insurance Co. v. Williams, 153 P.3d 798 (Utah App. 2006).

Virginia: Virginia Farm Bureau Mutual Insurance Co. v. Williams, 278 Va. 75, 677 S.E.2d 299 (2009); Seals v. Erie Insurance Exchange, 277 Va. 558, 674 S.E.2d 860 (2009).

Washington: Reliable Credit Association v. Progressive Direct Insurance Co., 2012 WL 5332477 (Wash. App. Oct. 30, 2012).

West Virginia: Blake v. State Farm Mutual Automobile Insurance Co., 224 W.Va. 317, 685 S.E.2d 895 (2009).

Wisconsin: Wadzinski v. Auto-Owners Insurance Co., 342 Wis.2d 311, 818 N.W.2d 819 (2012); Marotz v. Hallman, 302 Wis.2d 428, 734 N.W.2d 411 (2007).

[29] See:

First Circuit: OneBeacon America Insurance Co. v. Commercial Union Assurance Company of Canada, 684 F.3d 237 (1st Cir. 2012); Certain Interested Underwriters at Lloyd's, London v. Stolberg, 680 F.3d 61 (1st Cir. 2012); Financial Resources Network, Inc. v. Brown and Brown, Inc. 867 F. Supp.2d 153 (D. Mass 2012).

Second Circuit: Admiral Indemnity Co. v. Travelers Casualty and Surety Company of America, 881 F. Supp.2d 570 (S.D.N.Y. 2012); HSB Group, Inc. v. SVB Underwriting, Ltd., 664 F. Supp.2d 158 (D. Conn. 2009).

Third Circuit: Post v. St. Paul Travelers Insurance Co., 691 F.3d 500 (3d Cir. 2012); Premcor Refining Group v. National Fire Insurance Company of Hartford, 855 F. Supp.2d 237 (D. Del. 2012); *In re* Integrated Health Services, Inc., 375 B.R. 730 (D. Del. 2007).

Fourth Circuit: National Casualty Co. v. Lockheed Martin Corp., 415 F. Supp.2d 596 (D. Md. 2006).

Fifth Circuit: First American Bank v. First American Transportation Title Insurance Co., 585 F.3d 833 (5th Cir. 2009); Basic Energy Services, Inc. v. Liberty Mutual Insurance Co., 655 F. Supp.2d 666 (W.D. Tex. 2009); Charlton v. Evanston Insurance Co., 502 F. Supp.2d 553 (W.D. Tex. 2007); *In re* Katrina Canal Breaches Consolidated Litigation, 466 F. Supp.2d 729 (E.D. La. 2006).

Sixth Circuit: Pizza Magia International, LLC v. Assurance Company of America, 447 F. Supp.2d 766 (W.D. Ky. 2006).

Seventh Circuit: St. Paul Travelers Companies, Inc. v. Corn Island Shipyard, Inc., 495 F.3d 376 (7th Cir. 2007); National Casualty Co. v. Jewel's Bus Co., 880 F. Supp.2d 914 (N.D. Ill. 2012); Rockwell Automation, Inc. v. National Union Fire Insurance Co. of Pittsburgh, Pennsylvania, 494 F. Supp.2d 1009 (E.D. Wis. 2007).

Eighth Circuit: Friedberg v. Chubb & Sons, Inc., 691 F.3d 948 (8th Cir. 2012); TAMKO Building Products, Inc. v. Factual Mutual Insurance Co., 2012 WL 3596155 (E.D. Mo. Aug. 21, 2012); Carlson Marketing Group, Inc. v. Royal Indemnity Co., 517 F. Supp.2d 1089 (D. Minn. 2007); Fireman's Fund v. Structural Systems Technology, Inc., 426 F. Supp.2d 1009 (D. Neb. 2006).

Ninth Circuit: Century Surety Co. v. Casino West, Inc., 677 F.3d 903 (9th Cir. 2012); St. Paul Fire & Marine Insurance Co. v. Hebert Construction, Inc., 450 F. Supp.2d 1214 (W.D. Wash. 2006); Clarendon National Insurance Co. v. Insurance Company of the West, 442 F. Supp.2d 914 (E.D. Cal. 2006).

Tenth Circuit: EMC Insurance Cos. v. Mid-Continent Casualty Co., 2012 WL 3150528 (D. Colo. Aug. 2, 2012); Breaux v. American Family Mutual Insurance Co., 387 F. Supp.2d 1154 (D. Colo. 2005).

Eleventh Circuit: Ruderman *ex rel.* Schwartz v. Washington National Insurance Corp., 671 F.3d 1208 (11th Cir. 2012); Sinni v. Scottsdale Insurance Co., 676 F. Supp.2d 1319 (M.D. Fla. 2009); St. Paul Fire and Marine Insurance Co. v. Sea Quest International, Inc., 676 F. Supp.2d 1306 (M.D. Fla. 2009); Preis v. Lexington Insurance Co., 508 F. Supp.2d 1061 (S.D. Ala. 2007); Graphic Arts Mutual. Insurance Co. v. Essex Insurance Co., 465 F. Supp.2d 1290 (N.D. Ga. 2006).

State Courts:

Arizona: Tritschler v. Allstate Insurance Co., 144 P.3d 519 (Ariz. App. 2006).

California: Forecast Homes, Inc. v. Steadfast Insurance Co., 181 Cal. App.4th 1466, 105 Cal. Rptr.3d 200 (2010); Great Western Drywall, Inc. v. Interstate Fire and Casualty Co., 161 Cal. App.4th 1033, 74 Cal. Rptr.3d 657 (2008); ACS Systems, Inc. v. St. Paul Fire & Marine Insurance Co., 53 Cal. Rptr.3d 786 (Cal. App. 2007).

Colorado: Progressive Specialty Insurance Co. v. Hartford Underwriters Insurance Co., 148 P.3d 470 (Colo. App. 2006).

Connecticut: Arrowood Indemnity Co. v. King, 304 Conn. 179, 39 A.3d 712 (2012).

Florida: State Farm Mutual Automobile Insurance Co. v. Fischer, 16 So.3d 1028 (Fla. App. 2009); Lenhart v. Federated National Insurance Co., 950 So.2d 454 (Fla. Dist. App. 2007); The Doctors Co. v. Health Management Associates, Inc., 943 So.2d 807 (Fla. Dist. App. 2006).

Georgia: ALEA London Ltd. v. Woodcock, 286 Ga. App. 572, 649 S.E.2d 740 (2007); Coregis Insurance Co. v. Nelson, 639 S.E.2d 365 (Ga. App. 2006).

Illinois: Valley Forge Insurance Co. v. Swiderski Electronics, Inc., 860 N.E.2d 307 (Ill. 2006); American States Insurance Co. v. CFM Construction Co., 398 Ill. App.3d 994, 923 N.E.2d 299, 337 Ill. Dec. 740 (2010); DeSaga v. West Bend Mutual Insurance Co., 391 Ill. App.3d 1062, 910 N.E.2d 159, 331 Ill. Dec. 86 (2009); Knezovich v. Hallmark Insurance Co., 975 N.E.2d 1165, 363 Ill. Dec. 856 (Ill App. 2012), appeal pending (Nov. 1, 2012).

Louisiana: Fontenot v. Diamond B Marine Services, Inc., 937 So.2d 425 (La. App. 2006).

Massachusetts: Commerce Insurance Co. v. Blackburn, 81 Mass. App. Ct. 519, 964 N.E.2d 1005 (2012).

Michigan: Tenneco Inc. v. Amerisure Mutual Insurance Co., 281 Mich. App. 429, 761 N.W.2d 846 (2008).

Mississippi: Corban v. United Services Automobile Association, 20 So.3d 601 (Miss. 2009); Caldwell Freight Lines, Inc. v. Lumbermens Mutual Casualty Co., 947 So.2d 948 (Miss. 2007); Progressive Gulf Insurance Co. v. We Care Day Care Center, Inc., 2006 WL 2865495 (Miss. App. Oct. 10, 2006).

Missouri: Stone v. Farm Bureau Town & Country Insurance Company of Missouri, 203 S.W.3d 736 (Mo. App. 2006).

Nebraska: Harleysville Insurance Group v. Omaha Gas Appliance Co., 278 Neb. 547, 772 N.W.2d 88 (2009).

New York: Federal Insurance Co. v. International Business Machines Corp., 18 N.Y.3d 642, 965 N.E.2d 934, 942 N.Y.S.2d 432 (2012); Travelers Indemnity Co. v. Commerce & Industry Insurance Company of Canada, 828 N.Y.S.2d 658 (N.Y. App. Div. 2007).

North Carolina: Patel v. Scottsdale Insurance Co., 728 S.E.2d 394 (N.C. App. 2012).

Oregon: Marsh v. American Family Mutual Insurance Co., 231 Or. App. 332, 218 P.3d 573 (2009).

Pennsylvania: Mutual of Omaha Insurance Co. v. Bosses, 237 A.2d 218, 220 (Pa. 1968); Triplett v. Erie Insurance Exchange, 54 Pa. D. & C.2d 291, 292 (Pa. C.P. 1971).

South Carolina: Auto Owners Insurance Co. v. Newman, 385 S.C. 187, 684 S.E.2d 541 (2009).

Tennessee: Scheele v. Hartford Underwriters Insurance Co., 218 S.W.3d 636 (Tenn. 2007).

Texas: Fiess v. State Farm Lloyds, 202 S.W.3d 744 (Tex. 2006); SA-OMAX 2007, L.P. v. Certain Underwriters at Lloyd's, London, 374 S.W.3d 594 (Tex. App. 2012); Oceanus Insurance Co. v. White, 372 S.W.3d 700 (Tex. App. 2012); Coterill-Jenkins v. Texas Medical Association Health Care Liability Claim Trust, 2012 WL 3524985 (Tex. App. Aug. 16, 2012).

Virginia: PBM Nutritionals, L.L.C. v. Lexington Insurance Co., 283 Va. 624, 724 S.E.2d 707 (2012).

Washington: Ki Sin Kim v. Allstate Insurance Co., 153 Wash. App. 339, (2009); National Clothing Co. v. Hartford Casualty Insurance Co., 145 P.3d 394 (Wash. App. 2006).

Wisconsin: Veto v. American Family Mutual Insurance Co., 341 Wis.2d 390, 815 N.W.2d 713 (2012).

[30] See, e.g.:

First Circuit: Financial Resources Network, Inc. v. Brown and Brown, Inc. 867 F. Supp.2d 153 (D. Mass 2012); Picerne-Military Housing, L.L.C. v. American International Specialty Lines Insurance Co., 650 F. Supp.2d 135 (D.R.I. 2009).

Second Circuit: HSB Group, Inc. v. SVB Underwriting, Ltd., 664 F. Supp.2d 158 (D. Conn. 2009); North American Foreign Trading Corp. v. Mitsui Sumitomo Insurance USA, Inc., 499 F. Supp.2d 361 (S.D.N.Y. 2007).

Third Circuit: Allstate Insurance Co. v. Hopfer, 672 F. Supp.2d 682 (E.D. Pa. 2009).

Fourth Circuit: Premier Pet Products, L.L.C. v. Travelers Property Casualty Company. of America, 678 F. Supp.2d 409 (E.D. Va. 2010); Bao v. Liberty Mutual Fire Insurance Co., 535 F. Supp.2d 532 (D. Md. 2008).

Fifth Circuit: First American Bank v. First American Transportation Title Insurance Co., 585 F.3d 833 (5th Cir. 2009); Smith v. American Family Life Assurance Company of Columbus, 584 F.3d 212 (5th Cir. 2009).

Sixth Circuit: Bondex International, Inc. v. Hartford Accident and Indemnity Co., 667 F.3d 669 (6th Cir. 2011).

Seventh Circuit: BASF AG v. Great American Assurance Co., 522 F.3d 813 (7th Cir. 2008); Kimmel v. Western Reserve Life Assurance Company of Ohio, 678 F. Supp.2d 783 (N.D. Ind. 2010).

Eighth Circuit: Goddard v. South Dakota Public Assurance Alliance, 687 F.3d 965 (8th Cir. 2012); TAMKO Building Products, Inc. v. Factual Mutual Insurance Co., 2012 WL 3596155 (E.D. Mo. Aug. 21, 2012).

Ninth Circuit: Yue v. Conseco Life Insurance Co., 282 F.R.D. 469 (C.D. Cal. 2012); Matheny v. Unumprovident Corp., 594 F. Supp.2d 1212 (E.D. Wash. 2009); United Guaranty Mortgage Indemnity Co. v. Countrywide Financial Corp., 660 F. Supp.2d 1163 (C.D. Cal. 2009); Lukes v. American Family Mutual Insurance Co., 455 F. Supp.2d 1010 (D. Ariz. 2006).

Tenth Circuit: Boggs v. Great Northern Insurance Co., 659 F. Supp.2d 1199 (N.D. Okla. 2009).

Eleventh Circuit: HR Acquisition I Corp. v. Twin City Fire Insurance Co., 547 F.3d 1309 (11th Cir. 2008).

State Courts:

Alaska: Whittier Properties, Inc. v. Alaska National Insurance Co., 185 P.3d 84 (Alaska 2008); Nelson v. Progressive Casualty Insurance Co., 162 P.3d 1228 (Alaska 2007).

Arkansas: Nash v. American National Property and Casualty Co., 98 Ark. App. 258, 254 S.W.3d 758 (2007).

California: Philadelphia Indemnity Insurance Co. v. Montes-Harris, 40 Cal.4th 151, 146 P.3d 1251, 51 Cal. Rptr.3d 709 (Cal. 2006); State Farm General Insurance Co. v. JT's Frames, Inc., 181 Cal. App.4th 429, 104 Cal. Rptr.3d 573 (2010); Forecast Homes, Inc. v. Steadfast Insurance Co., 181 Cal. App.4th 1466, 105 Cal. Rptr.3d 200 (2010).

Colorado: Rocha v. Financial Indemnity Corp., 155 P.3d 602 (Colo. App. 2006).

Connecticut: Heyse v. Case, 114 Conn. App. 640, 971 A.2d 699 (2009).

Delaware: AT & T Corp. v. Faraday Capital Ltd., 918 A.2d 1104 (Del. 2007).

Florida: Certain Interested Underwriters at Lloyd's London v. Pitu, Inc., 95 So.2d 290 (Fla. App. 2012); Shaw v. State Farm Fire and Casualty Co., 918 A.2d 1104 (Fla. App. 2009).

Illinois: Nicor, Inc. v. Associated Electric and Gas Insurance Services Ltd., 223 Ill.2d 407, 860 N.E.2d 280, 307 Ill. Dec. 626 (2006); Knezovich v. Hallmark Insurance Co., 975 N.E.2d 1165, 363 Ill. Dec. 856 (Ill App. 2012), appeal pending (Nov. 1, 2012); Pekin Insurance Co. v. Equilon Enterprises L.L.C., 2012 IL App (1st) 111529 (Ill. App. Nov. 9, 2012).

Indiana: Buckeye State Mutual Insurance Co. v. Carfield, 914 N.E.2d 315 (Ind. App. 2009).

Kansas: American Special Risk Management Corp. v. Cahow, 286 Kan. 1134, 192 P.3d 614 (2008).

Maryland: State Farm Mutual Automobile Insurance Co. v. DeHaan, 393 Md. 163, 900 A.2d 208 (Md. 2006).

Massachusetts: LES Realty Trust "A" v. Landmark American Insurance Co., 82 Mass. App. Ct. 694, 977 N.E.2d 566 (2012).

Michigan: Tenneco Inc. v. Amerisure Mutual Insurance Co., 281 Mich. App. 429, 761 N.W.2d 846 (Mich. App. 2008).

Mississippi: Architex Association v. Scottsdale Insurance Co., 27 So.3d 1148 (Miss. 2010).

Missouri: Rice v. Shelter Mutual Insurance Co., 301 S.W.3d 43 (Mo. 2009).

Montana: Modroo v. Nationwide Mutual Fire Insurance Co., 345 Mont. 262, 191 P.3d 389 (2008).

New Hampshire: Great American Insurance Co. v. Christy, 164 N.H. 196, 53 A.3d 538 (2012).

New Mexico: United Nuclear Corp. v. Allstate Insurance Co., 285 P.3d 644 (N.M. 2012).

New York: Albany Medical Center v. Preferred Life Insurance Company of New York, 19 Misc.3d 209, 851 N.Y.S.2d 843 (N.Y. Supreme Ct. Albany Cnty. 2008).

Oregon: Capitol Specialty Insurance Corp. v. Chan & Lui, Inc., 248 Or. App. 674, 274 P.3d 238 (2012); Laird v. Allstate Insurance Co., 232 Or. App. 162, 221 P.3d 780 (2009); Marsh v. American Family Mutual Insurance Co., 231 Or. App. 332, 218 P.3d 573 (2009).

Pennsylvania: Continental Casualty Co. v. Pro Machine, 916 A.2d 1111 (Pa. Super. 2007).

Tennessee: Garrison v. Bickford, 377 S.W.3d 659 (Tenn. 2012); Scheele v. Hartford Underwriters Insurance Co., 218 S.W.3d 636 (Tenn. 2007).

Texas: Lancer Insurance Co. v. Perez, 308 S.W.3d 35 (Tex. App. 2009).

Washington: Ki Sin Kim v. Allstate Insurance Co., 153 Wash. App. 339, 223 P.3d 1180 (2009).

West Virginia: Blake v. State Farm Mutual Automobile Insurance Co., 224 W.Va. 317, 685 S.E.2d 895 (2009).

Wisconsin: Marotz v. Hallman, 302 Wis.2d 428, 734 N.W.2d 411 (2007); Veto v. American Family Mutual Insurance Co., 341 Wis.2d 390, 815 N.W.2d 713 (Wis. App. 2012); Bormann v. Sohns, 298 Wis.2d 250, 727 N.W.2d 341 (Wis. App. 2006).

[31] See:

First Circuit: Certain Interested Underwriters at Lloyd's, London v. Stolberg, 680 F.3d 61 (1st Cir. 2012); National Union Fire Insurance Company of Pittsburgh, PA v. West Lake Academy, 548 F.3d 8 (1st Cir. 2008); Central Mutual Insurance Co. v. Boston Telephone, Inc., 486 F. Supp.2d 180 (D. Mass. 2007).

Second Circuit: Vam Check Cashing Corp. v. Federal Insurance Co., 2012 WL 5416480 (2d Cir. Nov. 7, 2012); Parks Real Estate Purchasing Group v. St. Paul Fire & Marine Insurance Co., 472 F.3d 33 (2d Cir. 2006); United National Insurance Co. v. Granoff, Walker & Forlenza, P.C., 598 F. Supp.2d 540 (S.D.N.Y. 2009); Alamia v. Nationwide Mutual Fire Insurance Co., 495 F. Supp.2d 362 (S.D.N.Y. 2007).

Third Circuit: G-I Holdings, Inc. v. Reliance Insurance Co., 586 F.3d 247 (3d Cir. 2009); West v. Lincoln Benefit Life Co., 509 F.3d 160 (3d Cir. 2007); UPMC Health System v. Metropolitan Life Insurance Co., 391 F.3d 497, 502 (3d Cir. 2004); Reliance Insurance. Co. v. Moessner, 121 F.3d 895, 903 (3d Cir. 1997); Bensalem Township v. International Surplus Lines Insurance Co., 38 F.3d 1303, 1309 (3d Cir. 1994); Baughman v. United States Liability Insurance Co., 662 F. Supp.2d 386 (D.N.J. 2009).

Fourth Circuit: Lawson v. American General Assurance Co., 455 F. Supp.2d 526 (S.D. W. Va. 2006).

Fifth Circuit: Nautilus Insurance Co. v. Country Oaks Apartments Ltd., 566 F.3d 452 (5th Cir. 2009); *In re* Katrina Canal Breaches Litigation, 495 F.3d 191 (5th Cir. 2007).

Sixth Circuit: Scottsdale Insurance Co. v. Flowers, 513 F.3d 546 (6th Cir. 2008); Citizens Insurance Company of America v. MidMichigan Health ConnectCare Network Plan, 449 F.3d 688 (6th Cir. 2006); Caudill Seed and Warehouse Co. v. Houston Casualty Co., 835 F. Supp.2d 329 (W.D. Ky. 2011); Lifeline Health Group, Inc. v. National Union Fire Insurance Company of Pittsburgh, Pa., 665 F. Supp.2d 770 (W.D. Ky. 2009); Eckstein v. Cincinnati Insurance Co., 469 F.Supp.2d 455 (W.D. Ky. 2007).

Seventh Circuit: Ruttenberg v. United States Life Insurance Co. in the City of New York, 413 F.3d 652 (7th Cir. 2005); Kimmel v. Western Reserve Life Assurance Company of Ohio, 678 F.Supp.2d 783 (N.D. Ind. 2010).

Eighth Circuit: Grinnell Mutual Reinsurance Co. v. Schwieger, 685 F.3d 697 (8th Cir. 2012); Babinski v. American Family Insurance Group, 569 F.3d 349 (8th Cir. 2009); Fleishour v. Stewart Title Guaranty Co., 640 F. Supp.2d 1088 (E.D. Mo. 2009).

Ninth Circuit: Century Surety Co. v. Casino West, Inc., 677 F.3d 903 (9th Cir. 2012); Apana v. TIG Insurance Co., 574 F.3d 679 (9th Cir. 2009); Align Technology, Inc. v. Federal Insurance. Co., 673 F. Supp.2d 957 (N.D. Cal. 2009).

Tenth Circuit: Yaffe Companies, Inc. v. Great American Insurance Co., 499 F.3d 1182 (10th Cir. 2007); EMC Insurance Cos. v. Mid-Continent Casualty Co., 2012 WL 3150528 (D. Colo. Aug. 2, 2012); Kerber v. Qwest Group Life Insurance Plan, 544 F. Supp.2d 1187 (D. Colo. 2008); Fireman's Fund v. Structural System Technology, Inc., 426 F. Supp.2d 1009 (D. Neb. 2006).

Eleventh Circuit: Penzer v. Transportation Insurance Co., 509 F. Supp.2d 1278 (S.D. Fla. 2007).

District of Columbia Circuit: Essex Insurance Co. v. Cafe Dupont, L.L.C., 674 F. Supp.2d 166 (D.D.C. 2009); National Railroad Passenger Corp. v. Lexington Insurance Co., 445 F. Supp.2d 37 (D.D.C. 2006).

State Courts:

Alaska: State Farm Mutual Automobile Insurance Co. v. Dowdy, 192 P.3d 994 (Alaska 2008).

Arizona: State Farm Fire & Casualty Insurance Co. v. Grabowski, 150 P.3d 275 (Ariz. App. 2007).

California: State v. Continental Insurance Co., 55 Cal.4th 186, 281 P.3d 1000, 145 Cal. Rptr.3d 1 (2012); Delgado v. Interinsurance Exchange of Automobile Club of Southern California, 47 Cal.4th 302, 211 P.3d 1083, 97 Cal. Rptr.3d 298 (2009); American International Underwriters Insurance Co. v. American Guarantee and Liability Insurance Co., 181 Cal. App.4th 616, 105 Cal. Rptr.3d 64 (2010); State Farm General Insurance Co. v. JT's Frames, Inc., 181 Cal. App.4th 429, 104 Cal. Rptr.3d 573 (2010); ACS Systems, Inc. v. St. Paul Fire & Marine Insurance Co., 53 Cal. Rptr.3d 786 (Cal. App. 2007); London Market Insurers v. Superior Court, 53 Cal. Rptr.3d 154 (Cal. App. 2007).

Colorado: Hoang v. Assurance Company of America, 149 P.3d 798 (Colo. 2007); Lincoln General Insurance Co. v. Bailey, 224 P.3d 336 (Colo. App. 2009).

Connecticut: Vermont Mutual Insurance Co. v. Walukiewicz, 290 Conn. 582, 966 A.2d 672 (2009).

Delaware: Intel Corp. v. American Guarantee and Liability Insurance Co., 2012 WL 3889138 (Del. Sep. 7, 2012).

Florida: American Strategic Insurance Co. v. Lucas-Solomon, 927 So.2d 184 (Fla. Dist. App.), *review denied* 940 So.2d 1125 (Fla. 2006).

Georgia: Owners Insurance Co. v. Smith Mechanical Contractors, Inc., 294 Ga. App. 754, 670 S.E.2d 213 (2008).

Hawaii: Guajardo v. AIG Hawaii Insurance Co., 118 Haw. 196, 187 P.3d 580 (2008).

Kentucky: Bidwell v. Shelter Mutual Insurance Co., 367 S.W.3d 585 (Ky. 2012); Hugenberg v. West American Insurance Company/Ohio Casualty Group, 249 S.W.3d 174 (Ky. App. 2006); Lynch v. Claims Management Corp., 306 S.W.3d 93 (Ky. App. 2010).

Massachusetts: Boston Gas Co. v. Century Indemnity Co., 454 Mass. 337, 910 N.E.2d 290 (2009).

Minnesota: Kastning v. State Farm Insurance Cos., 821 N.W.2d 621 (Minn. App. 2012); RAM Mutual Insurance Co. v. Meyer, 768 N.W.2d 399 (Minn. App. 2009).

Missouri: Burns v. Smith, 303 S.W.3d 505 (Mo. 2010).

Montana: Giacomelli v. Scottsdale Insurance Co., 354 Mont. 15, 221 P.3d 666 (2009).

Nevada: Fourth Street Place, L.L.C. v. Travelers Indemnity Co., 270 P.3d 1235 (Nev. 2011).

New Hampshire: Colony Insurance Co. v. Dover Indoor Climbing Gym, 158 N.H. 628, 974 A.2d 399 (2009).

New Jersey: Selective Insurance Company of America v. Hudson East Pain Management Osteopathic Medicine, 210 N.J. 597, 46 A.3d 1272 (2012); Charles Beseler Co. v. O'Gorman & Young, Inc., 911 A.2d 47 (N.J. 2006); S.T. Hudson Engineers, Inc. v. Pennsylvania National Mutual Casualty Co., 909 A.2d 1156 (N.J. Super. App. Div. 2006), *cert. denied* (N.J. Feb. 15, 2007).

New Mexico: United Nuclear Corp. v. Allstate Insurance Co., 285 P.3d 644 (N.M. 2012); Rehders v. Allstate Insurance Co., 135 P.3d 237 (N.M. App. 2006).

New York: Federal Insurance Co. v. International Business Machines Corp., 18 N.Y.3d 642, 965 N.E.2d 934, 942 N.Y.S.2d 432 (2012); Commercial Insurance Company of Newark, New Jersey v. Popadich, 68 A.D.3d 401, 890 N.Y.S.2d 36 (N.Y. App. Div. 2009); City of New York v. Evanston Insurance Co., 830 N.Y.S.2d 299 (N.Y. App. Div. 2007).

Oklahoma: Andres v. Oklahoma Farm Bureau Mutual Insurance Co., 227 P.3d 1102 (Okla. Civ. App. Div. 4 2009).

Pennsylvania: Tonkovic v. State Farm Mutual Automobile Insurance Co., 521 A.2d 920, 925 (Pa. 1987); Bishops, Inc. v. Penn National Insurance Co., 984 A.2d 982 (Pa. Super. 2009); Donegal Mutual Insurance Co. v. Baumhammers, 893 A.2d 797 (Pa. Super.), *appeal granted* 908 A.2d 265 (Pa. 2006).

Vermont: Northern Security Insurance Co. v. Rosenthal, 980 A.2d 805 (Vt. 2009).

West Virginia: Blake v. State Farm Mutual Automobile Insurance Co., 224 W.Va. 317, 685 S.E.2d 895 (2009);

West Virginia: Jenkins v. State Farm Mutual Automobile Insurance Co., 632 S.E.2d 346 (W. Va. 2006).

Wisconsin: Wadzinski v. Auto-Owners Insurance Co., 342 Wis.2d 311, 818 N.W.2d 819 (2012); Veto v. American Family Mutual Insurance Co., 341 Wis.2d 390, 815 N.W.2d 713 (Wis. App. 2012); Bormann v. Sohns, 727 N.W.2d 341 (Wis. App. 2006).

Wyoming: Broderick v. Dairyland Insurance Co., 270 P.3d 684 (Wyo. 2012).

[32] See:

First Circuit: B & T Masonry Construction Co. v. Public Service Mutual Insurance Co., 382 F.3d 36 (1st Cir. 2004).

Second Circuit: D.C. USA Operating Co., LLC v. Indian Harbor Insurance Co., 2007 WL 945016 (S.D.N.Y. Mar. 27, 2007); *In re* Payroll Express Corp., 2005 WL 2438444 (Bankr. S.D.N.Y. Mar. 30, 2005).

Third Circuit: Scirex Corp. v. Federal Insurance Co., 313 F.3d 841, 850–851 (3d Cir. 2002); Pinkhasov v. Allstate Property and Casualty Co., 2012 WL 5197555 (M.D. Pa. Oct. 19, 2012); Great Northern Insurance Co. v. Greenwich Insurance Co., 2008 WL 2048354 (W.D. Pa. May 12, 2008); Hughes v. State Farm Fire and Casulaty Co., 2007 WL 2874849 (W.D. Pa. Sept. 27, 2007); St. Marys Area Water Authority v. St. Paul Fire and Marine Insurance Co., 472 F. Supp.2d 630 (M.D. Pa. 2007).

Fourth Circuit: Coleman v. Nationwide Life Insurance Co., 969 F.2d 54 (4th Cir. 1992); Imperial Casualty and Indemnity Co. v. Radiator Specialty Co., 862 F. Supp. 1437 (E.D.N.C. 1994).

Fifth Circuit: Coleman v. School Board of Richland Parish, 418 F.3d 511 (5th Cir. 2005); Aspen Specialty Insurance Co. v. Muniz Engineering, Inc., 514 F. Supp.2d 972 (S.D. Tex. 2007); Rimkus Consulting Group, Inc. v. Hartford Casualty Insurance Co., 552 F. Supp.2d 637 (S.D. Tex. 2007).

Sixth Circuit: Republic Services, Inc. v. Liberty Mutual Insurance Co., 2006 WL 3004014 (E.D. Ky. Oct. 20, 2006); Meijer, Inc. v. General Star Indemnity Co., 826 F. Supp. 241 (W.D. Mich. 1993).

Seventh Circuit: Liberty Mutual Fire Insurance Co. v. Statewide Insurance Co., 352 F.3d 1098 (7th Cir. 2003); Schilke v. Wachovia Mortgage, F.S.B., 820 F. Supp.2d 825 (N.D. Ill. 2011); Hall v. Travelers Property Casualty Company of America, 2009 WL 1148231 (S.D. Ind. Apr. 27, 2009); Employers' Fire Insurance Co. v. Berg, 2007 WL 273559 (N.D. Ill. Jan. 25, 2007).

Eighth Circuit: Grinnell Mutual Reinsurance Co. v. Schwieger, 685 F.3d 697 (8th Cir. 2012); H & R Block, Inc. v. American International Specialty Lines Insurance Co., 546 F.3d 937 (8th Cir. 2008); BancInsure, Inc. v. Marshall Bank, N.A., 453 F.3d 1073 (8th Cir. 2006).

Ninth Circuit: Research Corp. v. Westport Insurance Corp., 289 Fed. Appx. 989 (9th Cir. 2008); Progressive Casualty Insurance Co. v. Owen, 519 F.3d 1035 (9th Cir. 2008); McHenry v. Pacificsource Health Plans, 679 F. Supp.2d 1226 (D. Or. 2010); Amica Mutual Insurance Co. v. Fischer, 2008 WL 1970639 (E.D. Cal. May 5, 2008); Progressive Casualty Insurance Co. v. Owen, 456 F. Supp.2d 1205 (D. Mont. 2006).

Tenth Circuit: American Casualty Company of Reading PA v. Health Care Indemnity, Inc., 520 F.3d 1131 (10th Cir. 2008); Lee v. Enterprise Financial Group, 2009 WL 1362605 (W.D. Okla. May 14, 2009).

Eleventh Circuit: Twin City Fire Insurance Co. v. Ohio Casualty Insurance Co., 480 F.3d 1254 (11th Cir. 2007).

District of Columbia Circuit: Essex Insurance Co. v. Cafe Dupont, L.L.C., 674 F. Supp.2d 166 (D.D.C. 2009).

State Courts:

Alabama: Ex parte Cincinnati Insurance Co., 51 So.3d 298 (Ala. 2010); Shrader v. Employers Mutual Casualty Co., 907 So.2d 1026 (Ala. 2005).

Arizona: Phoenix Control Systems, Inc. v. Insurance Company of North America, 796 P.2d 463, 467 (Ariz. 1990); Mesino v. Clarendon America Insurance Co., 2008 WL 4173620 (Ariz. App. 2008).

California: Alpha Holdings, Ltd. v. Travelers Indemnity Co., 2006 WL 1916982 (Cal. App. July 13, 2006); Fresno Unified School District v. Coregis Insurance Co., 2006 WL 1633683 (Cal. App. June 14, 2006); R & B Auto Center, Inc. v. Farmers Group, Inc., 140 Cal. App.4th 327, 44 Cal. Rptr.3d 426 (2006).

Colorado: Mullen v. Allstate Insurance Co., 232 P.3d 168 (Colo. App. 2009); Fire Insurance Exchange v. Sullivan, 224 P.3d 348 (Colo. App. 2009); DeHerrera v. American Family Mutual Insurance Co., 219 P.3d 346 (Colo. App. 2009).

Connecticut: Wentland v. American Equity Insurance Co., 267 Conn. 592, 840 A.2d 1158 (2004).

Delaware: HLTH Corp. v. Clarendon National Insurance Co., 2009 WL 2849777 (Del. Super. Aug. 31, 2009).

Florida: Bell Care Nurses Registry, Inc. v. Continental Casualty Co., 25 So.3d 13 (Fla. App. 2009).

Idaho: Roylance v. John Alden Life Insurance Co., 2008 WL 4202018 (Idaho Dist. Kootenai Cnty. Aug. 22, 2008).

Illinois: W.E. Erickson Construction, Inc. v. Chicago Title Insurance Co., 641 N.E.2d 861 (Ill. App. 1994), *appeal denied* 647 N.E.2d 1018 (Ill. 1995).

Indiana: French v. State Farm Fire and Casualty Co., 881 N.E.2d 1031 (Ind. App. 2008); McGuire v. Century Surety Co., 861 N.E.2d 357 (Ind. App. 2007); Jones v. State Farm Mutual Automobile Insurance Co., 635 N.E.2d 200 (Ind. App. 1994).

Michigan: Ile v. Foremost Insurance Co., 293 Mich. App. 309, 809 N.W.2d 617 (2011); Abay v. DaimlerChrysler Insurance Co., 2009 WL 2477623 (Mich. App. Aug. 13, 2009).

Minnesota: West Bend Mutual Insurance Co. v. Allstate Insurance Co., 776 N.W.2d 693 (Minn. 2009); Johnson v. Cummiskey, 765 N.W.2d 652 (Minn. App. 2009).

Montana: Newbury v. State Farm Fire and Casualty Insurance Company of Bloomington, Ill., 343 Mont. 279, 184 P.3d 1021 (2008).

New Jersey: Pinto v. New Jersey Manufacturers Insurance Co., 874 A.2d 520 (N.J. 2005).

North Dakota: Tibert v. Nodak Mutual Insurance Co., 816 N.W.2d 31 (N.D. 2012).

Ohio: Coleman v. Progressive Preferred Insurance Co., 2008 WL 2779194 (Ohio App. July 18, 2008).

Pennsylvania: Heller v. Pennsylvania League of Cities and Municipalities, 32 A.3d 1213 (Pa. 2011); 401 Fourth Street, Inc. v. Investors Insurance Group, 583 Pa. 445, 879 A.2d 166 (2005); Lewinski v. Commonwealth, 852 A.2d 1270, 1274 (Pa. Commw. 2004).

South Carolina: South Carolina Farm Bureau Mutual Insurance Co. v. Kennedy, 730 So.2d 862 (S.C. 2012).

Tennessee: Morrison v. Allen, 338 S.W.3d 417 (Tenn. 2011).

Vermont: Pharmacists Mutual Insurance Co. v. Myer, 993 A.2d 413 (Vt. 2010).

Wisconsin: Teschendorf v. State Farm Insurance Cos., 717 N.W.2d 258 (Wis. 2006); Gillund v. Meridian Mutual Insurance Co., 323 Wis.2d 1, 778 N.W.2d 662 (Wis. App. 2009); Progressive Northern Insurance Co. v. Kirchoff, 313 Wis.2d 138, 756 N.W.2d 635 (Wis. App. 2008).

[33] See:

Second Circuit: New York Marine and General Insurance Co. v. Tradeline L.L.C., 266 F.3d 112 (2d Cir. 2001) (typed terms control over conflicting pre-printed forms); Acadia Insurance Co. v. American Crushing & Recycling, LLC, 475 F. Supp.2d 168 (D. Conn. 2007); Oldcastle Precast, Inc. v. United States Fidelity & Guaranty Co., 458 F. Supp.2d 131 (S.D.N.Y. 2006).

Third Circuit: In re Cendant Corp. Securities Litigation, 454 F.3d 235 (3d Cir. 2006); Whole Enchilada, Inc. v. Travelers Property Casualty Company of America, 581 F. Supp.2d 677 (W.D. Pa. 2008) (if there is a conflict between the terms of insurance endorsement and those in the body of the main policy, then the endorsement prevails); Nationwide Mutual Insurance Co. v. Schmidt, 307 F. Supp.2d 674 (W.D. Pa. 2004) (endorsements by their very nature are designed to trump general policy provisions where conflict exists between provisions in main policy and endorsement).

Fourth Circuit: Cordova v. Scottsdale Insurance Co., 5 Fed. Appx. 142 (4th Cir. 2001); Harleysville Mutual Insurance Co. v. Reliance National Insurance Co., 256 F. Supp.2d 413 (M.D.N.C. 2002).

Fifth Circuit: Mid-Continent Casualty Co. v. Bay Rock Operating Co., 614 F.3d 105 (5th Cir. 2010); Delta and Pine Land Co. v. Nationwide Agribusiness Insurance Co., 530 F.3d 395 (5th Cir. 2008) (riders or endorsements modify the general terms of a policy because they are, by definition, deemed more specific, they control the more general terms of the policy); Barnard Construction Co. v. City of Lubbock, 457 F.3d 425 (5th Cir. 2006).

Sixth Circuit: Aerel, S.R.L. v. PCC Airfoils, L.L.C., 448 F.3d 899 (6th Cir. 2006); Crutchfield v. Transamerica Occidental Life Insurance Co., 2012 WL 4212354 (W.D. Ky. Sept. 19, 2012); Whitt Machine, Inc. v. Essex Insurance Co., 631 F. Supp.2d 927 (S.D. Ohio 2009) (endorsement in conflict with pre-printed policy controls); Western World Insurance Co. v.

Lula Belle Stewart Center, Inc., 473 F. Supp.2d 776 (E.D. Mich. 2007) (sexual molestation endorsement's specific provisions, where applicable, would govern over the more general terms in commercial general liability policy).

Eighth Circuit: Grinnell Mutual Reinsurance Co. v. Schwieger, 685 F.3d 697 (8th Cir. 2012).

Ninth Circuit: Manzarek v. St. Paul Fire and Marine Insurance Co., 519 F.3d 1025 (9th Cir. 2008) (if conflict exists between main body of insurance policy and endorsement to policy, endorsement prevails); Idaho v. Shoshone-Bannock Tribes, 465 F.3d 1095 (9th Cir. 2006); Spa De Soleil, Inc. v. General Star Indemnity Co., 787 F.Supp.2d 1091 (C.D. Cal. 2011).

Tenth Circuit: Blackhawk-Central City Sanitation District v. American Guarantee and Liability Insurance Co., 214 F.3d 1183 (10th Cir. 2000).

Eleventh Circuit: Keenan Hopkins Schmidt and Stowell Contractors, Inc. v. Continental Casualty Co., 653 F. Supp.2d 1255 (M.D. Fla. 2009) (endorsement controls over pre-printed form); Fuddruckers, Inc. v. Fudpucker's, Inc., 436 F. Supp.2d 1260 (N.D. Fla. 2006).

State Courts:

Alabama: Commercial Standard Insurance Co. v. General Trucking Co., 423 So.2d 168 (Ala. 1982) (where there is added to printed insurance form a written or typewritten clause, that clause should be considered as superseding those clauses in conflict that are printed in form).

California: Haynes v. Farmers Insurance Exchange, 89 P.3d 381 (Cal. 2004); Venoco, Inc. v. Gulf Underwriters Insurance Co., 175 Cal. App.4th 750, 96 Cal. Rptr.3d 409 (Cal. App. 2009) (endorsement controls in conflict with pre-printed body of policy); Essex Insurance. Co. v. City of Bakersfield, 65 Cal. Rptr.3d 1 (Cal. App. 2007); Frontier Oil Corp. v. RLI Insurance Co., 63 Cal. Rptr.3d 816 (Cal. App. 2007).

Colorado: Weitz Co., LLC v. Mid-Century Insurance Co., 181 P.3d 309 (Colo. App. 2007).

Connecticut: Mount Vernon Fire Insurance Co. v. Morris, 877 A.2d 910 (Conn. App. 2005) (endorsements by their very nature alter and take precedence over the provisions of the policy to which they pertain).

Delaware: Mount Vernon Fire Insurance Co. v. Pied Piper Kiddie Rides, Inc., 445 A.2d 949 (Del. Super. 1982) (typewritten language of insurance contract generally controls printed language).

District of Columbia: Tillery v. District of Columbia Contract Appeals Board, 912 A.2d 1169 (D.C. 2006).

Florida: Kel Homes, LLC v. Burris, 933 So.2d 699 (Fla. Dist. App. 2006).

Georgia: RLI Insurance v. Highlands on Ponce, LLC, 635 S.E.2d 168 (Ga. App. 2006).

Illinois: Pekin Insurance Co. v. Recurrent Training Center, Inc., 409 Ill. App.3d 114, 948 N.E.2d 668, 350 Ill. Dec. 388 (2011); IMC Global v. Continental Insurance Co., 378 Ill. App.3d 797, 883 N.E.2d 68, 318 Ill. Dec. 234 (Ill. App. 2007).

Kansas: Lightner v. Centennial Life Insurance Co., 242 Kan. 29, 744 P.2d 840 (Kan. 1987) (handwritten provisions control over pre-printed confliction provisions).

Louisiana: Johnson v. Orleans Parish School Board, 80 So.3d 1175 (La. App. 2011); Chicago Property Interests, L.L.C. v. Broussard, 8 So.3d 42 (La. App. 2009) (exclusions that were set forth to modify the terms in an endorsement attached to parish's "public officials and employees liability insurance policy" narrowed the general obligations set forth in the endorsement, and controlled where they conflicted with such general obligations);

Louisiana: In re St. Louis Encephalitis Outbreak in Ouachita Parish No. 01-4224, 939 So.2d 563 (La. App. 2006).

Michigan: Besic v. Citizens Insurance Company of the Midwest, 290 Mich. App. 19, 800 N.W.2d 93 (2010).

Missouri: American Family Mutual Insurance Co. v. St. Clair, 295 S.W.3d 586 (Mo. App. 2009) (typed terms control over conflicting pre-printed forms); Grable v. Atlantic Casualty Insurance Co., 280 S.W.3d 104 (Mo. App. 2009) (if endorsement language conflicts with general provisions of the insurance policy, the endorsement will prevail).

Nebraska: Charley v. Farmers Mutual Insurance Company of Nebraska, 219 Neb. 765, 366 N.W.2d 417 (1985) (limits of liability specified in typed policy declarations control over lesser limits printed in uninsured motorist provision of policy).

New Jersey: Gabriele v. Lyndhurst Residential Community, L.L.C., 426 N.J. Super. 96, 43 A.3d 1169 (2012).

New York: Hunt v. Ciminelli-Cowper Co., 93 A.D.3d 1152, 939 N.Y.S.2d 781 (2012).

Ohio: American Hardware Mutual Insurance Co. v. Mansfield Auto Truck Plaza, 15 Ohio St.3d 367, 474 N.E.2d 310 (Ohio 1984) (typewritten provision controls pre-printed conflicting provision).

Oregon: Bresee Homes, Inc. v. Farmers Insurance Exchange, 227 Or. App. 587, 206 P.3d 1091 (Or. App. 2009) (to the extent that an endorsement conflicts with the rest of policy, the endorsement controls).

Pennsylvania: Trombetta v. Raymond James Financial Services, Inc., 907 A.2d 550 (Pa. Super. 2006); Maryland Casualty Co. v. Carolina Casualty Insurance Co., 445 A.2d 535 (Pa. Super. 1982) (as between typewritten and printed provisions of policy, typewritten provisions are controlling).

Rhode Island: Cheaters, Inc. v. United National Insurance Co., 41 A.3d 637 (R.I. 2012).

South Dakota: State v. Pursley, 729 N.W.2d 351 (S.D. 2007).

Texas: Wells Fargo Bank, Minnesota, N.A. v. North Central Plaza I, L.L.P., 194 S.W.3d 723 (Tex. App. 2006); TIG Insurance Co. v. San Antonio YMCA, 172 S.W.3d 652 (Tex. App. 2005) (endorsement provisions will only supersede the previous policy terms to the extent they are truly in conflict).

[34] See:

First Circuit: McGowan v. Warden, Maine State Prison, 2008 WL 4533901 (D. Me. Oct. 6, 2008).

Second Circuit: Cordiano v. Metacon Gun Club, Inc., 575 F.3d 199 (2d Cir. 2009); *In re* MF Global Holdings, Ltd., 481 B.R. 268 (Bankr. S.D.N.Y. 2012); Almeida v. United States Department of Housing and Urban Development, 2009 WL 873125 (S.D.N.Y. Feb. 11, 2009); Bernhard v. Dutchess Community College, 1982 WL 193 (S.D.N.Y. Feb. 19, 1982); *In re* Best Payphones, Inc., 2007 WL 1388103 (Bankr. S.D.N.Y. May 8, 2007).

Third Circuit: United States v. Cole, 567 F.3d 110 (3d Cir. 2009); Toffler Associates v. Hartford Fire Insurance Co., 651 F. Supp.2d 332 (E.D. Pa. 2009); Calyon New York Branch v. American Home Mortgage Corp., 383 B.R. 585 (Bankr. D. Del. 2008).

Fourth Circuit: PPG Industries Inc. v. International Chemical Workers Union Council of United Food and Commercial Workers, 587 F.3d 648 (4th Cir. 2009); Southern Walk at Broadlands Homeowner's Association, Inc. v. Openband at Broadlands, L.L.C., 2012 WL 3579605 (E.D. Va. Aug. 17, 2012); United States Chamber of Commerce v. National Labor Relations Board, 856 F. Supp.2d 778 (D.S.C. 2012); Vitullo v. Mancini, 684 F. Supp.2d 760 (E.D. Va. 2010); U.S. v. Okun, 2009 WL 2762620 (E.D. Va. Aug. 27, 2009); Hartford Fire Insurance Co. v. St. Paul Fire and Marine Insurance Co., 606 F. Supp.2d 602 (E.D.N.C. 2009).

Fifth Circuit: In re Seda France, Inc., 2011 WL 3022563 (W.D. Tex. July 22, 2011); Arnold By and Through Arnold v. Blue Cross & Blue Shield of Texas, Inc., 973 F. Supp. 726 (S.D. Tex. 1997).

Sixth Circuit: Andrews v. Columbia Gas Transmission Corp., 544 F.3d 618 (6th Cir. 2008); United Steel Workers Local Union 978 v. Packaging Corporation of America, 2010

WL 396353 (W.D. Tenn. Jan. 27, 2010); Gills v. Ford Motor Co., 829 F. Supp. 894 (W.D. Ky. 1993).

Seventh Circuit: Rickher v. Home Depot, Inc., 535 F.3d 661 (7th Cir. 2008); *In re* Hitch, 2009 WL 1542791 (Bankr. C.D. Ill. May 29, 2009).

Eighth Circuit: Dubinsky v. Mermart, L.L.C., 595 F.3d 812 (8th Cir. 2010); Shell v. Amalgamated Cotton Garment, 43 F.3d 364, 366 (8th Cir. 1994).

Ninth Circuit: Barnes v. Independent Automobile Dealers, 64 F.3d 1389 (9th Cir. 1995); Longview Fibre Co. v. Rasmussen, 980 F.2d 1307, 1312–1313 (9th Cir. 1992) (doctrine means that mention of one thing implies exclusion of the other); Hardware Mutual Insurance Co. v. Dunwoody, 194 F.2d 666, 668 (9th Cir. 1952).

Tenth Circuit: Via Christi Regional Medical Center, Inc. v. Leavitt, 509 F.3d 1259 (10th Cir. 2007); Air Methods Corp. v. Opeiu, 2008 WL 4614302 (D. Colo. Oct. 15, 2008); Kerber v. Qwest Group Life Insurance Plan, 544 F. Supp.2d 1187 (D. Colo. 2008).

Eleventh Circuit: Cliff v. Payco General American Credits, Inc., 363 F.3d 1113 (11th Cir. 2004); Bacon v. Stiefel Laboratories, Inc., 677 F. Supp.2d 1331 (S.D. Fla. 2010).

District of Columbia Circuit: Bynum v. Equitable Mortgage Group, 2005 WL 818619 (D.D.C. Apr. 7, 2005).

State Courts:

Alabama: Harper v. Coats, 988 So.2d 501 (Ala. 2008).

Arizona: Buckeye Pollution Control Corp. v. Maricopa County, 2007 WL 5517458 (Ariz. App. July 31, 2007).

Arkansas: National Life & Accident Insurance Co. v. Abbott, 455 S.W.2d 120 (Ark. 1970).

California: Steven v. Fidelity & Casualty Company of New York, 377 P.2d 284 (Cal. 1962); City of Corona v. Naulls, 166 Cal. App.4th 418, 83 Cal.Rptr.3d 1 (2008).

Colorado: Zab, Inc. v. Berenergy Corp., 136 P.3d 252 (Colo. 2006).

Connecticut: Honulik v. Town of Greenwich, 293 Conn. 641, 980 A.2d 845 (2009).

Delaware: Segovia v. Equities First Holdings, L.L.C., 2008 WL 2251218 (Del. Super. May 30, 2008).

Florida: Calhoun, Dreggors and Associates v. Volusia County, 26 So.3d 624 (Fla. App. 2009); Deen v. Wilson, 1 So.3d 1179 (Fla. App. 2009); United Automobile Insurance Co. v. Salgado, 22 So.3d 594 (Fla. App. 2009).

Georgia: Goddard v. City of Albany, 285 Ga. 882, 684 S.E.2d 635 (2009).

Idaho: Saint Alphonsus Diversified Care, Inc. v. MRI Associates, L.L.P., 148 Idaho 479, 224 P.3d 1068 (2009).

Illinois: People v. Lee, 397 Ill. App.3d 1067, 926 N.E.2d 402, 339 Ill. Dec. 170 (2010).

Indiana: Linton v. Davis, 887 N.E.2d 960 (Ind. App. 2008).

Iowa: State v. Hemphill, 771 N.W.2d 654 (Iowa App. 2009).

Kansas: Farmers Insurance Co., Inc. v. Jokan, 57 P.3d 24 (Kan. App. 2002).

Louisiana: Wooley v. Lucksinger, 14 So.3d 311 (La. App. 2008).

Maine: Foremost Insurance Co. v. Levesque, 926 A.2d 1185 (Me. 2007).

Maryland: Houghton v. Forrest, 412 Md. 578, 989 A.2d 223 (2010); Powell v. Breslin, 195 Md. App. 340, 6 A.3d 360 (2010).

Massachusetts: Souza v. Sheriff of Bristol County, 455 Mass. 573, 918 N.E.2d 823 (2010).

Michigan: Miller v. Allstate Insurance Co., 481 Mich. 601, 751 N.W.2d 463 (2008); Gray v. Chrostowski, 2012 WL 6062715 (Mich. App. Dec.6, 2012); Shaheen v. Michigan Public School Employees Retirement Board, 2008 WL 5076593 (Mich. App. Dec. 2, 2008).

Minnesota: Steps of Success Homes, L.L.C. v. Dowell, 2009 WL 5091936 (Minn. App. Dec. 29, 2009).

Missouri: Green v. Penn-America Insurance Co., 242 S.W.3d 374 (Mo. App. 2007); Versaw v. Versaw, 202 S.W.3d 638 (Mo. App. 2006).

Montana: In re Adoption of K.P.M., 349 Mont. 170, 201 P.3d 833 (2009).

Nebraska: Dowd Grain Co. v. County of Sarpy Board of Adjustment, 2008 WL 2511150 (Neb. App. June 24, 2008).

New Hampshire: State v. Fournier, 158 N.H. 441, 969 A.2d 434 (2009).

New Jersey: Saunders *ex rel.* Saunders v. Capital Health System at Mercer, 398 N.J. Super. 500, 942 A.2d 142 (N.J. Super. App. Dept. 2008).

New York: Hearst Corp. v. State, Office of State Comptroller, 24 Misc.3d 611, 882 N.Y.S.2d 862 (N.Y. Sup. Ct. Albany Cnty. 2009).

North Carolina: Mangum v. Raleigh Board of Adjustment, 196 N.C. App. 249, 674 S.E.2d 742 (2009).

Ohio: State *ex rel.* American Outdoor Advertising Co. v. Abell, 2010 WL 338226 (Ohio App. Jan. 29, 2010); Lawrence Township Board of Trustees v. Canal Fulton, 2008 WL 2572612 (Ohio App. 2008); Molnar v. Castle Bail Bonds, 2005 WL 3436923 (Ohio App. Dec. 13, 2005).

Oklahoma: In re Adoption of Baby G., 195 P.3d 377 (Okla. 2008).

Pennsylvania: Fletcher v. Pennsylvania Property and Casualty Insurance Guaranty Association, 985 A.2d 678 (Pa. 2009); Allegheny Inspection Service, Inc. v. North Union Township, 964 A.2d 878 (Pa. 2009); Commonwealth v. Ostrosky, 909 A.2d 1224 (Pa. 2006); Allegheny Inspection Service, Inc. v. North Union Township, 912 A.2d 380 (Pa. Commw. 2006).

South Carolina: Hughes v. Western Carolina Regional Sewer Authority, 386 S.C. 641, 689 S.E.2d 638 (S.C. App. 2010).

South Dakota: Rush v. U.S. Bancorp Equipment Finance, Inc., 742 N.W.2d 266 (S.D. 2007).

Tennessee: Tennessee River Collection Yacht Sales, L.L.C. v. P.F.C., Inc., 2009 WL 3103818 (Tenn. App. Sept. 29, 2009).

Texas: Texas Property and Casualty Insurance Guaranty Association for Reliance National Insurance Co. v. Toberny, 2010 WL 985170 (Tex. App. Mar. 19, 2010); *In re* Huag, 175 S.W.3d 449 (Tex. App. 2005).

Vermont: Kapusta v. Department of Health/Risk Management, 186 Vt. 276, 980 A.2d 236 (2009).

Washington: State v. Kelley, 168 Wash.2d 72, 226 P.3d 773 (2010); Clark County Public Utility District Number 1 v. State of Washington Department of Revenue, 153 Wash. App. 737, 222 P.3d 1232 (2009); State v. Wright, 774 P.2d 1265 (Wash. App. 1989).

35 See, e.g.:

First Circuit: OneBeacon America Insurance Co. v. Commercial Union Assurance Company of Canada, 684 F.3d 237 (1st Cir. 2012); Panagora Asset Management, Inc. v. St. Paul Mercury Insurance, 674 F. Supp.2d 315 (D. Mass. 2009); Vermont Mutual Insurance Co. v. Petit, 613 F. Supp.2d 154 (D. Mass. 2009).

Second Circuit: XL Specialty Insurance Co. v. Level Global Investors, L.P., 2012 WL 2138044 (S.D.N.Y. June 13, 2012); Macey v. Carolina Casualty Insurance Co., 585 F. Supp.2d 277 (D. Conn. 2008).

Third Circuit: American Automobile Insurance Co. v. Murray, 658 F.3d 311 (3d Cir. 2011); Wimberly Allison Tong & Goo, Inc. v. Travelers Property Casualty Company of America, 559 F. Supp.2d 504 (D.N.J. 2008).

Fourth Circuit: Bao v. Liberty Mutual Fire Insurance Co., 535 F. Supp.2d 532 (D. Md. 2008).

Fifth Circuit: Looney Ricks Kiss Architects, Inc. v. State Farm Fire and Casualty Co., 677 F.3d 250 (5th Cir. 2012); First American Bank v. First American Transportation Title Insurance Co., 585 F.3d 833 (5th Cir. 2009); Smith v. American Family Life Assurance Company of Columbus, 584 F.3d 212 (5th Cir. 2009).

Sixth Circuit: Continental Casualty Co. v. Auto Plus Insurance Agency, L.L.C., 676 F. Supp.2d 657 (N.D. Ohio 2009); Fulton Bellows, L.L.C. v. Federal Insurance Co., 107 Fair Empl. Prac. Cas. (BNA) 882 (E.D. Tenn. 2009).

Seventh Circuit: Levy v. Minnesota Life Insurance Co., 517 F.3d 519 (7th Cir. 2008).

Eighth Circuit: Goddard v. South Dakota Public Assurance Alliance, 687 F.3d 965 (8th Cir. 2012); TAMKO Building Products, Inc. v. Factual Mutual Insurance Co., 2012 WL 3596155 (E.D. Mo. Aug. 21, 2012); Orthopedic Resources, Inc. v. Nautilus Insurance Co., 654 F. Supp.2d 1307 (N.D. Okla. 2009); National Fire Insurance Company of Hartford v. NWM-Oklahoma, L.L.C., 546 F. Supp.2d 1238 (W.D. Okla. 2008).

Ninth Circuit: Century Surety Co. v. Casino West, Inc., 677 F.3d 903 (9th Cir. 2012); MidMountain Contractors, Inc. v. American Safety Indemnity Co., 2012 WL 3864901 (W.D. Wash. Sep. 5, 2012); Chartis Specialty Insurance Co. v. Queen Anne HS, L.L.C., 867 F. Supp.2d 1111 (W.D. Wash. 2012); California Dairies Inc. v. RSUI Indemnity Co., 617 F. Supp.2d 1023 (E.D. Cal. 2009); Matheny v. Unumprovident Corp., 594 F. Supp.2d 1212 (E.D. Wash. 2009).

Tenth Circuit: Admiral Insurance Co. v. Hosler, 626 F. Supp.2d 1105 (D. Colo. 2009).

Eleventh Circuit: Continental Casualty Co. v. City of Jacksonville, 654 F. Supp.2d 1338 (M.D. Fla. 2009).

State Courts:

Arkansas: Parker v. Southern Farm Bureau Casualty Insurance Co., 104 Ark. App. 301, 292 S.W.3d 311 (2009).

California: Carson v. Mercury Insurance Co., 210 Cal. App.4th 409, 148 Cal. Rptr.3d 518 (2012); American International Underwriters Insurance Co. v. American Guarantee and Liability Insurance Co., 181 Cal. App.4th 616, 105 Cal. Rptr.3d 64 (2010); Forecast Homes, Inc. v. Steadfast Insurance Co., 181 Cal. App.4th 1466, 105 Cal. Rptr.3d 200 (2010); Baker v. National Interstate Insurance Co., 180 Cal. App.4th 1319, 103 Cal. Rptr.3d 565 (2009); Mercury Insurance Co. v. Pearson, 169 Cal. App.4th 1064, 87 Cal. Rptr.3d 310 (2008).

Colorado: Massingill v. State Farm Mutual Automobile Insurance Co., 176 P.3d 816 (Colo. App. 2007).

Connecticut: Arrowood Indemnity Co. v. King, 304 Conn. 179, 39 A.3d 712 (2012); Connecticut Medical Insurance Co. v. Kulikowski, 286 Conn. 1, 942 A.2d 334 (2008).

Florida: Certain Interested Underwriters at Lloyd's London v. Pitu, Inc., 95 So.2d 290 (Fla. App. 2012); State Farm Mutual Automobile Insurance Co. v. Fischer, 16 So.3d 1028 (Fla. App. 2009); State Farm Mutual Automobile Insurance Co. v. Mashburn, 15 So.3d 701 (Fla. App. 2009).

Georgia: Murphy v. Ticor Title Insurance Co., 316 Ga. App. 97, 729 S.E.2d 21 (2012); GEICO General Insurance Co. v. Wright, 299 Ga. App. 280, 682 S.E.2d 369 (2009).

Illinois: Wolfensberger v. Eastwood, 382 Ill. App.3d 924, 889 N.E.2d 635, 321 Ill. Dec. 370 (2008).

Indiana: Motorists Mutual Insurance Co. v. Wroblewski, 898 N.E.2d 1272 (Ind. App. 2009).

Iowa: Thomas v. Progressive Casualty Insurance Co., 749 N.W.2d 678 (Iowa 2008).

Louisiana: Orleans Parish School Board v. Lexington Insurance Co., 99 So.3d 723 (La. App. 2012); McNamara v. Augustino Brothers, Inc., 13 So.3d 736 (La. App. 2009).

Massachusetts: Cable Mills, L.L.C. v. Coakley Pierpan Dolan and Collins Insurance Agency, Inc., 82 Mass. App. Ct. 415, 974 N.E.2d 1134 (2012); Commerce Insurance Co. v. Blackburn, 81 Mass. App. Ct. 519, 964 N.E.2d 1005 (2012).

Mississippi: Corban v. United Services Automobile Association, 20 So.3d 601 (Miss. 2009).

Missouri: Burns v. Smith, 303 S.W.3d 505 (Mo. 2010); Golden Rule Insurance Co. v. R.S., 368 S.W.3d 327 (Mo. App. 2012); Haulers Insurance Co., Inc. v. Pounds, 272 S.W.3d 902 (Mo. App. 2008).

Montana: United National Insurance Co. v. St. Paul Fire and Marine Insurance Co., 352 Mont. 105, 214 P.3d 1260 (2009).

New Jersey: Polarome International, Inc. v. Greenwich Insurance Co., 404 N.J. Super. 241, 961 A.2d 29 (N.J. Super. App. Dept. 2008).

New York: Antoine v. City of New York, 56 A.D.3d 583, 868 N.Y.S.2d 688 (N.Y. App. Div. 2008); Italian Designer Import Outlet, Inc. v. New York Central Mutual Fire Insurance Co., 26 Misc.3d 631, 891 N.Y.S.2d 260 (N.Y. Sup. Ct., King's Cnty. 2009).

North Dakota: Grinnell Mutual Reinsurance Co. v. Thies, 755 N.W.2d 852 (N.D. 2008).

Ohio: Bosserman Aviation Equipment, Inc. v. United States Liability Insurance Co., 183 Ohio App.3d 29, 915 N.E.2d 687 (2009).

Oklahoma: Andres v. Oklahoma Farm Bureau Mutual Insurance Co., 227 P.3d 1102 (Okla. App. 2009).

Oregon: Laird v. Allstate Insurance Co., 232 Or. App. 162, 221 P.3d 780 (2009).

Pennsylvania: Rood v. Commonwealth Land Title Insurance Co., 936 A.2d 488 (Pa. Super. 2007).

South Carolina: South Carolina Farm Bureau Mutual Insurance Co. v. Kennedy, 730 So.2d 862 (S.C. 2012).

South Dakota: Cole v. Wellmark of South Dakota, Inc., 776 N.W.2d 240 (S.D. 2009).

Tennessee: Garrison v. Bickford, 377 S.W.3d 659 (Tenn. 2012); Spears v. Tennessee Farmers Mutual Insurance Co., 300 S.W.3d 671 (Tenn. App. 2009).

Texas: Safeco Lloyds Insurance Co. v. Allstate Insurance Co., 308 S.W.3d 49 (Tex. App. 2009).

Utah: Doctors' Co. v. Drezga, 218 P.3d 598 (Utah 2009).

Washington: Vision One, L.L.C. v. Philadelphia Indemnity Insurance Co., 174 Wash.2d 501, 276 P.3d 300 (2012) (*en banc*); Campbell v. Ticor Title Insurance Co., 166 Wash.2d 466, 209 P.3d 859 (2009); Reliable Credit Association v. Progressive Direct Insurance Co., 2012 WL 5332477 (Wash. App. Oct. 30, 2012); Sauter *ex rel.* Sauter v. Houston Casualty Co., 168 Wash. App. 348, 276 P.3d 358 (2012); Ki Sin Kim v. Allstate Insurance Co., 153 Wash. App. 339, 223 P.3d 1180 (2009); S & K Motors, Inc. v. Harco National Insurance Co., 151 Wash. App. 633, 213 P.3d 630 (2009).

[36] See:

First Circuit: Certain Interested Underwriters at Lloyd's, London v. Stolberg, 680 F.3d 61 (1st Cir. 2012); Zurich American Insurance Co. v. Watts Regulator Co., 860 F. Supp.2d 78 (D. Mass. 2012).

Second Circuit: Acadia Insurance Co. v. American Crushing & Recycling, LLC, 2007 WL 610164 (D. Conn. Feb. 28, 2007).

Third Circuit: Travelers Property Casualty Company of America v. Chubb Custom Insurance Co., 864 F. Supp.2d 301 (E.D. Pa. 2012); Employers Mutual Casualty Co. v. Loos, 2007 WL 665841 (W.D. Pa. Feb. 28, 2007).

Fourth Circuit: Firemen's Insurance Company of Washington, D.C. v. Kline & Son Cement Repair, Inc., 2007 WL 519230 (E.D. Va. Feb. 13, 2007).

Fifth Circuit: ACE American Insurance Co. v. Freeport Welding and Fabricating, Inc., 2012 WL 5077688 (5th Cir. Oct. 19, 2012); First American Bank v. First American Transportation Title Insurance Co., 585 F.3d 833 (5th Cir. 2009).

Sixth Circuit: Pedicini v. Life Insurance Company of Alabama, 682 F.3d 522 (6th Cir. 2012); Smith v. Stonebridge Life Insurance Co., 2007 WL 466742 (W.D. Wis. Feb. 12, 2007).

Seventh Circuit: St. Paul Fire and Marine Insurance Co. v. Schilli Transportation Services, Inc., 672 F.3d 451 (7th Cir. 2012).

Eighth Circuit: Owners Insurance Co. v. European Auto Works, Inc., 2012 WL 4052406 (8th Cir. Sep. 17, 2012); TAMKO Building Products, Inc. v. Factual Mutual Insurance Co., 2012 WL 3596155 (E.D. Mo. Aug. 21, 2012); *In re* Acceptance Insurance Companies, 383 B.R. 128 (Bankr. 8th Cir. 2008).

Ninth Circuit: Century Surety Co. v. Casino West, Inc., 677 F.3d 903 (9th Cir. 2012); Chartis Specialty Insurance Co. v. Queen Anne HS, L.L.C., 867 F. Supp.2d 1111 (W.D. Wash. 2012); Scanlon v. Life Insurance Company of North America, 670 F. Supp.2d 1181 (W.D. Wash. 2009); Tri-Star Theme Builders, Inc./PCL Construction Services, Inc. v. Hawkeye-Security Insurance Co., 653 F. Supp.2d 973 (D. Ariz. 2009).

Tenth Circuit: Apartment Investment and Management Co. (AIMCO) v. Nutmeg Insurance Co., 593 F.3d 1188 (10th Cir. 2010).

Eleventh Circuit: James River Insurance Co. v. Oscar I. Garcia, Architect, P.A., 856 F. Supp.2d 1284 (S.D. Fla. 2012); Fabricant v. Kemper Independence Insurance Co., 2007 WL 458023 (S.D. Fla. Feb. 9, 2007).

District of Columbia Circuit: Essex Insurance Co. v. Cafe Dupont, L.L.C., 674 F. Supp.2d 166 (D.D.C. 2009).

State Courts:

California: State v. Continental Insurance Co., 55 Cal.4th 186, 281 P.3d 1000, 145 Cal. Rptr.3d 1 (2012); E.M.M.I Inc. v. Zurich American Insurance Co., 84 P.3d 385 (Cal. 2004); MacKinnon v. Truck Insurance Exchange, 73 P.3d 1205 (Cal. 2003); Pacific Gas & Electric. Co. v. G. W. Thomas Drayage & Rigging Co., 442 P.2d 641 (Cal. 1968); ACS Systems, Inc. v. St. Paul Fire & Marine Insurance Co., 53 Cal. Rptr.3d 786 (Cal. App. 2007); Benedek v. PLC Santa Monica, LLC, 129 Cal. Rptr.2d 197, 202 (Cal. App. 2002); Solis v. Kirkwood Resort Co., 114 Cal. Rptr.2d 265, 269 (Cal. App. 2001).

Colorado: Hecla Mining Co. v. New Hampshire Insurance Co., 811 P.2d 1083, 1090 (Colo. 1991); City of Englewood v. Commercial Union Assurance Co., 940 P.2d 948 (Colo. App. 1996).

Connecticut: Fiallo v. Allstate Insurance Co., 138 Conn. App. 325, 51 A.3d 1193 (2012).

Delaware: Intel Corp. v. American Guarantee and Liability Insurance Co., 51 A.3d 442 (Del. 2012); AT&T Corp. v. Faraday Capital Ltd., 2007 WL 329218 (Del. Super. Feb. 5, 2007).

Florida: Lenhart v. Federated National Insurance Co., 2007 WL 461335 (Fla. Dist. App. Feb. 14, 2007); Ward v. Nationwide Mutual Fire Insurance Co., 364 So.2d 73, 77 (Fla. Dist. App. 1978); Effort Enterprises of Florida v. Lexington Insurance Co., 666 So.2d 930, 931 (Fla. Dist. App. 1995); Airmanship, Inc. v. United States Aviation Underwriters, Inc., 559 So.2d 89, 91–92 (Fla. Dist. App.), *review denied* 576 So.2d 294 (Fla. 1990).

Idaho: Farm Bureau Mutual Insurance Company of Idaho v. Eisenman, 286 P.3d 185 (Idaho 2012).

Indiana: FLM, L.L.C. v. Cincinnati Insurance Co., 973 N.E.2d 1167 (Ind. App. 2012); McGuire v. Century Surety Co., 861 N.E.2d 357 (Ind. App. 2007).

Iowa: Bituminous Casualty Corp. v. Sand Livestock Systems, Inc., 728 N.W.2d 216 (Iowa 2007).

Louisiana: Robinson Brothers, Inc. v. Carter, 2007 WL 466586 (La. App. Feb. 14, 2007).

Massachusetts: Surabian Realty Co. v. NGM Insurance Co., 462 Mass. 715, 971 N.E.2d 268 (2012).

Michigan: Nickerson v. Citizens Mutual Insurance Co., 224 N.W.2d 896 (Mich. 1975).

Mississippi: Hankins v. Maryland Casualty Co./Zurich American Insurance Co., 2012 WL 4711437 (Miss. Oct. 4, 2012).

Missouri: Mendenhall v. Property and Casualty Insurance Company of Hartford, 375 S.W.3d 90 (Mo. 2012) (*en banc*); Seeck v. Geico General Insurance Co., 212 S.W.3d 129 (Mo. 2007).

Montana: Swank Enterprises, Inc. v. All Purpose Services, Ltd., 154 P.3d 52, (Mont. 2007).

New Mexico: United Nuclear Corp. v. Allstate Insurance Co., 285 P.3d 644 (N.M. 2012).

New York: Continental Casualty Co. v. Rapid-American Corp., 609 N.E.2d 506, 512 (N.Y. 1993).

Ohio: Professional Rental, Inc. v. Shelby Insurance Co., 599 N.E.2d 423, 427 (Ohio App. 1991).

Pennsylvania: Miller v. Poole, 45 A.3d 1143 (Pa. Super. 2012); Continental Casualty Co. v. Pro Machine, 916 A.2d 1111 (Pa. Super. 2007); Erie Insurance Exchange v. Transamerica Insurance Co., 533 A.2d 1363, 1368 (Pa. 1987).

Rhode Island: Riel v. Harleysville Worcester Insurance Co., 45 A.3d 561 (R.I. 2012).

South Carolina: Southern Glass & Plastics Co. v. Kemper, 732 S.E.2d 205 (S.C. App. 2012).

Texas: Farmers Insurance Exchange v. Greene, 376 S.W.3d 278 (Tex. App. 2012); SA-OMAX 2007, L.P. v. Certain Underwriters at Lloyd's, London, 374 S.W.3d 594 (Tex. App. 2012).

Washington: Greer v. Northwestern National Insurance Co., 743 P.2d 1244, 1249 (Wash. 1987); Reliable Credit Association v. Progressive Direct Insurance Co., 2012 WL 5332477 (Wash. App. Oct. 30, 2012).

[37] See, e.g.:

Third Circuit: *In re* Montgomery Ward and Co., Inc., 344 B.R. 256 (D. Del. 2006).

Eleventh Circuit: Lemy v. Direct General Finance Co., 2012 WL 239702 (M.D. Fla. June 19, 2012).

State Courts:

Alabama: Tindle v. State Farm General Insurance Co., 826 So.2d 144 (Ala. Civ. App. 2001).

California: Wayne v. Staples, Inc., 135 Cal. App.4th 466, 37 Cal. Rptr.3d 544 (2006).

Connecticut: Orkney v. Hanover Insurance Co., 248 Conn. 195, 727 A.2d 700 (1999).

Georgia: White v. State Farm Fire and Casualty Co., 291 Ga. 306, 728 S.E.2d 685 (2012).

Illinois: Lincoln Towers Insurance Agency, Inc. v. Boozell, 291 Ill. App.3d 965, 684 N.E.2d 900, 225 Ill. Dec. 909 (1997).

Iowa: Mueller v. Wellmark, Inc., 818 N.W.2d 244 (Iowa 2012).

Louisiana: Wooley v. State Farm Fire and Casualty Insurance Co., 893 So.2d 746 (La. 2005).

Michigan: Basic Property Insurance Association v. OFIR, 808 N.W.2d 456, 808 N.W.2d 456 (2010).

Minnesota: Illinois Farmers Insurance Co. v. Glass Service Co., 683 N.W.2d 792 (Minn. 2004).

Missouri: Angoff v. Holland-America Company Trust, 969 S.W.2d 351 (Mo. App. 1998).

New Jersey: In re Markel Insurance Companies, 319 N.J. Super. 23, 724 A.2d 848 (N.J. Super. App. Dept. 1999).

New York: A.M. Medical Services, P.C. v. Progressive Casualty Insurance Co., 101 A.D.3d 53, 953 N.Y.S.2d 219 (2012); Sclafani v. Allstate Insurance Co., 3 Misc.3d 634, 777 N.Y.S.2d 251 (N.Y. Sup. Ct. 2004).

Pennsylvania: Insurance Federation of Pennsylvania, Inc. v. Commissioner, Insurance Department, 601 Pa. 20, 970 A.2d 1108 (2009).

Texas: Canal Insurance Co. v. Hopkins, 238 S.W.3d 549 (Tex. App. 2007); Texas Department of Insurance v. Reconveyance Services, Inc., 240 S.W.3d 418 (Tex. App. 2007).

Washington: Pain Diagnostics and Rehabilitation Associates, P.S. v. Brockman, 97 Wash. App. 691, 988 P.2d 972 (1999).

West Virginia: Barefield v. DPIC Companies, 215 W.Va. 544, 600 S.E.2d 256 (2004).

[38] See §3.03[1][a] *infra.*

[39] Surplus lines insurance companies provide a market for insurance relating to risks the market of registered insurance companies may be unwilling to underwrite. Surplus lines insurance companies are generally exempt from the form and rate filing requirements, likely to induce them to fill the void in the market. See Flitner and Trupin, *AICPCU's Surplus Lines Products* (1st ed. 2006). See also, Lemy v. Direct General Finance Co., 2012 WL 239702 (M.D. Fla. June 19, 2012).

[40] See, e.g.:

Sixth Circuit: Kentucky Association of Health Plans, Inc. v. Nichols, 227 F.3d 352 (6th Cir. 2000).

State Court:

Kentucky: Davidson v. American Freightways, Inc., 25 S.W.3d 94 (Ky. 2000).

[41] 40 Pa. Cons. Stat. Ann. § 477b. See also:

Seventh Circuit: Edward E. Gillen Co. v. Insurance Company of the State of Pennsylvania, 747 F. Supp.2d 1058 (E.D. Wis. 2010).

Ninth Circuit: Stephan v. Unum Life Insurance Company of America, 697 F.3d 917 (9th Cir. 2012); Hinkle v. Crum & Forster Holding, Inc., 747 F. Supp.2d 1132 (D. Alaska 2010).

Eleventh Circuit: Lemy v. Direct General Finance Co., 2012 WL 239702 (M.D. Fla. June 19, 2012).

State Courts:

Maryland: St. Paul Travelers v. Millstone, 412 Md. 424, 987 A.2d 116 (Md. App. 2010).

Missouri: Central United Life Insurance Co. v. Huff, 358 S.W.3d 88 (Mo. App. 2011).

Ohio: Siegfried v. Farmers Insurance of Columbus, Inc., 187 Ohio App.3d 710, 933 N.E.2d 815 (2010).

Wisconsin: MercyCare Insurance Co. v. Wisconsin Commissioner of Insurance, 328 Wis.2d 110, 786 N.W.2d 785 (2010).

[42] See, e.g., Flitner and Trupin, *AICPU's Surplus Lines Products* (1st ed. 2006). See also:

Fifth Circuit: Steadfast Insurance Co. v. SMX 98, Inc., 2009 WL 890398 (S.D. Tex. Mar. 30, 2009).

Eleventh Circuit: Official Cargo Transport Co. v. Underwriters at Lloyd's of London, 143 Fed. Appx. 173 (11th Cir. 2005); Lemy v. Direct General Finance Co., 2012 WL 239702 (M.D. Fla. June 19, 2012); Vision I Homeowners Association v. Aspen Specialty Insurance Co., 643 F. Supp.2d 1356 (S.D. Fla. 2009); Essex Insurance Co. v. Zota, 607 F. Supp.2d 1340 (S.D. Fla. 2009).

State Courts:

Alabama: Burlington Insurance Co. v. Fluid Services, Inc., 13 So.3d 965 (Ala. App. 2008).

Georgia: Kay-Lex Co. v. Essex Insurance Co., 286 Ga. App. 484, 649 S.E.2d 602 (2007).

Louisiana: Edwards v. Daugherty, 883 So.2d 932 (La. 2004).

New Hampshire: Grand China, Inc. v. United National Insurance Co., 156 N.H. 429, 938 A.2d 905 (2007).

New Jersey: Piermount Iron Works, Inc. v. Evanston Insurance Co., 197 N.J. 432, 963 A.2d 818 (2009) (surplus lines insurance may involve risks that authorized or admitted insurers refuse to cover by reason of the nature of the risk).

Pennsylvania: Triage, Inc. v. Prime Insurance Syndicate, Inc., 887 A.2d 303 (Pa. Super. 2005).

Texas: Howard v. Burlington Insurance Co., 347 S.W.3d 783 (Tex. App. 2011); Yorkshire Insurance Co. v. Seger, 279 S.W.3d 755 (Tex. App. 2007).

43 *Id.*

44 See Yorkshire Insurance Co. v. Seger, 279 S.W.3d 755 (Tex. App. 2007). See also:

Ninth Circuit: Certain Underwriters at Lloyd's of London v. American Safety Insurance Services, Inc., 702 F.Supp.2d 1169 (C.D. Cal. 2010).

Eleventh Circuit: Lemy v. Direct General Finance Co., 2012 WL 239702 (M.D. Fla. June 19, 2012).

State Courts:

California: Silvers v. State Board of Equalization, 188 Cal. App.4th 1215, 116 Cal. Rptr.3d 355 (2010).

Texas: Howard v. Burlington Insurance Co., 347 S.W.3d 783 (Tex. App. 2011).

45 See § 3.03[1][a] *supra.*

46 In Workman v. Great Plains Insurance Co., 200 N.W.2d 8 (Neb. 1972), the insurance company had obtained approval from the state insurance department to use an automobile policy form that provided coverage for all persons that drive the vehicle with the policyholder's permission and for an exclusionary endorsement for use in that policy to exclude certain specifically named individuals. The insurance company sold a policy that contained the approved form and an altered version of the endorsement listing "all persons other than the policyholder" as persons excluded from coverage for accidents resulting from permissive use. The altered endorsement was never submitted for approval to the insurance department. The testimony of the person at the state insurance department who had approved the form indicated that if he had been asked to pass on such an endorsement, it would have been disapproved and rejected based upon guidelines in existence at the insurance department. The court held that in light of the fact that the insurance department would have rejected the language in the policy had it been submitted, the insured was covered for a driver using the car with his permission.

47 A number of cases have held that policy issuers may not rely on language expressly rejected by the state insurance department. In Hawkins Chemical, Inc. v. Westchester Fire Insurance Co., 159 F.3d 348 (8th Cir. 1998) (applying Minnesota law), the owner of a warehouse was sued by a class of claimants averring smoke inhalation from a fire on the premises. The owner sought insurance coverage for the class action suit for smoke inhalation, and its liability insurance company denied coverage on the basis of a "total pollution exclusion," which had no exception for hostile fires and which was included in its policy. The form of the "total pollution exclusion" relied on by the insurance company had been expressly rejected and disapproved for use by the Minnesota insurance department. The court held that regulatory disapproved language was void.

At issue in Linkens v. Furman, 201 N.E.2d 645 (Ill. App. 1964) was whether an endorsement excluding coverage for drivers under twenty-five applied to bar coverage. The policy was sold with the drivers under twenty-five endorsement ten days after the insurance department had expressly disapproved the use such an endorsement. The court ruled in favor of coverage.

> "We are not persuaded that [the Illinois statute] should be construed to allow casualty insurance companies to issue endorsements binding on their insureds, *after* the Director of Insurance has expressly found the endorsements to be 'not acceptable for use in this State.' If such a construction were to prevail, the filing and examination provisions of [the statute] would be rendered ineffective to accomplish their evident function of public protection. When construing statutes, courts must presume the legislature intended to enact an effective law. A construction which would make the statute ineffective in operation therefore must be avoided." 201 N.E.2d at 648.

In Golden Rule Insurance Co. v. Insurance Department, 641 A.2d 1255, 1259 (Pa. Commw. 1994), *appeal denied* 655 A.2d 994 (Pa. 1995), a health and accident insurance company sought large premium increases and submitted the request to the Pennsylvania Insurance Commissioner. The insurance company immediately started selling policies with the rate increases, even though the rates had not been approved. Eighty-five days after the request had been submitted, the Insurance Commissioner rejected the rate increase. The court held that policies issued after the date of express disapproval were "invalid" pursuant to 40 Pa. Cons. Stat. Ann. § 477b. 641 A.2d at 1259.

Similarly, in Hepler v. Liberty Mutual Fire Insurance Co., 13 Pa. D. & C.4th 528, 534 (Pa. C.P. 1992), the insurance company submitted for approval a clause allowing for arbitration only by mutual consent into its automobile insurance policies. The Insurance Commissioner initially approved the submission but later expressly withdrew its approval and rejected the mutual consent to arbitration provision. On the date of issuance of the policy in question, the Commissioner had already withdrawn its approval and expressly rejected the mutual consent to arbitration provision. Nonetheless, the insurance company sold a policy with the rejected mutual consent to arbitration provision. The court held that the mutual consent provision was "void" because it had been rejected and disapproved as of the date of issuance of the policy.

In Mutual Life Insurance Co. v. Daddy$ Money, Inc., 646 S.W.2d 255 (Tex. App. 1982), a life insurance company submitted an endorsement dealing with non-payment of premiums to the insurance department. The insurance department specifically rejected the endorsement as severable, but approved its use as part of two form policies with which it had been submitted. The insurance company subsequently used the endorsement on another form and sold it to the policyholder. After nonpayment of the premium, the policyholder died and the beneficiaries sought the proceeds of the policy, as if the severable endorsement had never been included in the policy. The insurance company offered a much smaller amount, assuming the severable endorsement had become a part of the policy. The court refused to effectuate the disapproved endorsement, and ruled in favor of the beneficiaries. "[W]e hold that the issuance of an unapproved endorsement to a life insurance policy, in violation of [the statute] constitutes a nullity when enforcement of its terms is sought against the insured." 646 S.W.2d at 258.

See also: Carrier v. Allstate Insurance Co., 702 So.2d 367 (La. App. 1997); Guidroz v. Lewis, 626 So.2d 736 (La. App. 1993) (disapproved language would be invalid from the date of disapproval).

Cf., AMEX Assurance Co. v. Caripides, 179 F. Supp.2d 309 (S.D.N.Y. 2002), *aff'd* 316 F.3d 154 (2d Cir. 2003), in which a husband and wife obtained group accident and death insurance through the purchase of airplane tickets with their credit card. When they died in a plane crash, the insurance company instituted an interpleader action to determine the rightful beneficiaries. The form at issue created the following order of default beneficiaries: spouse, dependent children, parents, siblings. The policies did not designate specific beneficiaries, and the dispute was over whether the estranged twenty-seven-year-old non-dependent daughter of the deceased parents, or the uncles, aunts, and grandparents (siblings and parents of decedents) would be entitled to the proceeds. The non-dependent daughter argued that although the policy form had been approved, it was mistakenly approved by the insurance department, offering the affidavit of the examiner who had approved the form. The affidavit stated that the insurer mistakenly used the term "dependent children" rather than just "children." He went on to state that if he had been made aware that the default beneficiary provision contained the dependent children limitation as part of the default beneficiary provision of the policy, he "would have asked the attorney reviewing the policy to notify [the insurer] of the inconsistent use of the 'dependent children' term and suggest that they correct the default beneficiary provision so as to make the provision consistent with the requirements of group accident and health policies." 179 F. Supp.2d at 319.

Nevertheless, the court refused to invalidate the provision in question, in part, because of the lack of evidence that the examiner would have rejected the form had he noticed the inclusion of dependent children in the endorsement. The court pointed out that the examiner in his affidavit failed to aver that he would not have approved the policy as submitted by the insurer. 179 F. Supp.2d at 319–320.

48 See, e.g.:

Seventh Circuit: Edward E. Gillen Co. v. Insurance Company of the State of Pennsylvania, 747 F. Supp.2d 1058 (E.D. Wis. 2010).

Eighth Circuit: Miller v. National Farmers Union Property & Casualty Co., 470 F.2d 700 (8th Cir. 1972).

State Courts:

Alabama: Aetna Insurance Co. v. Word, 611 So.2d 266, 268 (Ala. 1992).

Florida: Miami-Dade County v. Associated Aviation Underwriters, 840 So.2d 264 (Fla. Dist. App. 2002) (dissenting opinion), *review dismissed* 846 So.2d 1148 (Fla. 2003); American Mutual Fire Insurance Co. v. Illingworth, 213 So.2d 747 (Fla. Dist. App. 1968).

Wisconsin: Appleton Papers, Inc. v. Home Indemnity Co., 612 N.W.2d 760, 770 (Wis. App. 2000).

49 See, e.g.:

Third Circuit: Herman v. Mutual Life Insurance Co., 108 F.2d 678 (3d Cir. 1939); Reliance Insurance Co. v. V.E. Corp., 1995 WL 560024 at *6 (E.D. Pa. Sept. 19, 1995), *rev'd without addressing* 121 F.3d 895 (3d Cir. 1997); Cinkutis v. Confederation Life Insurance Co., 1990 WL 161260 (E.D. Pa. Oct. 19, 1990).

Fifth Circuit: Resolution Trust Corp. v. Hedden, 879 F. Supp. 600 (N.D. Miss. 1995).

Ninth Circuit: Stephan v. Unum Life Insurance Company of America, 697 F.3d 917 (9th Cir. 2012); Hinkle v. Crum & Forster Holding, Inc., 747 F. Supp.2d 1132 (D. Alaska 2010).

Eleventh Circuit: Lemy v. Direct General Finance Co., 2012 WL 239702 (M.D. Fla. June 19, 2012).

State Courts:

Connecticut: Cage v. Litchfield, 713 A.2d 281 (Conn. Super. 1997).

Georgia: Penn America Insurance Co. v. Miller, 492 S.E.2d 571 (Ga. App. 1997).

Illinois: Gaston v. Founders Insurance Co., 847 N.E.2d 523 (Ill. App.), *appeal denied* 852 N.E.2d 239 (Ill. 2006).

Louisiana: Carrier v. Allstate Insurance Co., 702 So.2d 367 (La. App. 1997); Guidroz v. Lewis, 626 So.2d 736 (La. App. 1993).

New York: National Union Fire Ins. Co. v. Ambassador Group, Inc., 556 N.Y.S.2d 549 (N.Y. App. Div. 1990), *appeal dismissed* 571 N.E.2d 85 (N.Y. 1991).

North Carolina: Home Indemnity Co. v. Hoechst Celanese Corp., 494 S.E.2d 768 (N.C. App.), *review denied* 505 S.E.2d 869 (N.C. 1998).

Ohio: Siegfried v. Farmers Insurance of Columbus, Inc., 187 Ohio App.3d 710, 933 N.E.2d 815 (2010).

Oklahoma: Hill v. Agri-Risk Services, 827 P.2d 904 (Okla. App. 1992).

Texas: Urrutia v. Decker, 992 S.W.2d 440 (Tex.), *cert. denied* 528 U.S. 1021 (1999); Pine Oak Builders, Inc. v. Great American Lloyds Insurance Co., 2006 WL 1892669 (Tex. App. July 6, 2006).

50 See Herman v. Mutual Life Insurance Co., 108 F.2d 678, 682 (3d Cir. 1939), in which a policyholder purchased an annuity policy that had not been formally approved by the insurance department. The insured sought to invalidate the policy on the basis that the form had not been formally approved. The court held that the statutory violation was a mere technicality, but explicitly recognized the distinction between unapproved policies and policies that are or would have been expressly disapproved or rejected.

> "The allegation here is that the new policy is wanting in formal approval, nothing more. It is not suggested that the issued policy offends against the substantive prescription of the statute. *By the same token there is nothing to show that the Commissioner's blessing would not have been conferred as of course or even that it could have been legally withheld.*" 108 F.2d at 682 (emphasis added).

The clear implication of the emphasized language is that the result would have been different if the insurance commissioner had disapproved the submitted policy form. Indeed, there are no reported decisions in which a court has held that a provision that is expressly rejected by a state insurance department or violates a specific state insurance department policy is valid and enforceable. In fact, in every decision in which the courts have determined that the statutory violations do not invalidate the policies, unapproved, as opposed to rejected, policies were at issue. See:

Connecticut: Cage v. Litchfield, 713 A.2d 281, 288–289 (Conn. Super. 1997).

Georgia: Penn America Insurance Co. v. Miller, 492 S.E.2d 571, 573 (Ga. App. 1997) ("In the absence of clear evidence showing the Commissioner would not have approved this exclusion, no reason exists to invalidate it as a matter of law.").

Louisiana: Guidroz v. Lewis, 626 So.2d 736 (La. App. 1993); Carrier v. Allstate Insurance Co., 702 So.2d 367, 370–371 (La. App. 1997).

North Carolina: Home Indemnity Co. v. Hoechst Celanese Corp., 494 S.E.2d 768, 773 (N.C. App.), *review denied* 505 S.E.2d 869 (N.C. 1998) ("In holding that the unapproved form here is not void, we do not address the situation where an unapproved form is never submitted for approval or is subsequently rejected for use by the Department of Insurance.").

But see, Hepler v. Liberty Mutual Fire Insurance Co., 13 Pa. D. & C.4th 528, 534 (Pa. C.P. Cumberland Cnty. 1992) (policies issued both before deemed approval and after rejection are invalid).

51 See:

Fifth Circuit: Roland v. Transamerica Life Insurance Co., 337 Fed. Appx. 389 (5th Cir. 2009) (policy at variance with approved form valid as differences were so minor that policyholder was not injured by such different language).

Ninth Circuit: Stephan v. Unum Life Insurance Company of America, 697 F.3d 917 (9th Cir. 2012); Hinkle v. Crum & Forster Holding, Inc., 747 F. Supp.2d 1132 (D. Alaska 2010).

Eleventh Circuit: Lemy v. Direct General Finance Co., 2012 WL 239702 (M.D. Fla. June 19, 2012).

State Courts:

Idaho: Hill v. American Family Mutual Insurance Co., 249 P.3d 812 (Idaho 2010).

Ohio: Siegfried v. Farmers Insurance of Columbus, Inc., 187 Ohio App.3d 710, 933 N.E.2d 815 (2010).

Oregon: Baylor v. Continental Casualty Co., 190 Or. App. 25, 78 P.3d 108 (2003).

52 See:

Seventh Circuit: Edward E. Gillen Co. v. Insurance Company of the State of Pennsylvania, 747 F. Supp.2d 1058 (E.D. Wis. 2010).

Ninth Circuit: Stephan v. Unum Life Insurance Company of America, 697 F.3d 917 (9th Cir. 2012).

State Courts:

Florida: AIU Insurance Co. v. Block Marina Investment, Inc., 544 So.2d 998 (Fla. 1989) (non-compliance acts as estoppel but cannot create or expand coverage).

Massachusetts: Clarendon National Insurance Co. v. Amica Mutual Insurance Co., 441 Mass. 248, 805 N.E.2d 8 (2004).

53 See:

Florida: American Mutual Fire Insurance Co. v. Illingworth, 213 So.2d 747 (Fla. App. 1968) (issuance of non-approved form makes form void).

Maryland: St. Paul Travelers v. Millstone, 412 Md. 424, 987 A.2d 116 (2010) (insurance department's approval of three-year contractual limitations provision did not preclude determination that policy did not comply with statute that voids a provision in an insurance contract that sets a shorter time to bring an action on the insurance contract than required by state law).

54 See:

Fourth Circuit: Howell v. State Farm Insurance Cos., 540 F. Supp.2d 621 (D. Md. 2008) (national flood policy should be reformed to policy mandated by law).

State Courts:

California: Fire Insurance Exchange v. Superior Court, 116 Cal. App.4th 446, 10 Cal. Rptr.3d 617 (2004).

Louisiana: Hoagboon v. Cannon, 54 So.3d 802 (La. App. 2010).

Minnesota: Watson v. United Services Automobile Association, 566 N.W.2d 683 (Minn. 1997).

55 See, e.g.:

Second Circuit: GB Marketing USA Inc. v. Gerolsteiner Brunnen GmbH & Co., 782 F. Supp. 763 (W.D.N.Y. 1991).

Third Circuit: Olefins Trading, Inc. v. Han Yang Chem Corp., 9 F.3d 282 (3d Cir. 1993).

State Courts:

District of Columbia: Kramer Associates, Inc. v. Ikam, Ltd., 888 A.2d 247 (D.C. App. 2005).

Missouri: In re Estate of Conkle, 982 S.W.2d 312 (Mo. App. 1998).

South Carolina: Armstrong v. Collins, 366 S.C. 204, 621 S.E.2d 368 (S.C. App. 2005).

Tennessee: In re Estate of Haskins, 224 S.W.3d 675 (Tenn. App. 2006).

Texas: Chambers v. Pruitt, 241 S.W.3d 679 (Tex. App. 2007).

These statutes of frauds generally apply to contracts that cannot be performed within one year or during a lifetime, contracts that pertain to real property, marriage and divorce agreements, settlement agreements, and contracts relating to trusts and estates, sales of goods in excess of $500, among other things. Whether an insurance policy fits within the various statutes of frauds is beyond the scope of this section. However, some contracts relating to insurance have been found subject to such statutes. See Binkowski v. Hartford

Accident and Indemnity Co., 60 A.D.3d 1473, 876 N.Y.S.2d 295 (N.Y. App. Div. 2009) (contract for offset of future workers' compensation benefits); Arnold and Associates, Inc. v. Misys Healthcare Systems, 275 F. Supp.2d 1013 (D. Ariz. 2003) (insurance broker agreement); Ellis v. Provident Life and Accident Insurance Co., 3 F. Supp.2d 399 (S.D.N.Y. 1998) (agreement to pay commission on policies). In all events, when or if an insurance policy is subject to the statute of frauds, there are recognized exceptions, such as promissory estoppel or partial/complete performance, which can operate to permit the enforcement of an oral contract that otherwise would be unenforceable under these statutes of frauds. See, e.g.:

Second Circuit: Momentive Performance Materials USA, Inc. v. AstroCosmos Metallurgical, Inc., 659 F. Supp.2d 332 (N.D.N.Y. 2009).

State Courts:

Connecticut: SS-II, LLC v. Bridge Street Associates, 293 Conn. 287, 977 A.2d 189 (2009).

Florida: Ala v. Chesser, 5 So.3d 715 (Fla. App. 2009).

Illinois: Anderson v. Kohler, 397 Ill. App.3d 773, 922 N.E.2d 8, 337 Ill. Dec. 150 (2009).

New York: McCormick v. Bechtol, 68 A.D.3d 1376, 891 N.Y.S.2d 188 (N.Y. App. Div. 2009).

Texas: Davis v. Sysco Food Services of Austin, L.P., 2009 WL 4458600 (Tex. App. Dec. 4, 2009).

56 See, e.g.:

Second Circuit: Torain v. Clear Channel Broadcasting, Inc., 651 F. Supp.2d 125 (S.D.N.Y. 2009).

Fifth Circuit: ARM Properties Management Group v. RSUI Indemnity Co., 642 F. Supp.2d 592 (W.D. Tex. 2009).

State Courts:

California: Iglesia Evangelica Latina, Inc. v. Southern Pacific Latin American District of Assemblies of God, 173 Cal. App.4th 420, 93 Cal. Rptr.3d 75 (2009).

Kentucky: Bobbitt v. Collins, 2010 WL 199308 (Ky. Jan. 22, 2010).

New York: Golden Gate Yacht Club v. Societe Nautique De Geneve, 12 N.Y.3d 248, 907 N.E.2d 276, 879 N.Y.S.2d 363 (2009).

North Dakota: Spitzer v. Bartelson, 773 N.W.2d 798 (N.D. 2009).

Ohio: Williams v. Spitzer Autoworld Canton, L.L.C., 122 Ohio St.3d 546, 913 N.E.2d 410 (2009).

Wisconsin: Town Bank v. City Real Estate Development, L.L.C., 322 Wis.2d 206, 777 N.W.2d 98 (Wis. App. 2009).

57 See, e.g.:

Fourth Circuit: Marble Bank v. Commonwealth Land Title Insurance Co., 914 F. Supp. 1252 (E.D.N.C. 1996).

Fifth Circuit: Time Insurance Co. v. Estate of White, 447 Fed. Appx. 561 (5th Cir. 2011); Trammell Crow Residential Co. v. Virginia Surety Co., 643 F. Supp.2d 844 (N.D. Tex. 2008).

Sixth Circuit: O'Brien v. Ed Donnelly Enterprises, Inc., 575 F.3d 567 (6th Cir. 2009).

Tenth Circuit: McInnis v. Fairfield Communities, Inc., 458 F.3d 1129 (10th Cir. 2006).

District of Columbia Circuit: U.S. *ex rel.* El-Amin v. George Washington University, 522 F. Supp.2d 135 (D.D.C. 2007).

State Courts:

Alabama: Byrd v. Bentley, 850 So.2d 232 (Ala. 2002).

Connecticut: Cadle Co. v. Errato, 71 Conn. App. 447, 802 A.2d 887 (2002).

Louisiana: Hoerner v. ANCO Insulations, Inc., 812 So.2d 45 (La. App. 2002); Abadie v. Metropolitan Life Insurance Co., 784 So.2d 46 (La. App. 2001).

Mississippi: Caver v. Brown, 818 So.2d 376 (Miss. App. 2002).

Washington: Eagle Group, Inc. v. Pullen, 114 Wash. App. 409, 58 P.3d 292 (2002).

[58] See, e.g.:

First Circuit: Southern Union Co. v. Liberty Mutual Insurance Co., 581 F. Supp.2d 120 (D. Mass. 2008).

Fifth Circuit: Railroad Management Co. v. CFS Louisiana Midstream Co., 428 F.3d 214 (5th Cir. 2005).

Sixth Circuit: Gabriel Ride Control Products, Inc. v. Wolverine Auto Supply, Inc., 35 Fed. Appx. 397 (6th Cir. 2002).

State Courts:

Georgia: DeGolyer v. Green Tree Servicing, L.L.C., 291 Ga. App. 444, 662 S.E.2d 141 (2008).

Missouri: Wheelhouse Marina Real Estate, L.L.C. v. Bommarito, 284 S.W.3d 761 (Mo. App. 2009).

New York: Schozer v. William Penn Life Insurance Company of New York, 84 N.Y.2d 639, 644 N.E.2d 1353, 620 N.Y.S.2d 797 (1994).

Pennsylvania: Hera v. McCormick, 425 Pa. Super. 432, 625 A.2d 682 (1993).

Washington: American Commerce Insurance Co. v. Ensley, 153 Wash. App. 31, 220 P.3d 215 (2009).

[59] See:

First Circuit: Kleenit, Inc. v. Sentry Insurance Co., 486 F. Supp.2d 121 (D. Mass. 2007); Metlife Capital Corp. v. Westchester Fire Insurance Co., 224 F. Supp.2d 374 (D.P.R. 2002).

Second Circuit: SR International Business Insurance Co. v. World Trade Center Properties, L.L.C., 467 F.3d 107 (2d Cir. 2006); Boyce Thompson Institute for Plant Research, Inc. v. Insurance Company of North America, 751 F. Supp. 1137, 1140–1141 (S.D.N.Y. 1990).

Third Circuit: Knoepfler v. Guardian Life Insurance Co. of America, 2009 WL 1834324 (D.N.J. June 26, 2009); Coregis Insurance Co. v. City of Harrisburg, 401 F. Supp.2d 398 (M.D. Pa. 2005); Remington Arms Co. v. Liberty Mutual Insurance Co., 810 F. Supp. 1420 (D. Del. 1992).

Fourth Circuit: Klopman v. Zurich American Insurance Co. of Illinois, 233 Fed. Appx. 256 (4th Cir. 2007); *In re* Wallace & Gale Co., 284 B.R. 553 (Bankr. D. Md.), *opinion amended* 2000 WL 32122507 (D. Md. Oct. 10, 2002).

Sixth Circuit: Century Indemnity Co. v. Aero-Motive Co., 336 F. Supp.2d 739 (W.D. Mich. 2004), *aff'd* 155 Fed. Appx. 833 (6th Cir. 2005).

Seventh Circuit: Coltec Industries Inc. v. Zurich Insurance Co., 33 Envtl. L. Rep. 20,084 (N.D. Ill. 2002).

Tenth Circuit: Continental Casualty Co. v. Hempel, 4 Fed. Appx. 703 (10th Cir. 2001); Servants of Paraclete, Inc. v. Great American Insurance Co., 857 F. Supp. 822 (D.N.M. 1994).

State Courts:

California: Dart Industries, Inc. v. Commercial Union Insurance Co., 52 P.3d 79 (Cal. 2002).

Connecticut: ACMAT Corp. v. Greater New York Mutual Insurance Co., 88 Conn. App. 471, 869 A.2d 1254 (2005).

Delaware: Boling v. All State Insurance Co., 2006 WL 3240008 (Del. Super. Oct. 30, 2006).

Florida: Lawyers Title Insurance Co. v. Novastar Mortgage, Inc., 862 So.2d 793 (Fla. App. 2003).

Georgia: Weiss v. Old Republic National Title Insurance Co., 262 Ga. App. 120, 584 S.E.2d 710 (2003).

Indiana: PSI Energy, Inc. v. Home Insurance Co., 801 N.E.2d 705 (Ind. App.), *transfer denied* 812 N.E.2d 805 (Ind. 2004).

Louisiana: Mateu v. State Farm Mutual Automobile Insurance Co., 13 So.3d 196 (La. App. 2009); Hoerner v. ANCO Insulations, Inc., 812 So.2d 45 (La. App. 2002).

Minnesota: St. Paul Fire and Marine Insurance Co. v. A.P.I., Inc., 738 N.W.2d 401 (Minn. App. 2007).

New Jersey: Borough of Sayreville v. Bellefonte Insurance Co., 728 A.2d 225, 228 (N.J. Super. App. Div. 1998).

New York: Kermanshah Oriental Rugs, Inc. v. Gollender, 47 A.D.3d 438, 850 N.Y.S.2d 47 (N.Y. App. Div. 2008); Gold Fields American Corp. v. Aetna Casualty and Surety Co., 661 N.Y.S.2d 948 (N.Y. Sup. 1997).

Ohio: Sharonville v. American Employers Insurance Co., 846 N.E.2d 833 (Ohio 2006); Henderson v. Lawyers Title Insurance Corp., 108 Ohio St.3d 265, 843 N.E.2d 152 (2006).

Rhode Island: Children's Friend and Service v. St. Paul Fire and Marine Insurance Co., 893 A.2d 222 (R.I. 2006).

Washington: Fraser v. Metropolitan Life Insurance Co., 5 P.2d 978, 979 (Wash. 1931).

[60] See, e.g.:

Second Circuit: GB Marketing USA Inc. v. Gerolsteiner Brunnen GmbH & Co., 782 F. Supp. 763 (W.D.N.Y. 1991).

Third Circuit: Olefins Trading, Inc. v. Han Yang Chem Corp., 9 F.3d 282 (3d Cir. 1993).

State Courts:

District of Columbia: Kramer Associates, Inc. v. Ikam, Ltd., 888 A.2d 247 (D.C. App. 2005).

Missouri: In re Estate of Conkle, 982 S.W.2d 312 (Mo. App. 1998).

South Carolina: Armstrong v. Collins, 366 S.C. 204, 621 S.E.2d 368 (S.C. App. 2005).

Tennessee: In re Estate of Haskins, 224 S.W.3d 675 (Tenn. App. 2006).

Texas: Chambers v. Pruitt, 241 S.W.3d 679 (Tex. App. 2007).

These statutes of frauds generally apply to contracts that cannot be performed within one year or during a lifetime, contracts that pertain to real property, marriage and divorce agreements, settlement agreements, contracts relating to trusts and estates, sales of goods in excess of $500, among other things. Whether an insurance policy fits within the various statutes of frauds is beyond the scope of this section. However, some contracts relating to insurance have been found subject to such statutes. See Binkowski v. Hartford Accident and Indemnity Co., 60 A.D.3d 1473, 876 N.Y.S.2d 295 (N.Y. App. Div. 2009) (contract for off-set of future workers' compensation benefits); Arnold and Associates, Inc. v. Misys Healthcare Systems, 275 F. Supp.2d 1013 (D. Ariz. 2003) (insurance broker agreement); Ellis v. Provident Life and Accident Insurance Co., 3 F. Supp.2d 399 (S.D.N.Y. 1998) (agreement to pay commission on policies). In all events, when or if an insurance policy is subject to the statute of frauds, there are recognized exceptions, such as promissory estoppel or partial/complete performance, which can operate to permit the enforcement of an oral contract that otherwise would be unenforceable under these statutes of frauds. See, e.g.:

Second Circuit: Momentive Performance Materials USA, Inc. v. AstroCosmos Metallurgical, Inc., 659 F. Supp.2d 332 (N.D.N.Y. 2009).

State Courts:

Connecticut: SS-II, LLC v. Bridge Street Associates, 293 Conn. 287, 977 A.2d 189 (2009).

Florida: Ala v. Chesser, 5 So.3d 715 (Fla. App. 2009).

Illinois: Anderson v. Kohler, 397 Ill. App.3d 773, 922 N.E.2d 8, 337 Ill. Dec. 150 (2009).

New York: McCormick v. Bechtol, 68 A.D.3d 1376, 891 N.Y.S.2d 188 (N.Y. App. Div. 2009).

Texas: Davis v. Sysco Food Services of Austin, L.P., 2009 WL 4458600 (Tex. App. Dec. 4, 2009).

61 *First Circuit:* Southern Union Co. v. Liberty Mutual Insurance Co., 581 F. Supp.2d 120 (D. Mass. 2008); Metlife Capital Corp. v. Westchester Fire Insurance Co., 224 F. Supp.2d 374 (D.P.R. 2002).

Second Circuit: Glew v. Cigna Group Insurance Co., 590 F. Supp.2d 395 (E.D.N.Y. 2008); Boyce Thompson Institute for Plant Research, Inc. v. Insurance Company of North America, 751 F. Supp. 1137, 1140–1141 (S.D.N.Y.1990).

Third Circuit: Flick v. Borg-Warner Corp., 892 F.2d 285 (3d Cir. 1989); Remington Arms Co. v. Liberty Mutual Insurance Co., 810 F. Supp. 1420 (D. Del. 1992).

Fourth Circuit: In re Wallace & Gale Co., 284 B.R. 553 (Bankr. D. Md.), *opinion amended* 2000 WL 32122507 (D. Md. Oct. 10, 2002).

Fifth Circuit: Estate of Vane v. The Fair, Inc., 849 F.2d 186 (5th Cir. 1988).

Sixth Circuit: T.H.E. Insurance Co. v. Naghtin, 916 F.2d 1082 (6th Cir. 1990); Century Indemnity Co. v. Aero-Motive Co., 336 F. Supp.2d 739 (W.D. Mich. 2004), *aff'd* 155 Fed. Appx. 833 (6th Cir. 2005).

Seventh Circuit: Coltec Industries Inc. v. Zurich Insurance Co., 33 Envtl. L. Rep. 20,084 (N.D. Ill. 2002).

State Courts:

California: Dart Industries, Inc. v. Commercial Union Insurance Co., 52 P.3d 79 (Cal. 2002).

Delaware: Boling v. All State Insurance Co., 2006 WL 3240008 (Del. Super. Oct. 30, 2006).

Georgia: Rhodes v. Amwest Surety Insurance Co., 207 Ga. App. 441, 428 S.E.2d 581 (1993).

Indiana: PSI Energy, Inc. v. Home Insurance Co., 801 N.E.2d 705 (Ind. App.), *transfer denied* 812 N.E.2d 805 (Ind. 2004).

Louisiana: Savoy v. Harris, 20 So.3d 1075 (La. App. 2009).

New Jersey: Borough of Sayreville v. Bellefonte Insurance Co., 728 A.2d 225, 228 (N.J. Super. App. Div. 1998).

New York: Commissioners of State Insurance Fund v. Munkacs Car Service Ltd., 11 Misc.3d 802, 809 N.Y.S.2d 868 (N.Y. City. Civ. 2006).

Ohio: Sharonville v. American Employers Insurance Co., 846 N.E.2d 833 (Ohio 2006).

Washington: Fraser v. Metropolitan Life Insurance Co., 5 P.2d 978, 979 (Wash. 1931); Torgerson v. State Farm Mutual Automobile Insurance Co., 91 Wash. App. 952, 957 P.2d 1283 (1998).

62 Borough of Sayreville v. Bellefonte Insurance Co., 728 A.2d 225, 228 (N.J. Super. App. Div. 1998) (citations and quotations omitted).

63 *Third Circuit:* Remington Arms Co. v. Liberty Mutual Insurance Co., 810 F. Supp. 1420 (D. Del. 1992).

Sixth Circuit: Century Indemnity Co. v. Aero-Motive Co., 336 F. Supp.2d 739 (W.D. Mich. 2004), *aff'd* 155 Fed. Appx. 833 (6th Cir. 2005).

Seventh Circuit: Coltec Industries Inc. v. Zurich Insurance Co., 2002 WL 31185789 (N.D. Ill. Sept. 30, 2002).

State Courts:

Indiana: PSI Energy, Inc. v. Home Insurance Co., 801 N.E.2d 705 (Ind. App.), *transfer denied* 812 N.E.2d 805 (Ind. 2004).

[64] *Second Circuit:* Boyce Thompson Institute for Plant Research, Inc. v. Insurance Company of North America, 751 F. Supp. 1137, 1140–1141 (S.D.N.Y. 1990).

Third Circuit: Compass Technology, Inc. v. Tseng Laboratories, Inc., 71 F.3d 1125, 1133 (3d Cir. 1995) (non-insurance contract); TIG Insurance Co. v. Meco Constructors, Inc., 30 Envtl. L. Rep. 20,360 (E.D. Pa. 2000) (insurance company granted summary judgment on basis of policyholder's failure to meet its burden regarding lost policy evidence).

Fourth Circuit: In re Wallace & Gale Co., 284 B.R. 553 (Bankr. D. Md.), *op. amended* 2000 WL 32122507 (D. Md. Oct. 10, 2002).

[65] See, e.g.:

Second Circuit: Liberty Mutual Insurance Co. v. Excel Imaging, P.C., 879 F. Supp.2d 243 (E.D.N.Y. 2012).

Eighth Circuit: Spine Imaging MRI, L.L.C. v. Liberty Mutual Insurance Co., 743 F. Supp.2d 1034 (D. Minn. 2010).

State Courts:

California: Housing Group v. PMA Capital Insurance Co., 123 Cal. Rptr.3d 603 (Cal. App. 2011).

Oregon: California Casualty Indemnity Exchange v. Federated Mutual Insurance Co., 286 P.3d 901 (Or. App. 2012).

[66] See, e.g., Form LEX-CM-EPLIT (09/00).

[67] See: Roland, "Arbitration—A Good Idea That Does Not Work," Ins. Advocate, 23 (June 8, 1996); Parloff, "Kaiser Arbitration: Waiting for Judge Godot," American Lawyer, July 1996, at 84; Masters, "Arbitration Clauses In Liability Policies: A Ticket To Ride?," John Liner Rev. 33 (Winter 1996); Jacobs, "Policies Requiring Arbitration Challenged," Wall St. J., Oct. 16, 1995, at B5; Anderson and Liben, "The Perfect Insurance or the Perfect Crime," Metro. Corp. Couns. (Jan. 1995).

[68] See:

Second Circuit: Bird Peak Corp. v. Lawyers Title Insurance Corp., 107 Fed. Appx. 240 (2d Cir. 2004) (enforced); Knickerbocker Dialysis, Inc. v. TrueBlue, Inc., 601 F. Supp.2d 502 (E.D.N.Y. 2009) (enforced); Best Concrete Mix Corp. v. Lloyd's of London Underwriters, 413 F. Supp.2d 182 (E.D.N.Y. 2006) (enforced); *In re* Quigley Co., 361 B.R. 723 (Bankr. S.D.N.Y. 2007) (enforced).

Third Circuit: Flexi-Van Leasing, Inc. v. Through Transport Mutual Insurance Association, Ltd., 108 Fed. Appx. 35 (3d Cir. 2004) (enforced); Liberty Mutual Fire Insurance Co. v. Yoder, 112 Fed. Appx. 826 (3d Cir. 2004) (not enforced); Wells v. Merit Life Insurance Co., 671 F. Supp.2d 570 (D. Del. 2009) (enforced); Radian Insurance, Inc. v. Deutsche Bank National Trust Co., 638 F. Supp.2d 443 (E.D. Pa. 2009) (enforced); Wells v. Merit Life Insurance Co., 671 F. Supp.2d 570 (D. Del. 2009) (enforced); Radian Insurance, Inc. v. Deutsche Bank National Trust Co., 638 F. Supp.2d 443 (E.D. Pa. 2009) (enforced); St. Paul Fire & Marine Insurance Co. v. Rhein, 484 F. Supp.2d 354 (E.D. Pa. 2007) (not enforced).

Fourth Circuit: American International Specialty Lines Insurance Co. v. A.T. Massey Coal Co., 628 F. Supp.2d 674 (E.D. Va. 2009) (not enforced); Brown v. Citifinancial, Inc., 414 F. Supp.2d 561 (D.S.C. 2006) (enforced).

Fifth Circuit: American Bankers Insurance Company of Florida v. Inman, 436 F.3d 490 (5th Cir. 2006) (not enforced); Wagoner v. Woodmen of the World, 2009 WL 2899050 (W.D. La. Sept. 9, 2009) (enforced); Kulpa v. OM Financial Life Insurance Co., 558 F. Supp.2d 676 (S.D. Miss. 2008) (enforced).

Sixth Circuit: National Home Insurance Co. v. King, 291 F. Supp.2d 518 (E.D. Ky. 2003) (not enforced).

Seventh Circuit: BCS Insurance Co. v. Wellmark, Inc., 410 F.3d 349 (7th Cir. 2005) (enforced); National Union Fire Insurance Company of Pittsburgh, PA. v. Westport

Insurance Corp., 2009 WL 528686 (N.D. Ill. Feb. 25, 2009) (enforced); Blue Cross Blue Shield of Tennessee v. BCS Insurance Co., 517 F. Supp.2d 1050 (N.D. Ill. 2007) (enforced).

Eighth Circuit: Guzhagin v. State Farm Mutual Automobile Insurance Co., 566 F. Supp.2d 962 (D. Minn. 2008) (enforced); Thrivent Financial For Lutherans v. Lakin, 322 F. Supp.2d 1017 (W.D. Mo. 2004) (enforced).

Ninth Circuit: Leonard *ex rel.* Leonard v. Equitable Life Assurance Society of the United States, 28 Fed. Appx. 686 (9th Cir. 2002) (enforced); Enger v. Allstate Insurance Co., 682 F. Supp.2d 1094 (E.D. Cal. 2009) (enforced).

Eleventh Circuit: Goshawk Dedicated v. Portsmouth Settlement Co. I, 466 F. Supp.2d 1293 (N.D. Ga. 2006) (enforced).

State Courts:

Alabama: Crews v. National Boat Owners Association Marine Insurance Agency, Inc., 2010 WL 336708 (Ala. Jan. 29, 2010) (enforced); Assurant, Inc. v. Mitchell, 26 So.3d 1171 (Ala. 2009) (enforced); Blue Cross Blue Shield of Alabama v. Rigas, 923 So.2d 1077 (Ala. 2005) (enforced).

California: Bouton v. USAA Casualty Insurance Co., 167 Cal. App.4th 412, 84 Cal. Rptr.3d 152 (Cal. App. 2008) (enforced); Rodriguez v. Blue Cross of California, 162 Cal. App.4th 330, 75 Cal. Rptr.3d 754 (Cal. App. 2008) (not enforced); Lambert v. Carneghi, 70 Cal. Rptr.3d 626 (Cal. App. 2008) (enforced); Medeiros v. Superior Court, 53 Cal. Rptr.3d 307 (Cal. App. 2007) (not enforced).

Colorado: Rocha v. Financial Indemnity Corp., 155 P.3d 602 (Colo. App. 2006) (not enforced).

District of Columbia: Menna v. Plymouth Rock Assurance Corp., 987 A.2d 458 (D.C. App. 2010) (enforced).

Florida: Lloyds Underwriters v. Netterstrom, 17 So.3d 732 (Fla. App. 2009) (enforced); Towers v. Clarendon National Insurance Co., 927 So.2d 913 (Fla. App. 2006) (not enforced); American International Group, Inc. v. Siemens Building Technologies, Inc., 881 So.2d 7 (Fla. App. 2004) (enforced).

Georgia: Love v. Money Tree, Inc., 614 S.E.2d 47 (Ga. 2005) (not enforced).

Michigan: Zales v. Habersham Funding, LLC, 2006 WL 664777 (Mich. App. Mar. 16, 2006) (enforced).

Minnesota: Charboneau v. American Family Insurance Co., 481 N.W.2d 19 (Minn. 1992) (not enforced).

Mississippi: Gulf Insurance Co. v. Neel-Schaffer, Inc., 904 So.2d 1036 (Miss. 2004) (enforced).

Missouri: Sturgeon v. Allied Professionals Insurance Co., 344 S.W.3d 205 (Mo. App. 2011) (not enforced).

Montana: Doctors' Co. v. Finney, 131 P.3d 572 (Mont. 2006) (not enforced).

New Jersey: Danchisko v. Harleysville Insurance Co., 2009 WL 395440 (N.J. Super. App. Div. Feb. 19, 2009) (enforced); Winner v. Revill, 889 A.2d 477 (N.J. Super. App. Div. 2006) (enforced).

New York: Progressive Casualty Insurance Co. v. New York State Insurance Fund, 850 N.Y.S.2d 478 (N.Y. App. Div. 2008) (enforced); Williams v. Progressive Northeastern Insurance Co., 839 N.Y.S.2d 381 (N.Y. App. Div. 2007) (enforced).

North Carolina: Capps v. Virrey, 645 S.E.2d 825 (N.C. App. 2007) (enforced).

Ohio: Banks v. Jennings, 184 Ohio App.3d 269, 920 N.E.2d 432 (2009) (enforced); West v. Household Life Insurance Co., 867 N.E.2d 868 (Ohio. App. 2007) (not enforced).

Pennsylvania: Koken v. Reliance Insurance Co., 846 A.2d 778 (Pa. Commw. 2004) (not enforced).

Rhode Island: Kraczkowski v. Quincy Mutual Fire Insurance Co., 898 A.2d 720 (R.I. 2006) (enforced).

Texas: In re Kepka, 178 S.W.3d 279 (Tex. App. 2005) (not enforced).

Washington: Kruger Clinic Orthopaedics, LLC v. Regence Blueshield, 138 P.3d 936 (Wash. 2006) (not enforced).

69 See § 3.05[1] *supra.*

70 See § 3.05[2][a] *infra.*

71 See § 3.05[2][b] *infra.*

72 See:

First Circuit: Phico Insurance Co. v. Pavia Health, Inc., 413 F. Supp.2d 76 (D.P.R. 2006).

Second Circuit: Greenberg v. Aetna Life Insurance Co., 421 Fed. Appx. 124 (2d Cir. 2011); Weiss v. La Suisse, 141 Fed. Appx. 31 (2d Cir. 2005); Hartford Fire Insurance Co. v. Mitlof, 193 F.R.D. 154 (S.D.N.Y. 2000).

Third Circuit: Harleysville Insurance Co. of New York v. Cerciello, 451 Fed. Appx. 110 (3d Cir. 2011); AGF Marine Aviation and Transport v. Cassin, 544 F.3d 255 (3d Cir. 2008) (enforced); Hammersmith v. TIG Insurance Co., 480 F.3d 220 (3d Cir. 2007); USX Corp. v. Adriatic Insurance Co., 64 F. Supp.2d 469 (W.D. Pa. 1998).

Fifth Circuit: Great Lakes Reinsurance P.L.C. v. Durham Auctions, Inc., 585 F.3d 236 (5th Cir. 2009) (enforced); Cantu v. Jackson National Life Insurance Co., 579 F.3d 434 (5th Cir. 2009) (enforced); Authenment v. Ingram Barge Co., 878 F. Supp.2d 672 (E.D. La. 2012); Burlington Resources, Inc. v. United National Insurance Co., 481 F. Supp.2d 567 (E.D. La. 2007); Arkwright-Boston Manufacturers Mutual Insurance Co. v. Energy Insurance Agency, Inc., 659 F. Supp. 97 (S.D. Tex. 1987).

Sixth Circuit: Asher v. Unarco Material Handling, Inc., 737 F. Supp.2d 662 (E.D. Ky. 2010).

Seventh Circuit: Auto-Owners Insurance Co. v. Websolv Computing, Inc., 580 F.3d 543 (7th Cir. 2009) (enforced); Edstrom Industries, Inc. v. Companion Life Insurance Co., 516 F.3d 546 (7th Cir. 2008) (enforced); Egan Marine Corp. v. Great American Insurance Co. of New York, 2007 WL 4801222 (N.D. Ill. June 13, 2007); Knoll Pharmaceutical Co. v. Automobile Insurance Company of Hartford, 152 F. Supp.2d 1026 (N.D. Ill. 2001) (choice of law upheld); Kubes v. American Medical Security, Inc., 895 F. Supp. 212 (S.D. Ill. 1995) (choice of law upheld).

Eighth Circuit: Allianz Insurance Company of Canada v. Sanftleben, 454 F.3d 853 (8th Cir. 2006) (choice of law provision enforced); Ceres Environmental Services, Inc. v. Arch Specialty Insurance Co., 853 F. Supp.2d 859 (D. Minn. 2012); Great Lakes Reinsurance (UK), P.L.C. v. Sea Cat I, L.L.C., 653 F. Supp.2d 1193 (W.D. Okla. 2009) (enforced).

Ninth Circuit: Gemini Insurance Co. v. Kukui'ula Development Co., 855 F. Supp.2d 1125 (D. Haw. 2012); Prime Insurance Syndicate, Inc. v. Damaso, 471 F. Supp.2d 1087 (D. Nev. 2007).

Tenth Circuit: TH Agriculture & Nutrition, L.L.C. v. Ace European Group Ltd., 416 F. Supp.2d 1054 (D. Kan. 2006) (upholding choice of law and forum clause); Arocho v. Goodyear Tire & Rubber Co., 88 F. Supp.2d 1175 (D. Kan. 2000) (choice of law upheld).

Eleventh Circuit: Capone v. Aetna Life Insurance Co., 592 F.3d 1189 (11th Cir. 2010) (enforced); Great American Fidelity Insurance Co. v. JWR Construction Services, Inc., 882 F. Supp.2d 1340 (S.D. Fla. 2012); Lemuel v. Admiral Insurance Co., 414 F. Supp.2d 1037 (M.D. Ala. 2006) (choice of law upheld).

State Courts:

Connecticut: Chen v. Nationwide Property and Casualty Insurance Co., 2010 WL 5158168 (Conn. Super., New Britain Nov. 19, 2010).

Delaware: AT and T Corp. v. Clarendon America Insurance Co., 2008 WL 2583007 (Del. Super. Feb. 11, 2008) (applied).

District of Columbia: Vaughan v. Nationwide Mutual Insurance Co., 702 A.2d 198 (D.C. 1997) (choice of law upheld).

Illinois: Old Republic Insurance Co. v. Ace Property and Casualty Insurance Co., 389 Ill. App.3d 356, 906 N.E.2d 630, 329 Ill. Dec. 432 (2009) (enforced).

Louisiana: Clark v. Legion Insurance Co., 947 So.2d 110 (La. Ct. App. 2006) (choice of law provision enforced); Lexington Insurance Co. v. M.W. Kellogg Constructors, Inc., 921 So.2d 1106 (La. Ct. App. 2006) (choice of law upheld).

Montana: Tenas v. Progressive Preferred Insurance Co., 347 Mont. 133, 197 P.3d 990 (2008) (enforced).

New Jersey: Chubb Custom Insurance Co. v. Prudential Insurance Company of America, 195 N.J. 231, 948 A.2d 1285 (2008) (enforced).

Wisconsin: Diocese of Superior v. Swan & Associates, Inc., 788 N.W.2d 383, 788 N.W.2d 383 (Wis. App. 2010).

[73] See, e.g.:

First Circuit: Acadia Insurance Co. v. Cunningham, 771 F. Supp.2d 172 (D. Mass. 2011).

Second Circuit: Fireman's Fund Insurance Co., Inc. v. Schuster Films, Inc., 811 F. Supp. 978 (S.D.N.Y. 1993) (choice of law provision is one factor to consider but is not dispositive).

Fourth Circuit: Riffe v. Magushi, 859 F. Supp. 220 (S.D. W. Va. 1994) (ignoring choice of law provision where chosen law was imprecise on issue at hand).

Fifth Circuit: In re Enron Corp. Securities, Derivative & "ERISA" Litigation, 391 F. Supp.2d 541 (S.D. Tex. 2005).

Sixth Circuit: Illinois Union Insurance Co. v. Shefchuk, 108 Fed. Appx. 294 (6th Cir. 2004); Allstate Insurance Co. v. My Choice Medical Plan for LDM Technologies, Inc., 298 F. Supp.2d 651 (E.D. Mich. 2004).

Seventh Circuit: Arch Insurance Co. v. R.A. Bright Construction, Inc., 2009 WL 1507574 (N.D. Ill. May 28, 2009) (not enforced).

State Courts:

Missouri: Sturgeon v. Allied Professionals Insurance. Co., 344 S.W.3d 205 (Mo. App. 2011).

New Jersey: Param Petroleum Corp. v. Commerce & Industry Insurance Co., 686 A.2d 377 (N.J. Super. Ct. App. Div. 1997) (choice of forum and choice of law agreements in liability insurance policies should generally be ignored, at least when the insured risk is in New Jersey and choice of forum or choice of law clauses require litigation in foreign state).

[74] See, e.g.:

Third Circuit: County of Monmouth v. Federal Emergency Management Agency, 2009 WL 3151331 (D.N.J. Sept. 24, 2009).

Sixth Circuit: Franklin County, Ky. v. Owners Insurance Co., 2008 WL 5273904 (E.D. Ky. Dec. 16, 2008).

State Courts:

Alabama: Ex parte Citizens Property Insurance Corp., 15 So.3d 511 (Ala. 2009).

Arizona: Bohreer v. Erie Insurance Exchange, 216 Ariz. 208, 165 P.3d 186 (Ariz. App. 2007).

California: Elkman v. National States Insurance Co., 173 Cal. App.4th 1305, 93 Cal. Rptr.3d 768 (2009).

Delaware: Daily Underwriters of America v. Maryland Automobile Insurance Fund, 2008 WL 3485807 (Del. Super. New Castle Cnty. July 31, 2008).

Illinois: Stonecrafters, Inc. v. Wholesale Life Insurance Brokerage, Inc., 393 Ill. App.3d 951, 915 N.E.2d 51, 333 Ill. Dec. 530 (2009).

Louisiana: Green v. Auto Club Group Insurance Co., 24 So.3d 182 (La. 2009); Tsaoussidis v. State Farm Mutual Automobile Insurance Co., 28 So.3d 311 (La. App. 2009).

Michigan: Psychosocial Service Associates, P.C. v. State Farm Mutual Automobile Insurance Co., 279 Mich. App. 334, 761 N.W.2d 716 (2008).

New Mexico: Baker v. BP America Production Co., 137 N.M. 334, 110 P.3d 1071 (2005).

New York: Transportation Insurance Co. v. Simplicity, Inc., 61 A.D.3d 963, 879 N.Y.S.2d 479 (N.Y. App. Div. 2009).

Pennsylvania: Petty v. Hospital Service Association of Northeastern Pennsylvania, 967 A.2d 439 (Pa. Commw. 2009).

South Carolina: Leggett v. Smith, 386 S.C. 63, 686 S.E.2d 699 (S.C. App. 2009).

Texas: Assurances Generales Banque Nationale v. Dhalla, 282 S.W.3d 688 (Tex. App. 2009).

Vermont: Northern Security Insurance Co. v. Mitec Electronics, Ltd., 184 Vt. 303, 965 A.2d 447 (2008).

Washington: Mutual of Enumclaw Insurance Co. v. T and G Construction, Inc., 165 Wash.2d 255, 199 P.3d 376 (2008).

West Virginia: Savarese v. Allstate Insurance Co., 223 W.Va. 119, 672 S.E.2d 255 (2008).

[75] See, e.g.:

Second Circuit: International Business Machines Corp. v. Liberty Mutual Fire Insurance Co., 303 F.3d 419 (2d Cir. 2002); Commercial Union Insurance Co. v. Flagship Marine Services, Inc., 190 F.3d 26 (2d Cir. 1999); Vermont Mutual Insurance Co. v. Ciccone, 2012 WL 5199688 (D. Conn. Oct. 22, 2012); Philadelphia Indemnity Insurance Co. v. Employers Insurance Company of Wausau, 318 F. Supp.2d 170 (S.D.N.Y. 2004).

Third Circuit: Travelers Property Casualty Company of America v. Chubb Custom Insurance Co., 864 F. Supp.2d 301 (E.D. Pa. 2012); Iko Monroe, Inc. v. Royal & Sun Alliance Insurance Co., 2001 WL 1568674 at *3 (D. Del. Dec. 7, 2001).

Fourth Circuit: St. Paul Fire & Marine Insurance Co. v. Jacobson, 826 F. Supp. 155, 158 (E.D. Va. 1993), *aff'd* 48 F.3d 778 (4th Cir. 1995); West American Insurance Co. v. Bank of Isle of Wight, 673 F. Supp. 760, 763 (E.D. Va. 1987).

Seventh Circuit: Massachusetts Bay Insurance Co. v. Vic Koenig Leasing, Inc., 136 F.3d 1116 (7th Cir. 1998); Continental Casualty Co. v. Duckson, 826 F. Supp.2d 1086 (N.D. Ill. 2011).

Eighth Circuit: Johnson International Co. v. Jackson National Life Insurance Co., 812 F. Supp. 966 (D. Neb. 1993).

Ninth Circuit: Axis Reinsurance Co. v. Telekenex, Inc., 2012 WL 6632180 (N.D. Cal. Dec. 19, 2012).

State Courts:

Arizona: Beckler v. State Farm Mutual Automobile Insurance Co., 195 Ariz. 282, 987 P.2d 768 (Ariz. App. 1999).

California: Stonewall Surplus Lines Ins. Co. v. Johnson Controls, Inc., 17 Cal. Rptr.2d 713 (Cal. App. 1993).

Connecticut: Reichold Chemicals, Inc. v. Hartford Accident & Indemnity Co., 703 A.2d 1132 (Conn. 1997); Anely v. Allstate Insurance Co., 2002 WL 173158, at *3 (Conn. Super. Jan. 9, 2002).

Illinois: Westchester Fire Insurance Co. v. G. Heileman Brewing Co., 321 Ill. App.3d 622, 747 N.E.2d 955, 254 Ill. Dec. 543 (2001).

Massachusetts: W.R. Grace v. Hartford Accident & Indemnity Co., 555 N.E.2d 214, 221 (Mass. 1990); Bushkin Associates, Inc. v. Raytheon Co., 473 N.E.2d 662, 668–669 (Mass. 1985) (in the absence of a choice of law agreement by parties, contract rights "are determined by the local law of the state which, with respect to that issue, has the most significant relationship to the transaction and the parties under the principles stated in Section 6 of the *Restatement of Conflict of Laws*"); Chicago Bridge & Iron Co. v. Certain Underwriters at Lloyd's, London, 1999 WL 1336605 at *2 (Mass. Super. Jan. 8, 1999), *aff'd* 797 N.E.2d 434 (Mass. App. 2003), *review denied* 803 N.E.2d 332 (Mass. 2004).

Utah: OneBeacon American Insurance Co. v. Huntsman Polymers Corp., 276 P.3d 1156 (Utah App. 2012).

Virginia: Erie Insurance Exchange v. Shapiro, 450 S.E.2d 144 (Va. 1994).

Washington: Baffin Land Corp. v. Monticello Motor Inn, Inc., 425 P.2d 623, 627 (Wash. 1967); Dairyland Insurance Co. v. State Farm Mutual Automobile Insurance Co., 701 P.2d 806, 808, *review denied* 104 Wash.2d 1016 (1985).

[76] See:

First Circuit: Baker v. St. Paul Travelers Insurance Co., 595 F.3d 391 (1st Cir. 2010).

Second Circuit: Luizzi v. Pro Transport Inc., 548 F. Supp.2d 1 (E.D.N.Y. 2008).

Third Circuit: Century Indemnity Co. v. Certain Underwriters at Lloyd's, London, subscribing to Retrocessional Agreement Nos. 950548, 950549, 950646, 584 F.3d 513 (3d Cir. 2009); Zaloga v. Provident Life and Accident Insurance Company of America, 671 F. Supp.2d 623 (M.D. Pa. 2009).

Fourth Circuit: CACI International, Inc. v. St. Paul Fire and Marine Insurance Co., 566 F.3d 150 (4th Cir. 2009); St. Paul Fire & Marine Insurance Co. v. Jacobson, 826 F. Supp. 155, 158 (E.D. Va. 1993), *aff'd* 48 F.3d 778 (4th Cir. 1995); West American Insurance Co. v. Bank of Isle of Wight, 673 F. Supp. 760, 763 (E.D. Va. 1987).

Fifth Circuit: Little v. USAA Casualty Insurance Co., 655 F. Supp.2d 625 (W.D. La. 2009).

Tenth Circuit: Valencia v. Colorado Casualty Insurance Co., 560 F. Supp.2d 1080 (D.N.M. 2007).

Eleventh Circuit: State Farm Mutual Automobile Insurance Co. v. Duckworth, 660 F. Supp.2d 1323 (M.D. Fla. 2009); Creative Hospitality Ventures, Inc. v. U.S. Liability Insurance Co., 655 F. Supp.2d 1316 (S.D. Fla. 2009).

District of Columbia Circuit: Thorpe v. Banner Life Insurance Co., 632 F. Supp.2d 8 (D.D.C. 2009).

State Courts:

Florida: State Farm Mutual Automobile Insurance Co. v. Roach, 945 So.2d 1160 (Fla. 2006).

Maryland: Continental Casualty Co. v. Kemper Insurance Co., 173 Md. App. 542, 920 A.2d 66 (2007).

North Carolina: Huber Engineered Woods, L.L.C. v. Canal Insurance Co., 690 S.E.2d 739 (N.C. App. 2010).

Tennessee: Charles Hampton's A-1 Signs, Inc. v. American States Insurance Co., 225 S.W.3d 482 (Tenn. App. 2006).

Virginia: Erie Insurance Exchange v. Shapiro, 450 S.E.2d 144 (Va. 1994).

[77] See, e.g.:

First Circuit: Acadia Insurance Co. v. Peerless Insurance Co., 679 F. Supp.2d 229 (D. Mass. 2010).

Second Circuit: Schwartz v. Liberty Mutual Insurance Co., 539 F.3d 135 (2d Cir. 2008); Vermont Mutual Insurance Co. v. Ciccone, 2012 WL 5199688 (D. Conn. Oct. 22, 2012); Crucible Materials Corp. v. Certain Underwriters at Lloyd's London and London Market Cos.,

681 F. Supp.2d 216 (N.D.N.Y. 2010); 2004 Stuart Moldaw Trust v. XE L.I.F.E., L.L.C., 642 F. Supp.2d 226 (S.D.N.Y. 2009).

Third Circuit: Travelers Property Casualty Company of America v. Chubb Custom Insurance Co., 864 F. Supp.2d 301 (E.D. Pa. 2012); Toffler Associates v. Hartford Fire Insurance Co., 651 F. Supp.2d 332 (E.D. Pa. 2009); Iko Monroe, Inc. v. Royal & Sun Alliance Insurance Co., 2001 WL 1568674 at *3 (D. Del. Dec. 7, 2001).

Fifth Circuit: Employers Mutual Casualty Co. v. Lennox International, Inc., 375 F. Supp.2d 500 (S.D. Miss. 2005).

Sixth Circuit: Flint v. Liberty Insurance Corp., 613 F. Supp.2d 899 (E.D. Ky. 2009).

Seventh Circuit: Auto-Owners Insurance Co. v. Websolv Computing, Inc., 580 F.3d 543 (7th Cir. 2009); Continental Casualty Co. v. Duckson, 826 F. Supp.2d 1086 (N.D. Ill. 2011); Ace Rent-A-Car, Inc. v. Empire Fire and Marine Insurance Co., 580 F. Supp.2d 678 (N.D. Ill. 2008).

Eighth Circuit: Fireman's Fund Insurance Co. v. Structural Systems Technology, Inc., 426 F. Supp.2d 1009 (D. Neb. 2006).

Ninth Circuit: Axis Reinsurance Co. v. Telekenex, Inc., 2012 WL 6632180 (N.D. Cal. Dec. 19, 2012); Costco Wholesale Corp. v. Liberty Mutual Insurance Co., 472 F. Supp.2d 1183 (S.D. Cal. 2007).

Tenth Circuit: Berry & Murphy, P.C. v. Carolina Casualty Insurance Co., 586 F.3d 803 (10th Cir. 2009).

State Courts:

California: Stonewall Surplus Lines Ins. Co. v. Johnson Controls, Inc., 17 Cal. Rptr.2d 713 (Cal. App. 1993).

Connecticut: Reichold Chemicals, Inc. v. Hartford Accident & Indemnity Co., 703 A.2d 1132 (Conn. 1997); Anely v. Allstate Insurance Co., 2002 WL 173158, at *3 (Conn. Super. Jan. 9, 2002).

District of Columbia: Adolph Coors Co. v. Truck Insurance Exchange, 960 A.2d 617 (D.C. 2008).

Indiana: Kentucky National Insurance Co. v. Empire Fire and Marine Insurance Co., 919 N.E.2d 565 (Ind. App. 2010).

Massachusetts: W.R. Grace v. Hartford Accident & Indemnity Co., 555 N.E.2d 214, 221 (Mass. 1990); Bushkin Associates, Inc. v. Raytheon Co., 473 N.E.2d 662, 668–669 (Mass. 1985) (in the absence of a choice of law agreement by parties, contract rights "are determined by the local law of the state which, with respect to that issue, has the most significant relationship to the transaction and the parties under the principles stated in Section 6 of the *Restatement of Conflict of Laws*"); Chicago Bridge & Iron Co. v. Certain Underwriters at Lloyd's, London, 1999 WL 1336605 at *2 (Mass. Super. Jan. 8, 1999), *aff'd* 797 N.E.2d 434 (Mass. App. 2003), *review denied* 803 N.E.2d 332 (Mass. 2004).

Mississippi: Zurich American Insurance Co. v. Goodwin, 920 So.2d 427 (Miss. 2006).

Missouri: Accurso v. Amco Insurance Co., 295 S.W.3d 548 (Mo. App. 2009).

Ohio: Byer v. Wright, 160 Ohio App.3d 472, 827 N.E.2d 835 (2005).

Pennsylvania: Budtel Associates, L.P. v. Continental Casualty Co., 915 A.2d 640 (Pa. Super. 2006).

Utah: OneBeacon American Insurance Co. v. Huntsman Polymers Corp., 276 P.3d 1156 (Utah App. 2012).

Washington: Baffin Land Corp. v. Monticello Motor Inn, Inc., 425 P.2d 623, 627 (Wash. 1967); Dairyland Insurance Co. v. State Farm Mutual Automobile Insurance Co., 701 P.2d 806, 808, *review denied* 104 Wash.2d 1016 (1985).

[78] See:

Third Circuit: Iko Monroe, Inc. v. Royal & Sun Alliance Insurance Co., 2001 WL 1568674 at *3 (D. Del. Dec. 7, 2001).

Sixth Circuit: Elliott Co. v. Liberty Mutual Insurance Co., 434 F. Supp.2d 483 (N.D. Ohio. 2006).

Seventh Circuit: Pulse Engineering, Inc. v. Travelers Indemnity Co., 679 F. Supp.2d 969 (S.D. Ind. 2009).

State Courts:

California: Stonewall Surplus Lines Ins. Co. v. Johnson Controls, Inc., 17 Cal. Rptr.2d 713 (Cal. App. 1993).

Connecticut: Reichold Chemicals, Inc. v. Hartford Accident & Indemnity Co., 703 A.2d 1132 (Conn. 1997); Anely v. Allstate Insurance Co., 2002 WL 173158, at *3 (Conn. Super. Jan. 9, 2002).

Indiana: National Union Fire Insurance Company of Pittsburgh, PA v. Standard Fusee Corp., 917 N.E.2d 170 (Ind. App. 2009).

Massachusetts: W.R. Grace v. Hartford Accident & Indemnity Co., 555 N.E.2d 214, 221 (Mass. 1990); Bushkin Associates, Inc. v. Raytheon Co., 473 N.E.2d 662, 668–669 (Mass. 1985) (in the absence of a choice of law agreement by parties, contract rights "are determined by the local law of the state which, with respect to that issue, has the most significant relationship to the transaction and the parties under the principles stated in Section 6 of the *Restatement of Conflict of Laws*"); Chicago Bridge & Iron Co. v. Certain Underwriters at Lloyd's, London, 1999 WL 1336605 at *2 (Mass. Super. Jan. 8, 1999), *aff'd* 797 N.E.2d 434 (Mass. App. 2003), *review denied* 803 N.E.2d 332 (Mass. 2004).

Washington: Baffin Land Corp. v. Monticello Motor Inn, Inc., 425 P.2d 623, 627 (Wash. 1967); Dairyland Insurance Co. v. State Farm Mutual Automobile Insurance Co., 701 P.2d 806, 808, *review denied* 104 Wash.2d 1016 (1985).

But see:

Fifth Circuit: Pennzoil-Quaker State Co. v. American International Specialty Lines Insurance Co., 653 F. Supp.2d 690 (S.D. Tex. 2009) (not applying laws of different states to multi-state peril policy); Employers Mutual Casualty Co. v. Lennox International, Inc., 375 F. Supp.2d 500 (S.D. Miss. 2005) (same).

Eighth Circuit: St. Paul Fire and Marine Insurance Co. v. Building Construction Enterprises, Inc., 526 F.3d 1166 (8th Cir. 2008) (same).

State Courts:

Indiana: American Employers Insurance Co. v. Coachmen Industries, Inc., 838 N.E.2d 1172 (Ind. App. 2005) (same).

New York: Liberty Surplus Insurance Corp. v. National Union Fire Insurance Company of Pittsburgh, PA, 67 A.D.3d 420, 888 N.Y.S.2d 35 (N.Y. App. Div. 2009) (applying law of policyholder's domicile where risk spread out over several states).

[79] See, e.g., Scratch Golf, L.L.C. v. Lexington Insurance Co., 2009 WL 1287963 (S.D. Fla. May 6, 2009).

[80] See ISO Form CP 00 90 07 88 (limitations period of two years from the date of loss). See also:

First Circuit: Santaliz-Rios v. Metropolitan Life Insurance Co., 693 F.3d 57 (1st Cir. 2012); DiMaio Family Pizza & Luncheonette, Inc. v. The Charter Oak Fire Insurance Co., 448 F.3d 460 (1st Cir. 2006); Nunheimer v. Continental Insurance Co., 68 F. Supp.2d 75 (D. Mass. 1999).

Second Circuit: Penna v. Peerless Insurance Co., 510 F. Supp.2d 199 (W.D.N.Y. 2007); North American Foreign Trading Corp. v. Mitsui Sumitomo Insurance USA, Inc., 499 F. Supp.2d 361 (S.D.N.Y. 2007).

Third Circuit: Knoepfler v. Guardian Life Insurance Co. of America, 438 F.3d 287 (3d Cir. 2006); Bowersox Truck Sales and Service, Inc. v. Harco National Insurance Co., 209 F.3d 273 (3d Cir. 2000).

Fourth Circuit: S. Wallace Edwards & Sons, Inc. v. Cincinnati Insurance Co., 353 F.3d 367 (4th Cir. 2003).

Fifth Circuit: Watson v. Allstate Texas Lloyd's, 224 Fed. Appx. 335 (5th Cir. 2007).

Sixth Circuit: Korn v. Paul Revere Life Insurance Co., 238 Fed. Appx. 109 (6th Cir. 2007); Smith v. Allstate Insurance Co., 403 F.3d 401 (6th Cir. 2005).

Seventh Circuit: Draper v. Wellmark, Inc., 478 F. Supp.2d 1101 (N.D. Iowa 2007).

Ninth Circuit: Lamb v. American Security Insurance Co., 131 Fed. Appx. 528 (9th Cir. 2005).

Tenth Circuit: Clipperton v. Allstate Insurance Co., 151 Fed. Appx. 652 (10th Cir. 2005).

Eleventh Circuit: Tri-State Consumer Insurance Co. v. LexisNexis Risk Solutions, Inc., 858 F. Supp.2d 1359 (N.D. Ga. 2012); Kocer v. New York Life Insurance Co., 340 F. Supp.2d 1351 (N.D. Ga. 2004).

District of Columbia Circuit: Martinez v. Hartford Casualty Insurance Co., 429 F. Supp.2d 52 (D.D.C. 2006).

State Courts:

Arizona: Nangle v. Farmers Insurance Company of Arizona, 73 P.3d 1252 (Ariz. App. 2003).

California: Superior Dispatch, Inc. v. Insurance Corp. of New York, 181 Cal. App.4th 175, 104 Cal. Rptr.3d 508 (2010).

Georgia: White v. State Farm Fire and Casualty Co., 291 Ga. 306, 728 S.E.2d 685 (2012).

Illinois: American Access Casualty Co. v. Tutson, 409 Ill. App.3d 233, 948 N.E.2d 309, 350 Ill. Dec. 240 (2011); Atwood v. St. Paul Fire & Marine Insurance Co., 845 N.E.2d 68 (Ill. App. 2006).

Louisiana: Estate of DeGraauw v. Travelers Insurance Co., 940 So.2d 858 (La. App. 2006), *writ denied* 948 So.2d 1088 (La. 2007).

New York: Blanar v. State Farm Insurance Cos., 824 N.Y.S.2d 702 (N.Y. App. Div. 2006).

Ohio: Figetakis v. Owners Insurance Co., 2006 WL 475271 (Ohio App. Mar. 1, 2006), *appeal denied* 850 N.E.2d 72 (Ohio 2006).

[81] See, e.g., Blanar v. State Farm Insurance Cos., 824 N.Y.S.2d 702 (N.Y. App. Div. 2006).

[82] See, e.g.:

Second Circuit: Gassiott v. Prudential Insurance Company of America, 2009 WL 3188428 (S.D.N.Y. Oct. 6, 2009).

Third Circuit: Bayer v. Fluor Corp., 682 F. Supp.2d 484 (E.D. Pa. 2010).

Fourth Circuit: Mirabile v. Life Insurance Company of North America, 293 Fed. Appx. 213 (4th Cir. 2008).

Sixth Circuit: Smith v. Allstate Insurance Co., 403 F.3d 410 (6th Cir. 2005).

Ninth Circuit: Shugerman v. Allstate Insurance Co., 594 F. Supp.2d 1131 (C.D. Cal. 2009); Malbco Holdings, L.L.C. v. AMCO Insurance Co., 629 F. Supp.2d 1185 (D. Or. 2009).

State Courts:

Georgia: Bullington v. Blakely Crop Hail, Inc., 294 Ga. App. 147, 668 S.E.2d 732 (2008).

Indiana: Bradshaw v. Chandler, 916 N.E.2d 163 (Ind. 2009).

Louisiana: Estate of DeGraauw v. Travelers Insurance Co., 940 So.2d 858 (La. App. 2006).

Maryland: St. Paul Travelers v. Millstone, 412 Md. 424, 987 A.2d 116 (2010).

Nebraska: Brodine v. Blue Cross Blue Shield of Nebraska, 272 Neb. 713, 724 N.W.2d 321 (2006).

Tennessee: Certain Underwriter's at Lloyd's of London v. Transcarriers, Inc., 107 S.W.3d 496 (Tenn. App. 2002).

Texas: Sheppard v. Travelers Lloyds of Texas Insurance Co., 2009 WL 3294997 (Tex. App. Oct. 15, 2009).

83 See, e.g.:

Third Circuit: Novinger Group, Inc. v. Hartford Insurance Co., 514 F. Supp.2d 662 (M.D. Pa. 2007).

Ninth Circuit: Campanelli v. Allstate Insurance Co., 322 F.3d 1086 (9th Cir. 2003); Shugerman v. Allstate Insurance Co., 594 F. Supp.2d 1131 (C.D. Cal. 2009).

State Courts:

Georgia: Encompass Insurance Company of America v. Friedman, 299 Ga. App. 429, 682 S.E.2d 694 (2009).

West Virginia: Noland v. Virginia Insurance Reciprocal, 224 W.Va. 372, 686 S.E.2d 23 (2009).

84 See:

First Circuit: Santaliz-Rios v. Metropolitan Life Insurance Co., 693 F.3d 57 (1st Cir. 2012); Island View Residential Treatment Center v. Blue Cross Blue Shield of Massachusetts, Inc., 548 F.3d 24 (1st Cir. 2008).

Second Circuit: Plon Realty Corp. v. Travelers Insurance Co., 533 F. Supp.2d 391 (S.D.N.Y. 2008).

Third Circuit: Koert v. GE Group Life Assurance Co., 231 Fed. Appx. 117 (3d Cir. 2007).

Fourth Circuit: S. Wallace Edwards & Sons, Inc. v. Cincinnati Insurance Co., 353 F.3d 367 (4th Cir. 2003).

Fifth Circuit: Fino v. Louisiana Citizens Fair Plan, 2009 WL 152535 (E.D. La. Jan. 22, 2009).

Sixth Circuit: Smith v. Allstate Insurance Co., 403 F.3d 410 (6th Cir. 2005).

Ninth Circuit: Lamb v. American Security Insurance Co., 131 Fed. Appx. 528 (9th Cir. 2005).

Eleventh Circuit: Tri-State Consumer Insurance Co. v. LexisNexis Risk Solutions, Inc., 858 F. Supp.2d 1359 (N.D. Ga. 2012); Scratch Golf, L.L.C. v. Lexington Insurance Co., 2009 WL 1287963 (S.D. Fla. May 6, 2009).

State Courts:

Arizona: Nangle v. Farmers Insurance Company of Arizona, 73 P.3d 1252 (Ariz. App. 2003).

California: Superior Dispatch, Inc. v. Insurance Corp. of New York, 181 Cal. App.4th 175, 104 Cal. Rptr.3d 508 (2010); CBS Broadcasting, Inc. v. Fireman's Fund Insurance Co., 70 Cal. App.4th 1075, 83 Cal. Rptr.2d 197 (1999).

Georgia: White v. State Farm Fire and Casualty Co., 291 Ga. 306, 728 S.E.2d 685 (2012); Morrill v. Cotton States Mutual Insurance Co., 293 Ga. App. 259, 666 S.E.2d 582 (2008).

Illinois: American Access Casualty Co. v. Tutson, 409 Ill. App.3d 233, 948 N.E.2d 309, 350 Ill. Dec. 240 (2011); Atwood v. St. Paul Fire & Marine Insurance Co., 845 N.E.2d 68 (Ill. App. 2006).

Indiana: Bradshaw v. Chandler, 916 N.E.2d 163 (Ind. 2009); Rockford Mutual Insurance Co. v. Pirtle, 911 N.E.2d 60 (Ind. App. 2009).

Iowa: Rolf v. Nationwide Mutual Insurance Co., 766 N.W.2d 648 (Iowa. App. 2009).

Louisiana: Louisiana Joint Underwriters of Audubon Insurance Co. v. Johnson, 20 So.3d 528 (La. App. 2009); Marsh Engineering, Inc. v. Parker, 2007 WL 397131 (La. App. Feb. 7,

2007); Estate of DeGraauw v. Travelers Insurance Co., 940 So.2d 858 (La. App. 2006), *writ denied* 948 So.2d 1088 (La. 2007).

Maine: Geyerhahn v. U.S. Fidelity and Guaranty Co., 724 A.2d 1258 (Me. 1999).

Michigan: Idalski v. Schwedt, 2009 WL 3118601 (Mich. App. Sept. 29, 2009).

New Jersey: Friscia v. Andrade, 2009 WL 3416058 (N.J. Super. App. Dept. Oct. 9, 2009).

New York: Snyder v. Allstate Insurance CO., 70 A.D.3d 670, 896 N.Y.S.2d 79, (N.Y. App. Div. 2010); Blanar v. State Farm Insurance Cos., 824 N.Y.S.2d 702 (N.Y. App. Div. 2006).

Ohio: Angel v. Reed, 119 Ohio St.3d 73, 891 N.E.2d 1179 (Ohio 2008); Figetakis v. Owners Insurance Co., 2006 WL 475271 (Ohio App. Mar. 1, 2006), *appeal denied* 850 N.E.2d 72 (Ohio 2006).

Pennsylvania: Prime Medica Associates v. Valley Forge Insurance Co., 970 A.2d 1149 (Pa. Super. 2009).

Rhode Island: Progressive Northern Insurance Co. v. Lyden, 986 A.2d 231 (R.I. 2010).

Texas: Spicewood Summit Office Condominiums Association, Inc. v. America First Lloyd's Insurance Co., 287 S.W.3d 461 (Tex. App. 2009).

85 See:

Second Circuit: North American Foreign Trading Corp. v. Mitsui Sumitomo Insurance USA, Inc., 413 F. Supp.2d 295, 302 (S.D.N.Y. 2006). ("An insurer has no duty to advise an insured of the limitations period.").

Ninth Circuit: SEMX Corp. v. Federal Insurance Co., 398 F. Supp.2d 1103 (S.D. Cal. 2005) (Under California law, insurer "did not have a duty to disclose the two-year contractual limitation . . . at the time the parties reached the settlement agreement.").

State Courts:

Vermont: Gilman v. Maine Mutual Fire Insurance Co., 830 A.2d 71 (Vt. 2003) (Vermont insurance regulation requiring notice to insured of time limitation in policy not applicable when insureds failed to show evidentiary support for the claim that negotiations between themselves and the insurer had not been concluded, or that the insurer had any knowledge of insured's dissatisfaction with the settlement of the claim).

But see:

Eleventh Circuit: Scratch Golf, L.L.C. v. Lexington Insurance Co., 2009 WL 1287963 (S.D. Fla. May 6, 2009).

State Courts:

California: Superior Dispatch, Inc. v. Insurance Corporation of New York, 181 Cal. App.4th 175, 104 Cal. Rptr.3d 508 (2010).

Maryland: St. Paul Travelers v. Millstone, 412 Md. 424, 987 A.2d 116 (2010).

86 See:

Supreme Court: Thompson v. Phenix Insurance Company of Brooklyn, New York, 136 U.S. 287, 298–299, 10 S.Ct. 1019, 34 L.Ed. 408 (1890).

First Circuit: Mendoza-Molostvov v. Vigilant Insurance Co., 392 F. Supp.2d 254 (D. Conn. 2005).

Second Circuit: New Image Roller Dome, Inc. v. Travelers Indemnity Company of Illinois, 310 Fed. Appx. 431 (2d Cir. 2009).

Third Circuit: McShane v. Merchants Insurance Co., 2009 WL 3837245 (W.D. Pa. Nov. 16, 2009).

Fifth Circuit: Lewis v. Allstate Insurance Co., 2009 WL 498509 (E.D. La. Feb. 26, 2009).

Sixth Circuit: Roberts v. Allstate Insurance Co., 2009 WL 2851017 (M.D. Tenn. Aug. 29, 2009).

Ninth Circuit: Shugerman v. Allstate Insurance Co., 594 F. Supp.2d 1131 (C.D. Cal. 2009); City of Ilwaco v. Affiliated FM Insurance Co., 2009 WL 2485393 (W.D. Wash. Aug. 10, 2009).

State Courts:

Arizona: Nangle v. Farmers Insurance Company of Arizona, 73 P.3d 1252 (Ariz. App. 2003).

California: Superior Dispatch, Inc. v. Insurance Corporation of New York, 181 Cal. App.4th 175, 104 Cal. Rptr.3d 508 (2010); City of Hollister v. Monterey Insurance Co., 165 Cal. App.4th 455, 81 Cal. Rptr.3d 72 (Cal. App. 2008).

Georgia: Thornton v. Georgia Farm Bureau Mutual Insurance Co., 297 Ga. App. 132, 676 S.E.2d 814 (2009).

Illinois: Mathis v. Lumbermen's Mutual Casualty Insurance Co., 822 N.E.2d 543 (Ill. App. 2004).

Louisiana: Estate of DeGraauw v. Travelers Insurance Co., 940 So.2d 858 (La. App. 2006).

Michigan: McDonald v. Farm Bureau Insurance Co., 480 Mich. 191, 747 N.W.2d 811 (2008).

New Jersey: Matos v. Farmers Mutual Fire Insurance Company of Salem County, 399 N.J. Super. 219, 943 A.2d 917 (N.J. Super. App. Dept. 2008).

New York: Snyder v. Allstate Insurance Co., 70 A.D.3d 670, 896 N.Y.S.2d 79 (N.Y. App. Div. 2010); Schachter v. Royal Insurance Company of America, 801 N.Y.S.2d 372 (App. Div. 2005).

Oregon: Wright v. State Farm Mutual Automobile Insursance Co., 223 Or. App. 357, 196 P.3d 1000 (2008).

Pennsylvania: Commonwealth v. Transamerica Insurance Co., 341 A.2d 74, 78 (Pa. 1975); Prime Medica Associates v. Valley Forge Insurance Co., 970 A.2d 1149 (Pa. Super. 2009); Baker v. Pennsylvania National Mutual Casualty Insurance Co., 536 A.2d 1357, 1358 (Pa. Super. 1987), *aff'd* 559 A.2d 914 (Pa. 1989); Sudnick v. Home Friendly Insurance Company of Maryland, 27 A.2d 468, 471 (Pa. Super. 1942) (collecting cases).

Wisconsin: Wieting Funeral Home of Chilton, Inc. v. Meridian Mutual Insurance Co., 277 Wis.2d 274, 690 N.W.2d 442 (Wis. App. 2004).

[87] See, e.g., State Farm Mutual Automobile Insurance Co. v. Illinois Farmers Insurance Co., 858 N.E.2d 519 (Ill. App. 2006), *appeal allowed* 862 N.E.2d 239 (Ill. 2007). Subrogation is distinguishable from contribution or indemnification based on equitable principles and "other insurance" clauses, whereby an insurance company that provides the policyholder with coverage for a loss is able to share the burden with other insurance companies that sold policies to the policyholder which also cover the same loss. *Id.* Contribution, indemnification, and "other insurance" are discussed in greater detail in §5.03[2] *infra*. In addition, access to others' insurance could allocate the loss among more parties and is discussed in greater detail in Chapter 13 *infra*.

[88] See, e.g., State Farm Mutual Automobile Insurance Co. v. Illinois Farmers Insurance Co., 858 N.E.2d 519 (Ill. App. 2006), *appeal allowed* 862 N.E.2d 239 (Ill. 2007). See also, § 5.03[2] and Chapter 13 *infra*.

[89] See:

First Circuit: Federal Insurance Co. v. Commerce Insurance Co., 597 F.3d 68 (1st Cir. 2010).

Second Circuit: Tropic Pollo I Corp. v. National Specialty Insurance Co., 818 F. Supp.2d 559 (E.D.N.Y. 2011); Liberty Mutual Fire Insurance Co. v. E.E. Cruz & Co., 2007 WL 582500 (S.D.N.Y Feb. 21, 2007); *In re* September 11 Property Damage and Business Loss Litigation, 468 F. Supp.2d 508 (S.D.N.Y. 2006).

Third Circuit: Wirth v. Aetna United States Healthcare, 469 F.3d 305 (3d Cir. 2006); *In re* Ricchi, 470 B.R. 715 (Bankr. D.N.J. 2012); Fidelity and Guaranty Insurance Underwriters, Inc. v. American Buildings Co., Inc., 14 F. Supp.2d 704 (M.D. Pa. 1998).

Fourth Circuit: Federal Insurance Co. v. Ward, 166 Fed. Appx. 24 (4th Cir. 2006).

Sixth Circuit: Commercial Money Center, Inc. v. Illinois Union Insurance Co., 508 F.3d 327 (6th Cir. 2007).

Seventh Circuit: Vanliner Insurance Co. v. Sampat, 320 F.3d 709 (7th Cir. 2003).

Eighth Circuit: Reliance Insurance Company in Liquidation v. Chitwood, 433 F.3d 660 (8th Cir. 2006); Wal-Mart Stores, Inc. v. RLI Insurance Co., 292 F.3d 583 (8th Cir. 2002); American Steamship Co. v. Hallett Dock Co., 862 F. Supp.2d 919 (D. Minn. 2012).

Ninth Circuit: Intri-Plex Technologies, Inc. v. Crest Group, Inc., 499 F.3d 1048 (9th Cir. 2007).

Tenth Circuit: Leprino Foods Co. v. Factory Mutual Insurance Co., 653 F.3d 1121 (10th Cir. 2011); D.R. Horton, Inc.-Denver v. Travelers Indemnity Company of America, 860 F. Supp.2d 1246 (D. Colo. 2012).

Eleventh Circuit: Millennium Partners, L.P. v. Colmar Storage, L.L.C., 494 F.3d 1293 (11th Cir. 2007).

State Courts:

Alabama: Ex parte State Farm Mutual Automobile Insurance Co., 105 So.3d 1199 (Ala. 2012).

California: State Farm General Insurance Co. v. Wells Fargo Bank, N.A., 49 Cal. Rptr.3d 785 (Cal. App. 2006).

Colorado: DeHerrera v. American Family Mutual Insurance Co., 219 P.3d 346 (Colo. App. 2009); Continental Divide Insurance Co. v. Western Skies Management, Inc., 107 P.3d 1145 (Colo. App. 2004).

Delaware: Levy v. HLI Operating Co., 924 A.2d 210 (Del. Ch. New Castle Cnty. 2007).

Florida: State Farm Florida Insurance Co. v. Loo, 27 So.3d 747 (Fla. App. 2010).

Georgia: AEW # 2 Corp. v. Federal Insurance Co., 603 S.E.2d 22 (Ga. App. 2004).

Illinois: Cincinnati Insurance Co. v. DuPlessis, 848 N.E.2d 220 (Ill. App.), *appeal denied* 857 N.E.2d 670 (Ill. 2006).

Indiana: Northern Indiana Public Service Co. v. Bloom, 847 N.E.2d 175 (Ind. 2006).

Iowa: Allied Mutual Insurance Co. v. Heiken, 675 N.W.2d 820 (Iowa 2004).

Louisiana: Shelter Mutual Insurance Co. v. State Farm Mutual Automobile Insurance Co., 993 So.2d 236 (La. App. 2008).

Maryland: Rausch v. Allstate Insurance Co., 882 A.2d 801 (Md. 2005).

Minnesota: RAM Mutual Insurance Co. v. Rohde, 820 N.W.2d 1 (Minn. 2012).

Missouri: Roberts v. BJC Health System, 2013 WL 331589 (Mo. Jan. 29, 2013) (*en banc*); Benton House, L.L.C. v. Cook & Younts Insurance, Inc., 249 S.W.3d 878 (Mo. App. 2008).

Nebraska: Hans v. Lucas, 703 N.W.2d 880 (Neb. 2005).

New Hampshire: Cambridge Mutual Fire Insurance Co. v. Crete, 846 A.2d 521 (N.H. 2004).

New Jersey: Universal Underwriters Group v. Heibel, 901 A.2d 398 (N.J. Super. App. Div. 2006).

New York: St. John's University v. Butler Rogers Baskett Architects, P.C., 92 A.D.3d 761, 938 N.Y.S.2d 578 (N.Y. App. Div. 2012); Armentano v. Broadway Mall Properties, Inc., 70 A.D.3d 614, 897 N.Y.S.2d 113 (N.Y. App. Div. 2010); Huthmacher v. Dunlop Tire Corp., 815 N.Y.S.2d 385 (N.Y. App. Div. 2006); Luna v. Hyundai Motor America, 808 N.Y.S.2d 38 (N.Y. App. Div. 2006).

North Dakota: Tri-State Insurance Company of Minnesota v. Commercial Group West, LLC, 698 N.W.2d 483 (N.D. 2005).

Ohio: Indiana Insurance Co. v. Barnes, 846 N.E.2d 73 (Ohio App. 2005).

Oregon: Koch v. Spann, 92 P.3d 146 (Or. App. 2004), *review denied* 100 P.3d 217 (Or. 2004).

Pennsylvania: Milton S. Hershey Medical Center of Pennsylvania State University v. Commonwealth of Pennsylvania Medical Professional Liability Catastrophe Loss Fund, 763 A.2d 945 (Pa. Commw. 2000).

South Dakota: American Family Mutual Insurance Co. v. Auto-Owners Insurance Co., 757 N.W.2d 584 (S.D. 2008).

Tennessee: Phoenix Insurance Co. v. Estate of Ganier, 212 S.W.3d 270 (Tenn. App. 2006).

Texas: State Farm Mutual Automobile Insurance Co. v. Perkins, 2006 WL 1914627 (Tex. App. July 13, 2006).

Utah: McEwan v. Mountain Land Support Corp., 116 P.3d 955 (Utah App. 2005).

Vermont: Town of Stowe v. Stowe Theatre Guild, 908 A.2d 447 (Vt. 2006).

Washington: Matsyuk v. State Farm Fire and Casualty Co., 155 Wash. App. 324, 229 P.3d 893 (2010).

[90] ISO Form CG 00 01 10 01. Liability policies also typically contain a cooperation clause that requires the policyholder to assist in recovery of subrogation from responsible tortfeasors:

> "You and any other involved insured must . . . [a]ssist us, upon our request, in the enforcement of any right against any person or organization which may be liable to the insured because of injury or damage to which this insurance may also apply."

[91] ISO Form CP 00 90 07 88.

[92] See, e.g.:

First Circuit: St. Paul Fire & Marine Insurance Co. v. Birch, Stewart, Kolasch & Birch, LLP., 379 F. Supp.2d 183 (D. Mass. 2005), *order confirmed* 408 F. Supp.2d 59 (D. Mass. 2006) (recognizing common-law and contractual rights to subrogation).

Second Circuit: Fireman's Fund Insurance Co. v. TD Banknorth Insurance Agency, Inc., 644 F.3d 166 (2d Cir. 2011); Stewart v. Atwood, 834 F. Supp.2d 171 (W.D.N.Y. 2012).

State Courts:

California: Dobbas v. Vitas, 119 Cal. Rptr.3d 798 (Cal. App. 2011).

Colorado: Ferrellgas, Inc. v. Yeiser, 247 P.3d 1022 (Colo. 2011) (*en banc*).

Florida: Lincoln National Health and Casualty Co. v. Mitsubishi Motor Sales, 778 So.2d 392 (Fla. Dist. App. 2001), *review denied* 805 So.2d 808 (Fla. 2001) (recognizing both common-law and contractual rights to subrogation).

Iowa: Allied Mutual Insurance Co. v. Heiken, 675 N.W.2d 820 (Iowa 2004) (subrogation derives from contract, statute, and/or common law).

Kentucky: Schwartz v. Hasty, 175 S.W.3d 621 (Ky. App. 2005) (subrogation derives from contract or common law).

Louisiana: Dickens v. Commercial Union Insurance Co., 762 So.2d 1193 (La. App. 2000) (subrogation can arise through statute, common law, and contract).

Massachusetts: Apthorp v. OneBeacon Insurance Group, L.L.C., 935 N.E.2d 365 (Mass. App. 2010); Safety Insurance Co. v. Massachusetts Bay Transportation Authority, 787 N.E.2d 1132 (Mass. App.), *review denied* 791 N.E.2d 346 (Mass. 2003) (subrogation derives from contract, statute, and/or common law).

New York: Blue Cross and Blue Shield of New Jersey, Inc. v. Philip Morris USA Inc., 818 N.E.2d 1140 (N.Y. 2004) (recognizing common-law right of subrogation); St. John's University v. Butler Rogers Baskett Architects, P.C., 938 N.Y.S.2d 578 (N.Y. App. Div. 2012).

Ohio: Warmack v. Arnold, 961 N.E.2d 1165 (Ohio App. 2011).

Pennsylvania: Mellon Bank, N.A. v. National Union Insurance Company of Pittsburgh, PA, 768 A.2d 865 (Pa. Super. 2001) (recognizing common-law and contractual rights to subrogation).

93 See, e.g., Dickens v. Commercial Union Insurance Co., 762 So.2d 1193 (La. App. 2000) (La. Rev. Stat. § 22:1406(D)(4) provides that "[i]n the event of payment to any person under the coverage required by this Section and subject to the terms and conditions of such coverage, the insurer making such payment shall, to the extent thereof, be entitled to the proceeds of any settlement or judgment resulting from the exercise of any rights of recovery of such person against any person or organization legally responsible for the bodily injury for which such payment is made, including the proceeds recoverable from the assets of the insolvent insurer").

94 See:

First Circuit: St. Paul Fire & Marine Insurance Co. v. Birch, Stewart, Kolasch & Birch, LLP., 379 F. Supp.2d 183 (D. Mass. 2005), *order confirmed* 408 F. Supp.2d 59 (D. Mass. 2006) (recognizing common-law and contractual rights to subrogation).

Third Circuit: Transportes Ferreos de Venezuela II CA v. NKK Corp., 239 F.3d 555 (3d Cir. 2001) ("insurer who has not paid its insured's claim or provided the insured with a defense has no right to obtain the benefit of the insured's claims against third parties").

Ninth Circuit: Barnes v. Independent Automobile Dealers, 64 F.3d 1389, 1292 (9th Cir. 1995) (subrogation is "the insurer's right to be put in the position of the insured, in order to recover from third parties who are legally responsible to the insured for a loss paid by the insurer").

Eleventh Circuit: Fidelity & Deposit Company of Maryland v. Williams, 699 F. Supp. 897 (N.D. Ga. 1988).

State Courts:

Alaska: Thomann v. Fouse, 93 P.3d 1048 (Alaska 2004) (subrogation recognized by operation of law and through contract).

California: Progressive West Insurance Co. v. Yolo County Superior Court, 37 Cal. Rptr.3d 434, 441 (Cal. App. 2005); Sapiano v. Williamsburg National Insurance Co., 33 Cal. Rptr.2d, 659 (Cal. App. 1994) (both cases stating that in addition to its source in equity, subrogation can "arise out of the contractual language of the insurance policy[,]" but "[t]he subrogation provisions of most insurance contracts typically are general and add nothing to the rights of subrogation that arise as a matter of law"); Plut v. Fireman's Fund Insurance Co., 102 Cal. Rptr.2d 36, 41–42 (Cal. App. 2000) (subrogation generally "requires that the person seeking its benefit must have paid a debt due to a third person before he can be substituted to that person's rights and it is not the liability to pay but an *actual payment* to the creditor which raises the actual right"; an insurance company may still receive a setoff for a payment that it has not paid if it "tenders payment" and assures "performance" or seeks declaratory relief).

Florida: Lincoln National Health and Casualty Co. v. Mitsubishi Motor Sales, 778 So.2d 392 (Fla. Dist. App. 2001), *review denied* 805 So.2d 808 (Fla. 2001) (recognizing both common-law and contractual rights to subrogation).

Iowa: Allied Mutual Insurance Co. v. Heiken, 675 N.W.2d 820 (Iowa 2004) (subrogation derives from contract, statute, and/or common law).

Kentucky: Schwartz v. Hasty, 175 S.W.3d 621 (Ky. App. 2005) (subrogation derives from contract or common law).

Louisiana: Dickens v. Commercial Union Insurance Co., 762 So.2d 1193 (La. App. 2000) (subrogation can arise through statute, common law, and contract).

Massachusetts: Safety Insurance Co. v. Massachusetts Bay Transportation Authority, 787 N.E.2d 1132 (Mass. App.), *review denied* 791 N.E.2d 346 (Mass. 2003) (subrogation derives from contract, statute, and/or common law).

Montana: St. Paul Fire & Marine Insurance Co. v. Glassing, 887 P.2d 218 (Mont. 1994) (subrogation rights attach by operation of law upon paying loss).

New Mexico: Amica Mutual Insurance Co. v. Maloney, 903 P.2d 834 (N.M. 1995) (recognizing subrogation by operation of law).

New York: Blue Cross and Blue Shield of New Jersey, Inc. v. Philip Morris USA Inc., 818 N.E.2d 1140 (N.Y. 2004) (recognizing common-law right of subrogation).

Pennsylvania: Mellon Bank, N.A. v. National Union Insurance Company of Pittsburgh, PA, 768 A.2d 865 (Pa. Super. 2001) (recognizing common-law and contractual rights to subrogation).

Texas: Latter v. Autry, 853 S.W.2d 836 (Tex. App. 1993) ("All insurers hold an absolute right to subrogation against any money an insured recovers from tortfeasor up to amount of benefits paid.").

Washington: Meas v. State Farm Fire & Casualty Co., 123 P.3d 519 (Wash. App. 2005), *review denied* 142 P.3d 607 (Wash. 2006); DeTurk v. State Farm Mutual Automobile Insurance Co., 967 P.2d 994 (Wash. App. 1998) (cases recognize equitable and contractual right to subrogation and no right to reimbursement until coverage is afforded).

95 See Ceres Environmental Services, Inc. v. Arch Specialty Insurance Co., 853 F. Supp.2d 859 (D. Minn. 2012).

96 See, e.g.:

Fifth Circuit: Admiral Insurance Co. v. Arrowood Indemnity Co., 471 B.R. 687 (Bankr. N.D. Tex. 2012).

Ninth Circuit: Oswalt v. Resolute Industries, Inc., 642 F.3d 856 (9th Cir. 2011).

State Courts:

California: Garbell v. Conejo Hardwoods, Inc., 193 Cal. App.4th 1563, 122 Cal. Rptr.3d 856 (2011).

Florida: McCabe v. Florida Power and Light Co., 68 So.3d 995 (Fla. App. 2011).

Washington: Averill v. Farmers Insurance Company of Washington, 155 Wash. App. 106, 229 P.3d 830 (2010).

97 See, e.g.:

First Circuit: In re McCabe Group, 424 B.R.1 (Bankr. D. Mass. 2010).

Fourth Circuit: Pharmacists Mutual Insurance Co. v. Cincinnati Insurance Co., 658 F. Supp.2d 745 (D.S.C. 2009); *In re* Houston, 409 B.R. 799 (Bankr. D.S.C. 2009).

Fifth Circuit: Bayou Steel Corp. v. Evanston Insurance Co., 2010 A.M.C. 296 (5th Cir. 2009).

Sixth Circuit: First American Title Insurance Co. v. Cumberland County Bank, 633 F. Supp.2d 566 (M.D. Tenn. 2009).

Eighth Circuit: In re Frankum, 399 B.R. 498 (Bankr. E.D. Ark. 2009).

Ninth Circuit: In re Deuel, 594 F.3d 1073 (9th Cir. 2010).

Tenth Circuit: Kinetic Co. v. Medtronic, Inc., 672 F. Supp.2d 933 (D. Minn. 2009).

Eleventh Circuit: In re Bill Heard Enterprises, Inc., 423 B.R. 771 (Bankr. N.D. Ala. 2010).

State Courts:

California: National Union Fire Insurance Company of Pittsburgh, PA v. Cambridge Integrated Services Group, Inc., 171 Cal. App.4th 35, 89 Cal. Rptr.3d 473 (2009).

Florida: State Farm Mutual Automobile Insurance Co. v. Johnson, 18 So.3d 1099 (Fla. App. 2009).

Illinois: Chicago Hospital Risk Pooling Program v. Illinois State Medical Inter-Insurance Exchange, 397 Ill. App.3d 512, 925 N.E.2d 1216, 339 Ill. Dec. 95 (2010).

Maryland: Bierman v. Hunter, 190 Md. App. 250, 988 A.2d 530 (2010).

Nebraska: Midwest PMS v. Olsen, 279 Neb. 492, 778 N.W.2d 727 (2010).

Pennsylvania: Pusl v. Means, 982 A.2d 550 (Pa. Super. 2009).

Texas: Bay Rock Operating Co. v. St. Paul Surplus Lines Insurance Co., 298 S.W.3d 216 (Tex. App. 2009).

Washington: Matsyuk v. State Farm Fire and Casualty Co., 155 Wash. App. 324, 229 P.3d 893 (2010).

[98] *Id.* See also:

Second Circuit: In re September 11 Litigation, 2012 WL 5954585 (S.D.N.Y. Nov. 27, 2012); Union Labor Life Insurance Co. v. Olsten Corporation Health and Welfare Benefit Plan, 617 F. Supp.2d 131 (E.D.N.Y. 2008).

Sixth Circuit: Safeco Insurance Company of America v. CPI Plastics Group, Ltd., 625 F. Supp.2d 508 (E.D. Mich. 2008).

State Courts:

California: Garbell v. Conejo Hardwoods, Inc., 193 Cal. App.4th 1563, 122 Cal. Rptr.3d 856 (2011); Interstate Fire and Casualty Insurance Co. v. Cleveland Wrecking Co., 182 Cal. App.4th 23, 105 Cal. Rptr.3d 606 (2010); State Bar of California v. Statile, 168 Cal. App.4th 650, 86 Cal. Rptr.3d 72 (2008).

Connecticut: Allstate Insurance Co. v. Palumbo, 109 Conn. App. 731, 952 A.2d 1235 (2008).

New Jersey: County of Bergen Employee Benefit Plan v. Horizon Blue Cross Blue Shield of New Jersey, 412 N.J. Super. 126, 988 A.2d 1230 (N.J. Super. App. Dept. 2010); Feigenbaum v. Guaracini, 402 N.J. Super. 7, 952 A.2d 511 (N.J. Super. App. Dept. 2008).

Pennsylvania: Wimer v. Pennsylvania Employees Benefit Trust Fund, 595 Pa. 627, 939 A.2d 843 (2007).

Texas: Frymire Engineering Co. *ex rel.* Liberty Mutual Insurance Co. v. Jomar International, Ltd., 259 S.W.3d 140 (Tex. 2008).

Washington: Averill v. Farmers Insurance Co. of Washington, 155 Wash. App. 106, 229 P.3d 830 (2010).

[99] *Id.*

[100] See, e.g.:

California: Hodge v. Kirkpatrick Development, Inc., 30 Cal. Rptr.3d 303 (Cal. App. 2005).

Florida: Kala Investments, Inc. v. Sklar, 538 So.2d 909 (Fla. App. 1989).

Minnesota: Citizens Security Mutual Insurance Co. of Red Wing v. General Electric Corp., 394 N.W.2d 167 (Minn. App. 1986).

Construction liability is discussed in greater detail in Chapters 5 and 6 *infra*.

[101] See:

Florida: Underwriters of Lloyds of London v. Cape Publications, Inc., 63 So.3d 892 (Fla. App. 2011).

Illinois: Auto Owners Insurance Co. v. Callaghan, 952 N.E.2d 119, 351 Ill. Dec. 746 (Ill. App.), *appeal denied* 955 N.E.2d 468 (Ill. 2011).

Indiana: LBM Realty, L.L.C. v. Mannia, 981 N.E.2d 569 (Ind. App. 2012).

Minnesota: RAM Mutual Insurance Co. v. Rohde, 820 N.W.2d 1 (Minn. 2012).

[102] See:

Third Circuit: Community Ass'n Underwriters of America v. Rhodes Development Group, Inc., 488 Fed. Appx. 547 (3d Cir. 2012) (cross-waiver of claims).

State Courts:

Illinois: Auto Owners Insurance Co. v. Callaghan, 952 N.E.2d 119, 351 Ill. Dec. 746 (Ill. App.), *appeal denied* 955 N.E.2d 468 (Ill. 2011) (contract made lessee co-insurer against whom subrogation was not permitted).

New York: St. John's University v. Butler Rogers Baskett Architects, P.C., 92 A.D.3d 761, 938 N.Y.S.2d 578 (N.Y. App. Div. 2012) (cross-waiver of claims).

Ohio: Westfield Insurance Group v. Affinia Development, L.L.C., 982 N.E.2d 132 (Ohio App. 2012) (cross-waiver of claims).

Texas: American Zurich Insurance Co. v. Barker Roofing, L.P., 387 S.W.3d 54 (Tex. App. 2012) (cross-waiver of claims).

103 See, e.g.: American Underwriters, Inc. v. Auto-Owners Mutual Insurance Co., 719 F.2d 900 (7th Cir. 1983) ("Private agreements, while they cannot expand insurance coverage, can foreclose insurer who had paid loss pursuant to its policy from pursuing others for indemnity or contribution."); Royal Insurance Company of America v. National Union Fire Insurance Corporation of Pittsburgh, 186 F. Supp.2d 895, 899 (N.D. Ind. 2002) (similar).

Additionally, at the time the insurance policy is purchased, the policyholder may be able to buy back the insurance company's subrogation rights for a relatively small amount of additional premium. This will eliminate the potential future problems caused by the insurance company's attempt to recoup its payment through a subrogation action, or to reduce its payment under the policy by selling its subrogation rights at a time when the policyholder is in no position to bargain.

104 See § 3.04[5][a] *supra*.

105 See:

Fifth Circuit: New Orleans Assets, LLC v. Woodward, 363 F.3d 372 (5th Cir. 2004); Hamilton v. Pilgrim's Pride Employee Group Health Plan, 37 F. Supp.2d 817 (E.D. Tex. 1998).

Sixth Circuit: Farris v. State Farm Insurance Co., 617 F. Supp.2d 654 (N.D. Ohio 2008).

Seventh Circuit: Principal Mutual Life Insurance Co. v. Baron, 964 F. Supp. 1221 (N.D. Ill. 1997).

Eighth Circuit: Wal-Mart Stores, Inc. Associates' Health and Welfare Plan v. Scott, 27 F. Supp.2d 1166 (W.D. Ark. 1998).

State Courts:

California: Progressive West Insurance Co. v. Yolo County Superior Court, 37 Cal. Rptr.3d 434, 441 (Cal. App. 2005).

Louisiana: Masters v. State Farm Mutual Automobile Insurance Co., 840 So.2d 665 (La. App.), *writ denied* 847 So.2d 1276 (La. 2003).

Nebraska: Continental Western Insurance Co. v. Swartzendruber, 570 N.W.2d 708 (Neb. 1997).

New Jersey: Perreira v. Rediger, 778 A.2d 429 (N.J. 2001).

Tennessee: Health Cost Controls, Inc. v. Gifford, 108 S.W.3d 227 (Tenn. 2003); Hamrick's, Inc. v. Roy, 115 S.W.3d 468 (Tenn. App. 2002).

Washington: Safeco Insurance Co. v. Woodley, 82 P.3d 660 (Wash. 2004); Winters v. State Farm Mutual Automobile Insurance Co., 31 P.3d 1164 (Wash. 2001), *opinion corrected* 63 P.3d 764 (Wash. 2002); Averill v. Farmers Insurance Co. of Washington, 155 Wash. App. 106, 229 P.3d 830 (2010).

106 *Id.*

107 *Id.*

108 See, e.g., Friedland v. TIC-THE Industrial Co., 566 F.3d 1203 (10th Cir. 2009).

109 Fireman's Fund Insurance Co. v. Maryland Casualty Co., 65 Cal. App.4th 1279, 1295, 77 Cal. Rptr.2d 296, 305 (1998).

> "The fact that several insurance policies may cover the same risk does not increase the insured's right to recover for the loss or give the insured the right to recover more than once. Rather, the insured's right of recovery is restricted to the actual amount of the loss. Hence, where there are several policies of insurance on the same risk and the insured has recovered the full amount of its loss from any one or more, but not all, of the insurance carriers, the insured has no further rights against the insurers who have not contributed to its recovery. Similarly, the liability of the remaining insurers to the insured ceases, even if they have done nothing to indemnify or defend the insured. They remain liable, however, for contribution to those insurers who have already paid on the loss or for the insured's behalf."

See also:

Second Circuit: Stonewell Insurance Co. v. Asbestos Claims Management, 73 F.3d 1178 (2d Cir. 1995), *modified and reh'g denied* 85 F.3d 49 (2d Cir. 1996) (prorating entire loss among all triggered policies).

Third Circuit: Koppers Co. v. Aetna Casualty& Surety Co., 98 F.3d 1440, 1451 (3d Cir. 1996) ("We begin with the principle of indemnity, a fundamental principle of insurance law which prohibits insurance contracts from conferring a benefit greater than the insured's loss.").

Eleventh Circuit: Fidelity and Deposit Company of Maryland v. C.E. Hall Construction, Inc., 2012 WL 100658 (S.D. Ga. Mar. 30, 2012).

State Courts:

Arkansas: Southern Farm Bureau Casualty Insurance Co. v. Tallant, 207 S.W.3d 468 (Ark. 2005).

California: Olympic Insurance Co. v. Employers Surplus Lines Insurance Co., 178 Cal. Rptr. 908 (Cal. App. 1981).

Florida: Citizens Property Insurance Corp. v. Ashe, 50 So.3d 645 (Fla. App. 2010); Schonau v. GEICO General Insurance Co., 903 So.2d 285 (Fla. Dist. App. 2005), *review denied* 934 So.2d 450 (Fla. 2006).

Indiana: State Automobile Insurance Co. v. DMY Realty Co., 977 N.E.2d 411 (Ind. App. 2012).

Massachusetts: Golchin v. Liberty Mutual Insurance Co., 460 Mass. 222, 950 N.E.2d 853 (2011).

Montana: Swanson v. Hartford Insurance Company of Midwest, 46 P.3d 584 (Mont. 2002).

Nebraska: Blue Cross and Blue Shield of Nebraska, Inc. v. Dailey, 687 N.W.2d 689 (Neb. 2004).

New Jersey: McShane v. New Jersey Manufacturers Insurance Co., 867 A.2d 1207 (N.J. Super. App. Div. 2005).

New York: Dina v. Aetna Life Insurance Co., 316 N.Y.S.2d 654, 656–657 (N.Y. Sup. 1970) (policy prevents double recoveries under insurance policies); Silinsky v. State-Wide Insurance Co., 289 N.Y.S.2d 541, 546 (App. Div. 1968).

Tennessee: Hamrick's, Inc. v. Roy, 115 S.W.3d 468 (Tenn. App. 2002).

Texas: State Farm Mutual Automobile Insurance Co. v. Perkins, 2006 WL 1914627 (Tex. App. July 13, 2006).

Although it follows the double indemnity rule, Washington holds that where a policyholder settles with other insurance companies and gives the settling insurance companies general releases, there is no setoff from any judgment against the non-settling insurance company. See Weyerhaeuser Co. v. Commercial Union Insurance Co., 15 P.3d 115, 125–127 (Wash. 2001).

> "[T]he insurers that chose to settle in this case received far more than a simple release of liability at specific sites. Rather these companies also purchased certainty by avoiding the risks of an adverse trial outcome—not to mention forgoing the expenses associated with a lengthy trial and appeal. As the insurers 'paid [plaintiff] for a release from an unquantifiable basket of risks and considerations,' . . . we cannot say the settlements simply constituted payment for [plaintiff's] cleanup costs."

See also, Pederson's Fryer Farms, Inc. v. Transamerica Insurance Co., 922 P.2d 126, 138–139 (Wash. App. 1996), *review denied* 932 P.2d 1255 (Wash. 1997) ("The settlement, however, was not mere payment for Pederson's cleanup costs; it was in exchange for a release of liability for all past, present and future environmental claims. Transamerica did not demonstrate what part, if any, of the settlement was attributable to cleanup costs. Thus, no showing of double recovery was made. The trial court acted appropriately by not reducing the award.").

[110] See, e.g.:

First Circuit: Haddad Motor Group, Inc. v. Karp, Ackerman, Skabowski & Hogan, P.C., 603 F.3d 1 (2010).

Fifth Circuit: Grand Acadian, Inc. v. Fluor Corp., 2010 WL 1253530 (W.D. La. Mar. 29, 2010).

Sixth Circuit: Klump v. Oglebay Norton Marine Services Co., 2010 WL 1463194 (E.D. Mich. Apr. 12, 2010).

Seventh Circuit: Green v. Goodyear Dunlop Tires North America, Ltd., 2010 WL 747503 (S.D. Ill. Mar. 2, 2010).

Eighth Circuit: Torres v. Cintas Corp., 707 F. Supp.2d 1284 (N.D. Okla. 2010).

Ninth Circuit: Deleon v. Astrue, 2010 WL 1531152 (C.D. Cal. Apr. 14, 2010).

Tenth Circuit: Marotta v. Cortez, 2010 WL 1286879 (D. Colo. Mar. 29, 2010).

Eleventh Circuit: Scharba v. Everett L. Braden, Ltd., 2010 WL 1380121 (M.D. Fla. Mar. 31, 2010).

State Courts:

California: Sabi v. Sterling, 183 Cal. App.4th 916, 107 Cal. Rptr.3d 805 (2010).

Florida: Parham v. Florida Health Sciences Center, Inc., 35 So.3d 920 (Fla. App. 2010).

Massachusetts: Nandy v. Allen, 76 Mass. App. Ct. 1124, 924 N.E.2d 779 (2010).

Minnesota: Do v. American Family Mutual Insurance Co., 779 N.W.2d 853 (Minn. 2010).

Missouri: Palmer v. Union Pacific Railroad Co., 311 S.W.3d 843 (Mo. App. 2010).

New Jersey: Ternier v. Smith, 2010 WL 1030461 (N.J. Super. App. Dept. Mar. 23, 2010).

Oklahoma: Salazar Roofing & Construction, Inc. v. Oklahoma City, 249 P.3d 950 (Okla. 2010).

Washington: Matsyuk v. State Farm Fire and Casualty Co., 155 Wash. App. 324, 229 P.3d 893 (2010).

[111] See New Orleans Assets, L.L.C. v. Woodward, 363 F.3d 372 (5th Cir. 2004).

[112] See § 3.05[4][c][iii][A] *infra*.

[113] See § 3.05[4][c][iii][B] *infra*.

[114] See § 3.05[4][c][iii][C] *infra*.

[115] See Plut v. Fireman's Fund Insurance Co., 85 Cal. App.4th 98, 102 Cal. Rptr.2d 36, 41 (2000).

[116] See Plut v. Fireman's Fund Insurance. Co., 85 Cal. App.4th 98, 102 Cal. Rptr.2d 36, 40 (2000).

See also:

Second Circuit: In re September 11 Litigation, 2012 WL 5954585 (S.D.N.Y. Nov. 27, 2012); Iron Workers Locals 40, 361 & 417 Health Fund v. Dinnigan, 2012 WL 5877426 (S.D.N.Y. Nov. 21, 2012).

Fourth Circuit: Sealy, Inc. v. Nationwide Mutual Insurance Co., 286 F. Supp.2d 625 (M.D.N.C. 2003).

Sixth Circuit: Hiney Printing Co. v. Brantner, 243 F.3d 956 (6th Cir. 2001) (made-whole rule applies as default rule).

Eighth Circuit: Ceres Environmental Services, Inc. v. Arch Specialty Insurance Co., 853 F. Supp.2d 859 (D. Minn. 2012).

Ninth Circuit: CGI Technologies and Solutions, Inc. v. Rose, 683 F.3d 1113 (9th Cir. 2012); Chong v. State Farm Mutual Automobile Insurance Co., 428 F. Supp.2d 1136 (S.D. Cal. 2006); Providence Health System-Washington v. Bush, 461 F. Supp.2d 1226 (W.D. Wash. 2006).

Eleventh Circuit: Cagle v. Bruner, 112 F.3d 1510 (11th Cir. 1997) (made-whole rule is default rule); Smith v. Life Insurance Company of North America, 466 F. Supp.2d 1275 (N.D. Ga. 2006).

District of Columbia Circuit: Moore v. CapitalCare, Inc., 461 F.3d 1 (D.C. Cir. 2006).

State Courts:

Alabama: Wolfe v. Alfa Mutual Insurance Co., 880 So.2d 1163 (Ala. Civ. App. 2003).

Arkansas: Riley v. State Farm Mutual Automobile Insurance Co., 381 S.W.3d 840 (Ark. 2011); Southern Farm Bureau Casualty Insurance Co. v. Tallant, 207 S.W.3d 468 (Ark. 2005).

California: Carson v. Mercury Insurance Co., 210 Cal. App.4th 409, 148 Cal. Rptr.3d 518 (2012); American Contractors Indemnity Co. v. Saladino, 9 Cal. Rptr.3d 835 (Cal. App. 2004).

Georgia: Georgia Casualty and Surety Co. v. Woodcraft by MacDonald, Inc., 315 Ga. App. 331, 726 S.E.2d 793 (2012); Simpson v. Southwire Co., 548 S.E.2d 660, 662 (Ga. App. 2001) ("In general, an insurer may not obtain reimbursement unless and until its insured has been completely compensated for his losses."); Duncan v. Integon General Insurance Corp., 482 S.E.2d 325 (Ga. 1997) (made-whole is a rule of default applying unless clearly contracted around).

Iowa: Brandon v. West Bend Mutual Insurance Co., 681 N.W.2d 633, 641 (Iowa 2004) ("'full recovery rule' requires that the insurance company's claim for reimbursement does not mature until the insured has been fully compensated for his or her damages").

Mississippi: Federated Mutual Insurance Co. v. McNeal, 943 So.2d 658 (Miss. 2006).

Montana: Swanson v. Hartford Insurance Company of Midwest, 46 P.3d 584 (Mont. 2002).

Nebraska: Blue Cross and Blue Shield of Nebraska, Inc. v. Dailey, 687 N.W.2d 689 (Neb. 2004).

New Jersey: O'Brien v. Two West Hanover Co., 795 A.2d 907 (N.J. Super. App. Div. 2002).

Nevada: Canfora v. Coast Hotels and Casinos, Inc., 121 P.3d 599 (Nev. 2005).

Ohio: Northern Buckeye Educational Council Group Health Benefits Plan v. Lawson, 814 N.E.2d 1210, 1217 (Ohio 2004) ("make-whole doctrine applies by default where a reimbursement or subrogation contract does not contain language providing otherwise").

Oklahoma: Manokoune v. State Farm Mutual Automobile Insurance Co., 145 P.3d 1081 (Okla. 2006); Reeds v. Walker, 2006 WL 1686739 (Okla. June 20, 2006) (made-whole rule controls unless language clearly overrides it).

Pennsylvania: Jones v. Nationwide Property and Casualty Insurance Co., 613 Pa. 219, 32 A.3d 1261 (2011).

Tennessee: Abbott v. Blount County, 207 S.W.3d 732 (Tenn. 2006).

Texas: Fortis Benefits v. Cantu, 170 S.W.3d 755 (Tex. App. 2005); AIG Life Insurance Co. v. Federated Mutual Insurance Co., 200 S.W.3d 280 (Tex. App. 2006) (subrogation rights are affected by the made-whole doctrine).

Utah: State Farm Mutual Automobile Insurance Co. v. Green, 89 P.3d 97 (Utah 2003); Birch v. Fire Insurance Exchange, 122 P.3d 696 (Utah App. 2005).

Vermont: Korda v. Chicago Insurance Co., 908 A.2d 1018 (Vt. 2006).

Washington: Safeco Insurance Co. v. Woodley, 82 P.3d 660 (Wash. 2004) ("Whether described as 'setoff' or 'offset' payments, insured must be fully compensated before the insurer may recoup benefits paid.").

West Virginia: Kanawha Valley Radiologists, Inc. v. One Valley Bank, N.A., 557 S.E.2d 277 (W. Va. 2001).

Wisconsin: Drinkwater v. American Family Mutual Insurance Co., 714 N.W.2d 568 (Wis. 2006).

117 See:

Second Circuit: In re September 11 Litigation, 2012 WL 5954585 (S.D.N.Y. Nov. 27, 2012) (uninsured losses within made-whole doctrine).

Eighth Circuit: Ceres Environmental Services, Inc. v. Arch Specialty Insurance Co., 853 F. Supp.2d 859 (D. Minn. 2012) (unreimbursed defense costs not within made-whole doctrine).

Ninth Circuit: Chong v. State Farm Mutual Automobile Insurance Co., 428 F. Supp.2d 1136, 1144 (S.D. Cal. 2006) (holding that "policyholder's litigation expenses must be taken into account when determining whether the policyholder has been made whole").

State Courts:

Georgia: Georgia Casualty and Surety Co. v. Woodcraft by MacDonald, Inc., 315 Ga. App. 331, 726 S.E.2d 793 (2012) (uninsured losses within made-whole doctrine).

Montana: Swanson v. Hartford Insurance Company of Midwest, 46 P.3d 584 (Mont. 2002) (policyholder must be completely reimbursed for all losses, including costs and attorney fees involved in recovering those losses, before the insurer can exercise any right of subrogation, regardless of contract language to the contrary).

118 Chong v. State Farm Mutual Automobile Insurance Co., 428 F. Supp.2d 1136, 1145 (S.D. Cal. 2006).

119 *Id.* See also:

Montana: Skauge v. Mountain States Telephone & Telegraph Co., 565 P.2d 628, 632 (Mont. 1977).

120 Progressive West Insurance Co. v. Yolo County Superior Court, 37 Cal. Rptr.3d 434, 443 (Cal. App. 2005). See also:

Fourth Circuit: Sealy, Inc. v. Nationwide Mutual Insurance Co., 286 F. Supp.2d 625 (M.D.N.C. 2003) (contract can override made-whole doctrine).

Eleventh Circuit: Summerlin v. Georgia-Pacific Corporation Life, Health and Accident Plan, 366 F. Supp.2d 1203 (M.D. Ga. 2005) (made-whole rule controls unless language clearly overrides it).

District of Columbia Circuit: Moore v. CapitalCare, Inc., 461 F.3d 1 (D.C. Cir. 2006) (made-whole rule controls unless language clearly overrides it).

State Courts:

Alabama: Wolfe v. Alfa Mutual Insurance Co., 880 So.2d 1163 (Ala. Civ. App. 2003) (parties are free to contract out of made-whole rule).

California: American Contractors Indemnity Co. v. Saladino, 9 Cal. Rptr.3d 835 (Cal. App. 2004); Sapiano v. Williamsburg National Insurance Co., 33 Cal. Rptr.2d 659 (Cal. App. 1994) (made-whole rule controls unless language clearly overrides it).

Ohio: Northern Buckeye Educational Council Group Health Benefits Plan v. Lawson, 814 N.E.2d 1210 (Ohio 2004) (made-whole rule controls unless language clearly overrides it).

Oklahoma: Manokoune v. State Farm Mutual Automobile Insurance Co., 145 P.3d 1081 (Okla. 2006); Reeds v. Walker, 2006 WL 1686739 (Okla. June 20, 2006) (made-whole rule controls unless language clearly overrides it).

Utah: State Farm Mutual Automobile Insurance Co. v. Green, 89 P.3d 97 (Utah 2003); Birch v. Fire Insurance Exchange, 122 P.3d 696 (Utah App. 2005) (made-whole rule controls unless language clearly overrides it).

West Virginia: Kanawha Valley Radiologists, Inc. v. One Valley Bank, N.A., 557 S.E.2d 277 (W. Va. 2001) (made-whole rule controls unless language clearly overrides it).

But see:

Montana: Swanson v. Hartford Insurance Company of Midwest, 46 P.3d 584 (Mont. 2002) (policyholder must be completely reimbursed for all losses, including costs and attorney fees involved in recovering those losses, before the insurer can exercise any right of subrogation, regardless of contract language to the contrary).

Nebraska: Blue Cross and Blue Shield of Nebraska, Inc. v. Dailey, 687 N.W.2d 689 (Neb. 2004) (any policy language attempting to contract around made-whole rule invalid).

Tennessee: Abbott v. Blount County, 207 S.W.3d 732 (Tenn. 2006) (made-whole doctrine applies regardless of the language found in the insurance contract).

Wisconsin: Drinkwater v. American Family Mutual Insurance Co., 714 N.W.2d 568 (Wis. 2006) (made-whole doctrine applies regardless of the language found in the insurance contract).

121 See § 3.02[1] *supra.*

122 See Progressive West Insurance Co. v. Yolo County Superior Court, 37 Cal. Rptr.3d 434, 443–444 (Cal. App. 2005).

123 See: ISO Form CG 00 01 10 01; ISO Form CP 00 90 07 88. See § 3.05[4][a] *supra.*

124 Progressive West Insurance Co. v. Yolo County Superior Court, 37 Cal. Rptr.3d 434, 444 (Cal. App. 2005) (policy provisions "do not clearly indicate that Progressive's rights are first in priority. In addition, these two provisions do not explain that Progressive may seek reimbursement regardless of whether the insured was made whole by his recovery from the third party").

125 See § 3.05[4][a] *supra.*

126 Sapiano v. Williamsburg National Insurance Co., 33 Cal. Rptr.2d 659 (Cal. App. 1994). See also:

Utah: State Farm Mutual Automobile Insurance Co. v. Green, 89 P.3d 97 (Utah 2003) (general language entitling insurance company to subrogation recovery to the extent of payment insufficient to override made-whole rule).

West Virginia: Kanawha Valley Radiologists, Inc. v. One Valley Bank, N.A., 557 S.E.2d 277 (W. Va. 2001) (made-whole doctrine is not overcome merely by including in the policy a general statement that the insurer is entitled to subrogation).

127 Sapiano v. Williamsburg National Insurance Co., 33 Cal. Rptr.2d 659 (Cal. App. 1994). See also, Samura v. Kaiser Foundation Health Plan, Inc., 22 Cal. Rptr.2d 20 (Cal. App. 1993), *cert. denied* 511 U.S. 1084 (1994).

128 *Id.*

[129] See:

Fourth Circuit: Sealy, Inc. v. Nationwide Mutual Insurance Co., 286 F. Supp.2d 625 (M.D.N.C. 2003).

Eleventh Circuit: Summerlin v. Georgia-Pacific Corporation Life, Health and Accident Plan, 366 F. Supp.2d 1203 (M.D. Ga. 2005).

District of Columbia Circuit: Moore v. CapitalCare, Inc., 461 F.3d 1 (D.C. Cir. 2006).

State Courts:

Alabama: Wolfe v. Alfa Mutual Insurance Co., 880 So.2d 1163 (Ala. Civ. App. 2003).

California: American Contractors Indemnity Co. v. Saladino, 9 Cal. Rptr.3d 835 (Cal. App. 2004); Progressive West Insurance Co. v. Yolo County Superior Court, 37 Cal. Rptr.3d 434, 443 (Cal. App. 2005); Sapiano v. Williamsburg National Insurance Co., 33 Cal. Rptr.2d 659 (Cal. App. 1994).

Montana: Swanson v. Hartford Insurance Company of Midwest, 46 P.3d 584 (Mont. 2002).

Nebraska: Blue Cross and Blue Shield of Nebraska, Inc. v. Dailey, 687 N.W.2d 689 (Neb. 2004).

Ohio: Northern Buckeye Educational Council Group Health Benefits Plan v. Lawson, 814 N.E.2d 1210 (Ohio 2004).

Oklahoma: Manokoune v. State Farm Mutual Automobile Insurance Co., 145 P.3d 1081 (Okla. 2006); Reeds v. Walker, 2006 WL 1686739 (Okla. June 20, 2006).

Tennessee: Abbott v. Blount County, 207 S.W.3d 732 (Tenn. 2006).

Utah: State Farm Mutual Automobile Insurance Co. v. Green, 89 P.3d 97 (Utah 2003); Birch v. Fire Insurance Exchange, 122 P.3d 696 (Utah App. 2005).

West Virginia: Kanawha Valley Radiologists, Inc. v. One Valley Bank, N.A., 557 S.E.2d 277 (W. Va. 2001).

Wisconsin: Drinkwater v. American Family Mutual Insurance Co., 714 N.W.2d 568 (Wis. 2006).

[130] *Id.*

[131] See:

Fourth Circuit: Sealy, Inc. v. Nationwide Mutual Insurance Co., 286 F. Supp.2d 625 (M.D.N.C. 2003) (contract can override made-whole doctrine).

Eleventh Circuit: Summerlin v. Georgia-Pacific Corporation Life, Health and Accident Plan, 366 F. Supp.2d 1203 (M.D. Ga. 2005) (made-whole rule controls unless language clearly overrides it).

District of Columbia Circuit: Moore v. CapitalCare, Inc., 461 F.3d 1 (D.C. Cir. 2006) (made-whole rule controls unless language clearly overrides it).

State Courts:

Alabama: Wolfe v. Alfa Mutual Insurance Co., 880 So.2d 1163 (Ala. Civ. App. 2003) (parties are free to contract out of made-whole rule).

California: American Contractors Indemnity Co. v. Saladino, 9 Cal. Rptr.3d 835 (Cal. App. 2004); Progressive West Insurance Co. v. Yolo County Superior Court, 37 Cal. Rptr.3d 434, 443 (Cal. App. 2005); Sapiano v. Williamsburg National Insurance Co., 33 Cal. Rptr.2d 659 (Cal. App. 1994) (made-whole rule controls unless language clearly overrides it).

Ohio: Northern Buckeye Educational Council Group Health Benefits Plan v. Lawson, 814 N.E.2d 1210 (Ohio 2004) (made-whole rule controls unless language clearly overrides it).

Oklahoma: Manokoune v. State Farm Mutual Automobile Insurance Co., 145 P.3d 1081 (Okla. 2006); Reeds v. Walker, 2006 WL 1686739 (Okla. June 20, 2006) (made-whole rule controls unless language clearly overrides it).

Utah: State Farm Mutual Automobile Insurance Co. v. Green, 89 P.3d 97 (Utah 2003); Birch v. Fire Insurance Exchange, 122 P.3d 696 (Utah App. 2005) (made-whole rule controls unless language clearly overrides it).

West Virginia: Kanawha Valley Radiologists, Inc. v. One Valley Bank, N.A., 557 S.E.2d 277 (W. Va. 2001) (made-whole rule controls unless language clearly overrides it).

But see:

Montana: Swanson v. Hartford Insurance Company of Midwest, 46 P.3d 584 (Mont. 2002) (policyholder must be completely reimbursed for all losses, including costs and attorney fees involved in recovering those losses, before the insurer can exercise any right of subrogation, regardless of contract language to the contrary).

Nebraska: Blue Cross and Blue Shield of Nebraska, Inc. v. Dailey, 687 N.W.2d 689 (Neb. 2004) (any policy language attempting to contract around "made-whole" rule is invalid).

Tennessee: Abbott v. Blount County, 207 S.W.3d 732 (Tenn. 2006) (made-whole doctrine applies regardless of the language found in the insurance contract).

Wisconsin: Drinkwater v. American Family Mutual Insurance Co., 714 N.W.2d 568 (Wis. 2006) (made-whole doctrine applies regardless of the language found in the insurance contract).

132 See:

California: Plut v. Fireman's Fund Insurance Co., 102 Cal. Rptr.2d 36, 41 (Cal. App. 2000).

Illinois: Trogub v. Robinson, 853 N.E.2d 59 (Ill. App. 2006).

133 *Id.*

134 See:

California: Plut v. Fireman's Fund Insurance Co., 102 Cal. Rptr.2d 36, 40 (Cal. App. 2000); Allstate Insurance Co. v. Mel Rapton, Inc., 92 Cal. Rptr.2d 151, 156 (Cal. App. 2000) ("When, as often happens, the insured is only partially compensated by the insurer for a loss (because of deductibles, policy limits, and exclusions), operation of the subrogation doctrine 'results in two or more parties having a right of action for recovery of damages based upon the same underlying cause of action.'"); Hodge v. Kirkpatrick Development, Inc., 30 Cal. Rptr.3d 303, 308, 310–311 (Cal. App. 2005) ("Partial payment to the insured results in partial subrogation; the insurer is subrogated in the amount of the insurance proceeds," and "the insured retains the right to sue the responsible party for any loss not fully compensated by insurance, and the insurer has the right to sue the responsible party for the insurer's loss in paying on the insurance policy.").

Florida: Monte de Oca v. State Farm Fire & Casualty Co., 897 So.2d 471 (Fla. Dist. App. 2004), *review denied* 934 So.2d 449 (Fla.2006) (insureds who were each found partially responsible for their automobile accidents were not entitled, under the made-whole doctrine, to full recovery of their collision loss deductible after automobile insurers recovered from third parties on subrogation claims; insureds, as comparative wrongdoers, were not entitled to be totally absolved from liability and remained liable for portion of deductible reflecting their comparative negligence).

Pennsylvania: Jones v. Nationwide Property and Casualty Insurance Co., 613 Pa. 219, 32 A.3d 1261 (2011) (where insurer recovered in subrogation 90% of what it paid insured for property damage, it properly returned 90% of the deductible to the insured).

South Dakota: Westfield Insurance Co. v. Rowe *ex rel.* Estate of Gallant, 631 N.W.2d 175 (S.D. 2001) (automobile insurer's payment of claim for collision loss entitled it to reimbursement out of liability insurance proceeds, whether or not the insureds were made whole; the policy required the insureds to hold the proceeds in trust and to reimburse the insurer).

135 16 *Couch on Insurance* § 61:43.

136 Hodge v. Kirkpatrick Development, Inc., 30 Cal. Rptr.3d 303, 309 (Cal. App. 2005).

137 *Id.*

138 *Id.*

139 See Travelers Indemnity Co. v. Ingebretsen, 113 Cal. Rptr. 679 (Cal. App. 1974) (allowing insurance company recovery notwithstanding that the policyholder was not made whole). Notably, however, this case dealt with an "executed a detailed subrogation agreement" with broad language abrogating the made-whole rule. The subrogation agreement was executed at the time the insurance company paid the policyholder and stated:

> "In consideration of and to the extent of said payment the undersigned hereby assigns and transfers to the said Company all rights, claims, demands and interest which the undersigned may have against any party through the occurrence of such loss."

See Travelers Indemnity Co. v. Ingebretsen, 113 Cal. Rptr. at 684. In addition, the insurance company's attorneys shared the expenses of recovering against the third party. Because of these facts, the court applied the intermediate approach allocating the recovery to both the policyholder and the insurance company.

140 See:

Second Circuit: In re Holocaust Victim Assets Litigation, 424 F.3d 150 (2d Cir. 2005), *cert. denied sub nom.* Weisshaus v. Union Bank of Switzerland, 126 S.Ct. 2901 (2006).

Fifth Circuit: Dear v. Union Central Life Insurance Co., 573 F. Supp.2d 958 (W.D. Tex. 2008).

Seventh Circuit: Ellis v. Allstate Insurance Co., 479 F. Supp.2d 782 (N.D. Ill. 2006).

Ninth Circuit: Chong v. State Farm Mutual Automobile Insurance Co., 428 F. Supp.2d 1136, 1145 (S.D. Cal. 2006) (inequitable to permit allocation if insurance company does not share in the costs of recovery).

Under that rule, a carrier that elected not to participate in the policyholder's tort action would be in effect allowed to engage in a risk free gamble with the policyholder's money. If the policyholder loses the tort action, the carrier has lost nothing because the carrier has not yet incurred any attorney fees and costs. If the policyholder wins, the carrier, knowing the outcome, may then offer to pay its *pro rata* portion of attorney fees and costs in exchange for reimbursement. Plainly, such a rule would not be in keeping with the equitable principles underlying the make-whole rule and the subrogation doctrine. See:

Tenth Circuit: Summerford v. Covenant Transportation, 370 F. Supp.2d 934 (D. Neb. 2005).

State Courts:

Alabama: Wolfe v. Alfa Mutual Insurance Co., 880 So.2d 1163 (Ala. Civ. App. 2003).

California: 21st Century Insurance Co. v. Superior Court, 47 Cal.4th 511, 213 P.3d 972, 98 Cal. Rptr.3d 516 (2009); Progressive West Insurance Co. v. Yolo County Superior Court, 37 Cal. Rptr.3d 434, 444 (Cal. App. 2005) ("Under this rule, an insurance company that does not participate in the underlying action must pay a *pro rata* share of the insured's attorney fees and costs when it seeks reimbursement from its insured out of funds obtained by the insured from the responsible third party."); Lee v. State Farm Mutual Automobile Insurance Co., 129 Cal. Rptr. 271 (Cal. App. 1976).

Delaware: Crowhorn v. Nationwide Mutual Insurance Co., 836 A.2d 558 (Del. Super. 2003).

Idaho: Boll v. State Farm Mutual Automobile Insurance Co., 92 P.3d 1081 (Idaho 2004).

Indiana: Indiana Union Mutual Insurance Group v. Smith, 656 N.E.2d 538 (Ind. App. 1995) (recognizing sharing in costs of recovery).

North Carolina: Farm Bureau Insurance Co. of North Carolina, Inc. v. Blong, 583 S.E.2d 307 (N.C. App.), *review denied* 589 S.E.2d 125 (N.C. 2003).

Pennsylvania: Couy v. Nardei Enterprises, 587 A.2d 345, 346 (Pa. Super. 1991).

Texas: Allstate Insurance Co. v. Edminster, 2007 WL 196433 (Tex. App. Jan. 26, 2007).

Washington: Meas v. State Farm Fire and Casualty Co., 130 Wash. App. 527, 123 P.3d 519 (2005).

Wisconsin: Grorud *ex rel.* Danielson v. Fencl, 2007 WL 584524 (Wis. App. Feb. 27, 2007) ("The common fund doctrine recognizes that a 'litigant or a lawyer who recovers a common fund for the benefit of persons other than himself or his client is entitled to a reasonable attorney's fee from the fund as a whole.'").

In Pennsylvania, the common fund doctrine has been expressly authorized by statute. See 42 Pa. Cons. Stat. Ann. § 2503.

"The following participants shall be entitled to a reasonable counsel fee as part of the taxable costs of the matter . . . [a]ny participant who is awarded counsel fees out of a fund within the jurisdiction of the court pursuant to any general rule relating to an award of counsel fees from a fund within the jurisdiction of the court."

141 *Id.*

CHAPTER 4

First-Party Insurance

Chapter Contents

§ 4.01 Overview

First-party insurance is an extremely complex and enormously interesting area of insurance coverage law.[1] Although there are many varieties of first-party insurance policies,[2] many of the coverage issues are common to all of them, diverse as they may be. Accordingly, an understanding of the inner workings of each of the types of first-party insurance policies is neither required nor necessary.

This chapter focuses on the first-party insurance most often associated with real estate-related entities—namely, property insurance and builders risk insurance. This chapter will first discuss the definition of first-party insurance.[3] In the context of property and builders risk coverage, the ensuing discussions will cover some of the most significant legal issues, including, among other things, the issues set forth in the insuring agreement:[4] (1) the meaning of "covered property," (2) "direct physical loss or damage," and (3) "covered causes of loss." It will conclude by looking at additional coverages,[5] conditions,[6] and exclusions in the insurance policy.[7]

§ 4.02 First-Party Insurance Defined

"First-party insurance" is a term of art.[8] As previously stated,[9] first-party insurance policies provide insurance coverage that compensates the policyholder for losses that are suffered to the person or to the property of the policyholder.[10]

In this vein—namely, in the sense of whose person or property suffers the injury—first-party insurance is distinguishable from third-party insurance.[11] Unlike first-party insurance, where the policyholder seeks reimbursement for losses suffered to the person or property of the policyholder, third-party insurance provides insurance coverage to the policyholder for liability related to losses suffered to the person or property of third parties, i.e., parties who are not part of the insurance contract between the policyholder (a.k.a, the "first party") and the insurance company (a.k.a., the "second party").[12]

For example, homeowners or renters insurance is a first-party insurance policy because it compensates the policyholder for damages to the policyholder's real and personal property at premises occupied by the policyholder. Likewise, commercial property and business interruption insurance is another form of first-party insurance because it compensates a business for both: (1) damages to its real and personal property; and (2) the consequential loss of its business income and continued operating expenses as a result of a covered accident during a period between the date the property damage started and the date the property is repaired to its pre-loss state. Additionally, builders risk insurance provides first-party insurance coverage for developers and contractors for losses that take place to the property they are developing or building until the project is completed. Of course, once operations are completed, the property should be covered by a residential or commercial property insurance policy.

§ 4.03 First-Party Property/Builders Risk Insurance Issues

[1]—Insuring Agreement

Insurance can be written in manuscript-form or standard-form policies. Under manuscript-form policies, each provision can be drafted from scratch or pre-approved language can be cut and pasted together to form a unique policy particular to the policyholder or risk at issue.

The majority of insurance policies are standard-form agreements in the sense that the agreements are contained in pre-printed forms that contain the same or substantially similar provisions. The Insurance Services Office, Inc. ("ISO") is an association of approximately 1400 domestic property and casualty insurers and operates as the "almost exclusive source of support services in this country for CGL [Comprehensive General Liability] insurance," drafing and submitting for approval these standard forms for the insurance companies it represents.[13]

A standard-form first-party property insurance policy may provide as follows:

> We will pay you for direct physical loss or damage to covered property at the premises described in the Declarations caused by or resulting from any Covered Cause of Loss.[14]

Builders risk insurance has the same basic insuring agreement designed to cover property that is damaged while under construction.[15]

Thus, there are three coverage issues that arise from the standard-form first-party property insurance policy's insuring agreement:

1. "Direct physical loss or damage";
2. "Covered property"; and
3. "Covered cause of loss."

[2]—"Covered Property"

The first issue derived from the insuring agreement is whether there has been a loss to "covered property."

[a]—Tangible Property

To determine whether there has been damage to "covered property," a policyholder should first look at the policy's definition of "covered property," which is ordinarily defined to include the policyholder's building, equipment, tangible personal property and stock, as well as the tangible personal property of others.[16] "Covered property" may also be defined more broadly, to include, for instance, "property owned, controlled, used, leased or intended for use by the insured."[17] However, land and landscaping are generally excluded.[18] Thus, "covered property" generally includes most forms of improvements to real property and of tangible personal property.[19] Therefore, in normal circumstances, it is a rather simple exercise to determine whether the damaged property is "covered property."

[b]—Intangible Personal Property

Intangible property, such as bonds, notes, money, and intellectual property, is generally excluded from the definition of "covered property,"[20] although careful review of the policy is necessary because some policies cover businesses for losses suffered to intangibles.

Computer losses present an interesting example where the "covered property" issue is not completely settled. In fact, in computer loss cases, courts are generally in agreement that computer hardware is considered "covered property."[21] It is "covered property" because it constitutes tangible personal property. However, where intangible property is excluded from the definition of "covered property," there is some disagreement as to whether electronic data and software is "covered property."[22]

Despite this disagreement, in loss of electronic data cases, a policyholder is often able to avoid the conflict altogether by couching the description of the damage as damage to the computer system itself, which, as previously stated, is universally considered "covered property." For instance, where there has been damage to electronic data, a policyholder often successfully argues that the loss of electronic data results in the shutdown or inability of operation of the computer hardware.[23] In such circumstances, the issue then becomes whether such "covered property" has suffered "direct physical loss or damage."[24]

[c]—"Blanket" and "Scheduled" or "Specific" Coverage

Another question with regard to the "covered property" issue is whether particular property needs to be specifically identified. For example, even where improved properties may be covered by the general definition of "insured property," large developers may be required to identify properties they want covered. In this vein, large developers with rapid and frequent turnover of real property will need to consider two general types of property insurance policies: (1) "blanket" and (2) "specific" or "scheduled" policies.

[i]—"Blanket" Insurance Policies

A "blanket" policy provides coverage for all locations of a policyholder without the requirement that the locations be specifically identified, or provides coverage for many locations without specifying the valuations of the items to be covered under the premise that coverage is afforded for each property up to the large "blanket" limits of the policy.[25]

[ii]—"Specific" or "Scheduled" Policies

On the other hand, a "specific" or "scheduled" policy covers specific locations identified by the policyholder or specific locations identified by the policyholder up to the values stated for each specific location.[26]

[d]—Newly Acquired and Unnamed Locations

Large developers with rapid and frequent turnover of real property who cannot purchase "blanket" coverage need to be aware of the "newly acquired locations" and "unnamed locations" provisions. Large developers who cannot access "blanket" coverage need to know about "newly acquired" and "unnamed locations" provisions because such provisions could impact the coverage available to locations they may inadvertently fail to identify.

[i]—Newly Acquired Locations

Policies generally provide either full or limited coverage for "newly acquired" locations for a specified period of time, with the requirement that the policyholder notify the insurance company of the "newly acquired" property within that specified time period.[27] Litigation often centers around the meaning of "newly acquired" location, with the vast majority of courts holding that a "newly acquired location" only includes property acquired after the onset of the policy period.[28]

Other issues may arise as to the effect of failure to follow the notice requirements. Failure to notify the insurance company of the acquisition likely causes the newly acquired property either to: (1) become an "unnamed location"[29] or (2) not be covered at all under the insurance policy.[30]

Losses that occur during the notice period present an interesting unresolved question as to the application of a reduced limit for "newly acquired" locations. Does the reduced limit apply until notice (and acceptance of the risk) occurs, or does the reduced limit apply where there is a failure of notice? No reported case has addressed this issue. Consequently, great care should be given to understanding the meaning of the particular contract at issue.

[ii]—Unnamed Locations

Policies might also contain reduced limits—in the form of sublimits—for "unnamed locations."[31] An "unnamed location" is generally not specifically defined in the policy forms, which makes it rife for litigation in the right case.[32] Common sense, however, dictates that the phrase could mean a newly acquired location for which no notice was given in the requisite notice period and/or an unidentified location that is not newly acquired.

Given this common-sense definition, a developer with a reduced limit for "unnamed locations" might want to consider ensuring that: (1) the sublimits for "unnamed locations" are adequate to cover losses for properties that might be inadvertently considered "unnamed locations;" and/or (2) all of its properties are "named locations." Otherwise, the policyholder might be forced to litigate the meaning of "unnamed locations" without any guidance on how courts have resolved the meaning of the term.

[3]—"Direct Physical Loss or Damage"

After establishing that the property at issue is "covered property,"[33] one would need to show "direct physical loss or damage" to the specified "covered property" to trigger coverage. The loss or damage question creates two subissues: (1) when is the "direct physical loss or damage" deemed to have taken place for purposes of applying the correct insurance policy;[34] and (2) has there been the requisite "direct physical loss or damage."[35]

[a]—Timing of Loss

With respect to the timing of the loss or damage, jurisdictions vary on the coverage trigger theory in first-party property insurance losses. Some states utilize the manifestation trigger, holding that the loss is deemed to occur in the policy period when it is first discovered.[36] Others follow an injury-in-fact trigger, holding that the policy in effect when the injury first takes place is required to respond to the loss.[37] Some jurisdictions may even apply a continuous trigger theory in latent and progressive injury contexts, holding that all policies between the date of the first exposure or injury until the date of discovery are responsible.[38]

[b]—Loss or Damage

The more difficult issue is whether there has even been "direct physical loss or damage." Resolution of the issue requires that the definitions in the insurance policy itself first be consulted. However, first-party property and builders risk insurance policies generally do not define the phrase "direct physical loss or damage," which would require reference and review of other sources to define the phrase.

[i]—Plain Meaning

When the policy does not define "direct physical loss or damage," consulting a dictionary is a good starting point. The dictionary definitions of the words in the phrase "direct physical loss or damage" leads to mixed results depending upon whether "physical" is deemed to modify only the word it precedes—"loss"—or whether it also is construed to modify the word "damage."

Webster's Ninth New Collegiate Dictionary defines "direct" as "without an intervening agency, instrumentality, or influence."[39] The same dictionary states that "physical" means "having a material existence: perceptible esp[ecially] through the senses and subject to the laws of nature."[40] "Loss" is the "act of losing possession . . . destruction, ruin,"[41] and "damage" is defined as "loss or harm resulting from injury to . . . property."[42]

Taken together, if "physical" modifies both "loss" and "damage," the dictionary definition of the terms within the phrase "direct physical loss or damage" suggests that "damage" within the phrase encompasses perceptible damage to or alteration of property. On the other hand, if "physical" is not deemed to modify "damage," then loss of use or function, without any perceptible injury to property, might qualify as "damage" within the phrase "direct physical loss or damage."

[ii]—Case Law

[A]—"Direct Physical Loss"

Consistent with the dictionary definitions, courts construe the phrase "direct physical loss" as the actual loss of property.[43] That "physical" modifies the word it immediately precedes should be of no moment to English scholars.

[B]—"Damage"

Moreover, nearly unanimously, courts define the phrase "direct physical damage" to include distinct and demonstrated physical alteration in property:

> "In ordinary parlance and widely accepted definition, physical damage to property means 'a distinct, demonstrable, and physical alteration' of its structure."[44]

Of course, within this construction is the assumption that "physical" modifies "damage," which merely begs the very question at issue. In construing the phrase, "direct physical loss or damage," the courts are divided as to whether there must be some perceptible alteration in the property ("physical" is deemed to modify "damage")[45] or whether loss of use or function is sufficient ("physical" is deemed not to modify "damage").[46]

[I]—Loss of Use or Function

One school of thought is that "physical loss or damage" is present when loss of use or function has resulted, even if no harmful or other physical change has occurred to the property. For example, one court found the presence of asbestos constituted a covered cause of loss if the asbestos rendered the premises uninhabitable:

> "When the presence of large quantities of asbestos in the air of a building is such as to make the structure uninhabitable and unusable, then there has been a distinct loss to its owner. However, if asbestos is present in components of a structure, but is not in such form or quantity as to make the building unusable, the owner has not suffered a loss. The structure continues to function—it has not lost its utility."[47]

There are numerous decisions from other jurisdictions in which the courts have similarly held that there was "direct physical loss or damage" when a building or other property becomes so contaminated that its function or use is effectively eliminated. For example, there are other cases involving asbestos contamination[48] and cases involving: misapplication of pesticide,[49] environmental contamination,[50] oil and gasoline contamination,[51] methamphetamine release,[52] lead paint,[53] carbon monoxide release,[54] food spoilage,[55] and mold contamination.[56]

Additionally, there are examples where even harmless contamination or other consequences to property, rendering the property unusable or non-operational, is "direct physical loss or damage."[57] For example, in one case, the policyholder was a manufacturer of cereal. When its contractor negligently treated its oats with an unapproved pesticide, the manufacturer recalled the product because Food and Drug Administration ("FDA") regulations prevented their sale. The manufacturer submitted a claim for first-party insurance coverage. The insurance company argued that there was no direct physical loss or damage. The court held that the product was damaged because it was rendered unusable as a result of the FDA regulations, even though the food was not unfit for human consumption.[58]

The cases discussed to this point either expressly or by implication are premised upon the view that "physical" does not modify "damage." Alternatively, they could be interpreted as taking the modern view of "physical," holding that loss of use or function in effect constitutes a perceptible loss or damage.

Nevertheless, there is some significant countervailing authority holding that loss of use or function, without more, does not constitute "physical loss or damage." The language of first-party property policies uses "physical," which has a dictionary definition meaning "having material existence perceptible esp[ecially] through the senses and subject to the laws of nature."[59] Thus, it could be argued that use of the adjective "physical" to describe "loss or damage" in the phrase at issue connotes that the "loss or damage" must be perceptible and measurable. There are some legal authorities supporting such a countervailing position:

> "When the structure of property itself is unchanged to the naked eye, however, and the insured alleges that its usefulness for its normal purposes has been destroyed or reduced, there are serious questions whether the alleged loss satisfies the policy trigger [of 'physical loss or damage']. . . . The requirement that the loss be "physical," given the ordinary definition of that term, is widely held

> to exclude alleged losses that are intangible or incorporeal, and, thereby, to preclude any claim against the property insurer when the insured merely suffers a detrimental economic impact unaccompanied by a distinct, demonstrable, physical alteration of the property."[60]

Indeed, although some of the cases use favorable language indicating coverage for loss of function[61] or loss of use,[62] with some exception,[63] most loss of use cases involve something "physical" happening to the property at issue.[64] Thus, while loss of use could constitute "direct physical loss or damage," there is significant authority suggesting that the issue is far from decided, and there are relatively few cases where loss of use without some physical manifestation of contamination or other alteration was present.[65]

[II]—Computer Loss Cases

With the increased use of computers, real estate-related entities may need to understand how first-party property policies might respond to a loss of computer software or hardware. In particular, engineering and architectural firms might have a significant amount of intellectual and business property in the form of drawings and plans stored on their computer systems. What happens if such property is deleted or otherwise becomes unusable?

In computer loss cases, the "direct physical loss or damage" issue is extremely interesting. The first and leading case in the area is *American Guarantee & Liability Insurance Co. v. Ingram Micro, Inc.*[66] In that case, a wholesale distributor of microcomputer products experienced a power outage that caused its computer system to become inoperable for eight hours. Because the distributor's business depended entirely upon operation of its computers, the distributor suffered eight hours of business interruption. Its first-party property insurance company denied coverage for the loss.

In subsequent coverage litigation, the sole issue was whether there was "direct physical loss or damage" to the computer system, which was unquestionably covered personal property. The insurance company argued that there was no such physical loss or damage because the computers at all times remained intact and capable of performing their intended functions, even though accidentally deleted programming needed to be reinstalled to make them operational. The distributor disagreed, arguing that loss of use and functionality itself constitutes "direct physical loss or damage." The court sided with the distributor:

> "At a time when computer technology dominates our professional as well as personal lives, the Court must side with Ingram's broader definition of 'physical damage.' The Court finds that 'physical damage' is not restricted to the physical destruction or harm of computer circuitry but includes loss of access, loss of use, and loss of functionality."[67]

Other cases, albeit in the third-party liability insurance context, suggest that damage to electronic data might not be covered because such property is "intangible."[68] By analogy to the first-party context, an argument could be made that "intangible" property is incapable of being "physically" damaged or injured because, by definition, it has no physical characteristics.[69] Non-coverage due to electronic data's being intangible was followed in California in a first-party property case in which human negligence resulted in a computer crash and loss of data.[70] The computer system was returned to functioning after a programmer restored the database. The policyholder sought the costs to bring the computer system to functionality and the loss of business income. The issue was whether the computer crash and loss of data constituted "direct physical loss or damage." The court held that loss of electronically stored data, without loss or damage to the storage media, did not constitute "direct physical loss or damage." The court based its holding on the use of the word "physical," which was defined to require a tangible loss or damage. Because computer data is generally considered "intangible property," there could be no "direct physical loss or damage."[71]

Thus, very few cases have construed the meaning of "direct physical loss or damage" in the first-party computer loss context, and the authority is split. Moreover, in the loss of use context in general, there is a split in authority regarding whether loss of use can constitute "physical loss or damage" under a first-party property insurance policy. Consequently, until the law is more developed, cases will continue to be unpredictable.

[4]—Covered Cause of Loss

Assuming there is "direct physical loss or damage" to "covered property," a policyholder will also need to demonstrate that the damage was caused by a "covered cause of loss."

[a]—Single Cause of Loss

Where there is only one cause of the loss, resolution of the "covered cause of loss" issue depends upon the type of policy involved in the dispute: (1) "All Risk"; or (2) "Named Peril." The reason that the type of policy controls in single causation cases is because: (a) one form covers losses from all causes unless specifically excluded while the other form only covers specifically enumerated causes; and (b) not every possible cause of loss is enumerated in these form policies.

[i]—Type of Policy

[A]—"All Risk"

"All risk" policies provide the broadest form of first-party property coverage. "All risk" insurance insures against all risks of direct physical loss or damage to insured property except those risks that are specifically excluded.[72] In an "all risk" policy, the list of excluded causes of loss generally is contained in a section entitled "excluded perils."

Thus, in an "all risk" policy, if the risk is one generally insured for, it is a covered risk unless it is specifically mentioned as being excluded.[73] For example, third-party negligence or policyholder/employee negligence that causes property damage is generally covered under an "all risk" policy unless it is specifically enumerated in the "excluded perils" section as excluded.[74] Additionally, "collapse" has historically been insured against, meaning that under an "all risk" policy, a "collapse" is covered unless it is specifically enumerated as excluded.[75] The meaning of "collapse" is a commonly litigated issue. As with all insurance coverage cases, the policy language itself governs. However, as is often the case, when the term is undefined in the policy, resort to case law is helpful, and the case law is divided. Some courts define the term as requiring the actual and abrupt caving in or falling down of a structure.[76] The majority are more liberal, only requiring the substantial impairment of the structural integrity.[77]

Other examples where the type of policy might control whether coverage is provided include the following. "Mysterious disappearance" and "unexplained losses" have been traditionally covered by first-party property insurance policies, meaning coverage for such losses is afforded under an "all risk" policy if such causes are not expressly excluded.[78] Further, absent an exclusion to the contrary, damages caused by earth movement are covered under "all risk" property policies.[79]

[B]—"Named Peril"

The other, more narrow type of first-party property insurance policy that is sold in the market is called a "named peril" policy, which insures against "direct physical loss or damage" to "covered property" or to "insured property," where the loss is caused by any of the specifically named "perils" or "causes of loss."[80] The policy will usually have a section called "covered perils," which will list the covered causes of loss.

Thus, if the cause of loss is not specifically named as a covered peril in the policy, the loss will not be covered.[81] In other words, under a "named peril" policy, the risk is insured against only if it is specifically listed.[82] For example, under a "named peril" policy, loss caused by "collapse" or by negligence of a third party or negligence of the policyholder or its employees may not be covered unless specifically enumerated as a "covered cause of loss" or a "named peril."[83]

[ii]—Excluded Causes of Loss

To ascertain whether the damage was caused by a "covered cause of loss," it is helpful to examine some typical excluded peril provisions.

[A]—Earth Movement and Settling

Most first-party property insurance policies exclude losses caused by: (1) "settling," "cracking," "shrinkage," or "expansion;" and (2) "earth movement."[84] Most policies have both exclusions; some have only one.

The starting place in determining applicability of these exclusions is the meaning of the terms used within the exclusions. One would need to first consult the policy itself. "Settling," "cracking," "shrinkage," and "expansion" are generally not defined terms. To understand the exclusion using such undefined terms, resort to a dictionary would help.

- "To settle" means "**a:** to sink gradually or to the bottom **b:** to become clear by the deposit of sediment or scum **c:** to become compact by sinking."[85]
- "To crack" means "to break, split, or snap apart."[86]
- "Shrinkage" means the process of "contract[ing] or curl[ing] up the body or part of it."[87]
- "Expansion" means the quality, state, act, or process of being "increase[d] in the extent, number, volume, or scope of" or enlarged.[88]

Thus, this first exclusion (for "settling," "cracking," "shrinkage," or "expansion") might apply to losses involving property that is damaged by movements in the earth or ground.

With respect to the "earth movement" exclusion, however, policies typically define "earth movement" as follows:

1. earthquake;
2. landslide;
3. volcanic eruption;
4. mudflow;
5. earth sinking, earth rising or shifting; or
6. subsidence.[89]

Unless otherwise provided in the policy, both of the aforementioned exclusions generally apply to damages caused by natural, as opposed to man-made, phenomenon.[90] However, the "settling, cracking, shrinkage, or expansion" exclusion is not limited to natural phenomena.[91] Additionally, the amount of land movement at issue will determine which exclusion might potentially apply. For example, "earth movement" may require greater movement than does "settling, cracking, shrinkage, or expansion."[92] Indeed, although inclusion of "mudflow," "earth sinking, earth rising or shifting" and "subsidence," within the definition of "earth movement," does not necessarily require a massive shift of earth, the inclusion of earthquake and landslide suggests something more than normal settlement.[93]

Moreover, any potential superfluity in the policy created by the use of the term "settling" or "settlement" in both an "earth movement expansion" and a "normal settling, shrinkage or expansion" exclusion can be avoided by construing "settlement" within the definition of "earth movement" as an unusual and abnormal settlement, which is in conformity with the prevailing authorities.[94] Indeed, several cases have construed damage caused by settlement beyond normal settlement to be encompassed within the meaning of "earth movement."[95] In addition, if earth movement results in a "collapse," the damage might be covered under the coverage afforded for "collapse."[96]

[B]—Faulty Workmanship and Latent Defect

First-party property insurance policies also typically contain exclusions for defective design or workmanship. For example, one exclusion is known as the "faulty material or workmanship" exclusion, which purports to exclude loss caused by:

> "The cost of making good faulty or defective workmanship, material, construction, designs, plans and/or specifications but this exclusion shall not apply to direct physical loss or direct physical damage resulting from such faulty or defective workmanship, material, construction, designs, plans and/or specifications."[97]

Thus, under the quoted language, the cost to repair or replace the work or material that is defective or faulty is generally excluded but any ensuing direct physical loss or damage would be covered. Thus, any damage to other property—namely, work or material that is not defective—is covered if such damage is caused by the defective work or materials.[98]

In addition or alternatively, policies might exclude losses caused by "inherent vice" or "latent defect." The cost to repair or replace such "inherent vice" or "latent defect," including any ensuing loss, is generally excluded.[99] Courts generally apply the "faulty workmanship" and "latent defect" exclusions to losses caused by defective construction or design.[100]

Even if the policy provides coverage, an ensuring loss might still not be compensable. If the ensuing loss results from the excluded peril, the ensuing loss may be excluded.[101] However, if the ensuing loss follows, but is not caused by, the excluded cause of loss, the ensuing loss may be covered.[102] Interestingly, the way the quoted provision (the "faulty workmanship" exclusion) is written suggests that damages to non-defective work caused by faulty workmanship would be a covered ensuing loss. However, the presence of a "latent defect" exclusion, which has no ensuing loss exception, would likely prevent coverage for damage to non-defective work caused by defective work or material.

The ensuing loss exception found in many forms of the "faulty workmanship" exclusion presents an interesting issue in the environmental area. For example, cases involving contamination may involve the purported use of "faulty material" or the alleged claim of "faulty workmanship."[103] In cases involving contamination, courts have mostly determined that faulty workmanship or a similarly worded exclusion does not apply because the cleanup of such contamination is usually an ensuing loss.[104] Such a result can be avoided by drafting—namely, by eliminating the "ensuing loss" exception.[105]

In one case, a university sought first-party insurance coverage for asbestos and lead paint released into its buildings.[106] The insurance company denied coverage, partly on the basis of a "defective material" exclusion, arguing that the loss resulted from the use of defective building materials (i.e., those containing asbestos or lead paint). In a subsequent insurance coverage action, the court held that the "faulty material" exclusion had no application:

> "[T]he 'physical loss of or damage to property' for which [plaintiff] seeks coverage is the contamination of its buildings by lead and asbestos. Although asbestos- and lead-containing building materials may certainly be rendered 'faulty' or 'defective' because of the presence of lead or asbestos, [plaintiff] is not seeking coverage for the costs to repair or replace the building materials with materials that do not contain asbestos or lead. Rather, [plaintiff] is seeking coverage for contamination of its buildings that resulted from the release of lead and asbestos in its buildings. Similarly, [plaintiff] does not seek coverage for damage caused by gradual wear and tear or deterioration of building materials containing lead and asbestos. Rather, it seeks coverage for the ensuing contamination, which contamination may itself have been caused by the wear and tear or deterioration of those materials. Thus, the plain language of the applicable exclusions would exclude coverage for any damage to the lead- or asbestos-containing building materials themselves caused by either the use of faulty materials or wear and tear, but would not exclude any damage to [plaintiff's] buildings caused by the resulting contamination."[107]

As this example demonstrates, under normal circumstances, a policyholder does not seek insurance coverage for the costs associated with replacing the faulty material or faulty workmanship with good material or good workmanship. Rather, the policyholder normally seeks coverage for some type of ensuing loss, such as contamination or other physical damage caused by the faulty material or faulty workmanship. Accordingly, as long as there remains an ensuing loss exception, coverage is likely to be provided.

[C]—Pollution or Contamination Exclusion

Another exclusion common in property policies is an exclusion for pollution or contamination,[108] which may purport to exclude coverage for:

> "Loss or damage caused by, resulting from, contributed to or made worse by actual alleged or threatened release, discharge, escape or dispersal of Contaminants and/or Pollutants, all whether direct or indirect, proximate or remote or in whole or in part caused by, contributed to or aggravated by any physical damage insured by this Policy."[109]

However, in normal circumstances, pollution or contamination is the result, not the cause. Hence, to determine whether the exclusion applies, one would want to review concurrent and efficient proximate causation, including provisions attempting to negotiate around the doctrines, all of which are discussed below.[110] For example, third-party negligence is usually not an excluded peril and, therefore, a pollution loss effectively caused by third-party negligence would be covered under an "all risk" property insurance policy.[111]

Illustrative of this point is the case of a farm that fought crop blight with a fungicide purchased from a third-party manufacturer. The farm applied the fungicide in the normal manner by flushing it through its aluminum irrigation pipes.[112] However, due to the copper components in the fungicide, the farm experienced damage to its irrigation pipes. The farm sought insurance coverage from its first-party property insurance company. The insurance company denied coverage on the basis of a contamination or deterioration exclusion. The Ninth Circuit held that the fungicide manufacturer's negligent failure to warn was the efficient proximate cause of the loss and, therefore, coverage existed for the loss caused concurrently by the third-party negligence and the deterioration.[113]

[D]—Law and Ordinance Exclusion

First-party property policies may also have a "law and ordinance" exclusion, which purports to exclude from coverage:

> "Loss or damage caused by or resulting from the enforcement of any ordinance or law, or any order of government or municipal authority; by suspension, lapse, termination and/or cancellation of any license, lease, permit, or any injunction or process of any court, unless otherwise endorsed hereon."[114]

The law and ordinance exclusion will apply only where the enforcement of the law or ordinance would itself be the primary cause of the loss.[115] This is distinguishable from situations in which enforcement of the law or ordinance occurs after a covered cause of loss results in damage to covered property. Similarly, in dealing with the opposite situation, namely provisions extending additional coverage for loss, cost, or expense occasioned by the enforcement of laws and ordinances, the additional coverage is triggered only if a covered loss occurs and does not apply merely by virtue of the enforcement of a law or ordinance.[116]

Courts construing law and ordinance exclusions have unanimously determined that they do not apply to voluntary cleanup of contamination, even if compelled by operation of state or federal environmental statutes, because the cleanup or ordered cleanup of the property takes place after the physical injury to the property, which was caused by something other than a law or ordinance.[117] In one case, asbestos fibers were released into an apartment building, necessitating asbestos abatement.[118] The insurance company denied coverage for the loss. The court found that the loss was caused by the release of a toxic substance in a building, not the law's requirements that the substance be removed.

> "A provision in [the] insurance policy excludes from coverage any damage resulting 'directly or indirectly' from the enforcement of any local or state ordinance or law regulating the construction, repair or demolition of buildings. *So long as extraneous forces cause physical damage to property, this type of exclusion does not defeat recovery when, as a result, a governmental body enforces an ordinance against the property.*"[119]

[E]—Flood or Surface Water

First-party property policies may also have certain "water" exclusions, including exclusions for all loss caused by: (1) "flood;" and/or (2) "surface water."

"Flood" has been defined to include the overflow of a natural or man-made body of water, such as a river, lake, or dam.[120] For example, damages caused by water's entry into a house from a burst water main would not be excluded by a "flood" exclusion, because water from the burst main is not an overflow of a body of water.[121]

"Surface water" means "water derived from falling rain or melting snow or that rises to the surface in springs and is diffused over the surface of the ground and follows no defined course or channel and does not form a natural body of water."[122] A similar definition of "surface water" is:

> "Water or natural precipitation diffused over the surface of the ground until it either evaporates, is absorbed by the land, or reaches channels where water naturally flows."[123]

Thus, "surface water" does not become "surface water" until it hits the ground, meaning rainwater's entry into a house from a crack in the roof would not be excluded by "surface water" exclusions.[124] Moreover, damages caused by water's entry into a house from a burst water main would not be excluded by a "surface water" exclusion, because water from the burst main is not natural precipitation that has hit the ground and is yet to become "surface water."[125]

Most of the interesting water issues arise in the context of multiple causation cases, such as where damage is caused by wind and flood.[126]

[F]—Ordinary Wear and Tear or Gradual Deterioration

Property policies also contain exclusions for losses caused by: (a) "ordinary wear and tear"; or (b) "gradual deterioration." Long-term corrosion or latent and gradual deterioration of property is generally excluded under either or both of these exclusions.[127]

[G]—Mysterious Disappearance or Unexplained Loss

Some property policies may also contain an exclusion for "mysterious disappearance," "inventory shortage," or "unexplained loss." Because property policies traditionally covered such losses, coverage for such losses will depend upon whether the policy is "all risk" or "named peril."[128] In particular, if the policy is of the "all risk" variety, a mysterious disappearance would be covered unless otherwise excluded, but under a "named peril" form, a mysterious disappearance would only be covered if it was specifically named as a "covered peril."[129] Where the policy in question has such an exclusion, it will generally apply only when the loss can be proven by inventory shortfalls solely or the loss cannot be proven by any reasonable explanation.[130]

Sometimes, losses involving mysterious disappearance require the policyholder to name the culprit.[131] An interesting issue arises in losses involving suggestions of theft or dishonesty—namely, whether a signed proof of loss specifically identifying a particular person as the culprit would subject the policyholder to a defamation claim by the named culprit. Some states recognize some sort of qualified privilege.[132] Thus, as long as the proof of loss statement identifying the culprit is made without malice and in good faith, any defamation claim is likely to fail under such a qualified privilege.[133] Moreover, the identified culprit would also likely have difficulty meeting his or her burden of proof on other elements of defamation, such as the existence of the requisite intent and damages.[134]

[H]—Mold

Property policies usually also contain some sort of "mold" exclusion or limitation, which purport to exclude or limit losses of or caused by "mold."[135] As with contamination, mold is often the result, not the cause, meaning any ensuing loss exception might apply.[136] Moreover, to determine whether the exclusion applies, one would want to review the doctrine of concurrent and efficient proximate causation, including provisions attempting to negotiate around the doctrines.[137] A mold loss might be covered under an "all risk" property insurance policy[138] if such mold loss were caused in whole, concurrently, or predominantly by a covered cause of loss, such as third-party negligence, and, if applicable, there was an absence of an enforceable anti-efficient proximate or anticoncurrent causation clause in the policy at issue. Even where the mold exclusion has been reviewed, enforceability of these mold exclusions has had mixed results.[139]

[I]—Terrorism

After September 11, 2001, terrorism exclusions started appearing in first-party property insurance policies. For example, policies excluded losses that were "caused by, or resulting from, or incurred as a result of: (a) (i) the detonation of an explosive and/or (ii) any weapon of war[;] and is caused by any person acting maliciously or from a political motive; [or] (b) [a]ny act for political or terrorist purposes of any persons, and whether or not agents of a sovereign power, and whether the physical loss, damage or expense resulting therefrom is accidental or intentional."[140] While not litigated extensively, the Boston Marathon bombings in 2013 demonstrate how terrorism sometimes can cause much more business interruption than actual property damage. Of course, the September 11, 2001, attacks and the Oklahoma City bombing demonstrate that large-scale property damage is also a strong possibility. In addition, some of the mass shootings seen in America recently, such as shootings in movie theatres, schools, and malls, raise an issue as to what actually constitutes "terrorism."

[b]—Multiple Causes of Loss

Interesting "covered cause of loss" issues may arise if there is more than one cause of a particular loss. Needless to say, where all causes of the particular loss are "covered causes of loss," coverage should be afforded under any multiple causation theory.[141] Similarly, where all causes of loss are excluded causes, coverage can never be afforded under any multiple causation theory.[142]

The litigation in this area occurs when the loss at issue is caused by *both* a covered cause and a non-covered cause.[143] If a policyholder has a loss that appears excluded under either an "all risk" or a "named peril" policy, the policyholder will need to determine whether the loss can be attributed to another, covered cause of loss. If so—namely, where there are several causes of loss one of which is a "covered cause of loss"—questions may still arise as to coverage.

This section deals with problems involving these multiple causation theories, including (1) concurrent causation,[144] and (2) efficient proximate causation,[145] and it also discusses insurance industry attempts to avoid the effects of these doctrines through clauses purporting to negate operation of these doctrines.[146]

[i]—Concurrent Causation

Under the doctrine of concurrent causation, where a loss is concurrently caused by both a covered and an excluded peril, the claim will be covered.[147]

[ii]—Efficient Proximate Cause Doctrine

Another multiple causation doctrine is the efficient proximate cause doctrine. In the vast majority of jurisdictions, the efficient proximate cause doctrine is utilized in adjudicating coverage where a covered and a non-covered peril contribute to a loss.[148] Indeed, the efficient proximate cause doctrine has been utilized to varying degrees in different jurisdictions.[149]

Under the efficient proximate cause doctrine, the status of the efficient proximate cause (also known as the predominant cause of the loss) will resolve whether coverage exists. If a covered peril is found to be the efficient proximate cause, then the loss is covered; but if a non-covered peril is found to be the efficient proximate cause, then the loss is not covered.[150]

> "The efficient proximate cause is 'the one that sets others in motion.' And while the efficient proximate cause is said to 'set into motion a chain of events,' it is not

necessarily the 'triggering cause' (assuming one could be identified). Rather the efficient proximate cause is the 'predominating cause.'

"The efficient proximate cause doctrine does not focus on a temporal place in the chain of events. For the last link (most immediate to the loss) may itself have been a natural or inevitable effect of the predominant cause, and therefore not the efficient proximate cause. Similarly, an earlier cause is not the efficient proximate cause if it was merely an 'antecedent circumstance' which 'set the stage for the loss' or 'made possible the subsequent loss.' The efficient proximate cause doctrine rather looks to the quality of the links in the chain to determine which is the predominant cause."[151]

The efficient proximate cause doctrine can apply to a loss under any type of policy. For example, under a "named peril" policy, the doctrine can apply where one cause of the loss is a "named peril" but other causes are not specifically enumerated as "named perils."[152] The doctrine can also apply to an "all risk" policy to establish coverage where one cause is excluded and the other is not.[153]

[A]—Hurricane

Hurricane losses illustrate the application of the efficient proximate cause doctrine. For example, in hurricane loss cases, the policyholder will generally claim that damage results from the covered peril of wind or third-party negligence, whereas insurance companies often claim that the damage results from the excluded peril of flood.[154]

In such cases, if the loss can be attributed solely to the covered peril of wind, there will be coverage for the entire loss.[155] Moreover, if portions of the loss can be attributed to wind, those portions will be covered.[156] Alternatively, if the policy provides hurricane coverage, the entire loss might be covered based upon a finding that the policy is ambiguous.[157]

[B]—Third-Party or Employee Negligence

As stated previously, third-party negligence or the negligence of the policyholder or of the policyholder's employee can be covered causes of loss.[158] In fact, if negligence of a third party, a policyholder, or an employee is not an excluded peril, loss caused by such third party, policyholder, or employee negligence is covered under an "all risk" property insurance policy.[159] Indeed, there is no question that physical loss or damage caused by negligence, even the negligence of the policyholder, is a covered risk under "all risk" property insurance policies.[160]

Interestingly, in multiple causes of loss cases where one of the causes is first-party or third-party negligence, courts have often determined that such first- or third-party negligence, rather than the other excluded causes of loss at issue (i.e., corrosion, pollution, earth movement), was the efficient proximate cause of the loss.[161]

[C]—Collapse

Another interesting multiple causation issue involves "collapse" coverage. Under "all risk" policies, "collapse" is deemed a covered cause of loss if it is not specifically excluded because, traditionally, collapse has always been deemed covered.[162] On the other hand, "collapse" would have to be a specifically "named peril" to be covered under a "named peril" policy.[163] Accordingly, in multiple causation cases, coverage for collapse may be governed by the type of policy at issue. Cases around the country are primarily in accord.[164]

What is a "collapse"? If a building actually falls down, no one would disagree that a "collapse" has occurred. What if an actual falling down does not occur? What if a building shows a crack or bulge and an engineer comes in and claims that it is unsafe. Is that a "collapse"?

The dictionary definition suggests alternative answers. "Collapse" means "a breakdown in vital energy, strength, or stamina" and "a sudden failure."[165] On the one hand, the "sudden failure" meaning would imply the need for a physical falling down of the structure. On the other hand, the "breakdown in vital energy, strength, or stamina" suggests that something less than actual falling down could constitute a "collapse."

Case law is split on the issue. The majority of cases hold that a collapse occurs if there is a substantial impairment of the structural integrity of a building.[166] The minority view requires the actual falling down of the building to constitute a "collapse."[167]

The majority view can be supported for the following reasons. First, insurance companies could have restricted coverage by use of a clear definition, but chose not to do so, despite numerous judicial warnings over the course of many decades.[168] In fact, some insurance companies have included restrictive definitions of "collapse."[169] That some insurance companies have used more restrictive definitions is evidence that the industry understood how to avoid any perceived ambiguity but chose not to. Moreover, requiring the actual falling down, when structural integrity of a building has been compromised, would be economically unsound.[170] It would provide economic incentives to wait for a falling down, rather than promoting the fixing of a building.

[iii]—Anti-Efficient Proximate Cause/Anticoncurrent Causation Clauses

An "anti-efficient proximate" cause or "anticoncurrent causation" clause attempts to draft around application of the efficient proximate cause and concurrent cause doctrines through the specific exclusion from coverage whenever a loss is caused by any excluded peril. As one court aptly stated: "Looking to contract around the concurrent-cause doctrine, the insurance industry has come up with anticoncurrent-cause clauses, which . . . bar coverage for damage caused by an excluded cause, regardless of whether a covered act also contributed to the damage."[171] For example, a policy might contain an exclusion for "loss resulting *directly or indirectly* from . . . water damage."[172] Similarly, a policy might exclude any loss "'caused *directly or indirectly'* by surface water *'regardless of any other cause or event contributing concurrently or in any sequence to the loss.'*"[173] Both of these clauses are examples of anti-efficient proximate cause or anticoncurrent cause clauses.

Some courts uphold these anti-efficient proximate or anticoncurrent cause clauses.[174] Other jurisdictions have not enforced such anti-efficient proximate causation or anticoncurrent causation clauses.[175] In a case from a jurisdiction that does not enforce such a clause, the court held that anticoncurrent causation language contained in a homeowners policy was ambiguous and unenforceable in the context of damage from a hurricane,[176] stating that enforcement of such so-called anticoncurrent causation language:

> "would mean that an insured whose dwelling lost its roof in high winds and at the same time suffered an incursion of even an inch of water could recover nothing under his . . . policy. Read literally, this provision would exclude all coverage when a windstorm did damage to both an insured dwelling (a covered loss) and adjacent 'screens, including their supports, around a pool, patio, or other areas.' (an excluded loss). I do not believe this is a reasonable interpretation of the policy."[177]

Taken together, cases refusing to enforce the anti-efficient proximate causation or anticoncurrent causation clauses demonstrate that coverage can only be determined following a fact-specific determination of causation.[178]

Variance in enforceability of the anti-efficient proximate cause and the anticoncurrent cause clauses, even if a minority does not enforce such clauses, has the effect of creating some uncertainty in an industry (insurance) that operates more effectively with certainty and predictability of outcomes. This uncertainty may have become problematic as mold losses started to mount in the 1990s. With mold losses the insurance industry crafted a provision that attempted to withstand jurisdictional variance of constructions under the efficient proximate cause and concurrent cause doctrines (and its rules regarding contracting such doctrines). Mold is caused by water and moisture. Therefore, in jurisdictions not permitting insurance companies to draft language around these doctrines or in jurisdictions refusing to enforce the exclusion for other reasons,[179] an outright exclusion for damages caused by mold would generally only apply where the water or moisture problem was caused exclusively by excluded causes of loss.[180] Recognizing that moisture infiltration often results from covered causes of loss and that jurisdictions are split on the enforceability of anticoncurrent/anti-efficient proximate causation causes,[181] insurers have added a clause that limits (rather than excludes) the amount of recovery for mold to a maximum dollar figure.[182] In this way, issues caused by mold can be controlled, even if the exclusion was not predictably enforced.[183]

§ 4.04 Additional Conditions and Provisions

[1]—Debris Removal

Property policies usually contain provisions for "debris removal." A typical provision may provide:

> "We will pay your expense to remove debris of Covered Property caused by or resulting from a Covered Cause of Loss that occurs during the policy period."[184]

The plain meaning of "debris removal" coverage is coverage for the necessary cost of clearing a loss site of debris so reconstruction or repair can take place.[185] Damage caused by debris removal activities is also usually covered.[186] Absent an express limitation, the provision has even been applied to the cost to clean up oil that leaked from an underground tank as a result of a covered loss.[187] Moreover, the clause has afforded coverage for cleaning and sanitizing kitchen equipment to eliminate contamination risks.[188] However, debris removal may be excluded if it is subsumed in the repair costs.[189]

[2]—Loss Mitigation and "Sue and Labor"

First-party property insurance policies may provide loss mitigation provisions. For instance, policies may state that "[i]n the event of loss or damage to Insured Property, which becomes known to the Named Insureds Risk Management Department, the Insured shall . . . [p]rotect the Insured Property from further loss or damage."[190]

The "Sue and Labor" clause similarly provides:

> "In case of loss or damage, it shall be lawful and necessary for the Insured, his or their factors, servants, or assigns to sue, labor, and travel for, in or about the defense, safeguard, and recovery of the Insured Property, or any part thereof, without prejudice to this insurance, nor shall the acts of the Insured or the Company, in recovering, saving, and preserving the Insured Property in case of loss be considered a waiver or an acceptance of abandonment."[191]

The loss mitigation and sue and labor provisions impose a duty on the policyholder to take steps to prevent and minimize a covered loss and provide for reimbursement of expenditures necessarily incurred in such efforts.[192] Resolution of the loss mitigation coverage issue will usually turn upon whether the expense was "reasonable" and "necessary" under the circumstances.[193]

[3]—Valuation

[a]—Valuation Methods

First-party property insurance policies provide that property damage may be paid on the basis of: (1) the cost of repair;[194] (2) the actual cash value;[195] (3) the replacement cost;[196] or (4) an agreed or stated value, which is an amount agreed on by the parties at the time of sale.[197]

While the "cost to repair" formula and the "agreed value" or "stated value" method of valuation are straightforward, "actual cost" and "replacement cost" valuation methods are not self-explanatory.

Under "actual cost" valuation, a policyholder suffering a total loss is entitled to the "actual cash value" of the property.[198] The phrase "actual cash value" may or may not be defined in the policy. If it is not defined, courts have defined it as the value of the property when it was damaged or destroyed—namely, either: (1) the market value or (2) the actual cost of repair or replacement less depreciation.[199]

Under "replacement cost" coverage, the policyholder is entitled to the current replacement cost of the totally lost or damaged property.[200] The phrase "replacement cost value" may or may not be defined in the policy. If it is not defined, courts have defined it as: "repair or replacement costs include any cost that an insured is reasonably likely to incur in repairing or replacing a covered loss."[201]

However, "replacement cost" coverage might require actual replacement. Under such circumstances, in the event of loss or damage to covered property as a result of a covered cause of loss, the policy might provide that the insurance company will pay the actual cost value of such lost or damaged property at the time of the loss. The insurance company will reimburse the policyholder for the depreciation that was held back once the policyholder actually repairs or replaces the item at issue.[202]

[b]—Replace vs. Repair

A policyholder may obtain a price or estimate to repair the damaged property and a separate price or estimate to replace the damaged property. Which one measures its recovery or reimbursement from its insurance company?

Some policies expressly provide an answer to the question. For example, some policy language values losses at the least of: (1) the limits set forth in the policy; (2) the replacement cost on the date of loss on the same premises; and (3) the actual amount spent "*to repair or replace*" the damaged property.[203] Obviously, using "least of" alternatives requires price comparisons without room for discussion.

Likewise, other policies state that the insurance company will pay the amount spent "*to replace or repair*" subject to the limits provision and the payment of actual cost value until repairs are completed.[204] This second option essentially allows the policyholder to choose between replacement and repair, paying the policyholder the depreciation held back after the repair or replacement is completed and paid for.

A third group of policies give the insurance company the option to pay: (1) the value of the damaged property; (2) the cost to *repair or replace*; (3) the appraised value; or (4) to undertake responsibility to *repair or replace*.[205] This third group clearly places the option in the insurer's hands subject to the conditions set forth in the policy.

Where the policy expressly leaves repair versus replacement an open issue, the courts may be required to resolve the question. Even where the repair versus replacement issue is expressly authorized by the language of the policy, courts will only permit repairs when the repairs can return the property to as good and/or as useful a condition as it was in before the loss or damage.[206]

For example, replacement has been permitted or awarded where the evidence revealed that the repair would not return the property to the same condition or usefulness that existed immediately before the loss occurred.[207] Similarly, where repair has been warranted, courts have determined that the pre-loss condition of the property could be restored through repair.[208]

Interestingly, in one case in which repair was found to be appropriate under the circumstances, the court based its determination on the uncontroverted evidence that the roof's "useful life" would not be affected by the repair of the loss.[209] Such reasoning suggests that if the "useful life" of property is diminished by a covered cause of loss and the repair thereof, replacement might be warranted.

One interesting repair or replace issue involves subrogation.[210] While an insurance company might be obligated to pay its policyholder's repair or replacement costs, or some other measure of recovery, under its policy with its insured, the insurer's right of subrogation might not be coterminous with what it pays out. In other words, under principles of subrogation, the insurer stands in its policyholder's shoes.[211] As such, it can assert against third parties only those claims that its policyholder could assert, meaning its recovery against third parties might be limited to tort recovery, which may not be the same as what it paid under its policy.[212]

[4]—Appraisal

Policies often contain appraisal provisions providing that if the parties disagree on the amount of loss, either may make a demand for an appraisal.[213] The appraisal process is generally limited to disagreement as to the amount of a loss and cannot include a dispute as to the existence or non-existence of coverage.[214] However, submission to the appraisal process may constitute a waiver as to coverage issues.[215]

Under the appropriate circumstance, each side generally chooses an appraiser, and the two chosen appraisers will select a third appraiser, who serves as an umpire. The appraiser's valuation agreed to by two of the three appraisers may be binding.

[5]—Notice and Proof of Loss

As condition precedent to the receipt of insurance coverage, the policyholder may be required to comply with the following: (1) notify the insurance company of the loss; (2) take all reasonable steps to protect the covered property from further damage; (3) cooperate with the insurance company, including permitting inspection of premises and submitting to examinations under oath; and (4) submit a signed proof of loss, which is a form specifying the items of the loss.[216]

[6]—Salvage

A property insurance policy may also provide that salvage value of damaged property belongs to the insurance company up to the amount of their payments.[217] This, of course, may be negotiated as part of the negotiation over the loss valuation.

[7]—Co-Insurance

A property insurance policy might contain co-insurance provisions, which require that the policyholder maintain insurance on the property equal to or greater than a certain percentage of the property's value.[218] For example, an 80% co-insurance clause on property valued at $5 million requires that the policyholder maintain insurance for at least 80% of the $5 million value or at least $4 million in insurance. The failure to comply will cause a proportionate decrease in recovery in the event of a loss.[219]

§ 4.05 Business Interruption and Extra Expense Coverage

[1]—Insuring Agreement

Another important coverage often provided by first-party property insurance policies is the promise to pay for "extra expenses" and losses of business income incurred in connection with damage to covered property.

An "extra expense" clause typically includes such expenses as are necessarily incurred for the purpose of reducing any loss under the policy, even though such expenses may exceed the amount by which the loss under the policy is reduced.[220]

Although many different forms are in use, a common business interruption clause provides:

> "We will pay for the actual loss of Business Income you sustain due to the necessary suspension of your 'operations' during the 'period of restoration.' The sus-

pension must be caused by direct physical loss of or damage to property. . . . The loss or damage must be caused by or result from a Covered Cause of Loss."[221]

Business income and extra expense coverage is designed to pay the extra expenses, loss of profits, and unavoidable continuing expenses caused by an interruption of the policyholder's business resulting from a covered cause of loss.[222] Business income coverage protects policyholders who have to suspend production or business due to covered property damage. It also reimburses policyholders for expenses that continue despite the cessation of business from a covered loss, such as salaries, certain utility charges and insurance premiums.[223]

[2]—Extra Expense

Extra expenses typically are necessary amounts spent to continue or resume normal operations during the period of restoration.[224] They cover costs of preserving the remains of the operations, of making preparations for re-opening of the business, of using other property or facilities, and of obtaining property for temporary use.[225] The expenses incurred must be "necessary" in the sense they are not gratuitous and are incurred solely for the purpose of avoiding business interruption during the restoration period.[226]

The expenses for a public adjuster are generally not "extra expenses" because they are not "necessary."[227] Moreover, the cost to build a new store is not an "extra expense" where the damaged facilities were a leasehold.[228] Further, "extra expenses" will not be covered unless there is a covered loss.[229]

[3]—"Business Income"

With regard to business interruption coverage, the first and most fundamental issue is whether there has been a loss of "business income." Coupled with this issue are issues concerning the calculation of the amount of business income lost per month and the determination of the appropriate period of restoration.

Property policies typically define "business income" to include "net income (net profit or loss before income taxes) that would have been earned or incurred" plus "continuing normal operating expenses incurred, including payroll."[230] Property policies generally provide little guidance as to how the amount of a business income loss is to be calculated. Essentially, they state that business income is to be calculated from historical figures.[231]

Generally, there are two tests when calculating lost earnings: (1) the "net profit" test; or (2) the "gross revenues" test.[232] Actual loss can be calculated by using either the "net profit" or the "gross revenues" method.[233] The "net profit" method calculates loss by adding a policyholder's continuing expenses (expenses that must be paid notwithstanding the interruption of the business) to the amount of the policyholder's estimated net profit that was prevented from being earned (lost profit) during the period the business was closed.[234] The sum equals the policyholder's actual loss sustained.[235]

In contrast, the "gross revenues" method calculates actual loss by subtracting the policyholder's non-continuing expenses (expenses that were saved by the interruption of the business), from the its estimated gross revenues, which were prevented from being earned by the interruption of the loss.[236] Either method, applied correctly, should give equivalent accurate loss measurements.[237] This is because profits equal revenues less variable costs and less taxed costs. Therefore, profits plus fixed costs equal revenues less variable costs.

A policy's lack of clarity leads to many sources of potential conflict, including: (1) whether the business as a whole or a small sector of the business is the focus in performing the calculation; (2) the extent of historical data that is required to set forth a business income loss;[238] (3) whether the claimed loss is too speculative in nature to be recoverable;[239] (4) whether new or unprofitable businesses can still recover loss of business income;[240] and (5) whether the cyclical nuances of a business should be considered, such as with Christmas light manufacturers for a loss at holiday time.[241]

[4]—"Suspension" or "Interruption"

The next issue is whether there was the requisite "suspension" or "interruption" of operations. For instance, is a suspension of part of the policyholder's operations sufficient? Although the answer to this question should be "yes," the insurance company will typically argue that there has been no suspension of the operations as a whole, or no "interruption," and thus that recovery is prohibited.[242] For large businesses—like a car manufacturer or a hotel chain—this argument would not be valid because no catastrophe, short of nuclear annihilation, could totally halt every facet of the operations of such a company.

Although there is some unfavorable law on this subject,[243] more reasoned cases have recognized that an "interruption" does not require a total halt to all operations but includes adverse effects on performance.[244] Further, the insurance industry's drafting organization, the Insurance Services Office ("ISO"), has described this argument as "unfortunate"[245] and has modified its new forms to ensure "slowdowns" are covered.[246]

[5]—Physical Loss or Damage

There may also be a question as to whether the loss of business income stemmed from physical loss or damage. This involves two questions: (1) Was there a physical loss or damage caused by a covered cause of loss? (2) Did that loss cause the business interruption?

First, a physical loss caused by a covered cause of loss is a prerequisite to a business interruption recovery.[247] The covered cause of loss issue has been previously discussed.[248] The additional issue is whether there was a physical loss or damage. For example, a concert hall cannot collect for lost ticket sales if a blizzard on the day of the performance keeps concertgoers away because there was no direct physical loss to covered property.[249]

Additionally, even if there is the requisite physical loss to covered property, the loss or damage must actually be the cause of a suspension or interruption in business operations.[250]

[6]—"Period of Restoration"

The "period of restoration" or "period of interruption" is typically defined to begin at the time of "direct physical loss or damage" and to end on the earlier of "the date when the property at the described premises should be repaired, rebuilt or replaced with reasonable speed and similar quality" or "the date when business is resumed at a new permanent location."[251]

Issues usually arise regarding the length of the period of interruption or period of restoration. As generally written in the policies, this period during which the loss of business income is covered is bounded by the shorter of (1) the hypothetical time in which the destroyed property could be repaired, rebuilt or replaced or (2) the actual time it takes to repair, rebuild or replace the property.[252]

A number of issues can arise surrounding the former, "hypothetical," date. For instance, does it start during the period when authorities will not let the policyholder on site due to ongoing investigation, e.g., by environmental authorities? In the context of the World Trade Center, there were issues regarding businesses that could technically "restart," but whose new business would be fundamentally of a different nature. For instance, could a business selling World Trade Center Observation Deck souvenirs really restart its business prior to the time the World Trade Center is rebuilt?

[7]—Wider Economic Effects of a Loss

Some property insurance companies have argued that business interruption recovery is diminished by the wider economic effects of the loss itself.[253] Typically, "Business Income" for a business interruption provision is defined to include "Net Income (net profit or loss before income taxes) that would have been earned or incurred."[254] Further, the profit component of lost business income is figured by computing the net income the policyholder was earning prior to the "physical loss or damage" and the net income that the policyholder would have earned "if no direct physical loss or damage occurred."[255] There is typically no provision permitting insurance companies to reduce estimates of their policyholder's lost business income on account of generalized lack of consumer demand because the "direct physical loss or damage occurred."[256] Nonetheless, this is what insurance companies have attempted to do.[257]

Courts have, however, consistently found that business income losses must be computed based on net profit expectancies *as they exist prior to the loss*.[258] More specifically, the insurance industry has been very successful in making the exact opposite of the argument insurance companies have made in the wake of the September 11, 2001, attacks.[259] Insurance companies have successfully contested business income claims where the policyholder seeks to increase the amount of lost income by including consideration of the widespread effect of the physical loss or damage.[260]

In one case, the policyholder owned a hotel that was destroyed by a hurricane.[261] The policy provided that business income was to be figured by including both "the earnings of the business before the date of damage or destruction and . . . the probable earnings thereafter, had no loss occurred."[262] Although the policyholder was operating at a net loss prior to the hurricane, it made a claim for "probable earnings resulting from accommodating the burgeoning demand due to the hurricane," which the insurance company contested.[263] The court considered the issue to be: "did the lost opportunity to house the influx of temporary residents after the hurricane constitute a loss of earnings cognizable under a policy that is designed to return [the policyholder] to the position it would have occupied had the hurricane not occurred."[264] The court rejected the policyholder's argument, finding that business income losses, both in general and under the terms of the policy, were to be figured based on the performance of the business prior to the loss. Further, the court found that the policyholder was not entitled to a windfall based on the happening of the insured peril.

> "[H]ad the hurricane not occurred (the policy's built-in premise for assessing profit expectancies during a business interruption), neither would the specifically claimed earnings source have come into being. To allow the claim therefore would be to confer a windfall upon the insured rather than merely to put it in the earnings position it would have been in had the insured peril not occurred."[265]

Notes

[1] Although this chapter is intended to set forth the significant and relevant issues thoroughly, such a task might be unattainable in the space allotted, given that many others have written multi-volume treatises on the topic. See, e.g.: Cozen, *Insuring Real Property* (2004); Lewis and Insua, *Business Income Insurance Disputes* (2006).

[2] For further discussion, see § 2.04 *supra*.

[3] See § 4.02 *infra*.

[4] See § 4.03 *infra*.

[5] See §§ 4.04 and 4.05 *infra*.

[6] See § 4.04 *infra*.

[7] See § 4.03[4] *infra*.

[8] See *Black's Law Dictionary* at 722 (5th ed. 1979).

[9] See Chapter 2 *supra*.

[10] See, e.g.:

First Circuit: deVries v. St. Paul Fire and Marine Insurance Co., 716 F.2d 939 (1st Cir. 1983); Utica Mutual Insurance Co. v. Hall Equipment, Inc., 73 F. Supp.2d 83 (D. Mass. Oct. 28, 1999), *aff'd* 292 F.3d 77 (1st Cir. 2002).

Second Circuit: Travelers Insurance Co. v. Henry, 470 F.3d 56 (2d Cir. 2006); Riordan v. Nationwide Mutual Fire Insurance Co., 756 F. Supp. 732 (S.D.N.Y. 1990), *aff'd in part, question certified* 977 F.2d 47 (2d Cir. 1992), *certified question withdrawn* 984 F.2d 69 (2d Cir. 1993).

Third Circuit: Port Authority v. Affiliated FM Insurance Co., 311 F.3d 226, 233 (3d Cir. 2002); Reinert v. Nationwide Insurance Co., 2013 WL 1311097 (E.D. Pa. Apr. 2, 2013); Daniel B. Fuss Builders-Contractors, Inc. v. Assurance Company of America, 2006 WL 2372226, at *4 n.2 (E.D. Pa. Aug. 11, 2006); *In re* Asousa Partnership, 2004 WL1043149, at *8 (Bankr. E.D. Pa. Apr. 26, 2004).

Fourth Circuit: A & E Supply Co. v. Nationwide Mutual Fire Insurance Co., 798 F.2d 669 (4th Cir. 1986), *cert. denied* 479 U.S. 1091 (1987); TIG Insurance Co. v. Alfa Laval, Inc., 2008 WL 639894 (E.D. Va. Mar. 5, 2008); 17th Street Associates, LLP v. Markel International Insurance Co., 373 F. Supp.2d 584 (E.D. Va. 2005); Provident Life and Accident Insurance Co. v. Cohen, 137 F. Supp.2d 631 (D. Md. 2001), *reconsideration granted* 2002 WL 500673 (D. Md. Mar. 28, 2002).

Fifth Circuit: Ross v. Citifinancial, Inc., 344 F.3d 458 (5th Cir. 2003), *cert. denied* 546 U.S. 813 (2005); Nautilus Insurance Co. v. International House of Pancakes, Inc., 622 F. Supp.2d 470 (S.D. Tex. 2009); Rx.Com Inc. v. Hartford Fire Insurance Co., 364 F. Supp.2d 609 (S.D. Tex. 2005); Felham Enterprises (Cayman) Ltd. v. Certain Underwriters at Lloyds, London Companies, 2004 WL 2984296 (E.D. La. Dec. 6, 2004), *reconsideration denied* 2005 WL 167585 (E.D. La. Jan. 24, 2005).

Sixth Circuit: Rawe v. Liberty Mutual Fire Insurance Co., 462 F.3d 521 (6th Cir. 2006); Barrow v. Amica Mutual Insurance Co., 2007 WL 3038031 (E.D. Mich. Oct. 17, 2007).

Seventh Circuit: Metropolitan Chicago Healthcare Council v. UNUM Life Insurance Co. of America, 149 F.3d 744 (7th Cir. 1998); Hall v. Travelers Property Casualty Company of America, 2009 WL 1148231 (S.D. Ind. Apr. 27, 2009); Spearman Industries, Inc. v. St. Paul Fire and Marine Insurance Co., 128 F. Supp.2d 1148 (N.D. Ill. Jan. 23, 2001).

Eighth Circuit: Dallas v. American General Life and Accident Insurance Co., 709 F.3d 734 (8th Cir. 2013); Siegfried v. B.I.A., 2007 WL 512876 (D.N.D. Feb. 12, 2007); Dairy Farmers of America, Inc. v. Ace American Insurance Co., 2006 WL 2850563 (W.D. Mo. Sept. 29, 2006); Metro Renovation, Inc. v. Allied Group, Inc., 389 F. Supp.2d 1131(D. Neb. Sept. 29, 2005).

Ninth Circuit: TIG Insurance Co. v. ACE American Insurance Co., 236 Fed. Appx. 336 (9th Cir. 2007); Oregon Mutual Insurance Co. v. Highland Court L.L.C., 2009 WL 779268 (W.D. Wash. Mar. 23, 2009); United States *ex rel.* North Star Terminal & Stevedore Co. v. Nugget Construction, Inc., 2006 WL 2251122 (D. Alaska July 28, 2006); Bernstein v. Travelers Insurance Co., 2006 WL 2567875 (N.D. Cal. Sept. 5, 2006).

Tenth Circuit: Colony Insurance Co. v. Burke, 698 F.3d 1222 (10th Cir. 2012); Fuller v. Nationwide Insurance Co., 2009 WL 723245 (D. Utah Mar. 16, 2009); Garcia v. Berkshire Life Insurance Co. of America, 2007 WL 4578333 (D. Colo. Dec. 27, 2007); Crabb v. State Farm Fire and Casualty Co., 2006 WL 1214998 (D. Utah May 4, 2006).

Eleventh Circuit: Mid-Continent Casualty Co. v. Royal Palm Estate Builders, Inc., 2007 WL 4225801 (S.D. Fla. Oct. 2, 2007).

District of Columbia Circuit: Athridge v. Aetna Casualty and Surety Co., 474 F. Supp.2d 102 (D.D.C. 2007), *reconsideration denied* 2007 WL 509224 (D.D.C. Feb. 13, 2007).

State Courts:

California: Cardio Diagnostic Imaging, Inc. v. Farmers Insurance Exchange, 212 Cal. App.4th 69, 150 Cal. Rptr.3d 798 (2012); Standard Fire Insurance Co. v. Spectrum Community Association, 141 Cal. App.4th 1117, 46 Cal. Rptr.3d 804, 818–819 (2006); Black Diamond Asphalt, Inc. v. Superior Court, 114 Cal. App.4th 109, 7 Cal. Rptr.3d 466, 470 n.2 (2003).

Florida: Subirats v. Fidelity National Property, 106 So.3d 997 (Fla. App. 2013); North Pointe Insurance Co. v. Tomas, 999 So.2d 728 (Fla. App. 2008).

Idaho: Dave's Inc. v. Linford, 291 P.3d 427 (Idaho 2012).

Illinois: Aurelius v. State Farm Fire and Casualty Co., 384 Ill. App.3d 969, 894 N.E.2d 765, 323 Ill. Dec. 739 (2008); Emerson Electric Co. v. Aetna Casualty & Surety Co., 815 N.E.2d 924 (Ill. App. 2004).

Indiana: Wagner v. Yates, 912 N.E.2d 805 (Ind. 2009).

Kansas: Lytle v. Pepsi Cola General Bottlers, Inc., 656 P.2d 786 (Kan. App. 1983).

Maryland: TravCo Insurance Co. v. Williams, 430 Md. 396, 61 A.3d 50 (Md. App. 2013).

Minnesota: Western World Insurance Co. v. Hall, 353 N.W.2d 221, 223 (Minn. App. 1984).

New Jersey: Universal Underwriters Group v. Heibel, 901 A.2d 398, 404 (N.J. Super. 2006).

New Mexico: Salas v. Mountain States Mutual Casualty Co., 145 N.M. 542, 202 P.3d 801 (2009).

North Dakota: Grinnell Mutual Reinsurance Co. v. Thies, 755 N.W.2d 852 (N.D. 2008).

Pennsylvania: Zimmerman v. Harleysville Mutual Insurance Co., 860 A.2d 167, 178 (Pa. Super. 2004), *appeal denied* 881 A.2d 820 (Pa. 2005).

Tennessee: Holt v. Pyles, 2007 WL 1217264 (Tenn. App. Apr. 24, 2007).

Texas: Lamar Homes, Inc. v. Mid-Continent Casualty Co., 242 S.W.3d 1 (Tex. 2007).

Utah: Tucker v. State Farm Mutual Auto. Insurance Co., 53 P.3d 947 (Utah 2002); Billings v. Union Bankers Insurance Co., 918 P.2d 461 (Utah 1996).

Virginia: McCullough v. Standard Pressing Machines. Co., 39 Va. Cir. 191, 39 Va. Cir. 191, 1996 WL 1065525, at *3 (Va. Cir. Apr. 18, 1996).

Washington: Cedell v. Farmers Insurance Company of Washington, 176 Wash.2d 686, 295 P.3d 239 (2013) (*en banc*); Staples v. Allstate Insurance Co., 176 Wash.2d 404, 295 P.3d 201 (2013) (*en banc*); Aluminum Co. of America v. Aetna Casualty & Surety Co., 998 P.2d 856 (Wash. 2000).

West Virginia: Miller v. Fluharty, 500 S.E.2d 310 (W. Va. 1997); Marshall v. Saseen, 450 S.E.2d 791, 797 (W. Va. 1994).

11 See, e.g., Aetna Casualty & Surety Co. v. Kentucky, 179 S.W.3d 830, 845 (Ky. 2005) ("Third party insurance involves protection for the policyholder for liability it incurs to someone else, while first party insurance involves protection for losses to the policyholder's own property."). See also § 2.06 *supra*.

12 Montrose Chemical Co. v. Admiral Insurance Co., 42 Cal. Rptr.2d 324, 332 (Cal. 1995). See also:

Third Circuit: In re Asousa Partnership, 2004 WL 1043149, at *8 (Bankr. E.D. Pa. Apr. 26, 2004); Marion v. Hartford Fire Insurance Co., 2012 WL 262650 (E.D. Pa. Jan. 27, 2012).

Fourth Circuit: Graham v. National Union Insurance Co. of Pittsburgh, PA, 2013 WL 870298, at *3 (S.D. W. Va. Mar. 7, 2013).

Sixth Circuit: White v. Insurance Company of State of Pennsylvania, 282 F. Supp.2d 618, 625 (N.D. Ohio 2003), vacated on other grounds 405 F.3d 455 (6th Cir. 2005) ("'Liability' insurance constitutes 'an agreement to cover a loss resulting from one's liability to a third party, such as a loss incurred by a driver who injures a pedestrian.' The claim under the policy 'arises once the insured's liability to a third party has been asserted.' In contrast to this 'third party insurance,' there is also 'indemnity' insurance which is characterized as 'first party insurance' and defined as '[a] policy that applies to oneself or one's own property, such as life insurance, health insurance, disability insurance, and fire insurance.'") (citations omitted).

Seventh Circuit: CitiMortgage, Inc. v. Absolute Title Services, Inc., 2012 WL 1108249 (N.D. Ill. Apr. 2, 2012) ("Each of the cited decisions involved third-party insurance, purchased by an insured from an insurer for protection against the claims of another party. This case deals with first-party insurance. The insured is to be paid by the insurer in the event of a loss.").

Eleventh Circuit: Breedlove v. Hartford Life and Accident Insurance Co., 2011 WL 6132254 (M.D. Fla. Dec. 9, 2011).

State Courts:

Alaska: United States *ex. rel.* North Star Terminal & Stevedore Co. v. Nuggett Insurance Construction Co., 2006 WL 2251122, at *2 n.3 (D. Alaska July 28, 2006).

California: Garvey v. State Farm Fire & Casualty Co., 48 Cal.3d 395, 770 P.2d 704, 257 Cal. Rptr. 292 (1989); California Insurance Guarantee Ass'n v. Workers' Compensation Appeals Board, 203 Cal. App.4th 1328, 138 Cal. Rptr.3d 24, 30–31 (2012) ("In the context of first party insurance, original claimant has been construed to mean the original insured. In the context of third party insurance, original claimant has been construed to mean a person who institutes a claim against an insured for liability.") (citations omitted); Pacific Civil Constructors, Inc. v. Western Heritage Insurance Co., 2011 WL 2112676, at *11 (Cal. App. May 27, 2011) ("The terms are defined as follows: 'First party' insurance policies provide coverage for loss or damage sustained by the insured (e.g., life, disability, health, fire, theft and casualty insurance). 'Third party' insurance policies provide coverage for liability of the insured to another (e.g., comprehensive general liability, directors and officers liability and errors and omissions insurance)."); Howard v. American National Fire Insurance Co., 187 Cal. App.4th 498, 115 Cal. Rptr.3d 42, 70 (2010) ("There are material differences in the purposes of first party insurance policies (that obligate the insurer to pay damages claimed by the insured itself) and third party insurance policies (that obligate the insurer to defend, settle, and pay damages claimed by a third party against the insured)."); Black Diamond Asphalt Co. v. Superior Court, 7 Cal. Rptr.3d 466, 470 n.2 (Cal. App. 2003) ("In first party insurance, a person insures himself or his property against loss. In third party insurance, a person insures himself against liability he may incur to others."); Century Indemnity Co. v. Hearrean, 120 Cal. Rptr.2d 66, 69 (Cal. App. 2002) ("'CGL policies are third party liability insurance policies which obligate insurers to pay money to third parties to whom their insureds are liable. In contrast to first party insurance policies which obligate an insurer to pay money directly to an insured for a loss sustained by the insured. . . .'").

Hawaii: Sentinel Insurance Co. v. First Insurance Co. of Hawaii, Ltd., 875 P.2d 894, 906 (Haw. 1994); Ferrer v. Ngo, 73 P.3d 73, 81 (Haw. App. 2003) ("a 'first party' policy provides coverage for *loss* or *damage* sustained by the *insured* (e.g., life, disability, health, fire, theft, and casualty insurance) whereby the insurer usually promises to pay money to the insured upon the happening of the risk insured against. A 'third party' policy, on the other hand, provides coverage for the insured's *liability to another* (e.g., CGL [comprehensive general liability], directors' and officers' liability, and errors and omissions insurance) wherein the carrier generally assumes a contractual duty to pay judgments recovered against the insured arising from the insured's negligence.") (emphasis in original).

Illinois: Emerson Electric Co. v. Aetna Casualty & Surety Co., 815 N.E.2d 924, 950 (Ill. App. 2004).

Indiana: Sanyo Laser Products, Inc. v. Royal Insurance Co., 2003 WL 23101793, at *3 n.2 (S.D. Ind. Nov. 7, 2003) ("'first party' insurance is a contract between the insurer and insured protecting the insured's own actual losses and expenses, while 'third party' insurance protects the insured from potential liability to a third party").

Kansas: Allstate Insurance Co. v. Johnston, 339 F. Supp.2d 1191, 1195 (D. Kan. 2004).

Kentucky: Aetna Casualty & Surety Co. v. Kentucky, 179 S.W.3d 830, 845 (Ky. 2005) ("Third party insurance involves protection for the policyholder for liability it incurs to someone else, while first party insurance involves protection for losses to the policyholder's own property.").

Louisiana: Niemann v. Crosby Development Co., 92 So.3d 1039, 1043 n.3 (La. App. 2012) ("'First-party' insurance covers a loss sustained by the insured, the first party to the insurance contract, as opposed to liability or 'third-party' insurance, which covers the insured's liability to a third party (a non-party to the insurance contract) for that party's loss."); Mangerchine v. Reaves, 63 So.3d 1049 (La. App. 2011) (similar); Felham Enterprises, Ltd. v. Certain Underwriters of Lloyds, 2004 WL 2984296, at *4 (E.D. La. Dec. 6, 2004) ("'[F]irst party insurance' generally is understood to provide coverage for the insured against loss or damage sustained by it, whereas 'third party insurance' covers liability of the insured to another person.").

Massachusetts: Quincy Mutual Fire Insurance Co. v. Crispo, 80 Mass. App. Ct. 484, 954 N.E.2d 27, 31 n.8 (2011) ("First-party insurance, such as protection against loss of an insured's property, is often treated differently than third-party insurance that protects the insured against liability to others.").

Mississippi: Watson Quality Ford, Inc. v. Great River Insurance Co., 909 So.2d 1196, 1199 (Miss. App. 2005) ("First party coverage is a promise by an insurer to pay its own insured, rather than a promise to its insured to pay a third party.").

Texas: Tellepsen Builders, L.P. v. Kendall/Heaton Associates, Inc., 325 S.W.3d 692 (Tex. App. 2010).

Utah: Black v. Allstate Insurance Co., 100 P.3d 1163, 1168 (Utah 2004) ("first-party coverage . . . refers to an insurance agreement where the insurer agrees to pay claims submitted to it by the insured for losses suffered by the insured, and third-party coverage . . . refers to an agreement wherein the insurer contracts to defend the insured against claims made by third parties against the insured").

Washington: State Farm Fire & Casualty Co. v. English Cove Association, Inc., 88 P.3d 986, 992 (Wash. App. 2004) ("Third party insurance provides protection for the policyholder for liability it incurs to someone else, while first party insurance provides protection for losses to the policyholder's own property."); Staples v. Allstate Insurance Co., 176 Wash.2d 404, 295 P.3d 201, 205 n.4 (2013) (*en banc*) ("Generally speaking, third-party insurance covers liability to a third party whereas first-party insurance covers personal loss.").

West Virginia: Loudin v. National Liability and Fire Insurance Co., 228 W. Va. 34, 716 S.E.2d 696 (2011).

13 Hartford Fire Insurance Co. v. California, 509 U.S. 764, 772, 113 S.Ct. 2891, 125 L.Ed.2d 612 (1993) ("ISO develops standard policy forms and files or lodges them with each State's insurance regulators; most CGL insurance written in the United States is written on these forms.").

See also:

State Courts:

New York: In re Hoechst Celanese Corp., 184 A.D.2d 223, 584 N.Y.S.2d 805, 806 (1992) (ISO is the "principal rating, statistical and drafting organization for the general liability insurance industry in the United States, whose primary function is to draft standard-form comprehensive general liability ("CGL") insurance policy language for the industry. . . .").

Washington: American Star Insurance Co. v. Grice, 854 P.2d 622, 627 n.19 (Wash. 1993) (ISO "is an insurance industry trade association which develops standard form insurance policies and often secures regulatory approval for their insurance").

Because of the widespread use of such standard-form language, courts should interpret the meaning of such standardized language uniformly by relying upon interpretations from other jurisdictions. See Anderson, Stanzler & Masters, *Insurance Coverage Litigation*, § 1.2, at 14 (1997).

14 See, e.g., ISO Form CP 00 10 04 02.

15 Builders risk coverage is a specialized form of first-party property insurance, providing coverage to a builder for risks of loss to the project during the construction phase. "A builders' risk policy is a species of [first party] property loss insurance by which the builder seeks to insulate himself from liability occasioned by damage to or loss of the structure which the builder has contracted to produce." The builders risk coverage can appear as a separate policy or as a rider on an "all risk" first-party property insurance policy. See 9 *Couch on Insurance*, § 132:20 (3d ed. 2004).

16 See ISO Form CP 00 10 04 02.

17 See Zurich American Insurance Co. v. ABM Industries, Inc., 397 F.3d 158 (2d Cir. 2005).

18 See ISO Form CP 00 10 04 02.

19 See, e.g.:

Second Circuit: Porco v. Lexington Insurance Co., 679 F. Supp.2d 432 (S.D.N.Y. 2009); Farrell v. Royal Insurance Co. of America, 989 F. Supp. 159 (D. Conn. 1997).

Third Circuit: Hartford Fire Insurance Co. v. B. Barks & Sons, Inc., 1999 WL 341972, at *1 (E.D. Pa. May 27, 1999).

Fourth Circuit: Icarom, PLC v. Howard County, 981 F. Supp. 379 (D. Md. 1997), *aff'd* 178 F.3d 1284 (4th Cir. 1999).

Fifth Circuit: First Baptist Church of Mauriceville, Texas v. GuideOne Mutual Insurance Co., 2009 WL 415482 (E.D. Tex. Feb. 17, 2009).

Seventh Circuit: Horning Wire Corp. v. Home Indemnity Co., 8 F.3d 587 (7th Cir. 1993).

Eighth Circuit: Farm Bureau Mutual Insurance Co. v. Wilcox, 500 F.3d 823 (8th Cir. 2007); TAMKO Building Products, Inc. v. Factual Mutual Insurance Co., 890 F. Supp.2d 1129 (E.D. Mo. 2012).

Ninth Circuit: Abbey Co. v. Lexington Insurance Co., 289 Fed. Appx. 161 (9th Cir. 2008); Port of Olympia v. Lexington Insurance Co., 73 Fed. Appx. 949 (9th Cir. 2003); Zurich American Insurance Co. v. Coeur Rochester, Inc., 720 F. Supp.2d 1223 (D. Nev. 2010); Grooms v. Liberty Mutual Fire Insurance Co., 2009 WL 2512408 (W.D. Wash. Aug. 13, 2009).

Tenth Circuit: Vista Ridge Development, L.L.C. v. Assurance Company of America, 2009 WL 1392077 (D. Colo. May 14, 2009); Fireman's Fund v. Structural Systems Technology, Inc., 426 F. Supp.2d 1009 (D. Neb. 2006).

Eleventh Circuit: Ajax Building Corp. v. Hartford Fire Insurance Co., 358 F.3d 795 (11th Cir. 2004); Royal Bahamian Ass'n v. QBE Insurance Corp., 750 F. Supp.2d 1346 (S.D. Fla. 2010).

State Courts:

Arizona: Aztar Corp. v. U.S. Fire Insurance Co., 223 Ariz. 463, 224 P.3d 960 (Ariz. App. 2010).

California: Palacin v. Allstate Insurance Co., 14 Cal. Rptr.3d 731 (Cal. App. 2004).

Georgia: Global Ship Systems, L.L.C. v. Continental Casualty Co., 292 Ga. App. 214, 663 S.E.2d 826 (2008).

Idaho: Arreguin v. Farmers Insurance Co. of Idaho, 2008 WL 246463 (Idaho Jan. 31, 2008).

Indiana: Bosecker v. Westfield Insurance Co., 724 N.E.2d 241 (Ind. 2000).

Louisiana: Mason v. Bankers Insurance Group, 90 So.3d 1088 (La. App. 2012); *In re* McDermott, 875 So.2d 863 (La. App. 2004).

Maryland: Nationwide Mutual Insurance Co. v. Regency Furniture, Inc., 183 Md. App. 710, 963 A.2d 253 (Md. Spec. App. 2009).

Michigan: Lazechko v. Auto Owners Insurance Co., 2008 WL 2697428 (Mich. App. July 10, 2008).

Mississippi: United States Fidelity and Guaranty Company of Mississippi v. Martin, 998 So.2d 956 (Miss. 2008); Trapani v. Treutel, 87 So.3d 1096 (Miss. App. 2012).

Nebraska: Craig v. Farmers Mutual Insurance Co. of Nebraska, 476 N.W.2d 529 (Neb. 1991).

Nevada: Fourth St. Place v. Travelers Indemnity Co., 270 P.3d 1235 (Nev. 2011).

New Jersey: Vantage Development Corp. v. American Environment Technologies Corp., 251 N.J. Super. 516, 598 A.2d 948 (1991).

New York: R.B. Woodcraft, Inc. v. Acadia Insurance Co., 60 A.D.3d 1447, 876 N.Y.S.2d 597 (N.Y. App. Div. 2009); Roland v. Nationwide Mutual Fire Insurance Co., 730 N.Y.S.2d 599 (N.Y. App. Div. 2001); Carden v. Allstate Insurance Co., 30 Misc.3d 479, 912 N.Y.S.2d 867 (N.Y. Sup. Ct., Westchester Cnty. 2010).

[20] See ISO Form CP 00 10 04 02. See also:

Second Circuit: Lumbermens Mutual Casualty Co. v. Flow International Corp., 844 F. Supp.2d 286 (N.D.N.Y. 2012).

Fifth Circuit: Hartford Insurance Co. of Midwest v. Mississippi Valley Gas Co., 181 Fed. Appx. 465 (5th Cir. 2006) (overpayment made to natural gas vendor by policyholder based upon repeated recirculation of the same gas through meter was not direct physical loss of or damage to covered property, but only an uncovered loss of money).

Eleventh Circuit: Omega Forensic Engineering, Inc. v. RLI Insurance Co., 682 F. Supp.2d 1336 (S.D. Fla. 2010).

State Courts:

California: MRI Healthcare Center of Glendale, Inc. v. State Farm General Insurance Co., 187 Cal. App.4th 766, 115 Cal. Rptr.3d 27 (2010).

Louisiana: Burmaster v. Plaquemines Parish Government, 64 So.3d 312 (La. App. 2011).

Texas: Venture Encoding Service, Inc. v. Atlantic Mutual Insurance Co., 107 S.W.3d 729 (Tex. App. 2003).

[21] See, e.g.:

Fourth Circuit: America Online, Inc. v. St. Paul Mercury Insurance Co., 347 F.3d 89 (4th Cir. 2003).

Ninth Circuit: American Guarantee & Liability Insurance Co. v. Ingram Micro, Inc., 2000 WL 726789 (D. Ariz. Apr. 18, 2000).

State Courts:

Minnesota: Retail Systems, Inc. v. CNA Insurance Cos., 469 N.W.2d 735, 737–738 (Minn. App. 1991).

Texas: Lambrecht & Associates, Inc. v. State Farm Lloyds, 119 S.W.3d 16 (Tex. App. 2003).

[22] *Compare,* American Guarantee & Liability Insurance Co. v. Ingram Micro, Inc., 2000 WL 726789 (D. Ariz. Apr. 18, 2000) (outage leading to erasure of electronic data and programming and disruption of computer system deemed damage to covered "property" under first-party property policy) *and* Retail Systems, Inc. v. CNA Insurance Cos., 469 N.W.2d 735, 737–738 (Minn. App. 1991) (electronic data is tangible property under third-party liability policy) *with* America Online, Inc. v. St. Paul Mercury Insurance Co., 347 F.3d 89 (4th Cir. 2003) (in third-party liability insurance context, electronic data is intangible property not covered but computers are tangible property that is covered).

See also:

Sixth Circuit: Southeast Mental Health Center, Inc. v. Pacific Insurance Co., 439 F. Supp.2d 831 (W.D. Tenn. 2006) (corruption of pharmacy computer system leading to nonfunctionality thereof deemed covered).

Seventh Circuit: Nationwide Insurance Co. v. Hentz, 2012 WL 734193 (S.D. Ill. Mar. 6, 2012) (loss of CD-ROM on which lost data is recorded is loss of tangible personalty even though loss of data itself would not be).

Eighth Circuit: Eyeblaster, Inc. v. Federal Insurance Co., 613 F.3d 797 (8th Cir. 2010) (loss of use of computer by freezing up, becoming inoperable, and crashing is loss of use of tangible property).

State Courts:

California: Greco and Traficante v. Fidelity and Guaranty Insurance Co., 2009 WL 162068 (Cal. App. Jan 26, 2009) (loss of billing data from corruption in computer not covered).

Connecticut: Recall Total Information Management, Inc. v. Federal Insurance Co., 2012 WL 469988 (Conn. Super. Hartford Jan. 17, 2012) (loss of use of data not tangible property).

Texas: Lambrecht & Associates, Inc. v. State Farm Lloyds, 119 S.W.3d 16 (Tex. App. 2003) (main server for computer system, pre-packaged software, and data stored on server were "physical" for purposes of coverage for accidental direct physical loss of business personal property after hacker invaded computer system and injected virus that ultimately caused system to fail and rendered server useless).

[23] See, e.g.:

Fourth Circuit: America Online, Inc. v. St. Paul Mercury Insurance Co., 347 F.3d 89 (4th Cir. 2003).

Seventh Circuit: Nationwide Insurance Co. v. Hentz, 2012 WL 734193 (S.D. Ill. Mar. 6, 2012).

Eighth Circuit: Eyeblaster, Inc. v. Federal Insurance Co., 613 F.3d 797 (8th Cir. 2010).

Ninth Circuit: American Guarantee & Liability Insurance Co. v. Ingram Micro, Inc., 2000 WL 726789 (D. Ariz. Apr. 18, 2000).

State Courts:

Connecticut: Recall Total Information Management, Inc. v. Federal Insurance Co., 2012 WL 469988 (Conn. Super. Hartford Jan. 17, 2012).

Minnesota: Retail Systems, Inc. v. CNA Insurance Cos., 469 N.W.2d 735, 737–738 (Minn. App. 1991).

Texas: Lambrecht & Associates, Inc. v. State Farm Lloyds, 119 S.W.3d 16 (Tex. App. 2003).

[24] See § 4.03[3] *infra.*

[25] See Abraxas Group, Inc. v. Guaranty National Insurance Co., 648 F. Supp. 304, 305 (W.D. Pa. 1986).

> "A blanket, compound or floater policy of insurance is written upon a risk as a whole, embracing whatever articles or items are included therein. [Blanket insurance] is one that invariably covers and attaches to every item of property described therein. If the loss of one item exhausts the whole amount of the policy, the entire insurance must be paid, and there can be no apportionment. Another definition is that a compound, or blanket, policy is one which insures property collectively without providing in the event of a loss for a distribution of insurance to each item."

See also:

Second Circuit: Core-Mark International Corp. v. Commonwealth Insurance Co., 2006 WL 2501884, at *5 n.3 (S.D.N.Y. Aug. 30, 2006) ("A scheduled policy may be contrasted with a 'blanket' policy, which 'attaches to, and covers to its full amount, every item of property described in it.' . . . Thus, pursuant to a blanket policy, '[i]f the loss upon one item exhausts the full amount of the policy, the whole insurance must be paid.'").

Third Circuit: Tucci v. Hartford Financial Services Group, Inc., 2011 WL 2555379 (D.N.J. June 27, 2011); Rich Maid Kitchens, Inc. v. Pennsylvania Lumbermens Mutual Insurance Co., 641 F. Supp. 297 (E.D. Pa. 1986), *aff'd without opinion* 833 F.2d 307 (3d Cir. 1987).

Fourth Circuit: First Centrum Corp. v. Landmark American Insurance Co., 237 Fed. Appx. 799 (4th Cir. 2007); Monumental Paving & Excavating, Inc. v. Pennsylvania Manufacturers' Association Insurance Co., 176 F.3d 794, 798 (4th Cir. 1999) ("A blanket policy by definition covers different types of property at one or more locations and does not specify the valuation of the items protected under the blanket, but allocates an overall limit to the policy, upon which premiums are based."); Medical Protective Company of Fort Wayne, Indiana v. South Carolina Medical Malpractice Liability Insurance Joint Underwriting Association, 648 F. Supp.2d 753 (D.S.C. 2009).

Fifth Circuit: Reliance Insurance Co. v. Orleans Parish School Board., 192 F. Supp. 524 (E.D. La. 1961), *rev'd on other grounds* 322 F.2d 803 (5th Cir. 1963), *cert. denied* 377 U.S. 916 (1964).

> "[A] blanket policy covers multiple pieces of property at an average rate, each piece being insured up to the total amount of insurance on all the property. A scheduled policy, on the other hand, relates to specifically described individual pieces of property, insuring each in an amount specifically designated at a rate justified by the risk on that property. A blanket policy is usually issued on the basis of a statement of values listing property included in the coverage. This statement of values does not become a part of the policy, and may not be used as a coverage limitation in adjusting losses. Since each piece of property is insured to the full extent of the total coverage, the actual value of the piece at the time of the loss is the only limitation. In a scheduled policy, each specific piece of property in the amount covered is listed in the policy itself, which listing not only is referred to in making adjustments for losses, but provides the limit of recovery under the policy."

See also, Rainbow USA, Inc. v. Crum & Forster Specialty Insurance Co., 711 F. Supp.2d 655 (E.D. La. 2010).

Sixth Circuit: Auto-Owners Insurance Co. v. Redland Insurance Co., 549 F.3d 1043 (6th Cir. 2008).

Seventh Circuit: Axis Specialty Insurance Corp. v. Simborg Development, Inc., 2009 WL 765298 (N.D. Ill. Mar. 20, 2009); Reliance National Indemnity Co. v. Lexington Insurance Co., 2002 WL 31409576, at *8 (N.D. Ill. Oct. 23, 2002) ("A distinction must be made between a policy which speaks in terms of a lump sum obligation or value of the property and one which separately schedules different items of property. In the latter case, each separately treated item of property is in effect covered by a separate contract of insurance and the amount recoverable with respect to a loss affecting such property is determined independently of the other items of property.").

Eighth Circuit: Best Buy Stores, L.P. v. Benderson-Wainberg Associates, L.P., 668 F.3d 1019 (8th Cir. 2012); State Auto Property and Casualty Insurance Co. v. Boardwalk Apartments, L.C., 572 F.3d 511 (8th Cir. 2009).

Ninth Circuit: Northrop Grumman Corp. v. Factory Mutual Insurance Co., 563 F.3d 777 (9th Cir. 2009); Gemini Insurance Co. v. Western Marine Insurance Services Corp., 2012 WL 2934657 (E.D. Cal. July 18, 2012); Fireman's Fund Insurance Co. v. Oregon Automobile Insurance Co., 2010 WL 1542552 (D. Or. Apr. 15, 2010); Allstate Insurance Co. v. Breeden, 2007 WL 4480759 (D. Or. Dec. 17, 2007); Northrop Grumman Corp. v. Factory Mutual Insurance Co., 2007 WL 2385134 (C.D. Cal. Aug. 16, 2007).

Eleventh Circuit: RSUI Indemnity Co. v. Benderson Development Co., 2011 WL 32318 (M.D. Fla. Jan. 5, 2011); Aerosonic Corp. v. Liberty Mutual Fire Insurance Co., 2009 WL 5068616 (M.D. Fla. Dec. 17, 2009); Lexington Insurance Co. v. Kash N' Karry Food Stores, Inc., 2008 WL 450035 (M.D. Fla. Feb. 15, 2008).

State Courts:

Arkansas: Bratton v. St. Paul Surplus Lines, Inc., 706 S.W.2d 189 (Ark. App. 1986) (presence of a schedule of values in a policy rendered the policy coverage specific).

Delaware: Those Certain Underwriters at Lloyd's London Who Subscribed Severally as Their Interests Appear Thereon and Not Jointly to Lloyd's Policy Number 390/J145210 v. National Installment Insurance Services, Inc., 2007 WL 4554453 (Del. Chancery Dec. 21, 2007).

Florida: Florida Insurance Guaranty Association v. B.T. of Sunrise Condominium Ass'n, Inc., 46 So.3d 1039 (Fla. App. 2010).

Indiana: Vernon Fire & Casualty Insurance Co. v. Sharp, 349 N.E.2d 173, 177 (Ind. 1976) (policies provided specific, rather than blanket, coverage because they separately scheduled values for individual pieces of property); Anderson Mattress Co. v. First State Insurance Co., 617 N.E.2d 932 (Ind. App. 1993).

Maine: Morse Brothers, Inc. v. Desmond & Payne, Inc., 2005 WL 1845167, at *1 n.3 (Me. Super. Apr. 22, 2005).

Massachusetts: LES Realty Trust "A" v. Landmark American Insurance Co., 82 Mass. App. Ct. 694, 977 N.E.2d 566 (2012).

Missouri: United Services Automobile Association v. United States Fidelity & Guaranty Co., 555 S.W.2d 38, 42 (Mo. App. 1977); Arch Insurance Co. v. Progressive Casualty Insurance Co., 294 S.W.3d 520 (Mo. App. 2009).

Nebraska: Schultz v. Western United Mutual Insurance Association, 2009 WL 1272390 (Neb. App. May 5, 2009).

New York: Core-Mark International v. Swett and Crawford, Inc., 71 A.D.3d 1072, 898 N.Y.S.2d 206 (N.Y. App. Div. 2010).

Texas: Lynd Co. v. RSUI Indemnity Co., 392 S.W.3d 319 (Tex. App. 2012).

Washington: Certain Underwriters at Lloyd's London v. Travelers Property Casualty Co. of America, 161 Wash. App. 265, 256 P.3d 368, 371 n.5 (2011) ("'*Blanket coverage*' insures *property* collectively without providing for a distribution of insurance to each item. In contrast, 'specific' insurance provides a specific amount of insurance for each item or each *property*.") (citations omitted) (emphasis added); Nationwide Mutual Insurance Co. v. Hayles, Inc., 150 P.3d 589 (Wash. App. 2007).

Wisconsin: Go Wireless, L.L.C. v. Maryland Casualty Co., 2013 WL 599761 (Wis. App. Feb. 29, 2013).

Wyoming: W.N. McMurry Construction Co. v. Community First Insurance, Inc. Wyoming, 160 P.3d 71 (Wyo. 2007).

See also, 15 *Couch on Insurance* 2d, § 54:83:

> "A distinction must be made between a policy which speaks in terms of a lump-sum obligation or value of the property and one which separately schedules different items of property. In the latter case, each separately treated item of property is in effect covered by a separate contract of insurance and the amount recoverable with respect to a loss affecting such property is determined independently of other items of property."

[26] See Abraxas Group, Inc. v. Guaranty National Insurance Co., 648 F. Supp. 304, 306 (W.D. Pa. 1986) ("A specific policy is one which allocates the amount of the risk in stated values upon the several items embraced in the coverage, or covers property at a designated location for a stated amount, or insures against a specific peril.").

See also:

Second Circuit: Royal Indemnity Co. v. Deep Sea International, 2007 WL 2059826 (S.D.N.Y. July 13, 2007).

Third Circuit: Tucci v. Hartford Financial Services Group, Inc., 2011 WL 2555379 (D.N.J June 27, 2011); Rich Maid Kitchens, Inc. v. Pennsylvania Lumbermens Mutual Insurance Co., 641 F. Supp. 297 (E.D. Pa. 1986), *aff'd without opinion* 833 F.2d 307 (3d Cir. 1987).

Fourth Circuit: First Centrum Corp. v. Landmark American Insurance Co., 237 Fed. Appx. 799 (4th Cir. 2007); Medical Protective Company of Fort Wayne, Indiana v. South Carolina Medical Malpractice Liability Insurance Joint Underwriting Association, 648 F. Supp.2d 753 (D.S.C. 2009).

Fifth Circuit: Rainbow USA, Inc. v. Crum & Forster Specialty Insurance Co., 711 F. Supp.2d 655 (E.D. La. 2010); Reliance Insurance Co. v. Orleans Parish School Board., 192 F. Supp. 524 (E.D. La. 1961), *rev'd on other grounds* 322 F.2d 803 (5th Cir. 1963), *cert. denied* 377 U.S. 916 (1964).

Sixth Circuit: Auto-Owners Insurance Co. v. Redland Insurance Co., 549 F.3d 1043 (6th Cir. 2008).

Seventh Circuit: Axis Specialty Insurance Corp. v. Simborg Development, Inc., 2009 WL 765298 (N.D. Ill. Mar. 20, 2009); Reliance National Indemnity Co. v. Lexington Insurance Co., 2002 WL 31409576, at *8 (N.D. Ill. Oct. 23, 2002).

Eighth Circuit: Best Buy Stores, L.P. v. Benderson-Wainberg Associates, L.P., 668 F.3d 1019 (8th Cir. 2012); State Auto Property and Casualty Insurance Co. v. Boardwalk Apartments, L.C., 572 F.3d 511 (8th Cir. 2009).

Ninth Circuit: Northrop Grumman Corp. v. Factory Mutual Insurance Co., 563 F.3d 777 (9th Cir. 2009); Gemini Insurance Co. v. Western Marine Insurance Services Corp., 2012 WL 2934657 (E.D. Cal. July 18, 2012); Fireman's Fund Insurance Co. v. Oregon Automobile Insurance Co., 2010 WL 1542552 (D. Or. Apr. 15, 2010); Calpine Corp. v. Ace American Insurance Co., 2007 WL 3010570 (N.D. Cal. Oct. 12, 2007).

Eleventh Circuit: RSUI Indemnity Co. v. Benderson Development Co., 2011 WL 32318 (M.D. Fla. Jan. 5, 2011); Aerosonic Corp. v. Liberty Mutual Fire Insurance Co., 2009 WL 5068616 (M.D. Fla. Dec. 17, 2009); Lexington Insurance Co. v. Kash N' Karry Food Stores, Inc., 2008 WL 450035 (M.D. Fla. Feb. 15, 2008).

State Courts:

Arkansas: Bratton v. St. Paul Surplus Lines, Inc., 706 S.W.2d 189 (Ark. App. 1986) (presence of a schedule of values in a policy rendered the policy coverage specific).

Florida: Florida Insurance Guaranty Ass'n v. B.T. of Sunrise Condominium Ass'n, Inc., 46 So.3d 1039 (Fla. App. 2010).

Indiana: Vernon Fire & Casualty Insurance Co. v. Sharp, 349 N.E.2d 173, 177 (Ind. 1976) (policies provided specific, rather than blanket, coverage because they separately scheduled values for individual pieces of property); Anderson Mattress Co. v. First State Insurance Co., 617 N.E.2d 932 (Ind. App. 1993).

Louisiana: Fair Grounds Corp. v. Travelers Indemnity Co., 742 So.2d 1069, 1074 (La. App. 1999), *writ denied* 753 So.2d 831 (La. 2000) ("Under a scheduled policy only listed risks are insured, and then only for the listed value.").

Massachusetts: LES Realty Trust "A" v. Landmark American Insurance Co., 82 Mass. App. Ct. 694, 977 N.E.2d 566 (2012).

Missouri: United Services Automobile Association v. United States Fidelity & Guaranty Co., 555 S.W.2d 38, 42 (Mo. App. 1977); Arch Insurance Co. v. Progressive Casualty Insurance Co., 294 S.W.3d 520 (Mo. App. 2009).

Texas: Lynd Co. v. RSUI Indemnity Co., 392 S.W.3d 319 (Tex. App. 2012).

Washington: Certain Underwriters at Lloyd's London v. Travelers Property Casualty Co. of America, 161 Wash. App. 265, 256 P.3d 368, 371 n.5 (2011) ("'Blanket coverage' insures property collectively without providing for a distribution of insurance to each item. In contrast, 'specific' insurance provides a specific amount of insurance for each item or each property.") (citations omitted).

Wisconsin: Go Wireless, L.L.C. v. Maryland Casualty Co., 2013 WL 599761 (Wis. App. Feb. 29, 2013).

[27] See:

First Circuit: TIG Insurance Co. v. Wembley USA, Inc., 75 Fed. Appx. 5 (1st Cir. 2003).

Second Circuit: McDermott v. Great American Alliance Insurance Co., 2005 WL 2437020 (N.D.N.Y. Sept. 30, 2005); GTM, Inc. v. Transcontinental Insurance Co., 5 F. Supp.2d 219, 224 (D. Vt. 1998); Katz Broadcasting of Atlanta, Inc. v. Alexander & Alexander of New York, Inc., 1990 WL 67433, at *5 (S.D.N.Y. May 16, 1990).

Sixth Circuit: Universal Image Productions, Inc. v. Chubb Corp., 2010 WL 1257770 (E.D. Mich. Mar. 29, 2010).

Tenth Circuit: Sharper Edge, Inc. v. Continental Insurance Co., 176 F.3d 489 (10th Cir. 1999).

Eleventh Circuit: Sherman International Corp. v. Liberty Mutual Insurance Co., 922 F.2d 729 (11th Cir.1991).

State Courts:

Arkansas: Clarendon National Insurance Co. v. Roberts, 82 Ark. App. 515, 120 S.W.3d 141 (2003).

California: S. Kornreich & Sons, Inc. v. Genesis Insurance Co., 65 Cal. Rptr.2d 418 (Cal. App. 1997).

Connecticut: Ryiz v. Federal Insurance Co., 497 A.2d 1001 (Conn. App. 1985).

Florida: On-Site Fasteners and Construction Supplies, Inc. v. Mapfre Insurance Company of Florida, 82 So.3d 1001 (Fla. App. 2011).

Georgia: Southern Trust Insurance Co. v. Dr. T's Nature Products Co., 584 S.E.2d 34, 36 (Ga. App. 2003).

Louisiana: Stan-Blast Abrasives Co. v. Lexington Insurance Co., 532 So.2d 861 (La. App. 1988), *writ denied* 536 So.2d 1240 (La. 1989).

Michigan: Hanlon v. State Farm Fire & Casualty Co., 1999 WL 33444362 (Mich. App. May 14, 1999).

Missouri: McNaul v. Kansas Power & Light Co., 770 S.W.2d 259, 261–262 (Mo. App. 1989).

Montana: Federated Mutual Insurance Co. v. Anderson, 920 P.2d 97, 102 (Mont. 1996).

New York: Warnock Capital Corp. v. Hermitage Insurance Co., 21 A.D.3d 1091, 803 N.Y.S.2d 606 (N.Y. App. Div. 2005).

Oregon: Vanderzanden Brothers, Inc. v. Mutual of Enumclaw Insurance Co., 601 P.2d 889, 891–892 (Or. App. 1979);

Pennsylvania: Budtel Associates, LP v. Continental Casualty Co., 2006 WL 3718238 (Pa. Super. Dec. 19, 2006).

[28] *Id.*

[29] For further discussion, see § 4.03[2][d] *infra.*

[30] See, e.g.:

First Circuit: TIG Insurance Co. v. Wembley, USA, Inc., 75 Fed. Appx. 5 (1st Cir. 2003).

Sixth Circuit: Universal Image Productions, Inc. v. Chubb Corp., 2010 WL 1257770 (E.D. Mich. Mar. 29, 2010).

Tenth Circuit: Barnard v. Fireman's Fund Insurance Co., 996 F.2d 246 (10th Cir. 1993).

State Courts:

Arkansas: Clarendon National Insurance Co. v. Roberts, 82 Ark. App. 515, 120 S.W.3d 141 (2003).

California: S. Kornreich & Sons, Inc. v. Genesis Insurance Co., 65 Cal. Rptr.2d 418 (Cal. App. 1997).

Florida: On-Site Fasteners and Construction Supplies, Inc. v. Mapfre Insurance Company of Florida, 82 So.3d 1001 (Fla. App. 2011); Reliance Insurance Co. v. D'Amico, 528 So.2d 533 (Fla. App. 1988).

Montana: Federated Mutual Insurance Co. v. Anderson, 920 P.2d 97 (Mont. 1996).

New York: Warnock Capital Corp. v. Hermitage Insurance Co., 803 N.Y.S.2d 606 (N.Y. App. Div. 2005).

[31] See, e.g., Toll Naval Associates v. Lexington Insurance Co., 2005 WL 1923836, at *3 (E.D. Pa. Aug. 10, 2005).

[32] See, e.g.:

Third Circuit: Royal Insurance Company of America v. KSI Trading Corp., 563 F.3d 68 (3d Cir. 2009); Toll Naval Associates v. Lexington Insurance Co., 2005 WL 1923836, at *3 (E.D. Pa. Aug. 10, 2005) (finding term ambiguous).

Fourth Circuit: Millennium Inorganic Chemicals Ltd. v. National Union Fire Insurance Co. of Pittsburgh, PA, 893 F. Supp.2d 715 (D. Md. 2012).

Fifth Circuit: Premier Entertainment Biloxi, L.L.C. v. James River Insurance Co., 2007 WL 2908791 (S.D. Miss. Oct. 3, 2007); Dillard University v. Lexington Insurance Co., 466 F. Supp.2d 723 (E.D. La. 2006).

Seventh Circuit: Bulkmatic Transport Co. v. National Union Fire Insurance Co., 1993 WL 437435 (N.D. Ill. Oct. 27, 1993).

Eighth Circuit: TAMKO Building Products, Inc. v. Factual Mutual Insurance Co., 890 F. Supp.2d 1129 (E.D. Mo. 2012).

Tenth Circuit: Continental Materials Corp. v. Affiliated FM Insurance Co., 2012 WL 5430955 (D. Colo. Nov. 7, 2012).

State Courts:

New York: Capital Mercury Shirt Corp. v. Arkwright Mutual Insurance Co., 195 A.D.2d 320, 600 N.Y.S.2d 34 (1993) (defined as "damage to plaintiff's property located off its premises").

South Carolina: Republic Textile Equipment Co. of South Carolina, Inc. v. Aetna Insurance Co., 360 S.E.2d 540 (S.C. App. 1987).

Washington: Monson Fruit Co., Inc. v. Marsh Advantage America, 120 Wash. App. 1045, 2004 WL 440842 (Wash. App. May 11, 2004) (finding term ambiguous).

33 See § 4.03[2] *supra*.

34 See § 4.03[3][a] *infra*.

35 See § 4.03[3][b] *infra*.

36 See, e.g.:

Fifth Circuit: Flores v. Allstate Texas Lloyds Co., 278 F. Supp.2d 810 (S.D. Tex. 2003).

Seventh Circuit: Atlantic Mutual Insurance Cos. v. Lotz, 384 F. Supp.2d 1292 (E.D. Wis. 2005).

Ninth Circuit: Duarte and Witting, Inc. v. Universal Underwriters Insurance Co., 291 Fed. Appx. 807 (9th Cir. 2008); Association of Unit Owners of Nestani v. State Farm Fire and Casualty Co., 670 F. Supp.2d 1156 (D. Or. 2009); Sapiro v. Encompass Insurance Co., 221 F.R.D. 513, 518–519 (N.D. Cal. 2004).

Tenth Circuit: Empire Underground Storage, Inc. v. Protective National Insurance Co., 685 F. Supp. 1187 (D. Kan. 1988).

State Courts:

California: Prudential-LMI Commercial Insurance Co. v. Superior Court, 798 P.2d 1230 (Cal. 1990).

District of Columbia: Hartford Financial Services Group, Inc. v. Hand, 30 A.3d 180 (D.C. App. 2011).

Louisiana: Mangerchine v. Reaves, 63 So.3d 1049 (La. App. 2011).

Nevada: Jackson v. State Farm Fire & Casualty Co., 835 P.2d 786 (Nev. 1992).

New Jersey: Winding Hills Condominium Association v. North American Specialty Insurance Co., 752 A.2d 837 (N.J. Super. 2000).

Texas: Allstate Insurance Co. v. Hunter, 2007 WL 4126055 (Tex. App. Nov. 21, 2007); Closner v. State Farm Lloyds, 64 S.W.3d 51 (Tex. App. 2001).

37 See, e.g.:

Third Circuit: Port Authority v. Affiliated FM Insurance Co., 311 F.3d 226 (3d Cir. 2002); PECO Energy Co. v. Boden, 64 F.3d 852 (3d Cir. 1995).

State Courts:

Idaho: Melichar v. State Farm Fire and Casualty Co., 152 P.3d 587 (Idaho 2007).

New York: Catucci v. Greenwich Insurance Co., 830 N.Y.S.2d 281 (N.Y. App. Div. 2007).

North Carolina: Nelson v. Hartford Underwriters Insurance Co., 630 S.E.2d 221, 229 (N.C. App. 2006);

Texas: Central Mutual Insurance Co. v. KPE Firstplace Land, L.L.C., 271 S.W.3d 454 (Tex. App. 2008).

Washington: Ellis Court Apartments. L.P. *ex rel.* Woodside Corp. v. State Farm Fire & Casualty Co., 72 P.3d 1086 (Wash. App. 2003).

38 See, e.g.:

Second Circuit: United Technologies Corp. v. American Home Assurance Co., 989 F. Supp. 128 (D. Conn. 1997).

Seventh Circuit: Miller v. Safeco Insurance Company of America, 683 F.3d 805 (7th Cir. 2012).

State Courts:

Illinois: Board of Education v. International Insurance Co., 720 N.E.2d 622 (Ill. App. 1999), *appeal denied* 729 N.E.2d 494 (Ill. 2000).

Ohio: Polk v. Landings of Walden Condominium Ass'n, 2005 WL 1862126, at *8 (Ohio App. Aug. 5, 2005).

39 *Webster's Ninth New Collegiate Dictionary* at 358.

40 *Id.,* at 887.

41 *Id.,* at 706.

42 *Id.,* at 323.

43 See:

First Circuit: Gaffey v. Acadia Insurance Co., 453 F. Supp.2d 236 (D. Mass. 2006) (theft).

Second Circuit: Horowitz v. American International Group, Inc., 498 Fed. Appx. 51 (2d Cir. 2012) (theft); Fleet Business Credit L.L.C. v. Global Aerospace Underwriting Managers Ltd., 646 F. Supp.2d 473 (S.D.N.Y. 2009) (theft); *In re* Balfour MacLaine International Ltd., 85 F.3d 68 (2d Cir. 1996) (mysterious disappearance); Fleet Business Credit L.L.C. v. Global Aerospace Underwriting Managers Ltd., 646 F. Supp.2d 473 (S.D.N.Y. 2009) (theft); North American Foreign Trading Corp. v. Mitsui Sumitomo Insurance USA, Inc., 499 F. Supp.2d 361 (S.D.N.Y. 2007) (disappearance).

Third Circuit: Gatti v. Hanover Insurance Co., 601 F. Supp. 210, 211–212 (E.D. Pa.), *aff'd* 774 F.2d 1151 (3d Cir. 1985) (loss of water into ground).

Fourth Circuit: Star Diamond, Inc. v. Underwriters at Lloyd's, London, 965 F. Supp. 763 (E.D. Va. 1997) (disappearance).

Sixth Circuit: Retail Ventures, Inc. v. National Union Fire Insurance Co. of Pittsburgh, Pa., 691 F.3d 821 (6th Cir. 2012) (theft); Westfield Insurance Co. v. Radcliff Auto, L.L.C., 2009 WL 859843 (W.D. Ky. Mar. 30, 2009) (theft).

Seventh Circuit: Coleman Cable, Inc. v. Travelers Indemnity Co., 790 F. Supp.2d 742 (N.D. Ill. 2011) (theft).

Eighth Circuit: O'Daniel v. NAU Country Insurance Co., 427 F.3d 1058 (8th Cir. 2005) (theft).

Ninth Circuit: Gem East Corp. v. Jewelers Mutual Insurance Co., 207 Fed. Appx. 820 (9th Cir. 2006) (theft).

Tenth Circuit: Farmland Industries, Inc. v. National Union Fire Insurance Co., 333 F. Supp.2d 1133 (D. Kan. 2004) (mysterious disappearance); Empire Underground Storage, Inc. v. Protective Nat'l Insurance Co., 685 F. Supp. 1187 (D. Kan. 1988) (mysterious disappearance of propane).

Eleventh Circuit: Seagull Enterprises, L.L.C. v. Travelers Property Casualty Company of America, 366 Fed. Appx. 979 (11th Cir. 2010) (mysterious disappearance); St. Paul Fire and Marine Insurance Co. v. Luke Ready Air, L.L.C., 880 F. Supp.2d 1299 (S.D. Fla. 2012) (conversion).

State Courts:

California: American Alternative Insurance Corp. v. Superior Court, 135 Cal. App.4th 1239, 37 Cal. Rptr.3d 918 (2006) (government seizure).

Delaware: National Grange Mutual Insurance Co. v. Elegant Slumming, Inc., 59 A.3d 928 (Del. 2013) (accidental disposal).

Georgia: Those Certain Underwriters at Lloyds London v. DTI Logistics, Inc., 300 Ga. App. 715, 686 S.E.2d 333 (2009) (theft); Certain Underwriters at Lloyd's of London v. Rucker Construction, Inc., 648 S.E.2d 170 (Ga. App. 2007) (theft).

Kansas: Snider v. American Family Mutual Insurance Co., 214 P.3d 1226 (Kan App. 2009) (theft).

Kentucky: Reynolds v. Travelers Indemnity Co. of America, 233 S.W.3d 197 (Ky. App. 2007) (theft).

Massachusetts: Schiappa v. National Marine Underwriters, Inc., 56 Mass. App. 161, 775 N.E.2d 791 (2002) (mysterious disappearance).

Mississippi: Corban v. United Services Automobile Association, 20 So.3d 601 (Miss. 2009) (deprivation of property).

New York: WestCom Corp. v. Greater New York Mutual Insurance Co., 839 N.Y.S.2d 19 (N.Y. App. Div. 2007) (disappearance); Anjay Corp. v. Those Certain Underwriters at Lloyd's of London subscribing to Certificate Number HN01AAF4393, 822 N.Y.S.2d 249 (N.Y. App. Div. 2006) (theft); Woods v. General Accident Insurance Co., 292 A.D.2d 802, 738 N.Y.S.2d 791 (N.Y. App. Div. 2002) (theft); Simplexdiam, Inc. v. Brockbank, 283 A.D.2d 34, 727 N.Y.S.2d 64 (N.Y. App. Div. 2001) (mysterious disappearance).

Ohio: Mastellone v. Lightning Rod Mutual Insurance Co., 175 Ohio App.3d 23, 884 N.E.2d 1130 (2008) (loss of structural integrity).

Tennessee: HCA, Inc. v. American Protection Insurance Co., 174 S.W.3d 184 (Tenn. App. 2005) (disappearance).

[44] Port Authority v. Affiliated FM Insurance Co., 311 F.3d 226, 235 (3d Cir. 2002). See also:

Sixth Circuit: Universal Image Productions, Inc. v. Federal Insurance Co., 475 Fed. Appx. 569 (6th Cir. 2012).

Eleventh Circuit: Fireman's Fund Insurance Co. v. Tropical Shipping & Construction Co., 254 F.3d 987,1004 (11th Cir. 2001) ("under the plain language of these provisions, the . . . policy provided . . . coverage for physical damage to equipment . . . owned or leased from a third party, unless the property was specifically excluded or the damage was caused by an uninsured peril").

State Courts:

California: MRI Healthcare Center of Glendale, Inc. v. State Farm General Insurance Co., 187 Cal. App.4th 766, 115 Cal. Rptr.3d 27 (2010) (same).

[45] See, e.g., Crestview Country Club, Inc. v. St. Paul Guardian Insurance Co., 321 F. Supp.2d 260 (D. Mass. 2004). See also:

Second Circuit: Dalton v. Harleysville Worcester Mutual Insurance Co., 557 F.3d 88 (2d Cir. 2009) (collapse).

Fifth Circuit: Watson v. Allstate Texas Lloyd's, 224 Fed. Appx. 335 (5th Cir. 2007) (physical damage); Arias-Benn v. State Farm Fire and Casualty Insurance Co., 495 F.3d 228 (5th Cir. 2007) (loss of use from power failure caused by hurricane damaging off site power source not covered); Southern Surgery Center, L.L.C. v. Fidelity and Guaranty Insurance Co., 2008 WL 4549871 (S.D. Miss. Oct. 10, 2008) (loss of use from power failure caused by hurricane damaging power pole off of premises not covered).

Sixth Circuit: Universal Image Productions, Inc. v. Federal Insurance Co., 475 Fed. Appx. 569 (6th Cir. 2012); Southeast Mental Health Center, Inc. v. Pacific Insurance Co., 439 F. Supp.2d 831 (W.D. Tenn. 2006).

Eighth Circuit: Pentair, Inc. v. American Guarantee and Liability Insurance Co., 400 F.3d 613 (8th Cir. 2005) (loss of use or function not sufficient to trigger coverage).

Ninth Circuit: Abbey Co. v. Lexington Insurance Co., 289 Fed. Appx. 161 (9th Cir. 2008) (damage in the form of storm-caused debris in a canal was covered because it was physical damage, rather than an intangible loss of navigability, for a company that leased landing in marina served by canal).

State Courts:

California: MRI Healthcare Center of Glendale, Inc. v. State Farm General Insurance Co., 187 Cal. App.4th 766, 115 Cal. Rptr.3d 27 (2010) ("A direct physical loss contemplates an actual change in insured property then in a satisfactory state, occasioned by accident or other fortuitous event directly upon the property causing it to become unsatisfactory for future use or requiring that repairs be made to make it so.").

Louisiana: Landmark American Ins. Co. v. Gulf Coast Analytical Laboratories, Inc., 2012 WL 1094761 (M.D. La. Mar. 30, 2012).

Mississippi: Corban v. United Services Automobile Association, 20 So.3d 601 (Miss. 2009) (physical damage).

Ohio: Mastellone v. Lightning Rod Mutual Insurance Co., 175 Ohio App.3d 23, 884 N.E.2d 1130 (2008) ("physical" loss required harm to property affecting its structural integrity; staining of wood caused by mold was not a physical loss).

Texas: Lambrect and Associates, Inc. v. State Farm Lloyds, 119 S.W.3d 16 (Tex. App. 2003).

[46] See, e.g.:

Second Circuit: United Technologies Corp. v. American Home Assurance Co., 989 F. Supp. 128 (D. Conn. 1997).

Third Circuit: Port Authority of New York and New Jersey v. Affiliated FM Insurance Co., 311 F.3d 226 (3d Cir. 2002).

Sixth Circuit: Ports of Indiana v. Lexington Insurance Co., 2011 WL5523419 (S.D. Ind. Nov. 14, 2011).

Ninth Circuit: Prudential Property and Casualty Co. v. Lillard–Roberts, 2002 WL 31495830 (D. Or. June 18, 2002); Columbiaknit, Inc. v. Affiliated FM Insurance Co., 1999 WL 619100 (D. Or. Aug. 4, 1999).

State Courts:

Colorado: West Fire Insurance Co. v. First Presbyterian Church, 437 P.2d 52 (Colo. 1968).

New Jersey: Wakefern Food Corp. v. Liberty Mutual Fire Insurance Co., 406 N.J. Super. 524, 968 A.2d 724 (N.J. Super. App. Dept. 2009) (loss of functionality deemed "physical damage").

West Virginia: Murray v. State Farm Fire and Casualty Co., 509 S.E.2d 1 (W. Va. 1998).

[47] Port Authority v. Affiliated FM Insurance Co., 311 F.3d 226, 235 (3d Cir. 2002) (emphasis added).

[48] *Second Circuit:* Yale University v. Cigna Insurance Co., 224 F. Supp.2d 402 (D. Conn. 2002) (lead and asbestos contamination in university buildings was direct physical loss or damage).

State Courts:

Minnesota: Sentinel Management Co. v. New Hampshire Insurance Co., 563 N.W.2d 296 (Minn. App. 1997) (asbestos contamination in apartment buildings constitutes direct physical loss or damage even though there is no tangible injury to the structure).

[49] See Auten v. Employers National Insurance Co., 722 S.W.2d 468 (Tex. App. 1986), *writ denied* 749 S.W.2d 497 (Tex. 1988) (loss from exterminator's misapplication of pesticide rendering house uninhabitable was a direct physical loss or damage).

[50] See United Technologies Corp. v. American Home Assurance Co., 989 F. Supp. 128 (D. Conn. 1997) (environmental contamination and moneys expended to remediate the problem are direct physical loss or damage).

51 See:

Second Circuit: Farrell v. Royal Insurance Co. of America, 989 F. Supp. 159 (D. Conn. 1997) (pollution exclusion did not apply to preclude coverage for a heating oil spill and cleanup because the efficient proximate cause of the loss was the negligence of the heating oil delivery company in pumping product into the wrong tank).

State Courts:

Colorado: Western Fire Insurance Co. v. First Presbyterian Church, 437 P.2d 52 (Colo. 1968) (infiltration of gasoline into church rendering it unsafe and resulting in fire department's ordering the church closed was "direct physical loss").

Massachusetts: Jussim v. Massachusetts Bay Insurance Co., 610 N.E.2d 954 (Mass. 1993) (pollution exclusion inapplicable to environmental contamination and the cleanup associated therewith because efficient proximate cause of the loss was a third-party oil company's negligent delivery of 500 gallons of oil to a disconnected tank).

52 See:

Fourth Circuit: Cleveland Construction, Inc. v. Fireman's Fund Insurance Co., 819 F. Supp.2d 477 (W.D.N.C. 2011).

State Courts:

Washington: Graff v. Allstate Insurance Co., 113 Wash. App. 799, 54 P.3d 1266 (2002), *review denied* 70 P.3d 964 (Wash. 2003) (cleanup of chemical release associated with methamphetamine lab used by tenant in apartment was direct physical loss or damage to the landlord).

53 See:

Second Circuit: Yale University v. Cigna Insurance Co., 224 F. Supp.2d 402 (D. Conn. 2002) (lead and asbestos contamination in university buildings was direct physical loss or damage).

Fifth Circuit: Widder v. Louisiana Citizens Property Insurance Corp., 82 So.3d 294 (La. App. 2011).

54 See Matzner v. Seaco Insurance Co., 9 Mass. L. Rptr. 41, 1998 WL 566658 (Mass. Super. Aug. 12, 1998) (carbon monoxide contamination in an apartment building requiring evacuation of tenants was direct physical loss or damage to apartment building owner).

55 See, e.g., Wakefern Food Corp. v. Liberty Mutual Fire Insurance Co., 406 N.J. Super. 524, 968 A.2d 724 (2009).

56 See, e.g., Prudential Property and Casualty Co. v. Lillard–Roberts, 2002 WL 31495830 (D. Or. June 18, 2002); Columbiaknit, Inc. v. Affiliated FM Insurance Co., 1999 WL 619100 (D. Or. Aug. 4, 1999).

57 *Second Circuit:* Allianz Insurance Co. v. RJR Nabisco Holdings Corp., 96 F. Supp.2d 253 (S.D.N.Y. 2000) (recall of food contaminated with trimethyl benzene, a harmless chemical that caused strong odors and bad flavor in the food products was covered under "all risk" property insurance).

Fifth Circuit: Flores v. Allstate Texas Lloyd's Cos., 229 F. Supp.2d 697 (S.D. Tex. 2002).

Eighth Circuit: Pillsbury Co. v. Underwriters of Lloyd's, London, 705 F. Supp. 1396 (D. Minn. 1989) (destruction of canned corn that was deemed undercooked was direct physical loss or damage).

Ninth Circuit: American Guarantee & Liability Insurance Co. v. Ingram Micro, Inc., 2000 WL 726789, at *2 (D. Ariz. Apr. 18, 2000) (outage leading to erasure of electronic data and programming and disruption of computer system deemed direct physical loss or damage under first-party property policy; "The Court finds that 'physical damage' is not restricted to the physical destruction or harm of computer circuitry but includes loss of access, loss of use, and loss of functionality.").

Tenth Circuit: Nelson v. Safeco Insurance Co. of North America, 396 F. Supp.2d 1274 (D. Utah. 2005).

State Courts:

Minnesota: General Mills, Inc. v. Gold Medal Insurance Co., 622 N.W.2d 147 (Minn. App. 2001) (oats that were consumable but rendered unusable under FDA regulations as a result of application of unapproved pesticide were covered by first-party property policy).

New York: Pepsico, Inc. v. Winterthur International America Insurance Co., 24 A.D.3d 743, 806 N.Y.S.2d 709 (2005) (non-merchantability of the products, due to faulty ingredients supplied by third parties, that the products' function and value had been seriously impaired, such that they could not be sold; constitutes "physical damage" even if products were not rendered non-consumable).

[58] General Mills, Inc. v. Gold Medal Insurance Co., 622 N.W.2d 147, 152 (Minn. App. 2001).

> "General Mills was unable to sell its products or use the contaminated oats, because of legal regulations. The business of manufacturing food products requires conforming to the appropriate FDA regulations. Whether or not the oats could be safely consumed, they legally could not be used in General Mills' business. The district court did not err in finding this to be an impairment of function and value sufficient to support a finding of physical damage."

[59] *Webster's Ninth New Collegiate Dictionary* at 887.

[60] 10 *Couch on Insurance,* § 148:46. See also:

First Circuit: Crestview Country Club, Inc. v. St. Paul Guardian Insurance Co., 321 F. Supp.2d 260, 262 (D. Mass. 2004) (coverage for "direct physical loss or damage" to golf course grounds caused by wind or hail did not include cost of redesigning or modifying hole as result of loss of tree that had served as obstacle on hole because "physical" was to be given its plain meaning, which was "material," such that intangible loss in value of golf course because of change in hole's difficulty did not fit within meaning).

Second Circuit: City of Burlington v. Indemnity Insurance Co. of North America, 332 F.3d 38 (2d Cir.), *aff'd* 346 F.3d 70 (2d Cir. 2003) (failed welds covered; defective welds that had not failed yet were not covered).

State Courts:

Washington: Washington Mutual Bank v. Commonwealth Insurance Co., 2006 WL 1731318, at *3 (Wash. App. June 26, 2006) (erred engineering report claiming bank was in imminent danger of collapse did not establish coverage for direct "physical loss or damage").

[61] See, e.g., Pepsico, Inc. v. Winterthur International America Insurance Co., 24 A.D.3d 743, 806 N.Y.S.2d 709 (2005).

[62] See, e.g., General Mills, Inc. v. Gold Medal Insurance Co., 622 N.W.2d 147 (Minn. App. 2001).

[63] *Eighth Circuit:* Pillsbury Co. v. Underwriters of Lloyd's, London, 705 F. Supp. 1396 (D. Minn. 1989) (destruction of canned corn that was deemed undercooked was direct physical loss or damage).

Ninth Circuit: American Guarantee & Liability Insurance Co. v. Ingram Micro, Inc., 2000 WL 726789 (D. Ariz. Apr. 18, 2000) (outage leading to erasure of electronic data and programming and disruption of computer system deemed damage to covered "property" under first-party property policy).

[64] See:

Second Circuit: Yale University v. Cigna Insurance Co., 224 F. Supp.2d 402 (D. Conn. 2002); Allianz Insurance Co. v. RJR Nabisco Holdings Corp., 96 F. Supp.2d 253 (S.D.N.Y. 2000); Farrell v. Royal Insurance Co. of America, 989 F. Supp. 159 (D. Conn. 1997); United Technologies Corp. v. American Home Assurance Co., 989 F. Supp. 128 (D. Conn. 1997).

Eighth Circuit: Pillsbury Co. v. Underwriters of Lloyd's, London, 705 F. Supp. 1396 (D. Minn. 1989).

Ninth Circuit: American Guarantee & Liability Insurance Co. v. Ingram Micro, Inc., 2000 WL 726789, at *2 (D. Ariz. Apr. 18, 2000).

State Courts:

Colorado: Western Fire Insurance Co. v. First Presbyterian Church, 437 P.2d 52 (Colo. 1968).

Massachusetts: Jussim v. Massachusetts Bay Insurance Co., 610 N.E.2d 954 (Mass. 1993); Matzner v. Seaco Insurance Co., 9 Mass. L. Rptr. 41, 1998 WL 566658 (Mass. Super. Aug. 12, 1998).

Minnesota: General Mills, Inc. v. Gold Medal Insurance Co., 622 N.W.2d 147 (Minn. App. 2001); Sentinel Management Co. v. New Hampshire Insurance Co., 563 N.W.2d 296 (Minn. App. 1997) (asbestos contamination in apartment buildings constitutes direct physical loss or damage even though there is no tangible injury to the structure).

New York: Pepsico, Inc. v. Winterthur International America Insurance Co., 24 A.D.3d 743, 806 N.Y.S.2d 709 (2005).

Texas: Auten v. Employers National Insurance Co., 722 S.W.2d 468 (Tex. App. 1986), *writ denied* 749 S.W.2d 497 (Tex. 1988.

Washington: Graff v. Allstate Insurance Co., 54 P.3d 1266 (Wash. App. 2002), *review denied* 70 P.3d 964 (Wash. 2003).

65 10 *Couch on Insurance,* § 148:46. See also:

First Circuit: Crestview Country Club, Inc. v. St. Paul Guardian Insurance Co., 321 F. Supp.2d 260, 262 (D. Mass. 2004) (coverage for "direct physical loss or damage" to golf course grounds caused by wind or hail did not include cost of redesigning or modifying hole as result of loss of tree that had served as obstacle on hole because "physical" was to be given its plain meaning, which was "material," such that intangible loss in value of golf course because of change in hole's difficulty did not fit within meaning).

Second Circuit: City of Burlington v. Indemnity Insurance Co. of North America, 332 F.3d 38 (2d Cir.), *aff'd* 346 F.3d 70 (2d Cir. 2003) (failed welds covered; defective welds that had not failed yet were not covered).

State Courts:

Washington: Washington Mutual Bank v. Commonwealth Insurance Co., 2006 WL 1731318, at *3 (Wash. App. June 26, 2006) (erred engineering report claiming bank was in imminent danger of collapse did not establish coverage for direct "physical loss or damage").

66 American Guarantee & Liability Insurance Co. v. Ingram Micro, Inc., 2000 WL 726789 (D. Ariz. Apr. 18, 2000).

67 *Id.*

68 See America Online, Inc. v. St. Paul Mercury Insurance Co., 347 F.3d 89 (4th Cir. 2003).

69 See *Webster's Ninth New Collegiate Dictionary* at 1205, defining "tangible" as "capable of being perceived esp[ecially] by the sense of touch" and "perceptible."

70 See Ward General Insurance Services, Inc. v. Employers Fire Insurance Co., 114 Cal. App.4th 548, 7 Cal. Rptr.3d 844 (2003).

71 Ward General Insurance Services, Inc. v. Employers Fire Insurance Co., 114 Cal. App.4th 548, 7 Cal. Rptr.3d 844, 848 (2003).

72 See: Parks Real Estate Purchasing Group v. St. Paul Fire & Marine Insurance Co., 472 F.3d 33, 48 (2d Cir. 2006) ("[I]n order to obtain coverage under a first-party property insurance policy, the insured must suffer a loss caused by a covered peril (in a named perils policy) or suffer a loss not caused by an excluded peril (in an all risk policy)."); Omni Berkshire Corp. v. Wells Fargo Bank, N.A., 307 F. Supp.2d 534, 538 (S.D.N.Y. 2004).

See also:

First Circuit: Markel American Insurance Co. v. Pajam Fishing Corp., 691 F. Supp.2d 260 (D. Mass. 2010).

Second Circuit: Dalton v. Harleysville Worcester Mutual Insurance Co., 557 F.3d 88 (2d Cir. 2009); Fleet Business Credit, L.L.C. v. Global Aerospace Underwriting Managers Ltd., 812 F. Supp.2d 342 (S.D.N.Y. 2011).

Third Circuit: Intermetal Mexicana, S.A. v. Insurance Company of North America, 866 F.2d 71, 75 (3d Cir. 1989); Plaza 61 v. North River Insurance Co., 446 F. Supp. 1168 (M.D. Pa.), *aff'd without opinion* 588 F.2d 822 (3d Cir. 1978).

Fourth Circuit: Cleveland Construction, Inc. v. Fireman's Fund Insurance Co., 819 F. Supp.2d 477 (W.D.N.C. 2011); John S. Clark Co. v. United National Insurance Co., 304 F. Supp.2d 758 (M.D.N.C. 2004).

Fifth Circuit: In re Katrina Canal Breaches Litigation, 495 F.3d 191 (5th Cir. 2007); *In re* Chinese Manufactured Drywall Products Liability Litigation, 759 F. Supp.2d 822 (E.D. La. 2010); Dow Chemical Co. v. Royal Indemnity Co., 635 F.2d 379, 386 (5th Cir. 1981); Johnson v. ZC Sterling Insurance Agency, Inc., 2007 WL 4553981 (E.D. La. Dec. 20, 2007); Arctic Slope Regional Corp. v. Affiliated FM Insurance Co., 2007 WL 4545894 (W.D. La. Dec. 18, 2007).

Sixth Circuit: Universal Image Productions, Inc. v. Federal Insurance Co., 475 Fed. Appx. 569 (6th Cir. 2012); HoneyBaked Foods, Inc. v. Affiliated FM Insurance Co., 757 F. Supp.2d 738 (N.D. Ohio 2010); Universal Image Productions, Inc. v. Chubb Corp., 703 F. Supp.2d 705 (E.D. Mich. 2010); Southeast Mental Health Center, Inc. v. Pacific Insurance Co., 439 F. Supp.2d 831 (W.D. Tenn. 2006).

Seventh Circuit: Superior Aluminum Alloys, LLC v. U.S. Fire Insurance Co., 2007 WL 1850838 (N.D. Ind. June 25, 2007).

Eighth Circuit: Macheca Transport v. Philadelphia Indemnity Insurance Co., 649 F.3d 661 (8th Cir. 2011); Sonstegard Foods Co. v. Wellington Underwriting, Inc., 2007 WL 1501278 (D. Minn. May 21, 2007).

Ninth Circuit: Gerawan Farming Partners, Inc. v. Westchester Surplus Lines Insurance Co., 2008 WL 80711 (E.D. Cal. Jan. 4, 2008).

Tenth Circuit: Switzer v. State Farm Fire and Casualty Co., 2007 WL 841111 (W.D. Okla. Feb. 7, 2007).

Eleventh Circuit: Preis v. Lexington Insurance Co., 508 F. Supp.2d 1061 (S.D. Ala. 2007); Church of the Palms-Presbyterian (U.S.A.), Inc. v. Cincinnati Insurance Co., 404 F. Supp.2d 1339, 1341 (M.D. Fla. 2005), *aff'd* 189 Fed. Appx. 932 (11th Cir. 2006); Fireman's Fund Insurance Co. v. Tropical Shipping & Construction Co., 254 F.3d 987, 1005 (11th Cir. 2001).

State Courts:

Alabama: State Department of Insurance v. Arthur J. Gallagher & Co., 622 So.2d 370, 372 (Ala. Civ. 1993).

California: Villa Los Alamos Homeowners Ass'n v. State Farm General Insurance Co., 198 Cal. App.4th 522, 130 Cal. Rptr.3d 374 (2011); Freedman v. State Farm Insurance Co., 173 Cal. App.4th 957, 93 Cal. Rptr.3d 296 (2009); Julian v. Hartford Underwriters Insurance Co., 110 P.3d 903 (Cal. 2005); De Bruyn v. Superior Court, 70 Cal. Rptr.3d 652 (Cal. App. 2008); Fire Insurance Exchange v. Superior Court, 10 Cal. Rptr.3d 617, 632 n.13 (Cal. App. 2004).

Connecticut: Fetzer v. Safeco Insurance Co., 2007 WL 4634728 (Conn. Super. Dec. 7, 2007).

Delaware: Sullivan v. Standard Fire Insurance Co., 2008 WL 361141 (Del. Super. Feb. 11, 2008).

Florida: Fayad v. Clarendon National Insurance Co., 899 So.2d 1082 (Fla. 2005); Liebel v. Nationwide Insurance Company of Florida, 22 So.3d 111 (Fla. App. 2009); Fisher v. Certain Underwriters of Lloyds, 930 So.2d 756, 758 (Fla. Dist. App. 2006).

Indiana: Hartford Casualty Insurance Co. v. Evansville Vanderburgh Public Library, 860 N.E.2d 636 (Ind. App. 2007).

Mississippi: Corban v. United Services Automobile Association, 20 So.3d 601 (Miss. 2009).

Nebraska: Poulton v. State Farm Fire & Casualty Cos., 675 N.W.2d 665, 670 (Neb. 2004).

New York: Renaissance Art Investors, L.L.C. v. AXA Art Insurance Corp., 102 A.D.3d 604, 961 N.Y.S.2d 31 (N.Y. App. Div. 2013); U.S. Dredging Corp. v. Lexington Insurance Co., 99 A.D.3d 695, 952 N.Y.S.2d 60 (N.Y. App. Div. 2012); Travelers Indemnity Co. v. Zeff Design, 60 A.D.3d 453, 875 N.Y.S.2d 456 (N.Y. App. Div. 2009).

Pennsylvania: Miller v. Boston Insurance Co., 218 A.2d 275, 278 (Pa. 1966); Spece v. Erie Insurance Co., 850 A.2d 679, 683 (Pa. Super. 2004).

Tennessee: HCA, Inc. v. American Protection Insurance Co., 174 S.W.3d 184, 187 (Tenn. App. 2005).

Texas: ECF North Ridge Associates, L.P. v. ORIX Capital Markets, L.L.C., 336 S.W.3d 400 (Tex. App. 2011); SMI Realty Management Corp. v. Underwriters at Lloyd's, 179 S.W.3d 619 (Tex. App. 2005).

Washington: Vision One, L.L.C. v. Philadelphia Indemnity Insurance Co., 174 Wash.2d 501, 276 P.3d 300 (2012) (*en banc*); Certain Underwriters at Lloyd's London v. Travelers Property Casualty Co. of America, 161 Wash. App. 265, 256 P.3d 368 (2011); Northwest Bedding Co. v. National Fire Insurance Company of Hartford, 154 Wash. App. 787, 225 P.3d 484 (2010); Frank Coluccio Construction Co. v. King County, 150 P.3d 1147 (Wash. App. 2007).

73 See Cozen, *Insuring Real Property*, § 1.06[7][d] (2004). See also, General Accident Insurance Co. v. Unity/Waterford-Fair Oaks, Ltd., 2000 WL 33979484, at *2 (W.D. Tex. Dec. 15, 2000) ("all risk" policy covers all risks of physical loss except those specifically excluded).

74 *Second Circuit:* Federal Insurance Co. v. PGG Realty, L.L.C., 538 F. Supp.2d 680 (S.D.N.Y. 2008).

Fourth Circuit: National Casualty Co. v. Lockheed Martin Corp., 764 F. Supp.2d 756 (D. Md. 2011).

Seventh Circuit: Arkwright-Boston Manufacturers Mutual Insurance Co. v. Wausau Paper Mills Co., 818 F.2d 591 (7th Cir. 1987) (policyholder's employee negligence); Basler Turbo Conversions L.L.C. v. HCC Insurance Co., 601 F. Supp.2d 1082 (E.D. Wis. 2009).

Ninth Circuit: Berry v. Commercial Union Insurance Co., 87 F.3d 387 (9th Cir. 1996) (manufacturer's negligence was covered cause of loss).

Eleventh Circuit: Northern Assurance Co. of America v. C&G Boat Works, Inc., 2012 WL 1712594 (S.D. Ala. May 15, 2012).

State Courts:

Alaska: Baugh-Belarde Construction Co. v. College Utilities Corp., 561 P.2d 1211 (Alaska 1977) (policyholder negligence).

California: Premier Insurance Co. v. Welch, 189 Cal. Rptr. 657 (Cal. App. 1983) (policyholder negligence).

Illinois: Triple-X Chemical Labs, Inc. v. Great American Insurance Co., 370 N.E.2d 70 (Ill. App. 1977) (policyholder negligence).

Iowa: Connor v. Thompson Construction & Development Co., 166 N.W.2d 109 (Iowa 1969) (policyholder negligence).

Louisiana: Walker v. Travelers Indemnity Co., 289 So.2d 864 (La. App. 1974) (employee negligence).

Oregon: ABCD Vision, Inc. v. Fireman's Fund Insurance Cos., 734 P.2d 1376 (Or. App. 1987) (policyholder negligence).

New York: J. Aron & Co. v. Chown, 231 A.D.2d 426, 647 N.Y.S.2d 8, 9 (1996) ("'all risk' policy insures risk that policyholder's own negligence might contribute to the loss"); David Danzeisen Realty Corp. v. Continental Insurance Co., 170 A.D.2d 432, 565 N.Y.S.2d 223, 224 (1991) ("Mere negligence of an insured is not a defense to coverage under an 'all risk' policy.").

North Carolina: Avis v. Hartford Fire Insurance Co., 195 S.E.2d 545 (N.C. 1973) (policyholder negligence).

Virginia: Fidelity & Guaranty Insurance Underwriters, Inc. v. Allied Realty Co., 384 S.E.2d 613 (Va. 1989) (policyholder negligence).

However, some deliberate conduct or misconduct, which results in loss may not be deemed a fortuitous event beyond the policyholder's control and therefore not covered under an "all risk" policy. See New York State Electric & Gas v. Lexington Insurance Co., 204 A.D.2d 226, 612 N.Y.S.2d 43 (1994).

75 See Cozen, *Insuring Real Property*, § 2.02[3][a], at 2–26 (2004) ("With the advent of all-risk policy forms, the peril of collapse was automatically a covered risk unless specifically excluded."). See also:

First Circuit: Mulhern v. Philadelphia Indemnity Insurance Co., 802 F. Supp.2d 317 (D. Mass. 2011); Middlesex Mutual Assurance Co. v. Puerta De La Esperanza, L.L.C., 723 F. Supp.2d 294 (D. Mass. 2010).

Second Circuit: Dalton v. Harleysville Worcester Mutual Insurance Co., 557 F.3d 88 (2d Cir. 2009); Residential Management, Inc. v. Federal Insurance Co., 884 F. Supp.2d 3 (E.D.N.Y. 2012).

Third Circuit: Holiday Village East Home Owners Association v. QBE Insurance Corp., 830 F. Supp.2d 24 (D.N.J. 2011).

Fourth Circuit: Insurance Company of North America v. United States Gypsum Co., 678 F. Supp. 138 (W.D. Va. 1988), *aff'd* 870 F.2d 148 (4th Cir. 1989).

Sixth Circuit: Huntingdon Ridge Townhouse Homeowners Association, Inc. v. QBE Insurance Corp., 2009 WL 4060458 (M.D. Tenn. Nov. 20, 2009).

Eighth Circuit: KAAPA Ethanol, L.L.C. v. Affiliated FM Insurance Co., 660 F.3d 299 (8th Cir. 2011); Macheca Transport v. Philadelphia Indenity Insurance Co., 649 F.3d 661 (8th Cir. 2001); Council Tower Ass'n v. Axis Specialty Insurance Co., 630 F.3d 725 (8th Cir. 2011).

Ninth Circuit: Association of Unit Owners of Nestani v. State Farm Fire and Casualty Co., 670 F. Supp.2d 1156 (D. Or. 2009); Mabco Holdings, L.L.C. v. AMCO Insurance Co., 629 F. Supp.2d 1185 (D. Or. 2009).

Tenth Circuit: Texas Eastern Transmission Corp. v. Marine Office-Appleton & Cox Corp., 579 F.2d 561, 565–566 (10th Cir. 1978) (applying Okla. law).

Eleventh Circuit: Johnston v. Companion Property and Casualty Insurance Co., 318 Fed. Appx. 861 (11th Cir. 2009); Kelly v. Balboa Insurance Co., 897 F. Supp.2d 1262 (M.D. Fla. 2012); Mount Zion Baptist Church of Marietta v. GuideOne Elite Insurance Co., 808 F. Supp.2d 1322 (N.D. Ga. 2011).

State Courts:

Connecticut: Beach v. Middlesex Mutual Assurance Co., 532 A.2d 1297 (Conn. 1987) (coverage for collapse, which itself was caused by excluded peril, was contemplated by the policy).

Georgia: Lipsitz v. Fireman's Fund Insurance Co., 358 S.E.2d 624, 625 (Ga. App. 1987).

Illinois: Gulino v. Economy Fire and Casualty Co., 971 N.E.2d 522, 361 Ill. Dec. 420 (Ill. App.), *appeal denied* 979 N.E.2d 876 (Ill. 2012).

Kansas: Sterling College v. GuideOne Insurance Co., 2005 WL 742065 (Kan. App. Apr. 1, 2005) (policy covered collapse loss because of failure to specifically exclude loss caused by collapse, even though collapse itself was likely caused by excluded peril).

Massachusetts: Audubon Hill South Condominium Ass'n v. Community Ass'n Underwriters of America, Inc., 82 Mass. App. Ct. 461, 975 N.E.2d 458 (2012).

Missouri: Missouri Community Insurance Co. v. Employers Mutual Casualty Insurance Co., 680 S.W.2d 397 (Mo. App. 1984) (risk of collapse within contemplation of "all risk" policy).

New York: Viscosi v. Preferred Mutual Insurance Co., 87 A.D.3d 1307, 930 N.Y.S.2d 165 (N.Y. App. Div. 2011); Rapp B. Properties, L.L.C. v. RLI Insurance Co., 65 A.D.3d 923, 885 N.Y.S.2d 283 (2009).

Oregon: Ruede v. City of Florence, 231 Or. App. 435, 220 P.3d 113 (Or. App. 2009).

Pennsylvania: Betz v. Erie Insurance Exchange, 957 A.2d 1244 (Pa. Super. 2008).

South Dakota: Zoo Properties, L.L.P. v. Midwest Family Mutual Insurance Co., 797 N.W.2d 779 (S.D. 2011).

Washington: Vision One, L.L.C. v. Philadelphia Indemnity Insurance Co., 174 Wash.2d 501, 276 P.3d 300 (2012) (*en banc*).

However, "collapse" is often analyzed under the "direct physical loss or damage" issue instead of the "covered cause of loss" issue. See, e.g.:

California: Palub v. Hartford Underwriters Insurance Co., 92 Cal. App.4th 645, 112 Cal. Rptr.2d 270, 276 (2001) (collapse is not a cause of loss but damage for which coverage is sought).

Massachusetts: Driscoll v. Providence Mutual Fire Insurance Co., 69 Mass. App. Ct. 341, 867 N.E.2d 806 (2007).

Washington: Washington Mutual Bank v. Commonwealth Insurance Co., 2006 WL 1731318, at *3 (Wash. App. June 26, 2006) (erred engineering report claiming bank was in imminent danger of collapse did not establish coverage for direct "physical loss or damage").

76 See, e.g.:

First Circuit: Mulhern v. Philadelphia Indemnity Insurance Co., 802 F. Supp.2d 317 (D. Mass. 2011); Middlesex Mutual Assurance Co. v. Puerta De La Esperanza, L.L.C., 723 F. Supp.2d 294 (D. Mass. 2010).

Second Circuit: Residential Management, Inc. v. Federal Insurance Co., 884 F. Supp.2d 3 (E.D.N.Y. 2012).

Third Circuit: Holiday Village East Home Owners Ass'n v. QBE Insurance Corp., 830 F. Supp.2d 24 (D.N.J. 2011).

Ninth Circuit: Mabco Holdings, L.L.C. v. AMCO Insurance Co., 629 F. Supp.2d 1185 (D. Or. 2009).

Eleventh Circuit: Mount Zion Baptist Church of Marietta v. GuideOne Elite Insurance Co., 808 F. Supp.2d 1322 (N.D. Ga. 2011).

State Courts:

Illinois: Gulino v. Economy Fire and Casualty Co., 971 N.E.2d 522, 361 Ill. Dec. 420 (Ill. App.), appeal denied 979 N.E.2d 876 (Ill. 2012).

Massachusetts: Audubon Hill South Condominium Association v. Community Association Underwriters of America, Inc., 82 Mass. App. Ct. 461, 975 N.E.2d 458 (2012).

New York: Viscosi v. Preferred Mutual Insurance Co., 87 A.D.3d 1307, 930 N.Y.S.2d 165 (N.Y. App. Div. 2011).

[77] See, e.g.:

Eighth Circuit: KAAPA Ethanol, L.L.C. v. Affiliated FM Insurance Co., 660 F.3d 299 (8th Cir. 2011); Macheca Transport v. Philadelphia Indenity Insurance Co., 649 F.3d 661 (8th Cir. 2001); Council Tower Ass'n v. Axis Specialty Insurance Co., 630 F.3d 725 (8th Cir. 2011).

Eleventh Circuit: Kelly v. Balboa Insurance Co., 2012 WL 4761905 (M.D. Fla. May 29, 2012).

State Courts:

Florida: Kings Ridge Community Ass'n v. Sagamore Insurance Co., 98 So.3d 74 (Fla. App. 2012).

South Dakota: Zoo Properties, L.L.P. v. Midwest Family Mutual Insurance Co., 797 N.W.2d 779 (S.D. 2011).

[78] See Empire Steel Trading Co. v. New York Marine Managers, Inc., 1989 WL 105846 (S.D.N.Y. Sept. 1, 1989).

See also:

Second Circuit: Fleet Business Credit L.L.C. v. Global Aerospace Underwriting Managers Ltd., 646 F. Supp.2d 473 (S.D.N.Y. 2009) (theft); North American Foreign Trading Corp. v. Mitsui Sumitomo Insurance USA, Inc., 499 F. Supp.2d 361 (S.D.N.Y. 2007) ("all risk" policy covers mysterious disappearance absent an exclusion therefore).

Eleventh Circuit: Seagull Enterprises, L.L.C. v. Travelers Property Casualty Co. of America, 366 Fed. Appx. 979 (11th Cir. 2010).

State Courts:

Delaware: National Grange Mutual Insurance Co. v. Elegant Slumming, Inc., 59 A.3d 928 (Del. 2013).

New York: WestCom Corp. v. Greater New York Mutual Insurance Co., 41 A.D.3d 224, 839 N.Y.S.2d 19 (N.Y. App. Div. 2007).

[79] See, e.g., Peters Township School District v. Hartford Accident & Indemnity Co., 833 F.2d 32 (3d Cir. 1987) (cracking of building as a result of mine subsidence when earth under the school moved in a downward sinking and shifting fashion into mine voids covered under an "all risk" property policy).

However, as will be discussed, policies generally contain settling and other earth movement exclusions, meaning coverage under "all risk" policies for losses caused by settling and other forms of earth movement has been effectively eliminated. See § 4.03[4][a][ii][A] *infra*.

[80] See Cozen, *Insuring Real Property*, § 1.06[7][d] (2004). See also:

Second Circuit: Parks Real Estate Purchasing Group v. St. Paul Fire & Marine Insurance Co., 472 F.3d 33, 48 (2d Cir. 2006) ("[I]n order to obtain coverage under a first-party property insurance policy, the insured must suffer a loss caused by a covered peril (in a named perils policy) or suffer a loss not caused by an excluded peril (in an all risk policy).").

Third Circuit: Ercolani v. Excelsior Insurance Co., 830 F.2d 31, 35 (3d Cir. 1987).

Fifth Circuit: French v. Allstate Indemnity Co., 637 F.3d 571 (5th Cir. 2011).

Sixth Circuit: Yarnell v. Transamerica Life Insurance Co., 447 Fed. Appx. 664 (6th Cir. 2011).

Eleventh Circuit: Northern Assurance Co. of America v. C&G Boat Works, Inc., 2012 WL 1712594 (S.D. Ala. May 15, 2012).

State Courts:

Alabama: State Department of Insurance v. Arthur J. Gallagher & Co., 622 So.2d 370, 372 (Ala. Civ. App. 1993).

California: E.M.M.I. Inc. v. Zurich American Insurance Co., 32 Cal.4th 465, 84 P.3d 385, 9 Cal. Rptr.3d 701 (2004); Barnett v. State Farm General Insurance Co., 200 Cal. App.4th 536, 132 Cal. Rptr.3d 742 (2011); Fire Insurance Exchange v. Superior Court, 116 Cal. App.4th 446, 10 Cal. Rptr.3d 617, 632 n.13 (2004).

Florida: Fisher v. Certain Underwriters of Lloyds, 930 So.2d 756, 758 (Fla. Dist. App. 2006).

Mississippi: Robichaux v. Nationwide Mutual Fire Insurance Co., 81 So.3d 1030 (Miss. 2011).

Nebraska: Poulton v. State Farm Fire & Casualty Cos., 675 N.W.2d 665, 670 (Neb. 2004).

New Jersey: Grossberg v. Chubb Insurance Co. of New Jersey, 2012 WL 3553002 (N.J. Super. App. Div. Aug. 20, 2012).

Pennsylvania: Peerless Dying Co. v. Industrial Risk Insurers, 573 A.2d 541, 544 (Pa. Super. 1990), *alloc. denied* 592 A.2d 1303 (Pa. 1991).

Tennessee: HCA, Inc. v. American Protection Insurance Co., 174 S.W.3d 184, 187 (Tenn. App. 2005).

Washington: Vision One, L.L.C. v. Philadelphia Indemnity Insurance Co., 174 Wash.2d 501, 276 P.3d 300 (2012) (*en banc*).

81 See:

First Circuit: Markel American Insurance Co. v. Pajam Fishing Corp., 691 F. Supp.2d 260 (D. Mass. 2010).

Second Circuit: Dalton v. Harleysville Worcester Mutual Insurance Co., 557 F.3d 88 (2d Cir. 2009); Parks Real Estate Purchasing Group v. St. Paul Fire & Marine Insurance Co., 472 F.3d 33, 48 (2d Cir. 2006) ("[I]n order to obtain coverage under a first-party property insurance policy, the insured must suffer a loss caused by a covered peril (in a named perils policy) or suffer a loss not caused by an excluded peril (in an all risk policy).").

Third Circuit: Ercolani v. Excelsior Insurance Co., 830 F.2d 31, 35 (3d Cir. 1987).

Fifth Circuit: French v. Allstate Indemnity Co., 637 F.3d 571 (5th Cir. 2011); *In re* Katrina Canal Breaches Litigation, 495 F.3d 191 (5th Cir. 2007); Johnson v. ZC Sterling Insurance Agency, Inc., 2007 WL 4553981 (E.D. La. Dec. 20, 2007).

Sixth Circuit: Yarnell v. Transamerica Life Insurance Co., 447 Fed. Appx. 664 (6th Cir. 2011); Universal Image Productions, Inc. v. Chubb Corp., 703 F. Supp.2d 705 (E.D. Mich. 2010).

Ninth Circuit: Butler v. Clarendon America Insurance Co., 494 F. Supp.2d 1112 (N.D. Cal. 2007).

Tenth Circuit: Switzer v. State Farm Fire and Casualty Co., 2007 WL 841111 (W.D. Okla. Feb. 7, 2007).

Eleventh Circuit: Northern Assurance Co. of America v. C&G Boat Works, Inc., 2012 WL 1712594 (S.D. Ala. May 15, 2012); Preis v. Lexington Insurance Co., 508 F. Supp.2d 1061 (S.D. Ala. 2007).

State Courts:

Alabama: State Department of Insurance v. Arthur J. Gallagher & Co., 622 So.2d 370, 372 (Ala. Civ. App. 1993).

California: E.M.M.I. Inc. v. Zurich Am. Insurance Co., 32 Cal.4th 465, 84 P.3d 385 (2004); Barnett v. State Farm General Insurance Co., 200 Cal. App.4th 536, 132 Cal. Rptr.3d 742 (2011); Freedman v. State Farm Insurance Co., 173 Cal. App.4th 957, 93 Cal. Rptr.3d 296 (2009); De Bruyn v. Superior Court, 70 Cal. Rptr.3d 652 (Cal. App. 2008); Fire Insurance Exchange v. Superior Court, 10 Cal. Rptr.3d 617, 632 n.13 (Cal. App. 2004).

Connecticut: Fetzer v. Safeco Insurance Co., 2007 WL 4634728 (Conn. Super. Dec. 7, 2007) (all risk).

Delaware: Sullivan v. Standard Fire Insurance Co., 2008 WL 361141 (Del. Super. Feb. 11, 2008) (unpublished) (all risk as to dwelling and named peril as to personal property).

Florida: Liebel v. Nationwide Insurance Company of Florida, 22 So.3d 111 (Fla. App. 2009); Fisher v. Certain Underwriters of Lloyds, 930 So.2d 756, 758 (Fla. Dist. App. 2006).

Indiana: Hartford Casualty Insurance Co. v. Evansville Vanderburgh Public Library, 860 N.E.2d 636 (Ind. App. 2007).

Mississippi: Robichaux v. Nationwide Mutual Fire Insurance Co., 81 So.3d 1030 (Miss. 2011); Corban v. United Services Automobile Association, 20 So.3d 601 (Miss. 2009).

Nebraska: Poulton v. State Farm Fire & Casualty Cos., 675 N.W.2d 665, 670 (Neb. 2004); Lind v. Clay County Mutual Insurance Co., 2007 WL 442248 (Neb. App. Feb. 6, 2007).

New Jersey: Grossberg v. Chubb Insurance Co. of New Jersey, 2012 WL 3553002 (N.J. Super. App. Div. Aug. 20, 2012).

New York: Travelers Indemnity Co. v. Zeff Design, 60 A.D.3d 453, 875 N.Y.S.2d 456 (2009).

Pennsylvania: Peerless Dying Co. v. Industrial Risk Insurers, 573 A.2d 541, 544 (Pa. Super. 1990), *alloc. denied* 592 A.2d 1303 (Pa. 1991).

Tennessee: HCA, Inc. v. American Protection Insurance Co., 174 S.W.3d 184, 187 (Tenn. App. 2005).

Texas: Kelly v. Travelers Lloyds of Texas Insurance Co., 2007 WL 527911 (Tex. App. Feb. 22, 2007).

Vermont: Sperling v. Allstate Indemnity Co., 182 Vt. 521, 944 A.2d 210 (Vt. 2007).

Washington: Northwest Bedding Co. v. National Fire Insurance Company of Hartford, 154 Wash. App. 787, 225 P.3d 484 (2010); Frank Coluccio Construction Co. v. King County, 150 P.3d 1147 (Wash. App. 2007).

[82] *Id.*

[83] *Id.*

[84] See ISO Form CP 10 30 04 02.

[85] *Meriam-Webster's Online Dictionary,* available at http://www.m-w.com (last visited June 26, 2007).

[86] *Id.*

[87] *Id.*

[88] *Id.*

[89] See, e.g., ISO Form CP 10 30 04 02.

[90] See:

First Circuit: Espedito Realty, L.L.C. v. National Fire Insurance Co. of Hartford, 849 F. Supp.2d 179 (D. Mass. 2012) (exclusion inapplicable where floor sunk because of burst water pipe).

Second Circuit: Alamia v. Nationwide Mutual Fire Insurance Co., 495 F. Supp.2d 362 (S.D.N.Y. 2007) (settlement or erosion constitutes "earth movement").

Third Circuit: Peters Township School District v. Hartford Accident and Indemnity Co., 833 F.2d 32 (3d Cir. 1987); T.H.E. Insurance Co. v. Charles Boyer Children's Trust, 455 F. Supp.2d 284 (M.D. Pa. 2006); Totty v. Chubb Corp., 455 F. Supp.2d 376 (W.D. Pa. 2006).

Fourth Circuit: Great American Insurance Co. v. Rose Marie Bogley, 837 F. Supp.2d 570 (E.D. Va. 2011); Sentinel Associates v. American Manufacturers Mutual Insurance Co., 804 F. Supp. 815 (E.D. Va. 1992).

Tenth Circuit: Davis-Travis v. State Farm Fire and Casualty Co., 336 Fed. Appx. 770 (10th Cir. 2009); Winters v. Charter Oak Fire Insurance Co., 4 F. Supp.2d 1288 (D.N.M. 1998).

State Courts:

Alaska: West v. Umialik Insurance Co., 8 P.3d 1135 (Alaska 2000) (loss caused by erosion of soil from water leaking from broken plumbing not excluded).

Florida: Fayad v. Clarendon National Insurance Co., 899 So.2d 1082 (Fla. 2005) (exclusion inapplicable to loss caused by blasting).

Massachusetts: Kelley v. Iantosca, 78 Mass. App. Ct. 147, 935 N.E.2d 783 (2010).

Nevada: Powell v. Liberty Mutual Fire Insurance Co., 252 P.3d 668 (Nev. 2011).

New York: Wilner v. Allstate Insurance Co., 99 A.D.3d 700, 953 N.Y.S.2d 49 (N.Y. App. Div. 2012); Insurance Co. of Greater New York v. Clermont Armory, L.L.C., 84 A.D.3d 1168, 923 N.Y.S.2d 661 (N.Y. App. Div. 2011); 242–244 E. 77th Street, LLC v. Greater New York Mutual Insurance Co., 31 A.D.3d 100, 815 N.Y.S.2d 507 (2006) (limited applicability of exclusion to damage caused by natural phenomenon; damage from demolition work taking place on adjoining property not excluded).

Oregon: Ruede v. City of Florence, 231 Or. App. 435, 220 P.3d 113 (2009).

Tennessee: Rankin v. Generali-U.S. Branch, 986 S.W.2d 237 (Tenn. App. 1998) (exclusion inapplicable to damage caused by earth movement resulting from heavy machinery used nearby).

Texas: Dimotsis v. State Farm Lloyds, 5 S.W.3d 808 (Tex. App. 1999) (exclusion inapplicable to foundation damage caused by earth movement/cracking resulting from leakage from plumbing system).

West Virginia: Murray v. State Farm Fire & Casualty Insurance Co., 509 S.E.2d 1 (W. Va. 1998).

But see:

Second Circuit: Brice v. State Farm Fire and Casualty Co., 761 F. Supp.2d 96 (S.D.N.Y. 2010).

Tenth Circuit: Arkansas Valley Drilling, Inc. v. Continental Western Insurance Co., 703 F. Supp.2d 1232 (D. Colo. 2010).

State Courts:

Florida: Liebel v. Nationwide Insurance Co. of Florida, 22 So.3d 111 (Fla. App. 2009); State Farm Fire & Casualty Insurance Co. v. Castillo, 829 So.2d 242 (Fla. Dist. App. 2002), *review denied* 846 So.2d 1147 (Fla. 2003) (loss caused by earth movement resulting from blasting activities excluded).

Massachusetts: Audubon Hill South Condominium Ass'n v. Community Ass'n Underwriters of America, Inc., 82 Mass. App. Ct. 461, 975 N.E.2d 458 (2012).

Mississippi: Boteler v. State Farm Casualty Insurance Co., 876 So.2d 1067 (Miss. App. 2004) (exclusion applied to pipe leak or man-made cause of earth movement).

New York: Bentoria Holdings, Inc. v. Travelers Indemnity Co., 20 N.Y.3d 65, 980 N.E.2d 504, 956 N.Y.S.2d 456 (2012) (exclusion applied to natural and man-made events).

91 See:

First Circuit: Amherst Country Club, Inc. v. Harleysville Worcester Insurance Co., 561 F. Supp.2d 138 (D.N.H. 2008).

Second Circuit: Alamia v. Nationwide Mutual Fire Insurance Co., 495 F. Supp.2d 362 (S.D.N.Y. 2007).

Ninth Circuit: Federated Rural Electric Insurance Corp. v. Certain Underwriters at Lloyds, 293 Fed. Appx. 539 (9th Cir. 2008).

Tenth Circuit: Davis-Travis v. State Farm Fire and Casualty Co., 336 Fed. Appx. 770 (10th Cir. 2009); Arkansas Valley Drilling, Inc. v. Continental Western Insurance Co., 703 F. Supp.2d 1232 (D. Colo. 2010).

State Courts:

California: Roberts v. Assurance Co. of America, 163 Cal. App.4th 1398, 78 Cal. Rptr.3d 361 (2008).

Florida: Liebel v. Nationwide Insurance Co. of Florida, 22 So.3d 111 (Fla. App. 2009).

New York: Pioneer Tower Owners Ass'n v. State Farm Fire and Casualty Co., 12 N.Y.3d 302, 908 N.E.2d 875, 880 N.Y.S.2d 885 (2009).

Oregon: Ruede v. City of Florence, 231 Or. App. 435, 220 P.3d 113 (2009).

Tennessee: Walker v. Beasley, 2009 WL 4801480 (Tenn. App. Dec. 15, 2009).

[92] *Merriam-Webster's Online Dictionary* (available at www.m-w.com). See ISO Form CP 10 30 04 02. See also:

Second Circuit: Alamia v. Nationwide Mutual Fire Insurance Co., 495 F. Supp.2d 362 (S.D.N.Y. 2007) (settlement or erosion constitutes "earth movement").

Third Circuit: Totty v. Chubb Corp., 455 F. Supp.2d 376 (W.D. Pa. 2006) (earth movement exclusion inapplicable to damage resulting from earth movement caused by vibrations emanating from construction equipment).

Fifth Circuit: Eaker v. State Farm Fire & Casualty Insurance Co., 216 F. Supp.2d 606, 622 (S.D. Miss. 2001) (exclusion applied to damage caused by home's settlement); Rhoden v. State Farm Fire & Casualty Insurance Co., 32 F. Supp.2d 907, 913 (S.D. Miss. 1998), *aff'd* 200 F.3d 815 (5th Cir. 1999) (exclusion applied to loss caused by settlement regardless of whether settlement also resulted from builder's negligence or some other natural or external cause).

Ninth Circuit: Tacoma Electric Supply, Inc. v. Atlantic Mutual Insurance Co., 40 Fed. Appx. 567 (9th Cir. 2002) (damage caused by sinking of slab excluded by "earth movement" exclusion); Century Park East Homeowners Ass'n v. Northbrook Property & Casualty Insurance Co., 21 Fed. Appx. 708, 709 (9th Cir. 2001) ("earth movement" exclusion applied to damage caused by sinking of slab; "earth movement" includes all types of movement, both sudden and sluggish, and both natural and artificial); Schroeder v. State Farm Fire & Casualty Insurance Co., 770 F. Supp. 558 (D. Nev. 1991) (damage caused by settlement when broken water main saturated soil beneath was excluded by "earth movement" exclusion).

State Courts:

Louisiana: Nida v. State Farm Fire & Casualty Insurance Co., 454 So.2d 328 (La. App.), *writ denied* 458 So.2d 486 (La. 1984) ("earth movement" exclusion applied to bar coverage for loss caused by settlement, shrinking, and rising of the clay upon which the home was built).

Massachusetts: Driscoll v. Providence Mutual Fire Insurance Co., 867 N.E.2d 806 (Mass. App. 2007) (leaning outside walls, interior ceiling and wall cracks, and drop in roof resulting from snow and ice on roof did not involve "settling, cracking, shrinking, or expansion" excluded from coverage).

New York: Labate v. Liberty Mutual Insurance Co., 45 A.D.3d 811, 847 N.Y.S.2d 128 (2007) (damage resulting from cracking of walls and settling of and falling in of concrete basement floor excluded); Sheehan v. State Farm Fire & Casualty Insurance Co., 239 A.D.2d 486, 658 N.Y.S.2d 61 (1977) (damage caused by excessive sinking of concrete slab, even if the cause of such sinking was decomposition of organic material under the ground, was included within ambit of "earth movement" exclusion).

Utah: Village Inn Apartments v. State Farm Fire & Casualty Insurance Co., 790 P.2d 581 (Utah App. 1990) (damage caused by excessive settlement within "earth movement" exclusion).

[93] See, e.g., ISO Form CP 10 30 04 02.

[94] See Brazener, "Property Insurance: Construction and Effect of Provision Excluding Loss Caused By Earth Movement or Earthquake," 44 A.L.R.3d 1316, at n.2 (2004) (earth movement encompasses extraordinary settlement).

[95] *Fifth Circuit:* Eaker v. State Farm Fire & Casualty Insurance Co., 216 F. Supp.2d 606, 622 (S.D. Miss. 2001) (exclusion applied to damage caused by home's settlement); Rhoden v. State Farm Fire & Casualty Insurance Co., 32 F. Supp.2d 907, 913 (S.D. Miss. 1998), *aff'd* 200 F.3d 815 (5th Cir. 1999) (exclusion applied to loss caused by settlement regardless of whether settlement also resulted from builder's negligence or some other natural or external cause).

Ninth Circuit: Century Park East Homeowners Ass'n v. Northbrook Property & Casualty Insurance Co., 21 Fed. Appx. 708, 709 (9th Cir. 2001) ("earth movement" exclusion applied to damage caused by sinking of slab; "earth movement" includes all types of movement, both sudden and sluggish, and both natural and artificial); Schroeder v. State Farm Fire & Casualty Insurance Co., 770 F. Supp. 558 (D. Nev. 1991) (damage caused by settlement when broken water main saturated soil beneath was excluded by "earth movement" exclusion).

State Courts:

Louisiana: Nida v. State Farm Fire & Casualty Insurance Co., 454 So.2d 328 (La. App.), *writ denied* 458 So.2d 486 (La. 1984) ("earth movement" exclusion applied to bar coverage for loss caused by settlement, shrinking, and rising of the clay upon which the home was built).

New York: Sheehan v. State Farm Fire & Casualty Insurance Co., 239 A.D.2d 486, 658 N.Y.S.2d 61 (1977) (damage caused by excessive sinking of concrete slab, even if the cause of such sinking was decomposition of organic material under the ground, was included within ambit of "earth movement" exclusion).

Utah: Village Inn Apartments v. State Farm Fire & Casualty Insurance Co., 790 P.2d 581 (Utah App. 1990) (damage caused by excessive settlement within "earth movement" exclusion).

But see, Boston Company Real Estate Counsel, Inc. v. Home Insurance Co., 887 F. Supp. 369 (D. Mass. 1995) (loss caused by settling was not within "earth movement" exclusion).

[96] See § 4.03[4][b][ii][C] *infra*. See also:

Delaware: Olde Colonial Village Condominium Council v. Millers Mutual Insurance Co., 2002 WL 122885 (Del. Super. Jan. 28, 2002).

Florida: Nationwide Mutual Insurance Co. v. Bates, 840 So.2d 349 (Fla. App. 2003).

North Carolina: Erie Insurance Exchange v. Bledsoe, 540 S.E.2d 57 (N.C. App. 2000).

Pennsylvania: 401 Fourth Street, Inc. v. Investors Insurance Group, 879 A.2d 166 (Pa. 2005).

Tennessee: Walker v. Beasley, 2009 WL 4801480 (Tenn. App. Dec. 18, 2009).

[97] See, e.g., ISO Form CP 10 30 04 02.

[98] Some policies also exclude ensuing losses caused by faulty or defective work or materials. See:

First Circuit: Gargano v. Vigilant Insurance Co., 494 Fed. Appx. 98 (1st Cir. 2012).

Second Circuit: 1765 First Associates, L.L.C. v. Continental Casualty Co., 817 F. Supp.2d 374 (S.D.N.Y. 2011).

Fourth Circuit: TRAVCO Insurance Co. v. Ward, 715 F. Supp.2d 699 (E.D. Va. 2010) (ensuing loss not covered).

Fifth Circuit: Bishop v. Alfa Mutual Insurance Co., 796 F. Supp.2d 814 (S.D. Miss. 2011).

Sixth Circuit: TMW Enterprises, Inc. v. Federal Insurance Co., 619 F.3d 574 (6th Cir. 2010).

Eighth Circuit: Friedberg v. Chubb and Sons, Inc., 691 F.3d 948 (8th Cir. 2012); Michigan Millers Mutual Insurance Co. v. DG & G Co., 569 F.3d 807 (8th Cir. 2009).

Ninth Circuit: Terminal Freezers Inc. v. U.S. Fire Insurance, 345 Fed. Appx. 305 (9th Cir. 2009).

Tenth Circuit: Kesling v. American Family Mutual Insurance Co., 861 F. Supp.2d 1274 (D. Colo. 2012) (ensuing loss covered).

State Courts:

California: Freedman v. State Farm Insurance Co., 173 Cal. App.4th 957, 93 Cal. Rptr.3d 296 (2009); Roberts v. Assurance Co. of America, 163 Cal. App.4th 1398, 78 Cal. Rptr.3d 361 (Cal. App. 2008).

Florida: Kings Ridge Community Ass'n v. Sagamore Insurance Co., 98 So.3d 74 (Fla. App. 2012).

Louisiana: Ross v. C. Adams Construction and Design, L.L.C., 70 So.3d 949 (La. App. 2011).

Massachusetts: Driscoll v. Providence Mutual Fire Insurance Co., 69 Mass. App. Ct. 341, 867 N.E.2d 806 (2007).

Nevada: Fourth Street Place v. Travelers Indemnity Co., 270 P.3d 1235 (Nev. 2011).

Virginia: TravCo Insurance Co. v. Ward, 284 Va. 547, 736 S.E.2d 321 (2012) (ensuing loss not covered).

Washington: Vision One, L.L.C. v. Philadelphia Indemnity Insurance Co., 174 Wash.2d 501, 276 P.3d 300 (2012) (*en banc*) (ensuing loss covered); City of Oak Harbor v. St. Paul Mercury Insurance Co., 139 Wash. App. 68, 159 P.3d 422 (2007).

99 See, e.g., ISO Form CP 10 30 10 00.

100 *Third Circuit:* GTE Corp. v. Allendale Mutual Insurance Co., 372 F.3d 598 (3d Cir. 2004) (Y2K repairs excluded by latent defect or inherent vice exclusion because they resulted from defective design); St. Marys Area Water Authority v. St. Paul Fire and Marine Insurance Co., 472 F. Supp.2d 630 (M.D. Pa. 2007).

Fourth Circuit: Carney v. Assurance Company of America, 177 Fed. Appx. 282 (4th Cir. 2006) (loss caused by failure to properly stain wood excluded).

Sixth Circuit: Atlantic Mutual Insurance Cos. v. Lotz, 384 F. Supp.2d 1292 (E.D. Wis. 2005) (mold caused by faulty work on shower and plumbing excluded).

Eighth Circuit: Royal Insurance Co. v. Dumahel Broadcasting Entertainment, Inc., 170 Fed. Appx. 438 (8th Cir. 2006) ("workmanship" means process of producing something as well as the furnished product itself).

Ninth Circuit: Sapiro v. Encompass Insurance Co., 221 F.R.D. 513 (N.D. Cal. 2004) (damage caused by faulty construction excluded).

Tenth Circuit: Ash Grove Cement Co. v. Employers Insurance of Wausau, 513 F. Supp.2d 1200 (D. Kan. 2007), *vacated in part* 2008 WL 151239 (D. Kan. Jan. 15, 2008).

State Courts:

California: Butki v. United Services Automobile Ass'n, 274 Cal. Rptr. 909 (Cal. App. 1990) (cracking in slab caused by high level of sulfites in soil excluded by latent defect exclusion); Brodkin v. State Farm Fire & Casualty Co., 265 Cal. Rptr. 710 (Cal. App. 1989) (foundation damage resulting from corrosion in soil excluded by latent defect exclusion).

Indiana: Hartford Casualty Insurance Co. v. Evansville Vanderburgh Public Library, 860 N.E.2d 636 (Ind. App. 2007) (loss caused by contractor negligence excluded).

Massachusetts: Driscoll v. Providence Mutual Fire Insurance Co., 867 N.E.2d 806 (Mass. App. 2007) (coverage afforded for roof damage because it was caused jointly by excluded cause [faulty design] and by non-excluded cause [weight of snow and ice]).

Minnesota: Bloom v. Western National Mutual Insurance Co., 2006 WL 1806415 (Minn. App. July 3, 2006).

Montana: State v. Allendale Mutual Insurance Co., 154 P.3d 1233 (Mont. 2007) (Y2K field code in computer software was "faulty design" that excluded coverage for costs to prevent loss).

New York: Wider v. Heritage Maintenance, Inc., 827 N.Y.S.2d 837 (N.Y. Sup. 2007) (damage caused by maintenance worker's negligence excluded).

North Carolina: Magnolia Manufacturing of North Carolina, Inc. v. Erie Insurance Exchange, 639 S.E.2d 443 (N.C. 2007) (losses from collapse caused by faulty or inadequate maintenance or during construction were expressly excluded from coverage).

Ohio: Walker v. McKinnis, 2005 WL 1864144 (Ohio App. Aug. 8, 2005) (loss from basement flood caused by rainwater's penetration into basement from faulty geometry of roof and faulty gutter system excluded).

Washington: City of Oak Harbor v. St. Paul Mercury Insurance Co., 159 P.3d 422 (Wash. App. 2007) (coverage for damage to liner of wastewater treatment lagoon excluded by faulty workmanship exclusion).

But see, Ariston Airline & Catering Supply, Inc. v. Forbes, 511 A.2d 1278 (N.J. Super. 1986) (exclusion did not encompass design or construction defects: exclusion is ambiguous as applied to construction defects, because: (1) the term was undefined; (2) the dictionary definition of "latent"; (3) the use of other exclusions for other seemingly "latent" problems, such as earth movement, surface water, water below the surface, and settling, cracking, and shrinking; and (4) the failure to include standard exclusion for faulty workmanship or design defects found in other policies).

101 See Arnold v. Cincinnati Insurance Co., 688 N.W.2d 708 (Wis. App. 2004). See also:

First Circuit: Gargano v. Vigilant Insurance Co., 494 Fed. Appx. 98 (1st Cir. 2012).

Second Circuit: 1765 First Associates, L.L.C. v. Continental Casualty Co., 817 F. Supp.2d 374 (S.D.N.Y. 2011); Montefiore Medical Center v. American Protection Insurance Co., 226 F. Supp.2d 470 (S.D.N.Y. 2002).

Third Circuit: GTE Corp. v. Allendale Mutual Insurance Co., 372 F.3d 598 (3d Cir. 2004).

Fifth Circuit: Bishop v. Alfa Mutual Insurance Co., 796 F. Supp.2d 814 (S.D. Miss. 2011).

Seventh Circuit: Atlantic Mutual Insurance Cos. v. Lotz, 384 F. Supp.2d 1292 (E.D. Wis. 2005).

Eighth Circuit: Friedberg v. Chubb and Sons, Inc., 691 F.3d 948 (8th Cir. 2012).

Ninth Circuit: Continental Casualty Co. v. Landmark Hotels, LLC, 184 Fed. Appx. 649 (9th Cir. 2006); Costco Wholesale Corp. v. Commonwealth Insurance Co., 45 Fed. Appx. 646 (9th Cir. 2002).

Tenth Circuit: Kesling v. American Family Mutual Insurance Co., 861 F. Supp.2d 1274 (D. Colo. 2012).

State Courts:

Alabama: Phillips v. National Security Fire and Casualty Co., 59 So.3d 711 (Ala. App. 2010).

California: Acme Galvanizing Co. v. Fireman's Fund Insurance Co., 270 Cal. Rptr. 405 (Cal. App. 1990).

Florida: Kings Ridge Community Ass'n v. Sagamore Insurance Co., 98 So.3d 74 (Fla. App. 2012).

Louisiana: Ross v. C. Adams Construction and Design, L.L.C., 70 So.3d 949 (La. App. 2011).

Minnesota: Bloom v. Western National Mutual Insurance Co., 2006 WL 1806415 (Minn. App. July 3, 2006) (rot and mold damage to home caused by water infiltration resulting from faulty design and installation of windows was not covered under ensuing loss provision because damage was not "otherwise covered" as required by the policy's ensuing loss provision).

Nevada: Fourth Street Place v. Travelers Indemnity Co., 270 P.3d 1235 (Nev. 2011).

New Hampshire: Weeks v. Co-Operative Insurance Cos., 817 A.2d 292 (N.H. 2003).

Ohio: Schrock v. Feazel Roofing Co., 2003 WL 21652162 (Ohio App. July 9, 2003) (rot damage to house resulting from faulty roof repair was not covered as ensuing loss because rot was separately excluded).

Virginia: TravCo Insurance Co. v. Ward, 284 Va. 547, 736 S.E.2d 321 (2012) (ensuing loss not covered).

Washington: Vision One, L.L.C. v. Philadelphia Indemnity Insurance Co., 174 Wash.2d 501, 276 P.3d 300 (2012) (*en banc*).

102 *Id.*

103 See:

Second Circuit: Yale University v. Cigna Insurance Co., 224 F. Supp.2d 402 (D. Conn. 2002) (cost to clean up asbestos contamination released from faulty asbestos-containing building materials was ensuing loss not excluded by faulty material exclusion); United Technologies Corp. v. American Home Assurance Co., 989 F. Supp. 128 (D. Conn. 1997) (environmental contamination may be an ensuing loss not excluded by the wear and tear exclusion).

Eighth Circuit: Pillsbury Co. v. Underwriters of Lloyd's, London, 705 F. Supp. 1396 (D. Minn. 1989) (destruction of canned corn deemed undercooked is an ensuing loss that was caused by the defect and was thus not excluded by faulty workmanship exclusion).

State Courts:

Minnesota: Sentinel Management Co. v. New Hampshire Insurance Co., 563 N.W.2d 296 (Minn. App. 1997) (asbestos contamination was ensuing loss not excluded by wear and tear exclusion).

104 *Id.*

105 See, e.g.:

Fifth Circuit: Lopez v. Shelter Insurance Co., 833 F. Supp.2d 613 (S.D. Miss. 2011); Bishop v. Alfa Mutual Insurance Co., 796 F. Supp.2d 814 (S.D. Miss. 2011); *In re* Chinese Manufactured Drywall Products Liability Litigation, 759 F. Supp.2d 822 (E.D. La. 2010) (cases holding that contamination from defective drywall excluded).

State Courts:

Louisiana: Ross v. C. Adams Construction and Design, L.L.C., 70 So.3d 949 (La. App. 2011) (contamination from defective drywall excluded).

Virginia: TravCo Insurance Co. v. Ward, 736 S.E.2d 321 (Va. 2012) (contamination from defective drywall excluded).

106 Yale University v. Cigna Insurance Co., 224 F. Supp.2d 402 (D. Conn. 2002).

107 *Id.*, 224 F. Supp.2d at 418.

108 The pollution exclusion is in fact common in all types of policies and discussed more extensively in Chapter 8 *infra*. Other exclusions are discussed in Chapter 7 *infra*.

109 Yale University v. Cigna Insurance Co., 224 F. Supp.2d 402, 418 (D. Conn. 2002).

110 See discussion at § 4.03[4][b] *infra*.

111 See Berry v. Commercial Union Insurance Co., 87 F.3d 387, 392 (9th Cir. 1996); Allstate Insurance Co. v. Smith, 929 F.2d 447, 451 (9th Cir. 1991).

112 Berry v. Commercial Union Insurance Co., 87 F.3d 387 (9th Cir. 1996).

[113] *Id.*, 87 F.3d at 391–392. See also:

Second Circuit: Parks Real Estate Purchasing Group v. St. Paul Fire and Marine Insurance Co., 472 F.3d 33 (2d Cir. 2006) ("contamination" held ambiguous because it would allow contamination exclusion to be boundless and the parties should be allowed to introduce evidence of what was intended by the use of the term); Farrell v. Royal Insurance Company of America, 989 F. Supp. 159 (D. Conn. 1997) (pollution exclusion did not apply to preclude coverage for a heating oil spill and cleanup because the efficient proximate cause of the loss was the negligence of the heating oil delivery company in pumping product into the wrong tank).

Fourth Circuit: TRAVCO Insurance Co. v. Ward, 715 F. Supp.2d 699 (E.D. Va. 2010) (pollution from defective drywall not covered).

Fifth Circuit: Lopez v. Shelter Insurance Co., 833 F. Supp.2d 613 (S.D. Miss. 2011); Bishop v. Alfa Mutual Insurance Co., 796 F. Supp.2d 814 (S.D. Miss. 2011); *In re* Chinese Manufactured Drywall Products Liability Litigation, 759 F. Supp.2d 822 (E.D. La. 2010) (cases holding that contamination from defective drywall excluded).

Sixth Circuit: Whitt Machine, Inc. v. Essex Insurance Co., 377 Fed. Appx. 492, 2010 WL 1924709 (6th Cir. 2010) (pollution exclusion barred coverage for asbestos removal following a fire).

Eighth Circuit: Macheca Transport v. Philadelphia Indemnity Insurance Co., 649 F.3d 661 (8th Cir. 2011) (collapse of refrigerated warehouse that led to release of ammonia pipe was covered because weight of ice is a covered cause of loss and the pollution exclusion did not apply when release of pollutants was caused by any of the specified causes of loss).

Tenth Circuit: Gerdes v. American Family Mutual Insurance Co., 713 F. Supp.2d 1290 (D. Kan. 2010) (mercury contamination from house fire not covered).

Eleventh Circuit: Maxine Furs, Inc. v. Auto-Owners Insurance Co., 426 Fed.Appx. 687 (11th Cir. 2011) (costs for cleaning furs after they began to smell like curry due to sharing air-conditioning ducts with neighboring restaurant were excluded).

State Courts:

California: Villa Los Alamos Homeowners Ass'n v. State Farm General Insurance Co., 198 Cal. App.4th 522, 130 Cal. Rptr.3d 374 (2011) (pollution exclusion excluded coverage for asbestos remediation).

Massachusetts: Jussim v. Massachusetts Bay Insurance Co., 610 N.E.2d 954 (Mass. 1993) (pollution exclusion inapplicable to environmental contamination and the cleanup associated therewith because efficient proximate cause of the loss was a third party oil company's negligent delivery of 500 gallons of oil to a disconnected tank).

New York: White v. Rhodes, 34 A.D.3d 951, 823 N.Y.S.2d 786 (2006) (cleanup costs following oil contamination resulting from motorist's crashing into above-ground oil tank covered). Obviously, if the pollution results from an uncovered cause of loss, coverage therefore is more difficult to find. In addition, some courts come to different conclusions. See, e.g.:

Virginia: PBM Nutritionals, L.L.C. v. Lexington Insurance Co., 283 Va. 624, 724 S.E.2d 707 (2012) (contaminated baby formula resulting from defective manufacturing machine not excluded due to concurrent causation); TravCo Insurance Co. v. Ward, 284 Va. 547, 736 S.E.2d 321 (2012) (negligent installation of defective drywall resulting in release of sulfuric acid into the atmosphere was excluded).

Wisconsin: Hirschhorn v. Auto-Owners Insurance Co., 338 Wis.2d 761, 809 N.W.2d 529 (2012) (pollution exclusion barred coverage for house made uninhabitable by bat guano between siding and interior wall).

[114] See, e.g., Sentinel Management Co. v. New Hampshire Insurance Co., 563 N.W.2d 296 (Minn. App. 1997).

115 See, e.g.:

Ninth Circuit: Sierra Pacific Power Co. v. Hartford Steam Boiler Inspection and Insurance Co., 490 Fed. Appx. 871 (9th Cir. 2012).

State Courts:

California: Reichert v. State Farm General Insurance Co., 212 Cal. App.4th 1543, 152 Cal. Rptr.3d 6 (2012).

Louisiana: Estopinal v. Parish of St. Bernard, 32 So.3d 991 (La. App. 2010); Royal Cloud Nine, L.L.C. v. Lafayette Insurance Co., 987 So.2d 355 (La. App. 2008).

116 See, e.g.:

Second Circuit: Farrell v. Royal Insurance Company of America, 989 F. Supp. 159 (D. Conn. 1997) (law and ordinance exclusion applied to cost to remove inactive fuel tank because removal was required by ordinance and unrelated to fuel oil spill by delivery of fuel oil to wrong tank).

Third Circuit: Regents of Mercersburg College v. Republic Franklin Insurance Co., 458 F.3d 159 (3d Cir. 2006) (repairs to undamaged portions of premises not covered by law and ordinance coverage extension because law and ordinance came into play only once the owner decided to upgrade the facilities; however, to the extent the Americans with Disabilities Act regulated alterations to hall after lightning strike and fire, such alterations would be covered under the law and ordinance extension).

Fourth Circuit: John S. Clark Co., Inc. v. United National Insurance Co., 304 F. Supp.2d 758 (M.D.N.C. 2004) (law and ordinance clause covered loss occasioned by enforcement of building codes only if the loss was first covered by policy and did not operate to cover costs incurred by insured to correct defectively built project).

Eighth Circuit: Rias v. Safeco Insurance Company of America, 594 F. Supp.2d 1090 (E.D. Mo. 2009).

Ninth Circuit: Sierra Pacific Power Co. v. Hartford Steam Boiler Inspection and Insurance Co., 490 Fed. Appx. 871 (9th Cir. 2012).

Tenth Circuit: Trinity Baptist Church v. GuideOne Elite Insurance Co., 2009 WL 2972502 (W.D. Okla. Sept. 14, 2009).

State Courts:

California: Fire Insurance Exchange v. Superior Court, 10 Cal. Rptr.3d 617 (Cal. App. 2004) (law and ordinance exclusion inapplicable to increased costs of repair to buildings damaged by earthquake when such increased costs were caused by the need to conform to changes in the building codes).

Florida: Jossfolk v. United Property and Casualty Insurance Co., 110 So.3d 110 (Fla. App. 2013).

New Jersey: DEB Associates v. Greater New York Mutual Insurance Co., 970 A.2d 1074 (N.J. Super. App. Div. 2009).

New York: Seward Park Housing Corp. v. Greater New York Mutual Insurance Co., 43 A.D.3d 23, 836 N.Y.S.2d 99 (2007) (demolition of portion of garage by ordinance after other portion collapsed was covered by law and ordinance extension).

Washington: Certain Underwriters at Lloyd's London v. Travelers Property Casualty Co. of America, 161 Wash. App. 265, 256 P.3d 368 (2011); Commonwealth Insurance Company of America v. Grays Harbor County, 84 P.3d 304 (Wash. App. 2004) (earthquake policy covered safety upgrades if earthquake damage caused official to enforce such upgrades).

But see:

Fifth Circuit: Prytania Park Hotel v. General Star Indemnity Co., 896 F.Supp. 618 (E.D. La. 1995) (sprinkler system required by ordinance to be in place after restoration from fire loss not covered by virtue of exclusion).

State Courts:

Oklahoma: Spears v. Shelter Mutual Insurance Co., 73 P.3d 865 (Okla. 2003) (exclusion barred coverage for cost to rewire entire home to meet current construction codes after lightning strike damaged part of electrical system).

117 *Id.* Other cases are in accord, either focusing on the lack of governmental order (and thus the voluntary abatement) or the proximate cause of the loss. See:

Second Circuit: Farrell v. Royal Insurance Co., 989 F. Supp. 159 (D. Conn. 1997) (law and ordinance exclusion applied only where governmental order was issued, not to voluntary cleanup of oil spill).

Third Circuit: Townsends of Arkansas, Inc. v. Millers Mutual Insurance Co., 823 F. Supp. 233 (D. Del. 1993), *aff'd* 26 F.3d 123 (3d Cir. 1994) (heptachlor contamination to food resulted in food company's voluntary recall and destruction of the product in compliance with EPA regulations; law and ordinance exclusion not applicable because no governmental order).

Sixth Circuit: Henri's Food Products Co. v. Home Insurance Co., 474 F. Supp. 889 (E.D. Wis. 1979) (loss occasioned by edible goods in factory that were voluntarily destroyed under governmental regulations because they came in contact with a toxic chemical residue were not excluded by civil authority exclusion).

Eighth Circuit: Hampton Foods, Inc. v. Aetna Casualty & Surety Co., 787 F.2d 349, 353 (8th Cir. 1986) (property owner's loss resulted from weather damage to building and resulting evacuation, and condemnation decree did not cause or increase loss).

Tenth Circuit: MarkWest Hydrocarbon, Inc. v. Liberty Mutual Insurance Co., 558 F.3d 1184 (10th Cir. 2009).

State Courts:

Louisiana: Haas v. Audubon Indemnity Co., 722 So.2d 1022 (La. App. 1998) (exclusion for loss caused directly or indirectly by enforcement of any ordinance or law did not apply to cost of asbestos abatement necessitated by theft of pipes and subsequent flood when water was turned back on; vandalism, not enforcement of ordinance, caused damage to the buildings).

Montana: Farmers Union Mutual Insurance Co. v. Oakland, 825 P.2d 554, 556 (Mont. 1992) (physical damage to insured property was caused by fire and higher cost of debris removal due to asbestos regulations did not bring loss within exclusion for loss caused directly or indirectly by enforcement of ordinance).

Virginia: Fidelity & Guaranty Insurance Underwriters, Inc. v. Allied Realty Co., 384 S.E.2d 613, 617 (Va. 1989) (ordinance exclusion did not apply where earth pressure resulted in structural failure of warehouse, and property owner was forced to evacuate tenants before city condemned property).

118 Sentinel Management Co. v. New Hampshire Insurance Co., 563 N.W.2d 296 (Minn. App. 1997).

119 *Id.*, 563 N.W.2d at 302 (citations omitted) (emphasis added).

120 *Fifth Circuit:* Bayle v. Allstate Insurance Co., 615 F.3d 350 (5th Cir. 2010); Arctic Slope Regional Corp. v. Affiliated FM Insurance Co., 564 F.3d 707 (5th Cir. 2009); *In re* Katrina Canal Breaches Litigation, 495 F.3d 191 (5th Cir. 2007).

Eleventh Circuit: Preis v. Lexington Insurance Co., 508 F. Supp.2d 1061 (S.D. Ala. 2007).

State Courts:

Arkansas: Ebbing v. State Farm Fire & Casualty Co., 1 S.W.3d 459 (Ark. App. 1999).

Colorado: Kane v. Royal Insurance Co., 768 P.2d 678 (Colo. 1989) (overflow from dam); Bartlett v. Continental Divide Insurance Co., 697 P.2d 412 (Colo. App. 1984), *aff'd* 730 P.2d 308 (Colo. 1986) (dam failure).

Illinois: Wallis v. Country Mutual Insurance Co., 723 N.E.2d 376 (Ill. App.), *appeal denied* 731 N.E.2d 772 (Ill. 2000) (overflow from man-made water course that entered and damaged home).

Louisiana: Rosen v. United Services Automobile Ass'n, 104 So.3d 633 (La. App. 2012).

Mississippi: Robichaux v. Nationwide Mutual Fire Insurance Co., 81 So.3d 1030 (Miss. 2011).

New Hampshire: Bates v. Phenix Mutual Fire Insurance Co., 2008 WL 375221 (N.H. Feb. 13, 2008).

New York: Steve's Pier One, Inc. v. Insurance Co. of North America, 131 A.D.2d 834, 517 N.Y.S.2d 194 (1987) (overflow of water from Long Island Sound).

North Dakota: Western National Mutual Insurance Co. v. University of North Dakota, 643 N.W.2d 4, 9 (N.D. 2002) ("The plain, ordinary meaning of 'flood' is 'an overflowing of water on an area normally dry.'").

Texas: Valley Forge Insurance Co. v. Hicks, Thomas, & Lilienstern, LLP, 174 S.W.3d 254 (Tex. App. 2004) (overflow from bayou's banks resulting in water intrusion into basement); State Farm Lloyds v. Marchetti, 962 S.W.2d 58, 61 (Tex. App. 1997).

Washington: Northwest Bedding Co. v. National Fire Insurance Co. of Hartford, 225 P.3d 484 (Wash. App. 2010).

Wyoming: State Farm Fire & Casualty Co. v. Paulson, 756 P.2d 764 (Wyo. 1988) (flood constitutes a body of water overflowing or inundating land not usually covered with water).

121 See Ebbing v. State Farm Fire & Casualty Co., 1 S.W.3d 459 (Ark. App. 1999). See also:

New York: Rovelli v. Allstate Insurance Co., 38 A.D.3d 241, 831 N.Y.S.2d 150 (N.Y. App. Div. 2007). See also:

Massachusetts: Surabian Realty Co. v. NGM Insurance Co., 462 Mass. 715, 971 N.E.2d 268 (2012).

New York: Platek v. Town of Hamburg, 97 A.D.3d 1118, 948 N.Y.S.2d 797 (N.Y. App. Div. 2012); K.J.D.E. Corp. v. Hartford Fire Insurance Co., 89 A.D.3d 1531, 932 N.Y.S.2d 778 (N.Y. App. Div. 2011).

122 Selective Way Insurance Co. v. Litigation Technology, Inc., 606 S.E.2d 68, 70–71 (Ga. App. 2004).

123 *Third Circuit:* Gold v. State Farm Fire and Casualty Co., 880 F. Supp.2d 587 (E.D. Pa. 2012); T.H.E. Insurance Co. v. Charles Boyer Children's Trust, 455 F. Supp.2d 284 (M.D. Pa. 2006).

Fifth Circuit: Cali v. Republic Fire and Casualty Insurance Co., 2009 WL 5064469 (E.D. La. Dec. 16, 2009) (water damage from accumulated rainfall entering through brick holes excluded).

Sixth Circuit: Front Row Theatre, Inc. v. American Manufacturer's Mutual Insurance Cos., 18 F.3d 1343 (6th Cir. 1994).

Seventh Circuit: Atlantic Mutual Insurance Cos. v. Lotz, 384 F. Supp.2d 1292 (E.D. Wis. 2005).

Eleventh Circuit: Living Legends Retirement Center, Inc. v. Lexington Insurance Co., 208 Fed. Appx. 805 (11th Cir. 2006).

State Courts:

Arkansas: Ebbing v. State Farm Fire & Casualty Co., 1 S.W.3d 459 (Ark. App. 1999).

Colorado: Heller v. Fire Insurance Exchange, 800 P.2d 1006, 1008–1009 (Colo. 1990).

District of Columbia: Cameron v. United Services Automobile Ass'n Casualty Insurance Co., 733 A.2d 965 (D.C. App. 1999).

Florida: Florida Residential Property & Casualty Joint Underwriting Association v. Kron, 721 So.2d 825 (Fla. Dist. App. 1998).

Georgia: Selective Way Insurance Co. v. Litigation Technology, Inc., 606 S.E.2d 68 (Ga. App. 2004).

Illinois: Smith v. Union Auto. Indemnity Co., 752 N.E.2d 1261, 1267 (Ill. App. 2001), *appeal denied* 763 N.E.2d 778 (Ill. 2000).

Louisiana: Cochran v. Travelers Insurance Co., 606 So.2d 22, 24 (La. App. 1992).

Massachusetts: Surabian Realty Co. v. NGM Insurance Co., 462 Mass. 715, 971 N.E.2d 268 (2012).

Nebraska: Thorell v. Union Insurance Co., 492 N.W.2d 879 (Neb. 1992); Georgetowne Square v. United States Fiduciary & Guarantee Co., 523 N.W.2d 380, 384–385 (Neb. App. 1994).

New York: Casey v. General Accident Insurance Co., 178 A.D.2d 1001, 578 N.Y.S.2d 337, 338 (1991).

North Dakota: State *ex rel.* State Fire and Tornado Fund of North Dakota Insurance Department v. North Dakota State University, 694 N.W.2d 225 (N.D. 2005).

Ohio: Myers v. Encompass Indemnity Co., 863 N.E.2d 1083 (Ohio App. 2006).

Texas: Crocker v. American National General Insurance Co., 211 S.W.3d 928 (Tex. App. 2007); State Farm Lloyds v. Marchetti, 962 S.W.2d 58, 61 (Tex. App. 1997).

Wyoming: State Farm Fire & Casualty Co. v. Paulson, 756 P.2d 764, 768 (Wyo. 1988).

[124] See:

Third Circuit: T.H.E. Insurance Co. v. Charles Boyer Childrens Trust, 269 Fed. Appx. 220 (3d Cir. 2008); Gold v. State Farm Fire and Casualty Co., 880 F. Supp.2d 587 (E.D. Pa. 2012).

Fourth Circuit: Bao v. Liberty Mutual Fire Insurance Co., 535 F. Supp.2d 532 (D. Md. 2008).

Fifth Circuit: Cali v. Republic Fire and Casualty Insurance Co., 2009 WL 5064469 (E.D. La. Dec. 16, 2009).

State Courts:

Delaware: Brandywine Smyrna, Inc. v. Millennium Builders, L.L.C., 2010 WL 1380252 (Del. Super. New Castle Cnty. Apr. 8, 2010).

Louisiana: Cochran v. Travelers Insurance Co., 606 So.2d 22, 24 (La. App. 1992).

Michigan: Legal Services Plan of Eastern Michigan v. Citizens Insurance Co. of America, 2009 WL 1175514 (Mich. App. Apr. 30, 2009).

Washington: Northwest Bedding Co. v. National Fire Insurance Co. of Hartford, 225 P.3d 484 (Wash. App. 2010).

[125] See Ebbing v. State Farm Fire & Casualty Co., 1 S.W.3d 459 (Ark. App. 1999). See also:

Third Circuit: Gold v. State Farm Fire and Casualty Co., 880 F. Supp.2d 587 (E.D. Pa. 2012).

State Courts:

Massachusetts: Surabian Realty Co. v. NGM Insurance Co., 971 N.E.2d 268 (Mass. 2012); Boazova v. Safety Insurance Co., 968 N.E.2d 385 (Mass. 2012).

New York: Platek v. Town of Hamburg, 948 N.Y.S.2d 797 (N.Y. App. Div. 2012); K.J.D.E. Corp. v. Hartford Fire Insurance Co., 932 N.Y.S.2d 778 (N.Y. App. Div. 2011).

[126] See, e.g., Seacor Holdings, Inc. v. Commonwealth Insurance Co., 635 F.3d 675 (5th Cir. 2011). For further discussion on multiple causation issues, see §4.03[4][b], *infra.*

[127] *Fourth Circuit:* TRAVCO Ins. Co. v. Ward, 715 F. Supp.2d 699 (E.D. Va. 2010).

Fifth Circuit: Bishop v. Alfa Mutual Insurance Co., 796 F. Supp.2d 814 (S.D. Miss. 2011); *In re* Chinese Manufactured Drywall Products Liability Litigation, 759 F. Supp.2d 822 (E.D. La. 2010).

Sixth Circuit: Meridian Leasing, Inc. v. Associated Aviation Underwriters, Inc., 409 F.3d 342 (6th Cir. 2005).

Seventh Circuit: Atlantic Mutual Insurance Cos. v. Lotz, 384 F. Supp.2d 1292 (E.D. Wis. 2005) (mold damage from faulty work on shower excluded by "gradual deterioration" exclusion).

Ninth Circuit: Jardine v. Maryland Casualty Co., 823 F. Supp.2d 955 (N.D. Cal. 2011).

State Courts:

California: Alex R. Thomas, Inc. v. Mutual Service Casualty Insurance Co., 119 Cal. Rptr.2d 394, 399 (Cal. App. 2002) (deterioration means to make worse or become worse, to lower in quality or value, or to depreciate; damage to refrigeration's aluminum coils caused by chloride in refrigeration system excluded by gradual deterioration or corrosion exclusions); Brodkin v. State Farm Fire & Casualty Co., 265 Cal. Rptr. 710 (Cal. App. 1989) (deterioration refers to slow moving disintegration or corrosion of the insured material because of external forces; foundation damage from cow urine in the fill material excluded by "wear and tear" and "gradual deterioration" exclusions); Butki v. United Services Automobile Ass'n, 225 Cal.App.3d 464, 274 Cal. Rptr. 909 (1990) (cracking and slow deterioration of concrete slab caused by high level of sulfates in soil excluded by "wear and tear" and "gradual deterioration" exclusions); Murray v. State Farm Fire & Casualty Co., 268 Cal. Rptr. 33 (Cal. App. 1990) (damage caused by break in copper water pipe caused by corrosion from electrolysis excluded by "wear and tear" and "gradual deterioration" exclusions).

Indiana: Association Aviation Underwriters v. George Koch Sons, Inc., 712 N.E.2d 1071, 1076 (Ind. App. 1989) (wear and tear and deterioration exclusions inapplicable to damage from airplane crash because wear and tear/deterioration of engine that caused the crash resulted from negligent maintenance).

Louisiana: Ross v. C. Adams Construction and Design, L.L.C., 70 So.3d 949 (La. App. 2011) (contamination from defective drywall excluded).

Massachusetts: 529 East Broadway Condominium Trust v. Vermont Mutual Insurance Co., 73 Mass. App. Ct. 1121, 900 N.E.2d 913 (Mass. App. 2009).

New York: Garson Management Co., LLC v. Travelers Indemnity Co., 300 A.D.2d 538, 752 N.Y.S.2d 696 (2002) (costs to repair corrosion of structural steel beams excluded under deterioration or corrosion exclusion); Kent Centre Associates v. Greater New York Mutual Insurance Co., 139 A.D.2d 630, 527 N.Y.S.2d 269 (1988) (damage to retaining wall that had deteriorated over time excluded "wear and tear" or "gradual deterioration").

Oklahoma: Bank of Oklahoma, N.A. v. Continental Casualty Co., 849 P.2d 1091 (Okla. Civ. App. 1992) (damage from deterioration caused by lack of or inadequate maintenance is covered).

Virginia: TravCo Insurance Co. v. Ward, 284 Va. 547, 736 S.E.2d 321 (2012).

[128] See Empire Steel Trading Co. v. New York Marine Managers, Inc., 1989 WL 105846 (S.D.N.Y. Sept. 1, 1989). See also §4.03[4][a][i] *supra*.

[129] See:

First Circuit: Astoria Jewelry Manufacturing Co. v. N. Barquet, Inc., 291 F. Supp.2d 16 (D.P.R. 2003).

Second Circuit: Fleet Business Credit L.L.C. v. Global Aerospace Underwriting Managers Ltd., 646 F. Supp.2d 473 (S.D.N.Y. 2009); North American Foreign Trading Corp. v. Mitsui Sumitomo Insurance USA, Inc., 499 F. Supp.2d 361 (S.D.N.Y. 2007).

Sixth Circuit: C.T.S.C. Boston, Inc. v. Continental Insurance Co., 25 Fed. Appx. 320 (6th Cir. 2001).

Eighth Circuit: Sphere Drake Insurance PLC v. Trisko, 24 F. Supp.2d 985 (D. Minn. 1998).

Tenth Circuit: Farmland Industries, Inc. v. National Union Fire Insurance Co. of Pittsburgh, Pennsylvania, 333 F. Supp.2d 1133 (D. Kan. 2004).

Eleventh Circuit: Seagull Enterprises, L.L.C. v. Travelers Property Casualty Co. of America, 366 Fed. Appx. 979 (11th Cir. 2010).

State Courts:

Delaware: National Grange Mutual Insurance Co. v. Elegant Slumming, Inc., 59 A.3d 928 (Del. 2013) (accidental disposal).

Massachusetts: Schiappa v. National Marine Underwriters, Inc., 775 N.E.2d 791 (Mass. App. 2002) (good faith explanation of loss can avoid exclusion).

New York: WestCom Corp. v. Greater New York Mutual Insurance Co., 41 A.D.3d 224, 839 N.Y.S.2d 19 (2007); S. Bellara Diamond Corp. v. First Specialty Insurance Corp., 287 A.D.2d 368, 731 N.Y.S.2d 185 (2001) (surmised explanation as to loss of diamonds avoided application of exclusion).

Tennessee: HCA, Inc. v. American Protection Insurance Co., 174 S.W.3d 184 (Tenn. App. 2005) (purpose of inventory exclusion is to exclude losses proven solely by inventory records).

Texas: Betco Scaffolds Co. v. Houston United Casualty Insurance Co., 29 S.W.3d 341 (Tex. App. 2000) (exclusion applies where loss can be explained solely by reason of inventory).

130 *Id.*

131 *Seventh Circuit:* International Administrators, Inc. v. Life Insurance Company of North America, 753 F.2d 1373 (7th Cir. 1985).

Eleventh Circuit: In re Prime Commercial Corp., 187 B.R. 785, 803 (N.D. Ga. 1995).

State Courts:

Georgia: Tetrault v. Shelton, 347 S.E.2d 636 (Ga. App. 1986).

New York: Dano v. Royal Globe Insurance Co., 89 A.D.2d 817, 453 N.Y.S.2d 528 (1982), *aff'd* 464 N.Y.S.2d 741 (N.Y. 1983).

Texas: Moore & Associates v. Metropolitan Life Insurance Co., 604 S.W.2d 487 (Tex. App. 1980).

132 For example, Georgia statutes recognize a qualified privilege for either: (1) "[s]tatements made in good faith in the performance of a legal or moral private duty;" or (2) "[s]tatements made with good faith intent on the part of the speaker to protect his or her interest in a matter in which it is concerned." Ga. Code. Ann. § 51-5-7(2)-(3). A federal bankruptcy court has construed these statutory provisions to "presumably provide a privilege for reporting events believed to be covered by fidelity bonds." *In re* Prime Commercial Corp., 187 B.R. 785, 803 (N.D. Ga. 1995). See also, Tetrault v. Shelton, 347 S.E.2d 636 (Ga. App. 1986) (statement made in good faith to insurance agent with respect to possible claim for vandalism by former employee was conditionally privileged).

Other jurisdictions also provide for a limited privilege. See:

Seventh Circuit: International Administrators, Inc. v. Life Insurance Company of North America, 753 F.2d 1373 (7th Cir. 1985).

State Courts:

New York: Dano v. Royal Globe Insurance Co., 89 A.D.2d 817, 453 N.Y.S.2d 528 (1982), *aff'd* 464 N.Y.S.2d 741 (N.Y. 1983).

Texas: Moore & Associates v. Metropolitan Life Insurance Co., 604 S.W.2d 487 (Tex. App. 1980).

133 *Id.*

134 See, e.g.:

Second Circuit: Cweklinsky v. Mobil Chemical Co., 364 F.3d 68 (2d Cir, 2004).

State Courts:

Ohio: Davis v. Jacobs, 710 N.E.2d 1185 (Ohio App. 1998).

Washington: Caruso v. Local Union 690, 730 P.2d 1299 (Wash. 1987).

135 See ISO Forms CP 10 30 10 00; ISO Form CG-7219.

136 See discussion at § 4.03[4][a][ii][C] *supra*.

137 See discussion at § 4.03[4][b] *infra*.

138 See Berry v. Commercial Union Insurance Co., 87 F.3d 387, 392 (9th Cir. 1996); Allstate Insurance Co. v. Smith, 929 F.2d 447, 451 (9th Cir. 1991).

139 See:

Third Circuit: Kemmerer v. State Farm Insurance Co., 2004 WL 87017, at *2 (E.D. Pa. Jan. 19, 2004) ("If the leak from the powder room caused the mold infestation, that leak would fall within the peril [sudden and accidental discharge or overflow of water] outlined in the homeowner's insurance policy.").

Fifth Circuit: Salinas v. State Farm Lloyds, 267 Fed. Appx. 381 (5th Cir. 2008) (exclusion applied to real property, not personalty); Watson v. Allstate Texas Lloyd's, 224 Fed. Appx. 335 (5th Cir. 2007) (exclusion applied); Pierre v. Potomac Insurance Company of Illinois, 583 F. Supp.2d 806 (N.D. Tex. 2008) (exclusion applied).

Sixth Circuit: Eckstein v. Cincinnati Insurance Co., 618 F. Supp.2d 707 (W.D. Ky. 2007) (exclusion inapplicable).

Ninth Circuit: Sapiro v. Encompass Insurance Co., 221 F.R.D. 513 (N.D. Cal. 2004) (exclusion applied); Prudential Property & Casualty Insurance Co. v. Lillard-Roberts, 2002 WL 31495830, at *9–10 (D. Or. June 18, 2002) (in a named-perils policy, the "accidental discharge or overflow of water" peril provided for coverage of physical mold damage caused by a water leak).

Tenth Circuit: Kelly v. Farmers Insurance Co., 281 F. Supp.2d 1290 (W.D. Okla. 2003) (exclusion not applied).

Eleventh Circuit: Church of the Palms-Presbyterian (U.S.A.), Inc. v. Cincinnati Insurance Co., 404 F. Supp.2d 1339 (M.D. Fla. 2005) (exclusion applied).

State Courts:

Arizona: Liristis v. American Family Mutual Insurance Co., 61 P.3d 22, 25 (Ariz. App. 2002) (homeowner's policy did not exclude mold damage caused by a covered event).

California: Freedman v. State Farm Insurance Co., 173 Cal. App.4th 957, 93 Cal. Rptr.3d 296 (Cal. App. 2009) (loss excluded); De Bruyn v. Superior Court, 70 Cal. Rptr.3d 652 (Cal. App. 2008) (loss excluded).

Florida: Fisher v. Certain Underwriters of Lloyds, 930 So.2d 756 (Fla. Dist. App. 2006) (exclusion not applied).

Illinois: DeVore v. American Family Mutual Insurance Co., 383 Ill. App.3d 266, 891 N.E.2d 505, 322 Ill. Dec. 490 (2008) (loss excluded).

Iowa: Williams v. Pekin Insurance Co., 778 N.W.2d 218 (Iowa. App. 2009) (loss excluded).

Kentucky: Reynolds v. Travelers Indemnity Co. of America, 233 S.W.3d 197 (Ky. App. 2007) (exclusion inapplicable).

Louisiana: Morgan v. Auto Club Family Insurance Co., 899 So.2d 135 (La. App. 2005) (exclusion applied).

Michigan: Feinbloom v. American International Insurance Co., 2008 WL 1836563 (Mich. App. Apr. 24, 2008) (exclusion applied); Ortiz v. Allstate Insurance Co., 2006 WL 889378

(Mich. App. July 3, 2006) (exclusion applied); Hayley v. Allstate Insurance Co., 686 N.W.2d 273 (Mich. App. 2004), *appeal denied* 697 N.W.2d 155 (Mich. 2005) (exclusion applied).

Minnesota: Bloom v. Western National Mutual Insurance Co., 2006 WL 1806415 (Minn. App. July 3, 2006) (exclusion applied).

New Jersey: Chadwell v. New Jersey Manufacturers Insurance Co., 2011 WL 31353 (N.J. Super. App. Div. Jan. 6, 2011) (exclusion applied); Simonetti v. Selective Insurance Co., 859 A.2d 694 (N.J. Super. 2004) (mold loss covered).

New York: Siegel v. Chubb Corp., 33 A.D.3d 565, 825 N.Y.S.2d 441 (N.Y. App. Div. 2006) (exclusion applied for failure to attribute loss to a leak); Hritz v. Saco, 18 A.D.3d 377, 795 N.Y.S.2d 236 (2005) (exclusion applied).

Ohio: Polk v. Landings of Walden Condominium Association, 2005 WL 1862126 (Ohio App. Aug. 5, 2005) (exclusion applied).

Pennsylvania: Tatalovich v. Pennsylvania National Mutual Casualty Insurance Co., 2003 WL 22844173, at *1–2 (Pa. C.P. Oct. 10, 2003) (exclusion applied).

Texas: Fiess v. State Farm Lloyds, 202 S.W.3d 744 (Tex. 2006) (homeowners policy which excluded "loss caused by mold" did not provide coverage for mold stemming from small roof and window leaks); Justice v. State Farm Lloyds Insurance Co., 2008 WL 123857 (Tex. App. Jan. 15, 2008) (exclusion applied); Lundstrom v. United Services Automobile Association-CIC, 192 S.W.3d 78 (Tex. App. 2006) (exclusion applied); de Laurentis v. United Services Automobile Ass'n, 162 S.W.3d 714 (Tex. App. 2005) (mold damage covered); Keenan v. Wausau Lloyds Insurance Co., 1998 WL 652332, at *3 (Tex. App. Sept. 23, 1998) (named-perils policy covered cost for accessing defectively constructed plumbing lines after named peril caused damage to homeowner's property).

Wisconsin: Arnold v. Cincinnati Insurance Co., 688 N.W.2d 708 (Wis. App. 2004) (mold covered).

140 Houston Exploration Co. v. Wellington Underwriting Agencies, Ltd., 352 S.W.3d 462 (Tex. 2011).

141 See Stewart Enterprises, Inc. v. RSUI Indemnity Co., 614 F.3d 117 (5th Cir. 2010).

142 *Id.* See also, Fourth Street Place v. Travelers Indemnity Co., 270 P.3d 1235 (Nev. 2011).

143 See, e.g.: Berry v. Commercial Union Insurance Co., 87 F.3d 387, 392 (9th Cir. 1996); Allstate Insurance Co. v. Smith, 929 F.2d 447, 451 (9th Cir. 1991).

144 For further discussion, see § 4.03[4][b][i] *infra.*

145 For further discussion, see § 4.03[4][b][ii] *infra.*

146 For further discussion, see § 4.03[4][b][iii] *infra.*

147 See, e.g.:

Second Circuit: American National Fire Insurance Co. v. Mirasco, Inc., 249 F. Supp.2d 303, 325–326 (S.D.N.Y. 2003), *vacated in part* 144 Fed. Appx. 171 (2d Cir. 2005); ABI Asset Corp. v. Twin City Fire Insurance Co., 1997 WL 724568, at *2 (S.D.N.Y. Nov. 18, 1997).

Fifth Circuit: Lexington Insurance Co. v. Unity/Waterford-Fair Oaks, Ltd., 2002 WL 356756, at *2 (N.D. Tex. Mar. 5, 2002).

Sixth Circuit: Davidson Hotel Co. v. St. Paul Fire & Marine Insurance Co., 136 F. Supp.2d 901, 909 (W.D. Tenn. 2001) (discussing concurrent causation generally).

Ninth Circuit: Terminal Freezers Inc. v. U.S. Fire Insurance Co., 345 Fed. Appx. 305 (9th Cir. 2009); Ass'n of Apartment Owners of Imperial Plaza v. Fireman's Fund Insurance Co., 2013 WL 1442465 (D. Haw. Apr. 9, 2013).

Tenth Circuit: Estate of Pennington v. Wolfe, 262 F. Supp.2d 1254 (D. Kan. 2003).

State Courts:

Kansas: Newton v. Nicholas, 887 P.2d 1158 (Kan. App. 1995).

Mississippi: Corban v. United Services Automobile Association, 20 So.3d 601 (Miss. 2009).

New York: Continental Casualty Co. v. Rapid-American Corp., 609 N.E.2d 506, 513 (N.Y. 1993); Potoff v. Chubb Indemnity Insurance Co., 60 A.D.3d 477, 874 N.Y.S.2d 124 (2009); Reynolds v. Standard Fire Insurance Co., 221 A.D.2d 616, 634 N.Y.S.2d 163, 164 (1995); Casey v. General Accident Insurance Co., 178 A.D.2d 1001, 578 N.Y.S.2d 337, 338 (1991); Cooperative Fire Insurance Co. of Catskill, New York v. Vondrak, 346 N.Y.S.2d 965, 970 (N.Y. Sup. 1973).

Rhode Island: Textron, Inc. v. Aetna Casualty & Surety Co., 754 A.2d 742, 755 (R.I. 2000) ("Where contamination could occur in a variety of ways, only one of which is potentially excluded, [the insurance company] cannot meet the heavy burden of showing that the exclusion applies.").

148 See:

Second Circuit: Gelwan v. Vermont Mutual Insurance Co., 2013 WL 48951 (2d Cir. Jan. 14, 2013).

Sixth Circuit: Union Savings Bank v. Allstate Indemnity Co., 830 F. Supp.2d 623 (S.D. Ind. 2011).

Eighth Circuit: Friedberg v. Chubb and Sons, Inc., 691 F.3d 948 (8th Cir. 2012).

Ninth Circuit: Pioneer Chlor Alkali Co. v. National Union Fire Insurance Co., 863 F. Supp. 1226, 1230 (D. Nev. 1994) ("A majority of jurisdictions use the efficient proximate cause doctrine in adjudicating all risk insurance policies where a covered and a non-covered peril contribute to a loss.").

State Courts:

California: Brown v. Mid-Century Insurance Co., 215 Cal. App.4th 841, 156 Cal. Rptr.3d 56 (2013).

Louisiana: Rosen v. United Services Automobile Ass'n, 104 So.3d 633 (La. App. 2012).

Massachusetts: Standard Electric Supply Co. v. Norfolk & Dedham Mutual Fire Insurance Co., 307 N.E.2d 11 (Mass. App. 1973).

Oklahoma: National American Insurance Co. v. Gerlicher Co., 260 P.3d 1279 (Okla. Civ. App. 2011).

Washington: Vision One, L.L.C. v. Philadelphia Indemnity Insurance Co., 174 Wash.2d 501, 276 P.3d 300 (2012) (*en banc*); Villella v. Public Employees Mutual Insurance Co., 106 Wash.2d 806, 725 P.2d 957, 962 (1986) (*en banc*).

See also: Appleman, *5 Insurance Law and Practice,* § 3083 (1970); Couch, 18 *Cyclopedia of Insurance Law*, §§ 74:696–717 (2d ed. rev. 1983).

149 See, e.g.:

Second Circuit: Gelwan v. Vermont Mutual Insurance Co., 2013 WL 48951 (2d Cir. Jan. 14, 2013); Parks Real Estate Purchasing Group v. St. Paul Fire and Marine Insurance Co., 472 F.3d 33 (2d Cir. 2006).

Third Circuit: Cher-D, Inc. v. Great American Alliance Insurance Co., 2009 WL 943530 (E.D. Pa. Apr. 7, 2009); Zurich American Insurance Co. v. Keating Building Corp., 513 F. Supp.2d 55 (D.N.J. 2007); Younis Brothers & Co. v. CIGNA Worldwide Insurance Co., 899 F. Supp. 1385, 1394 (E.D. Pa. 1995), *aff'd* 91 F.3d 13 (3d Cir. 1996), *cert. denied* 519 U.S. 1077 (1997); New Market Investment Co. v. Fireman's Fund Insurance Co., 774 F. Supp. 909, 915 (E.D. Pa. 1991).

Fifth Circuit: Stewart Enterprises, Inc. v. RSUI Indemnity Co., 614 F.3d 117 (5th Cir. 2010); Tuepker v. State Farm Fire & Casualty Co., 507 F.3d 346 (5th Cir. 2007).

Sixth Circuit: Union Savings Bank v. Allstate Indemnity Co., 830 F. Supp.2d 623 (S.D. Ind. 2011).

Eighth Circuit: Friedberg v. Chubb and Sons, Inc., 691 F.3d 948 (8th Cir. 2012).

Ninth Circuit: Terminal Freezers Inc. v. U.S. Fire Insurance Co., 345 Fed. Appx. 305 (9th Cir. 2009); Berry v. Commercial Union Insurance Co., 87 F.3d 387, 392 (9th Cir. 1996); Loughney v. Allstate Insurance Co., 465 F. Supp.2d 1039 (S.D. Cal. 2006); Allstate Insurance Co. v. Smith, 929 F.2d 447, 451 (9th Cir. 1991).

Tenth Circuit: Ash Grove Cement Co. v. Employers Insurance of Wausau, 513 F. Supp.2d 1200 (D. Kan. 2007), *vacated in part* 2008 WL 151239 (D. Kan. Jan. 15, 2008).

Eleventh Circuit: Burgess v. Allstate Insurance Co., 334 F. Supp.2d 1351 (N.D. Ga. 2003).

State Courts:

Alabama: State Farm Fire & Casualty Co. v. Slade, 747 So.2d 293, 313 (Ala. 1999).

California: Brown v. Mid-Century Insurance Co., 215 Cal. App.4th 841, 156 Cal. Rptr.3d 56 (2013); De Bruyn v. Superior Court, 58 Cal. App.4th 1213, 70 Cal. Rptr.3d 652 (2008).

Florida: Fisher v. Certain Interested Underwriters at Lloyds Subscribing to Contract # 242/99, 930 So.2d 756 (Fla. App. 2006).

Indiana: Hartford Casualty Insurance Co. v. Evansville Vanderburgh Public Library, 860 N.E.2d 636 (Ind. App. 2007).

Kentucky: Reynolds v. Travelers Indemnity Co. of America, 233 S.W.3d 197 (Ky. App. 2007).

Louisiana: Rosen v. United Services Automobile Ass'n, 104 So.3d 633 (La. App. 2012); Landry v. Louisiana Citizens Property Insurance Co., 964 So.2d 463 (La. App. 2007).

New York: Potoff v. Chubb Indemnity Insurance Co., 60 A.D.3d 477, 874 N.Y.S.2d 124 (2009).

Oklahoma: National American Insurance Co. v. Gerlicher Co., 260 P.3d 1279 (Okla. Civ. App. 2011).

Pennsylvania: DiFabio v. Centaur Insurance Co., 531 A.2d 1141 (Pa. Super. 1997); Tatalovich v. Pennsylvania National Mutual Casualty Insurance Co., 2003 WL 22844173, at *1–2 (Pa. C.P. Oct. 10, 2003).

Texas: Warrilow v. Norrell, 791 S.W.2d 515, 527–528 (Tex. App. 1989); Fidelity Fire Insurance Co. v. Crow, 390 S.W.2d 788, 793–794 (Tex. App. 1965).

Washington: Vision One, L.L.C. v. Philadelphia Indemnity Insurance Co., 174 Wash.2d 501, 276 P.3d 300 (2012) (*en banc*).

150 See Pioneer Chlor Alkali Co. v. National Union Fire Insurance Co., 863 F. Supp. 1226, 1230 (D. Nev. 1994).

151 *Id.* (citations omitted).

152 See, e.g.:

Second Circuit: Gelwan v. Vermont Mutual Insurance Co., 2013 WL 48951 (2d Cir. Jan. 14, 2013).

Third Circuit: Younis Bros. & Co. v. CIGNA Worldwide Insurance Co., 899 F. Supp. 1385, 1394 (E.D. Pa. 1995), *aff'd* 91 F.3d 13 (3d Cir. 1996), *cert. denied* 519 U.S. 1077 (1997); New Market Investment Co. v. Fireman's Fund Insurance Co., 774 F. Supp. 909, 915 (E.D. Pa. 1991).

Sixth Circuit: Union Savings Bank v. Allstate Indemnity Co., 830 F. Supp.2d 623 (S.D. Ind. 2011).

Eighth Circuit: Friedberg v. Chubb and Sons, Inc., 691 F.3d 948 (8th Cir. 2012).

Ninth Circuit: Berry v. Commercial Union Insurance Co., 87 F.3d 387, 392 (9th Cir. 1996); Allstate Insurance Co. v. Smith, 929 F.2d 447, 451 (9th Cir. 1991).

State Courts:

Alabama: State Farm Fire & Casualty Co. v. Slade, 747 So.2d 293, 313 (Ala. 1999).

California: Brown v. Mid-Century Insurance Co., 215 Cal. App.4th 841, 156 Cal. Rptr.3d 56 (2013).

Louisiana: Rosen v. United Services Automobile Ass'n, 104 So.3d 633 (La. App. 2012).

Oklahoma: National American Insurance Co. v. Gerlicher Co., 260 P.3d 1279 (Okla. Civ. App. 2011).

Pennsylvania: DiFabio v. Centaur Insurance Co., 531 A.2d 1141 (Pa. Super. 1997); Tatalovich v. Pennsylvania Nat. Mutual Casualty Insurance Co., 2003 WL 22844173, at *1–2 (Pa. C.P. Oct. 10, 2003).

Texas: Warrilow v. Norrell, 791 S.W.2d 515, 527–528 (Tex. App. 1989); Fidelity Fire Insurance Co. v. Crow, 390 S.W.2d 788, 793–794 (Tex. App. 1965).

Washington: Vision One, L.L.C. v. Philadelphia Indemnity Insurance Co., 174 Wash.2d 501, 276 P.3d 300 (2012) (*en banc*).

153 *Id.*

154 *Fifth Circuit:* GBP Partners, Ltd. v. Maryland Casualty Co., 2013 WL 57905 (5th Cir. Jan. 4, 2013); Styron v. State Farm Fire and Casualty Co., 479 Fed. Appx. 604 (5th Cir. 2012); Seacor Holdings, Inc. v. Commonwealth Insurance Co., 635 F.3d 675 (5th Cir. 2011); ARM Properties Management Group v. RSUI Indemnity Co., 400 Fed. Appx. 938 (5th Cir. 2010); Bayle v. Allstate Insurance Co., 615 F.3d 350 (5th Cir. 2010); Smith v. Allstate Indemnity Co., 2007 WL 4259194 (5th Cir. Dec. 4, 2007); Tuepker v. State Farm Fire & Casualty Co., 507 F.3d 346 (5th Cir. 2007); Leonard v. Nationwide Mutual Insurance Co., 499 F.3d 419 (5th Cir. 2007); *In re* Katrina Canal Breaches Litigation, 495 F.3d 191 (5th Cir. 2007); Great American Insurance Co. of New York v. Lowry Development, LLC, 524 F. Supp.2d 778 (S.D. Miss. 2007); Buente v. Allstate Insurance Co., 422 F. Supp.2d 690 (S.D. Miss. 2006).

Eleventh Circuit: Preis v. Lexington Insurance Co., 508 F. Supp.2d 1061 (S.D. Ala. 2007).

State Courts:

Alabama: Western Assurance Co. v. Hann, 78 So. 232, 236 (Ala. 1917).

California: MRI Healthcare Center of Glendale, Inc. v. State Farm General Insurance Co., 187 Cal. App.4th 766, 115 Cal. Rptr.3d 27 (2010).

Florida: Citizens Property Insurance Corp. v. Ueberschaer, 956 So.2d 483 (Fla. App. 2007).

Louisiana: Roach-Strayhan-Holland Post No. 20, American Legion Club, Inc. v. Continental Insurance Co., 112 So.2d 680, 683 (La. 1959); Rosen v. United Services Automobile Ass'n, 104 So.3d 633 (La. App. 2012); Young v. United States Automotive Association Casualty Co., 15 So.3d 327 (La. App. 2009); Landry v. Louisiana Citizens Property Insurance Co., 964 So.2d 463 (La. App. 2007).

Mississippi: Robichaux v. Nationwide Mutual Fire Insurance Co., 81 So.3d 1030 (Miss. 2011); Corban v. United Services Automobile Association, 20 So.3d 601 (Miss. 2009); Glens Falls Insurance Co. v. Linwood Elevator, 130 So.2d 262, 270 (Miss. 1961); Evana Plantation, Inc. v. Yorkshire Insurance Co., 58 So.2d 797, 798 (Miss. 1952); Chevis v. Mississippi Farm Bureau Mutual Insurance Co., 76 So.3d 187 (Miss. App. 2011).

155 *Id.*

156 *Id.*

157 See Buente v. Allstate Insurance Co., 422 F. Supp.2d 690 (S.D. Miss. 2006).

158 See § 4.03[4][a][i][A] *supra*.

159 See:

First Circuit: Farrell v. Royal Insurance Co. of America, 989 F. Supp. 159 (D. Conn. 1997).

Sixth Circuit: Essex House v. St. Paul Fire and Marine Insurance Co., 404 F. Supp. 978 (S.D. Ohio 1975).

160 See:

Seventh Circuit: Arkwright-Boston Manufacturers Mutual Insurance Co. v. Wausau Paper Mills Co., 818 F.2d 591 (7th Cir. 1987) (policyholder's employee negligence); Basler Turbo Conversions L.L.C. v. HCC Insurance Co., 601 F. Supp.2d 1082 (E.D. Wis. 2009).

Eighth Circuit: Fireman's Fund v. Structural Systems Technology, Inc., 426 F. Supp.2d 1009 (D. Neb. 2006).

Ninth Circuit: Berry v. Commercial Union Insurance Co., 87 F.3d 387, 392 (9th Cir. 1996); Allstate Insurance Co. v. Smith, 929 F.2d 447, 451 (9th Cir. 1991).

State Courts:

Alaska: Baugh-Belarde Construction Co. v. College Utilities Corp., 561 P.2d 1211 (Alaska 1977) (policyholder negligence).

California: Premier Insurance Co. v. Welch, 189 Cal. Rptr. 657 (Cal. App. 1983) (policyholder negligence).

Illinois: Triple-X Chemical Laboratories, Inc. v. Great American Insurance Co., 370 N.E.2d 70 (Ill. App. 1977) (policyholder negligence).

Iowa: Connor v. Thompson Construction & Development Co., 166 N.W.2d 109 (Iowa 1969) (policyholder negligence).

Louisiana: Walker v. Travelers Indemnity Co., 289 So.2d 864 (La. App. 1974) (employee negligence).

Massachusetts: Chow v. Merrimack Mutual Fire Insurance Co., 83 Mass. App. Ct. 622, 987 N.E.2d 1275 (2013).

New York: J. Aron & Co. v. Chown, 231 A.D.2d 426, 647 N.Y.S.2d 8, 9 (1996) ("'all risk' policy insures risk that policyholder's own negligence might contribute to the loss"); David Danzeisen Realty Corp. v. Continental Insurance Co., 170 A.D.2d 432, 565 N.Y.S.2d 223, 224 (1991) ("mere negligence of an insured is not a defense to coverage under an 'all risk' policy").

North Carolina: Avis v. Hartford Fire Insurance Co., 195 S.E.2d 545 (N.C. 1973) (policyholder negligence).

Oregon: ABCD . . . Vision, Inc. v. Fireman's Fund Insurance Cos., 734 P.2d 1376 (Or. App. 1987), *rev'd in part* 744 P.2d 998 (Or. 1987) (policyholder negligence).

Virginia: Fidelity & Guaranty Insurance Underwriters, Inc. v. Allied Realty Co., 384 S.E.2d 613 (Va. 1989) (policyholder negligence).

161 See:

First Circuit: Farrell v. Royal Insurance Company of America, 989 F. Supp. 159 (D. Conn. 1997) (pollution exclusion did not apply to preclude coverage for a heating oil spill and cleanup because the efficient proximate cause of the loss was the negligence of the heating oil delivery company in pumping product into the wrong tank).

Sixth Circuit: Essex House v. St. Paul Fire & Marine Insurance Co., 404 F. Supp. 978 (S.D. Ohio 1975) (builder's negligence in failing to provide proper drainage).

Eighth Circuit: Fireman's Fund v. Structural Systems Technology, Inc., 426 F. Supp.2d 1009 (D. Neb. 2006).

Ninth Circuit: Berry v. Commercial Union Insurance Co., 87 F.3d 387 (9th Cir. 1996) (fungicide's manufacturer's negligence was proximate efficient cause of loss due to corrosion that occurred as a result of flushing aluminum irrigation pipes with fungicide); Loughney v. Allstate Insurance Co., 465 F. Supp.2d 1039 (S.D. Cal. 2006).

State Courts:

California: Garvey v. State Farm Fire & Casualty Co., 257 Cal. Rptr. 292 (Cal. 1989) (negligence of builder was efficient proximate cause of damage to foundation); Sabella v. Wisler, 27 Cal. Rptr. 689 (Cal. 1963) (negligence of builder was efficient proximate cause of damage to house caused by mudslide); Century Surety Co. v. Polisso, 43 Cal. Rptr.3d 468, 491–492 (Cal. App. 2006) (glass damaged from negligence of contractor who attempted to remove film off of glass caused by flood not excluded because negligence, not flood, was efficient proximate cause of loss); Premier Insurance Co. v. Welch, 189 Cal. Rptr. 657 (Cal. App. 1983) (negligence of builder was efficient proximate cause where damage to policyholder's house was caused by heavy rains).

Illinois: Mattis v. State Farm Fire & Casualty Co., 454 N.E.2d 1156 (Ill. App. 1983).

Indiana: Associated Aviation Underwriters v. George Koch Sons, 712 N.E.2d 1071,1076 (Ind. App. 1999) (airplane crash resulted from negligence of maintenance provider; "wear and tear" and "gradual deterioration" of engine were effects, not the cause, of the loss).

Massachusetts: Jussim v. Massachusetts Bay Insurance Co., 610 N.E.2d 954 (Mass. 1993) (pollution exclusion inapplicable to environmental contamination and the cleanup associated therewith because efficient proximate cause of the loss was a third party oil company's negligent delivery of 500 gallons of oil to a disconnected tank).

New York: J. Aron & Co. v. Chown, 231 A.D.2d 426, 647 N.Y.S.2d 8 (1996).

But see:

Fifth Circuit: In re Katrina Canal Breaches Litigation, 495 F.3d 191 (5th Cir. 2007) (determining loss excluded because efficient proximate cause was flood, not negligence).

162 See Cozen, *Insuring Real Property,* § 2.02[3][a], at 2–26 (2004) ("With the advent of all-risk policy forms, the peril of collapse was automatically a covered risk unless specifically excluded."). Of note, collapse coverage is triggered by the event rather than the cause. See Palub v. Hartford Underwriters Insurance Co., 92 Cal. App.4th 645, 112 Cal. Rptr.2d 270 (2001).

163 *Id.*

164 See:

First Circuit: Mulhern v. Philadelphia Indemnity Insurance Co., 802 F. Supp.2d 317 (D. Mass. 2011); Middlesex Mutual Assurance Co. v. Puerta De La Esperanza, L.L.C., 723 F. Supp.2d 294 (D. Mass. 2010).

Second Circuit: Dalton v. Harleysville Worcester Mutual Insurance Co., 557 F.3d 88 (2d Cir. 2009); Residential Management, Inc. v. Federal Insurance Co., 884 F. Supp.2d 3 (E.D.N.Y. 2012).

Third Circuit: Holiday Village East Home Owners Ass'n v. QBE Insurance Corp., 830 F. Supp.2d 24 (D.N.J. 2011); Zurich American Insurance Co. v. Keating Building Corp., 513 F. Supp.2d 55 (D.N.J. 2007); T.H.E. Insurance Co. v. Charles Boyer Children's Trust, 455 F. Supp.2d 284 (M.D. Pa. 2006); Wurst v. State Farm Fire and Casualty Co., 431 F. Supp.2d 501 (D.N.J. 2006).

Fourth Circuit: Insurance Company of North America v. United States Gypsum Co., 678 F. Supp. 138 (W.D. Va. 1988), *aff'd* 870 F.2d 148 (4th Cir. 1989).

Sixth Circuit: Huntingdon Ridge Townhouse Homeowners Association v. QBE Insurance Corp., 2009 WL 4060458 (M.D. Tenn. Nov. 20, 2009).

Eighth Circuit: KAAPA Ethanol, L.L.C. v. Affiliated FM Insurance Co., 660 F.3d 299 (8th Cir. 2011); Macheca Transport v. Philadelphia Indemnity Insurance Co., 649 F.3d 661 (8th Cir. 2011); Council Tower Ass'n v. Axis Specialty Insurance Co., 630 F.3d 725 (8th Cir. 2011).

Ninth Circuit: Malbco Holdings, L.L.C. v. AMCO Insurance Co., 719 F. Supp.2d 1311 (D. Or. 2010); Schray v. Fireman's Fund Insurance Co., 402 F. Supp.2d 1212 (D. Or. 2005).

Tenth Circuit: Texas Eastern Transmission Corp. v. Marine Office-Appleton & Cox Corp., 579 F.2d 561, 565–566 (10th Cir. 1978) (applying Oklahoma law).

Eleventh Circuit: Nix v. State Farm Fire and Casualty Co., 444 Fed. Appx. 388 (11th Cir. 2011); Kelly v. Balboa Insurance Co., 897 F. Supp.2d 1262 (M.D. Fla. 2012); Mount Zion

Baptist Church of Marietta v. GuideOne Elite Insurance Co., 808 F. Supp.2d 1322 (N.D. Ga. 2011).

State Courts:

Connecticut: Beach v. Middlesex Mutual Assurance Co., 532 A.2d 1297 (Conn. 1987) (coverage for collapse, which itself was caused by excluded peril, was contemplated by the policy).

Florida: Kings Ridge Community Ass'n v. Sagamore Insurance Co., 98 So.3d 74 (Fla. App. 2012).

Georgia: Lipsitz v. Fireman's Fund Insurance Co., 358 S.E.2d 624, 625 (Ga. App. 1987).

Illinois: Gulino v. Economy Fire and Casualty Co., 971 N.E.2d 522, 361 Ill. Dec. 420 (Ill. App.), *appeal denied* 979 N.E.2d 876 (Ill. 2012).

Kansas: Sterling College v. GuideOne Insurance Co., 2005 WL 742065 (Kan. App. Apr. 1, 2005) (policy covered collapse loss because of failure to specifically exclude loss caused by collapse, even though collapse itself was likely caused by excluded peril).

Missouri: Missouri Commercial Insurance Co. v. Employers Mutual Casualty Insurance Co., 680 S.W.2d 397 (Mo. App. 1984) (risk of collapse within contemplation of all risk policy).

New York: Viscosi v. Preferred Mutual Insurance Co., 87 A.D.3d 1307, 930 N.Y.S.2d 165 (N.Y. App. Div. 2011); Seward Park Housing Corp. v. Greater New York Mutual Insurance Co., 43 A.D.3d 23, 836 N.Y.S.2d 99 (2007).

North Carolina: Magnolia Manufacturing of North Carolina, Inc. v. Erie Insurance Exchange, 639 S.E.2d 443 (N.C. 2007).

But see:

California: Palub v. Hartford Underwriters Insurance Co., 92 Cal. App.4th 645, 112 Cal. Rptr.2d 270, 276 (2001) (collapse is not a cause of loss but damage for which coverage is sought).

Massachusetts: Driscoll v. Providence Mutual Fire Insurance Co., 867 N.E.2d 806 (Mass. App. 2007).

Oregon: Chou v. Farmers Insurance Exchange, 253 Or. App. 552, 291 P.3d 784 (2012).

South Dakota: Zoo Properties, L.L.P. v. Midwest Family Mutual Insurance Co., 797 N.W.2d 779 (S.D. 2011).

Washington: Vision One, L.L.C. v. Philadelphia Indemnity Insurance Co., 174 Wash.2d 501, 276 P.3d 300 (2012) (*en banc*).

165 *Webster's Ninth New Collegiate Dictionary* at 259.

166 See, e.g.:

Second Circuit: Dalton v. Harleysville Worcester Mutual Insurance Co., 557 F.3d 88 (2d Cir. 2009).

Third Circuit: Ercolani v. Excelsior Insurance Co., 830 F.2d 31, 34–35 (3d Cir. 1987).

Eighth Circuit: KAAPA Ethanol, L.L.C. v. Affiliated FM Insurance Co., 660 F.3d 299 (8th Cir. 2011); Macheca Transport v. Philadelphia Indemnity Insurance Co., 649 F.3d 661 (8th Cir. 2011); Council Tower Ass'n v. Axis Specialty Insurance Co., 630 F.3d 725 (8th Cir. 2011).

Eleventh Circuit: Kelly v. Balboa Insurance Co., 897 F. Supp.2d 1262 (M.D. Fla. 2012).

State Courts:

Florida: Kings Ridge Community Ass'n v. Sagamore Insurance Co., 98 So.3d 74 (Fla. App. 2012).

Nebraska: Morton v. Travelers Indemnity Co., 106 N.W.2d 710 (Neb. 1960).

Oregon: Hennessy v. Mutual of Enumclaw Insurance Co., 228 Or. App. 186, 206 P.3d 1184 (2009).

South Dakota: Zoo Properties, L.L.P. v. Midwest Family Mutual Insurance Co., 797 N.W.2d 779 (S.D. 2011).

See also, "What Constitutes 'Collapse' of a Building Within Coverage of a Property Insurance Policy," 71 A.L.R.3d 1072 (2004).

Alabama seems to follow the majority view, although such conclusion is not definitive. See: State Farm Fire & Casualty v. Slade, 747 So.2d 293, 325–326 & n.11 (Ala. 1999); Fidelity & Casualty Co. v. Mitchell, 503 So.2d 870, 871 (Ala. Civ. App. 1987).

[167] See, e.g.:

First Circuit: Mulhern v. Philadelphia Indemnity Insurance Co., 802 F. Supp.2d 317 (D. Mass. 2011).

Second Circuit: Residential Management, Inc. v. Federal Insurance Co., 884 F. Supp.2d 3 (E.D.N.Y. 2012).

Third Circuit: Holiday Village East Home Owners Ass'n v. QBE Insurance Corp., 830 F. Supp.2d 24 (D.N.J. 2011).

Eighth Circuit: Council Tower Association v. Axis Specialty Insurance Co., 2009 WL 3806994 (E.D. Mo. Nov. 12, 2009) (partial failure of brick veneer not a "collapse").

Eleventh Circuit: Mount Zion Baptist Church of Marietta v. GuideOne Elite Insurance Co., 808 F. Supp.2d 1322 (N.D. Ga. 2011).

State Courts:

Illinois: Gulino v. Economy Fire and Casualty Co., 971 N.E.2d 522, 361 Ill. Dec. 420 (Ill. App.), *appeal denied* 979 N.E.2d 876 (Ill. 2012).

Pennsylvania: Dominick v. Statesman Insurance Co., 692 A.2d 188, 190 (Pa. Super. 1997), *alloc. denied* 723 A.2d 671 (Pa. 1998).

To attempt to avoid the majority rule of coverage for substantial impairment of the structural integrity of a building or part thereof, some insurance companies have altered the policy language to require a sudden or abrupt falling down of a structure to constitute a "collapse." See, e.g.:

First Circuit: Middlesex Mutual Assurance Co. v. Puerta De La Esperanza, L.L.C., 723 F. Supp.2d 294 (D. Mass. 2010); Mulhern v. Philadelphia Indemnity Insurance Co., 802 F. Supp.2d 317 (D. Mass. 2011).

Second Circuit: Residential Management, Inc. v. Federal Insurance Co., 884 F. Supp.2d 3 (E.D.N.Y. 2012).

Third Circuit: Holiday Village East Home Owners Ass'n v. QBE Insurance Corp., 830 F. Supp.2d 24 (D.N.J. 2011).

Sixth Circuit: Huntingdon Ridge Townhouse Homeowners Ass'n v. QBE Insurance Corp., 2009 WL 4060458 (M.D. Tenn. Nov. 20, 2009).

Ninth Circuit: Malbco Holdings, L.L.C. v. AMCO Insurance Co., 719 F. Supp.2d 1311 (D. Or. 2010); Ass'n of Unit Owners of Nestani v. State Farm Fire and Casualty Co., 670 F. Supp.2d 1156 (D. Or. 2009).

Eleventh Circuit: Mount Zion Baptist Church of Marietta v. GuideOne Elite Insurance Co., 808 F. Supp.2d 1322 (N.D. Ga. 2011).

State Courts:

Illinois: Gulino v. Economy Fire and Casualty Co., 971 N.E.2d 522, 361 Ill. Dec. 420 (Ill. App.), *appeal denied* 979 N.E.2d 876 (Ill. 2012).

New York: Viscosi v. Preferred Mutual Insurance Co., 87 A.D.3d 1307, 930 N.Y.S.2d 165 (N.Y. App. Div. 2011); Rapp B. Properties, L.L.C. v. RLI Insurance Co., 65 A.D.3d 923, 885 N.Y.S.2d 283 (2009).

168 See, e.g.:

Third Circuit: Ercolani v. Excelsior Insurance Co., 830 F.2d 31, 34–35 (3d Cir. 1987).

State Courts:

Nebraska: Morton v. Travelers Indemnity Co., 106 N.W.2d 710 (Neb. 1960).

169 See Rosen v. State Farm General Insurance Co., 70 P.3d 351 (Cal. 2003) (defining "collapse" as "actually falling down or falling into pieces"). See also:

First Circuit: Mulhern v. Philadelphia Indemnity Insurance Co., 802 F. Supp.2d 317 (D. Mass. 2011); Middlesex Mutual Assurance Co. v. Puerta De La Esperanza, L.L.C., 723 F. Supp.2d 294 (D. Mass. 2010).

Second Circuit: Residential Management, Inc. v. Federal Insurance Co., 884 F. Supp.2d 3 (E.D.N.Y. 2012).

Third Circuit: Holiday Village East Home Owners Ass'n v. QBE Insurance Corp., 830 F. Supp.2d 24 (D.N.J. 2011).

Sixth Circuit: Huntingdon Ridge Townhouse Homeowners Ass'n v. QBE Insurance Co., 2009 WL 4060458 (M.D. Tenn. Nov. 20, 2009).

Ninth Circuit: Malbco Holdings, L.L.C. v. AMCO Insurance Co., 719 F. Supp.2d 1311 (D. Or. 2010); Ass'n of Unit Owners of Nestani v. State Farm Fire and Casualty Co., 670 F. Supp.2d 1156 (D. Or. 2009).

Eleventh Circuit: Mount Zion Baptist Church of Marietta v. GuideOne Elite Insurance Co., 808 F. Supp.2d 1322 (N.D. Ga. 2011).

State Courts:

Illinois: Gulino v. Economy Fire and Casualty Co., 971 N.E.2d 522, 361 Ill. Dec. 420 (Ill. App.), *appeal denied* 979 N.E.2d 876 (Ill. 2012).

170 See, e.g.:

Third Circuit: Ercolani v. Excelsior Insurance Co., 830 F.2d 31, 34–35 (3d Cir. 1987).

State Courts:

Nebraska: Morton v. Travelers Indemnity Co., 106 N.W.2d 710 (Neb. 1960).

See also, "What Constitutes 'Collapse' of a Building Within Coverage of a Property Insurance Policy," 71 A.L.R.3d 1072 (2004).

Alabama seems to follow the majority view, although such conclusion is not definitive. See: State Farm Fire & Casualty v. Slade, 747 So.2d 293, 325–326 & n.11 (Ala. 1999); Fidelity & Casualty Co. v. Mitchell, 503 So.2d 870, 871 (Ala. Civ. App. 1987).

171 See Stor/Gard, Inc. v. Strathmore Insurance Co., 2013 WL 2364168 (1st Cir. May 31, 2013).

172 Reynolds v. Standard Fire Insurance Co., 221 A.D.2d 616, 634 N.Y.S.2d 163, 164 (1995) (upholding application of clause) (emphasis added).

173 Casey v. General Accident Insurance Co., 178 A.D.2d 1001, 578 N.Y.S.2d 337, 338 (1991) (emphasis added) (anti-efficient proximate or concurrent causation clause excluded coverage where the loss was caused, in part, by surface water, even if other factors, such as a clogged drain and a sloped roof, may have contributed to the loss).

See also:

Second Circuit: ABI Asset Corp. v. Twin City Fire Insurance Co., 1997 WL 724568, at *2 (S.D.N.Y. Nov. 18, 1997) ("New York courts have interpreted [anticoncurrent causation] clauses to mean that where a loss results from multiple contributing causes, coverage is excluded if the insurer can demonstrate that any of the concurrent or contributing causes of loss are excluded by the policy.").

Fifth Circuit: Leonard v. Nationwide Mutual Insurance Co., 438 F. Supp.2d 684 (S.D. Miss. 2006) (in hurricane loss case, court upholds anti-efficient proximate cause clause excluding all portions of loss caused in part by flood).

[174] See:

First Circuit: Stor/Gard, Inc. v. Strathmore Insurance Co., 2013 WL 2364168 (1st Cir. May 31, 2013); Amherst Country Club, Inc. v. Harleysville Worcester Insurance Co., 561 F. Supp.2d 138 (D.N.H. 2008); Preferred Mutual Insurance Co. v. Travelers Cos., 955 F. Supp. 9 (D. Mass. 1997).

Second Circuit: Gelwan v. Vermont Mutual Insurance Co., 2013 WL 48951 (2d Cir. Jan. 14, 2013); Alamia v. Nationwide Mutual Fire Insurance Co., 495 F. Supp.2d 362 (S.D.N.Y. 2007); ABI Asset Corp. v. Twin City Fire Insurance Co., 1997 WL 724568, at *2 (S.D.N.Y. Nov. 18, 1997) ("New York courts have interpreted [anticoncurrent causation] clauses to mean that where a loss results from multiple contributing causes, coverage is excluded if the insurer can demonstrate that any of the concurrent or contributing causes of loss are excluded by the policy."); Farrell v. Royal Insurance Company of America, 789 F. Supp. 159 (D. Conn. 1997).

Third Circuit: Colella v. State Farm Fire and Casualty Co., 407 Fed. Appx. 616 (3d Cir. 2011); Hamm v. Allstate Property and Casualty Insurance Co., 2012 WL 5451523 (W.D. Pa. Nov. 7, 2012); T.H.E. Insurance Co. v. Charles Boyer Children's Trust, 455 F. Supp.2d 284 (M.D. Pa. 2006); Assurance Company of America, Inc. v. Jay-Mar, Inc., 38 F. Supp.2d 349 (D.N.J. 1999).

Fourth Circuit: Bao v. Liberty Mutual Fire Insurance Co., 535 F. Supp.2d 532 (D. Md. 2008).

Fifth Circuit: ARM Properties Management Group v. RSUI Indemnity Co., 400 Fed. Appx. 938 (5th Cir. 2010); Stewart Enterprises, Inc. v. RSUI Indemnity Co., Inc., 614 F.3d 117 (5th Cir. 2010); Arctic Slope Regional Corp. v. Affiliated FM Insurance Co., 564 F.3d 707 (5th Cir. 2009); Bilbe v. Belsom, 530 F.3d 314 (5th Cir. 2008); Tuepker v. State Farm Fire & Casualty Co., 507 F.3d 346 (5th Cir. 2007) (upheld); Leonard v. Nationwide Mutual Insurance Co., 499 F.3d 419 (5th Cir. 2007).

Sixth Circuit: Atlantic Mutual Insurance Cos. v. Lotz, 384 F. Supp.2d 1292 (E.D. Wis. 2005).

Eighth Circuit: TNT Speed and Sport Center, Inc. v. American States Insurance Co., 114 F.3d 731 (8th Cir. 1997); Swenson v. State Farm Fire and Casualty Co., 891 F. Supp.2d 1101 (D.S.D. 2012).

Ninth Circuit: Cooper v. American Family Mutual Insurance Co., 184 F. Supp.2d 960 (D. Ariz. 2002); Schroeder v. State Farm Fire and Casualty Co., 770 F. Supp. 558 (D. Nev. 1991).

Tenth Circuit: Arkansas Valley Drilling, Inc. v. Continental Western Insurance Co., 703 F. Supp.2d 1232 (D. Colo. 2010); Winters v. Charter Oak Fire Insurance Co., 4 F. Supp.2d 1288 (D.N.M. 1998).

Eleventh Circuit: Paulucci v. Liberty Mutual Fire Insurance Co., 190 F. Supp.2d 1312 (M.D. Fla. 2002).

State Courts:

Alabama: State Farm Fire & Casualty Co. v. Slade, 747 So.2d 293 (Ala. 1999).

Alaska: State Farm Fire & Casualty Co. v. Bongen, 925 P.2d 1042 (Alaska 1996).

Colorado: Colorado Intergovernmental Risk Sharing Agency v. Northfield Insurance Co., 207 P.3d 839 (Colo. App. 2008).

District of Columbia: Chase v. State Farm Fire & Casualty Co., 780 A.2d 1123 (D.C. App. 2001).

Louisiana: La Louisiane Bakery Co. v. Lafayette Insurance Co., 61 So.3d 17 (La. App. 2011).

Massachusetts: Surabian Realty Co. v. NGM Insurance Co., 462 Mass. 715, 971 N.E.2d 268 (2012); Boazova v. Safety Insurance Co., 462 Mass. 346, 968 N.E.2d 385 (2012).

Mississippi: Robichaux v. Nationwide Mutual Fire Insurance Co., 81 So.3d 1030 (Miss. 2011); Corban v. United Services Automobile Association, 20 So.3d 601 (Miss. 2009).

Missouri: Toumayan v. State Farm General Insurance Co., 970 S.W.2d 822 (Mo. App. 1998); Pakmark Corp. v. Liberty Mutual Insurance Co., 943 S.W.2d 256 (Mo. App. 1997).

New York: Lattimore Road Surgicenter, Inc. v. Merchants Group, Inc., 71 A.D.3d 1379, 898 N.Y.S.2d 741 (2010); Fairchild v. Gennessee Patrons Co-op Insurance Co., 234 A.D.2d 392, 651 N.Y.S.2d 544 (1997); Reynolds v. Standard Fire Insurance Co., 221 A.D.2d 616, 634 N.Y.S.2d 163, 164 (1995) (upholding application of clause) (emphasis added); Casey v. General Accident Insurance Co., 178 A.D.2d 1001, 578 N.Y.S.2d 337, 338 (1991) (upholding application of anti-efficient proximate or concurrent causation clause).

Ohio: Polk v. Landings of Walden Condominium Association, 2005 WL 1862126 (Ohio App. Aug. 5, 2005).

Oklahoma: Duensing v. State Farm Fire & Casualty Co., 131 P.3d 127 (Okla. Civ. App. 2005) (applied for earth movement exclusion).

Pennsylvania: Spece v. Erie Insurance Group, 850 A.2d 679 (Pa. Super. 2004).

South Carolina: South Carolina Farm Bureau Mutual Insurance Co. v. Durham, 380 S.C. 506, 671 S.E.2d 610 (2009).

Texas: Wong v. Monticello Insurance Co., 2003 WL 1522938 (Tex. App. Mar. 26, 2003).

175 See:

Fifth Circuit: Leonard v. Nationwide Mutual Insurance Co., 438 F. Supp.2d 684 (S.D. Miss. 2006); Tuepker v. State Farm Fire & Casualty Co., 2006 WL 1442489 (S.D. Miss. May 24, 2006); Buente v. Allstate Insurance Co., 422 F. Supp.2d 690 (S.D. Miss. 2006).

Tenth Circuit: Kelly v. Farmers Insurance Co., 281 F. Supp. 1290 (W.D. Okla. 2003).

State Courts:

Louisiana: La Louisiane Bakery Co. v. Lafayette Insurance Co., 61 So.3d 17 (La. App. 2011).

Mississippi: Grace v. Lititz Mutual Insurance Co., 257 So.2d 217 (Miss. 1972).

North Dakota: Western National Mutual Insurance Co. v. University of North Dakota, 643 N.W.2d 4 (N.D. 2002).

Oklahoma: Duensing v. State Farm Fire & Casualty Co., 131 P.3d 127 (Okla. Civ. App. 2005) (not applied for settlement exclusion).

Pennsylvania: Bishops, Inc. v. Penn National Insurance Co., 984 A.2d 982 (Pa. Super. 2009).

Washington: Safeco Insurance Company of America v. Hirschmann, 773 P.2d 413 (Wash. 1989); Villella v. Public Employers Mutual Insurance Co., 725 P.2d 957 (Wash. 1986); Graham v. Public Employers Mutual Insurance Co., 656 P.2d 1077 (Wash. 1983).

West Virginia: Murray v. State Farm Fire & Casualty Co., 509 S.E.2d 1 (W. Va. 1998).

In California, the court in Howell v. State Farm Fire & Casualty Co., 218 Cal. App.3d 1446, 267 Cal. Rptr. 708 (1990), refused to permit an insurance company to contract out of the efficient proximate cause doctrine on the basis of California Insurance Code Sections 530 and 532. However, in Julian v. Hartford Underwriters Insurance Co., 35 Cal.4th 747, 110 P.3d 903, 27 Cal. Rptr.3d 648 (2005), the clause that excluded a loss which was proximately caused by excluded cause of loss was upheld as not violating statutory provisions. See also, De Bruyn v. Superior Court, 158 Cal. App.4th 1213, 70 Cal. Rptr.3d 652 (2008).

In contrast to the previously cited Washington cases, see Findlay v. United Pacific Insurance Co., 129 Wash.2d 368, 917 P.2d 116 (1996), which upheld a clause that excluded a loss that was proximately caused by excluded cause of loss.

176 Leonard v. Nationwide Mutual Insurance Co., 438 F. Supp.2d 684 (S.D. Miss. 2006).

177 *Id.*, 438 F. Supp.2d at 694, denying coverage for much of the loss claimed because "[a]lmost all of the damage to the Leonard residence" was attributable to water and, therefore, excluded under the policy. 438 F. Supp.2d at 695. See also, Tuepker v. State Farm Fire & Casualty Co., 2006 WL 1442489 (S.D. Miss. May 24, 2006).

The *Leonard* case is unique. In fact, in similar situations where very little physical evidence existed to determine causation following a hurricane-related loss, Mississippi courts held that coverage existed under the efficient proximate cause doctrine. For example, in Grace v. Lititz Mutual Insurance Co., 257 So.2d 217 (Miss. 1972), the Mississippi Supreme Court affirmed a jury verdict finding coverage for the policyholder for windstorm damages in the aftermath of Hurricane Camille. The insurance policy in that case covered windstorm damages but excluded coverage for loss caused or aggravated by tidal water. There was very little physical evidence to substantiate the alleged causes of loss because the building was destroyed and, in the absence of such physical evidence, the parties relied on a combination of scientific and circumstantial evidence to substantiate causation. The jury returned a verdict in favor of the policyholder, finding that the building had been destroyed by wind, not by flood, despite the lack of physical evidence to substantiate the cause of loss. The insurance company appealed, but the appellate court affirmed the verdict, holding that "the material facts in the record were disputed therefore the jury was entitled to accept the policyholder's assertion that his office building was destroyed by wind before the tidal waters reach his property."

178 *First Circuit:* Stor/Gard, Inc. v. Strathmore Insurance Co., 2013 WL 2364168 (1st Cir. May 31, 2013).

Fifth Circuit: Leonard v. Nationwide Mutual Insurance Co., 438 F. Supp.2d 684 (S.D. Miss. 2006); Tuepker v. State Farm Fire & Casualty Co., 2006 WL 1442489 (S.D. Miss. May 24, 2006).

State Courts:

California: Howell v. State Farm Fire & Casualty Co., 218 Cal. App.3d 1446, 267 Cal. Rptr. 708 (1990) (refusing to permit insurance company to contract out of efficient proximate cause doctrine on the basis of California Insurance Code Sections 530 and 532).

Mississippi: Grace v. Lititz Mutual Insurance Co., 257 So.2d 217 (Miss. 1972).

179 See:

Third Circuit: Kemmerer v. State Farm Insurance Co., 2004 WL 87017, at *2 (E.D. Pa. Jan. 19, 2004) ("If the leak from the powder room caused the mold infestation, that leak would fall within the peril [sudden and accidental discharge or overflow of water] outlined in the homeowner's insurance policy.").

Ninth Circuit: Prudential Property & Casualty Insurance Co. v. Lillard-Roberts, 2002 WL 31495830, at *9–10 (D. Or. June 18, 2002) (in a named-perils policy, the "accidental discharge or overflow of water" peril provided for coverage of physical mold damage caused by a water leak); Sapiro v. Encompass Insurance Co., 221 F.R.D. 513 (N.D. Cal. 2004) (exclusion applied).

Tenth Circuit: Kelly v. Farmers Insurance Co., 281 F. Supp.2d 1290 (W.D. Okla. 2003) (exclusion not applied).

Eleventh Circuit: Church of the Palms-Presbyterian (U.S.A.), Inc. v. Cincinnati Insurance Co., 404 F. Supp.2d 1339 (M.D. Fla. 2005) (exclusion applied).

State Courts:

Arizona: Liristis v. American Family Mutual Insurance Co., 61 P.3d 22, 25 (Ariz. App. 2002) (homeowner's policy did not exclude mold damage caused by a covered event).

Florida: Fisher v. Certain Underwriters of Lloyds, 930 So.2d 756 (Fla. Dist. App. 2006) (exclusion not applied).

Louisiana: Morgan v. Auto Club Family Insurance Co., 899 So.2d 135 (La. App. 2005) (exclusion applied).

Michigan: Ortiz v. Allstate Insurance Co., No. 25477, 2006 WL 889378 (Mich. App. July 3, 2006) (exclusion applied); Hayley v. Allstate Insurance Co., 686 N.W.2d 273 (Mich. App. 2004), ***appeal denied*** 697 N.W.2d 155 (Mich. 2005) (exclusion applied).

Minnesota: Bloom v. Western National Mutual Insurance Co., 2006 WL 1806415 (Minn. App. July 3, 2006) (exclusion applied).

New Jersey: Simonetti v. Selective Insurance Co., 372 N.J. Super. 421, 859 A.2d 694 (2004) (mold loss covered).

New York: Siegel v. Chubb Corp., 33 A.D.3d 565, 825 N.Y.S.2d 441 (2006) (exclusion applied for failure to attribute loss to a leak); Hritz v. Saco, 18 A.D.3d 377, 795 N.Y.S.2d 236 (2005) (exclusion applied).

Ohio: Polk v. Landings of Walden Condominium Association, 2005 WL 1862126 (Ohio App. Aug. 5, 2005) (exclusion applied).

Pennsylvania: Tatalovich v. Pennsylvania National Mutual Casualty Insurance Co., 2003 WL 22844173, at *1–2 (Pa. C.P. Oct. 10, 2003) (exclusion applied).

Texas: Fiess v. State Farm Lloyds, 202 S.W.3d 744 (Tex. 2006) (homeowners policy which excluded "loss caused by mold" did not provide coverage for mold stemming from small roof and window leaks); Lundstrom v. United Services Automobile Ass'n-CIC, 192 S.W.3d 78 (Tex. App. 2006) (exclusion applied); de Laurentis v. United Services Automobile Association, 162 S.W.3d 714 (Tex. App. 2005) (mold damage covered); Keenan v. Wausau Lloyds Insurance Co., 1998 WL 652332, at *3 (Tex. App. Sept. 23, 1998) (named-perils policy covered cost for accessing defectively constructed plumbing lines after named peril caused damage to homeowner's property).

Wisconsin: Arnold v. Cincinnati Insurance Co., 276 Wis.2d 762, 688 N.W.2d 708 (2004) (mold covered).

But see:

Fifth Circuit: Rooters v. State Farm Lloyds, 428 Fed. Appx. 441 (5th Cir. 2011) (upholding mold exclusion).

Eighth Circuit: Swenson v. State Farm Fire and Casualty Co., 891 F. Supp.2d 1101 (D.S.D. 2012) (mold exclusion applied after anti-efficient proximate cause and anticoncurrent cause clauses upheld).

State Courts:

North Carolina: Builders Mutual Insurance Co. v. Glascarr Properties, Inc., 202 N.C. App. 323, 688 S.E.2d 508 (2010) (mold exclusion applied in light of anti-efficient proximate cause and anticoncurrent cause clauses).

180 See:

Third Circuit: Kemmerer v. State Farm Insurance Co., 2004 WL 87017, at *2 (E.D. Pa. Jan. 19, 2004) ("If the leak from the powder room caused the mold infestation, that leak would fall within the peril [sudden and accidental discharge or overflow of water] outlined in the homeowner's insurance policy.").

Ninth Circuit: Prudential Property & Casualty Insurance Co. v. Lillard-Roberts, 2002 WL 31495830, at *9–10 (D. Or. June 18, 2002) (in a named-perils policy, the "accidental discharge or overflow of water" peril provided for coverage of physical mold damage caused by a water leak); Sapiro v. Encompass Insurance Co., 221 F.R.D. 513 (N.D. Cal. 2004) (exclusion applied).

Tenth Circuit: Kelly v. Farmers Insurance Co., 281 F. Supp.2d 1290 (W.D. Okla. 2003) (exclusion not applied).

Eleventh Circuit: Church of the Palms-Presbyterian (U.S.A.), Inc. v. Cincinnati Insurance Co., 404 F. Supp.2d 1339 (M.D. Fla. 2005) (exclusion applied).

State Courts:

Arizona: Liristis v. American Family Mutual Insurance Co., 61 P.3d 22, 25 (Ariz. App. 2002) (homeowner's policy did not exclude mold damage caused by a covered event).

Florida: Fisher v. Certain Underwriters of Lloyds, 930 So.2d 756 (Fla. Dist. App. 2006) (exclusion not applied).

Louisiana: Morgan v. Auto Club Family Insurance Co., 899 So.2d 135 (La. App. 2005) (exclusion applied).

Michigan: Ortiz v. Allstate Insurance Co., No. 25477, 2006 WL 889378 (Mich. App. July 3, 2006) (exclusion applied); Hayley v. Allstate Insurance Co., 686 N.W.2d 273 (Mich. App. 2004), *appeal denied* 697 N.W.2d 155 (Mich. 2005) (exclusion applied).

Minnesota: Bloom v. Western National Mutual Insurance Co., 2006 WL 1806415 (Minn. App. July 3, 2006) (exclusion applied).

New Jersey: Simonetti v. Selective Insurance Co., 372 N.J. Super. 421, 859 A.2d 694 (2004) (mold loss covered).

New York: Siegel v. Chubb Corp., 33 A.D.3d 565, 825 N.Y.S.2d 441 (2006) (exclusion applied for failure to attribute loss to a leak); Hritz v. Saco, 18 A.D.3d 377, 795 N.Y.S.2d 236 (2005) (exclusion applied).

Ohio: Polk v. Landings of Walden Condominium Association, 2005 WL 1862126 (Ohio App. Aug. 5, 2005) (exclusion applied).

Pennsylvania: Tatalovich v. Pennsylvania National Mutual Casualty Insurance Co., 2003 WL 22844173, at *1–2 (Pa. C.P. Oct. 10, 2003) (exclusion applied).

Texas: Fiess v. State Farm Lloyds, 202 S.W.3d 744 (Tex. 2006) (homeowners policy that excluded "loss caused by mold" did not provide coverage for mold stemming from small roof and window leaks); Lundstrom v. United Services Automobile Ass'n-CIC, 192 S.W.3d 78 (Tex. App. 2006) (exclusion applied); de Laurentis v. United Services Automobile Association, 162 S.W.3d 714 (Tex. App. 2005) (mold damage covered); Keenan v. Wausau Lloyds Insurance Co., 1998 WL 652332, at *3 (Tex. App. Sept. 23, 1998) (named-perils policy covered cost for accessing defectively constructed plumbing lines after named peril caused damage to homeowner's property).

Wisconsin: Arnold v. Cincinnati Insurance Co., 276 Wis.2d 762, 688 N.W.2d 708 (2004) (mold covered).

But see:

Fifth Circuit: Rooters v. State Farm Lloyds, 428 Fed. Appx. 441 (5th Cir. 2011) (upholding mold exclusion).

Eighth Circuit: Swenson v. State Farm Fire and Casualty Co., 891 F. Supp.2d 1101 (D.S.D. 2012) (mold exclusion applied after anti-efficient proximate cause and anticoncurrent cause clauses upheld).

State Courts:

North Carolina: Builders Mutual Insurance Co. v. Glascarr Properties, Inc., 202 N.C. App. 323, 688 S.E.2d 508 (2010) (mold exclusion applied in light of anti-efficient proximate cause and anticoncurrent cause clauses).

[181] See Ns. 144–145 *supra* and accompanying text.

[182] See ISO Form CP 10 30 04 02.

[183] The mold endorsement limiting coverage to a certain dollar amount is relatively new and sparsely litigated. See Certain Interested Underwriters at Lloyd's London v. Pitu, Inc., 95 So.3d 290 (Fla. App. 2012).

[184] See ISO Form CP 00 10 04 02.

[185] See, e.g.:

Second Circuit: Fireman's Fund Insurance Co. v. Great American Insurance Company of New York, 2013 WL 1195277 (S.D.N.Y. Mar. 25, 2013); Lionshead 110 Dev. v. The Insurance Corporation of New York, 2010 WL 743277 (S.D.N.Y. Feb. 24, 2010).

Third Circuit: Davis v. Peerless Indemnity Insurance Co., 2013 WL 2147796 (M.D. Pa. May 16, 2013); Williams v. Allstate Insurance Co., 2010 WL 1979299 (W.D. Pa. May 17, 2010).

Fourth Circuit: New Jerusalem Rebirth and Restoration Ministries, Inc. v. Meyer, 2012 WL 2704251 (W.D.N.C. July 6, 2012); American Resources Insurance Co. v. Palmer, 2010 WL 3282579 (D.S.C. Aug. 19, 2010).

Fifth Circuit: Diamond Beach, VP, L.P. v. Lexington Insurance Co., 2010 WL 3732092 (S.D. Tex. Sept. 20, 2010).

Sixth Circuit: Whitt Machine, Inc. v. Essex Insurance Co., 477 Fed. Appx. 492 (6th Cir. 2010); Hartford Insurance Co. v. Miller, 2006 WL 2844124, at *6–7 (E.D. Mich. Sept. 30, 2006).

Seventh Circuit: Dombrowski v. Administrator, Federal Emergency Management Agency, 2010 WL 3671976 (N.D. Ind. Sept. 13, 2010).

Eighth Circuit: Mason v. Safeco Insurance Co. of America, 2010 WL 3340501 (E.D. Mo. Aug. 23, 2010).

Ninth Circuit: A-1 Transmission Automotive Technology, Inc. v. AMCO Insurance Co., 2012 WL 1534466 (C.D. Cal. Apr. 27, 2012); Montana Rail Link v. Lexington Insurance Co., 175 F. Supp.2d 1248 (D. Mont. 2001); Brandt v. American Bankers Insurance Co. of Florida, 2010 WL 3220620 (W.D. Wash. Aug. 13, 2010).

Tenth Circuit: James River Insurance Co. v. Rapid Funding, L.L.C., 2010 WL 965523 (D. Colo. Mar. 16, 2010).

Eleventh Circuit: Mattox v. State Farm Fire and Casualty Co., 2012 WL 3870392 (S.D. Ala. Aug. 15, 2012); Southern Realty Management, Inc. v. Aspen Specialty Inc., 2009 WL 1174661 (N.D. Ga. Apr. 28, 2009).

State Courts:

Florida: Citizens Property Insurance Corp. v. Manning, 966 So.2d 486 (Fla. App. 2007).

Idaho: Manduca Datsun, Inc. v. Universal Underwriters Insurance Co., 676 P.2d 1274 (Idaho App. 1984).

Michigan: Acorn Investment v. Michigan Basic Property Insurance Ass'n, 298 Mich. App. 558, 828 N.W.2d 94 (2012); Utica Mutual Insurance Co. v. Hastings Mutual Insurance Co., 2009 WL 2605407 (Mich. App. Aug. 25, 2009).

New Jersey: LGC Investments, Inc. v. Merchants Mutual Insurance Co., 2006 WL 1508708, at *2–4 (N.J. Super. App. Div. June 2, 2006).

New York: Carden v. Allstate Insurance Co., 30 Misc.3d 479, 912 N.Y.S.2d 867 (N.Y. Sup. Ct., Westchester Cnty. 2010).

South Dakota: Henry v. American Concept Insurance Co., 498 N.W.2d 657 (S.D. 1993).

[186] See Manduca Datsun, Inc. v. Universal Underwriters Insurance Co., 676 P.2d 1274 (Idaho App. 1984).

[187] See Lexington Insurance Co. v. Ryder Systems, Inc., 142 Ga. App. 36, 234 S.E.2d 839 (1977).

[188] See Interstate Gourmet Coffee Roasters, Inc. v. Seaco Insurance Co., 794 N.E.2d 607 (Mass. App. 2003).

[189] See Starczewski v. Unigard Insurance Co., 810 P.2d 58 (Wash. App.), *review denied* 818 P.2d 1099 (Wash. 1991).

[190] See ISO Form CP 00 10 04 02.

[191] See, e.g., Insurance Company of North America v. United States Gypsum Co., 870 F.2d 148, 154 (4th Cir. 1989).

[192] See:

First Circuit: Demers Brothers Trucking, Inc. v. Certain Underwriters at Lloyd's, London, Subscribing to Certificate Number SRS IM MA 04-124, 600 F. Supp.2d 265 (D. Mass. 2009).

Second Circuit: American Home Assurance Co. v. Merck & Co., 386 F. Supp.2d 501 (S.D.N.Y. 2005).

Third Circuit: Buczek v. Continental Casualty Insurance Co., 378 F.3d 284 (3d Cir. 2004); GTE Corp. v. Allendale Mutual Insurance Co., 372 F.3d 598 (3d Cir. 2004); Dickler v. CIGNA Property and Casualty Co., 957 F.2d 1088 (3d Cir. 1992); El Bor Corp. v. Fireman's Fund Insurance Co., 787 F. Supp.2d 341 (E.D. Pa. 2011).

Fourth Circuit: Insurance Company of North America v. United States Gypsum Co., 870 F.2d 148, 154 (4th Cir. 1989) (policyholder could recover "sue and labor" damages for expenditures that were reasonably incurred in attempting to reduce the losses suffered following subsidence of earth beneath the plant, whether or not those attempts were successful).

Fifth Circuit: Carrizales v. State Farm Lloyds, 2008 WL 467097 (5th Cir. Feb. 22, 2008); C.D. Henderson, Inc. v. Commercial Union Insurance Co., 2004 WL 67669 (N.D. Tex. Jan. 13, 2004).

Sixth Circuit: Jackson v. State Farm Fire and Casualty Co., 461 Fed. Appx. 422 (6th Cir. 2012); Union Savings Bank v. Allstate Indemnity Co., 830 F. Supp.2d 623 (S.D. Ind. 2011).

Seventh Circuit: Miller v. Safeco Insurance Company of America, 761 F. Supp.2d 813 (E.D. Wis. 2010).

Eighth Circuit: United Fire and Casualty Co. v. Historic Preservation Trust, 265 F.3d 722 (8th Cir. 2001).

Eleventh Circuit: Swire Pacific Holdings, Inc. v. Zurich Insurance Co., 139 F. Supp.2d 1374 (S.D. Fla. 2001).

State Courts:

Florida: Swire Pacific Holdings, Inc. v. Zurich Insurance Co., 845 So.2d 161 (Fla. 2003).

Louisiana: Maloney Cinque, L.L.C. v. Pacific Insurance Co., 89 So.3d 12 (La. App. 2012).

Massachusetts: American Commercial Finance Corp. v. Seneca Insurance Co., 850 N.E.2d 1114 (Mass. App. 2006).

Minnesota: Witcher Construction Co. v. St. Paul Fire & Marine Insurance Co., 550 N.W.2d 1, 7–8 (Minn. App. 1996) (duty to mitigate loss and entitlement to indemnity for reasonable and necessary expenses incurred to prevent an imminent covered loss).

Montana: State v. Allendale Mutual Insurance Co., 154 P.3d 1233 (Mont. 2007).

Nebraska: Curtis O. Griess & Sons, Inc. v. Farm Bureau Insurance Co., 528 N.W.2d 329, 334 (Neb. 1995) (veterinarian fees expended to prevent death to hogs and refunds made by policyholder to purchasers of infected swine were recoverable as mitigation expenses in loss under farm policy).

New York: NIACC, L.L.C. v. Greenwich Insurance Co., 51 A.D.3d 883, 857 N.Y.S.2d 723 (2008); Benjamin Shapiro Realty Co. v. Agricultural Insurance Co., 287 A.D.2d 389, 731 N.Y.S.2d 453, 454 (2001) (loss mitigation provisions entitled policyholder to reimbursement of costs of demolishing and repairing that portion of a concrete slab that had not fallen).

Washington: Port of Seattle v. Lexington Insurance Co., 111 Wash. App. 901, 48 P.3d 334 (2002).

193 See Cozen, *Insuring Real Property*, § 51.01 (2004) (policyholder is obligated to take all reasonable steps to avert or minimize a loss, and the right to reimbursement for expenditures related to such efforts depends upon whether they were reasonable and necessary).

194 See:

Third Circuit: Zurich American Insurance Co. v. Keating Building Corp., 513 F. Supp.2d 55 (D.N.J. 2007).

Sixth Circuit: Society of St. Vincent De Paul in Archdiocese of Detroit v. Mount Hawley Insurance Co., 49 F. Supp.2d 1011 (E.D. Mich. 1999).

Eleventh Circuit: Matthews v. State Farm Fire and Casualty Co., 500 Fed. Appx. 836 (11th Cir. 2012).

State Courts:

Arkansas: St. Paul Fire & Marine Insurance Co. v. Griffin Construction Co., 993 S.W.2d 485 (Ark. 1999) (uncertainty of the value of the insured property distinguishes an open policy from a valued policy).

Florida: Slayton v. Universal Property and Casualty Insurance Co., 103 So.3d 934 (Fla. App. 2012); Florida Farm Bureau Casualty Insurance Co. v. Cox, 943 So.2d 823 (Fla. Dist. App. 2006) (purpose of a valued policy law is to fix the measure of damages under an insurance policy when there is a total loss).

Georgia: Royal Capital Development L.L.C. v. Maryland Casualty Co., 291 Ga. 262, 728 S.E.2d 234 (2012).

Illinois: Young v. Allstate Insurance Co., 812 N.E.2d 741, 748 (Ill. App.), *appeal denied* 823 N.E.2d 980 (Ill. 2004) ("A stated value policy differs from an actual cash value policy because the parties predetermine the insurance company's liability, whereas the company's liability under an actual cash value policy is determined after the loss based on the vehicle's actual cash value immediately before the loss.").

195 See, e.g.:

Second Circuit: Woodhams v. Allstate Fire and Casualty Co., 453 Fed. Appx. 108 (2d Cir. 2012); SR International Business Insurance Co. v. World Trade Center Properties, LLC, 445 F. Supp.2d 320 (S.D.N.Y. 2006).

Fifth Circuit: French v. Allstate Indemnity Co., 637 F.3d 571 (5th Cir. 2011); Bradley v. Allstate Insurance Co., 620 F.3d 509 (5th Cir. 2010); Real Asset Management, Inc. v. Lloyd's of London, 61 F.3d 1223 (5th Cir. 1995); Tolar v. Allstate Texas Lloyd's Co., 772 F. Supp.2d 825 (N.D. Tex. 2011); Cameron Parish School Board v. RSUI Indemnity Co., 2008 WL 5082136 (W.D. La. Nov. 25, 2008); Ghoman v. New Hampshire Insurance Co., 159 F. Supp.2d 928 (N.D. Tex. 2001).

Eighth Circuit: Buddy Bean Lumber Co. v. Axis Surplus Insurance Co., 2013 WL 2248464 (8th Cir. May 23, 2013); Harris v. American Modern Home Insurance Co., 571 F. Supp.2d 1066 (E.D. Mo. 2008).

Ninth Circuit: Sierra Pacific Power Co. v. Hartford Steam Boiler Inspection and Insurance Co., 490 Fed. Appx. 871 (9th Cir. 2012); Lukes v. American Family Mutual Insurance Co., 455 F. Supp.2d 1010 (D. Ariz. 2006).

Tenth Circuit: Davis v. Mid-Century Insurance Co., 311 F.3d 1250 (10th Cir. 2002); Farmland Industries, Inc. v. National Union Fire Insurance Co., 359 F. Supp.2d 1144 (D. Kan. 2005).

Eleventh Circuit: Mills v. Foremost Insurance Co., 511 F.3d 1300 (11th Cir. 2008).

State Courts:

Alabama: Ballard v. Lee, 671 So.2d 1368, 1374 (Ala. 1995), *overruled on other grounds* State Farm Fire & Casualty Co. v. Owen, 729 So.2d 834 (Ala. 1998); Pritchett v. State Farm Mutual Automobile Insurance Co., 834 So.2d 785 (Ala. Civ. App. 2002).

Arizona: Tritschler v. Allstate Insurance Co., 144 P.3d 519, 529 (Ariz. App. 2006).

California: Doan v. State Farm General Insurance Co., 195 Cal. App.4th 1082, 125 Cal. Rptr.3d 793 (2011); Fire Insurance Exchange v. Superior Court, 10 Cal. Rptr.3d 617 (Cal. App. 2004).

Florida: American Reliance Insurance Co. v. Perez, 689 So.2d 290 (Fla. Dist. App.), *review denied* 698 So.2d 840 (Fla. 1997); Goff v. State Farm Florida Insurance Co., 999 So.2d 684 (Fla. App. 2008).

Idaho: Hall v. Farmers Alliance Mutual Insurance Co., 145 Idaho 313, 179 P.3d 276 (Idaho 2008).

Illinois: Carey v. American Family Brokerage, Inc., 391 Ill. App.3d 273, 909 N.E.2d 255, 330 Ill. Dec. 542 (2009); Young v. Allstate Insurance Co., 812 N.E.2d 741, 748 (Ill. App.), *appeal denied* 823 N.E.2d 980 (Ill. 2004); General Casualty Co. v. Tracer Industries, Inc., 674 N.E.2d 473 (Ill. App. 1996), *appeal denied* 679 N.E.2d 379 (Ill. 1997).

Indiana: Rockford Mutual Insurance Co. v. Pirtle, 911 N.E.2d 60 (Ind. App. 2009).

Louisiana: Jouve v. State Farm Fire and Casualty Co., 74 So.3d 220 (La. App. 2011).

Massachusetts: O'Connor v. Merrimack Mutual Fire Insurance Co., 73 Mass. App. Ct. 205, 897 N.E.2d 593 (2008).

Nebraska: D & S Realty, Inc. v. Markel Insurance Co., 284 Neb. 1, 816 N.W.2d 1 (2012); Olson v. Le Mars Mutual Insurance Co., 696 N.W.2d 453 (Neb. 2005).

New Hampshire: Nicolaou v. Vermont Mutual Insurance Co., 155 N.H. 724, 931 A.2d 1265 (2007).

New York: D.R. Watson Holdings, LLC v. Caliber One Indemnity Co., 789 N.Y.S.2d 787 (N.Y. App. Div. 2005).

Ohio: Jenkins v. State Farm Fire and Casualty Co., 2012 WL 6681882 (Ohio App. Dec. 20, 2012).

Oklahoma: Tyler v. Shelter Mutual Insurance Co., 184 P.3d 496 (Okla. 2008); Branch v. Farmers Insurance Co., 55 P.3d 1023 (Okla. 2002).

Pennsylvania: Mee v. Safeco Insurance Co., 908 A.2d 344, 350–351 (Pa. Super. 2006); Kane v. State Farm Fire & Casualty Co., 841 A.2d 1038 (Pa. Super. 2003), *appeal denied* 871 A.2d 192 (Pa. 2005); Gilderman v. State Farm Insurance Co., 649 A.2d 941, 943 (Pa. Super. 1994), *appeal denied* 661 A.2d 874 (Pa. 1995).

Washington: Holden v. Farmers Insurance Company of Washington, 239 P.3d 344, (Wash. 2010); DePhelps v. Safeco Insurance Co., 65 P.3d 1234 (Wash. App. 2003).

[196] See, e.g.:

Second Circuit: Executive Plaza L.L.C. v. Peerless Insurance Co., 2013 WL 2249134 (2d Cir. May 23, 2013).

Fifth Circuit: Cameron Parish School Board v. RSUI Indemnity Co., 2008 WL 5082136 (W.D. La. Nov. 25, 2008).

State Courts:

Colorado: Dupre v. Allstate Insurance Co., 62 P.3d 1024 (Colo. App. 2002).

Florida: Goff v. State Farm Florida Insurance Co., 999 So.2d 684 (Fla. App. 2d Dist. 2009).

Idaho: Hall v. Farmers Alliance Mutual Insurance Co., 145 Idaho 313, 179 P.3d 276 (2008).

Indiana: Rockford Mutual Insurance Co. v. Pirtle, 911 N.E.2d 60 (Ind. App. 2009).

Kansas: Burchett v. Kansas Mutual Insurance Co., 48 P.3d 1290 (Kan. App. 2002).

New Hampshire: Nicolaou v. Vermont Mutual Insurance Co., 155 N.H. 724, 931 A.2d 1265 (2007).

Pennsylvania: Gilderman v. State Farm Insurance Co., 649 A.2d 941, 945 (Pa. Super. 1994), *appeal denied* 661 A.2d 874 (Pa. 1995); Rotell v. Erie Insurance Group, 53 Pa. D. & C.4th 533 (Pa. C.P. 2001).

197 See:

Sixth Circuit: Society of St. Vincent De Paul in Archdiocese of Detroit v. Mount Hawley Insurance Co., 49 F. Supp.2d 1011 (E.D. Mich. 1999).

State Courts:

Arkansas: St. Paul Fire & Marine Insurance Co. v. Griffin Construction Co., 993 S.W.2d 485 (Ark. 1999) (uncertainty of the value of the insured property distinguishes an open policy from a valued policy).

Florida: Florida Farm Bureau Casualty Insurance Co. v. Cox, 943 So.2d 823 (Fla. Dist. App. 2006) (purpose of a valued policy law is to fix the measure of damages under an insurance policy when there is a total loss).

Illinois: Young v. Allstate Insurance Co., 812 N.E.2d 741, 748 (Ill. App.), *appeal denied* 823 N.E.2d 980 (Ill. 2004) ("A stated value policy differs from an actual cash value policy because the parties predetermine the insurance company's liability, whereas the company's liability under an actual cash value policy is determined after the loss based on the vehicle's actual cash value immediately before the loss.").

Minnesota: Auto-Owners Insurance Co. v. Second Chance Investments, L.L.C., 827 N.W.2d 766 (Minn. 2103).

198 See, e.g.:

Second Circuit: Woodhams v. Allstate Fire and Casualty Co., 453 Fed. Appx. 108 (2d Cir. 2012); SR International Business Insurance Co. v. World Trade Center Properties, LLC, 445 F. Supp.2d 320 (S.D.N.Y. 2006).

Fifth Circuit: French v. Allstate Indemnity Co., 637 F.3d 571 (5th Cir. 2011); Bradley v. Allstate Insurance Co., 620 F.3d 509 (5th Cir. 2010); Real Asset Management, Inc. v. Lloyd's of London, 61 F.3d 1223 (5th Cir. 1995); Tolar v. Allstate Texas Lloyd's Co., 772 F. Supp.2d 825 (N.D. Tex. 2011); Cameron Parish School Board v. RSUI Indemnity Co., 2008 WL 5082136 (W.D. La. Nov. 25, 2008); Ghoman v. New Hampshire Insurance Co., 159 F. Supp.2d 928 (N.D. Tex. 2001).

Eighth Circuit: Buddy Bean Lumber Co. v. Axis Surplus Insurance Co., 2013 WL 2248464 (8th Cir. May 23, 2013); Harris v. American Modern Home Insurance Co., 571 F. Supp.2d 1066 (E.D. Mo. 2008).

Ninth Circuit: Sierra Pacific Power Co. v. Hartford Steam Boiler Inspection and Insurance Co., 490 Fed. Appx. 871 (9th Cir. 2012); Lukes v. American Family Mutual Insurance Co., 455 F. Supp.2d 1010 (D. Ariz. 2006).

Tenth Circuit: Davis v. Mid-Century Insurance Co., 311 F.3d 1250 (10th Cir. 2002); Farmland Industries, Inc. v. National Union Fire Insurance Co., 359 F. Supp.2d 1144 (D. Kan. 2005).

Eleventh Circuit: Mills v. Foremost Insurance Co., 511 F.3d 1300 (11th Cir. 2008).

State Courts:

Alabama: Ballard v. Lee, 671 So.2d 1368, 1374 (Ala. 1995), *overruled on other grounds* State Farm Fire & Casualty Co. v. Owen, 729 So.2d 834 (Ala. 1998); Pritchett v. State Farm Mutual Automobile Insurance Co., 834 So.2d 785 (Ala. Civ. App. 2002).

Arizona: Tritschler v. Allstate Insurance Co., 144 P.3d 519, 529 (Ariz. App. 2006).

California: Doan v. State Farm General Insurance Co., 195 Cal. App.4th 1082, 125 Cal. Rptr.3d 793 (2011); Fire Insurance Exchange v. Superior Court, 10 Cal. Rptr.3d 617 (Cal. App. 2004).

Florida: Goff v. State Farm Florida Insurance Co., 999 So.2d 684 (Fla. App. 2008); American Reliance Insurance Co. v. Perez, 689 So.2d 290 (Fla. Dist. App.), *review denied* 698 So.2d 840 (Fla. 1997).

Idaho: Hall v. Farmers Alliance Mutual Insurance Co., 145 Idaho 313, 179 P.3d 276 (2008).

Illinois: Carey v. American Family Brokerage, Inc., 391 Ill. App.3d 273, 909 N.E.2d 255, 330 Ill. Dec. 542 (2009); Young v. Allstate Insurance Co., 812 N.E.2d 741, 748 (Ill. App.), *appeal denied* 823 N.E.2d 980 (Ill. 2004); General Casualty Co. v. Tracer Industries, Inc., 674 N.E.2d 473 (Ill. App. 1996), *appeal denied* 679 N.E.2d 379 (Ill. 1997).

Indiana: Rockford Mutual Insurance Co. v. Pirtle, 911 N.E.2d 60 (Ind. App. 2009).

Louisiana: Jouve v. State Farm Fire and Casualty Co., 74 So.3d 220 (La. App. 2011).

Massachusetts: O'Connor v. Merrimack Mutual Fire Insurance Co., 897 N.E.2d 593 (Mass. App. 2008).

Nebraska: D & S Realty, Inc. v. Markel Insurance Co., 284 Neb. 1, 816 N.W.2d 1 (2012); Olson v. Le Mars Mutual Insurance Co., 696 N.W.2d 453 (Neb. 2005).

New Hampshire: Nicolaou v. Vermont Mutual Insurance Co., 155 N.H. 724, 931 A.2d 1265 (2007).

New York: D.R. Watson Holdings, LLC v. Caliber One Indemnity Co., 789 N.Y.S.2d 787 (N.Y. App. Div. 2005).

Ohio: Jenkins v. State Farm Fire and Casualty Co., 2012 WL 6681882 (Ohio App. Dec. 20, 2012).

Oklahoma: Tyler v. Shelter Mutual Insurance Co., 184 P.3d 496 (Okla. 2008); Branch v. Farmers Insurance Co., 55 P.3d 1023 (Okla. 2002).

Pennsylvania: Mee v. Safeco Insurance Co., 908 A.2d 344, 350–351 (Pa. Super. 2006); Kane v. State Farm Fire & Casualty Co., 841 A.2d 1038 (Pa. Super. 2003), *appeal denied* 871 A.2d 192 (Pa. 2005); Gilderman v. State Farm Insurance Co., 649 A.2d 941, 943 (Pa. Super. 1994), *appeal denied* 661 A.2d 874 (Pa. 1995).

Washington: Holden v. Farmers Insurance Company of Washington, 239 P.3d 344, (Wash. 2010); DePhelps v. Safeco Insurance Co., 65 P.3d 1234 (Wash. App. 2003).

[199] See, e.g.:

Second Circuit: SR International Business Insurance Co. v. World Trade Center Properties, LLC, 445 F. Supp.2d 320 (S.D.N.Y. 2006).

Fifth Circuit: French v. Allstate Indemnity Co., 637 F.3d 571 (5th Cir. 2011); Bradley v. Allstate Insurance Co., 620 F.3d 509 (5th Cir. 2010); Real Asset Management, Inc. v. Lloyd's of London, 61 F.3d 1223 (5th Cir. 1995); Tolar v. Allstate Texas Lloyd's Co., 772 F. Supp.2d 825 (N.D. Tex. 2011); Ghoman v. New Hampshire Insurance Co., 159 F. Supp.2d 928 (N.D. Tex. 2001).

Eighth Circuit: Buddy Bean Lumber Co. v. Axis Surplus Insurance Co., 2013 WL 2248464 (8th Cir. May 23, 2013); Harris v. American Modern Home Insurance Co., 571 F. Supp.2d 1066 (E.D. Mo. 2008).

Ninth Circuit: Sierra Pacific Power Co. v. Hartford Steam Boiler Inspection and Insurance Co., 490 Fed. Appx. 871 (9th Cir. 2012); Lukes v. American Family Mutual Insurance Co., 455 F. Supp.2d 1010 (D. Ariz. 2006).

Tenth Circuit: Davis v. Mid-Century Insurance Co., 311 F.3d 1250 (10th Cir. 2002); Farmland Industries, Inc. v. National Union Fire Insurance Co., 359 F. Supp.2d 1144 (D. Kan. 2005).

Eleventh Circuit: Mills v. Foremost Insurance Co., 511 F.3d 1300 (11th Cir. 2008).

State Courts:

Alabama: Ballard v. Lee, 671 So.2d 1368, 1374 (Ala. 1995), *overruled on other grounds* State Farm Fire & Casualty Co. v. Owen, 729 So.2d 834 (Ala. 1998); Pritchett v. State Farm Mutual Automobile Insurance Co., 834 So.2d 785 (Ala. Civ. App. 2002).

Arizona: Tritschler v. Allstate Insurance Co., 144 P.3d 519, 529 (Ariz. App. 2006).

California: Doan v. State Farm General Insurance Co., 195 Cal. App.4th 1082, 125 Cal. Rptr.3d 793 (2011); Fire Insurance Exchange v. Superior Court, 10 Cal. Rptr.3d 617 (Cal. App. 2004).

Florida: Goff v. State Farm Florida Insurance Co., 999 So.2d 684 (Fla. App. 2008); American Reliance Insurance Co. v. Perez, 689 So.2d 290 (Fla. Dist. App.), *review denied* 698 So.2d 840 (Fla. 1997).

Idaho: Hall v. Farmers Alliance Mutual Insurance Co., 145 Idaho 313, 179 P.3d 276 (2008).

Illinois: Carey v. American Family Brokerage, Inc., 391 Ill. App.3d 273, 909 N.E.2d 255, 330 Ill. Dec. 542 (2009); Young v. Allstate Insurance Co., 812 N.E.2d 741, 748 (Ill. App.), *appeal denied* 823 N.E.2d 980 (Ill. 2004); General Casualty Co. v. Tracer Industries, Inc., 674 N.E.2d 473 (Ill. App. 1996), *appeal denied* 679 N.E.2d 379 (Ill. 1997).

Indiana: Rockford Mutual Insurance Co. v. Pirtle, 911 N.E.2d 60 (Ind. App. 2009).

Louisiana: Jouve v. State Farm Fire and Casualty Co., 74 So.3d 220 (La. App. 2011).

Massachusetts: O'Connor v. Merrimack Mutual Fire Insurance Co., 897 N.E.2d 593 (Mass. App. 2008).

Nebraska: D & S Realty, Inc. v. Markel Insurance Co., 284 Neb. 1, 816 N.W.2d 1 (2012); Olson v. Le Mars Mutual Insurance Co., 696 N.W.2d 453 (Neb. 2005).

New Hampshire: Nicolaou v. Vermont Mutual Insurance Co., 155 N.H. 724, 931 A.2d 1265 (2007).

New York: D.R. Watson Holdings, LLC v. Caliber One Indemnity Co., 789 N.Y.S.2d 787 (N.Y. App. Div. 2005).

Ohio: Jenkins v. State Farm Fire and Casualty Co., 2012 WL 6681882 (Ohio App. Dec. 20, 2012).

Oklahoma: Tyler v. Shelter Mutual Insurance Co., 184 P.3d 496 (Okla. 2008); Branch v. Farmers Insurance Co., 55 P.3d 1023 (Okla. 2002).

Pennsylvania: Mee v. Safeco Insurance Co., 908 A.2d 344, 350–351 (Pa. Super. 2006); Kane v. State Farm Fire & Casualty Co., 841 A.2d 1038 (Pa. Super. 2003), *appeal denied* 871 A.2d 192 (Pa. 2005); Gilderman v. State Farm Insurance Co., 649 A.2d 941, 943 (Pa. Super. 1994), *appeal denied* 661 A.2d 874 (Pa. 1995).

Washington: Holden v. Farmers Insurance Company of Washington, 239 P.3d 344, (Wash. 2010); DePhelps v. Safeco Insurance Co., 65 P.3d 1234 (Wash. App. 2003).

[200] See, e.g.:

Second Circuit: Executive Plaza L.L.C. v. Peerless Insurance Co., 2013 WL 2249134 (2d Cir. May 23, 2013).

Fifth Circuit: Cameron Parish School Board v. RSUI Indemnity Co., 2008 WL 5082136 (W.D. La. Nov. 25, 2008).

State Courts:

Colorado: Dupre v. Allstate Insurance Co., 62 P.3d 1024 (Colo. App. 2002).

Kansas: Burchett v. Kansas Mutual Insurance Co., 48 P.3d 1290 (Kan. App. 2002).

Pennsylvania: Gilderman v. State Farm Insurance Co., 649 A.2d 941, 945 (Pa. Super. 1994), *appeal denied* 661 A.2d 874 (Pa. 1995); Rotell v. Erie Insurance Group, 53 Pa. D. & C.4th 533 (Pa. C.P. 2001).

[201] *Id.*

[202] *Id.* See also:

Eleventh Circuit: Langhorne v. Fireman's Fund Insurance Co., 432 F. Supp.2d 1274 (N.D. Fla. 2006).

State Courts:

Kansas: Burchett v. Kansas Mutual Insurance Co., 48 P.3d 1290 (Kan. App. 2002).

New York: Todd v. Wayne Co-op. Insurance Co., 819 N.Y.S.2d 179 (N.Y. App. Div. 2006).

Pennsylvania: Burton v. Republic Insurance Co., 845 A.2d 889 (Pa. Super. 2004); Rotell v. Erie Insurance Group, 53 Pa. D. & C.4th 533 (Pa. C.P. 2001).

203 See, e.g.:

California: Alex R. Thomas & Co. v. Pacific Indemnity Co., 2002 WL 737478 (Cal. App. Apr. 26, 2002).

Louisiana: Higginbotham v. New Hampshire Indemnity Co., 498 So.2d 1149 (La. App. 1986), *writ denied* 501 So.2d 236 (La. 1987).

Nebraska: Eledge v. Farmers Mutual Home Insurance Co., 571 N.W.2d 105 (Neb. App. 1997).

204 See, e.g.:

Alabama: Padgett v. State Farm Fire Insurance Co., 714 So.2d 302 (Ala. Civ. App. 1997).

California: Alex R. Thomas & Co. v. Pacific Indemnity Co., 2002 WL 737478 (Cal. App. Apr. 26, 2002) (promising to pay cost to repair or replace subject to the least of the three choices listed above).

205 See, e.g.:

Fourth Circuit: Tidewater Equipment Co. v. Reliance Insurance Co., 650 F.2d 503 (4th Cir. 1981).

State Courts:

Florida: Northbrook Property & Casualty Insurance Co. v. R. & J. Crane Service, Inc., 765 So.2d 836 (Fla. Dist. App. 2000).

206 See, e.g., Cozen, *Insuring Real Property*, § 25.04[6] (2004) (courts generally hold that insurance company is required to replace damaged property unless it can be shown that the repair will fully compensate the policyholder).

207 See, e.g.:

Fourth Circuit: Tidewater Equipment Co. v. Reliance Insurance Co., 650 F.2d 503 (4th Cir. 1981) (evidence that crane could not be returned to its pre-loss condition warranted replacement over repair).

State Courts:

Florida: Northbrook Property & Casualty Insurance Co. v. R. & J. Crane Service, Inc., 765 So.2d 836, 839–846 (Fla. Dist. App. 2000) (replacement of crane warranted because OSHA required that damaged crane could not be repaired and placed back in use).

Louisiana: Becnel v. Lafayette Insurance Co., 773 So.2d 247 (La. App. 2000), *writ denied* 785 So.2d 827 (La. 2001) (repair would not necessarily return roof to pre-loss condition); Higginbotham v. New Hampshire Indemnity Co., 498 So.2d 1149, 1152 (La. App. 1986), *writ denied* 501 So.2d 236 (La. 1987) (uncontroverted evidence establishing that repaired roof would not guarantee against leakage supported conclusion that replacement was warranted).

208 See, e.g.:

Alabama: Padgett v. State Farm Fire Insurance Co., 714 So.2d 302, 303–304 (Ala. Civ. App. 1997) (expert established that roof could be returned to pre-loss condition through repair).

California: Alex R. Thomas & Co. v. Pacific Indemnity Co., 2002 WL 737478 (Cal. App. Apr. 26, 2002) (repair warranted because there was no evidence to support conclusion that replacement was the only effective solution).

Iowa: Hulsing v. Iowa National Mutual Insurance Co., 329 N.W.2d 5 (Iowa 1983) (repair is permitted where damaged property, when repaired, is in as good a condition as it was before the loss).

Nebraska: Eledge v. Farmers Mutual Home Insurance Co., 571 N.W.2d 105, 147–148 (Neb. App. 1997) (replacement of the whole is not required where evidence shows that it can be satisfactorily repaired by replacement of a part so long as the building is returned to like construction and use as a result of the repair).

209 See Padgett v. State Farm Fire Insurance Co., 714 So.2d 302, 303–304 (Ala. Civ. App. 1997).

210 For further discussion, see § 3.05[4] *supra*.

211 *Id.* See also:

Second Circuit: Wachovia Bank, N.A. v. EnCap Golf Holdings, L.L.C., 690 F. Supp.2d 311 (S.D.N.Y. 2010).

Fifth Circuit: Amerisure Insurance Co. v. Navigators Insurance Co., 611 F.3d 299 (5th Cir. 2010).

Eighth Circuit: Travelers Property Casualty Insurance Company of America v. National Union Insurance Company of Pittsburg, PA, 621 F.3d 697 (8th Cir. 2010); Kinetic Co. v. Medtronic, Inc., 672 F. Supp.2d 933 (D. Minn. 2009).

Ninth Circuit: Chandler v. State Farm Mutual Automobile Insurance Co., 596 F. Supp.2d 1314 (C.D. Cal. 2008).

State Courts:

Arizona: Desert Mountain Properties Limited Partnership v. Liberty Mutual Fire Insurance Co., 225 Ariz. 194, 236 P.3d 421 (Ariz. App. 2010).

California: 21st Century Insurance Co. v. Superior Court, 47 Cal.4th 511, 213 P.3d 972, 98 Cal. Rptr.3d 516 (2009); Amerigas Propane, L.P. v. Landstar Ranger, Inc., 184 Cal. App.4th 981, 109 Cal. Rptr.3d 686 (2010).

Colorado: American Family Mutual Insurance Co. v. DeWitt, 218 P.3d 318 (Colo. 2009); United Fire Group *ex rel.* Metamorphosis Salon v. Powers Electric, Inc., 240 P.3d 569 (Colo. App. 2010).

Florida: State Farm Florida Insurance Co. v. Loo, 27 So.3d 747 (Fla. App. 2010).

Iowa: Wilson v. Farm Bureau Mutual Insurance Co., 770 N.W.2d 324 (Iowa 2009).

Nebraska: Thrower v. Anson, 752 N.W.2d 555 (Neb. 2008).

New York: NYP Holdings, Inc. v. McClier Corp., 65 A.D.3d 186, 881 N.Y.S.2d 407 (2009).

Ohio: Corn v. Whitmere, 183 Ohio App.3d 204, 916 N.E.2d 838 (2009).

Rhode Island: Credit Union Central Falls v. Groff, 966 A.2d 1262 (R.I. 2009).

Texas: Bay Rock Operating Co. v. St. Paul Surplus Lines Insurance Co., 298 S.W.3d 216 (Tex. App. 2009).

Wisconsin: Fischer v. Steffen, 325 Wis.2d 382, 783 N.W.2d 889 (Wis. App. 2010).

212 *Id.*

213 See ISO Form CP 00 10 04 02. See also:

First Circuit: D'Agostino v. Federal Insurance Co., 2013 WL 3106203 (D. Mass. June 17, 2013).

Third Circuit: Williamson v. Chubb Indemnity Insurance Co., 2013 WL 3009911 (E.D. Pa. June 17, 2013).

Fifth Circuit: Smith v. Employers Mutual Insurance Co., No. 06-1440, 2006 WL 3533126 (W.D. La. Dec. 7, 2006) (appraisal process is permissive not mandatory).

Sixth Circuit: Hartford Insurance Co. v. Miller, 2006 WL 2844124 (E.D. Mich. Sept. 30, 2006).

Ninth Circuit: Moncada v. Allstate Insurance Co., No. C 05-4762, 2006 WL 3782835, at *5 (N.D. Cal. Dec. 20, 2006) ("either party may request that disputes over the amount of a loss be decided by appraisal by an independent umpire").

Eleventh Circuit: Moore v. Travelers, 321 Fed. Appx. 911 (11th Cir. 2009).

State Courts:

California: Community Assisting Recovery, Inc. v. Aegis Security Insurance Co., 112 Cal. Rptr.2d 304 (Cal. App. 2001).

Georgia: Thornton v. Georgia Farm Bureau Mutual Insurance Co., 287 Ga. 379, 695 S.E.2d 642 (2010).

Michigan: Auto-Owners Insurance Co. v. Kwaiser, 476 N.W.2d 467, 469 (Mich. App. 1991) (the appraisal process is a "substitute for judicial determination of a dispute concerning the amount of loss, which is a simple and inexpensive method for the prompt adjustment and settlement of the claims" [internal quotations and citations omitted]; although the process is not subject to the strict standard of review associated with statutory arbitration, "[j]udicial review of the [umpire's] award is limited to instances of bad faith, fraud, misconduct, or manifest mistake," citing Davis v. National Am. Insurance Co., 259 N.W.2d 433 (Mich. App. 1977)).

214 See, e.g.:

Sixth Circuit: Hartford Insurance Co. v. Miller, 2006 WL 2844124 at *6 (E.D. Mich. Sept. 30, 2006) ("The umpire generally is limited to determining the amount of loss based on competing claims of the parties.").

Eleventh Circuit: Moore v. Travelers, 321 Fed. Appx. 911 (11th Cir. 2009).

State Courts:

California: Safeco Insurance Company of America v. Sharma, 160 Cal. App.3d 1060, 1063 (1984).

Georgia: Thornton v. Georgia Farm Bureau Mutual Insurance Co., 287 Ga. 379, 695 S.E.2d 642 (2010).

Michigan: Auto-Owners Insurance Co. v. Kwaiser, 476 N.W.2d 467, 469–470 (Mich. App. 1991) ("The umpire generally is limited to determining the amount of loss based on competing claims of the parties. As a result, '[m]atters of insurance coverage are . . . for a court and not for appraisers.'"; "In fact, '[t]he appraisal process cannot legally settle coverage issues.'"; "Where the parties cannot agree on coverage, a court is to determine coverage in a declaratory action before an appraisal of the damage to the property.").

215 See, e.g.:

Sixth Circuit: Hartford Insurance Co. v. Miller, 2006 WL 2844124 at *7 (E.D. Mich. Sept. 30, 2006) ("failure to assert a coverage issue may constitute waiver once the appraisal process begins").

State Courts:

Michigan: Angott v. Chubb Group Insurance, 717 N.W.2d 341, 347 (Mich. App.), *appeal denied* 723 N.W.2d 825 (Mich. 2006) (rejecting coverage claim because "by indicating that the court should not be involved with the case and that the appraisal process was the only appropriate avenue for relief, defendant was necessarily conceding that there were no coverage issues to be judicially resolved. The issue of coverage under the policy was waived.").

216 See ISO Form CP 00 10 04 02. See also:

Fifth Circuit: Fanning v. American Reliable Insurance Co., 2010 WL 724130 (E.D. La. Feb. 19, 2010); Boone v. Safeco Insurance Company of Indiana, 2009 WL 3063320 (S.D. Tex. Sept. 22, 2009).

Eleventh Circuit: El Dorado Towers Condominium Association v. QBE Insurance Corp., 2010 WL 2400082 (S.D. Fla. June 16, 2010); Swaebe v. Federal Insurance Co., 374 Fed. Appx. 855 (11th Cir. 2010).

State Courts:

California: Village of Northridge Homeowners Association v. State Farm Fire and Casualty Co., 50 Cal.4th 913, 237 P.3d 598, 114 Cal. Rptr.3d 280 (2010).

Florida: Menendez v. Progressive Express Insurance Co., Inc., 35 So.3d 873 (Fla. 2010); Kramer v. State Farm Florida Insurance Co., 95 So.3d 303 (Fla. App. 2012); First Home Insurance Co. v. Fleurimond, 36 So.3d 172 (Fla. App. 2010).

Georgia: Resource Life Insurance Co. v. Buckner, 304 Ga. App. 719, 698 S.E.2d 19 (Ga. 2010).

Illinois: *MHM Services, Inc. v. Assurance Company of America,* 975 N.E.2d 1139, 363 Ill. Dec. 830 (Ill. App. 2012).

Michigan: Tenneco, Inc. v. Amerisure Mutual Insurance Co., 281 Mich. App. 429, 761 N.W.2d 846 (2008).

New York: Henner v. Everdry Marketing and Management, Inc., 74 A.D.3d 1776, 902 N.Y.S.2d 765 (2010).

Pennsylvania: Ario v. Underwriting Members of Lloyd's of London Syndicates 33, 205 and 506, 996 A.2d 588 (Pa. Commw. 2010).

Texas: U.S. Fire Insurance Co. v. Lynd Co., 2012 WL 3326344 (Tex. App. Aug. 15, 2012).

217 See ISO Form CP 00 10 04 02.

218 *Id.*

219 See:

District of Columbia Circuit: Carley Capital Group v. Fireman's Fund Insurance Co., 877 F.2d 78 (D.C. Cir. 1989).

State Courts:

Florida: General Star Indemnity Co. v. West Florida Village Inn, Inc., 874 So.2d 26 (Fla. App. 2004).

Kansas: Wenrich v. Employers Mutual Insurance Cos., 132 P.3d 970 (Kan. App. 2006).

Maine: Boudreau v. Manufacturers and Merchants Mutual Insurance Co., 588 A.2d 286 (Me. 1991).

Michigan: Royal Property Group, LLC v. Prime Insurance Syndicate, Inc., 706 N.W.2d 426 (Mich. App. 2005).

New York: Rochester and Southern Railroad, Inc. v. Utica Mutual Insurance Co., 156 A.D.2d 1000, 550 N.Y.S.2d 761 (1989); Aldrich v. Great American Insurance Co., New York, 195 A.D. 174, 186 N.Y.S. 569 (1921).

Washington: Wetmore v. Unigard Insurance Co., 125 Wash. App. 938, 107 P.3d 123 (2005).

220 See ISO Form CP 00 30 04 02.

221 *Id.*

222 *Id.* See also:

First Circuit: Vermont Mutual Insurance Co. v. Petit, 613 F. Supp.2d 154 (D. Mass. 2009).

Second Circuit: Duane Reade, Inc. v. St. Paul Fire and Marine Insurance Co., 600 F.3d 190 (2d Cir. 2010); Eurospark Industries, Inc. v. Underwriters at Lloyds Subscribing to Risk on Cover No. 97FA0071010A, 567 F. Supp.2d 345 (E.D.N.Y. 2008).

Third Circuit: Ski Shawnee, Inc. v. Commonwealth Insurance Co., 2010 WL 2696782 (M.D. Pa. July 6, 2010).

Fourth Circuit: Breton, L.L.C. v. Graphic Arts Mutual Insurance Co., 2010 WL 678128 (E.D. Va. Feb. 24, 2010).

Fifth Circuit: GBP Partners, Ltd. v. Maryland Casualty Co., 505 Fed. Appx. 389 (5th Cir. 2013); Dillard University v. Lexington Insurance Co., 2009 WL 1565943 (E.D. La. June 3, 2009).

Eighth Circuit: George's, Inc. v. Allianz Global Risks U.S. Insurance Co., 596 F.3d 989 (8th Cir. 2010).

Ninth Circuit: Polymer Plastics Corp. v. Hartford Casualty Insurance Co., 389 Fed. Appx. 703 (9th Cir. 2010); Zurich American Insurance Co. v. Coeur Rochester, Inc., 720 F. Supp.2d 1223 (D. Nev. 2010).

Eleventh Circuit: Bartram, L.L.C. v. Landmark American Insurance Co., 864 F. Supp.2d 1229 (N.D. Fla. 2012).

State Courts:

Arizona: Aztar Corp. v. U.S. Fire Insurance Co., 223 Ariz. 463, 224 P.3d 960 (Ariz. App. 2010).

California: Amerigraphics, Inc. v. Mercury Casualty Co., 182 Cal. App.4th 1538, 107 Cal. Rptr.3d 307 (2010).

Georgia: Lavoi Corp., Inc. v. National Fire Insurance of Hartford, 293 Ga. App. 142, 666 S.E.2d 387 (2008).

Illinois: Baxter International, Inc. v. American Guaranty and Liability Insurance Co., 861 N.E.2d 263 (Ill. App. 2006); Lyon Metal Products, LLC v. Protection Mutual Insurance Co., 747 N.E.2d 495 (Ill. App. 2001).

Louisiana: Maloney Cinque, L.L.C. v. Pacific Insurance Co., 89 So.3d 12 (La. App. 2012); Chalmette Retail Center, L.L.C. v. LaFayette Insurance Co., 974 So.2d 822 (La. App. 2008).

Michigan: Farm Bureau General Insurance Co. of Michigan v. Dynamic Land, L.L.C., 2009 WL 454961 (Mich. App. Feb. 24, 2009).

Nevada: Fourth Street Place v. Travelers Indemnity Co., 270 P.3d 1235 (Nev. 2011).

New Jersey: Wakefern Food Corp. v. Liberty Mutual Fire Insurance Co., 406 N.J. Super. 524, 968 A.2d 724 (2009).

New York: Bi-Economy Market, Inc. v. Harleysville Insurance Company of New York, 10 N.Y.3d 187, 886 N.E.2d 127, 856 N.Y.S.2d 505 (2008).

North Carolina: Defeat The Beat, Inc. v. Underwriters at Lloyd's London, 194 N.C. App. 108, 669 S.E.2d 48 (2008).

Ohio: Trautman v. Union Insurance Co., 2010 WL 1267217 (Ohio App. Apr. 5, 2010).

Pennsylvania: Bishops, Inc. v. Penn National Insurance Co., 984 A.2d 982 (Pa. Super. 2009); Berkeley Inn, Inc. v. Centennial Insurance Co., 422 A.2d 1078, 1080–1081 (Pa. Super. 1980).

[223] See Berkeley Inn, Inc. v. Centennial Insurance Co., 422 A.2d 1078, 1080–1081 (Pa. Super. 1980). See also, Lyon Metal Products, LLC v. Protection Mutual Insurance Co., 747 N.E.2d 495 (Ill. App. 2001).

[224] See ISO Form CP 00 30 04 02. See also, N. 3 *supra.*

[225] See Travelers Indemnity Co. v. Pollard Friendly Ford Co., 512 S.W.2d 375 (Tex. App. 1974). See also, N. 3 *supra.*

[226] See:

Fifth Circuit: GBP Partners, Ltd. v. Maryland Casualty Co., 505 Fed. Appx. 389 (5th Cir. 2013).

Eighth Circuit: Midwest Regional Allergy, Asthma, Arthritis and Osteoporosis Center, P.C. v. Cincinnati Insurance Co., 2013 WL 4400823 (W.D. Mo. Aug. 15, 2013).

State Courts:

Illinois: Chatham Corp. v. Dann Insurance, 812 N.E.2d 483 (Ill. App. 2004). See also, Lyon Metal Prods., LLC v. Protection Mutual Insurance Co., 747 N.E.2d 495 (Ill. App. 2001) (extra expenses necessary to prevent lost earnings).

Louisiana: Maloney Cinque, L.L.C. v. Pacific Insurance Co., 89 So.3d 12 (La. App. 2012).

[227] See Butwin Sportswear Co. v. St. Paul Fire & Marine Insurance Co., 534 N.W.2d 565 (Minn. App. 1995). See also, N. 3 *supra*.

[228] See Thompson v. Threshermen's Mutual Insurance Co., 493 N.W.2d 734 (Wis. App. 1992), *review denied* 497 N.W.2d 132 (Wis. 1993). See also, N. 3 *supra*.

[229] See Port Murray Dairy Co. v. Providence Washington Insurance Co., 145 A.2d 504 (N.J. Super. 1958). See also, N. 3 *supra*.

[230] See ISO Form CP 00 30 04 02.

[231] See, e.g., American Medical Imaging Corp. v. St. Paul Fire & Marine Insurance Co., 949 F.2d 690, 693–694 (3d Cir. 1991).

[232] See *In re* S.N.A. Nut Co., 210 B.R. 140, 144 (N.D. Ill. 1997).

[233] *Id.*

[234] *Id.*

[235] *Id.,* 210 B.R. at 144–145.

[236] *Id.,* 210 B.R. at 145.

[237] See Borghesi, "Business Interruption Insurance—A Business Perspective," 17 Nova L.R. 1147, 1153–1156 (1993).

[238] Proof of lost profits, many times, is difficult with respect to a business that does not have a long "track record." Past experience in a similar business and/or some profit experience since operations began can be enough to gauge profit expectancies. See Cozen, *Insuring Real Property*, § 3.05[5][c] (1994).

[239] See, e.g., American Medical Imaging Corp. v. St. Paul Fire & Marine Insurance Co., 949 F.2d 690, 693–694 (3d Cir. 1991).

[240] See, e.g.:

Arkansas: Liberty Mutual Insurance Co. v. Sexton Foods Co., 854 S.W.2d 365 (Ark. App. 1993).

Tennessee: Continental Insurance Co. v. DNE Corp., 834 S.W.2d 930 (Tenn. 1992).

[241] See Finger Furniture Co. v. Commonwealth Ins. Co., 404 F.3d 312 (5th Cir. 2005).

[242] *Third Circuit:* Ski Shawnee, Inc. v. Commonwealth Insurance Co., 2010 WL 2696782 (M.D. Pa. July 6, 2010).

Fifth Circuit: Dillard University v. Lexington Insurance Co., 2009 WL 1565943 (E.D. La. June 3, 2009).

Ninth Circuit: Zurich American Insurance Co. v. Coeur Rochester, Inc., 720 F. Supp.2d 1223 (D. Nev. 2010).

State Courts:

Arizona: Aztar Corp. v. U.S. Fire Insurance Co., 223 Ariz. 463, 224 P.3d 960 (Ariz. App. 2010).

Minnesota: Forestview The Beautiful, Inc. v. All Nation Insurance Co., 704 N.W.2d 773 (Minn. App. 2005) (total cessation).

New York: Broad Street, LLC v. Gulf Insurance Co., 2006 WL 3593049 (N.Y. App. Div. Dec. 12, 2006) ("Necessary suspension" of operations, required as condition of business interruption coverage of apartment building owner's commercial property insurance policy, meant total cessation of insured's business operations, not mere suspension of normal business activities.).

[243] *Id.*

[244] See, e.g., American Medical Imaging Corp. v. St. Paul Fire & Marine Insurance Co., 949 F.2d 690, 692–693 (3d Cir. 1991). See also:

Third Circuit: Ski Shawnee, Inc. v. Commonwealth Insurance Co., 2010 WL 2696782 (M.D. Pa. July 6, 2010).

Fifth Circuit: Dillard University v. Lexington Insurance Co., 2009 WL 1565943 (E.D. La. June 3, 2009).

Ninth Circuit: Zurich American Insurance Co. v. Coeur Rochester, Inc., 720 F. Supp.2d 1223 (D. Nev. 2010).

State Courts:

Arizona: Aztar Corp. v. U.S. Fire Insurance Co., 223 Ariz. 463, 224 P.3d 960 (Ariz. App. 2010).

245 Lewis and Insua, *Business Income Insurance Disputes*, § 3.0[B][3] (2006).

246 *Id.*

247 See ISO Form CP 00 30 04 02. See also:

Second Circuit: Rapid Park Industries v. Great Northern Insurance Co., 502 Fed. Appx. 40 (2d Cir. 2012); United Air Lines, Inc. v. Insurance Company of the State of Pennsylvania, 439 F.3d 128 (2d Cir. 2006).

Fifth Circuit: Dickie Brennan & Co. v. Lexington Insurance Co., 636 F.3d 683 (5th Cir. 2011).

Sixth Circuit: Southeast Mental Health Center, Inc. v. Pacific Insurance Co., 439 F. Supp.2d 831 (W.D. Tenn. 2006).

Eighth Circuit: Source Food Technology, Inc. v. United States Fidelity and Guaranty Co., 465 F.3d 834 (8th Cir. 2006).

State Courts:

Arizona: Aztar Corp. v. U.S. Fire Insurance Co., 223 Ariz. 463, 224 P.3d 960 (Ariz. App. 2010).

Nevada: Fourth Street Place v. Travelers Indemnity Co., 270 P.3d 1235 (Nev. 2011).

New Jersey: Arthur Andersen L.L.P. v. Federal Insurance Co., 416 N.J. Super. 334, 3 A.3d 1279 (2010).

248 See § 4.03[4] *supra*.

249 See, e.g., 54th Street Limited Partnership v. Fidelity & Guaranty Insurance Co., 763 N.Y.S.2d 243 (N.Y. App. Div. 2003). See also:

State Courts:

Arizona: Aztar Corp. v. U.S. Fire Insurance Co., 223 Ariz. 463, 224 P.3d 960 (Ariz. App. 2010).

New Jersey: Arthur Andersen L.L.P. v. Federal Insurance Co., 416 N.J. Super. 334, 3 A.3d 1279 (2010).

250 See, e.g., Harry's Cadillac-Pontiac-GMC Truck Center v. Motors Insurance Co., 486 S.E.2d 249 (N.C. App. 1997) (no business income loss because evidence revealed that loss resulted from inaccessibility to reach premises during snowstorm rather than from damage to roof caused by snowstorm).

251 See: Duane Reade, Inc. v. St. Paul Fire & Marine Insurance Co., 411 F.3d 384 (2d Cir. 2005); Lava Trading, Inc. v. Hartford Fire Insurance Co., 365 F. Supp.2d 434 (S.D.N.Y. 2005).

252 *Id.*

253 See Broad Street, LLC v. Gulf Insurance Co., 2006 WL 3593049 (N.Y. App. Div. Dec. 12, 2006). See also, Lewis and Insua, *Business Income Insurance Disputes*, § 3.03[D] (2006).

254 See ISO Form CP 00 30 04 02.

255 See Prudential LMI Commercial Insurance Co. v. Colleton Enterprises, Inc., 1992 WL 252507 (4th Cir. 1992). See also, Lewis and Insua, *Business Income Insurance Disputes*, § 3.03[D] (2006).

[256] See Prudential LMI Commercial Insurance Co. v. Colleton Enterprises, Inc., 1992 WL 252507 (4th Cir. 1992). See also, Lewis and Insua, *Business Income Insurance Disputes*, § 3.03[D] (2006).

[257] See Prudential LMI Commercial Insurance Co. v. Colleton Enterprises, Inc., 1992 WL 252507 (4th Cir. 1992). See also, Lewis and Insua, *Business Income Insurance Disputes*, § 3.03[D] (2006).

[258] See Prudential LMI Commercial Insurance Co. v. Colleton Enterprises, Inc., 1992 WL 252507 (4th Cir. 1992). See also, Lewis and Insua, *Business Income Insurance Disputes*, § 3.03[D] (2006).

[259] See Prudential LMI Commercial Insurance Co. v. Colleton Enterprises, Inc., 1992 WL 252507 (4th Cir. 1992). See also, Lewis and Insua, *Business Income Insurance Disputes*, § 3.03[D] (2006).

[260] See Prudential LMI Commercial Insurance Co. v. Colleton Enterprises, Inc., 1992 WL 252507 (4th Cir. 1992). See also, Lewis and Insua, *Business Income Insurance Disputes*, § 3.03[D] (2006).

[261] Prudential LMI Commercial Insurance Co. v. Colleton Enterprises, Inc., 1992 WL 252507 (4th Cir. 1992).

[262] *Id.*, 1992 WL 252507, at *1.

[263] *Id.*

[264] *Id.*, 1992 WL 252507, at *2.

[265] *Id.*, 1992 WL 252507, at *4. See also, American Automobile Insurance Co. v. Fisherman's Paradise Boats, Inc., 1994 WL 1720238 (S.D. Fla. Oct. 3, 1994) (policyholder, a boat seller, whose business was interrupted by a hurricane, could not include in its business income claim the increased business it would have done after the hurricane because of increased need for marine equipment, on the grounds that "windfall profits are not within the scope of the policy" which, like the policy, based business income projections on "the likely Net Income of the business if no loss or damage occurred").

CHAPTER 5

Comprehensive or Commercial General Liability (CGL) Insurance: Coverage A for "Bodily Injury" or "Property Damage" Liabilities

Chapter Contents

§ 5.01 Overview of CGL Insurance

Comprehensive or commercial general liability insurance, known as "CGL" insurance, is a form of third-party insurance that is commonly known as "litigation insurance."[1] CGL insurance deals with insurance coverage for situations in which a third party has suffered a loss in the form of bodily injury,[2] property damage,[3] or injuries related to a list of enumerated intentional torts known as personal or advertising injuries,[4] and is seeking monetary or other damages from the policyholder by way of a civil action or demand. The policyholder then uses the CGL insurance (in particular, the defense and indemnity provisions) to protect himself, herself, or itself against third-party litigation costs and damages awarded for or related to the bodily injury, property damage, or personal or advertising injury suffered by the claimant(s).[5]

CGL insurance contains two principal coverage parts, one for "bodily injury" and "property damage" liabilities, known as "Coverage A," and one for "personal and advertising injury" liabilities, known as "Coverage B." Both Coverage A and Coverage B have separate, albeit similar, insuring agreements and exclusions and are subject to similar terms and conditions.[6]

This chapter focuses upon the insuring agreement under Coverage A, along with General Conditions applicable to Coverage A.[7] In particular, this chapter focuses on the CGL Coverage A insuring agreement issues most relevant to real estate-related businesses, including, without limitation, ownership of land issues and design, development, and construction liability issues.

Most of the relevant exclusions for Coverage A are the primary focus of a subsequent chapter.[8] The pollution exclusion of Coverage A (and of almost any other insurance policy) is the focus of a separate chapter.[9] Coverage B, which deals with "personal and advertising injury" liabilities, including the insuring agreement, exclusions, and conditions applicable thereto, is the subject of yet another subsequent chapter.[10] Finally, the duty to defend, which is part of Coverage A and coverage B, is the subject of the next chapter.[11]

§ 5.02 Coverage A Insuring Agreement

In Coverage A, CGL insurance policies generally contain promises by the insurance company to defend and indemnify the policyholder for certain "bodily injury" or "property damage" claims asserted by third parties. A typical provision states:

> "a. We will pay those sums that the insured becomes legally obligated to pay as damages because of 'bodily injury' or 'property damage' to which this insurance applies. We will have the right and duty to defend the insured against any 'suit' seeking those damages.

b. This insurance applies to 'bodily injury' and 'property damage' only if:

(1) The 'bodily injury' or 'property damage' is caused by an 'occurrence' that takes place in the 'coverage territory';

(2) The 'bodily injury' or 'property damage' occurs during the policy period."[12]

Thus, the Coverage A insuring agreement issues are as follows:

1. the identity of the insurance company ("we" or "the company");[13]
2. allocation ("all sums" or "those sums");[14]
3. the identity of the policyholder ("you" or "the insured");[15]
4. "legally obligated to pay as damages";[16]
5. "bodily injury" or "property damage";[17]
6. "occurrence";[18] and
7. the duty to defend.[19]

Within each of these issues are a myriad of subissues, which are discussed herein.

§ 5.03 Coverage A Issues

[1]—Identity of the Insurance Company—Meaning of "We" or "The Company"

"We" or "the company" as used in the Coverage A insuring agreement of CGL policies means the insurance company providing the insurance. This is usually identified in the policy or in the declarations pages attached to the policy. The identity of the insurer is particularly relevant to long-tail claims, described in the immediately subsequent paragraph.

[a]—Latent Defect Liabilities

The identity of the insurance company is important in the environmental, toxic tort, and construction liability areas. In these subjects, policyholders generally experience latent defect problems that often are hidden with the damage first becoming apparent years after the happening of initial conditions or conduct that caused, and/or is continuing to cause, the damage to take place. This results in litigation that often may take place years after the occurrence of the precise conduct that ultimately is proven to be the cause of the third-party damage.[20]

In these latent injury cases, courts generally hold that, among others, policies purchased near in time to the injury-causing conduct provide coverage for the loss.[21] Consequently, a policyholder may very well need insurance it purchases today to pay for future liabilities and costs of third-party litigation. In the same vein, a policyholder may need insurance policies it, or its predecessors, purchased years ago to cover litigation commenced today. Accordingly, a policyholder will want to consider carefully the insurance company's financial rating, as well as the rating of all affiliated companies, before deciding whether to purchase the policy in the first place. If the policyholder purchases insurance from an entity that later fails, the policyholder might be in the unenviable position of having no insurance capable of responding, forcing the policyholder effectively, to self-insure itself at a time after knowledge that a claim will be made and therefore too late to purchase other, alternative insurance.

Brokers may be helpful in selecting financially sound insurers, although a broker's loyalties could be divided based on compensation it receives in the form of commissions and bonuses. There are also insurance rating organizations available in libraries and on the Internet. However, reliance on these organizations is no guarantee, because these agencies often do not find the financial difficulties until it is too late.[22]

Perhaps the best way to deal with insurance company insolvency is through diversification, i.e., purchasing insurance from different companies for different coverages, among various layers in any particular year, and from year to year at all levels.

[b]—Policy Buyouts and General Releases

Another interesting issue that arises in the long-tail coverage context concerns settlements under and buyouts of policies. For instance, whenever a policyholder and insurance company get involved in a coverage dispute, even a dispute over a simple non-long-tail claim, the policyholder needs to think carefully when the insurance company offer pays some amount under the policy in exchange for a release. Policyholders need to be keenly aware and vigilant of attempts by the insurance company to obtain a general release or policy buyout, even where the policy appears to have "expired." The reason for this, of course, concerns the possibility that unknown and latent damage claims might arise in the future and those latent claims might trigger the policy under which the insurance company had sought to obtain a general release.

[2]—Allocation: The Meaning of "Those Sums" or "All Sums"

"Allocation" means apportionment and relates to the meaning of "those sums" or "all sums" in the insuring agreement. The allocation issue arises most acutely in a situation in which a policyholder has an underlying claim or liability that implicates more than one insurance company at the same level. For example, in environmental, asbestos, toxic tort, and construction defect contexts, some courts have determined that multiple policies over the course of several consecutive years are all responsible to defend and indemnify the policyholder.[23]

In such situations, the issues include: (1) which insurance company must pay; and (2) how much must each pay. What must be determined in these instances are (1) allocation among all responsible insurance companies; and (2) allocation between the policyholder, on the one hand, and the insurance companies, on the other hand.

[a]—Allocation among Responsible Insurance Companies

[i]—"Other Insurance" Provisions

Allocation among the responsible insurance companies is generally governed by principles of equitable contribution and the "other insurance" provisions in the policies at issue. There are three types of "other insurance" clauses: (1) *pro rata*; (2) excess; and (3) escape. They provide as follows:

Pro rata clauses provide that the insurer will pay a prorated share of a loss, usually in the proportion the policy limits bear to the total limits of all valid and collectible insurance.

Excess clauses provide that the insurer's liability will be only the amount by which the loss exceeds the coverage of all other valid and collectible insurance.

Escape clauses provide that the policy affords no coverage when there is other valid and collectible insurance.[24]

If the "other insurance" provisions, read in conjunction with each other, provide for an order of payment, courts attempt to effectuate the presumed intent of the parties by following the allocation provisions set forth in the various triggered policies.[25]

However, "other insurance" provisions might conflict and, if construed literally, provide no order or effectively eliminate all coverage for the policyholder. For example, all triggered policies might contain "excess other insurance" provisions, which make the triggered insurance policy excess insurance over all other triggered policies. A sample "excess other insurance" provision states:

"This insurance shall be in excess of . . . any other valid and collectible insurance available to the insured whether such other insurance is stated to be primary, *pro rata*, contributory, excess, contingent or otherwise unless such other insurance is written only as specific excess insurance over the limits of liability provided in this policy."[26]

When such a conflict among "other insurance" provisions exists, it becomes impossible to effectuate the parties' intentions without eliminating primary coverage for the policyholder. For example, if all policies contain "excess clauses" and those clauses are all given effect, no policy can possibly be primary because they would all be deemed excess of all others. Likewise, if all policies contain "escape clauses" and such clauses are given full force and effect, no policy can apply because they would all be deemed as inapplicable given the existence of other insurance. Under such circumstances—namely, the existence of excess escape "other insurance" provisions in all triggered policies of the same level—the law in most, if not all, jurisdictions provides that each insurance company must contribute. As stated by one court, "Where policies each contain excess or escape clauses, they are declared mutually repugnant, and each insurer is required to contribute to the loss, for to give effect to both clauses would result in no coverage for the insured."[27]

[ii]—Joinder of Other Insurance Companies

When there is more than one triggered policy for a particular loss, and thus other responsible insurance company(ies), an issue arises as to whether the defendant insurance companies can force the policyholder to join all such "other insurers" in a coverage suit. Under the Federal Rules of Civil Procedure, plaintiffs are required to join all "necessary" and "indispensable" parties.[28] There are similar requirements in many state civil procedure rules.[29]

Courts have come to different results as to whether "other insurers" are necessary and indispensable parties that are required to be joined in an insurance coverage declaratory judgment action.[30] Moreover, even if the defendant insurance companies attempt to join a non-diverse "other insurer," such joinder will not deprive a federal court of diversity of citizenship jurisdiction, as long as the policyholder does not amend its complaint to assert a claim against the non-diverse party.[31] Indeed, a plaintiff generally enjoys the right to select a forum, and the defendant(s) cannot add parties to oust the court of jurisdiction.[32]

[iii]—Stacking Policies

Where more than one insurance policy is triggered by a particular occurrence, the policyholder will attempt to use all triggered policies to the extent of his, her, or its loss. This might mean the policyholder needs to use the indemnity limits from more than one policy. This is called stacking.[33] Stacking is generally permitted unless stated otherwise in the policies.[34] A typical antistacking provision provides as follows: "The total limit of our liability under all policies issued to [the policyholder] by [the insurance company] shall not exceed the highest limit of liability under any one policy."[35] These provisions are generally enforced if unambiguous and not against public policy.[36] Anti-stacking typically involves multiple policies sold by one insurance company, albeit language could be drafted to apply to other insurers' policies as well.

[b]—Policyholder Contribution

Regardless of how the triggered insurers allocate liability among themselves, a question arises as to allocation between the policyholder and the insurers. The question is important where there are gaps in coverage over a policyholder's history, either due to lack of insurance, lack of enough insurance, or insolvency of an insurer. Courts have applied two principal approaches or theories to resolve this allocation issue: (1) *pro rata*; and (2) joint and several.

*[i]—*Pro Rata *Approach*

Some courts have adopted a *pro rata* allocation approach, dividing liability for a particular claim among all triggered policies in the first instance.[37] Under the *pro rata* approach, these courts have held that principles of equity and/or *pro rata* the "other insurance" language effectively modifies the promise to pay "all sums" language, which means that the policyholder can recover only a share of its overall loss from any one of its insurance companies.[38] That share, called the "*pro rata* share," is determined by either the insurance company's proportionate share of time on the risk or proportionate share of total policy limits.[39]

Additionally, under the "*pro rata* approach," all "uninsured" time periods—namely, all periods during which there is no insurance because none is purchased, because that which is purchased has been exhausted, or because the insurance company has filed for bankruptcy—are allocated on a *pro rata* basis to the policyholder.[40]

With regard to uninsured periods attributable to years when insurance was unavailable in the marketplace, there is a split.[41] Some courts decline to place a policyholder on the risk when insurance was unavailable.[42] Others reject this unavailability rule altogether and treat such periods as uninsured periods.[43]

[ii]—Joint and Several Approach

In contrast to the "*pro rata*" allocation theory, other courts utilize a "joint and several approach," finding that the "all sums" language should be interpreted as written to hold that each triggered policy is jointly and severally liable for the policyholder's liability.[44] The courts that adopt the "joint and several approach" find it significant that there is a promise to pay "all sums," and they discount a *pro rata* or other "other insurance" provision.[45] Under this approach, the policyholder "picks and chooses" which triggered policy pays "all sums" for a given loss, subject only to the limits of liability under the policy chosen.[46] After the "picked and chosen" insurance company pays the claim, it is free to seek contribution/setoff from other insurance companies/the policyholder standing in the other insurance companies' shoes. However, the insurance companies, not the policyholder, bear the risk of insurer insolvency, and the policyholder is not allocated any portion of liability for periods during which it was uninsured.[47]

Moreover, under the "joint and several approach," in the contribution proceeding among the various insurance companies, liability is allocated *pro rata* among the various insurance companies in a number of ways, such as insurance company's proportionate share of time on the risk or proportionate share of total policy limits, which are quite similar to allocation schemes used under the "*pro rata* approach."[48] Alternatively, Massachusetts requires all insurance companies to contribute equally up to the limits of the lower-limited policy and, thereafter, the insurance company that sold the higher limited policy must contribute 100% up to the limits of its policy.[49] Additionally, in Massachusetts, each insurance company would be permitted to subtract its deductible from its total liability.[50]

As a third method, with respect to apportionment of indemnification costs among the various jointly and severally liable insurance companies, Washington has adopted the maximum loss rule, meaning that the loss is shared equally among the insurance companies up to the maximum limits of the policy with the smaller maximum limit, and then paid under the larger policy until either the larger policy is exhausted or full compensation for the loss is made.[51] However, in Washington, defense costs are allocated equally among primary insurance companies responsible for the defense of the underlying action.[52]

The majority of jurisdictions follow the "joint and several" allocation approach.[53] In fact, since the late 1990s, most courts have supported the "joint and several approach."[54]

[iii]—Distinctions

Under either the "*pro rata* approach" or "joint and several approach," an insurance company is ultimately liable only for its allocable share, however calculated, of the entire loss. The difference between the approaches arises when such allocation occurs. Under the "*pro rata* approach," allocation occurs when the loss is paid so all primary policies will exhaust simultaneously. Under the "joint and several approach," in contrast, allocation occurs in a second proceeding, when the loss becomes the subject of contribution among policies and insurers. Although allocation occurs under both approaches, the particular approach selected does have economic consequences. In particular, the risk of insurer insolvency is borne by the policyholder under the "*pro rata* approach" and by the insurance companies under the "joint and several approach." Additionally, under the "*pro rata* approach," there may be a larger pro-insurance company bias through application of more policies to each claim, including the effect of deductibles, retroactive premiums, and self-insured retentions that might apply to each claim.[55]

[3]—The Identity of the Policyholder—Meaning of "You" or "The Insured"

The insuring agreement contains a promise to pay amounts that "*you*" become or "*the insured*" becomes legally obligated to pay as damages.[56] The identity of the policyholder, as delineating "the insured," or "you" in other policy forms widely in use, generally refers to the "named insured." Consultation with the declarations page, definitions in the policy form, and other provisions regarding who is insured define the exact scope of "you" or "the insured."

The standard-form CGL insurance policy usually defines "you" as a "named insured" listed in the declarations or endorsements and any person or entity qualifying as a "named insured" under the policy.[57] The policy form itself usually will have a separate provision dealing with who qualifies as an insured.[58] In fact, in that separate section, the policy may qualify a named insured's spouse and dependent children as insureds.[59] It may also qualify a named insured entity's members, partners, managers, executive officers, directors, shareholders, and employees, while acting in the course and scope of employment or in furtherance of the entity, as named insureds.[60] It may further qualify newly acquired or formed entities as named insureds.[61]

Generally speaking, a policyholder should take great care in naming all entities it owns or controls because only if an entity is named will that entity be entitled to the benefits of the policy in the event it is sued or a claim is otherwise made against it. Consultation with appropriate insurance specialists and coverage counsel is advisable if the purchasing entity has any questions in this regard. Examples where the liable party was not insured under the CGL policy are abundant.[62]

Moreover, "additional insured" status may or may not provide the same benefits as "named insured" status.[63] A review of the policy will elucidate whether and what rights the additional insured might have.

[4]—"Legally Obligated to Pay as Damages"

The insuring agreement contains a promise to pay amounts that the policyholder or insured become(s) "*legally obligated to pay as damages.*"[64] The issues encompassed within the construction of "legally obligated to pay as damages" in the insuring agreement involve a number of interesting problems for real estate-related businesses, including: (1) what the phrase means and includes;[65] (2) certain types of settlements in question;[66] (3) elimination of the right to enforce a settlement or judgment;[67] (4) zero-sum net settlements;[68] (5) overhead and personnel costs;[69] (6) environmental liabilities;[70] and (7) construction defect liabilities: contract vs. tort.[71]

[a]—What the Phrase Encompasses—Judgments, Verdicts, and Settlements

"Legally obligated to pay as damages" can include judgments, awards, verdicts, and settlements entered against or agreed to by the policyholder in an action or a court of law or in an alternative dispute resolution or arbitration proceeding.[72] A Maryland court's decision explained the rationale as to why "legally obligated" does not require the entry of a judgment in all circumstances.

> "The term 'legally liable' to pay damages depends not upon when, and if, a judicial determination is made, but, generally, upon the creation of circumstances by and/or between parties, whereby the parties, or one or the other of them, can enforce rights through legal process. Parties often become legally obligated ('liable') to pay by way of contract, i.e., construction contracts, leases, insurance contracts, etc., or by committing tortious acts. The verdict of a jury and the judgment of a court are merely a determination that a legal obligation existed, and continues to exist. The verdict of a jury and the judgment of the court do not, of themselves, create the underlying legal obligation. The underlying legal obligation changes into judgment form—but the legal obligation pre-existed the judgment or the judgment would not have been possible. If a 'legal obligation' does not exist until there is a judgment, there would never be a judgment because a judgment of necessity arises out of legal obligations, liabilities, and legal duties."[73]

Sometimes, a question may be raised as to when the legal obligation to pay damages arises. The answer, of course, depends upon the nature of the legal obligation. The obligation to pay may attach at any of the following times: (1) the time the underlying legal obligation attaches under a contract or through tort; (2) the time a verdict or award is entered; (3) the time for appeal ends; (4) the conclusion of an appeal; or (5) the date a settlement is executed.[74]

[b]—Certain Settlements in Question

Issues may also arise as to whether certain settlements are legal obligations to pay damages. Insurance companies may question the basis for the legal obligation of the policyholder. For instance, when there is a dispute over the scope of insurance coverage, the policyholder often must defend or settle the underlying case without the help of its insurance company. If the underlying case is resolved by settlement, the insurance company may contend that the policyholder was not liable to the underlying claimant. Thus, the insurance company may try to force re-litigation of the underlying case to prove its policyholder's lack of legal liability.

The authorities generally hold that a settlement is a covered legal obligation if there is potential liability of the policyholder to the claimant, and the settlement is reasonable, prudent, and made in good faith.[75]

The issue arose in a case in which a bank entered into a non-binding settlement with the Federal Deposit Insurance Corporation ("FDIC") over the actions of its officers, with a sizeable portion of the settlement apportioned to the miscreant officer.[76] The bank's directors and officers (D&O) liability insurance policy provided insurance coverage for a "loss" which was described as "any amount which the Insureds are legally obligated to pay for a claim . . . and shall include damages, judgments, [and] settlements."[77] The court held that even though the settlement was non-binding, the FDIC would have pursued legal remedies in court. Accordingly, the "settlement" was a sum that the bank was "legally obligated to pay," because to decide otherwise would eviscerate the protection of all policyholders, and would undermine the public policy in favor of settlements.[78] The court also ruled that the D&O policy was required to indemnify the entire amount allocated to cover the liability of the culpable officer in the underlying settlement.[79] This ruling is an important rejection of the argument that the policyholder must retry the underlying claim in order to obtain coverage. The court ruled that all that the policyholder must show is that "the settlement allocation reasonably reflected [the policyholder's] potential exposure in the underlying litigation." In conclusion, the court held that:

> "Where a reluctant insurer fails to participate in an insured's settlement discussions, and the insured becomes party to a global settlement agreement, the insured may be indemnified for any amount of the total settlement package for which it can establish a reasonable anticipation of liability."[80]

[c]—Elimination of the Right to Enforce

Cases are often settled, or consent judgments are entered, under which the liability and amount of damages are stipulated but the plaintiff agrees not to enforce or execute on that judgment.[81] Such agreement may even include an assignment of rights under a CGL insurance policy.[82]

With respect to a settlement or consent judgment, an issue may arise if the agreement releases the policyholder from liability or otherwise eliminates the claimant's right to execute on the settlement or consent judgment. Insurance companies have argued that such a release or limitation on the right to enforce the judgment strips it of its legal obligation to pay damages and, therefore, eliminates coverage therefor. Case law is split on the issue, with the majority of cases holding that the elimination of the right to enforce does not cause the policyholder to forfeit its rights to coverage therefor.[83] However, even under the majority view, courts sometimes, albeit not always, distinguish between covenants not to execute and releases, finding that a release extinguishes the policyholder's legal obligation to pay and therefore should likewise release the coverage obligation therefor.[84]

Given that some jurisdictions find no coverage in such circumstances,[85] great care should be taken before entering into a settlement agreement of the underlying action which attempts to limit the claimants' rights against the policyholder. Consultation with skilled coverage counsel is advisable.

[d]—Zero-Sum Net Settlements

Architects, engineers, contractors, and others in the construction trade profession are sometimes involved in disputes with their clients concerning allegedly defective construction. These disputes can involve claims ranging from strict product liability,[86] to breach of warranty,[87] to negligence, including professional negligence.[88] Often, the clients withhold payment of moneys owed to these building professionals until the defective construction disputes are resolved.[89]

When the parties enter into a settlement agreement in which the building professional agrees to forego a claim it has against the underlying claimant for unpaid fees, a question arises as to whether the entire settlement, including the portion representing the unpaid fees that are waived by the settlement agreement, is covered under the building professional's relevant liability insurance policy.

Insurance companies have universally treated such zero-sum and other net settlements[90] as a zero-sum game, to which it refuses to be the net economic loser. In particular, insurance companies typically take the position that waivers of unpaid fees are not covered because they represent the outlay of no new value.[91]

However, such settlements should be fully covered because there is no functional difference between paying cash or foregoing a chose in action. In fact, the few cases that have addressed the issue have unanimously determined that the portion of a settlement constituting the waiver of the unpaid fees or chose in action is covered.[92]

Despite the unanimity of result in these reported decisions, insurance companies continue to take the position that such unpaid fees are not covered, arguing that the settlement of unpaid fees is excluded from the definition of damages, that the settlement represents a collusive attempt by the policyholder, with the assistance of his client or other third party, to obtain an unwarranted insurance recovery, or that the settlement is unfair or unreasonable.

Insurance companies have argued that the settlement is collusive and that the definition of "damages" excludes claims for unpaid fees. These arguments are related. Professional liability insurance policies may define "damages" as any amount that a policyholder is "legally obligated to pay" for any covered claim, including judgments, settlements, and interest on judgments.[93] In some professional liability insurance policies, "damages" may expressly exclude the "return or withdrawal of professional fees."[94] This provision has been construed to prevent a policyholder and its client—the claimant—from colluding and obtaining an unwarranted insurance recovery.[95] Thus, as long as the settlement is not a collusive effort by the policyholder and the client to extract the payment of unwarranted fees from the insurance company, the "withdrawal of fees" exclusion should not operate as a bar to insurance coverage for the portion of the settlement that includes the waiver of the unpaid fees.[96]

Additionally, the insurance company might attempt to argue that the settlement is unfair and unreasonable. An insurance company that breaches its duty to defend bears the burden of proving that the claims that were settled were outside the policy's coverage.[97] If the insurance company fails to meet this burden, the insurance company is liable for a fair and reasonable settlement.[98]

Thus, zero-sum and other net settlements should be fully covered. Accordingly, as long as the settlement is fair, reasonable, and non-collusive, the agreement to forego the collection of fees should be recoverable under the indemnity provisions of the relevant liability insurance policy.[99]

[e]—Overhead and Personnel Costs

General contractors may choose to undertake the repair of defects and consequential damage because they can be fixed less expensively when done internally and because the contractor can control any harm to its reputation by standing behind its product.

This raises an issue as to the availability of coverage for the contractor's incurring overhead and personnel costs in repairing defective construction and damages caused thereby. Case law is sparse and split on the issue, with some courts holding that such internal costs are "legal obligations to pay damages" covered by the CGL policy,[100] while others have held that they are not covered.[101]

[f]—Environmental Liabilities

In the environmental liability context, which is important for anyone that owns any type of real property, an issue has arisen as to whether amounts spent in compliance with state or federal agency administrative enforcement actions constitute legal obligations to pay damages. The majority of courts that have addressed the issue hold that environmental response costs constitute legal obligations to pay damages.[102]

The term "damages," within the meaning of standard-form CGL insurance policies, could certainly be construed as ambiguous with respect to whether it is limited to legal damages or whether it also includes equitable remedies, such as certain response costs under the Comprehensive Environmental Response, Compensation, and Liability Act ("CERCLA"). Like the term "suit," the standard-form CGL insurance policies do not define the term "damages." One dictionary defines "damages" to mean "the estimated reparation in money for detriment or injury sustained."[103] Such a definition does not, *ipso facto*, exclude equitable remedies.

> "This definition does not distinguish between legal compensatory damages or the costs of complying with a mandatory injunction. It merely indicates that 'damages' stands for the money required to be expended in order to right a wrong. To the popular mind, to most people, to ordinary laypersons, 'damages' connotes money one must expend to remedy an injury for which he or she is responsible, irrespective of whether that expenditure is compelled by a court of law in the form of compensatory damages or by a court of equity in the form of compliance with mandatory injunctions. Whether [a policyholder] expends the money and conducts the cleanup itself or pays the money to the government as the injured public's representative and the government conducts the cleanup is of little consequence. In either case, [a policyholder] would have to expend money to remedy the environmental damage it has caused. For precisely this purpose, [a policyholder] insured itself by purchasing CGL policies."[104]

Indeed, as stated above, the overwhelming majority of federal and state courts have found environmental cleanup costs incurred, or for which liability is imposed, under government enforcement actions, such as those at issue, are "damages" covered under standard-form CGL policies.[105] Indeed, a strong nationwide trend has emerged in the case law favoring a common sense interpretation of policy terms such as "damages." That trend is entirely consistent with a long line of cases dating back to at least 1956 on insurance policy construction.[106]

The minority view—namely that response costs are not damages—is based upon a hypertechnical distinction between equitable and legal damages that has been rejected by many courts.[107] For example, the New Jersey Supreme Court, in rejecting the argument that environmental cleanup costs were not covered as damages held that:

> "The clear weight of authority, however, among both federal and state courts adopts the view that the undefined term 'damages' in CGL policies should be accorded its plain, non-technical meaning, thereby encompassing response costs imposed to remediate environmental damage."[108]

The distinction between those cases that find environmental cleanup costs are covered "damages" and those that find the opposite, turns on whether the law of the particular state accords undefined terms in an insurance policy their plain, non-technical meaning.[109] In states in which ordinary terms are given their ordinary, non-technical meaning, the courts have uniformly found that environmental cleanup costs are damages.[110]

If the "equitable" versus "legal" damages distinction urged by many insurance companies were upheld, "[t]he utility of the policy would be seriously called into question."[111] Furthermore, "it would come as an unexpected, if not incomprehensible, shock to the insureds to discover that their insurance coverage was being denied because the plaintiff chose to frame his complaint in equity rather than in law."[112]

That "damages" includes environmental cleanup costs is manifestly evident from the insurance industry's own sworn testimony during congressional environmental legislation hearings.[113] During 1969 hearings on the Federal Water Pollution Control Act, a witness from the insurance industry testified that "[i]t is perfectly true that underwriters consider that the cost of *cleaning up* an oil spill . . . is covered under existing policies, provided the spill is one for which the ship owner is legally liable under existing law."[114]

[g]—Construction Defect Liabilities: Contract vs. Tort

The courts are unanimous in holding that in construction defect cases, tort liability constitutes a legal obligation to pay damages.[115] There is, however, a difference of opinion as to whether contractual liability also constitutes a legal obligation to pay damages. Some courts have held that contractual liabilities can constitute legal obligations to pay damages,[116] while others have taken the opposite position.[117]

The position that contractual liabilities are within the ambit of "legally obligated to pay as damages" appears more intellectually honest. Certainly, judgments in a lawsuit can be based on contract, tort, or statutes. Logic and common sense dictate such because there are other provisions in the CGL policy forms that provide coverage for contractual liabilities, such as the contractual liability coverage grant and the inclusion of warranty claims in the products-completed operations coverage grant.[118] Further, many of the exclusions would be rendered as unnecessary surplus and therefore against standard contract construction if the CGL policy provided no contractual liability coverage.[119] In addition, there are other provisions and exclusions that adequately address the concerns of the cases holding otherwise—namely, that a CGL insurance policy is not meant to be a performance bond.[120] Moreover, noted commentators have written that contractual liabilities certainly can fit within the meaning of "legally obligated to pay as damages."[121]

[5]—"Bodily Injury" or "Property Damage"

Coverage A of the CGL insuring agreement only requires the existence of a third party's claim of either "bodily injury" or "property damage."[122] Both need not be present for there to be triggered coverage under Coverage A of the CGL policy. Moreover, the "bodily injury" or "property damage" must be suffered by a third party—namely, a person other than the policyholder.[123] Of course, there are other requirements, which are discussed in other sections of this chapter.

[a]—"Bodily Injury"

[i]—General

As stated above, a third party must not suffer either "bodily injury" or "property damage" as a result of the policyholder's action such that the policyholder is legally obligated to pay damages to compensate the third party for the "bodily injury" or "property damage" harm that the third party suffered.

The standard-form CGL insurance policy defines "bodily injury" as "bodily injury, sickness or disease sustained by a person, including death resulting from any of these at any time."[124] With this definition, it should be relatively easy to ascertain whether "bodily injury" has been suffered or allegedly suffered by a third party.

[ii]—Emotional Distress

While most injuries will be easy to characterize as within or outside the definition of "bodily injury," mental and emotional distress injuries are more difficult to resolve. The majority of cases have held that in order for claims for emotional distress to fall within the definition of "bodily injury" they must arise out of actual physical injuries or such emotional distress is not specifically excluded from the definition of bodily injury.[125] However, where such injuries are unaccompanied by physical manifestations or symptoms, the majority of courts,[126] albeit not all courts,[127] hold that there is no "bodily injury."

[b]—"Property Damage"

"Property damage" is typically defined as:

"(1) physical injury to or destruction of tangible property which occurs during the policy period, including loss of use thereof at any time resulting therefrom; or

"(2) loss of use of tangible property that has not been physically injured or destroyed, provided the loss of use is caused by an occurrence during the policy period."[128]

Thus, there are two types of "property damage." One type of "property damage" is any physical injury or destruction of tangible property.[129] The second type is "loss of use" of tangible property.[130] Both types involve tangible property,[131] meaning that any damage to "intangible property" is generally not covered under Coverage A of the standard-form CGL insurance policy.[132]

[i]—Defective Construction

In construction cases, physical injury involving tangible property is clearly present if the construction defect causes damage to non-defective work or personal property. However, there is a split of authority as to whether the construction defect itself constitutes physical injury or destruction of tangible property. The majority view is that the defect itself must damage non-defective work or other property for there to be "property damage."[133] Costs incurred to ascertain existence of property damage will also be covered.[134] The minority view is that the defect itself can constitute "property damage," as long as the elements of the definition are satisfied, i.e., physical injury or loss of use of tangible property.[135] The more analytically accurate view is the minority view because it is consistent with the definition of "property damage." There are other portions of the policy that might otherwise exclude coverage for the work product of the policyholder, and the minority view does not sacrifice accuracy to arrive at what may be viewed as the correct result. Irrespective, the construction defect may still constitute the loss of use form of "property damage" to the extent it causes property to be uninhabitable or unusable.[136]

[ii]—Economic Losses, Loss of Use, and Diminution in Value

Purely economic losses generally do not constitute "property damage."[137] However, when a claimant avers loss of use of tangible property, such "loss of use" constitutes "property damage" within the meaning of the CGL policy.[138] When such loss of use is caused by purely economic losses, the losses are covered.[139] The damages for "loss of use" generally include the cost to rent similar property during the period where use is lost.[140] Similarly, diminution in value is often considered "property damage," especially if it is accompanied by physical injury.[141]

[iii]—Computer Losses

Real estate-related companies engage in business activities that might cause computer losses to third parties. For example, if an engineering or construction company performs work on an occupied building, the company could conceivably engage in some activity that results in loss of computer data vital to a third-party occupant.

Whether loss of computer software and data constitute "property damage" is undecided.[142] Moreover, there are only a few decisions that deal with the somewhat analogous claims by third parties for loss of data or software. Case law is somewhat evenly divided on the issue. The question turns on whether the software and data are tangible property, which is covered, or intangible property, which is not covered.[143] A couple of courts have opted to hold that computer data and software are covered tangible property,[144] while others have declared that they are intangible and not subject to coverage.[145]

[6]—"Occurrence"

The Coverage A insuring agreement requires that the bodily injury or property damage be caused by an "occurrence" that takes place in the policy's coverage territory and during its policy period.[146]

[a]—Definition

Liability policies typically define "occurrence" as "an accident, including continuous or repeated exposure to substantially the same general harmful conditions."[147] Courts have construed this definition to include actions of a policyholder resulting in potential liability based on common or statutory law, including ordinary acts, negligence, recklessness, warranty, breach of contract, and strict liability.[148]

[b]—Construction Defect Claims

There is a split in authority as to whether construction defects or faulty workmanship claims can constitute "occurrences." Some courts hold that construction defects causing unexpected, unintended, and accidental "property damage," even damage to other, completed, non-defective portions of the project, can constitute an "occurrence" regardless of the legal theory asserted against the contractor.[149] Other courts hold the opposite and refuse to find that an "occurrence" can ever result from defective construction.[150]

Before late 2006,[151] courts applying Pennsylvania law, including the state's intermediate courts, were also split, mirroring the split nationally. One line followed the majority approach.[152] Another line of authority held that construction defect claims could never constitute "occurrences."[153] Some courts applying Pennsylvania law simply found that construction defects were never fortuitous because they were in the control of the policyholder.[154] While others held that construction defects could never arise from an "occurrence" because: (1) under the "gist-of-the-action" doctrine, construction defect claims are breach of contract claims irrespective of whether negligence is alleged; and (2) breach of contract claims could never amount to "occurrences."[155]

Resolution of this conflict was decided by the Pennsylvania Supreme Court in late 2006 when the court held that a claim solely for the repair of faulty workmanship does not constitute an "occurrence."[156] The Pennsylvania Supreme Court based this holding on: (1) the policy definition of "occurrence" as an "accident"; (2) the plain meaning of "accident" as an unexpected and unintended event; and (3) its conclusion that a claim for defective or faulty workmanship to the work product itself can never be an "accident."[157]

In reaching its determination, the court specifically differentiated between two types of claims: (1) breach of contract claims for the repair of faulty or defective workmanship, which encompasses the specific economic loss that was the basis of the contract at issue; and (2) claims based upon tort for unexpected and unintended damages to other persons or property caused by the faulty or defective workmanship, which do not involve the very basis of the bargain contracted for.[158] The court held that the first set can never arise from an "occurrence," because the loss at issue is not fortuitous and is a risk more aptly responded to by a performance bond.[159] On the other hand, the court recognized that in other jurisdictions and in prior Pennsylvania authority, the second set of claims could arise from an "occurrence."[160]

[i]—Contract vs. Tort

Courts holding that faulty workmanship can never constitute an "occurrence" often draw a distinction between claims based in contract and claims based in tort.[161] These courts reason as follows: claims sounding in contract can never arise from an "occurrence" because such claims involving construction liability generally manifest themselves as claims for repair of defective workmanship alone—the very work product promised to be free of defects in the original contract, which is more appropriately guaranteed by a performance bond than by a CGL insurance policy. On the other hand, claims for construction liability that are based in tort generally involve damage to other property caused by faulty workmanship, which are the types of claims meant to be covered by CGL insurance policies.[162]

The distinctions mirror the debate nationally. In fact, case law around the country is split as to this distinction. Some courts hold that breach of contract claims can never arise from an "occurrence,"[163] whereas others hold that breach of contract claims that result in unexpected and unintended damage can arise from an "occurrence."[164]

A contractor who works on a home owes a tort duty of care to any present or future homeowner, even if he is not in contractual privity with the homeowner.[165] Courts sometimes use the gist-of-the-action doctrine to preclude a tort claim. However, "that doctrine only applies when the plaintiff and the defendant have a contract."[166] Hence, if a homeowner not in contractual privity with a builder has a claim against the builder, the gist-of-the-action doctrine cannot re-characterize a tort claim as a contract claim, and the tort versus contract distinction should be of no moment regardless of the jurisdiction in which the claim has been asserted.

However, courts have been known to invoke the economic-loss doctrine to preclude tort claims.[167] The economic-loss rule bars "negligence claims seeking recovery for 'economic damages' or 'losses' *unless there has also been physical injury either to a person or property*."[168] Thus, as long as the economic-loss and gist-of-the action doctrines can be avoided, a claim against a builder with whom the claimant is not in contractual privity should be sustainable in tort and the contract versus tort distinction should be irrelevant even in a pro-insurance company jurisdiction.

The gist-of-the-action and economic-loss rules might explain a court's central distinction between: (1) claims based upon contract for the repair of defects; and (2) claims based in tort for the repair of damage caused by defects.[169] When only economic losses (i.e., losses involving defective workmanship that result in damage solely to the defective work product itself) are at issue, the gist-of-the-action and/or economic-loss rules state that the only claim that can exist arises in contract because that is the basis of what was promised by the contractor and what is not insurable by a CGL insurance policy.[170] However, where defective workmanship damages other property, including non-defective portions of the contractor's completed work, the economic-loss and/or gist-of-the-action doctrines will not preclude the tort claim and CGL coverage may exist.[171]

[ii]—Faulty Workmanship vs. Damage to Other Property Caused by Faulty Workmanship

The second, but related, distinction is the distinction between claims solely for the repair of faulty workmanship and claims that encompass damage to other property caused by faulty workmanship.[172] Claims solely for repairs of faulty or defective work are not themselves an "occurrence" because such claims are more properly addressed by performance bonds dealing with the quality of the work supplied.[173] However, when the defective work malfunctions and unintentionally and unexpectedly causes damage to other property, including completed, non-defective work product, there is an "occurrence."[174]

Nationally, case law is split as to coverage for damages to non-defective completed operations caused by faulty workmanship, although the majority approach uses the distinction between repair of faulty workmanship and repair of damages caused thereby as the basis for denying/finding a covered "occurrence."[175]

[iii]—Insurance Industry Literature

The insurance industry itself recognizes that property damage results from an "occurrence" when defective workmanship causes unexpected and unintended damage to other property, including other non-defective, completed portions of the same work product. In fact, insurance industry literature, the *FC&S Bulletin* (*Fire, Casualty, & Surety Bulletin*), has illustrated, by way of an example, that coverage exists when defective workmanship results in damage to completed, non-defective portions of the policyholder's same work product. The *Bulletin* has been cited by at least one court in finding coverage for defective workmanship causing damage to a non-defective area.[176]

> "An insurance industry bulletin analyzes exclusion (j)(5) as follows: 'To illustrate the effect of this exclusion, say that a plumbing subcontractor working for a *home builder* accidentally starts one of the *builder's projects* on fire while soldering copper pipes, and the entire structure is burned down. If the owner of the house sues *the builder* for the loss, the exclusion . . . will apply only to "that particular part" of the structure on which the plumber was working. Thus, *the named insured would be covered . . . for damage to all parts of the building other than the plumbing and all parts of the plumbing system other than the particular part being worked on at the time of the loss.* The coverage forms do not define "that particular part," . . . [but] in the final analysis, the use of the word "particular" indicates that the exclusion should be applied narrowly. In the example above, the exclusion should then apply only to the two portions of pipe being soldered together; the damage to the rest of the plumbing system should not be excluded.'"[177]

Although the *Bulletin* deals with application of a specific exclusion, it makes clear that the insurance industry itself recognizes that insurance coverage exists for damage to non-defective, completed portions of the work product of a general contractor caused by faulty workmanship on another portion of the work product. In fact, in the illustration, the policyholder was the builder in charge of the entire project, and the author of the *FC&S Bulletin* made it clear that the builder would be entitled to insurance coverage for all damage to the completed, non-defective work product (the home) except the particular pipes on which the plumbing subcontractor was soldering at the time of the accident, even though there was faulty workmanship performed on a portion of the project.

[iv]—Rules of Construction: Contract vs. Tort Revisited

In faulty workmanship coverage matters where a jurisdiction does not recognize an "occurrence" or is undecided on the issue, a policyholder could advance several strong arguments in favor of the existence of an "occurrence." First, under settled rules on insurance policy construction, the language of the insurance policy itself demonstrates that the insurance policy contemplates coverage for breach of contract and/or faulty workmanship claims, which undercuts a central premise behind the line of cases that hold that breach of contract claims can never constitute "occurrences."[178]

[A]—Contractual Liability Exclusion Is Limited—Contractual Indemnity Coverage Exists

The first relevant rule of construction is that insurance policies are to be construed as a whole.[179] In construing the policy as a whole, one could argue that the insurance policy itself contemplates insurance coverage for certain contractual liabilities. For instance, the contractual liability exclusion does not exclude all contractual liability. Rather, by its express terms, it merely excludes liability arising from certain indemnity or contribution agreements—namely, contractual claims relating to the assumption of liability.

> "This insurance does not apply to . . . 'property damage' or 'bodily injury' for which the insured is obligated to pay damages by reason of the assumption of liability in a contract or agreement."[180]

Because it only excludes some contractual liabilities, it could be argued that other contractual liabilities are not excluded and are therefore covered.

In fact, insurance companies know how to exclude claims for breach of contract. Indeed, in Coverage B of standard liability insurance policies, the "personal and advertising injury" coverage part, insurance companies exclude coverage for not only (1) the contractual assumption of liability in connection with "personal and advertising injury" claims, but also (2) "personal and advertising injury" claims arising from breach of contract. A typical exclusion reads: "This insurance does not apply to . . . 'personal and advertising injury' arising out of a breach of contract."[181] Because insurance companies do not include a similar "breach of contract" exclusion in Coverage A—the "bodily injury" and "property damage" coverage—and instead only include the contractual assumption of liability exclusion in such coverage part, it can be inferred that they never intended to exclude coverage for all claims for breach of contract.

Moreover, the policy itself provides some explicit insurance coverage for certain contractual liabilities. In particular, the contractual liability exclusion quoted above and below (in the non-highlighted portion) expressly has an exception for equitable or contractual indemnity claims, which is highlighted for ease of reference below:

> "Bodily injury" or "property damage" for which the insured is obligated to pay damages by reason of the assumption of liability in a contract or agreement. **This exclusion does not apply to liability for damages:**
>
> **(1) That the insured would have in the absence of a contract or agreement; or**
>
> **(2) Assumed in a contract or agreement that is an "Insured Contract" provided the "bodily injury" or "property damage" occurs subsequent to the execution of the contract or agreement.**[182]

By virtue of the exception to the contractual liability exclusion, the policy provides coverage for certain contractually assumed liabilities—namely, liabilities that would nonetheless exist in the absence of a contract or agreement and liability under certain types of written contribution or indemnity agreements.[183]

[B]—Warranty Coverage Exists

Likewise, products-completed operations coverage includes coverage for breach of certain warranties. A typical policy provides coverage for bodily injury or property damage within the "products-completed operations hazard," which is defined as including:

"... all 'bodily injury' and 'property damage' occurring away from premises you own or rent and arising out of 'your product' or 'your work' except:

(1) Products that are still in your physical possession; or

(2) Work that has not yet been completed or abandoned. However, 'your work' will be deemed completed at the earliest of the following times:

(a) When all of the work called for in your contract has been completed.

(b) When all of the work to be done at the job site has been completed if your contract calls for work at more than one job site.

(c) When that part of the work done at the job site has been put to its intended use by any person or organization other than another contractor or subcontractor working on the same project."

"Work that may need service, maintenance, correction, repair or replacement, but which is otherwise complete, will be treated as completed.

b. Does not include 'bodily injury' and 'property damage' arising out of:

▼

(3) Products or operations for which the classification, listed in the Declarations or in the policy schedule, states that products-completed operations are subject to the general aggregate limit."[184]

"'Your work' is typically defined as:

(1) Work or operations performed by you or on your behalf; and

(2) Materials, parts and equipment furnished in connection with such work or operations.

▼

b. ['Your work' i]ncludes

(1) Warranties or representations made at any time with respect to the fitness, quality, durability, performance or use of 'your work,' and

(2) The providing of or failure to provide warnings or instructions."[185]

Thus, "your work" includes all labor and materials performed by the policyholder or on the policyholder's behalf, *including "warranties or representations made at any time with respect to the fitness, quality, durability, performance or use" of such labor and materials* (emphasis added).[186] As a result, under the plain meaning of products-completed operations coverage, if "property damage" arises away from the policyholder's premises and occurs as a result of the labor, materials, or *warranties* related to such labor or materials involved in the construction of homes built by the policyholder, such "property damage" would be covered.[187] Accordingly, the products-completed operations coverage affords coverage for another contractual claim—namely, breach of warranties.

[C]—Exclusions Rendered Meaningless or Redundant

Moreover, an insurance policy should be construed to give effect to all of its provisions and to avoid any part being rendered redundant.[188] Here, if breach of contract claims could never constitute "occurrences," then certain exclusions that expressly exclude coverage for contract liabilities would be redundant. For instance, the contractual liability exclusion[189] previously quoted would be redundant and unnecessary because all contractually assumed liabilities would already be excluded by virtue of the rule that contractual liability is excluded from the meaning of "occurrence." Therefore, the intent of the drafter must have been to provide some coverage for contractual liabilities, and an insurance policy interpretation to avoid surplusage of the contractual liability exclusion would require a finding that breach of contract could constitute an "occurrence."[190]

Similarly, if breach of contract claims could never constitute "occurrences," a portion of the impaired property exclusion would be unnecessary.[191] In fact the "impaired property" excludes coverage for:

> "'Property damage' to 'impaired property' or property that has not been physically injured, arising out of:
>
> (1) A defect, deficiency, inadequacy or dangerous condition in 'your product' or 'your work'; or
>
> (2) A *delay or failure by you or anyone acting on your behalf to perform a contract or agreement in accordance with its terms* (emphasis added).
>
> "This exclusion does not apply to the loss of use of other property arising out of sudden and accidental physical injury to 'your product' or 'your work' after it has been put to its intended use."[192]

If breach of contract claims could never constitute "occurrences," there would be no need to exclude "property damage" to "impaired property" or property that has not been physically injured arising out of a breach of contract (subparagraph (2) above). Such "property damage" would already be excluded by the postulated rule—namely, no coverage for breach of contract claims.[193]

Moreover, if there could be no "occurrence" for defective construction damaging a contractor's own work, the "business risk" exclusions—"Your Work" Exclusion and Exclusions J(5) and J(6)[194]—would be rendered meaningless surplusage.[195] These "business risk" exclusions are intended to eliminate coverage for traditional business risks not contemplated by insurance, such as the risk of producing deficient products or work that does not live up to the contract.[196] These exclusions are unnecessary and redundant if an occurrence could ever arise from a contract or faulty craftsmanship claim. As one court aptly and succinctly explained:

> "There are two kinds of risks that are incurred by a contractor. The first is the business risk borne by the contractor to replace or repair defective work to make the building project conform to the agreed contractual requirements. This type of risk is not covered by the [insurance] policy, and the business risk exclusions in

> the policy make this clear. The second is the risk that the defective or faulty workmanship will cause injury to people or damage to other property. Because of the potentially limitless liability associated with this risk, it is the type for which . . . commercial general liability coverage is contemplated. . . . The risk intended to be insured is the possibility that the . . . work of the insured, once relinquished or completed, will cause bodily injury or damage to property other than to the . . . completed work itself, and for which the insured may be found liable."[197]

Additionally, as will be discussed, the subcontractor exception to the "Your Work" Exclusion provides coverage for "property damage" to the work of a subcontractor or "property damage" arising out of the work of a subcontractor.[198] "Accordingly, finding no occurrence for defective construction resulting in damage to the insured's work would render the subcontractor exception superfluous and meaningless."[199] Otherwise, why even have the exception for work performed by a subcontractor?

[D]—Performance Bond Analogy Imperfect

Furthermore, the central premise behind the no "occurrence" line of cases is that the CGL policy was not meant to be a performance bond.[200] However, even if this premise were correct, there would be no reason to negate coverage on the basis of lack of "occurrence." There are numerous business risk exclusions in place to prevent the evil contemplated by the performance bond rationale.[201]

[E]—Illusory Coverage for Contracts

Additionally, a policy is construed to comport with the policyholder's reasonable expectations.[202] Insurance policies are also construed to provide some coverage for the premium paid, to avoid the possibility of purchasing coverage deemed "illusory."[203] Here, if a policyholder that is involved in home building and development purchased products-completed operations coverage, a determination that breach of contract and breach of warranty claims could never constitute an "occurrence" would be tantamount to providing no "property damage" coverage for the products-completed operations coverage purchased.[204] Moreover, most commentators have taken the position that contractual liabilities can constitute "occurrences."[205]

[c]—Trigger of Coverage

[i]—Timing of "Occurrence"

Assuming the existence of an "occurrence," the next issue concerns the appropriate "trigger of coverage"—namely, the event that "triggers" or causes a policy to cover or respond to a particular loss, liability, or suit.[206] All cases hold that the coverage trigger is the existence of covered damage (usually property damage or bodily injury suffered by a third party) caused by an occurrence.[207] There are four theories of "occurrence" triggers that courts apply in determining when damage has occurred so as to trigger insurance coverage under CGL policies in the context of long-tail claims, such as environmental contamination, construction and toxic tort cases:[208]

1. Exposure—a policy is triggered on the first exposure to the injury-causing event. Under the "exposure theory," the triggering occurrence takes place on "the date of exposure to the injury producing agent."[209]

2. Manifestation—a policy is triggered on the first manifestation of injury. Under the "manifestation theory," the policy is triggered "when the injury became reasonably apparent or known to the claimant."[210]
3. Injury in fact—a policy is triggered when the first injury takes place. Under the "injury in fact" theory, a policy is triggered only "if the claimant was actually injured during the policy period."[211]
4. Continuous—all policies between the date of first exposure and the date of manifestation are triggered. The "continuous trigger theory" provides that "all policies in effect during the aggregate trigger period, for example, during the period of exposure or injury in fact, are activated and may be called on to respond to a loss."[212]

Cases around the country apply different theories of the appropriate trigger of coverage for construction defect claims, although the most prevalent theories are manifestation, injury in fact, and continuous.[213]

[ii]—Ownership at the Time of "Occurrence"

Insurance companies have taken the position that there is no coverage for damage to property if the damage takes place at a time when the policyholder owns the property at issue.[214] Similarly, insurance companies have argued there is no coverage unless the injured party owned the damaged property at the time the damage actually occurred or during the relevant policy period.[215] The theory behind such an approach is that CGL insurance is "third-party" insurance that only covers a policyholder for liabilities attributed to a loss to property owned by a third party or a loss that harms a third party during the policy period.[216] Such concepts are incorporated into the CGL policy both through a central, implicit premise behind the concept of third-party liability coverage (i.e., coverage for liabilities resulting from damage suffered by a third party) and as an exclusion—the owned property exclusion.[217]

Case law is split on the issue. In California[218] and some other jurisdictions,[219] courts unequivocally hold that "occurrence" of "property damage" is determined at the time of trigger. The crucial inquiry is when the damage occurs, not when the claimant is actually injured, and the "owned property" exclusion is tested at the time the claim is made. In other words, in these jurisdictions, an "occurrence" of "property damage" is deemed to take place at all times between the first exposure to the harmful conditions and the first manifestation of "property damage," irrespective of ownership by the policyholder at any time during the trigger period, as long as it is ultimately owned by a third-party claimant at the time the claim is made.

Elsewhere, courts apply the concept of damage during the policy period or the owned property exclusion to bar coverage, reasoning that at the time the property damage takes place, it cannot be covered "property damage" if it is then owned by the policyholder.[220]

[d]—Number of Occurrences

For large developers with many construction defect claims, an issue may arise as to whether each property or instance of property damage would constitute one "occurrence" or multiple "occurrences." This is important for "per occurrence" deductibles and "per occurrence" indemnity limits.

As an initial matter, the vast majority of courts that have attempted to ascertain the "number of occurrences" have followed the cause test—namely, an occurrence is determined by the cause or causes of the resulting injury.[221] The minority approach looks at the effects, focusing upon the number of individual claims or injuries.[222] The test adopted in New York has been denominated the "unfortunate events test,"[223] which is quite similar to the "cause test." "In most instances, they probably will be identical, since the liability triggering event ordinarily will be the 'cause' of the damage or injury to each of the claimants."[224]

[i]—Construction Defect Claims

Regardless of the approach to the number of occurrences, there will need to be a fact-based inquiry in each circumstance. Not surprisingly, courts have construed nearly identical policy language and reached inconsistent results when applying the cause or effect test to insurance coverage actions involving similar liabilities. A few cases have addressed the "number of occurrences" issue in the context of construction defect liabilities.[225] In fact, in one jurisdiction, there is a split of authority on the issue.[226]

[ii]—Asbestos Claims

Likewise, courts have construed nearly identical policy language and reached inconsistent results when applying the cause test to an insurance coverage action for asbestos-related bodily injury liabilities. In fact, there does not even appear to be a majority approach to this issue.

Some courts hold that there can be only one cause of all of the individual claims—namely, the manufacture and production of the same asbestos-containing products—even though there may be thousands of different claimants exposed to products at different times and different locations.[227] Other courts have held that under virtually identical insurance policy language applied to virtually identical facts, there are multiple occurrences, focusing on each sale of each asbestos-containing product or each exposure by each claimant.[228] Still a third set of cases have addressed the issue but not resolved it, either because the procedural posture (denying a motion for summary judgment based upon a finding of a genuine issue of material fact) or because the court asked for clarity from the state's highest court.[229]

Pennsylvania is undecided. There do not appear to be any published Pennsylvania state court decisions on the issue as applied to an asbestos coverage action. However, there are four relevant decisions from the United States District Court for the Eastern District of Pennsylvania. Not surprisingly, these decisions reach opposite results. Three of them hold that there is one occurrence—the manufacture of the asbestos-containing products.[230] A fourth case held opposite—namely, that there are multiple occurrences.[231]

§ 5.04 General Conditions

[1]—Notice

CGL policies generally require the policyholder to give notice of a claim or "suit" as soon as practicable.[232] Real estate-related entities and professionals should provide notice as soon as they have any inkling of a claim, to avoid any risk of forfeiture of coverage.

[a]—Late Notice

When notice is untimely under an occurrence-based insurance policy, the vast majority of jurisdictions require a showing of prejudice before late notice will justify denial of coverage.[233] This is known as the notice-prejudice rule.[234]

Various jurisdictions may differ on the burden of proof with respect to prejudice. In Florida, for example, late notice raises a rebuttable presumption of prejudice, requiring the policyholder to offer evidence of lack of prejudice, and the burden of proof on lack of prejudice remains with the policyholder.[235] A similar rule applies in Indiana.[236] In contrast, some other jurisdictions place the burden of proving prejudice caused by late notice of an underlying suit on the insurance company.[237]

Mere passage of time does not demonstrate prejudice. Rather, the late notice must substantially impair the insurance company's ability to investigate the claim adequately or otherwise protect itself.[238] Moreover, even if substantial prejudice is proven, if the policyholder acted reasonably in giving late notice, late notice may not necessarily act as a bar to coverage.[239]

To establish actual prejudice, an insurance company must demonstrate how an earlier notice would have changed the outcome of the underlying case or its coverage determination.[240] In most jurisdictions, prejudice does not occur if the purpose of the notice provision is satisfied despite being late.[241] In most jurisdictions, the purpose of the notice provision in an insurance policy is to provide the insurance company with adequate time to investigate the file in order to prepare an adequate defense on behalf of the policyholder against the underlying claimant.[242] Some courts have held that the entry of a default judgment or a settlement before notice is given does not automatically establish prejudice,[243] while others have decided that under such circumstances, prejudice arises as a matter of law.[244]

[b]—Knowledge to Key Employees

Some notice clauses are concerned with the problem of a policyholder's low-level employee acquiring knowledge of a loss and forgetting to notify the appropriate persons. These policies are triggered only when any insured in a key management position or department, such as the risk management or counsel departments, receives notice of a claim or suit.[245]

[2]—Cooperation Clause

CGL policies also contain cooperation clauses that require the policyholders to "cooperate with [the insurer] in the investigation or settlement of the claim or defense against the 'suit.'"[246] These clauses are generally valid and enforceable.[247]

The purpose of the cooperation clause is to allow the insurance company to adequately defend the policyholder in the underlying action.[248] To substantiate a denial of coverage for breach of the cooperation clause, the insurance company must suffer substantial prejudice as a result of the breach, with the burden of proving such prejudice resting with the insurance company.[249] Actual, not potential, prejudice must be shown to justify denial on the basis of non-cooperation.[250]

The prejudice that must be shown correlates with the purpose behind the clause. Thus, at a minimum, the insurance company would need to demonstrate that absent the breach of cooperation, there is a substantial likelihood it would have achieved a better result in the underlying action.[251] A collusive settlement may be prejudicial breach of cooperation clause.[252]

When an insurance company denies coverage for reasons other than breach of a condition, such as the cooperation clause, it waives compliance with such a condition. By denying coverage, the insurance company admits that satisfaction of the condition would not have altered its coverage position and therefore the breach was immaterial.[253]

[3]—Voluntary Payments

CGL policies contain "consent to settlement" or voluntary payments provisions that typically state that:

> "No insured will, except at that insured's own cost, voluntarily make a payment, assume any obligation, or incur any expense, other than for first aid, without our consent."[254]

Developers, contractors, and other real estate professionals often find that maintenance of their business reputation is paramount to their present and future success, choosing to make repairs themselves to problems brought to their attention by their customers. In addition, it may be less expensive for a real estate entity to repair the work itself, as it eliminates a third-party contractor's profit and overhead costs and possible legal expenses likely to be incurred if a client's complaints are ignored.

An issue to consider is whether expenditures of funds to remediate some problems before putting the insurance company on notice could be excluded under this "voluntary payments" or "consent to settle" provision. In order to avoid liability under the policy for breach of the voluntary payments provision, the majority of courts require a showing of prejudice caused by the breach.[255]

There are some courts that hold otherwise, albeit the distinction might be one without a real difference. In Pennsylvania, for example, the courts have uniformly upheld the "consent to settlement" provisions without any showing of prejudice to the insurance company.[256] However, an insurer that withholds consent must do so reasonably, and absent prejudice, withholding consent would be unreasonable.[257]

[4]—Non-Cumulation of Liability Provisions

Some policies have "non-cumulation of liability" provisions, sometimes referred to as a "telescope clause" or antistacking provision, which provides as follows:

> "If collectible insurance under any other policy issued through [another insurer] is available to the Insured covering a loss also covered hereunder, the Insurer's total liability shall in no event exceed the greater or greatest limit of liability applicable to such loss under this or any other such policy."[258]

One court construed similar language in the context of an asbestos bodily injury insurance coverage action.[259] The case involved a policyholder who was being sued by thousands of claimants for asbestos bodily injuries. The excess liability insurance company sought to limit its exposure on the basis of a telescoping clause that the insurer claimed limited its total liability for multiple triggered policies to the aggregate limits of one policy.

The insurer argued that all of the asbestos claims arose from one "occurrence," the manufacture and sale of asbestos-containing products. The court, however, refused to apply the telescoping clause in that manner and held that the word "occurrence" as used in the policy was ambiguous and construed it to mean that each claim was a separate occurrence, thereby limiting application of the telescoping clause to large individual claims (where two or more policies are required to pay indemnity to satisfy a judgment or settlement).[260]

The term "loss" in the telescoping/non-cumulation of liability clauses is similarly undefined in standard policies.[261] One court, in the environmental liability context, construed the identical language of the clause previously quoted and held that such a clause only limits stacking for claims involving one "loss."[262]

[5]—Supplementary Payments

[a]—Policyholder Benefits

CGL policies typically contain a "supplementary payments" provision requiring reimbursement to the policyholder for investigation costs, interest on judgments, and the cost of appeal bonds, among other things. Like duty-to-defend expenditures, these "supplementary payments" are in addition to, and do not count against, indemnity limits. A classic such provision provides as follows:

> "We will pay, with respect to any claim we investigate or settle, or any "suit" against an insured we defend:
>
> a. All expenses [the insured] incurs.
>
> b. Up to $250 for the cost of bail bonds required because of accidents or traffic law violations arising out of the use of any vehicle to which the Bodily Injury Liability Coverage applies. We do not have to furnish these bonds.
>
> c. The cost of bonds to release attachments, but only for bond amounts within the applicable limit of insurance. We do not have to furnish these bonds.
>
> d. All reasonable expenses incurred by the insured at our request to assist us in the investigation or defense of the claim or 'suit.' Including actual loss of earnings up to $250 a day because of time off from work.
>
> e. All costs taxed against the insured in the 'suit.'
>
> f. Prejudgment interest awarded against the insured on that part of the judgment we pay. If we make an offer to pay the applicable limit of insurance, we will not pay any prejudgment interest based on that period of time after the offer.

g. All interest on the full amount of any judgment that accrues after entry of the judgment and before we have paid, offered to pay, or deposited in court part of the judgment that is within the applicable limit of insurance.

"These payments will not reduce the limits of insurance."[263]

An interesting issue is whether prevailing party attorneys' fees are "costs taxed against the insured." Some courts hold that supplementary payments do not include prevailing party attorneys' fees awarded in the underlying action.[264] Others hold they do include such fees and may include any increased fees awarded where the court uses a multiplier to boost to the lodestar calculation.[265]

[b]—Policyholder's Indemnitee Benefits

In addition, the "supplementary payments" provision may entitle an indemnitee of the policyholder to a paid defense under certain circumstances. A typical clause provides:

"If we defend an insured against a 'suit' and an indemnitee of the insured is also named as a party to the 'suit,' we will defend that indemnitee if all of the following conditions are met:

a. The 'suit' against the indemnitee seeks damages for which the insured has assumed the liability of the indemnitee in a contract or agreement that is an 'Insured Contract';

b. This insurance applies to such liability assumed by the insured;

c. The obligation to defend, or the cost of the defense of, that indemnitee, has also been assumed by the insured in the same 'Insured Contract.'

d. The allegations in the 'suit' and the information we know about the "occurrence" are such that no conflict appears to exist between the interests of the insured and the interests of the indemnitee;

e. The indemnitee and the insured ask us to conduct and control the defense of that indemnitee against such 'suit' and agree that we can assign the same counsel to defend the insured and the indemnitee.

f. The indemnitee:

(1) Agrees in writing to

(a) Cooperate with us in the investigation, settlement or defense of the 'suit;'

(b) Immediately send us copies of any demands, notices, summonses or legal papers received in connection with the 'suit';

(c) Notify any other insurer whose coverage is available to the indemnitee; and

(d) Cooperate with us with respect to coordinating other applicable insurance available to the indemnitee; and

(2) Provides us with written authorization to:

(a) Obtain records and other information related to the 'suit';

(b) Conduct and control the defense of the indemnitee in such 'suit.'

"So long as the above conditions are met, attorneys' fees incurred by us in the defense of that indemnitee, necessary litigation expenses incurred by us and necessary litigation expenses incurred by the indemnitee at our request will be paid as Supplementary Payments. . . . [S]uch payments will not be deemed to be damages for 'bodily injury' or 'property damage' and will not reduce the limits of insurance."[266]

Thus, defense costs of a policyholder's indemnitee are potentially covered under two places. First, under the plain meaning of this supplementary payments provision, the indemnitee's defense costs would not count against limits as long as they qualify as "supplementary payments." Alternatively, if they do not qualify as a "supplementary payment because the requirements set forth in the provision are not satisfied, such defense costs would likely constitute "damages" that count against limits.[267] In addition, amounts incurred in connection with seeking to enforce indemnity rights have been held to be "supplementary payments," where such amounts were awarded pursuant to a fee-shifting statute.[268]

[6]—Apportionment Regarding Covered and Uncovered Claims and Policyholders

Interesting issues arise as to allocation between covered and uncovered (a) claims and (b) policyholders/insureds.[269] For example, insurance companies may argue that they are entitled to apportion the costs of defense, settlement, or judgment in the underlying lawsuit between insured and uninsured parties or between insured and uninsured claims. In essence, the arguments suggest that where there are covered and uncovered claims or persons in a suit, the duty to defend and/or indemnify should be apportioned as follows. Payment of defense costs and indemnity should follow the covered claims or persons, but such payments should not follow uncovered claims or persons.

Thus the companies may argue for two different types of "allocation" as appropriate, and these arguments can occur at two different times. First, they may argue for "allocation" of defense costs and expenses at the time the underlying claims against the policyholder are pending.[270] Second, insurance companies may argue for "allocation" of indemnity payments at the time of any settlement or judgment.[271]

[a]—Settlements and Judgments

Several courts have rejected insurance company attempts to limit insurance for the indemnity of settlements and/or judgments through "allocation" arguments. These courts have adapted the "larger settlement" rule, holding that the insurer must pay the settlement except insofar as uninsured claims or parties increased the liability.[272] For example, allocation was an issue in a Tenth Circuit case because the policy only provided insurance for the individual officers and directors,[273] but not for the corporate defendant.[274] The court rejected the insurance company's allocation argument and held that the insurance company had to pay the entire amount, unless defense or liability payments were increased as a result of the presence of uninsured parties or entities in the lawsuits. The court followed the "larger settlement rule," recognizing that the principal wrongdoers, as alleged, were the officers and directors and that the D&O policy was ambiguous on the allocation issue.[275]

Other courts come to the opposite conclusion, apply the "relative exposure rule," and allocate according to the relative risk of exposure between covered and uncovered claims and/or parties.[276]

[b]—Defense Costs

On the issue of allocation of defense costs, results differ depending on the type of policy. For instance, in standard duty-to-defend policies, the nearly universal rule is that an insurance company cannot pick and choose which claims to defend, but, instead, is required to defend all claims—whether excluded or potentially covered—that arise from the same occurrence as long as a potentially covered claim is alleged in the underlying complaint. The rationale behind this rule is the duty-to-defend language in the policies, which provides a promise to defend a suit, not some *pro rata* portion of the suit.[277] The same rule applies where there may be claims asserted against uninsured parties.[278]

With respect to defense-cost reimbursement policies—where defense costs are included in what is indemnified, such as is the case in many E&O and D&O policies—allocation of defense costs between covered and uncovered claims and/or parties is generally permitted.[279]

In the leading case on indemnity or defense-cost reimbursement policies, the court held that defense costs "reasonably related" to the defense of the covered claims should be covered by the policy, even if those services and expenses would also be of use in defending the non-covered claims.[280] This "reasonably related" standard also has been applied to allocation between covered and non-covered parties.[281]

[c]—Other Insurance

Where more than one insurance company is required to defend or reimburse for defense costs, allocation issues arise as to how that defense is paid for. There are two possible results. First, the policyholder picks and chooses which insurance company defends it or pays for its defense, and later the co-obligor insurers divide up the costs among themselves either through agreement or in litigation. Alternatively, defense costs could be allocated in the first instance on a *pro rata* basis or with the insurance companies and the policyholder coming to an agreement or litigating how the division occurs.[282]

Notes

[1] See:

First Circuit: New England Environmental Technologies Corp. v. American Safety Risk Retention Group, Inc., 810 F. Supp.2d 390 (D. Mass. 2011).

Second Circuit: Barney Greengrass, Inc. v. Lumbermens Mutual Casualty Co., 445 Fed. Appx. 411 (2d Cir. 2011); International Chemical Corp. v. Nautilus Insurance Co., 2012 WL 32963 (W.D.N.Y. Jan. 6, 2012); Continental Casualty Co. v. JBS Construction Management, Inc., 2010 WL 2834898 (S.D.N.Y. July 1, 2010).

Fourth Circuit: Baker's Express, L.L.C. v. Arrowpoint Capital Corp., 2012 WL 437065 (D. Md. Sept. 20, 2012); Trice, Geary & Myers, L.L.C. v. CAMICO Mutual Insurance Co., 2010 WL 1375389 (D. Md. Mar., 25, 2010), *rev'd on other grounds*, 459 Fed. Appx. 266 (4th Cir.

2011); Capital Environmental Services, Inc. v. North River Insurance Co., 536 F. Supp.2d 633 (E.D. Va. 2008).

Fifth Circuit: Illinois Union Insurance Co. v. NRI Construction, Inc., 846 F. Supp.2d 1366 (N.D. Ga. 2012); Purcel v. Advanced Bionics Holding Corp., 2008 WL 4790998 (N.D. Tex. Oct. 27, 2008).

Sixth Circuit: Keely v. Fire Insurance Exchange, 833 F. Supp.2d 722 (E.D. Mich. 2011).

Eighth Circuit: Pekin Insurance Co. v. Tysa, Inc., 2006 WL 3827232 (S.D. Iowa Dec. 27, 2006).

Ninth Circuit: Newmont USA Ltd. v. American Home Assurance Co., 676 F. Supp.2d 1146 (E.D. Wash. 2009); Dong Ah Tire & Rubber Co. v. Glasforms, Inc., 2009 WL 667171 (N.D. Cal. Mar. 10, 2009).

Tenth Circuit: Hurtado v. Passmore & Sons, L.L.C., 2011 WL 2533698 (D. Colo. June 27, 2011); Westport Insurance Corp. v. Ong, 2008 WL 892941 (D. Utah Mar. 28, 2008).

District of Columbia Circuit: Fireman's Fund Insurance Co. v. CTIA, 480 F. Supp.2d 7 (D.D.C. 2007).

State Courts:

Connecticut: Community Healthcare Credit Union, Inc. v. Cuna Mutual Group, 2007 WL 1827837 (Conn. Super. June 1, 2007).

Delaware: ASB Allegiance Real Estate Fund v. Scion Breckenridge Managing Member, L.L.C., 2013 WL 5152295 (Del. Ch. Sept. 16, 2013).

Kansas: Miller v. Westport Insurance Corp., 200 P.3d 419 (Kan. 2009).

Massachusetts: Hingham Mutual Fire Insurance Co. v. DeWolfe, 2008 WL 4290919 (Mass. App. Sept. 16, 2008); Celanese Corp. v. One-Beacon America Insurance Co., 2008 WL 5784444 (Mass. Super. Ct. Suffolk Cnty. Dec. 29, 2008).

Michigan: Hastings Mutual Insurance Co. v. Mosher Dolan Cataldo & Kelly, Inc., 2013 WL 1149790 (Mich. App. Feb. 14, 2013).

New York: New York University v. American Building Maintenance, 25 Misc.3d 1217(A), 901 N.Y.S.2d 908 (Table) (2009).

North Carolina: SPX Corp. v. Liberty Mutual Insurance Co., 709 S.E.2d 441 (N.C. App. 2011).

Pennsylvania: American and Foreign Insurance Co. v. Jerry's Sport Center, Inc., 948 A.2d 834 (Pa. Super. 2008).

Washington: National Surety Corp. v. Immunex Corp., 176 Wash.2d 872, 297 P.3d 688 (2013) (*en banc*).

[2] See § 5.03[5][a] *infra*.

[3] See § 5.03[5][b] *infra*.

[4] See Chapter 9 *infra*.

[5] See Chapter 2 *supra*. See White v. Insurance Company of State of Pennsylvania, 282 F. Supp.2d 618, 625 (N.D. Ohio 2003), *vacated on other grounds* 405 F.3d 455 (6th Cir. 2005).

> "'Liability' insurance constitutes 'an agreement to cover a loss resulting from one's liability to a third party, such as a loss incurred by a driver who injures a pedestrian.' The claim under the policy 'arises once the insured's liability to a third party has been asserted.' In contrast to this 'third-party insurance,' there is also 'indemnity' insurance which is characterized as 'first-party insurance' and defined as '[a] policy that applies to oneself or one's own property, such as life insurance, health insurance, disability insurance, and fire insurance.'" (citations omitted)

See also:

First Circuit: Ryan v. Royal Insurance Co., 916 F.2d 731 (1st Cir. 1990); Liberty Mutual Insurance Co. v. Black & Decker Corp., 383 F. Supp.2d 200, 219 (D. Mass. 2004); American Employers' Insurance Co. v. DeLorme Publishing Co., 39 F. Supp.2d 64 (D. Me. 1999); City of West Haven v. Liberty Mutual Insurance Co., 639 F. Supp. 1012 (D. Conn. 1986).

Second Circuit: Allianz Insurance Co. v. Lerner, 416 F.3d 109, 116 (2d Cir. 2005).

Third Circuit: NL Industries, Inc. v. Commercial Union Insurance Co., 926 F. Supp. 446 (D.N.J. 1996); Harristown Development Corp. v. International Insurance Co., 1988 WL 123149, at *12 (M.D. Pa. Nov. 15, 1988); *In re* Asousa Partnership, 2004 WL 1043149, at *8 (Bankr. E.D. Pa. Apr. 26, 2004).

Fourth Circuit: Perdue Farms, Inc. v. Travelers Casualty & Surety Co., 448 F.3d 252, 258 (4th Cir. 2006) ("'Although the type of policy here considered is most often referred to as liability insurance, it is 'litigation insurance' as well, protecting the insured from the expense of defending suits brought against him.'"); Provident Bank v. Travelers Property Casualty Corp., 236 F.3d 138 (4th Cir. 2000).

Fifth Circuit: Felham Enterprises, Ltd. v. Certain Underwriters of Lloyd's London, 2004 WL 2984296, at *4 (E.D. La. Dec. 6, 2004) ("'[F]irst party insurance' generally is understood to provide coverage for the insured against loss or damage sustained by it, whereas 'third party insurance' covers liability of the insured to another person.").

Sixth Circuit: Ndabishuriye v. Albert Schweitzer Society, USA, Inc., 136 Fed. Appx. 795, 796, 2005 WL 1386475 (6th Cir. 2005); Taylor v. Temple & Cutler, 192 F.R.D. 552, 558 (E.D. Mich. 1999) ("'In a sense, liability insurance is nothing more than litigation insurance.'").

Seventh Circuit: Sanyo Laser Products, Inc. v. Royal Insurance Co., 2003 WL 23101793, at *3 n.2 (S.D. Ind. Nov. 7, 2003) ("'first-party' insurance is a contract between the insurer and insured protecting the insured's own actual losses and expenses, while 'third-party' insurance protects the insured from potential liability to a third party").

Ninth Circuit: Kla-Tencor Corp. v. National Union Fire Insurance Co., 2006 WL 2479106 (N.D. Cal. Aug. 28, 2006); United States *ex rel.* North Star Terminal & Stevedore Co. v. Nuggett Construction Co., 2006 WL 2251122, at *2 n.3 (D. Alaska July 28, 2006).

Tenth Circuit: Allstate Insurance Co. v. Johnston, 339 F. Supp.2d 1191, 1195 (D. Kan. 2004); American States Insurance Co. v. Ridco, Inc., 1996 WL 33401184, at *3 (D. Wyo. Feb. 8, 1996); Weitzman v. Blazing Pedals, Inc., 151 F.R.D. 125 (D. Colo. 1993).

Eleventh Circuit: Colonial Oil Industries, Inc. v. Underwriters, 1995 WL 692691, at *10–11 (S.D. Ga. Nov. 6, 1995), *vacated on other grounds* 910 F. Supp. 655 (S.D. Ga.).

District of Columbia Circuit: Pierce Associates, Inc. v. St. Paul Mercury Insurance Co., 421 F. Supp.2d 11, 17 (D.D.C. 2006), *vacated on other grounds* 437 F. Supp.2d 16 (D.D.C. 2006).

State Courts:

Alaska: Langdon v. Champion, 752 P.2d 999 (Alaska 1988).

California: Montrose Chemical Co. v. Admiral Insurance, Inc., 10 Cal.4th 645, 42 Cal. Rptr.2d 324, 332, 913 P.2d 878 (Cal. 1995); Garvey v. State Farm Fire & Casualty Co., 48 Cal.3d 395, 257 Cal.Rptr. 292, 770 P.2d 704 (Cal. 1989); Black Diamond Asphalt Co. v. Superior Court, 114 Cal. App.4th 109, 7 Cal. Rptr.3d 466, 470 n.2 (Cal. App. 2003) ("In first party insurance, a person insures himself or his property against loss. In third party insurance, a person insures himself against liability he may incur to others."); Century Indemnity Co. v. Hearrean, 98 Cal. App.4th 734, 120 Cal. Rptr.2d 66, 69 (Cal. App. 2002) ("'CGL policies are third party liability insurance policies which obligate insurers to pay money to third parties to whom their insureds are liable. In contrast to first party insurance policies which obligate an insurer to pay money directly to an insured for a loss sustained by the insured. . . .'").

Connecticut: Community Healthcare Credit Union, Inc. v. Cuna Mutual Group, 2007 WL 1827837 (Conn. Super. June 1, 2007).

Delaware: Liggett Group, Inc. v. Ace Property & Casualty Insurance Co., 798 A.2d 1024, 1031 (Del. 2002).

Hawaii: Sentinel Insurance Co. v. First Insurance Company of Hawaii, Ltd., 875 P.2d 894, 906 (Haw. 1994); Ferrer v. Ngo, 73 P.3d 73, 81 (Haw. App. 2003) ("a 'first-party' policy provides coverage for loss or damage sustained by the insured (e.g., life, disability, health, fire, theft, and casualty insurance) whereby the insurer usually promises to pay money to the insured upon the happening of the risk insured against. A 'third-party' policy, on the other hand, provides coverage for the insured's liability to another (e.g., CGL [comprehensive general liability], directors' and officers' liability, and errors and omissions insurance) wherein the carrier generally assumes a contractual duty to pay judgments recovered against the insured arising from the insured's negligence.") (emphasis in original).

Illinois: Emerson Electric Co. v. Aetna Casualty & Surety Co., 352 Ill. App.3d 399, 287 Ill. Dec. 280, 815 N.E.2d 924, 950 (Ill. App. 2004).

Indiana: Transamerica Insurance Services v. Kopko, 559 N.E.2d 322 (Ind. App. 1990).

Kentucky: Aetna Casualty & Surety Co. v. Kentucky, 179 S.W.3d 830, 845 (Ky. 2005) ("Third party insurance involves protection for the policyholder for liability it incurs to someone else, while first party insurance involves protection for losses to the policyholder's own property.").

Maryland: BGE Home Products & Services, Inc. v. Owens, 833 A.2d 8, 14 (Md. 2003); Sherwood Brands, Inc. v. Hartford Accident & Indemnity Co., 698 A.2d 1078, 1083 (Md. 1997); Brohawn v. Transamerica Insurance Co., 347 A.2d 842, 851 (Md. 1975).

Massachusetts: Hanover Insurance Co. v. Golden, 766 N.E.2d 838, 841 (Mass. 2002).

Michigan: Allstate Insurance Co. v. Freeman, 443 N.W.2d 734 (Mich. 1989).

Mississippi: Watson Quality Ford, Inc. v. Great River Insurance Co., 909 So.2d 1196, 1199 (Miss. App. 2005) ("First party coverage is a promise by an insurer to pay its own insured, rather than a promise to its insured to pay a third party.").

New York: BP Air Conditioning Corp. v. One Beacon Insurance Group, 8 N.Y.3d 708, 840 N.Y.S.2d 302, 871 N.E.2d 1128 (N.Y. 2007); Automobile Insurance Co. v. Cook, 7 N.Y.3d 131, 818 N.Y.S.2d 176, 850 N.E.2d 1152, 1155 (N.Y. 2006) ("For this reason, when a policy represents that it will provide the insured with a defense, we have said that it actually constitutes 'litigation insurance' in addition to liability coverage."); BP Air Conditioning Corp. v. One Beacon Insurance Group, 821 N.Y.S.2d 1, 33 A.D.3d 116, 120 (N.Y. App. Div. 2006); City of New York v. Certain Underwriters of Lloyd's London, 790 N.Y.S.2d 82, 15 A.D.3d 228, 230 (N.Y. App. Div. 2005).

North Carolina: Brown v. Lumbermens' Mutual Insurance Co., 369 S.E.2d 367 (N.C. App.), *review denied* 373 S.E.2d 541 (N.C. 1988).

Texas: Lamar Homes, Inc. v. Mid-Continent Casualty Co., 242 S.W.3d 1 (Tex. 2007).

Virginia: Veney v. Duke, 2005 WL 3476760, at *2 (Va. Cir. Oct. 26, 2005) ("'liability insurance' essentially constitutes 'litigation insurance'").

Washington: State Farm Fire & Casualty Co. v. English Cove Association, Inc., 88 P.3d 986, 992 (Wash. App. 2004) ("Third party insurance provides protection for the policyholder for liability it incurs to someone else, while first party insurance provides protection for losses to the policyholder's own property.").

Wyoming: Shoshone First Bank v. Pacific Employers Insurance Co., 2 P.3d 510, 516 (Wyo. 2000); First Wyoming Bank, N.A. v. Continental Ins. Co., 860 P.2d 1064 (Wyo.), *vacated in part* 860 P.2d 1094 (Wyo. 1993).

[6] See ISO Form CG 00 01 10 01. See also: § 5.02 *supra*, and Chapter 8 *infra*.

[7] Some or all of the General Conditions are also applicable to Coverage B and other third-party insurance policies. However, for sake of convenience, they will be discussed in § 5.04 *infra* and referred to later in this treatise.

[8] See Chapter 7 *infra.*

[9] See Chapter 8 *infra.*

[10] See Chapter 9 *infra.*

[11] See Chapter 6 *infra.*

[12] See ISO Form CG 00 01 10 01. That agreement was unchanged in the 2007 and 2013 versions. See ISO Forms CG 00 01 12 07 and 00 01 04 13.

[13] See § 5.03[1] *infra.*

[14] See § 5.03[2] *infra.*

[15] See § 5.03[3] *infra.*

[16] See § 5.03[4] *infra.*

[17] See § 5.03[5] *infra.*

[18] See § 5.03[6] *infra.*

[19] See Chapter 6 *infra.*

[20] See, e.g.:

First Circuit: Emhart Industries, Inc. v. Century Indemnity Co., 559 F.3d 57 (1st Cir. 2009) (environmental).

Second Circuit: Stonewell Insurance Co. v. Asbestos Claims Management, 73 F.3d 1178 (2d Cir. 1995), *modified and rehearing denied* 85 F.3d 49 (2d Cir. 1996) (asbestos bodily injury).

Third Circuit: Koppers Co. v. Aetna Casualty & Surety Co., 158 F.3d 170, 176 (3d Cir. 1998) (underlying environmental claims).

Fifth Circuit: Wilshire Insurance Co. v. RJT Construction, L.L.C., 581 F.3d 222 (5th Cir. 2009) (construction loss); Maxum Indemnity Co. v. Wilson, 707 F. Supp.2d 683 (S.D. Miss. 2010) (construction loss).

Eighth Circuit: West Bend Mutual Insurance Co. v. Valley Forge Insurance Co., 651 F. Supp.2d 983 (D. Minn. 2009) (construction loss).

Ninth Circuit: Pacific Coast Building Products, Inc. v. AIU Insurance Co., 300 Fed. Appx. 546 (9th Cir. 2008) (construction); Axis Surplus Insurance Co. v. James River Insurance Co., 2009 WL 675938 (W.D. Wash. Mar. 13, 2009) (construction).

Tenth Circuit: American Family Mutual Insurance Co. v. Teamcorp, Inc., 659 F. Supp.2d 1115 (D. Colo. 2009) (construction loss).

Eleventh Circuit: Mid-Continent Casualty Co. v. Frank Casserino Construction, Inc., 721 F. Supp.2d 1209 (M.D. Fla. 2010) (construction loss); Keenan Hopkins Schmidt and Stowell Contractors, Inc. v. Continental Casualty Co., 653 F. Supp.2d 1255 (M.D. Fla. 2009) (construction loss).

State Courts:

California: Pennsylvania General Insurance Co. v. American Safety Indemnity Co., 185 Cal. App.4th 1515, 111 Cal. Rptr.3d 403 (2010) (construction loss); Pepperell v. Scottsdale Insurance Co., 73 Cal. Rptr.2d 164, 167 (Cal. App. 1998) (construction defect property damage); Montrose Chemical Corp. v. Admiral Insurance Co., 42 Cal. Rptr.2d 324, 347 (Cal. 1995) (environmental property damage).

Delaware: Viking Pump, Inc. v. Century Indemnity Co., 2 A.3d 76 (Del. Ch. 2009) (asbestos).

Florida: Pennsylvania Lumbermens Mutual Insurance Co. v. Indiana Lumbermens Mutual Insurance Co., 43 So.3d 182 (Fla. App. 2010) (construction loss).

Louisiana: Ricks v. Kentwood Oil Co., 38 So.3d 363 (La. App. 2010) (environmental).

Massachusetts: Boston Gas Co. v. Century Indemnity Co., 454 Mass. 337, 910 N.E.2d 290 (2009) (environmental); Maestranzi Brothers, Inc. v. American Employers' Insurance Co., 2010 WL 1427352 (Mass. Super. Apr. 9, 2010) (environmental loss).

Minnesota: Donnelly Brothers Construction Co. v. State Auto Property and Casualty Insurance Co., 759 N.W.2d 651 (Minn. App. 2009) (construction).

Missouri: D.R. Sherry Construction, Ltd. v. American Family Mutual Insurance Co., 316 S.W.3d 899 (Mo. 2010) (construction loss).

New Jersey: Polarome International, Inc. v. Greenwich Insurance Co., 404 N.J. Super. 241, 961 A.2d 29 (2008) (environmental).

New York: Continental Casualty Co. v. Employers Insurance Co. of Wausau, 60 A.D.3d 128, 871 N.Y.S.2d 48 (2008) (asbestos).

Pennsylvania: J.H. France Refractories Co. v. Allstate Insurance Co., 626 A.2d 502, 508–509 (Pa. 1993) (asbestos bodily injury).

Texas: Pine Oak Builders, Inc. v. Great American Lloyd's Insurance Co., 279 S.W.3d 650 (Tex. 2009) (construction).

Washington: Walla Walla College v. Ohio Casualty Insurance Co., 149 Wash. App. 726, 204 P.3d 961 (2009) (environmental loss).

Wisconsin: Plastics Engineering Co. v. Liberty Mutual Insurance Co., 315 Wis.2d 556, 759 N.W.2d 613 (2009) (asbestos).

[21] See, e.g.:

First Circuit: Emhart Industries, Inc. v. Century Indemnity Co., 559 F.3d 57 (1st Cir. 2009) (environmental).

Second Circuit: Stonewell Insurance Co. v. Asbestos Claims Management, 73 F.3d 1178 (2d Cir. 1995), *modified and rehearing denied* 85 F.3d 49 (2d Cir. 1996) (asbestos bodily injury).

Third Circuit: Koppers Co. v. Aetna Casualty & Surety Co., 158 F.3d 170, 176 (3d Cir. 1998) (underlying environmental claims).

Fifth Circuit: Wilshire Insurance Co. v. RJT Construction, L.L.C., 581 F.3d 222 (5th Cir. 2009) (construction loss); Maxum Indemnity Co. v. Wilson, 707 F. Supp.2d 683 (S.D. Miss. 2010) (construction loss).

Eighth Circuit: West Bend Mutual Insurance Co. v. Valley Forge Insurance Co., 651 F. Supp.2d 983 (D. Minn. 2009) (construction loss).

Ninth Circuit: Pacific Coast Building Products, Inc. v. AIU Insurance Co., 300 Fed. Appx. 546 (9th Cir. 2008) (construction); Axis Surplus Insurance Co. v. James River Insurance Co., 2009 WL 675938 (W.D. Wash. Mar. 13, 2009) (construction).

Tenth Circuit: American Family Mutual Insurance Co. v. Teamcorp, Inc., 659 F. Supp.2d 1115 (D. Colo. 2009) (construction loss).

Eleventh Circuit: Mid-Continent Casualty Co. v. Frank Casserino Construction, Inc., 721 F. Supp.2d 1209 (M.D. Fla. 2010) (construction loss); Keenan Hopkins Schmidt and Stowell Contractors, Inc. v. Continental Casualty Co., 653 F. Supp.2d 1255 (M.D. Fla. 2009) (construction loss).

State Courts:

California: Pennsylvania General Insurance Co. v. American Safety Indemnity Co., 185 Cal. App.4th 1515, 111 Cal. Rptr.3d 403 (2010) (construction loss); Pepperell v. Scottsdale Insurance Co., 73 Cal. Rptr.2d 164, 167 (Cal. App. 1998) (construction defect property damage); Montrose Chemical Corp. v. Admiral Insurance Co., 42 Cal. Rptr.2d 324, 347 (Cal. 1995) (environmental property damage).

Delaware: Viking Pump, Inc. v. Century Indemnity Co., 2 A.3d 76 (Del. Ch. 2009) (asbestos).

Florida: Pennsylvania Lumbermens Mutual Insurance Co. v. Indiana Lumbermens Mutual Insurance Co., 43 So.3d 182 (Fla. App. 2010) (construction loss).

Louisiana: Ricks v. Kentwood Oil Co., 38 So.3d 363 (La. App. 2010) (environmental).

Massachusetts: Boston Gas Co. v. Century Indemnity Co., 454 Mass. 337, 910 N.E.2d 290 (2009) (environmental); Maestranzi Brothers, Inc. v. American Employers' Insurance Co., 2010 WL 1427352 (Mass. Super. Apr. 9, 2010) (environmental loss).

Minnesota: Donnelly Brothers Construction Co. v. State Auto Property and Casualty Insurance Co., 759 N.W.2d 651 (Minn. App. 2009) (construction).

Missouri: D.R. Sherry Construction, Ltd. v. American Family Mutual Insurance Co., 316 S.W.3d 899 (Mo. 2010) (construction loss).

New Jersey: Polarome International, Inc. v. Greenwich Insurance Co., 404 N.J. Super. 241, 961 A.2d 29 (2008) (environmental).

New York: Continental Casualty Co. v. Employers Insurance Co. of Wausau, 60 A.D.3d 128, 871 N.Y.S.2d 48 (2008) (asbestos).

Pennsylvania: J.H. France Refractories Co. v. Allstate Insurance Co., 626 A.2d 502, 508–509 (Pa. 1993) (asbestos bodily injury).

Texas: Pine Oak Builders, Inc. v. Great American Lloyds Insurance Co., 279 S.W.3d 650 (Tex. 2009) (construction).

Washington: Walla Walla College v. Ohio Casualty Insurance Co., 149 Wash. App. 726, 204 P.3d 961 (2009) (environmental loss).

Wisconsin: Plastics Engineering Co. v. Liberty Mutual Insurance Co., 315 Wis.2d 556, 759 N.W.2d 613 (2009) (asbestos).

[22] The Reliance Insurance Company insolvency presents an interesting example as to the lack of notice that can be afforded to policyholders owning policies covered by insolvent insurance companies. On May 29, 2001, the Pennsylvania Insurance Department took over Reliance Insurance Company and its affiliated insurance companies, placing them in rehabilitation. In June 2001, Reliance Group Holdings—the parent of the Reliance insurance companies—filed for bankruptcy protection. On October 3, 2001, Reliance was placed into liquidation. See Associated Press, "Pennsylvania Sues Steinberg, Others Over Reliance," *The Wall Street Journal* (June 26, 2002).

The liquidation dashed policyholder expectations of coverage. Although guaranty associations are designed to provide a safety net when insurance companies become insolvent, not all policyholders and not all claims are subject to such protection. Even when claims are covered by a guaranty association, statutory limits apply to each claim. Some policyholders were shocked to find out that the guaranty associations would not voluntarily pay them anything because they had been sold "surplus lines" insurance—insurance from a company that was not admitted to do business in their state. Although some recovery might have been or was forthcoming ultimately to policyholders in the liquidation proceedings, the liquidation proceedings usually take an inordinately long period of time. Policyholders usually should not expect even a partial recovery for a number of years. When the claim payment arrives, it will be pennies on the dollar.

Interestingly, the insurance press indicates that Reliance's difficulties first became public in the middle of 1999. See Christopher Oster, "At A Premium: Insurance Costs Loom As A Cloud Over The Economy," *The Wall Street Journal* at 2 (Apr, 11, 2002).

Other signs of problems emerged in 1999, such as Reliance's backing out of a deal with Business Backers Management Corporation. See Alan Kline, "From Private Sector, A Challenger To SBA," *American Banker* at 2 (June 7, 2001). Reliance posted a net loss of $123 million in the fourth quarter of 1999 and took a $117 million after-tax charge to settle a dispute over workers' compensation relating to Unicover Managers, Inc. See Meg Green, "Pennsylvania Regulators Consider Suing Reliance Officers," *Best's Insurance News* at 2 (Dec. 19, 2001). Ratings for Reliance were reduced beginning in late 1999 but it was not until late 2000 that a rating necessitating a need to move a policyholder's insurance appeared, which would be too late for most policyholders' one-year policies. In 1999, Best's rated Reliance at A- (Excellent), which had been its rating since at least 1995. See Reliance Insurance Group Best's Company Reports (July 12, 1999). In October, 1999, Best's placed Reliance under review with negative implications. See Reliance Insurance Group Best's Company Reports (Dec. 8, 1999). It was not until August 2000 that Reliance's Best rating was significantly reduced, and even then, it was reduced to a rating of C (weak), which does not indicate ultimate financial insolvency. Best's ultimately reduced Reliance's rating to E (Under Regulatory Supervision) in January 2001 and to F (In Liquidation) in October, 2001. See: Reliance Insurance Group Best's Company Reports (Aug. 23, 2000); "A.M. Best Downgrades Reliance Rating," *Best's Insurance News* (Jan. 31, 2001); "A.M. Best Downgrades Reliance Rating," *Best's Insurance News* (Oct. 10, 2001).

[23] See, e.g.:

First Circuit: Travelers Casualty and Surety Co. v. Providence Washington Insurance Co., 685 F.3d 22 (1st Cir. 2012).

Second Circuit: Stonewell Insurance Co. v. Asbestos Claims Management, 73 F.3d 1178 (2d Cir. 1995), *modified and rehearing denied* 85 F.3d 49 (2d Cir. 1996) (asbestos bodily injury).

Third Circuit: Koppers Co. v. Aetna Casualty & Surety Co., 158 F.3d 170, 176 (3d Cir. 1998) (underlying environmental claims).

Fourth Circuit: Liberty Mutual Fire Insurance Co. v. J.T. Walker Industries, Inc., 835 F. Supp.2d 104 (D.S.C. 2011).

Fifth Circuit: Louisiana Generating L.L.C. v. Illinois Union Insurance Co., 719 F.3d 328 (5th Cir. 2013)

Sixth Circuit: Burlington Insurance Co. v. PMI America, Inc., 862 F. Supp.2d 719 (S.D. Ohio 2012).

Seventh Circuit: Trinity Homes L.L.C. v. Ohio Casualty Insurance Co., 864 F. Supp.2d 744 (S.D. Ind. 2012).

Eighth Circuit: Genesis Insurance Co. v. City of Council Bluffs, 677 F.3d 806 (8th Cir. 2012).

Ninth Circuit: City of San Buenaventura v. Insurance Company of the State of Pennsylvania, 719 F.3d 1115 (9th Cir. 2013).

Eleventh Circuit: Axis Surplus Insurance Co. v. Contravest Construction Co., 921 F. Supp.2d 1338 (M.D. Fla. 2012).

State Courts:

California: State v. Continental Insurance Co., 55 Cal.4th 186, 281 P.3d 1000, 145 Cal. Rptr.3d 1 (2012); Pepperell v. Scottsdale Insurance Co., 73 Cal. Rptr.2d 164, 167 (Cal. App. 1998) (construction defect property damage); Montrose Chemical Corp. v. Admiral Insurance Co., 42 Cal. Rptr.2d 324, 347 (Cal. 1995) (environmental property damage).

Louisiana: Arceneaux v. Amstar Corp., 66 So.3d 438 (La. 2011).

Massachusetts: New England Insulation Co. v. Liberty Mutual Insurance Co., 83 Mass. App. Ct. 631, 988 N.E.2d 450 (2013).

New Jersey: Farmers Mutual Fire Insurance Company of Salem v. New Jersey Property Liability Insurance Guaranty Ass'n, 2013 WL 5311272 (N.J. Sept. 24, 2013).

New York: U.S. Fidelity & Guaranty Co. v. American Re-Insurance Co., 20 N.Y.3d 407, 985 N.E.2d 876, 962 N.Y.S.2d 566 (2013).

Pennsylvania: J.H. France Refractories Co. v. Allstate Insurance Co., 626 A.2d 502, 508–509 (Pa. 1993) (asbestos bodily injury).

Texas: Lennar Corp. v. Merkel American Insurance Co., 2013 WL 4492800 (Tex. Aug. 23, 2013); Geico General Insurance Co. v. Austin Power, Inc., 357 S.W.3d 821 (Tex. App. 2012).

Utah: One Beacon American Insurance Co. v. Huntsman Polymers Corp., 276 P.3d 1156 (Utah App. 2012).

Vermont: Bradford Oil Co. v. Stonington Insurance Co., 190 Vt. 330, 54 A.3d 983 (2011).

[24] See:

Third Circuit: TIG Insurance Co. v. Tyco International Ltd., 919 F. Supp.2d 439 (M.D. Pa. 2013).

Ninth Circuit: Axis Surplus Insurance Co. v. St. Paul Fire and Marine Insurance Co., 2013 WL 2318847 (W.D. Wash. May 24, 2013).

State Courts:

Kansas: Western Casualty and Surety Co. v. Trinity Universal Insurance Co. of Kansas, Inc., 13 Kan. App.2d 133, 764 P.2d 1256 (1988).

Missouri: Planet Insurance Co. v. Ertz, 920 S.W.2d 591 (Mo. App. 1996).

New York: Utica Mutual Insurance Co. v. Erie Insurance Co., 107 A.D.3d 1522, 966 N.Y.S.2d 790 (N.Y. App. 2013).

South Carolina: Bardsley v. Government Employees Insurance Co., 405 S.C. 68, 747 S.E.2d 436 (2013).

[25] See, e.g., Mission Insurance Co. v. United States Fire Insurance Co., 517 N.E.2d 463, 466 (Mass. 1988).

See also:

Second Circuit: Federal Insurance Co. v. American Home Assurance Co., 664 F. Supp.2d 397 (S.D.N.Y. 2009).

Third Circuit: TIG Insurance Co. v. Tyco International Ltd., 919 F. Supp.2d 439 (M.D. Pa. 2013); Mega Construction Corp. v. Quincy Mutual Fire Insurance Co., 2012 WL 3994473 (E.D. Pa. Sept. 12, 2012).

Fourth Circuit: Horace Mann Insurance Co. v. General Star National Insurance Co., 514 F.3d 327 (4th Cir. 2008); Executive Risk Indemnity, Inc. v. Charleston Area Medical Center, Inc., 681 F. Supp.2d 694 (S.D.W. Va. 2009).

Fifth Circuit: Travelers Lloyd's Insurance Co. v. Pacific Employers Insurance Co., 602 F.3d 677 (5th Cir. 2010); Trinity Universal Insurance Co. v. Employers Mutual Casualty Co., 592 F.3d 687 (5th Cir. 2010); Millis Development & Construction, Inc. v. America First Lloyd's Insurance Co., 809 F. Supp.2d 616 (S.D. Tex. 2011).

Ninth Circuit: Axis Surplus Insurance Co. v. St. Paul Fire and Marine Insurance Co., 2013 WL 2318847 (W.D. Wash. May 24, 2013); Clarendon America Insurance Co. v. Steadfast Insurance Co., 2008 WL 5221048 (S.D. Cal. Dec. 12, 2008).

State Courts:

Arizona: Regal Homes, Inc. v. CNA Insurance Co., 217 Ariz. 159, 171 P.3d 610 (2007).

California: OneBeacon America Insurance Co. v. Fireman's Fund Insurance Co., 175 Cal. App.4th 183, 95 Cal. Rptr.3d 808 (2009).

Missouri: Farm Bureau Town and Country Insurance Company of Missouri v. American Alternative Insurance Corp., 347 S.W.3d 525 (Mo. App. 2011).

Texas: Mid-Continent Insurance Co. v. Liberty Mutual Insurance Co., 236 S.W.3d 765 (Tex. 2007); Truck Insurance Exchange v. Mid-Continent Casualty Co., 320 S.W.3d 613 (Tex. App. 2010).

[26] Alternatively, conflicts can arise where all triggered policies have "escape" clauses or where all triggered policies have some combination of "escape" and "excess" clauses and the court views those two clauses as irreconcilable and conflicting. Sometimes, however, a court might consider an excess clause to apply over an escape clause, thereby finding no mutual repugnancy. See, e.g., American Casualty Company of Reading, PA v. Health Care Indemnity, Inc., 520 F.3d 1131 (10th Cir. 2008). In all events, where such a conflict is found to exist, courts almost universally construe them as mutually repugnant and give effect to none of the clauses. The reason for this is that effectuating all of these "mutually repugnant" clauses would, in essence, eliminate all coverage for the policyholder. See, e.g., Home Insurance Co. v. St. Paul Fire & Marine Insurance Co., 229 F.3d 56, 62 (1st Cir. 2000).

See also:

Second Circuit: Avondale Industries, Inc. v. Travelers Indemnity Co., 774 F. Supp. 1416 (S.D.N.Y. 1991); Evanston Insurance Co. v. Affiliated FM Insurance Co., 556 F. Supp. 135 (D. Conn. 1983).

Third Circuit: Landmark American Insurance Co. v. Rider University, 2009 WL 1905107 (D.N.J. June 30, 2009); General Accident Insurance Company of America v. Safety National Casualty Corp., 825 F. Supp. 705 (E.D. Pa. 1993); Covington Township v. Pacific Employers Insurance Co., 639 F. Supp. 793 (M.D. Pa. 1986); American Home Assurance Co. v. American Employers Insurance Co., 384 F. Supp. 3 (E.D. Pa. 1974).

Fifth Circuit: Willbros RPI, Inc. v. Continental Casualty Co., 601 F.3d 306 (5th Cir. 2010).

Seventh Circuit: Continental Casualty Co. v. Armstrong World Industries, Inc., 776 F. Supp. 1296 (N.D. Ill. 1991).

Eighth Circuit: Great West Casualty Co. v. General Casualty Co. of Wisconsin, 2010 WL 3269900 (D. Minn. Aug. 16, 2010).

Ninth Circuit: Peerless Insurance Co. v. St. Paul Surplus Lines Insurance Co., 2010 WL 2486795 (S.D. Cal. June 15, 2010); Flintkote Co. v. General Accident Assurance Co. of Canada, 2008 WL 3270922 (N.D. Cal. Aug. 6, 2008).

Tenth Circuit: American Casualty Co. of Reading, PA v. Health Care Indemnity, Inc., 520 F.3d 1131 (10th Cir. 2008); Attorneys Liability Protection Society v. Reliance Insurance Co., 117 F. Supp.2d 1114 (D. Kan. 2000); Carriers Insurance Co. v. American Home Assurance Co., 512 F.2d 360 (10th Cir. 1975).

Eleventh Circuit: Towne Realty, Inc. v. Safeco Insurance Company of America, 854 F.2d 1264 (11th Cir. 1988).

State Courts:

Arizona: Fremont Indemnity Co. v. New England Reinsurance Co., 168 Ariz. 476, 815 P.2d 403 (1991).

California: Shell Oil Co. v. Winterthur Swiss Insurance Co., 12 Cal. App.4th 715, 15 Cal. Rptr.2d 815 (1993).

Connecticut: England v. Reliance Insurance Co., 2004 WL 425139 (Conn. Super. Feb. 24, 2004).

Florida: Travelers Insurance Co. v. Lexington Insurance Co., 478 So.2d 363 (Fla. App. 1985), *review denied* 488 So.2d 69 (Fla. 1986).

Indiana: Citizens Insurance Co. v. Ganschow, 859 N.E.2d 786 (Ind. App. 2007); United Farm Bureau Mutual Insurance Co. v. Nationwide Mutual Fire Insurance Co., 678 N.E.2d 1165 (Ind. App. 1997); Indiana Insurance Co. v. Federated Mutual Insurance Co., 415 N.E.2d 80 (Ind. App. 1981).

Louisiana: Penton v. Hotho, 601 So.2d 762 (La. App. 1992).

Michigan: South Macomb Disposal Authority v. National Surety Corp., 608 N.W.2d 814 (Mich. App.), *appeal denied* 613 N.W.2d 726 (Mich. 2000).

Minnesota: Cargill, Inc. v. Evanston Insurance Co., 642 N.W.2d 80 (Minn. App. 2002).

New York: In re Liquidation of Midland Insurance Co., 709 N.Y.S.2d 24 (N.Y. App. Div. 2000).

Ohio: Jennings v. Mohawk Fireworks Display Co., 1990 WL 237410 (Ohio App. Dec. 19, 1990).

Oregon: Thurman v. Signal Insurance Co., 260 Or. 524, 491 P.2d 1002 (1971).

Texas: Safeco Lloyds Insurance Co. v. Allstate Insurance Co., 308 S.W.3d 49 (Tex. App. 2009); National Union Fire Insurance Company of Pittsburgh, Pa. v. United L.P. Gas Corp., 2002 WL 396533 (Tex. App. Mar. 14, 2002); Liberty Mutual Insurance Co. v. General Insurance Corp., 517 S.W.2d 791 (Tex. Civ. App. 1974).

Wisconsin: Johnson Controls, Inc. v. London Market, 325 Wis.2d 176, 784 N.W.2d 579 (Wis. 2010); International Surplus Lines Insurance Co. v. Monticello Insurance Co., 526 N.W.2d 280 (Wis. App. Oct. 5, 1994).

See also, ISO Form CG 00 01 07 98, providing a somewhat different version of an "other" insurance provision.

27 Mission Insurance Co. v. United States Fire Insurance Co., 517 N.E.2d 463, 466 n.4 (Mass. 1988). See also:

First Circuit: Aviles v. Burgos, 783 F.2d 270 (1st Cir. 1986).

Second Circuit: National Casualty Co. v. Vigilant Insurance Co., 466 F. Supp.2d 533 (S.D.N.Y. 2006).

Third Circuit: TIG Insurance Co. v. Tyco International Ltd., 919 F. Supp.2d 439 (M.D. Pa. 2013); Mega Construction Corp. v. Quincy Mutual Fire Insurance Co., 2012 WL 3994473 (E.D. Pa. Sept. 12, 2012).

Fifth Circuit: Travelers Lloyd's Insurance Co. v. Pacific Employers Insurance Co., 602 F.3d 677 (5th Cir. 2010); American Indemnity Lloyds v. Travelers Property & Casualty Insurance Co., 335 F.3d 429 (5th Cir. 2003); Millis Development & Construction, Inc. v. America First Lloyd's Insurance Co., 809 F. Supp.2d 616 (S.D. Tex. 2011); Hill v. General Insurance Company of America, 456 F. Supp.2d 757 (N.D. Miss. 2006).

Sixth Circuit: Central Michigan Board of Trustees v. Employers Reinsurance Corp., 117 F. Supp.2d 627 (E.D. Mich. 2000).

Seventh Circuit: American Alliance Insurance Co. v. IARW Insurance Co., Ltd., 165 F.3d 558 (7th Cir. 1999); Public Service Mutual Insurance Co. v. Capitol Transamerica Corp., 756 F. Supp.2d 920 (N.D. Ill 2010).

Tenth Circuit: MIC Property & Casualty Insurance Corp. v. International Insurance Co., 990 F.2d 573 (10th Cir. 1993); Baker v. Allied Property and Casualty Insurance Co., 2013 WL 1397297 (D. Colo. June 12, 2013).

State Courts:

Alabama: Nationwide Mutual Insurance Co. v. Hall, 643 So.2d 551 (Ala. 1994).

Arizona: Western Agricultural Insurance Co. v. Industrial Indemnity Insurance Co., 838 P.2d 1353 (Ariz. App. 1992).

California: Dart Industries, Inc. v. Commercial Union Insurance Co., 28 Cal.4th 1059, 52 P.3d 79, 124 Cal. Rptr.2d 142 (2002); American International Specialty Lines Insurance Co. v. Continental Casualty Insurance Co., 142 Cal. App.4th 1342, 49 Cal. Rptr.3d 1 (2006); Employers Insurance Company of Wausau v. Travelers Indemnity Co., 141 Cal. App.4th 398, 46 Cal. Rptr.3d 1 (2006); Travelers Casualty and Surety Co. v. Century Surety Co., 118 Cal. App.4th 1156, 13 Cal. Rptr.3d 526 (2004).

Colorado: Colonial Insurance Company of California v. American Hardware Mutual Insurance Co., 969 P.2d 796 (Colo. App. 1998).

Illinois: Home Insurance Co. v. Cincinnati Insurance Co., 213 Ill.2d 307, 821 N.E.2d 269, 290 Ill. Dec. 218 (2004); State Farm Mutual Automobile Insurance Co. v. Illinois Farmers Insurance Co., 368 Ill. App.3d 914, 858 N.E.2d 519, 306 Ill. Dec. 722 (2006).

Iowa: Aid Insurance Co. v. United Fire & Casualty Co., 445 N.W.2d 767 (Iowa 1989).

Louisiana: Hull v. Louisiana Indemnity, 606 So.2d 923 (La. App. 1992).

Maryland: Pacific Employers Insurance Co. v. Eig, 864 A.2d 240 (Md. App. 2004).

Massachusetts: Aetna Casualty & Surety Co. v. Home Insurance Co., 689 N.E.2d 1355, 1358–1359 (Mass. App.), *review denied* 707 N.E.2d 1076 (Mass. 1998).

Michigan: Arco Industries Corp. v. American Motorists Insurance Co., 594 N.W.2d 61 (Mich. App. 1998).

Minnesota: Continental Casualty Insurance Co. v. Teachers Insurance Co., 532 N.W.2d 275 (Minn. App. 1995).

Missouri: Farm Bureau Town and Country Insurance Co. of Missouri v. American Alternative Insurance Corp., 347 S.W.3d 525 (Mo. App. 2011); Heartland Payment Systems, L.L.C. v. Utica Mutual Insurance Co., 185 S.W.3d 225 (Mo. App. 2006).

New York: Utica Mutual Insurance Co. v. Erie Insurance Co., 107 A.D.3d 1522, 966 N.Y.S.2d 790 (N.Y. App. 2013); State Farm Fire & Casualty Co. v. LiMauro, 65 N.Y.2d 369, 482 N.E.2d 13, 492 N.Y.S.2d 534 (1985).

North Carolina: Nationwide Mutual Insurance Co. v. State Farm Mutual Automobile Insurance Co., 470 S.E.2d 556 (N.C. App. 1996).

Oklahoma: Mustain v. United States Fidelity & Guaranty Co., 925 P.2d 533 (Okla. 1996).

South Carolina: State Automobile Property & Casualty Insurance Co. v. Gibbs, 444 S.E.2d 504 (S.C. 1994).

See also: Appleman and Appleman, 8A *Insurance Law and Practice*, § 4909 (1981); *Couch on Insurance*, § 219:33.

[28] Fed. R. Civ. P. 19.

> "(a) Persons to be Joined if Feasible. A person who is subject to service of process and whose joinder will not deprive the court of jurisdiction over the subject matter of the action shall be joined as a party in the action if (1) in the person's absence complete relief cannot be accorded among those already parties, or (2) the person claims an interest relating to the subject of the action and is so situated that the disposition of the action in the person's absence may (i) as a practical matter impair or impede the person's ability to protect that interest or (ii) leave any of the persons already parties subject to a substantial risk of incurring double, multiple, or otherwise inconsistent obligations by reason of the claimed interest. If the person has not been so joined, the court shall order that the person be made a party. If the person should join as a plaintiff but refuses to do so, the person may be made a defendant, or, in a proper case, an involuntary plaintiff. If the joined party objects to venue and joinder of that party would render the venue of the action improper, that party shall be dismissed from the action.
>
> "(b) Determination by Court Whenever Joinder not Feasible. If a person as described in subdivision (a)(1)-(2) hereof cannot be made a party, the court shall determine whether in equity and good conscience the action should proceed among the parties before it, or should be dismissed, the absent person being thus regarded as indispensable. The factors to be considered by the court include: first, to what extent a judgment rendered in the person's absence might be prejudicial to the person or those already parties; second, the extent to which, by protective provisions in the judgment, by the shaping of relief, or other measures, the prejudice can be lessened or avoided; third, whether a judgment rendered in the person's absence will be adequate; fourth, whether the plaintiff will have an adequate remedy if the action is dismissed for nonjoinder."

29 See, e.g., Vale Chemical Co. v. Hartford Accident & Indemnity Co., 516 A.2d 684 (Pa. 1986) (mandatory joinder of indispensable parties).

30 See:

Second Circuit: St. Paul Fire and Marine Insurance Company v. Universal Builders Supply, 409 F.3d 73 (2d Cir. 2005) (not indispensable).

Third Circuit: General Refractories Co. v. First State Insurance Co., 500 F.3d 306 (3d Cir. 2007) (not necessary party); Koppers Co. v. Aetna Casualty & Surety Co., 158 F.3d 170, 176 (3d Cir. 1998) (not indispensable in underlying environmental claims); Equivest Development, Inc. v. Travelers Indemnity Co., 1994 WL 675191, at *3 (E.D. Pa. Nov. 23, 1994) (not indispensable in first-party property claim); Reading Co. v. Travelers Indemnity Co., 1988 WL 13242, at *3–4 (E.D. Pa. Feb. 18, 1988) (not indispensable in underlying asbestos claims); Special Jet Services, Inc. v. Federal Insurance Co., 83 F.R.D. 596, 600 (W.D. Pa. 1979) (not indispensable in underlying airplane liability claim).

Fourth Circuit: Pennsylvania National Mutual Casualty Insurance Co. v. Perlberg, 268 F.R.D. 218 (D. Md. 2010) (not indispensable party).

Fifth Circuit: Collegiate Licensing Co. v. American Casualty Company of Reading, Pa., 842 F. Supp.2d 1360 (N.D. Ga. 2012) (not indispensable).

Sixth Circuit: Continental Casualty Co. v. Taco Bell Corp., 127 F. Supp.2d 864 (W.D. Mich. 2001) (necessary joinder).

Seventh Circuit: Sta-Rite Industries, Inc. v. Allstate Insurance Co., 96 F.3d 281 (7th Cir. 1996); Rhone-Poulenc, Inc. v. International Insurance Co., 877 F. Supp. 1170 (N.D. Ill.), *vacated on other grounds* 71 F.3d 1299 (7th Cir. 1995) (primary and/or underlying insurance companies are necessary and indispensable parties in coverage lawsuit brought by insured against its excess or contingent insurance companies).

Ninth Circuit: SCI California Funeral Services, Inc. v. Westchester Fire Insurance Co., 288 F.R.D. 450 (C.D. Cal. 2013) (not indispensable); Gemini Insurance Co. v. Clever Construction, Inc., 2009 WL 3378593 (D. Haw. Oct. 21, 2009) (not indispensable).

District of Columbia Circuit: Brinco Mining, Ltd. v. Federal Insurance Co., 552 F. Supp. 1233 (D.D.C. 1982) (not indispensable).

31 See:

Third Circuit: Sheppard v. Atlantic States Gas Co., 167 F.2d 841, 845 (3d Cir. 1948) ("where the plaintiff seeks no recovery against the third party defendants, we think the inclusion of the third party claim is justified though it does not of itself meet the diversity test"); White v. Pulver Systems, Inc., 1997 WL 5184, at *1 (E.D. Pa. Jan. 6, 1997) ("an identity of citizenship between an original plaintiff and a third party defendant does not destroy diversity jurisdiction"); Woods v. Laidlaw Transit, 1989 WL 69494, at *1 (E.D. Pa. June 19, 1989) ("'it is well settled that there need be no independent jurisdictional basis for such a claim if diversity of citizenship exists between the original parties'").

Eighth Circuit: St. Louis Trade Diverters, Inc. v. Constitution State Insurance Co., 738 F. Supp. 1269 (E.D. Mo. 1990).

Tenth Circuit: Garcia v. Hall, 624 F.2d 150 (10th Cir. 1980).

State Courts:

New York: David Christa Construction, Inc. v. American Home Assurance Co., 41 A.D.3d 1211, 837 N.Y.S.2d 447 (2007) (not necessary party).

32 See:

Supreme Court: Owen Equipment & Erection Co. v. Kroger, 437 U.S. 365, 375 n.17, 98 S. Ct. 2396, 57 L.Ed.2d 274 (1978) ("there is nothing necessarily collusive about a plaintiff's selectively suing only those tortfeasors of diverse citizenship").

Fourth Circuit: Pennsylvania National Mutual Casualty Insurance Co. v. Perlberg, 268 F.R.D. 218 (D. Md. 2010).

Tenth Circuit: Garcia v. Hall, 624 F.2d 150 (10th Cir. 1980); Amerada Petroleum Corp. v. Rio Oil Co., 225 F. Supp. 907, 910 (D. Wyo. 1964) ("it is elementary that a plaintiff has the right to select his own forum and that a defendant may not alter the substantial controversy or add parties so as to oust the court of its jurisdiction over the original parties").

33 See:

Colorado: Rivera v. American Family Insurance Group, 292 P.3d 1181 (Colo. App. 2012) ("'stacking' is the process of obtaining benefits from a second policy on the same claim when recovery from the first policy alone would be inadequate.").

Connecticut: Lane v. Metropolitan Property and Casualty Insurance Co., 125 Conn. App. 424, 7 A.3d 950 (2010) ("'Stacking' is the ability of the insured, when covered by more than one insurance policy, to obtain benefits from a second policy, on the same claim, when recovery from the first policy alone would be inadequate").

Kansas: Riley v. Allstate Insurance Co., 48 Kan. App.2d 60, 281 P.3d 591 (2012) ("'Stacking' is the right to recover on two or more policies in an amount not to exceed the total of the limits of liability of all policies up to the full amount of the damages sustained.").

Missouri: Long v. Shelter Insurance Cos., 351 S.W.3d 692 (Mo. App. 2011) ("'Stacking' is an insured's ability to obtain multiple insurance coverage benefits for an injury either from more than one policy, as where the insured has two or more separate vehicles under separate policies, or from multiple coverages provided for within a single policy, as when an insured has one policy which covers more than one vehicle.").

South Carolina: Nationwide Mutual Insurance Co. v. Rhoden, 728 S.E.2d 477 (S.C. 2012) ("'[S]tacking' is defined as the insured's recovery of damages under more than one policy until all of his damages are satisfied or the limits of all available policies are met."); Nakatsu v. Encompass Indemnity Co., 700 S.E.2d 283 (S.C. App. 2010) ("'Stacking' refers to an insured's recovery of damages under more than one insurance policy in succession until all of his damages are satisfied or until the total limits of all policies have been exhausted.").

34 See:

Third Circuit: TIG Insurance Co. v. Tyco International Ltd., 919 F. Supp.2d 439 (M.D. Pa. 2013).

Fifth Circuit: French v. Allstate Indemnity Co., 637 F.3d 571 (5th Cir. 2011).

Eighth Circuit: DeMeo v. State Farm Mutual Automobile Insurance Co., 639 F.3d 413 (8th Cir. 2011).

State Courts:

Arizona: American Family Mutual Insurance Co. v. Sharp, 277 P.3d 192 (Ariz. 2012) (*en banc*).

California: Howard v. American National Fire Insurance Co., 187 Cal. App.4th 498, 115 Cal. Rptr.3rd 42 (2010).

Colorado: Rivera v. American Family Insurance Group, 292 P.3d 1181 (Colo. App. 2012).

Connecticut: Lane v. Metropolitan Property and Casualty Insurance Co., 125 Conn. App. 424, 7 A.3d 950 (2010).

Kansas: Riley v. Allstate Insurance Co., 281 P.3d 591 (Kan. App. 2012).

Louisiana: Prest v. Louisiana Citizens Property Insurance Corp., 2012 WL 6015594 (La. App. Dec. 4, 2012); Wegener v. Lafayette Insurance Co., 60 So.3d 1220 (La. 2011).

Missouri: Bush v. Shelter Mutual Insurance Co., 2013 WL 4052876 (Mo. App. Aug. 13, 2013); Long v. Shelter Insurance Cos., 351 S.W.3d 692 (Mo. App. 2011); Stewart v. Liberty Mutual Fire Insurance Co., 349 S.W.3d 381 (Mo. App. 2011).

New York: Fidelity and Guaranty Co. v. American Re-Insurance Co., 93 A.D.3d 14, 939 N.Y.S.2d 307 (N.Y. App. Div. 2012).

South Carolina: Nationwide Mutual Insurance Co. v. Rhoden, 398 S.C. 393, 728 S.E.2d 477 (2012); Beaufort County School District v. United National Insurance Co., 392 S.C. 506, 709 S.E.2d 85 (S.C. App. 2011).

35 Chamness v. American Family Mutual Insurance Co., 226 S.W.3d 199 (Mo. App. 2007). See also, Long v. Shelter Insurance Cos., 351 S.W.3d 692 (Mo. App. 2011).

36 See:

Eighth Circuit: DeMeo v. State Farm Mutual Automobile Insurance Co., 639 F.3d 413 (8th Cir. 2011).

State Courts:

Missouri: Chamness v. American Family Mutual Insurance Co., 226 S.W.3d 199 (Mo. App. 2007); Long v. Shelter Insurance Cos., 351 S.W.3d 692 (Mo. App. 2011); Durbin v. Deitrick, 323 S.W.3d 122 (Mo. App. 2010).

37 See:

Second Circuit: Stonewell Insurance Co. v. Asbestos Claims Management, 73 F.3d 1178, 1203 (2d Cir. 1995), *modified and rehearing denied* 85 F.3d 49 (2d Cir. 1996); United States Fidelity & Guaranty Co. v. Treadwell Corp., 58 F. Supp.2d 77, 96 (S.D.N.Y. 1999); Uniroyal, Inc. v. Home Insurance Co., 707 F. Supp. 1368, 1392 (E.D.N.Y. 1988).

Fourth Circuit: In re Wallace & Gale Corp., 385 F.3d 820 (4th Cir. 2004); Lafarge Corp. v. National Union Fire Insurance Co., 935 F. Supp. 675, 687–688 (D. Md. 1996).

Fifth Circuit: cf., Gulf Chemical & Metallurgical Corp. v. Associated Metals & Minerals Corp., 1 F.3d 365, 371–373 (5th Cir. 1993) (allocating defense costs *pro rata*).

Sixth Circuit: Insurance Company of North America v. Forty-Eight Insulations, Inc., 633 F.2d 1212, 1224–1225 (6th Cir. 1980), *clarified* 657 F.2d 814, 816 (6th Cir.), *cert. denied* 454 U.S. 1109 (1981).

Eighth Circuit: United States Fidelity & Guarantee Insurance Co. v. Commercial Union Midwest Insurance Co., 430 F.3d 929 (8th Cir. 2005).

State Courts:

Connecticut: Metropolitan Life Insurance Co. v. Aetna Casualty & Surety Co., 1999 WL 244642, at *6–9 (Conn. Super. Apr. 16, 1999), *aff'd* 765 A.2d 891 (Conn. 2001).

Delaware: E.I. duPont de Nemours & Co. v. Allstate Insurance Co., 879 A.2d 929 (Del. Super. 2004).

Minnesota: Wooddale Builders, Inc. v. Maryland Casualty Co., 722 N.W.2d 283 (Minn. 2006); Northern States Power Co. v. Fidelity & Casualty Company of New York, 523 N.W.2d 657, 662–664 (Minn. 1994).

New Jersey: Owens-Illinois, Inc. v. United Insurance Co., 650 A.2d 974, 995–996 (N.J. 1994); *In re* Liquidation of Integrity Insurance Co./Sepco Corp., 427 N.J. Super. 521, 49 A.3d 428 (N.J. Super. App. Div. 2012); Morrone v. Harleysville Mutual Insurance Co., 662 A.2d 562 (N.J. Super. 1995).

New York: Roman Catholic Diocese of Brooklyn v. National Union Fire Insurance Company of Pittsburgh, Pa., 21 N.Y.3d 139, 991 N.E.2d 666, 969 N.Y.S.2d 808 (2013).

Texas: Truck Insurance Exchange v. Mid-Continent Casualty Co., 320 S.W.3d 613 (Tex. App. 2010).

38 *Id.*

39 *Id.*

40 See, e.g.: Stonewell Insurance Co. v. Asbestos Claims Management Corp., 73 F.3d 1178, 1202–1203 (2d Cir. 1995), *modified and rehearing denied* 85 F.3d 49 (2d Cir. 1996); United States Fidelity & Guaranty Co. v. Treadwell Corp., 58 F. Supp.2d 77, 96–97 (S.D.N.Y. 1999).

[41] See, e.g., KeySpan Gas East Corp. v. Munich reinsurance America, Inc., 96 N.E.3d 209 (N.Y. 2018).

[42] *Id.*

[43] *Id.*

[44] See:

First Circuit: Stonewall Insurance Co. v. Travelers Casualty and Surety Co., 677 F. Supp.2d 420 (D. Mass. 2010).

Second Circuit: United States Fidelity & Guaranty Co. v. Treadwell Corp., 58 F. Supp.2d 77, 96–97 (S.D.N.Y. 1999) (good discussion of both approaches).

Third Circuit: Koppers Co. v. Aetna Casualty & Surety Co., 98 F.3d 1440 (3d Cir. 1996).

Fifth Circuit: Dayton Independent School District v. National Gypsum Co., 682 F. Supp. 1403, 1410–1411 (E.D. Tex. 1988), *rev'd on other grounds sub nom.* W.R. Grace & Co. v. Continental Casualty Co., 896 F.2d 865 (5th Cir. 1990).

Sixth Circuit: GenCorp, Inc. v. AIU Insurance Co., 297 F. Supp.2d 995 (N.D. Ohio 2003), *aff'd* 138 Fed. Appx. 732 (6th Cir. 2005).

Ninth Circuit: Fireman's Fund Insurance Co. v. Ed Niemi Oil Co., 436 F. Supp.2d 1174 (D. Or. 2006).

Tenth Circuit: Adolph Coors Co. v. American Insurance Co., 1993 WL 1302957 (D. Colo. Sept. 9, 1993).

District of Columbia Circuit: Keene Corp. v. Insurance Company of North America, 667 F.2d 1034, 1057–1058 (D.C. Cir. 1981), *cert. denied* 455 U.S. 1007 (1982).

State Courts:

California: Howard v. American National Fire Insurance Co., 187 Cal. App.4th 498, 115 Cal. Rptr.3d 42 (2010); Scottsdale Insurance Co. v. Century Surety Co., 182 Cal. App.4th 1023, 105 Cal. Rptr.3d 896 (2010); Armstrong World Industries, Inc. v. Aetna Casualty & Surety Co., 45 Cal. App.4th 1, 52 Cal. Rptr.2d 690 (1996).

Colorado: National Insurance Co. v. Great Southwest Fire Insurance Co., 833 P.2d 741 (Colo. 1992); Empire Casualty Co. v. St. Paul Fire & Marine Insurance Co., 764 P.2d 1191 (Colo. 1988); Dairyland Insurance Co. v. Drum, 568 P.2d 459 (Colo. 1977).

Delaware: Viking Pump, Inc. v. Century Indemnity Co., 2 A.3d 76 (Del. Ch. 2009).

Illinois: Chicago Hospital Risk Pooling Program v. Illinois State Medical Inter-Insurance Exchange, 397 Ill. App.3d 512, 925 N.E.2d 1216, 339 Ill. Dec. 95 (2010); North River Insurance Co. v. Grinnell Mutual Reinsurance Co., 369 Ill. App.3d 563, 860 N.E.2d 460, 307 Ill. Dec. 806 (2006).

Massachusetts: Rubenstein v. Royal Insurance Co., 694 N.E.2d 381, 388 (Mass. App. 1998); High Voltage Engineering Corp. v. American Employers Insurance Co., 1995 WL 809577, at *5 (Mass. Super. July 7, 1995) ("[T]his Court holds that AE's liability under its duty to defend the Brecher, Blanchard, and RHI actions is joint and several, without proration.").

Ohio: Pennsylvania General Insurance Co. v. Park-Ohio Industries, 126 Ohio St.3d 98, 930 N.E.2d 800 (2010).

Oregon: Cascade Corp. v. American Home Assurance Co., 135 P.3d 450 (Or. App. 2006).

Pennsylvania: J.H. France Refractories Co. v. Allstate Insurance Co., 626 A.2d 502 (Pa. 1993).

Washington: American National Fire Insurance Co. v. B & L Trucking & Construction Co., 920 P.2d 192 (Wash. App. 1996), *aff'd* 951 P.2d 250 (Wash. 1998); Gruol Construction Co. v. Insurance Company of North America, 524 P.2d 427 (Wash. App.), *review denied* 1974 WL 45336 (Wash. 1974).

[45] *Id.*

[46] *Id.*

[47] *Id.*

[48] See:

Third Circuit: Koppers Co. v. Certain Underwriters at Lloyd's, 1997 U.S. Dist. LEXIS 16123 (W.D. Pa. June 23, 1997).

State Courts:

California: Armstrong World Industries, Inc. v. Aetna Casualty & Surety Co., 45 Cal. App.4th 1, 52 Cal. Rptr.2d 690 (1996).

Pennsylvania: American Casualty Co. v. Phico Insurance Co., 702 A.2d 1050 (Pa. 1997).

[49] See, e.g.: Mission Insurance Co. v. United States Fire Insurance Co., 517 N.E.2d 463, 468 (Mass. 1988) ("[I]n the absence of language controlling the issue, the better approach is to require the insurers to contribute equally until the policy with the lower limit is exhausted. Any remaining amounts due would be paid by the remaining insurer until its policy limit is also exhausted."); Aetna Casualty & Surety Co. v. Home Insurance Co., 689 N.E.2d 1355, 1359 (Mass. App.), *review denied* 707 N.E.2d 1076 (Mass. 1998) (similar).

[50] See Insurance Company of North America v. Protection Mutual Insurance Co., 939 F. Supp. 79, 89 (D. Mass. 1996) ("Each party may subtract from its total liability any applicable deductible under its respective policy.").

[51] Mission Insurance Co. v. Allendale Mutual Insurance Co., 626 P.2d 505 (Wash. 1981).

[52] Perez Trucking, Inc. v. Ryder Truck Rental, Inc., 886 P.2d 196 (Wash. App. 1994).

[53] See Monsanto Co. v. C.E. Health Compensation & Liability Insurance Co., 652 A.2d 30, 35 n.6 (Del. 1994) ("joint and several" approach is majority rule). See also, Rose and Bagga, "The Law of Allocation—Who's Winning the Battle Anyway," *Coverage*, v.12, no. 4, at 12 and n.2 (ABA July/Aug. 2002) (stating that as of 2002, fourteen jurisdictions have adopted "joint and several," eight have adopted a "*pro rata*" variant, and twenty-nine are undecided or unclear).

[54] See:

California: Aerojet-General Transportation Corp. v. Transport Indemnity Co., 948 P.2d 909 (Cal. 1997).

Delaware: Hercules, Inc. v. AIU Insurance Co., 784 A.2d 481, 489–491 (Del. 2001).

Indiana: Allstate Insurance Co. v. Dana Corp., 759 N.E.2d 1049, 1057–1058 (Ind. 2001).

Michigan: Dow Corning Corp. v. Continental Casualty Co., 1999 WL 33435067, at *6–8 (Mich. App. Oct. 12, 1999) (*per curiam*), *appeal denied* 617 N.W.2d 554 (Mich. 2000).

Ohio: Goodyear Tire & Rubber Co. v. Aetna Casualty & Surety Co., 769 N.E.2d 835 (Ohio 2002).

Washington: American National Fire Insurance Co. v. B & L Trucking & Construction Co., 951 P.2d 250, 253–257 (Wash. 1998).

See also, Rose and Bagga, "The Law of Allocation—Who's Winning the Battle Anyway," *Coverage*, v.12, no. 4, at 12 (ABA July/Aug. 2002).

[55] See:

Second Circuit: United States Fidelity & Guaranty Co. v. Treadwell Corp., 58 F. Supp.2d 77, 97 (S.D.N.Y. 1999) (good discussion of both approaches).

Third Circuit: Koppers Co. v. Aetna Casualty & Surety Co., 98 F.3d 1440, 1449 n.9 (3d Cir. 1996).

State Courts:

Delaware: Viking Pump, Inc. v. Century Indemnity Co., 2 A.3d 76 (Del. Ch. 2009).

New Jersey: In re Liquidation of Integrity Insurance Co./Sepco Corp., 427 N.J. Super. 521, 49 A.3d 428 (N.J. Super. App. Div. 2012).

[56] See § 5.02 *supra*.

[57] See ISO Form CG 00 01 10 01.

[58] *Id.* See also:

First Circuit: Middlesex Mutual Assurance Co. v. Fish, 2010 WL 3342207 (D. Me. Aug. 24, 2010) (officer in performance of corporate duties).

Third Circuit: Baughman v. U.S. Liability Insurance Co., 662 F. Supp.2d 386 (D.N.J. 2009) (employee in course and scope).

Fourth Circuit: Parts Inc. v. Utica Mutual Insurance Co., 602 F. Supp.2d 617 (D. Md. 2009) (course and scope).

Fifth Circuit: Medford v. Lavergne, 727 F. Supp.2d 512 (W.D. La. 2010) (officer in performance of corporate duties).

Sixth Circuit: Employers Mutual Casualty Co. v. Al-Mashhadi, 2009 WL 2711963 (E.D. Mich. Aug. 24, 2009) (course and scope).

Eleventh Circuit: XL Insurance America, Inc. v. Ortiz, 673 F. Supp.2d 1331 (S.D. Fla. 2009) (course and scope).

State Courts:

California: Sprinkles v. Associated Indemnity Corp., 188 Cal. App.4th 69, 114 Cal. Rptr.3d 887 (2010) (employee in course and scope).

Georgia: Geiger v. Georgia Farm Bureau Mutual Insurance Co., 305 Ga. App. 399, 699 S.E.2d 571 (2010) (relative living in policyholder's home).

South Carolina: Auto-Owners Insurance Co. v. Rhodes, 405 S.C. 584, 748 S.E.2d 781 (S.C. 2013) (course and scope).

Texas: Chrysler Insurance Co. v. Greenspoint Dodge of Houston, Inc., 297 S.W.3d 248 (Tex. 2009) (executive officer).

[59] See ISO Form CG 00 01 10 01.

[60] *Id.*

[61] *Id.*

[62] See:

Third Circuit: Koons v. XL Insurance America, Inc., 516 Fed. Appx. 217 (3d Cir. 2013).

Ninth Circuit: National Fire Insurance Company of Hartford v. Lewis, 898 F. Supp.2d 1132 (D. Ariz. 2012).

State Courts:

Missouri: Dry v. United Fire and Casualty Co., 2013 WL 3147341 (Mo. App. June 21, 2013).

New York: Southern Queens Park Association v. Capitol Insurance Co., 107 A.D.3d 1006, 969 N.Y.S.2d 84 (N.Y. App. Div. 2013).

Texas: Mid-Continent Casualty Co. v. Castagna, 2013 WL 4432353 (Tex. App. Aug. 10, 2013).

[63] See Bruner and O'Connor, *Construction Law* § 11:63 (2006). Depending on the jurisdiction, the cases go both ways as to whether an "additional insured" has the same rights as a "named insured." See, e.g., Page v. Mountain West Farm Bureau Mutual Insurance Co., 2 P.3d 506 (Wyo. 2000) ("you" as used in the policy referred only to the named insureds). See also:

First Circuit: Wyner v. North American Specialty Insurance Co., 78 F.3d 752, 756 (1st Cir. 1996) (rejecting additional insured's argument that "you" as used in the policy only applied to "named insured").

Seventh Circuit: Prisco Serena Sturm Architects, Ltd. v. Liberty Mutual Insurance Co., 126 F.3d 886, 892 (7th Cir. 1997) (rejecting insurance company's argument that "your" refers only to "named insured").

Eighth Circuit: SFH, Inc. v. Millard Refrigerated Services, Inc., 339 F.3d 738, 744 (8th Cir. 2003) (additional insured constituted a named insured).

Tenth Circuit: Marathon Ashland Pipe Line LLC v. Maryland Casualty Co., 243 F.3d 1232 (10th Cir. 2001) (additional insureds are "named insureds").

State Courts:

Illinois: Pekin Insurance Co. v. Roszak/ADC, L.L.C., 402 Ill. App.3d 1055, 931 N.E.2d 799, 341 Ill. Dec. 902 (2010) (not same status).

Massachusetts: Massachusetts Turnpike Authority v. Perini Corp., 208 N.E.2d 807, 812 (Mass. 1965) ("[t]he naming of additional insureds does not extend the nature of the substantive coverage originally given by the policy but merely gives to other persons the same protection afforded to the principal insured").

New York: William Floyd School District v. Maxner, 68 A.D.3d 982, 892 N.Y.S.2d 115 (2009) (same protection absent a contrary intention in the policy).

Ohio: Efficient Lighting Sales Co. v. Neverman, 2009 WL 348826 (Ohio App. Feb. 12, 2009) (not same status).

Texas: Chrysler Insurance Co. v. Greenspoint Dodge of Houston, Inc., 297 S.W.3d 248 (Tex. 2009) (different status).

Virginia: K & W Builders, Inc. v. Merchants & Business Men's Mutual Insurance Co., 495 S.E.2d 473, 476 (Va. 1998) (interpreting "you" to refer to "additional insureds" and "named insureds").

Wisconsin: Greene v. General Casualty Co., 576 N.W.2d 56, 60 (Wis. 1997), *review denied* 579 N.W.2d 44 (Wis. 1998) ("you" refers to "additional insured" and "named insured").

[64] See § 5.02 *supra.*

[65] See § 5.03[4][a] *infra.*

[66] See § 5.03[4][b] *infra.*

[67] See § 5.03[4][c] *infra.*

[68] See § 5.03[4][d] *infra.*

[69] See § 5.03[4][e] *infra.*

[70] See § 5.03[4][f] *infra.*

[71] See § 5.03[4][g] *infra.*

[72] See: Turner, *Insurance Coverage for Construction Disputes* § 5.07, at 66 (1st ed. 1992); 11 *Couch on Insurance 2d* § 44:271 (1982). See also:

Second Circuit: General Star National Insurance Co. v. Universal Fabricators, Inc., 585 F.3d 662 (2d Cir. 2009) (arbitration, judgment, or settlement).

Third Circuit: Permasteelisa CS Corp. v. Columbia Casualty Co., 377 Fed. Appx. 260 (3d Cir. 2010) (entry of judgment); General Refractories Co. v. First State Insurance Co., 862 F. Supp.2d 382 (E.D. Pa. 2012) (settlement).

Fourth Circuit: Pennsylvania National Mutual Casualty Insurance Co. v. City Homes, Inc., 719 F. Supp.2d 605 (D. Md. 2010) (judgments); Erie Insurance Exchange v. First United Methodist Church, 690 F. Supp.2d 410 (W.D.N.C. 2010) (judgments and verdicts); Builders Mutual Insurance Co. v. Dragas Management Corp., 709 F. Supp.2d 441 (E.D. Va. 2010) (settlements or damages); National Union Fire Insurance Company of Pittsburgh, PA v. Porter Hayden Co., 408 B.R. 66 (D. Md. 2009) (liability in tort).

Fifth Circuit: Federal Insurance Co. v. Hanover Insurance Co., 2013 WL 5339210 (N.D. Tex. Sept. 24, 2013) (settlement or judgment); Building Specialties, Inc. v. Liberty Mutual

Fire Insurance Co., 712 F. Supp.2d 628 (S.D. Tex. 2010) (settlements); Gilbane Building Co. v. Empire Steel Erectors, L.P., 691 F. Supp.2d 712 (S.D. Tex. 2010) (settlements and judgments).

Sixth Circuit: Martin County Coal Corp. v. Universal Underwriters Insurance Co., 727 F.3d 589 (6th Cir. 2013) (settlement or judgment); Detroit Water Team Joint Venture v. Agricultural Insurance Co., 371 F.3d 336 (6th Cir. 2004) (settlement or judgment); Missouri Public Entity Risk Management Fund v. Investors Insurance Company of America, 338 F. Supp.2d 1046 (W.D. Mo. 2004), *aff'd* 451 F.2d 925 (8th Cir. 2006) (policy, which provided coverage for losses incurred as a result of contract, clearly contemplated coverage for settled disputes, not just litigated disputes).

Seventh Circuit: Maxum Indemnity Co. v. Eclipse Manufacturing Co., 848 F. Supp.2d 871 (N.D. Ill. 2012) (settlement).

Eighth Circuit: UnitedHealth Group Inc. v. Hiscox Dedicated Corporate Member Ltd., 2010 WL 550991 (D. Minn. Feb. 9, 2010) (settlements).

Ninth Circuit: Texas Farmer's Insurance Co. v. Lexington Insurance Co., 380 Fed. Appx. 604 (9th Cir. 2010) (settlements); Align Technology, Inc. v. Federal Insurance Co., 673 F. Supp.2d 957 (N.D. Cal. 2009) (sustained liability or paid damages); Hawaiian Isle Adventures, Inc. v. North American Capacity Insurance Co., 623 F. Supp.2d 1189 (D. Haw. 2009) (loss or injury); Teck Metals, Ltd. v. Certain Underwriters at Lloyd's, London, 2010 WL 3211949 (E.D. Wash. Aug. 10, 2010) (settlement agreement); Reliance Insurance Co. v. Doctors Co., 299 F. Supp.2d 1131 (D. Haw. 2003), *aff'd* 132 Fed. Appx. 730 (9th Cir. 2005) (physicians were "legally obligated" to pay damages in underlying medical malpractice action when suit settled).

Tenth Circuit: Vitkus v. Beatrice Co., 127 F.3d 936 (10th Cir. 1997) (settlement constitutes legal obligation to pay damages); American Family Mutual Insurance Co. v. Teamcorp, Inc., 659 F. Supp.2d 1115 (D. Colo. 2009) (judgment); Peoples Mortgage Corp. v. Kansas Bankers Surety Trust Co., 176 F. Supp.2d 1199 (D. Kan. 2001), *aff'd* 62 Fed. Appx. 232 (10th Cir. 2003) (settlement constitutes legal obligation to pay damages).

State Courts:

Arizona: Desert Mountain Properties Limited Partnership v. Liberty Mutual Fire Insurance Co., 236 P.3d 421 (Ariz. App. 2010) (repair costs paid by developer were legal obligations under tort and contract law, amounting to settlements made in connection therewith).

California: Executive Risk Indemnity, Inc. v. Jones, 171 Cal. App.4th 319, 89 Cal. Rptr.3d 747 (2009) (arbitration award).

Georgia: Owners Insurance Co. v. Smith Mechanical Contractors, Inc., 285 Ga. 807, 683 S.E.2d 599 (2009) (payment for damages unquestionably caused by negligence).

Illinois: Central Illinois Light Co. v. Home Insurance Co., 795 N.E.2d 412 (Ill. App. 2003), *aff'd* 821 N.E.2d 206 (Ill. 2004) (suit against insured was not required for indemnity obligation to arise under excess liability policies that covered liability imposed by law or assumed by the insured under contract or agreement for damages as a result of property damage); Guillen *ex rel.* Guillen v. Potomac Insurance Company of Illinois, 785 N.E.2d 1 (Ill. 2003) (settlement is a "legal obligation" that is covered).

Kansas: Kansas Health Care Stabilization Fund v. St. Francis Hospital, 41 Kan. App.2d 488, 203 P.3d 33 (2009) (judgment or settlement).

Minnesota: Wanzek Construction, Inc. v. Employers Insurance of Wausau, 667 N.W.2d 473 (Minn. App. 2003), *aff'd* 679 N.E.2d 322 (Minn. 2004) (when an insurance policy provides coverage for sums that the insured is "legally obligated to pay as damages," the insured need not have had litigation commenced against it for the policy to be triggered, but is entitled to coverage based solely on a contractual duty to replace faulty building materials).

Missouri: D.R. Sherry Construction, Ltd. v. American Family Mutual Insurance Co., 316 S.W.3d 899 (Mo. 2010) (settlements); Penn-Star Insurance Co. v. Griffey, 306 S.W.3d 591 (Mo. App. 2010) (judgments or verdicts).

New York: Prave v. New York Central Mutual Fire Insurance Co., 104 A.D.3d 1139, 961 N.Y.S.2d 651, (N.Y. App. Div. 2013) (judgment); Stellar Mechanical Services of New York, Inc. v. Merchants Insurance of New Hampshire, 74 A.D.3d 948, 903 N.Y.S.2d 471 (2010) (settlements); Bovis Lend Lease LMB, Inc. v. Garito Contracting, Inc., 65 A.D.3d 872, 885 N.Y.S.2d 59 (2009) (judgment); Richmond Farms Dairy, L.L.C. v. National Grange Mutual Insurance Co., 60 A.D.3d 1411, 875 N.Y.S.2d 681 (2009) (liable for a loss); Gap, Inc. v. Fireman's Fund Insurance Co., 782 N.Y.S.2d 242 (N.Y. App. Div. 2004) (CGL policy pays a third-party claimant according to a judgment or settlement against the insured).

North Carolina: Harleysville Mutual Insurance Co. v. Buzz Off Insect Shield, L.L.C., 364 N.C. 1, 692 S.E.2d 605 (2010) (verdicts and judgments); Lida Manufacturing Co. v. United States Fire Insurance Co., 448 S.E.2d 854 (N.C. App. 1994) (settlement constitutes legal obligation to pay damages).

Pennsylvania: Regis Insurance Co. v. All American Rathskeller, Inc., 976 A.2d 1157 (Pa. Super. 2009) (settlements).

Texas: Lancer Insurance Co. v. Perez, 308 S.W.3d 35 (Tex. App. 2009) (judgments); Lennar Corp. v. Great American Insurance Co., 200 S.W.3d 651 (Tex. App.), *substituted concurring and dissenting opinions* 2006 WL 909937 (Tex. App. Apr. 11, 2006) ("The policies do not include a definition of 'legally obligated to pay.' However, giving the phrase its ordinary meaning, it means an obligation imposed by law, such as an obligation to pay pursuant to a judgment, settlement, contract, or statute."); Comsys Information Technology Services, Inc. v. Twin City Fire Insurance Co., 130 S.W.3d 181, 189 n.3 (Tex. App. 2003) ("a court judgment is not the only manner by which [insurer] could become legally obligated to pay [insured's] claim. A legal obligation can also arise out of a contract, such as a settlement."); Grimes Construction, Inc. v. Great American Lloyds Insurance Co., 188 S.W.3d 805 (Tex. App. 2006) (insurance company's "duty to indemnify arises only after the insured has been adjudicated legally responsible for damages in a lawsuit by judgment or settlement"); Texas Property & Casualty Insurance Guaranty Association v. Boy Scouts of America, 947 S.W.2d 682, 691 (Tex. App. 1997) (similar).

Wisconsin: Johnson Controls, Inc. v. London Market, 325 Wis.2d 176, 784 N.W.2d 579 (2010) (damages or losses); Bloomfield Road, L.L.C. v. DeMichele, 315 Wis.2d 769, 762 N.W.2d 863 (2008) (judgment for money damages).

73 Megonnell v. United Services Automobile Ass'n, 796 A.2d 758, 765–766 (Md. 2002).

74 *Id.*

75 See, e.g.:

Fifth Circuit: Federal Insurance Co. v. Hanover Insurance Co., 2013 WL 5339210 (N.D. Tex. Sept. 24, 2013).

Eleventh Circuit: Mid-Continent Casualty Co. v. American Pride Building Co., 2013 WL 4472288 (11th Cir. Aug. 22, 2013).

State Courts:

Arizona: Colorado Casualty Insurance Co. v. Safety Control Co., 230 Ariz. 560, 288 P.3d 764 (Ariz. App. 2012).

Connecticut: Capstone Building Corp. v. American Motorists Insurance Co., 308 Conn. 760, 67 A.3d 961 (2013).

Missouri: Columbia Casualty Co. v. HIAR Holding, L.L.C., 2013 WL 4080770 (Mo. Aug. 13, 2103) (*en banc*).

Pennsylvania: Babcock & Wilcox Co. v. American Nuclear Insurers, 2013 Pa. Super 174, 76 A.3d 1 (2013).

Texas: U.S. Fire Insurance Co. v. Scottsdale Insurance Co., 264 S.W.3d 160 (Tex. App. 2008).

Washington: Bird v. Bert Plumbing Group, L.L.C., 175 Wash.2d 756, 287 P.3d 551 (2013) (*en banc*).

76 Vitkus v. Beatrice Co., 127 F.3d 936 (10th Cir. 1997).

77 *Id.*, 127 F.3d at 942.

78 *Id.*, 127 F.3d at 942–943.

79 *Id.*, 127 F.3d at 944.

> "Actual liability . . . is not our guide in evaluating whether a settlement allocation is enforceable. It would be wholly impractical to charge the district court with trying the Silverado litigation after a successful settlement in order to ascertain Vitkus' and the other settling parties relative culpabilities."

80 *Id.*, 127 F.3d at 945. See also:

Second Circuit: General Star National Insurance Co. v. Universal Fabricators, Inc., 585 F.3d 662 (2d Cir. 2009) (settlements are covered legal obligations).

Third Circuit: General Refractories Co. v. First State Insurance Co., 862 F. Supp.2d 382 (E.D. Pa. 2012) (settlement is covered).

Fourth Circuit: Builders Mutual Insurance Co. v. Dragas Management Corp., 709 F. Supp.2d 441 (E.D. Va. 2010) (settlements are covered legal obligations).

Fifth Circuit: Federal Insurance Co. v. Hanover Insurance Co., 2013 WL 5339210 (N.D. Tex. Sept. 24, 2013) (settlement is covered); Building Specialties, Inc. v. Liberty Mutual Fire Insurance Co., 712 F. Supp.2d 628 (S.D. Tex. 2010) (settlements are covered legal obligations); Gilbane Building Co. v. Empire Steel Erectors, L.P., 691 F. Supp.2d 712 (S.D. Tex. 2010) (settlements are covered legal obligations).

Sixth Circuit: Martin County Coal Corp. v. Universal Underwriters Insurance Co., 727 F.3d 589 (6th Cir. 2013) (settlement is covered); Missouri Public Entity Risk Management Fund v. Investors Insurance Company of America, 338 F. Supp.2d 1046 (W.D. Mo. 2004) (policy, which provided coverage for losses incurred as a result of contract, clearly contemplated coverage for settled disputes, not just litigated disputes).

Seventh Circuit: Maxum Indemnity Co. v. Eclipse Manufacturing Co., 848 F. Supp.2d 871 (N.D. Ill. 2012) (settlement is covered).

Eighth Circuit: UnitedHealth Group Inc. v. Hiscox Dedicated Corporate Member Ltd., 2010 WL 550991 (D. Minn. Feb. 9, 2010) (settlements are covered legal obligations).

Ninth Circuit: Texas Farmers Insurance Co. v. Lexington Insurance Co., 380 Fed. Appx. 604 (9th Cir. 2010) (settlements are covered legal obligations); Teck Metals, Ltd. v. Certain Underwriters at Lloyd's, London, 2010 WL 3211949 (E.D. Wash. Aug. 10, 2010) (settlements are covered legal obligations).

State Courts:

Arizona: Desert Mountain Properties Limited Partnership v. Liberty Mutual Fire Insurance Co., 236 P.3d 421 (Ariz. App. 2010) (repair costs paid by developer were legal obligations under tort and contract law, amounting to settlements made in connection therewith).

Georgia: Owners Insurance Co. v. Smith Mechanical Contractors, Inc., 285 Ga. 807, 683 S.E.2d 599 (Ga. 2009) (payment for damages that were unquestionably caused by policyholder's negligence amounts to a settlement that is covered).

Kansas: Kansas Health Care Stabilization Fund v. St. Francis Hospital, 41 Kan. App.2d 488, 203 P.3d 33 (2009) (settlements are covered legal obligations).

Missouri: D.R. Sherry Construction, Ltd. v. American Family Mutual Insurance Co., 316 S.W.3d 899 (Mo. 2010) (settlements are covered legal obligations).

New York: Stellar Mechanical Services of New York, Inc. v. Merchants Insurance of New Hampshire, 74 A.D.3d 948, 903 N.Y.S.2d 471 (2010) (settlements are covered legal obligations).

Pennsylvania: Regis Insurance Co. v. All American Rathskeller, Inc., 976 A.2d 1157 (Pa. Super. 2009) (settlements are covered legal obligations).

But see:

Sixth Circuit: XXL of Ohio, Inc. v. City of Broadview Heights, 341 F. Supp.2d 825 (N.D. Ohio 2004) (settlement of claim not covered where no covered damages were averred).

State Courts:

Nevada: United National Insurance Co. v. Frontier Insurance Co., 99 P.3d 1153 (Nev. 2004) (settlement not covered where claim was clearly not covered).

81 See, e.g., Griggs v. Bertram, 443 A.2d 163 (N.J. 1982).

82 See, e.g., Reliance Insurance Co. v. Moessner, 121 F.3d 895, 903 (3d Cir. 1997) (applying Pennsylvania law).

83 See:

Second Circuit: General Star National Insurance Co. v. Universal Fabricators, Inc., 585 F.3d 662 (2d Cir. 2009) (settlements are covered legal obligations).

Third Circuit: General Refractories Co. v. First State Insurance Co., 862 F. Supp.2d 382 (E.D. Pa. 2012) (settlement is covered).

Fourth Circuit: Builders Mutual Insurance Co. v. Dragas Management Corp., 709 F. Supp.2d 441 (E.D. Va. 2010) (settlements are covered legal obligations).

Fifth Circuit: Endserch v. Shand Morahan & Co., 952 F.2d 12485 (5th Cir. 1992); Coblentz v. American Surety Company of New York, 416 F.2d 1059 (5th Cir. 1969) (consent judgment or agreement not to execute does not excuse insurance company from coverage obligation); Building Specialties, Inc. v. Liberty Mutual Fire Insurance Co., 712 F. Supp.2d 628 (S.D. Tex. 2010) (settlements are covered legal obligations); Gilbane Building Co. v. Empire Steel Erectors, L.P., 691 F. Supp.2d 712 (S.D. Tex. 2010) (settlements are covered legal obligations); National Union Fire Insurance Company of Pittsburgh, PA v. Puget Plastics Corp., 649 F. Supp.2d 613 (S.D. Tex. 2009) (majority).

Sixth Circuit: Martin County Coal Corp. v. Universal Underwriters Insurance Services, Inc., 792 F. Supp.2d 958 (E.D. Ky. 2011) (minority).

Seventh Circuit: Midwestern Indemnity Co. v. Laikin, 119 F. Supp.2d 831, 853 (S.D. Ind. 2000) (consent judgment or agreement not to execute does not excuse insurance company from coverage obligation).

Eighth Circuit: U.S. Bank, N.A. v. Federal Insurance Co., 2010 WL 3928123 (W.D. Mo. Oct. 4, 2010) (predicting Missouri would follow majority); UnitedHealth Group Inc. v. Hiscox Dedicated Corporate Member Ltd., 2010 WL 550991 (D. Minn. Feb. 9, 2010) (settlements are covered legal obligations).

Ninth Circuit: Texas Farmers Insurance Co. v. Lexington Insurance Co., 380 Fed. Appx. 604 (9th Cir. 2010) (settlements are covered legal obligations); Teck Metals, Ltd. v. Certain Underwriters at Lloyd's, London, 2010 WL 3211949 (E.D. Wash. Aug. 10, 2010) (settlements are covered legal obligations).

Eleventh Circuit: Mid-Continent Casualty Co. v. American Pride Building Co., 2013 WL 4472288 (11th Cir. Aug. 22, 2013) (majority); Twin City Fire Insurance Co. v. Ohio Casualty Insurance Co., 480 F.3d 1254 (11th Cir.2007) (consent judgment or agreement not to execute does not excuse insurance company from coverage obligation).

District of Columbia Circuit: Gray v. Grain Dealers Mutual Insurance Co., 871 F.2d 1128 (D.C. Cir. 1989) (following majority).

State Courts:

Alabama: Liberty Mutual Insurance Co. v. Wheelwright Trucking Co., 851 So.2d 466 (Ala. 2002) (bankrupt insured was legally obligated to pay consent judgment entered against it, even though the debtor had agreed to collect only from liability insurers).

Arizona: Globe Indemnity Co. v. Blomfield, 562 P.2d 1372 (Ariz. 1977); State Farm Mutual Automobile Insurance Co. v. Paynter, 593 P.2d 948 (Ariz. 1979) (consent judgment or agreement not to execute does not excuse insurance company from coverage obligation); Desert Mountain Properties Limited Partnership v. Liberty Mutual Fire Insurance Co., 236 P.3d 421 (Ariz. App. 2010) (repair costs paid by developer were legal obligations under tort and contract law, amounting to settlements made in connection therewith); Flood Control District of Maricopa County v. Paloma Investment Limited Partnership, 230 Ariz. 29, 279 P.3d 1191 (Ariz. App. 2012) (majority); Colorado Casualty Insurance Co. v. Safety Control Co., 230 Ariz. 560, 288 P.3d 764 (Ariz. App. 2012) (majority).

Connecticut: Esposito v. CPM Insurance Services, Inc., 50 Conn. Supp. 283, 922 A.2d 343 (2006) (following majority approach).

Florida: Lageman v. Frank H. Furman Inc., 697 So.2d 981 (Fla. App. 1997) (following majority).

Georgia: Owners Insurance Co. v. Smith Mechanical Contractors, Inc., 285 Ga. 807, 683 S.E.2d 599 (2009) (payment for damages that were unquestionably caused by policyholder's negligence amounts to a settlement that is covered); Dowse v. Southern Guaranty Insurance Co., 588 S.E.2d 234 (Ga. App. 2003), *aff'd* 605 S.E.2d 27 (Ga. 2004) (consent judgment or agreement not to execute does not excuse insurance company from coverage obligation).

Hawaii: McLellan v. Atchison Insurance Agency, Inc., 912 P.2d 559 (Haw. App. 1996) (agreement not to execute does not eliminate duty to indemnify).

Illinois: Guillen *ex rel.* Guillen v. Potomac Insurance Company of Illinois, 785 N.E.2d 1 (Ill. 2003) (consent judgment or agreement not to execute does not excuse insurance company from coverage obligation).

Indiana: American Family Mutual Insurance Co. v. Kivela, 408 N.E.2d 805 (Ind. App. 1980) (consent judgment or agreement not to execute does not excuse insurance company from coverage obligation).

Iowa: Red Giant Oil Co. v. Lawlor, 528 N.W.2d 524 (Iowa 1995) (consent judgment or agreement not to execute does not excuse insurance company from coverage obligation).

Kansas: Kansas Health Care Stabilization Fund v. St. Francis Hospital, 41 Kan. App.2d 488, 203 P.3d 33 (2009) (settlements are covered legal obligations).

Kentucky: Associated Insurance Service, Inc. v. Garcia, 307 S.W.3d 58 (Ky. 2010) (following majority view).

Massachusetts: Campione v. Wilson, 422 Mass. 185, 661 N.E.2d 658 (1996) (majority).

Missouri: D.R. Sherry Construction, Ltd. v. American Family Mutual Insurance Co., 316 S.W.3d 899 (Mo. 2010) (settlements are covered legal obligations).

Nebraska: Metcalf v. Hartford Accident & Indemnity Co., 126 N.W.2d 471 (Neb. 1964) (consent judgment or agreement not to execute does not excuse insurance company from coverage obligation).

New Hampshire: Stateline Steel Erectors, Inc. v. Shields, 150 N.H. 332, 837 A.2d 285 (2003) (following majority approach).

New Jersey: Griggs v. Bertram, 443 A.2d 163 (N.J. 1982) (consent judgment or agreement not to execute does not excuse insurance company from coverage obligation).

New York: Stellar Mechanical Services of New York, Inc. v. Merchants Insurance of New Hampshire, 74 A.D.3d 948, 903 N.Y.S.2d 471 (2010) (settlements are covered legal obligations).

North Dakota: Wangler v. Lerol, 670 N.W.2d 830 (N.D. 2003) (majority approach).

Oregon: Brownstone Homes Condominium Ass'n v. Brownstone Forest Heights, L.L.C., 255 Or. App. 390, 298 P.3d 1228 (2013) (minority approach).

Pennsylvania: Regis Insurance Co. v. All American Rathskeller, Inc., 976 A.2d 1157 (Pa. Super. 2009) (settlements are covered legal obligations).

South Dakota: Kobbeman v. Oleson, 574 N.W.2d 633 (S.D. 1998) (settlement with agreement not to execute must still be indemnified).

Tennessee: Tip's Package Store, Inc. v. Commercial Insurance Managers, Inc., 86 S.W.3d 543 (Tenn. App. 2001) (majority approach).

Washington: Bird v. Bert Plumbing Group, L.L.C., 175 Wash.2d 756, 287 P.3d 551 (2013) (*en banc*); Unigard Insurance Co. v. Mutual of Enumclaw Insurance Co., 160 Wash. App. 912, 250 P.3d 121 (2011) (majority).

Wyoming: Gainsco Insurance Co. v. Amoco Production Co., 53 P.3d 1051 (Wyo. 2002) (agreement not to execute does not eliminate duty to indemnify).

[84] *Id.*

[85] See:

First Circuit: Holmes Group, Inc. v. Federal Insurance Co., 2005 WL 4134556 (D. Mass. Oct. 5, 2005) (minority).

Eighth Circuit: Freeman v. Schmidt Real Estate & Insurance, 755 F.2d 135 (8th Cir. 1985) (consent judgment or agreement not to execute excuses insurance company from coverage obligation).

Tenth Circuit: American Manufacturers Mutual Insurance Co. v. Seco/Warwick Corp., 266 F. Supp.2d 1259 (D. Colo. 2003) (consent judgment or agreement not to execute excuses insurance company from coverage obligation).

Eleventh Circuit: Bendall v. White, 511 F. Supp. 793 (N.D. Ala. 1981) (consent judgment or agreement not to execute excuses insurance company from coverage obligation).

State Courts:

North Carolina: Terrell v. Lawyers Mutual Liability Insurance Company of North Carolina, 507 S.E.2d 923, 927 (N.C. App. 1998); Lida Manufacturing Co. v. United States Fire Insurance Co., 448 S.E.2d 854 (N.C. App. 1994); Huffman v. Peerless Insurance Co., 193 S.E.2d 773 (N.C. App.), *cert. denied* 195 S.E.2d 689 (N.C. 1973) (consent judgment or agreement not to execute excuses insurance company from coverage obligation).

Oregon: Stubblefield v. St. Paul Fire & Marine Insurance Co., 517 P.2d 262 (Or. 1973) (consent judgment or agreement not to execute excuses insurance company from coverage obligation); Oregon Mutual Insurance Co. v. Gibson, 88 Or. App. 574, 746 P.2d 245 (1987) (agreement not to execute makes settlement non-recoverable under a CGL policy).

Pennsylvania: Dennis v. New Amsterdam Casualty Co., 264 A.2d 436 (Pa. Super. 1970) (consent judgment or agreement not to execute excuses insurance company from coverage obligation).

Texas: State Farm Fire and Casualty Co. v. Gandy, 925 S.W.2d 696 (Tex. 1996) (minority view).

Utah: Christiansen v. Holiday Rent-A-Car, 845 P.2d 1316 (Utah App. 1992) (minority).

[86] See:

Arkansas: Blagg v. Fred Hunt Co., 612 S.W.2d 321 (Ark. 1981).

Connecticut: Leahey v. Lawrence D. Coon & Sons, Inc., 2006 WL 2130438 (Conn. Super. July 14, 2006).

Mississippi: Oliver v. City Builders, Inc., 303 So.2d 466 (Miss. 1974).

Nevada: Calloway v. City of Reno, 993 P.2d 1259 (Nev. 2000).

Washington: Gay v. Cornwall, 494 P.2d 1371 (Wash. App. 1974).

87 *Id.*

88 *Id.*

89 See, e.g.:

First Circuit: Brown Daltas & Associates, Inc. v. General Accident Insurance Co., 844 F. Supp. 58, 66 (D. Mass. 1994), *rev'd on other grounds* 48 F.3d 30 (1st Cir.), *cert. denied* 516 U.S. 822 (1995).

Third Circuit: Stargatt v. Fidelity & Casualty Company of New York, 67 F.R.D. 689, 690–691 (D. Del. 1975), *aff'd* 578 F.2d 1375 (3d Cir. 1978).

State Courts:

California: Earth Elements, Inc. v. National American Insurance Co., 48 Cal. Rptr.2d 399, 402 (Cal. App. 1995).

Michigan: Lynn v. Detroit Edison, 2006 WL 1408443 (Mich. App. May 23, 2006); Detroit Edison Co. v. Comcast Cablevision of Taylor, Inc., No. 00-020276-CK, slip op. at 4 (Mich. Cir. Apr. 17, 2002).

90 A "zero-sum settlement" results if no money changes hands in the settlement because the parties value the policyholder's claim for unpaid fees equally with the underlying claimant's claim. Alternatively, an "other net settlement" results if some money changes hands in the settlement, but the amount of money that changes hands is less than the value of the claimant's claim because the parties value the claimant's claim as greater than the policyholder's claim for unpaid fees.

91 See, e.g., Brown Daltas & Associates, Inc. v. General Accident Insurance Co., 844 F. Supp. 58, 66 (D. Mass. 1994), *rev'd on other grounds* 48 F.3d 30 (1st Cir.), *cert. denied* 516 U.S. 822 (1995).

92 See, e.g.:

California: Earth Elements, Inc. v. National American Insurance Co., 41 Cal. App.4th 110, 48 Cal. Rptr.2d 399, 402 (1995).

> "A chose in action was given as consideration for a settlement. There is no analytical distinction between surrendering money in exchange for a settlement and exchanging any other item of value. While the value of money is apparent on its face, an intangible item is equally capable of being evaluated. Whether the insured gave up money or a chose in action, the consideration for the settlement had a value which is compensable because of the breach of the contractual duty to indemnify."

See also:

First Circuit: Brown Daltas & Associates, Inc. v. General Accident Insurance Co., 844 F. Supp. 58, 66 (D. Mass. 1994), *rev'd on other grounds* 48 F.3d 30 (1st Cir.), *cert. denied* 516 U.S. 822 (1995).

Third Circuit: Stargatt v. Fidelity & Casualty Company of New York, 67 F.R.D. 689, 690–691 (D. Del. 1975), *aff'd* 578 F.2d 1375 (3d Cir. 1978).

Seventh Circuit: Platinum Technology, Inc. v. Federal Insurance Co., 282 F.3d 927 (7th Cir. 2002).

Ninth Circuit: Morgan v. Chicago Title Insurance Co., 230 Fed. Appx. 656 (9th Cir. 2007); Thane International, Inc. v. Hartford Fire Insurance Co., 2009 WL 453106 (C.D. Cal. Feb. 19, 2009).

State Courts:

California: Feurzeig v. Insurance Company of the West, 2003 WL 21003733 (Cal. App. May 5, 2003); Atlantic Mutual Insurance Co. v. J. Lamb, Inc., 100 Cal. App.4th 1017, 123 Cal. Rptr.2d 256 (2002).

Michigan: Lynn v. Detroit Edison, 2006 WL 1408443 (Mich. App. May 23, 2006); Detroit Edison Co. v. Comcast Cablevision of Taylor, Inc., No. 00-020276-CK, slip op. at 4 (Mich. Circuit Ct., Wayne Cnty. Apr. 17, 2002) (waiver of workers' compensation lien considered a contribution toward settlement).

93 See § 10.03[2] *infra*.

94 Brown Daltas & Associates, Inc. v. General Accident Insurance Company of America, 844 F. Supp. 58, 66 (D. Mass. 1994), *rev'd on other grounds* 48 F.3d 30 (1st Cir.), *cert. denied* 516 U.S. 822 (1995).

95 *Id.*

96 *Id.*

97 Brown Daltas & Associates, Inc. v. General Accident Insurance Company of America, 844 F. Supp. 58, 66 (D. Mass. 1994), *rev'd on other grounds* 48 F.3d 30 (1st Cir.), *cert. denied* 516 U.S. 822 (1995).

98 *Id.*, 844 F. Supp. at 65 n.8.

99 *Id.*, 844 F. Supp. at 66. In this case an architectural firm was sued by a bank for errors in the design and supervision of the construction of certain buildings. The parties settled the underlying action by entering into a zero-sum settlement whereby the bank withdrew its claims for faulty design and supervision in exchange for the architectural firm's foregoing claims for unpaid invoices. The architectural firm sought insurance coverage for such settlement, and the insurance company denied on the basis that the policy excluded from the definition of "damages" the "return or withdrawal of fees." The court rejected the insurance company arguments that the zero-sum settlement constituted the "return or withdrawal of fees."

> "The withdrawal of fees exclusion exists to prevent an insured and a claimant from colluding and obtaining an unwarranted insurance recovery. No evidence of collusion exists in this case. Further, Defendants' argument rests in formality and not logic. Defendants argue that no money changed hands in the zero-sum settlement, and therefore a withdrawal of fees occurred. However, the zero-sum settlement functions as if each paid the other." 844 F. Supp. at 66.

100 See:

Fourth Circuit: Builders Mutual Insurance Co. v. Dragas Management Corp., 709 F. Supp.2d 441 (E.D. Va. 2010) (builder's remediation costs covered).

Ninth Circuit: Megavail, Inc. v. Illinois Union Insurance Co., 2007 WL 3232605 (D. Or. Nov. 1, 2007) (in-house legal costs covered under policy).

State Courts:

Arizona: Desert Mountain Properties Limited Partnership v. Liberty Mutual Fire Insurance Co., 236 P.3d 421 (Ariz. App. 2010) (repair costs incurred are covered); Tritschler v. Allstate Insurance Co., 144 P.3d 519 (Ariz. App. 2006) (overhead and profit recoverable in first-party claim).

California: Geddes & Smith, Inc. v. St. Paul Mercury Indemnity Co., 63 Cal.2d 602, 407 P.2d 868, 47 Cal. Rptr. 564 (1965) (personnel, overhead, and administrative costs properly recoverable under liability policy).

Oregon: Employers Insurance of Wausau v. Tektronix, Inc., 156 P.3d 105 (Or. App. 2007) (salaries of employees covered).

101 See:

Third Circuit: Permasteelisa CS Corp. v. Columbia Casualty Co., 377 Fed. Appx. 260 (3d Cir. 2010) (repairs performed by contractor not covered).

Sixth Circuit: *Cincinnati Insurance Co. v. Crossmann Communities Partnership,* 2008 WL 852133 (E.D. Ky. Mar. 28, 2008).

State Courts:

California: Globe Indemnity Co. v. State of California, 43 Cal. App.3d 745, 118 Cal. Rptr. 75 (1974) (increased overhead and lost profits not recoverable).

Illinois: Fremont Indemnity Co. v. Special Earth Equipment Corp., 131 Ill. App.3d 108, 474 N.E.2d 926, 86 Ill. Dec. 12 (1985) (fixed overhead not covered).

Maryland: Nationwide Mutual Insurance Co. v. Regional Electric Contractors, Inc., 111 Md. App. 80, 680 A.2d 547 (1996).

Texas: Lennar Corp. v. Great American Insurance Co., 200 S.W.3d 651 (Tex. App.), *substituted concurring and dissenting opinions* 2006 WL 909937 (Tex. App. Apr. 11, 2006) (overhead and personnel costs not covered).

102 *Third Circuit:* Centennial Insurance Co. v. Lumbermens Mutual Casualty Co., 677 F. Supp. 342 (E.D. Pa. 1987).

Fifth Circuit: Mid-Continent Casualty Co. v. Eland Energy, Inc., 2009 WL 3074618 (N.D. Tex. Mar. 30, 2009) (environmental responses costs covered).

Seventh Circuit: Keystone Consolidated Industries, Inc. v. Employers Insurance Company of Wausau, 456 F.3d 758 (7th Cir. 2006).

Eighth Circuit: Coffeyville Resources Refining & Marketing, L.L.C. v. Liberty Surplus Insurance Corp., 714 F. Supp.2d 1119 (D. Kan. 2010) (cleanup costs covered).

Ninth Circuit: Teck Metals, Ltd. v. Certain Underwriters at Lloyd's, London, 2010 WL 3211949 (E.D. Wash. Aug. 10, 2010) (remedial costs are "damages").

State Courts:

Alabama: Alabama Plating Co. v. United States Fidelity & Guaranty Co., 690 So.2d 331 (Ala. 1996).

California: AIU Insurance Co. v. Superior Court (FMC Corp.), 51 Cal.3d 807, 799 P.2d 1253, 274 Cal. Rptr. 820 (1990).

Iowa: A.Y. McDonald Industries, Inc. v. Insurance Company of North America, 475 N.W.2d 607 (Iowa 1991).

Kentucky: Aetna Casualty & Surety Co. v. Commonwealth of Kentucky, 179 S.W.3d 830 (Ky. 2005).

New Jersey: Morton International, Inc. v. General Accident Insurance Co., 629 A.2d 831 (N.J. 1993), *cert. denied* 512 U.S. 1245 (1994).

Oregon: Certain Underwriters at Lloyd's London and Excess Insurance Co. v. Massachusetts Bonding and Insurance Co., 235 Or. App. 99, 230 P.3d 103 (2010) (response costs covered).

South Carolina: Helena Chemical Co. v. Allianz Underwriters Insurance Co., 594 S.E.2d 455 (S.C. 2004) (environmental response costs covered).

Washington: Boeing Co. v. Aetna Casualty & Surety Co., 784 P.2d 507 (Wash. 1990).

But see:

Eighth Circuit: Grisham v. Commercial Union Insurance Co., 951 F.2d 872 (8th Cir. 1991).

State Courts:

California: County of San Diego v. Ace Property & Casualty Insurance Co., 37 Cal.4th 406,118 P.3d 607, 33 Cal. Rptr.3d 583 (2005); Powerine Oil Co. v. Superior Court, 37 Cal.4th 377, 118 P.3d 589, 33 Cal. Rptr.3d 562 (2005); Certain Underwriters At Lloyd's London v. Superior Court, 24 Cal.4th 945, 16 P.3d 94, 103 Cal. Rptr.2d 672 (2001); Ortega Rock Quarry v. Golden Eagle Insurance Corp., 141 Cal. App.4th 969, 46 Cal. Rptr.3d 517 (2006).

103 *Webster's Ninth Collegiate Dictionary* at 571.

104 Outboard Marine Corp. v. Liberty Mutual Insurance Co., 607 N.E.2d 1204, 1216 (Ill. 1992) (citation omitted) Accordingly, "damages" can actually be construed as ambiguous with

respect to whether it includes CERCLA response costs, and this ambiguity could be construed in favor of coverage. See Metro Wastewater Reclamation District v. Continental Casualty Co., 834 F. Supp. 1254, 1259 (D. Colo. 1993) (construing "damages" as including CERCLA response costs partially on the basis of the dictionary definition of "damages").

105 See:

Second Circuit: Olin Corp. v. Insurance Company of North America, 221 F.3d 307 (2d Cir. 2000); Texaco A/S (Denmark) v. Commercial Insurance Company of Newark, NJ, 160 F.3d 124 (2d Cir. 1998).

Third Circuit: Centennial Insurance Co. v. Lumbermens Mutual Casualty Co., 677 F. Supp. 342 (E.D. Pa. 1987).

Fourth Circuit: Morrow Corp. v. Harleysville Mutual Insurance Co., 101 F. Supp.2d 422 (E.D. Va. 2000).

Seventh Circuit: Keystone Consolidated Industries, Inc. v. Employers Insurance Company of Wausau, 456 F.3d 758 (7th Cir. 2006) (CERCLA response costs are "damages").

Ninth Circuit: Monarch Greenback, LLC v. Monticello Insurance Co., 118 F. Supp.2d 1068 (D. Idaho 1999).

Tenth Circuit: Metro Wastewater Reclamation District v. Continental Casualty Co., 834 F. Supp. 1254, 1258 (D. Colo. 1993) (recognizing that the majority position is that CERCLA response costs are "damages"); Gahagen Iron & Metal Co. v. Transportation Insurance Co., 1992 U.S. Dist. LEXIS 20817, at *10 (D. Colo. Nov. 9, 1992) (citing West American Insurance Co. v. Baumgartner, No. 89CA1751, slip op. at 3 (Colo. App. Aug. 8, 1991)).

Eleventh Circuit: Briggs & Stratton Corp. v. Royal Globe Insurance Co., 64 F. Supp.2d 1340 (M.D. Ga. 1999).

State Courts:

Alabama: Alabama Plating Co. v. United States Fidelity & Guaranty Co., 690 So.2d 331 (Ala. 1996).

California: AIU Insurance Co. v. Superior Court (FMC Corp.), 51 Cal.3d 807, 799 P.2d 1253, 274 Cal. Rptr. 820 (1990).

Delaware: Monsanto Co. v. Aetna Casualty & Surety Co., Del. Super. LEXIS 463 (Del. Super. Dec. 21, 1993), *aff'd* 1994 Del. LEXIS 192, slip op. at 15 (Del. June 13, 1994).

Illinois: Central Illinois Light Co. v. Home Insurance Co., 213 Ill.2d 141, 821 N.E.2d 206, 290 Ill. Dec. 155 (2004); Outboard Marine Corp. v. Liberty Mutual Insurance Co., 154 Ill.2d 90, 607 N.E.2d 1204, 1216, 180 Ill. Dec. 691 (1992); Emerson Electric Co. v. Aetna Casualty & Surety Co., 319 Ill. App.3d 218, 743 N.E.2d 629, 252 Ill. Dec. 761 (2001) (applying Missouri law).

Indiana: Travelers Indemnity Co. v. Summit Corporation of America, 715 N.E.2d 926 (Ind. App. 1999).

Iowa: A.Y. McDonald Industries, Inc. v. Insurance Company of North America, 475 N.W.2d 607 (Iowa 1991).

Kentucky: Aetna Casualty & Surety Co. v. Commonwealth of Kentucky, 179 S.W.3d 830 (Ky. 2005).

Maryland: Bausch & Lomb, Inc. v. Utica Mutual Insurance Co., 625 A.2d 1021 (Md. 1993).

Massachusetts: Hazen Paper Co. v. United States Fidelity & Guaranty Co., 407 Mass. 689, 555 N.E.2d 576 (1990).

Minnesota: Minnesota Mining & Manufacturing Co. v. Travelers Indemnity Co., 457 N.W.2d 175 (Minn. 1990).

Missouri: Hocker Oil Co. v. Barker-Phillips-Jackson, Inc., 997 S.W.2d 510 (Mo. App. 1999).

New Hampshire: Coakley v. Maine Bonding & Casualty Co., 136 N.H. 402, 618 A.2d 777 (1992).

New Jersey: Morton International, Inc. v. General Accident Insurance Co., 134 N.J. 1, 629 A.2d 831 (1993), *cert. denied* 512 U.S. 1245 (1994).

New York: Griffith Oil Co. v. National Union Fire Insurance Company of Pittsburgh, Pa., 15 A.D.3d 982, 789 N.Y.S.2d 352 (2005).

North Carolina: C.D. Spangler Construction Co. v. Industrial Crankshaft & Engineering Co., 388 S.E.2d 557 (N.C. 1990).

Rhode Island: Insurance Company of North America v. Kayser-Roth Corp., 770 A.2d 403 (R.I. 2001).

South Carolina: Helena Chemical Co. v. Allianz Underwriters Insurance Co., 357 S.C. 631, 594 S.E.2d 455 (2004).

Vermont: Hardwick Recycling & Salvage, Inc. v. Acadia Insurance Co., 177 Vt. 421, 869 A.2d 82 (2004); State v. CNA Insurance Cos., 172 Vt. 318, 779 A.2d 662 (2001).

Washington: Boeing Co. v. Aetna Casualty & Surety Co., 113 Wash.2d 869, 784 P.2d 507 (1990); Puget Sound Energy v. Certain Underwriters At Lloyd's London, 134 Wash. App. 228, 138 P.3d 1068 (2006).

Wisconsin: Johnson Controls, Inc. v. Employers Insurance of Wausau, 264 Wis.2d 60, 665 N.W.2d 257 (2003).

Wyoming: Compass Insurance Co. v. Cravens, Dargan & Co., 748 P.2d 724 (Wyo. 1988).

But see: Certain Underwriters At Lloyd's London v. Superior Court, 24 Cal.4th 945, 16 P.3d 94, 103 Cal. Rptr.2d 672 (2001); Ortega Rock Quarry v. Golden Eagle Insurance Corp., 141 Cal. App.4th 969, 46 Cal. Rptr.3d 517 (2006); CDM Investors v. Travelers Casualty & Surety Co., 139 Cal. App.4th 1251, 43 Cal. Rptr.3d 669 (2006).

106 See, e.g.:

Third Circuit: Moffat v. Metropolitan Casualty Insurance Co., 238 F. Supp. 165, 172 (M.D. Pa. 1964).

Ninth Circuit: City of Myrtle Point v. Pacific Indemnity Co., 233 F. Supp. 193, 198 (D. Or. 1963).

State Courts:

Alabama: Employers Insurance Company of Alabama v. Rives, 87 So.2d 653 (Ala. 1955), *cert. denied* 87 So.2d 658 (Ala. 1956).

107 *Second Circuit:* Gerrish Corp. v. Universal Underwriters Insurance Co., 947 F.2d 1023 (2d Cir.1991), *cert. denied* 504 U.S. 973 (1992) (applying Vermont law); Avondale Industries, Inc. v. Travelers Indemnity Co., 887 F.2d 1200, 1207 (2d Cir.1989), *cert. denied* 496 U.S. 906 (1990) (applying New York law).

Third Circuit: New Castle County v. Hartford Accident & Indemnity Co., 933 F.2d 1162, 1184–1191 (3d Cir.1991) (applying Delaware law); Township of Gloucester v. Maryland Casualty Co., 668 F. Supp. 394, 400 (D.N.J. 1987) (applying New Jersey law).

Ninth Circuit: Aetna Casualty & Surety Co. v. Pintlar Corp., 948 F.2d 1507, 1513 (9th Cir. 1991) (applying Idaho law).

District of Columbia Circuit: Independent Petrochemical Corp. v. Aetna Casualty & Surety Co., 944 F.2d 940, 947 (D.C. Cir. 1991), *cert. denied sub nom.* Certain Underwriters at Lloyd's, London v. Independent Petrochemical Corp., 503 U.S. 1011 (1992) (applying Missouri law).

State Courts:

California: AIU Insurance Co. v. Superior Court, 51 Cal.3d 807, 799 P.2d 1253, 1267–1278, 274 Cal. Rptr. 820 (1990); Aerojet-General Corp. v. Superior Court, 211 Cal. App.3d 216, 257 Cal. Rptr. 621, 628 (1989).

Iowa: A.Y. McDonald Industries v. Insurance Company of North America, 475 N.W.2d 607, 615–622 (Iowa 1991).

Massachusetts: Hazen Paper Co. v. United States Fidelity & Guaranty Co., 407 Mass. 689, 555 N.E.2d 576, 582–584 (1990).

Michigan: United States Aviex Co. v. Travelers Insurance Co., 125 Mich. App. 579, 336 N.W.2d 838, 842–843 (1983).

Minnesota: Minnesota Mining & Manufacturing Co. v. Travelers Indemnity Co., 457 N.W.2d 175, 179–184 (Minn. 1990).

North Carolina: C.D. Spangler Construction Co. v. Industrial Crankshaft & Engineering Co., 326 N.C. 133, 388 S.E.2d 557, 565–569 (1990).

Washington: Boeing Co. v. Aetna Casualty & Surety Co., 113 Wash.2d 869, 784 P.2d 507, 510–515 (1990).

Wyoming: Compass Insurance Co. v. Cravens, Dargan & Co., 748 P.2d 724, 729–730 (Wyo. 1988).

[108] Morton International, Inc. v. General Accident Insurance Co., 134 N.J. 1, 629 A.2d 831, 845 (1993), *cert. denied* 512 U.S. 1245 (1994).

[109] *Eighth Circuit:* Continental Insurance Co. v. Northeastern Pharmaceutical & Chemical Co., 842 F.2d 977, 990 (8th Cir.) (dissenting opinion), *cert. denied sub nom.* Missouri v. Continental Insurance Cos., 488 U.S. 821 (1988).

State Courts:

Iowa: A.Y. McDonald Industries, Inc. v. Insurance Company of North America, 475 N.W.2d 607, 621 (Iowa 1991).

[110] See, e.g.:

District of Columbia Circuit: Independent Petrochemical Corp. v. Aetna Casualty & Surety Co., 944 F.2d 940, 946 (D.C. Cir. 1991), *cert. denied* 503 U.S. 1011 (1992) ("Liability for environmental cleanup costs quite naturally fits th[e] common and ordinary understanding of damages.").

State Courts:

Iowa: A.Y. McDonald Industries, Inc. v. Insurance Company of North America, 475 N.W.2d 607, 619 (Iowa 1991).

New Jersey: Morton International, Inc. v. General Accident Insurance Co., 134 N.J. 1, 629 A.2d 831, 845 (1993), *cert. denied* 512 U.S. 1245 (1994).

North Carolina: C.D. Spangler Construction Co. v. Industrial Crankshaft & Engineering Co., 388 S.E.2d 557, 563 (N.C. 1990).

Washington: Boeing Co. v. Aetna Casualty & Surety Co., 113 Wash.2d 869, 784 P.2d 507, 511 (1990).

Even in Continental Insurance Co. v. Northeastern Pharmaceutical & Chemical Co., 842 F.2d 977, 985 (8th Cir.), *cert. denied sub nom.* Missouri v. Continental Insurance Cos., 488 U.S. 821 (1988), the most-cited court espousing the minority view that cleanup costs are not covered damages, the majority conceded that the plain, ordinary, and generally accepted meaning of "damages" makes no distinction between "legal" or "equitable" damages and, that "from the viewpoint of the lay insured, the term 'damages' could reasonably include all monetary claims. . . ."

[111] A.Y. McDonald Industries, Inc. v. Insurance Company of North America, 475 N.W.2d 607, 621 (Iowa 1991).

[112] *Id.*, 475 N.W.2d at 620–621. See also, Aerojet-General Corp. v. Superior Ct., 211 Cal. App.3d 216, 257 Cal. Rptr. 621, 628, *opinion supplemented* 258 Cal. Rptr. 684 (Cal. App. 1989).

113 See generally, Stanzler and Yuen, "Coverage for Environmental Cleanup Cost: The History of the Word 'Damages' in the Standard Form Comprehensive General Liability Insurance Policy," 1990 Columbia Bus. L. Rev. 449, 462–465 (1990).

114 *Id.*, 1990 Columbia Bus. L. Rev. at 481 (citations and quotations omitted).

115 See:

Fifth Circuit: Data Specialties, Inc. v. Transcontinental Insurance Co., 125 F.3d 909 (5th Cir. 1997).

Ninth Circuit: Gulf Insurance Co. v. LA Effects Group, Inc., 827 F.2d 574, 577 (9th Cir. 1987); Willmar Development, L.L.C. v. Illinois National Insurance Co., 726 F. Supp.2d 1280 (D. Or. 2010) (negligence claim is covered occurrence).

Tenth Circuit: VBF, Inc. v. Chubb Group of Insurance Cos., 263 F.3d 1226 (10th Cir. 2001).

Eleventh Circuit: Key Custom Homes, Inc. v. Mid-Continent Casualty Co., 450 F. Supp.2d 1311, 1314 (M.D. Fla. 2006).

State Courts:

California: Vandenberg v. Superior Court, 21 Cal.4th 815, 982 P.2d 229, 88 Cal. Rptr.2d 366 (1999).

Georgia: McDonald Construction Co. v. Bituminous Casualty Corp., 279 Ga. App. 757, 632 S.E.2d 420 (2006); Custom Planning & Development, Inc. v. American National Fire Insurance Co., 270 Ga. App. 8, 606 S.E.2d 39 (2004).

Illinois: Viking Construction Management, Inc. v. Liberty Mutual Insurance Co., 358 Ill. App.3d 34, 831 N.E.2d 1, 294 Ill. Dec. 478 (2005).

Indiana: Amerisure, Inc. v. Wurster Construction Co., 818 N.E.2d 998 (Ind. App. 2004), *clarified* 822 N.E.2d 1115 (Ind. App. 2005); Jim Barna Log Systems Midwest, Inc. v. General Casualty Insurance Company of Wisconsin, 791 N.E.2d 816 (Ind. App. 2003).

Kansas: Lee Builders, Inc. v. Farm Bureau Mutual Insurance Co., 281 Kan. 844, 137 P.3d 486 (2006).

Minnesota: Wanzek Construction, Inc. v. Employers Insurance of Wausau, 667 N.W.2d 473 (Minn. App. 2003), *aff'd* 679 N.W.2d 322 (Minn. 2004).

New Jersey: Atlantic Mutual Insurance Co. v. Hillside Bottling Co., 387 N.J. Super. 224, 903 A.2d 513, *certif. denied* 912 A.2d 1264 (N.J. 2006).

New York: Perras Excavating, Inc. v. Transportation Insurance Co., 291 A.D.2d 643, 737 N.Y.S.2d 692, *appeal denied* 773 N.E.2d 1017 (N.Y. 2002); Bonded Concrete, Inc. v. Transcontinental Insurance Co., 12 A.D.3d 761, 784 N.Y.S.2d 212 (2004).

North Dakota: ACUITY v. Burd & Smith Construction, Inc., 721 N.W.2d 33 (N.D. 2006).

Pennsylvania: Kvaerner Metals v. Commercial Union Insurance Co., 908 A.2d 888 (Pa. 2006); Pennsylvania Manufacturers' Association Insurance Co. v. L.B. Smith, Inc., 831 A.2d 1178 (Pa. Super. 2003).

Texas: Lennar Corp. v. Great American Insurance Co., 200 S.W.3d 651 (Tex. App.), *substituted concurring and dissenting opinions* 2006 WL 909937 (Tex. App. Apr. 11, 2006).

Wisconsin: American Family Mutual Insurance Co. v. American Girl, Inc., 268 Wis.2d 16, 673 N.W.2d 65 (2004).

116 See:

Fifth Circuit: Westchester Surplus Lines Insurance Co. v. Maverick Tube Corp., 590 F.3d 316 (5th Cir. 2009) (breach of warranty claim can arise from a covered occurrence).

Seventh Circuit: Sigma Chi Corp. v. Westchester Fire Insurance Co., 587 F. Supp.2d 891 (N.D. Ill. 2008) (breach of contract claims not automatically excluded).

Ninth Circuit: Gulf Insurance Co. v. LA Effects Group, Inc., 827 F.2d 574, 577 (9th Cir. 1987) (inadequate performance of contract may result in a covered claim); Willmar Development, L.L.C. v. Illinois National Insurance Co., 726 F. Supp.2d 1280 (D. Or. 2010) (occurrence can arise from contract if the deficient work damages other portions).

Tenth Circuit: Continental Western Insurance Co. v. Shay Construction, Inc., 805 F. Supp.2d 1125 (D. Colo. 2011).

State Courts:

Arizona: Desert Mountain Properties Limited Partnership v. Liberty Mutual Fire Insurance Co., 236 P.3d 421 (Ariz. App. 2010) (policy can cover contractual claim in construction coverage context).

California: Vandenberg v. Superior Court, 21 Cal.4th 815, 982 P.2d 229, 88 Cal. Rptr.2d 366 (1999), *overruling* International Surplus Lines Insurance Co. v. Devonshire Group, 155 Cal. Rptr. 870, 874 (Cal. App. 1979) (CGL policy that provides coverage for sums the insured is "legally obligated to pay as damages" does not necessarily preclude coverage for losses pleaded as contractual damages).

Indiana: T.R. Bulger, Inc. v. Indiana Insurance Co., 901 N.E.2d 1110 (Ind. App. 2009) (coverage turns on whether the workmanship itself was faulty and needed to be replaced or whether the faulty workmanship damaged other portions of the home).

Kansas: Lee Builders, Inc. v. Farm Bureau Mutual Insurance Co., 281 Kan. 844, 137 P.3d 486 (2006) (coverage for contract and tort claims).

Minnesota: Wanzek Construction, Inc. v. Employers Insurance of Wausau, 667 N.W.2d 473 (Minn. App. 2003), *aff'd* 679 N.W.2d 322 (Minn. 2004) (When an insurance policy provides coverage for sums that the insured is "legally obligated to pay as damages," the insured need not have had litigation commenced against it for the policy to be triggered, but is entitled to coverage based solely on a contractual duty to replace faulty building materials.).

Missouri: D.R. Sherry Construction, Ltd. v. American Family Mutual Insurance Co., 316 S.W.3d 899 (Mo. 2010) (breach of contract claim can be covered).

New York: J. Lucarelli & Sons, Inc. v. Mountain Valley Indemnity Co., 64 A.D.3d 856, 881 N.Y.S.2d 708 (2009) (suggesting that policy only covers tort liability but case may be distinguishable because only damages sought were to repair defective workmanship [as opposed to damage to non-defective work]).

North Dakota: ACUITY v. Burd & Smith Construction, Inc., 721 N.W.2d 33 (N.D. 2006) (breach of contract claims are within scope of coverage of CGL policy that was sold to general contractor; CGL policy could provide coverage for tort claims, contract claims, and claims for statutory violations as long as requisite accidental occurrence and property damage were present).

Texas: Lennar Corp. v. Great American Insurance Co., 200 S.W.3d 651 (Tex. App.), *substituted concurring and dissenting opinions* 2006 WL 909937 (Tex. App. Apr. 11, 2006) (construction defect claims sounding in contact and in tort can be covered by CGL policy if the claims result in "property damage" that is unexpected and unintended).

Wisconsin: American Family Mutual Insurance Co. v. American Girl, Inc., 268 Wis.2d 16, 673 N.W.2d 65 (2004) (language of CGL policy and the purpose of the CGL insuring agreement will provide coverage for claims sounding in part in breach of contract/breach of warranty under some circumstances).

117 See:

First Circuit: Lopez and Medina Corp. v. Marsh USA, Inc., 667 F.3d 58 (1st Cir. 2012).

Second Circuit: Transportation Insurance Co. v. AARK Construction Group, Ltd., 526 F. Supp.2d 350 (E.D.N.Y. 2007) (Under New York law, CGL insurance policies do not cover claims sounding in contract).

Third Circuit: Nationwide Mutual Insurance Co. v. CPB International, Inc., 562 F.3d 591 (3d Cir. 2009) (Pennsylvania law does not recognize coverage for breach of contract and breach of warranty claims); Meridian Mutual Insurance Co. v. James Gilligan Builders, 2009 WL 1704474 (E.D. Pa. June 18, 2009) (only tort liability can result from a covered occurrence).

Fifth Circuit: Federal Insurance Co. v. New Hampshire Insurance Co., 439 Fed. Appx. 287 (5th Cir. 2011); Data Specialties, Inc. v. Transcontinental Insurance Co., 125 F.3d 909 (5th Cir. 1997) (CGL policy does not cover contract liabilities).

Seventh Circuit: Benefit Systems & Services, Inc. v. Travelers Casualty & Surety Co. of America, 2009 WL 1106948 (N.D. Ill. Apr. 22, 2009) (contractual liability not covered).

Ninth Circuit: State Farm Fire and Casualty Co. v., Willison, 833 F. Supp.2d 1200 (D. Haw. 2011); Burlington Insurance Co. v. United Coatings Manufacturing Co., 518 F. Supp.2d 1241 (D. Haw. 2007) (Under Hawaii law, contractual claims are not covered.).

Tenth Circuit: VBF, Inc. v. Chubb Group of Insurance Cos., 263 F.3d 1226 (10th Cir. 2001) (as used in provisions of CGL, phrases "legally obligated to pay" and "liability imposed by law" referred only to tort claims asserted against insured, and not contract claims).

Eleventh Circuit: Key Custom Homes, Inc. v. Mid-Continent Casualty Co., 450 F. Supp.2d 1311, 1314 (M.D. Fla. 2006) ("legally obligated to pay as damages" only encompasses tort based liabilities).

State Courts:

Georgia: McDonald Construction Co. v. Bituminous Casualty Corp., 632 S.E.2d 420 (Ga. App. 2006) (replacement of defective tiles not covered); Custom Planning & Development, Inc. v. American National Fire Insurance Co., 606 S.E.2d 39 (Ga. App. 2004) (coverage applicable under CGL policy is for tort liability for injury to persons and damage to other property, not for contractual liability of the insured for economic loss because the product or completed work is not that for which the damaged person bargained).

Illinois: Viking Construction Management, Inc. v. Liberty Mutual Insurance Co., 358 Ill. App.3d 34, 831 N.E.2d 1, 294 Ill. Dec. 478 (Ill. App. 2005) (CGL policy does not cover underlying claim for breach of contract).

Indiana: Amerisure, Inc. v. Wurster Construction Co., 818 N.E.2d 998 (Ind. App. 2004), *clarified* 822 N.E.2d 1115 (Ind. App. 2005) (coverage for property damage under CGL policy is for tort liability for physical damages to others, not for contractual liability of the insured for economic loss); Jim Barna Log Systems Midwest, Inc. v. General Casualty Insurance Company of Wisconsin, 791 N.E.2d 816 (Ind. App. 2003) (CGL insurance policy is for tort liability for physical damages to others and not for the business risk of contractual liability of the insured for economic loss because the product or completed work is not that for which the damaged person bargained).

Nebraska: Federated Service Insurance Co. v. Alliance Construction, L.L.C., 282 Neb. 638, 805 N.W.2d 468 (2011).

New Jersey: Atlantic Mutual Insurance Co. v. Hillside Bottling Co., 387 N.J. Super. 224, 903 A.2d 513, *cert. denied* 912 A.2d 1264 (N.J. 2006) (coverage is for tort liability for physical damages to others and not for contractual liability of the insured for economic loss because the product or completed work is not that for which the damaged person bargained).

New York: J. Lucarelli & Sons, Inc. v. Mountain Valley Indemnity Co., 64 A.D.3d 856, 881 N.Y.S.2d 708 (2009) (suggesting that policy only covers tort liability but case may be distinguishable because only damages sought were to repair defective workmanship [as opposed to damage to non-defective work]); Perras Excavating, Inc. v. Transportation Insurance Co., 291 A.D.2d 643, 737 N.Y.S.2d 692, *appeal denied* 773 N.E.2d 1017 (N.Y. 2002) (breach of contract claim not covered under CGL policy); Bonded Concrete, Inc. v. Transcontinental Insurance Co., 784 N.Y.S.2d 212 (N.Y. App. Div. 2004) (purpose of CGL policy is to provide coverage for tort liability for physical damage to others, and not for insured's contractual liability for economic loss because its product is not what the damaged party bargained for).

Pennsylvania: Kvaerner Metals v. Commercial Union Insurance Co., 908 A.2d 888 (Pa. 2006) (no coverage for contractual liability for repair of work product); Erie Insurance Exchange v. Abbott Furnace Co., 972 A.2d 1232 (Pa. Super. 2009) (no coverage for contractual liability); Pennsylvania Manufacturers' Association Insurance Co. v. L.B. Smith, Inc., 831 A.2d 1178 (Pa. Super. 2003) (no coverage for contractual liability).

[118] See § 5.03[6] *infra.*

[119] See § 5.03[6] *infra.*

[120] See, e.g., Kvaerner Metals v. Commercial Union Insurance Co., 908 A.2d 888, 898–899 (Pa. 2006) ("a CGL policy may provide coverage where faulty workmanship caused bodily injury or damage to another property, but not in cases where faulty workmanship damages the work product alone. . . . To permit coverage in such instances would convert CGL policies into performance bonds, which guarantee the work, rather than like an insurance policy, which is intended to insure against accidents.").

[121] Malecki and Flitner, *Commercial General Liability,* at 6 (6th ed. 1995):

> "The expression 'legally obligated' connotes legal responsibility that is broad in scope. It is directed at civil liability [which] can arise . . . under common law, statute *or contract. . . .*
>
> "The insurer's promise to 'pay those sums that the insured becomes legally obligated to pay' requires only that the insured have an *obligation* to pay." (emphasis added)

Arthur L. Flitner is the Senior Director of Curriculum Design at the American Institute of Chartered Property Casualty Underwriters (the insurance organization actually charged with training and certifying underwriters).

See also, Wielinski, "Selected Insurance Coverage Issues in a Construction Defect Claim," at B-1, B-23, 1998 Construction Law Seminar (1998).

> "[A coverage] denial based upon the proposition that a breach of contract does not give rise to liability for which the insured is 'legally obligated' flies in the face of the ordinary meaning of 'legal obligation.' *An obligation arising out of breach of contract is as legally enforceable as a liability arising out of breach of a tort duty in the eyes of most insureds, let alone most attorneys and insurance professionals.*" (emphasis added)

Patrick J. Wielinski is an insurance industry commentator and co-author of several insurance industry commentaries. See, e.g., Wielinski and Gibson, *Broad Form Property Damage Coverage* (3d ed. 1992).

See Kornblum and Cerillo, *Litigating Insurance Claims: Coverage, Bad Faith, and Business Disputes,* § 3.11, at 95 (1993).

> "There is another alternative which [the cases cited by insurance companies for contract v. tort distinction] ignore—that a policy covering sums that the insured may become 'legally obligated to pay' may be given an interpretation that does not rest upon the distinction between tort and contractual liabilities. One commentator writes 'Liability imposed by law for damages' or damages which the insured becomes 'legally obligated' to pay, excludes the concept of liability which the insured may have voluntarily assumed. . . .' In other words, limiting the 'legally obligated to pay' language to liabilities voluntarily assumed by an insured is not only easier to pinpoint and apply but makes subjective sense. That is, *an insured is as 'legally obligated to pay' a judgment based on a breach of contract as a judgment based on a commission of a tort.*" (emphasis added)

Guy Kornblum is also the first named co-author of Kornblum *et al.*, *California Practice Guide: Bad Faith* (Rutter Group 1988–1992).

Scott Turner, author of a treatise on insurance coverage for construction liabilities, writes that "[l]iabilities based on contract rather than tort should nevertheless qualify for coverage under this term ['legally obligated to pay'] absent disqualification under some other term or provision of the policy." See Turner, *Insurance Coverage of Construction Disputes*, §§ 5.07–5.08, at 66–74 (1st ed. 1992).

122 See ISO Form CG 00 01 10 01.

123 See, e.g., Port Authority of New York and New Jersey v. Affiliated FM Insurance Co., 311 F.3d 226, 233 (3d Cir. 2002).

The primary aim of third-party insurance is to defend and indemnify insureds against liability for claims made against them as a result of their own conduct. First-party coverage, on the other hand, protects against loss caused by injury to the insured's own property. See:

Third Circuit: In re Asousa Partnership, 2004 WL 1043149, at *8 (Bankr. E.D. Pa. Apr. 26, 2004).

Fifth Circuit: America First Lloyd's Insurance Co. v. Global Experience Specialists, Inc., 2013 WL 6164293 (N.D. Tex. Nov. 21, 2013); Diamond Services Corp. v. British European and Overseas P & I Insurance Co., 2013 WL 5410133 (W.D. La. Sept. 24, 2013); Felham Enterprises, Ltd. v. Certain Underwriters at Lloyd's, London, 2004 WL 2984296, at *4 (E.D. La. Dec. 6, 2004) ("'[F]irst party insurance' generally is understood to provide coverage for the insured against loss or damage sustained by it, whereas 'third party insurance' covers liability of the insured to another person.").

Sixth Circuit: White v. Insurance Company of the State of Pennsylvania, 282 F. Supp.2d 618, 625 (N.D. Ohio 2003) (citations omitted), *vacated on other grounds* 405 F.3d 455 (6th Cir. 2005):

> "'Liability' insurance constitutes 'an agreement to cover a loss resulting from one's liability to a third party, such as a loss incurred by a driver who injures a pedestrian.' The claim under the policy 'arises once the insured's liability to a third party has been asserted.' In contrast to this 'third-party insurance,' there is also 'indemnity' insurance which is characterized as 'first-party insurance' and defined as '[a] policy that applies to oneself or one's own property, such as life insurance, health insurance, disability insurance, and fire insurance.'"

Seventh Circuit: Sanyo Laser Products, Inc. v. Royal Insurance Co., 2003 WL 23101793, at *3 n.2 (S.D. Ind. Nov. 7, 2003) ("'first party' insurance is a contract between the insurer and insured protecting the insured's own actual losses and expenses, while 'third party' insurance protects the insured from potential liability to a third party").

Ninth Circuit: United States *ex. rel.* North Star Terminal & Stevedore Co. v. Nuggett Construction Co., 2006 WL 2251122, at *2 n.3 (D. Alaska July 28, 2006).

Tenth Circuit: Wells v. Hartford Insurance Company of Midwest, 2013 WL 5962961 (D. Utah Nov. 7, 2013); Allstate Insurance Co. v. Johnston, 339 F. Supp.2d 1191, 1195 (D. Kan. 2004).

State Courts:

Alabama: Titan Indemnity Co. v. Riley, 679 So.2d 701, 706 (Ala. 1996) (citations omitted; emphasis added).

"Murphy involved a 'first-party' insurance contract, that is, a policy providing for the payment of proceeds to the insured. More specifically, Murphy involved allegations that the insured, who owned a ship, had conspired 'with others . . . to sink and . . . destroy the vessel and cargo for the purpose of collecting the insurance upon the ship and also for the purpose of defrauding [the insurer] in causing it to repay [the insured] any sum paid by him to the owner of the cargo.' In short, Titan has not cited a case in which this Court has held that an insurer who, as in this case, agrees—in exchange for receipt of premiums—to pay for the harm or loss suffered by a third party arising out of the intentional acts of its insured, may, nevertheless, avoid the contract on the ground of public policy."

California: Montrose Chemical Co. v. Admiral Insurance Co., 10 Cal.4th 645, 913 P.2d 878, 886 42 Cal. Rptr.2d 324 (1995).

> "[A] first party insurance policy provides coverage for loss or damage sustained directly by the insured (e.g., life, disability, health, fire, theft and casualty insurance). A third party liability policy, in contrast, provides coverage for liability of the insured to a 'third party' (e.g., a CGL policy, a directors' and officers' liability policy, or an errors and omissions policy). In the usual first party policy, the insurer promises to pay money to the insured upon the happening of an event, the risk of which has been insured against. In the typical third party liability policy, the carrier assumes a contractual duty to pay judgments the insured becomes legally obligated to pay as damages because of bodily injury or property damage caused by the insured."

See also: Black Diamond Asphalt Co. v. Superior Court, 114 Cal. App.4th 109, 7 Cal. Rptr.3d 466, 470 n.2 (2003) ("In first party insurance, a person insures himself or his property against loss. In third party insurance, a person insures himself against liability he may incur to others."); Century Indemnity Co. v. Hearrean, 120 Cal. Rptr.2d 66 (Cal. App. 2002) ("'CGL policies are third party liability insurance policies which obligate insurers to pay money to third parties to whom their insureds are liable. In contrast to first party insurance policies which obligate an insurer to pay money directly to an insured for a loss sustained by the insured. . . .'"); Garvey v. State Farm Fire & Casualty Co., 48 Cal.3d 395, 770 P.2d 704, 257 Cal. Rptr. 292 (1989).

Georgia: Taylor Morrison Services, Inc. v. HDI-Gerling America Insurance Co., 293 Ga. 456, 746 S.E.2d 587 (2013).

Hawaii: Sentinel Insurance Co. v. First Insurance Company of Hawaii, Ltd., 875 P.2d 894, 906 (Haw. 1994); Ferrer v. Ngo, 73 P.3d 73, 81 (Haw. App. 2003).

> "A 'first-party' policy provides coverage for loss or damage sustained by the insured (e.g., life, disability, health, fire, theft, and casualty insurance) whereby the insurer usually promises to pay money to the insured upon the happening of the risk insured against. A 'third-party' policy, on the other hand, provides coverage for the insured's liability to another (e.g., CGL [comprehensive general liability], directors' and officers' liability, and errors and omissions insurance) wherein the carrier generally assumes a contractual duty to pay judgments recovered against the insured arising from the insured's negligence."

Illinois: Emerson Electric Co. v. Aetna Casualty & Surety Co., 815 N.E.2d 924, 950 (Ill. App. 2004).

Kentucky: Aetna Casualty & Surety Co. v. Kentucky, 179 S.W.3d 830, 845 (Ky. 2005) ("Third party insurance involves protection for the policyholder for liability it incurs to someone else, while first party insurance involves protection for losses to the policyholder's own property.").

Mississippi: Watson Quality Ford, Inc. v. Great River Ins. Co., 909 So.2d 1196, 1199 (Miss. App. 2005) ("'First party coverage is a promise by an insurer to pay its own insured, rather than a promise to its insured to pay a third party.'").

New Mexico: Cohen v. Continental Casualty Co., 2013 WL 5741841 (N.M. App. Sept. 23, 2013).

Pennsylvania: Zimmerman v. Harleysville Mutual Insurance Co., 860 A.2d 167, 178 (Pa. Super. 2004), *alloc. denied* 881 A.2d 820 (Pa. 2005) (Joyce, J., dissenting) (citations and quotations omitted).

Texas: In re First Mercury Insurance Co., 2013 WL 6056665, Tex. App. Nov. 13, 2013); National American Insurance Co. v. Texas Property and Casualty Insurance Guaranty Association for Paula Insurance Co., 2013 WL 4817637 (Tex. App. Aug. 28, 2013).

Washington: International Marine Underwriters v. ABCD Marine, L.L.C. 2013 WL 6212026 (Wash. Nov. 27, 2013) (*en banc*); State Farm Fire & Casualty Co. v. English Cove

Association, Inc., 121 Wash. App. 358 88 P.3d 986, 992 (2004) ("Third party insurance provides protection for the policyholder for liability it incurs to someone else, while first party insurance provides protection for losses to the policyholder's own property.").

[124] See ISO Form CG 00 01 10 01.

[125] See, e.g., State Farm Fire & Casualty Co. v. Wilson, 153 Fed. Appx. 952, 957 (6th Cir. 2005) ("policy specifically exclude[d] coverage for 'emotional distress, mental anguish, humiliation, mental distress, mental injury, or any similar injury unless it arises out of actual physical injury'").

See also:

Second Circuit: Jewish Community Center of Staten Island v. Trumbull Insurance Co., 2013 WL 3936204 (E.D.N.Y. July 22, 2013).

State Courts:

Indiana: Grinnell Mutual Reinsurance Co. v. Ault, 918 N.E.2d 619 (Ind. App. 2009).

New Jersey: Bucca v. Hartford Insurance Co., 2008 WL 2852485 (N.J. Super. App. Dept. July 25, 2008).

Ohio: Granger v. Auto Owners Insurance Co., 991 N.E.2d 1254 (Ohio App. 2013); Westfield Insurance Co. v. Porchervina, 2008 WL 5205662 (Ohio App. Dec. 12, 2008).

Texas: Evanston Insurance Co. v. Legacy of Life, Inc., 370 S.W.3d 377 (Tex. 2012).

[126] See Keri Farrell-Kolb, "General Liability Coverage for Claims of Emotional Distress—An Insurance Nightmare," 45 Drake L. Rev. 981 (1997).

See also:

Second Circuit: Allstate Insurance Co. v. Burnard, 2010 WL 1332002 (D. Conn. Mar. 31, 2010); Peck v. Public Service Mutual Insurance Co., 363 F. Supp.2d 137 (D. Conn. 2005) (emotional distress is not bodily injury).

Third Circuit: Babalola v. Donegal Group, Inc., 2008 WL 4006721 (M.D. Pa. Aug. 26, 2008); Coregis Insurance Co. v. City of Harrisburg, 401 F. Supp.2d 398, 406 (M.D. Pa. 2005) ("emotional injury . . . does not constitute 'bodily injury' under Pennsylvania insurance law").

Sixth Circuit: Sherwin-Williams Co. v. Certain Underwriters at Lloyd's, London, 813 F. Supp. 576, 584 (N.D. Ohio 1993) (mental distress from ingesting lead paint constitutes bodily injury).

Eighth Circuit: National Fire Insurance Co. of Hartford v. NWM-Oklahoma, L.L.C., 546 F. Supp.2d 1238 (W.D. Okla. 2008).

Ninth Circuit: General Star Indemnity Co. v. Schools Excess Liability Fund, 888 F. Supp. 1022, 1027 (N.D. Cal. 1995) ("'bodily injury' is generally limited to 'physical injury, sickness or disease and their consequences.' . . . It does not encompass nonphysical, emotional or mental harm. . . . Physical injury resulting from emotional distress, however, constitutes 'bodily injury.'").

Tenth Circuit: Admiral Insurance Co. v. Hosler, 626 F. Supp.2d 1105 (D. Colo. 2009).

Eleventh Circuit: Home Insurance Co. v. Hartford Fire Insurance Co., 379 F. Supp.2d 1282 (M.D. Ala. 2005), *aff'd* 164 Fed. Appx. 950 (11th Cir. 2006) (intentional infliction of emotional distress is not covered as an "accident").

State Courts:

California: Original Joe's, Inc. v. Golden Eagle Insurance Corp., 2002 WL 192737 at *2 (Cal. App. Feb. 7, 2002) ("bodily injury" "does not include emotional distress in the absence of *physical* injury") (emphasis in original).

District of Columbia: Adolph Coors Co. v. Truck Insurance Exchange, 960 A.2d 617 (D.C. 2008).

Kansas: Rockgate Management Co. v. CGU Insurance, Inc./PG Insurance Company of New York, 32 Kan. App.2d 743, 88 P.3d 798, 804 (2004) ("Where the policy defines bodily injury as bodily injury, it seems to imply that actual physical injury must occur for policy coverage.").

Montana: Allstate Insurance Co. v. Wagner-Ellsworth, 344 Mont. 445, 188 P.3d 1042 (2008).

New Jersey: United States Liability Insurance Group v. Security Insurance Company of Hartford, 381 N.J. Super. 211, 885 A.2d 477, 481 (2005) ("'bodily injury' coverage does not include purely emotional injuries without physical manifestations").

Ohio: Hawthorne v. Migoni, 2004 WL 177439 at *2 (Ohio App. Jan. 26, 2004), *appeal denied* 809 N.E.2d 1158 (Ohio 2004) ("plaintiffs' claim for emotional distress does not constitute a separate 'bodily injury' as that term is defined in the insurance policy"); Dickens v. General Accident Insurance Co., 695 N.E.2d 1168, 1169 (Ohio App.), *appeal denied* 684 N.E.2d 91 (Ohio 1997) ("Ohio law does not extend insurance coverage to injuries stemming from emotional distress where 'bodily injury' is the term interpreted by the courts in the policy provisions.").

Pennsylvania: Philadelphia Contributionship Insurance Co. v. Shapiro, 798 A.2d 781, 787 (Pa. Super. 2002) (emotional distress or humiliation due to employment termination does not constitute "bodily injury").

Texas: Evanston Insurance Co. v. Legacy of Life, Inc., 370 S.W.3d 377 (Tex. 2012).

West Virginia: Cherrington v. Erie Insurance Property and Casualty Co., 745 S.E.2d 508 (W. Va. 2013).

127 See:

Second Circuit: Jewish Community Center of Staten Island v. Trumbull Insurance Co., 2013 WL 3936204 (E.D.N.Y. July 22, 2013).

Seventh Circuit: Washington v. Krahn, 440 F. Supp.2d 911, 913 (E.D. Wis. 2006) ("an allegation of emotional distress is sufficient to trigger bodily injury coverage 'when there is no physical impact, fear of physical harm, or physical manifestation of emotional distress'").

Ninth Circuit: Manzarek v. St. Paul Fire & Marine Insurance Co., 519 F.3d 1025 (9th Cir. 2008).

State Courts:

Louisiana: Johnson v. Orleans Parish School Board, 975 So.2d 698 (La. App. 2008).

Massachusetts: Fuller v. First Financial Insurance Co., 448 Mass. 1, 858 N.E.2d 288, 292 n.6 (2006) ("damages, including . . . emotional injuries and [the] need for psychotherapeutic care fall under the definition of 'bodily injury' for the purposes of an insurance contract. . . . The nonphysical harm . . . constitutes 'bodily injury' because it directly resulted from the corporeal harm that she suffered at the hands of her attacker.").

New York: Tortoso v. MetLife Automobile & Home Insurance Co., 21 A.D.3d 276, 799 N.Y.S.2d 506, 508 (2005) ("Where a policy provides coverage for 'bodily injury,' such coverage encompasses a claim for 'purely emotional distress.'").

Texas: GuideOne Elite Insurance Co. v. Fielder Road Baptist Church, 197 S.W.3d 305 (Tex. 2006) ("emotional and psychological injuries as a consequence of sexual assault and abuse were 'bodily injury' within the meaning of the policy's coverage").

128 See ISO Form CG 00 01 10 01.

129 *Id.*

130 *Id.*

131 *Id.*

132 America Online, Inc. v. St. Paul Mercury Insurance Co., 347 F.3d 89 (4th Cir. 2003) (in third-party liability insurance context, electronic data is not covered intangible property, although the computers are covered).

[133] See:

First Circuit: Friel Luxury Home Construction, Inc. v. ProBuilders Specialty Insurance Company RRG, 2009 WL 5227893 (D. Mass. Dec. 22, 2009).

Second Circuit: Transportation Insurance Co. v. AARK Construction Group, Ltd., 526 F. Supp.2d 350 (E.D.N.Y. 2007).

Fourth Circuit: NAS Surety Group v. Precision Wood Products, Inc., 271 F. Supp.2d 776, 781 (M.D.N.C. 2003) ("damages for repair or replacement of faulty or defective workmanship *standing alone* are not covered under the terms of standard CGL policies") (emphasis in original).

Fifth Circuit: Building Specialties, Inc. v. Liberty Mutual Fire Insurance Co., 712 F. Supp.2d 628 (S.D. Tex. 2010); *In re* ML & Associates, Inc., 302 B.R. 857 (Bankr. N.D. Tex. 2003).

Sixth Circuit: Forrest Construction Co. v. Cincinnati Insurance Co., 703 F.3d 359 (6th Cir. 2013); New Hampshire Insurance Co. v. Knoxville Cast Stone, Inc., 433 F. Supp.2d 879 (E.D. Tenn. 2004), *aff'd sub nom.* American & Foreign Insurance Co. v. Sequatchie Concrete Services, Inc., 441 F.3d 341 (6th Cir. 2006).

Seventh Circuit: East Coast Fasteners & Closures, Inc. v. Employers Mutual Casualty Co., 93 Fed. Appx. 948 (7th Cir. 2004); Hartford Casualty Insurance Co. v. Construction Builders in Motion, Inc. 2013 WL 4478758 (N.D. Ill. Aug. 19, 2013) (need damage beyond scope of work).

Eighth Circuit: Modern Equipment Co. v. Continental Western Insurance Co., Inc., 355 F.3d 1125 (8th Cir. 2004).

Ninth Circuit: MW Builders, Inc. v. Safeco Insurance Co. of America, 267 Fed. Appx. 552 (9th Cir. 2008); Big-D Construction Corp. v. Take it for Granite Too, 917 F. Supp.2d 1096 (D. Nev. 2013).

Eleventh Circuit: Mid-Continent Casualty Co. v. Frank Casserino Construction, Inc., 721 F. Supp.2d 1209 (M.D. Fla. 2010).

State Courts:

Alabama: United States Fidelity & Guaranty Co. v. Andalusia Ready Mix, Inc., 436 So.2d 868, 870 (Ala. 1983) (coverage for repair and remodeling of water sewage plant where defective grout was used in the construction; "if [an] occurrence or accident causes damage to some other property than the insured's product, the insured's liability for such damage becomes the liability of the insurer under the policy").

California: F & H Construction Co. v. ITT Hartford Insurance Company of Midwest, 118 Cal. App.4th 364, 12 Cal. Rptr.3d 896 (Cal. App. 2004); Maryland Casualty Co. v. Reeder, 221 Cal. App.3d 961, 270 Cal. Rptr. 719 (Cal. App. 1990).

Connecticut: Capstone Building Corp. v. American Motorists Insurance Co., 308 Conn. 760, 67 A.3d 961 (2013) (physical damage to or loss of use of policyholder's non-defective property is within the grant of coverage for property damage under CGL policy).

Florida: Nationwide Mutual Fire Insurance Co. v. Advanced Cooling and Heating, Inc., 2013 WL 5807880 (Fla. App. Oct. 30, 2013) (no coverage for defective work/materials); United States Fire Insurance Co. v. J.S.U.B., Inc., 2007 WL 4440232 (Fla. Dec. 20, 2007); Auto-Owners Insurance Co. v. Pozzi Window Co., 267 Fla. Appx. 552 (Fla. 2008).

Georgia: Taylor Morrison Services, Inc. v. HDI-Gerling America Insurance Co., 293 Ga. 456, 746 S.E.2d 587 (2013) (damage beyond policyholder's work is covered); SawHorse, Inc. v. Southern Guaranty Insurance Company of Georgia, 604 S.E.2d 541 (Ga. App. 2004).

Illinois: Country Mutual Insurance Co. v. Carr, 372 Ill. App.3d 335, 311 Ill. Dec. 171, 867 N.E.2d 1157 (Ill. App. 2007).

Indiana: Amerisure, Inc. v. Wurster Construction Co., 818 N.E.2d 998 (Ind. App. 2004), *clarified* 822 N.E.2d 1115 (Ind. App. 2005).

Louisiana: Stewart Interior Contractors, L.L.C. v. Metalpro Industries, L.L.C., 969 So.2d 653 (La. App. 2007).

Massachusetts: New Hampshire Insurance Co. v. Arpin, 842 N.E.2d 995 (Mass. App.), *review denied* 848 N.E.2d 1212 (Mass. 2006).

Missouri: Columbia Mutual Insurance Co. v. Epstein, 239 S.W.3d 667 (Mo. App. 2007).

New Hampshire: Webster v. Acadia Insurance Co., 934 A.2d 567 (N.H. 2007).

New Jersey: Firemen's Insurance Company of Newark v. National Union Fire Insurance Co., 904 A.2d 754 (N.J. Super. App. Div. 2006).

New York: I.J. White Corp. v. Columbia Casualty Co., 105 A.D.3d 531, 964 N.Y.S.2d 21 (N.Y. App. Div. 2013) (damage to property other than policyholder's work); Bonded Concrete, Inc. v. Transcontinental Insurance Co., 784 N.Y.S.2d 212, 12 A.D.3d 761 (N.Y. App. Div. 2004).

North Carolina: Erie Insurance Exchange v. Builders Mutual Insurance Co., 742 S.E.2d 803 (N.C. App. 2013) (faulty workmanship does not constitute property damage); Production Systems, Inc. v. Amerisure Insurance Co., 605 S.E.2d 663 (N.C. App. 2004).

Ohio: Erie Insurance Exchange v. Colony Development Corp., 2003 WL 23096010 (Ohio App. Dec. 31, 2003).

South Carolina: Auto Owners Insurance Co. v. Newman, 684 S.E.2d 187 (S.C. 2009).

Tennessee: Travelers Indemnity Company of America v. Moore & Associates, Inc., 216 S.W.3d 302 (Tenn. 2007).

Texas: Lennar Corp. v. Markel American Insurance Co., 2013 WL 4492800 (Tex. Aug. 23, 2013) (water damage from defective stucco covered); Lamar Homes, Inc. v. Mid-Continent Casualty Co., 242 S.W.3d 1 (Tex. 2007); Lennar Corp. v. Great American Insurance Co., 200 S.W.3d 651 (Tex. App. 2006), *substituted concurring and dissenting opinions* 2006 WL 909937 (Tex. App. 2006); Summit Custom Homes, Inc. v. Great American Lloyds Insurance Co., 202 S.W.3d 823 (Tex. App. 2006).

[134] See Lennar Corp. v. Markel American Insurance Co., 2013 WL 4492800 (Tex. Aug. 23, 2013).

[135] See:

Ninth Circuit: Willmar Development, L.L.C. v. Illinois National Insurance Co., 726 F. Supp.2d 1280 (D. Or. 2010).

State Courts:

Illinois: Viking Construction Management, Inc. v. Liberty Mutual Insurance Co., 358 Ill. App.3d 34, 831 N.E.2d 1, 294 Ill. Dec. 478 (2005) (discussing majority and minority positions).

Minnesota: Hauenstein v. St. Paul-Mercury Indemnity Co., 65 N.W.2d 122 (Minn. 1954).

Ohio: Erie Insurance Exchange v. Colony Development Corp., 2003 WL 23096010 (Ohio App. Dec. 31, 2003).

Wisconsin: American Family Mutual Insurance Co. v. American Girl, Inc., 673 N.W.2d 65 (Wis. 2004).

[136] See Turner, *Insurance Coverage for Construction Disputes*, § 5.28, at 129.

[137] See:

First Circuit: Berkshire-Cranwell Limited Partnership v. Tokio Marine and Nichido Fire Insurance Co., 874 F. Supp.2d 41 (D. Mass. 2012).

Second Circuit: Bridge Metal Industries, L.L.C. v. Travelers Indemnity Co., 812 F. Supp.2d 527 (S.D.N.Y. 2011).

Third Circuit: 21st Century North American Insurance Co. v. Wolfington, 892 F. Supp.2d 692 (E.D. Pa. 2012).

Fourth Circuit: Builders Mutual Insurance Co. v. OakTree Homes, Inc., 867 F. Supp.2d 800 (D.S.C. 2012).

Fifth Circuit: PPI Technology Services, L.P. v. Liberty Mutual Insurance Co., 515 Fed. Appx. 310 (5th Cir. 2013); DeLoach v. HGI Catastrophe Services, L.L.C., 460 Fed. Appx. 314 (5th Cir. 2012); *Audubon Insurance Co. v. Stefancik,* 98 F. Supp.2d 751 (S.D. Miss. 1999); Snug Harbor, Ltd. v. Zurich Insurance Co., 968 F.2d 538 (5th Cir. 1992).

Seventh Circuit: Amerisure Mutual Insurance Co. v. Microplastics, Inc., 622 F.3d 806 (7th Cir. 2010).

Ninth Circuit: Genesis Insurance Co. v. BRE Properties, 916 F. Supp.2d 1058 (N.D. Cal. 2013).

Tenth Circuit: Sterling Construction Management, L.L.C. v. Steadfast Insurance Co., 280 F.R.D. 576 (D. Colo. 2011).

Eleventh Circuit: Scottsdale Insurance Co. v. Pursley, 487 Fed. Appx. 508 (11th Cir. 2012).

State Courts:

Arizona: Nucor Corp. v. Employers Insurance Company of Wausau, 231 Ariz. 411, 296 P.3d 74 (Ariz. App. 2012).

California: Chatton v. National Union Fire Insurance Co., 10 Cal. App.4th 846, 13 Cal. Rptr.2d 318 (1992) ("economic damages" do not constitute "property damage" where there is no allegation of physical damage to tangible property); Giddings v. Industrial Indemnity Co., 112 Cal. App.3d 213, 169 Cal. Rptr. 278 (1980) (same).

Georgia: Maxum Indemnity Co. v. Jimenez, 318 Ga. App. 669, 734 S.E.2d 499 (2012).

Illinois: Universal Underwriters Insurance Co. v. LKQ Smart Parts, Inc., 963 N.E.2d 930, 357 Ill. Dec. 532 (Ill. App. 2011); West Bend Mutual Insurance Co. v. People, 401 Ill. App.3d 857, 929 N.E.2d 606, 340 Ill. Dec. 955 (2010); Viking Construction Management, Inc. v. Liberty Mutual Insurance Co., 358 Ill. App.3d 34, 831 N.E.2d 1, 7, 294 Ill. Dec. 478 (2005); Country Mutual Insurance Co. v. Carr, 2007 WL 899486 (Ill. App. Mar. 19, 2007).

Maine: Langevin v. Allstate Insurance Co., 66 A.3d 585 (Me. 2013).

Michigan: Krueger Seed Farms, Inc. v. Szlarczyk, 1999 WL 33453867, at *4–5 (Mich. App. Mar. 9, 1999) (since the underlying claims did not allege physical damage to tangible property, there was no "property damage"); Fitch v. State Farm Fire and Casualty Co., 536 N.W.2d 273, 275–276 (Mich. App. 1995) (same).

Minnesota: Farm Bureau Mutual Insurance Co. v. Earthsoils, Inc., 812 N.W.2d 873 (Minn. App. 2012).

Mississippi: W.R. Berkley Corp. v. Rea's Country Lane Construction, Inc., 2013 WL 3884909 (Miss. App. July 30, 2013) (purely pecuniary or economic losses are not property damage).

Texas: Evanston Insurance Co. v. Legacy of Life, Inc., 370 S.W.3d 377 (Tex. 2012).

138 See ISO Form CG 00 01 10 01.

139 See Hartzell Industries, Inc. v. Federal Insurance Co., 168 F. Supp.2d 789 (S.D. Ohio 2001) (partial loss of use of boiler house and resultant loss of worker productivity as a result of accident resulting in inability to use roof fan that caused house to become too hot was loss of use type of "property damage" even though damages represented purely economic losses).

140 See F & H Construction Co. v. ITT Hartford Insurance Company of Midwest, 118 Cal. App.4th 364, 12 Cal. Rptr.3d 896, 903 (2004).

141 See:

Seventh Circuit: W.E. O'Neil Construction Co. v. National Union Fire Insurance Co., 721 F. Supp. 984 (N.D. Ill. 1989).

Eighth Circuit: Western Casualty & Surety Co. v. Polar Panel Co., 457 F.2d 957 (8th Cir. 1972).

Ninth Circuit: Aetna Casualty & Surety Co. v. PPG Industries, Inc., 554 F. Supp. 290, 293–294 (D. Ariz. 1983).

State Courts:

California: F&H Construction Co. v. ITT Hartford Insurance Company of Midwest, 12 Cal. Rptr.3d 896, 903 (Cal. App. 2004).

Ohio: Akkon Brick & Block v. Travelers Insurance Co., 1983 WL 3931, at *5 (Ohio App. Nov. 30, 1983).

But see:

Ninth Circuit: New Hampshire Insurance Co. v. Viera, 930 F.2d 696 (9th Cir. 1991).

State Courts:

Iowa: Kartridg Pak Co. v. Travelers Indemnity Co., 425 N.W.2d 687 (Iowa App. 1988).

142 See *Couch on Insurance,* § 126:40 (3d ed.).

143 See, e.g., America Online, Inc. v. St. Paul Mercury Insurance Co., 347 F.3d 89 (4th Cir. 2003) (in third-party liability insurance context, electronic data is not covered intangible property, although the computers are covered).

144 See:

Seventh Circuit: Centenial Insurance Co. v. Applied Health Care Systems, Inc., 710 F.2d 1288 (7th Cir. 1983).

State Courts:

Minnesota: Retail Systems, Inc. v. CNA Insurance Cos., 469 N.W.2d 735, 737 (Minn. App. 1991) ("computer tape and data are tangible property under this policy. The data on the tape was of permanent value and was integrated completely with the physical property of the tape. Like a motion picture, where the information and the celluloid medium are integrated, so too were the tape and data integrated at the moment the tape was lost.").

145 *Fourth Circuit:* America Online, Inc. v. St. Paul Mercury Insurance Co., 347 F.3d 89, 95 (4th Cir. 2003) (applying Virginia law) ("the conclusion that physical magnetic material on the hard drive is tangible property is quite separate from the question of whether the data, information, and instructions, which are codified in a binary language for storage on the hard drive, are tangible property. . . . If the arrangement of the data and information stored on the hard drive were to become disordered or the instructions were to come into conflict with each another, the physical capabilities and properties of the hard drive would not be affected. Such disordering or conflicting instructions would amount to damage to the data and information and to the instructions (i.e., the software) but not to the hard drive. The magnetic material on the hard drive could be reoriented and reordered with reinstallation of the instructions. So it is that we make the distinction between hardware and software.").

Tenth Circuit: Cincinnati Insurance Co. v. Professional Data Services, Inc., 2003 WL 22102138 at *7 (D. Kan. July 18, 2003) ("Neither the . . . Software nor the data incorporated therein constitute tangible property because neither has any physical substance and neither is perceptible to the senses."); State Auto Property & Casualty Insurance Co. v. Midwest Computers & More, 147 F. Supp.2d 1113, 1116 (W.D. Okla. 2001) ("Although the medium that holds the information can be perceived, identified or valued, the information itself cannot be. Alone, computer data cannot be touched, held, or sensed by the human mind; it has no physical substance. It is not tangible property.").

146 See ISO Form CG 00 01 10 01. The location of the occurrence is rarely at issue. But it certainly is feasible that the location can be an issue because, as quoted above, the insuring agreement requires that the "occurrence" take place within the "coverage territory." If it is an issue, the "coverage territory" is usually defined in the policy. See, e.g.:

Fourth Circuit: CACI International, Inc. v. St. Paul Fire and Marine Insurance Co., 566 F.3d 150 (4th Cir. 2009).

Seventh Circuit: Ace American Insurance Co. v. RC2 Corp., 600 F.3d 763 (7th Cir. 2010);

Ninth Circuit: Hewlett-Packard Co. v. Ace Property and Casualty Insurance Co., 378 Fed. Appx. 739 (9th Cir. 2010).

If it is an issue, such as in the cases cited immediately before this sentence, the location of the accident/injury will usually answer the question. Hence, for defective construction, the location of the property at issue would be deemed to be the location of where the "occurrence" is deemed to have taken place.

147 See ISO Form CG 00 01 10 01.

148 See:

Third Circuit: Koppers Co. v. Aetna Casualty and Surety Co., 158 F.3d 170 (3d Cir. 1998); State Farm Fire & Casualty Co. v. Corry, 324 F. Supp.2d 666, 672 (E.D. Pa. 2004).

Fourth Circuit: USF Insurance Co. v. Orion Development RA XXX, L.L.C., 756 F. Supp.2d 749 (N.D. W. Va. 2010); Builders Mutual Insurance Co. v. Dragas Management Corp., 709 F. Supp.2d 441 (E.D. Va. 2010).

Fifth Circuit: Royal Insurance Company of America v. Caliber One Indemnity Co., 465 F.3d 614 (5th Cir. 2006).

Sixth Circuit: American Family Mutual Insurance Co. v. Bower, 752 F. Supp.2d 957 (N.D. Ind. 2010).

Seventh Circuit: Trinity Homes L.L.C. v. Ohio Casualty Insurance Co., 629 F.3d 653 (7th Cir. 2010); Jackson v. McKay-Davis Funeral Home, Inc., 717 F. Supp.2d 809 (E.D. Wis. 2010).

Eighth Circuit: Lexicon, Inc. v. ACE American Insurance Co., 634 F.3d 423 (8th Cir. 2010).

Ninth Circuit: Great American Insurance Co. v. Woodside Homes Corp., 448 F. Supp.2d 1275 (D. Utah. 2006).

State Courts:

California: Vandenberg v. Superior Court, 982 P.2d 229 (Cal. 1999); Medill v. Westport Insurance Corp., 49 Cal. Rptr.3d 570 (Cal. App. 2006); Roger H. Proulx & Co. v. Crest-Liners, Inc., 119 Cal. Rptr.2d 442 (Cal. App. 2002).

Connecticut: Colony Insurance Co. v. Walnut Beach, L.L.C., 2010 WL1224364 (Conn. Super. Feb. 25, 2010).

Indiana: Sheehan Construction Co. v. Continental Casualty Co., 935 N.E.2d 160 (Ind. 2010).

Kansas: Dickerson v. Schroeder, 132 P.3d 929 (Kan. 2006).

Minnesota: Wooddale Builders, Inc. v. Maryland Casualty Co., 722 N.W.2d 283 (Minn. 2006).

Missouri: D.R. Sherry Construction, Ltd. v. American Family Mutual Insurance Co., 316 S.W.3d 899 (Mo. 2010).

Nebraska: Dutton-Lainson Co. v. Continental Insurance Co., 778 N.W.2d 433 (Neb. 2010).

New Hampshire: Preferred National Insurance Co. v. Docusource, Inc., 829 A.2d 1068 (N.H. 2003).

New Jersey: D.R. v. Allstate Insurance Co., 2010 WL 289082 (N.J. Super. App. Dept. Jan. 27, 2010).

New York: Massa v. Nationwide Mutual Fire Insurance Co., 74 A.D.3d 1661, 904 N.Y.S.2d 531 (N.Y. App. 2010).

Oregon: ZRZ Realty Co. v. Beneficial Fire and Casualty Insurance Co., 349 Or. 117, 241 P.3d 710 (2010).

Tennessee: Travelers Indemnity Company of America v. Moore & Associates, Inc., 216 S.W.3d 302 (Tenn. 2007).

149 See:

Second Circuit: Scottsdale Insurance Co. v. R.I. Pools, Inc., 742 F. Supp.2d 239 (D. Conn. 2010) (no coverage but recognizing possibility if damage to non-defective work).

Third Circuit: Wassau Underwriters Insurance Co. v. State Automobile Mutual Insurance Co., 557 F. Supp.2d 502 (D.N.J. 2008) (applying Pennsylvania law and diustinguishing Kvaerner Metals v. Commercial Union Insurance Co., 908 A.2d 888 (Pa. 2006)).

Fourth Circuit: Builders Mutual Insurance Co. v. Dragas Management Corp., 709 F. Supp.2d 441 (E.D. Va. 2010); Builders Mutual Insurance Co. v. R Design Construction Co. 2010 WL 2079741 (D.S.C. May 24, 2010).

Fifth Circuit: Advanced Environmental Recycling Technologies, Inc. v. American International Specialty Lines Insurance Co., 399 Fed. Appx. 869 (5th Cir. 2010) (no occurrence because no damage to property other than defective material itself); Admiral Insurance Co. v. Little Big Inch Pipeline Co., Inc., 523 F. Supp.2d 524 (W.D. Tex. 2007).

Seventh Circuit: Trinity Homes L.L.C. v. Ohio Casualty Insurance Co., 629 F.3d 653 (7th Cir. 2010); Hartford Casualty Insurance Co. v. Construction Builders in Motion, Inc. 996 F. Supp.2d 777 (N.D. Ill. 2013).

Eighth Circuit: Lexicon, Inc. v. ACE American Insurance Co., 634 F.3d 423 (8th Cir. 2010); Cincinnati Insurance Co. v. Stolzer, 2010 WL 481298 (E.D. Mo. Feb. 5, 2010); Aten v. Scottsdale Insurance Co., 511 F.3d 818 (8th Cir. 2008).

Ninth Circuit: MW Builders, Inc. v. Safeco Insurance Co. of America, 2008 WL 422222 (9th Cir. Feb. 15, 2008); Willmar Development, L.L.C. v. Illinois National Insurance Co., 726 F. Supp.2d 1280 (D. Or. 2010); PMA Capital Insurance Co. v. American Safety Indemnity Co., 695 F. Supp.2d 1124 (E.D. Cal. 2010).

Tenth Circuit: Adair Group, Inc. v. St. Paul Fire & Marine Insurance Co., 477 F.3d 1186 (10th Cir. 2007); United Fire and Casualty Co. v. Boulder Plaza Residential, L.L.C., 2010 WL 420046 (D. Colo. Feb. 1, 2010).

Eleventh Circuit: Amerisure Mutual Insurance Co. v. Auchter Co., 2010 WL 457386 (M.D. Fla. Feb 4, 2010).

State Courts:

Alabama: Owners Insurance Co. v. Jim Carr Homebuilder, L.L.C., 157 So.3d 148 (Ala. 2014); United States Fidelity & Guaranty Co. v. Andalusia Ready Mix, Inc., 436 So.2d 868, 870 (Ala. 1983).

Arizona: Desert Mountain Properties Limited Partnership v. Liberty Mutual Fire Insurance Co., 236 P.3d 421 (Ariz. App. 2010); Lennar Corp. v. Auto-Owners Insurance Co., 151 P.3d 538 (Ariz. App. 2007) (differentiating between damage caused by defective construction and defective construction itself).

California: F & H Construction Co. v. ITT Hartford Insurance Company of Midwest, 12 Cal. Rptr.3d 896 (Cal. App. 2004); Maryland Casualty Co. v. Reeder, 270 Cal. Rptr. 719 (Cal. App. 1990).

Florida: Auto-Owners Insurance Co. v. Pozzi Window Co., 984 So.2d 1241 (Fla. 2008).

Georgia: Taylor Morrison Services, Inc. v. HDI-Gerling America Insurance Co., 746 S.E.2d 587 (Ga. 2013).

Illinois: Viking Construction Management, Inc. v. Liberty Mutual Insurance Co., 831 N.E.2d 1 (Ill. App. 2005).

Indiana: Amerisure, Inc. v. Wurster Construction Co., 818 N.E.2d 998 (Ind. App. 2004), *clarified* 822 N.E.2d 1115 (Ind. 2006); Jim Barna Log Systems Midwest, Inc. v. General Casualty Insurance Company of Wisconsin, 791 N.E.2d 816 (Ind. App. 2003).

Mississippi: W.R. Berkley Corp. v. Rea's Country Lane Construction, Inc., 2013 WL 3884909 (Miss. App. July 30, 2013).

Ohio: Erie Insurance Exchange v. Colony Development Corp., 2003 WL 23096010, at *5 (Ohio App. Dec. 31, 2003).

Tennessee: Travelers Indemnity Company of America v. Moore & Associates, Inc., 216 S.W.3d 302 (Tenn. 2007).

Texas: Grimes Construction, Inc. v. Great American Lloyds Insurance Co., 248 S.W.3d 171 (Tex. 2008); Lennar Corp. v. Great American Insurance Co., 200 S.W.3d 651 (Tex. App.), *substituted concurring and dissenting opinions* 2006 WL 909937 (Tex. App. 2006).

West Virginia: Cherrington v. Erie Insurance Property and Casualty Co., 745 S.E.2d 508 (W. Va. 2013); Webster County Solid Waste Authority v. Brackenrich & Associates, Inc., 617 S.E.2d 851 (W. Va. 2005).

See also, Turner, *Insurance Coverage of Construction Disputes*, §§ 5.43–5.47, at 154–159; Bruner and O'Connor, *Bruner & O'Connor on Construction Law*, § 11:213 (2018).

150 See, e.g., Turner, *Insurance Coverage for Construction Disputes*, §§ 5.43–5.47, at 154–159; Bruner and O'Connor, *Bruner & O'Connor on Construction Law*, § 11:213 (2018).

See also:

Sixth Circuit: Liberty Mutual Fire Insurance Co. v. Kay and Kay Contracting, L.L.C., 2013 WL 6084276 (6th Cir. Nov. 19, 2013).

Eleventh Circuit: Owners Insurance Co. v. James, 295 F. Supp.2d 1354 (N.D. Ga. 2003).

State Courts:

Nebraska: Auto-Owners Insurance Co. v. Home Pride Cos., 684 N.W.2d 571 (Neb. 2004).

Pennsylvania: Kvaerner Metals v. Commercial Union Insurance Co., 908 A.2d 888 (Pa. 2006).

South Carolina: L-J, Inc. v. Bituminous Fire and Marine Insurance Co., 621 S.E.2d 33 (S.C. 2005).

151 Of course, the law has now been clarified in Pennsylvania. Now, claims for damage caused by faulty workmanship are not covered by the CGL policy. See, e.g., Specialty Surfaces International, Inc. v. Continental Casualty Co., 609 F.3d 223 (3d Cir. 2010); Pennsylvania National Mutual Casualty Insurance Co. v. Parkshore Development Corp., 403 Fed. Appx. 770 (3d Cir. 2010) (applying New Jersey law); Bomgardner v. State Farm Fire and Casualty Insurance Co., 2010 WL 3657084 (E.D. Pa. Sept. 14, 2010) (applying Pennsylvania law); Erie Insurance Exchange v. Abbott Furnace Co., 972 A.2d 1232 (Pa. Super. 2009); Millers Capital Insurance Co. v. Gambone Brothers Development Co., 941 A.2d 706 (Pa. Super. 2007).

152 See:

Third Circuit: West American Insurance Co. v. Lindepuu, 128 F. Supp.2d 220 (E.D. Pa. 2000) (applying Pennsylvania law) (refusing to find no "occurrence" in claim by owner against contractor for defective installation of windows and doors).

Fourth Circuit: Limbach Co. v. Zurich American Insurance Co., 396 F.3d 358 (4th Cir. 2005) (applying Pennsylvania law) (damages caused by defective construction that led to a pipe leak, including damage to non-defective backfill work, non-defective piping, and cost to remove and redo the concrete and landscaping work to get to the problem was a covered "occurrence").

State Courts:

Pennsylvania: Kvaerner Metals v. Commercial Union Insurance Co., 825 A.2d 641 (Pa. Super. 2003) (claim by owner for damage to coke oven battery caused by defective construction and torrential rains after work was completed was an "occurrence" under the builder's CGL insurance policy); Barber v. Harleysville Mutual Insurance Co., 450 A.2d 718

(Pa. Super. 1982) (claim by owner for negligent breach of contract was an "occurrence" under the contractor's CGL insurance policy); Nitterhouse Concrete Products v. Pennsylvania Manufacturers' Association Insurance Co., 67 Pa. D. & C.4th 225 (Pa. C.P. 2004) (breach of contract claim by school district against contractor for defective pre-cast concrete work that caused unintended structural problems to the school was an "occurrence" under the contractor's CGL insurance policy).

[153] See:

Fifth Circuit: Data Specialties, Inc. v. Transcontinental Insurance Co., 125 F.3d 909 (5th Cir. 1997).

Tenth Circuit: VBF, Inc. v. Chubb Group of Insurance Cos., 263 F.3d 1226 (10th Cir. 2001); Adair Group, Inc. v. St. Paul Fire & Marine Insurance Co., 477 F.3d 1186 (10th Cir. 2007).

Eleventh Circuit: Key Custom Homes, Inc. v. Mid-Continent Casualty Co., 450 F. Supp.2d 1311 (M.D. Fla. 2006).

State Courts:

Alabama: United States Fidelity & Guaranty Co. v. Andalusia Ready Mix, Inc., 436 So.2d 868, 870 (Ala. 1983).

Arizona: Lennar Corp. v. Auto-Owners Insurance Co., 151 P.3d 538 (Ariz. App. 2007) (differentiating between damage caused by defective construction and defective construction itself).

California: F & H Construction Co. v. ITT Hartford Insurance Company of Midwest, 12 Cal. Rptr.3d 896 (Cal. App. 2004); Maryland Casualty Co. v. Reeder, 270 Cal. Rptr. 719 (Cal. App. 1990).

Georgia: McDonald Construction Co. v. Bituminous Casualty Corp., 632 S.E.2d 420 (Ga. App. 2006); Custom Planning & Development, Inc. v. American National Fire Insurance Co., 606 S.E.2d 39 (Ga. App. 2004).

Illinois: Viking Construction Management, Inc. v. Liberty Mutual Insurance Co., 831 N.E.2d 1 (Ill. App. 2005).

Indiana: Amerisure, Inc. v. Wurster Construction Co., 818 N.E.2d 998 (Ind. App. 2004), *clarified* 822 N.E.2d 1115 (Ind. 2006); Jim Barna Log Systems Midwest, Inc. v. General Casualty Insurance Company of Wisconsin, 791 N.E.2d 816 (Ind. App. 2003).

New Jersey: Atlantic Mutual Insurance Co. v. Hillside Bottling Co., 903 A.2d 513 (N.J. Super. App. Div. 2006).

New York: Perras Excavating, Inc. v. Transportation Insurance Co., 737 N.Y.S.2d 692 (N.Y. App. Div. 2002); Bonded Concrete, Inc. v. Transcontinental Insurance Co., 784 N.Y.S.2d 212 (N.Y. App. Div. 2004).

Ohio: Erie Insurance Exchange v. Colony Development Corp., 2003 WL 23096010, at *5 (Ohio App. Dec. 31, 2003).

Pennsylvania: Kvaerner Metals v. Commercial Union Insurance Co., 908 A.2d 888 (Pa. 2006); Pennsylvania Manufacturers' Association Insurance Co. v. L.B. Smith, Inc., 831 A.2d 1178 (Pa. Super. 2003).

Tennessee: Travelers Indemnity Company of America v. Moore & Associates, Inc., 216 S.W.3d 302 (Tenn. 2007).

Texas: Lennar Corp. v. Great American Insurance Co., 200 S.W.3d 651 (Tex. App.), *substituted concurring and dissenting opinions* 2006 WL 909937 (Tex. App. 2006).

West Virginia: Webster County Solid Waste Authority v. Brackenrich & Associates, Inc., 617 S.E.2d 851 (W. Va. 2005).

See also, Turner, *Insurance Coverage of Construction Disputes*, §§ 5.43–5.47, at 154–159.

[154] See, e.g., Brosnahan Builders, Inc. v. Harleysville Mutual Insurance Co., 137 F. Supp.2d 517 (D. Del. 2001), *aff'd* 2003 WL 146486 (3d Cir.), *cert. denied* 540 U.S. 820 (2003) (applying Pennsylvania law).

[155] See:

Third Circuit: ProDent, Inc. v. Zurich U.S., 33 Fed. Appx. 32 (3d Cir. 2002) (applying Pennsylvania law) (claim against plumbing contractor for installation of wrong pipes resulting in a jury verdict for negligence was not an "occurrence" under contractor's CGL insurance policy); Jerry Davis, Inc. v. Maryland Insurance Co., 38 F. Supp.2d 387 (E.D. Pa. 1999) (claim for faulty electrical work was not an "occurrence" under the electrical contractor's CGL insurance policy).

State Courts:

Pennsylvania: Freestone v. New England Log Homes, Inc., 819 A.2d 550 (Pa. Super.), *alloc. denied* 847 A.2d 1286 (Pa. 2003) (claims for breach of contract, breach of warranty, and negligence by purchaser of log home building kit for defective product was not an "occurrence"); Solcar Equipment Leasing Corp. v. Pennsylvania Manufacturers' Association Insurance Co., 606 A.2d 522 (Pa. Super. 1992) (claim against contractor for negligence and breach of contract causing structural damage was not an "occurrence").

See also, Turner, *Insurance Coverage for Construction Disputes*, §§ 5.43–5.47, at 154–159.

[156] Kvaerner Metals v. Commercial Union Insurance Co., 908 A.2d 888 (Pa. 2006).

[157] *Id.*, 908 A.2d at 899.

> "We hold that the definition of 'accident' required to establish an 'occurrence' under the policies cannot be satisfied by claims based upon faulty workmanship. Such claims simply do not present the degree of fortuity contemplated by the ordinary definition of 'accident' or its common judicial construction in this context."

[158] *Id.*

[159] *Id.*

[160] *Id.*, 908 A.2d at 898–899 (Pa. 2006), quoting Snyder Heating v. Pennsylvania Manufacturer's Association Insurance Co., 715 A.2d 483, 487 (Pa. Super. 1998) (occurrence exists if policyholder's work or products actively malfunctions resulting in damage to another's property). See also, L-J, Inc. v. Bituminous Fire & Marine Insurance Co., 621 S.E.2d 33, 36 n.4 (S.C. 2005).

As stated above, the law appeared to have been clarified in Pennsylvania that claims for damage caused by faulty workmanship do not arise from an "occurrence" and are therefore not covered by the CGL policy. See, e.g.: Specialty Surfaces International, Inc. v. Continental Casualty Co., 609 F.3d 223 (3d Cir. 2010); Pennsylvania National Mutual Casualty Insurance Co. v. Parkshore Development Corp., 403 Fed. Appx. 770 (3d Cir. Dec. 10, 2010) (applying New Jersey law); Bomgardner v. State Farm Fire and Casualty Insurance Co., 2010 WL 3657084 (E.D. Pa. Sept. 14, 2010) (applying Pennsylvania law); Erie Insurance Exchange v. Abbott Furnace Co., 972 A.2d 1232 (Pa. Super. 2009); Millers Capital Insurance Co. v. Gambone Brothers Development Co., 941 A.2d 706 (Pa. Super. 2007). However, a subsequent decision has opened the door to damage to property not within the work product itself. See Pennsylvania National Mutual Casualty Insurance Co. v. St. John, 106 A.3d 1 (Pa. 2014) (coverage for damage to herd by negligent installation of plumbing system by plumbing contractor, thereby limiting *Kvaerner* to claims for damage to the work product itself).

[161] See, e.g., Kvaerner Metals v. Commercial Union Insurance Co., 908 A.2d 888 (Pa. 2006).

[162] *Id.*, 908 A.2d at 900, n.10

[163] See:

Second Circuit: Scottsdale Insurance Co. v. R.I. Pools, Inc., 742 F. Supp.2d 239 (D. Conn. 2010).

Third Circuit: Specialty Surfaces International, Inc. v. Continental Casualty Co., 609 F.3d 223 (3d Cir. 2010); Nationwide Mutual Insurance Co. v. CPB International, Inc., 562 F.3d 591 (3d Cir. 2009); Bomgardner v. State Farm Fire and Casualty Insurance Co., 2010 WL 3657084 (E.D. Pa. Sept. 14, 2010); Century Surety Co. v. QSC Painting, Inc., 2010 WL 891245 (W.D. Pa. Mar. 8, 2010).

Fifth Circuit: Data Specialties, Inc. v. Transcontinental Insurance Co., 125 F.3d 909 (5th Cir. 1997) (CGL policy does not cover contract liabilities).

Sixth Circuit: Lenning v. Commercial Union Insurance Co., 260 F.3d 574 (6th Cir. 2001).

Ninth Circuit: Burlington Insurance Co. v. United Coatings Manufacturing Co., 518 F. Supp.2d 1241 (D. Haw. 2007); WDC Venture v. Hartford Accident and Indemnity Co., 938 F. Supp. 671 (D. Haw. 1996).

Tenth Circuit: Great Divide insurance Co. v. Bitterroot Timberframes of Wyoming, L.L.C., 2006 WL 3933078 (D. Wyo. Oct. 20, 2006); VBF, Inc. v. Chubb Group of Insurance Cos., 263 F.3d 1226 (10th Cir. 2001) (CGL policy only covers tort claims asserted against insured, and not contract claims).

Eleventh Circuit: The Burt Co. v. Clarendon National Insurance Co., 385 Fed. Appx. 892 (11th Cir. 2010); State Farm Fire and Casualty Co. v. Diner Concepts, Inc., 370 Fed. Appx. 56 (11th Cir. 2010); Key Custom Homes, Inc. v. Mid-Continent Casualty Co., 450 F. Supp.2d 1311 (M.D. Fla. 2006) (CGL policy only covers tort based liabilities).

State Courts:

Georgia: McDonald Construction Co. v. Bituminous Casualty Corp., 632 S.E.2d 420 (Ga. App. 2006) (replacement of defective tiles not covered); Custom Planning & Development, Inc. v. American National Fire Insurance Co., 606 S.E.2d 39 (Ga. App. 2004) (business risk borne by the contractor to replace or repair defective work to make the building project conform to the agreed contractual requirements is not covered under contractor's CGL policy; coverage applicable under CGL policy is for tort liability for injury to persons and damage to other property, not for contractual liability of the insured for economic loss because the product or completed work is not that for which the damaged person bargained); Hathaway Development Co. v. American Empire Surplus Lines Insurance Co., 301 Ga. App. 65, 686 S.E.2d 855 (2009).

Hawaii: Group Builders, Inc. v. Admiral Insurance Co., 123 Haw. 142, 231 P.3d 67 (Haw. App. 2010).

Illinois: Viking Construction Management, Inc. v. Liberty Mutual Insurance Co., 831 N.E.2d 1 (Ill. App. 2005) (CGL policy does not cover underlying claim for breach of contract).

Indiana: Amerisure, Inc. v. Wurster Construction Co., 818 N.E.2d 998 (Ind. App. 2004), *clarified* 822 N.E.2d 1115 (Ind. App. 2005) (coverage for property damage under CGL policy is for tort liability for physical damages to others, not for contractual liability of the insured for economic loss); Jim Barna Log Systems Midwest, Inc. v. General Casualty Insurance Company of Wisconsin, 791 N.E.2d 816 (Ind. App. 2003) (CGL insurance policy is for tort liability for physical damages to others and not for the business risk of contractual liability of the insured for economic loss because the product or completed work is not that for which the damaged person bargained).

Massachusetts: National Union Fire Insurance Company of Pittsburgh, PA v. Modern Continental Construction Co., 2009 WL 6376180 (Mass. Super. Dec. 11, 2009).

New Jersey: Atlantic Mutual Insurance Co. v. Hillside Bottling Co., 903 A.2d 513 (N.J. Super. App. Div. 2006) (risk intended to be insured by a CGL policy is the possibility that the goods, products, or work of the insured, once relinquished or completed, will cause bodily injury or damage to property other than to the product or completed work itself; the coverage is for tort liability for physical damages to others and not for contractual liability of the insured for economic loss because the product or completed work is not that for which the damaged person bargained).

New York: Perras Excavating, Inc. v. Transportation Insurance Co., 737 N.Y.S.2d 692 (N.Y. App. Div. 2002) (breach of contract claim not covered under CGL policy); Bonded Concrete, Inc. v. Transcontinental Insurance Co., 784 N.Y.S.2d 212 (N.Y. App. Div. 2004) (purpose of CGL policy is to provide coverage for tort liability for physical damage to others, and not for insured's contractual liability for economic loss because its product is not what the damaged party bargained for).

Pennsylvania: Kvaerner Metals v. Commercial Union Insurance Co., 908 A.2d 888 (Pa. 2006) (no coverage for contractual liability for repair of work product); Pennsylvania Manufacturers' Association Insurance Co. v. L.B. Smith, Inc., 831 A.2d 1178 (Pa. Super. 2003) (no coverage for contractual liability).

164 See:

Fourth Circuit: Builders Mutual Insurance Co. v. Dragas Management Corp., 709 F. Supp.2d 441 (E.D. Va. 2010).

Fifth Circuit: Westchester Surplus Lines Insurance Co. v. Maverick Tube Corp., 590 F.3d 316 (5th Cir. 2009).

Sixth Circuit: Houseman Construction Co. v. Cincinnati Insurance Co., 2010 WL 1658959 (W.D. Mich. Apr. 23, 2010).

Ninth Circuit: Gulf Insurance Co. v. L.A. Effects Group, Inc., 827 F.2d 574, 577 (9th Cir. 1987) (inadequate performance of contract may result in a covered claim).

Tenth Circuit: Great American Insurance Co. v. Woodside Homes Corp., 448 F. Supp.2d 1275 (D. Utah 2006).

State Courts:

Arizona: Desert Mountain Properties Limited Partnership v. Liberty Mutual Fire Insurance Co., 225 Ariz. 194, 236 P.3d 421 (Ariz. App. 2010).

California: Vandenberg v. Superior Court, 982 P.2d 229 (Cal. 1999) (CGL policy can provide coverage for tort and contract claims).

Illinois: CMK Development Corp. v. West Bend Mutual Insurance Co., 395 Ill. App.3d 830, 917 N.E.2d 1155, 335 Ill. Dec. 91 (2009).

Kansas: Lee Builders, Inc. v. Farm Bureau Mutual Insurance Co., 137 P.3d 486 (Kan. 2006) (coverage for contract and tort claims).

Minnesota: Wanzek Construction, Inc. v. Employers Insurance of Wausau, 667 N.W.2d 473 (Minn. App. 2003), *aff'd* 679 N.E.2d 322 (Minn. 2004) (When an insurance policy provides coverage for sums that the insured is "legally obligated to pay as damages," the insured need not have had litigation commenced against it for the policy to be triggered, but is entitled to coverage based solely on a contractual duty to replace faulty building materials.).

North Dakota: ACUITY v. Burd & Smith Construction, Inc., 721 N.W.2d 33 (N.D. 2006) (breach of contract claims are within scope of coverage of CGL policy that was sold to general contractor; CGL policy could provide coverage for tort claims, contract claims, and claims for statutory violations as long as requisite accidental occurrence and property damage were present).

Texas: Lennar Corp. v. Great American Insurance Co., 200 S.W.3d 651 (Tex. App.), *substituted concurring and dissenting opinions* 2006 WL 909937 (Tex. App. Apr. 11, 2006) (construction defect claims sounding in contact and in tort can be covered by CGL policy if the claims result in "property damage" that is unexpected and unintended).

Wisconsin: American Family Mutual Insurance Co. v. American Girl, Inc., 673 N.W.2d 65 (Wis. 2004) (language of CGL policy and the purpose of the CGL insuring agreement will provide coverage for claims sounding in part in breach of contract/breach of warranty under some circumstances).

165 See, e.g., Prost v. Caldwell Store, Inc., 187 A.2d 273, 275, 277 (Pa. 1963):

> "[A] party to a contract by the very nature of his contractual undertaking may place himself in such a position that the law will impose upon him a duty to perform his contractual undertaking in such manner that third persons—strangers to the contract—will not be injured thereby. . . . Where a builder creates a hazard which, without the need of a prophetic telescope, proclaims potential injury to the public, he may not plead immunity from liability for resulting damage on the basis that his responsibility ceased with the insertion of the last bolt and the driving of the final nail."

See also: DeTillo v. Carlyn Construction, Inc., 206 A.2d 376, 378 (Pa. 1965) (contractor's negligence in constructing home improvements was a sufficient basis for a subsequent homeowner to recover, despite the absence of privity, because it is foreseeable that third-party homeowners would subsequently take possession of the home); Woodward v. Dietrich, 548 A.2d 301, 314–315 (Pa. Super. 1988) (homeowner may sue a prior homeowner and the contractor the prior homeowner hired, despite the lack of privity with the contractor, for intentional misrepresentations where subsequent homeowners' reliance on those misrepresentations is "specially foreseeable").

166 Pennsylvania State Employees Credit Union v. Fifth 3rd Bank, 398 F. Supp.2d 317, 329 n.5 (M.D. Pa. 2005).

167 *Id.*, 398 F. Supp.2d at 327.

168 *Id.*, at 327 (M.D. Pa. 2005) (emphasis added), citing Adams v. Copper Beach Townhome Communities, L.P., 816 A.2d 301, 305 (Pa. Super. 2003). See also, Spivack v. Berks Ridge Corp., 586 A.2d 402, 405 (Pa. Super. 1990).

169 Kvaerner Metals v. Commercial Union Insurance Co., 908 A.2d 888 (Pa. 2006).

170 See:

Third Circuit: Pennsylvania State Employees Credit Union v. Fifth 3rd Bank, 398 F. Supp.2d 317 (M.D. Pa. 2005).

State Courts:

Pennsylvania: Adams v. Copper Beach Townhome Communities, L.P., 816 A.2d 301, 305 (Pa. Super. 2003); Spivack v. Berks Ridge Corp, 586 A.2d 402, 405 (Pa. Super. 1990); Kvaerner Metals v. Commercial Union Insurance Co., 908 A.2d 888 (Pa. 2006).

171 *Id.*

172 Kvaerner Metals v. Commercial Union Insurance Co., 908 A.2d 888 (Pa. 2006).

173 *Id.*, 908 A.2d at 898–899 ("a CGL policy may provide coverage where faulty workmanship caused bodily injury or damage to another property, but not in cases where faulty workmanship damages the work product alone. . . . To permit coverage in such instances would convert CGL policies into performance bonds, which guarantee the work, rather than like an insurance policy, which is intended to insure against accidents.").

174 *Id.*, 908 A.2d at 897–900 (Pa. 2006). The *Kvaerner* decision is consistent with prior Pennsylvania authorities, which hold that damage to other property, including non-defective completed operations, caused by faulty workmanship results from an "occurrence." See, e.g.:

Fourth Circuit: Limbach Co. v. Zurich American Insurance Co., 396 F.3d 358 (4th Cir. 2005) (applying Pennsylvania law) (contractor was entitled to coverage for damage to non-defective, completed portions of work product damaged by faulty or defective workmanship that was also part of the contracted work product).

State Courts:

Pennsylvania: Gene & Harvey Builders, Inc. v. Pennsylvania Manufacturer's Association Insurance Co., 517 A.2d 910 (Pa. 1986) (homeowner's claim against builder for damages to non-defective, completed portions of work product caused by specific defects arises from an "occurrence" but was excluded by certain exclusions not applicable here); Snyder Heating v. Pennsylvania Manufacturer's Association Insurance Co., 715 A.2d 483, 494 (Pa. Super. 1998); Carpenter v. Federal Insurance Co., 637 A.2d 1008 (Pa. Super. 1994), *alloc. denied* 655 A.2d 982 (Pa. 1995) (defective electrical work that resulted in a fire that destroyed the home was a covered "occurrence" under the general contractor's liability insurance policy).

Other decisions applying Pennsylvania law hold that where damage occurs to non-defective completed operations arising from defective workmanship, an "occurrence" exists. See:

Fourth Circuit: Limbach Co. v. Zurich American Insurance Co., 396 F.3d 358 (4th Cir. 2005) (applying Pennsylvania law) (contractor was entitled to coverage for damage to non-defective, completed portions of work product damaged by faulty or defective workmanship that was also part of the contracted work product).

State Courts:

Pennsylvania: Carpenter v. Federal Insurance Co., 637 A.2d 1008 (Pa. Super. 1994), *alloc. denied* 655 A.2d 982 (Pa. 1995) (defective electrical work which resulted in a fire that destroyed the home was a covered "occurrence" under the general contractor's liability insurance policy).

In addition, authorities elsewhere but relied upon by the *Kvaerner* court elucidate this distinction and make clear that *Kvaerner* never intended to change the law. See:

Fourth Circuit: Harleysville Mutual Insurance Co. v. Cambridge Building Corp., 2006 WL 2038302 (D.S.C. July 19, 2006) (applying South Carolina law) ("where the complaint alleged negligent construction that resulted in property damage caused by continuous exposure to moisture, and not merely negligent construction damaging only the work product, the CGL policy provided coverage").

State Courts:

New Hampshire: High Country Associates v. New Hampshire Insurance Co., 648 A.2d 474, 477 (N.H. 1994); McAllister v. Peerless Insurance Co., 474 A.2d 1033, 1036–1037 (N.H. 1984) ("defective work, standing alone, [does] not result from an occurrence, and indeed [is] not property damage within the meaning of the policy").

Nebraska: Auto-Owners Insurance Co. v. Home Pride Cos., 684 N.W.2d 571 (Neb. 2004) (damage was caused by an "occurrence" because there were claims of property damage caused by the alleged defects).

South Carolina: L-J, Inc. v. Bituminous Fire & Marine Insurance Co., 621 S.E.2d 33 (S.C. 2005).

175 See:

Second Circuit: Scottsdale Insurance Co. v. R.I. Pools, Inc., 742 F. Supp.2d 239 (D. Conn. 2010) (no coverage but recognizing possibility if damage to non-defective work).

Fourth Circuit: French v. Assurance Company of America, 448 F.3d 693 (4th Cir. 2006) (repair of defect not a covered occurrence but repair of damage caused by the defect, even damage to non-defective completed portions of work product, is a covered occurrence); Builders Mutual Insurance Co. v. Dragas Management Corp., 709 F. Supp.2d 441 (E.D. Va. 2010); Builders Mutual Insurance Co. v. R Design Construction Co. 2010 WL 2079741 (D.S.C. May 24, 2010); Harleysville Mutual Insurance Co. v. Cambridge Building Corp., 2006 WL 2038302 (D.S.C. July 19, 2006) (noting distinction between a claim for faulty workmanship and a claim for damages in the work product caused by the negligence of a third party); Auto-Owners Insurance Co. v. Zurich US, 377 F. Supp.2d 496 (D.S.C. 2004) (similar).

Fifth Circuit: Advanced Environmental Recycling Technologies, Inc. v. American International Specialty Lines Insurance Co., 399 Fed. Appx. 869 (5th Cir. 2010) (no occurrence because no damage to property other than defective material itself); Federated Mutual Insurance Co. v. Grapevine Excavation, Inc., 197 F.3d 720 (5th Cir. 1999) (parking lot damage from installation of substandard fill is a covered occurrence).

Seventh Circuit: Trinity Homes L.L.C. v. Ohio Casualty Insurance Co., 629 F.3d 653 (7th Cir. 2010); Durbrow v. Mike Check Builders, Inc., 442 F. Supp.2d 676 (E.D. Wis. 2006) (property damage to house caused by moisture seepage due to faulty work constituted occurrence under contractor's CGL policy).

Eighth Circuit: Lexicon, Inc. v. ACE American Insurance Co., 634 F.3d 423 (8th Cir. 2010); Transcontinental Insurance Co. v. W.G. Samuels Co., 370 F.3d 755 (8th Cir. 2004) (carpet installation negligence resulting in delamination of carpet was covered occurrence); Cincinnati Insurance Co. v. Stolzer, 2010 WL 481298 (E.D. Mo. Feb. 5, 2010).

Ninth Circuit: Willmar Development, L.L.C. v. Illinois National Insurance Co., 726 F. Supp.2d 1280 (D. Or. 2010); PMA Capital Insurance Co. v. American Safety Indemnity Co., 695 F. Supp.2d 1124 (E.D. Cal. 2010); Gary G. Day Construction Co. v. Clarendon America Insurance Co., 459 F. Supp.2d 1039 (D. Nev. 2006) (water intrusion caused by faulty workmanship in connection with window caulking arose from covered occurrence).

Tenth Circuit: Adair Group, Inc. v. St. Paul Fire & Marine Insurance Co., 477 F.3d 1186 (10th Cir. 2007) (defective construction alone is not a covered occurrence; damage resulting from defective construction is a covered occurrence); United Fire and Casualty Co. v. Boulder Plaza Residential, L.L.C., 2010 WL 420046 (D. Colo. Feb. 1, 2010).

Eleventh Circuit: Amerisure Mutual Insurance Co. v. Auchter Co., 2010 WL 457386 (M.D. Fla. Feb 4, 2010); IDC Construction, LLC. v. Admiral Insurance Co., 339 F. Supp.2d 1342 (S.D. Fla. 2004) (water intrusion damage caused by faulty workmanship is a covered occurrence in a claim against a general contractor).

State Courts:

Arizona: Desert Mountain Properties Limited Partnership v. Liberty Mutual Fire Insurance Co., 225 Ariz. 194, 236 P.3d 421 (Ariz. App. 2010); Lennar Corp. v. Auto-Owners Insurance Co., 151 P.3d 538 (Ariz. App. 2007) (developer owed a defense in claim by homeowners for damage to completed, non-defective home caused by soil subsidence as a result of developer's negligence was potentially covered "occurrence;" distinguishing between faulty workmanship and damages caused thereby).

Colorado: Hoang v. Assurance Company of America, 129 P.3d 1028 (Colo. App. 2005), *rev'd on other grounds* 149 P.3d 798 (Colo. 2007) (damage to homes caused by soil problems arose from a covered occurrence); American Employer's Insurance Co. v. Pinkard Construction Co., 806 P.2d 954 (Colo. App. 1990) (roof corrosion caused by use of improper fill material arose from occurrence).

Georgia: QBE Insurance Co. v. Couch Pipeline and Grading, Inc., 303 Ga. App. 196, 692 S.E.2d 795 (2010).

Illinois: Monticello Insurance Co. v. Wil-Freds Construction, Inc., 661 N.E.2d 451, 456 (Ill. App. 1996) ("natural results of negligent and unworkmanlike construction of a building do not constitute an occurrence").

Indiana: Sheehan Construction Co. v. Continental Casualty Co., 935 N.E.2d 160 (Ind. 2010).

Kansas: Lee Builders, Inc. v. Farm Bureau Mutual Insurance Co., 137 P.3d 486 (Kan. 2006) (claim against general contractor for water intrusion damages from faulty installation of windows by subcontractor arose from a covered occurrence).

Louisiana: Rando v. Top Notch Properties, L.L.C., 879 So.2d 821 (La. App. 2004) (faulty pile driving work resulting in structural damages was a covered occurrence).

Maryland: Lerner Corp. v. Assurance Company of America, 707 A.2d 906 (Md. App. 1998) (repair of defect not a covered occurrence but repair of damage caused by the defect, even damage to non-defective completed portions of work product are a covered occurrence).

Minnesota: Kootenia Homes, Inc. v. Federated Mutual Insurance Co., 2006 WL 224162 (Minn. App. Jan. 31, 2006) (general contractor entitled to coverage for moisture intrusion damages caused by faulty stucco work); Westfield Insurance Co. v. Kroiss, 694 N.W.2d 102 (Minn. App. 2005) (water damage resulting from defective construction was a covered occurrence); Parr v. Gonzalez, 669 N.W.2d 401 (Minn. App. 2003) (roofing contractor's negligence resulting in damage to heating system vent cap was covered occurrence).

Mississippi: Architex Association, Inc. v. Scottsdale Insurance Co., 27 So.3d 1148 (Miss. 2010).

Missouri: D.R. Sherry Construction, Ltd. v. American Family Mutual Insurance Co., 316 S.W.3d 899 (Mo. 2010).

Montana: Swank Enterprises, Inc. v. All Purpose Services, Ltd., 154 P.3d 52 (Mont. 2007) (subcontractor's selection and application of improper paint for water treatment plant pipes and tanks was covered occurrence).

Nebraska: Auto-Owners Insurance Co. v. Home Pride Cos., 684 N.W.2d 571 (Neb. 2004) (roofing contractor's faulty workmanship in installation of new shingles on an apartment building resulting in suit by the owner averring damage to the roof structure and other portions of the buildings was covered).

New Hampshire: Concord General Mutual Insurance Co. v. Green and Company Building and Development Corp., 160 N.H. 690, 8 A.3d 24 (2010); High Country Associates v. New Hampshire Insurance Co., 648 A.2d 474, 477 (N.H. 1994) (finding coverage for water damage to non-defective completed portions of homes caused by certain defects in the exterior cladding); McAllister v. Peerless Insurance Co., 474 A.2d 1033, 1036–1037 (N.H. 1984) ("defective work, standing alone, [does] not result from an occurrence, and indeed [is] not property damage within the meaning of the policy").

New Jersey: Firemen's Insurance Company of Newark v. National Union Fire Insurance Co., 904 A.2d 754 (N.J. Super. App. Div. 2006) (repair of defective workmanship is not an occurrence; there must be damage to non-defective work); Atlantic Mutual Insurance Co. v. Hillside Bottling Co., 903 A.2d 513 (N.J. Super. App. Div.), *certif. denied* 912 A.2d 1264 (N.J. 2006) (CGL policy does not cover an accident of faulty workmanship, but covers faulty workmanship which causes an accident).

North Carolina: Harleysville Mutual Insurance Co. v. Berkley Insurance Company of Carolinas, 610 S.E.2d 215 (N.C. App. 2005) (water damage from defective stucco arises from covered occurrence).

North Dakota: ACUITY v. Burd & Smith Construction, Inc., 721 N.W.2d 33 (N.D. 2006) (alleged water damage to interior of apartment building during replacement of building's roof constituted an occurrence under general contractor's CGL insurance policy because faulty workmanship allegedly caused damage to property other than general contractor's work product).

Ohio: Erie Insurance Exchange v. Colony Development Corp., 2003 WL 23096010, at *5 (Ohio App. Dec. 31, 2003) (negligent construction resulting in damage to non-defective portions of property is a covered occurrence).

Pennsylvania: Kvaerner Metals v. Commercial Union Insurance Co., 908 A.2d 888 (Pa. 2006) (no coverage for repair of defectively built coke oven battery because damages involved solely the repair of a defect as opposed to the repair of damages caused thereby).

South Carolina: L-J, Inc. v. Bituminous Fire & Marine Insurance Co., 621 S.E.2d 33, 36 (S.C. 2005) ("We find the analysis used by the New Hampshire Supreme Court helpful in distinguishing between a claim for faulty workmanship versus a claim for damage to the work product caused by the negligence of a third party.").

Tennessee: Travelers Indemnity Company of America v. Moore & Associates, Inc., 216 S.W.3d 302 (Tenn. 2007) (claim against general contractor for alleged water penetration from faulty window installation by subcontractor was an occurrence).

Texas: Lennar Corp. v. Great American Insurance Co., 200 S.W.3d 651(Tex. App.), *substituted concurring and dissenting opinions* 2006 WL 909937 (Tex. App. Apr. 11, 2006) (water damage caused by defective construction arises from covered occurrence); Pine Oak Builders, Inc. v. Great American Lloyds Insurance Co., 2006 WL 1892669 (Tex. App. July 6, 2006) (moisture infiltration damage caused by faulty workmanship arises from covered occurrence); Gehan Homes, Ltd. v. Employers Mutual Casualty Co., 146 S.W.3d 833 (Tex. App. 2004) (damage caused by faulty workmanship is covered occurrence); Summit Custom Homes, Inc. v. Great American Lloyds Insurance Co., 202 S.W.3d 823 (Tex. App. 2006) (negligently created defective construction resulting in damage to the insured's own work that is unintended and unexpected can constitute an occurrence).

Wisconsin: American Family Mutual Insurance Co. v. American Girl, Inc., 673 N.W.2d 65 (Wis. 2004) (damage from soil settlement as a result of inadequate site preparation advice was covered occurrence); Mantz Automation, Inc. v. Navigators Insurance Co., 326 Wis.2d 266, 787 N.W.2d 60 (Wis. App. 2010); Glendenning's Limestone & Ready-Mix Co. v. Reimer, 721 N.W.2d 704 (Wis. App. 2006) (negligent construction alone is not an occurrence); Kalchthaler v. Keller Construction Co., 591 N.W.2d 169 (Wis. App. 1999) (damage from leaking windows resulting from negligent window installation is a covered occurrence).

176 C.O.D. Gas & Oil Co. v. Ace American Insurance Co., 2004 WL 1245759 (Cal. App. June 8, 2004).

177 *Id.*, 2004 WL 1245759, at *5, citing *Fire Casualty & Surety Bull.*, The Nat'l Underwriter Co., Sept. 1998, § A.3-12. (Emphasis added).

178 See § 3.02[2][b] *supra.*

179 *Id.* See also:

Third Circuit: J.C. Penney Life Insurance Co. v. Pilosi, 393 F.3d 356, 363 (3d Cir. 2004).

Fourth Circuit: Trigo v. Travelers Commercial Insurance Co., 2010 WL 5153399 (W.D. Va. Dec. 17, 2010).

Fifth Circuit: American International Specialty Lines Insurance Co. v. Rentech Steel L.L.C., 620 F.3d 558 (5th Cir. 2010).

Eighth Circuit: R & J Enterprizes v. General Casualty Company of Wisconsin, 627 F.3d 723 (8th Cir. 2010); Gulf Underwriters Insurance Co. v. City of Council Bluffs, 755 F. Supp.2d 988 (S.D. Iowa 2010).

Eleventh Circuit: El-Ad Enclave at Miramar Condominium Association v. Mt. Hawley Insurance Co., 2010 WL 4722288 (S.D. Fla. Nov. 18, 2010).

State Courts:

Alabama: Phillips v. National Security Fire and Casualty Co., 59 So.3d 711 (Ala. App. 2010).

Arizona: Hamill v. Mid-Century Insurance Co., 225 Ariz. 386, 238 P.3d 654 (Ariz. App. 2010).

California: Advanced Network, Inc. v. Peerless Insurance Co., 190 Cal. App.4th 1054, 119 Cal. Rptr.3d 17 (2010).

Colorado: Farmers Insurance Exchange v. Anderson, 2010 WL 4241596 (Colo. App. Oct. 28, 2010).

Illinois: West American Insurance Co. v. Yorkville National Bank, 238 Ill.2d 177, 939 N.E.2d 288, 345 Ill. Dec. 445 (2010).

Indiana: Haag v. Castro, 934 N.E.2d 189 (Ind. App. 2010).

Kansas: Thornburg v. Schweitzer, 44 Kan. App.2d 611, 240 P.3d 969 (2010).

Louisiana: Succession of Barreca v. Weiser, 53 So.3d 481, (La. App. 2010).

Massachusetts: Boazova v. Safety Insurance Co., 78 Mass. App. Ct. 438, 939 N.E.2d 793 (Mass. App. 2010).

Missouri: Dodson International Parts, Inc. v. National Union Fire Insurance Company of Pittsburg Pennsylvania, 2010 WL 4823272 (Mo. App. Nov. 30, 2010).

New Hampshire: Concord General Mutual Insurance Co. v. Doe, 161 N.H. 73, 8 A.3d 154 (2010).

North Carolina: Smith v. Heath, 703 S.E.2d 194 (N.C. App. 2010).

Oregon: Fred Shearer & Sons, Inc. v. Gemini Ins. Co., 237 Or. App. 468, 240 P.3d 67 (2010).

Pennsylvania: Burton v. Republic Insurance Co., 845 A.2d 889, 893 (Pa. Super. 2004).

Rhode Island: Bliss Mine Road Condominium Association v. Nationwide Property and Casualty Insurance Co., 11 A.3d 1078 (R.I. 2010).

South Carolina: South Carolina Farm Bureau Mutual Insurance Co. v. Kennedy, 390 S.C. 125, 700 S.E.2d 258 (S.C. App. 2010).

South Dakota: Western National Mutual Insurance Co. v. Decker, 791 N.W.2d 799 (S.D. 2010).

Texas: Gilbert Texas Construction, L.P. v. Underwriters at Lloyd's London, 327 S.W.3d 118 (Tex. 2010).

Washington: Holden v. Farmers Insurance Company of Washington, 169 Wash.2d 750, 239 P.3d 344 (2010).

[180] ISO Form CG 00 01 10 01.

[181] See ISO Form CG 00 01 10 01.

[182] See *Id.* (emphasis added).

[183] See Turner, *Insurance Coverage of Construction Disputes* § 9.01, at 213–214 (CGL insurance policy provides contractual liability coverage by virtue of an exception to an exclusion). See also:

Fourth Circuit: Capital Environmental Services, Inc. v. North River Insurance Co., 536 F. Supp.2d 633 (E.D. Va. 2008).

Fifth Circuit: Kirschenbaum v. Spraggins, 752 F. Supp.2d 728 (E.D. La. 2010); McGinnis v. Union Pacific Railroad Co., 612 F. Supp.2d 776 (S.D. Tex. 2009).

Sixth Circuit: Martin County Coal Corp. v. Universal Underwriters Insurance Services, Inc., 2010 WL 55926 (E.D. Ky. Jan. 4, 2010); Stryker Corp. v. National Union Fire Insurance Company of Pittsburgh, PA, 2009 WL 56292 (W.D. Mich. Jan. 8, 2009).

Ninth Circuit: Teck Metals, Ltd. v. Certain Underwriters at Lloyd's, London, 2010 WL 3211949 (E.D. Wash. Aug. 10, 2010).

Eleventh Circuit: Twin City Fire Insurance Co. v. Ohio Casualty Insurance Co., 480 F.3d 1254 (11th Cir. 2007); Birmingham Fire Insurance Company of Pennsylvania v. Comcar Industries, Inc., 551 F. Supp.2d 1340 (M.D. Fla. 2008).

State Courts:

Minnesota: Soo Line Railroad Co. v. Brown's Crew Car of Wyoming, 694 N.W.2d 109 (Minn. App. 2005).

New Mexico: Krieger v. Wilson Corp., 139 N.M. 274, 131 P.3d 661 (N.M. App. 2005).

Wisconsin: 1325 North Van Buren, LLC v. T-3 Group, Ltd., 716 N.W.2d 822 (Wis. 2006) (policy can provide coverage for contractual liabilities).

[184] ISO Form CG 00 01 10 01.

[185] *Id.*

[186] *Id.*

[187] See:

Sixth Circuit: Secura Insurance Co. v. Gray Construction, Inc., 717 F. Supp.2d 710 (W.D. Ky. 2010).

Ninth Circuit: Willmar Development, L.L.C. v. Illinois National Insurance Co., 726 F. Supp.2d 1280 (D. Or. 2010).

State Courts:

Florida: U.S. Fire Insurance Co. v. J.S.U.B., Inc., 979 So.2d 871 (Fla. 2007).

Indiana: T.R. Bulger, Inc. v. Indiana Insurance Co., 901 N.E.2d 1110 (Ind. App. 2009).

North Dakota: Emcasco Insurance Co. v. L & M Development Co., 372 N.W.2d 908 (N.D. 1985) (finding coverage for breach of warranty claims based upon similar policy language).

But see, Owings v. Gifford, 697 P.2d 865 (Kan. 1985) (property damage from breach of warranty is not covered where loss resulted from policyholder's own work).

188 See § 3.02[2][b] *supra*. See also: Mutual of Omaha Insurance Co. v. Bosses, 237 A.2d 218, 220 (Pa. 1968); Triplett v. Erie Insurance Exchange, 54 Pa. D. & C.2d 291, 292 (Pa. C.P. 1971).

189 ISO Form CG 00 01 10 01.

190 Likewise, the breach of contract exclusion under Coverage B would be redundant if a breach of contract claim could never constitute an "occurrence."

191 See Hartzell Industries, Inc. v. Federal Insurance Co., 168 F. Supp.2d 789, 795–796 (S.D. Ohio 2001) (impaired property exclusion would be meaningless if loss of productivity from partial loss of use were not "property damage").

192 See ISO Form CG 00 01 10 01 (emphasis added).

193 See Hartzell Industries, Inc. v. Federal Insurance Co., 168 F. Supp.2d 789 (S.D. Ohio 2001).

194 See ISO Form CG 00 01 10 01. These exclusions are discussed in detail in § 7.04 *infra.*

195 See:

Texas: Lennar Corp. v. Great American Insurance Co., 200 S.W.3d 651 (Tex. App.), *substituted concurring and dissenting opinions* 2006 WL 909937 (Tex. App. Apr. 11, 2006).

Wisconsin: American Family Mutual Insurance Co. v. American Girl, Inc., 673 N.W.2d 65, 78 (Wis. 2004):

If, as *American Family* contends, losses actionable in contract are never CGL "occurrences" for purposes of the initial coverage grant, then the business risk exclusions are entirely unnecessary. The business risk exclusions eliminate coverage for liability for property damage to the insured's own work or product—liability that is typically actionable between the parties pursuant to the terms of their contract, not in tort. If the insuring agreement never confers coverage for this type of liability as an original definitional matter, then there is no need to specifically exclude it. Why would the insurance industry exclude damage to the insured's own work or product if the damage could never be considered to have arisen from a covered "occurrence" in the first place?

As will be discussed, if a policy contains a subcontractor exception to the "your work" exclusion, the "business risk" exclusions may not eliminate coverage that would normally constitute facets of performance bond damages not generally covered by CGL policies. See 7.06[4] *infra*.

196 See, e.g., Saw Horse, Inc. v. Southern Guaranty Insurance Company of Georgia, 604 S.E.2d 541 (Ga. App. 2004).

197 Saw Horse, Inc. v. Southern Guaranty Insurance Company of Georgia, 604 S.E.2d 541 (Ga. App. 2004).

198 See § 7.06[4] *infra*. See also:

Texas: Lennar Corp. v. Great American Insurance Co., 200 S.W.3d 651(Tex. App.), *substituted concurring and dissenting opinions* 2006 WL 909937 (Tex. App. Apr. 11, 2006); Mid-United Contractors, Inc. v. Providence Lloyds Ins. Co., 754 S.W.2d 824, 827 (Tex. App. 1988).

Wisconsin: American Family Mutual Insurance Co. v. American Girl, Inc., 673 N.W.2d 65, 82–83 (Wis. 2004).

[199] Lennar Corp. v. Great American Insurance Co., 200 S.W.3d 651, 673 (Tex. App.), *substituted concurring and dissenting opinions* 2006 WL 909937 (Tex. App. Apr. 11, 2006). See also:

Fourth Circuit: Limbach Co. v. Zurich American Insurance Co., 396 F.3d 358, 362–363 (4th Cir. 2005) (applying Pennsylvania law).

State Courts:

Kansas: Lee Builders, Inc. v. Farm Bureau Mutual Insurance Co., 104 P.3d 997, 1001–1003 (Kan. App. 2005).

Wisconsin: American Family Mutual Insurance Co. v. American Girl, Inc., 673 N.W.2d 65, 78 (Wis. 2004).

[200] See, e.g., Kvaerner Metals v. Commercial Union Insurance Co., 908 A.2d 888, 898–899 (Pa. 2006).

[201] Erie Insurance Exchange v. Colony Development Corp., 2003 WL 23096010, at *5 (Ohio App. Dec. 31, 2003).

[202] See § 3.02[2][b] *supra*. See also, Reliance Insurance Co. v. Moessner, 121 F.3d 895, 903 (3d Cir. 1997) (applying Pennsylvania law).

[203] See § 3.02[2][b] *supra*. See also:

Third Circuit: Scirex Corp. v. Federal Insurance Co., 313 F.3d 841, 850–851 (3d Cir. 2002) (applying Pennsylvania law).

State Courts:

Pennsylvania: Lewinski v. Commonwealth, 852 A.2d 1270, 1274 (Pa. Commw. 2004).

[204] See Bruner and O'Connor, *Bruner & O'Connor on Construction Law*, § 11:26 (2004) (an "occurrence" should be met in most construction defect cases because to provide any meaningful coverage, the focus should be on the accidental nature of the injury rather than the act causing the injury).

[205] See, for example Malecki, "Breach of Contract: Can It Be the Subject of Liability Coverage?" in *Malecki on Insurance*, at 5, 7 (May 1995), an article specifically focused on the tort vs. contract issue.

> "The wording found in liability policies does not alert even the most sophisticated insured to the potential elimination of coverage for injury or damage otherwise covered by the policy, but emanating from breach of contract."

Mr. Malecki has been described by one court as "the father of many of the insurance policies' forms." See *In re* Dow Corning Corp., 198 B.R. 214, 232 (Bankr. E.D. Mich. 1996).

See also, Windt, 2 *Insurance Claims and Disputes*, § 11.07, at 228–229 (3d ed. 1995).

> "The question also arises as to how far the 'no coverage for breach of contract rules,' set forth above can be extended. . . . The foregoing rule is not justifiable. If there has been an occurrence of property damage, and no exclusion applies, there should be coverage."

Edward J. Zulkey, a coverage attorney for insurance companies writing in an insurance industry publication, Zulkey, "Note," 1 *CGL Reporter*, at 310–8 through 310–10 (1983) states:

> "A frequent source of confusion in the field of insurance coverage interpretation has to do with whether causes of action which sound solely in breach of contract are covered by a CGL policy. The confusion is compounded when the issue is discussed generically (i.e., without reference to policy language). Unfortunately, certain courts have added to the confusion by rendering decisions without reference to policy language. Simply stated, whether breach of contract is covered depends, not on the

nature of the cause of action, but whether there was . . . 'property damage' caused by an 'occurrence,' and not otherwise excluded.

▼

"In summary, CGL policies, do not differentiate claims based on the cause of action, but rather provide or do not provide coverage based on whether the alleged event fits within its terms. Cases which attempt to premise coverage on general principles rather than contract language, or the lack thereof, must be reviewed carefully."

See also, Bruner and O'Connor, ***Bruner & O'Connor on Construction Law***, § 11:26 (2004) ("finding of no coverage simply because of poor workmanship is not an accident is an insufficient analysis of the issue"; an "occurrence" should be met in most construction defect cases because to provide any meaningful coverage, the focus should be on the accidental nature of the injury rather than the act causing the injury).

[206] See:

First Circuit: Peabody Essex Museum, Inc. v. U.S. Fire Insurance Co., 2010 WL 3895172 (D. Mass. Sept. 30, 2010).

Third Circuit: Jack Daniels Motors, Inc. v. Universal Underwriters Insurance Co., 2011 WL 346500 (D.N.J. Feb. 1, 2011).

Sixth Circuit: American Family Mutual Insurance Co. v. Bower, 2010 WL 4630486 (N.D. Ind. Nov. 5, 2010).

Seventh Circuit: R.C. Wegman Construction Co. v. Admiral Insurance Co., 634 F.3d 371 (7th Cir. 2011); Northfield Insurance Co. v. City of Waukegan, 761 F. Supp.2d 766 (N.D. Ill. 2010).

Ninth Circuit: Bayley Construction Co. v. American Guarantee and Liability Insurance Co., 2010 WL 4272454 (W.D. Wash. Oct. 15, 2010).

Tenth Circuit: United Fire & Casualty Co. v. Boulder Plaza Residential, L.L.C., 2011 WL 240520 (10th Cir. Jan. 27, 2011); Dish Network Corp. v. Arch Specialty Insurance Co., 734 F. Supp.2d 1173 (D. Colo. 2010).

Eleventh Circuit: Amerisure Mutual Insurance Co. v. Albanese Popkin The Oaks Development Group, L.P. 2010 WL 4942972 (S.D. Fla. Nov. 30, 2010).

State Courts:

California: Safeco Insurance Company of America v. Fireman's Fund Insurance Co., 55 Cal. Rptr.3d 844 (Cal. App. 2007) ("trigger of coverage" is a term of convenience used to describe that which, under the specific terms of an insurance policy, must happen in the policy period in order for the potential of coverage to arise).

Colorado: Village Homes of Colorado, Inc. v. Travelers Casualty & Surety Co., 148 P.3d 293 (Colo. App. 2006) ("trigger of coverage" refers to circumstances that activate coverage under a CGL policy and is determined based on the language of the policy).

Florida: Pennsylvania Lumbermens Mutual Insurance Co. v. Indiana Lumbermens Mutual Insurance Co., 43 So.3d 182 (Fla. App. 2010).

Massachusetts: Fitchburg Gas & Electric Light Co. v. One Beacon American Insurance Co., 2010 WL 5490148 (Mass. Super. Nov. 26, 2010).

New Hampshire: Concord General Mutual Insurance Co. v. Doe, 161 N.H. 73, 8 A.3d 154 (2010).

[207] See:

Missouri: City of Lee's Summit v. Missouri Public Entity Risk Management, 390 S.W.3d 214 (Mo. App. 2012).

Pennsylvania: Vurimindi v. LandAmerica Financial Group, Inc., 2012 WL 8700440 (Pa. Commw. Nov. 29, 2012).

208 See generally:

Fourth Circuit: National Union Fire Insurance Company of Pittsburgh, PA v. Reichhold, Inc., 2009 WL 3125483 (M.D.N.C. Sept. 30, 2009).

Sixth Circuit: Generali U.S. Branch v. National Trust Insurance Co., 2009 WL 2762273 (W.D. Ky. Aug. 27, 2009).

Eleventh Circuit: Amerisure Mutual Insurance Co. v. Albanese Popkin The Oaks Development Group, L.P., 2010 WL 4942972 (S.D. Fla. Nov. 30, 2010); Mid-Continent Casualty Co. v. Frank Casserino Construction, Inc., 721 F. Supp.2d 1209 (M.D. Fla. 2010).

State Courts:

California: Montrose Chemical Corp. v. Admiral Insurance Co., 42 Cal. Rptr.2d 324 (Cal. 1995); Grimsley v. Mid-Century Insurance Co., 2011 WL 321004 (Cal. App. Feb. 2, 2011).

Florida: Pennsylvania Lumbermens Mutual Insurance Co. v. Indiana Lumbermens Mutual Insurance Co., 43 So.3d 182 (Fla. App. 2010); Fidelity and Guarantee Insurance Co. v. Polk County, 20 So.3d 383 (Fla. App. 2009).

Massachusetts: Boston Gas Co. v. Century Indemnity Co., 454 Mass. 337, 910 N.E.2d 290 (2009); Hernandez v. Scottsdale Insurance Co., 2009 WL 2603361 (Mass. Super. Aug. 6, 2009).

New Jersey: Quincy Mutual Fire Insurance Co. v. Borough of Bellmawr, 799 A.2d 499, 417 (N.J. 2002); Polarome International, Inc. v. Greenwich Insurance Co., 404 N.J. Super. 241, 961 A.2d 29 (N.J. Super. App. Div. 2008).

209 Fischer, "Insurance Coverage For Mass Exposure Tort Claims: The Debate Over the Appropriate Trigger Rule," 45 Drake L. Rev. 625, 643 (1997). See:

Sixth Circuit: Insurance Co. of North America v. Forty-Eight Insulations, Inc., 451 F. Supp. 1230, 1238 (E.D. Mich. 1978), *aff'd* 633 F.2d 1212 (6th Cir. 1980).

Eighth Circuit: Continental Insurance Co. v. Northeastern Pharmaceutical & Chemical Co., 811 F.2d 1180, 1189 (8th Cir. 1987).

210 Fischer, "Insurance Coverage For Mass Exposure Tort Claims: The Debate Over the Appropriate Trigger Rule," 45 Drake L. Rev. 625, 644 (1997). See:

First Circuit: New Hampshire Ball Bearings v. Aetna Casualty & Surety Co., 848 F. Supp. 1082, 1092–1093 (D.N.H. 1994), *rev'd on other grounds*, 43 F.3d 749 (1st Cir. 1995); Honeycomb Systems, Inc. v. Admiral Insurance Co., 567 F. Supp. 1400, 1405 (D. Me. 1983).

Tenth Circuit: United Fire & Casualty Co. v. Boulder Plaza Residential, L.L.C., 2011 WL 240520 (10th Cir. Jan. 27, 2011).

Eleventh Circuit: Mid-Continent Casualty Co. v. Frank Casserino Construction, Inc., 721 F. Supp.2d 1209 (M.D. Fla. 2010); Bray & Gillespie IX, L.L.C. v. Hartford Fire Insurance Co., 2009 WL 1953649 (M.D. Fla. July 6, 2009).

State Courts:

Florida: Pennsylvania Lumbermens Mutual Insurance Co. v. Indiana Lumbermens Mutual Insurance Co., 43 So.3d 182 (Fla. App. 2010).

Louisiana: Eagle Pipe and Supply, Inc. v. Amerada Hess Corp., 47 So.3d 428 (La. App. 2010).

Maryland: Harford County v. Harford Mutual Insurance Co., 610 A.2d 286, 293–294 (Md. 1992).

Michigan: Transamerica Insurance Co. v. Safeco Insurance Co., 472 N.W.2d 5, 7 (Mich. App. 1991).

Pennsylvania: Pennsylvania National Mutual Casualty Insurance Co. v. St. John, 106 A.3d 1 (Pa. 2014).

211 Fischer, "Insurance Coverage For Mass Exposure Tort Claims: The Debate Over the Appropriate Trigger Rule," 45 Drake L. Rev. 625, 641 (1997). See, Royal Globe Insurance Co. v. Great American Insurance Corp., 325 N.W.2d 556, 558 (Mich. App. 1982).

See also:

First Circuit: Emhart Industries, Inc. v. Century Indemnity Co., 559 F.3d 57 (1st Cir. 2009); Berkshire-Cranwell Limited Partnership v. Tokio Marine and Nichido Fire Insurance Co., 874 F. Supp.2d 41 (D. Mass. 2012).

Fourth Circuit: National Union Fire Insurance Company of Pittsburgh, PA v. Reichhold, Inc., 2009 WL 3125483 (M.D.N.C. Sept. 30, 2009).

Sixth Circuit: Wehr Constructors, Inc. v. Assurance Company of America, 2013 WL 6331666 (W.D. Ky. Dec. 5, 2013); Continental Casualty Co. v. Indian Head Industries, Inc., 2010 WL 188083 (E.D. Mich. Jan. 15, 2010).

Ninth Circuit: Charter Oak Fire Insurance Co. v. Interstate Mechanical, Inc., 2013 WL 3809466 (D. Or. July 23, 2013).

Tenth Circuit: American Family Mutual Insurance Co. v. Teamcorp., Inc., 659 F. Supp.2d 1115 (D. Colo. 2009).

Eleventh Circuit: Axis Surplus Insurance Co. v. Contravest Construction Co., 921 F. Supp.2d 1338 (M.D. Fla. 2012); Mid-Continent Casualty Co. v. Frank Casserino Construction, Inc., 721 F. Supp.2d 1209 (M.D. Fla. 2010).

State Courts:

Florida: Pennsylvania Lumbermens Mutual Insurance Co. v. Indiana Lumbermens Mutual Insurance Co., 43 So.3d 182 (Fla. App. 2010).

Minnesota: Donnelly Brothers Construction Co. v. State Auto Property and Casualty Insurance Co., 759 N.W.2d 651 (Minn. App. 2009).

New York: Downey v. 10 Realty Co., 78 A.D.3d 575, 911 N.Y.S.2d 67 (N.Y. App. Dept. 2010); Continental Casualty Co. v. Employers Insurance Company of Wausau, 60 A.D.3d 128, 871 N.Y.S.2d 48 (N.Y. App. Dept. 2008).

Texas: Vines-Herrin Custom Homes, L.L.C. v. Great American Lloyds Insurance Co., 357 S.W.3d 166 (Tex. App. 2011).

212 Fischer, "Insurance Coverage For Mass Exposure Tort Claims: The Debate Over the Appropriate Trigger Rule," 45 Drake L. Rev. 625, 646 (1997). See, Owens-Illinois, Inc. v. United Insurance Co., 650 A.2d 974 (N.J. 1994).

See also:

First Circuit: Emhart Industries, Inc. v. Century Indemnity Co., 559 F.3d 57 (1st Cir. 2009).

Ninth Circuit: Bayley Construction Co. v. American Guarantee and Liability Insurance Co., 2010 WL 4272454 (W.D. Wash. Oct. 15, 2010).

Eleventh Circuit: Mid-Continent Casualty Co. v. Frank Casserino Construction, Inc., 721 F. Supp.2d 1209 (M.D. Fla. 2010)

State Courts:

California: Employers Insurance Company of Wausau v. Pacific Employers Insurance Co., 2009 WL 1363475 (Cal. App. May 18, 2009).

Delaware: American Guarantee & Liability Insurance Co. v. Intel Corp., 2009 WL 2589597 (Del. Super. July 24, 2009).

Illinois: Federal Insurance Co. v. Binney & Smith, Inc., 393 Ill. App.3d 277, 913 N.E.2d 43, 332 Ill. Dec. 448 (2009).

New Jersey: Farmers Mutual Fire Insurance Company of Salem v. New Jersey Property-Liability Insurance Guaranty Association, 215 N.J. 522, 74 A.3d 860 (N.J. 2013); Polarome International, Inc. v. Greenwich Insurance Co., 404 N.J. Super. 241, 961 A.2d 29 (N.J. Super. App. Div. 2008).

Ohio: Pennsylvania General Insurance Co. v. Park-Ohio Industries, Inc., 179 Ohio App.3d 385, 902 N.E.2d 53 (2008).

Texas: Lennar Corp. v. Merkel American Insurance Co., 2013 WL 4492800 (Tex. Aug. 23, 2013) (continuous).

[213] See:

Third Circuit: West American Insurance Co. v. Lindepuu, 128 F. Supp.2d 220, 226 (E.D. Pa. 2000) (manifestation); Caln Village Associates, L.P. v. Home Indemnity Co., 75 F. Supp.2d 404, 411 (E.D. Pa. 1999) (manifestation).

Fifth Circuit: Wilshire Insurance Co. v. RJT Construction, L.L.C., 581 F.3d 222 (5th Cir. 2009) (manifestation); Maxum Indemnity Co. v. Wilson, 707 F. Supp.2d 683 (S.D. Miss. 2010) (injury in fact); OneBeacon Insurance Co. v. Don's Building Supply, Inc., 516 F. Supp.2d 615 (N.D. Tex. 2006) (manifestation).

Eighth Circuit: Liberty Mutual Insurance Co. v. Pella Corp., 631 F. Supp.2d 1125 (S.D. Iowa 2009) (injury in fact); West Bend Mutual v. Valley Forge Insurance Co., 651 F. Supp.2d 983 (D. Minn. 2009) (injury in fact).

Ninth Circuit: Axis Surplus Insurance Co. v. James River Insurance Co., 2009 WL 675938 (W.D. Wash. Mar. 13, 2009) (injury in fact); USF Insurance Co. v. Clarendon America Insurance Co., 452 F. Supp.2d 972 (C.D. Cal. 2006) (manifestation).

Tenth Circuit: American Family Mutual Insurance Co. v. Teamcorp., Inc., 659 F. Supp.2d 1115 (D. Colo. 2009) (injury in fact).

Eleventh Circuit: Mid-Continent Casualty Co. v. Frank Casserino Construction, Inc., 721 F. Supp.2d 1209 (M.D. Fla. 2010) (manifestation); Keenan Hopkins Schmidt and Stowell Contractors, Inc. v. Continental Casualty Co., 653 F. Supp.2d 1255 (M.D. Fla. 2009) (manifestation); Essex Builders Group, Inc. v. Amerisure Insurance Co., 485 F. Supp.2d 1302 (M.D. Fla. 2006) (manifestation).

State Courts:

California: Pepperell v. Scottsdale Insurance Co., 73 Cal. Rptr.2d 164 (Cal. App. 1998) (continuous).

Florida: Pennsylvania Lumbermens Mutual Insurance Co. v. Indiana Lumbermens Mutual Insurance Co., 43 So.3d 182 (Fla. App. 2010) (injury in fact).

Hawaii: Sentinel Insurance Co. v. First Insurance Company of Hawaii, 875 P.2d 894, 917 (Haw. 1994) (injury in fact or continuous).

Louisiana: Rando v. Top Notch Properties, LLC, 879 So.2d 821, 826 n.2 (La. App. 2004) (manifestation).

Minnesota: Wooddale Builders, Inc. v. Maryland Casualty Co., 722 N.W.2d 283 (Minn. 2006) (injury in fact); Tony Eiden Co. v. State Auto Property and Casualty Insurance Co., 2009 WL 233883 (Minn. App. Jan. 26, 2009) (continuous).

Missouri: D.R. Sherry Construction, Ltd. v. American Family Mutual Insurance Co., 316 S.W.3d 899 (Mo. 2010) (continuous).

Montana: Swank Enterprises, Inc. v. All Purpose Services, Ltd., 154 P.3d 52 (Mont. 2007) (injury in fact).

New York: Downey v. 10 Realty Co., 78 A.D.3d 575, 911 N.Y.S.2d 67 (N.Y. App. Div. 2010) (injury in fact).

North Carolina: Harleysville Mutual Insurance Co. v. Berkley Insurance Company of Carolinas, 610 S.E.2d 215 (N.C. App. 2005) (injury in fact or date of defect).

Ohio: Plum v. West American Insurance Co., 2006 WL 256881 (Ohio App. Feb. 3, 2006) (continuous).

Pennsylvania: Pennsylvania National Mutual Casualty Insurance Co. v. St. John, 106 A.3d 1 (Pa. 2014).

South Carolina: Joe Harden Builders, Inc. v. Aetna Casualty & Surety Co., 486 S.E.2d 89 (S.C. 1997) (continuous).

Texas: Summit Custom Homes, Inc. v. Great American Lloyds Insurance Co., 202 S.W.3d 823 (Tex. App. 2006) (manifestation).

Washington: Gruol Construction Co. v. Insurance Company of North America, 524 P.2d 427 (Wash. App.), *review denied* 84 Wash.2d 1014 (Wash. 1974) (continuous).

214 See:

Ninth Circuit: Axis Surplus Insurance Co. v. James River Insurance Co., 2009 WL 675938 (W.D. Wash. Mar. 13, 2009); Scottsdale Insurance Co. v. OU Interests, Inc., 2005 WL 2893865 (N.D. Cal. Nov 2, 2005).

State Courts:

California: Housing Group v. Great American Insurance Co., 2008 WL 2421706 (Cal. App. June 16, 2008); Standard Fire Insurance Co. v. Spectrum Community Ass'n, 46 Cal. Rptr.3d 804 (Cal. App. 2006); Century Indemnity Co. v. Cannery Row Plaza Associates, 2002 WL 317915, at *5 (Cal. App. Feb. 28, 2002); Pepperell v. Scottsdale Insurance Co., 73 Cal. Rptr.2d 164 (Cal. App. 1998).

Colorado: Travelers Casualty & Surety Co. v. Village Homes of Colorado, Inc., 155 P.3d 369 (Colo. 2007); Hoang v. Assurance Company of America, 149 P.3d 798 (Colo. 2007).

Massachusetts: Trustees of Tufts University v. Commercial Union Insurance Co., 616 N.E.2d 69 (Mass. 1993) (proper inquiry is whether damage took place during the policy period, not whether the claimant owned the property during the policy period).

Washington: National Clothing Co. v. Hartford Casualty Insurance Co. 135 Wash. App. 578, 145 P.3d 394 (Wash. App. 2006) (ownership of damaged property applies only to policy exclusions and is irrelevant to determination of an "occurrence").

215 See:

First Circuit: *Hoppy's Oil Service, Inc. v. Insurance Company of North America,* 783 F. Supp. 1505, 1508 (D. Mass.1992).

Second Circuit: E.R. Squibb & Sons, Inc. v. Lloyd's, 241 F.3d 154, 170 (2d Cir. 2001); Burt Rigid Box Inc. v. Travelers Property Casualty Corp., 126 F. Supp.2d 596, 636–637 (W.D.N.Y. 2001), *aff'd in relevant part* 302 F.3d 83 (2d Cir. 2002).

Fifth Circuit: Mid-Continent Casualty Co. v. Academy Development, Inc., 476 Fed. Appx. 316, 321 (5th Cir.2012) (*per curiam*); Mid-Continent Casualty Co. v. Bay Rock Operating Co., 614 F.3d 105, 111 (5th Cir. 2010).

Seventh Circuit: Great Lakes Dredge & Dock Co. v. City of Chicago, 260 F.3d 789, 795 (7th Cir. 2001).

Eighth Circuit: Bergen v. Grinnell Mutual Reinsurance Co., 2013 WL 2278113 (D. Minn. May 6, 2013); Johnson v. Studyvin, 828 F. Supp. 877, 882–883 (D. Kan. 1993).

Ninth Circuit: Bradley v. Continental Casualty Co., 2011 WL 1748672 (N.D. Cal. Apr. 22, 2011).

State Courts:

California: Standard Fire Insurance Co. v. Spectrum Community Association, 46 Cal. Rptr.3d 804, 811–816 (Cal. App. 2006).

Colorado: Hoang v. Assurance Company of America, 149 P.3d 798, 803–804 (Colo. 2007); Village Homes of Colorado, Inc. v. Travelers Casualty & Surety Co., 148 P.3d 293 (Colo. App. 2006).

Indiana: Great Lakes Chemical Corp. v. International Surplus Lines Insurance Co., 638 N.E.2d 847, 854 (Ind. App.1994).

Massachusetts: Trustees of Tufts University v. Commercial Union Insurance Co., 616 N.E.2d 68, 72 (Mass. 1993).

Missouri: Renco Group, Inc. v. Certain Underwriters at Lloyd's, London, 362 S.W.3d 472, 480 (Mo. App. 2012).

North Dakota: Grinnell Mutual Reinsurance Co. v. Thies, 755 N.W.2d 852 (N.D. 2008).

216 See Chapter 2 *supra*.

217 See § 7.04[1] *infra*.

218 Standard Fire Insurance Co. v. Spectrum Community Ass'n, 46 Cal. Rptr.3d 804 (Cal. App. 2006); Century Indemnity Co. v. Cannery Row Plaza Associates, 2002 WL 317915, at *5 (Cal. App. Feb. 28, 2002); Pepperell v. Scottsdale Insurance Co., 73 Cal. Rptr.2d 164 (Cal. App. 1998).

In Century Indemnity Co. v. Hearrean, 98 Cal. App.4th 734, 741, 120 Cal. Rptr.2d 66 (2002), the policyholder developed and improved a hotel. Ten years later, a subsequent purchaser of the hotel discovered property damage caused by faulty workmanship in connection with the policyholder's development activities. The subsequent purchaser sued the policyholder for the damage caused by the faulty work. The insurance company that sold insurance to the policyholder during the period of construction and development and a few years thereafter defended and settled, under reservation of rights, the policyholder in the suit by the purchaser. In a subsequent declaratory judgment action, the insurance company argued that at the time of the occurrence of property damage the property damage was to property of the policyholder, which is not covered by CGL insurance. The trial court awarded summary judgment to the policyholder. On appeal, the California intermediate appellate court affirmed, holding that trigger of coverage for injury to the property allegedly from defective design and construction was property damage during the policy period and did not require injury to the purchaser during the policy period.

> "the trigger of coverage, the continuous and progressive injury to the hotel property caused by defective design and construction, occurred during the policy period and activated Century's defense and indemnity obligations. To require the claim of the third party, Kang Family Partners, to arise during the policy period, "would unduly transform [an occurrence-based CGL policy] into a 'claims made' policy."120 Cal. Rptr.2d at 72.

Of course, the mere fact that an "occurrence" is found to have taken place does not definitively establish that coverage exists. In fact, a fairly recent California decision held that the owned property exclusion applied to bar coverage in this scenario. See Housing Group v. Great American Insurance Co., 2008 WL 2421706 (Cal App. June 16, 2008).

219 See:

Second Circuit: E.R. Squibb & Sons, Inc. v. Lloyd's, 241 F.3d 154, 170 (2d Cir. 2001); Burt Rigid Box Inc. v. Travelers Property Casualty Corp., 126 F. Supp.2d 596, 636–637 (W.D.N.Y. 2001), *aff'd in relevant part* 302 F.3d 83 (2d Cir. 2002).

Fifth Circuit: Mid-Continent Casualty Co. v. Academy Development, Inc., 476 Fed. Appx. 316, 321 (5th Cir. 2012) (*per curiam*) ("Nothing in the Policies require[s] the claimant . . . to have an ownership interest in the property that was damaged for coverage to exist."); Mid-Continent Casualty Co. v. Bay Rock Operating Co., 614 F.3d 105, 111 (5th Cir. 2010).

Eighth Circuit: Bergen v. Grinnell Mutual Reinsurance Co., 2013 WL 2278113 (D. Minn. May 6, 2013).

Ninth Circuit: Bradley v. Continental Casualty Co., 2011 WL 1748672, at *5 n.3 (N.D. Cal. Apr. 22, 2011).

State Courts:

California: Standard Fire Insurance Co. v. Spectrum Community Ass'n, 141 Cal. App.4th 1117, 46 Cal. Rptr.3d 804, 811–816 (2006).

Colorado: Travelers Casualty & Surety Co. v. Village Homes of Colorado, Inc., 155 P.3d 369 (Colo. 2007); Hoang v. Assurance Company of America, 149 P.3d 798 (Colo. 2007).

Indiana: Great Lakes Chemical Corp. v. International Surplus Lines Insurance Co., 638 N.E.2d 847, 854 (Ind. App.1994) ("[The insurers] argue that no damage to the [underlying plaintiff] occurred until 1989, long after the policies had expired. . . . [The insurers], however, confuse damage to the [plaintiff] and damage to [property]. The policies provide coverage for damage to property, as long as that damage occurs during the policy period. . . . When the [underlying plaintiff] incurred 'damages' . . . is not relevant to when damage to property occurred for purposes of determining coverage under the policies.").

Massachusetts: Trustees of Tufts University v. Commercial Union Insurance Co., 616 N.E.2d 69 (Mass. 1993) (proper inquiry is whether damage took place during the policy period, not whether the claimant owned the property during the policy period).

Missouri: Renco Group, Inc. v. Certain Underwriters at Lloyd's, London, 362 S.W.3d 472, 480 (Mo. App. 2012).

220 *First Circuit:* Dryden Oil Co. v. Travelers Indemnity Co., 91 F.3d 278, 284 (1st Cir. 1996); Hoppy's Oil Service, Inc. v. Insurance Company of North America, 783 F. Supp. 1505, 1508 (D. Mass. 1992).

Second Circuit: Burt Rigid Box, Inc. v. Travelers Property Casualty Insurance Co., 126 F. Supp.2d 596 (W.D.N.Y. 2001), *aff'd in part, rev'd in part* 302 F.3d 83 (2d Cir. 2002).

Seventh Circuit: Great Lakes Dredge & Dock Co. v. City of Chicago, 260 F.3d 789 (7th Cir. 2001), *cert. denied* 535 U.S. 1012 (2002).

Eighth Circuit: Johnson v. Studyvin, 828 F. Supp. 877, 882–883 (D. Kan. 1993).

State Courts:

Colorado: Browder v. United States Fidelity & Guaranty Co., 893 P.2d 132 (Colo. 1995).

New Jersey: Morrone v. Harleysville Mutual Insurance Co., 662 A.2d 562, 565 (N.J. Super. App. Div. 1995).

North Dakota: Grinnell Mutual Reinsurance Co. v. Thies, 755 N.W.2d 852 (N.D. 2008).

Texas: Lennar Corp. v. Great American Insurance Co., 200 S.W.3d 651 (Tex. App.), *substituted concurring and dissenting opinions* 2006 WL 909937 (Tex. App. Apr. 11, 2006).

221 See:

Second Circuit: Champion International Corp. v. Continental Casualty Co., 546 F.2d 502, 505–506 (2d Cir. 1976), *cert. denied* 434 U.S. 819 (1977).

Third Circuit: Real Legacy Assurance Co. v. Afif, 409 Fed. Appx. 558 (3d Cir. 2011); Liberty Mutual Insurance Co. v. Treesdale, Inc., 418 F.3d 330 (3d Cir. 2005); Appalachian Insurance Co. v. Liberty Mutual Insurance Co., 676 F.2d 56 (3d Cir. 1982).

Fourth Circuit: Norfolk & Western Railroad Co. v. Accident & Casualty Insurance Co., 796 F. Supp. 929, 936–937 (W.D. Va. 1992), *aff'd in part, appeal dismissed in part, remanded,* 41 F.3d 928 (4th Cir. 1994); American Casualty Co. v. Heary, 432 F. Supp. 995, 997 (E.D. Va. 1977).

Fifth Circuit: Maurice Pincoffs Co. v. St. Paul Fire & Marine Insurance Co., 447 F.2d 204, 206–207 (5th Cir. 1971); St. Paul-Mercury Indemnity Co. v. Rutland, 225 F.2d 689, 692 (5th Cir. 1955); West Chester Surplus Lines Insurance Co. v. Maverick Tube Corp., 722 F. Supp.2d 787 (S.D. Tex. 2010).

Sixth Circuit: Babcock & Wilcox Co. v. Arkwright-Boston Manufacturing Mutual Insurance Co., 53 F.3d 762, 767–768 (6th Cir. 1995), *cert. denied* 516 U.S. 1140 (1996); Michigan Chemical Corp. v. American Home Assurance Co., 728 F.2d 374, 379 (6th Cir. 1984); Elston-

Richards Storage Co. v. Indemnity Insurance Co., 194 F. Supp. 673, 681 (W.D. Mich. 1960), *aff'd* 291 F.2d 627 (6th Cir. 1961).

Seventh Circuit: Ace American Insurance Co. v. RC2 Corp., 600 F.3d 763 (7th Cir. 2010); Aetna Casualty & Surety Co. v. Medical Protective Co., 575 F. Supp. 901, 903 (N.D. Ill. 1983).

Eighth Circuit: North River Insurance Co. v. Huff, 628 F. Supp. 1129, 1133–1134 (D. Kan. 1985).

Ninth Circuit: Mead Reinsurance Co. v. Granite State Insurance Co., 873 F.2d 1185, 1188 (9th Cir. 1988); Chemstar, Inc. v. Liberty Mutual Insurance Co., 797 F. Supp. 1541, 1546–1548 (C.D. Cal. 1992), *aff'd* 41 F.3d 429 (9th Cir. 1994), *cert. denied* 517 U.S. 1219 (1996).

Tenth Circuit: Business Interiors, Inc. v. Aetna Casualty & Surety Co., 751 F.2d 361, 363 (10th Cir. 1984).

Eleventh Circuit: Home Indemnity Co. v. City of Mobile, 749 F.2d 659, 662–663 (11th Cir. 1984).

State Courts:

Alabama: United States Fire Insurance Co. v. Safeco Insurance Co., 444 So.2d 844, 846–847 (Ala. 1983).

Arizona: Arizona Property & Casualty Insurance Guarantee Fund v. Helme, 735 P.2d 451, 457–458 (Ariz. 1987).

Florida: Maddox v. Florida Farm Bureau General, 121 So.3d 652 (Fla. App. 2013).

Georgia: State Auto Property and Casualty Co. v. Matty, 286 Ga. 611, 690 S.E.2d 614 (2010).

Illinois: Aetna Casualty & Surety Co. v. O'Rourke Brothers, Inc., 776 N.E.2d 588, 597 (Ill. App. 2002); Village of Camp Point v. Continental Casualty Co., 578 N.E.2d 1363, 1371 (Ill. App. 1991), *appeal denied* 587 N.E.2d 1012 (Ill. 1992); Mason v. Home Insurance Co., 532 N.E.2d 526, 528–530 (Ill. App. 1988), *appeal denied* 537 N.E.2d 811 (Ill. 1989).

Louisiana: Cole v. Celotex Corp., 588 So.2d 376, 390 (La. App. 1991), *aff'd* 599 So.2d 401 (La. 1992).

Maryland: CSX Transportation, Inc. v. Continental Insurance Co., 680 A.2d 1082, 1091 (Md. 1996).

Massachusetts: Worcester Insurance Co. v. Fells Acres Day School, Inc., 558 N.E.2d 958, 973 (Mass. 1990).

New Jersey: Doria v. Insurance Company of North America, 509 A.2d 220, 223 (N.J. Super. App. Div. 1986).

Pennsylvania: Donegal Mutual Insurance Co. v. Baumhammers, 938 A.2d 286 (Pa. 2007); D'Auria v. Zurich Insurance Co., 507 A.2d 857, 860 (Pa. Super. 1986).

Washington: Certain Underwriters at Lloyd's London v. Valiant Insurance Co., 155 Wash. App. 469, 229 P.3d 930 (2010).

See Windt, *Insurance Claims and Disputes*, § 11:24.

In analyzing the cause test, the court determines "if 'there is but one proximate, uninterrupted, and continuing cause which resulted in all of the injuries or damage.'" See Appalachian Insurance Co. v. Liberty Mutual Insurance Co., 676 F.2d 56, 61 (3d Cir. 1982) See also, CSX Transportation, Inc. v. Continental Insurance Co., 680 A.2d 1082, 1091 (Md. 1996).

[222] *Fifth Circuit:* Anchor Casualty Co. v. McCaleb, 178 F.2d 322, 324–325 (5th Cir. 1949).

State Courts:

Louisiana: Lombard v. Sewerage & Water Board of New Orleans, 284 So.2d 905, 915–916 (La. 1973).

New York: Arthur A. Johnson Corp. v. Indemnity Insurance Company of North America, 164 N.E.2d 704, 707–708 (N.Y. 1959).

West Virginia: Shamblin v. Nationwide Mutual Insurance Co., 332 S.E.2d 639, 643–644 (W. Va. 1985).

See Windt, *Insurance Claims and Disputes*, § 11:24.

223 So referred to in CSX Transportation, Inc. v. Continental Insurance Co., 680 A.2d 1082, 1092 n.12 (Md. 1996). See also, Mount McKinley Insurance Co. v. Corning, Inc., 28 Misc.3d 893, 903 N.Y.S.2d 709 (N.Y. Sup. Ct. N.Y. Cnty. 2010).

224 *Id.*

225 See, e.g.:

First Circuit: Colonial Gas Co. v. Aetna Casualty & Surety Co., 823 F. Supp. 975, 983–984 (D. Mass. 1993) (use of insulation in 390 homes which was later barred by law from use was one occurrence).

Sixth Circuit: Dow Chemical Co. v. Associated Indemnity Corp., 727 F. Supp. 1524 (E.D. Mich. 1989) (multiple occurrences).

Seventh Circuit: Irving Materials, Inc. v. Zurich American Insurance Co., 2007 WL 1035098 (S.D. Ind. Mar. 30, 2007) (each contract for sale of concrete constituted separate occurrence); Household Manufacturing, Inc. v. Liberty Mutual Insurance Co., 1987 WL 6611, at *4–7 (N.D. Ill. Feb. 11, 1987), *vacated in part* 1987 WL 20137 (N.C. Ill. Nov. 16, 1987) (sale of defective plumbing systems installed in numerous homes constituted one occurrence).

Ninth Circuit: Chemstar, Inc. v. Liberty Mutual Insurance Co., 797 F. Supp. 1541 (C.D. Cal. 1992), *aff'd* 41 F.3d 429 (9th Cir. 1994), *cert. denied* 517 U.S. 1219 (1996) (28 homeowners' claims for defective plaster deemed one occurrence).

Eleventh Circuit: Mid-Continent Casualty Co. v. Basdeo, 477 Fed. Appx. 702 (11th Cir. 2012) (damage to home from three separate acts of negligence by roofers constituted three occurrences).

State Courts:

California: Insurance Company of North America v. National American Insurance Co., 43 Cal. Rptr.2d 518 (Cal. App. 1995) (faulty roof work resulting in property damage at each of nine phases of a condominium project was not a single "occurrence," even though roofs were constructed the same way with the same plans, same installation methods, and same contractor and even though there were the same or similar defects causing the same or similar damage to buildings in each phase).

New Jersey: Wilkinson & Son, Inc. v. Providence Washington Insurance Co. 307 A.2d 639 (N.J. Super. 1973) (contractor's employee's negligence leading to damage to carpeting in thirty-four different apartments over a two-day span constituted a single occurrence).

South Carolina: Owners Insurance Co. v. Salmonsen, 622 S.E.2d 525 (S.C. 2005) (class action complaint against stucco distributor for water intrusion from defective stucco was deemed one occurrence).

Texas: Don's Building Supply Co. v. OneBeacon Insurance Co., 267 S.W.3d 20 (Tex. 2008); Lennar Corp. v. Great American Insurance Co., 200 S.W.3d 651(Tex. App.), *substituted concurring and dissenting opinions* 2006 WL 909937 (Tex. App. Apr. 11, 2006) (Exterior Insulation and Finish System (EIFS) claims for each of 400 homes constituted a separate "occurrence" using the cause test).

Washington: Certain Underwriters at Lloyd's London v. Valiant Insurance Co., 155 Wash. App. 469, 229 P.3d 930 (2010).

226 *Compare,* Chemstar, Inc. v. Liberty Mutual Insurance Co., 797 F. Supp. 1541 (C.D. Cal. 1992), *aff'd* 41 F.3d 429 (9th Cir. 1994), *cert. denied* 517 U.S. 1219 (1996), *with* Insurance Company of North America v. National American Insurance Co., 43 Cal. Rptr.2d 518 (Cal. App. 1995).

[227] See, e.g.:

Fifth Circuit: Fina, Inc. v. Travelers Indemnity Co., 184 F. Supp.2d 547, 552–553 (N.D. Tex. 2002). (three asbestos exposure occurrences at each of the policyholder's three plants constituted separate occurrences; nonetheless all of the bodily injury claims arising from products manufactured at the same facility were deemed one occurrence).

Sixth Circuit: International Surplus Lines Insurance Co. v. Certain Underwriters & Underwriting Syndicates at Lloyd's London, 868 F. Supp. 917, 920–922 (S.D. Ohio 1994).

District of Columbia Circuit: Owens-Illinois, Inc. v. Aetna Casualty & Surety Co., 597 F. Supp. 1515, 1527–1528 (D.D.C. 1984).

State Courts:

New Jersey: Owens-Illinois, Inc. v. United Insurance Co., 625 A.2d 1, 21–24 (N.J. Super. App. Div. 1993), *rev'd in part on other grounds* 650 A.2d 974 (N.J. 1994).

Texas: Certain Underwriters at Lloyd's, London v. Chicago Bridge and Iron Co., 406 S.W.3d 326 (Tex. App. 2013) (workers' inhalation of asbestos constituted a single occurrence).

[228] See, e.g.:

Second Circuit: In re Prudential Lines, Inc., 158 F.3d 65, 82 (2d Cir. 1998).

Sixth Circuit: Babcock & Wilcox Co. v. Arkwright-Boston Manufacturing Mutual Insurance Co., 53 F.3d 762 (6th Cir. 1995), *cert. denied* 516 U.S. 1140 (1996); LuK Clutch Systems, L.L.C. v. Century Indemnity Co., 850 F. Supp.2d 370 (N.D. Ohio 2011) (asbestos inhalation by each claimant constituted separate occurrences).

State Courts:

Connecticut: Metropolitan Life Insurance Co. v. Aetna Casualty & Surety Co., 765 A.2d 891, 896, 899 (Conn. 2001).

Maryland: Commercial Union Insurance Co. v. Porter Hayden Co., 698 A.2d 1167, 1210 (Md. App.), *cert. denied* 703 A.2d 147 (Md. 1997).

Ohio: Cincinnati Insurance Co. v. ACE INA Holdings, Inc., 175 Ohio App.3d 266, 886 N.E.2d 876 (2007).

[229] See, e.g.:

Seventh Circuit: Plastics Engineering Co. v. Liberty Mutual Insurance Co., 514 F.3d 651 (7th Cir. 2008).

State Courts:

New York: Mount McKinley Insurance Co. v. Corning, Inc., 28 Misc.3d 893, 903 N.Y.S.2d 709 (N.Y. Sup. Ct. N.Y. Cty. June 14, 2010); Continental Casualty Co. v. Employers Insurance of Wausau, 60 A.D.3d 128, 871 N.Y.S.2d 48 (N.Y App. Div. 2008).

[230] Air Products & Chemicals, Inc. v. Hartford Accident & Indemnity Co., 707 F. Supp. 762, 772–774 (E.D. Pa. 1989), *aff'd in part and rev'd in part on other grounds* 25 F.3d 177 (3d Cir. 1994); Colt Industries, Inc. v. Aetna Casualty & Surety Co., 1989 WL 147615, at *5–6 (E.D. Pa. Dec. 6, 1989); General Refractories Co. v. American Mutual Liability Insurance Co., No. 88–2250, slip op. (E.D. Pa. Dec. 15, 1988).

[231] See Pittsburgh Corning Corp. v. Travelers Indemnity Co., 1988 WL 5302 (E.D. Pa. Jan. 21, 1988).

[232] See ISO Form CG 00 01 10 01.

[233] The rule is different for claims made policies. See § 9.03[4] *infra*. But see, Sherwood Brands, Inc. v. Great American Insurance Co., 418 Md. 300, 13 A.3d 1268 (Md. App. 2011) (notice-prejudice rule applies to claims made policies).

[234] See:

First Circuit: IDC Properties, Inc. v. Chicago Title Insurance Co., 974 F. Supp.2d 87 (D.R.I. 2013).

Third Circuit: Berko Investments, L.L.C. v. State National Insurance Co., 2010 WL 2853731 (E.D. Pa. July 21, 2010).

Fourth Circuit: Minnesota Lawyers Mutual Insurance Co. v. Baylor & Jackson, L.L.C., 531 Fed. Appx. 312 (4th Cir. 2013).

Fifth Circuit: A3M Vacuum Services, L.L.C. v. HUB International Midwest, Ltd., 17 F. Supp.3d 554 (E.D. La. 2014).

Seventh Circuit: National Union Fire Insurance Co. of Pittsburgh, PA v. Mead Johnson & Co., 735 F.3d 539 (7th Cir. 2013).

Ninth Circuit: Trishan Air, Inc. v. Federal Insurance Co., 635 F.3d 422 (9th Cir. 2011); Terhune Homes, Inc. v. Nationwide Mutual Insurance Co., 2014 U.S. Dist. LEXIS 60939 (W.D. Wash. May 9, 2014).

Tenth Circuit: Leadville Corp. v. United States Fidelity & Guaranty Co., 55 F.3d 537, 540 (10th Cir. 1995).

Eleventh Circuit: Lane v. Provident Life & Accident Insurance Co., 178 F. Supp.2d 1281, 1287–1288 (S.D. Fla. 2001).

State Courts:

Florida: Bankers Insurance Co. v. Macias, 475 So.2d 1216, 1218 (Fla. 1985).

Illinois: Rice v. AAA Aerostar, Inc., 294 Ill. App.3d 801, 690 N.E.2d 1067, 1072, 229 Ill. Dec. 20 (1998).

Indiana: Sheehan Construction Co. v. Columbia Casualty Co., 938 N.E.2d 635 (Ind. 2010).

Louisiana: State v. National Union Fire Insurance Co. of Louisiana, 56 So.3d 1236 (La. App. 2011).

Maryland: Sherwood Brands, Inc. v. Great American Insurance Co., 418 Md. 300, 13 A.3d 1268 (Md. App. 2011).

Massachusetts: Darcy v. Hartford Insurance Co., 407 Mass. 481, 554 N.E.2d 28 (1990).

New Mexico: Foundation Reserve Insurance Co. v. Esquibel, 94 N.M. 132, 607 P.2d 1150, 1152 (1980).

Oregon: Lusch v. Aetna Casualty & Surety Co., 538 P.2d 902 (Or. 1975).

Texas: Hudson v. City of Houston, 2011 WL 1376168 (Tex. App. Jan. 13, 2011); Struna v. Concord Insurance Services, Inc., 11 S.W.3d 355, 359 (Tex. App. 2000).

But see:

Second Circuit: Pactrans Air & Seas, Inc. v. New York Marine and General Insurance Co., 387 Fed. Appx. 43 (2d Cir. 2010).

Fourth Circuit: State Farm Fire and Casualty Co. v. Wallace, 997 F. Supp.2d 439 (W.D. Va. Feb. 3, 2014) (prolonged delay without prejudice may be enough to justify forfeiture).

State Courts:

New York: Power Authority v. Westinghouse Electric Co., 117 A.D.2d 336, 502 N.Y.S.2d 420 (N.Y. App. Div. 1986) (under New York law, late notice may be an absolute defense to coverage, irrespective of actual prejudice suffered).

In 2008, New York law was amended to adopt the notice-prejudice rule for policies issued in New York after January 17, 2009. See: N.Y. Insurance Law § 3420(b); Rockland Exposition, Inc. v. Great American Assurance Co., 445 Fed. Appx. 387 (2d Cir. 2011); Indian Harbor Insurance Co. v. City of San Diego, 972 F. Supp.2d 634 (S.D.N.Y. 2013).

[235] See:

Eleventh Circuit: Lane v. Provident Life & Accident Insurance Co., 178 F. Supp.2d 1281, 1287–1288 (S.D. Fla. 2001) (applying Florida law).

State Courts:

Florida: Bankers Insurance Co. v. Macias, 475 So.2d 1216, 1218 (Fla. 1985).

236 See National Union Fire Insurance Co. of Pittsburgh, PA v. Mead Johnson & Co., 735 F.3d 539 (7th Cir. 2013).

237 See:

First Circuit: IDC Properties, Inc. v. Chicago Title Insurance Co., 974 F. Supp.2d 87 (D.R.I. 2013).

Fourth Circuit: Financial Industry Regulatory Authority, Inc. v. Axis Insurance Co., 951 F. Supp.2d 826 (D. Md. 2013).

Fifth Circuit: A3M Vacuum Services, L.L.C. v. HUB International Midwest, Ltd., 17 F. Supp.3d 554 (E.D. La. 2014).

Ninth Circuit: Terhune Homes, Inc. v. Nationwide Mutual Insurance Co., 2014 U.S. Dist. LEXIS 60939 (W.D. Wash. May 9, 2014).

State Courts:

Illinois: Rice v. AAA Aerostar, Inc., 294 Ill. App.3d 801, 690 N.E.2d 1067, 1072, 229 Ill. Dec. 20 (1998).

Massachusetts: Darcy v. Hartford Insurance Co., 407 Mass. 481, 554 N.E.2d 28 (1990).

New Mexico: Foundation Reserve Insurance Co. v. Esquibel, 94 N.M. 132, 607 P.2d 1150, 1152 (1980).

Oregon: Lusch v. Aetna Casualty & Surety Co., 538 P.2d 902 (Or. 1975); Halsey v. Fireman's Fund Insurance Co., 681 P.2d 168 (Or. App.), *review denied* 687 P.2d 795 (Or. 1984).

Texas: Struna v. Concord Insurance Services, Inc., 11 S.W.3d 355, 359 (Tex. App. 2000).

238 *Massachusetts:* Darcy v. Hartford Insurance. Co., 407 Mass. 481, 554 N.E.2d 28 (1990) (actual prejudice exists by loss of critical evidence or witnesses).

Oregon: Lusch v. Aetna Casualty & Surety Co., 538 P.2d 902 (Or. 1975).

239 *Id.*

240 See, e.g., Halsey v. Fireman's Fund Insurance Co., 681 P.2d 168 (Or. App.), *review denied* 687 P.2d 795 (Or. 1984).

241 See:

Florida: Tiedtke v. Fidelity & Casualty Company of New York, 222 So.2d 206, 209 (Fla. 1969).

Illinois: Rice v. AAA Aerostar, Inc., 294 Ill. App.3d 801, 690 N.E.2d 1067, 1071–1072, 229 Ill. Dec. 20 (1998).

New Mexico: Roberts Oil Co. v. Transamerica Insurance Co., 833 P.2d 222, 232 (N.M. 1992).

Texas: Duzich v. Marine Office of America Corp., 980 S.W.2d 857, 865 (Tex. App. 1998).

242 See:

Florida: Tiedtke v. Fidelity & Casualty Company of New York, 222 So.2d 206, 209 (Fla. 1969).

Illinois: Rice v. AAA Aerostar, Inc., 294 Ill. App.3d 801, 690 N.E.2d 1067, 1071–1072, 229 Ill. Dec. 20 (1998).

New Mexico: Roberts Oil Co. v. Transamerica Insurance Co., 833 P.2d 222, 232 (N.M. 1992).

Texas: Duzich v. Marine Office of America Corp., 980 S.W.2d 857, 865 (Tex. App. 1998)

243 See:

Fifth Circuit: Brown v. State Farm Automobile Casualty Insurance Co., 506 F.2d 976, 978–979 (5th Cir. 1979) (applying Florida law).

Tenth Circuit: Hunt v. Ford Motor Co., 65 F.3d 168 (10th Cir. 1995) (notice after entry of default may not be prejudicial if the default can be vacated).

State Courts:

Florida: American Fire & Casualty Co. v. Collura, 163 So.2d 784, 786 (Fla. Dist. App.), *cert. denied* 171 So.2d 389 (Fla. 1964).

Illinois: Rice v. AAA Aerostar, Inc., 294 Ill. App.3d 801, 690 N.E.2d 1067, 1072, 229 Ill. Dec. 20 (1998) ("In some cases notice of suit even after a default is entered might enable the insurer to satisfactorily defend the suit, if the insurer would be able to persuade the court to vacate the default.").

Texas: Lennar Corp. v. Great American Insurance Co., 200 S.W.3d 651 (Tex. App.), *substituted concurring and dissenting opinions.* 2006 WL 909937 (Tex. App. Apr. 11, 2006); Duzich v. Marine Office of America Corp., 980 S.W.2d 857, 866 (Tex. App. 1998) ("there is a fact question as to (1) whether insurers were actually prejudiced at the time they learned of default, given [policyholder's] success at that point in challenging its validity, and (2) whether the prejudice they suffered derived from [the policyholder's] negligence, or from some other source [such as the underlying claimants' failure to properly serve the policyholder]").

244 See:

Illinois: Vega v. Gore, 313 Ill. App.3d 632, 730 N.E.2d 587, 589, 246 Ill. Dec. 562 (2000) ("An insurer may demonstrate prejudice where it does not receive notice of a suit until after a default judgment is entered, as the insurer is deprived of the opportunity to present evidence and engage in cross-examination of the opposing witnesses on the issues of liability and damages."); American Country Insurance Co. v. Cash, 171 Ill. App.3d 9, 524 N.E.2d 1016, 1017–1018, 120 Ill. Dec. 834 (1988) ("failure to provide notice until after the entry of a default judgment would be sufficient to justify the assertion of a policy defense . . . since the insurer is deprived of an opportunity to present evidence and cross-examine plaintiff's witnesses on the issues of liability and damages. We conclude that the delayed compliance in the instant case constituted a breach of the policy provision as a matter of law."); Reisman v. Delgado, 117 Ill. App.3d 331, 453 N.E.2d 902, 905, 73 Ill. Dec. 77 (1983) ("An insurer is prejudiced when it does not receive notice of a lawsuit until after entry of a default judgment because, in such cases, it 'did not have an opportunity to appear and defend the action on liability, was not given an opportunity to cross-examine plaintiffs' witnesses on damages and was not given an opportunity to present its own evidence relative to liability and damages.'").

Texas: Liberty Mutual Insurance Co. v. Cruz, 883 S.W.2d 164, 165 (Tex. 1993) (failure to give notice to the insurance company of a claim, until after a default judgment is entered, is prejudicial to the insurance company as a matter of law); Kimble v. Aetna Casualty & Surety Co., 767 S.W.2d 846, 850 (Tex. App. 1989) (same)

245 See Montgomery Ward & Co. v. Home Insurance Co., 324 Ill. App.3d 441, 753 N.E.2d 999, 257 Ill. Dec. 373 (2001) (notice was not untimely because knowledge by the insured's insurance department is what triggered the policyholder's duty to provide notice to the insurance company).

> "[The insurance company] contends that to allow [the policyholder] to hide behind the literal terms of the notice provision would encourage insureds to purposely keep the designated department uninformed so as to defeat insurance carrier defenses to coverage. First, we note that [the insurance company] easily could have refused to have included this type of notice requirement in the policy. Insurance carriers are certainly sophisticated enough and wield sufficient bargaining power to protect their interests, and [the insurance company] cannot claim that the notice provision in issue was forced on it by [the policyholder]." 753 N.E.2d 999 at 1004.

246 See ISO Form CG 00 01 10 01.

[247] See, e.g.:

Third Circuit: Goddard v. State Farm Mutual Automobile Insurance Co., 992 F. Supp.2d 473 (E.D. Pa. 2014).

Sixth Circuit: The Medical Assurance Co. v. 779 F. Supp.2d 902 (N.D. Ind. 2011).

Seventh Circuit: Employers Mutual Casualty Co. v. Skoutaris, 453 F.3d 915 (7th Cir. 2006).

Eighth Circuit: Heubel Materials Handling Co. v. Universal Underwriters Insurance Co., 704 F.3d 558 (8th Cir. 2013); Medical Protective Co. v. Bubenik, 594 F.3d 1047 (8th Cir. 2010).

Ninth Circuit: Allstate Insurance Co. v. Herron, 634 F.3d 1101 (9th Cir. 2011).

Eleventh Circuit: Mid-Continent Casualty Co. v. American Pride Building Co., 601 F.3d 1143 (11th Cir. 2010).

State Courts:

California: Belz v. Clarendon America Insurance Co., 158 Cal. App.4th 615, 69 Cal. Rptr.3d 864 (2007).

Connecticut: Double G.G. Leasing, L.L.C. v. Underwriters at Lloyd's, London, 116 Conn. App. 417, 978 A.2d 83 (2009).

Illinois: Founders Insurance Co. v. Shaikh, 405 Ill. App.3d 367, 937 N.E.2d 1186, 344 Ill. Dec. 845 (2010).

Massachusetts: Hanover Insurance Co. v. Cape Cod Custom Home Theater, Inc., 72 Mass. App. Ct. 331, 891 N.E.2d 703 (2008).

New York: Hunter Roberts Construction Group, L.L.C. v. Arch Insurance Co., 75 A.D.3d 404, 904 N.Y.S.2d 52 (N.Y. App. Div. 2010).

[248] See Truck Insurance Exchange v. Unigard Insurance Co., 79 Cal. App.4th 966, 94 Cal. Rptr.2d 516, 523 (2000).

[249] *California:* Berman v. Gulf Insurance Co., 2004 WL 909239, at *5 (Cal. App. Apr. 29, 2004); Campbell v. Allstate Insurance Co., 384 P.2d 155 (Cal. 1963); Insua v. Scottsdale Insurance Co., 129 Cal. Rptr.2d 138, 144 (Cal. App. 2002).

[250] See:

Third Circuit: Goddard v. State Farm Mutual Automobile Insurance Co., 992 F. Supp.2d 473 (E.D. Pa. 2014).

Sixth Circuit: The Medical Assurance Co. v. Miller, 779 F. Supp.2d 902 (N.D. Ind. 2011).

Seventh Circuit: Employers Mutual Casualty Co. v. Skoutaris, 453 F.3d 915 (7th Cir. 2006).

Eighth Circuit: Heubel Materials Handling Co. v. Universal Underwriters Insurance Co., 704 F.3d 558 (8th Cir. 2013); Medical Protective Co. v. Bubenik, 594 F.3d 1047 (8th Cir. 2010).

Ninth Circuit: Allstate Insurance Co. v. Herron, 634 F.3d 1101 (9th Cir. 2011).

Eleventh Circuit: Mid-Continent Casualty Co. v. American Pride Building Co., 601 F.3d 1143 (11th Cir. 2010).

State Courts:

California: Belz v. Clarendon America Insurance Co., 158 Cal. App.4th 615, 69 Cal. Rptr.3d 864 (2007); Great American Insurance Co. v. Short, 2001 WL 1264944, at *8 (Cal. App. Oct. 23, 2001).

Connecticut: Double G.G. Leasing, L.L.C. v. Underwriters at Lloyd's, London, 116 Conn. App. 417, 978 A.2d 83 (2009).

Illinois: Founders Insurance Co. v. Shaikh, 405 Ill. App.3d 367, 937 N.E.2d 1186, 344 Ill. Dec. 845 (2010).

Massachusetts: Hanover Insurance Co. v. Cape Cod Custom Home Theater, Inc., 72 Mass. App. Ct. 331, 891 N.E.2d 703 (2008).

New York: Hunter Roberts Construction Group, L.L.C. v. Arch Insurance Co., 75 A.D.3d 404, 904 N.Y.S.2d 52 (N.Y. App. Div. 2010).

251 See Great American Insurance Co. v. Short, 2001 WL 1264944, at *8 (Cal. App. Oct. 23, 2001); Truck Insurance Exchange v. Unigard Insurance Co., 79 Cal. App.4th 966, 94 Cal. Rptr.2d 516, 523 (2000) (if cooperation clause is breached, insurance company's performance is excused if its ability to provide a defense has been substantially prejudiced).

252 See Andrade v. Jennings, 54 Cal. App.4th 307, 62 Cal. Rptr.2d 787 (1997).

253 See Select Insurance Co. v. Superior Court, 226 Cal. App.3d 631, 276 Cal. Rptr. 598, 601 (1990).

254 See ISO Form CG 00 01 10 01.

255 See, e.g., Ohaus v. Continental Casualty Insurance Co., 292 N.J. Super. 501, 679 A.2d 179, 184 (1996) (requiring that an insurance company establish prejudice to advance a "voluntary payments" defense).

> "[I]n New Jersey, where the insured has acted in good faith, an exclusion barring coverage for the insured's voluntary assumption of an obligation only applies where the insurer can establish 'appreciable prejudice.'"

See also:

Second Circuit: PB Americas, Inc. v. Continental Casualty Co., 690 F. Supp.2d 242 (S.D.N.Y. 2010).

Third Circuit: Wheeler v. Nationwide Mutual Insurance Co., 749 F. Supp. 660, 663 (E.D. Pa. 1990); Prudential Property & Casualty Insurance Co. v. Nayerahamadi, 593 F. Supp. 216, 218 (E.D. Pa. 1984).

Sixth Circuit: Demolition Contractors, Inc. v. Westchester Surplus Lines Insurance Co., 381 Fed. Appx. 526 (6th Cir. 2010).

Seventh Circuit: Kmart Corp. v. Footstar, Inc., 2010 WL 1541296 (N.D. Ill. Apr. 14, 2010).

Ninth Circuit: Trishan Air, Inc. v. Federal Insurance Co., 635 F.3d 422 (9th Cir. 2011); Charter Oak Fire Insurance Co. v. Interstate Mechanical, Inc., 958 F. Supp.2d 1188 (D. Or. 2013); Raisin Bargaining Ass'n v. Hartford Casualty Insurance Co., 715 F. Supp.2d 1079 (N.D. Cal. 2010).

Eleventh Circuit: Rolyn Cos., Inc. v. R & J Sales of Texas, Inc., 671 F. Supp.2d 1314, (11th Cir. 2011); Thompson v. American States Insurance Co., 687 F. Supp. 559, 564 (M.D. Ala. 1988).

State Courts:

Arizona: Leflet v. Redwood Fire and Casualty Insurance Co., 247 P.3d 180 (Ariz. App. 2011).

Arkansas: Shelter Mutual Insurance Co. v. Bough, 834 S.W.2d 637, 640 (Ark. 1992).

California: OneBeacon American Insurance Co. v. Fireman's Fund Insurance Co., 175 Cal. App.4th 183, 95 Cal. Rptr.3d 808 (2009).

Delaware: Hilco Capital, L.P. v. Federal Insurance Co., 978 A.2d 174 (Del. 2009).

Florida: Tucker v. Seward, 400 So.2d 505, 506 (Fla. App. 1981); Rafferty v. Progressive American Insurance Co., 558 So.2d 432, 433 (Fla. App. 1990).

Illinois: Hoel v. Crum & Forster Insurance Co., 366 N.E.2d 901 (Ill. App. 1977); Marsh v. Prestige Insurance Group, 374 N.E.2d 1268, 1270 (Ill. App. 1978).

Iowa: Kapadia v. Preferred Risk Mutual Insurance Co., 418 N.W.2d 848, 851–852 (Iowa 1988).

Kentucky: Newark Insurance Co. v. Ezell, 520 S.W.2d 318, 321 (Ky. 1975).

Maine: Bazinet v. Concord General Mutual Insurance Co., 513 A.2d 279, 282 (Me. 1986).

Massachusetts: MacInnis v. Aetna Life & Casualty Co., 403 Mass. 220, 526 N.E.2d 1255, 1257–1258 (1988).

Missouri: Tegtmeyer v. Snellen, 791 S.W.2d 737, 740 (Mo. App. 1990) (insurer who refused to consent to a settlement for the full limits of a tortfeasor's liability policy was not prejudiced and therefore could not escape liability under a settlement-without-consent exclusion).

North Carolina: Branch v. Travelers Indemnity Co., 90 N.C. App. 116, 367 S.E.2d 369, 371 (1988), *aff'd* 378 S.E.2d 748 (N.C. 1989); Silvers v. Horace Mann Insurance Co., 378 S.E.2d 21, 27 (N.C. 1989).

Texas: Hernandez v. Gulf Group Lloyds, 875 S.W.2d 691, 693 & n.4 (Tex. 1994).

Washington: Thiringer v. American Motor Insurance Co., 91 Wash.2d 215, 588 P.2d 191, 193 (1978) (showing of prejudice required in order for insurer to deny personal injury protection coverage on the basis that an insured's settlement failed to comply with a subrogation provision).

Wisconsin: Westport Insurance Co. v. Appleton Papers, Inc., 327 Wis.2d 120, 787 N.W.2d 894 (Wis. App. 2010).

But see:

Second Circuit: Travelers Indemnity Co. v. Northrop Grumman Corp., 4 F. Supp.3d 599 (S.D.N.Y. 2014).

Third Circuit: Fisher v. USAA Casualty Insurance Co., 973 F.2d 1103, 1106–1107 (3d Cir. 1992); Coregis Insurance Co. v. Carol F. Kafrissen, P.C., 140 F. Supp.2d 461, 463 (E.D. Pa. 2001).

Fourth Circuit: Perini/Tompkins Joint Venture v. Ace American Insurance Co., 738 F.3d 95 (4th Cir. 2013).

Seventh Circuit: West Bend Mutual Insurance Co. v. Arbor Homes, L.L.C., 703 F.3d 1092 (7th Cir. 2013);

Eleventh Circuit: Piedmont Office Realty Trust v. XL Specialty Insurance Co., 11 F. Supp.3d 1184 (N.D. Ga. 2014).

State Courts:

Georgia: Trinity Outdoor, L.L.C. v. Central Mutual Insurance Co., 285 Ga. 583, 679 S.E.2d 10 (2009).

New Hampshire: Stevens v. Merchants Mutual Insurance Co., 135 N.H. 26, 599 A.2d 490 (1991) (enforcement of settlement-without-consent term did not depend upon showing of prejudice to insurer).

Pennsylvania: Resource America, Inc. v. Certain Underwriters, 2004 WL 2580554, at *4 (Pa. C.P. Philadelphia Cnty. Nov. 12, 2004); Boyle v. Erie Insurance Co., 656 A.2d 941, 944 (Pa. Super.), *alloc. denied* 668 A.2d 1120 (Pa. 1995); Archer v. State Farm Automobile Insurance Co., 615 A.2d 779 (Pa. Super. 1992), *alloc. denied* 629 A.2d 1375 (Pa. 1993); Hockenberry v. Horace Mann Insurance Co., 19 Pa. D. & C.4th 567, 571 (Pa. C.P. Cumberland Cnty. 1993).

256 *Third Circuit:* Fisher v. USAA Casualty Insurance Co., 973 F.2d 1103, 1106–1107 (3d Cir. 1992) (applying Pennsylvania law); Coregis Insurance Co. v. Carol F. Kafrissen, P.C., 140 F. Supp.2d 461, 463 (E.D. Pa. 2001) (applying Pennsylvania law).

State Courts:

Pennsylvania: Boyle v. Erie Insurance Co., 656 A.2d 941, 944 (Pa. Super.), *alloc. denied* 668 A.2d 1120 (Pa. 1995); Archer v. State Farm Automobile Insurance Co., 615 A.2d 779 (Pa. Super. 1992), *alloc. denied* 629 A.2d 1375 (Pa. 1993); Resource America, Inc. v. Certain Underwriters, 2004 WL 2580554, at *4 (Pa. C.P. Philadelphia Cnty. Nov. 12, 2004); Hockenberry v. Horace Mann Insurance Co., 19 Pa. D. & C.4th 567, 571 (Pa. C.P. Cumberland Cnty 1993).

257 *Id.*

258 See, e.g., Federal Insurance Co. v. Purex Industries, Inc., 972 F. Supp. 872, 892 (D.N.J. 1997). See also:

First Circuit: Liberty Mutual Insurance Co. v. Black and Decker Corp., 383 F. Supp.2d 200 (D. Mass. 2004).

Second Circuit: Endicott Johnson Corp. v. Liberty Mutual Insurance Co., 928 F. Supp. 176 (N.D.N.Y. 1996).

Third Circuit: Liberty Mutual Insurance Co. v. Treesdale, Inc., 418 F.3d 330 (3d Cir. 2005).

Seventh Circuit: Plastics Engineering Co. v. Liberty Mutual Insurance Co., 514 F.3d 651 (7th Cir. 2008).

Eighth Circuit: Carlson Marketing Group, Inc. v. Royal Indemnity Co., 517 F. Supp.2d 1089 (D. Minn. 2007).

Ninth Circuit: Northwest Pipe Co. v. RLI Insurance Co., 734 F. Supp.2d 1122 (D. Or. 2010).

State Courts:

California: A.B.S. Clothing Collection, Inc. v. Home Insurance Co., 34 Cal. App.4th 1470, 41 Cal. Rptr.2d 166 (1995).

Delaware: Hercules, Inc. v. AIU Insurance Co., 784 A.2d 481 (Del. 2001).

Illinois: Outboard Marine Corp. v. Liberty Mutual Insurance Co., 283 Ill. App.3d 630, 670 N.E.2d 740, 219 Ill. Dec. 62 (1996).

New Jersey: Spaulding Composites Co. v. Aetna Casualty and Surety Co., 176 N.J. 25, 819 A.2d 410 (2003); Polarome International, Inc. v. Greenwich Insurance Co., 404 N.J. Super. 241, 961 A.2d 29 (2008).

Pennsylvania: Reliance Insurance Co. v. IRPC, Inc., 904 A.2d 912 (Pa. Super. 2006).

Wisconsin: Westport Insurance Corp. v. Appleton Papers, Inc., 327 Wis.2d 120, 787 N.W.2d 894 (2010).

259 Pittsburgh Corning Corp. v. Travelers Indemnity Co., 1988 WL 5302 (E.D. Pa. Jan. 21, 1988).

260 *Id.*

261 See Federal Insurance Co. v. Purex Industries, Inc., 972 F. Supp. 872, 892 (D.N.J. 1997) (applying New Jersey law). There are other cases that similarly refuse to enforce this provision. See Mennen Co. v. Atlantic Mutual Insurance Co., 1999 U.S. Dist. LEXIS 21916 (D.N.J. Oct. 26, 1999).

262 *Id.*

263 See ISO Form CG 00 01 10 01.

264 See, e.g., Alea London Ltd. v. American Home Services, Inc., 638 F.3d 768 (11th Cir. 2011).

265 See:

Seventh Circuit: Carolina Casualty Insurance Co. v. Merge Healthcare Solutions, Inc., 728 F.3d 615 (7th Cir. 2013).

266 *Id.*

267 *Ninth Circuit:* R.W. Beck & Associates v. City & Borough of Sitka, 27 F.3d 1475, 1484 (9th Cir. 1994).

Eleventh Circuit: United Rentals, Inc. v. Mid-Continent Casualty Co., 843 F. Supp.2d 1309 (S.D. Fla. 2012).

State Courts:

California: Golden Eagle Insurance Co. v. Insurance Company of the West, 99 Cal. App.4th 837, 121 Cal. Rptr.2d 682, 690–691 (2002).

[268] See R.W. Beck & Associates v. City & Borough of Sitka, 27 F.3d 1475, 1484 (9th Cir. 1994) (attorneys' fees of indemnitee in seeking indemnity awarded under Alaska prevailing plaintiff fee shifting statute were "supplementary payments").

[269] For a fuller discussion on allocation, see initial discussion on allocation in § 5.03 ***supra***.

[270] See Anderson and Paar, "What's Wrong With D&O Insurance?," ***Risk Mgmt.***, Jan. 1995, at 29.

[271] *Id.*

[272] See, e.g.:

Sixth Circuit: Telxon Corp. v. Federal Insurance Co., 309 F.3d 386 (6th Cir. 2002); Bank One, N.A. v. Echo Acceptance Corp., 522 F. Supp.2d 959 (S.D. Ohio 2007).

Seventh Circuit: Santa's Best Craft, L.L.C. v. St. Paul Fire and Marine Insurance Co., 611 F.3d 339 (7th Cir. 2010); Harbor Insurance Co. v. Continental Bank Corp., 922 F.2d 357, 368 (7th Cir. 1990) ("To allow insurance companies an allocation between the director's liability and the corporation's derivative liability for the director's acts would rob the [policyholder] of the insurance protection that it sought and bought."); Caterpillar, Inc. v. Great American Insurance Co., 62 F.3d 955 (7th Cir. 1995).

Eighth Circuit: Piper Jaffray Cos. v. National Union Fire Insurance Co., 38 F. Supp.2d 771 (D. Minn. 1999).

Ninth Circuit: Nordstrom, Inc. v. Chubb & Son, Inc., 54 F.3d 1424 (9th Cir. 1995); Safeway Stores, Inc. v. National Union Fire Insurance Co., 64 F.3d 1282 (9th Cir. 1995); Clackamas County v. Midwest Employers Casualty Co., 2009 WL 4916364 (D. Or. Dec. 14, 2009).

Tenth Circuit: Stauth v. Federal Insurance Co., 1997 WL 33558656 (W.D. Okla. Nov. 12, 1997), ***aff'd in part, rev'd in part*** 185 F.3d 875 (10th Cir. 1999).

See also, Celebrezze and Potter, "Allocation Cases Expand D&O Cover," ***Nat'l Underwriter***, Nov. 13, 1995, at 3.

[273] As most real estate businesses use the corporate form and many are publicly traded entities, Directors and Officers liability insurance is topical for real estate-related businesses. For a further discussion on relevant E&O or D&O issues, see Chapter 10 ***infra***.

[274] Stauth v. Federal Insurance Co., 1997 WL 33558656 (W.D. Okla. Nov. 12, 1997), ***aff'd in part, rev'd in part*** 185 F.3d 875 (10th Cir. 1999).

[275] Insurance companies have responded to this line of authority by including policy provisions that explicitly set forth an allocation formula. Alternatively, some insurance companies selling D&O policies avoid the allocation issue by selling express "entity coverage," insurance for the corporate entity itself, for the most frequently asserted claims. Despite the recent cases ruling in favor of policyholders, D&O insurance companies continue to try to assert allocation arguments when the policy language appears ambiguous, according to one commentator. See Lenckus, "D&O Insurer Loss on Allocations Is Third Straight," ***Business Ins.***, Sept. 4, 1995, at 1, 27.

[276] See, e.g.:

Second Circuit: Pepsico v. Continental Casualty Co., 640 F. Supp. 656 (S.D.N.Y. 1986).

Sixth Circuit: Owens Corning v. National Union Fire Insurance Company of Pittsburgh, PA, 257 F.3d 484 (6th Cir. 2001).

Seventh Circuit: Caterpillar, Inc. v. Great American Insurance Co., 62 F.3d 955 (7th Cir. 1995).

Eighth Circuit: Piper Jaffray Companies v. National Union Fire Insurance Company of Pittsburgh, PA, 38 F. Supp.2d 771 (D. Minn. 1999).

Ninth Circuit: Clackamas County v. Midwest Employers Casualty Co., 2009 WL 4916364 (D. Or. Dec. 14, 2009); Commercial Capital Bankcorp. Inc. v. St. Paul Mercury Insurance Co., 419 F. Supp.2d 1173 (C.D. Cal. 2006).

Tenth Circuit: Stauth v. National Union Fire Insurance Company of Pittsburgh, PA, 1999 WL 420401 (10th Cir. June 24, 1999).

State Courts:

New York: Clifford Chance Limited Liability Partnership v. Indian Harbor Insurance Co., 2006 WL 3821841 (N.Y. Sup. Ct. N.Y. Cty. Dec. 27, 2006).

277 See:

First Circuit: Oxford Aviation, Inc. v. Global Aerospace, Inc., 680 F.3d 85 (1st Cir. 2012); Centennial Insurance Co. v. Patterson, 564 F.3d 46 (1st Cir. 2009); Acadia Insurance Co. v. Peerless Insurance Co., 679 F. Supp.2d 229 (D. Mass. 2010); MIB Group, Inc. v. Federal Insurance Co., 473 F. Supp.2d 142 (D. Mass. 2006).

Second Circuit: Admiral Indemnity Co. v. Travelers Casualty and Surety Co. of America, 881 F. Supp.2d 570 (S.D.N.Y. 2012); Burlington Insurance Co. v. De Vesta, 511 F. Supp.2d 231 (D. Conn. 2007).

Third Circuit: Post v. St. Paul Travelers Insurance Co., 691 F.3d 500 (3d Cir. 2012); Nationwide Mutual Insurance Co. v. CPB International, Inc., 562 F.3d 591 (3d Cir. 2009); American Legacy Foundation v. National Union Fire Insurance Company of Pittsburgh, Pennsylvania, 640 F. Supp.2d 524 (D. Del. 2009); Westport Insurance Corp. v. Hanft & Knight, P.C., 523 F. Supp.2d 444 (M.D. Pa. 2007).

Fourth Circuit: Nautilus Insurance Co. v. BSA Limited Partnership, 602 F. Supp.2d 641 (D. Md. 2009); American Select Insurance Co. v. Taylor, 445 F. Supp.2d 681 (N.D. W. Va. 2006).

Fifth Circuit: Trinity Universal Insurance Co. v. Employers Mutual Casualty Co., 592 F.3d 687 (5th Cir. 2010); Gilbane Building Co. v. Empire Steel Erectors, L.P., 691 F. Supp.2d 712 (S.D. Tex. 2010); Classic Performance Cars, Inc. v. Acceptance Indemnity Insurance Co., 464 F. Supp.2d 652 (S.D. Tex. 2006).

Sixth Circuit: Cincinnati Insurance Co. v. Zen Design Group, Ltd., 329 F.3d 546 (6th Cir. 2003); Aearo Corp. v. American International Specialty Lines Insurance Co., 676 F. Supp.2d 738 (S.D. Ind. 2009).

Seventh Circuit: ProLink Holdings Corp. v. Federal Insurance Co., 688 F.3d 828 (7th Cir. 2012); Plastics Engineering Co. v. Liberty Mutual Insurance Co., 2008 WL 170040 (7th Cir. Jan. 22, 2008); Krueger International, Inc. v. Federal Insurance Co., 647 F. Supp.2d 1024 (E.D. Wis. 2009).

Eighth Circuit: Interstate Bakeries Corp. v. OneBeacon Insurance Co., 686 F.3d 539 (8th Cir. 2012); Westchester Fire Insurance Co. v. Wallerich, 2007 WL 2821656 (D. Minn. Sept. 25, 2007).

Ninth Circuit: Align Technology, Inc. v. Federal Insurance Co., 673 F. Supp.2d 957 (N.D. Cal. 2009); Burlington Insurance Co. v. United Coatings Manufacturing Co., 518 F. Supp.2d 1241 (D. Haw. 2007).

Tenth Circuit: Ohio Casualty Insurance Co. v. Cloud Nine, LLC, 464 F. Supp.2d 1161 (D. Utah. 2006).

Eleventh Circuit: HDI-Gerling America Insurance Co. v. Morrison Homes, Inc., 701 F.3d 662 (11th Cir. 2012); Lime Tree Village Community Club Ass'n v. State Farm General Insurance Co., 980 F.2d 1402, 1405 (11th Cir. 1993); Trizec Properties, Inc. v. Biltmore Construction Co., 767 F.2d 810, 811 (11th Cir. 1985); Eastpointe Condominium I Association, Inc. v. Travelers Casualty and Surety Company of America, 664 F. Supp.2d 1281 (S.D. Fla. 2009).

State Courts:

California: Fire Insurance Exchange v. Superior Court, 181 Cal. App.4th 388, 104 Cal. Rptr.3d 534 (2010).

Colorado: TerraMatrix, Inc. v. United States Fire Insurance Co., 939 P.2d 483, 486 (Colo. App. 1997); City of Englewood v. Commercial Union Assurance Co., 940 P.2d 948 (Colo. App. 1996).

Illinois: Illinois State Bar Association Mutual Insurance Co. v. Mondo, 392 Ill. App.3d 1032, 911 N.E.2d 1144, 331 Ill. Dec. 914 (2009).

Iowa: First Newton National Bank v. General Casualty Company of Wisconsin, 426 N.W.2d 618, 630 (Iowa 1988) (noting that partial defense is minority rule).

Louisiana: Adams v. Frost, 990 So.2d 751 (La. App. 2008).

Minnesota: Jarvis & Sons, Inc. v. International Marine Underwriters, 768 N.W.2d 365 (Minn. App. 2009).

New York: QBE Insurance Corp. v. Jinx-Proof Inc., 102 A.D.3d 508, 959 N.Y.S.2d 19 (N.Y. App. Div. 2013); Natural Organics, Inc. v. OneBeacon America Insurance Co., 102 A.D. 756, 959 N.Y.S.2d 204 (N.Y. App. Div. 2013); Barkan v. New York Schools Insurance Reciprocal, 65 A.D.3d 1061, 886 N.Y.S.2d 414 (N.Y. App. Div. 2009).

Ohio: Sanborn Plastics Corp. v. St. Paul Fire & Marine Insurance Co., 616 N.E.2d 988, 996 (Ohio App. 1993).

Oregon: Bresee Homes, Inc. v. Farmers Insurance Exchange, 353 Or. 112, 293 P.3d 1036 (2012); Mutual of Enumclaw Insurance Co. v. Gutman, 21 P.3d 101 (Or. App.), *review denied* 39 P.3d 192 (Or. 2001).

Pennsylvania: General Accident Insurance Co. v. Allen, 692 A.2d 1089, 1095 (Pa. 1997); Erie Insurance Exchange v. Transamerica Insurance Co., 533 A.2d 1363, 1368 (Pa. 1987).

Texas: AccuFleet, Inc. v. Hartford Fire Insurance Co., 2009 WL 2961351 (Tex. App. Sept. 17, 2009).

Washington: Waite v. Aetna Casualty & Surety Co., 467 P.2d 847, 851 (Wash. 1970).

West Virginia: Camden-Clark Memorial Hospital Association v. St. Paul Fire and Marine Insurance Co., 224 W.Va. 228, 682 S.E.2d 566 (2009).

Wisconsin: Plastics Engineering Co. v. Liberty Mutual Insurance Co., 315 Wis.2d 556, 759 N.W.2d 613 (Wis. 2009).

But see:

Fifth Circuit: Employers Mutual Casualty Co. v. Lennox International, Inc., 375 F. Supp.2d 500 (S.D. Miss. 2005) (under Mississippi law, an insurer's duty to defend applies only to covered claims and there is no duty to defend noncovered claims, unless there is no reasonable way to allocate defense costs between covered and noncovered claims).

Ninth Circuit: Quigley v. Travelers Property Casualty Insurance Co., 630 F. Supp.2d 1204 (E.D. Cal. 2009) (allowing allocation).

State Courts:

New Jersey: William H. Hall Co. v. Harleysville Insurance Company of New Jersey, 2009 WL 3416050 (N.J. Super. App. Dept. Oct. 13, 2009) (allowing allocation).

[278] See, e.g.:

Fifth Circuit: Texaco Exploration and Production Inc. v. AmClyde Engineered Products, Inc., 2009 WL 2567190 (E.D.La. Aug. 17, 2009).

[279] See, e.g.:

Fifth Circuit: Gabarick v. Laurin Maritime (America) Inc., 635 F. Supp.2d 499 (E.D. La. 2009).

Sixth Circuit: City of Sterling Heights, Michigan v. United Nat'l Insurance Co., 319 Fed. Appx. 357 (6th Cir. 2009).

Eighth Circuit: Liberty Mutual Insurance Co. v. Pella Corp., 633 F. Supp.2d 714 (S.D. Iowa 2009).

Ninth Circuit: Jeff Tracy, Inc. v. U.S. Specialty Insurance Co., 636 F. Supp.2d 995 (C.D. Cal. 2009); Acacia Research Corp. v. National Union Fire Insurance Company of Pittsburgh, PA, 2008 WL 4179206 (C.D. Cal. Feb. 8, 2008).

State Courts:

California: State Farm General Insurance Co. v. Mintarsih, 175 Cal. App.4th 274, 95 Cal. Rptr.3d 845 (2009).

New Jersey: Polarome International, Inc. v. Greenwich Insurance Co., 404 N.J. Super. 241, 961 A.2d 29 (N.J. Super. App., Dept. 2008).

New York: Federal Insurance Co. v. Tyco International Ltd., 57 A.D.3d 335, 871 N.Y.S.2d 9 (N.Y. App. Div. 2008); Millennium Partners, L.P. v. Select Insurance Co., 24 Misc.3d 212, 882 N.Y.S.2d 849 (N.Y. Sup. Ct. N.Y. Cty. 2009).

Texas: Ulico Casualty Co. v. Allied Pilots Association, 262 S.W.3d 773 (Tex. 2008).

But see:

Second Circuit: Julio and Sons Co. v. Travelers Casualty and Surety Company of America, 591 F. Supp.2d 651 (S.D.N.Y. 2008) (insurer required to advance defense costs if any claim were potentially covered).

[280] Continental Casualty Co. v. Board of Education of Charles County, 489 A.2d 536, 544 (Md. 1985). See also, Weinstein & Riley PS v. Westport Insurance Corp., 484 Fed. Appx. 121 (9th Cir. 2012).

[281] See, e.g., Nodaway Valley Bank v. Continental Casualty Co., 715 F. Supp. 1458, 1460–1461 (W.D. Mo. 1989), *aff'd* 916 F.2d 1362 (8th Cir. 1990).

The "reasonably related" standard also has found acceptance in common law jurisdictions outside the United States. See New Zealand Forest Product Ltd. v. New Zealand Insurance Company Ltd., 1 WLR 1237 (Privy Council, 21 July 1997). In that case, which involved D&O policy language similar to U.S. policies, New Zealand's highest appellate court (then the Privy Council in England) embraced the "reasonably related" approach, reasoning:

"On the ordinary meaning of the words which have been used it is reasonable to understand that the cover would extend to the whole costs incurred in the defense where the officer was the sole defendant. Why then should the meaning of the words change simply because there is another defendant who is not covered by the policy." *Id.,* at *7

[282] See § 5.03[2] *infra*. See also:

First Circuit: Emhart Industries, Inc. v. Century Indemnity Co., 559 F.3d 57 (1st Cir. 2009).

Fifth Circuit: Continental Casualty Co. v. North American Capacity Insurance Co., 683 F.3d 79 (5th Cir. 2012); Mid-Continent Casualty Co. v. Academy Development, Inc., 476 Fed. Appx. 316 (5th Cir. 2012); Willbros RPI, Inc. v. Continental Casualty Co., 601 F.3d 306 (5th Cir. 2010); Trinity Universal Insurance Co. v. Employers Mutual Casualty Co., 592 F.3d 687 (5th Cir. 2010).

Sixth Circuit: Alticor, Inc. v. National Union Fire Insurance Company of Pennsylvania, 2013 WL 135157 (W.D. Mich. Jan. 4, 2013).

Seventh Circuit: Coca-Cola Enterprises, Inc. v. ATS Enterprises, Inc., 670 F.3d 771 (7th Cir. 2012).

Ninth Circuit: MGA Entertainment, Inc. v. Hartford Insurance Group, 869 F. Supp.2d 1117 (C.D. Cal. 2012).

State Courts:

Arizona: Nucor Corp. v. Employers Insurance Company of Wausau, 2012 WL 5893485 (Ariz. App. Nov. 23, 2012).

California: Lisa Risely v. Interinsurance Exchange of the Automobile Club, 183 Cal. App.4th 196, 107 Cal. Rptr.3d 343 (2010); American States Insurance Co. v. Progressive Casualty Insurance Co., 180 Cal. App.4th 18, 102 Cal. Rptr.3d 591 (2009).

Illinois: United National Insurance Co. v. 200 North Dearborn Partnership, 979 N.E.2d 920, 366 Ill. Dec. 119 (Ill. App. 2012), *appeal dismissed* 982 N.E.2d 775 (Ill. 2013); Illinois School District Agency v. St. Charles Community Unit School District 303, 971 N.E.2d 1099, 361 Ill. Dec. 577 (Ill. App.), *appeal denied* 979 N.E.2d 877 (Ill. 2012); Chicago Hospital Risk Pooling Program v. Illinois State Medical Inter-Insurance Exchange, 397 Ill. App.3d 512, 925 N.E.2d 1216, 339 Ill. Dec. 95 (2010); Statewide Insurance Co. v. Houston General Insurance Co., 397 Ill. App.3d 410, 920 N.E.2d 611, 336 Ill. Dec. 402 (2009).

North Carolina: SPX Corp. v. Liberty Mutual Insurance Co., 709 S.E.2d 441 (N.C. App. 2011).

Texas: Safeco Lloyds Insurance Co. v. Allstate Insurance Co., 308 S.W.3d 49, (2009).

Washington: Ledcor Industries (USA), Inc. v. Mutual of Enumclaw Insurance Co., 150 Wash. App. 1, 206 P.3d 1255 (2009).

CHAPTER 6

Duty to Defend and Insured Litigation

Chapter Contents

§ 6.01 Overview

Liability insurance is also known as litigation insurance because it provides for defense and indemnity obligations.[1] This chapter discusses the issues surrounding the defense obligations. First, it looks at the central policy language issue—whether a "suit" exists requiring commencement of an insurance company paid or reimbursed defense.[2] It then looks at the general rules concerning the duty to defend,[3] issues concerning independent counsel,[4] settlement after breach,[5] tender,[6] umbrella insurance,[7] and reimbursement of defense costs.[8] Finally, it addresses the topic of insured litigation.[9]

§ 6.02 Duty to Defend

The second sentence of the standard-form insuring agreement states that "we will have the right and duty to defend the insured against any 'suit' seeking those ['bodily injury' or 'property damage'] damages."[10] This is the duty-to-defend language, which is the promise by the insurance company to defend the policyholder in a "suit" potentially covered by the indemnity provisions of the policy. The coverage issues include the existence of a "suit" and allegations potentially within the policy's coverage grant.

[1]—"Suit"

Nowhere in CGL insurance policies is the term "suit" defined. In most cases, a legal action needs to be filed to constitute a "suit." In the environmental context, there is a dispute as to whether a "potentially responsible party" ("PRP") letter constitutes a "suit" triggering the defense obligation.[11] The insurance companies argue that "suit" is limited to actions filed in a court of law,[12] while policyholders maintain that the term includes out-of-court legal proceedings, such as administrative enforcement actions initiated by the Environmental Protection Agency ("EPA").[13]

It is undisputed that the term "suit" includes a court proceeding. Similarly, the term "suit" has also been defined in terms of legal process outside a court of law. For example, *Webster's Dictionary*, on which courts have relied for definitions of undefined insurance policy terms,[14] "suit" is "the attempt to gain an end by legal process: prosecution of right before any tribunal."[15] The existence of such alternative dictionary definitions establishes that the term "suit" is ambiguous at minimum.[16]

In addition, the majority of courts that have addressed this issue have determined that a PRP letter[17] constitutes a "suit."[18] Indeed, the majority of state courts (including the majority of courts of last resort) that have addressed the "suit" issue have held government enforcement actions are "suits" that insurance companies must defend.[19] Likewise, the majority of federal courts applying state law have also determined that a PRP letter constitutes a "suit."[20] There is only a small minority of decisions holding that PRP letters are not "suits."[21] Conflicting judicial viewpoints reinforce this ambiguity:

> "The determination that 'sudden and accidental' [as used in the "qualified" pollution exclusion] is an ambiguous phrase is supported by a large amount of conflicting authority. Although the mere existence of conflicting authority does not establish the ambiguity of a contract term, 'this type of comprehensive debate dispels the insurer's contention that the exclusionary language is clear.'"[22]

Under most states' laws, insurance policy ambiguities are resolved in favor of coverage.[23] Thus, the term "suit" should be construed broadly and in favor of coverage, including as applying to legal proceedings other than court actions initiated by complaints, such as EPA enforcement actions initiated by PRP letters.

The majority view is in fact supported by sound reasoning or namely, that an EPA enforcement action initiated by a PRP letter is akin to a lawsuit initiated by complaint:

> "The EPA processes for the enforcement of obligations to aid in the cleaning up of environmental pollution have moved away from the use of lawsuits toward the use of agency demands for participation in remedial action. Those requests

> are dangerous for the alleged polluter to ignore because they often result in dispositive, extrajudicial solutions. The consequences of the receipt of [an] EPA [demand] letter [are] so substantially equivalent to the commencement of a lawsuit that a duty to defend [arises] immediately.
>
> "The EPA demand letter is not the same as a conventional demand letter based on a personal injury claim. The identification of an insured as a 'potentially responsible party' (PRP) has more serious consequences than a demand letter in a personal injury case. For example, the insured can be fined for failure to cooperate in the EPA's process of cleanup. In addition, if the EPA ultimately recovers the costs of cleanup, the insured's failure to settle before any legal action by the EPA could increase the amount of recovery against the insured.
>
> "The insured's obligation to respond positively to the [EPA's demand] letter [is] strong. The prospects of avoiding financial responsibility [are] minimal because liability is not based on fault. Moreover, the risk to which [the insured is] exposed [is] substantial because, as a practical matter, its liability is joint and several. Early involvement in the settlement discussions is thus often crucial to protect one's interests. Any court action by EPA is limited to the administrative record, and judicial review considers only whether the EPA 'decision was arbitrary and capricious or otherwise not in accordance with law.' Thus participation in the development of that record can be crucial. Settlement of EPA claims against potentially responsible parties, with protection against claims for contribution, is a desired goal. The situation [is] such that opportunity to protect [the insured's] interests could well [be] lost, long before any lawsuit would be brought. It would be naive to characterize [an] EPA [demand] letter as a request for voluntary action. [The insured has] no practical choice other than to respond actively to the letter."[24]

Such reasoning is supported by important public policy interests. Any distinction between "claim" and "suit" would place perverse incentives on non-cooperation with the EPA, because non-cooperation would be the only mechanism through which a policyholder could ensure insurance coverage.[25] Non-cooperation would force the EPA to initiate a lawsuit and thereby trigger a policyholder's right to a defense. Such a position would obviously impede environmental cleanup efforts, and it would effectively amount to a waste of precious judicial resources. Further, permitting policyholders to do indirectly that which they could not do directly flies in the face of all logic and reason. As stated by the Michigan Supreme Court:

> "[F]rom a policy perspective, . . . the position urged by [the insurance companies] would only increase the litigiousness of this already extensively litigated area of the law. Limiting an insurer's duty to defend to an actual court proceeding preceded by a complaint would merely encourage PRPs to decline voluntary involvement in site cleanups, waiting instead for an actual lawsuit to be brought in order to receive insurance coverage. This would have the effect of substantially protracting the cleanup of contaminated sites."[26]

[2]—General Rules Regarding the Duty to Defend

Once a suit is found to exist, there are a number of rules to aid in ascertaining whether the duty has been implicated by such "suit." An insurance company's duty to defend is interpreted expansively. Indeed, the duty to defend is independent of, and broader than, the duty to indemnify, meaning the duty to defend might be owed even in circumstances where the duty to indemnify is not owed.[27]

Initially, the duty to defend is determined exclusively from the insurance policy and the allegations made against the policyholder in the underlying action.[28] However, even when the underlying complaint's allegations do not trigger an insurance company's duty to defend, the insurance company must nonetheless defend its policyholder if it later discovers facts establishing a possibility of coverage.[29] On the other hand, in some jurisdictions, when the underlying complaint establishes a duty to defend, an insurance company may not deny that defense based on *actual facts* that it later discovers in the underlying action.[30]

An insurance company is also under a duty to defend its policyholder whenever the allegations or the actual facts in the underlying action ***potentially*** or ***even arguably*** come within the scope of the policy coverage.[31] Significantly, it is the facts alleged, not the theories asserted, that determine the existence of a duty to defend.[32] For example, if a complaint "contains ambiguous or incomplete allegations and does not state facts sufficient to bring a case clearly within or without the coverage," the insurance company is obligated to defend its policyholder.[33]

When the duty to defend attaches, the insurance company cannot pick and choose which claims to defend, but is required to defend all claims—whether excluded or potentially covered—that arise from the same occurrence in which the potentially covered claim arises.[34]

Any doubts regarding the allegations of the underlying action or the scope of coverage are construed in favor of finding a duty to defend.[35] This rule follows the more general rule of insurance policy construction that any ambiguities in the interpretation of insurance policy terms are resolved in favor of the policyholder.[36]

The duty to defend may also include a duty to settle within policy limits if it is reasonable to do so. The insurance company has an affirmative duty to seek to protect its policyholder against any excess liability by making reasonable effort to settle within the policy limits, and the insurance company's failures in this regard, to the extent it has acted unreasonably, may expose it to liability in excess of the indemnity limits set forth in the policy.[37]

[3]—Independent Counsel

[a]—Right to Control Defense

Generally, where a true duty to defend is present in a policy,[38] the insurance company has the right to control the selection of and actions by defense counsel in defense of the underlying claims.[39] Some courts, on the other hand, hold that an insurance company's defense under "reservation of rights" transfers control of the defense to the policyholder.[40]

[b]—Conflicts of Interest

Conflicts of interest can arise in a few contexts. For instance, as stated above,[41] the vast majority of courts hold that when the duty to defend attaches, the insurance company cannot pick and choose which claims to defend, but, instead, is required to defend all claims—whether excluded or potentially covered—that arise from the same occurrence in which the potentially covered claim arises.[42]

In this circumstance—namely, when some claims are covered and some are not in the underlying action—a conflict of interest is present because the insurance company has the opposite economic incentive to litigate the underlying action in a way that eliminates all covered claims, while the policyholder has economic incentive to litigate to eliminate uncovered claims. In such situations, the policyholder may be entitled to independent counsel paid for by the insurance company.[43]

Independent counsel may also be required in other conflict of interest situations, such as the insurance companies' defending under a "reservation of rights" or where there are two policyholders, each entitled to a defense, but the joint representation of which would create a conflict of interest for defense counsel.[44]

A defense under a "reservation of rights" usually occurs only when there are some covered and some uncovered claims. The Fourth Circuit has set forth one position of the relevant law in the "reservation of rights" area, stating: "Several courts have adopted a *per se* rule that where an insurance company reserves the right to deny coverage for a particular claim, then a conflict of interest between the insurance company and insured exists."[45] The court went on to say that:

> "These courts conclude that where an insurance company defends its insured under a reservation of rights concerning coverage, a conflict exists. These courts have identified the following conflicts: if an insurance company contends that a particular loss will not be covered under the policy, the lawyer hired by the insurance company may offer only a token defense of the potentially non-covered claim or conduct the defense in such a manner as to make the likelihood of the plaintiff's verdict greater on the non-covered claim. Additionally, the lawyer hired by the insurance company might gain access to confidential information during the defense that the lawyer might provide to the insurance company to contest coverage. Further, the lawyer retained to defend the insured might tend to favor the insurance company over the insured due to a desire to receive future legal work from the insurance company."[46]

In contrast, other courts have held that defending an insured with a "reservation of rights" concerning coverage does not create a *per se* conflict.[47] In rejecting a *per se* rule, these courts have held that not every "reservation of rights" creates a conflict. Instead a case-by-case assessment must be made.[48]

Regardless of whether a court applies a *per se* conflict rule, once a court does find that a conflict of interest exists, it must determine how to remedy the conflict. Under duty-to-defend policies (as opposed to reimbursement policies),[49] the courts universally require that the insured receive counsel, but are divided over who should control the selection of counsel.[50] Some courts hold that if a conflict exists, the insured has the right to select its own counsel to be paid for by the insurance company.[51] Others hold that the insurance company has the right to provide counsel or to allow the insured to choose counsel.[52] In either case, the insurance company pays the legal bills.[53] A third set of courts has held that an insurance company retains the right to select counsel on the insured's behalf or acknowledge the insured's right to counsel without specifying who is entitled to make the selection.[54]

[4]—Settlement after Breach

During pendency of the defense of the underlying action it may be premature to delineate the policyholder's entitlement to indemnification from its CGL insurance company for any liability that might be assessed or incurred against the policyholder in the underlying action. However, if the policyholder must defend itself as the result of the insurance company's breach of its duty to defend, and, in that defense, the policyholder settles the underlying action before the action can be confined solely to claims outside the scope of coverage of all policies, the policyholder may be able to establish an entitlement to indemnification for the settlement, without any obligation to contribute.[55] One court has held:

> "An insurer who refuses to defend a claim potentially within the scope of the policy does so at its own peril. . . . Therefore, the [insurance company], which has refused to provide any defense for [the policyholder], may not now protest that it was deprived of an opportunity to litigate and establish that the underlying claims fell outside its policy coverage. Those insurers that did contribute to the [policyholder's] defense are also precluded from arguing that the underlying claims fell outside their policies since they had the opportunity and declined to litigate the claims to conclusion."[56]

[5]—Tender

Tender of the claim for defense is another interesting issue. It arises when an insurance company insists on the policyholder's formal tendering of the claim for a defense. This requires an understanding of what constitutes a proper "tender" of a suit for the purpose of seeking a defense.

CGL insurance policies generally do not mention the word "tender."[57] Rather, they ordinarily have "notice" requirements, compelling a policyholder to provide notice of any claim or circumstances likely to lead to a claim as soon as practicable and to forward copies of all "suit" papers.[58]

The subissues include: (1) whether a policyholder need specifically demand or request a defense; (2) whether a policyholder needs to tender under specifically identified policies; and (3) whether a policyholder can pick and choose which policies to use or target its tender.

[a]—Need for Specific Demand for Defense

Based on this policy language, there is a split in authority as to what constitutes "tender" for purposes of triggering an insurer's duties. Most courts appropriately hold that "tender" of a claim is accomplished merely by placing an insurance company on notice of a claim.[59] Other courts hold that tender is accomplished by, in addition to notice, the policyholder's specifically requesting coverage for the claim.[60]

[b]—Specification of Policy under Which Coverage Is Sought

In either case, there is generally no requirement that a policyholder specify under which particular policy it is tendering a claim.[61] In fact, courts have almost unanimously held that notice of a claim under one policy constitutes notice of the same claim under other policies sold by the same insurance company.[62] These courts have based their holding, in part, on the notice language in the policies, which merely requires notice of the claim and its particulars, not a specification of the applicable policy.[63] Moreover, an insurance company's duty to defend is usually triggered by actual knowledge of a cause of action being asserted against its policyholder and that the claim potentially fits within the scope of any of the policies that had been sold to the policyholder.[64]

Furthermore, virtually every state has adopted, through statute or administrative regulation, rules placing an affirmative duty on an insurance company to disclose all coverages available to a policyholder and pertinent to a submitted claim. For example, many states have adopted the Uniform Unfair Claims Settlement Practices Act, which places an affirmative duty upon the insurance company to disclose fully all insurance coverages available to a policyholder with respect to a particular claim.[65] Similarly, other states have adopted the Uniform Unfair and Deceptive Practices Act, which expressly prohibits misrepresentation of pertinent facts and policy provisions concerning coverages applicable to claims at issue, and implicitly requires insurance companies affirmatively to apprise policyholders of all coverage applicable to a claim.[66]

Thus, given the standard "notice" language, virtually unanimous case law on notice under one policy constituting notice under all policies, and statutes and/or regulations that place on the insurance company an affirmative duty to disclose other coverages available to respond to a particular claim, "tender" is accomplished through normal notice, without specifically requesting a defense under a specific insurance policy.

[c]—"Targeted Tender Rule"

The "targeted tender rule" allows the policyholder to pick and choose under which policy it shall receive a defense and/or indemnity. Of course, such a choice, even if followed, has no impact on the chosen insurance company's rights to contribution or indemnity and cannot cause an excess or umbrella policy to provide first-level coverage over a primary insurance policy.[67]

[6]—Umbrella Insurance

Excess and umbrella insurance policies also provide defense obligations to policyholders in the following circumstances: (i) "drop down" coverage; and (ii) exhaustion of primary coverage.

[a]—"Drop Down" Clauses

Umbrella insurance policies may provide a defense under a "drop down" provision. In fact, such provisions generally obligate the umbrella insurance company to defend the policyholder in underlying actions when no other underlying insurance is so obligated. For example, a standard provision often provides as follows:

> "With respect to such insurance as is afforded by this form and, if there is no underlying insurer obligated to do so, the Company shall have the right and duty

to defend any suit against the policyholder, even if any of the allegations of the suit are groundless, false or fraudulent."[68]

Thus, for suits that aver claims that are potentially covered by the terms of the umbrella policies, the umbrella insurance company should be required to defend the policyholder if no underlying insurance company is "obligated" to provide a defense to the policyholder.

The term "obligated," in the above-quoted provision, is usually undefined in the policies. However, the dictionary defines "obligate" as "to bind legally" and to "oblige" or "commit (as funds) to meet an obligation."[69] Under the plain meaning of the quoted policy provision, the umbrella insurance company would be required to defend the policyholder in suits that are potentially covered under the terms of the umbrella policies if there is no underlying insurance company that is either legally bound to defend or obliged to commit funds to defend the policyholder in such suit.[70]

Logically, an underlying insurance company would not be "obligated" to defend the policyholder in situations where the suit is somehow excluded by the terms of the underlying insurance policy or policies. Indeed, courts have held that an umbrella insurance company with virtually identical duty-to-defend language must defend a policyholder when the claims were excluded under the terms of the underlying insurance company's policy.[71]

[b]—Exhaustion of Primary Coverage

By the same logic, no underlying insurance company would be obligated to defend an underlying action asserted against the policyholder if the indemnity limits of such underlying insurance had been exhausted. Many jurisdictions have stated that upon exhaustion of the primary policy limits, the primary policy cannot be obligated to defend or indemnify any claims, thereby obligating the express or umbrella carrier to undertake the defense.[72]

In fact, umbrella policies may contain a provision that obligates the insurance company to defend the policyholder upon exhaustion of the indemnity limits of the underlying primary policy. Umbrella liability insurance policies usually contain a provision that states that upon exhaustion of the underlying primary policy, the umbrella company is required to act as the underlying primary insurance company, subject to the terms of the underlying primary policy (which usually includes a duty to defend):

> "In the event of reduction or exhaustion of the aggregate limits of liability under underlying insurance by reason of losses paid thereunder, this policy shall, subject to this Limits of Liability provision, and to the terms and conditions of the underlying insurance:
>
> "(a) in the event of reduction, continue in force as excess of the reduced underlying insurance;
>
> "(b) in the event of exhaustion, continue in force as underlying insurance."[73]

Courts have determined that the phrase "continue in force as underlying insurance," obligates an umbrella insurance company to act as the primary insurance company and to defend its policyholder on exhaustion of the primary policy limits.[74]

[7]—Reimbursement of Defense Costs

A relatively recent phenomenon is the insurance companies' right to recoup defense costs from their policyholders. The insurance companies have attempted, and sometimes successfully, obtained this right to recoupment by reserving such rights in "reservation of rights" letters where they agree to undertake the defense of the policyholder. A minority of courts permit recoupment of defense costs.[75] A majority of courts, on the other hand, do not permit an insurance company to seek and/or obtain reimbursement of defense costs from its policyholder even if coverage is later determined not to exist for the loss or liability at issue, reasoning that such a position would unilaterally amend the contract, narrow the duty to defend to equate it with the duty to indemnify, and eliminate one of the central benefits of liability coverage—namely, the "litigation insurance" it provides.[76]

§ 6.03 Insured Litigation

Real estate-related entities may have a subset of insured litigation, which is just a name for litigation covered by its insurance policies' defense obligations.[77] The main difference is that this category of insurance generally includes claims where coverage issues are not in dispute, such as automobile liabilities, workers' compensation liabilities, and bodily injury and property damage claims allegedly caused by the policyholder's purported negligence.

With regard to general liability and automobile liability insurance, the issues addressed under liability insurance apply and there is no need for a separate discussion here.[78] Of note, however, many large companies use third-party administrators to manage this subset of litigation and oversee insurance defense litigation counsel. To save on premiums, some large companies self-insure at a low layer, having large self-insured retentions and/or deductibles.[79] This allows these companies to manage the routine litigation and insure against catastrophic losses above the per claim/aggregate retention level and/or deductible.

Any entity that employs workers is generally governed by workers' compensation laws. Workers' compensation laws are statutory, ensuring that workers who are injured in the course and scope of their jobs suffer no adverse economic consequences as the result of such injuries irrespective of fault. This means that employees receive medical care necessitated by such accident and lost wages during any period of disability, and employers receive immunity from damages to their employees under tort law.[80] Employers purchase various types of insurance to pay for these liabilities. Coverage fights over liabilities owed under these policies are rare and to the extent there are disputes, they are not industry specific to real estate. Accordingly, workers' compensation insurance coverage is beyond the scope of this treatise.

Notes

[1] See §§ 2.03, 5.01 *supra*.

[2] See § 6.02[1] *infra*.

[3] See § 6.02[2] *infra*.

[4] See § 6.02[3] *infra*.

[5] See § 6.02[4] *infra*.

6 See § 6.02[5] *infra*.

7 See § 6.02[6] *infra*.

8 See § 6.02[7] *infra*.

9 See § 6.03 *infra*.

10 See ISO Form CG 00 01 10 01. Of course, there are also insurance policies that do not provide for a duty to defend but instead may provide coverage solely for liability against the policyholder and/or reimburse the policyholder for defense costs incurred in defense of covered or potentially covered claims. For further discussion, see § 10.03[2][b] *infra*.

11 PRP stands for "potentially responsible party." The letter is a demand letter and the recipient is under a strong obligation to respond to it. See Avondale Industries, Inc. v. Travelers Indemnification Co, 697 F. Supp 1314, 1321 (S.D.N.Y. 1988).

See, e.g.:

Second Circuit: Avondale Industries, Inc. v. Travelers Indemnity Co., 887 F.2d 1200, 1206 (2d Cir. 1989); EDO Corp. v. Newark Insurance Co., 898 F. Supp. 952 (D. Conn. 1995).

Third Circuit: New Castle County v. Hartford Accident & Indemnity Co, 673 F. Supp. 1359, 1366 (D. Del. 1987), *aff'd in part, rev'd in part* 933 F.2d 1162 (3d Cir. 1991), *cert. denied* 507 U.S. 1030 (1993); Simon Wrecking Co. v. AIU Insurance Co., 350 F. Supp.2d 624 (E.D. Pa. 2004).

Eighth Circuit: Land O' Lakes, Inc. v. Employers Insurance Co. of Wausau, 728 F.3d 822 (8th Cir. 2013) (PRP letter was a "suit").

Ninth Circuit: Anderson Brothers, Inc. v. St. Paul Fire and Marine Insurance Co., 729 F.3d 923 (9th Cir. 2013) (PRP letter triggered duty).

State Courts:

Alabama: Travelers Casualty and Surety Co. v. Alabama Gas Corp., 117 So.3d 695 (Ala. 2012) (PRP letter constitutes "suit").

Arizona: Nucor Corp. v. Employers Insurance Co. of Wausau, 296 P.3d 74 (Ariz. App. 2012) (PRP letter is "suit").

California: Powerine Oil Co. v. Superior Court, 118 P.3d 589 (Cal. 2005); Ortega Rock Quarry v. Golden Eagle Insurance Corp., 46 Cal. Rptr.3d 517 (Cal. App. 2006); CDM Investors v. Travelers Casualty & Surety Co., 43 Cal. Rptr.3d 669 (Cal. App. 2006).

Indiana: Thomson, Inc. v. Continental Casualty Co., 982 N.E.2d 4 (Ind. App. 2012) (PRP letter was not a "suit").

Massachusetts: Hazen Paper Co. v. United States Fidelity & Guaranty Co., 555 N.E.2d 576, 581 (Mass. 1990); Preferred Mutual Insurance Co. v. Gordon, 2003 WL 21077026 (Mass. Super. May 13, 2003).

Michigan: American Bumper & Manufacturing Co. v. Hartford Fire Insurance Co., 550 N.W.2d 475, 481 (Mich. 1996); Michigan Millers Mutual Insurance Co. v. Bronson Plating Co., 519 N.W.2d 864, 869 (Mich. 1994); Polkow v. Citizens Insurance Company of America, 447 N.W.2d 853, 855–56 (Mich. App. 1989), *rev'd in part on other grounds* 476 N.W.2d 382 (Mich. 1991).

12 See, e.g.:

Second Circuit: Avondale Industries, Inc. v. Travelers Indemnity Co., 887 F.2d 1200, 1206 (2d Cir. 1989); EDO Corp. v. Newark Insurance Co., 898 F. Supp. 952 (D. Conn. 1995).

Third Circuit: New Castle County v. Hartford Accident & Indemnity Co, 673 F. Supp. 1359, 1366 (D. Del. 1987), *aff'd in part, rev'd in part* 933 F.2d 1162 (3d Cir. 1991), *cert. denied* 507 U.S. 1030 (1993); Simon Wrecking Co. v. AIU Insurance Co., 350 F. Supp.2d 624 (E.D. Pa. 2004).

State Courts:

California: Powerine Oil Co. v. Superior Court, 118 P.3d 589 (Cal. 2005); Ortega Rock Quarry v. Golden Eagle Insurance Corp., 46 Cal. Rptr.3d 517 (Cal. App. 2006); CDM Investors v. Travelers Casualty & Surety Co., 43 Cal. Rptr.3d 669 (Cal. App. 2006).

Massachusetts: Hazen Paper Co. v. United States Fidelity & Guaranty Co., 555 N.E.2d 576, 581 (Mass. 1990); Preferred Mutual Insurance Co. v. Gordon, 2003 WL 21077026 (Mass. Super. May 13, 2003).

Michigan: American Bumper & Manufacturing Co. v. Hartford Fire Insurance Co., 550 N.W.2d 475, 481 (Mich. 1996); Michigan Millers Mutual Insurance Co. v. Bronson Plating Co., 519 N.W.2d 864, 869 (Mich. 1994); Polkow v. Citizens Insurance Company of America, 447 N.W.2d 853, 855–856 (Mich. App. 1989), *rev'd in part on other grounds* 476 N.W.2d 382 (Mich. 1991).

13 See, e.g.:

First Circuit: Century Indemnity Co. v. Liberty Mutual Insurance Co., 708 F. Supp.2d 202 (D.R.I. 2010); Whittaker Corp. v. American Nuclear Insurers, 671 F. Supp.2d 242 (D. Mass. 2009).

Second Circuit: Avondale Industries, Inc. v. Travelers Indemnity Co., 887 F.2d 1200, 1206 (2d Cir. 1989); EDO Corp. v. Newark Insurance Co., 898 F. Supp. 952 (D. Conn. 1995).

Third Circuit: New Castle County v. Hartford Accident & Indemnity Co, 673 F. Supp. 1359, 1366 (D. Del. 1987), *aff'd in part, rev'd in part* 933 F.2d 1162 (3d Cir. 1991), *cert. denied* 507 U.S. 1030 (1993); Simon Wrecking Co. v. AIU Insurance Co., 350 F. Supp.2d 624 (E.D. Pa. 2004).

Fourth Circuit: National Union Fire Insurance Company of Pittsburgh, PA v. Porter Hayden Co., 408 B.R. 66 (D. Md. 2009).

State Courts:

California: Ameron International Corp. v. Insurance Company of the State of Pennsylvania, 50 Cal.4th 1370, 242 P.3d 1020, 118 Cal. Rptr.3d 95 (2010); Powerine Oil Co. v. Superior Court, 37 Cal.4th 377, 118 P.3d 589, 33 Cal. Rptr.3d 562 (2005); Ortega Rock Quarry v. Golden Eagle Insurance Corp., 46 Cal. Rptr.3d 517 (Cal. App. 2006); CDM Investors v. Travelers Casualty & Surety Co., 43 Cal. Rptr.3d 669 (Cal. App. 2006).

Massachusetts: Hazen Paper Co. v. United States Fidelity & Guaranty Co., 555 N.E.2d 576, 581 (Mass. 1990); Preferred Mutual Insurance Co. v. Gordon, 2003 WL 21077026 (Mass. Super. May 13, 2003).

Michigan: American Bumper & Manufacturing Co. v. Hartford Fire Insurance Co., 550 N.W.2d 475, 481 (Mich. 1996); Michigan Millers Mutual Insurance Co. v. Bronson Plating Co., 519 N.W.2d 864, 869 (Mich. 1994); Polkow v. Citizens Insurance Company of America, 447 N.W.2d 853, 855–856 (Mich. App. 1989), *rev'd in part on other grounds* 476 N.W.2d 382 (Mich. 1991).

Nebraska: Dutton-Lainson Co. v. Continental Insurance Co., 279 Neb. 365, 778 N.W.2d 433 (2010).

Oregon: Certain Underwriters at Lloyd's London and Excess Insurance Co. v. Massachusetts Bonding and Insurance Co., 235 Or. App. 99, 230 P.3d 103 (2010).

14 See Hecla Mining Co. v. New Hampshire Insurance Co., 811 P.2d 1083, 1091 (Colo. 1991).

15 *Webster's Third New International Dictionary* at 2286 (1986) (emphasis added).

16 See:

Colorado: Hecla Mining Co. v. New Hampshire Insurance Co., 811 P.2d 1083, 1091 (Colo. 1991) (ambiguity exists if term is susceptible to more than one reasonable interpretation).

Iowa: A.Y. McDonald Industries, Inc. v. Insurance Company of North America, 475 N.W.2d 607, 627–628 (Iowa 1991) (finding "suit" ambiguous on basis of dictionary definitions).

Michigan: Michigan Millers Mutual Insurance Co. v. Bronson Plating Co., 519 N.W.2d 864, 869 (Mich. 1994) (finding "suit" ambiguous on basis of dictionary definitions).

New Hampshire: Coakley v. Maine Bonding & Casualty Co., 618 A.2d 777, 786–787 (N.H. 1992) (finding "suit" ambiguous on basis of dictionary definitions).

North Carolina: C.D. Spangler Construction Co. v. Industrial Crankshaft & Engineering Co., 388 S.E.2d 557, 569–570 (N.C. 1990) (finding "suit" ambiguous on basis of dictionary definitions).

17 As stated above, PRP stands for "potentially responsible party." The letter is a demand letter and the recipient is under a strong obligation to respond to it. See Avondale Industries, Inc. v. Travelers Indemnification Co, 697 F. Supp 1314, 1321 (S.D.N.Y. 1988).

"Unlike the garden variety demand letter, which only exposes one to a potential threat of future litigation, a PRP notice carries with it immediate and severe implications. Generally, a party asserting a claim can do nothing between the occurrence of the tort and the filing of the complaint that can adversely affect the insureds' rights. However, in a CERCLA case, the PRP's substantive rights and ultimate liability are affected from the start of the administrative process."

18 See, e.g.:

Second Circuit: Avondale Industries, Inc. v. Travelers Indemnity Co., 887 F.2d 1200, 1206 (2d Cir. 1989); EDO Corp. v. Newark Insurance Co., 898 F. Supp. 952 (D. Conn. 1995).

Third Circuit: New Castle County v. Hartford Accident & Indemnity Co, 673 F. Supp. 1359, 1366 (D. Del. 1987), *aff'd in part, rev'd in part* 933 F.2d 1162 (3d Cir. 1991), *cert. denied* 507 U.S. 1030 (1993).

Eighth Circuit: Land O' Lakes, Inc. v. Employers Insurance Co. of Wausau, 728 F.3d 822 (8tth Cir. 2013) (PRP letter was a "suit").

Ninth Circuit: Anderson Brothers, Inc. v. St. Paul Fire and Marine Insurance Co., 729 F.3d 923 (9th Cir. 2013) (PRP letter triggered duty).

State Courts:

Alabama: Travelers Casualty and Surety Co. v. Alabama Gas Corp., 117 So.3d 695 (Ala. 2012) (PRP letter constitutes "suit").

Arizona: Nucor Corp. v. Employers Insurance Co. of Wausau, 296 P.3d 74 (Ariz. App. 2012) (PRP letter is "suit").

Massachusetts: Hazen Paper Co. v. United States Fidelity & Guaranty Co., 555 N.E.2d 576, 581 (Mass. 1990); Preferred Mutual Insurance Co. v. Gordon, 2003 WL 21077026 (Mass. Super. May 13, 2003).

Michigan: American Bumper & Manufacturing Co. v. Hartford Fire Insurance Co., 550 N.W.2d 475, 481 (Mich. 1996); Michigan Millers Mutual Insurance Co. v. Bronson Plating Co., 519 N.W.2d 864, 869 (Mich. 1994); Polkow v. Citizens Insurance Company of America, 447 N.W.2d 853, 855–856 (Mich. App. 1989), *rev'd in part on other grounds* 476 N.W.2d 382 (Mich. 1991).

19 See, e.g.:

Alabama: Travelers Casualty and Surety Co. v. Alabama Gas Corp., 117 So.3d 695 (Ala. 2012) (PRP letter constitutes "suit").

Arizona: Nucor Corp. v. Employers Insurance Co. of Wausau, 296 P.3d 74 (Ariz. App. 2012) (PRP letter is "suit").

Connecticut: R.T. Vanderbilt Co. v. Continental Casualty Co., 273 Conn. 448, 870 A.2d 1048 (Conn. 2005).

Iowa: A.Y. McDonald Industries, Inc. v. Insurance Company of North America, 475 N.W.2d 607, 627–628 (Iowa 1991).

Kentucky: Aetna Casualty & Surety Co. v. Commonwealth of Kentucky, 179 S.W.3d 830 (Ky. 2005).

Maryland: Bausch & Lomb, Inc. v. Utica Mutual Insurance Co., 330 Md. 758, 625 A.2d 1021 (Md. 1993).

Massachusetts: Hazen Paper Co. v. United States Fidelity & Guaranty Co., 407 Mass. 689, 555 N.E.2d 576, 581 (1990); Preferred Mutual Insurance Co. v. Gordon, 2003 WL 21077026 (Mass. Super. May 13, 2003).

Michigan: American Bumper & Manufacturing Co. v. Hartford Fire Insurance Co., 550 N.W.2d 475, 481 (Mich. 1996); Michigan Millers Mutual Insurance Co. v. Bronson Plating Co., 519 N.W.2d 864, 869 (Mich. 1994); Polkow v. Citizens Insurance Company of America, 447 N.W.2d 853, 855–856 (Mich. App. 1989), *rev'd in part on other grounds* 476 N.W.2d 382 (Mich. 1991).

Minnesota: SCSC Corp. v. Allied Mutual Insurance Co., 536 N.W.2d 305, 315 (Minn. 1995); Minnesota Mining & Manufacturing Co. v. Travelers Indemnity Co., 457 N.W.2d 175, 182 (Minn. 1990).

New Hampshire: Coakley v. Maine Bonding & Casualty Co., 136 N.H. 402, 618 A.2d 777, 786–787 (1992).

New Jersey: Metex Corp. v. Federal Insurance Co., 90 N.J. Super. 95, 675 A.2d 220, 225–226 (N.J. Super. App. Div. 1996); Lansco, Inc. v. New Jersey Department of Environmental Protection, 138 N.J. Super. 275, 350 A.2d 520 (1975), *aff'd* 368 A.2d 363 (N.J. Super. App. Div. 1976), *cert. denied* 372 A.2d 322 (N.J. 1977).

North Carolina: C.D. Spangler Construction Co. v. Industrial Crankshaft & Engineering Co., 388 S.E.2d 557, 569–570 (N.C. 1990).

Oregon: Schnitzer Investment Corp. v. Certain Underwriters at Lloyd's London, 197 Or. App. 147, 104 P.3d 1162 (2005), *aff'd* 137 P.3d 1282 (Or. 2006).

Vermont: State of Vermont v. CNA Insurance Companies, 172 Vt. 318, 779 A.2d 662 (2001).

Wisconsin: Johnson Controls, Inc. v. Employers Insurance of Wausau, 264 Wis.2d 60, 665 N.W.2d 257, 263 (2003), *cert. denied* 541 U.S. 1027 (2004).

Wyoming: Compass Insurance Co. v. Cravens, Dargen & Co., 748 P.2d 724 (Wyo. 1988).

But see:

California: Powerine Oil Co. v. Superior Court, 37 Cal.4th 377, 118 P.3d 589, 33 Cal. Rptr.3d 562 (2005); Ortega Rock Quarry v. Golden Eagle Insurance Corp., 141 Cal. App.4th 969, 46 Cal. Rptr.3d 517 (2006); CDM Investors v. Travelers Casualty & Surety Co., 139 Cal. App.4th 1251, 43 Cal. Rptr.3d 669 (2006).

[20] See, e.g.:

Second Circuit: Avondale Industries, Inc. v. Travelers Indemnity Co., 887 F.2d 1200, 1206 (2d Cir. 1989); EDO Corp. v. Newark Insurance Co., 898 F. Supp. 952 (D. Conn. 1995).

Third Circuit: New Castle County v. Hartford Accident & Indemnity Co, 673 F. Supp. 1359, 1366 (D. Del. 1987), *aff'd in part, rev'd in part* 933 F.2d 1162 (3d Cir. 1991), *cert. denied* 507 U.S. 1030 (1993).

Sixth Circuit: Harrow Products, Inc. v. Liberty Mutual Insurance Co., 64 F.3d 1015, 1025 (6th Cir. 1995).

Eighth Circuit: Land O' Lakes, Inc. v. Employers Insurance Co. of Wausau, 728 F.3d 822 (8th Cir. 2013) (PRP letter was a "suit").

Ninth Circuit: Anderson Brothers, Inc. v. St. Paul Fire and Marine Insurance Co., 729 F.3d 923 (9th Cir. 2013) (PRP letter triggered duty); Aetna Casualty & Surety Co. v.

Pintlar Corp., 948 F.2d 1507, 1511–1515 (9th Cir. 1991); Intel Corp. v. Hartford Accident & Indemnity Co., 692 F. Supp. 1171, 1188 (N.D. Cal. 1988), *rev'd in part on other grounds* 952 F.2d 1551 (9th Cir. 1991); Pacific Employers Insurance Co. v. Servco Pacific, Inc., 273 F. Supp.2d 1149 (D. Haw. 2003).

Tenth Circuit: City of Lakewood v. United States Fire Insurance Co., No. 90-Z-880 (D. Colo. Mar. 30, 1993), reported in 7 Mealey's Litigation Reports (Insurance), No. 30 (June 8, 1993). But see, Metro Wastewater Reclamation District v. Continental Casualty Co., 834 F. Supp. 1254 (D. Colo. 1993).

But see:

Third Circuit: Simon Wrecking Co. v. AIU Insurance Co., 350 F. Supp.2d 624 (E.D. Pa. 2004).

Eighth Circuit: Liberty Mutual Insurance Co. v. FAG Bearings Corp., 335 F.3d 752 (8th Cir. 2003).

21 See:

Third Circuit: Simon Wrecking Co. v. AIU Insurance Co., 350 F. Supp.2d 624 (E.D. Pa. 2004).

State Courts:

California: Powerine Oil Co. v. Superior Court, 118 P.3d 589 (Cal. 2005); Ortega Rock Quarry v. Golden Eagle Insurance Corp., 46 Cal. Rptr.3d 517 (Cal. App. 2006); CDM Investors v. Travelers Casualty & Surety Co., 43 Cal. Rptr.3d 669 (Cal. App. 2006).

Indiana: Thomson, Inc. v. Continental Casualty Co., 982 N.E.2d 4 (Ind. App. 2012) (PRP letter was not a "suit").

22 Hecla Mining Co. v. New Hampshire Insurance Co., 811 P.2d 1083, 1092 n.13 (Colo. 1991).

23 See, e.g.:

Colorado: Hecla Mining Co. v. New Hampshire Insurance Co., 811 P.2d 1083, 1090 (Colo. 1991).

Georgia: Claussen v. Aetna Casualty & Surety Co., 259 Ga. 333, 380 S.E.2d 686 (1989).

Illinois: United States Fidelity & Guaranty v. Specialty Coatings Co., 180 Ill. App.3d 378, 129 Ill. Dec. 306, 535 N.E.2d 1071, 1077 (1989).

Michigan: Upjohn Co. v. New Hampshire Ins. Co., 178 Mich. App. 706, 444 N.W.2d 813, 817 (1989).

New Jersey: Broadwell Realty Services, Inc. v. Fidelity & Casualty Co. of N.Y., 218 N.J. Super. 516, 528 A.2d 76, 84–85 (1987).

New York: Allstate Insurance Co. v. Klock Oil Co., 73 A.D.2d 486, 426 N.Y.S.2d 603, 605 (1980).

Ohio: Kipin Industries, Inc. v. American Universal Insurance Co., 41 Ohio App.3d 228, 535 N.E.2d 334, 338 (1987); United Pacific Insurance Co. v. Van's Westlake Union, Inc., 34 Wash. App. 708, 664 P.2d 1262 (1983).

Wisconsin: Just v. Land Reclamation, Ltd., 155 Wis.2d 737, 157 Wis.2d 507, 456 N.W.2d 570, 575–576 (1990).

24 A.Y. McDonald Industries, Inc. v. Insurance Company of North America, 475 N.W.2d 607, 628 (Iowa 1991) (citations and internal quotations omitted). See also, Michigan Millers Mutual Insurance Co. v. Bronson Plating Co., 519 N.W.2d 864, 870–871 (Mich. 1994).

> "We also note that a broader definition of the term 'suit' reflects more accurately the modern realities of our legal system. As the legal community and state and federal legislatures struggle to relieve the ever-increasing burdens on our courts and the constantly rising costs of litigation, a gravitation is evident toward less formal and more expeditious means of dispute resolution. This movement has manifested itself in the growing use of arbitration, as well as increased authority given to administrative agencies to resolve disputes, so that the functional equivalents of suits brought

in a court of law have developed. . . . [T]his point is particularly valid in the context of CERCLA actions, where the Legislature has deliberately and painstakingly developed a system in which a PRP has every incentive to 'voluntarily' cooperate with the EPA, before actual litigation, and where significant legal prejudice may develop if the PRP fails to do so." (footnotes omitted).

25 Michigan Millers Mutual Insurance Co. v. Bronson Plating Co., 519 N.W.2d 864, 871, n.13 (Mich. 1994). In drawing a distiction between a claim by the EPA as distinguished from ordinary types of claims, the court said:

"In making this determination, we are cognizant of the concern raised by the insurers that a decision in plaintiff's favor might blur the distinction between "claim" and "suit" evidenced in their insurance policies. While the policies reserve for the insurer the *right* to investigate any '*claim,*' the insurers' *duty to defend* extends only to a '*suit.*' In response to this concern, we wish to emphasize that this opinion should in no way be viewed as intimating that every request for relief should be considered the initiation of a suit that the insurers are obliged to defend. Rather, our determination on this issue is made primarily based on the unique aspects of CERCLA actions and the authority given to EPA under the statute." (emphasis in original).

26 *Id.*, 519 N.W.2d at 872.

27 See, e.g.:

First Circuit: Prime Tanning Co. v. Liberty Mutual Insurance Co., 750 F. Supp.2d 198 (D. Me. 2010).

Second Circuit: CGS Industries, Inc. v. Charter Oak Fire Insurance Co., 720 F.3d 71 (2d Cir. 2013).

Third Circuit: Haines v. State Auto Property and Casualty Insurance Co., 417 Fed. Appx. (3d Cir. 2011).

Fourth Circuit: Pennsylvania National Mutual Casualty Insurance Co. v. Block Roofing Corp., 754 F. Supp.2d 819 (E.D. Va. 2010).

Fifth Circuit: City of College Station, Tex. v. Star Insurance Co., 735 F.3d 332 (5th Cir. 2013); Looney Ricks Kiss Architects, Inc. v. Bryan, 761 F. Supp.2d 399 (W.D. La. 2010).

Eighth Circuit: Bethel v. Darwin Select Insurance Co., 735 F.3d 1035 (8th Cir. 2013); Raines v. Safeco Insurance Company of America, 637 F.3d 872 (8th Cir. 2011); FACE, Festivals and Concert Events, Inc. v. Scottsdale Insurance Co., 632 F.3d 417 (8th Cir. 2011); Behrens v. Arch Insurance Co., 631 F.3d 895 (8th Cir. 2011).

Ninth Circuit: Michael Taylor Designs, Inc. v. Travelers Property Casualty Company of America, 761 F. Supp.2d 90 (N.D. Cal. 2011).

Tenth Circuit: Automax Hyundai South, L.L.C. v. Zurich American Insurance Co., 720 F.3d 798 (10th Cir. 2013); United Fire and Casualty Co. v. Boulder Plaza Residential L.L.C., 633 F.3d 951 (10th Cir. 2011).

Eleventh Circuit: Lime Tree Village Community Club Association v. State Farm General Insurance Co., 980 F.2d 1402, 1405 (11th Cir. 1993); Trizec Properties, Inc. v. Biltmore Construction Co., 767 F.2d 810, 811 (11th Cir. 1985).

State Courts:

California: Liberty National Enterprises, L.P. v. Chicago Title Insurance Company, 217 Cal. App.4th 62, 157 Cal. Rptr.3d 664 (2013).

Colorado: Constitution Associates v. New Hampshire Insurance Co., 930 P.2d 556, 563 (Colo. 1996); Hecla Mining Co. v. New Hampshire Insurance Co., 811 P.2d 1083, 1086 n.5, 1089 (Colo. 1991).

Florida: Hale v. State Farm Florida Insurance Co., 51 So.3d 1169 (Fla. App. 2010); Baron Oil Co. v. Nationwide Mutual Fire Insurance Co., 470 So.2d 810, 813–814 (Fla. App. 1985).

Illinois: Maxum Indemnity Co. v. Gillette, 405 Ill. App.3d 881, 940 N.E.2d 78, 346 Ill. Dec. 78 (2010).

Louisiana: American Home Assurance Co. v. Czarniecki, 230 So.2d 253, 259 (La. 1969); West Brothers of DeRidder, Louisiana, Inc. v. Morgan Roofing Co., 376 So.2d 345, 348 (La. App. 1979).

Michigan: American Bumper & Manufacturing Co. v. Hartford Fire Insurance Co., 550 N.W.2d 475, 481 (Mich. 1996).

Montana: State Farm Fire and Casualty Co. v. Schwan, 371 Mont. 192, 308 P.3d 48 (2013).

New York: Frontier Insulation Contractors, Inc. v. Merchants Mutual Insurance Co., 667 N.Y.S.2d 982, 986 (N.Y. 1997); Auriemma v. Biltmore Theatre, L.L.C., 82 A.D.3d 1, 917 N.Y.S.2d 130 (2011).

Ohio: W. Lyman Case & Co. v. National City Corp., 667 N.E.2d 978, 979–980 (Ohio 1996).

Oregon: Ledford v. Gutoski, 877 P.2d 80 (Or. 1994).

Pennsylvania: General Accident Insurance Co. v. Allen, 692 A.2d 1089, 1095 (Pa. 1997).

Texas: Mid-Continent Casualty Co. v. Krolczyk, 408 S.W.3d 896 (Tex. App. 2013).

Washington: Travelers Insurance Cos. v. North Seattle Christian & Missionary Alliance, 650 P.2d 250, 254 (Wash. App. 1982).

[28] See, e.g.:

First Circuit: Clark School for Creative Learning, Inc. v. Philadelphia Indemnity Insurance Co., 734 F.3d 51 (1st Cir. 2013); Vermont Mutual Insurance Co. v. Zamsky, 732 F.3d 37 (1st Cir. 2013).

Second Circuit: CGS Industries, Inc. v. Charter Oak Fire Insurance Co., 720 F.3d 71 (2d Cir. 2013).

Third Circuit: Illinois Union Insurance Co. v. Hydro International, P.L.C., 929 F. Supp.2d 365 (M.D. Pa. 2013).

Fourth Circuit: Pennsylvania National Mutual Casualty Insurance Co. v. Block Roofing Corp., 754 F. Supp.2d 81 (E.D. Va. 2010).

Fifth Circuit: City of College Station, Tex. v. Star Insurance Co., 735 F.3d 332 (5th Cir. 2013); Cal-Dive International, Inc. v. Seabright Insurance Co., 627 F.3d 110 (5th Cir. 2010); VRV Development L.P. v. Mid-Continent Casualty Co., 630 F.3d 451 (5th Cir. 2011); Liberty Surplus Insurance Corp. v. Allied Waste Systems, Inc., 758 F. Supp.2d 414 (S.D. Tex. 2010).

Sixth Circuit: Atlantic Casualty Insurance Co. v. Cheyenne Country, 515 Fed. Appx. 398 (6th Cir. 2013).

Seventh Circuit: Atlantic Casualty Insurance Co. v. Paszko Masonry, Inc., 718 F.3d 721 (7th Cir. 2013); Hartford Casualty Insurance Co. v. Construction Builders in Motion, Inc. 2013 WL 4478758 (N.D. Ill. Aug. 19, 2013).

Eighth Circuit: Bethel v. Darwin Select Insurance Co., 735 F.3d 1035 (8th Cir. 2013); Raines v. Safeco Insurance Company of America, 637 F.3d 872 (8th Cir. 2011); FACE, Festivals and Concert Events, Inc. v. Scottsdale Insurance Co., 632 F.3d 417 (8th Cir. 2011).

Ninth Circuit: Anderson Brothers, Inc. v. St. Paul Fire and Marine Insurance Co., 729 F.3d 923 (9th Cir. 2013); Time Oil Co. v. Cigna Property & Casualty Co., 743 F. Supp. 1400, 1419 (W.D. Wash. 1990).

Tenth Circuit: United Fire and Casualty Co. v. Boulder Plaza Residential L.L.C., 633 F.3d 951 (10th Cir. 2011).

Eleventh Circuit: Lime Tree Village Community Club Association v. State Farm General Insurance Co., 980 F.2d 1402, 1405 (11th Cir. 1993); Trizec Properties, Inc. v. Biltmore Construction Co., 767 F.2d 810, 811 (11th Cir. 1985).

State Courts:

California: Shanahan v. State Farm General Insurance Co., 193 Cal. App.4th 780, 122 Cal. Rptr.3d 572 (2011).

Colorado: Constitution Associates v. New Hampshire Insurance Co., 930 P.2d 556, 563 (Colo. 1996); Hecla Mining Co. v. New Hampshire Insurance Co., 811 P.2d 1083, 1086 n.5, 1089 (Colo. 1991).

Florida: Essex Insurance Co. v. Big Top of Tampa, Inc., 53 So.3d 1220 (Fla. App. 2011); Baron Oil Co. v. Nationwide Mutual Fire Insurance Co., 470 So.2d 810, 813–814 (Fla. App. 1985); Effort Enterprises v. Lexington Insurance Co., 666 So.2d 930, 931 (Fla. Dist. App. 1995); Psychiatric Associates v. St. Paul Fire & Marine Insurance Co., 647 So.2d 134, 137 (Fla. Dist App. 1994).

Georgia: Landmark America Insurance Co. v. Kahn, 307 Ga. App. 609, 705 S.E.2d 707 (2011).

Illinois: Maxum Indemnity Co. v. Gillette, 405 Ill. App.3d 881, 940 N.E.2d 78, 346 Ill. Dec. 78 (2010).

Louisiana: American Home Assurance Co. v. Czarniecki, 230 So.2d 253, 259 (La. 1969); West Brothers of DeRidder, Louisiana, Inc. v. Morgan Roofing Co., 376 So.2d 345, 348 (La. App. 1979); Audubon Coin & Stamp Co. v. Alford Safe & Lock Co., 230 So.2d 278, 279 (La. App. 1969).

Maryland: Back Creek Partners, L.L.C. v. First American Title Insurance Co., 213 Md. App. 703, 75 A.3d 394 (2013).

Michigan: American Bumper & Manufacturing Co. v. Hartford Fire Insurance Co., 550 N.W.2d 475, 481 (Mich. 1996).

New York: Frontier Insulation Contractors, Inc. v. Merchants Mutual Insurance Co., 667 N.Y.S.2d 982, 986 (N.Y. 1997).

Ohio: W. Lyman Case & Co. v. National City Corp., 667 N.E.2d 978, 979–980 (Ohio 1996).

Oregon: Ledford v. Gutoski, 877 P.2d 80 (Or. 1994); Mutual of Enumclaw Insurance Co. v. Gutman, 21 P.3d 101 (Or. App.), *review denied* 39 P.3d 192 (Or. 2001); North Pacific Insurance Co. v. Wilson's Distributing Service, Inc., 908 P.2d 827 (Or. App. 1995), *appeal denied* 916 P.2d 312 (Or. 1996); Gebrayel v. Transamerica Title Insurance Co., 888 P.2d 83 (Or. App.), *appeal denied* 892 P.2d 1024 (Or. 1995).

Pennsylvania: General Accident Insurance Co. v. Allen, 692 A.2d 1089, 1095 (Pa. 1997).

Texas: Burlington Northern and Santa Fe Railway Co. v. National Union Insurance Co. of Pittsburgh, PA, 334 S.W.3d 217 (Tex. 2011).

Washington: Holland American Insurance Co. v. National Indemnity Co., 454 P.2d 383, 385 (Wash. 1969); Travelers Insurance Cos. v. North Seattle Christian & Missionary Alliance, 650 P.2d 250, 254 (Wash. App. 1982).

29 See:

First Circuit: Clark School for Creative Learning, Inc. v. Philadelphia Indemnity Insurance Co., 734 F.3d 51 (1st Cir. 2013); Financial Resources Network, Inc. v. Brown and Brown, Inc. 754 F. Supp.2d 128 (D. Mass. 2010); Prime Tanning Co. v. Liberty Mutual Insurance Co., 750 F. Supp.2d 198 (D. Me. 2010).

Second Circuit: Westport Insurance Corp. v. Napoli, Kaiser & Burn, 746 F. Supp.2d 502 (S.D.N.Y. 2010).

Third Circuit: Air Products & Chemicals, Inc. v. Hartford Accident & Indemnity Co., 25 F.3d 177, 179–180 (3d Cir. 1994).

Fourth Circuit: Auto Owners Insurance Co. v. Personal Touch Med Spa, L.L.C., 763 F. Supp.2d 769 (D.S.C. 2011).

Sixth Circuit: Alticor, Inc. v. National Union Fire Insurance Co. of Pennsylvania, 916 F. Supp.2d 813 (W.D. Mich. 2013); Rose Acre Farms, Inc. v. Columbia Casualty Co., 772 F. Supp.2d 99 (S.D. Ind. 2011).

Eighth Circuit: Raines v. Safeco Insurance Company of America, 637 F.3d 872 (8th Cir. 2011); FACE, Festivals and Concert Events, Inc. v. Scottsdale Insurance Co., 632 F.3d 417 (8th Cir. 2011); Behrens v. Arch Insurance Co., 631 F.3d 895 (8th Cir. 2011).

Ninth Circuit: City of San Buenaventura v. Insurance Co. of the State of Pennsylvania, 719 F.3d 1115 (9th Cir. 2013); Michael Taylor Designs, Inc. v. Travelers Property Casualty Company of America, 761 F. Supp.2d 904 (N.D. Cal. 2011).

State Courts:

California: Ameron International Corp. v. Insurance Co. of the State of Pennsylvania, 50 Cal.4th 1370, 242 P.3d 1020, 118 Cal. Rptr.3d 95 (2010); San Miguel Community Ass'n v. State Farm General Insurance Co., 220 Cal. App.4th 798, 163 Cal. Rptr.3d 358 (2013); Advanced Network, Inc. v. Peerless Insurance Co., 190 Cal. App.4th 1054, 119 Cal. Rptr.3d 17 (2010).

Illinois: Illinois Emcasco Insurance Co. v. Waukegan Steel Sales, Inc., 996 N.E.2d 247, 374 Ill. Dec. 800 (Ill. App. 2013).

Kansas: Thornburg v. Schweitzer, 44 Kan. App.2d 611, 240 P.3d 969 (2010).

Massachusetts: Billings v. Commerce Insurance Co., 458 Mass. 194, 936 N.E.2d 408 (2010).

New York: Fitzpatrick v. American Honda Motor Co., 571 N.Y.S.2d 672, 674 (N.Y. 1991); Auriemma v. Biltmore Theatre, L.L.C., 82 A.D.3d 1, 917 N.Y.S.2d 130 2011); Exeter Building Corp. v. Scottsdale Insurance Co., 79 A.D.3d 927, 913 N.Y.S.2d 733 (2010).

Oregon: Fred Shearer and Sons, Inc. v. Gemini Insurance Co., 237 Or. App. 468, 240 P.3d 67 (2010).

But see:

Fifth Circuit: VRV Development L.P. v. Mid- Continent Casualty Co., 630 F.3d 451 (5th Cir. 2011); Looney Ricks Kiss Architects, Inc. v. Bryan, 677 F.3d 250 (5th Cir. 2012); Liberty Surplus Insurance Corp. v. Allied Waste Systems, Inc., 758 F. Supp.2d 414 (S.D. Tex. 2010).

Seventh Circuit: Amerisure Mutual Insurance Co. v. Microplastics, Inc., 622 F.3d 806 (7th Cir. 2010).

Tenth Circuit: United Fire and Casualty Co. v. Boulder Plaza Residential L.L.C., 633 F.3d 951 (10th Cir. 2011).

State Courts:

Colorado: Fire Insurance Exchange v. Sullivan, 224 P.3d 349 (Colo. App. 2009); Carl's Italian Restaurant v. Truck Insurance Exchange, 183 P.3d 636 (Colo. App. 2007).

Louisiana: Louisiana Stadium & Exposition District v. BFS Diversified Products, L.L.C., 49 So.3d 49 (La. App. 2010).

30 See, e.g.:

Eighth Circuit: Ritter v. United States Fidelity & Guaranty Co., 573 F.2d 539, 542 (8th Cir. 1978); United States v. Conservation Chemical Co., 653 F. Supp. 152, 205 (W.D. Mo. 1986).

District of Columbia Circuit: Independent Petrochemical Corp. v. Aetna Casualty & Surety Co., 654 F. Supp. 1334 (D.D.C.1986).

State Courts:

Colorado: Constitution Associates v. New Hampshire Insurance Co., 930 P.2d 556, 563 (Colo. 1996) (an insurance company may not deny a defense based upon actual facts that are later discovered in the underlying action); Hecla Mining Co. v. New Hampshire Insurance Co., 811 P.2d 1083, 1089–1090 & n.10 (Colo. 1991) (an insurance company may not deny a defense based upon actual facts that are later discovered in the underlying action).

New York: Fitzpatrick v. American Honda Motor Co., 571 N.Y.S.2d 672, 674 (N.Y. 1991) ("the courts of this State have refused to permit insurers to look beyond the complaint's allegations to avoid their obligation to defend").

Maine: Travelers Indemnity Co. v. Dingwell, 414 A.2d 220, 227 (Me. 1980).

Massachusetts: Omega Flex, Inc. v. Pacific Employers Insurance Co., 78 Mass. App. Ct. 262, 937 N.E.2d 52 (2010).

Michigan: Wright v. White Birch Park, Inc., 325 N.W.2d 524, 527 (Mich. App. 1982); Dochod v. Central Mutual Insurance Co., 264 N.W.2d 122, 123–24 (Mich. App. 1978) (insurance company cannot go beyond the allegations in the complaint in attempting to avoid its duty to defend).

Ohio: Preferred Risk Insurance Co. v. Gill, 507 N.E.2d 1118, 1123–1124 (Ohio 1987) (insurance company's duty to defend does not depend solely on allegations in the underlying complaint, unless the company agrees to defend groundless, false, or fraudulent claims); Sanborn Plastics Corp. v. St. Paul Fire & Marine Insurance Co., 616 N.E.2d 988, 995 (Ohio App. 1993) (although further investigation into the basis of the underlying action could reveal that indemnification is improper, the subsequent investigation has no relevance to the duty to defend).

But see:

Fifth Circuit: Liberty Surplus Insurance Corp. v. Allied Waste Systems, Inc., 758 F. Supp.2d 414 (S.D. Tex. 2010) (recognizing exception to eight corners rule for collusion between policyholder and litigant suing policyholder).

31 See, e.g.:

First Circuit: Financial Resources Network, Inc. v. Brown and Brown, Inc. 754 F. Supp.2d 128 (D. Mass. 2010); Prime Tanning Co. v. Liberty Mutual Insurance Co., 2010 WL 4553531 (D. Me. 2010).

Second Circuit: CGS Industries, Inc. v. Charter Oak Fire Insurance Co., 751 F. Supp.2d 444 (E.D.N.Y. 2010).

Third Circuit: American Legacy Foundation v. National Union Fire Insurance Co. of Pittsburgh, PA, 623 F.3d 135 (3d Cir. 2010).

Fourth Circuit: Federal Insurance Co. v. Firemen's Insurance Company of Washington, D.C., 769 F. Supp.2d 865 (D. Md. 2011).

Fifth Circuit: Scarborough v. Northern Assurance Company of America, 718 F.2d 130, 134–135 (5th Cir. 1983).

Sixth Circuit: Rose Acre Farms, Inc. v. Columbia Casualty Co., 772 F. Supp.2d 994 (S.D. Ind. 2011).

Seventh Circuit: Amerisure Mutual Insurance Co. v. Microplastics, Inc., 622 F.3d 806 (7th Cir. 2010).

Eighth Circuit: Raines v. Safeco Insurance Company of America, 637 F.3d 872 (8th Cir. 2011).

Ninth Circuit: Hudson Insurance Co. v. Colony Insurance Co., 624 F.3d 1264 (9th Cir. 2010); Time Oil Co. v. Cigna Property & Casualty Co., 743 F. Supp. 1400, 1419 (W.D. Wash. 1990).

Tenth Circuit: Allstate Insurance Co. v. Von Metzger, 774 F. Supp.2d 1157 (D. Colo. Feb. 28, 2011).

Eleventh Circuit: Lime Tree Village Community Club Association v. State Farm General Insurance Co., 980 F.2d 1402, 1405 (11th Cir. 1993); Trizec Properties, Inc. v. Biltmore Construction Co., 767 F.2d 810, 811 (11th Cir. 1985); Liberty Mutual Insurance Co. v. Lone Star Building Centers (Eastern), Inc., No. 95-7041-CIV-MARCUS, slip op. at 25 (S.D. Fla. Mar. 19, 1997).

State Courts:

California: Shanahan v. State Farm General Insurance Co., 193 Cal. App.4th 780, 122 Cal. Rptr.3d 572 (2011).

Colorado: Constitution Associates v. New Hampshire Insurance Co., 930 P.2d 556, 563 (Colo. 1996); Hecla Mining Co. v. New Hampshire Insurance Co., 811 P.2d 1083, 1086 n.5, 1089 (Colo. 1991); Sachs v. American Family Mutual Insurance Co., 2010 WL 3259822 (Colo. App. Aug. 19, 2010).

Florida: Baron Oil Co. v. Nationwide Mutual Fire Insurance Co., 470 So.2d 810, 813–814 (Fla. App. 1985); Effort Enterprises v. Lexington Insurance Co., 666 So.2d 930, 931 (Fla. Dist. App. 1995); Psychiatric Associates v. St. Paul Fire & Marine Insurance. Co., 647 So.2d 134, 137 (Fla. Dist App. 1994).

Georgia: Landmark America Insurance Co. v. Kahn, 307 Ga. App. 609, 705 S.E.2d 707 (2011).

Louisiana: American Home Assurance Co. v. Czarniecki, 230 So.2d 253, 259 (La. 1969); West Brothers of DeRidder, Louisiana, Inc. v. Morgan Roofing Co., 376 So.2d 345, 348 (La. App. 1979); Audubon Coin & Stamp Co. v. Alford Safe & Lock Co., 230 So.2d 278, 279 (La. App. 1969).

Michigan: American Bumper & Manufacturing Co. v. Hartford Fire Insurance Co., 550 N.W.2d 475, 481 (Mich. 1996); Polkow v. Citizens Insurance Company of America, 476 N.W.2d 382, 384 (Mich. 1991).

Montana: Horace Mann Insurance Co. v. Hanke, 312 P.3d 429 (Mont. 2013).

New York: Frontier Insulation Contractors, Inc. v. Merchants Mutual Insurance Co., 667 N.Y.S.2d 982, 986 (N.Y. 1997).

Ohio: W. Lyman Case & Co. v. National City Corp., 667 N.E.2d 978, 979–980 (Ohio 1996); City of Willoughby Hills v. Cincinnati Insurance Co., 459 N.E.2d 555, 558 (Ohio 1984).

Oregon: Ledford v. Gutoski, 877 P.2d 80 (Or. 1994); Mutual of Enumclaw Insurance Co. v. Gutman, 21 P.3d 101 (Or. App.), *review denied* 39 P.3d 192 (Or. 2001); North Pacific Insurance Co. v. Wilson's Distributing Service, Inc., 908 P.2d 827 (Or. App. 1995), *appeal denied* 916 P.2d 312 (Or. 1996); Gebrayel v. Transamerica Title Insurance Co., 888 P.2d 83 (Or. App.), *appeal denied* 892 P.2d 1024 (Or. 1995).

Pennsylvania: General Accident Insurance Co. v. Allen, 692 A.2d 1089, 1095 (Pa. 1997); Erie Insurance Exchange v. Transamerica Insurance Co., 533 A.2d 1363, 1368 (Pa. 1987).

Washington: Holland American Insurance Co. v. National Indemnity Co., 454 P.2d 383, 385 (Wash. 1969); Travelers Insurance Cos. v. North Seattle Christian & Missionary Alliance, 650 P.2d 250, 254 (Wash. App. 1982).

32 See, e.g.:

Fifth Circuit: Liberty Surplus Insurance Corp. v. Allied Waste Systems, Inc., 758 F. Supp.2d 414 (S.D. Tex. 2010).

Ninth Circuit: Michael Taylor Designs, Inc. v. Travelers Property Casualty Company of America, 761 F. Supp.2d 904 (N.D. Cal. 2011).

Tenth Circuit: United Fire and Casualty Co. v. Boulder Plaza Residential L.L.C., 633 F.3d 951 (10th Cir. 2011).

Eleventh Circuit: Northland Casualty Co. v. HBE Corp., 160 F. Supp.2d 1348, 1362 (M.D. Fla. 2001) ("the court must look to the facts alleged, rather than any particular legal theory, when determining whether a claim falls within the scope of insurance coverage").

State Courts:

California: Shanahan v. State Farm General Insurance Co., 193 Cal. App.4th 780, 122 Cal. Rptr.3d 572 (2011).

Florida: Scarlet O'Hara's, Inc. v. Sphere Drake Insurance Co., 715 So.2d 317, 319 (Fla. App. 1998) ("Florida courts, in construing insurance coverages, have consistently looked at the operative facts and not the nomenclature placed on the action by the lawyers.").

Pennsylvania: Step Plan Services, Inc. v. Koresko, 12 A.3d 401 (Pa. Super. 2010).

But see:

First Circuit: Prime Tanning Co. v. Liberty Mutual Insurance Co., 750 F. Supp.2d 198 (D. Me. 2010).

33 See:

Commercial Pipe & Supply Corp. v. Allstate Insurance Co., 321 N.Y.S.2d 219, 221 (N.Y. App. Div. 1971), *aff'd* 331 N.Y.S.2d 42 (N.Y. 1972). See also:

Fifth Circuit: Liberty Surplus Insurance Corp. v. Allied Waste Systems, Inc., 758 F. Supp.2d 414 (S.D. Tex. 2010).

Seventh Circuit: American Safety Casualty Insurance Co. v. City of Waukegan, 776 F. Supp.2d 670 (N.D. Ill. 2011).

Ninth Circuit: Hartford Fire Insurance Co. v. Leahy, 774 F. Supp.2d 1104 (W.D. Wash. 2011).

Eleventh Circuit: Mount Hawley Insurance Co. v. Dania Distribution Centre, Ltd., 763 F. Supp.2d 1359 (S.D. Fla. 2011).

State Courts:

Colorado: Constitution Associates v. New Hampshire Insurance Co., 930 P.2d 556, 563 (Colo. 1996); Hecla Mining Co. v. New Hampshire Insurance Co., 811 P.2d 1083, 1090 (Colo. 1991); TerraMatrix, Inc. v. United States Fire Insurance Co., 939 P.2d 483, 486 (Colo. App. 1997); City of Englewood v. Commercial Union Assurance Co., 940 P.2d 948 (Colo. App. 1996) (insurance company can avoid its defense obligation only by establishing that: (1) the underlying action complaint solely and exclusively describes a non-covered event; and (2) there is no factual or legal basis under which the insurance company might eventually be held liable).

Louisiana: Michel v. Ryan, 373 So.2d 985, 988 (La. App.), *writ denied* 376 So.2d 319 (La. 1979) (only if the allegations in the plaintiff's complaint unambiguously and absolutely exclude coverage is the insurer relieved of its duty to defend).

New Hampshire: Northern Security Insurance Co. v. Connors, 161 N.H. 645, 20 A.3d 912 (2011).

Pennsylvania: General Accident Insurance Co. v. Allen, 692 A.2d 1089, 1095 (Pa. 1997); Erie Insurance Exchange v. Transamerica Insurance Co., 533 A.2d 1363, 1368 (Pa. 1987) (duty to defend continues indefinitely, until such time as the insurance company can affirmatively confine the underlying claims to a recovery that the insurance policy does not cover).

34 See:

First Circuit: Financial Resources Network, Inc. v. Brown and Brown, Inc. 754 F. Supp.2d 128 (D. Mass. 2010);

Second Circuit: Westport Insurance Corp. v. Napoli, Kaiser & Burn, 746 F. Supp.2d 502 (S.D.N.Y. 2010).

Third Circuit: American Legacy Foundation v. National Union Fire Insurance Company of Pittsburgh, PA, 623 F.3d 135 (3d Cir. 2010).

Fourth Circuit: Federal Insurance Co. v. Firemen's Insurance Company of Washington, D.C., 769 F. Supp.2d 865 (D. Md. 2011).

Seventh Circuit: American Safety Casualty Insurance Co. v. City of Waukegan, 776 F. Supp.2d 670 (N.D. Ill. 2011).

Eighth Circuit: Interstate Bakeries Corp. v. OneBeacon Insurance Co., 773 F. Supp.2d 799 (W.D. Mo. 2011).

Ninth Circuit: U.S. Fidelity and Guarantee Co. v. Lee Investments, L.L.C., 641 F.3d 1126 (9th Cir. 2011); Hudson Insurance Co. v. Colony Insurance Co., 624 F.3d 1264 (9th Cir. 2010).

Eleventh Circuit: Lime Tree Village Community Club Ass'n v. State Farm General Insurance Co., 980 F.2d 1402, 1405 (11th Cir. 1993); Trizec Properties, Inc. v. Biltmore Construction Co., 767 F.2d 810, 811 (11th Cir. 1985).

State Courts:

Colorado: TerraMatrix, Inc. v. United States Fire Insurance Co., 939 P.2d 483, 486 (Colo. App. 1997); City of Englewood v. Commercial Union Assurance Co., 940 P.2d 948 (Colo. App. 1996).

Illinois: Maxum Indemnity Co. v. Gillette, 405 Ill. App.3d 881, 940 N.E.2d 78, 346 Ill. Dec. 78 (2010).

Ohio: Sanborn Plastics Corp. v. St. Paul Fire & Marine Insurance Co., 616 N.E.2d 988, 996 (Ohio App. 1993).

Oregon: Fred Shearer & Sons, Inc. v. Gemini Ins. Co., 237 Or. App. 468, 240 P.3d 67 (2010).

Pennsylvania: General Accident Insurance Co. v. Allen, 692 A.2d 1089, 1095 (Pa. 1997); Erie Insurance Exchange v. Transamerica Insurance Co., 533 A.2d 1363, 1368 (Pa. 1987).

But see:

Iowa: First Newton National Bank v. General Casualty Company of Wisconsin, 426 N.W.2d 618, 630 (Iowa 1988) (noting that partial defense is minority rule).

Oregon: Mutual of Enumclaw Insurance Co. v. Gutman, 21 P.3d 101 (Or. App.), *review denied* 39 P.3d 192 (Or. 2001).

Washington: Waite v. Aetna Casualty & Surety Co., 467 P.2d 847, 851 (Wash. 1970).

[35] See:

Fifth Circuit: Liberty Surplus Insurance Corp. v. Allied Waste Systems, Inc., 758 F. Supp.2d 414 (S.D. Tex. 2010).

Seventh Circuit: American Safety Casualty Insurance Co. v. City of Waukegan, 776 F. Supp.2d 670 (N.D. Ill. Mar. 3, 2011).

Ninth Circuit: Hartford Fire Insurance Co. v. Leahy, 774 F. Supp.2d 1104 (W.D. Wash. 2011); Berkeley v. Fireman's Fund Insurance Co., 407 F. Supp. 960, 966–967 (W.D. Wash. 1975).

Eleventh Circuit: Lime Tree Village Community Club Association v. State Farm General Insurance Co., 980 F.2d 1402, 1405 (11th Cir. 1993); Trizec Properties, Inc. v. Biltmore Construction Co., 767 F.2d 810, 811–812 (11th Cir. 1985); Mount Hawley Insurance Co. v. Dania Distribution Centre, Ltd., 763 F. Supp.2d 1359 (S.D. Fla. 2011); Maryland Casualty Co. v. Florida Atlantic Orthopedics P.L.C., 771 F. Supp.2d 1328 (S.D. Fla. 2011); Liberty Mutual Insurance Co. v. Lone Star Building Centers (Eastern), Inc., No. 95-7041-CIV-MARCUS, slip op. at 26 (S.D. Fla. Mar. 19, 1997).

State Courts:

California: Shanahan v. State Farm General Insurance Co., 193 Cal. App.4th 780, 122 Cal. Rptr.3d 572 (2011).

Colorado: Constitution Associates v. New Hampshire Insurance Co., 930 P.2d 556, 563 (Colo. 1996); Hecla Mining Co. v. New Hampshire Insurance Co., 811 P.2d 1083, 1090 (Colo. 1991); TerraMatrix, Inc. v. United States Fire Insurance Co., 939 P.2d 483, 486 (Colo. App. 1997); City of Englewood v. Commercial Union Assurance Co., 940 P.2d 948 (Colo. App. 1996).

Florida: Baron Oil Co. v. Nationwide Mutual Fire Insurance Co., 470 So.2d 810, 814 (Fla. App. 1985); Effort Enterprises v. Lexington Insurance Co., 666 So.2d 930, 931 (Fla. Dist. App. 1995); Psychiatric Associates v. St. Paul Fire & Marine Insurance. Co., 647 So.2d 134, 137 (Fla. Dist App. 1994).

New Hampshire: Northern Security Insurance Co. v. Connors, 161 N.H. 645, 20 A.3d 912 (2011).

Michigan: Polkow v. Citizens Insurance Company of America, 476 N.W.2d 382, 384 (Mich. 1991).

New York: Travelers Indemnity Co. v. Town of Highland, 456 N.Y.S.2d 516, 517 (N.Y. App. Div. 1982).

Ohio: W. Lyman Case & Co. v. National City Corp., 667 N.E.2d 978, 979–980 (Ohio 1996).

Pennsylvania: Erie Insurance Exchange v. Transamerica Insurance Co., 533 A.2d 1363, 1368 (Pa. 1987).

Washington: National Steel Construction Co. v. National Union Fire Insurance Co., 543 P.2d 642, 644 n.1 (Wash. App. 1975).

Oregon: Ledford v. Gutoski, 877 P.2d 80 (Or. 1994); Blohm v. Glenn Falls Insurance Co., 373 P.2d 412 (Or. 1962).

36 See:

First Circuit: School Union No. 37 v. United National Insurance Co., 617 F.3d 554 (1st Cir. 2010).

Second Circuit: Acadia Insurance Co. v. American Crushing & Recycling, LLC, 475 F. Supp.2d 168 (D. Conn. 2007).

Third Circuit: Employers Mutual Casualty Co. v. Loos, 476 F. Supp.2d 478 (W.D. Pa. 2007).

Fourth Circuit: Firemen's Insurance Company of Washington, D.C. v. Kline & Son Cement Repair, Inc., 474 F. Supp.2d 779 (E.D. Va. 2007).

Sixth Circuit: Smith v. Stonebridge Life Insurance Co., 473 F. Supp.2d 903 (W.D. Wis. 2007).

Eighth Circuit: Wintermute v. Kansas Bankers Surety Co., 630 F.3d 1063 (8th Cir. 2011); Baker v. Catlin Specialty Insurance Co., 769 F. Supp.2d 1157 (N.D. Iowa 2011).

Eleventh Circuit: Fabricant v. Kemper Independence Insurance Co., 474 F. Supp.2d 1328 (S.D. Fla. 2007).

State Courts:

California: ACS Systems, Inc. v. St. Paul Fire & Marine Insurance Co., 53 Cal. Rptr.3d 786 (Cal. App. 2007).

Colorado: Hecla Mining Co. v. New Hampshire Insurance Co., 811 P.2d 1083, 1090 (Colo. 1991); City of Englewood v. Commercial Union Assurance Co., 940 P.2d 948 (Colo. App. 1996).

Delaware: AT&T Corp. v. Faraday Capital Ltd., 918 A.2d 1104 (Del. Super. 2007).

Florida: Lenhart v. Federated National Insurance Co., 950 So.2d 454 (Fla. App. 2007); Ward v. Nationwide Mutual Fire Insurance Co., 364 So.2d 73, 77 (Fla. Dist. App. 1978); Effort Enterprises v. Lexington Insurance Co., 666 So.2d 930, 931 (Fla. Dist. App. 1995); Airmanship, Inc. v. United States Aviation Underwriters, Inc., 559 So.2d 89, 91–92 (Fla. Dist. App.), *review denied* 576 So.2d 294 (Fla. 1990).

Indiana: McGuire v. Century Surety Co., 861 N.E.2d 357 (Ind. App. 2007).

Iowa: Bituminous Casualty Corp. v. Sand Livestock Systems, Inc., 782 N.W.2d 216 (Iowa 2007).

Kentucky: Motorists Mutual Insurance Co. v. Hartley, 2011 WL 474944 (Ky. App. Feb. 11, 2011).

Louisiana: Robinson Brothers, Inc. v. Carter, 962 So.2d 446 (La. App. 2007).

Michigan: Nickerson v. Citizens Mutual Insurance Co., 224 N.W.2d 896 (Mich. 1975).

Missouri: Seeck v. Geico General Insurance Co., 212 S.W.3d 129 (Mo. 2007).

Montana: Swank Enterprises, Inc. v. All Purpose Services, Ltd., 154 P.3d 52 (Mont. 2007).

New Jersey: New Jersey Lawyers' Fund for Client Protection v. Stewart Title Guarantee Co., 203 N.J. 208, 1 A.3d 632 (2010).

New York: Continental Casualty Co. v. Rapid-American Corp., 593 N.Y.S.2d 966, 972 (N.Y. 1993).

Pennsylvania: Continental Casualty Co. v. Pro Machine, 916 A.2d 1111 (Pa. Super. 2007); Erie Insurance Exchange v. Transamerica Insurance Co., 533 A.2d 1363, 1368 (Pa. 1987).

Washington: Greer v. Northwestern National Insurance Co., 743 P.2d 1244, 1249 (Wash. 1987).

37 See, e.g., Radcliffe v. Franklin National Insurance Co., 298 P.2d 1002 (Or. 1956); Goddard v. Farmers Insurance Co., 22 P.3d 1224 (Or. App.), *review denied* 34 P.3d 1178 (Or. 2001). See also:

Second Circuit: Windmill Distributing Co. v. Hartford Fire Insurance Co., 742 F. Supp.2d 247 (D. Conn. 2010).

Seventh Circuit: R.C. Wegman Construction Co. v. Admiral Insurance Co., 629 F.3d 724 (7th Cir. 2011).

Eighth Circuit: Valle v. State Farm Mutual Automobile Insurance Co., 395 Fed. Appx. 555 (8th Cir. 2010).

Ninth Circuit: Allstate Insurance Co. v. Herron, 634 F.3d 1101 (9th Cir. 2011).

Eleventh Circuit: Noonan v. Vermont Mutual Insurance Co., 761 F. Supp.2d 1330 (M.D. Fla. 2010).

State Courts:

California: Howard v. American National Fire Insurance Co., 187 Cal. App.4th 498, 115 Cal. Rptr.3d 42 (2010).

Colorado: Nunn v. Mid-Century Insurance Co., 244 P.3d 116 (Colo. 2010).

Illinois: Founders Insurance Co. v. Shaikh, 405 Ill. App.3d 367, 937 N.E.2d 1186, 344 Ill. Dec. 845 (2010).

New York: Federal Insurance Co. v. North American Specialty Insurance Co., 83 A.D.3d 401, 921 N.Y.S.2d 28 (N.Y. App. Div. 2011).

Pennsylvania: Step Plan Services, Inc. v. Koresko, 12 A.3d 401 (Pa. Super. 2010).

38 A true duty to defend is what is discussed in this chapter and contained in the standard-form policy. That is to be distinguished from a duty to indemnify for defense costs incurred, such as is often found in umbrella policies. See § 6.02[6] *infra*.

39 See:

First Circuit: Mutual Insurance Co. v. Murphy, 630 F. Supp.2d 158 (D. Mass. 2009).

Second Circuit: In re Quigley Co., 391 F. Supp.2d 695 (Bankr. S.D.N.Y. 2008).

Seventh Circuit: R.C. Wegman Construction Co. v. Admiral Insurance Co., 629 F.3d 724 (7th Cir. 2011).

Ninth Circuit: Medical Protective Co. v. Pang, 606 F. Supp.2d 1049 (D. Ariz. 2008).

State Courts:

California: Gray v. Begley, 182 Cal. App.4th 1509, 106 Cal. Rptr.3d 729 (2010).

Mississippi: Progressive Gulf Insurance Co. v. Dickerson and Bowen, Inc., 965 So.2d 1050 (Miss. 2007).

New York: Staats v. Wegmans Food Markets, Inc., 48 A.D.3d 1115, 852 N.Y.S.2d 514 (N.Y. App. Div. 2008).

Ohio: Bruce v. Junghun, 182 Ohio App.3d 341, 912 N.E.2d 1144 (2009).

[40] See:

Eleventh Circuit: Mid-Continent Casualty Co. v. American Pride Building Co., 601 F.3d 1143 (11th Cir. 2010).

But see:

California: Gray v. Begley, 182 Cal. App.4th 1509, 106 Cal. Rptr.3d 729 (2010).

[41] See §6.02[2] *supra*.

[42] See:

First Circuit: Financial Resources Network, Inc. v. Brown and Brown, Inc. 754 F. Supp.2d 128 (D. Mass. 2010);

Second Circuit: Westport Insurance Corp. v. Napoli, Kaiser & Burn, 746 F. Supp.2d 502 (S.D.N.Y. Sept. 27, 2010).

Third Circuit: American Legacy Foundation v. National Union Fire Insurance Company of Pittsburgh, PA, 623 F.3d 135 (3d Cir. 2010).

Fourth Circuit: Federal Insurance Co. v. Firemen's Insurance Company of Washington, D.C., 769 F. Supp.2d 865 (D. Md. 2011).

Seventh Circuit: American Safety Casualty Insurance Co. v. City of Waukegan, 776 F. Supp.2d 670 (N.D. Ill. 2011).

Eighth Circuit: Interstate Bakeries Corp. v. OneBeacon Insurance Co., 773 F. Supp.2d 799 (W.D. Mo. 2011).

Ninth Circuit: U.S. Fidelity and Guarantee Co. v. Lee Investments, L.L.C., 641 F.3d 1126 (9th Cir. 2011); Hudson Insurance Co. v. Colony Insurance Co., 624 F.3d 1264 (9th Cir. 2010).

Eleventh Circuit: Lime Tree Village Community Club Association v. State Farm General Insurance Co., 980 F.2d 1402, 1405 (11th Cir. 1993); Trizec Properties, Inc. v. Biltmore Construction Co., 767 F.2d 810, 811 (11th Cir. 1985).

State Courts:

Colorado: TerraMatrix, Inc. v. United States Fire Insurance Co., 939 P.2d 483, 486 (Colo. App. 1997); City of Englewood v. Commercial Union Assurance Co., 940 P.2d 948 (Colo. App. 1996).

Illinois: Maxum Indemnity Co. v. Gillette, 405 Ill. App.3d 881, 940 N.E.2d 78, 346 Ill. Dec. 78 (2010).

Ohio: Sanborn Plastics Corp. v. St. Paul Fire & Marine Insurance Co., 616 N.E.2d 988, 996 (Ohio App. 1993).

Oregon: Fred Shearer & Sons, Inc. v. Gemini Ins. Co., 237 Or. App. 468, 240 P.3d 67 (2010).

Pennsylvania: General Accident Insurance Co. v. Allen, 692 A.2d 1089, 1095 (Pa. 1997); Erie Insurance Exchange v. Transamerica Insurance Co., 533 A.2d 1363, 1368 (Pa. 1987).

But see:

Iowa: First Newton National Bank v. General Casualty Company of Wisconsin, 426 N.W.2d 618, 630 (Iowa 1988) (noting that partial defense is minority rule).

Oregon: Mutual of Enumclaw Insurance Co. v. Gutman, 21 P.3d 101 (Or. App.), *review denied* 39 P.3d 192 (Or. 2001).

Washington: Waite v. Aetna Casualty & Surety Co., 467 P.2d 847, 851 (Wash. 1970).

[43] See, e.g.:

Eighth Circuit: Howard v. Russell Stover Candies, Inc. 649 F.2d 620, 625 (8th Cir. 1981); Union Insurance Co. v. Knife Co., 902 F. Supp. 877, 880 (W.D. Ark. 1995).

State Courts:

California: Dynamic Concepts, Inc. v. Truck Insurance Exchange, 71 Cal. Rptr.2d 882, 887–888 (Cal. App. 1998).

Iowa: First Newton National Bank v. General Casualty Company of Wisconsin, 426 N.W.2d 618, 630 (Iowa 1988).

See also § 5.04[6] *supra*.

[44] See:

Third Circuit: Cay Divers, Inc. v. Raven, 812 F.2d 866 (3d Cir. 1987) (provision of independent counsel or reimbursement of policyholder's choice of counsel and expenses ordinarily fulfills the insurance company's duty to defend, and is particularly appropriate where a conflict of interest exists); St. Paul Fire & Marine Insurance Co. v. Roach Brothers Co., 639 F. Supp. 134, 138 (E.D. Pa. 1986) (insurance company breaches its duty to defend if it does not provide independent counsel in conflict of interest situations); Bituminous Insurance Cos. v. Pennsylvania Manufacturers' Association Insurance Co., 427 F. Supp. 539, 555 (E.D. Pa. 1976) (conflict of interest between two policyholders required insurance company to hire separate counsel for each such policyholder).

Seventh Circuit: R.C. Wegman Construction Co. v. Admiral Insurance Co., 629 F.3d 724 (7th Cir. 2011).

Ninth Circuit: Michael Taylor Designs, Inc. v. Travelers Property Casualty Company of America, 761 F. Supp.2d 9042011 WL 221658 (N.D. Cal. Jan. 20, 2011).

State Courts:

Illinois: Santa's Best Craft, L.L.C. v. Zurich American Insurance Co., 408 Ill. App.3d 173, 941 N.E.2d 291, 346 Ill. Dec. 733 (Ill. App. 2010).

Louisiana: Emery v. Progressive Casualty Insurance Co., 49 So.3d 17 (La. App. 2010).

Massachusetts: Northern Security Insurance Co. v. R.H. Realty Trust, 78 Mass. App. Ct. 691, 941 N.E.2d 688 (Mass. App. 2011).

See also, Smyth, "Duty of the Insurer to Pay for Independent Counsel When Conflict of Interest Exists Between Insured and Insurer," 50 A.L.R.4th 932 (1986).

[45] Twin City Fire Insurance Co. v. Ben Arnold-Sunbelt Beverage Co., 433 F.3d 365, 370 (4th Cir. 2005).

[46] *Id.*, 433 F.3d at 371 (4th Cir. 2005). See also:

Fifth Circuit: Rhodes v. Chicago Insurance Co., 719 F.2d 116, 120 (5th Cir. 1983) (applying Texas law).

Eighth Circuit: Union Insurance Co. v. Knife Co., 902 F. Supp. 877, 880 (W.D. Ark. 1995) (predicting Arkansas law); Howard v. Russell Stover Candies, Inc., 649 F.2d 620, 625 (8th Cir. 1981) (predicting Missouri law).

State Courts:

Alaska: CHI of Alaska, Inc. v. Employers Reinsurance Corp., 844 P.2d 1113, 1118 (Alaska 1993).

California: Kroll & Tract v. Paris & Paris, 72 Cal. App.4th 1537, 86 Cal. Rptr.2d 78, 82 (1999) (citing Cal. Civ. Code § 2860).

Illinois: Nandorf, Inc. v. CNA Insurance Cos., 134 Ill. App.3d 134, 479 N.E.2d 988, 994, 88 Ill. Dec. 968 (1985) (finding conflict when punitive damages not covered by policy).

Massachusetts: Herbert A. Sullivan, Inc. v. Utica Mutual Insurance Co., 439 Mass. 387, 788 N.E.2d 522, 539 (2003).

Mississippi: Moeller v. American Guaranty & Liability Insurance Co., 707 So.2d 1062, 1069 (Miss. 1996).

47 See, e.g.:

Fourth Circuit: Twin City Fire Insurance Co. v. Ben Arnold-Sunbelt Beverage Co., 433 F.3d 365, 370–372 (4th Cir. 2005); Driggs Corp. v. Pennsylvania Manufacturers' Association Insurance Co., 3 F. Supp.2d 657, 659 (D. Md. 1998), *aff'd* 181 F.3d 87 (4th Cir. 1999) (applying Maryland law).

Fifth Circuit: Trinity Universal Insurance Co. v. Stevens Forestry Service, Inc., 335 F.3d 353, 356 (5th Cir. 2003) (applying Louisiana law).

Sixth Circuit: Central Michigan Board of Trustees v. Employers Reinsurance Corp., 117 F. Supp.2d 627, 634–635 (E.D. Mich. 2000) (applying Michigan law); Federal Insurance Co. v. X-Rite, Inc., 748 F. Supp. 1223, 1229 (W.D. Mich. 1990) (same).

Seventh Circuit: Armstrong Cleaners, Inc. v. Erie Insurance Exchange, 364 F. Supp.2d 797, 816 (S.D. Ind. 2005) (applying Indiana law); HK Systems, Inc. v. Admiral Insurance Co., 2005 WL 1563340, at *8–10 (E.D. Wis. June 27, 2005) (applying Wisconsin law).

Eleventh Circuit: Travelers Indemnity Company of Illinois v. Royal Oak Enterprises, Inc., 344 F. Supp.2d 1358, 1374 (M.D. Fla. 2004), *aff'd* 171 Fed. Appx. 831 (11th Cir. 2006) (predicting Florida law).

State Courts:

Alabama: L & S Roofing Supply Co. v. St. Paul Fire & Marine Insurance Co., 521 So.2d 1298, 1304 (Ala. 1987).

Hawaii: Finley v. Home Insurance Co., 90 Haw. 25, 975 P.2d 1145, 1150–1155 (Haw. 1998).

Oklahoma: Nisson v. American Home Assurance Co., 917 P.2d 488, 490 (Okla. App. 1996).

Washington: Tank v. State Farm Fire & Casualty Co., 105 Wash.2d 381, 715 P.2d 1133, 1137–1138 (1986).

48 *Id.*

49 See § 10.03[2][b][ii] *infra*.

50 See, e.g., Twin City Fire Insurance Co. v. Ben Arnold-Sunbelt Beverage Co., 433 F.3d 365, 370–372 (4th Cir. 2005).

51 *Id.* See also:

Fifth Circuit: Rhodes v. Chicago Insurance Co., 719 F.2d 116, 120 (5th Cir. 1983) (applying Texas law).

Seventh Circuit: Armstrong Cleaners, Inc. v. Erie Insurance Exchange, 364 F. Supp.2d 797, 816 (S.D. Ind. 2005) (applying Indiana law).

Eighth Circuit: Union Insurance Co. v. Knife Co., 902 F. Supp. 877, 880 (W.D. Ark. 1995) (predicting Arkansas law).

Eleventh Circuit: American Family Life Assurance Company of Columbus, Georgia v. United States Fire Co., 885 F.2d 826, 831–832 (11th Cir. 1989) (applying Georgia law).

State Courts:

Alaska: CHI of Alaska, Inc. v. Employers Reinsurance Corp., 844 P.2d 1113, 1118 (Alaska 1993).

California: Kroll & Tract v. Paris & Paris, 72 Cal. App.4th 1537, 86 Cal. Rptr.2d 78, 82 (Cal. App. 1999).

Illinois: Nandorf, Inc. v. CNA Insurance Cos., 134 Ill. App.3d 134, 479 N.E.2d 988, 994, 88 Ill. Dec. 968 (1985).

Massachusetts: Herbert A. Sullivan, Inc. v. Utica Mutual Insurance Co., 439 Mass. 387, 788 N.E.2d 522, 539 (2003).

Mississippi: Moeller v. American Guaranty & Liability Insurance Co., 707 So.2d 1062, 1069 (Miss. 1996).

[52] See, e.g., Twin City Fire Insurance Co. v. Ben Arnold-Sunbelt Beverage Co., 433 F.3d 365, 370–372 (4th Cir. 2005).

[53] See, e.g.:

Fourth Circuit: Twin City Fire Insurance Co. v. Ben Arnold-Sunbelt Beverage Co., 433 F.3d 365, 370–372 (4th Cir. 2005).

Seventh Circuit: HK Systems, Inc. v. Admiral Insurance Co., 2005 WL 1563340, at *8–10 (E.D. Wis. June 27, 2005) (applying Wisconsin law).

[54] See, e.g.:

Third Circuit: Consolidated Rail Corp. v. Hartford Accident & Indemnity Co., 676 F. Supp. 82, 86 (E.D. Pa. 1987) (predicting Pennsylvania law).

Fourth Circuit: Twin City Fire Insurance Co. v. Ben Arnold-Sunbelt Beverage Co., 433 F.3d 365, 370–372 (4th Cir. 2005).

Sixth Circuit: Central Michigan Board of Trustees v. Employers Reinsurance Corp., 117 F. Supp.2d 627, 634–635 (E.D. Mich. 2000) (applying Michigan law).

Eighth Circuit: Howard v. Russell Stover Candies, Inc., 649 F.2d 620, 625 (8th Cir. 1981).

State Courts:

Hawaii: Finley v. Home Insurance Co., 975 P.2d 1145, 1150–55 (Haw. 1998).

Kansas: Patrons Mutual Insurance Association v. Harmon, 732 P.2d 741, 745 (Kan. 1987).

New Mexico: American Employers Insurance Co. v. Crawford, 533 P.2d 1203, 1208–1209 (N.M. 1975).

Oklahoma: Nisson v. American Home Assurance Co., 917 P.2d 488, 490 (Okla. App. 1996).

Utah: Chatterton v. Walker, 938 P.2d 255, 262 (Utah 1997).

[55] See, e.g.,

First Circuit: Peabody Essex Museum, Inc. v. U.S. Fire Insurance Co., 623 F. Supp.2d 98 (D. Mass. 2009).

Third Circuit: Pacific indemnity Co. v. Linn, 590 F. Supp. 643, 651 n.8 (E.D. Pa. 1984), *aff'd* 766 F.2d 754 (3d Cir. 1985); Princeton Insurance Co. v. LaHoda, D.C., 1996 U.S. Dist LEXIS 169 at *14 (E.D. Pa. Jan. 4, 1996); Bracciale v. Nationwide Mutual Fire Insurance Co., No. 92-7190, 1993 U.S. Dist. LEXIS 11606 (E.D. Pa. Aug. 20, 1993).

Eighth Circuit: American Guarantee & Liability Insurance Co. v. U.S. Fidelity & Guarantee Co., 693 F. Supp.2d 1038 (E.D. Mo. 2010).

Ninth Circuit: Stone v. Hartford Casualty Co., 470 F. Supp.2d 1088 (C.D. Cal. 2006).

Eleventh Circuit: Mid-Continent Casualty Co. v. Basdeo, 742 F. Supp.2d 1293 (S.D. Fla. 2010).

State Courts:

California: Richards v. Sequoia Insurance Co. 195 Cal. App.4th 431, 124 Cal. Rptr.3d 637 (2011); Intergulf Development v. Superior Court, 183 Cal. App.4th 16, 107 Cal. Rptr.3d 162 (2010); Gray v. Begley, 182 Cal. App.4th 1509, 106 Cal. Rptr.3d 729 (2010).

Colorado: Nunn v. Mid-Century Insurance Co., 244 P.3d 116 (Colo. 2010).

Connecticut: Capstone Building Corp. v. American Motorists Insurance Co., 308 Conn. 760, 67 A.3d 961 (2013).

Georgia: McGregor v. Columbia National Insurance Co., 298 Ga. App. 491, 680 S.E.2d 559 (2009).

Indiana: Grinnell Mutual Reinsurance Co. v. Ault, 918 N.E.2d 619 (Ind. App. 2009).

North Carolina: Erie Insurance Exchange v. Builders Mutual Insurance Co., 742 S.E.2d 803 (N.C. App. 2013).

Pennsylvania: Cadwallader v. New Amsterdam Casualty Co., 152 A.2d 484, 488 (Pa. 1959).

Virginia: School Board of City of Newport News v. Commonwealth, 279 Va. 460, 689 S.E.2d 731 (2010).

Wisconsin: James Cape & Sons Co. v. Streu Construction Co., 321 Wis.2d 604, 775 N.W.2d 117 (Wis. App. 2009).

But see:

Second Circuit: CSG Industries, Inc. v. Charter Oak Fire Insurance Co., 720 F.3d 71 (2d Cir. 2013) (breach of duty to defend under New York law did not obligate insurer to pay settlement amount in absence of duty to indemnify.).

Ninth Circuit: Regence Group v. TIG Specialty Insurance Co., 903 F. Supp.2d 1152 (D. Or. 2012) (similar).

56 Pacific Indemnity Co. v. Linn, 590 F. Supp. 643, 651 n.8 (E.D. Pa. 1984), *aff'd* 766 F.2d 754 (3d Cir. 1985). See also:

Michigan: Michigan Department of Transportation v. CNA Insurance, 2002 WL 31296641, at *3 (Mich. App. Oct. 11, 2002); Alyas v. Gillard, 446 N.W.2d 610 (Mich. App. 1989); Elliott v. Casualty Association of America, 236 N.W. 782 (Mich. App. 1931); Detroit Edison Co. v. Michigan Mutual Insurance Co., 301 N.W.2d 832, 836 (Mich. App. 1981) (similar).

Oregon: Northwest Pump & Equipment Co. v. American States Insurance Co., 917 P.2d 1025, 1028 (Or. App.) ("When an insurer wrongfully refuses to defend its insured on a claim that could impose liability covered by the policy and the insured, acting in its own defense, reasonably settles the claim, the insurer is liable for the amount of the settlement."), *modified* 925 P.2d 1241 (Or. App. 1996).

But see, American States Insurance Co. v. State Automobile Insurance Co., 721 A.2d 56, 62–64 (Pa. Super. 1998) (only if settlement of underlying action makes it impossible to ascertain on which theories the underlying claimant would have recovered will application of the rule that the duty to indemnify follows the duty to defend be justified).

57 See ISO Form CG 00 01 10 01.

58 See § 5.04[1] *supra*.

59 See, e.g.:

First Circuit: Acadia Insurance Co. v. Peerless Insurance Co., 679 F. Supp.2d 229 (D. Mass. 2010).

Fourth Circuit: Medical Mutual Insurance Company of North Carolina v. American Casualty Company of Reading, PA, 721 F. Supp.2d 447 (E.D.N.C. 2010).

Fifth Circuit: Jones v. Francis Drilling Fluids, Ltd., 642 F. Supp.2d 643 (S.D. Tex. 2009).

Sixth Circuit: Travelers Property Casualty Company of America v. Hillerich & Bradsby Co., 598 F.3d 257 (6th Cir. 2010); Stryker Corp. v. National Union Fire Insurance Company of Pittsburgh, PA, 2009 WL 56671 (W.D. Mich Jan. 8, 2009).

Eighth Circuit: Continental Casualty Co. v. National Union Fire Insurance Co. of Pittsburgh, PA, 940 F. Supp.2d 898 (D. Minn. 2013); Ortega-Maldonado v. Allstate Insurance Co., 519 F. Supp.2d 981 (D. Minn. 2007).

Eleventh Circuit: Mid-Continent Casualty Co. v. Basdeo, 742 F. Supp.2d 1293 (S.D. Fla. 2010).

State Courts:

California: The Housing Group v. PMA Capital Insurance Co., 193 Cal. App.4th 1150, 123 Cal. Rptr.3d 603 (2011).

Illinois: American Service Insurance Co. v. China Ocean Shipping Co., 402 Ill. App.3d 513, 932 N.E.2d 8, 342 Ill. Dec. 117 (2010); E.W. Corrigan Construction Co., 247 Ill. App.3d 326, 617 N.E.2d 228, 233–234, 187 Ill. Dec. 20 (Ill. App.), *appeal denied* 622 N.E.2d 1201 (Ill. 1993).

Massachusetts: High Voltage Engineering Corp. v. American Employer's Insurance Co., 1995 WL 809577, at *3 (Mass. Super. July 7, 1995).

Minnesota: Hornberger v. Wendel, 764 N.W.2d 371 (Minn. App. 2009).

New Mexico: Garcia v. Underwriters at Lloyd's London, 156 P.3d 712 (N.M. App. 2007).

North Carolina: Kubit v. MAG Mutual Insurance Co., 708 S.E.2d 138 (N.C. App. 2011).

Pennsylvania: Widener University v. F.S. James & Co., 537 A.2d 829 (Pa. Super. 1988).

[60] See:

Second Circuit: U.S. Underwriters Insurance Co. v. Kum Gang, Inc., 443 F. Supp.2d 348 (E.D.N.Y. 2006).

Seventh Circuit: Castronovo v. National Union Fire Insurance Company of Pittsburgh, PA, 571 F.3d 667 (7th Cir. 2009); Hartford Accident and Indemnity Co. v. Gulf Insurance Co., 776 F.2d 1380 (7th Cir. 1985).

Ninth Circuit: Goodstein v. Continental Casualty Co., 509 F.3d 1042 (9th Cir. 2007).

State Courts

Illinois: Kajima Construction Services, Inc. v. St. Paul Fire and Marine Insurance Co., 227 Ill.2d 102, 316 Ill. Dec. 238, 879 N.E.2d 305 (Ill. 2007).

Mississippi: Progressive Gulf Insurance Co. v. Dickerson and Bowen, Inc., 965 So.2d 1050 (Miss. 2007).

New Hampshire: White Mountain Cable Construction Co. v. Transamerica Insurance Co., 631 A.2d 907, 910 (N.H. 1993).

Texas: Jenkins v. State & County Mutual Fire Insurance Co., 287 S.W.3d 891 (Tex. App. 2009).

Washington: National Surety Corp. v. Immunex Corp., 176 Wash.2d 872, 297 P.3d 688 (2013) (*en banc*); Mutual of Enumclaw Insurance Co. v. USF Insurance Co., 164 Wash.2d 411, 191 P.3d 866 (2008).

Wisconsin: Maxwell v. Hartford Union High School District, 341 Wis.2d 238, 814 N.W.2d 484 (2012); Towne Realty, Inc. v. Zurich Insurance Co., 201 Wis.2d 260, 548 N.W.2d 64, 66–67 (1996).

[61] *Illinois:* Casualty Insurance Co. v. E.W. Corrigan Construction Co., 247 Ill. App.3d 326, 617 N.E.2d 228, 232, 187 Ill. Dec. 20 (Ill. App.), *appeal denied* 622 N.E.2d 1201 (Ill. 1993) ("In view of the 'plain language' of the provision which requires that notice include 'particulars sufficient to identify the insured,' we must initially agree with [the insured] that failure to include the name of the additional insured and the relevant policy number is not, in and of itself, fatal to the adequacy of the notice.").

Massachusetts: High Voltage Engineering Corp. v. American Employer's Insurance Co., 1995 WL 809577, at *3 (Mass. Super. July 7, 1995) ("The Policy requires only that [the insured] 'immediately forward to [insurer] every demand, notice, summons or other process received by him.' There is no requirement that [the insured] specifically reference which policy, if any, is implicated by the claim against [the insured].").

[62] *First Circuit:* Duggan v. Travelers Indemnity Co., 383 F.2d 871, 873–875 (1st Cir. 1967).

Seventh Circuit: Mangol v. Metropolitan Life Insurance Co., 103 F.2d 14, 18 (7th Cir. 1939).

State Courts:

Alabama: Mutual Life Industry Association of Georgia v. Scott, 170 Ala. 420, 54 So. 182, 183 (1911).

California: Dietlin v. General American Life Insurance Co., 4 Cal.2d 336, 49 P.2d 590, 598 (1935).

Colorado: Rose Medical Center v. State Farm Mutual Automobile Insurance Co., 903 P.2d 15, 17–18 (Colo. App. 1994).

Georgia: Caldwell v. Life & Casualty Insurance Co., 38 Ga. App. 589, 144 S.E. 678, 679 (1928).

Illinois: LeGrange Memorial Hospital v. St. Paul Insurance Company of Tennessee, 317 Ill. App.3d 863, 740 N.E.2d 21, 29, 251 Ill. Dec. 191 (2000); Northbrook Property & Casualty Insurance Co. v. Applied System, Inc., 313 Ill. App.3d 457, 729 N.E.2d 915, 920, 246 Ill. Dec. 264 (Ill. App.), *appeal denied* 738 N.E.2d 928 (Ill. 2000); Casualty Insurance Co. v. E.W. Corrigan Construction Co., 247 Ill. App.3d 326, 617 N.E.2d 228, 232, 187 Ill. Dec. 20 (Ill. App.), *appeal denied* 622 N.E.2d 1201 (Ill. 1993).

Maryland: Automobile Insurance Company of Hartford, Connecticut v. Thomas, 138 A. 33 (Md. 1927).

Massachusetts: High Voltage Engineering Corp. v. American Employer's Insurance Co., 1995 WL 809577, at *3 (Mass. Super. July 7, 1995).

New Hampshire: Canney v. Massachusetts Bonding & Insurance Co., 88 N.H. 325, 189 A. 168 (1937).

New York: Lindblom v. Metropolitan Life Insurance Co., 210 A.D. 177, 205 N.Y.S. 505 (N.Y. App. Div. 1924).

Pennsylvania: Telesky v. Fidelity Guaranty Fire Corp., 140 Pa. Super. 457, 13 A.2d 899 (1940).

Texas: Anchor Casualty Co. v. Brewers, 385 S.W.2d 568 (Tex. App. 1964), *rev'd on other grounds* 393 S.W.2d 168 (Tex. 1965); International Travelers' Association v. Francis, 260 S.W. 938 (Tex. App. 1924), *aff'd* 23 S.W.2d 282 (Tex. 1930).

See also, Director, "Notice or Proof of Loss Under One Policy as Notice or Proof of Loss Under Another Provision of Same Policy or Another Policy Issued by Same Insurer," 29 A.L.R.3d 856, §§ 2–7.

63 *Id.* See, e.g., High Voltage Engineering Corp. v. American Employer's Insurance Co., 1995 WL 809577, at *3 (Mass. Super. July 7, 1995).

> "[Insurer] contends that it has no duty to defend against the . . . action due to [the insured's] failure to give timely notice. Under the Policy, [the insured] must "immediately forward to [insurer] every demand, notice, summons or other process received by him." [The insured] first gave [insurer] notice of the . . . action by a letter dated September 28, 1988, claiming coverage under certain excess policies. [The insured] correctly informed [insurer] that these excess policies did not cover the . . . action. It was not until August 11, 1992 that [the insured] discovered and sought the primary and comprehensive coverage of the . . . action under the Policy. [Insurer] has acknowledged that the . . . action is covered under the Policy. However, since it did not claim coverage under the Policy itself until nearly four years after the [underlying] suit was initiated, [insurer] contends that [the insured] failed to provide the immediate notice required by the Policy. [The insured] responds that the letter of September 28, 1988 gave [insurer] sufficient and timely notice of the [underlying] claim, even though the letter incorrectly claimed coverage under the excess policies.
>
> "This issue may be resolved by examining the plain meaning of the relevant language in the Policy, construing all ambiguities against the insurer. The Policy requires only that [the insured] "immediately forward to [insurer] every demand,

> notice, summons or other process received by him." There is no requirement that [the insured] specifically reference which policy, if any, is implicated by the claim against [the insured]. The Policy is therefore ambiguous with respect to which party, the insured or the insurer, bears the burden of identifying the correct policies once the insured has forwarded a claim against it to the insurer. Construing this ambiguity against the insurer . . . , this Court holds that [the insured] satisfied the notice provision of the Policy through the September 28, 1988 letter, notwithstanding [the insured's] failure to reference the correct policy."

See also, Casualty Insurance Co. v. E.W. Corrigan Construction Co., 247 Ill. App.3d 326, 617 N.E.2d 228, 233–234, 187 Ill. Dec. 20 (Ill. App.), *appeal denied* 622 N.E.2d 1201 (Ill. 1993).

> "[W]e note that the policy requires that notice be given 'to the company or any of its authorized agents.' It does not require that notice be given to a specific department of the company. Therefore, if an insured notifies its insurer of an occurrence and references its workers' compensation policy, it should be considered notice in regards to any general liability policy the insured might have with the same insurer.
>
> ▼
>
> ". . . An insurer should not be able to claim prejudice . . . simply because the insured referenced his workers' compensation file and not any general liability policies he may have had with the insurer when he sent notice. The requirement that notice of an occurrence be given to the company and include 'particulars sufficient to identify the insured' does not require that, if the insured holds more than one policy with the insurer, that he identify to the insurer which of the two policies, general liability or workers' compensation, covers the particular accident nor that the notice be directed to a particular department. . . ."

64 See, e.g., Home Insurance Co. v. United States Fidelity & Guaranty Co., 324 Ill. App.3d 981, 755 N.E.2d 122, 132, 258 Ill. Dec. 41 (2001).

> "'[I]n order to have actual notice sufficient to locate and defend a suit, the insurer must know both that the cause of action has been filed [against its insured] and that the complaint falls within the scope of the coverage of one of its policies."

See also: Employers Insurance Company of Wausau v. Ehlco Liquidation Trust, 186 Ill.2d 127, 708 N.E.2d 1122, 1131, 237 Ill. Dec. 82 (1999); Cincinnati Cos. v. West American Insurance Co., 183 Ill.2d 317, 701 N.E.2d 499, 505, 233 Ill. Dec. 649 (1998); Employers Reinsurance Corp. v. E. Miller Insurance Agency, Inc., 332 Ill. App.3d 326, 773 N.E.2d 707, 265 Ill. Dec. 943 (2002); Illinois Founders Insurance Co. v. Barnett, 304 Ill. App.3d 602, 710 N.E.2d 28, 33, 237 Ill. Dec. 605 (Ill. App.), *appeal denied* 720 N.E.2d 1092 (Ill. 1999) (all cases with similar quotations).

65 See, e.g.:

Alaska: 3 Alaska Admin. Code § 26.06(1).

Arizona: Ariz. Admin. Code § R20-6-801.D.2.

Arkansas: Ark. Ins. R. & Reg. 43, § 9(h).

California: 10 Cal. Admin. Code § 2695.4(a).

Illinois: 50 Ill. Admin. Code § 919.50(c).

Kansas: Kan. Admin. Regs. 40-1-34.

Kentucky: 106 Ky. Admin. Regs. 12:095, § 4(1).

Maryland: Md. Ins. Admin. Code § 31-15.07.03.

Minnesota: Minn. Stat. Ann. § 72A201, subd. 4(b).

Missouri: 20 Mo. Admin. Code § 100-1.020(2).

Nebraska: 210 Neb. Admin. R. & Regs., Ch. 20, § 4.01.

Nevada: Nev. Admin. Regs. § 686A.660(2).

New Jersey: N.J. Admin. Code § 11:2-17.5(1), (2).

New York: 11 N.Y. Comp. Codes R. § 216.3.

Ohio: Ohio Admin. Code § 3901-1-54(E)(1), (2).

Oklahoma: Okla. Admin. Code § 365:15-3-4(a), (b).

Oregon: Or. Admin. Code § 836-080-0220(1), (2).

Pennsylvania: 31 Pa. Admin. Code § 146.4 ("An insurer or agent may not fail to fully disclose to first-party claimants benefits, coverages or other provisions of an insurance policy or an insurance contract when the benefits, coverages or other provisions are pertinent to a claim.").

Rhode Island: R.I. Admin. Code § 02-030-073, § 5.

Texas: 28 Tex. Admin. Code § 21.203.

Utah: Utah Admin. Code § R590-190-5.

Virginia: 14 Va. Admin. Code § 5-400-40(A) ("No person shall knowingly obscure or conceal from first-party claimants, either directly or by omission, benefits, coverages or other provisions of any insurance policy or insurance contract when such benefits, coverages or other provisions are pertinent to a claim.").

Washington: Wash. Admin. Code §§ 284-30-330, 284-30-350.

West Virginia: W. Va. Code St. Regs. §114-14-4.2.

[66] *Colorado:* Colo. Rev. Stat. § 10-3-1104(h)(I).

Connecticut: Conn. Gen. Stat. Ann. § 38a-816(1).

Delaware: 18 Del. Admin. Code Reg. 902, § 2(a).

Florida: Fla. Stat. Ann. § 626.9541.

Georgia: Ga. Code Ann. § 33-6-33.

Hawaii: Haw. Rev. L. § 431:13-103(1)(A).

Idaho: Idaho Code § 41-1329(1).

Indiana: Ind Code § 27-4-1-4.5(1).

Iowa: Iowa Code 507B.4, § 9a.

Louisiana: La. Rev. Stat. Ann. § 22:1214(14)(a).

Maine: Me. Rev. Stat. Ann. § 2164-D, § 3.A.

Massachusetts: Mass. Gen. L. Ann. Ch. 176D, § 3(9)(a).

North Carolina: N.C. Gen. Stat. § 58-63-15(11)(a).

[67] See, e.g.:

Seventh Circuit: Coca-Cola Enterprises, Inc. v. ATS Enterprises, Inc., 670 F.3d 771 (7th Cir. 2012).

State Courts:

Illinois: American Service Insurance Co. v. China Ocean Shipping Co., 2014 IL App (1st) 121895, 7 N.E.3d 161, 379 Ill. Dec. 735 (Ill. App. Mar., 4, 2014); Vedder v. Continental Western Insurance Co., 2012 IL App (5th) 110583, 978 N.E.2d 1111, 365 Ill. Dec. 608 (2012); United National Insurance Co. v. 200 North Dearborn Partnership, 2012 IL App (1st) 100569, 979 N.E.2d 920, 366 Ill. Dec. 119 (2012); Illinois School District Agency v. St. Charles Community Unit School District 303, 2012 IL App (1st) 100088, 971 N.E.2d 1099, 361 Ill. Dec. 577 (2012).

For further discussion of allocation, see § 5.03[2] *supra*.

[68] For cases dealing with comparable language, see:

Fifth Circuit: Harrison v. Ohio Casualty Insurance Co., 199 F. Supp.2d 518, 521 (S.D. Miss. 2000).

State Courts:

Pennsylvania: American States Insurance Co. v. Maryland Casualty Co., 628 A.2d 880, 886–887 (Pa. Super. 1993).

[69] *Webster's Ninth New Collegiate Dictionary* at 814 (1991).

[70] Two interesting "drop down" questions emerge from the foregoing discussion: (1) What if the underlying insurer, although obligated to defend, refuses to undertake the defense?; and (2) What if the obligated underlying insurance company is insolvent or otherwise unable to defend? The policy language will usually control. See, e.g.:

Fifth Circuit: Lumar Marine, Inc. v. Insurance Company of North America, 910 F.2d 1267 (5th Cir. 1990).

Sixth Circuit: Federal-Mogul U.S. Asbestos Personal Injury Trust v. Continental Casualty Co., 666 F.3d 384 (6th Cir. 2011).

Seventh Circuit: Zurich Insurance Co. v. Heil Co., 815 F.2d 1172 (7th Cir. 1987).

State Courts:

Alabama: Certain Underwriters at Lloyd's London v. Southern Natural Gas Co., 142 So.3d 436 (Ala. 2013)

Delaware: Playtex FP, Inc. v. Columbia Casualty Co., 622 A.2d 1074 (Del. Super. 1992).

Louisiana: Louisiana Insurance Guaranty Association v. Interstate Fire and Casualty Co., 630 So.2d 759 (La. 1994); Kelly v. Weil, 563 So.2d 221 (La. 1990); Nasello v. Transit Casualty Co., 530 So.2d 1114 (La. 1998).

Massachusetts: Gulezian v. Lincoln Insurance Co., 399 Mass. 606, 506 N.E.2d 123 (1987).

Ohio: Granger v. Auto Owners Insurance Co., 991 N.E.2d 1254 (Ohio App. 2013).

Pennsylvania: Donegal Mutual Insurance Co. v. Cory, 528 Pa. 295, 597 A.2d 1124 (1991).

Wisconsin: Lechner v. Scharrer, 145 Wis.2d 667, 429 N.W.2d 491 (Wis. App. 1988).

[71] *Fifth Circuit:* Harrison v. Ohio Casualty Insurance Co., 199 F. Supp.2d 518, 521 (S.D. Miss. 2000) (plain meaning of not "obligated" includes absence of underlying insurance by virtue of an exclusion or declaratory judgment).

State Courts:

Ohio: Granger v. Auto Owners Insurance Co., 991 N.E.2d 1254 (Ohio App. 2013).

Pennsylvania: American States Insurance Co. v. Maryland Casualty Co., 628 A.2d 880, 886–887 (Pa. Super. 1993) (plain meaning of not "covered" in provision of umbrella policy requiring umbrella insurance company to defend suits not "covered" by underlying insurance includes absence of insurance by reason of an exclusion).

[72] See:

Ninth Circuit: Washington Insurance Guaranty Association v. Guaranty National Insurance Co., 685 F. Supp. 1160, 1165 (W.D. Wash. 1988) ("the excess carrier [is relieved] of any duty to defend or to indemnify until or unless the damages or judgment exceed the limits of the primary policy").

State Courts:

California: Community Redevelopment Agency v. Aetna Casualty & Surety Co., 50 Cal. App.4th 329, 57 Cal. Rptr.2d 755, 761 (1996) (construing similar clause obligating umbrella insurer to defend where no other underlying insurance is *available* to mean that duty to defend will attach upon exhaustion of the limits of underlying insurance).

Illinois: Zurich Insurance Co. v. Raymark Industries, Inc., 118 Ill.2d 23, 514 N.E.2d 150, 163, 112 Ill. Dec. 684 (1987) ("Where the [primary] insurer has exhausted its indemnity limits, however, the [primary] insurer cannot ultimately *be obligated* to indemnify the insured.") (emphasis added).

Missouri: Miller Mutual Insurance Association of Illinois v. Shell Oil Co., 959 S.W.2d 864, 871 (Mo. App. 1997) ("Upon exhaustion of the indemnity limits of the [underlying primary insurance policy], however, the [underlying primary] insurer cannot ultimately *be obligated* to indemnify the insured.") (emphasis added).

Washington: Weyerhauser Co. v. Commercial Union Insurance Co., 142 Wash.2d 654, 15 P.3d 115, 134–136 (2001) (when an umbrella liability insurance policy provides for a duty to defend upon exhaustion of the underlying limits, an umbrella liability insurance company is required to defend its policyholder immediately on exhaustion of the underlying limits).

73 For cases dealing with comparable language, see:

Fifth Circuit: Texas Employers Insurance Association v. Underwriting Members of Lloyds, 836 F. Supp. 398, 409–410 (S.D. Tex. 1993); Mission National Insurance Co. v. Duke Transportation Co., 792 F.2d 550, 553 (5th Cir. 1986).

Seventh Circuit: Zurich Insurance Co. v. Heil Co., 815 F.2d 1122, 1126 (7th Cir. 1987).

State Courts:

Alaska: Grace v. Insurance Company of North America, 944 P.2d 460, 465–466 (Alaska 1997).

California: Housing Group v. California Insurance Guarantee Ass'n, 47 Cal. App.4th 528, 56 Cal. Rptr.2d 378, 380–381 (1996).

Wisconsin: Republic Insurance Co. v. Harnischfeger Co., 151 Wis.2d 557, 445 N.W.2d 58 (Wis. App.), *review denied* 449 N.W.2d 276 (Wis. 1989).

Some umbrella policies combine the provision quoted in the text with an obligation to defend the policyholder in claims where the underlying primary policy has been exhausted or where the underlying primary policy did not provide coverage for the particular suit. See ISO Form CU 00 01 04 13:

> "We will pay on behalf of the insured the 'ultimate net loss' in excess of the 'retained limit' because of 'bodily injury' or 'property damage' to which this insurance applies. We will have the right and duty to defend the insured against any 'suit' seeking damages for such 'bodily injury' or 'property damage' when the 'underlying insurance' does not provide coverage or the limits of 'underlying insurance' have been exhausted. When we have no duty to defend, we will have the right to defend, or to participate in the defense of, the insured against any other 'suit' seeking damages to which this insurance may apply. However, we will have no duty to defend the insured against any 'suit' seeking damages for 'bodily injury' or 'property damage' to which this insurance does not apply."

74 See:

Fifth Circuit: Mission National Insurance Co. v. Duke Transportation Co., 792 F.2d 550, 553 (5th Cir. 1986) ("[T]he policy specifically provides that it functions as the underlying insurance only when the exhaustion occurs by reason of losses paid under the policy."); Texas Employers Insurance Association v. Underwriting Members of Lloyds, 836 F. Supp. 398, 409–410 (S.D. Tex. 1993) (primary policy exhaustion triggers umbrella insurance company's duty to defend under similarly worded provision).

Seventh Circuit: Zurich Insurance Co. v. Heil Co., 815 F.2d 1122, 1126 (7th Cir. 1987) ("[T]he excess insurer functions as the primary insurer only when the exhaustion occurs by reason of losses paid under the policy.").

State Courts:

Alaska: Grace v. Insurance Company of North America, 944 P.2d 460, 465–466 (Alaska 1997).

California: Housing Group v. California Insurance Guarantee Association, 56 Cal. Rptr.2d 378, 380–381 (Cal. App. 1996) (exhaustion triggers an umbrella insurance company's duty to defend under similarly worded policy).

Wisconsin: Republic Insurance Co. v. Harnischfeger Co., 445 N.W.2d 58 (Wis. App.), *review denied* 449 N.W.2d 276 (Wis. 1989) ("umbrella policy attaches when the underlying insurance is exhausted").

[75] See, e.g.:

Fifth Circuit: American International Specialty Lines Insurance Co. v. Res-Care, Inc., 529 F.3d 649 (5th Cir. 2008).

Seventh Circuit: Maxum Indemnity Co. v. Eclipse Manufacturing Co., 848 F. Supp.2d 871 (N.D. Ill. 2012).

Ninth Circuit: Evanston Insurance Co. v. OEA, Inc., 566 F.3d 915 (9th Cir. 2009); Park Townsend, L.L.C. v. Clarendon America Insurance Co., 916 F. Supp.2d 1045 (N.D. Cal. 2013); Markel American Insurance Co. v. G.L. Anderson Insurance Services, Inc., 715 F. Supp.2d 1068 (E.D. Cal. 2010); Seagate Technology L.L.C. v. National Union Fire Insurance Company of Pittsburgh, PA, 737 F. Supp.2d 1013 (N.D. Cal. 2010); Zurich Specialties London Ltd. v. Bickerstaff, Whatley, Ryan & Burkhalter, Inc., 650 F. Supp.2d 1064 (C.D. Cal. 2009); Century Surety Co. v. 350 W.A., LLC, 2008 WL 4402919 (S.D. Cal. Sept. 26, 2008).

Tenth Circuit: Yousuf v. Cohlmia, 741 F.3d 31 (10th Cir. 2014); Valley Forge Insurance Co. v. Health Care Management Partners, Ltd., 616 F.3d 1086 (10th Cir. 2010); EMC Insurance Cos. v. Mid-Continent Casualty Co., 884 F. Supp.2d 1147 (D. Colo. 2012).

Eleventh Circuit: Nationwide Mutual Fire Insurance Co. v. Royall, 588 F. Supp.2d 1306 (M.D. Fla. 2008).

State Courts:

Arizona: Beckler v. State Farm Mutual Automobile Insurance Co., 195 Ariz. 282, 987 P.2d 768 (Ariz. App. 1999).

California: Toll Brothers, Inc. v. OneBeacon Insurance Co., 2011 WL 883000 (Cal. App. Mar. 15, 2011); American States Insurance Co. v. Progressive Casualty Insurance Co., 180 Cal. App.4th 18, 102 Cal. Rptr.3d 591 (2009); Great American Insurance Co. v. Superior Court, 178 Cal. App.4th 221, 100 Cal. Rptr.3d 258 (2009); Griffin Dewatering Corp. v. Northern Insurance Company of New York, 176 Cal. App.4th 172, 97 Cal. Rptr.3d 568 (2009); State Farm General Insurance Co. v. Mintarsih, 175 Cal. App.4th 274, 95 Cal. Rptr.3d 845 (2009).

Indiana: Allianz Insurance Co. v. Guidant Corp., 884 N.E.2d 405 (Ind. App. 2008).

Montana: Horace Mann Insurance Co. v. Hanke, 372 Mont. 350, 312 P.3d 429 (2013).

New Jersey: Passaic Valley Sewerage Commissioners v. St. Paul Fire and Marine Insurance Co., 206 N.J. 596, 21 A.3d 1151 (2011); Polarome International, Inc. v. Greenwich Insurance Co., 404 N.J. Super. 241, 961 A.2d 29 (N.J. Super. App. Dept. 2008).

[76] See, e.g.:

First Circuit: Century Indemnity Co. v. Liberty Mutual Insurance Co., 708 F. Supp.2d 202 (D.R.I. 2010).

Second Circuit: Narragansett Electric Co. v. American Home Assurance Co., 999 F. Supp.2d 511 (S.D.N.Y. 2014).

Third Circuit: Terra Nova Insurance Co. v. 900 Bar, Inc., 887 F.2d 1213 (3d Cir.1989); Access Insurance Co. v. Carpio, 861 F. Supp.2d 539 (E.D. Pa. 2012); Utica Mutual Insurance Co. v. Rohm and Haas Co., 683 F. Supp.2d 368 (E.D. Pa. 2010); General Star Indemnity Co. v. Virgin Islands Port Authority, 564 F. Supp.2d 473 (D.V.I. 2008).

Fourth Circuit: Capital Environmental Services, Inc. v. North River Insurance Co., 536 F. Supp.2d 633 (E.D. Va. 2008) (A duty to defend limited to and coextensive with the duty to indemnify would be essentially meaningless; insureds pay a premium for what is partly "litigation insurance" designed to "protect the insured from the expense of defending suits brought against him."); Zurich American Insurance Co. v. Public Storage Co., 743 F. Supp.2d 548 (E.D. Va. 2010).

Fifth Circuit: Liberty Mutual Insurance Co. v. Tedford, 658 F. Supp.2d 786 (N.D. Miss. 2009).

Eighth Circuit: Westchester Fire Insurance Co. v. Wallerich, 563 F.3d 707 (8th Cir. 2009).

Ninth Circuit: Blue Cross of Idaho Health Service, Inc. v. Atlantic Mutual Insurance Co., 734 F. Supp.2d 1107 (D. Idaho 2010); St. Paul Fire & Marine Insurance Co. v. Holland Realty, Inc., 2008 WL 3255645 (D. Idaho Aug. 6, 2008); Ohio Casualty Insurance Co. v. Biotech Pharmacy, Inc., 547 F. Supp.2d 1158 (D. Nev. 2008).

Tenth Circuit: Employers Mutual Casualty Co. v. Bartile Roofs, Inc., 618 F.3d 1153 (10th Cir. 2010); Westport Insurance Corp. v. Ong, 2008 WL 892941 (D. Utah Mar. 28, 2008).

State Courts:

Arkansas: Medical Liability Mutual Insurance Co. v. Alan Curtis Enterprises, Inc., 373 Ark. 525, 285 S.W.3d 233 (2008).

Illinois: General Agents Insurance Company of America, Inc. v. Midwest Sporting Goods Co., 215 Ill.2d 146, 828 N.E.2d 1092, 293 Ill. Dec. 594 (2005).

Pennsylvania: American and Foreign Insurance Co. v. Jerry's Sport Center, Inc., 606 Pa. 584, 2 A.3d 526 (2010); American and Foreign Insurance Co. v. Jerry's Sport Center, Inc., 948 A.2d 834 (Pa. Super. 2008).

Washington: National Surety Corp. v. Immunex Corp., 176 Wash.2d 872, 297 P.3d 688 (2013) (*en banc*).

[77] See §§ 2.03 and 6.02 *supra*.

[78] See Chapter 5 *supra* and Chapters 7–8 *infra*.

[79] See § 2.2 *supra*.

[80] See, e.g.:

Alaska: Burke v. Raven Electric, Inc., 2018 WL 2173938 (Alaska May 11, 2018).

District of Columbia: Dent v. District of Columbia Department of Employment Services, 158 A.3d 886 (D.C. App. 2017).

Kansas: Coincinnati Insurance Co. v. Karns, 379 P.3d 399 (Kan. App. 2016).

Louisiana: Borja v. FARA, 218 So.3d 1 (La. 2016).

New Mexico: Benavides v. Eastern New Mexico Medical Center, 338 P.3d 1265 (N.M. 2014).

CHAPTER 7

Comprehensive General Liability Exclusions for Coverage A

Chapter Contents

§ 7.01 Overview

The preceding chapters discussed the CGL insurance coverage agreement—promises, conditions, terms, and limitations for Coverage A (bodily injury and property damage) and the duty to defend. This chapter focuses on the exclusions applicable to Coverage A, paying particular emphasis on those most relevant to real estate entities and real estate-related entities. In discussing these Coverage A exclusions, reference is made to standard exclusions by letter and number, such as Exclusion J(1), J(2), J(6), K, etc. These are references to the exclusion used in the standard-form ISO CGL insurance policy.[1]

In particular, this chapter analyzes the exclusions for or related to fortuity,[2] contractual liability,[3] damage to property (Exclusions J(1), J(2), J(3), J(4), J(5), and J(6)),[4] "your product" (Exclusion K),[5] "your work" (Exclusion L),[6] impaired property (Exclusion M),[7] work or product recalls (Exclusion N),[8] professional services,[9] and mold.[10] The pollution exclusion is discussed in Chapter 8.[11]

§ 7.02 Fortuity Doctrine

[1]—Definition and Specific Exclusions

Rooted in the common law, the fortuity doctrine provides that insurance protects against contingent, unknown, and fortuitous events, not certainties.[12] The fortuity doctrine manifests itself in at least two ways. First, it can take the form of the judicially created "known-loss" doctrine and/or the "loss-in-progress" doctrine,[13] which provides that one may not obtain insurance for a loss known to have already occurred or a loss already in progress.[14] Most policies do not have an explicit exclusion for "known losses," but courts have adopted it as an unwritten exclusion.[15] Alternatively, the doctrine can arise as a contractually created "expected or intended" exclusion, derived from the requirements of an "occurrence" which provides that coverage is not afforded for losses that are "expected or intended from the standpoint of the insured."[16]

[2]—Scope

[a]—Narrow and Expansive Approaches

Courts are divided on the scope of the fortuity doctrine. The vast majority has construed various manifestations of fortuity extremely narrowly, excluding coverage only when the policyholder subjectively knows with certainty, at the time of purchasing the insurance in question, of the legal liability for which coverage is sought.[17] The minority view is to construe the doctrine broadly, barring coverage when the policyholder either objectively should know, or was substantially aware of, the risk of loss.[18] A plurality of the Pennsylvania Supreme Court, for example, adopted the known-loss doctrine with an expansive scope that holds policyholders to something akin to a negligence standard.[19] Interestingly, a defense to the known-loss doctrine is that the insurance company also knew of the loss but chose to sell the policy without explicitly excluding the loss.[20]

[b]—Problems with Expansive Approach

If the minority view were to prevail, resulting in a wholesale adoption of the expansive interpretation of fortuity, serious problems for policyholders might surface.

One consequence in adopting a broad known-loss doctrine is that it would essentially swallow up the insurance fraud defense.[21] In essence, the known-loss doctrine is a specific application of the insurance fraud defense because a known but undisclosed loss is merely one example of something already excluded by insurance fraud provisions.[22] Under well-settled law, insurance fraud is a defense that requires an insurance company to prove its elements, including knowledge of wrongdoing, or a specific intent to deceive, by clear and convincing evidence.[23] A broadly construed known-loss doctrine essentially lowers the standard of proof for insurance fraud from clear and convincing evidence to a preponderance of the evidence, and it lowers the requisite knowledge/intent from actual knowledge of the wrongdoing or specific intent to deceive to a negligence standard—namely, *should* the policyholder have been aware of the loss at the time of purchasing the insurance in question?[24]

More importantly, the broad interpretation of "known loss," if universally adopted and taken to its logical conclusion, would implicitly ring the death knell for liability insurance. Even under an expansive minority approach previously adopted elsewhere, coverage is not excluded simply because the policyholder is aware of the possibility of loss, especially since the possibility of loss is the reason a person purchases insurance in the first place.[25] In fact, it would be irresponsible for anyone to purchase insurance for conduct without acknowledging the possibility of loss occurring.[26] However, if the approach adopted by the Pennsylvania court is universally adopted, or even if it signifies a trend, it would create a version of fortuity that seems to exclude coverage if the policyholder should have been aware of the mere potential for a loss. The expansive interpretation of fortuity, if literally applied, would seem to exclude coverage for any foreseeable loss.[27]

[3]—Application to Construction Defect Litigation

In coverage litigation involving construction liabilities, fortuity would preclude coverage if there were evidence that the policyholder actually knew of the problem before purchasing the insurance. This could happen if, for instance, the problem manifested itself before the commencement of the policy period. The question that arises is: Does the loss only become known when there is a wide-scale problem?[28] To the extent coverage is available at all, there would likely be some time during which coverage was triggered and knowledge of the problem would not eliminate coverage. Under such circumstances, the policyholder should be able to recover.[29]

[4]—Estoppel: Loss Control as a Shield

Policyholders can, and have, used insurance company loss-control reports to estop the insurance companies from relying on the expected, intended, or known-loss defenses.[30] The policyholder's position is that the insurance company had the same knowledge as the policyholder concerning the likelihood of the loss and chose to nevertheless insure the policyholder and accept premiums without taking any steps to eliminate coverage for such losses or notify the policyholder of a desire to discontinue insuring its operations without a reduction in coverage to exclude the foreseeable loss. "[T]he known-loss rule . . . states that an insurer need not cover a loss known to the insured at the time the parties enter into an insurance contract, *unless the loss was also known to the insurer at the time of the formation of an insurance contract.*"[31]

The expansive language chosen by a minority of courts, that the fortuity doctrine be broadly interpreted to deny coverage when the policyholder either should know, or was substantially aware of, the risk of loss,[32] if applied literally, could be used to argue for the exclusion of all products and completed operations coverage for all businesses. For instance, assume XYZ Corporation has an outstandingly low level of defects per unit manufactured, and based on prior experience, can fairly accurately estimate that it produces one defect in every fifty million units manufactured. Does the fortuity doctrine prevent insurance coverage for unknown but foreseeable losses to third parties from that one defect?

Under a literal application of this minority standard, it could be argued that XYZ Corporation should have been aware of the defect and, hence, the resultant loss. If the loss-control report correctly advised the policyholder of the potential loss for which the insurance company will invoke the known-loss doctrine (i.e., the one defect in fifty million units produced), the policyholder will be able to follow the loss-control expert's guidance on how to minimize or avoid the loss, which will probably improve the policyholder's operations, help avoid or minimize the number and severity of accidents or occurrences, and positively impact the policyholder's insurance costs in the long run.

To the extent the policyholder is unsuccessful in preventing the loss and then after the insurance company denies coverage for the loss gets involved in a coverage dispute, the policyholder should be able to invoke the estoppel doctrine to prevent the insurance company's reliance on the knowledge defenses.[33] Further, even if the policyholder is unsuccessful in its attempt to advance the estoppel argument, the policyholder may have a tort claim against the insurance company for failure to provide an effective loss prevention or loss mitigation recommendation, if the loss is as severe as predicted by the loss-control engineer.[34]

On the other hand, if the loss-control report makes no mention of the potential losses that are at issue in the future litigation—i.e., the one defect in fifty million units produced—the policyholder will likely be able to defeat the expansive fortuity defense by pointing to the report's deficiency as proof that when it purchased the policy, it could not be expected to have suspected, foreseen, or known of the losses. If an expert trained in loss-control engineering hired for the specific purpose of assessing likely areas of losses fails to foresee the loss for which the insurance company is attempting to exclude coverage under the expansive reading of the known-loss doctrine, then the policyholder—a mere layman in loss control—cannot be reasonably expected to know or foresee the loss.[35] Even in the unlikely event that a policyholder is unsuccessful in its attempt to defeat the fortuity doctrine, it should nonetheless have a valid cause of action against its insurance company for negligent provision of loss control services based on the engineer's failure to identify and warn against the particular loss.[36]

[5]—Punitive Damages

One interesting issue is whether punitive damages are excluded under the fortuity doctrine. The question arises because punitive damages are generally not permitted to be awarded absent some knowledge, intent, or other culpable scienter on the part of the party against whom they are assessed.[37] The standard CGL policy is silent; and it neither expressly states that punitive damages are covered nor does it expressly exclude punitive damages from coverage.[38]

Insurance companies argue that punitive damages are excluded because of public policy or the fortuity doctrine. Case law is split on the insurability of punitive damages. Some courts hold that punitive damages are always uninsurable on the basis of general public policy.[39] Others hold otherwise and find that public policy either favors insurability or does not prevent their insurability.[40] A third set of jurisdictions analyze public policy after determining whether the insurance policy even covers the punitive damages and look at each case on an ad hoc basis.[41] Yet another set of jurisdictions have held that public policy requires that directly assessed punitive damages are not insurable, but vicariously assessed punitive damages are insurable.[42] In these jurisdictions, the insurance company may bear the burden of proving that the policyholder's liability is direct, rather than vicarious, in order to show that punitive damages are excluded from coverage.[43]

The fortuity doctrine has limited applicability in this context. In cases involving intentional conduct by the policyholder, the doctrine will likely apply to prevent coverage for all damages, including punitive damages, assessed against the policyholder.[44] However, fortuity likely will not apply to prevent coverage for punitive damages assessed for reckless behavior.[45] Indeed, one court refused to apply the fortuity defense, holding it was ambiguous.[46]

§ 7.03 Contractual Liability Exclusion

[1]—Contractually Assumed Liabilities

CGL insurance policies generally provide contractual liability insurance coverage by virtue of an exception to an exclusion.[47] The exclusion provides:

> "This insurance does not apply to:
>
> 'Bodily injury' or 'property damage' for which the insured is obligated to pay damages by reason of the assumption of liability in a contract or agreement. This exclusion does not apply to liability for damages:
>
> (1) That the insured would have in the absence of the contract or agreement; or
>
> (2) Assumed in a contract or agreement that is an 'Insured Contract' provided the 'bodily injury' or 'property damage' occurs subsequent to the execution of the contract or agreement."[48]

As the clause makes clear, not all liability in a contract is excluded. Rather, the policyholder's indemnity or contractual assumption of liability is generally excluded. However, the contractual liability exclusion has two specifically enumerated exceptions: (1) liability for "damages that the insured would have in the absence of the contract or agreement"; or (2) liability for "damages assumed in a contract or agreement that is" (a) an "'insured contract' provided the (b) "'bodily injury' or 'property damage' occurs subsequent to the execution of the contract or agreement."[49]

[2]—Liability in the Absence of Agreement

The first exception provides that the exclusion for contractually assumed liabilities does not apply to liability that the policyholder would have in the absence of a contract or an agreement.[50] In other words, tort or statutory liability asserted directly against the policyholder would not be excluded under this provision.[51]

Although the indemnitee may only initially assert claims for contractual indemnification, a policyholder should be vigilant of the possibility of non-contractual liability in the future, such as a later assertion of any statutory or tort claims or a claim of equitable indemnification or contribution. In cases involving allegations of bodily injuries caused by negligence, the potentially responsible parties generally attempt to apportion liability among themselves based on their respective fault.[52] A forum's law generally recognizes claims for equitable indemnification and contribution, both of which are tort claims.[53]

Mandatory joinder rules and/or jurisprudence on *res judicata* often bar any claims for equitable indemnification or contribution if they are not asserted in the underlying action.[54] As a result, it is likely that before any underlying action is completed, claims for equitable indemnification and contribution would be asserted against a potentially responsible policyholder; otherwise, such claims would be barred. If such claims are asserted, they would constitute claims for liability that the policyholder would have in the absence of an agreement, and would be potentially covered under the policy, thereby requiring the insurance company to defend or indemnify the policyholder.[55]

[3]—"Insured Contract" Executed Prior to the Injury

Alternatively, the insurance company might owe the policyholder a duty to defend or indemnify under the second enumerated exception to the contractual liability exclusion, which contemplates the existence of an "insured contract" that satisfies the requirements of the policy.[56]

The second exception to the contractual liability exclusion, provides for two discreet elements that must be met for the claim to fall within that exception: (1) the "bodily injury" must occur subsequent to the execution of the contract or agreement; and (2) the contract must be an "insured contract."[57]

[a]—Injury Occurs after Agreement's Execution

Determining whether a bodily injury occurred subsequent to the execution of the agreement is a rather straightforward exercise of comparing the date of execution with the date of/alleged date of injury.[58]

[b]—"Insured Contract"

The second exclusion requirement is that the agreement must be an "insured contract." CGL insurance policies define "insured contract" as:

> "That part of any . . . contract or agreement pertaining to your business under which you assume the tort liability of another party to pay for 'bodily injury' or 'property damage' to a third person or organization. Tort liability means a liability that would be imposed by law in the absence of any contract or agreement."[59]

Under the provision, there are four requirements: (1) the contract or agreement must be entered into by "you" and must pertain to "your" business; (2) the contract must contain a promise to pay for bodily injury or property damage to a third party; (3) the contract must contain the assumption of the liability of "another;" and (4) the contract must involve the assumption of "tort liability."[60]

Determination of the first element requires confirmation that the signatory of the agreement be a "named insured" or otherwise qualify as "you" under the policy and that the agreement be written and "pertains to" the entity's business.[61]

Likewise, determination of the second and third elements is a simple exercise of construing the agreement and the insurance policy to determine whether the policyholder assumed the liability of "another" for "bodily injury" or "property damage" suffered by a third party.[62] A few issues may arise in this exercise. For example, who is a "third party" who suffers injury or "another" whose liability is assumed in the contract? One case held that the general partner of a partnership that was the policyholder did not qualify.[63] Additionally, if there is no duty to indemnify another for defense costs, the insurance company can deny the claim.[64]

Finally, an issue may arise with respect to indemnification of an indemnitee's indemnitee.[65] It should not matter whether the other party is the indemnitee of the policyholder or the indemnitee of the indemnitee of the policyholder. An insurance company may argue that "another party" constitutes only the indemnitee in an indemnification agreement. However, "another party" is not so limited based on the express language of the insurance policy, rules of insurance policy construction, and relevant case law construing identical language.[66]

The plain language of the CGL insurance policy suggests "another party" can be any other person or entity and is not limited to the indemnitee of the policyholder. The policy defines "insured contract" as an agreement by which a "named insured" assumes liability of "another party."[67] Nowhere in the policy is "another party" defined.[68] The plain meaning of "another party" suggests it can be any other person or entity, and is not limited to an indemnitee under a written contract. In fact, case law has construed this language and held that "another party" can include a party that an indemnitee has itself agreed to indemnify.[69]

Rules of insurance policy construction are in accord.[70] In fact, if the insurance company had intended to limit the meaning of "another party" to an indemnitee of the policyholder, it could have easily done so explicitly in the policy. The insurance company's failure to limit the meaning of "another party" evinces an intent not to limit the definition.[71]

The fourth element requires that the agreement at issue must involve the assumption of "tort liability," which means that "liability that would be imposed by law in the absence of any contract or agreement."[72] Liability imposed by law in the absence of agreement would be statutory or tort liability.[73] Numerous cases have held that indemnification agreements involve the assumption of liability in tort, as opposed to contract.[74] One interesting issue that has arisen is whether unenforceability of a written indemnity agreement would cause the contract to lose its status as an "insured contract." Case law has held that enforceability was irrelevant.[75]

[4]—Indemnitee's Indemnitee

[a]—Indemnitee's Liability

An interesting issue arises where coverage is sought for an indemnitee's liability or an indemnitee's contractual assumption of another entity's liability. Insurance companies generally argue that such liability is not covered. The central premise behind this position is that the policyholder's claim for indemnification sounds in contract, rather than in tort, because it involves the policyholder's assumption of an indemnitee's contractual liability to a third party in the underlying action.

The insurance companies' position, however, fails to recognize that the underlying claims arise from the contractual assumption of tort liability that the indemnitee would have in the absence of any contract, rather than the breach of any contractual obligation. In fact, indemnification has been deemed nothing more than a derivative claim.[76] As a result, the existence of a contract for indemnification between the indemnitee and the third party should not change the underlying characteristics of the underlying tort liability of the third party in the underlying action, which is what the policyholder is ultimately being asked to indemnify. In virtually identical circumstances, courts have held that a policyholder is entitled to insurance coverage for the assumption of another party's contractual assumption of a fourth party's tort liability.[77]

[b]—Indemnitee's Defense Costs

There are at least three ways for an indemnitee to obtain an insurance company-funded defense from its indemnitor's insurance company. First, an indemnitee may seek defense costs as an insured under the indemnitor's CGL insurance policy. However, such an effort may fail if the policyholder fails to name the indemnitee as an additional "named insured" as required by the insurance policy. Of course, these defense costs would be covered under the duty-to-defend provisions and likely not erode indemnity limits of the policy.[78]

Alternatively, if, in the indemnity agreement, the policyholder has agreed to fund the defense, such costs might be covered as indemnity payments to the policyholder, but such amounts will count against limits under the policy.[79] Under the terms of CGL insurance policies, an insurance company is obligated to indemnify the policyholder for "all sums" the policyholder is "legally obligated to pay as damages."[80] Thus, even if the indemnitee cannot claim coverage for a defense as a "named insured" under the policyholder's policy, its defense costs might constitute damages that the policyholder is legally obligated to pay (meaning its defense costs would be an indemnity payment within limits).[81]

As discussed previously,[82] a third option is to resort to the "supplementary payments" provisions of the policy, which might obligate the insurance company to fund the indemnitee's defense costs.[83] Under the "supplementary payments" provisions of CGL policies, insurance companies must pay, in addition to the limits of liability, amounts included as "costs" and "interest" taxed against the policyholder by a court in the underlying action and, in certain circumstances, defense costs of the indemnitee.[84] The "supplementary payment" provisions obligate the insurance company to fund a defense of the policyholder's indemnitee under the following circumstances:

> "If we defend an insured against a 'suit' and an indemnitee of the insured is also named as a party to the 'suit,' we will defend that indemnitee if all of the following conditions are met:
>
> a. The 'suit' against the indemnitee seeks damages for which the insured has assumed the liability of the indemnitee in a contract or agreement that is an 'Insured Contract';
>
> b. This insurance applies to such liability assumed by the insured;
>
> c. The obligation to defend, or the cost of the defense of, that indemnitee, has also been assumed by the insured in the same 'Insured Contract.'
>
> d. The allegations in the 'suit' and the information we know about the "occurrence" are such that no conflict appears to exist between the interests of the insured and the interests of the indemnitee;

e. The indemnitee and the insured ask us to conduct and control the defense of that indemnitee against such 'suit' and agree that we can assign the same counsel to defend the insured and the indemnitee."[85]

Applicability of the "supplementary payment" provisions often will hinge upon conditions (d) and (e), i.e., the perceived conflict of interest between the policyholder and its indemnitee and whether the policyholder and its indemnitee request a joint defense.[86]

§ 7.04 Damage to Property Exclusions [Exclusions J(1) through J(6)]

There are six "damage to property" exclusions in the standard-form CGL insurance policy—Exclusions J(1) through J(6)—any of which may be applicable in construction defect insurance recovery litigation. Typically, the standard-form CGL insurance policy provides that:

"This insurance does not apply to:

▼

"J. 'Property damage' to:

(1) Property you own, rent, or occupy, including any costs or expenses incurred by you, or any other person, organization or entity, for repair, replacement, enhancement, restoration or maintenance of such property for any reason, including prevention of injury to a person or damage to another's property;

(2) Premises you sell, give away or abandon, if the 'property damage' arises out of any part of those premises;

(3) Property loaned to you;

(4) Personal property in the care, custody or control of the insured;

(5) That particular part of real property on which you or any contractors or subcontractors working directly or indirectly on your behalf are performing operations, if the "property damage" arises out of those operations; or

(6) That particular part of any property that must be restored, repaired or replaced because 'your work' was incorrectly performed on it."

"Paragraphs (1), (3) and (4) of this exclusion do not apply to 'property damage' (other than damage by fire) to premises, including the contents of such premises, rented to you for a period of 7 or fewer consecutive days. . . .

"Paragraph (2) of this exclusion does not apply if the premises are 'your work' and were never occupied, rented or held for rental by you.

▼

"Paragraph (6) of this exclusion does not apply to "property damage" included in the "products-completed operations hazard."[87]

[1]—Exclusions for Damage to Property Owned, Leased, or Controlled by Policyholder [J(1), J(3), and J(4)]

Application of Exclusions J(1), J(3), and J(4) requires that the damaged property be: (1) "owned, rented, or occupied" by the policyholder [J(1)]; (2) "loaned" to the policyholder [J(3)]; or (3) personal property in the policyholder's "care, custody or control" [J(4)].[88] There is also an express exception for property rented to the policyholder for a period of seven or fewer consecutive days.[89] Whether the facts implicate these exclusions will be fairly evident. Applicability of these exclusions usually presents a straightforward analysis, looking at the ownership, lease, or control of the damaged property.[90] The purpose of the "care, custody and control" [J(4)] exclusion has been described as a means of preventing coverage for damage to a contractor's own work.[91]

Interestingly, albeit obviously, Exclusion J(1) can only apply to an entity that actually owns the property in question. Hence, while Exclusion J(1) may apply to a seller/developer, a contractor who never owns, occupies, or rents the property should never have to worry about this exclusion. Likewise, a partner should not be concerned about application of Exclusion J(1) to property damage to property owned by a partnership since the exclusion applies strictly to the partnership itself.[92]

With respect to Exclusions J(1), J(3), and J(4), there is some disagreement as to when the "control" begins. The issue is whether it occurs at the time that ownership, occupation, renting, loaning, and under "care, custody, and control" are occurring or at the time a claim is made against the insured. The language of the policy suggests that control begins at the time the claim is asserted since it excludes coverage for liability resulting from damage to "[p]roperty you [currently] own, rent, or occupy."[93] Use of the present tense suggests that the relevant date is the present, which is the date from which coverage is tested and would be synonymous with the date the claim is asserted.

Courts are split on the issue. Some courts take the position that such "control" begins at the time the "property damage" is deemed to take place,[94] while others hold that "control" starts at the time the claim is made against the policyholder.[95]

[2]—Alienated Premises Exclusion [J(2)]

The alienated premises Exclusion [J(2)] potentially applies to sellers of real property. The exclusion provides that insurance does not apply to property damage to "[p]remises you sell, give away or abandon, if the 'property damage' arises out of any part of those premises."[96] Thus, by its own terms, the alienated premises exclusion can only apply to preclude coverage for an entity that owned the property in question, meaning it should have no application to a general contractor.[97]

However, some versions of Exclusion J(2) have an express exception if the alienated "premises are 'your work' and were never occupied, rented or held for rental by" the policyholder.[98] Thus, unless the damaged premises were ever occupied, rented, or held for rental by the developer/builder/seller, the alienated premises exclusion is likely inapplicable in construction defect litigation.[99]

In fact, the alienated premises exclusion has been applied by courts in situations in which the exception did not apply because the building in question was an apartment building that was held for rental by the policyholder/prior owner of the building.[100] Application of this exclusion or the exception to the exclusion to other situations will depend on the facts of a given situation. What is likely to be litigated is the meaning of "occupied, rented, or held for rental" by the policyholder.[101]

There is also an issue as to whether the phrase "occupied, rented, or held for rental" encompasses a situation where a structure serves as a model home and/or sales office. It would appear that the issue has not yet been litigated in a reported decision.[102]

[3]—Performing Operations Exclusion [J(5)]

Exclusion J(5) excludes coverage for "property damage" to:

> "That particular part of real property on which you or any contractors or subcontractors working directly or indirectly on your behalf are performing operations, if the 'property damage' arises out of those operations."[103]

Three issues arise under Exclusion J(5). First, does the property damage arise out of the policyholder's construction operations? Second, does the property damage occur while the policyholder is performing construction activity or after the work is completed? Third, does the property damage occur to a portion of the construction project or to other property?

[a]—Arising Out of Policyholder's Operations

The first issue concerns whether the property damage at issue arose out of the policyholder's construction operations. This issue is one of causation and involves a factual inquiry into the cause of the damage.[104]

[b]—During Operations

The next issue concerns the timing of the occurrence of property damage—namely, whether it arises during construction operations or after completion of the work contracted for. Courts construing the language of Exclusion J(5) have held that as a result of the use of the present tense ("are performing operations"),[105] the exclusion is inapplicable to claims involving "property damage" arising after operations are completed and is limited to "property damage" occurring during ongoing construction operations.[106] Performance of operations has been held to include affirmative acts and omissions.[107]

[c]—Damage to "That Particular Part"

The final issue concerns the location of the property damage—namely, whether the damage is to the portion of the project under construction or other real property. There is a question as to the meaning of the phrase "[t]hat particular part of real property on which you or any contractors or subcontractors working directly or indirectly on your behalf are performing operations."[108] Although a policyholder may be able to avoid application of Exclusion J(5) by arguing that the damage did not occur to "that particular part," of a building under renovation, but "occurred to . . . parts of the building that were never intended to be renovated," several courts have rejected this interpretation and held that the exclusion applies,[109] but it has been accepted by others.[110] In the words of one court:

"An insurer relying on the exclusion is not entitled to summary judgment unless it proves all of the alleged damage was to the *particular part* of the real property on which the insured *was performing operations.*"[111]

Interestingly, an explanation of Exclusion J(5) in an insurance industry bulletin sides with the latter view.[112]

[4]—Faulty Workmanship Exclusion [J(6)]

The faulty workmanship exclusion, Exclusion J(6), excludes coverage for "property damage" to "[t]hat particular part of any property that must be restored, repaired or replaced because 'your work' was incorrectly performed on it."[113] Exclusion J(6), as explained in more detail below, has an exception for completed operations.[114] Thus, taken together, Exclusion J(6), and the completed operations exception, thus involves consideration of two primary issues: (1) whether the damage occurred during construction operations; and (2) whether the damage occurred to property other than the defective work itself.

[a]—During Operations—The Completed Operations Exception

Like Exclusion J(5), Exclusion J(6) only applies to damage that occurs or arises during ongoing construction operations. This is because Exclusion J(6) has an exception, stating that it "does not apply to 'property damage' included in the 'products-completed operations hazard.'"[115] Courts have upheld the exception, holding that Exclusion J(6) does not apply to "property damage" arising away from the policyholder's own premises and out of its completed operations.[116] In fact, one court stated:

"Exclusion [J] (6) is commonly known as the faulty workmanship exclusion. The purpose of exclusion [J](6) is to preclude coverage for the costs to repair or replace particular work discovered while the insured is still performing its work. According to the policy, the [J](6) exclusion does not apply to property damage included in the products completed operations hazard exception to the exclusion. Thus, if the claim arises from defective work that is discovered after the contractor has completed its work, exclusion [J](6) does not apply. Stated otherwise, because of the completed operations exception, the exclusion only applies to losses occurring within the course of construction."[117]

[b]—Damage to Defective Work Itself

As with Exclusion J(5), a second issue arises as to whether "it," the last word in Exclusion J(6), refers to the "particular part" that must be repaired or replaced or to "any property."[118] The issue is whether "your work" was incorrectly performed on any property that must be restored, repaired, or replaced or whether it was incorrectly performed on that particular part that must be restored, repaired, or replaced.

Courts have nearly unanimously held that "it" refers to the "particular part" on which "your work" was performed, which limits application of the exclusion, holding that it excludes damage only to the faulty or defective work itself, and does not operate to exclude damage to other property or to non-defective work caused by the faulty or defective work. In other words, most courts hold that Exclusion J(6) only excludes coverage for repair or replacement of the defective work itself.[119]

§ 7.05 "Your Product" Exclusion [Exclusion K]

Exclusion K excludes coverage for "'[p]roperty damage' to 'your product' arising out of it or any part of it."[120] Insurance companies often rely upon this Exclusion K or the "your product" exclusion to deny coverage to developers for claims related to defective construction.

In the context of building supply manufacturers, the "Your Product" exclusion has relevance to defectively manufactured products and supplies that result in damage solely to the defective product itself. Where the defective products damage non-defective pieces of property, the exclusion likely does not apply.[121]

In the context of new home developers, general contractors, and some subcontractors, reliance upon Exclusion K is often misplaced. CGL policies typically define "your product" specifically to exclude real property.

> "'Your product' means . . . [a]ny good or services, *other than real property,* manufactured, sold, handled, distributed or disposed of by . . . You"[122]

"Real property" includes both land and any improvements erected thereon, according to both an ordinary English[123] and a legal dictionary.[124] In fact, "real property" means "[l]and, and generally whatever is erected or growing upon or affixed to land."[125]

Moreover, other portions of the CGL insurance policy suggest that "real property" encompasses improvements erected on land. For instance, Exclusion J(5) excludes coverage for "property damage" to "[t]hat particular part of *real property* on which you or any contractors or subcontractors working directly or indirectly on your behalf are performing operations, if the 'property damage' arises out of those operations."[126] Use of contractors' and subcontractors' operations in the language of Exclusion J(5) demonstrates that "real property" includes improvements or structures erected onto land because contractors and subcontractors generally perform operations on such improvements and structures, rather than on the land itself. In fact, cases construing Exclusion J(5) hold that "real property" includes improvements on land.[127]

Cases are split on the issue of whether a contractor's "work" would be "your product" under Exclusion K, but the majority of cases hold, and the insurance industry itself specifically believes, that the "your product" exclusion is inapplicable to real estate or construction work of a developer or contractor.[128] The confusion results from some case law construing an earlier version of the CGL policy that failed to specifically exclude real property from the definition of "your product."[129] The majority approach distinguished between services performed and products sold in determining that completed work was not a "product."[130]

§ 7.06 "Your Work" Exclusion [Exclusion L]

The standard-form CGL insurance policy also contains Exclusion L, known as the "your work" exclusion, which excludes coverage for:

"'Property damage' to 'your work' arising out of it or any part of it and included in the 'products-completed operations hazard.'"[131]

This exclusion has an express exception for subcontractor work, providing that it does not apply if the damaged work or the work out of which the damage arises was performed on your behalf by a subcontractor.[132]

[1]—"Your Work"

By definition in the policy itself, "your work" includes, among other things, all labor, materials, parts, equipment, and warranties included in a project performed by the policyholder itself, and it also includes all of the aforementioned items in work performed by subcontractors hired by the policyholder:

"a. 'Your work' means:

(1) Work or operations performed by you or on your behalf; and

(2) Materials, parts and equipment furnished in connection with such work or operations.

"b. ['Your work'] includes

(1) Warranties or representations made at any time with respect to the fitness, quality, durability, performance or use of 'your work,' and

(2) The providing of or failure to provide warnings or instructions."[133]

Thus, if the policyholder utilizes a subcontractor to perform part of his "work," the work of both the policyholder and any subcontractors it uses is included in the policyholder's "work."[134] Without consideration of the other elements, such as the completed operations requirement,[135] the issue of damage to others' work,[136] and/or the subcontractor exception,[137] any damage to all such policyholder's work, if caused by any portion of policyholder's work, would likely be excluded.[138]

[2]—Damages Occurring after Operations Are Complete

"Your Work" Exclusion L only applies to damage taking place after operations are completed because there is an express exception for "property damage" that is not included in the "products-completed operations hazard."[139] In other words, if the "property damage" occurs during operations, "Your Work" Exclusion L is inapplicable.[140]

[3]—Damage to Others' Work

Under the express language of Exclusion L, any damage to other property (i.e., others' non-defective work or personal property) would not be encompassed by the exclusion.[141] Cases are in accord with this interpretation.[142] However, by definition in the policy itself, work performed by subcontractors hired by the policyholder would be included in "your work,"[143] meaning that damage to a contractor's subcontractor's work would not be damage to others' work.[144] Under such circumstances, the subcontractor exception to the "your work" exclusion might apply to negate its application and allow coverage for the damage.

[4]—Subcontractor Work

[a]—Subcontractor Exception

In cases in which the property damage occurred after operations were completed and were therefore within the "products-completed operations hazard," analysis of the exception is required. Many versions of Exclusion L have express exceptions "if the damaged work or the work out of which the damage arises was performed on your behalf by a subcontractor."[145] Courts have held that "Your Work" Exclusion L has no application to property damage to the part of "your work" performed by subcontractors. In such cases, the CGL policy does indeed operate as a performance bond.[146] Some insurance policies have deleted the subcontractor exception.[147]

One court described the scope of the exclusion and its applicability to various scenarios involving damage to the policyholder's work, the subcontractor's work, and property of a third party:[148]

> "Application of the completed operations work exclusion in the context of a construction project often entails categorizing damages that flow from defective work into five groups: (1) the insured's work causes damage to the insured's work—to which the exclusion applies; (2) the insured's work is damaged by a subcontractor—to which the exclusion does not apply; (3) a subcontractor's work is damaged by the insured['s] improperly performed its work—to which the exclusion does not apply; (4) a subcontractor's work damaged by improperly performed work by one or more subcontractors—to which the exclusion does not apply; and (5) damage to third-party property is caused by improperly performed work of the insured or others working on its behalf—to which the exclusion does not apply."[149]

[b]—Burden of Proof

The question with respect to the subcontractor exception is: Who bears the burden of proof? Wisconsin is the only jurisdiction that explicitly provides that the burden to prove the exception to the "your work" exclusion lies with the policyholder.[150] In an unpublished opinion, the Wisconsin Court of Appeals held that "when a policy contains an exception within an exception, the insurer need not negate the internal exception; rather the insured must show that the exception from the exemption from liability applies."[151] The court found that "once [the CGL insurance company] makes a *prima facie* showing that no coverage existed because an exclusion applied (here, the exclusion set forth in (2)1 of the policy), the burden shifts to [the policyholder] to show that an exception to the exclusion (that the allegedly negligent construction was performed by subcontractors) applies."[152]

According to one commentator addressing the "your work" exclusion and its burden of proof, "[i]n general, when there is an exception to an exclusion and the insurer establishes that the exclusion applies, the burden of proof shifts to the insured to perfect the exception."[153] Another commentary states that the burden of proof question can be answered through the following analysis: (1) whether the plaintiff objected to assuming the burden of proof; (2) which party asserted the affirmative of the issue; (3) which party would lose in the absence of any evidence on the issue; and (4) what sort of relief is sought.[154]

§ 7.07 Impaired Property Exclusion [Exclusion M]

Standard-form CGL insurance policies contain an "impaired property" exclusion, known as Exclusion M, purporting to exclude coverage for:

"'Property damage' to 'impaired property' or property that has not been physically injured, arising out of:

(1) A defect, deficiency, inadequacy or dangerous condition in 'your product' or 'your work'; or

(2) A delay or failure by you or anyone acting on your behalf to perform a contract or agreement in accordance with its terms."[155]

This exclusion does not apply to the loss of use of other property arising out of sudden and accidental physical injury to "your product" or "your work" after it has been put to its intended use.[156]

Policies typically contain the following definition of "impaired property":

"[T]angible property other than 'your product' or "your work,' that cannot be used or is less useful because:

a. It incorporates 'your product' or 'your work' that is known or thought to be defective, deficient, inadequate or dangerous; or

b. You have failed to fulfill the terms of a contract or agreement;

if such property can be restored to use by:

a. The repair, replacement, adjustment or removal of 'your product' or 'your work'; or

b. Your fulfilling the terms of the contract or agreement."[157]

Exclusion M narrows coverage for claims involving the reduced usefulness or impairment of property other than the policyholder's property.[158] The exclusion "targets situations where a defective product, after being incorporated into the property of another, must be replaced or removed at great expense thereby causing loss of use of the property."[159] The effect of the "impaired property" exclusion is to "bar coverage for loss of use claims (1) when the loss was caused solely by the insured's failure to provide work of the quality or performance capabilities called for by the contract and (2) when there has been no physical injury to property other than the insured's work itself."[160]

Based on the plain language of the policy, Exclusion M is applicable only if: (1) the "property damage" at issue occurred to "property that has not been physically injured" or to property that is "impaired property"; and the exception to Exclusion M does not apply.[161]

[1]—Property Physically Injured

Initially, Exclusion M can apply if the damages at issue involve "property that has not been physically injured."[162] Thus, Exclusion M is likely only applicable where the defect has caused a loss-of-use type of "property damage."[163] Acordingly, where the underlying action involves allegations of faulty construction, which, in and of itself may be "property damage" and/or allegations of either damage to other property caused by the faulty construction, this first prong of Exclusion M is inapplicable (except, perhaps, for the repair of the defect itself).[164] Similarly, Exclusion M "does not apply . . . if the insured's work cannot be repaired or replaced without causing physical injury to other property."[165]

[2]—"Impaired Property"

Exclusion M, known as the "impaired property" exclusion, may apply if the "property damage" at issue constitutes "impaired property," which is defined as "tangible property other than . . . 'your work,' that cannot be used or is less useful" for certain enumerated reasons if such property can be restored by the repair of "your work."[166] Because the damaged property at issue is generally a developer's or contractor's "work," the damaged property usually cannot constitute "impaired property."[167] Additionally, property might not constitute "impaired property" if the repair will not restore the property injured by incorporation.[168]

[3]—Exception

The "impaired property exclusion" has an exception, stating that it does not apply to the "loss of use of other property arising out of sudden and accidental physical injury to . . . 'your work' after it has been put to its intended use."[169] As a result, if there are allegations of loss of use of other property that took place after the property had been put to its intended use, the exclusion does not apply.[170] The exception has been considered ambiguous by some, meaning that rules of insurance policy construction favor a finding of coverage.[171]

§ 7.08 Product Recall Exclusion [Exclusion N]

Standard-form CGL insurance policies contain "product recall" or "sistership" exclusions, known or enumerated as Exclusion N, which excludes claims for:

> "Damages claimed by you for any loss, cost or expense incurred by you or others for the loss of use, withdrawal, recall, inspection, repair, replacement, adjustment, removal or disposal of:
>
> (1) 'Your product'
>
> (2) 'Your work' or
>
> (3) 'Impaired property';
>
> if such product, work, or property is withdrawn or recalled from the market or from use by any person or organization because of a known or suspected defect, deficiency, inadequacy or dangerous condition in it."[172]

In construction defect contexts, insurance companies often reserve their rights as to the "product recall" or "sistership" exclusion to the extent of "impaired property" and "your work." In this section, there are two relevant issues to discuss under Exclusion N: (1) whether the type of property damage involves the loss-of-use type or physical injury type; and (2) whether the damages at issue involve a recall of work or products or a repair of property damage.

[1]—Loss of Use

Exclusion N only applies to the "loss-of-use" form of property damage, meaning if an actual injury or destruction form of "property damage" is discovered, Exclusion N should not apply.[173]

[2]—Recall of Work

Exclusion N's applicability presupposes a recall of undamaged products or work, as opposed to repair of "property damage."[174] Courts have construed Exclusion N to be applicable only in cases involving the recall of sister products or those products that are recalled because they are similar to those that caused damage and raised the suspicion leading to the recall, not to items actually damaged and in need of repairs.[175]

One court succinctly set forth Exclusion N's purpose:

> "When a product is withdrawn because of defective performance, a 'sistership' provision excludes coverage for costs incurred when a related, 'sister' product is also withdrawn because its relationship to the defective product renders its quality suspect. *Sistership provisions are not intended to exclude from coverage damages arising from the withdrawal of the product that raised suspicions. A fortiori,* they do not exclude coverage of damages arising from a defective product when no sister products are involved.
>
> ▼
>
> "Stated another way, the intent of this exclusion is to 'exclude from coverage the cost of preventative or curative action by withdrawal of a product in which a danger is to be apprehended because of a common defect in a sister product.'"[176]

§ 7.09 Professional Services Exclusion

CGL policies for building and construction professionals may contain a "professional services" exclusion which provides that:

> "This insurance does not apply to 'bodily injury' or "property damage" . . . arising out of the rendering or failure to render any professional services by or for you, including:
>
> 1. The preparing, approving, or failing to prepare or approve maps, drawings, opinions, reports, surveys, change orders, designs or specifications; and
> 2. Supervisory, inspection or engineering services."[177]

CGL policies usually do not define "professional services."[178] However, the "professional services" exclusion has been applied narrowly to activities of a policyholder when the policyholder is functioning solely in its professional capacity, which may include specialized skill or knowledge.[179]

§ 7.10 Mold Losses

There are a couple of exclusions that are potentially applicable for mold losses, which are discussed herein: (1) pollution exclusions; and (2) mold exclusions.

[1]—Pollution Exclusion

Bodily injuries or property damage caused by mold infestation are likely not excluded by the various pollution exclusions.[180] In fact, only a very few cases have addressed the precise issue—whether bodily injuries caused by mold are excluded by operation of an absolute pollution exclusion.[181]

In the standard-form CGL policy, losses caused by or related to pollution or pollutants are generally excluded.[182] The standard-form CGL policy defines "pollutants" as "any solid, liquid, gaseous or thermal irritant or contaminant, including smoke, vapor, soot, fumes, acids, alkalis, chemicals and waste. Waste includes materials to be recycled, reconditioned or reclaimed."[183] The dictionary defines "mold" as a "superficially often woolly growth produced on a damp or decaying organic matter or on living organisms,"[184] which, in and of itself, would not qualify mold as a pollutant. Because there is nothing in the definition of "mold" to indicate that it is an irritant or contaminant or that it is akin to "smoke, vapor, soot, fumes, acids, alkalis, chemicals and waste,"[185] the dictionary likely supports the notion that mold is not commonly understood as a "pollutant." On the other hand, of course, mold infestation can result in irritant-type bodily injuries. Hence, whether mold would operate as a "pollutant" is unanswered by resort to the dictionary and common understanding of mold injuries.

Additionally, mold is not listed as a hazardous air pollutant in the federal Clean Air Act.[186] On the other hand, in an unpublished decision, a trial court determined that the EPA lists biological organisms to be indoor air pollutants, but still held that "pollutant" was ambiguous as applied to mold.[187]

Furthermore, the use of a mold exclusion[188] now militates against pollution exclusions' applicability to mold losses. The current mold exclusion shows the insurance industry knows how to exclude mold. The absence of a mold exclusion in older policies, when one easily could have been included suggests an intent not to exclude mold losses in the older policies.[189]

Although there is a dearth of authority on point, the majority of courts that have decided whether mold is a pollutant under the pollution exclusion have found that mold is not a "pollutant" and, thus, coverage for bodily injury claims caused by exposure to mold is not excluded by the absolute pollution exclusion.[190] One court, finding that the pollution exclusion was intended to prevent businesses from escaping responsibility for polluting behavior held that application of the pollution exclusion to a loss is determined by the following factors:

1. whether the insured is a "polluter" within the meaning of the exclusion;
2. whether the injury-causing substance is a "pollutant" within the meaning of the exclusion; and
3. whether there was a "discharge, dispersal, seepage, migration, release or escape" of a pollutant by the insured within the meaning of the policy.[191]

To determine whether a company is a polluter with the meaning of the pollution exclusion clause the court identified the following factors as relevant to the inquiry:

1. whether the type of business in which they operate is one that carries a risk of pollution;

2. whether the policyholder should have known that a separate policy covering pollution would have been necessary for the business; who the insurance company usually insures;

3. any other claims submitted under the policy; and

4. any other factor the trier of fact deems relevant to the question.[192]

To determine whether a substance is a "pollutant" within the meaning of the pollution exclusion the court identified the following factors:

1. the nature of the injury-causing substance;

2. the quantity of the discharge, whether the substance was being used for its intended purpose when the injury took place;

3. whether the substance is one that would be viewed as a pollutant as the term is generally understood; and

4. any other factor that the trier of fact deems relevant to that conclusion.[193]

[2]—Mold Exclusion

Another exclusion often relied upon by insurance companies in connection with mold losses is the mold exclusion. The mold exclusion typically states that:

> "This insurance does not apply to . . . 'property damage' . . . directly or indirectly arising out of, caused by, resulting from, contributed to, attributed to, or aggravated by any type of 'fungi,' including, but not limited to, any species of fungus, mold, yeast, mildew or mushrooms, and any resulting allergens.
>
> "We shall have no obligation under this insurance:
>
> 1. to investigate, settle or defend any claim or 'suit' against any insured alleging actual or threatened injury or damage of any nature or kind to persons or property which arises out of or would not have occurred but for the 'fungi hazard'; or
>
> 2. to pay, contribute to or indemnify another for any damages, judgments, settlements, loss, costs or expenses, including any obligation to share with or repay any person, organization or entity, that may be awarded or incurred by reason of any such claim or "suit" or any injury or damage, or in complying with any action authorized by law and relating to such injury or damage; or
>
> 3. to pay, contribute to or indemnify another for any costs or expenses associated, in any way, with the abatement, mitigation, remediation, containment, detoxification, neutralization, monitoring, removal, disposal or any obligation to investigate or assess the presence or effects of any 'fungi,' or any resulting allergens.
>
> "As used in this exclusion:
>
> "'Fungi hazard' means:
>
> (a) an actual exposure or threat of exposure to the harmful properties of 'fungi,' including, but not limited to fungus, mold, yeast, mildew or mushrooms; or

(b) the presence of 'fungi' in any place, whether or not within a building or structure; or

(c) any disease associated with the harmful effects of 'fungi.'

"'Fungi' means the organism in any form, including but not limited to dust, spores, gas, vapor, mycotoxins, fungal metabolites, microbial volatile organic compounds, glucans, or fungal cell wall components."[194]

A few cases have construed this exclusion (or similarly worded exclusions) and enforced them as purportedly unambiguously written.[195] The existence of a mold exclusion means at least two important things. First, as discussed above, with regard to mold losses, the less specific exclusions (i.e., pollution exclusions) likely have no application.[196] Second, the absence of a Mold Exclusion militates in favor of coverage for such mold losses.

One recognized method to challenge the applicability of the mold exclusion, albeit in the first-party property context, is through recognition of the distinction between mold as a loss and mold as a cause of loss:

"[T]he growth of mold is usually sparked by some moisture-related trigger, whether a covered event or not. Therefore, the [question rooted in linear analysis is]: are there any damages along the sequential chain of losses caused wholly or in part by mold? In other words, once mold appears—for whatever reason—what additional damages can be attributed in some way to the presence of the mold? It is these damages that . . . the mold exclusion prohibiting recovery for damages "caused by" mold are designed to address.

▼

"Mold can presumably always be attributed to something. The moisture sparking the growth of mold has to come from somewhere. What the mold exclusion instead limits is coverage for damage that is attributed to the mold itself, rather than to the initially covered peril.

"Using this analysis, once mold develops, the question of whether mold, as the damage itself, is covered is an inquiry into whether what led to the development of mold is a covered loss under the policy. If the event triggering the growth of mold is a covered loss under the insurance policy, then the mold is also covered and the question becomes: what other damages have resulted solely as a result of the mold which would not have been present but-for the presence of mold. Conversely, if the triggering event is not a covered loss, then both the mold itself, and any resulting damages would likely be excluded from coverage."[197]

This argument seems to hold up in the CGL policy, assuming the policy contains an exclusion worded like the one quoted in the beginning of this section. Of course, drafting the exclusion in a similar way to the total pollution exclusion[198] or by providing low indemnity limits for mold losses[199] are ways insurance companies have used to draft around what they view as bad decisional results.[200]

If mold is at issue and a policyholder is unsuccessful challenging applicability or enforceability of the mold exclusion, it might consider trying to avoid the mold exclusion by arguing that it is improperly part of the policy. There are several doctrines at the policyholder's disposal, including: (1) binder law;[201] (2) the renewal doctrine;[202] (3) the unilateral mistake rule;[203] and (4) reasonable expectations.[204]

[a]—Binder Law

If the mold exclusion was not mentioned in a pre-policy binder, a policyholder may try to avoid application of the mold exclusion through use of the law on binders. A binder is the enforceable insurance contract until cancelled or replaced by the insurance policy.[205] "A preliminary contract of insurance, evidenced by a written memorandum or binder, is valid and effective, even though a loss occurs before a formal policy is issued."[206] In fact, when a loss occurs before the formal issuance of an insurance policy and while the binder is in effect, the terms of the binder control if there is a material conflict with the after-issued policy.[207] Put another way, when a policy is delivered after a loss, which is a fairly common occurrence, material changes from the binder are ineffective with respect to the loss because the policyholder's rights are deemed to have vested on the date of the loss.[208] For this reason, if the binder fails to mention the mold exclusion, a policyholder may be able to avoid application of it to any mold losses at issue.

[b]—Renewal Doctrine

The removal doctrine is another possible mechanism to avoid application of the mold exclusion. Under the renewal doctrine, the terms and conditions of a renewal insurance policy will be the same as those in the original policy, unless the insurance company provides its policyholder with notice, separate and apart from any notice in the renewal policy itself, about: (1) the fact that the terms of the renewal policy have been altered; and (2) the ramifications of such alterations.[209] The policyholder need not read the renewal policy to discover any such changes; rather, the burden rests entirely with the insurance company to establish that it fulfilled its notice requirements.[210] This rule, which places on insurance companies a burden of notifying the policyholder of changes in the terms of renewal policies, applies irrespective of whether the insurance company or the policyholder initiates the offer to renew, and regardless of whether the policyholder ever read the policy when it was delivered.[211]

[c]—Unilateral Mistake Doctrine

In addition to binders and renewal doctrines, the unilateral mistake rule might help a policyholder avoid application of the mold exclusion. Under the unilateral mistake doctrine,[212] an insurance company is estopped from relying on a mistake in an insurance policy when the insurance company knows the coverage that the policyholder requests and either intentionally or inadvertently fails to integrate such requested coverage into the written policy.[213] The policyholder's failure to read the policy and discover the error prior to an occurrence does not bar recovery under this doctrine.[214]

[d]—Reasonable Expectations

Finally, the reasonable expectations doctrine might aid a policyholder in an attempt to avoid the mold exclusion. Some policyholders have avoided other exclusions under the reasonable expectations doctrine.

When the language of an insurance policy is clear and unambiguous, courts are generally required to give effect to that language.[215] However, the parties' reasonable expectations are the touchstone of any inquiry into the meaning of an insurance policy.[216] Accordingly, in certain circumstances, the policyholder's reasonable expectations will be allowed to defeat the express language of an insurance policy.[217] One court explained the use of the reasonable expectations doctrine as follows. "In certain limited situations, the reasonable expectations doctrine permits courts to depart from the literal terms and conditions of an insurance policy in order to protect the reasonable expectations of the insured with respect to coverage. The doctrine is extremely narrow. It applies only to resolving ambiguity in policy terms and for correcting extreme situations, such as where a party's coverage is significantly different from what the party reasonably believes it has paid for and where the only notice the party has of that difference is an obscure and unexpected provision."[218]

For example, where, without prior notice to the policyholder, an insurance company issues a renewal policy that changes the terms of the original policy, courts have held that the original policy's terms, which represent the policyholder's reasonable expectations, will prevail over the express language of the renewal policy.[219] Likewise, where an insurance company issues an insurance policy that differs from what the policyholder requested, without ensuring that the policyholder is notified and has comprehension of the changes made, the expected terms of the requested policy, which represent the policyholder's reasonable expectations, will control over the express terms of the issued policy.[220]

It is not the policyholder's duty to read the policy and discover any changes. Rather, in all cases, the burden of proof rests with the insurance company to establish the required notice to, and understanding by, the policyholder of the nature of the change, apart from reading about it in the policy.[221] While policyholder sophistication does not negate operation of the reasonable expectations doctrine, it is a factor to consider in determining whether the policyholder truly did not have any reason to know of the inclusion of the more restrictive covenant.[222]

A policyholder who has renewed with the same insurance company for many years will want to develop a record as to when the mold exclusion was first added to its policies and what notice was provided to it of the change in coverage. Such a record will enable the policyholder to analyze and perhaps apply some of these doctrines to help avoid a application of the Mold Exclusion.[223]

Notes

1 See ISO Form CG 0001 10 01.

2 See § 7.02 *infra.*

3 See § 7.03 *infra.*

4 See § 7.04 *infra.*

5 See § 7.05 *infra.*

6 See § 7.06 *infra.*

7 See § 7.07 *infra.*

8 See § 7.08 *infra.*

9 See § 7.09 *infra.*

10 See § 7.10 *infra.*

[11] For a broad discussion of the pollution exclusions, see Chapter 8 *infra*.

[12] See *Black's Law Dictionary* at 589 (5th ed. 1979). See also:

Second Circuit: Known Litigation Holdings, L.L.C. v. Navigators Insurance Co., 934 F. Supp.2d 409 (D. Conn. 2013); North American Foreign Trading Corp. v. Mitsui Sumitomo Insurance USA, Inc., 413 F. Supp.2d 295 (S.D.N.Y. 2006); 40 Gardenville, LLC v. Travelers Property Casualty Company of America, 387 F. Supp.2d 205 (W.D.N.Y. 2005).

Third Circuit: Specialty Surfaces International, Inc. v. Continental Casualty Co., 609 F.3d 223 (3d Cir. 2010); Kirkpatrick v. AIU Insurance Co., 204 F. Supp.2d 850 (E.D. Pa. 2002).

Fourth Circuit: ABT Building Products Corp. v. National Union Fire Insurance Company of Pittsburgh, 472 F.3d 99 (4th Cir. 2006); Insurance Company of North America v. United States Gypsum Co., 678 F. Supp. 138 (W.D. Va. 1988), *aff'd* 870 F.2d 148 (4th Cir. 1989).

Fifth Circuit: RLI Insurance Co. v. Maxxon Southwest, Inc., 108 Fed. Appx. 194, 2004 WL 1941757 (5th Cir. 2004); Trammell Crow Residential Co. v. Virginia Surety Co., Inc., 643 F. Supp.2d 844 (N.D. Tex. 2008).

Sixth Circuit: Fifth Third Mortgage Co. v. Chicago Title Insurance Co., 692 F.3d 507 (6th Cir. 2012); University of Cincinnati v. Arkwright Mutual Insurance Co., 51 F.3d 1277 (6th Cir. 1995).

Seventh Circuit: Sarac v. Minnesota Life Insurance Co., 529 F. Supp.2d 924 (N.D. Ill. 2007).

Eighth Circuit: J.E. Jones Construction Co. v. Chubb & Sons, Inc., 486 F.3d 337 (8th Cir. 2007).

Ninth Circuit: Pacific Insurance Co. v. Catholic Bishop of Spokane, 450 F. Supp.2d 1186 (E.D. Wash. 2006).

Tenth Circuit: Ash Grove Cement Co. v. Employers Insurance of Wausau, 513 F. Supp.2d 1200 (D. Kan. 2007), *vacated in part on other grounds* 530 F. Supp.2d 1199 (D. Kan. 2008).

Eleventh Circuit: Owners Insurance Co. v. James, 295 F. Supp.2d 1354 (N.D. Ga. 2003).

State Courts:

California: Delgado v. Interinsurance Exchange of Automobile Club of Southern California, 47 Cal.4th 302, 211 P.3d 1083, 97 Cal. Rptr.3d 298 (2009).

Colorado: General Security Indemnity Co. of Arizona v. Mountain States Mutual Casualty Co., 205 P.3d 529 (Colo. App. 2009).

Illinois: Rich v. Principal Life Insurance Co., 226 Ill.2d 359, 314 Ill. Dec. 795, 875 N.E.2d 1082, (Ill. 2007).

Indiana: Thompson, Inc. v. Insurance Co. of North America, 11 N.E.3d 982 (Ind. App. 2014); Newnam Manufacturing, Inc. v. Transcontinental Insurance Co., 871 N.E.2d 396 (Ind. App. 2007).

Kentucky: Cincinnati Insurance Co. v. Motorists Mutual Insurance Co., 306 S.W.3d 69 (Ky. 2010).

Massachusetts: Massachusetts Electric Co. v. Commercial Union Insurance Co., 2005 Mass. Super. LEXIS 542 (Mass. Super. Oct. 18, 2005).

New York: National Union Fire Insurance Company of Pittsburgh, PA v. Turner Construction Co., 119 A.D.3d 103, 986 N.Y.S.2d 74 (N.Y. App. Div. 2014).

Oregon: ZRZ Realty Co. v. Beneficial Fire and Casualty Insurance Co., 241 P.3d 710 (Or. 2010) (*en banc*).

Pennsylvania: Donegal Mutual Insurance Co. v. Baumhammers, 938 A.2d 286 (Pa. 2007).

South Carolina: Crossmann Communities of North Carolina, Inc. v. Harleysville Mutual Insurance Co., 2011 S.C. LEXIS 2 (S.C. Jan. 7, 2011), *rehearing granted* (Mar. 9, 2011).

South Dakota: North Star Mutual Insurance Co. v. Rasmussen, 734 N.W.2d 352 (S.D. 2007).

Texas: Lennar Corp. v. Great American Insurance Co., 200 S.W.3d 651 (Tex. App.), *substituted concurring and dissenting opinions* 2006 WL 909937 (Tex. App. Apr. 11, 2006).

Wisconsin: Fetherston v. Parks, 352 Wis.2d 472, 842 N.W.2d 481 (Wis. App. 2013); State of Wisconsin v. Hydrite Chemical Co., 695 N.W.2d 816 (Wis. App. 2005).

[13] However, the loss-in-progress doctrine has not been universally adopted. See, e.g.:

Second Circuit: Peck v. Public Service Mutual Insurance Co., 363 F. Supp.2d 137 (D. Conn. 2005).

State Courts:

Pennsylvania: Diamond State Insurance Co. v. Bosco, 57 Pa. D. & C.4th 129 (Pa. C.P. 2002) (loss-in-progress doctrine rejected because not adopted in Pennsylvania).

[14] See:

First Circuit: Ferguson v. General Star Indemnity Co., 582 F. Supp.2d 91 (D. Mass. 2008).

Second Circuit: Known Litigation Holdings, L.L.C. v. Navigators Insurance Co., 934 F. Supp.2d 409 (D. Conn. 2013); Bodewes v. Ulico Casualty Co., 336 F. Supp.2d 263 (W.D.N.Y. 2004).

Fourth Circuit: ABT Building Products Corp. v. National Union Fire Insurance Company of Pittsburgh, 472 F.3d 99 (4th Cir. 2006).

Fifth Circuit: National Casualty Co. v. Franklin County, Miss., 718 F. Supp.2d 785 (S.D. Miss. 2010); Sentry Insurance Co. v. DFW Alliance Corp., 2007 WL 669418 (N.D. Tex. Mar. 6, 2007).

Sixth Circuit: Fifth Third Mortgage Co. v. Chicago Title Insurance Co., 692 F.3d 507 (6th Cir. 2012); American & Foreign Insurance Co. v. Sequatchie Concrete Services, Inc., 441 F.3d 341 (6th Cir. 2006); Inland Waters Pollution Control, Inc. v. National Union Fire Insurance Company of Pittsburgh, Pennsylvania, 997 F.2d 172, 177–178 (6th Cir. 1993); State Automobile Mutual Insurance Co. v. R.H.L., Inc., 2010 WL 909073 (W.D. Tenn. Mar. 12, 2010); Pizza Magia International, LLC v. Assurance Company of America, 447 F. Supp.2d 766 (W.D. Ky. 2006).

Seventh Circuit: Grey Direct, Inc. v. Erie Insurance Exchange, 460 F.3d 895 (7th Cir. 2006); Wolf Lake Terminals, Inc. v. Mutual Marine Insurance Co., 433 F. Supp.2d 933 (N.D. Ind. 2005); Central Mutual Insurance Co. v. Useong International, Ltd., 394 F. Supp.2d 1043 (N.D. Ill. 2005).

Eighth Circuit: Ohio Casualty Insurance Co. v. Union Pacific Railroad Co., 469 F.3d 1158 (8th Cir. 2006).

Tenth Circuit: Lone Star Steakhouse & Saloon, Inc. v. Liberty Mutual Insurance Group, 343 F. Supp.2d 989 (D. Kan. 2004).

Eleventh Circuit: Keenan Hopkins Schmidt and Stowell Contractors, Inc. v. Continental Casualty Co., 653 F. Supp.2d 1255 (M.D. Fla. 2009).

State Courts:

California: Root v. American Equity Specialty Insurance Co., 30 Cal. Rptr.3d 631 (Cal. App. 2005).

Colorado: Hunt v. Aetna Casualty & Surety Co., 387 P.2d 405, 406 (Colo. 1963).

Indiana: Thompson, Inc. v. Insurance Co. of North America, 11 N.E.3d 982 (Ind. App. 2014); Crawfordsville Square, LLC v. Monroe Guaranty Insurance Co. 906 N.E.2d 934 (Ind. App. 2009).

Kansas: American Special Risk Management Corp. v. Cahow, 192 P.3d 614 (Kan. 2008).

Massachusetts: Massachusetts Electric Co. v. Commercial Union Insurance Co., 2005 WL 3490756 (Mass. Super. Oct. 18, 2005).

Michigan: American Bumper & Manufacturing Co. v. Hartford Fire Insurance Co., 550 N.W.2d 475, 484 n.19 (Mich. 1996); Chrysler Corp. v. Wel-Tek International, 2002 WL 1897666, at *2 (Mich. App. Aug. 16, 2002); South Macomb Disposal Authority v. American Insurance Co., 572 N.W.2d 686, 693 (Mich. App. 1997).

Minnesota: Wooddale Builders, Inc. v. Maryland Casualty Co., 722 N.W.2d 283 (Minn. 2006).

New Jersey: Scottsdale Insurance Co. v. Woolsulate Corp., 2008 WL 5233662 (N.J. Super. App. Div. Dec. 17, 2008).

Ohio: Buckeye Ranch, Inc. v. Northfield Insurance Co., 839 N.E.2d 94 (Ohio C.P. 2005).

Texas: Warrantech Corp. v. Steadfast Insurance Co., 210 S.W.3d 760 (Tex. App. 2006).

Wisconsin: State of Wisconsin v. Hydrite Chemical Co., 695 N.W.2d 816 (Wis. App. 2005).

[15] *Id.*

[16] See ISO Form CG 00 01 10 01. See also:

Massachusetts: Massachusetts Electric Co. v. Commercial Union Insurance Co., 2005 WL 3490756 (Mass. Super. Oct. 18, 2005).

Wisconsin: Becker by Kasieta v. State Farm Mutual Automobile Insurance Co., 582 N.W.2d 499 (Wis. App. 1998).

In fact, as will be discussed, fraud exclusions encompass the concept underpinning the doctrine. See § 7.02[2] *infra*. See also:

State Courts:

Maryland: Moscarillo v. Professional Risk Management Services, Inc., 398 Md. 529, 921 A.2d 245 (2007).

New York: National Union Fire Insurance Co. of Pittsburgh, PA v. Turner Construction Co., 119 A.D.3d 103, 986 N.Y.S.2d 74 (N.Y. App. Div. 2014).

Ohio: Buckeye Ranch, Inc. v. Northfield Insurance Co., 839 N.E.2d 94 (Ohio C.P. 2005).

Pennsylvania: Rohm & Haas Co. v. Continental Casualty Co., 781 A.2d 1172, 1183–1184 (Pa. 2001) (Castille, J. dissenting).

[17] See, e.g.:

First Circuit: United States Liability Insurance Co. v. Selman, 70 F.3d 684 (1st Cir. 1995).

Second Circuit: 84 Albany Avenue Realty Corp. v. The Standard Fire Insurance Co., 13 F. Supp.3d 241 (E.D.N.Y. 2014) (actual knowledge of loss, as opposed to knowledge of risk, required); Known Litigation Holdings, L.L.C. v. Navigators Insurance Co., 934 F. Supp.2d 409 (D. Conn. 2013) (actual knowledge required); Hartford Steam Boiler Group, Inc. v. SVB Underwriting, Ltd., 2011 WL 1899392 (D. Conn. May 19, 2011); Fleet Business Credit LLC v. Global Aerospace Underwriting Managers Ltd., 646 F. Supp.2d 473 (S.D.N.Y 2009); North American Foreign Trading Corp. v. Mitsui Sumitomo Insurance USA, Inc., 413 F. Supp.2d 295 (S.D.N.Y. 2006); 40 Gardenville, LLC v. Travelers Property Casualty Company of America, 387 F. Supp.2d 205 (W.D.N.Y. 2005).

Third Circuit: Intermetal Mexicana, S.A. v. Insurance Company of North America, 866 F.2d 71, 77 (3d Cir. 1989); Campagnie Des Bauxites De Guinee v. Insurance Company of North America, 724 F.2d 369, 372–373 (3d Cir. 1983); Kirkpatrick v. AIU Insurance Co., 204 F. Supp.2d 850 (E.D. Pa. 2002).

Fourth Circuit: ABT Building Products Corp. v. National Union Fire Insurance Company of Pittsburgh, 472 F.3d 99 (4th Cir. 2006); Stonehenge Engineering Corp. v. Employers Insurance of Wausau, 201 F.3d 296 (4th Cir. 2001).

Sixth Circuit: Fifth Third Mortgage Co. v. Chicago Title Insurance Co., 692 F.3d 507 (6th Cir. 2012) (mere poor underwriting of a loan and therefore substantial likelihood of default is not enough); American & Foreign Insurance Co., Inc. v. Sequatchie Concrete Services, Inc., 441 F.3d 341 (6th Cir. 2006); Inland Waters Pollution Control, Inc. v. National Union Fire Insurance Co., 997 F.2d 172, 179 (6th Cir. 1993); Generali U.S. Branch v. National Trust Insurance Co., 2009 WL 2762273 (W.D. Ky. Aug. 27, 2009); Pizza Magia International, LLC v. Assurance Company of America, 447 F. Supp.2d 766 (W.D. Ky. 2006).

Seventh Circuit: West Bend Mutual Insurance Co. v. U.S. Fidelity and Guaranty Co., 598 F.3d 918 (7th Cir. 2010); Sarac v. Minnesota Life Insurance Co., 529 F. Supp.2d 924 (N.D. Ill. 2007); Wolf Lake Terminals, Inc. v. Mutual Marine Insurance Co., 433 F. Supp.2d 933 (N.D. Ind. 2005).

Eighth Circuit: Pins v. State Farm Fire and Casualty Co., 476 F.3d 581 (8th Cir. 2007); Ohio Casualty Insurance Co. v. Union Pacific Railroad Co., 469 F.3d 1158 (8th Cir. 2006).

Ninth Circuit: Chale v. Allstate Life Insurance Co., 353 F.3d 742 (9th Cir. 2003); Trident Seafoods Corp. v. Commonwealth Insurance Co., 850 F. Supp.2d 1189 (W.D. Wash. 2012) (subjective knowledge required); Pacific Insurance Co. v. Catholic Bishop of Spokane, 450 F. Supp.2d 1186 (E.D. Wash. 2006).

Tenth Circuit: Greystone Construction, Inc. v. National Fire and Marine Insurance Co., 661 F.3d 1272 (10th Cir. 2011) (actual knowledge); Kinniburgh v. Safeco Insurance Company of America, 164 F. Supp.2d 1213 (D. Mont. 2001).

Eleventh Circuit: Owners Insurance Co. v. James, 295 F. Supp.2d 1354 (N.D. Ga. 2003).

State Courts:

California: Montrose Chemical Corp. v. Admiral Insurance Co., 913 P.2d 878 (Cal. 1995) (in continuous, progressive injury cases, even though subsequent damage or loss may be inevitable, it is insurable if there is at least some contingency or risk that the event might or might not occur) (receipt of PRP notice did not make environmental liability a known loss without definitive establishment of liability); Stonewall Insurance. Co. v. City of Palos Verdes Estates, 54 Cal. Rptr.2d 176 (Cal. App. 1996) (inevitable loss is not a known loss if, at the time of purchase of the insurance, there is a lack of definitive establishment of the policyholder's liability same); IMCERA Group, Inc. v. Liberty Mutual Insurance Co., 50 Cal. Rptr.2d 583, 597–598 (Cal. App.) (inevitable loss is not a known loss if, at the time of purchase of the insurance, there is a lack of definitive establishment of the policyholder's liability).

Illinois: Rich v. Principal Life Insurance Co., 226 Ill.2d 359, 314 Ill. Dec. 795, 875 N.E.2d 1082 (2007).

Indiana: Thompson, Inc. v. Insurance Company of North America, 11 N.E.3d 982 (Ind. App. 2014) (actual knowledge); Crawfordsville Square, LLC v. Monroe Guaranty Insurance Co., 906 N.E.2d 934 (Ind. App. 2009); General Housewares Corp. v. National Surety Corp., 741 N.E.2d 408 (Ind. App. 2000).

Massachusetts: Allmerica Financial Corp. v. Certain Underwriters at Lloyd's, London, 871 N.E.2d 418 (Mass. 2007).

Minnesota: Domtar, Inc. v. Niagara Fire Insurance Co., 563 N.W.2d 724 (Minn. 1997).

Missouri: United Capitol Insurance Co. v. Hoodco, Inc., 974 S.W.2d 572 (Mo. App. 1998).

New Hampshire: State Farm Insurance Co. v. Bruns, 942 A.2d 1275 (N.H. 2008).

New Jersey: High Point Insurance Co. v. J.M., 942 A.2d 804 (N.J. Super. App. Div. 2008).

New York: National Union Fire Insurance Company of Pittsburgh, Pennsylvania v. Xerox Corp., 807 N.Y.S.2d 344, 346 (N.Y. App. Div. 2006).

Pennsylvania: Donegal Mutual Insurance Co. v. Baumhammers, 938 A.2d 286 (Pa. 2007).

Texas: Lennar Corp. v. Great American Insurance Co., 200 S.W.3d 651 (Tex. App.), *substituted concurring and dissenting opinions* 2006 WL 909937 (Tex. App. Apr. 11, 2006).

Vermont: Anderson v. Cooperative Insurance Cos., 895 A.2d 155 (Vt., 2006).

Washington: Mutual of Enumclaw Insurance Co. v. USF Insurance Co., 153 P.3d 877 (Wash. App. 2007).

Wisconsin: American Family Mutual Insurance Co. v. Bateman, 726 N.W.2d 678 Wis. App. 2006); State v. Hydrite Chemical Co., 695 N.W.2d 816 (Wis. App.), *review denied* 700 N.W. 2d 271 (Wis. 2005).

[18] See, e.g.:

Third Circuit: Pittston Company Ultramar America Ltd. v. Allianz Insurance Co., 124 F.3d 508 (3d Cir.1997).

Fifth Circuit: Summers v. Harris, 573 F.2d 869 (5th Cir. 1978) (mere threat of loss justified application of doctrine); RLI Insurance Co. v. Maxxon Southwest, Inc., 265 F. Supp.2d 727 (N.D. Tex. 2003).

Sixth Circuit: New Hampshire Insurance Co. v. Knoxville Cast Stone, Inc., 433 F. Supp.2d 879 (E.D. Tenn. 2004).

Seventh Circuit: Grey Direct, Inc. v. Erie Insurance Exchange, 460 F.3d 895 (7th Cir. 2006); Zaragon Holdings, Inc. v. Indian Harbor Insurance Co., 2011 U.S. Dist. LEXIS 39378 (N.D. Ill. Apr. 12, 2011); International Environmental Corp. v. National Union Fire Insurance Company of Pittsburgh, Pennsylvania, 860 F. Supp. 511 (N.D. Ill. 1994).

State Courts:

Maine: Acadia Insurance Co. v. Keiser Industries, Inc., 793 A.2d 495, 498 (Me. 2002) (upholding verdict for an insurance company under a fortuity principle, adopting a "reasonably should have known" test).

Pennsylvania: Rohm & Haas Co. v. Continental Casualty Co., 781 A.2d 1172, 1177 (Pa. 2001).

Texas: Certain Underwriters at Lloyd's Subscribing to Policy No. WDO-10000 v. KKM Inc., 215 S.W.3d 486 (Tex. App. 2006) (knew or reasonably should have known); Hartrick v. Great American Lloyds Insurance Co., 62 S.W.3d 270, 277 (Tex. App. 2001) (adopting the objective test to the "expected or intended" defense, finding no coverage when the policyholder reasonably and objectively should have expected the loss to occur).

Washington: Overton v. Consolidated Insurance Co., 38 P.3d 322 (Wash. 2002) (policyholder knew of soil contamination caused by others at the time that it purchased the insurance policy but could not have predicted the absolute liability associated with being the mere owner of contaminated property as a result of the subsequent enactment of federal and state environmental statutes).

Wisconsin: State of Wisconsin v. City of Rhinelander, 2001 WL 1155667, at *3 (Wis. App. Oct. 2, 2001) ([A]n "objective standard should be applied when analyzing known loss. The question is whether the City knew or should have known that a claim was likely.").

[19] Rohm & Haas Co. v. Continental Casualty Co., 781 A.2d 1172, 1177 (Pa. 2001)

> "We agree, therefore, with the Superior Court's conclusion that the standard for the known loss defense in this case should be 'whether the evidence shows that the insured was charged with knowledge which reasonably shows that it was, *or should [have been],* aware of a likely exposure to losses which would reach the level of coverage' [at issue]." (emphasis added).

[20] See, e.g., Crawfordsville Square, LLC v. Monroe Guaranty Insurance Co., 906 N.E.2d 934 (Ind. App. 2009). For further discussion, see § 7.02[4] *infra.*

[21] *Id.*, 781 A.2d at 1183–1184 (dissenting opinion).

[22] *Maryland:* Moscarillo v. Professional Risk Management Services, Inc., 2007 WL 1109216 (Md. Apr. 16, 2007).

Ohio: Buckeye Ranch, Inc. v. Northfield Insurance Co., 839 N.E.2d 94 (Ohio C. P. 2005).

Pennsylvania: Rohm & Haas Co. v. Continental Casualty Co., 781 A.2d 1172, 1183–1184 (Pa. 2001) (dissenting opinion).

[23] *Id.*

[24] *Id.*

[25] See Rohm & Haas Co. v. Continental Casualty Co., 732 A.2d 1236, 1256 (Pa. Super. 1999), *aff'd* 781 A.2d1172 (Pa. 2001).

[26] *Illinois:* Missouri Pacific. Railroad Co. v. American Home Assurance Co., 675 N.E.2d 1378, 1386 (Ill. App.), *appeal denied* 684 N.E.2d 1336 (Ill 1997) (known loss cannot extend to known risks because purchase of insurance involves need to protect against known risks).

New York: National Union Fire Insurance Co. of Pennsylvania v. Xerox Corp., 807 N.Y.S.2d 344, 346 (N.Y. App. Div. 2006) (rejecting application of doctrine to a known risk situation).

[27] *Id.*

[28] See, e.g., Lennar Corp. v. Great American Insurance Co., 200 S.W.3d 651 (Tex. App.), *substituted concurring and dissenting opinions* 2006 WL 909937 (Tex. App. Apr. 11, 2006) (issue of material fact as to when large-scale problem became known to policyholder to the extent fortuity applied to bar coverage).

See also:

Second Circuit: 84 Albany Avenue Realty Corp. v. The Standard Fire Insurance Co., 13 F. Supp.3d 241 (E.D.N.Y. 2014).

Fourth Circuit: ABT Building Products Corp. v. National Union Fire Insurance Company of Pittsburgh, PA, 472 F.3d 99 (4th Cir. 2006).

Sixth Circuit: American & Foreign Insurance Co. v. Sequatchie Concrete Services, Inc., 441 F.3d 341 (6th Cir. 2006); New Hampshire Insurance Co. v. Knoxville Cast Stone, Inc., 433 F. Supp.2d 879 (E.D. Tenn. 2004).

Seventh Circuit: Central Mutual Insurance Co. v. Useong International, Ltd., 394 F. Supp.2d 1043 (N.D. Ill. 2005).

Tenth Circuit: Glacier Construction Co. v. Travelers Property Casualty Company of America, 2014 U.S. Dist. LEXIS 73652 (10th Cir. June 20, 2014); Greystone Construction, Inc. v. National Fire and Marine Insurance Co., 661 F.3d 1272 (10th Cir. 2011).

State Courts:

New York: National Union Fire Insurance Co. of Pittsburgh, PA v. Turner Construction Co., 119 A.D.3d 103, 986 N.Y.S.2d 74 (N.Y. App. Div. 2014).

[29] *Id.*

[30] See:

Third Circuit: Nestle Foods Corp. v. Aetna Casualty & Surety Co., 842 F. Supp. 125, 128 (D.N.J. 1993); J.T. Baker, Inc. v. Aetna Casualty & Surety Co., No. 86-4794, slip op. at 42–43 (D.N.J. Sept. 23, 1993), reprinted in 7 Mealey's Litigation Reports (Insurance) No. 48, at A-21–A-22 (Oct. 28, 1993).

Seventh Circuit: Affiliated FM Insurance Co. v. Board of Education of Chicago, 1992 WL 409442, at *16 (N.D. Ill. Oct. 6, 1992), *rev'd on other grounds*1993 WL 189808 (N.D. Ill. June 3, 1993), *aff'd* 23 F.3d 1261 (7th Cir.), *cert. denied* 513 U.S. 963 (1994).

State Courts:

Illinois: Missouri Pacific Railroad Co. v. American Home Assurance Co., 286 Ill. App.3d 305, 675 N.E.2d 1378, 221 Ill. Dec. 648 (Ill. App.), *appeal denied* 684 N.E.2d 1336 (Ill. 1997).

Indiana: Crawfordsville Square, L.L.C. v. Monroe Guaranty Insurance Co., 906 N.E.2d 934 (Ind. App. 2009); General Housewares Corp. v. National Surety Corp., 741 N.E.2d 408 (Ind. App. 2000).

Vermont: Anderson v. Cooperative Insurance Cos., 895 A.2d 155 (Vt. 2006).

Washington: Joseph Simon & Sons, Inc. v. Aetna Fire Underwriters Insurance Co., No. 90-2-14568-9, slip op. 2-3 (Wash. Super. May 14, 1991), reprinted in 5 Mealey's Litigation Reports (Insurance) No. 28, at D-1–D-2 (May 28, 1991).

31 Anderson v. Cooperative Insurance Cos., 895 A.2d 155 (Vt. 2006) (emphasis added). See also:

Third Circuit: Nestle Foods Corp. v. Aetna Casualty & Surety Co., 842 F. Supp. 125, 128 (D.N.J. 1993) (if an insurance company has the same knowledge as the policyholder and continues to renew coverage and accept premiums, the insurance company is estopped from relying upon the expected or intended defense); J.T. Baker, Inc. v. Aetna Casualty & Surety Co., No. 86-4794, slip op. at 42–43 (D.N.J. Sept. 23, 1993), reprinted in 7 Mealey's Litigation Reports (Insurance) No. 48, at A-21–A-22 (Oct. 28, 1993) ("insurers may be estopped from asserting . . . non-coverage if [the insured] can establish that the insurer in question had knowledge of essentially the same facts possessed by the insured and continued to renew coverage and collect premiums").

Seventh Circuit: Affiliated FM Insurance Co. v. Board of Education of Chicago, 1992 WL 409442, at *16 (N.D. Ill. Oct. 6, 1992), *rev'd on other grounds* 1993 WL 189808 (N.D. Ill. June 3, 1993), *aff'd* 23 F.3d 1261 (7th Cir.), *cert. denied* 513 U.S. 963 (1994).

State Courts:

Illinois: Missouri Pacific Railroad Co. v. American Home Assurance Co., 675 N.E.2d 1378 (Ill. App.), *appeal denied* 684 N.E.2d 1336 (Ill. 1997) ("an insurer does not have the duty to defend or indemnify a known loss *unless the parties intended the known loss to be covered*") (emphasis in original).

Washington: Joseph Simon & Sons, Inc. v. Aetna Fire Underwriters Insurance Co., No. 90-2-14568-9, slip op. 2-3 (Wash. Super. May 14, 1991), reprinted in 5 Mealey's Litigation Reports (Insurance) No. 28, at D-1–D-2 (May 28, 1991).

32 See:

Third Circuit: Pittston Company Ultramar America Ltd. v. Allianz Insurance Co., 124 F.3d 508 (3d Cir.1997).

Fifth Circuit: Summers v. Harris, 573 F.2d 869 (5th Cir. 1978) (mere threat of loss justified application of doctrine).

Seventh Circuit: International Environmental Corp. v. National Union Fire Insurance Company of Pittsburgh, Pennsylvania, 860 F. Supp. 511 (N.D. Ill. 1994).

State Courts:

Indiana: Crawfordsville Square, L.L.C. v. Monroe Guaranty Insurance Co., 906 N.E.2d 934 (Ind. App. 2009); General Housewares Corp. v. National Surety Corp., 741 N.E.2d 408 (Ind. App. 2000).

Maine: Acadia Insurance Co. v. Keiser Industries, Inc., 793 A.2d 495, 498 (Me. 2002) (upholding verdict for an insurance company under a fortuity principle, adopting a "reasonably should have known" test).

Pennsylvania: Rohm & Haas Co. v. Continental Casualty Co., 781 A.2d 1172, 1177 (Pa. 2001).

Texas: Certain Underwriters at Lloyd's Subscribing to Policy No. WDO-10000 v. KKM Inc., 215 S.W.3d 486 (Tex. App. 2006) (knew or reasonably should have known); Hartrick v. Great American Lloyds Insurance Co., 62 S.W.3d 270, 277 (Tex. App. 2001) (adopting the objective test to the "expected or intended" defense, finding no coverage when the policyholder reasonably and objectively should have expected the loss to occur).

Washington: Overton v. Consolidated Insurance Co., 38 P.3d 322 (Wash. 2002) (policyholder knew of soil contamination caused by others at the time that it purchased the insurance policy but could not have predicted the absolute liability associated with being the mere owner of contaminated property as a result of the subsequent enactment of federal and state environmental statutes).

Wisconsin: State of Wisconsin v. City of Rhinelander, 2001 WL 1155667, at *3 (Wis. App. Oct. 2, 2001) ("objective standard should be applied when analyzing known loss. The question is whether the City knew or should have known that a claim was likely.").

[33] See:

Third Circuit: Nestle Foods Corp. v. Aetna Casualty & Surety Co., 842 F. Supp. 125, 128 (D.N.J. 1993); J.T. Baker, Inc. v. Aetna Casualty & Surety Co., No. 86-4794, slip op. at 42–43 (D.N.J. Sept. 23, 1993), reprinted in 7 Mealey's Litigation Reports (Insurance) No. 48, at A-21–A-22 (Oct. 28, 1993).

Seventh Circuit: Affiliated FM Insurance Co. v. Board of Education of Chicago, 1992 WL 409442, at *16 (N.D. Ill. Oct. 6, 1992), *rev'd on other grounds* 1993 WL 189808 (N.D. Ill. June 3, 1993), *aff'd* 23 F.3d 1261 (7th Cir.), *cert. denied* 513 U.S. 963 (1994).

State Courts:

Illinois: Missouri Pacific Railroad Co. v. American Home Assurance Co., 675 N.E.2d 1378 (Ill. App.), *appeal denied* 684 N.E.2d 1336 (Ill. 1997).

Indiana: Crawfordsville Square, L.L.C. v. Monroe Guaranty Insurance Co., 906 N.E.2d 934 (Ind. App. 2009); General Housewares Corp. v. National Surety Corp., 741 N.E.2d 408 (Ind. App. 2000).

Pennsylvania: See Diamond State Insurance Co. v. Most Reverend Anthony G. Bosco, No. 5170 of 1999, slip op. (Pa. C.P. May 28, 2002).

Vermont: Anderson v. Cooperative Insurance Cos., 895 A.2d 155 (Vt. 2006) (emphasis added).

Washington: Joseph Simon & Sons, Inc. v. Aetna Fire Underwriters Insurance Co., No. 90-2-14568-9, slip op. 2-3 (Wash. Super. May 14, 1991), reprinted in 5 Mealey's Litigation Reports (Insurance) No. 28, at D-1–D-2 (May 28, 1991).

[34] See Chapter 14 *infra.*

[35] See Diamond State Insurance Co. v. Most Reverend Anthony G. Bosco, No. 5170 of 1999, slip opinion (Pa. C.P. May 28, 2002) (denying insurer's motion for summary judgment on the known-loss doctrine because, *inter alia,* lack of a loss-control report is evidence raising an issue of material fact that the policyholder should not have expected the loss).

[36] See Chapter 14 *infra.*

[37] See, e.g.: State Farm Mutual Automobile Insurance Co. v. Campbell, 538 U.S. 408, 123 S.Ct. 1513, 155 L.Ed.2d 585 (2003); BMW of North America, Inc. v. Gore, 517 U.S. 559, 116 S.Ct. 1589, 134 L.Ed.2d 809 (1996).

[38] See ISO Form CG 00 01 10 01.

[39] See:

Third Circuit: Regent Insurance Co. v. Strausser Enterprises, Inc., 902 F. Supp.2d 628 (E.D. Pa. 2012).

Eighth Circuit: Carlson Marketing Group, Inc. v. Royal Indemnity Co., 517 F. Supp.2d 1089 (D. Minn. 2007).

Tenth Circuit: Wardrip v. Hart, 28 F. Supp.2d 1213 (D. Kan. 1998).

Eleventh Circuit: Penzer v. Transportation Insurance Co., 545 F.3d 1303 (11th Cir. 2008)

State Courts:

California: Carter v. Entercom Sacramento, L.L.C., 219 Cal. App.4th 337, 161 Cal. Rptr.3d 782 (2013).

Colorado: Bohrer v. Church Mutual Insurance Co., 12 P.3d 854 (Colo. App. 2000).

Minnesota: Wojciak v. Northern Package Corp., 310 N.W.2d 675 (Minn. 1981).

Missouri: Brand v. Kansas City Gastroenterology & Hepatology, L.L.C., 414 S.W.3d 546 (Mo. App. 2013).

New York: J.P. Morgan Securities, Inc. v. Vigilant Insurance. Co., 992 N.E.2d 1076 (N.Y. 2013).

Ohio: Neal-Pettit v. Lahman, 125 Ohio St.3d 327, 928 N.E.2d 421 (2010).

[40] See:

Third Circuit: In re Mariner Health Group, 300 B.R. 610 (Bankr. D. Del 2003).

Seventh Circuit: Harris v. County of Racine, 512 F. Supp. 1273 (E.D. Wis.1981).

State Courts:

Arizona: Price v. Hartford Accident and Indemnity Co., 108 Ariz. 485, 502 P.2d 522 (1972); Irvin v. Lexington Insurance Co., 2010 WL 3450986 (Ariz. App. Sept. 2, 2010).

Washington: Fluke Corp. v. Hartford Accident and Indemnity Co., 145 Wash.2d 137, 34 P.3d 809 (2001) (*en banc*).

[41] See, e.g.:

Fifth Circuit: American International Specialty Lines Insurance Co. v. Res-Care Inc., 529 F.3d 649 (5th Cir. 2008).

State Courts:

Texas: Fairfield Insurance Company v. Stephens Martin Paving, L.P., 246 S.W.3d 653 (Tex. 2008).

[42] See:

Second Circuit: In re September 11th Litigation, 494 F. Supp.2d 232 (S.D.N.Y. 2007).

Third Circuit: Pennbank v. St. Paul Fire & Marine Insurance Co., 669 F. Supp. 122, 126 (W.D. Pa. 1987).

Ninth Circuit: Continental Casualty Corp. v. Fibreboard Corp., 762 F. Supp. 1368 (N.D. Cal. 1991), *aff'd* 953 F.2d 1386 (9th Cir.), *cert. denied, judgment vacated on other grounds* 506 U.S. 948 (1992).

Tenth Circuit: Carlson Marketing Group, Inc. v. Royal Indemnity Co., 517 F. Supp.2d 1089 (D. Minn. 2007).

State Courts:

California: Peterson v. Superior Court, 642 P.2d 1305 (Cal. 1982).

Connecticut: Avis Rent A Car System, Inc. v. Liberty Mutual Insurance Co., 526 A.2d 522 (Conn. 1987).

Delaware: Whalen v. On-Deck, Inc., 514 A.2d 1072 (Del. 1986).

Kansas: Pugh v. Munguia, 146 P.3d 1108 (Kan. App. 2006).

Pennsylvania: Butterfield v. Giuntoli, 670 A.2d 646 (Pa. Super. 1995), *alloc. denied* 683 A.2d 875 (Pa.1996); Aetna Casualty & Surety Co. v. Roe, 650 A. 2d 94, 100 (Pa. Super. 1994); Edmond v. Liscio, 224 A.2d 793, 799 (Pa. Super. 1966).

In Butterfield v. Giuntoli, 670 A.2d 646, 653 (Pa. Super. 1994), the court concluded that the policy in that case, containing standard language of insurance for damages caused by medical malpractice, was ambiguous because that language neither included nor excluded coverage for punitive damages. Hence, the court determined that some punitive damages were covered. See *Id.*

Even when an insurance policy does not exclude coverage for punitive damages, public policy precludes coverage for punitive damages that are incurred directly. See, e.g., Aetna Casualty & Surety Co. v. Roe, 650 A. 2d 94, 100 (Pa. Super. 1994). Because punitive damages are imposed as a punishment and deterrent to the defendant and others, rather than as mere compensation to the plaintiff, allowing insurance coverage for such damages would thwart the purpose behind a punitive damage award. See Esmond v. Liscio, 224 A.2d 793, 799 (Pa. Super. 1966).

As set forth above, some jurisdictions do not bar insurance coverage for punitive damages where the policyholder's liability is vicarious rather than dire. See, e.g., Butterfield, 670 A.2d at 655 (Pa. Super. 1995). The rationale for this distinction in these jurisdictions is:

> "Where corporate management commits an outrageous act, punishment is appropriate. Where the act is committed by . . . an agent, not pursuant to corporate policy or plan, the corporation, though vicariously liable for punitive damages, is entitled to insure against such damages." See Pennbank v. St. Paul Fire & Marine Insurance Co., 669 F. Supp. 122, 126 (W.D. Pa. 1987).

Texas: Fairfield Insurance Co. v. Stephens Martin Paving, LP, 246 S.W.3d 653 (Tex. 2008).

Virginia: United Services Automobile Association v. Webb, 369 S.E.2d 196 (Va. 1988); United States Fire Insurance Co. v. Aspen Building. Corp., 367 S.E.2d 478 (Va. 1988).

43 Butterfield v. Giuntoli, 670 A.2d 646 (Pa. Super. 1995).

44 See ISO Form CG 00 01 10 01. See also, United States Fire Insurance Co. v. Aspen Building Corp., 367 S.E.2d 478 (Va. 1988) (punitive damages are insurable when assessed for bodily injury caused by unintentional acts).

45 See, e.g., United States Fire Insurance Co. v. Aspen Building Corp., 367 S.E.2d 478 (Va. 1988) (punitive damages are insurable when assessed for bodily injury caused by unintentional acts).

46 Aetna Casualty & Surety Co. v. Roe, 650 A. 2d 94, 100 (Pa. Super. 1994).

> "This Court has construed insurance policy provisions excluding coverage for 'expected or intended injuries' in other disputes and, after a thorough exegesis of the 'expected or intended harm' clause, this Court has held that these clauses are ambiguous as a matter of law and must be construed against the insurer. In addition, this Court has held that the words 'expected' and 'intended' are synonymous when interpreting insurance exclusionary clauses."

47 See Turner, *Insurance Coverage of Construction Disputes* § 9.01, at 213–214 (CGL insurance policy provides contractual liability coverage by virtue of an exception to an exclusion). See also, 1325 North Van Buren, LLC v. T-3 Group, Ltd., 716 N.W.2d 822 (Wis. 2006) (policy can provide coverage for contractual liabilities).

48 See ISO Form CG 00 01 10 01.

49 *Id.*

50 *Id.*

51 See:

First Circuit: Lopez and Medina Corp. v. Marsh USA, Inc., 694 F. Supp.2d 119 (D.P.R. 2010).

Third Circuit: Penn National Insurance v. HNI Corp., 482 F. Supp.2d 568 (M.D. Pa. 2007).

Fourth Circuit: Cowan Systems, Inc. v. Harleysville Mutual Insurance Co., 457 F.3d 368 (4th Cir. 2006); Capital Environmental Services, Inc. v. North River Insurance Co., 536 F. Supp.2d 633 (E.D. Va. 2008); Energy Corporation of America v. Bituminous Casualty Corp., 543 F. Supp.2d 536 (S.D. W. Va. 2008); Harleysville Mutual Insurance Co. v. Reliance National Insurance Co., 256 F. Supp.2d 413 (M.D.N.C. 2002).

Fifth Circuit: Henry's Marine Service, Inc. v. Fireman's Fund Insurance Co., 193 Fed. Appx. 267 (5th Cir. 2006); Kirschenbaum v. Spraggins, 752 F. Supp.2d 728 (E.D. La. 2010); McGinnis v. Union Pacific Railroad Co., 612 F. Supp.2d 776 (S.D. Tex. 2009); Burlington Resources, Inc. v. United National Insurance Co., 481 F. Supp.2d 567 (E.D. La. 2007).

Sixth Circuit: Martin County Coal Corp. v. Universal Underwriters Insurance Services, Inc., 2010 WL 55926 (E.D. Ky. Jan. 4, 2010); Stryker Corp. v. National Union Fire Insurance Company of Pittsburgh, PA, 2009 WL 56292 (W.D. Mich. Jan. 8, 2009).

Eighth Circuit: Spirtas Co. v. Federal Insurance Co., 481 F. Supp.2d 993 (E.D. Mo. 2007).

Ninth Circuit: Teck Metals, Ltd. v. Certain Underwriters at Lloyd's London, 735 F. Supp.2d 1260 (E.D. Wash. 2010).

Tenth Circuit: VBF, Inc. v. Chubb Group of Insurance Cos., 263 F.3d 1226 (10th Cir. 2001).

Eleventh Circuit: Ring Power Corp. v. Amerisure Insurance Co., 326 Fed. Appx. 502 (11th Cir. 2009); Twin City Fire Insurance Co., Inc. v. Ohio Casualty Insurance Co., 480 F.3d 1254 (11th Cir. 2007); Birmingham Fire Insurance Company of Pennsylvania v. Comcar Industries, Inc., 551 F. Supp.2d 1340 (M.D. Fla. 2008).

State Courts:

Arkansas: United States Fidelity & Guaranty Co. v. Continental Casualty Co., 120 S.W.3d 556 (Ark. 2003).

Louisiana: Alwell v. Meadowcrest Hospital, Inc., 971 So.2d 411 (La. App. 2007); Stewart Interior Contractors, L.L.C. v. Metalpro Industries, L.L.C., 969 So.2d 653 (La. App. 2007).

Maryland: Chang v. Brethren Mutual Insurance Co., 897 A.2d 854 (Md. Spec. App. 2006).

Massachusetts: Garnet Construction Co. v. Acadia Insurance Co., 814 N.E.2d 23 (Mass. App. 2004), *appeal denied* 816 N.E.2d 1223 (Mass. 2004).

Michigan: Lynn v. Detroit Edison, 2006 WL 1408443 (Mich. App. May 23, 2006).

Minnesota: Soo Line Railroad Co. v. Brown's Crew Car of Wyoming, 694 N.W.2d 109 (Minn. App. 2005).

New Hampshire: White Mountain Cable Construction Co. v. Transamerica Insurance Co., 631 A.2d 907 (N.H. 1993).

New Jersey: Epic Management, Inc. v. v. Harleysville Insurance Company of New Jersey, 2010 WL 3516902 (N.J. Super. App. Div. Aug. 31, 2010).

New York: J. Lucarelli & Sons, Inc. v. Mountain Valley Indemnity Co., 64 A.D.3d 856, 881 N.Y.S.2d 708 (N.Y. App. Div. 2009); Aetna Casualty & Surety Co. v. Lumbermens Mutual Casualty. Co., 527 N.Y.S.2d 143 (N.Y. App. Div.), appeal denied 532 N.E.2d 101 (N.Y. 1988).

North Carolina: Pennsylvania National Mutual Casualty Insurance Co. v. Associated Scaffolders & Equipment Co., 579 S.E.2d 404 (N.C. App. 2003).

North Dakota: ACUITY v. Burd & Smith Construction, Inc., 721 N.W.2d 33 (N.D. 2006).

Tennessee: York v. Vulcan Materials Co., 63 S.W.3d 384 (Tenn. App.).

Texas: Underwriters at Lloyd's of London v. Gilbert Texas Construction, L.P., 245 S.W.3d 29 (Tex. App. 2007); Lennar Corp. v. Great American Insurance Co., 200 S.W.3d 651 (Tex. App. 2006).

West Virginia: Marlin v. Wetzel County Board of Education, 569 S.E.2d 462 (W. Va. 2002).

Wisconsin: United Co-op. v. Frontier FS Co-op., 738 N.W.2d 578 (Wis. App. 2007).

[52] See, e.g., La. Rev. Stat. Ann., Art. 1804 (contribution among joint tortfeasors). See also: Hamway v. Braud, 838 So.2d 803, 806 (La. App. 2002) (indemnity may arise under a tort theory); Farbe v. Casualty Reciprocal Exchange, 765 So.2d 994, 996 (La. 2000) (source of the right to claim contribution is subrogation to the plaintiff's rights against the remaining tortfeasors).

[53] *Id.*

[54] See, e.g., La. La. Rev. Stat. Ann., Art. 425A (mandatory joinder rule for all claims arising out of the common nucleus of operative facts). See also, Tate v. Prewitt, 769 So.2d 800, 808 (La.

App. 2000) (*res judicata* bars relitigation of any subject matter arising from same transaction or occurrence).

55 See American Home Assurance Co. v. Czarniecki, 230 So.2d 253, 259 (La. 1969).

56 See:

First Circuit: Lopez and Medina Corp. v. Marsh USA, Inc., 694 F. Supp.2d 119 (D.P.R. 2010).

Fourth Circuit: Capital Environmental Services, Inc. v. North River Insurance Co., 536 F. Supp.2d 633 (E.D. Va. 2008); Harleysville Mutual Insurance Co. v. Reliance National Insurance Co., 256 F. Supp.2d 413 (M.D.N.C. 2002).

Fifth Circuit: Musgrove v. Southland Corp., 898 F.2d 1041 (5th Cir. 1990); Kirschenbaum v. Spraggins, 752 F. Supp.2d 728 (E.D. La. 2010); McGinnis v. Union Pacific Railroad Co., 612 F. Supp.2d 776 (S.D. Tex. 2009); Burlington Resources, Inc. v. United National Insurance Co., 481 F. Supp.2d 567 (E.D. La. Feb. 13, 2007).

Sixth Circuit: Martin County Coal Corp. v. Universal Underwriters Insurance Services, Inc., 2010 WL 55926 (E.D. Ky. Jan. 4, 2010); Stryker Corp. v. National; Union Fire Insurance Company of Pittsburgh, PA, 2009 WL 56292 (W.D. Mich. Jan. 8, 2009).

Eighth Circuit: Harleysville Insurance Co. v. Physical Distribution Services, Inc., 716 F.3d 451 (8th Cir. 2013).

Ninth Circuit: USF Insurance Co. v. Smith's Food and Drug Center, Inc., 921 F. Supp.2d 1082 (D. Nev. 2013); Teck Metals, Ltd. v. Certain Underwriters at Lloyd's London, 735 F. Supp.2d 1260 (E.D. Wash. 2010).

Tenth Circuit: VBF, Inc. v. Chubb Group of Insurance Cos., 263 F.3d 1226 (10th Cir. 2001).

Eleventh Circuit: Ring Power Corp. v. Amerisure Insurance Co., 326 Fed. Appx. 502 (11th Cir. 2009); Twin City Fire Insurance Co. v. Ohio Casualty Insurance Co., 480 F.3d 1254 (11th Cir. 2007); Birmingham Fire Insurance Company of Pennsylvania v. Comcar Industries, Inc., 551 F. Supp.2d 1340 (M.D. Fla. 2008).

State Courts:

Arkansas: United States Fidelity & Guaranty Co. v. Continental Casualty Co., 120 S.W.3d 556 (Ark. 2003).

California: Loyola Marymount University v. Hartford Accident & Indemnity Co., 271 Cal. Rptr. 528 (Cal. App. 1990).

Delaware: Office Structures, Inc. v. Home Insurance Co., 503 A.2d 193 (Del. 1985).

Indiana: West Bend Mutual Insurance Co. v. MacDougall Pierce Construction, Inc., 11 N.E.3d 531 (Ind. App. 2014).

Massachusetts: Garnet Construction Co. v. Acadia Insurance Co., 814 N.E.2d 23 (Mass. App. 2004), *appeal denied* 816 N.E.2d 1223 (Mass. 2004).

Minnesota: Soo Line Railroad Co. v. Brown's Crew Car of Wyoming, 694 N.W.2d 109 (Minn. App. 2005).

Missouri: Holland Corp. v. Maryland Casualty Co., 775 S.W.2d 531 (Mo. App. 1989).

New Hampshire: White Mountain Cable Construction Co. v. Transamerica Insurance Co., 631 A.2d 907 (N.H. 1993).

New Jersey: Epic Management, Inc. v. v. Harleysville Insurance Co. of New Jersey, 2010 WL 3516902 (N.J. Super. App. Div. Aug. 31, 2010).

New York: Hunt v. Viminelli-Cowper Co., 93 A.D.3d 1152, 939 N.Y.S.2d 781 (N.Y. App. Div. 2012); J. Lucarelli & Sons, Inc. v. Mountain Valley Indemnity Co., 64 A.D.3d 856, 881 N.Y.S.2d 708 (N.Y. App. Div. 2009); Aetna Casualty & Surety Co. v. Lumbermens Mutual Casualty Co., 136 A.D.2d 246, 527 N.Y.S.2d 143 (N.Y. App. Div.), *appeal denied* 532 N.E.2d 101 (N.Y. 1988).

North Carolina: Pennsylvania National Mutual Casualty Insurance Co. v. Associated Scaffolders and Equipment Co., 579 S.E.2d 404 (N.C. App. 2003).

57 See ISO Form CG 00 01 10 01.

58 *Id.*

59 *Id.*

60 *Id.*

61 *Id.*

62 *Id.*

63 See, e.g., International Marine Undersriters v. ABCD Marine, L.L. C., 179 Wash.2d 274, 313 P.3d 395 (2013) (*en banc*).

64 See, e.g., Martin K. Eby Construction Co. v. One Beacon Insurance Co., 926 F. Supp.2d 1237 (D. Kan. 2013).

65 For a more detailed discussion, see § 7.03[4] *infra*.

66 *Fifth Circuit:* Premiere, Inc. v. Commercial Underwriters Insurance Co., 2003 WL 21634953 (E.D. La. July 9, 2003) (applying Louisiana law) ("another party" encompasses an indemnitee of the policyholder's indemnitee).

Sixth Circuit: Legge Associates, Inc. v. Dayton Power & Light Co., 113 F.3d 1235 (Table), 1997 WL 199491, at *6 (6th Cir. Apr. 22, 1997).

67 See ISO Form CG 00 01 10 01.

68 *Id.*

69 Legge Associates, Inc. v. Dayton Power & Light Co., 113 F.3d 1235 (Table), 1997 WL 199491, at *6 (6th Cir. Apr. 22, 1997).

> "Nothing in the policy's definition of insured contract requires that 'another' and [the policyholder] deal with each other directly, as long as [the policyholder] has agreed to assume 'another's' tort liability. [The policyholder] assumed responsibility for the harm caused in some part by [the equipment supplier]. Therefore, under the policy the hold harmless clause is an insured contract."

See also, Premiere, Inc. v. Commercial Underwriters Insurance Co., 2003 WL 21634953 (E.D. La. July 9, 2003) (applying Louisiana law) ("another party" encompasses an indemnitee of the policyholder's indemnitee). But see, Alea London Ltd. v. Central Gulf Shipyard, L.L.C. 2006 U.S. Dist. LEXIS 22512 (W.D. La. Mar. 30, 2006).

70 *Fifth Circuit:* Premiere, Inc. v. Commercial Underwriters Insurance Co., 2003 WL 21634953, at *8 (E.D. La. July 9, 2003) (applying Louisiana law) ("another party" was not limited to the policyholder's indemnitee because the insurance company "could have written [the] exclusions to expressly and unambiguously preclude coverage for underlying indemnification agreements"). But see, Alea London Ltd. v. Central Gulf Shipyard, L.L.C. 2006 U.S. Dist. LEXIS 22512 (W.D. La. Mar. 30, 2006).

Sixth Circuit: Legge Associates, Inc. v. Dayton Power & Light Co., 113 F.3d 1235 (Table), 1997 WL 199491, at *6 (6th Cir. Apr. 22, 1997) ("another party" not limited to policyholder's indemnitee because "[i]f this result is unexpected to [the insurance company], it could have been avoided by better draftmanship").

71 *Fifth Circuit:* Premiere, Inc. v. Commercial Underwriters Insurance Co., 2003 WL 21634953, at *8 (E.D. La. July 9, 2003) (applying Louisiana law) ("another party" was not limited to the policyholder's indemnitee because the insurance company "could have written [the] exclusions to expressly and unambiguously preclude coverage for underlying indemnification agreements"). But see, Alea London Ltd. v. Central Gulf Shipyard, L.L.C. 2006 U.S. Dist. LEXIS 22512 (W.D. La. Mar. 30, 2006).

Sixth Circuit: Legge Associates, Inc. v. Dayton Power & Light Co., 113 F.3d 1235 (Table), 1997 WL 199491, at *6 (6th Cir. Apr. 22, 1997) ("another party" not limited to policyholder's indemnitee because "[i]f this result is unexpected to [the insurance company], it could have been avoided by better draftsmanship").

72 See ISO Form CG 00 01 10 01.

73 See:

First Circuit: Lopez and Medina Corp. v. Marsh USA, Inc., 694 F. Supp.2d 119 (D.P.R. 2010).

Fourth Circuit: Capital Environmental Services, Inc. v. North River Insurance Co., 536 F. Supp.2d 633 (E.D. Va. 2008); Harleysville Mutual Insurance Co. v. Reliance National Insurance Co., 256 F. Supp.2d 413 (M.D.N.C. 2002).

Fifth Circuit: Deville v. Conmaco Rector, L.P., 516 Fed. Appx. 296 (5th Cir. 2012); Kirschenbaum v. Spraggins, 752 F. Supp.2d 728 (E.D. La. 2010); McGinnis v. Union Pacific Railroad Co., 612 F. Supp.2d 776 (S.D. Tex. 2009); Burlington Resources, Inc. v. United National Insurance Co., 481 F. Supp.2d 567 (E.D. La. 2007).

Sixth Circuit: Martin County Coal Corp. v. Universal Underwriters Insurance Services, Inc., 2010 WL 55926 (E.D. Ky. Jan. 4, 2010); Stryker Corp. v. National; Union Fire Insurance Company of Pittsburgh, PA, 2009 WL 56292 (W.D. Mich. Jan. 8, 2009).

Ninth Circuit: Teck Metals, Ltd. v. Certain Underwriters at Lloyd's London, 735 F. Supp.2d 1260 (E.D. Wash. 2010).

Tenth Circuit: VBF, Inc. v. Chubb Group of Insurance Cos., 263 F.3d 1226 (10th Cir. 2001).

Eleventh Circuit: Ring Power Corp. v. Amerisure Insurance Co., 326 Fed. Appx. 502 (11th Cir. 2009); Twin City Fire Insurance Co. v. Ohio Casualty Insurance Co., 480 F.3d 1254 (11th Cir. 2007); Birmingham Fire Insurance Company of Pennsylvania v. Comcar Industrie, Inc., 551 F. Supp.2d 1340 (M.D. Fla. 2008).

State Courts:

Arkansas: United States Fidelity & Guaranty Co. v. Continental Casualty Co., 120 S.W.3d 556 (Ark. 2003).

Massachusetts: Garnet Construction Co. v. Acadia Insurance Co., 814 N.E.2d 23 (Mass. App. 2004), *appeal denied* 816 N.E.2d 1223 (Mass. 2004).

Minnesota: Soo Line Railroad Co. v. Brown's Crew Car of Wyoming, 694 N.W.2d 109 (Minn. App. 2005).

New Hampshire: White Mountain Cable Construction Co. v. Transamerica Insurance Co., 631 A.2d 907 (N.H. 1993).

New Jersey: Epic Management, Inc. v. v. Harleysville Insurance Company of New Jersey, 2010 WL 3516902 (N.J. Super. App. Div. Aug. 31, 2010).

New York: J. Lucarelli & Sons, Inc. v. Mountain Valley Indemnity Co., 64 A.D.3d 856, 881 N.Y.S.2d 708 (N.Y. App. Div. 2009); Aetna Casualty & Surety Co. v. Lumbermens Mutual Casualty. Co., 136 A.D.2d 246, 527 N.Y.S.2d 143 (N.Y. App. Div.), *appeal denied* 532 N.E.2d 101 (N.Y. 1988).

North Carolina: Pennsylvania National Mutual Casualty Insurance Co. v. Associated Scaffolders & Equipment Co., 579 S.E.2d 404 (N.C. App. 2003).

74 Gibson & Associates, Inc. v. Home Insurance Co., 966 F. Supp. 468 (N.D. Tex. 1997).

> "The assumption by contract of the liability of another is distinct conceptually from the breach of one's contract with another. Liability on the part of the insured for the former is triggered by contractual performance; for the latter liability is triggered by contractual breach. Contractual liability coverage provisions are specifically designed to provide coverage for indemnification actions."

See also:

Alaska: Continental Insurance Co. v. Bussell, 498 P.2d 706, 709–710 (Alaska 1972) (finding no coverage for breach of contract to purchase insurance because contractual liability insurance is intended to apply to hold harmless provisions).

Delaware: Office Structures, Inc. v. Home Insurance Co., 503 A.2d 193, 197 (Del. Supr. 1985) (same).

Florida: Amertec-Grenada, Inc v. Old Republic Insurance Co., 421 So.2d 722 (Fla. App. 1982) ("The contractual liability endorsement provides coverage for the purpose of indemnifying a third party for damages in tort, not for business expenses directly incurred by the insured as a result of its contractual obligations.").

Washington: West Waterway Lumber Co. v. Aetna Insurance Co., 545 P.2d 564, 566–567 (Wash. App.), *review denied* 87 Wash. 2d 1007 (1976) (the contractual liability endorsement is not intended to provide coverage for any liability that the policyholder is subject to under a contract, but to provide coverage in the event the policyholder is held liable under a "hold harmless" or "save harmless" clause).

Wyoming: First Wyoming Bank, N.A. v. Continental Insurance Co., 860 P.2d 1064, 1071–73 (Wyo.), *vacated in part* 860 P.2d 1094 (Wyo. 1993) (contractual liability coverage covers the assumption of liability of another, not first-party obligations for the breach of their own contract).

75 See: Clayton Williams Energy, Inc. v. National Union Fire Insurance Co. of Louisiana, 2004 U.S. Dist. LEXIS 22094 (E.D. La. Nov. 1, 2004); Premiere, Inc. v. Commercial Underwriters Insurance Co., 2003 U.S. Dist. LEXIS 11998 (E.D. La. July 9, 2003).

76 See Premiere, Inc. v. Commercial Underwriters Insurance Co., 2003 WL 21634953, at *8 (E.D. La. July 9, 2003).

77 *Id.* See also:

Fifth Circuit: American Employers' Insurance Co. v. DynMcDermott Petroleum Operations Co., 2009 WL 1814124 (S.D. Tex. Mar. 25, 2009); Gibson & Associates v. Home Insurance Co., 966 F. Supp. 468 (N.D. Tex 1997).

Sixth Circuit: Legge Associates, Inc. v. Dayton Power and Light Co., 113 F.3d 1235 (Table), 1997 WL 199491 (6th Cir. Apr. 22, 1997).

State Courts:

New Hampshire: White Mountain Construction Co. v. Transamerica Insurance Co., 631 A.2d 907 (N.H. 1993) (insured was entitled to insurance coverage for liabilities assumed by its indemnitee under a separate indemnification agreement between its indemnitee and a public utility).

See also, Bruner and O'Conner, *Bruner and O'Conner On Construction Law* §§ 11:52-11:53 "Scope of Contractual Liability Coverage." But see, Alea London Ltd. v. Central Gulf Shipyard, L.L.C., 2006 WL 845752 (W.D. La. Mar. 30, 2006).

78 See ISO Form CG 00 01 10 01.

79 *Seventh Circuit*: Wausau Underwriters Insurance Co. v. Mount Vernon Fire Insurance Co., 507 F. Supp.2d 898 (N.D. Ill. 2007).

Ninth Circuit: R.W. Beck & Associates v. City & Borough of Sitka, 27 F.3d 1475, 1484 (9th Cir. 1994) (attorneys' fees of the indemnitee in defense of the underlying action are "damages" which would count against limits, where the indemnification agreement included defense costs).

State Courts:

California: Golden Eagle Insurance Co. v. Insurance Company of the West, 121 Cal. Rptr.2d 682, 690–691 (Cal. App. 2002) (attorneys' fees of the indemnitee in defense of the underlying action are "damages" which would count against limits, where the indemnification agreement included defense costs).

[80] See ISO Form CG 00 01 10 01.

[81] *Ninth Circuit:* R.W. Beck & Associates v. City & Borough of Sitka, 27 F.3d 1475, 1484 (9th Cir. 1994) (attorneys' fees of the indemnitee in defense of the underlying action are "damages" which would count against limits, where the indemnification agreement included defense costs).

State Courts:

California: Golden Eagle Insurance Co. v. Insurance Company of the West, 121 Cal. Rptr.2d 682, 690–691 (Cal. App. 2002) (attorneys' fees of the indemnitee in defense of the underlying action are "damages" that would count against limits, where the indemnification agreement included defense costs).

[82] See § 5.04[5] *supra*.

[83] *Ninth Circuit:* R.W. Beck & Associates v. City & Borough of Sitka, 27 F.3d 1475, 1484 (9th Cir. 1994).

State Courts:

California: Golden Eagle Insurance Co. v. Insurance Company of the West, 121 Cal. Rptr.2d 682, 690–691 (Cal. App. 2002).

[84] See ISO Form CG 00 01 10 01.

[85] See ISO Form CG 00 01 10 01.

[86] *Cf.*, R.W. Beck & Associates v. City & Borough of Sitka, 27 F.3d 1475, 1484 (9th Cir. 1994) (attorneys' fees of indemnitee in seeking indemnity awarded under Alaska prevailing plaintiff fee shifting statute were "supplementary payments").

[87] See ISO Form CG 00 01 10 01.

[88] See ISO Form CG 00 01 10 01.

[89] See ISO Form CG 00 01 10 01.

[90] See:

First Circuit: Narragansett Jewelry Co. v. St. Paul Fire and Marine Insurance Co., 526 F. Supp.2d 245 (D.R.I. 2007); First Specialty Insurance Corp. v. Maine Coast Marine Construction, Inc., 497 F. Supp.2d 11 (D. Me. 2007).

Second Circuit: Curran v. Merrimack Mutual Fire Insurance Co., 1995 WL 104100 (S.D.N.Y. Mar. 8, 1995).

Third Circuit: Sunoco, Inc. v. Illinois National Insurance Co., 2007 WL 127737 (E.D. Pa. Jan. 11, 2007).

Fourth Circuit: Industrial Enterprises, Inc. v. Penn America Insurance Co., 637 F.3d 481 (4th Cir. 2011); Harbor Court Associates v. Kiewit Construction Co., 6 F. Supp.2d 449 (D. Md. 1998) (owned property exclusion did not bar coverage for insureds other than landowners and did not apply to claim against steel subcontractor for property damage to masonry or claim against masonry subcontractor for damage to steel).

Fifth Circuit: Shelter Mutual Insurance Co. v. Brown, 345 F. Supp.2d 645 (S.D. Miss. 2004) (homeowner's liability insurance policy's "owned property" exclusion applied to purchaser's negligent misrepresentation and intentional non-disclosure action against insured vendor, alleging that insured had known of but had failed to disclose house's failing foundation).

Sixth Circuit: Lenning v. Commercial Union Insurance Co., 260 F.3d 574 (6th Cir. 2001).

Seventh Circuit: Wausau Underwriters Insurance v. United Plastics Group, 512 F.3d 953 (7th Cir. 2008); Essex Insurance Co. v. Soy City Sock Co., 503 F. Supp.2d 1068 (C.D. Ill. 2007).

Eighth Circuit: Land O'Lakes, Inc. v. Employers Insurance Co. of Wausau, 728 F.3d 822 (8th Cir. 2013); Essex Insurance Co. v. Inland Marine Sales, LLC, 387 F. Supp.2d 978 (W.D. Ark. 2005).

Ninth Circuit: Travelers Casualty and Surety Co. v. American International Surplus Lines Insurance Co., 465 F. Supp.2d 1005 (S.D. Cal. 2006).

Tenth Circuit: Panico v. State Farm Fire and Casualty Co., 410 Fed. Appx. 160 (10th Cir. 2011).

Eleventh Circuit: New Hampshire Insurance Co. v. Hill, 516 Fed. Appx. 803 (11th Cir. 2013).

State Courts:

Alabama: Certain Underwriters at Lloyd's, London v. Southern Natural Gas Co., 142 So.3d 436 (Ala. 2013).

Arizona: California Casualty Insurance Co. v. American Family Mutual Insurance Co., 94 P.3d 616 (Ariz. App. 2004).

California: Subkoski v. Standard Fire Insurance Co., 2010 WL 2840091 (Cal. App. July 21, 2010).

Colorado: Hoang v. Assurance Co. of America, 149 P.3d 798 (Colo. 2007) (*en banc*).

Florida: Danny's Backhoe Service, L.L.C. v. Auto Owners Insurance Co., 116 S.3d 508 (Fla. App. 2013).

Georgia: Rampey v. Grange Mutual Casualty Co., 629 S.E.2d 525 (Ga. App. 2006) (exclusion for damage to property in control of named insured's employee, its bookkeeper, applied only to portion of house owned by named insured's employee and in employee's control when she started fire in kitchen).

Indiana: Selective Insurance Co. of South Carolina v. Erie Insurance Exchange, 14 N.E.3d 105 (Ind. App. 2014).

Massachusetts: Fitchburg Gas & Electric Light Co. v. OneBeacon American Insurance. Co., 27 Mass. L. Rptr. 556 (Mass. Super. Ct. 2010).

Missouri: Shelter Mutual Insurance Co. v. Ballew, 203 S.W.3d 789 (Mo. App. 2006) (exclusion of liability coverage for damage to property owned by insured applied to purchasers' claim against insured vendors for negligent misrepresentation that house was free of defects).

New Hampshire: First Londonderry Development Corp. v. CNA Insurance Cos., 669 A.2d 232 (N.H. 1995) (condominium developer, which owned three condo units at time of lawsuit, was an insured under commercial umbrella excess insurance policy's limitation endorsement, which provided that each co-owner of insured condominium was an insured with respect to liability arising out of ownership of common areas, brought it within the universe of "any insured" contained in owned property exclusion for damage to property owned by any insured).

New Jersey: Strnad v. North River Insurance Co., 679 A.2d 166 (N.J. Super. App. Div. 1996) (application of "owned property" exclusions in policies turns on insured's relationship to damaged property).

New York: Castle Village Owners Corp. v. Greater New York Mutual Insurance Co., 64 A.D.3d 44, 878 N.Y.S.2d 311 (N.Y. App. Div. 2009).

Oregon: ZRZ Realty Co. v. Beneficial Fire and Casualty Insurance Co., 241 P.3d 710 (Or. 2010) (*en banc*).

Vermont: Towns v. Northern Security Insurance Co., 184 Vt. 322, 964 A.2d 1150 (2008).

Washington: State Farm Fire & Casualty Co. v. English Cove Association, 88 P.3d 986 (Wash. App. 2004) ("owned property" exclusion applied to the insured developer of a 160-unit condominium project, for purposes of adjudicating coverage based on alleged construction defects, inasmuch as the developer retained ownership of 43 of the units that had not yet been sold; by virtue of its ownership of the unsold units, the insured had an undivided interest in the common areas of the condominium, and since the word "own" was not ambiguous in this context, the policy exclusion applied).

Wisconsin: Watertown Tire Recyclers, L.L.C. v. Nortman, 331 Wis.2d 730, 795 N.W.2d 493 (Wis. App. 2011).

91 See, e.g., Boelman v. Grinnell Mutual Reinsurance Co., 826 N.W.2d 494 (Iowa 2013) ("The care, custody, or control exclusion functions specifically to prevent the insurance company from becoming a guarantor of the insured's work.").

92 See:

Fourth Circuit: Auto-Owners Insurance Co. v. Madison at Park West Property Owners Ass'n, 834 F. Supp.2d 437 (D.S.C. 2011) (exclusion not applicable to homeowners association); Harbor Court Associates v. Kiewit Construction Co., 6 F. Supp.2d 449 (D. Md. 1998) (owned property exclusion did not bar coverage for insureds other than landowners and did not apply to claim against steel subcontractor for property damage to masonry or claim against masonry subcontractor for damage to steel).

Ninth Circuit: Scottsdale Insurance Co. v. Ou Interests, Inc., 2005 WL 2893865, at *5–6 (N.D. Cal. Nov. 2, 2005).

State Courts:

California: Century Indemnity Co. v. Hearrean, 98 Cal. App.4th 734, 741 (Cal. App. 2002); Century Indemnity Co. v. Cannery Row Plaza Associates, 2002 WL 317915, at *5 (Cal. App. Feb. 28, 2002).

New Hampshire: First Londonderry Development Corp. v. CNA Insurance Cos., 669 A.2d 232 (N.H. 1995) (condominium developer, which owned three condo units at time of lawsuit, was an insured under commercial umbrella excess insurance policy's limitation endorsement, which provided that each co-owner of insured condominium was an insured with respect to liability arising out of ownership of common areas, brought it within the universe of "any insured" contained in owned property exclusion for damage to property owned by any insured).

South Dakota: Dakota Fire Insurance Co. v. J & J McNeil, L.L.C., 849 N.W.2d 648 (S.D. 2014).

93 See ISO Form CG 00 01 10 01.

94 See:

First Circuit: Dryden Oil Co. of New England v. Travelers Indemnity Co., 91 F.3d 278, 284 (1st Cir. 1996).

Fourth Circuit: Stull v. American States Insurance Co., 963 F. Supp. 492 (D. Md. 1997).

Fifth Circuit: South Louisiana Ethanol, L.L.C. v. Messer, 932 F. Supp.2d 735 (E.D. La. 2013) (at time of damage).

Sixth Circuit: Lenning v. Commercial Union Insurance Co., 260 F.3d 574 (6th Cir. 2001).

Seventh Circuit: Wausau Underwriters Insurance v. United Plastics Group, 512 F.3d 953 (7th Cir. 2008).

Ninth Circuit: Genesis Insurance Co. v. BRE Properties, 916 F. Supp.2d 1058 (N.D. Cal. 2013) (at time of damage).

State Courts:

Minnesota: Domtar, Inc. v. Niagara Fire Insurance Co., 563 N.W.2d 724 (Minn. 1997).

New Jersey: Morrone v. Harleysville Mutual Insurance Co., 662 A.2d 562, 565 (N.J. Super. App. Div. 1995).

Ohio: Erie Insurance Exchange v. Colony Development Corp., 2003 WL 23096010 (Ohio. App. Dec. 31, 2003).

Texas: Lennar Corp. v. Great American Insurance Co., 200 S.W.3d 651 (Tex. App.), *substituted concurring and dissenting opinions.* 2006 WL 909937 (Tex. App. Apr. 11, 2006).

95 Century Indemnity Co. v. Hearrean, 98 Cal. App.4th 734, 741 (Cal. App. 2002); Century Indemnity Co. v. Cannery Row Plaza Associates, 2002 WL 317915, at *5 (Cal. App. Feb. 28, 2002).

96 ISO Form CG 00 01 10 01.

97 See Discover Specialty Insurance Co. v. Certain Underwriters at Lloyd's London, 2008 WL 4225885 (Cal. App. Sept. 27, 2008); Maryland Casualty Co. v. Reeder, 221 Cal. App.3d 961, 270 Cal. Rptr. 719 (1990).

98 See ISO Form CG 00 01 10 01. A developer's or builder's construction project is likely to be construed as coming under "your work," which is defined in the ISO Form as:

"'Your work':

a. Means:

(1) Work or operations performed by you or on your behalf; and

(2) Materials, parts and equipment furnished in connection with such work or operations.

b. Includes:

(1) Warranties or representations made at any time with respect to the fitness, quality, durability, performance or use of 'your work,' and

(2) The providing of or failure to provide warnings or instructions."

99 See:

Second Circuit: Savoy Medical Supply Co. v. F & H Manufacturing Corp., 776 F. Supp. 703 (E.D.N.Y. 1991).

Fourth Circuit: Stull v. American States Insurance Co., 963 F. Supp. 492 (D. Md. 1997).

Fifth Circuit: American States Insurance Co. v. Hanson Industries, 873 F. Supp. 17 (S.D. Tex. 1995).

Sixth Circuit: Aetna Casualty & Surety Co. v. Dow Chemical Co., 28 F. Supp.2d 448 (E.D. Mich. 1998).

Eighth Circuit: Taylor-Morley-Simon, Inc. v. Michigan Mutual Insurance Co., 645 F. Supp. 596 (E.D. Mo. 1986).

State Courts:

Alaska: Fejes v. Alaska Insurance Co., 984 P.2d 519 (Alaska 1999) (alienated property exclusion inapplicable to claim against general contractor arising out of damage to septic system caused by subcontractor's defective installation of curtain drain, after premises were conveyed to homeowner).

California: Insurance Commissioner of the State of California v. Golden Eagle Insurance Co., 2010 WL 3688427 (Cal. App. Sept. 22, 2010); Discover Specialty Insurance Co. v. Certain Underwriters at Lloyd's London, 2008 WL 4225885 (Cal. App. Sept. 27, 2008); Prudential-LMI Commercial Insurance Co. v. Reliance Insurance Co., 22 Cal. App.4th 1508, 27 Cal. Rptr.2d 841 (1994) ("premises alienated" exclusion inapplicable to preclude coverage for construction defects in condominium complex that policyholder purchased after construction, where policyholder completed its work of converting and marketing units, defects were caused by work of persons other than policyholder, and condominiums had not been rented or occupied before sold by policyholder).

Louisiana: Oxner v. Montgomery, 794 So.2d 86 (La. App.), *writ denied* 803 So.2d 36 (La. 2001) ("premises alienated" exclusion in home builders' policies applied to damage to house in which they had lived for more than twelve months before selling it).

Minnesota: Auto-Owners Insurance Co. v. NewMech Cos., 678 N.W.2d 477 (Minn. App. 2004) (coverage for property damage to condominium units caused by faulty mechanical systems was not excluded under "property damage to sold premises" provision of developer's CGL policy, where premises were developer's "work" that was exception to sold premises exclusion).

Ohio: GRE Insurance Group v. Normandy Pointe Associates, 2002 WL 360646 (Ohio App. Mar. 8, 2002) ("alienated" property exclusion inapplicable to policyholder, who was not builder but was in business of developing and marketing homes, against negligence claim by homeowners that homes were built in 100-year flood plain, even though policy excluded coverage for property damage "to property you sell, give away or abandon, if the property damages arise out of any part of those premises"; contract could be construed to include work on land or property itself, and not just construction of home or premises, therefore, exception to exclusion applied because development of property was insured's "work" but such property was never occupied, rented, or held for rent by insured).

But see Korossy v. Sunrise Homes, Inc., 653 So.2d 1215 (La. App.), *writ denied* 660 So.2d 878 (La. 1995) (exclusion appied to claim against developer because no exception to exclusion was in the policy).

100 General Star National Insurance Co. v. Paley, 1993 WL 89759, at *6 (E.D. Pa. Mar. 25), *aff'd* 14 F.3d 47 (3d Cir. 1993); Rieder v. Cherokee Insurance Co., 635 F. Supp. 699 (E.D. Pa. 1986), *aff'd* 813 F.2d 398 (3d Cir.), *cert. denied* 484 U.S. 823 (1987).

101 See Century Indemnity Co. v. Cannery Row Plaza Associates, 2002 WL 317915 (Cal. App. Feb. 28, 2002) (hotel was occupied by partnership that owned and operated hotel but not occupied by the general partner of the partnership).

102 Certainly, to the extent coverage is eliminated by these exclusions in the liability policy, coverage may be restored by a first-party property policy covering the model home. See Chapter 4 *supra*.

103 See ISO Form CG 00 01 10 01.

104 See, e.g.:

Fifth Circuit: Carl E. Woodward, L.L.C. v. Acceptance Indemnity Insurance Co., 743 F.3d 91 (5th Cir. 2014); Gore Design Completions, Ltd. v. Hartford Fire Insurance Co., 538 F.3d 365 (5th Cir. 2008).

Tenth Circuit: A.W. Interiors, Inc. v. The Travelers Indemnity Co., 2014 U.S. Dist. LEXIS 71065 (D. Colo. May 23, 2014).

State Courts:

California: Toll Brothers, Inc. v. OneBeacon Insurance Co., 2011 WL 883000 (Cal. App. Mar. 15, 2011); Clarendon America Insurance Co. v. General Security Indemnity Company of Arizona, 193 Cal. App.4th 1311, 124 Cal. Rptr.3d 1 (2011).

Colorado: Stresscon Corp. v. Travelers Property Casualty Insurance Co. of America, 2013 Colo. App. LEXIS 1451 (Colo. App. Sept. 12, 2013).

Connecticut: Barber v. Berthiaume, 48 Conn. L. Rptr. 662 (Conn. Super. New Haven 2009).

Georgia: Hathaway Development Co. v. American Empire Surplus Lines Insurance Co., 301 Ga. App. 65, 686 S.E.2d 855 (2009).

Massachusetts: National Union Fire Insurance Company of Pittsburgh, PA v. Modern Continental Construction Co., 27 Mass. L. Rptr. 16 (Mass. Super. Suffolk Cnty. 2009).

Minnesota: Integrity Mutual Insurance Co. v. Klampe, 2008 WL 5335690 (Minn. App. Dec. 23, 2008).

Nebraska: Copple Construction, L.L.C. v. Columbia National Insurance Co., 776 N.W.2d 503 (Neb. 2009).

New Jersey: Ohio Casualty Insurance Co. v. Island Pool & Spa, Inc, 418 N.J. Super. 162, 12 A.3d 719 (N.J. Super. App. Div. 2011).

New York: Tower Insurance Company of New York v. BCS Construction Services Corp., 118 A.D.3d 527, 988 N.Y.S.2d 145 (N.Y. App. Div. 2014).

South Carolina: Bennett & Bennett Construction, Inc. v. Auto Owners Insurance Co., 405 S.C. 1, 747 S.E.2d 426 (S.C. 2013).

Texas: Evanston Insurance Co. v. D & L Masonry of Lubbock, Inc., 2011 WL 1465776 (Tex. App. Apr. 18, 2011).

Washington: Western National Assurance Co. v. Shelcon Construction Group L.L.C., 182 Wash. App. 256, 332 P.3d 986 (Wash. App. 2014); Mutual of Enumclaw Insurance Co. v. OneBeacon Insurance Co., 158 Wash. App. 1006 (2010).

Wisconsin: Camelot Development Group, L.L.C. v. Jim Karrels Trucking Sand & Gravel, Inc., 322 Wis.2d 736, 778 N.W.2d 172 (Wis. App. 2009).

105 *Id.*

106 See:

Fifth Circuit: Boss Management Services, Inc. v. Acceptance Insurance Co., 2007 WL 2752700 (S.D. Tex. Sept. 19, 2007).

Ninth Circuit: Dewitt Construction, Inc. v. Charter Oak Fire Insurance Co., 307 F.3d 1127 (9th Cir. 2002).

Tenth Circuit: Advantage Homebuilding, LLC v. Maryland Casualty Co., 470 F.3d 1003 (10th Cir. 2006); EMC Insurance Cos. v. Mid-Continent Casualty Co., 884 F. Supp.2d 1147 (D. Colo. 2012); American States Insurance Co. v. Powers, 262 F. Supp.2d 1245, 1250–1251 (D. Kan. 2003).

Eleventh Circuit: Pinkerton & Laws, Inc. v. Royal Insurance Co., 227 F. Supp.2d 1348, 1356 (N.D. Ga. 2002).

State Courts:

California: Toll Brothers, Inc. v. OneBeacon Insurance Co., 2011 WL 883000 (Cal. App. Mar. 15, 2011); Clarendon America Insurance Co. v. General Security Indemnity Company of Arizona, 193 Cal. App.4th 1311, 124 Cal. Rptr.3d 1 (2011); Garamendi v. Golden Eagle Insurance Co., 2006 WL 337599, at *16 (Cal. App. Feb. 15, 2006).

Connecticut: Barber v. Berthiaume, 48 Conn. L. Rptr. 662 (Conn. Super. New Haven 2009).

Florida: Mansfield Industrial Coatings, Inc. v. Employers National Insurance Corp., 557 So.2d 221 (Fla. App. 1990).

Georgia: Maxum Indemnity Co. v. Jimenez, 318 Ga. App. 669, 734 S.E.2d 499 (2012); Hathaway Development Co. v. American Empire Surplus Lines Insurance Co., 301 Ga. App. 65, 686 S.E.2d 855 (2009).

Illinois: Pekin Insurance Co. v. Willett, 704 N.E.2d 923 (Ill. App. 1998).

Louisiana: McMath Construction Co. v. Dupuy, 897 So.2d 677 (La. App. 2004), *writ denied* 896 So.2d 40 (La. 2005).

Massachusetts: National Union Fire Insurance Company of Pittsburgh, PA v. Modern Continental Construction Co., 27 Mass. L. Rptr. 16 (Mass. Super. Suffolk Cnty. 2009).

Minnesota: Integrity Mutual Insurance Co. v. Klampe, 2008 WL 5335690 (Minn. App. Dec. 23, 2008).

Nebraska: Copple Construction, L.L.C. v. Columbia National Insurance Co., 776 N.W.2d 503 (Neb. 2009).

New Jersey: Ohio Casualty Insurance Co. v. Island Pool & Spa, Inc., 12 A.3d 719 (N.J. Super. App. Div. 2011).

New York: Brawdy v. National Grange Mutual Insurance Co., 616 N.Y.S.2d 846 (N.Y. App. Div. 1994) (exclusion applied to damage to wall that collapsed during wall building operations).

North Dakota: Grinnell Mutual Reinsurance Co. v. Lynne, 686 N.W.2d 118 (N.D. 2004); Fisher v. American Family Mutual Insurance Co., 579 N.W.2d 599, 604 (N.D. 1998).

Ohio: Spears v. Smith, 690 N.E.2d 557, 559 (Ohio App. 1996).

Texas: Lennar Corp. v. Great American Insurance Co., 200 S.W.3d 651 (Tex. App.), *substituted concurring and dissenting opinions* 2006 WL 909937 (Tex. App. Apr. 11, 2006); CU Lloyd's of Texas v. Main Street Homes, Inc., 79 S.W.3d 687, 696 (Tex. App. 2002).

Washington: Mutual of Enumclaw Insurance Co. v. OneBeacon Insurance Co., 158 Wash. App. 1006 (2010).

Wisconsin: Camelot Development Group, L.L.C. v. Jim Karrels Trucking Sand & Gravel, Inc., 322 Wis.2d 736, 778 N.W.2d 172 (Wis. App. 2009).

[107] See, e.g., A.W. Interiors, Inc. v. The Travelers Indemnity Co., 2014 U.S. Dist. LEXIS 71065 (D. Colo. May 23, 2014).

[108] See ISO Form CG 00 01 10 01.

[109] See:

Fifth Circuit: Advance Electric, Inc. v. United States Fidelity & Guaranty Co., 818 F.2d 378 (5th Cir. 1987) (exclusion applied for damages that arose when fire occurred on jobsite while insured was repairing electric motor for third party, even though fire occurred during middle of night when none of insured's employees were on duty, where fire occurred during necessary cooling phase of repair project).

Sixth Circuit: Action Auto Stores, Inc. v. United Capitol Insurance Co., 845 F. Supp. 417 (W.D. Mich. 1993) (exclusion prevented coverage for damage done to land or other property that insured physically worked on in course of installing gasoline containment systems at service stations).

Eleventh Circuit: Hathaway Development Co. v. Illinois Union Insurance Co., 274 Fed. Appx. 787, 2008 WL 1773307 (11th Cir. 2008).

State Courts:

Massachusetts: Jet Line Services, Inc. v. American Employers Insurance Co., 537 N.E.2d 107 (Mass. 1989) (no coverage for damage to petroleum storage tank caused by an explosion that occurred while tank was being cleaned by insured's employees because "that particular part" referred to entire tank and not just to bottom of tank that insured's employees were cleaning at moment of explosion).

Minnesota: Integrity Mutual Insurance Co. v. Klampe, 2008 WL 5335690 (Minn. App. Dec. 23, 2008).

New York: Brawdy v. National Grange Mutual Insurance Co., 616 N.Y.S.2d 846 (N.Y. App. Div. 1994) (exclusion applied to damage to wall that collapsed during wall building operations).

[110] See:

Fifth Circuit: *Gore Design Completions, Ltd. v. Hartford Fire Insurance Co.,* 538 F.3d 365 (5th Cir. 2008).

Seventh Circuit: Minergy Neenah, LLC v. Rotary Dryer Parts, Inc., 2008 WL 1869040 (E.D. Wis. Apr. 24, 2008)

Ninth Circuit: Clear, LLC v. American and Foreign Insurance Co., 2008 WL 818978 (D. Alaska Mar. 24, 2008).

State Courts:

California: Clarendon America Insurance Co. v. General Security Indemnity Company of Arizona, 193 Cal. App.4th 1311, 124 Cal. Rptr.3d 1 (2011); C.O.D. Gas & Oil Co. v. Ace American Insurance Co., 2004 WL 1245759, at *5–6 (Cal. App. June 8, 2004).

Connecticut: Barber v. Berthiaume, 48 Conn. L. Rptr. 662 (Conn. Super. New Haven 2009).

Georgia: Hathaway Development Co. v. American Empire Surplus Lines Insurance Co., 301 Ga. App. 65, 686 S.E.2d 855 (2009); SawHorse, Inc. v. Southern Guarantee Insurance Co. of Georgia, 604 S.E.2d 541, 545 (Ga. App. 2004) (damage to portions of premises on which operations were not being performed were not excluded by Exclusion J(5)).

Missouri: Columbia Mutual Insurance Co. v. Schauf, 967 S.W.2d 74 (Mo. 1998) (kitchen cabinets sprayed by insured just before fire started from cleaning sprayer were "particular part of real property" on which insured was performing operations within meaning of exclusion; thus, exclusion was inapplicable to fire damage to remainder of house and was not limited to damage to paint work on cabinets).

Nebraska: Copple Construction, L.L.C. v. Columbia National Insurance Co., 776 N.W.2d 503 (Neb. 2009).

North Dakota: ACUITY v. Burd & Smith Construction, Inc., 721 N.W.2d 33 (N.D. 2006) (roof was "that particular part" so that exclusion did not apply to damage to interior caused by faulty roof work).

Texas: Evanston Insurance Co. v. D & L Masonry of Lubbock, Inc., 2011 WL 1465776 (Tex. App. Apr. 18, 2011).

Wisconsin: Camelot Development Group, L.L.C. v. Jim Karrels Trucking Sand & Gravel, Inc., 778 N.W.2d 172 (Wis. App. 2009); 1325 North Van Buren., LLC v. T-3 Group, Ltd., 701 N.W.2d 13, 30 (Wis. App.), *aff'd in part, reversed in part on other grounds* 716 N.W.2d 822 (Wis. 2006) ("damage occurred to work that had already been completed or parts of the building that were never intended to be renovated. . . . [T]hese exclusions raise questions of fact that have not been considered below, and thus, should be addressed by the trial court.").

111 C.O.D. Gas & Oil Co. v. Ace American Insurance Co., 2004 WL 1245759, at *5–6 (Cal. App. June 8, 2004).

112 *Fire, Casualty & Surety Bulletin*, The Nat'l Underwriter Co., Sept. 1998, § A.3-12.

> "To illustrate the effect of this exclusion, say that a plumbing subcontractor working for a home builder accidentally starts one of the builder's projects on fire while soldering copper pipes, and the entire structure is burned down. If the owner of the house sues the builder for the loss, the exclusion . . . will apply only to 'that particular part' of the structure on which the plumber was working. Thus, the named insured would be covered . . . for damage to all parts of the building other than the plumbing and all parts of the plumbing system other than the particular part being worked on at the time of the loss.
>
> "The coverage forms do not define 'that particular part,' . . . [but] in the final analysis, the use of the word 'particular' indicates that the exclusion should be applied narrowly. In the example above, the exclusion should then apply only to the two portions of pipe being soldered together; the damage to the rest of the plumbing system should not be excluded."

113 See ISO Form CG 00 01 10 01.

114 See ISO Form CG 00 01 10 01. See also, § 7.04[4][a] *infra*.

115 *Id.*

116 See, e.g.:

Second Circuit: Harleysville Worcester Insurance Co. v. Paramount Concrete, Inc., 10 F. Supp.3d 252 (D. Conn. 2014).

Third Circuit: Allegheny Design Management, Inc. v. Travelers Indemnity Co. of America, 2013 U.S. Dist. LEXIS 137748 (W.D. Pa. Sept. 25, 2013).

Fifth Circuit: Boss Management Services, Inc. v. Acceptance Insurance Co., 2007 WL 2752700 (S.D. Tex. Sept. 19, 2007); Essex Insurance Co. v. Patrick, 2006 WL 3779812 (W.D. Tex. Oct. 16, 2006).

Sixth Circuit: The Stansley Group v. Fru-Con Construction Corp., 2006 WL 2711795 (N.D. Ohio Sept. 21, 2006).

Ninth Circuit: Arroyo v. Uniguard Insurance Company, 2014 U.S. Dist. LEXIS 131191 (N.D. Cal. Sept. 17, 2014); St. Paul Fire and Marine Insurance Co. v. ACE American Insurance Co., 2014 U.S. Dist. LEXIS 113295 (E.D. Cal. Aug. 14, 2014); Western Heritage Insurance Co. v. Cannon, 2014 U.S. Dist. LEXIS 101382 (E.D. Wash. July 24, 2014); Canal Indemnity Co. v. Adair Homes Inc., 737 F. Supp.2d 1294 (W.D. Wash. 201), *aff'd* 45 Fed. Appx. 938 (9th Cir. 2011).

Tenth Circuit: Advantage Homebuilding, LLC v. Maryland Casualty Co., 470 F.3d 1003 (10th Cir. 2006).

State Courts:

Arizona: Desert Mountain Properties Limited Partnership v. Liberty Mutual Fire Insurance Co., 225 Ariz. 194, 236 P.3d 421 (Ariz. App. 2010), *aff'd* 250 P.3d 196 (Ariz. 2011).

California: Toll Brothers, Inc. v. OneBeacon Insurance Co., 2011 WL 883000 (Cal. App. Mar. 15, 2011); Clarendon America Insurance Co. v. General Security Indemnity Company of Arizona, 193 Cal. App.4th 1311, 124 Cal. Rptr.3d 1 (2011); Garamendi v. Golden Eagle Insurance Co., 2006 WL 337599, at *16 (Cal. App. Feb. 15, 2006).

Georgia: Hathaway Development Co. v. American Empire Surplus Lines Insurance Co., 686 S.E.2d 855 (Ga. App. 2009).

Louisiana: Stewart Interior Contractors, L.L.C. v. Metalpro Industries, L.L.C., 969 So.2d 653 (La. App. 2007); McMath Construction Co. v. Dupuy, 897 So.2d 677, 682 (La. App. 2004), *writ denied* 896 So.2d 40 (La. 2005).

Minnesota: Integrity Mutual Insurance Co. v. Klampe, 2008 WL 5335690 (Minn. App. Dec. 23, 2008); Acceptance Insurance Co. v. Ross Contractors, Inc., 2005 WL 1870688, at *4–5 (Minn. App. Aug. 9, 2005).

Nebraska: Alsobrook v. Jim Earp Chrysler-Plymouth, Ltd., 740 N.W.2d 785 (Neb. 2007).

New York: Brawdy v. National Grange Mutual Insurance Co., 616 N.Y.S.2d 846 (N.Y. App. Div. 1994) (exclusion applied to damage to wall that collapsed during wall building operations).

North Carolina: Builders Mutual Insurance Co. v. Mitchell, 2011 WL 1238373 (N.C. App. Apr. 5, 2011).

Pennsylvania: Nitterhouse Concrete Products v. Pennsylvania Manufacturers' Association Insurance Co., 67 Pa. D. & C.4th 225, 237 (Pa. C.P. Franklin Cnty. 2004).

Texas: Mid-Continent Casualty Co. v. Krolczyk, 408 S.W.3d 896 (Tex. App. 2013).

Washington: Vandivort Construction Co. v. Seattle Tennis Club, 11 Wash. App. 303, 522 P.2d 198 (1974).

Wisconsin: 1325 North Van Buren, LLC v. T-3 Group, Ltd., 701 N.W.2d 13, 29 (Wis. App. 2005), *aff'd in part, rev'd in part on other grounds* 716 N.W.2d 822 (Wis. 2006).

[117] Garamendi v. Golden Eagle Insurance Co., 2006 WL 337599, at *16 (Cal. App. Feb. 15, 2006) (internal quotes and citations omitted).

[118] See ISO Form CG 00 01 10 01. See also, § 7.04[3][c] *supra*.

[119] See:

Third Circuit: Wausau Underwriters Insurance Co. v. State Automobile Mutual Insurance Co., 2008 WL 2315706 (D.N.J. June 6, 2008).

Fifth Circuit: Mid-Continent Casualty Co. v. J.H.P. Development, Inc., 557 F.3d 207 (5th Cir. 2009).

Sixth Circuit: Fortney & Weygandt, Inc. v. American Manufacturers Mutual Insurance Co., 595 F.3d 308 (6th Cir. 2010); The Stansley Group v. Fru-Con Construction Corp., 2006

WL 2711795 (N.D. Ohio Sept. 21, 2006); Action Auto Stores, Inc. v. United Capitol Insurance Co., 845 F. Supp. 428 (W.D. Mich. 1993).

Seventh Circuit: Minergy Neenah, LLC v. Rotary Dryer Parts, Inc., 2008 WL 1869040 (E.D. Wis. Apr. 24, 2008).

Ninth Circuit: Dewitt Construction, Inc. v. Charter Oak Fire Insurance Co., 307 F.3d 1127 (9th Cir. 2002).

Tenth Circuit: Advantage Homebuilding, LLC v. Maryland Casualty Co., 470 F.3d 1003 (10th Cir. 2006); Lukes v. Mid-Continent Casualty Co., 2013 U.S. Dist. LEXIS 17979 (D. Mont. Feb. 11, 2013).

State Courts:

Alaska: Fejes v. Alaska Insurance Co., 984 P.2d 519, 524 (Alaska 1999).

Arizona: Desert Mountain Properties Limited Partnership v. Liberty Mutual Fire Insurance Co., 236 P.2d 421 (Ariz. App. 2010), *aff'd* 250 P.3d 196 (Ariz. 2011).

Florida: Auto-Owners Insurance Co. v. Pozzi Window Co., 2008 WL 2369244 (Fla. June 12, 2008); Biltmore Construction Co. v. Owners Insurance Co., 842 So.2d 947, 949 (Fla. App. 2003).

Georgia: Hathaway Development Co. v. American Empire Surplus Lines Insurance Co., 301 Ga. App. 65, 686 S.E.2d 855 (2009).

Louisiana: Stewart Interior Contractors, L.L.C. v. Metalpro Industries, L.L.C., 969 So.2d 653 (La. App. 2007).

Massachusetts: Essex Insurance Co. v. David's Floor Service, Inc., 23 Mass. L. Rptr. 325 (Mass. Super. Oct. 22, 2007); United States Fire Insurance Co. v. Peerless Insurance Co., 2004 WL 1515591, at *8 (Mass. Super. June. 15, 2004).

Minnesota: Integrity Mutual Insurance Co. v. Klampe, 2008 WL 5335690 (Minn. App. Dec. 23, 2008).

Nebraska: Alsobrook v. Jim Earp Chrysler-Plymouth, Ltd., 740 N.W.2d 785 (Neb. 2007).

New York: Brawdy v. National Grange Mutual Insurance Co., 616 N.Y.S.2d 846 (N.Y. App. Div. 1994) (exclusion applied to damage to wall that collapsed during wall building operations).

North Carolina: Builders Mutual Insurance Co. v. Mitchell, 2011 WL 1238373 (N.C. App. Apr. 5, 2011).

North Dakota: ACUITY v. Burd & Smith Construction, Inc., 721 N.W.2d 33 (N.D. 2006) (exclusion did not apply to damage to interior caused by faulty roof work).

Ohio: Beaverdam Contracting v. Erie Insurance Co., 2008 WL 4378153 (Ohio App. Sept. 29, 2008).

Pennsylvania: Snyder Heating Co. v. Pennsylvania Manufacturers' Association Insurance Co., 715 A.2d 483, 495 (Pa. Super. 1998) (Popovich, J, dissenting) (refusing to apply Exclusion J(6), despite existence of maintenance contract on entire boiler, because it was "not 'patently' clear [from the underlying complaint asserted by the School District] whether the School District claimed damage *only* to those parts of the boiler upon which Snyder worked") (emphasis in original).

Rhode Island: Employers Mutual Casualty Co. v. Pires, 723 A.2d 295, 299 n.1 (R.I. 1999).

Texas: Mid-Continent Casualty Co. v. Krolczyk, 408 S.W.3d 896 (Tex. App. 2013); Dorchester Development Corp. v. Safeco Insurance Co., 737 S.W.2d 380, 382 (Tex. App. 1987).

Wisconsin: Camelot Development Group, L.L.C. v. Jim Karrels Trucking Sand & Gravel, Inc., 322 Wis.2d 736, 778 N.W.2d 172 (Wis. App. 2009); 1325 North Van Buren, LLC v. T-3 Group, Ltd., 701 N.W.2d 13, 29 (Wis. App. 2005), *aff'd in part and rev'd in part on other grounds* 716 N.W.2d 822 (Wis. 2006) ("this exclusion requires a determination of whether the work was 'incorrectly performed on' the damaged property").

See also, Turner, *Insurance Coverage of Construction Disputes* §§ 30.05, 31.01, at 354–357.

But see:

Fifth Circuit: Essex Insurance Co. v. Patrick, 2006 WL 3779812 (W.D. Tex. Oct. 16, 2006).

Ninth Circuit: Arroyo v. Uniguard Insurance Company, 2014 U.S. Dist. LEXIS 131191 (N.D. Cal. Sept. 17, 2014) (recognizing distinction between general contractor and subcontractor and holding entire project was general contractor's "particular part"); St. Paul Fire and Marine Insurance Co. v. ACE American Insurance Co., 2014 U.S. Dist. LEXIS 113295 (E.D. Cal. Aug. 14, 2014) (when general contractor is additional insured under subcontractors' policies, coverage is afforded to general contractor for damage to non-defective portions of general contractor's project); Western Heritage Insurance Co. v. Cannon, 2014 U.S. Dist. LEXIS 101382 (E.D. Wash. July 24, 2014).

State Courts:

California: Toll Brothers, Inc. v. OneBeacon Insurance Co., 2011 WL 883000 (Cal. App. Mar. 15, 2011); Clarendon America Insurance Co. v. General Security Indemnity Company of Arizona, 193 Cal. App.4th 1311, 124 Cal. Rptr.3d 1 (2011).

New York: J. Lucarelli & Sons, Inc. v. Mountain Valley Indemnity Co., 64 A.D.3d 856, 881 N.Y.S.2d 708 (N.Y. App. Div. 2009).

Ohio: Welfle, Inc. v. Motorist Insurance Group, 2007 WL 1174652 (Ohio App. Apr. 23, 2007) (negligent removal of asphalt resulting in damage to concrete bridge deck excluded by J(6)).

South Carolina: Century Indemnity Co. v. Golden Hills Builders, Inc., 561 S.E.2d 355, 358–359 (S.C. 2002) (damage to non-defective work caused by defective stucco was excluded by faulty workmanship exclusion).

Wisconsin: Arnold v. Cincinnati Insurance Co., 276 Wis.2d 762, 688 N.W.2d 708 (Wis. App. 2004).

[120] See ISO Form CG 00 01 10 01.

[121] See, e.g.:

Second Circuit: Harleysville Worcester Insurance Co. v. Paramount Concrete, Inc., 10 F. Supp.3d 252 (D. Conn. 2014).

Fifth Circuit: Valmont Energy Steel, Inc. v. Commercial Union Insurance Co., 359 F.3d 770 (5th Cir. 2004); National Union Fire Insurance Co. v. Puget Plastics Corp., 450 F. Supp.2d 682 (S.D. Tex. 2006).

Ninth Circuit: Big-D Construction Corp. v. Take it for Granite Too, 917 F. Supp.2d 1096 (D. Nev. 2013).

State Courts:

Florida: Liberty Mutual Fire Insurance Co. v. MI Windows & Doors, Inc., 131 So.3d 15 (Fla. App. 2013).

Massachusetts: National Union Fire Insurance Company of Pittsburgh, PA v. Modern Continental Construction Co., 27 Mass. L. Rptr. 16 (Mass. Super. Suffolk Cnty. 2009).

North Carolina: Builders Mutual Insurance Co. v. Mitchell, 2011 WL 1238373 (N.C. App. Apr. 5, 2011).

Ohio: Home Insurance Company of Illinois v. OM Group, Inc., 2003 WL 21569154 (Ohio App. July 11, 2003).

Texas: Zurich American Insurance Co. v. Nokia, Inc., 268 S.W.3d 487 (Tex. 2008).

Utah: America First Credit Union v. Kier Construction Corp., 314 P.3d 1055 (Utah App. 2013).

[122] See ISO Form CG 00 01 10 01.

[123] See *Webster's II New College Dictionary* at 907, 944 (3d ed 2005), (defining "property" as "[s]omething tangible or intangible to which its owner holds legal title" and defining "real" as "[o]f or relating to fixed or stationary property, as buildings or land") (defining "real estate" as "[l]and owned as property, along with natural resources and permanent buildings on it").

[124] *Black's Law Dictionary* at 1096 (5th ed. 1989).

[125] *Id.*

[126] See ISO Form CG 00 01 10 01 (emphasis added). For a discussion of Exclusion J(5), see § 7.04[3] *supra.*

[127] See:

Ninth Circuit: Dewitt Construction, Inc. v. Charter Oak Fire Insurance Co., 307 F.3d 1127 (9th Cir. 2002).

Tenth Circuit: Advantage Homebuilding, LLC v. Maryland Casualty Co., 470 F.3d 1003 (10th Cir. 2006); American States Insurance Co. v. Powers, 262 F. Supp.2d 1245, 1250–1251 (D. Kan. 2003).

Eleventh Circuit: Pinkerton & Laws, Inc. v. Royal Insurance Company of America, 227 F. Supp.2d 1348, 1356 (N.D. Ga. 2002).

State Courts:

California: Garamendi v. Golden Eagle Insurance Co., 2006 WL 337599, at *16 (Cal. App. Feb. 15, 2006); C.O.D. Gas & Oil Co. v. Ace American Insurance Co., 2004 WL 1245759, at *5–6 (Cal. App. June 8, 2004).

Florida: Mansfield Industrial Coatings, Inc. v. Employers National Insurance Corp., 557 So.2d 221 (Fla. App. 1990).

Georgia: Hathaway Development Co. v. American Empire Surplus Lines Insurance Co., 301 Ga. App. 65, 686 S.E.2d 855 (Ga. App. 2009).

Illinois: Pekin Insurance Co. v. Willett, 704 N.E.2d 923 (Ill. App. 1998).

Louisiana: McMath Construction Co. v. Dupuy, 897 So.2d 677 (La. App. 2004), *writ denied* 896 So.2d 40 (La. 2005).

Massachusetts: Pacific Indemnity Co. v. Lampro, 86 Mass. App. Ct. 60, 12 N.E.3d 1037 (2014); National Union Fire Insurance Company of Pittsburgh, PA v. Modern Continental Construction Co., 27 Mass. L. Rptr. 16 (Mass. Super. Suffolk Cnty. 2009).

Missouri: Columbia Mutual Insurance Co. v. Epstein, 239 S.W.3d 667 (Mo. App. 2007).

New York: Brawdy v. National Grange Mutual Insurance Co., 616 N.Y.S.2d 846 (N.Y. App. Div. 1994) (exclusion applied to damage to wall that collapsed during wall building operations).

North Dakota: Grinnell Mutual Reinsurance Co. v. Lynne, 686 N.W.2d 118 (N.D. 2004); Fisher v. American Family Mutual Insurance Co., 579 N.W.2d 599, 604 (N.D. 1998).

Ohio: The Cincinnati Insurance Co. v. G.L.H., Inc., 2008 WL 2940663 (Ohio App. Aug. 1, 2008); Dublin Building Systems v. Selective Insurance Co., 172 Ohio App.3d 196, 874 N.E.2d 788 (2007); Spears v. Smith, 690 N.E.2d 557, 559 (Ohio App. 1996).

Texas: Lennar Corp. v. Great American Insurance Co., 200 S.W.3d 651 (Tex. App.), *substituted concurring and dissenting opinions* 2006 WL 909937 (Tex. App. Apr. 11, 2006); CU Lloyd's of Texas v. Main Street Homes, Inc., 79 S.W.3d 687, 696 (Tex. App. 2002).

[128] See:

First Circuit: American Home Assurance Co. v. AGM Marine Contractors, Inc., 467 F.3d 810 (1st Cir. 2006).

Second Circuit: Harleysville Worcester Insurance Co. v. Paramount Concrete, Inc., 10 F. Supp. 3d 252 (D. Conn. 2014).

Third Circuit: Brosnahan Builders v. Harleysville Mutual Insurance Co., 137 F. Supp.2d 517 (D. Del. 2001), *aff'd* 2003 WL 146486 (3d Cir. Jan. 21, 2003), *cert. denied* 540 U.S. 820 (2003).

Sixth Circuit: Trinity Homes LLC v. Ohio Casualty Insurance Co., 864 F. Supp.2d 744 (S.D. Ind. 2012).

Seventh Circuit: Prisco Serena Sturm Architects Limited v. Liberty Mutual Insurance Co., 126 F.3d 886, 892 (7th Cir.1997); Edward E. Gillen Co. v. Insurance Co. of Pennsylvania, 874 F. Supp.2d 755 (E.D. Wis. 2012); Green v. National Union Fire Insurance Co., 771 F. Supp. 1000 (W.D. Mo. 1991).

Eighth Circuit: Scottsdale Insurance Co. v. Tri-State Insurance Company of Minnesota, 302 F. Supp.2d 1100 (D.N.D. 2004).

Ninth Circuit: Fireguard Sprinkler Systems v. Scottsdale Insurance Co., 864 F.2d 648 (9th Cir. 1988); Northern Insurance Company of New York v. Allied Mutual Insurance Co., 1995 WL 599024, at *4–5 (N.D. Cal. Oct. 2, 1995), *aff'd* 107 F.3d 877 (9th Cir. 1997); Big-D Construction Corp. v. Take It for Granite Too, 917 F. Supp.2d 1096 (D. Nev. 2013).

Tenth Circuit: American States Insurance Co. v. Powers, 262 F. Supp.2d 1245 (D. Kan. 2003).

Eleventh Circuit: Great American Fidelity Insurance Co. v. JWR Construction Services, Inc., 882 F. Supp.2d 1340 (S.D. Fla. 2012).

State Courts:

Alaska: Fejes, Inc. v. Alaska Insurance Co., 984 P.2d 519, 526 (Alaska 1999).

California: Collett v. Insurance Company of the West, 75 Cal. Rptr.2d 165 (Cal. App. 1998); Maryland Casualty Co. v. Reeder, 270 Cal. Rptr. 719, 727–728 (Cal. App. 1990) (discussing insurance bulletin).

Florida: Liberty Mutual Fire Insurance Co. v. MI Windows & Doors, Inc., 131 So.3d 15 (Fla. App. 2013).

Georgia: Hathaway Development Co. v. American Empire Surplus Lines Insurance Co., 301 Ga. App. 65, 686 S.E.2d 855 (2009); Stratton & Co. v. Argonaut Insurance Co., 469 S.E.2d 545 (Ga. App. 1996).

Kansas: Lee Builders, Inc. v. Farm Bureau Mutual Insurance Co., 104 P.3d 997, 1004 (Kan. App. 2005), *aff'd* 137 P.3d 486 (Kan. 2006) ("'This [specific exception of real property under the "your product" exclusion] provides meaningful clarification that work performed by contractors on dwellings, buildings, structures, and other realty is not considered to be the named insured's product.'").

Massachusetts: National Union Fire Insurance Company of Pittsburgh, PA v. Modern Continental Construction Co., 27 Mass. L. Rptr. 16 (Mass. Super. Suffolk Cnty. 2009).

Minnesota: Remodeling Dimensions, Inc. v. Integrity Mutual Insurance Co., 819 N.W.2d 602 (Minn. 2012); Wanzek Construction, Inc. v. Employers Insurance of Wausau, 679 N.W.2d 322 (Minn. 2004).

Missouri: Columbia Mutual Insurance Co. v. Epstei, 239 S.W.3d 667 (Mo. App. 2007).

Ohio: The Cincinnati Insurance Co. v. G.L.H., Inc., 2008 WL 2940663 (Ohio App. Aug. 1, 2008); Dublin Building Systems v. Selective Insurance Co., 172 Ohio App.3d 196, 874 N.E.2d 788 (2007); Panzica Construction Co. v. Ohio Casualty Insurance Co., 1996 WL 257470, at *4 (Ohio App. May 16, 1996), *appeal denied* 673 N.E.2d 142 (Ohio 1996).

Texas: CU Lloyd's of Texas v. Main Street Homes, Inc., 79 S.W.3d 687 (Tex. App. 2002); Mid-United Contractors v. Providence Lloyds Insurance Co., 754 S.W.2d 824 (Tex. App. 1988).

Utah: America First Credit Union v. Kier Construction Corp., 314 P.3d 1055 (Utah App. 2013).

Wisconsin: 1325 North Van Buren, LLC v. T-3 Group, Ltd., 701 N.W.2d 13 (Wis. App. 2005), *aff'd in part, rev'd in part on other grounds* 716 N.W.2d 822 (Wis. 2006).

See also, 9A *Couch on Insurance* §129:19 (3d ed. 2006) (Based on the above-quoted express exception for "real property" in the definition of "your product," the "work performed by contractors on dwellings, buildings, structures, and any other form of realty is . . . not considered to be the product of the insured.").

But see:

Maryland: Century I Joint Venture v. United States Fidelity & Guarantee Insurance Co., 493 A.2d 370 (Md. App.), *cert. denied* 498 A.2d 1183 (Md. 1985).

Washington: Westman Industrial Co. v. Hartford Insurance Group, 751 P.2d 1242 (Wash. App.), *review denied* 110 Wash. 2d 1036 (1988).

[129] See:

California: Maryland Casualty Co. v. Reeder, 270 Cal. Rptr. 719, 727–728 (Cal. App. 1990).

Ohio: The Cincinnati Insurance Co. v. G.L.H., Inc., 2008 WL 2940663 (Ohio App. Aug. 1, 2008); *Dublin Building Systems v. Selective Insurance Co.,* 172 Ohio App.3d 196, 874 N.E.2d 788 (Ohio App. 2007).

[130] *Id.*

[131] See ISO Form CG 00 01 10 01.

[132] See ISO Form CG 00 01 10 01.

[133] See ISO Form CG 00 01 10 01.

[134] See ISO Form CG 00 01 10 01.

[135] See § 7.06[2] *infra.*

[136] See § 7.06[3] *infra.*

[137] See § 7.06[4][a] *infra.*

[138] See ISO Form CG 00 01 10 01.

[139] The policy actually says that the exclusion applies if the damage is "within the products completed operations hazard." *Id.*

[140] *Id. Accord,* § 7.04[4][a], *supra.* See also:

Fifth Circuit: Assurance Company of America v. Admiral Insurance Co., 2011 WL 1897589 (S.D. Ala. May 18, 2011); Auto-Owners Insurance Co. v. L. Thomas Development, Inc., 2010 WL 2308190 (M.D. Ala. June 9, 2010).

Tenth Circuit: Fidelity & Deposit Company of Maryland v. Hartford Casualty Insurance Co., 189 F. Supp.2d 1212 (D. Kan. 2002) ("your work" exclusion inapplicable to damage occurring during operations).

State Courts:

Florida: U.S. Fire Insurance Co. v. J.S.U.B., Inc., 979 So.2d 871, 879 (Fla. 2007).

Indiana: Sheehan Construction Co. v. Continental Casualty Co., 935 N.E.2d 160 (Ind. 2010).

Louisiana: Sibley v. Deer Valley Homebuilders, Inc., 32 So.3d 1034 (La. App. 2010).

Massachusetts: Pacific Indemnity Co. v. Lampro, 86 Mass. App. Ct. 60, 12 N.E.3d 1037 (2014); National Union Fire Insurance Company of Pittsburgh, PA v. Modern Continental Construction Co., 27 Mass. L. Rptr. 16 (Mass. Super. Suffolk Cnty. 2009).

Minnesota: Wanzek Construction, Inc. v. Employers Insurance of Wausau, 679 N.W.2d 322 (Minn. 2004).

New Hampshire: Brown v. Concord Group Insurance Co., 163 N.H. 522, 44 A.3d 586 (2012).

Ohio: Auto Owners Mutual Insurance Co. v. Kendrick, 2009 WL 1263967 (Ohio App. May 4, 2009); The Cincinnati Insurance Co. v. G.L.H., Inc., 2008 WL 2940663 (Ohio App. Aug. 1, 2008).

Texas: Lennar Corp. v. Great American Insurance Co., 200 S.W.3d 651 (Tex. App.), *substituted concurring and dissenting opinions* 2006 WL 909937 (Tex. App. Apr. 11, 2006) ("In short, the 'your work' exclusion precludes coverage for 'property damage' to the insured's work arising after a construction project is finished and in the owner's possession.").

Washington: Mutual of Enumclaw Insurance Co. v. T & G Construction, Inc., 165 Wash.2d 255, 199 P.3d 376 (2008) (*en banc*).

Wisconsin: General Casualty Company of Wisconsin v. Rainbow Insulators, Inc., 2011 WL 1162088 (Wis. App. Mar. 31, 2011).

[141] See ISO Form CG 00 01 10 01.

[142] *Fifth Circuit*: Assurance Company of America v. Admiral Insurance Co., 2011 U.S. Dist. LEXIS 54498 (S.D. Ala. May 18, 2011); Auto–Owners Insurance Co. v. L. Thomas Development, Inc., 2010 U.S. Dist. LEXIS 56801 (M.D. Ala. June 9, 2010).

Seventh Circuit: Edward E. Gillen Co. v. Insurance Co. of Pennsylvania, 874 F. Supp.2d 755 (E.D. Wis. 2012).

Eighth Circuit: Corn Plus Co-op. v. Continental Casualty Co., 516 F.3d 674 (8th Cir. 2008).

Ninth Circuit: MW Builders, Inc. v. Safeco Insurance Company of America, 267 Fed. Appx. 552, 2008 WL 422222 (9th Cir. Feb. 15, 2008).

State Courts:

Alabama: Fitness Equipment Co. v. Pennsylvania General Insurance Co., 493 So.2d 1337, 1341 (Ala. 1985); United States Fidelity & Guaranty Co. v. Andalusia Ready Mix, Inc., 436 So.2d 868, 870 (Ala. 1983) ("if [an] occurrence or accident causes damage to some *other* property than the insured's product, the insured's liability for such damage becomes the liability of the insurer under the policy").

Florida: U.S. Fire Insurance Co. v. J.S.U.B., Inc., 979 So.2d 871, 879 (Fla. 2007).

Georgia: Glens Falls Insurance Co. v. Donmac Golf Shaping, 417 S.E.2d 197 (Ga. App. 1992) ("your work" exclusion inapplicable to damage to other trades' work).

Indiana: Sheehan Construction Co. v. Continental Casualty Co., 935 N.E.2d 160 (Ind. 2010).

Massachusetts: National Union Fire Insurance Company of Pittsburgh, PA v. Modern Continental Construction Co., 27 Mass. L. Rptr. 16 (Mass. Super. Suffolk Cnty. 2009).

Missouri: Assurance Co. of America v. Secura Insurance Co., 384 S.W.3d 224 (Mo. App. 2012).

Nebraska: Auto-Owners Insurance Co. v. Home Pride Cos., Inc., 684 N.W.2d 571 (Neb. 2004) ("your work" exclusion inapplicable to damage to other trades' work).

North Carolina: Builders Mutual Insurance Co. v. Mitchell, 2011 WL 1238373 (N.C. App. Apr. 5, 2011).

Ohio: Auto Owners Mutual Insurance Co. v. Kendrick, 2009 WL 1263967 (Ohio App. May 4, 2009); The Cincinnati Insurance Co. v. G.L.H., Inc., 2008 WL 2940663 (Ohio App. Aug. 1, 2008).

South Carolina: Crossmann Communities of North Carolina, Inc. v. Harleysville Mutual Insurance Co., 2011 WL 93716 (S.C. Jan. 7, 2011).

Tennessee: Standard Fire Insurance Co. v. Chester O'Donley & Associates, 972 S.W.2d 1 (Tenn. App. 1998) ("your work" exclusion inapplicable to claims involving losses resulting from failure of the policyholder's work).

Texas: Mid-Continent Casualty Co. v. Krolczyk, 408 S.W.3d 896 (Tex. App. 2013).

Utah: America First Credit Union v. Kier Construction Corp., 314 P.3d 1055 (Utah App. 2013).

Washington: Mutual of Enumclaw Insurance Co. v. T & G Construction, Inc., 165 Wash.2d 255, 199 P.3d 376 (2008) (*en banc*).

143 See ISO Form CG 00 01 10 01.

144 See ISO Form CG 00 01 10 01.

145 See ISO Form CG 00 01 10 01.

146 See:

Third Circuit: Allegheny Design Management, Inc. v. Travelers Indemnity Co. of America, 572 Fed. Appx. 98 (3d Cir. 2014).

Fifth Circuit: Admiral Insurance Co. v. Little Big Inch Pipeline Co., 523 F. Supp.2d 524 (W.D. Tex. 2007).

Fourth Circuit: Limbach Co. v. Zurich American Insurance Co., 396 F.3d 358 (4th Cir. 2005).

Fifth Circuit: Pennsylvania National Mutual Casualty Insurance Co. v. St. Catherine of Siena Parish, 16 F. Supp.3d 1370 (S.D. Ala. 2014).

Sixth Circuit: Forest Construction, Inc. v. Cincinnati Insurance Co., 703 F.3d 359 (6th Cir. 2013); Salomon v. Cincinnati Insurance Co., 954 F. Supp.2d 828 (N.D. Ind. 2013).

Seventh Circuit: Durbrow v. Mike Check Builders, Inc., 442 F. Supp.2d 676 (E.D. Wis. 2006) (subcontractor exception applied where damage was to work performed by a subcontractor).

Ninth Circuit: Willmar Development, L.L.C. v. Illinois National Insurance Co., 464 Fed. Appx. 594 (9th Cir. 2011).

Eleventh Circuit: J.B.D. Construction, Inc. v. Mid-Continent Casualty Co., 571 Fed. Appx. 918 (11th Cir. 2014); Essex Builders Group, Inc. v. Amerisure Insurance Co., 429 F. Supp.2d 1274 (M.D. Fla. 2005) (applying subcontractor exception).

State Courts:

California: Garamerdi v. Golden Eagle Insurance Co., 2006 WL 337599 (Cal. App. Feb. 15, 2006) (Exclusion L is inapplicable to defective work that was not performed by the policyholder itself); Insurance Company of North America v. National American Insurance Co., 43 Cal. Rptr.2d 518, 522–523 (Cal. App. 1995); Maryland Casualty Co. v. Reeder, 270 Cal. Rptr. 719, 727–728 (Cal. App. 1990) (modified language designed to provide policyholder with coverage for damage to policyholder's work that resulted from negligence of policyholder's subcontractors).

Connecticut: Capstone Building Corp. v. American Motorists Insurance Co., 308 Conn. 760, 67 A.3d 961 (2013).

Delaware: AE-Newark Associates, L.P. v. CNA Insurance Cos., 2001 WL 1198930 (Del. Super. Oct. 2, 2001) (a subcontractor exception applied to moisture intrusion damage caused by faulty installation of roof by subcontractor).

Florida: J.S.U.B., Inc. v. United States Fire Insurance Co., 906 So.2d 303 (Fla. App. 2005) (subcontractor exception applied to allow coverage for damage to home caused by faulty soil work).

Indiana: Sheehan Construction Co. v. Continental Casualty Co., 935 N.E.2d 160 (Ind. 2010).

Louisiana: Sibley v. Deer Valley Homebuilders, Inc., 32 So.3d 1034 (La. App. 2010); Broadmoor Anderson v. National Union Fire Insurance Company of Louisiana, 912 So.2d 400 (La. App. 2005) (subcontractor exception applied).

Minnesota: Wanzek Construction, Inc. v. Employers Insurance of Wausau, 679 N.W.2d 322 (Minn. 2004) (as a result of application of the subcontractor exception, general contractor for construction of swimming pool was entitled to coverage for the cost to repair failure of overflow coping stones provided by a supplier).

Ohio: Erie Insurance Exchange v. Colony Development Corp., 2003 WL 23096010, (Ohio App. Dec. 31, 2003) (subcontractor exception applied).

Pennsylvania: Kvaerner Metals v. Commercial Union Insurance Co., 825 A.2d 641, 656 (Pa. Super. 2003), *rev'd on other grounds* 908 A.2d 888 (Pa. 2006) (noting that general contractors who subcontract out all work and remain on the job in a supervisory capacity can now insure complete coverage for faulty workmanship); Nitterhouse Concrete Products v. Pennsylvania Manufacturers' Association Insurance Co., 67 Pa. D. & C.4th 225, 237 (Pa. C.P. Franklin Cnty. 2004).

Tennessee: Travelers Indemnity Company of America v. Moore & Associates, Inc., 216 S.W.3d 302 (Tenn. 2007) (general contractor's liability for water intrusion damages from faulty window installation done by a subcontractor not excluded by "your work" exclusion as a result of subcontractor exception).

Texas: Lennar Corp. v. Great American Insurance Co., 200 S.W.3d 651 (Tex. App.), *substituted concurring and dissenting opinions* 2006 WL 909937 (Tex. App. Apr. 11, 2006) (subcontractor exception applied).

Utah: America First Credit Union v. Kier Construction Corp., 314 P.3d 1055 (Utah App. 2013).

West Virginia: Cherrington v. Erie Insurance Property and Casualty Co., 231 W. Va. 470, 745 S.E.2d 508 (2013).

Wisconsin: American Family Mutual Insurance Co. v. American Girl, Inc., 673 N.W.2d 65 (Wis.) (subcontractor exception applied); Kalchthaler v. Keller Construction Co., 591 N.W.2d 169 (Wis. App. 1999); Rzepkowski v. Schuenke, 599 N.W.2d 666 (Wis. App. 1999) (subcontractor exception applied).

In *Kalchthaler*, the court affirmed the lower court's determination that coverage existed under the CGL policy because of the exception to the "your work" exclusion. The defendant, Keller Construction, sought coverage from its insurance company, Aetna, under its CGL policy for any liability imposed upon it arising out of a leaky building it built for the *Kalchthaler* plaintiffs. Citing case law from other jurisdictions, the court affirmed the trial court's finding that "[t]he person who acquired this insurance policy with the product-completed operations hazard provisions would reasonably expect coverage in such a situation." Kalchthaler v. Keller Construction Co., 591 N.W.2d 169, 171 (Wis. App. 1999) (citing O'Shaughnessy v. Smuckler Corp., 543 N.W.2d 99 (Minn. App. 1996), *abrogated on other grounds* 645 N.W.2d 393 (Minn. 2002)).

147 See, e.g.:

Fourth Circuit: Builders Mutual Insurance Co. v. OakTree Homes, Inc., 867 F. Supp.2d 800 (D.S.C. 2012).

Eleventh Circuit: J.B.D. Construction, Inc. v. Mid-Continent Casualty Co., 571 Fed. Appx. 918 (11th Cir. 2014).

148 Erie Insurance Exchange v. Colony Development Corp., 2003 WL 23096010 (Ohio App. Dec. 31, 2003).

149 *Id.*, 2003 WL 23096010 at *7.

150 See Dells Club Condominium Owners Ass'n v. Bergman, 1993 WL 393118, 514 N.W.2d 723 (Table of Unpublished Opinions) (Wis. App. Oct. 7, 1993).

151 *Id.*, at *2 (quoting Just v. Land Reclamation, Ltd., 445 N.W.2d 683, 688 (Wis. App. 1989), *rev'd on other grounds* 456 N.W.2d 570 (1990)).

152 *Id.* See also:

Louisiana: Massey v. Parker, 733 So.2d 74 (La. App.), *writ denied* 745 So.2d 30 (La. 1999) (remanding case to trial court without elaboration for fact finding on the exception to the "your work" exclusion, suggesting that the burden is on plaintiffs to demonstrate facts tending to show that the exclusion in fact applied to provide it with insurance coverage for the construction defects).

Minnesota: O'Shaughnessy v. Smuckler Corp., 543 N.W.2d 99 (Minn. App. 1996) ("your work" exclusion does not preclude coverage when the exception to the exclusion applies; so-called "business risk doctrine," which had influenced the development of the "your work" exception to commercial general liability insurance policies, did not operate to discourage good workmanship on the part of those who performed it; subcontractor's burden to purchase performance bond was proper, since the subcontractor is the one actually performing the work and assuming the risk).

153 Franco, "Insurance Coverage for Faulty Workmanship Claims under Commercial General Liability Policies," 30 Tort & Ins. L.J. 785 (Spring 1995). See also: Aydin Corp. v. First State Insurance Co., 959 P.2d 1213, 1215–1216 (Cal. 1998); Garamendi v. Golden Eagle Insurance Co., 2006 WL 337599, at *16 (Cal. App. Feb. 15, 2006).

154 See Annotation, 23 A.L.R. 2d 1243 (1952).

155 See ISO Form CG 00 01 10 01.

156 See ISO Form CG 00 01 10 01.

157 See ISO Form CG 00 01 10 01.

158 Hamlin, Inc. v. Hartford Accident & Indemnity Co., 86 F.3d 93, 96 (7th Cir. 1996).

159 Standard Fire Insurance Co. v. Chester O'Donley & Associates, 972 S.W.2d 1, 10 (Tenn. App. 1998).

160 *Id.*

161 See ISO Form CG 00 01 10 01.

162 See ISO Form CG 00 01 10 01.

163 Indeed, to trigger coverage in the first place, there must be "property damage," which requires that property be physically injured or its use lost. See ISO Form CG 00 01 10 01. Here, since physical injury property damage is expressly excepted, the only type of property damage to which Exclusion M can apply is the loss-of-use type.

164 See:

First Circuit: Essex Insurance Co. v. BloomSouth Flooring Corp., 562 F.3d 399 (1st Cir. 2009).

Second Circuit: Harleysville Worcester Insurance Co. v. Paramount Concrete, Inc., 10 F. Supp.3d 252 (D. Conn. 2014).

Third Circuit: Imperial Casualty & Indemnity Co. v. High Concrete Structures, Inc., 858 F.2d 128, 136 (3d Cir.1988) (Exclusion M does not apply if there is damage to property other than policyholder's work); Lang Tendons, Inc. v. Northern Insurance Company of New York, 2001 WL 228920 (E.D. Pa. Mar. 7, 2001) (impaired property exclusion inapplicable if there is physical injury to property other than the policyholder's work or if policyholder's work cannot be repaired without physical injury to other property).

Fourth Circuit: National Union Fire Insurance Company of Pittsburgh, PA v. Reichhold, Inc., 2009 WL 3125483 (M.D.N.C. Sep. 30, 2009).

Fifth Circuit: Blanton v. Continental Insurance Co., 565 Fed. Appx. 330 (5th Cir. 2014); Fox Electric I, Ltd. v. Amerisure Insurance Co., 252 Fed. Appx. 579, 2007 WL 2693633 (5th Cir. 2007); MAPP Construction, L.L.C. v. Paragon Steel Services, Inc., 2011 WL 572425 (M.D. La. Feb. 15, 2011); Admiral Insurance Co. v. H & W Industries Services, Inc., 2011 WL 318277 (W.D. Tex. Feb. 1, 2011); National Union Fire Insurance Company of Pittsburgh, Pennsylvania v. Puget Plastics Corp., 735 F. Supp.2d 650 (S.D. Tex. 2010); Admiral Insurance Co. v. Little Big Inch Pipeline Co., 523 F. Supp.2d 524 (W.D. Tex. 2007).

Seventh Circuit: Sokol and Co. v. Atlantic Mutual Insurance. Co., 430 F.3d 417 (7th Cir. 2005).

Eighth Circuit: Eyeblaster, Inc. v. Federal Insurance Co., 613 F.3d 797 (8th Cir. 2010); Missouri Terrazzo Co. v. Iowa National Mutual Insurance Co., 740 F.2d 647, 651–652 (8th Cir. 1984) (holding that cracking in a terrazzo floor constituted physical injury, thus making the "loss-of-use" exclusion inapplicable); North Star Mutual Insurance Co. v. Rose, 27 F. Supp.3d 1250 (W.D. Okla. 2014).

Ninth Circuit: SWA Painting, Inc. v. Golden Eagle Insurance Co., 268 Fed. Appx. 521, 2008 WL 510535 (9th Cir. Feb. 26, 2008); Indian Harbor Insurance Co. v. Transform L.L.C., 2010 WL 3584412 (W.D. Wash. Sept. 8, 2010); Centillium Communications, Inc. v. Atlantic Mutual Insurance Co., 528 F. Supp.2d 940 (N.D. Cal. 2007).

Tenth Circuit: American Family Mutual Insurance Co. v. Teamcorp, Inc., 659 F. Supp.2d 1115 (D. Colo. 2009); Fidelity & Deposit Company of Maryland v. Hartford Casualty Insurance Co., 189 F. Supp.2d 1212 (D. Kan. 2002) ("impaired property" exclusion inapplicable where there is physical injury).

Eleventh Circuit: Hathaway Development Co. v. Illinois Union Insurance Co., 274 Fed. Appx. 787, 2008 WL 1773307 (11th Cir. Apr. 18, 2008); Transcontinental Insurance Co. v. Ice Systems of America, Inc., 847 F. Supp. 947, 950 (M.D. Fla. 1994) (Exclusion M inapplicable if there is damage to property other than policyholder's work).

State Courts:

California: Regional Steel Corporation v. Liberty Surplus Insurance Corp., 226 Cal. App.4th 1377, 173 Cal. Rptr.3d 91 (2014); Watts Industries v. Zurich American Insurance Co., 18 Cal. Rptr.3d 61, 73 (Cal. App. 2004) (Exclusion M is inapplicable where the property damage is to "your work" or "your product" and "where other property [which incorporates allegedly faulty work or product] has been physically injured").

Florida: J.S.U.B., Inc. v. United States Fire Insurance Co., 906 So.2d 303, 310–311 (Fla. App. 2005) (home built by policyholder was not excluded by Exclusion M because it was physically injured and constituted "your work").

Louisiana: D & D Pipe and Rentals, Inc. v. Century Exploration New Orleans, Inc., 10 So.3d 361 (La. App. 2009).

Massachusetts: National Union Fire Insurance Company of Pittsburgh, PA v. Modern Continental Construction Co., 27 Mass. L. Rptr. 16 (Mass. Super. Suffolk Cnty. 2009).

Michigan: Kent Cos. v. Wausau Insurance Cos., 2011 WL 1687676 (Mich. App. May 3, 2011).

Pennsylvania: Nitterhouse Concrete Products v. Pennsylvania Manufacturers' Association Insurance Co., 67 Pa. D. & C. 4th 225, 238 (Pa. C.P. Franklin Cnty. 2004) ("impaired property" exclusion inapplicable to structural damage to a school allegedly caused by contractor's faulty pre-cast concrete work).

Tennessee: Standard Fire Insurance Co. v. Chester O'Donley & Associates, 972 S.W.2d 1, 10 (Tenn. App. 1998) ("exclusion does not apply if there is damage to property other than the insured's work").

Texas: Lennar Corp. v. Great American Insurance Co., 200 S.W.3d 651 (Tex. App.), *substituted concurring and dissenting opinions* 2006 WL 909937 (Tex. App. Apr. 11, 2006) (impaired property exclusion applicable, if at all, only to repair of the defect itself and not to damage caused by the defect).

Washington: Truck Insurance Exchange v. Vanport Homes, Inc., 58 P.3d 276 (Wash. 2002) ("impaired property" exclusion inapplicable where there is physical injury).

165 Standard Fire Insurance Co. v. Chester O'Donley & Associates, 972 S.W.2d 1, 10 (Tenn. App. 1998). See also:

Sixth Circuit: Oscar W. Larson Co. v. United Capitol Insurance Co., 845 F. Supp. 445, 448–449 (W.D. Mich. 1993), *aff'd* 64 F.3d 1010 (6th Cir. 1995); Action Auto Stores, Inc. v. United Capitol Insurance Co., 845 F. Supp. 417, 425–426 (W.D. Mich. 1993).

State Courts:

Illinois: Elco Industries v. Liberty Mutual Insurance Co., 361 N.E.2d 589, 591 (Ill. App. 1977).

166 See ISO Form CG 00 01 10 01.

167 See:

First Circuit: Essex Insurance Co. v. BloomSouth Flooring Corp., 562 F.3d 399 (1st Cir. 2009).

Third Circuit: Washington Energy Co. v. Century Surety Co., 407 F. Supp.2d 680, 690–691 (W.D. Pa. 2005) ("However, [the impaired property and sistership] exclusions generally do not preclude coverage where the insured's work or product causes damage to a third party's person or property.").

Fourth Circuit: National Union Fire Insurance Company of Pittsburgh, PA v. Reichhold, Inc., 2009 WL 3125483 (M.D.N.C. Sept. 30, 2009).

Fifth Circuit: MAPP Construction, L.L.C. v. Paragon Steel Services, Inc., 2011 WL 572425 (M.D. La. Feb. 15, 2011); Admiral Insurance Co. v. H & W Industries Services, Inc., 2011 WL 318277 (W.D. Tex. Feb. 1, 2011); National Union Fire Insurance Company of Pittsburgh, Pennsylvania v. Puget Plastics Corp., 735 F. Supp.2d 650 (S.D. Tex. 2010); *In re* ML & Associates, Inc., 302 B.R. 857 (Bankr. N.D. Tex. 2003) (damage to home not excluded by "impaired property" exclusion because home was "your work," which could not be "impaired property").

Seventh Circuit: Durbrow v. Mike Check Builders, Inc., 442 F. Supp.2d 676 (E.D. Wis. 2006) ("impaired property" exclusion inapplicable to home builder because home constituted builder's work).

Eighth Circuit: Eyeblaster, Inc. v. Federal Insurance Co., 613 F.3d 797 (8th Cir. 2010); Corn Plus Co-op. v. Continental Casualty Co., 516 F.3d 674 (8th Cir. 2008).

Ninth Circuit: Indian Harbor Insurance Co. v. Transform L.L.C., 2010 WL 3584412 (W.D. Wash. Sept. 8, 2010).

Tenth Circuit: American Family Mutual Insurance Co. v. Teamcorp, Inc., 659 F. Supp.2d 1115 (D. Colo. 2009); Fidelity & Deposit Company of Maryland v. Hartford Casualty Insurance Co., 189 F. Supp.2d 1212 (D. Kan. 2002) ("impaired property" exclusion inapplicable where the damage occurred to the work of the policyholder).

Eleventh Circuit: Essex Builders Group, Inc. v. Amerisure Insurance Co., 429 F. Supp.2d 1274 (M.D. Fla. 2005) ("impaired property" exclusion cannot apply to damage to policyholder's "work").

State Courts:

California: Watts Industries v. Zurich American Insurance Co., 18 Cal. Rptr.3d 61, 73 (Cal. App. 2004) (Exclusion M is inapplicable where the property damage is to "your work" or "your product" and "where other property [which incorporates allegedly faulty work or product] has been physically injured.").

Florida: J.S.U.B., Inc. v. United States Fire Insurance Co., 906 So.2d 303, 310–311 (Fla. App. 2005) (home built by policyholder was not excluded by Exclusion M because it was physically injured and constituted "your work").

Louisiana: D & D Pipe and Rentals, Inc. v. Century Exploration New Orleans, Inc., 10 So.3d 361 (La. App. 2009).

Massachusetts: National Union Fire Insurance Company of Pittsburgh, PA v. Modern Continental Construction Co., 27 Mass. L. Rptr. 16 (Mass. Super. Suffolk Cty. 2009).

Michigan: Kent Cos. v. Wausau Insurance Cos., 2011 WL 1687676 (Mich. App. May 3, 2011).

Minnesota: Auto-Owners Insurance Co. v. NewMech Cos., Inc., 678 N.W.2d 477, 485 (Minn. App. 2004).

Texas: Lennar Corp. v. Great American Insurance Co., 200 S.W.3d 651, 687 n.46 (Tex. App. 2006).

168 Auto-Owners Insurance Co. v. Home Pride Cos., 684 N.W.2d 571 (Neb. 2004) ("impaired property" exclusion inapplicable to damage to other trades' work because property cannot be restored by repair of "your work").

169 See ISO Form CG 00 01 10 01.

170 See ISO Form CG 00 01 10 01. See also:

Eighth Circuit: St. Paul Fire & Marine Insurance Co. v. American Chemical Co., 1996 WL 1054302 (D. Minn. Feb. 29, 1996) (Exclusion M "exception only applies to the loss of use of property not physically damaged").

Ninth Circuit: Indiana Lumbermens Insurance Co. v. PrimeWood, Inc., 1999 WL 33283343 (D.N.D. Jan. 8, 1999) (replacement of yellowing cabinets not excluded by "impaired property" exclusion).

Eleventh Circuit: Hathaway Development Co. v. Illinois Union Insurance Co., 2008 WL 1773307 (11th Cir. Apr. 18, 2008).

171 See Turner, *Insurance Coverage of Construction Disputes* § 25.20, at 316–318. See also § 3.02[b] *supra*.

172 See ISO Form CG 00 01 10 01.

173 See ISO Form CG 00 01 10 01. See also:

Third Circuit: Washington Energy Co. v. Century Surety Co., 407 F. Supp.2d 680, 690–691 (W.D. Pa. 2005) ("However, [the impaired property and sistership] exclusions generally do not preclude coverage where the insured's work or product causes damage to a third party's person or property.").

Fourth Circuit: National Union Fire Insurance Company of Pittsburgh, PA v. Reichhold, Inc., 2009 WL 3125483 (M.D.N.C. Sept. 30, 2009).

Seventh Circuit: Fireman's Fund Insurance Co. v. Amstek Metal, L.L.C., 2008 WL 4066096 (N.D. Ill. Aug. 27, 2008).

Eighth Circuit: Cincinnati Insurance Co. v. Transport Graphics, Inc., 2011 WL 2083960 (W.D. Mo. May 19, 2011).

Ninth Circuit: Security National Insurance Co. v. GloryBee Foods, Inc., 2011 WL 902635 (D. Or. Mar. 15, 2011); Mid-Continent Casualty Co. v. Titan Construction Corp., 2009 WL 1587215 (W.D. Wash. June 5, 2009).

Eleventh Circuit: Auto-Owners Insurance Co. v. American Building Materials, Inc., 2011 WL 1878236 (M.D. Fla. May 17, 2011); Gentry Machine Works, Inc. v. Harleysville Mutual Insurance Co., 621 F. Supp.2d 1288 (M.D. Ga. 2008).

State Courts:

Alabama: Commercial Union Assurance Co. v. Glass-Lined Pipe Co., 372 So.2d 1305, 1307–1308 (Ala. 1979) (lack of physical injury form of property damage warranted application of exclusion to replacement of defective glass lined pipes in construction project).

Georgia: Hathaway Development Co. v. American Empire Surplus Lines Insurance Co., 686 S.E.2d 855 (Ga. App. 2009).

Illinois: United National Insurance Co. v. Faure Brothers Corp., 2011 WL 1902126 (Ill. App. May 17, 2011).

Massachusetts: National Union Fire Insurance Company of Pittsburgh, PA v. Modern Continental Construction Co., 27 Mass. L. Rptr. 16 (Mass. Super. Suffolk Cnty. 2009).

Michigan: Hastings Mutual Insurance Co. v. Mosher Dolan Cataldo & Kelly, Inc., 2014 Mich. App. LEXIS 138 (Mich. App. Jan. 23, 2014); Amerisure Mutual Insurance Co. v. Hall Steel Co., 2009 WL 4724303 (Mich App. Dec. 10, 2009).

South Carolina: Auto-Owners Insurance Co. v. Rhodes, 385 S.C. 83, 682 S.E.2d 857 (S.C. App. 2009).

Texas: Lennar Corp. v. Great American Insurance Co., 200 S.W.3d 651 (Tex. App.), *substituted concurring and dissenting opinions* 2006 WL 909937 (Tex. App. Apr. 11, 2006) ("sistership" exclusion would only apply, if at all, to repair of the defect, which is not the physical injury form of "property damage").

Washington: Olympic Steamship Co., Inc. v. Centennial Insurance Co., 811 P.2d 673 (Wash. 1991) (intent of "sistership" exclusion is to cover the cost of preventative or curative action taken by the policyholder).

174 See ISO Form CG 00 01 10 01.

175 *First Circuit:* Honeycomb Systems, Inc. v. Admiral Insurance Co., 567 F. Supp. 1400 (D. Me. 1983).

Third Circuit: Imperial Casualty & Indemnity Co. v. High Concrete Structures, Inc., 858 F.2d 128, 136 n.9 (3d Cir. 1988) ("a fortiori, [Exclusion N does] not exclude coverage of damages arising from a defective product when no sister products are involved"); Lang Tendons, Inc. v. Northern Insurance Co. of New York, 2001 WL 228920, at *10 (E.D. Pa. Mar. 7, 2001) ("It is well settled that [the product recall exclusion] applies only if the product or property of which it is a part is withdrawn from the market or from use by the insured, and even in such situations, the policy still covers damages caused by the product that failed."); Washington Energy Co. v. Century Surety Co., 407 F. Supp.2d 680, 691 (W.D. Pa. 2005).

Fourth Circuit: National Union Fire Insurance Company of Pittsburgh, PA v. Reichhold, Inc., 2009 WL 3125483 (M.D.N.C. Sept. 30, 2009).

Sixth Circuit: North Star Mutual Insurance Co. v. Rose, 27 F. Supp.3d 1250 (W.D. Okla. 2014).

Seventh Circuit: Fireman's Fund Insurance Co. v. Amstek Metal, L.L.C., 2008 WL 4066096 (N.D. Ill. Aug. 27, 2008).

Eighth Circuit: Cincinnati Insurance Co. v. Transport Graphics, Inc., 2011 WL 2083960 (W.D. Mo. May 19, 2011); Corn Plus Co-operative v. Continental Casualty Co., 444 F. Supp.2d 981 (D. Minn. 2006).

Ninth Circuit: Security National Insurance Co. v. GloryBee Foods, Inc., 2011 WL 902635 (D. Or. Mar. 15, 2011); Indian Harbor Insurance Co. v. Transform L.L.C., 2010 WL 3584412 (W.D. Wash. Sept. 8, 2010); Mid-Continent Casualty Co. v. Titan Construction Corp., 2009 WL 1587215 (W.D. Wash June 5, 2009); Indiana Lumbermens Insurance Co. v. PrimeWood, Inc., 1999 WL 33283343 (D.N.D. Jan. 8, 1999) (replacement of yellowing cabinets not excluded by "sistership" exclusion).

Eleventh Circuit: Auto-Owners Insurance Co. v. American Building Materials, Inc., 2011 WL 1878236 (M.D. Fla. May 17, 2011); Gentry Machine Works, Inc. v. Harleysville Mutual Insurance Co., 621 F. Supp.2d 1288 (M.D. Ga. 2008).

State Courts:

Florida: Aetna Casualty & Surety Co. v. Monsanto Co., 487 So.2d 398 (Fla. App. 1986).

Georgia: Hathaway Development Co. v. American Empire Surplus Lines Insurance Co., 301 Ga. App. 65, 686 S.E.2d 855 (2009).

Illinois: United National Insurance Co. v. Faure Brothers Corp., 949 N.E.2d 1185 (Ill. App. 2011); United States Fire Insurance Co. v. CNA Insurance Cos., 213 Ill. App.3d 568,

572 N.E.2d 1124, 157 Ill. Dec. 660 (1991); United States Fidelity & Guaranty Co. v. Wilkin Insulation Co., 144 Ill.2d 64, 578 N.E.2d 926, 161 Ill. Dec. 280 (1991).

Massachusetts: National Union Fire Insurance Company of Pittsburgh, PA v. Modern Continental Construction Co., 27 Mass. L. Rptr. 16 (Mass. Super. Suffolk Cnty. 2009).

Michigan: Hastings Mutual Insurance Co. v. Mosher Dolan Cataldo & Kelly, Inc., 2014 Mich. App. LEXIS 138 (Mich. App. Jan. 23, 2014); Amerisure Mutual Insurance Co. v. Hall Steel Co., 2009 Mich. App. LEXIS 2545 (Mich App. Dec. 10, 2009).

Minnesota: Auto-Owners Insurance Co. v. NewMech Cos., Inc., 678 N.W.2d 477, 485 (Minn. App. 2004) ("Some of the units sustained damage due to the defective make-up air system. Brighton agreed to repair the damage. The units were never *withdrawn* from the market in the sense of the policy; rather, they were just repaired. If you took Auto-Owners literally, there would never be coverage for any loss as, arguably, nothing needing repairs from a covered loss is "impaired." Exclusion n does not apply.") (emphasis in original).

South Carolina: Auto-Owners Insurance Co. v. Rhodes, 385 S.C. 83, 682 S.E.2d 857 (S.C. App. 2009).

Texas: Venture Encoding Service, Inc. v. Atlantic Mutual Insurance Co., 107 S.W.3d 729 (Tex. App. 2003).

Washington: Olympic Steamship Co. v. Centennial Insurance Co., 811 P.2d 673 (Wash. 1991) (intent of "sistership" exclusion is to cover the cost of preventative or curative action taken by the policyholder).

West Virginia: Cherrington v. Erie Insurance Property and Casualty Co., 231 W. Va. 470, 745 S.E.2d 508 (2013).

Wisconsin: Pamperin Rentals II, L.L.C. v. R.G. Hendricks and Sons Construction, Inc., 344 Wis.2d 518, 822 N.W.2d 736 (Wis. App. 2012).

See also, Turner, *Insurance Coverage of Construction Disputes* §§ 33.01–33.03, 34.01, at 369–374.

But see:

Delaware: Charles E. Brohawn & Brothers, Inc. v. Employers Commercial Union Insurance Co., 409 A.2d 1055 (Del. Super. 1979).

[176] Washington Energy Co. v. Century Surety Co., 407 F. Supp.2d 680, 691 (W.D. Pa. 2005), quoting Imperial Casualty & Indemnity Co. v. High Concrete Structures, Inc., 858 F.2d 128, 136 n. 9 (3d Cir. 1988) (emphasis added).

[177] See Hartford Accident & Indemnity Co. v. Regent Nursing Home, 413 N.Y.S.2d 195 (N.Y. App. Div. 1979). See also, ISO Form CG 22 79 07 98.

[178] See ISO Form CG 00 01 10 01.

[179] *First Circuit:* GRE Insurance Group v. Metropolitan Boston Housing Partnership, Inc., 61 F.3d 79 (1st Cir. 1995).

Second Circuit: Vermont Mutual Insurance Co. v. Ciccone, 900 F. Supp.2d 249 (D. Conn. 2012).

Third Circuit: Wimberly Allison Tong & Goo, Inc. v. Travelers Property Casualty Company of America, 352 Fed. Appx. 642 (3d Cir. 2009); Continental Casualty Co. v. Hartford Accident & Indemnity Co., 836 F. Supp. 246 (E.D. Pa. 1993) (professional services exclusion depends on a fact-based analysis).

Fourth Circuit: Nautilus Insurance Co. v. Strongwell Corp., 968 F. Supp.2d 807 (W.D. Va. 2013).

Fifth Circuit: Wisznia Co. v. General Star Indemnity Co., 759 F.3d 446 (5th Cir. 2014); Admiral Insurance Co. v. Ford, 607 F.3d 420 (5th Cir. 2010); Willbros RPI, Inc. v. Continental Casualty Co., 601 F.3d 306 (5th Cir. 2010); QBE Insurance Corp. v. Brown and Mitchell, Inc.,

591 F.3d 439 (5th Cir. 2009); Essex Insurance Co. v. McFadden, 2010 WL 2246293 (E.D. Tex. June 3, 2010).

Sixth Circuit: Neighborhood Housing Services of America, Inc. v. Turner-Ridley, 742 F. Supp.2d 964 (N.D. Ind. 2010).

Seventh Circuit: U.S. Fidelity and Guaranty Co. v. Shorenstein Realty Services, L.P., 700 F. Supp.2d 1003 (N.D. Ill. 2010); Chapman v. Mutual Service Casualty Insurance Co., 35 F. Supp.2d 693 (E.D. Wis. 1999) (exclusion narrowly construed against insurer).

Eighth Circuit: Westfield Insurance Co. v. Weis Builders, Inc., 2004 U.S. Dist. LEXIS 13658 (D. Minn. July 1, 2004).

Ninth Circuit: National Fire Insurance Company of Hartford v. Lewis, 898 F. Supp.2d 1132 (D. Ariz. 2012).

Eleventh Circuit: Auto-Owners Insurance Co. v. E.N.D. Services, Inc., 506 Fed. Appx. 920 (11th Cir. 2013); Maryland Casualty Co. v. Florida Atlantic Orthopedics, P.L., 2011 WL 1085184 (S.D. Fla. Feb. 24, 2011).

State Courts:

California: North Counties Engineering, Inc. v. State Farm General Insurance Co., 224 Cal. App.4th 902, 169 Cal. Rptr.3d 726 (2014).

Louisiana: Louisiana Stadium & Exposition District v. BFS Diversified Products, L.L.C., 49 So.2d 49 (La. App. 2010).

Minnesota: Western National Mutual Insurance Co. v. Structural Restoration, Inc., 2010 WL 1753336 (Minn. App. May 4, 2010).

New York: Hartford Accident & Indemnity Co. v. Regent Nursing Home, 413 N.Y.S.2d 195 (N.Y. App. Div. 1979).

Ohio: Burlington Insurance Co. v. PMI America, Inc., 862 F. Supp.2d 719 (S.D. Ohio 2012); Eastley v. Volkman, 2010 WL 3835666 (Ohio App. Sept. 23, 2010).

Oklahoma: Brown v. Oklahoma Farm Bureau Mutual Insurance Co., 261 P.3d 622 (Okla. App. 2011).

Pennsylvania: Lexington Insurance Co. v. Charter Oak Fire Insurance Co., 81 A.3d 903 (Pa. Super. 2013).

West Virginia: Boggs v. Camden-Clark Memorial Hospital Corp., 225 W. Va. 300, 693 S.E.2d 53 (2010).

180 See Chapter 8 *infra* for a discussion of various pollution exclusions.

181 *Seventh Circuit:* Droegkamp v. Langdon, C.A. WL 21749514, at *7 (Wis. App. July 30, 2003) (mold not a pollutant).

Eighth Circuit: American Western Home Insurance Co. v. Utopia Acquisition L.P., 2009 WL 792483 (W.D. Mo. Mar. 24, 2009).

State Courts:

Arizona: Keggi v. Northbrook Property & Casualty Insurance Co., 13 P.3d 785 (Ariz. App. 2000) (purpose of the pollution exclusion, public policy, and the facts of the case, demonstrate that the language should not be interpreted to preclude coverage for bacterial contamination absent any evidence that the actual contamination arose from traditional environmental pollution).

California: Johnson v. Clarendon National Insurance Co., 2009 WL 252619 (Cal. App. Feb. 4, 2009) (pollution exclusion inapplicable).

Louisiana: State Farm Fire & Casualty Co. v. MLT Construction Co., 849 So.2d 762, 770–771 (La. App.), *writ denied* 857 So.2d 483 (La. 2003) (mold is neither a "pollutant" nor a "discharge").

Michigan: Hastings Mutual Insurance Co. v. Mosher Dolan Cataldo & Kelly, Inc., 2014 WL 265506 (Mich. App. Jan. 23, 2014).

Minnesota: Larson v. Composting Concepts, Inc., 2008 WL 2020489 (Minn. App. May 13, 2008) (pollution exclusion applied).

But see, Lexington Insurance Co. v. Unity/Waterford-Fair Oaks, Ltd., 2002 WL 356756 (N.D. Tex. Mar. 5 2002) (since the pollution exclusion explicitly listed fungi as a "pollutant," the policyholder's claim for mold coverage was excluded).

In Stillman v. Travelers Insurance Co., 88 F.3d 911 (11th Cir. 1996) (reversing "final" judgment but leaving trial court's determination on application of pollution exclusion to mold-related bodily injury claims undisturbed), molds, fungi, and yeasts were released into the air in an office building. Workers sued the owner of the building for various health impairments resulting from negligent design, maintenance, installation, and repair of the HVAC system. The owner's CGL insurance company refused to defend, claiming coverage on the basis of an absolute pollution exclusion. The trial court found in favor of the owner on the pollution exclusion. On appeal, the Eleventh Circuit reversed solely on a procedural issue, leaving the determination with respect to the pollution exclusion intact.

See also, Wielinski, "Insurance Coverage for Mold Arising Out of Defective Workmanship," IRMI.com (Feb. 2001) (discussing trial court decision in *Stillman*).

[182] See Chapter 8 *infra*. See also, ISO Form CG 00 01 10 01.

[183] See ISO Form CG 00 01 10 01.

[184] *Webster's Ninth New Collegiate Dictionary* at 764 (1991).

[185] See ISO Form CG 00 01 10 01.

[186] See 42 U.S.C. § 7412.

[187] The appellate court reversed the trial court on other grounds in Stillman v. Travelers Insurance Co., 88 F.3d 911 (11th Cir. 1996). See Wielinski, "Insurance Coverage for Mold Arising Out of Defective Workmanship," IRMI.com (Feb. 2001), discussing the trial court's holding.

[188] See § 7.10[2] *infra*.

[189] See § 3.02[2] *supra*. But see, American Western Home Insurance Co. v. Utopia Acquisition, L.P., 2009 WL 792483 (W.D. Mo. Mar. 24, 2009).

[190] See:

Sixth Circuit: Universal Image Productions, Inc. v. Chubb Corp., 703 F. Supp.2d 705 (E.D. Mich. 2010) (pollution exclusion inapplicable to mold loss under first-party policy).

Seventh Circuit: Droegkamp v. Langdon, C.A. WL 21749514, at *7 (Wis. App. July 30, 2003) (mold not a pollutant).

Eighth Circuit: American Western Home Insurance Co. v. Utopia Acquisition L.P., 2009 WL 792483 (W.D. Mo. Mar. 24, 2009).

State Courts:

Arizona: Keggi v. Northbrook Property & Casualty Insurance Co., 13 P.3d 785 (Ariz. App. 2000) (purpose of the pollution exclusion, public policy, and the facts of the case, demonstrate that the language should not be interpreted to preclude coverage for bacterial contamination absent any evidence that the actual contamination arose from traditional environmental pollution).

California: Johnson v. Clarendon National Insurance Co., 2009 WL 252619 (Cal. App. Feb. 4, 2009) (pollution exclusion inapplicable).

Louisiana: State Farm Fire & Casualty Co. v. MLT Construction Co., 849 So.2d 762, 770–771 (La. App.), *writ denied* 857 So.2d 483 (La. 2003) (mold is neither a "pollutant" nor a "discharge").

Michigan: Hastings Mutual Insurance Co. v. Mosher Dolan Cataldo & Kelly, Inc., 2014 Mich. App. LEXIS 138 (Mich. App. Jan. 23, 2014).

Minnesota: Larson v. Composting Concepts, Inc., 2008 WL 2020489 (Minn. App. May 13, 2008) (pollution exclusion applied).

But see, Lexington Insurance Co. v. Unity/Waterford-Fair Oaks, Ltd., 2002 WL 356756 (N.D. Tex. Mar. 5, 2002) (since the pollution exclusion explicitly listed fungi as a "pollutant," the policyholders claim for mold coverage was excluded).

191 State Farm Fire & Casualty Co. v. MLT Construction Co., 849 So.2d 762, 770–771 (La. App.), *writ denied* 857 So.2d 483 (La. 2003). See also, Doerr v. Mobil Oil Corp., 774 So.2d 119, 135 (La. 2000).

192 *Id.*

193 *Id.* See also, Doerr v. Mobil Oil Corp., 774 So.2d 119, 135 (La. 2000).

194 See ISO Form CG 21 67 04 02.

195 See:

Third Circuit: Alea London Ltd. v. Rudley, 2004 WL 1563002, at *3 (E.D. Pa. July 13, 2004).

Fourth Circuit: Mount Vernon Fire Insurance Co. v. Adamson, 2010 WL 3937336 (E.D. Va. Sept. 15, 2010); Union Insurance Co. v. Williams Contracting Inc., 2006 WL 1582405 (W.D. Va. June 2, 2006).

Fifth Circuit: Clarendon American Insurance Co. v. Southern States Plumbing, Inc., 2011 WL 1103385 (W.D. La. Mar. 23, 2011); Nationwide Mutual Fire Insurance Co. v. Hayes, 2010 WL 3603797 (S.D. Miss. Sept. 7, 2010); State Farm Lloyds v. Chandler, 2005 WL 2467071 (E.D. Tex. Oct. 6, 2005).

Ninth Circuit: Canal Indemnity Co. v. Adair Homes, Inc., 737 F. Supp.2d 1294 (W.D. Wash. 2010).

Eleventh Circuit: Empire Indemnity Insurance Co. v. Winsett, 325 Fed. Appx. 849 (11th Cir. 2009); Mid-Continent Casualty Co. v. Basdeo, 742 F. Supp.2d 1293 (S.D. Fla. 2010).

State Courts:

Michigan: Hometowne Building Co. v. Amerisure Mutual Insurance Co., 2009 WL 3276509 (Mich. App. Oct. 13, 2009).

196 See § 3.02[2] *supra*. But see, American Western Home Insurance Co. v. Utopia Acquisition, L.P., 2009 WL 792483 (W.D. Mo. Mar. 24, 2009).

197 Orleans Parish School Board v. Lexington Insurance Co., 123 So.3d 787, 797 (La. App. 2013). See also:

Fifth Circuit: Hayes v. Southern Fidelity Insurance Co., 2014 U.S. Dist. LEXIS 146962 (E.D. La. Oct. 15, 2014).

State Courts:

Arizona: Liristis v. American Family Mutual Insurance Co., 204 Ariz. 140, 61 P.3d 22 (Ariz. App. 2002).

Kentucky: Reynolds v. Travelers Indemnity Company of America, 233 S.W.3d 197 (Ky. App. 2007).

New Jersey: Simonetti v. Selective Insurance Co., 372 N.J. Super. 421, 859 A.2d 694 (2004).

198 See § 7.04 *infra*.

199 See §§ 3.02[1], 4.03[4][a][H] *supra*.

200 See Certain Underwriters at Lloyds of London Subscribing to Policy No. SMP3791 v. Creagh, 563 Fed. Appx. 209 (3d Cir. 2014) (excluding claims "'directly or indirectly arising out of or relating to: mold, mildew, fungus, spores or other microorganism of any type, nature,

or description, including but not limited to any substance whose presence poses an actual or potential threat to human health'").

201 See § 7.10[2][a] *infra*.

202 See § 7.10[2][b] *infra*.

203 See § 7.10[2][c] *infra*.

204 See § 7.10[2][d] *infra*.

205 See:

First Circuit: Grande v. St. Paul Fire & Marine Insurance Co., 436 F.3d 277 (1st Cir. 2006).

Second Circuit: B & A Demolition and Removal, Inc. v. Markel Insurance Co., 941 F. Supp.2d 307 (E.D.N.Y. 2013); *In re* September 11th Liability Insurance Coverage Cases, 458 F. Supp.2d 104 (S.D.N.Y.), *subsequent determination* 2006 WL 1876672 (S.D.N.Y. June 27, 2006).

Third Circuit: AGF Marine Aviation & Transport v. Cassin, 544 F.3d 255 (3d Cir. 2008); Fire & Casualty Insurance Co. v. Ligon, 86 Fed. Appx. 517, 519 (3d Cir. 2004) (applying Pennsylvania law) ("a binder constitutes evidence that insurance has attached at a specific time, and continues in effect until either the policy is issued or the risk is declined and notice thereof is given").

Fourth Circuit: Whiting-Turner Contracting Co. v. Liberty Mutual Insurance Co., 912 F. Supp.2d 321 (D. Md. 2012); C.B. Fleet Co. v. Aspen Insurance UK Ltd., 743 F. Supp.2d 575 (W.D. Va. 2010).

Sixth Circuit: Anton v. National Union Fire Insurance Company of Pittsburgh, Pennsylvania, 634 F.3d 364 (6th Cir. 2011).

Ninth Circuit: O'Keefe v. Allstate Indemnity Co., 953 F. Supp.2d 1111 (S.D. Cal. 2013).

Eleventh Circuit: Underwriters at Lloyds London v. STD Enterprises, Inc., 395 F. Supp.2d 1142 (M.D. Fla. 2005).

State Courts:

California: Chicago Title Insurance Co. v. AMZ Insurance Services, Inc., 188 Cal. App.4th 401, 115 Cal. Rptr.3d 707 (2010).

Connecticut: Jimdee, L.L.C. v. Flanagan Associates, 2010 WL 561 0889 (Conn. Super. New Haven Dec. 17, 2010).

Florida: Medley Warehouses, L.C. v. Scottsdale Insurance Co, 39 So.3d 440 (Fla. App. 2010).

Georgia: Georgia Farm Bureau Mutual Insurance Co. v. T & G Enterprises, Inc., 324 Ga. App. 445, 751 S.E.2d 99 (2013).

Louisiana: Safeguard Storage Properties, L.L.C. v. Donahue Favret Contractors, Inc., 2011 WL 1226419 (La. App. Mar. 31, 2011); All Crane Rental of Georgia, Inc. v. Vincent, 47 So.3d 1024 (La. 2010).

Maine: Pine Ridge Realty, Inc. v. Massachusetts Bay Insurance Co., 752 A.2d 595 (Me. 2000).

Mississippi: Coastal Hardware and Rental Co., L.L.C. v. Certain Underwriters at Lloyds, London, 120 So.3d 1017 (Miss. App. 2013).

Missouri: Alea London Ltd. v. Bono-Soltysiak Enterprises, 186 S.W.3d 403 (Mo. App. 2006).

New Jersey: EPIX Holdings Corp. v. Marsh & McLennan Companies, 982 A.2d 1194 (N.J. Super. App. Div. 2009).

Ohio: Midland Enterprises, Inc. v. St. Paul Fire & Marine Insurance Co., 745 N.E.2d 455 (Ohio App. 2000).

Oregon: Stuart v. Pittman, 2011 WL 2162919 (Or. June 3, 2011); Baylor v. Continental Casualty Co., 78 P.3d 108 (Or. App. 2003).

Pennsylvania: Erie Insurance Exchange v. Lake, 671 A.2d 681, 685 n.7 (Pa. 1996) ("A binder offers temporary protection for the insured pending the investigation of the risk by the insurance company until a formal policy of insurance is issued.").

Tennessee: Scheele v. Hartford Underwriters Insurance Co., 218 S.W. 3d 636 (Tenn. 2007).

206 Peele v. Atlantic Express Transportation Group, Inc., 840 A.2d 1008, 1011 (Pa. Super. 2003). See also:

First Circuit: Grande v. St. Paul Fire & Marine Insurance Co., 436 F.3d 277 (1st Cir. 2006).

Second Circuit: B & A Demolition and Removal, Inc. v. Markel Insurance Co., 941 F. Supp.2d 307 (E.D.N.Y. 2013); *In re* September 11th Liability Insurance Coverage Cases, 458 F. Supp.2d 104 (S.D.N.Y. 2006), *subsequent determination* 2006 WL 1876672 (S.D.N.Y. June 27, 2006).

Fourth Circuit: Whiting-Turner Contracting Co. v. Liberty Mutual Insurance Co., 912 F. Supp.2d 321 (D. Md. 2012).

Ninth Circuit: O'Keefe v. Allstate Indemnity Co., 953 F. Supp.2d 1111 (S.D. Cal. 2013).

Eleventh Circuit: Underwriters at Lloyds London v. STD Enterprises, Inc., 395 F. Supp.2d 1142 (M.D. Fla. 2005).

State Courts:

Georgia: Georgia Farm Bureau Mutual Insurance Co. v. T & G Enterprises, Inc., 324 Ga. App. 445, 751 S.E.2d 99 (2013).

Maine: Pine Ridge Realty, Inc. v. Massachusetts Bay Insurance Co., 752 A.2d 595 (Me. 2000).

Mississippi: Coastal Hardware and Rental Co., L.L.C. v. Certain Underwriters at Lloyds, London, 120 So.3d 1017 (Miss. App. 2013).

Missouri: Alea London Ltd. v. Bono-Soltysiak Enterprises, 186 S.W.3d 403 (Mo. App. 2006).

Ohio: Midland Enterprises, Inc. v. St. Paul Fire & Marine Insurance Co., 745 N.E.2d 455 (Ohio App. 2000).

Oregon: Baylor v. Continental Casualty Co., 78 P.3d 108 (Or. App. 2003).

Tennessee: Scheele v. Hartford Underwriters Insurance Co., 2007 WL 609004 (Tenn. Feb. 28, 2007).

207 See:

First Circuit: Grande v. St. Paul Fire & Marine Insurance Co., 436 F.3d 277 (1st Cir. 2006).

Second Circuit: *In re* September 11th Liability Insurance Coverage Cases, 458 F. Supp.2d 104 (S.D.N.Y. 2006), *subsequent determination* 2006WL 1876672 (S.D.N.Y. June 27, 2006).

Third Circuit: AGF Marine Aviation & Transport v. Cassin, 544 F.3d 255 (3d Cir. 2008); Fire & Casualty Insurance Co. v. Ligon, 86 Fed. Appx. 517, 519–520 (3d Cir. 2004) (binder providing "statutory" limits controlled over policy issued after the loss, which had $35,000 limits; policyholder's rights under the binder vested on the date of the accident, and replacement of the binder with an after-issued policy cannot retroactively strip the policyholder of his rights under the binder).

Fourth Circuit: C.B. Fleet Co. v. Aspen Insurance UK Ltd., 743 F. Supp.2d 575 (W.D. Va. 2010).

Sixth Circuit: Anton v. National Union Fire Insurance Company of Pittsburgh, Pennsylvania, 634 F.3d 364 (6th Cir. 2011).

Eleventh Circuit: Underwriters at Lloyds London v. STD Enterprises, Inc., 395 F. Supp.2d 1142 (M.D. Fla. 2005).

State Courts:

California: Chicago Title Insurance Co. v. AMZ Insurance Services, Inc., 188 Cal. App.4th 401, 115 Cal. Rptr.3d 707 (2010).

Connecticut: Jimdee, L.L.C. v. Flanagan Associates, 2010 WL 561 0889 (Conn. Super. New Haven Dec. 17, 2010).

Florida: Medley Warehouses, L.C. v. Scottsdale Insurance Co, 39 So.3d 440 (Fla. App. 2010).

Louisiana: Safeguard Storage Properties, L.L.C. v. Donahue Favret Contractors, Inc., 2011 WL 1226419 (La. App. Mar. 31, 2011); All Crane Rental of Georgia, Inc. v. Vincent, 47 So.3d 1024 (La. 2010).

Maine: Pine Ridge Realty, Inc. v. Massachusetts Bay Insurance Co., 752 A.2d 595 (Me. 2000).

Missouri: Alea London Ltd. v. Bono-Soltysiak Enterprises, 186 S.W.3d 403 (Mo. App. 2006).

New Jersey: EPIX Holdings Corp. v. Marsh & McLennan Companies, 410 N.J. Super. 453, 982 A.2d 1194 (N.J. Super. App. Div. 2009).

Ohio: Midland Enterprises, Inc. v. St. Paul Fire & Marine Insurance Co., 745 N.E.2d 455 (Ohio App. 2000).

Oregon: Stuart v. Pittman, 2011 WL 2162919 (Or. June 3, 2011); Baylor v. Continental Casualty Co., 78 P.3d 108 (Or. App. 2003).

Pennsylvania: Peele v. Atlantic Express Transportation Group, Inc., 840 A.2d 1008, 1011 (Pa. Super. 2003) (binder that provided limits of $2 million in coverage controlled over terms of policy issued after the loss that had $35,000 limits; retroactive change of terms and conditions are ineffective as to an accident taking place before the changes).

[208] *Id.*

[209] Overholt v. Reliance Insurance Co. of Philadelphia, 179 A. 554, 556–557 (Pa. 1935).

> "When the defendant [insurance] company inquired through its agent whether the policy was to be renewed, this was an offer to make a new contract. In the absence of circumstances to indicate that a different meaning was intended, this meant a contract chronologically 'new,' but in *form* and *substance* identical with the original; no other interpretation is reasonable and can be maintained. . . . If the [insurance] company intended in the new policy to alter the terms of this old one, it should have made its intentions evident. When [the insured] accepted the offer as made, by instructing [the insurance company's agent] to renew the policy and paying the premium therefor, the minds of the contracting parties met on a new policy identical in form and substance with the one it superseded."

See Schock v. Penn Township Mutual Fire Insurance Association of Lancaster County, 24 A.2d 741, 743 (Pa. Super. 1942).

> "The delivery of the policy as a renewal, in the absence of notice or explanation that the terms of the policy had been altered, contemplated the same terms and conditions as the existing insurance. A renewal of a policy of fire insurance is, in effect, a new contract of insurance, and, unless otherwise expressed, on the same terms and conditions as the original policy."

See also:

First Circuit: Whittaker Corp. v. First Nuclear Insurers, 671 F. Supp.2d 242 (D. Mass. 2009).

Third Circuit: Stowe Township v. Standard Life Insurance Co., 507 F.2d 1332, 1336–1337 (3d Cir. 1975) ("When an insurance renewal contract curtails benefits from those provided by the original policy, insurers have been held to the terms of the original policy. . . . In the insurance renewal cases, the crucial elements were the existence of the first policy and the terms of its coverage; the renewal; the lessened coverage of the second policy; and finally, evidence regarding the lack of warning by the insurance company about the diminished protection."); Haines v. State Auto Property and Casualty Insurance Co., 2009 WL 1767534 (E.D. Pa. June 22, 2009).

Fourth Circuit: Benner v. Nationwide Mutual Insurance Co., 93 F.3d 1228 (4th Cir. 1996); Wysong & Miles Co. v. Employers of Wausau, 4 F. Supp.2d 421 (M.D.N.C. 1998).

Fifth Circuit: Great American Insurance Company of New York v. Lowry Development, L.L.C., 576 F.3d 251 (5th Cir. 2009).

Sixth Circuit: MDC Acquisition Co. v. Travelers Property Casualty Company of America, 545 Fed. Appx. 398 (6th Cir. 2013); Amway Distributors Benefits Association v. Northfield Insurance Co., 323 F.3d 386 (6th Cir. 2003).

Seventh Circuit: Essex Insurance Co. v. Kasten Railcar Services, Inc., 129 F.3d 947 (7th Cir. 1997).

Eighth Circuit: Hawkins Chemical, Inc. v. Westchester Fire Insurance Co., 159 F.3d 348 (8th Cir. 1998).

Ninth Circuit: Metropolitan Business Management, Inc. v. Allstate Insurance Co., 448 Fed. Appx. 677 (9th Cir. 2011); Meunier v. Northwestern Mutual Life Insurance Co., 2014 U.S. Dist. LEXIS 137740 (D. Or. Sept. 24, 2014); American Casualty Company of Reading, Pennsylvania v. Baker, 22 F.3d 880 (9th Cir. 1994); Ventana Medical Systems, Inc. v. St. Paul Fire & Marine Insurance Co., 709 F. Supp.2d 744 (D. Ariz. 2010).

Tenth Circuit: American Casualty Co. v. Glaskin, 805 F. Supp. 866 (D. Colo. 1992).

Eleventh Circuit: Shelton v. Liberty Mutual Fire Insurance Co., 578 Fed. Appx. 841 (11th Cir. Aug. 21, 2014); Allen v. State Farm Fire & Casualty Co., 59 F. Supp.2d 1217 (S.D. Ala. 1999).

State Courts:

California: Everett v. State Farm General Insurance Co., 162 Cal. App.4th 649, 75 Cal. Rptr.3d 812 (2008); Tompkins v. California Insurance Group, 2002 WL 187085 (Cal. App. Feb. 6, 2002).

Colorado: Ken Caryl Ranch Master Association v. Granite State Insurance Co., 155 P.3d 457 (Colo. App. 2006), *cert. granted* 2007 WL 883515 (Colo. Mar. 26, 2007); Tepe v. Rocky Mountain Hospital & Medical Services, 893 P.2d 1323 (Colo. App. 1994).

Florida: JN Auto Collection Corp. v. U.S. Security Insurance Co., 59 So.3d 256 (Fla. App. 2011); Zenith Insurance Co. v. Commercial Forming Corp., 850 So.2d 568, 570 (Fla. App. 2003).

Illinois: Windmill Nursing Pavilion, Ltd. v. Cincinnati Insurance Co., 2013 IL App (1st) 122431, 2 N.E.3d 582, 377 Ill. Dec. 666 (2013); Burmac Metal Finishing Co. v. West Bend Mutual Insurance Co., 825 N.E.2d 1246 (Ill. App. 2005).

Kentucky: Adkins v. Kentucky National Insurance Co., 220 S.W.3d 296 (Ky. App. 2007).

Louisiana: Gaylord Container Corp. v. CNA Insurance Cos., 807 So.2d 864 (La. App.), *writ denied* 803 So.2d 31 (La. 2001).

Maryland: CIGNA Property & Casualty Cos. v. Zeitler, 730 A.2d 248 (Md. App. 1999).

Michigan: Casey v. Auto Owners Insurance Co. 729 N.W.2d 277 (Mich. App. 2006), *appeal denied* 2007 WL 1550959 (Mich. May 30, 2007).

Minnesota: Schupp v. United Fire and Casualty Co., 821 N.W.2d 824 (Minn. App. 2012); Bast v. Capitol Indemnity Corp., 562 N.W.2d 24 (Minn. App. 1997).

Montana: Robertus v. Farmers Union Mutual Insurance Co., 344 Mont. 157, 189 P.3d 582 (Mont. 2008); Thomas v. Northwestern National Insurance Co., 973 P.2d 804 (Mont. 1998).

New Jersey: Nova Development Group, Inc. v. J.J. Farber-Lottman Co., 2010 WL 680859 (N.J. Super. App. Div. Mar. 1, 2010); McClellan v. Feit, 870 A.2d 644 (N.J. Super. App. Div. 2005).

New York: Essex Insurance Co. v. Vickers, 103 A.D.3d 684, 959 N.Y.S.2d 525 (N.Y. App. Div. 2013); Bloom v. St. Paul Travelers Companies, 57 A.D.3d 819, 870 N.Y.S.2d 400 (N.Y. App. Div. 2008); Farmbrew Realty Corp. v. Tower Insurance Company of New York, 734 N.Y.S.2d 592 (N.Y. App. Div. 2001), ***appeal denied*** 771 N.E.2d 834 (N.Y. 2002).

Pennsylvania: Pressley v. Travelers Property & Casualty Corp., 817 A.2d 1131 (Pa. Super. 2003).

South Carolina: Todd v. Federated Mutual Insurance Co., 409 S.E.2d 361 (S.C. 1991).

Texas: Safeway Managing General Agency for State & County Mutual Fire Insurance Co. v. Cooper, 952 S.W.2d 861 (Tex. App. 1997).

210 Schock v. Penn Township Mutual Fire Insurance Association of Lancaster County, 24 A.2d 741, 743 (Pa. Super. 1942).

See also:

First Circuit: Whittaker Corp. v. First Nuclear Insurers, 671 F. Supp.2d 242 (D. Mass. 2009).

Third Circuit: Haines v. State Auto Property and Casualty Insurance Co., 2009 WL 1767534 (E.D. Pa. June 22, 2009).

Fourth Circuit: Benner v. Nationwide Mutual Insurance Co., 93 F.3d 1228 (4th Cir. 1996); Wysong & Miles Co. v. Employers of Wausau, 4 F. Supp.2d 421 (M.D.N.C. 1998).

Fifth Circuit: Great American Insurance Company of New York v. Lowry Development, L.L.C., 576 F.3d 251 (5th Cir. 2009).

Sixth Circuit: MDC Acquisition Co. v. Travelers Property Casualty Co. of America, 545 Fed. Appx. 398 (6th Cir. 2013); Amway Distributors Benefits Association v. Northfield Insurance Co., 323 F.3d 386 (6th Cir. 2003).

Seventh Circuit: Essex Insurance Co. v. Kasten Railcar Services, Inc., 129 F.3d 947 (7th Cir. 1997).

Eighth Circuit: Hawkins Chemical, Inc. v. Westchester Fire Insurance Co., 159 F.3d 348 (8th Cir. 1998).

Ninth Circuit: Metropolitan Business Management, Inc. v. Allstate Insurance Co., 448 Fed. Appx. 677 (9th Cir. 2011); Meunier v. Northwestern Mutual Life Insurance Co., 2014 U.S. Dist. LEXIS 137740 (D. Or. Sept. 24, 2014); American Casualty Company of Reading, Pennsylvania v. Baker, 22 F.3d 880 (9th Cir. 1994); Ventana Medical Systems, Inc. v. St. Paul Fire & Marine Insurance Co., 709 F. Supp.2d 744 (D. Ariz. 2010).

Tenth Circuit: American Casualty Co. v. Glaskin, 805 F. Supp. 866 (D. Colo. 1992).

Eleventh Circuit: Shelton v. Liberty Mutual Fire Insurance Co., 2014 578 Fed. Appx. 841 (11th Cir. Aug. 21, 2014); Allen v. State Farm Fire & Casualty Co., 59 F. Supp.2d 1217 (S.D. Ala. 1999).

State Courts:

California: Everett v. State Farm General Insurance Co., 162 Cal. App.4th 649, 75 Cal. Rptr.3d 812 (2008); Tompkins v. California Insurance Group, 2002 WL 187085 (Cal. App. Feb. 6, 2002).

Colorado: Ken Caryl Ranch Master Association v. Granite State Insurance Co., 155 P.3d 457 (Colo. App. 2006), ***cert. granted*** 2007 WL 883515 (Colo. Mar. 26, 2007); Tepe v. Rocky Mountain Hospital & Medical Services, 893 P.2d 1323 (Colo. App. 1994).

Florida: JN Auto Collection Corp. v. U.S. Security Insurance Co., 59 So.3d 256 (Fla. App. 2011).

Illinois: Windmill Nursing Pavilion, Ltd. v. Cincinnati Insurance Co., 2013 IL App (1st) 122431, 2 N.E.3d 582, 377 Ill. Dec. 666 (2013); Burmac Metal Finishing Co. v. West Bend Mutual Insurance Co., 356 Ill. App.3d 471, 825 N.E.2d 1246, 292 Ill. Dec. 235 (2005).

Kentucky: Adkins v. Kentucky National Insurance Co., 220 S.W.3d 296 (Ky. App. 2007).

Louisiana: Gaylord Container Corp. v. CNA Insurance Cos., 807 So.2d 864 (La. App.), *writ denied* 803 So.2d 31 (La. 2001).

Maryland: CIGNA Property & Casualty Cos. v. Zeitler, 730 A.2d 248 (Md. App. 1999).

Michigan: Casey v. Auto Owners Insurance Co. 729 N.W.2d 277 (Mich. App. 2006), *appeal denied* 2007 WL 1550959 (Mich. May 30, 2007).

Minnesota: Schupp v. United Fire and Casualty Co., 821 N.W.2d 824 (Minn. App. 2012); Bast v. Capitol Indemnity Corp., 562 N.W.2d 24 (Minn. App. 1997).

Montana: Robertus v. Farmers Union Mutual Insurance Co., 344 Mont. 157, 189 P.3d 582 (Mont. 2008); Thomas v. Northwestern National Insurance Co., 973 P.2d 804 (Mont. 1998).

New Jersey: Nova Development Group, Inc. v. J.J. Farber-Lottman Co., 2010 WL 680859 (N.J. Super. App. Div. Mar. 1, 2010); McClellan v. Feit, 870 A.2d 644 (N.J. Super. App. Div. 2005).

New York: Essex Insurance Co. v. Vickers, 959 N.Y.S.2d 525 (N.Y. App. Div. 2013); Bloom v. St. Paul Travelers Companies, 57 A.D.3d 819, 870 N.Y.S.2d 400 (N.Y. App. Div. 2008); Farmbrew Realty Corp. v. Tower Insurance Company of New York, 734 N.Y.S.2d 592 (N.Y. App. Div. 2001), *appeal denied* 771 N.E.2d 834 (N.Y.2002).

South Carolina: Todd v. Federated Mutual Insurance Co., 409 S.E.2d 361 (S.C. 1991).

Texas: Safeway Managing General Agency for State & County Mutual Fire Insurance Co. v. Cooper, 952 S.W.2d 861 (Tex. App. 1997).

211 See, e.g., Schock v. Penn Township Mutual Fire Insurance Association of Lancaster County, 24 A.2d 741, 743 (Pa. Super. 1942).

212 Mutual mistake, misrepresentation, or fraud may also justify reformation. For further discussion, see § 3.03[2] *supra*, where a policy fails to comply with or include statutorily mandated provisions, it may be reformed. However, evidence of such circumstances may be difficult to prove in most instances. See:

First Circuit: Tucard, L.L.C. v. Fidelity National Property and Casualty Insurance Co., 567 F. Supp.2d 215 (D. Mass. 2008).

Second Circuit: O'Brien v. Argo Partners, Inc., 736 F. Supp.2d 528 (E.D.N.Y. 2010); Creative Waste Management, Inv. v. Capitol Environmental Services, Inc., 429 F. Supp.2d 582 (S.D.N.Y.), *opinion supplemented* 458 F. Supp.2d 178 (S.D.N.Y. 2006).

Fourth Circuit: West Virginia Mutual Insurance Co. v. Vargas, 933 F. Supp.2d 847 (N.D. W. Va. 2013).

Fifth Circuit: Fruge v. Amerisure Mutual Insurance Co., 663 F.3d 743 (5th Cir. 2011); American International Specialty Lines Insurance Co. v. Blakesmore, 776 F. Supp.2d 215 (W.D. La. 2011), *reversed on other grounds and remanded* 462 Fed. Appx. 434 (5th Cir. 2012); Bordelon Marine, Inc. v. F/V Kenny Boy, 2011 WL 317744 (E.D. La. Feb. 1, 2011); Underwriters at Lloyds, Syndicate 242 v. Turtle Creek Partnership, Ltd., 716 F. Supp.2d 633 (S.D. Tex. 2010).

Sixth Circuit: Westfield Insurance Co. v. Enterprise 522, L.L.C., 2014 U.S. Dist. LEXIS 102961 (E.D. Mich. July 29, 2014); Ball v. Versar, Inc., 454 F. Supp.2d 783 (S.D. Ind. 2006).

Seventh Circuit: Milwaukee Metropolitan Sewerage District v. American International Specialty Lines Insurance Co., 598 F.3d 311 (7th Cir. 2010).

Eighth Circuit: Harleysville Worchester Insurance Co. v. Diamondhead Property Owners Ass'n, Inc., 741 F.3d 1336 (8th Cir. 2014); Cascades Development of Minnesota, L.L.C. v. National Specialty Insurance Co., 675 F.3d 1095 (8th Cir. 2012).

Ninth Circuit: Axis Surplus Insurance Co. v. St. Paul Fire and Marine Insurance Co., 947 F. Supp.2d 1129 (W.D. Wash. 2013).

Tenth Circuit: Reid v. Geico General Insurance Co., 499 F.3d 1163 (10th Cir. 2008).

State Courts:

California: Cedars-Sinai Medical Center v. Shewry, 41 Cal. Rptr.3d 48 (Cal. App. 2006).

Louisiana: Haddad v. Elkhateeb, 46 So.3d 244 (La. App. 2010); Palmer v. Martinez, 42 So.3d 1147 (La. App. 2010).

Missouri: Husch & Eppenberger, LLC v. Eisenberg, 213 S.W.3d 124 (Mo. App. 2006).

New York: Greater New York Mutual Insurance Co. v. United States Underwriters Insurance Co., 827 N.Y.S.2d 147 (N.Y. A.D. 2007).

North Carolina: Carter v. West American Insurance Co., 190 N.C. App. 532, 661 S.E.2d 264 (2008).

Oklahoma: Cox v. Kaiser-Francis Oil Co., 152 P.3d 274 (Okla. App. 2006).

Pennsylvania: Line Lexington Lumber & Millwork Co. v. Pennsylvania Publishing Corp., 301 A.2d 684, 687–688 (Pa. 1973).

Tennessee: Sikora v. Vanderploeg, 212 S.W.3d 277 (Tenn. App. 2006).

Washington: Oliver v. Flow International Corp., 155 P.3d 140 (Wash. App. 2006).

Wyoming: Broderick v. Dairyland Insurance Co., 270 P.3d 684 (Wyo. 2012).

[213] General Electric Credit Corp. v. Aetna Casualty & Surety Co., 263 A.2d 448, 455 (Pa. 1970).

> "[W]here one with an insurable interest . . . at the time of applying for a policy, advises the agent of the insurance company . . . of the desired coverage and truthfully states to such agent the facts involved in the risk, and the agent, acting within his real or apparent authority and without the actual or constructive knowledge of the applicant, fails to insert a requested provision, the insurer cannot set up such mistake in avoidance of the policy."

See also:

First Circuit: Tucard, L.L.C. v. Fidelity National Property and Casualty Insurance Co., 567 F. Supp.2d 215 (D. Mass. 2008).

Second Circuit: O'Brien v. Argo Partners, Inc., 736 F. Supp.2d 528 (E.D.N.Y. 2010); Creative Waste Management, Inv. v. Capitol Environmental Services, Inc., 429 F. Supp.2d 582 (S.D.N.Y.), *op. supplemented* 458 F. Supp.2d 178 (S.D.N.Y. 2006).

Third Circuit: Special Jet Services, Inc. v. Federal Insurance Co., 643 F.2d 977 (3d Cir. 1981).

Fourth Circuit: Charter Oak Fire Insurance Co. v. American Capital, Ltd., 2011 WL 856374 (D. Md. Mar. 9, 2011).

Fifth Circuit: American International Specialty Lines Insurance Co. v. Blakesmore, 776 F. Supp.2d 215 (W.D. La. 2011), *reversed on other grounds and remanded* 462 Fed. Appx. 434 (5th Cir. 2012).

Sixth Circuit: Ball v. Versar, Inc., 454 F. Supp.2d 783 (S.D. Ind. 2006).

Seventh Circuit: Milwaukee Metropolitan Sewerage District v. American International Specialty Lines Insurance Co., 598 F.3d 311 (7th Cir. 2010).

Eighth Circuit: Cascades Development of Minnesota, L.L.C. v. National Specialty Insurance, 675 F.3d 1095 (8th Cir. 2012).

Ninth Circuit: Davis v. Liberty Mutual Group, 2011 WL 809793 (W.D. Wash. Feb. 28, 2011).

Eleventh Circuit: Essex Insurance Co. v. Tina Marie Entertainment, L.L.C., 13 F. Supp.3d 1234 (M.D. Fla. 2014).

State Courts:

California: Cedars-Sinai Medical Center v. Shewry, 41 Cal. Rptr.3d 48 (Cal. App. 2006).

Louisiana: Haddad v. Elkhateeb, 46 So.3d 244 (La. App. 2010).

New York: Essex Insurance Co. v. Vickers, 103 A.D.3d 684, 959 N.Y.S.2d 525 (N.Y. App. Div. 2013); EGW Temporaries, Inc. v. RLI Insurance Co., 83 A.D.3d 1481, 919 N.Y.S.2d 752 (N.Y. App. Div. 2011); Greater New York Mutual Insurance Co. v. United States Underwriters Insurance Co., 36 A.D.3d 441 827 N.Y.S.2d 147 (N.Y. App. Div. 2007); John John, LLC v. Exit 63 Development, LLC, 35 A.D.3d 538, 826 N.Y.S.2d 656 (N.Y. App. Div. 2006).

North Carolina: Branch Banking and Trust Co. v. Chicago Title Insurance Co., 2011 WL 2207563 (N.C. App. June 7, 2011); Carter v. West American Insurance Co., 190 N.C. App. 532, 661 S.E.2d 264 (2008).

Oklahoma: Cox v. Kaiser-Francis Oil Co., 152 P.3d 274 (Okla. App. 2006).

Pennsylvania: Line Lexington Lumber & Millwork Co. v. Pennsylvania Publishing Corp., 301 A.2d 684, 687–688 (Pa. 1973).

Tennessee: Sikora v. Vanderploeg, 212 S.W.3d 277 (Tenn. App. 2006).

Washington: Oliver v. Flow International Corp., 155 P.3d 140 (Wash. App. 2006).

214 See, e.g., General Electric Credit Corp. v. Aetna Casualty & Surety Co., 263 A.2d 448, 458 (Pa. 1970).

215 See, e.g.: Reliance Insurance Co. v. Moessner 121 F.3d 895, 899 (3d Cir. 1997); Bensalem Township v. International Surplus Lines Insurance Co., 38 F.3d 1303, 1309 (3d Cir. 1994). See also, § 3.02[b] *supra*.

216 See:

First Circuit: Blais v. Hartford Fire Insurance Co., 2011 WL 1303135 (D. Mass. Mar. 30, 2011).

Second Circuit: Parks Real Estate Purchasing Group v. St. Paul Fire & Marine Insurance Co., 472 F.3d 33 (2d Cir. 2006); Endurance American Specialty Insurance Co. v. Century Surety Co., 2014 U.S. Dist. LEXIS 129628 (S.D.N.Y. Sept. 15, 2014).

Third Circuit: UPMC Health System v. Metropolitan Life Insurance Co., 391 F.3d 497, 502 (3d Cir. 2004); Reliance Insurance. Co. v. Moessner, 121 F.3d 895, 903 (3d Cir. 1997); Bensalem Township v. International Surplus Lines Insurance Co., 38 F.3d 1303, 1309 (3d Cir. 1994); Fry v. Phoenix Insurance Co., 2014 U.S. Dist. LEXIS 131504 (E.D. Pa. Sept. 19, 2014); Haines v. State Auto Property and Casualty Insurance Co., 2009 WL 1767534 (E.D. Pa. June 22, 2009).

Fourth Circuit: Lawson v. American General Assurance Co., 455 F. Supp.2d 526 (S.D. W. Va. 2006).

Fifth Circuit: Bradley v. Allstate Insurance Co., 620 F.3d 509 (5th Cir. 2010).

Sixth Circuit: Citizens Insurance Company of America v. MidMichigan Health Connect-Care Network Plan, 449 F.3d 688 (6th Cir. 2006); Eckstein v. Cincinnati Insurance Co., 469 F. Supp.2d 455 (W.D. Ky. 2007).

Seventh Circuit: Kimmel v. Western Reserve Life Assurance Company of Ohio, 678 F. Supp.2d 783 (N.D. Ind. 2010).

Eighth Circuit: Occidental Fire and Casualty Co. v. Soczynski, 765 F.3d 931 (8th Cir. 2014); Bethel v. Darwin Select Insurance Co., 735 F.3d 1035 (8th Cir. 2014); W3i Mobile, L.L.C. v. Westchester Fire Insurance Co., 632 F.3d 432 (8th Cir. 2011); R & J Enterprises v. General Casualty Company of Wisconsin, 627 F.3d 723 (8th Cir. 2011); North Star Mutual Insurance Co. v. Rose, 27 F. Supp.3d 1250 (W.D. Okla. 2014); American Economy Insurance Co. v. Rutledge, 2011 WL 2215019 (W.D. Okla. June 6, 2011).

Ninth Circuit: Apana v. TIG Insurance Co., 574 F.3d 679 (9th Cir. 2009); Nautilus Insurance Co. v. Hawk Transport Services, L.L.C., 2011 WL 2456376 (D. Haw. June 20, 2011).

Tenth Circuit: Fireman's Fund Insurance Co. v. Structural System Technology, Inc., 426 F. Supp.2d 1009 (D. Neb. 2006).

Eleventh Circuit: Office Depot, Inc. v. National Union Fire Insurance Company of Pittsburgh, Pa., 734 F. Supp.2d 1304 (S.D. Fla. 2010).

State Courts:

Arizona: Beaver v. American Family Mutual Insurance Co., 234 Ariz. 584, 324 P.3d 870 (Ariz. App. 2014); State Farm Fire & Casualty Insurance Co. v. Grabowski, 150 P.3d 275 (Ariz. App. 2007).

California: RNT Holdings, LLC v. United General Title Insurance Co., 179 Cal. Rptr.3d 175 (Cal. App. 2014); California Traditions, Inc. v. Claremont Liability Insurance Co., 2011 WL 2452684 (Cal. App. June 21, 2011); ACS Systems, Inc. v. St. Paul Fire & Marine Insurance Co., 53 Cal. Rptr.3d 786 (Cal. App. 2007); London Market Insurers v. Superior Court, 53 Cal. Rptr.3d 154 (Cal. App. 2007).

Colorado: Bailey v. Lincoln General Insurance Co., 255 P.3d 1039 (Colo. 2011); Hoang v. Assurance Company of America, 149 P.3d 798 (Colo. 2007).

Connecticut: Travelers Casualty and Surety Co. of America v. Netherlands Insurance Co., 312 Conn. 714, 95 A.3d 1031 (2014).

Florida: American Strategic Insurance Co. v. Lucas-Solomon, 927 So.2d 184 (Fla. Dist. App.), *review denied* 940 So.2d 1125 (Fla. 2006).

Georgia: American Strategic Insurance Corp. v. Helm, 327 Ga. App. 482, 759 S.E.2d 563 (2014).

Kentucky: Adkins v. Kentucky National Insurance Co., 220 S.W.3d 296 (Ky. App. 2007); Hugenberg v. West American Insurance Company/Ohio Casualty Group, 2006 WL 891074 (Ky. App. Apr. 7, 2006).

Massachusetts: Boston Gas Co. v. Century Indemnity Co, 454 Mass. 337, 910 N.E.2d 290 (2009).

Montana: Winter v. State Farm Mutual Automobile Insurance Co., 375 Mont. 351, 328 P.3d 665 (2014); Giacomelli v. Scottsdale Insurance Co., 354 Mont. 15, 221 P.3d 666 (2009).

Nevada: Powell v. Liberty Mutual Fire Insurance Co., 252 P.3d 668 (Nev. 2011).

New Jersey: Abouzaid v. Mansard Gardens Associates, L.L.C., 207 N.J. 67, 23 A.3d 338 (2011); Passaic Valley Sewerage Commissioners v. St. Paul Fire and Marine Insurance Co., 206 N.J. 596, 21 A.3d 1151 (2011); Charles Beseler Co. v. O'Gorman & Young, Inc., 911 A.2d 47 (N.J. 2006); S.T. Hudson Engineers, Inc. v. Pennsylvania National Mutual Casualty Co., 909 A.2d 1156 (N.J. Super. App. Div. 2006), *cert. denied* 917 A.2d 787 (N.J. 2007).

New Mexico: Rehders v. Allstate Insurance Co., 135 P.3d 237 (N.M. App.), *cert. granted* 136 P.3d 569 (N.M. 2006).

New York: ACC Construction Corp. v. Tower Insurance Co. of New York, 83 A.D.3d 443, 921 N.Y.S.2d 218 (N.Y. App. Div. 2011); City of New York v. Evanston Insurance Co., 830 N.Y.S.2d 299 (N.Y. App. Div. 2007).

Oklahoma: Porter v. Oklahoma Farm Bureau Mutual Insurance Co., 330 P.3d 511 (Okla. 2014); Andres v. Oklahoma Farm Bureau Mutual Insurance Co., 227 P.3d 1102 (Okla. App. 2009).

Pennsylvania: Tonkovic v. State Farm Mutual Automobile Insurance Co., 521 A.2d 920, 925 (Pa. 1987); Donegal Mutual Insurance Co. v. Baumhammers, 893 A.2d 797 (Pa. Super.), *alloc. granted* 908 A.2d 265 (Pa. 2006).

Vermont: Northern Security Insurance Co. v. Rosenthal, 186 Vt. 578, 980 A.2d 805 (2009).

Washington: No Boundaries, Ltd. v. Pacific Indemnity Co., 160 Wash. App. 951, 249 P.3d 689 (2011).

West Virginia: Jenkins v. State Farm Mutual Automobile Insurance Co., 632 S.E.2d 346 (W. Va. 2006).

Wisconsin: Bormann v. Sohns, 727 N.W.2d 341 (Wis. App. 2006).

See also, § 3.02[b] *supra*.

[217] *Id.*

[218] Bethel v. Darwin Select Insurance Co., 735 F.3d 1035 (8th Cir. 2014).

See also:

Eighth Circuit: Babinski v. American Family Insurance Group, 569 F.3d 349 (8th Cir.2009).

State Courts:

Minnesota: West Bend Mutual Insurance Co. v. Allstate Insurance Co., 776 N.W.2d 693 (Minn. 2009).

[219] See: Reliance Insurance Co. v. Moessner, 121 F.3d 895, 906 (3d Cir. 1997); Bensalem Township v. International Surplus Lines Ins. Co., 38 F.3d 1303, 1311–1312 (3d Cir. 1994).

[220] See Tonkovic v. State Farm Mutual Automobile Insurance Co., 521 A.2d 920, 925 (Pa. 1987).

[221] See:

Third Circuit: Bensalem Township v. International Surplus Lines Ins. Co., 38 F.3d 1303, 1311 (3d Cir. 1994).

State Court:

Colorado: Bailey v. Lincoln General Insurance Co., 255 P.3d 1039 (Colo. 2011).

Montana: Giacomelli v. Scottsdale Insurance Co., 354 Mont. 15, 221 P.3d 666 (2009).

Pennsylvania: Tonkovic v. State Farm Mutual Automobile Insurance Co., 521 A.2d 920, 922, 925 (Pa. 1987).

[222] See Reliance Insurance Co. v. Moessner, 121 F.3d 895, 906 (3d Cir. 1997). See also, § 3.02[2][a] *supra*; G-I Holdings, Inc. v. Reliance Insurance Co., 586 F.3d 247 (3d Cir. 2009).

[223] See § 7.10[2][b] *supra*.

CHAPTER 8

Comprehensive General Liability Insurance— The Pollution Exclusions

Chapter Contents

§ 8.01 Overview

Real estate-related entities need to be familiar with the various types of pollution exclusions used and in use in the marketplace. In fact, ownership, use, development, construction, operation, and sale of real estate can involve significant environmental issues and risks. Accordingly, it behooves the real estate-related entity to understand how its insurance policies might respond to these environmental issues.

This chapter focuses on forms of pollution exclusions historically used and currently in use in the insurance policies that a real estate-related entity might use, such as pollution exclusions in first-party property policies,[1] comprehensive general liability insurance policies,[2] and directors and officers or professional liability insurance policies.[3]

With regard to the forms no longer in use, those exclusions are still relevant and applicable. Indeed, many environmental claims involve latent losses that may not manifest themselves until years after the damages first commence, and many jurisdictions apply the continuous trigger theory to coverage, meaning all policies between the date the damages first commenced until the damages are discovered are responsible to respond to the loss.[4]

The distinction between first-party and third-party insurance policies[5] is important to remember because, as mentioned above, the exclusions discussed in this chapter are usually included in all types of first-party and third-party insurance policies. Accordingly, one should focus on the environmental exposure, claim, or liability at issue to determine which type would be the appropriate policy under which to consider submission of a claim. For example, a governmentally initiated cleanup action might require a third-party insurance policy if the cleanup efforts are directed at the groundwater. Additionally, a cleanup action initiated by a neighboring landowner or a bodily injury claim initiated by one exposed to materials emanating from one's property or operations would require consideration of submission to a third-party liability policy. On the other hand, a cleanup action initiated to clean up pollution confined to one's own property might require submission to one's first-party property insurance company.

This chapter first reviews the "qualified" pollution exclusion, including the "sudden and accidental" exception from which its "qualified" label has emanated,[6] its regulatory and drafting history,[7] and the case law construing it.[8] This chapter then reviews the so-called "absolute" pollution exclusion, including the policy language,[9] its regulatory and drafting history,[10] and the case law construing it.[11] This chapter further reviews the so-called "total" pollution exclusion, including the policy language,[12] its regulatory and drafting history,[13] and the case law construing it.[14]

§ 8.02 The "Qualified" Pollution Exclusion

Beginning in the early 1970s, most comprehensive general liability insurance policies contained a "qualified" pollution exclusion, which was limited in scope and attempted to exclude coverage for "releases" and "discharges" of "pollutants."[15] One such exclusionary provision that has been used provides:

> "This insurance does not apply to bodily injury or property damage arising out of the discharge, dispersal, release or escape of smoke, vapors, soots, fumes, acids, alkalis, toxic chemicals, liquids or gases, waste materials or other irritants, contaminants or pollutants into or upon land, the atmosphere or any water course or body of water, but this exclusion does not apply if such discharge, dispersal, release or escape is sudden and accidental."[16]

[1]—"Sudden and Accidental" Exception

The "qualified" pollution exclusion is denoted as "qualified" because it is limited in scope to wit, it contains an express exception for discharges or releases that are "sudden and accidental."[17] This "sudden and accidental" exception is the central litigated issue under the "qualified" pollution exclusion.

As a result of stringent enforcement of state and federal environmental statutes,[18] the insurance industry often took the position that the "qualified" pollution exclusion relieved its members of any coverage obligations for such liabilities.[19]

The principal disputes between policyholders and insurance companies over the exclusion are: (1) the meaning of "sudden" in the "sudden and accidental" exception;[20] and (2) whether "sudden and accidental" refers to the initial dumping of hazards or to the release into the environment.[21]

[2]—The Construction of "Sudden"

The first issue concerns the meaning of "sudden" within the "sudden and accidental" exception. The dispute over the meaning of "sudden" is whether the word connotes a temporal or time-related element requiring something "abrupt, immediate, or of short duration" or whether it merely rehashes the "occurrence" or fortuity requirement of "unexpected" and "unintended." If a court reads a temporal component into the exception, then damage occurring over an extended period of time, which would be typical of government-mandated cleanup under the various state and federal environmental statutes, would not be covered even if the pollution is unexpected and unintended. However, if no temporal limitation is imputed to the word "sudden," then as long as the damage was unexpected and unintended, the "qualified" pollution exclusion should not apply to bar coverage.[22]

Case law is split as to the meaning of "sudden" in the "qualified" pollution exclusion. Some courts hold the insurance company to their regulatory representations that the "qualified" pollution was meant to clarify pre-existing insurance coverage and did not restrict coverage for gradual pollution damage and apply the "sudden and accidental" exception to all unintended and unexpected pollution losses irrespective of the abruptness of the release.[23]

In its seminal case, using principles of regulatory estoppel, the New Jersey Supreme Court determined that the insurance industry misrepresented that the "sudden and accidental" polluters exclusion merely clarified pre-existing insurance coverage.[24] The court found that the insurance industry had failed to disclose its intent to restrict coverage for gradual pollution damage and determined that "[h]aving profited from that nondisclosure by maintaining pre-existing rates for substantially-reduced coverage, the industry justly should be required to bear the burden of its omission by providing coverage at a level consistent with its representations to regulatory authorities."[25]

In so holding, the court defined "sudden" as "connoting an event that begins abruptly or without prior notice or warning, but the duration of the event—whether it lasts an instant, a week, or a month—is not necessarily relevant to whether the inception of the event is sudden."[26]

Several courts have concurred with this position.[27] A number of courts, however, have found the "qualified" pollution exclusion requires that pollutant releases be temporally quick, typically holding that excluding the temporal aspect of "sudden" renders the term "mere surplusage."[28]

[3]—What Does "Sudden and Accidental" Modify?

The other main area of contention between policyholders and insurance companies with regard to the "sudden and accidental" pollution exclusion is whether it is the initial dumping of the pollutant or the subsequent release of that contaminant into the environment that must be "sudden and accidental." Some courts hold that "the relevant polluting event for purposes of the pollution exclusion clause is the release of pollutants from a containment area and not the initial placement of waste in that containment area."[29] This distinction is significant because if the relevant "release" of the pollutant is the initial deposit of material into the area of containment, no coverage would ever be afforded when a policyholder intentionally places wastes into a containment area, even if that party neither expected nor intended for the pollutants to escape from that containment area.[30] Other courts have found the exception ambiguous.[31] In contrast, a number of courts look to the initial "release" of the pollutant as the relevant point to test whether it was "sudden and accidental."[32]

§ 8.03 The "Absolute" Pollution Exclusion

[1]—Language

As litigation surrounding the scope of the "qualified" pollution exclusion continued, the insurance industry, through ISO, an insurance industry trade organization which drafts and revises standard-form liability insurance policies and endorsements (the successor to the Insurance Rating Bureau ("IRB") and the Mutual Insurance Rating Bureau ("MIRB")), drafted another pollution exclusion: the so-called "absolute" pollution exclusion. ISO specifically crafted this exclusion to exclude liability for government-directed cleanup of damage to the natural environment. The language of the standard form exclusion providing as follows:

"This insurance does not apply to:

▼

f. (1) 'Bodily injury' or 'property damage' arising out of the actual, alleged or threatened discharge, dispersal, seepage, migration, release or escape of pollutants:

(a) At or from any premises, site or location which is or was at any time owned or occupied by, or rented or loaned to, any insured;

(b) At or from any premises, site or location which is or was at any time used by or for any insured or others for the handling, storage, disposal, processing or treatment of waste;

(c) Which are or were at any time transported, handled, stored, treated, disposed of, or processed as waste by or for any insured or any person or organization for whom you may be legally responsible; or

(d) At or from any premises, site or location on which any insured or any contractors or subcontractors working directly or indirectly on any insured's behalf are performing operations:

(i) if the pollutants are brought on or to the premises, site or location in connection with such operations by such insured, contractor or subcontractor; or

(ii) if the operations are to test for, monitor, clean up, remove, contain, treat, detoxify or neutralize, or in any way respond to, or assess the effects of pollutants.

(2) Any loss, cost or expense arising out of any:

(a) Request, demand or order that any insured or others test for, monitor, clean up, remove, contain, treat, detoxify or neutralize, or in any way respond to, or assess the effects of pollutants; or

(b) Claim or suit by or on behalf of a governmental authority for damages because of testing for, monitoring, cleaning up, removing, containing, treating, detoxifying or neutralizing, or in any way responding to, or assessing the effects of pollutants.

"'Pollutants' means any solid, liquid, gaseous or thermal irritant or contaminant, including smoke, vapor, soot, fumes, acids, alkalis, chemicals and waste. Waste includes materials to be recycled, reconditioned or reclaimed."[33]

[2]—Regulatory and Drafting History

The name "absolute" pollution exclusion is a misnomer because it was never intended to exclude all pollution liabilities. Indeed, the insurance industry has so acknowledged. A senior analyst and representative of one of the largest insurance companies in the world testified that the name "absolute" pollution exclusion is an oxymoron, and is so characterized in company-sponsored training programs for claims representatives.[34] ISO has similarly admitted that the so-called "absolute" pollution exclusion was not absolute and that there were certain circumstances where coverage was afforded for pollution liabilities.[35]

At the time the "absolute" pollution exclusion was introduced to the nation's insurance regulators, the industry also submitted a companion pollution liability insurance buyback policy representing it as a designed restoration of the insurance coverage purportedly eliminated by the exclusion. However, as noted by a former Louisiana Insurance Commissioner, this companion policy only restored insurance coverage for injury or damage caused by a "pollution incident."[36] That term is defined in the policy as:

"'Pollution incident' means emission, discharge, release or escape of pollutants into or upon land, the atmosphere, or any watercourse or body of water, provided that such emission, discharge, release or escape results in 'environmental damage.'"[37]

In turn, "environmental damage" is defined as:

"'Environmental damage' means the injurious presence (injurious to the environment, not just the claimant) in or upon land, the atmosphere, or any watercourse or body of water of solid, liquid, gaseous or thermal contaminants, irritants or pollutants."[38]

The commissioner further noted that "[t]he exclusion should not be read more broadly than the policy which restores the deleted coverage," and suggested that the insurance industry should be estopped from asserting an interpretation of the "absolute" pollution exclusion that is contrary to the one given to the nation's insurance regulators.[39] In the commissioner's words:

> "When the ISO package was presented to regulators, it was represented that the buyback restored the coverage excluded by the ["absolute" pollution exclusion]; it was not represented that the buyback was more limited in scope than the exclusion."[40]

The "absolute" pollution exclusion was never intended to apply to products/completed-operations claims. ISO, which drafted the exclusion, represented that it does not bar coverage for products-completed operations claims.[41]

Nonetheless, the "absolute" pollution exclusion was written in such broad terms that it is susceptible to abuse. Insurance companies may argue that its language is broad enough to apply in situations far removed from government environmental enforcement actions. "The supposed definition [of the "absolute" pollution exclusion] has been expanded even further [by insurance companies] to mean if any potential pollutant, i.e. household bleach, is involved in the accident, the [insurance] company can rely on the [exclusion] to be relieved of responsibility."[42] These interpretations come despite the fact that the insurance industry secured approval of the "absolute" pollution exclusion by representing to regulators that it would not read the exclusion to bar coverage in situations outside those of typical, industrial pollution.[43]

[3]—Case Law

Some courts have construed the "absolute" pollution exclusion literally and applied it to non-environmental circumstances, ignoring the regulatory representations of the industry.[44] Other courts have limited application of the "absolute" pollution exclusion to traditional environmental losses.[45] These courts recognize that many of the key terms in the "absolute" pollution exclusion (i.e., "release," "discharge," "disposal," and "escape")[46] are environmental terms of art. Many of the terms are key terms for the imposition of liability under the Comprehensive Environmental Response, Compensation, and Liability Acct ("CERCLA").[47] For instance, the exclusion incorporates the concept of a "*threatened* discharge, disposal, release or a surge of pollutants." Liability for a mere *threat* of an injury is fundamental to modern environmental statutes, but is foreign to normal tort liability.[48] The incorporation of these environmental liability terms and concepts into the "absolute" pollution exclusion demonstrates that the exclusion was designed to be limited to injury for typical, industrial environmental damage.[49]

§ 8.04 The "Total" Pollution Exclusion

The "total" pollution exclusion, introduced in 1988, differs from the "absolute" pollution exclusion only in that it removes coverage for releases from products and for certain, off-site releases of pollutants. The exclusion excludes insurance for losses involving:

"(1) 'Bodily Injury' or 'property damage' which would not have occurred in whole or part but for the actual, alleged or threatened discharge, dispersal, seepage, migration, release or escape of pollutants at any time;

"(2) Any loss, or expense arising out of any:

(a) Request, demand or order that any insured or others test for, monitor, clean up, remove, contain, treat, detoxify or neutralize, or in any way respond to, or assess the effects of pollutants; or

(b) Claim or 'suit' by or on behalf of a governmental authority for damages because of testing for, monitoring, cleaning up, removing, containing, treating, detoxifying or neutralizing, or in any way responding to, or assessing the effects of pollutants.

"'Pollutants' means any solid, liquid, gaseous or thermal irritant or contaminant, including smoke, vapor, soot, fumes, acids, alkalis, chemicals and waste. Waste includes materials to be recycled, reconditioned or reclaimed."[50]

ISO, in setting forth the effect of the "Total Pollution Exclusion Endorsement," stated:

"[T]he endorsement eliminates the pollution coverage left in the policy by the [1985 so-called "absolute" pollution exclusion]—products/completed operations coverage and certain off-site discharges."[51]

Further, the National Association of Insurance Commissioners working group described the "total" pollution exclusion as "an option to delete the pollution coverage from the products and completed operations coverage. . . ."[52]

Case law construing the "total" pollution exclusion is somewhat mixed as to whether the exclusion applies solely to circumstances involving traditional environmental harm.[53] Some courts enforce it against liabilities not generally considered environmental, such as ingestion, inhalation, operations, and premises claims.[54] Other courts refuse to apply the exclusion to non-environmental liabilities.[55]

Notes

[1] See Chapter 4 *supra.*

[2] See Chapters 5–7 *supra*, and Chapter 9 *infra.*

[3] See Chapter 10 *infra.*

[4] See, e.g.:

Second Circuit: Sarinsky's Garage Inc. v. Erie Insurance Co., 691 F. Supp.2d 483 (S.D.N.Y. 2010).

Third Circuit: Koppers Co. v. Aetna Casualty & Surety Co., 158 F.3d 170, 176 (3d Cir. 1998).

Fifth Circuit: DPC Industries, Inc. v. American International Specialty Lines Insurance Co., 615 F.3d 609 (5th Cir. 2010).

Ninth Circuit: Hinkle v. Crum & Forster Holding, Inc., 747 F. Supp.2d 1132 (D. Alaska 2010).

Eleventh Circuit: Mears Transportation Group, Inc. v. Zurich American Insurance Co., 660 F. Supp.2d 1297 (M.D. Fla. 2009).

State Courts:

California: Montrose Chemical Corp. v. Admiral Insurance Co., 42 Cal. Rptr.2d 324, 347 (Cal. 1995); Frontier Oil Corp. v. RLI Insurance Co., 153 Cal. App.4th 1436, 63 Cal. Rptr.3d 816 (2007).

Montana: Montana Petroleum Tank Release Compensation Board v. Crumleys, Inc., 341 Mont. 33, 174 P.3d 948 (2008).

New Jersey: See, e.g., Morton International, Inc. v. General Accident Insurance Company of America, 629 A.2d 831 (N.J. 1993), *cert. denied* 512 U.S. 1245 (1994).

New York: Denihan Ownership Co. v. Commerce and Industry Insurance Co., 830 N.Y.S.2d 128 (N.Y. App. Div. 2007).

Oregon: Certain Underwriters at Lloyd's London and Excess Insurance Co. v. Massachusetts Bonding and Insurance Co., 235 Or. App. 99, 230 P.3d 103 (2010).

Washington: Puget Sound Energy, Inc. v. Alba General Insurance Co., 149 Wash.2d 135, 68 P.3d 1061 (2003) (*en banc*); Grey v. Leach, 158 Wash. App. 837, 244 P.3d 970 (2010).

5 See § 2.06 *supra*.

6 See § 8.02[1] *infra*.

7 See § 8.02[2] *infra*.

8 See § 8.02[3] *infra*.

9 See § 8.03[1] *infra*.

10 See § 8.03[2] *infra*.

11 See § 8.03[3] *infra*.

12 See § 8.04[1] *infra*.

13 See § 8.04[2] *infra*.

14 See § 8.04[3] *infra*.

15 See, e.g., Morton International, Inc. v. General Accident Insurance Company of America, 629 A.2d 831 (N.J. 1993), *cert. denied* 512 U.S. 1245 (1994).

16 Textron, Inc. v. Aetna Casualty And Surety Co., 754 A.2d 742, 744 (R.I. 2000). The court also discussed a comparable clause which provided:

"This insurance does not cover liability for:

(1) Personal Injury or Bodily Injury or loss of, damage to, or loss of use of property directly or indirectly caused by seepage, pollution or contamination, provided always that this paragraph (1) shall not apply to liability for Personal Injury or Bodily Injury or loss of or physical damage to or destruction of tangible property, or loss of use of such property damaged or destroyed where such seepage, pollution or contamination is caused by a sudden, unintended and unexpected happening during the period of this Insurance.

(2) The cost of removing, nullifying or cleaning-up seeping, polluting or contaminating substances unless the seepage, pollution or contamination is caused by a sudden, unintended and unexpected happening during the period of this Insurance." 754 A.2d at 745.

17 See, e.g., Morton International, Inc. v. General Accident Insurance Company of America, 629 A.2d 831 (N.J. 1993), *cert. denied* 512 U.S. 1245 (1994).

18 See, e.g., Comprehensive Environmental Response, Compensation, Liability Act ("CERCLA"), 42 U.S.C. §§ 9601 *et seq.* The statutes typically impose joint and several, retroactive, and significant liability on people and businesses in any way involved in the environmental problem. The scope of the statutes include distributors, manufacturers, producers, haulers, and disposers of any substance released into the environment and operators of disposal facilities.

19 See, e.g., Morton International, Inc. v. General Accident Insurance Company of America, 629 A.2d 831, 852–853 (N.J. 1993), *cert. denied* 512 U.S. 1245 (1994).

20 *Id.*, 629 A.2d at 847–848 (N.J. 1993).

21 See, e.g., Compass Insurance Co. v. City of Littleton, 984 P.2d 606 (Colo. 1999).

22 In fact, based on the insurance industry's representations to regulators that this exclusion would only bar intentional pollution—and, thus, that the word "sudden" would impose no temporal limitation to coverage under general liability insurance policies—a number of courts throughout the country rejected the insurance industry's attempts to escape these

liabilities. See, e.g., Morton International, Inc. v. General Accident Insurance Company of America, 629 A.2d 831, 852–853 (N.J. 1993), *cert. denied* 512 U.S. 1245 (1994) (estopping insurance companies from contradicting its regulatory position when seeking approval of the language).

[23] Morton International, Inc. v. General Accident Insurance Company of America, 629 A.2d 831, 852–853 (N.J. 1993), *cert. denied* 512 U.S. 1245 (1994) (estopping insurance companies from contradicting its regulatory position when seeking approval of the language). The courts in previous cases also found the industry's representations to state insurance regulators to be "dishonest." See:

Eleventh Circuit: Claussen v. Aetna Casualty & Surety Co., 676 F. Supp. 1571, 1573 n.4 (S.D. Ga. 1987), *rev'd on other grounds* 888 F.2d 747 (11th Cir. 1989).

State Courts:

California: AIU Insurance Co. v. Superior Court, 799 P.2d 1253 (Cal. 1990).

[24] Morton International, Inc. v. General Accident Insurance Company of America, 629 A.2d 831, 852–853 (N.J. 1993), *cert. denied* 512 U.S. 1245 (1994).

[25] *Id.*, 629 A.2d at 876.

[26] *Id.*, 629 A.2d at 847.

[27] See:

Third Circuit: Simon Wrecking Co. v. AIU Insurance Co., 530 F. Supp.2d 706 (E.D. Pa. 2008); Simon Wrecking Co. v. AIU Insurance Co., 350 F. Supp.2d 624 (E.D. Pa. 2004); *In re* Tutu Water Wells Contamination Litigation, 78 F. Supp.2d 456 (D.V.I. Nov. 29, 1999).

Fourth Circuit: Ross Development Corp. v. PCS Nitrogen, Inc., 526 Fed. Appx. 299 (4th Cir. 2013).

Seventh Circuit: Huntzinger v. Hastings Mutual Insurance Co., 143 F.3d 302 (7th Cir. 1998); Keystone Consolidated Industries, Inc. v. Employers Insurance Company of Wausau, 470 F. Supp.2d 873 (C.D. Ill. 2007).

Ninth Circuit: Teck Metals, Ltd. v. Certain Underwriters at Lloyd's, London, 735 F. Supp.2d 1246 (E.D. Wash. 2010); MAPCO Alaska Petroleum, Inc. v. Central National Insurance Company of Omaha, 795 F. Supp. 941 (D. Alaska 1991); Pacific Employers Insurance Co. v. Servco Pacific, Inc., 273 F. Supp.2d 1149 (D. Haw. 2003).

Tenth Circuit: Blackhawk-Central City Sanitation District v. American Guarantee & Liability Insurance Co., 214 F.3d 1183 (10th Cir. 2000); American Universal Insurance Co. v. Whitewood Custom Treaters, Inc., 707 F. Supp. 1140 (D.S.D. 1989).

State Courts:

Alabama: Alabama Plating Co. v. United States Fidelity & Guaranty Co., 690 So.2d 331 (Ala. 1996).

Alaska: Sauer v. Home Indemnity Co., 841 P.2d 176 (Alaska 1992).

Colorado: Cotter Corp. v. American Empire Surplus Lines Insurance Co., 90 P.3d 814 (Colo. 2004) (*en banc*); Public Service Company of Colorado v. Wallis & Companies, 986 P.2d 924 (Colo. 1999); Hecla Mining Co. v. New Hampshire Insurance Co., 811 P.2d 1083 (Colo. 1991).

Georgia: Claussen v. Aetna Casualty & Surety Co., 380 S.E.2d 686 (Ga. 1989), *rev'd on other grounds* 888 F.2d 747 (11th Cir. 1989); Lumbermens Mutual Casualty Co. v. Plantation Pipeline Co., 447 S.E. 2d 89 (Ga. App. 1994).

Illinois: Outboard Marine Corp. v. Liberty Mutual Insurance Co., 607 N.E.2d 1204 (Ill. 1992); St. Paul Fire & Marine Insurance Co. v. Lefton Iron & Metal Co., 694 N.E.2d 1049 (Ill. App.), *appeal denied* 705 N.E.2d 449 (Ill. 1998).

Indiana: American States Insurance Co. v. Kiger, 662 N.E.2d 945 (Ind. 1996).

New Hampshire: Hudson v. Farm Family Mutual Insurance Co., 697 A.2d 501 (N.H. 1997).

Oregon: Employers Insurance of Wausau v. Tektronix, Inc., 156 P.3d 105 (Or. App. 2007); St. Paul Fire Insurance Co. v. McCormick & Baxter Creosoting Co., 923 P.2d 1200 (Or. 1996).

Pennsylvania: Sunbeam Corp. v. Liberty Mutual Insurance Co., 781 A.2d 1189, 1195 (Pa. 2001).

Rhode Island: Textron, Inc. v. Aetna Casualty & Surety Co., 754 A.2d 742 (R.I. 2000).

South Carolina: Helena Chemical Corp. v. Allianz Underwriters Insurance Co., 594 S.E.2d 455 (S.C. 2004); Greenville County v. Insurance Reserve Fund, 443 S.E.2d 552 (S.C. 1994).

Washington: Queen City Farms, Inc. v. Central National Insurance Company of Omaha, 882 P.2d 703 (Wash. 1994).

West Virginia: Joy Technologies, Inc. v. Liberty Mutual Insurance Co., 421 S.E.2d 493 (W. Va. 1992).

Wisconsin: Just v. Land Reclamation, Ltd., 456 N.W.2d 570 (Wis. 1990).

[28] See, e.g.:

First Circuit: Barrett Paving Materials, Inc. v. Continental Insurance Co., 488 F.3d 59 (1st Cir. 2007); A. Johnson & Co. v. Aetna Casualty & Surety Co., 933 F.2d 66 (1st Cir. 1991); Prime Tanning Co. v. Liberty Mutual Insurance Co., 750 F. Supp.2d 198 (D. Me. 2010); House of Clean, Inc. v. St. Paul Fire and Marine Insurance Co., 705 F. Supp.2d 102 (D. Mass. 2010).

Second Circuit: Bedford Affiliates v. Manheimer, 205 F.3d 1321 (2d Cir. 2000); Century Indemnity Co. v. Liberty Mutual Insurance Co., 708 F. Supp.2d 202 (D.R.I. 2010); Mahl Brothers Oil Co. v. St. Paul Fire & Marine Insurance Co., 307 F. Supp.2d 474 (W.D.N.Y. 2004).

Fourth Circuit: Asbestos Removal Corporation of America, Inc. v. Guaranty National Insurance Co., 846 F. Supp. 33 (E.D. Va. 1994), *aff'd* 48 F.3d 1215 (4th Cir. 1995).

Fifth Circuit: Fair Operating, Inc. v. Mid-Continent Casualty Co., 193 Fed. Appx. 302, 2006 WL 2242547 (5th Cir. 2006); Primrose Operating Co. v. National American Insurance Co., 382 F.3d 546 (5th Cir. 2004).

Sixth Circuit: Mueller Copper Tube Products, Inc. v. Pennsylvania Manufacturers Association Insurance Co., 254 Fed. Appx. 491, 2007 WL 3390942 (6th Cir. 2007); Transamerica Insurance Co. v. Duro Bag Manufacturing Co., 50 F.3d 370 (6th Cir. 1995).

Eighth Circuit: Aetna Casualty & Surety Co. v. General Dynamics Corp., 968 F.2d 707 (8th Cir. 1992).

Ninth Circuit: Smith v. Hughes Aircraft Co., 22 F.3d 1432 (9th Cir. 1993); Nammo Talley, Inc. v. Allstate Insurance Co., 99 F. Supp.3d 999 (D. Ariz. 2015); MAPCO Alaska Petroleum, Inc. v. Central National Insurance Company of Omaha, 795 F. Supp. 941 (D. Alaska 1991).

Tenth Circuit: Mesa Oil, Inc. v. Insurance Company of North America, 123 F.3d 1333 (10th Cir. 1997); Coffeyville Resources Refining & Marketing, L.L.C. v. Liberty Surplus Insurance Corp., 714 F. Supp.2d 1119 (D. Kan. 2010).

State Courts:

California: Frontier Oil Corp. v. RLI Insurance Co., 153 Cal. App.4th 1436, 63 Cal. Rptr.3d 816 (2007); Travelers Casualty & Surety Co. v. Superior Court of Santa Clara County, 75 Cal. Rptr.2d 54 (Cal. App. 1998).

Connecticut: Buell Industries, Inc. v. Greater New York Mutual Insurance Co., 791 A.2d 489, 498–499 (Conn. 2002); Zero-Max, Inc. v. Liberty Mutual Insurance Co., 1999 WL 1246922 (Conn. Super. Dec. 6, 1999).

Delaware: E.I. du Pont de Nemours & Co. v. Allstate Insurance Co., 693 A.2d 1059 (Del. 1997).

Florida: Dimmitt Chevrolet, Inc. v. Southeastern Fidelity Insurance Co., 636 So.2d 700 (Fla. 1994).

Illinois: Emerson Electric Co. v. Aetna Casualty & Surety Co., 815 N.E.2d 924 (Ill. App. 2004) (applying Missouri Law).

Idaho: North Pacific Insurance Co. v. Mai, 939 P.2d 570 (Idaho 1997).

Iowa: Iowa Comprehensive Petroleum Underground Storage Tank Fund Board v. Farmland Mutual Insurance Co., 568 N.W.2d 815 (Iowa 1997).

Kansas: Farm Bureau Mutual Insurance Co. v. Laudick, 859 P.2d 410 (Kan. App. 1993).

Louisiana: Hinds v. Clean Land Air Water Corp., 693 So.2d 321 (La. App. 1997).

Massachusetts: Nashua Corp. v. First State Insurance Co., 648 N.E.2d 1272 (Mass. 1995); Lumbermens Mutual Casualty Co. v. Belleville Industries, Inc., 555 N.E.2d 568 (Mass. 1990).

Michigan: Upjohn Co. v. New Hampshire Insurance Co., 476 N.W.2d 392 (Mich. 1991); Auto-Owners Insurance Co. v. Clare, 521 N.W.2d 480 (Mich. 1994).

Minnesota: Anderson v. Minnesota Insurance Guarantee Association, 534 N.W.2d 706 (Minn. 1995); Westling Manufacturing Co. v. Western National Mutual Insurance Co., 581 N.W.2d 39 (Minn. App. 1998); Board of Regents of University of Minnesota v. Royal Insurance Company of America, 517 N.W.2d 888 (Minn. 1994).

Montana: Travelers Casualty & Surety Co. v. Ribi Immunochem Research, Inc., 108 P.3d 469, (Mont. 2005); Sokoloski v. American West Insurance Co., 980 P.2d 1043 (Mont. 1999).

New Mexico: United Nuclear Corp. v. Allstate Insurance Co., 149 N.M. 574, 252 P.3d 798 (N.M. App. 2011) (temporal limitation).

New York: Northville Industries Corp. v. National Union Fire Insurance Co., 679 N.E.2d 1044 (N.Y. 1997).

North Carolina: Home Indemnity Co. v. Hoechst Celanese Corp., 494 S.E.2d 774 (N.C. App. 1998); Waste Management of Carolinas, Inc. v. Peerless Insurance Co., 340 S.E.2d 374 (N.C. 1986).

Ohio: Hybud Equipment Corp. v. Sphere Drake Insurance Co., 597 N.E.2d 1096 (Ohio 1992), *cert. denied* 507 U.S. 987 (1993).

Oklahoma: Kerr-McGee Corp. v. Admiral Insurance Co., 905 P.2d 760 (Okla. 1995).

Tennessee: Drexel Chemical Co. v. Bituminous Insurance Co., 933 S.W.2d 471 (Tenn. App. 1996).

Texas: Gulf Metals Industries, Inc. v. Chicago Insurance Co., 993 S.W.2d 800 (Tex. App. 1999).

Utah: Sharon Steel Corp. v. Aetna Casualty & Surety Co., 931 P.2d 127 (Utah 1997).

Wyoming: Sinclair Oil Corp. v. Republic Insurance Co., 929 P.2d 535 (Wyo. 1996).

[29] See, e.g., Compass Insurance Co. v. City of Littleton, 984 P.2d 606, 617 (Colo. 1999).

[30] See:

Sixth Circuit: City of Albion v. Guaranty National Insurance Co., 73 F. Supp.2d 846 (W.D. Mich. 1999).

Seventh Circuit: Huntzinger v. Hastings Mutual Insurance Co., 143 F.3d 302 (7th Cir. 1998); Patz v. St. Paul Fire & Marine Insurance Co., 15 F.3d 699 (7th Cir. 1994).

Eighth Circuit: Bell Lumber & Pole Co. v. United States Fire Insurance Co., 60 F.3d 437 (8th Cir. 1995).

Ninth Circuit: Nammo Talley, Inc. v. Allstate Insurance Co., 99 F. Supp.3d 999 (D. Ariz. 2015).

Tenth Circuit: Broderick Investment Co. v. Hartford Accident & Indemnity Co., 954 F.2d 601 (10th Cir.), *cert. denied* 506 U.S. 856 (1992).

State Courts:

California: California v. Allstate Insurance Co., 45 Cal.4th 1008, 201 P.3d 1147, 90 Cal. Rptr.3d 1 (2009).

Colorado: Compass Insurance Co. v. City of Littleton, 984 P.2d 606, 617 (Colo. 1999); Cotter Corp. v. American Empire Surplus Lines Insurance Co., 90 P.3d 814 (Colo. 2004) (*en banc*).

Illinois: Kim v. State Farm Fire & Casualty Co., 728 N.E.2d 530 (Ill. App. 2000).

Massachusetts: OneBeacon America Insurance Co. v. Narragansett Electric Co., 2010 Mass. Super. LEXIS 230 (Mass Super. Suffolk Cty. Aug. 25, 2010).

Michigan: South Macomb Disposal Authority v. American Insurance Co., 572 N.W.2d 686 (Mich. App. 1997), *appeal denied* 586 N.W.2d 919 (Mich. 1998); Traverse City Light & Power Board v. Home Insurance Co., 530 N.W.2d 150 (Mich. App. 1995), *appeal denied* 549 N.W.2d 563 (Mich. 1996).

Minnesota: Wakefield Pork, Inc. v. Ram Mutual Insurance Co., 731 N.W.2d 154 (Minn. App. 2007).

Rhode Island: Textron, Inc. v. Aetna Casualty & Surety Co., 754 A.2d 742, 750 (R.I. 2000).

[31] See, e.g., Hudson v. Farm Family Mutual Insurance Co., 697 A.2d 501 (N.H. 1997).

[32] See:

First Circuit: St. Paul Fire & Marine Insurance Co. v. Warwick Dyeing Corp., 26 F.3d 1195 (1st Cir. 1994).

Second Circuit: Emerson Enterprises, LLC v. Kenneth Crosby-New York, Inc., 386 F. Supp.2d 151 (W.D.N.Y. 2005).

Fourth Circuit: Ross Development Corp. v. PCS Nitrogen, Inc., 526 Fed. Appx. 299 (4th Cir. 2013).

Fifth Circuit: United States Fidelity & Guarantee Co. v. B & B Oil Well Service, Inc., 910 F. Supp. 1172 (S.D. Miss. 1995).

Sixth Circuit: Mueller Copper Tube Products, Inc. v. Pennsylvania Manufacturers Association Insurance Co., 254 Fed. Appx. 491 2007 WL 3390942 (6th Cir. 2007); Transamerica Insurance Co. v. Duro Bag Manufacturing Co., 50 F.3d 370 (6th Cir. 1995).

Ninth Circuit: Teck Metals, Ltd. v. Certain Underwriters at Lloyd's, London, 735 F. Supp.2d 1246 (E.D. Wash. 2010).

State Courts:

California: Standun, Inc. v. Fireman's Fund Insurance Co., 73 Cal. Rptr.2d 116 (Cal. App. 1998); Travelers Casualty & Surety Co. v. Superior Court of Santa Clara County, 75 Cal. Rptr.2d 54 (Cal. App. 1998).

Delaware: E.I. du Pont de Nemours & Co. v. Allstate Ins. Co., 693 A.2d 1059 (Del. 1997).

Maine: Travelers Indemnity Co. v. Dingwell, 414 A.2d 220 (Me. 1980).

Ohio: M&M Metals, Inc. v. Continental Casualty Co., 2008 Ohio App. LEXIS 973 (Ohio App. Mar. 14, 2008).

[33] See ISO Form CG 00 01 10 01. See also, Reliance Insurance Co. v. Moessner, 121 F.3d 895 (3d Cir. 1997).

[34] Deposition testimony of James G. King, Senior Analyst, Aetna Casualty & Surety Co., taken July 17, 1991 at 25–28.

> "I . . . talk about what is called the, quote, absolute pollution exclusion. . . . [M]ore than anything else I'm trying to get across the fact that even though it's called a pollution exclusion, there are still things that are covered. . . . '[P]ollution exclusion'

is another oxymoron because it's not a total exclusion, because there are situations where coverage could be available."

See Hi-Mill Manufacturing Co. v. Aetna Casualty & Surety Co., 884 F. Supp. 1109 (E.D. Mich. 1995), *aff'd* 98 F.3d 1341 (6th Cir. 1996).

35 Statement of Robert Miller, ISO Regional Vice President for the Southern Region, to the Louisiana Insurance Commissioner, Sept. 6, 1995, Tr., p. 57.

"In the aftermath of the elimination of the sudden and accidental qualification, the new exclusion has been at times mislabeled as absolute. This is an unfortunate misnomer. Given the coverage exceptions I mentioned earlier, this is not an absolute pollution exclusion."

36 James H. Brown, Louisiana Insurance Commissioner, Letter to the Editor, *National Underwriter Property & Casualty Edition,* April 22, 1996, p. 30.

"When the Insurance Services Office submitted the [absolute pollution exclusion to insurance regulators] in the mid-1980s, it also submitted a buyback policy to restore the coverage carved out by the exclusion. The pollution liability buyback policy covers bodily injury and property damage resulting only from a 'pollution incident.'"

37 *Id.*

38 *Id.*

39 *Id.*

40 *Id.*, at 54.

41 ISO Submission to Pennsylvania Insurance Department of 11/3/88, 1989-1 NAIC Proc. 860, 869.

"Under the current program, the basic CGL policy—both in its simplified and pre-simplified versions—contains an exclusion for pollution emissions from the insured's premises and from waste facilities. That exclusion does not run to the products liability/completed operations exposure, nor does it preclude coverage for certain contracting operations. Cleanup costs are also specifically excluded. That's the provision that has been approved for use countrywide for over three years."

42 James H. Brown, Louisiana Insurance Commissioner, Letter to the Editor, *National Underwriter Property & Casualty Edition,* May 1996, p. 16.

43 "Hearing to Consider, Discuss, and Act on Commercial General Liability Forms Filed by the Insurance Services Office, Inc.," (Oct. 31, 1985).

44 See:

First Circuit: United States Liability Insurance Co. v. Bourbeau, 49 F.3d 786 (1st Cir. 1995); Clark's Cars & Parts, Inc. v. Monticello Insurance Co., 2005 WL 2972988 (D. Me. Nov. 4, 2005); Essex Insurance Co. v. Tri-Town Corp., 863 F. Supp. 38 (D. Mass. 1994).

Second Circuit: Gotham Insurance Co. v. GLNX, Inc., 1993 WL 312243 (S.D.N.Y. Aug. 6, 1993).

Third Circuit: United States Fidelity & Guaranty Association v. Lehigh Valley Ice Arena, Inc., 121 Fed. Appx 976 (3d Cir. 2005); Mark I Restoration SVC v. Assurance Company of America, 112 Fed. Appx. 153 (3d Cir. 2004); Edwards & Caldwell LLC v. Gulf Insurance Co., 2005 WL 2090636 (D.N.J. Aug. 29, 2005); Kaytes v. Scottsdale Insurance Co., 1997 WL 763022 (E.D. Pa. Dec. 9, 1997) (absolute pollution exclusion barred coverage for bodily injury from ingestion of lead paint); Brown v. American Motorists Insurance Co., 930 F. Supp. 207 (E.D. Pa. 1996); St. Leger v. American Fire & Casualty Insurance Co., 870 F. Supp. 641 (E.D. Pa. 1994), *aff'd* 111 F.3d 125 (3d Cir.), *cert. denied* 522 U.S. 950 (1997); Townsends of Arkansas, Inc. v. Millers Mutual Insurance Co., 823 F. Supp. 233 (D. Del. 1993), *aff'd* 26 F.3d 123 (3d Cir. 1994); Prudential-LMI Commercial Insurance Co. v. Meadowood Condominium Association, 1992 WL 189490 (E.D. Pa. Aug. 3, 1992).

Fourth Circuit: National Electric Manufacturers Association v. Gulf Underwriters Insurance Co., 162 F.3d 821 (4th Cir. 1998); Assicurazioni Generali, S.p.A. v. Neil, 160 F.3d 997 (4th Cir. 1998); New NGC, Inc. v. Ace American Insurance Co., 105 F. Supp.3d 552 (W.D.N.C. 2015); Firemen's Insurance Company of Washington, D.C. v. Kline & Son Cement Repair, Inc., 474 F. Supp.2d 779 (E.D. Va. 2007); Whiteville Oil Co. v. Federated Mutual Insurance Co., 889 F. Supp. 241 (E.D.N.C. 1995), *aff'd* 87 F.3d 1310 (4th Cir. 1996).

Fifth Circuit: Columbia Casualty Co. v. Georgia & Florida RailNet, Inc., 542 F.3d 106 (5th Cir. 2008); Noble Energy, Inc. v. Bituminous Casualty Co., 529 F.3d 642 (5th Cir. 2008); United National Insurance Co. v. Hydro Tank, Inc., 525 F.3d 400 (5th Cir. 2008); National Union Fire Insurance Company of Pittsburgh, Pennsylvania v. United States Liquids, Inc., 88 Fed. Appx. 725 (5th Cir. 2004); Certain Underwriters at Lloyd's London v. C.A. Turner Construction Co., 112 F.3d 184 (5th Cir. 1997); Constitution State Insurance Co. v. Iso-Tex, Inc., 61 F.3d 405 (5th Cir. 1995); American States Insurance Co. v. Nethery, 79 F.3d 473 (5th Cir. 1996); Nautilus Insurance Co. v. Country Oaks Apartments, Ltd., 556 F. Supp.2d 611 (W.D. Tex. 2008); Acceptance Insurance Co. v. Powe Timber Co., 403 F. Supp.2d 552 (S.D. Miss. 2005), *aff'd* 2007 WL 624992 (5th Cir. Feb. 21, 2007); American States Insurance Co. v. F.H.S., Inc., 843 F. Supp. 187 (S.D. Miss. 1994); United National Insurance Co. v. Motiva Enterprises, L.L.C., 2006 WL 83482 (S.D. Tex. Jan. 12, 2006); Mt. Hawley Insurance Co. v. Wright Materials, Inc., 2005 WL 2805565 (N.D. Tex. Oct. 27, 2005); West Texas Agriplex v. Mid-Continent Casualty Co., 2004 WL 1515122 (N.D. Tex. July 7, 2004); Williams v. Brown's Dairy, 2003 WL 22717718 (E.D. La. Nov. 14, 2003); Hamm v. Allstate Insurance Co., 286 F. Supp.2d 790 (N.D. Tex. 2003); Amoco Production Co. v. Hydroblast Corp., 90 F. Supp.2d 727 (N.D. Tex. 1999), *aff'd* 226 F.3d 642 (5th Cir. 2000) (finding that absolute pollution exclusions barred coverage for claims of accidental workplace exposure to chemicals); Crown Central Petroleum Corp. v. Rust Scaffold Builders, Inc., 951 F. Supp. 636 (S.D. Tex. 1996).

Sixth Circuit: United States Fire Insurance Co. v. Warren, 87 Fed. Appx. 487 (6th Cir. 2003); United States Fidelity & Guaranty Co. v. Jones Chemicals, Inc., 194 F.3d 1315 (6th Cir. 1999); Park-Ohio Industries, Inc. v. Home Indemnity Co., 975 F.2d 1215 (6th Cir. 1992); Bituminous Casualty Corp. v. RPS Co., 915 F. Supp. 882 (W.D. Ky. 1996); Transportation Insurance Co. v. Valentine Investments, L.L.C., 2005 WL 2218913 (E.D. Mich. Sept. 12, 2005), *aff'd* 205 Fed. Appx. 362 (6th Cir. 2006); United Longaberger Co. v. United States Fidelity & Guaranty Co., 31 F. Supp.2d 595 (S.D. Ohio 1998), *aff'd* 201 F.3d 441 (6th Cir. 1999).

Seventh Circuit: Housing Authority Risk Retention Group, Inc. v. Chicago Housing Authority, 378 F.3d 596 (7th Cir. 2004); Pipefitters Welfare Educational Fund v. Westchester Fire Insurance Co., 976 F.2d 1037 (7th Cir. 1992).

Eighth Circuit: United Fire and Casualty Co. v. Titan Contractors Service, Inc., 751 F.3d 880 (8th Cir. 2014); Continental Insurance Co. v. Shapiro Sales Co., 2005 U.S. Dist. LEXIS 43015 (E.D. Mo. Sept. 26, 2005).

Ninth Circuit: City of Yakima v. Lexington Insurance Co., 80 Fed. Appx. 7 (9th Cir. 2003); Lewis v. Hartford Casualty Insurance Co., 2006 WL 249516 (N.D. Cal. Jan. 31, 2006); East Quincy Services District v. Continental Insurance Co., 864 F. Supp. 976 (E.D. Cal. 1994); Allen v. Scottsdale Insurance Co., 307 F. Supp.2d 1170 (Haw. 2004).

Tenth Circuit: Blackhawk-Central City Sanitation District v. American Guarantee & Liability Insurance Co., 214 F.3d 1183 (10th Cir. 2000); Bituminous Casualty Corp. v. St. Clair Lime Co., 69 F.3d 547 (10th Cir. 1995); City of Salina v. Maryland Casualty Co., 856 F. Supp. 1467 (D. Kan. 1994).

Eleventh Circuit: Admiral Insurance Co. v. Feit Management Co., 321 F.3d 1326 (11th Cir. 2003); Auto Owners Insurance Co. v. City of Tampa Housing Authority, 231 F.3d 1298 (11th Cir. 2000); Technical Coating Applicators, Inc. v. United States Fidelity & Guaranty Co., 157 F.3d 843 (11th Cir. 1998); West American Insurance Co. v. Band & Desenberg, 138 F.3d 1428 (11th Cir. 1998); Haman, Inc. v. St. Paul Fire & Marine Insurance Co., 18 F. Supp.2d 1306 (N.D. Ala. 1998); Shalimar Contractors, Inc. v. American States Insurance Co., 975 F. Supp. 1450 (M.D. Ala. 1997), *aff'd 158* F.3d 588 (11th Cir. 1998); Kruger Commodities, Inc. v. United States Fidelity & Guaranty Co., 923 F. Supp. 1474 (M.D. Ala. 1996); American Home Assurance Co. v. Devcon International, Inc., 1993 WL 401872 (S.D. Fla. Sept. 28, 1993), *aff'd* 28 F. 3d 118 (11th Cir. 1994); Owners Insurance Co. v. Farmer, 173 F. Supp.2d 1330 (N.D. Ga. 2001).

State Courts:

California: Garamendi v. Golden Eagle Insurance Co., 25 Cal. Rptr.3d 642 (Cal. App. 2005); Bechtel Petroleum Operations, Inc. v. Continental Insurance Co., 117 Cal. Rptr.2d 399 (Cal. App. 2002); MacKinnon v. Truck Insurance Exchange, 115 Cal. Rptr.2d 369 (Cal. App. 2002), *rev'd, vacated on other grounds* 3 Cal. Rptr.3d 228 (Cal. 2003); Employers Casualty Co. v. St. Paul Fire & Marine Insurance Co., 52 Cal. Rptr.2d 17 (Cal. App. 1996).

Colorado: TerraMatrix, Inc. v. United States Fire Insurance Co., 939 P.2d 483 (Colo. App. 1997).

Florida: Deni Associates v. State Farm Fire & Casualty Insurance Co., 711 So.2d 1135 (Fla. 1998).

Georgia: Reed v. Auto-Owners Insurance Co., 667 S.E.2d 90 (Ga. 2008); American States Insurance Co. v. Zippro Construction Co., 455 S.E.2d 133 (Ga. App. 1995); Perkins Hardwood Lumber Co. v. Bituminous Casualty Corp., 378 S.E.2d 407 (Ga. App. 1989).

Illinois: Connecticut Specialty Insurance Co. v. Loop Paper Recycling, Inc., 824 N.E. 2d 1125 (Ill. App 2005); Economy Preferred Insurance Co. v. Grandadam, 656 N.E.2d 787 (Ill. App. 1995).

Iowa: Bituminous Casualty Corp. v. Sand Livestock Systems, Inc., 728 N.W.2d 216 (Iowa 2007).

Kansas: Atlantic Avenue Associates v. Central Solutions, Inc., 24 P.3d 188 (Kan. App. 2001).

Louisiana: Ducote v. Koch Pipeline Co., 730 So.2d 432 (La. 1999); Grefer v. Travelers Insurance Co., 919 So.2d 758 (La. App. 2005); Crabtree v. Hayes-Dockside, Inc., 612 So.2d 249 (La. App. 1992), *writ denied* 614 So.2d 1257 (La. 1993); *In re* American Cyanamid Co., 1991 WL 242184 (E.D. La. Nov. 7, 1991).

Maryland: Bernhardt v. Hartford Fire Insurance Co., 648 A.2d 1047 (Md. App. 1994).

Michigan: City of Grosse Pointe Park v. Michigan Municipal Liability & Property Pool, 702 N.W.2d 106 (Mich. 2005); Watson v. Travelers Indemnity Co., 2005 WL 839504 (Mich. App. Apr. 12, 2005); Michigan Municipal Risk Management Authority v. Seaboard Surety Co., 2003 WL 21854655 (Mich. App. Aug. 7, 2003), *appeal denied* 687 N.W. 2d 292 (Mich. 2004); Carpet Workroom v. Auto Owners Insurance Co., 2002 WL 1747884 (Mich. App. July 23, 2002), *appeal denied sub nom.* Meridian Mutual Insurance Co. v. Handrinos, 661 N.W.2d 236 (Mich. 2003); McKusick v. Travelers Indemnity Co., 632 N.W.2d 525 (Mich. App. 2001), *appeal denied* 661 N.W.2d 236 (Mich. 2003).

Missouri: Heringer v. American Family Mutual Insurance Co., 140 S.W.3d 100 (Mo. App. 2004); Boulevard Investment Co. v. Capitol Indemnity Corp., 27 S.W.3d 856 (Mo. App. 2000); Casualty Indemnity Exchange v. City of Sparta, 997 S.W.2d 545 (Mo. App. 1999).

Nebraska: State Farm Fire and Casualty Co. v. Dantzler, 852 N.W.2d 918 (Neb. 2014); Cincinnati Insurance Co. v. Becker Warehouse, Inc., 635 N.W.2d 112 (Neb. 2001); Ferrell v. State Farm Insurance Co., 2003 Neb. App. LEXIS 123 (Neb. App. May 13, 2003).

New York: White v. Freedman, 643 N.Y.S.2d 160 (N.Y. App. Div. 1996); Demakos v. Travelers Insurance Co., 613 N.Y.S.2d 709 (N.Y. App. Div. 1994); Oates v. State, 597 N.Y.S.2d 550 (N.Y. Claims 1993).

Ohio: I.G.H. II, Inc. v. Selective Insurance Company of South Carolina, 2007 WL 1378379 (Ohio App. May 11, 2007); Danis v. Great American Insurance Co., 823 N.E.2d 59 (Ohio App. 2004); Rybacki v. Allstate Insurance Co., 2004 WL 894406 (Ohio. App. Apr. 28, 2004); Selm v. American States Insurance Co., 2001 WL 1103509 (Ohio App. Sept. 21, 2001); Air Products & Chemicals v. Indiana Insurance Co., 2000 WL 955600 (Ohio App. Dec. 23, 1999);

Owners Insurance Co. v. Singh, 1999 WL 976249 (Ohio App. Sept. 21, 1999); Zell v. Aetna Casualty & Surety Insurance Co., 683 N.E.2d 1154 (Ohio App. 1996).

Oklahoma: Bituminous Casualty Corp. v. Cowen Construction, Inc., 55 P.3d 1030 (Okla. 2002).

Pennsylvania: Madison Construction Co. v. Harleysville Mutual Insurance Co., 735 A.2d 100 (Pa. 1999); Matcon Diamond, Inc. v. Penn National Insurance Co., 815 A.2d 1109 (Pa. Super. 2003); Fayette County Housing Authority v. Housing & Redevelopment Insurance Exchange, 771 A.2d 11 (Pa. Super. 2001); Ford City Borough Municipal Sewage Disposal Authority v. EMC Insurance Cos., 73 Pa. D. & C.4th 225 (Pa. C.P. 2005).

South Dakota: South Dakota State Cement Plant Commission v. Wausau Underwriters Insurance Co., 616 N.W.2d 397 (S.D. 2000).

Texas: National Union Fire Insurance Co. v. CBI Industries, Inc., 907 S.W.2d 517 (Tex. 1995); Zaiontz v. Trinity Universal Insurance Co., 87 S.W.3d 565 (Tex. App. 2002).

Vermont: Cincinnati Specialty Underwriters Insurance Co. v. Energy Wise Homes, Inc., 120 A.3d 1160 (Vt. 2015).

Washington: Quadrant Corp. v. American States Insurance Co., 110 P.3d 733 (Wash. 2005) (*en banc*); City of Bremerton v. Harbor Insurance Co., 963 P.2d 194 (Wash. App. 1998); Cook v. Evanson, 920 P.2d 1223 (Wash. App. 1996), *review denied* 936 P.2d 416 (Wash. 1997).

Wisconsin: Peace v. Northwestern National Insurance Co., 596 N.W.2d 429 (Wis. 1999); Landshire Fast Foods of Milwaukee, Inc. v. Employers Mutual Casualty Co., 676 N.W.2d 528 (Wis. App.), *review denied* 679 N.W.2d 546 (Wis. 2004); Norks v. American Family Mutual Insurance Co., 551 N.W.2d 62 (Wis. App. 1996); Brown v. Mosser Lee Co., 419 N.W.2d 573 (Wis. App. 1987), *review denied* 422 N.W.2d 860 (Wis. 1988).

45 See:

First Circuit: Titan Holdings Syndicate, Inc. v. Keene, 898 F.2d 265 (1st Cir. 1990); Maritime Energy, Inc. v. Continental Insurance Co., 2005 WL 2365317, at *1 (D. Me. Sept. 26, 2005), *vacated on other grounds* 2005 WL 3132309 (D. Me. Nov. 22, 2005); Eastern Reproduction Corp. v. Seaco Insurance Co., 2004 WL 1932640 (D. Mass. July 19, 2004).

Second Circuit: Stoney Run Co. v. Prudential-LMI Commercial Insurance Co., 47 F.3d 34 (2d Cir. 1995); WTC Captive Insurance Co. v. Liberty Mutual Fire Insurance Co., 549 F. Supp.2d 555 (S.D.N.Y. 2008); Herald Square Loft Corp. v. Merrimack Mutual Fire Insurance Co., 344 F. Supp.2d 915 (S.D.N.Y. 2004); Maryland Casualty Co. v. W.R. Grace & Co., 1998 WL 729648 (S.D.N.Y. Oct. 15, 1998); Garfield Slope Housing Corp. v. Public Service Mutual Insurance Co., 973 F. Supp. 326 (E.D.N.Y. 1997); Sphere Drake Insurance Co. v. Y.L. Realty Co., 990 F. Supp. 240 (S.D.N.Y. 1997); Lefrak Organization, Inc. v. Chubb Custom Insurance Co., 942 F. Supp. 949 (S.D.N.Y. 1996); National Union Fire Insurance Company of Pittsburg, Pennsylvania v. America Re-Insurance Co., 351 F. Supp.2d 201 (S.D.N.Y. 2005).

Third Circuit: Amerada Hess Corp. v. Zurich Insurance Co., 29 Fed. Appx. 800 (3d Cir. 2002); *In re* Hub Recycling, Inc., 106 B.R. 372 (D.N.J. 1989); Sunoco, Inc. v. Illinois National Insurance Co., 2005 WL 2077258 (E.D. Pa. Aug. 29, 2005); Atlantic Casualty Insurance Co. v. Epstein, 2004 WL 2075038 (E.D. Pa. Sept. 15, 2004); Island Associates, Inc. v. Eric Group, Inc., 894 F. Supp. 200 (W.D. Pa. 1995); Mahogany Run Condominium Ass'n v. Certain Underwriters at Lloyds London 2004 WL 1987236 (D.V.I. Aug. 30, 2004); Evanston Insurance Co. v. Treister, 794 F. Supp. 560 (D.V.I. 1992).

Fourth Circuit: Auto-Owners Insurance Co. v. Potter, 105 Fed. Appx. 484 (4th Cir. 2004); State Auto Property & Casualty Insurance Co. v. Gorsuch, 323 F. Supp.2d 746 (W.D. Va. 2004) (uncontaminated water did not constitute pollutant under pollution exclusion).

Fifth Circuit: Northfield Insurance Co. v. George E. Buisson Realty Co., 1999 WL 680391 (E.D. La. Aug. 26, 1999).

Sixth Circuit: Center for Creative Studies v. Aetna Life & Casualty Co., 871 F. Supp. 941 (E.D. Mich. 1994); Bailey PVS Oxide LLC v. Plas-Tanks Industries, Inc., 2003 WL 22182555 (N.D. Ohio Sept. 4, 2003).

Seventh Circuit: Great American Insurance Company of New York v. Helwig, 2006 WL 618590 (N.D. Ill. Mar. 9, 2006).

Eighth Circuit: First Realty, Ltd. v. Frontier Insurance Co., 378 F.3d 729 (8th Cir. 2004); Employers Mutual Casualty Co. v. Industrial Rubber Products, Inc., 2006 WL 453207 (D. Minn. Feb. 23, 2006); Continental Casualty Co. v. Advance Terrazzo & Tile Co., 2005 WL 1923661 (D. Minn. Aug. 11, 2005), *aff'd* 462 F.3d 1002 (8th Cir. 2006); American States Insurance Co. v. Technical Surfacing, Inc., 50 F. Supp.2d 888 (D. Minn. 1999); Sargent Construction Co. v. State Auto Insurance Co., 23 F.3d 1324 (8th Cir. 1994) (applying Missouri law).

Ninth Circuit: Manus v. Ranger Insurance Co., 142 Fed. Appx. 280 (9th Cir. 2005); Cooper v. Travelers Indemnity Company of Illinois, 113 Fed. Appx. 198 (9th Cir. 2004); Nicholson v. Allstate Insurance Co., 979 F. Supp.2d 1054 (E.D. Cal. 2013); Apana v. TIG Insurance Co., 504 F. Supp.2d 998 (D. Haw. 2007); SEMX Corp. v. Federal Insurance Co., 398 F. Supp.2d 1103 (S.D. Cal. 2005).

Tenth Circuit: Regional Bank of Colorado, N.A. v. St. Paul Fire & Marine Insurance Co., 35 F.3d 494 (10th Cir. 1994); Regent Insurance Co. v. Holmes, 835 F. Supp. 579 (D. Kan. 1993); Westchester Fire Insurance Co. v. City of Pittsburg, Kansas, 794 F. Supp. 353 (D. Kan. 1992), *aff'd* 987 F.2d 1516 (10th Cir. 1993).

Eleventh Circuit: Bituminous Casualty Corp. Advanced Adhesive Technology, Inc., 73 F.3d 335 (11th Cir. 1996).

State Courts:

Alabama: Porterfield v. Audubon Indemnity Co., 856 So.2d 789 (Ala. 2002); Essex Insurance Co. v. Avondale Mills, Inc., 639 So.2d 1339 (Ala. 1994).

Alaska: Whittier Properties, Inc. v. Alaska National Insurance Co., 185 P.3d 84 (Alaska 2008).

Arizona: Keggi v. Northbrook Property & Casualty Insurance Co., 13 P.3d 785 (Ariz. App. 2000).

Arkansas: State Auto Property & Casualty Insurance Co. v. Arkansas Department of Environmental Quality, 258 S.W.3d 736 (Ark. 2007); Minerva Enterprises, Inc. v. Bituminous Casualty Corp., 851 S.W.2d 403 (Ark. 1993).

California: MacKinnon v. Truck Insurance Exchange, 73 P.3d 1205 (Cal. 2003); American Casualty Company of Reading, Pennsylvania v. Miller, 159 Cal. App.4th 501, 71 Cal. Rptr.3d 571 (2008); Cold Creek Compost, Inc. v. State Farm Fire and Casualty Co., 156 Cal. App.4th 1469, 68 Cal. Rptr.3d 216 (2007); C.O.D. Gas & Oil Co. v. Ace American Insurance Co., 2004 WL 1245759 (Cal. App. June 8, 2004).

Colorado: Roinestad v. Kirkpatrick, 2010 Colo. App. LEXIS 1508 (Colo. App. Oct. 14, 2010).

Connecticut: National Grange Mutual Insurance Co. v. Caraker, 2006 WL 853153 (Conn. Super. Feb. 28, 2006).

Idaho: Esterovich v. City of Kellogg, 80 P.3d 1040 (Idaho 2003).

Illinois: American States Insurance Co. v. Koloms, 687 N.E.2d 72 (Ill. 1997); Insurance Company of Illinois v. Stringfield, 685 N.E.2d 980 (Ill. App. 1997).

Indiana: Freidline v. Shelby Insurance Co., 774 N.E.2d 37 (Ind. 2002); American States Insurance Co. v. Kiger, 662 N.E.2d 945 (Ind. 1996); Great Lakes Chemical Corp. v. International Surplus Lines Insurance Co., 638 N.E.2d 847 (Ind. App. 1994).

Iowa: West Bend Mutual Insurance Co. v. Iowa Iron Works, Inc., 503 N.W.2d 596 (Iowa 1993).

Kansas: Associated Wholesale Grocers, Inc. v. Americold Corp., 934 P.2d 65 (Kan. 1997).

Kentucky: Motorists Mutual Insurance Co. v. RSJ, Inc., 926 S.W.2d 679 (Ky. App. 1996).

Louisiana: Sandbom v. BASF Wyandotte, Corp., 674 So.2d 349 (La. App. 1996); Avery v. Commercial Union Insurance Co., 621 So.2d 184 (La. App. 1993); West v. Board of Commissioners of Port of New Orleans, 591 So.2d 1358 (La. App. 1991); Thompson v. Temple, 580 So.2d 1133 (La. App. 1991).

Massachusetts: McGregor v. Allamerica Insurance Co., 868 N.E.2d 1225 (Mass. 2007); Western Alliance Insurance Co. v. Gill, 686 N.E.2d 997 (Mass. 1997); Atlantic Mutual Insurance Co. v. McFadden, 595 N.E.2d 762 (Mass. 1992).

Minnesota: Minnesota Mining & Manufacturing Co. v. Walbrook Insurance Co., 1996 WL 5787 (Minn. App. Jan. 9, 1996); Auto-Owners Insurance Co. v. Hanson, 588 N.W.2d 777 (Minn. App. 1999); League of Minnesota Cities Insurance Trust v. Coon Rapids, 446 N.W.2d 419 (Minn. App. 1989).

Missouri: Hocker Oil Co. v. Barker-Phillips-Jackson, Inc., 997 S.W.2d 510 (Mo. App. 1999).

New Hampshire: Weaver v. Royal Insurance Co., 674 A.2d 975 (N.H. 1996).

New Jersey: Nav-Its, Inc. v. Selective Insurance Company of America, 869 A.2d 929 (N.J. 2005); Estate of Mini v. Metro Supply & Service, Inc., 2004 WL 1284173 (N.J. Super. App. Div. June 8, 2004); Byrd v. Blumenreich, 722 A.2d 598 (N.J. Super. App. Div. 1999); S.N. Golden Estates, Inc. v. Continental Casualty Co., 680 A.2d 1114 (N.J. Super. 1996); Jackson v. Atlantic, 2005 WL 2757134 (N.J. Super. App. Div. Oct. 26, 2005) (*per curiam*).

New York: Tower Insurance Company of New York v. Breyter, 830 N.Y.S.2d 122, 37 A.D.3d 309, (2007); Westview Associates v. Guaranty National Insurance Co., 740 N.E.2d 220 (N.Y. 2000); Incorporated Village of Cedarhurst v. Hanover Insurance Co., 675 N.E.2d 822 (N.Y. 1996); Pepsico, Inc. v. Winterthur International America Insurance Co., 788 N.Y.S.2d 142 (N.Y. App. Div. 2004); Village Mall at Hillcrest Condominium v. Merrimack Mutual Fire Insurance Co., 766 N.Y.S.2d 70 (N.Y. App. Div. 2003); Republic Franklin Insurance Co. v. L & J Realty Corp., 720 N.Y.S.2d 473 (N.Y. App. Div.), *appeal denied* 730 N.Y.S.2d 790 (N.Y. 2001); Cepeda v. Varveris, 651 N.Y.S.2d 185 (N.Y. App. Div. 1996) (claims for bodily injury to child from ingesting lead-based paint not barred by "absolute" pollution exclusion); General Accident Insurance Company of America v. Naimberg Realty Associates, 650 N.Y.S.2d 246 (N.Y. App. Div. 1996); General Accident Insurance Company of America v. IDBAR Realty Corp., 646 N.Y.S.2d 138 (N.Y. App. Div. 1996); Miano v. Hehn, 614 N.Y.S.2d 829 (N.Y. App. Div. 1994); Karroll v. Atomergic Chemetals Corp., 600 N.Y.S.2d 101 (N.Y. App. Div. 1993); Vigilant Insurance Co. v. V.I. Technologies, Inc., 676 N.Y.S.2d 596 (N.Y. App. Div. 1998).

North Carolina: West American Insurance Co. v. Tufco Flooring East, Inc., 409 S.E.2d 692 (N.C. App. 1991), *overruled on other grounds* Gaston County Dyeing Machinery Co. v. Northfield Insurance Co., 524 S.E.2d 558 (N.C. 2000).

Ohio: Anderson v. Highland House Co., 757 N.E.2d 329 (Ohio 2001); Bosserman Aviation Equipment, Inc. v. United States Liability Insurance, Co., 183 Ohio App.3d 29, 915 N.E.2d 687 (Ohio App. 2009).

Pennsylvania: Lititz Mutual Insurance Co. v. Steely, 785 A.2d 975 (Pa. 2001); Mistick, Inc. v. Northwestern National Casualty Co., 806 A.2d 39 (Pa. Super. 2002); Municipality of Mt. Lebanon v. Reliance Insurance Co., 778 A.2d 1228 (Pa. Super. 2001); Gamble Farm Inn, Inc. v. Selective Insurance Co., 656 A.2d 142 (Pa. Super. 1995).

Texas: Urethane International Products v. Mid-Continent Casualty Co., 2006 WL 242459 (Tex. App. Feb. 1, 2006).

Washington: Kent Farms, Inc. v. Zurich Insurance Co., 998 P.2d 292 (Wash. 2000).

Wisconsin: Donaldson v. Urban Land Interests, Inc., 564 N.W.2d 728 (Wis. 1997); Langone v. American Family Mutual Insurance Co., 731 N.W.2d 334 (Wis. App. 2007); Arnold v. Cincinnati Insurance Co., 688 N.W.2d 708 (Wis. App. 2004).

[46] See ISO Form CG 00 01 10 01.

[47] See 42 U.S.C. § 9607(a).

[48] See 42 U.S.C. § 9607(a).

[49] See Porterfield v. Audubon Indemnity Co., 2002 WL 31630705, at *7 (Ala. Nov. 22, 2002) ("Also, the absolute pollution-exclusion clause incorporates the concept of a 'threatened discharge, disposal, release or a surge of pollutants.' 'Liability for a mere threat of an injury is a concept that is fundamental to modern environmental statutes, including CERCLA, but is foreign to normal tort liability,' and '[t]he incorporation of environmental liability terms and concepts into the absolute pollution exclusion illustrates that the exclusion was designed to be limited to injury for typical, industrial environmental damage.'").

[50] See Reliance Insurance Co. v. Moessner, 121 F.3d 895 (3d Cir. 1997).

[51] ISO Explanatory Memorandum at 2. See Reliance Insurance Co. v. Moessner, 121 F.3d 895 (3d Cir. 1997).

[52] NAIC, Report of the ISO/CGL Working Group of the Commercial Lines—Property and Casualty (D) Committee (New Orleans, La., Dec. 12, 1988), at 3.

[53] See, e.g.:

Fourth Circuit: Firemen's Insurance Co. v. Kline & Son Cement Repair, 474 F. Supp.2d 779, 792 ns. 5–6 (E.D. Va. 2007) (listing cases on both sides of the issue).

Ninth Circuit: Apana v. TIG Insurance Co., 504 F. Supp.2d 998, 1003–1004 (D. Haw. 2007) (listing cases on both sides of the issue).

State Courts:

California: MacKinnon v. Truck Insurance Exchange, 73 P.3d 1205, 1209 ns.1–2 (Cal. 2003) (listing cases on both sides of the issue).

[54] See:

Second Circuit: Lapolla Industries, Inc. v. Aspen Specialty Insurance Co., 962 F. Supp.2d 479 (E.D.N.Y. 2013) ("total" pollution exclusion applied to losses caused by gaseous release of noxious fumes from insulation materials).

Third Circuit: Mark I Restoration SVC v. Assurance Company of America, 112 Fed. Appx. 153, 2004 WL 2297145 (3d Cir. 2004) (injury from deodorizing chemicals used in home excluded by pollution exclusion); Reliance Insurance Co. v. Moessner, 121 F.3d 895 (3d Cir. 1997) ("total" pollution exclusion unambiguously excluded coverage for carbon monoxide poisoning); State Auto Insurance Cos. v. Summy, 83 F. Supp.2d 530 (E.D. Pa. 2000), *vacated on other grounds* 234 F.3d 131 (3d Cir. 2000) (injuries stemming from ingestion of lead paint barred by "total" pollution exclusion).

Fourth Circuit: National Electric Manufacturers v. Gulf Underwriters Insurance Co., 162 F.3d 821 (4th Cir. 1998) (inhalation injuries from magnese fumes excluded by pollution exclusion).

Fifth Circuit: Nautilus Insurance Co. v. Country Oaks Apartments, Ltd., 566 F.3d 452 (5th Cir. 2009); Certain Underwriters at Lloyd's v. C.A. Turner Construction Co., 112 F.3d 184 (5th Cir. 1997) (injury from exposure to phenol gas at work site excluded by pollution exclusion); Eott Energy Pipeline Limited Partnership v. Hattiesburg Speedway, Inc., 303 F. Supp.2d 819 (S.D. Miss. 2004) ("total" pollution exclusion inapplicable to claim for repair of oil pipeline accidentally severed by road grader, or for lost profits during course of oil cleanup, but did exclude cost of oil cleanup itself); American Equity Insurance Co. v. Castlemane Farms, Inc., 220 F. Supp.2d 809, 814 (S.D. Tex. 2002) (property damages caused by accidental rupture of salt water disposal pipeline excluded by "total" pollution exclusion);

Clarendon America Insurance Co. v. Bay, Inc., 10 F. Supp.2d 736 (S.D. Tex. 1998) (exclusion applied to bar coverage for claims for bodily injury from inhalation of dust, sand and other substances containing silica, and fumes emanating from cement and additives, but the exclusion would not apply to claims of damage from exposure to wet cement if that cement and its ingredients were in their intended location).

Sixth Circuit: Pure Tech Systems, Inc. v. Mt. Hawley Insurance Co., 95 Fed. Appx. 132 (6th Cir. 2004) (contamination of water reclamation system with PCBs excluded by "total" pollution exclusion).

Eighth Circuit: Continental Casualty Co. v. Advance Terrazzo & Tile Co., 462 F.3d 1002 (8th Cir. 2006) (carbon monoxide inhalation excluded by pollution exclusion); Hartford Underwriter's Insurance Co. v. Estate of Turks, 206 F. Supp.2d 968 (E.D. Mo. 2002) ("total" pollution exclusion barred coverage for lead poisoning from lead paint).

Ninth Circuit: City of Spokane v. United National Insurance Co., 190 F. Supp.2d 1209 (E.D. Wash. 2002) ("total" pollution exclusion applied to claims for injury from odors released by city composting plant).

Eleventh Circuit: Scottsdale Insurance Co. v. Pursley, 487 Fed. Appx. 508 (11th Cir. 2012) ("total" pollution exclusion excluded coverage for losses caused by carbon monoxide poisoning from boat motor); General Fidelity Insurance Co. v. Foster, 808 F. Supp.2d 1315 (S.D. Fla. 2011) (claims from inhalation of noxious materials from defective drywall excluded under "total" pollution exclusion); West American Insurance Co. v. Band & Desenberg, 138 F.3d 1428 (11th Cir. 1998) (airborne contaminants moving from attic space to office space excluded by pollution exclusion); Nova Casualty Co. v. Waserstein, 2006 WL 833081 (S.D. Fla. Mar. 24, 2006) ("total" pollution exclusion applied to injuries from "living organisms," "microbial pollutions," "microbial contaminants," and "indoor allergens").

District of Columbia Circuit: Nationwide Mutual Insurance Co. v. National REO Management, Inc., 205 F.R.D. 1 (D.D.C. 2000) ("total" pollution exclusion barred coverage for carbon monoxide ingestion claims).

State Courts:

Alabama: Porterfield v. Audubon Indemnity Co., 856 So.2d 789 (Ala. 2003).

California: The Villa Los Alamos Homeowners Ass'n v. State Farm General Insurance Co., 198 Cal. App.4th 522; 130 Cal. Rptr.3d 374 (2011); Bechtel Petroleum Operations, Inc. v. Continental Insurance Co., 2006 WL 531277 (Cal. App. Mar. 6, 2006) (claims of workplace exposure to toxic substances and claims based on unsanitary and dangerous work conditions excluded by "total" pollution exclusion); Insurance Commissioner v. Golden Eagle Insurance Co., 2000 WL 968215 (Cal. App. May 8, 2000) ("total" pollution exclusion barred coverage for bodily injury to employees caused by carbon monoxide from gas engine); Panda Management Co. v. Wausau Underwriters Insurance Co., 73 Cal. Rptr.2d 160 (Cal. App. 1998) ("total" pollution exclusion excluded claim for property damage caused by discharge of grease and cooking oils into sewer system).

Delaware: Farm Family Casualty Co. v. Cumberland Insurance Co., 2013 Del. Super. LEXIS 427 (Del. Super. Oct. 2, 2013) ("total" pollution exclusion applied to residential lead pain ingestion claim).

Louisiana: Matheny v. Ludwig, 742 So.2d 1029 (La. App. 1999) (property damage to neighboring landowner from discharge of waste grease barred by "total" pollution exclusion).

Minnesota: Board of Regents of University of Minnesota v. Royal Insurance Company of America, 517 N.W.2d 888 (Minn. 1994) ("total" pollution exclusion applied to claim for costs of asbestos abatement in buildings).

Missouri: Cincinnati Insurance Co. v. German St. Vincent Orphan Association, 54 S.W.3d 661 (Mo. App. 2001) ("total" pollution exclusion applied to claim for property damage to building caused by release of friable asbestos fibers from vinyl flooring by abrasion with floor scraper).

Nebraska: Harleysville Insurance Group v. Omaha Gas Appliance Co., 278 Neb. 547, 772 N.W.2d 88 (2009).

New York: Space v. Farm Family Mutual Insurance Co., 652 N.Y.S.2d 357 (N.Y. App. Div. 1997) ("total" pollution exclusion barred coverage for property damage from natural organic fertilizer applied to cropland); Bruckner Realty, LLC v. County Oil Co., 2006 WL 756090 (N.Y. Sup. Feb. 27, 2006), *aff'd* 2007 WL 1502254 (N.Y. App. Div. May 22, 2007) ("total" pollution exclusion precluded coverage for discharge of heating oil from apartment building).

Pennsylvania: Municipal Authority of the Town of Bloomsburg v. Pennsylvania Pooled Risk Insurance for Municipal Entities, 73 Pa. D. & C.4th 152 (Pa. C.P. 2005) (claim arising from alleged chemical emissions excluded by "total" pollution exclusion).

Wisconsin: State Farm Fire & Casualty Co. v. Acuity, 695 N.W. 2d 883 (Wis. App. 2005) (property damage caused by fumes stemming from residential oil spill excluded by "total" pollution exclusion).

55 See:

First Circuit: Nascimento v. Preferred Mutual Insurance Co., 513 F.3d 273 (1st Cir. 2008); Nautilus Insurance Co. v. Jabar, 188 F.3d 27 (1st Cir. 1999) ("total" pollution exclusion inapplicable to bodily injury claim for inhalation of hazardous fumes at place of employment); Zurich American Insurance Co. v. Lord Electric Company of Puerto Rico, 986 F. Supp.2d 104 (D.P.R. 2013) (diesel fuel from backup generators that spilled entirely inside of building was not excluded by "total" pollution exclusion); Boise Cascade Corp. v. Reliance National Indemnity Co., 99 F. Supp.2d 87 (D. Me. 2000) ("total" pollution exclusion not applicable to claims by workers exposed at workplace to accidental release of chlorine gas).

Second Circuit: Calvert Insurance Co. v. S & L Realty Corp., 926 F. Supp. 44 (S.D.N.Y. 1996) ("total" pollution exclusion inapplicable to fumes ingestion claim).

Third Circuit: Merchants Insurance Company of New Hampshire, Inc. v. Hessler, 2005 WL 2009902 (D.N.J. Aug. 18, 2005) ("total" pollution exclusion did not apply to claim for "request by the health department to remediate the lead paint chips by removing the top layer of soil off the property and laying down fresh soil").

Fourth Circuit: Auto-Owners Insurance Co. v. Potter, 105 Fed. Appx. 484, 2004 WL 1662454 (4th Cir. 2004) (pollution exclusion is not applicable to claims "more akin to an instance in which an adulterated product has been supplied to consumers").

Fifth Circuit: In re Chinese Manufactured Drywall Products Liability Litigation, 759 F. Supp.2d 822 (E.D. La. 2010) (defective drywall claims causing property damage not excluded by "total" pollution exclusion in all-risk property policy); Eott Energy Pipeline Limited Partnership v. Hattiesburg Speedway, Inc., 303 F. Supp.2d 819 (S.D. Miss. 2004) ("total" pollution exclusion inapplicable to claim for repair of oil pipeline accidentally severed by road grader, or for lost profits during course of oil cleanup, but did exclude cost of oil cleanup itself); Clarendon America Insurance Co. v. Bay, Inc., 10 F. Supp.2d 736 (S.D. Tex. 1998) ("total" pollution exclusion barred coverage for claims of plaintiffs for bodily injury from inhalation of dust, sand, and other substances containing silica, and fumes emanating from cement and additives, but exclusion would not apply to claims of damage from exposure to wet cement if that cement and its ingredients were in their intended location).

Sixth Circuit: Meridian Mutual Insurance Co. v. Kellman, 197 F.3d 1178 (6th Cir. 1999) ("total" pollution exclusion did not bar coverage for fume ingestion claim from chemicals used to seal floor).

Ninth Circuit: Enron Oil Trading & Transportation Co. v. Walbrook Insurance Co., 132 F.3d 526 (9th Cir. 1997) ("total" pollution exclusion inapplicable to claims of injury from injection of foreign materials into oil pipeline); EFK Investments, L.L.C. v. Peerless Insurance Co., 2014 U.S. Dist. LEXIS 137864 (N.D. Cal. Sept. 26, 2014) (sandblasting leading to damage of neighboring store's electronic equipment not excluded by "total" pollution exclusion).

Tenth Circuit: The New Salida Ditch Co. v. United Fire and Casualty Insurance Co., 400 Fed. Appx. 338 (10th Cir. 2010); Red Panther Chemical Co. v. Insurance Company of the State of Pennsylvania, 43 F.3d 514 (10th Cir. 1994) ("total" pollution exclusion did not necessarily bar coverage for bodily injury to a mechanic resulting from workplace ingestion or inhalation of insecticide).

Eleventh Circuit: Bituminous Casualty Corp. v. Advance Adhesive Technology, Inc., 73 F.3d 335 (11th Cir. 1996) (inhalation of fumes from carpet machine not excluded by pollution exclusion).

State Courts:

Arkansas: Anderson Gas & Propane, Inc. v. Westport Insurance Co., 140 S.W.3d 504 (Ark. App. 2004) ("total" pollution exclusion ambiguous as applied to claims of injury from leaking gasoline from an underground pipe).

California: Gonzales v. Western Mutual Insurance Co., 2004 WL 3019113 (Cal. App. Dec. 30, 2004) ("total" pollution exclusion in homeowners policy inapplicable to costs to remove asbestos from house damaged by fire).

Connecticut: Camp Delaware, Inc. v. Markel Insurance Co., 2001 WL 541451 (Conn. Super. May 4, 2001) ("total" pollution exclusion inapplicable to claim for damages caused by backup of sewage).

Illinois: American States Insurance Co. v. Koloms, 177 Ill.2d 473, 227 Ill.Dec. 149, 687 N.E.2d 72, (1997) (injury from carbon monoxide leak from apartment furnace not excluded).

Indiana: American States Insurance Co. v. Kiger, 662 N.E.2d 945 (Ind. 1996) (injury resulting from gas leak from commercial gas station not excluded).

Kansas: Associated Wholesale Grocers, Inc. v. Americold Corp., 934 P.2d 65 (Kan. 1997) (property losses from smoke emanating from a fire not excluded).

Louisiana: Doerr v. Mobil Oil Corp., 774 So.2d 119 (La. 2000) ("total" pollution exclusion inapplicable to claim for damage to water system caused by releases of hydrocarbons from an oil company's wastewater facility); State Farm Fire & Casualty Co. v. M.L.T. Construction Co., 849 So.2d 762 (La. App. 2003) (mold and mildew damages not excluded by "total" pollution exclusion); Smith v. Reliance Insurance Company of Illinois, 807 So.2d 1010 (La. App. 2002) ("total" pollution exclusion inapplicable to claims for personal injuries from noxious odors).

Maryland: Clendenin Brothers, Inc. v. United States Fire Insurance Co., 889 A.2d 387 (Md. 2006) ("total" pollution exclusion inapplicable to claims for alleged injuries arising from manganese welding fumes because claims were for localized, workplace injuries, and not for environmental pollution).

Massachusetts: McGregor v. Allamerica Insurance Co., 2005 WL 3722412 (Mass. Super. 2005) (rejecting application of "total" pollution exclusion to claim for broken oil burner), *rev'd* 868 N.E.2d 1225 (Mass. 2007); Eastern Casualty Insurance Co. v. Home Store, Inc., 2005 WL 1477619 (Mass. Super. May 20, 2005) (leakage of oil from home furnace sold by policyholder-home store to owner of modular home was not excluded under "total" pollution exclusion).

Michigan: Hobson v. Indian Harbor Insurance Co., 2015 Mich. App. LEXIS 486 (Mich. App. Mar. 10, 2015) (bodily injuries caused by inhalation of smoke from negligently caused fire not excluded by "total" pollution exclusion).

Missouri: American National Property and Casualty Co. v. Wyatt, 400 S.W.3d 417 (Mo. App. 2013) ("total" pollution exclusion inapplicable to injuries caused by car's discharge of carbon monoxide).

New York: Belt Painting Corp. v. TIG Insurance Co., 795 N.E.2d 15 (N.Y. 2003) ("total" pollution exclusion did not apply to claim for injuries from ingestion of paint fumes in building); Roofers' Joint Trading, Apprentice & Education Committee v. General Accident Insurance Company of America, 713 N.Y.S.2d 615 (N.Y. App. Div. 2000) ("total" pollution exclusion not applied to claim for ingestion-of-fumes bodily injuries).

Ohio: Bosserman Aviation Equipment, Inc. v. United States Liability Insurance Co., 183 Ohio App.3d 29, 915 N.E.2d 687 (2009).

Wisconsin: Guenther v. City of Onalaska, 588 N.W.2d 375 (Wis. App. 1998), *review denied* 640 N.W.2d 571 (Wis. 1999) ("total" pollution exclusion did not bar coverage for damage resulting from the liquid, non-toxic domestic sewage, which backed up into basement); Beahm v. Pautsch, 510 N.W.2d 702 (Wis. App. 1993) ("total" pollution exclusion did not apply to claim for injuries in traffic accident caused by poor visibility due to fire to burn off winter grass).

Wyoming: Gainsco Insurance Co. v. Amoco Product Co., 53 P.3d 1051 (Wyo. 2002) ("total" pollution exclusion inapplicable to claim for injury caused by exposure of worker to poisonous hydrogen sulfide gas).

CHAPTER 9

Coverage B for "Personal Injuries" and "Advertising Injuries"

Chapter Contents

§ 9.01 Overview

As previously discussed, CGL insurance is commonly known as "litigation insurance,"[1] because it provides insurance coverage in the form of reimbursement for defense and indemnity obligations in connection with litigation asserted against the policyholder by third parties. As also previously discussed, CGL insurance has two prinicipal coverage parts—Coverage A and Coverage B.[2] Coverage A provides such "litigation" insurance attributable to third-party claims for "property damage" or "bodily injury."[3] Coverage B, on the other hand, affords the same "litigation insurance" for liability of the policyholder for "personal injury" and "advertising injury" suffered by third parties. Since Coverage B also provides litigation insurance, the duty to defend discussed previsouly is equally applicable.[4]

This chapter focuses on the Coverage B issues likely to be faced by real estate-related entities. In particular, it sets forth the relevant insuring agreements, including the 1973, 1986, and 1998 form agreements.[5] Then, it discusses the various coverage issues, including: (a) the business or advertising activity;[6] (b) the offense committed in the coverage territory during the policy period;[7] and (c) the enumerated "personal injury" offenses[8] and "advertising injury" offenses,[9] including application to statutory claims likely faced by real estate-related entities.[10] Finally, it discusses some common exclusions, including those for intentional acts[11] and breach of contract.[12]

§ 9.02 Insuring Agreement

Although the Coverage B insuring agreement has changed over time, the standard-form agreement has always contained a promise by the insurance company to defend and indemnify the policyholder for liabilities associated with certain offenses committed in the course of advertising or business activities.[13] There are three forms that are generally in use or have been used: (1) the 1998 personal and advertising injury coverage form ("1998 Form"); (2) the 1986 personal and advertising injury coverage form ("1986 Form"); and (3) the 1973 personal and advertising injury coverage form ("1973 Form").[14] The 1986 and 1998 Forms are now more prevalent, but all three forms are generally still in use and remain the subject of litigation.[15] Generally, insurance companies currently tend to use the more recent forms (1986 or 1998 Form), although that practice is far from absolute.[16]

[1]—The 1998 Personal and Advertising Injury Form

The 1998 Form contains the following insuring agreement, with emphasis (italicized language) provided to highlight the relevant coverage issues for this treatise:

"a. We will pay those sums that the insured becomes legally obligated to pay as damages because of '*personal and advertising injury*' to which this insurance applies. We will have the right and duty to defend the insured against any 'suit' seeking those damages. . . .

"b. This insurance applies to 'personal and advertising injury' caused by an offense arising out of your business but only if the offense was committed in the 'coverage territory' during the policy period."[17]

The 1998 Form defined the following terms, again with emphasis (italicized language) provided to highlight the relevant coverage issues for this treatise:

"'Advertisement' means a notice that is broadcast or published to the general public or specific market segments about your goods, products or services for the purpose of attracting customers or supporters. For purposes of this definition:

a. Notices that are published include material placed on the internet or on similar electronic means of communication; and

b. Regarding web-sites, only that part of a web-site that is about your goods, products or services for the purpose of attracting customers or supporters is considered an advertisement.

▼

"'Personal and advertising injury' means injury, including consequential 'bodily injury', arising out of one or more of the following offenses:

a. False arrest, detention or imprisonment;

b. Malicious prosecution;

c. The wrongful eviction from, wrongful entry into, or invasion of the right of private occupancy of a room, dwelling or premises that a person occupies, committed by or on behalf of its owner, landlord or lessor;

d. Oral or written publication, in any manner, of material that slanders or libels a person or organization or disparages a person's or organization's goods, products or services;

e. Oral or written publication, in any manner, of material that violates a person's right of privacy;

f. The use of another's advertising idea in your 'advertisement'; or

g. Infringing upon another's copyright, trade dress or slogan in your 'advertisement.'"[18]

[2]—The 1986 Personal and Advertising Injury Form

The 1986 personal and advertising injury coverage form ("1986 Form") contains the following insuring agreement, with emphasis (italicized language) provided to amplify the coverage issues:

"a. We will pay those sums that the insured becomes legally obligated to pay as damages because of *'personal injury'* or *'advertising injury'* to which this insurance applies. We will have the right and duty to defend the insured against any 'suit' seeking those damages.

▼

"b. This insurance applies to:

(1) 'Personal injury' caused by an *offense arising out of your business,* excluding advertising, publishing, broadcasting or telecasting done by or for you;

(2) 'Advertising injury' caused by an *offense committed in the course of advertising* your goods, products or services; but only if the *offense is committed in the 'coverage territory' during the policy period.*"[19]

The 1986 Form defined the following terms:

"'Advertising injury' means injury arising out of one or more of the following offenses:

a. Oral or written publication of material that slanders or libels a person or organization or disparages a person's or organization's goods, products or services;

b. Oral or written publication of material that violates a person's right of privacy;

c. Misappropriation of advertising ideas or style of doing business; or

d. Infringement of copyright, title or slogan.

▼

"'Personal injury' means injury, other than 'bodily injury,' arising out of one or more of the following offenses:

a. False arrest, detention or imprisonment;

b. Malicious prosecution;

c. The wrongful eviction from, wrongful entry into, or invasion of the right of private occupancy of a room, dwelling or premises that a person occupies by or on behalf of its owner, landlord or lessor;

d. oral or written publication of material that slanders or libels a person or organization or disparages a person's or organization's goods, products or services; or

e. Oral or written publication of material that violates a person's right of privacy."[20]

[3]—The 1973 Personal and Advertising Injury Form

An earlier version, the 1973 personal and advertising injury coverage form ("1973 Form"), contains the following agreement with emphasis provided to highlight the coverage issues:

"The company will pay on behalf of the insured all sums which the insured shall become legally obligated to pay as damages because of '*personal injury*' or '*advertising injury*' to which this insurance applies, sustained by any person or organization and *arising out of the conduct of the named insured's business, within the policy territory*, and the company shall have the right and duty to defend any suit against the insured seeking damages on account of such injury."[21]

The 1973 Form defined the following terms:

"'Advertising injury' means injury arising out of *an offense committed during the policy period* occurring in the course of the named insured's advertising activities, if such injury arises out of libel, slander, defamation, violation of right of privacy, piracy, unfair competition, or infringement of copyright, title or slogan.

"'Personal injury' means injury arising out of one or more of the following offenses *committed during the policy period:*

(1) false arrest, detention, imprisonment or malicious prosecution;

(2) wrongful entry or eviction or other invasion of the right of private occupancy;

(3) a publication or utterance

(a) of libel or slander or other defamatory or disparaging material; or

(b) in violation of an individual's right of privacy except publications or utterances in the course of or related to advertising, broadcasting, publishing or telecasting activities conducted by or on behalf of the named insured shall not be deemed personal injury."[22]

[4]—Distinctions between the 1973 and the 1986/1998 Forms

The 1998 Form made some rather minimal modifications to the 1986 Form.[23] In particular, the 1998 Form combined "personal injury" and "advertising injury" into one definition in the standard agreement.[24] Likewise, in the definition section, it eliminated the redundancy to make one defined term instead of two.[25] In addition, the 1998 Form combined sections b.1 and b.2 of the insuring agreement into one section (section b), continuing to require that the relevant offense arise from one's business and be committed in the relevant coverage territory.[26] Moreover, the 1998 Form created an exclusion for advertising, publishing, telecasting, and broadcasting businesses by pulling such language from section b.1 of the 1986 Form's insuring agreement.[27]

Further, the 1998 Form clarified what was meant by advertising activities by defining "advertisement" (to the extent "advertising" was previously undefined).[28] Finally, the 1998 Form defined "personal and advertising injury" to include consequential bodily injury, and the 1998 Form replaced the enumerated offense of: (a) "misappropriation of advertising ideas or style of doing business" with "use of another's advertising idea in your 'advertisement'"; and (b) infringement of "title" with infringement of "trade dress."[29]

There are very few material differences in "personal injury" coverage between the 1973 and 1986/1998 Forms. However, with respect to "advertising injury" coverage, the 1973 Form includes the offenses of "unfair competition" and "piracy," and the 1986 and 1998 Forms replaced such offenses with "misappropriation of advertising ideas or styles of doing business" or "use of another's advertising idea in your 'advertisement.'"[30]

§ 9.03 Coverage Issues

[1]—Business or Advertising Activity

One issue involves whether the specific conduct for which coverage is sought is committed or accomplished as a business or advertising activity. In particular, to be covered, the "personal injury" offense[31] must arise out of an offense committed in the operation of the policyholder's business and not involve advertising, publication, broadcasting, and telecasting.[32] Similarly, for the "advertising injury" offense[33] to be covered, the offense must be committed in furtherance of advertising, publication, broadcasting, and telecasting activities.[34]

It should be relatively easy to discern whether the activities at issue are committed in the requisite context. With regard to advertising activities, "advertising" is sometimes undefined in CGL insurance policies.[35] Other policies define "advertisement" as "notice that is broadcast or published to the general public or specific market segments about [the policyholder's] goods, products or services for the purpose of attracting customers or supporters."[36] Consistent with dictionary and policy definitions, many courts define it as "affirmative self-promotion" or "solicitation of business."[37] Courts will generally apply the policy definition to determine whether widespread dissemination or one-on-one solicitation satisfies the definition of "advertising activity."[38] Absent a clear indication in the policy language, there is a split of authority, however, on how widespread the activities must be. A few courts consider direct, one-on-one solicitation to be "advertising."[39] The majority, on the other hand, requires widespread promotion or solicitation.[40]

[2]—Offense Committed in Coverage Territory during Policy Period

The offenses that are deemed to constitute "personal injury" or advertising injury" offenses must also be committed in the coverage territory and during the policy period.[41] The "coverage territory" is usually defined as the United States, but can be defined more broadly as anywhere in the world.[42] Determination of the timing and situs of the offense will usually be a fairly straightforward exercise. Indeed, the date the offense is committed will ordinarily be the date by which coverage should be measured.[43] Similarly, although there is very little case law on the issue, the location where the offense is committed should determine the "coverage territory" issue.[44]

[3]—Enumerated Offenses

Although the location and timing of the offenses and the characterization of the activity (business or advertising activity) are important matters, the central coverage issue will ordinarily be whether an "advertising injury" or "personal injury" offense has occurred.

[a]—"Personal Injury" Offenses

One form of offense is a "personal injury" offense, which is expressly defined as injury arising from certain enumerated torts. The 1973 and 1986 Forms define "personal injury" in the same basic way as:

> "injury, other than 'bodily injury,' arising out of one or more of the following offenses:
>
> a. False arrest, detention or imprisonment;
>
> b. Malicious prosecution;

c. The wrongful eviction from, wrongful entry into, or invasion of the right of private occupancy of a room, dwelling or premises that a person occupies by or on behalf of its owner, landlord or lessor;

d. oral or written publication of material that slanders or libels a person or organization or disparages a person's or organization's goods, products or services; or

e. Oral or written publication of material that violates a person's right of privacy."[45]

The 1998 Form merely eliminated some redundancy by combining the separate defined-terms "personal injury" and "advertising injury" into one defined-term—"personal and advertising injury."[46] As for the "personal injury" offenses set forth in the 1973 and 1986 Forms, the 1998 Form makes no significant changes.[47]

Thus under all the forms generally in use, if the underlying plaintiff asserts, could assert, or even appears to assert a claim against the policyholder for or akin to false arrest or imprisonment,[48] malicious prosecution and/or wrongful use of civil proceeding,[49] trespass, nuisance, wrongful entry or eviction,[50] libel, slander, commercial disparagement, or defamation,[51] or invasion of privacy,[52] the policyholder should be entitled to coverage.[53]

The enumerated offenses of nuisance, trespass, and wrongful entry or eviction should be of interest to real estate-related entities, as these are "real property" torts. In the environmental context, there have been mixed results when a policyholder contends that claims for cleanup by an environmental authority or neighboring landowner trigger these "real property" enumerated offenses.[54] Moreover, with the advent of modern telecommunications, invasion of privacy torts, particularly in the context of advertising and marketing, involving pre-recorded phone solicitations or mass facsimile or email solicitations, take on renewed importance for all businesses.[55]

[b]—"Advertising Injury" Offenses

Coverage is afforded for "advertising injury," which is defined in the 1986 Form as follows:

"injury arising out of one or more of the following offenses:

a. Oral or written publication of material that slanders or libels a person or organization or disparages a person's or organization's goods, products or services;

b. Oral or written publication of material that violates a person's right of privacy;

c. Misappropriation of advertising ideas or style of doing business; or

d. Infringement of copyright, title or slogan."[56]

The 1973 Form specified the offenses of "unfair competition" and "piracy" in lieu of offense "c" ("misappropriation of advertising ideas and style of doing business.").[57] In addition to combining "personal injury" and "advertising injury" into one defined term, the 1998 Form replaced "misappropriation of" with "use of another's" and deleted "style of doing business" from enumerated offense "c" quoted above.[58] The 1998 Form also replaced infringement of "title" with infringement of "trade dress" in enumerated offense "d" quoted above.[59]

Despite these slight differences among the 1973, 1986, and 1998 Forms, claims for defamation, libel, slander, or commercial disparagement,[60] invasion of privacy,[61] infringement of copyright, title, trade dress or slogan,[62] piracy,[63] unfair competition,[64] or use of or misappropriation of advertising ideas or style of doing business[65] are covered "advertising injury" offenses.[66]

Real estate-related entities that engage in advertising and solicitation, especially now through use of modern telecommunications, should pay particular attention to Coverage B. For instance, if a real estate-related entity is sued for solicitations in connection with pre-recorded telephone calls or engagement in mass telephone, facsimile, text message, or email solicitations, that entity could potentially be covered for such conduct under the enumerated "invasion of privacy" tort in Coverage B, and it behooves that entity to engage appropriate experts in coverage to ascertain its insurance rights.[67] Likewise, if in the course of advertising, a real estate-related entity uses a website or automated telephone system, any claim for patent infringement in connection with such use of its website or telephone system, could be potentially covered as "misappropriation of advertising idea or style of doing business."[68]

[c]—Statutory and Constitutional Claims

Interesting issues arise where claims, which are not specifically enumerated as "personal injury" or "advertising injury" offenses, such as statutory or constitutional claims, are asserted against the policyholder. For example, a realtor or other real estate-related business could be sued for antitrust or anticompetitive behavior or under another statute for deceptive business practices.[69] Likewise, a zoning board or other governmental entity could be sued by a developer not permitted to develop what it wants or for improper compensation in a condemnation action, possibly asserting those claims as constitutional violations.[70] Similarly, a real estate-related entity could be sued for mass solicitations in violation of state and federal consumer protections or "do not call" statutes.[71] In these circumstances, coverage is generally afforded where the statutory or constitutional claim can be likened to an enumerated offense.[72]

[i]—Anticompetitive Behavior

The extent of coverage afforded for claims of anticompetitive behavior depends on the list of enumerated "personal injury" or "advertising injury" offenses and the ability to liken the claims to the enumerated offenses. For example, the anticompetitive and predatory conduct averred could include conduct that also amounts to state law torts enumerated in the definitions, such as libel, slander, or commercial disparagement of the competitor.[73] Sometimes, statements of superiority of services or product to even unnamed competitors have been held to constitute commercial disparagement for purposes of triggering insurance coverage.[74] Moreover, the conduct complained of could include use of predatory litigation tactics, raising the possibility of an abuse of process or malicious prosecution offense having been committed.[75] When the definition of "advertising injury" includes injury arising out of "unfair competition," such as in the 1973 Form, courts have construed that term to mean anticompetitive conduct, including antitrust claims and tortious interference with a contract between the competitor and a third party.[76]

[ii]—Claims against Government

In the context of zoning eminent domain, regulatory, and other governmental actions, there may be an averment of restraint on alienation of real property. Such averments may constitute an invasion of the right of private occupancy and ownership. In fact, courts have often held that similar interferences with rights of ownership constitute "invasions of the rights of private occupancy," as used in Coverage B of CGL insurance policies.[77]

[iii]—Telephone Consumer Protection Act Claims

As discussed above, business entities, including real estate-related entities, that use modern telecommunications to solicit, either through mass telephone calls, facsimiles, or emails, could be sued for violation of state and federal consumer protections or "do not call" statutes. Such "do not call" claims are often covered, although there is a split as to whether such acts are covered "invasion of privacy" offenses.[78]

§ 9.04 Common Exclusions

There are some common exclusions that are relevant here.

[1]—Intentional Acts Exclusion

The intentional act or fortuity exclusion is often raised by insurance companies as a means to seek to avoid coverage for the claims that might otherwise fit under Coverage B as a "personal injury" or "advertising injury." However, the intentional act or fortuity exclusion should not apply to bar coverage under the personal and advertising injury coverage part. The rationale for this hypothesis is that Coverage B enumerates covered acts that include numerous intentional torts, such as defamation, wrongful entry or eviction, malicious prosecution, and false arrest, among others.[79] Courts have generally refused to apply such exclusions to bar coverage on the following bases: (1) to exclude coverage for such intentional conduct would be tantamount to providing illusory coverage because any interpretation that there is an exclusion for intentional acts would negate the very coverage that appears to be afforded by Coverage B of the policy; (2) the coverage grant and intentional action exclusion create an ambiguity; and (3) the claim at issue can be sustained without a finding of specific intent and therefore does not fit squarely within the express terms of the exclusion. Courts have consistently refused to allow such over-reaching and strained interpretations of contracts.[80]

[2]—Breach of Contract Exclusion

Moreover, in Coverage B of standard-form CGL insurance policies, insurance companies exclude coverage not only for (a) the contractual assumption of liability in connection with "personal and advertising injury" claims but also for (b) "personal and advertising injury" claims arising from breach of contract. A typical exclusion reads: "This insurance does not apply to . . . 'personal and advertising injury' arising out of a breach of contract. . . ."[81] This "breach of contract" exclusion has been generally enforced, albeit not in every circumstance.[82]

Of significance, here, is the fact that such an exclusion does not appear in Coverage A exclusions.[83] Because insurance companies do not include a similar "breach of contract" exclusion in Coverage A—the "bodily injury" and "property damage" coverage at issue—it can be inferred that they never intended to exclude coverage for all claims for breach of contract in Coverage A.[84]

[3]—Statutory Violation Exclusion

Some policies contain a statutory violation exclusion that has been used by insurance companies to deny coverage for statutory claims that are similar to common-law torts. These exclusions appear to be an attempt to draft around some unfavorable results from cases finding coverage for statutory violations of all sorts.[85] Insurance companies have had some success in enforcing these exclusions.[86]

Notes

[1] See § 2.03 *supra*. See also, e.g.:

First Circuit: Ryan v. Royal Insurance Co., 916 F.2d 731 (1st Cir. 1990); Barletta Heavy Division, Inc. v. Travelers Insurance Co., 2013 U.S. Dist. LEXIS 153555 (D. Mass. Oct. 25, 2013); New England Environmental Technologies Corp. v. American Safety Risk Retention Group, Inc., 810 F. Supp.2d 390 (D. Mass. 2011); Liberty Mutual Insurance Co. v. Black & Decker Corp., 383 F. Supp.2d 200, 219 (D. Mass. 2004); American Employers' Insurance Co. v. DeLorme Publishing Co., 39 F. Supp.2d 64 (D. Me. 1999).

Second Circuit: Barney Greengrass, Inc. v. Lumbermens Mutual Casualty Co., 445 Fed. Appx. 411 (2d Cir. 2011); Continental Casualty Co. v. JBS Construction Management, Inc., 2010 U.S. Dist. LEXIS 85467 (S.D.N.Y. July 1, 2010); Allianz Insurance Co. v. Lerner, 416 F.3d 109, 116 (2d Cir. 2005); Specialty National Insurance Co. v. English Brothers Funeral Home, 606 F. Supp.2d 466 (S.D.N.Y. 2009); City of West Haven v. Liberty Mutual Insurance Co., 639 F. Supp. 1012 (D. Conn. 1986).

Third Circuit: NL Industries, Inc. v. Commercial Union Insurance Co., 926 F. Supp. 446 (D.N.J. 1996); Harristown Development Corp. v. International Insurance Co., 1988 WL 123149, at *12 (M.D. Pa. Nov. 15, 1988).

Fourth Circuit: Perdue Farms, Inc. v. Travelers Casualty & Surety Company of America, 448 F.3d 252, 258 (4th Cir. 2006) ("'Although the type of policy here considered is most often referred to as liability insurance, it is 'litigation insurance' as well, protecting the insured from the expense of defending suits brought against him.'"); Provident Bank of Maryland v. Travelers Property Casualty Corp., 236 F.3d 138 (4th Cir. 2000); Lott v. Scottsdale Insurance Co., 827 F. Supp.2d 626 (E.D. Va. 2013); Stewart Title Guaranty Co. v. Sanford Title Services, L.L.C., 2013 WL 5566493 (D. Md. Oct. 8, 2013); Baker's Express, L.L.C. v. Arrowpoint Capital Corp., 2012 WL 4370265 (D. Md. Sept. 20, 2012); New England Environmental Technologies Corp. v. American Safety Risk Retention Group, Inc., 810 F. Supp.2d 390 (D. Mass. 2011); Capital Environmental Services, Inc. v. North River Insurance Co., 536 F. Supp.2d 633 (E.D. Va. 2008); Zurich American Insurance Co. v. Fieldstone Mortgage Co., 2007 WL 3268460 (D. Md. Oct. 26, 2007).

Sixth Circuit: Ndabishuriye v. Albert Schweitzer Society, USA, Inc., 136 Fed. Appx. 795, 796 (6th Cir. 2005); Keely v. Fire Insurance Exchange, 833 F. Supp.2d 722 (E.D. Mich. 2011); Taylor v. Temple & Cutler, 192 F.R.D. 552, 558 (E.D. Mich. 1999) ("'In a sense, liability insurance is nothing more than litigation insurance.'").

Seventh Circuit: Sampson v. Western Sierra Acceptance Corp., 2004 U.S. Dist. LEXIS 11779 (N.D. Ill. July 1, 2004).

Eighth Circuit: Pekin Insurance Co. v. Tysa, Inc., 2006 U.S. Dist. LEXIS 93525 (S.D. Iowa Dec. 27, 2006); Schipp v. General Motors Corp., 457 F. Supp.2d 917 (E.D. Ark. 2006).

Ninth Circuit: Newmont USA Ltd. v. American Home Assurance Co., 676 F. Supp.2d 1146 (E.D. Wash. 2009); Intel Corp. v. Insurance Company of Pennsylvania, 2009 WL 81393 (N.D. Cal. Jan. 9, 2009); Kla-Tencor Corp. v. National Union Fire Insurance Co., 2006 WL 2479106 (N.D. Cal. Aug. 28, 2006).

Tenth Circuit: Hurtado v. Passmore & Sons, L.L.C., 2011 U.S. Dist. LEXIS 68795 (D. Colo. June 27, 2011); Westport Insurance Corp. v. Ong, 2008 WL 892941 (D. Utah Mar. 28, 2008); American States Insurance Co. v. Ridco, Inc., 1996 WL 33401184, at *3 (D. Wyo. Feb. 8, 1996); Weitzman v. Blazing Pedals, Inc., 151 F.R.D. 125 (D. Colo. 1993).

Eleventh Circuit: Illinois Union Insurance Co. v. NRI Construction Inc., 846 F. Supp.2d 1366 (N.D. Ga. 2012); Smith v. Williams, 819 F. Supp.2d 1264 (M.D. Fla. 2011); Colonial Oil Industries, Inc. v. Underwriters Subscribing to Policy Nos. T031504670, 1995 WL 692691, at *10–11 (S.D. Ga. Nov. 6, 1995), ***vacated and modified*** 910 F. Supp. 655 (S.D. Ga. 1995).

District of Columbia Circuit: Pierce Associates, Inc. v. St. Paul Mercury Insurance Co., 421 F. Supp.2d 11, 17 (D.D.C.), ***vacated on other grounds*** 437 F. Supp.2d 16 (D.D.C. 2006).

State Courts:

Alaska: Langdon v. Champion, 752 P.2d 999 (Alaska 1988).

Connecticut: Ferri v. Powell-Ferri, 2014 Conn. Super. LEXIS 1377 (Conn. Super. June 5, 2014); Community Healthcare Credit Union, Inc. v. CUNA Mutual Group, 2007 Conn. Super. LEXIS 1415 (Conn. Super. June 1, 2007).

Delaware: Liggett Group, Inc. v. Ace Property & Casualty Insurance Co., 798 A.2d 1024, 1031 (Del. 2002); Deutsche Bank Trust Co. v. Royal Surplus Lines Insurance Co., 2012 WL 2898478 (Del. Super. Ct., Sept. 12, 2012).

Florida: Contreras v. 21st Century Insurance Co., 52 So.2d 1194 (Fla. App. 2011).

Illinois: Illinois Tool Works Inc. v. Travelers Casualty and Surety Co., 2015 IL App (1st) 132350, 26 N.E.3d 421, 389 Ill. Dec. 331 (2015).

Indiana: Transamerica Insurance Services v. Kopco, 559 N.E.2d 322 (Ind. App. 1990).

Kansas: Miller v. Westport Insurance Corp., 200 P.3d 419 (Kan. 2009).

Maryland: BGE Home Products & Services, Inc. v. Owens, 833 A.2d 8, 14 (Md. 2003); Sherwood Brands, Inc. v. Hartford Accident & Indemnity Co., 698 A.2d 1078, 1083 (Md. 1997); Brohawn v. Transamerica Insurance Co., 347 A.2d 842, 851 (Md. 1975); Back Creek Partners, L.L.C. v. First American Title Insurance. Co., 213 Md. App. 703, 75 A.3d 394 (2013).

Massachusetts: Hanover Insurance Co. v. Golden, 766 N.E.2d 838, 841 (Mass. 2002); Hingham Mutual Fire Insurance Co. v. De Wolfe, 2008 WL 4290919 (Mass. App. Sept. 16, 2008); Celanase Corp. v. OneBeacon America Insurance Co., 2008 WL 5784444 (Mass. Super. Dec. 9, 2008).

Michigan: Allstate Insurance Co. v. Freeman, 443 N.W.2d 734 (Mich. 1989).

New York: K2 Investment Group, L.L.C. v. American Guarantee & Liability Insurance Co., 22 N.Y.3d 578, 6 N.E.3d 1117, 983 N.Y.S.2d 761 (2014); Bovis Lend Lease LMB, Inc. v. Garito Contracting, Inc., 65 A.D.3d 872, 885 N.Y.S.2d 59 (N.Y. App. Div. 2009); BP Air Conditioning Corp. v. One Beacon Insurance Group, 33 A.D.3d 116, 821 N.Y.S.2d 1 (N.Y. App. Div. 2006) ("For this reason, when a policy represents that it will provide the insured with a defense, we have said that it actually constitutes 'litigation insurance' in addition to liability coverage."); Automobile Insurance Company of Hartford v. Cook, 850 N.E.2d 1152, 1155 (N.Y. 2006) ("when a policy represents that it will provide the insured with a defense, . . . it actually constitutes 'litigation insurance' in addition to liability coverage"); City of New

York v. Certain Underwriters of Lloyd's of London, England, 15 A.D.3d 228, 790 N.Y.S.2d 82, 2005 WL 319709, at *2 (N.Y. App. Div. Feb. 10, 2005).

North Carolina: SPX Corp. v. Liberty Mutual Insurance Co., 210 N.C. App. 562, 709 S.E.2d 441 (2011); Brown v. Lumbermens Mutual Insurance Co., 90 N.C. App. 464, 369 S.E.2d 367 (1988), *review denied* 373 S.E.2d 541 (N.C. 1988).

Texas: Lamar Homes, Inc. v. Mid-Continent Casualty Co., 242 S.W.3d 1 (Tex. 2007).

Virginia: Veney v. Duke, 2005 WL 3476760, at *2 (Va. Cir. Oct. 26, 2005) ("'liability insurance' essentially constitutes 'litigation insurance'").

Washington: National Surety Corp. v. Immunex Corp., 176 Wash.2d 872, 297 P.3d 688 (Wash. 2013) (*en banc*).

Wyoming: Shoshone First Bank v. Pacific Employers Insurance Co., 2 P.3d 510, 516 (Wyo. 2000); First Wyoming Bank, N.A. v. Continental Insurance Co., 860 P.2d 1064 (Wyo.), *vacated in part* 860 P.2d 1094 (Wyo. 1993).

2 See § 5.01 *supra.*

3 See Chapter 5 *supra.*

4 See Chapter 6 *supra.*

5 See § 9.02 *infra.*

6 See § 9.03[1] *infra.*

7 See § 9.03[2] *infra.*

8 See § 9.03[3][a] *infra.*

9 See § 9.03[3][b] *infra.*

10 See § 9.03[3][c] *infra.*

11 See § 9.04[1] *infra.*

12 See § 9.04[2] *infra.*

13 See ISO Form CG 00 01 10 01. See also, David B. Goodwin & A. Mari Mazour, "Insuring Corporate Competitive Practices" 661 PLI/Comm 69 (1993).

14 Elizabeth Lauzon, "Advertising Injury Insurance," 98 A.L.R.5th 1 (2009) (discussing the 1973, 1986, and 1998 Forms); Goodwin and Mazour, "Insuring Corporate Competitive Practices" 661 PLI/Comm 69, 72–76 (1993) (discussing the 1973 and 1986 Forms).

15 *Id.*

16 *Id.*

17 See ISO Form CG 00 01 12 07.

18 See ISO Form CG 00 01 12 07.

19 Goodwin and Mazour, "Insuring Corporate Competitive Practices" 661 PLI/Comm 69, 72–76 (1993) (discussing the 1973 and 1986 Forms).

20 *Id.*, at 75–76.

21 *Id.*, at 72–76.

22 *Id.*, at 72–76.

23 Compare ISO Form CG 00 01 12 07 with ISO Form CG 00 01 10 01.

24 Goodwin and Mazour, "Insuring Corporate Competitive Practices" 661 PLI/Comm 69, 72–76 (1993) (discussing the 1973 and 1986 Forms).

25 *Id.*

26 *Id.*

27 *Id.*

28 *Id.*

[29] *Id.*

[30] *Id.* See also ISO Form CG 00 01 12 07.

[31] See § 9.03[3][a] *infra.*

[32] See ISO Form CG 00 01 10 01. See also, Goodwin and Mazour, "Insuring Corporate Competitive Practices" 661 PLI/Comm 69, 72–76 (1993).

The 1998 Form includes a limited exclusion for some enumerated traditionally "advertising injury" offenses committed by policyholders in the business of advertising, publishing, broadcasting, or telecasting. See §§ 9.02[1] and [4] *supra.*

[33] See § 9.03[3][b] *infra.*

[34] See § 9.03[3][b] *infra.*

[35] Goodwin and Mazour, "Insuring Corporate Competitive Practices" 661 PLI/Comm 69, 72–76 (1993).

[36] See ISO Form CG 00 01 10 01.

[37] See, e.g., Liberty Life Insurance Co. v. Commercial Union Insurance Co., 857 F.2d 945 (9th Cir. 1988).

[38] See, e.g., Air Engineering, Inc. v. Industrial Air Power, L.L.C., 346 Wis.2d 9, 828 N.W.2d 565 (Wis. App. 2013).

[39] See:

Fifth Circuit: Merchants Co. v. American Motorists Insurance Co., 794 F. Supp. 611 (S.D. Miss. 1992).

Sixth Circuit: Amway Distributions Benefits Association v. Federal Insurance Co., 990 F. Supp. 936 (W.D. Mich. 1997) (finding as ambiguous "advertising activities" because they "can be reasonably interpreted to encompass widespread distribution of materials to the public as well as direct solicitation of small groups or individuals").

Seventh Circuit: Attorneys' Title Guaranty Fund, Inc. v. Maryland Casualty Co., 1991 WL 171339 (N.D. Ill. Aug. 23, 1991).

Eighth Circuit: Owners Insurance Co. v. European Auto Works, Inc., 695 F.3d 814 (8th Cir. 2012); John Deere Insurance Co. v. Shamrock Industries, Inc., 696 F. Supp. 434 (D. Minn. 1988), *aff'd* 929 F.2d 413 (8th Cir. 1991).

Tenth Circuit: Park University Enterprises, Inc. v. American Casualty Company of Reading, Pennsylvania, 442 F.3d 1239 (10th Cir. 2006).

State Courts:

Minnesota: General Casualty Company of Wisconsin v. Wozniak Travel, Inc., 762 N.W.2d 572 (Minn. 2009).

Washington: Amazon.com International, Inc. v. American Dynasty Surplus Lines Insurance Co., 120 Wash. App. 610, 85 P.3d 974, *review denied* 103 P.3d 200 (Wash. 2004).

Wisconsin: Acuity v. Bagadia, 310 Wis.2d 197, 750 N.W.2d 817 (2008); Air Engineering, Inc. v. Industrial Air Power, L.L.C., 346 Wis.2d 9, 828 N.W.2d 565 (Wis. App. 2013).

[40] See:

Fourth Circuit: Teletronics International, Inc. v. CNA Insurance Company/Transportation Insurance Co., 120 Fed. Appx. 440 (4th Cir. 2005); Solers, Inc. v. Hartford Casualty Insurance Co., 146 F. Supp.2d 785 (E.D. Va. 2001).

Fifth Circuit: Mid-Continent Casualty Co. v. Kipp Flores Architects, L.L.C., 602 Fed. Appx. 985 (5th Cir. 2015); Continental Casualty Co. v. Consolidated Graphics, Inc., 646 F.3d 210 (5th Cir. 2011).

Seventh Circuit: Playboy Enterprises, Inc. v. St. Paul Fire & Marine Insurance Co., 769 F.2d 425, 429 (7th Cir. 1985); Attorneys' Title Guaranty Fund, Inc. v. Maryland Casualty Co., 1991 WL 171339 (N.D. Ill. Aug. 23, 1991).

Ninth Circuit: Hayward v. Centennial Insurance Co., 430 F.3d 989 (9th Cir. 2005).

State Courts:

California: Hameid v. National Fire Insurance of Hartford, 31 Cal.4th 16, 71 P.3d 761, 1 Cal. Rptr.3d 401 (2003); Rombe Corp. v. Allied Insurance Co., 27 Cal. Rptr.3d 99 (Cal. App. 2005).

Georgia: North Metro Directories Publication, LLC v. Cotton States Mutual Insurance Co., 631 S.E.2d 726 (Ga. App. 2006).

Illinois: People v. Beaulieu Realtors, Inc., 494 N.E.2d 504, 508 (Ill. App. 1986).

Kansas: MGM, Inc. v. Liberty Mutual Insurance Co., 839 P.2d 537, 540 (Kan. App. 1992), *aff'd* 855 P.2d 77 (Kan. 1993).

Maryland: Monumental Life Insurance Co. v. United States Fidelity & Guaranty Co., 617 A.2d 1163, 1173 (Md. App.), *cert. denied* 624 A.2d 491 (Md. 1993).

Massachusetts: Smartfoods, Inc. v. Northbrook Property & Casualty Co., 618 N.E.2d 1365, 1368 (1993).

Michigan: Citizens Insurance Co. v. Pro-Seal Service Group, Inc., 2007 WL 1229099 (Mich. Apr. 25, 2007).

Minnesota: Fox Chemical Co. v. Great American Insurance Co., 264 N.W.2d 385, 386 (Minn. 1978).

Missouri: American States Insurance Co. v. Vortherms, 5 S.W.3d 538 (Mo. App. 1999).

New Hampshire: First Bank & Trust Co. v. New Hampshire Insurance Group, 469 A.2d 1367, 1368 (N.H. 1983).

Vermont: Select Designs, Ltd. v. Union Mutual Fire Insurance Co., 674 A.2d 798 (Vt. 1996).

[41] See ISO Form CG 00 01 10 01.

[42] See ISO Form CG 00 01 10 01.

[43] See, e.g.:

Second Circuit: Park Place Entertainment Corp. v. Transcontinental Insurance Co., 2003 WL 1913709 (S.D.N.Y. Apr. 18, 2003) (date of defamatory statement); County of Suffolk v. Travelers Insurance Co., 267 F. Supp.2d 288 (E.D.N.Y. 2003) (date of trespass/nuisance).

Third Circuit: CGU v. Travelers Property & Casualty Co., 121 F. Supp.2d 819 (E.D. Pa. 2000) (date of defamation).

Ninth Circuit: Ecology Works, Inc. v. Essex Insurance Co., 58 Fed. Appx. 714 (9th Cir. 2003) (date of infringement).

Tenth Circuit: Scottsdale Insurance Co. v. James L. Gardner Trust, 53 Fed. Appx. 882 (10th Cir. 2002) (date of wrongful entry or eviction).

State Courts:

Illinois: National Fire and Indemnity Exchange v. Ali & Sons Co., 346 Ill. App.3d 107, 281 Ill. Dec. 232, 803 N.E.2d 636 (Ill. App. 2004) (date of trespass).

Missouri: Hampton v. Carter Enterprises, Inc., 238 S.W.3d 170 (Mo. App. 2007) (date of filing malicious prosecution claim).

New Hampshire: Broom v. Continental Casualty Co., 152 N.H. 749, 887 A.2d 1128 (N.H. 2005) (date of defamatory statement).

Texas: KLN Steel Products Co. v. CNA Insurance Cos., 2008 WL 5423148 278 S.W.3d 429 (Tex. App. Dec. 31, 2008) (date of libelous statement).

[44] See, e.g., Industrial Indemnity Co. v. Apple Computer, Inc., 79 Cal. App.4th 817, 95 Cal. Rptr.2d 528 (Cal. App. 1999). Of course, as case law develops, the location of the offenses could be the location where the actor committed the offense or the location where the victim suffered the injury emanating from the offense.

[45] *Id.* See also, Goodwin and Mazour, "Insuring Corporate Competitive Practices" 661 PLI/ Comm 69, 72–76 (1993).

[46] See ISO Form CG 00 01 12 07. See also §§ 9.02[1] and [4] *supra.*

[47] See ISO Form CG 00 01 12 07.

[48] See ISO Forms CG 00 01 10 01 and CG 00 01 12 07. See also:

Fourth Circuit: Selective Insurance Co. v. Oglebay, 242 Fed. Appx. 104 (4th Cir. 2007); Erie Insurance Property and Casualty Co., Inc. v. Edmond, 785 F. Supp.2d 561 (N.D. W. Va. 2011).

Fifth Circuit: Cornhill Insurance PLC v. Valsamis, Inc., 106 F.3d 80 (5th Cir.), *cert. denied* 522 U.S. 818 (1997).

Seventh Circuit: Colton v. Swain, 527 F.2d 296 (7th Cir. 1975); American Safety Casualty Insurance Co. v. City of Waukegan, 776 F. Supp.2d 670 (N.D. Ill. 2011).

Eighth Circuit: Gulf Underwriters Insurance Co. v. City of Council Bluffs, 755 F. Supp.2d 988 (S.D. Iowa 2010).

Tenth Circuit: Cole v. State Farm Fire & Casualty Co., 25 Fed. Appx. 791 (10th Cir. 2002).

Eleventh Circuit: First Specialty Insurance Corp. v. 633 Partners Ltd., 300 Fed. Appx. 777 (11th Cir. 2008); State Farm Fire and Casualty Co. v. G.H.W., 56 F. Supp.3d 1210 (N.D. Ala. 2014).

State Courts:

California: City of Newport Beach v. Sasse, 88 Cal. Rptr. 476 (Cal. App. 1970); State Farm General Insurance Co. v. Mintarsih, 175 Cal. App.4th 274, 95 Cal. Rptr.3d 845 (2009).

Colorado: Mountain States Mutual Casualty Co. v. Hauser, 221 P.3d 56 (Colo. App. 2009).

Illinois: Allstate Insurance Co. v. Amato, 372 Ill. App.3d 139, 310 Ill. Dec. 192, 865 N.E.2d 516 (Ill. App. 2007).

New Hampshire: Northern Security Insurance Co. v. Connors, 161 N.H. 645, 20 A.3d 912 (2011); State Farm Insurance Co. v. Bruns, 942 A.2d 1275 (N.H. 2008).

New Jersey: City of Newark v. Hartford Accident & Indemnity Co., 342 A.2d 513 (N.J. Super. App. Div. 1975).

Oregon: Minnis v. Oregon Mutual Insurance Co., 48 P.3d 137 (Or. 2002).

South Dakota: Biegler v. American Family Mutual Insurance Co., 621 N.W.2d 592 (S.D. 2001).

Utah: Benjamin v. Amica Mutual Insurance Co., 140 P.3d 1210 (Utah 2006).

See also, Goodwin and Mazour, "Insuring Corporate Competitive Practices" 661 PLI/ Comm 69, 72–76 (1993).

[49] See ISO Forms CG 00 01 10 01 and CG 00 01 12 07. See also:

First Circuit: Global Naps, Inc. v. Federal Insurance Co., 336 F.3d 59 (1st Cir. 2003).

Second Circuit: Ethicon, Inc. v. Aetna Casualty & Surety Co., 737 F. Supp. 1320 (S.D.N.Y. 1990).

Third Circuit: Brotherhood Mutual Insurance Co. v. Salem Baptist Church of Jenkintown, 985 F. Supp.2d 624 (E.D. Pa. 2013); Regent Insurance Co. v. Strausser Enterprises, Inc., 902 F. Supp.2d 628 (E.D. Pa. 2012).

Sixth Circuit: Smith & Nephew, Inc. v. Federal Insurance Co, 113 Fed. Appx. 99 (6th Cir. 2004).

Seventh Circuit: Heil Co. v. Hartford Accident & Indemnity Co., 937 F. Supp. 1355 (E.D. Wis. 1996).

Eighth Circuit: Chicago Insurance Co. v. City of Council Bluffs, 713 F.3d 963 (8th Cir. 2013).

Ninth Circuit: Petrochem Marketing, Inc. v. Mt. Hawley Insurance Co., 131 Fed. Appx. 100 (9th Cir. 2005); Lunsford v. American Guarantee & Liability Insurance Co., 18 F.3d 653 (9th Cir. 1994); St. Paul Mercury Insurance Co. v. Tessera, Inc., 908 F. Supp.2d 1054 (N.D. Cal. 2012).

Tenth Circuit: Carolina Casualty Insurance Co. v. Nanodetex Corp., 733 F.3d 1018 (10th Cir. 2013).

State Courts:

California: Butcher v. Truck Insurance Exchange, 92 Cal. Rptr.2d 521 (Cal. App. 2000).

Connecticut: QSP, Inc. v. Aetna Casualty & Surety Co., 773 A.2d 906 (Conn. 2001).

Florida: St. Paul Fire & Marine Insurance Co. v. Naples Community Hospital, Inc., 585 So.2d 374 (Fla. App. 1991).

Illinois: William J. Templeman Co. v. Liberty Mutual Insurance Co., 735 N.E.2d 669 (Ill. App. 2000); Spiegel v. Zurich Insurance Co., 687 N.E.2d 1099 (Ill. App. 1997).

Iowa: Employers Mutual Casualty Co. v. Cedar Rapids Television Co., 552 N.W.2d 639 (Iowa 1996).

Louisiana: Regency Motors of Metairie, L.L.C. v. Hibernia-Rosenthal Insurance Agency, L.L.C., 868 So.2d 905 (La. App.), *writ denied* 872 So.2d 1087 (La. 2004); Finnie v. LeBlanc, 856 So.2d 208 (La. App. 2003), *writ denied* 869 So.2d 849 (La. 2004).

New Mexico: Hinkle v. State Farm Fire and Casualty Co., 308 P.3d 1009 (N.M. App. 2013).

Pennsylvania: High Concrete Structures, Inc. v. National Union Fire Insurance Company of Pittsburgh, Pennsylvania, 65 Pa. D. & C.4th 143 (Pa. C.P. 2004).

South Carolina: Town of Duncan v. State Budget & Control Board, Division of Insurance Services, 482 S.E.2d 768 (S.C. 1997).

Texas: Pennsylvania Pulp & Paper Co. v. Nationwide Mutual Insurance Co., 100 S.W.3d 566 (Tex. App. 2003).

Washington: Fluke Corp. v. Hartford Accident & Indemnity Co., 34 P.3d 809 (Wash. 2001).

See also Goodwin & Mazour, "Insuring Corporate Competitive Practices" 661 PLI/Comm 69, 72–76 (1993).

50 See ISO Forms CG 00 01 10 01 and CG 00 01 12 07. See also:

Second Circuit: Rosenberg Diamond Development Corp. v. Wausau Insurance Co., 326 F. Supp.2d 472 (S.D.N.Y. 2004), *aff'd* 144 Fed. Appx. 122 (2d Cir. 2005).

Fifth Circuit: Lexington Insurance Co. v. St. Bernard Parish Government, 548 Fed. Appx. 176 (5th Cir. 2013); Mid-Continent Casualty Co. v. Camaley Energy Co., 364 F. Supp.2d 600 (N.D. Tex. 2005).

Seventh Circuit: Supreme Laundry Service, L.L.C. v. Hartford Casualty Insurance Co., 521 F.3d 743 (7th Cir. 2008); Great American Insurance Company of New York v. Helwig, 419 F. Supp.2d 1017 (N.D. Ill. 2006); Wolf Lake Terminals, Inc. v. Mutual Marine Insurance Co., 433 F. Supp.2d 933 (N.D. Ind. 2005).

Ninth Circuit: Sell v. Nationwide Mutual Insurance Co., 492 Fed. Appx. 740 (9th Cir. 2012); *In re* Captain Blyther's, Inc., 152 Fed. Appx. 669 (9th Cir. 2005).

Tenth Circuit: Chimera Investment Co. v. State Farm Fire and Casualty Co., 268 Fed. Appx. 793 (10th Cir. 2008); Hartford Fire Insurance Co. v. Gandy Dancer, L.L.C., 981 F. Supp.2d 981 (D.N.M. 2013); National Fire Insurance Company of Hartford v. NWM-Oklahoma, LLC, 546 F. Supp.2d 1238 (W.D. Okla. 2008).

Eleventh Circuit: Nationwide Mutual Fire Insurance Co. v. Royall, 588 F. Supp.2d 1306 (M.D. Fla. 2008).

State Courts:

Alaska: Whittier Properties, Inc. v. Alaska National Insurance Co., 185 P.3d 84 (Alaska 2008).

California: Golden Eagle Insurance Corp. v. Cen-Fed, Ltd., 148 Cal. App.4th 976, 56 Cal. Rptr.3d 279 (Cal. App. 2007).

Delaware: Westfield Insurance Group v. J.P.'s Wharf, Ltd, 859 A.2d 74 (Del. 2004).

Georgia: Nationwide Mutual Fire Insurance Co. v. Somers, 264 Ga. App. 421, 591 S.E.2d 430 (Ga. App. 2003).

Illinois: John T. Doyle Trust v. Country Mutual Insurance Co., 2014 IL App (2d) 121238, 8 N.E.3d 490, 380 Ill. Dec. 320 (2014).

Indiana: Thomson, Inc. v. Insurance Co. of North America, 11 N.E.3d 982 (Ind. App. 2014); Chubb Custom Insurance Co. v. Standard Fusee Corp., 2 N.E.3d 752 (Ind. App. 2014); Newnam Manufacturing, Inc. v. Transcontinental Insurance Co., 871 N.E.2d 396 (Ind. App. 2007).

Kansas: Rockgate Management Co. v. CGU Insurance, Inc./PG Insurance Company of New York, 32 Kan. App.2d 743 88 P.3d 798 (Kan. App. 2004).

Louisiana: Regency Motors of Metairie, L.L.C. v. Hibernia-Rosenthal Insurance Agency, L.L.C., 868 So.2d 905 (La. App.), *writ denied* 872 So.2d 1087 (La. 2004).

Massachusetts: Dilbert v. Hanover Insurance Co., 63 Mass. App.Ct. 327, 825 N.E.2d 1071 (Mass. App. 2005).

Ohio: Meyers Lake Sportsman's Club, Inc. v. Auto-Owners Mutual Insurance Co., 2013 LEXIS 3164 (Ohio App. July 15, 2013).

Pennsylvania: Penn's Market I, L.P. v. Harlesyville Mutual Insurance Co., 2007 WL 5124011 (Pa. Super. Apr. 3, 2007).

North Carolina: Hobbs Realty & Construction Co. v. Scottsdale Insurance Co., 163 N.C. App. 285, 593 S.E.2d 103 (N.C. App.), *cert. denied* 599 S.E.2d 907 (N.C. 2004).

Texas: Hettler v. Travelers Lloyds Insurance Co., 190 S.W.3d 52 (Tex. App. 2005).

Wisconsin: Liebovich v. Minnesota Insurance Co., 299 Wis.2d 331, 728 N.W.2d 357 (Wis. App. 2007).

See also, Goodwin & Mazour, "Insuring Corporate Competitive Practices" 661 PLI/Comm 69, 72–76 (1993).

[51] See ISO Forms CG 00 01 10 01 and CG 00 01 12 07. See also:

First Circuit: Hansen v. Sentry Insurance Co., 756 F.3d 53 (1st Cir. 2014); Great American Insurance Co. v. Riso, Inc., 479 F.3d 158 (1st Cir. 2007).

Third Circuit: Charter Oak Insurance Co. v. Maglio Fresh Food, 979 F. Supp.2d 581 (E.D. Pa. 2013).

Fifth Circuit: Nationwide Mutual Insurance Co. v. Gum Tree Property Management, L.L.C., 597 Fed. Appx. 241 (5th Cir. 2015); Lamar Advertising Co. v. Continental Casualty Co., 396 F.3d 654 (5th Cir. 2005); Uretek (USA), Inc. v. Continental Casualty Co., 92 F. Supp.3d 589 (S.D. Tex. 2015).

Sixth Circuit: Smith & Nephew, Inc. v. Federal Insurance Co, 113 Fed. Appx. 99 (6th Cir. 2004); Dave's Detailing, Inc. v. Catlin Insurance Co., 13 F. Supp.3d 935 (S.D. Ind. 2014); Michigan Municipal Risk Management Authority v. State Farm Fire and Casualty Co., 559 F. Supp.2d 794 (E.D. Mich. 2008).

Seventh Circuit: National Union Fire Insurance Co. of Pittsburgh, Pa. v. Mead Johnson & Co., 735 F.3d 539 (7th Cir. 2013); BASF AG v. Great American Assurance Co., 522 F.3d 813 (7th Cir. 2008).

Eighth Circuit: Sletten and Brettin Orthodontics, L.L.C. v. Continental Casualty Co., 782 F.3d 931 (8th Cir. 2015).

Ninth Circuit: Bullpen Distribution, Inc. v. Sentinel Insurance Co., 584 Fed. Appx. 769 (9th Cir. 2014); ABM Industries, Inc. v. National Union Fire Insurance Co. of Pittsburgh, PA, 291 Fed. Appx. 800 (9th Cir. 2008); Primiani v. Federal Insurance Co., 203 Fed. Appx. 902 (9th Cir. 2006); E.piphany, Inc. v. St. Paul Fire & Marine Insurance Co., 590 F. Supp.2d 1244 (N.D. Cal. 2008).

Tenth Circuit: Chimera Investment Co. v. State Farm Fire and Casualty Co., 268 Fed. Appx. 793 (10th Cir. 2008).

Eleventh Circuit: Vector Products, Inc. v. Hartford Fire Insurance Co., 397 F.3d 1316 (11th Cir. 2005).

State Courts:

California: Hartford Casualty Insurance Co. v. Swift Distribution, Inc., 59 Cal.4th 277, 326 P.3d 253, 172 Cal. Rptr.3d 653 (2014).

Colorado: Thompson v. Maryland Casualty Co., 84 P.3d 496 (Colo. 2004).

Florida: Khatib v. Old Dominion Insurance Co., 153 So.3d 943 (Fla. App. 2014); St. Paul Fire & Marine Insurance Co. v. Naples Community Hospital, Inc., 585 So.2d 374 (Fla. App. 1991).

Illinois: Cincinnati Insurance Co. v. American Hardware Manufacturers Association, 387 Ill. App.3d 85, 325 Ill. Dec. 483, 898 N.E.2d 216 (Ill. App. 2008).

Indiana: Barnard v. Menard, Inc., 25 N.E.3d 750 (Ind. App. 2015).

Kansas: Rockgate Management Co. v. CGU Insurance, Inc./PG Insurance Company of New York, 32 Kan. App.2d 743, 88 P.3d 798 (Kan. App. 2004).

Louisiana: Finnie v. LeBlanc, 856 So.2d 208 (La. App. 2003), *writ denied* 869 So.2d 849 (La. 2004).

New Hampshire: Broom v. Continental Casualty Co., 152 N.H. 749, 887 A.2d 1128 (N.H. 2005).

New York: Natural Organics, Inc. v. OneBeacon America Insurance Co., 102 A.D.3d 756, 959 N.Y.S.2d 204, (N.Y. App. Div. 2013); JMZ USA, Inc. v. Lumbermens Mutual Casualty Co., 36 A.D.3d 555, 828 N.Y.S.2d 385 (N.Y. App. Div. 2007).

North Carolina: Harleysville Mutual Insurance Co. v. Buzz Off Insect Shield, L.L.C., 664 S.E.2d 317 (N.C. App. 2008).

South Carolina: Owners Insurance Co. v. Clayton, 364 S.C. 555, 614 S.E.2d 611 (S.C. 2005).

Tennessee: Ralph v. Pipkin, 183 S.W.3d 362 (Tenn. App. 2005).

Texas: KLN Steel Products Co. v. CNA Insurance Companies, 278 S.W.3d 429 (Tex. App. 2008); Hettler v. Travelers Lloyds Insurance Co., 190 S.W.3d 52 (Tex. App. 2005).

Washington: Grange Insurance Ass'n v. Roberts, 179 Wash. App. 739, 320 P.3d 77 (2013).

Wisconsin: Baumann v. Elliott, 286 Wis.2d 667, 704 N.W.2d 361 (Wis. App. 2005).

See also, Goodwin and Mazour, "Insuring Corporate Competitive Practices" 661 PLI/Comm 69, 72–76 (1993).

[52] See ISO Forms CG 00 01 10 01 and CG 00 01 12 07. See also:

Third Circuit: OneBeacon America Insurance Co. v. Urban Outfitters, Inc., 21 F. Supp.3d 426 (E.D. Pa. 2014).

Fourth Circuit: Travelers Indemnity Co. of America v. Portal Healthcare Solutions, L.L.C., 35 F. Supp.3d 765 (E.D. Va. 2014).

Fifth Circuit: Nationwide Mutual Insurance Co. v. Gum Tree Property Management, L.L.C., 597 Fed. Appx. 241 (5th Cir. 2015); Ticknor v. Rouse's Enterprises, L.L.C., 2 F. Supp.3d 882 (E.D. La. 2014).

Sixth Circuit: National Union Fire Insurance Co. of Pittsburgh, Pa. v. Papa John's International, Inc., 29 F. Supp.3d 961 (W.D. Ky. 2014).

Seventh Circuit: Indiana Insurance Co. v. CE Design Ltd., 6 F. Supp.3d 858 (N.D. Ill. 2013).

Eighth Circuit: Owners Insurance Co. v. European Auto Works, Inc., 695 F.3d 814 (8th Cir. 2012); State Farm Fire & Casualty Co. v. National Research Center for College & University Admissions, 445 F.3d 1100 (8th Cir. 2006).

Ninth Circuit: Cort v. St. Paul Fire & Marine Insurance Cos., 311 F.3d 979 (9th Cir. 2002); National Union Fire Insurance Co. of Pittsburgh, Pa. v. Coinstar, Inc., 39 F. Supp.3d 1149 (W.D. Wash. 2014); Big 5 Sporting Goods Corp. v. Zurich American Insurance Co., 957 F. Supp.2d 1135 (C.D. Cal. 2013).

Tenth Circuit: National Fire Insurance Co. of Hartford v. NWM-Oklahoma, LLC, 546 F. Supp.2d 1238 (W.D. Okla. 2008); Lextron, Inc. v. Travelers Casualty & Surety Company of America, 267 F. Supp.2d 1041 (D. Colo. 2003).

Eleventh Circuit: Allstate Insurance Co. v. Ginsberg, 351 F.3d 473 (11th Cir. 2003).

State Courts:

California: Stein-Brief Group, Inc. v. Home Indemnity Co., 76 Cal. Rptr.2d 3 (Cal. App. 1998).

Connecticut: Recall Total Information Management, Inc. v. Federal Insurance Co., 147 Conn. App. 450, 83 A.3d 664 (2014).

Florida: Allstate Insurance Co. v. Ginsberg, 863 So.2d 156 (Fla. 2003).

Illinois: Standard Mutual Insurance Co. v. Lay, 2014 IL App (4th) 110527-B, 2 N.E.3d 1253, 377 Ill. Dec. 972 (2014); Valley Forge Insurance Co. v. Swiderski Electronics, Inc., 834 N.E.2d 562 (Ill. App. 2005), *aff'd* 860 N.E.2d 307 (Ill. 2006).

Indiana: Allstate Insurance Co. v. Dana Corp., 759 N.E.2d 1049 (Ind. 2001).

Kansas: State Farm Fire & Casualty Co. v. Martinez, 995 P.2d 890 (Kan. App. 2000).

Maine: Maine State Academy of Hair Design, Inc. v. Commercial Union Insurance Co., 699 A.2d 1153 (Me. 1997).

Massachusetts: Norfolk & Dedham Mutual Fire Insurance Co. v. Cleary Consultants, Inc., 81 Mass. App. Ct. 40, 958 N.E.2d 853 (2011); Transamerica Insurance Co. v. KMS Patriots, L.P., 752 N.E.2d 777 (Mass. App. 2001).

Missouri: Columbia Casualty Co. v. HIAR Holding, L.L.C., 411 S.W.3d 258 (Mo. 2013) (*en banc*).

New Hampshire: State Farm Insurance Co. v. Bruns, 156 N.H. 708, 942 A.2d 1275 (N.H. 2008).

New York: Sportsfield Specialties, Inc. v. Twin City Fire Insurance Co., 116 A.D.3d 1270, 984 N.Y.S.2d 447 (N.Y. App. Div. 2014).

Ohio: Owners Insurance Co. v. William Benjamin Trucking, Inc., 2005 WL 1398836 (Ohio App. June 15, 2005).

Oregon: Marleau v. Truck Insurance Exchange, 37 P.3d 148 (Or. 2001).

Utah: Benjamin v. Amica Mutual Insurance Co., 140 P.3d 1210 (Utah 2006).

West Virginia: Bowyer v. Hi-Lad, Inc., 609 S.E.2d 895 (W. Va. 2004).

Wisconsin: Sawyer v. West Bend Mutual Insurance Co., 343 Wis.2d 714, 821 N.W.2d 250 (Wis. App. 2012).

See also, Goodwin and Mazour, "Insuring Corporate Competitive Practices" 661 PLI/Comm 69, 72–76 (1993).

53 See ISO Forms CG 00 01 10 01 and CG 00 01 12 07. See also, Goodwin and Mazour, "Insuring Corporate Competitive Practices" 661 PLI/Comm 69, 72–76 (1993).

54 See, e.g.:

Third Circuit: Devcon International Corp. v. Reliance Insurance Co., 609 F.3d 214 (3d Cir. 2010).

Seventh Circuit: Wolf Lake Terminals, Inc. v. Mutual Marine Insurance Co., 433 F. Supp.2d 933 (N.D. Ind. 2005).

Ninth Circuit: Newmont U.S.A. Limited and Dawn Mining Co. v. American Home Assurance Co., 787 F. Supp.2d 1208 (E.D. Wash. 2011).

State Courts:

Alaska: Whittier Properties, Inc. v. Alaska National Insurance Co., 185 P.3d 84 (Alaska 2008).

California: Cold Creek Compost, Inc. v. State Farm Fire and Casualty Co., 156 Cal. App.4th 1469, 68 Cal. Rptr.3d 216 (2007); Lockheed Corp. v. Continental Insurance Co., 134 Cal. App.4th 187, 35 Cal. Rptr.3d 799 (Cal. App. 2005), *disapproved on other grounds by* State v. Allstate Insurance Co., 45 Cal.4th 1008, 90 Cal. Rptr.3d 1, 201 P.3d 1147 (Cal. 2009).

Indiana: Thomson, Inc. v. Insurance Company of North America, 11 N.E.3d 982 (Ind. App. 2014); Chubb Custom Insurance Co. v. Standard Fusee Corp., 2 N.E.3d 752 (Ind. App. 2014); Newnam Manufacturing, Inc. v. Transcontinental Insurance Co., 871 N.E.2d 396 (Ind. App. 2007).

Louisiana: Johnson v. Orleans Parish School Board, 975 So.2d 698 (La. App. 2008).

Ohio: Sherwin-Williams Co. v. Travelers Casualty and Surety Co., 2003 Ohio App. Lexis 5357 (Ohio App. Nov. 13, 2003).

55 See discussion of invasion of privacy torts in the "advertising injury" section—§9.03[3][b] *infra*.

56 See ISO Forms CG 00 01 10 01 and CG 00 01 12 07. See also, Goodwin and Mazour, "Insuring Corporate Competitive Practices" 661 PLI/Comm 69, 72–76 (1993).

57 *Id.* In fact, the 1973 Form provided:

> "'Advertising injury' means injury arising out of an offense committed during the policy period occurring in the course of the named insured's advertising activities, if such injury arises out of libel, slander, defamation, violation of right of privacy, piracy, unfair competition, or infringement of copyright, title or slogan."

58 See ISO Form CG 00 01 12 07. See also §§ 9.02[1] and [4] *supra*.

59 See ISO Form CG 00 01 12 07.

60 See ISO Forms CG 00 01 10 01 and CG 00 01 12 07. See also:

First Circuit: Hansen v. Sentry Insurance Co., 756 F.3d 53 (1st Cir. 2014).

Second Circuit: Elite Brands, Inc. v. Pennsylvania General Insurance Co., 164 Fed. Appx. 60 (2d Cir. 2006); Amerisure Insurance Co. v. Laserage Technology Corp., 2 F. Supp.2d 296 (W.D.N.Y. 1998).

Third Circuit: Transportation Insurance Co. v. Pennsylvania Manufacturers' Ass'n Insurance Co., 346 Fed. Appx. 862 (3d Cir. 2009); Charter Oak Insurance Co. v. Maglio Fresh Food, 979 F. Supp.2d 581 (E.D. Pa. 2013); DecisionOne Corp. v. ITT Hartford Insurance Group, 942 F. Supp. 1038 (E.D. Pa. 1996).

Fifth Circuit: Nationwide Mutual Insurance Co. v. Gum Tree Property Management, L.L.C., 597 Fed. Appx. 241 (5th Cir. 2015); Uretek (USA), Inc. v. Continental Casualty Co.,

92 F. Supp.3d 589 (S.D. Tex. 2015); Nutmeg Insurance Co. v. Clear Lake City Water Authority, 229 F. Supp.2d 668 (S.D. Tex. 2002).

Sixth Circuit: Duramax Marine LLC v. Travelers Indemnity Company of Illinois, 107 Fed. Appx. 465 (6th Cir. 2004); Dave's Detailing, Inc. v. Catlin Insurance Co., 13 F. Supp.3d 935 (S.D. Ind. 2014).

Seventh Circuit: National Union Fire Insurance Co. of Pittsburgh, Pa. v. Mead Johnson & Co., 735 F.3d 539 (7th Cir. 2013); BASF AG v. Great American Assurance Co., 522 F.3d 813 (7th Cir. 2008); Skylink Technologies, Inc. v. Assurance Company of America, 400 F.3d 982 (7th Cir. 2005); Knoll Pharmaceutical Co. v. Automobile Insurance Co., 152 F. Supp.2d 1026 (N.D. Ill. 2001); Winklevoss Consultants, Inc. v. Federal Insurance Co., 11 F. Supp.2d 995 (N.D. Ill. 1998).

Eighth Circuit: Sletten and Brettin Orthodontics, L.L.C. v. Continental Casualty Co., 782 F.3d 931 (8th Cir. 2015); Home Insurance Co. v. Waycrosse, Inc., 990 F. Supp. 720 (D. Minn. 1996), *aff'd* 131 F.3d 143 (8th Cir. 1997).

Ninth Circuit: Bullpen Distribution, Inc. v. Sentinel Insurance Co., 584 Fed. Appx. 769 (9th Cir. 2014); ABM Industries, Inc. v. National Union Fire Insurance Co. of Pittsburgh, PA, 291 Fed. Appx. 800 (9th Cir. 2008); Clear Logic, Inc. v. Federal Insurance Co., 244 Fed. Appx. 164 (9th Cir. 2007); Primiani v. Federal Insurance Co., 203 Fed. Appx. 902 (9th Cir. 2006); Aurafin-OroAmerica, LLC v. Federal Insurance Co., 188 Fed. Appx. 565 (9th Cir. 2006); Philips Oral Healthcare, Inc. v. Federal Insurance Co., 83 Fed. Appx. 963 (9th Cir. 2003); E.piphany, Inc. v. St. Paul Fire & Marine Insurance Co., 590 F. Supp.2d 1244 (N.D. Cal. 2008).

Tenth Circuit: Chimera Investment Co. v. State Farm Fire and Casualty Co., 268 Fed. Appx. 793 (10th Cir. 2008).

Eleventh Circuit: Vector Products, Inc. v. Hartford Fire Insurance Co., 397 F.3d 1316 (11th Cir. 2005).

State Courts:

California: Hartford Casualty Insurance Co. v. Swift Distribution, Inc., 59 Cal.4th 277, 326 P.3d 253, 172 Cal. Rptr.3d 653 (2014); Engine Clean Technology v. Continental Insurance Co., 2002 WL 1010102 (Cal. App. May 20, 2002).

Florida: Khatib v. Old Dominion Insurance Co., 153 So.3d 943 (Fla. App. 2014); Amerisure Insurance Co. v. Gold Coast Marine Distributors, Inc., 771 So.2d 579 (Fla. App. 2000).

Illinois: Cincinnati Insurance Co. v. American Hardware Manufacturers Ass'n, 387 Ill. App.3d 85, 325 Ill. Dec. 483, 898 N.E.2d 216 (Ill. App. 2008); Pekin Insurance Co. v. Phelan, 343 Ill. App.3d 1216, 278 Ill. Dec. 805, 799 N.E.2d 523 (Ill. App. 2003), *appeal denied* 807 N.E.2d 976 (Ill. 2004).

Indiana: Barnard v. Menard, Inc., 25 N.E.3d 750 (Ind. App. 2015).

Kansas: State Farm Fire & Casualty Co. v. Martinez, 26 Kan. App.2d 869, 995 P.2d 890 (Kan. App. 2000).

Maine: Foundation of Blood Research v. St. Paul Fire & Marine Insurance Co., 730 A.2d 175 (Me. 1999).

New York: Natural Organics, Inc. v. OneBeacon America Insurance Co., 102 A.D.3d 756, 959 N.Y.S.2d 204, (N.Y. App. Div. 2013); JMZ USA, Inc. v. Lumbermens Mutual Casualty Co., 36 A.D.3d 555, 828 N.Y.S.2d 385 (N.Y. App. Div. 2007); Bonded Concrete, Inc. v. Transcontinental Insurance Co., 12 A.D.3d 761, 784 N.Y.S.2d 212 (N.Y. App. Div. 2004).

North Carolina: Harleysville Mutual Insurance Co. v. Buzz Off Insect Shield, L.L.C., 664 S.E.2d 317 (N.C. App. 2008).

Ohio: Acme Construction Co. v. Continental National Indemnity Co., 2003 WL 194879 (Ohio App. Jan. 30, 2003), *appeal denied* 788 N.E.2d 648 (Ohio 2003).

Texas: KLN Steel Products Co. v. CNA Insurance Companies, 278 S.W.3d 429, (Tex. App. Dec. 31, 2008); Atlantic Lloyd's Insurance Company of Texas v. Susman Godfrey LLP, 982 S.W.2d 472 (Tex. App. 1998).

See also, Goodwin and Mazour, "Insuring Corporate Competitive Practices" 661 PLI/ Comm 69, 72–76 (1993).

61 See ISO Form CG 00 01 10 01. See also:

Third Circuit: OneBeacon America Insurance Co. v. Urban Outfitters, Inc., 21 F. Supp.3d 426 (E.D. Pa. 2014); Melrose Hotel, Co. v. St. Paul Fire & Marine Insurance Co., 432 F. Supp.2d 488 (E.D. Pa. 2006).

Fourth Circuit: Resource Bankshares Corp. v. St. Paul Mercury Insurance Co., 407 F.3d 631 (4th Cir.), *cert. denied* 126 S. Ct. (2005); Travelers Indemnity Co. of America v. Portal Healthcare Solutions, L.L.C., 35 F. Supp.3d 765 (E.D. Va. 2014); Prime TV, LLC v. Travelers Insurance Co., 223 F. Supp.2d 744 (M.D.N.C. 2002).

Fifth Circuit: Nationwide Mutual Insurance Co. v. Gum Tree Property Management, L.L.C., 597 Fed. Appx. 241 (5th Cir. 2015); Ticknor v. Rouse's Enterprises, L.L.C., 2 F. Supp.3d 882 (E.D. La. 2014); Western Rim Investment Advisors, Inc. v. Gulf Insurance Co., 269 F. Supp.2d 836 (N.D. Tex. 2003), *aff'd* 96 Fed. Appx. 960 (5th Cir. 2004).

Sixth Circuit: National Union Fire Insurance Co. of Pittsburgh, Pa. v. Papa John's International, Inc., 29 F. Supp.3d 961 (W.D. Ky. 2014); Heritage Mutual Insurance Co. v. Advanced Polymer Technology, Inc., 97 F. Supp.2d 913 (S.D. Ind. 2000).

Seventh Circuit: American States Insurance Co. v. Capital Associates of Jackson County, Inc., 392 F.3d 939 (7th Cir. 2004); Indiana Insurance Co. v. C.E. Design Limited, 6 F. Supp.3d 858 (N.D. Ill. 2013); Ace Rent-A-Car, Inc. v. Empire Fire & Marine Insurance Co., 580 F. Supp.2d 678 (N.D. Ill. 2008); American Home Assurance Co. v. McLeod USA, Inc., 475 F. Supp.2d 766 (N.D. Ill. 2007); St. Paul Fire & Marine Insurance Co. v. Brunswick Corp., 405 F. Supp.2d 890 (N.D. Ill. 2005).

Eighth Circuit: Owners Insurance Co. v. European Auto Works, Inc., 695 F.3d 814 (8th Cir. 2012).

Ninth Circuit: National Union Fire Insurance Co. of Pittsburgh, Pa. v. Coinstar, Inc., 39 F. Supp.3d 1149 (W.D. Wash. 2014); Big 5 Sporting Goods Corp. v. Zurich American Insurance Co., 957 F. Supp.2d 1135 (C.D. Cal. 2013); San Diego National Bank v. Aetna Casualty & Surety Company of Illinois, 807 F. Supp. 95 (S.D. Cal. 1992).

Tenth Circuit: Park University Enterprises, Inc. v. American Casualty Company of Reading, Pennsylvania, 442 F.3d 1239 (10th Cir. 2006).

Eleventh Circuit: Hooters of Augusta, Inc. v. American Global Insurance Co., 157 Fed. Appx. 201 (11th Cir. 2005); Penzer v. Transportation Insurance Co., 509 F. Supp.2d 1278 (S.D. Fla. 2007).

State Courts:

California: ACS Systems, Inc. v. St. Paul Fire & Marine Insurance Co., 147 Cal. App.4th 137, 53 Cal. Rptr.3d 786 (Cal. App. 2007).

Connecticut: Recall Total Information Management, Inc. v. Federal Insurance Co., 147 Conn. App. 450, 83 A.3d 664 (2014).

Illinois: Standard Mutual Insurance Co. v. Lay, 2014 IL App (4th) 110527-B, 2 N.E.3d 1253, 377 Ill. Dec. 972 (2014); Valley Forge Insurance Co. v. Swiderski Electronics, Inc., 359 Ill. App.3d 872, 296 Ill. Dec. 5, 834 N.E.2d 562 (Ill. App. 2005), *aff'd* 860 N.E.2d 307 (Ill. 2006).

Kansas: State Farm Fire & Casualty Co. v. Martinez, 26 Kan. App.2d 869, 995 P.2d 890 (Kan. App. 2000).

Massachusetts: Terra Nova Insurance Co. v. Fray-Witzer, 449 Mass. 406, 869 N.E.2d 565 (Mass. 2007); Norfolk & Dedham Mutual Fire Insurance Co. v. Cleary Consultants, Inc., 81 Mass. App. Ct. 40, 958 N.E.2d 853 (2011).

Missouri: Columbia Casualty Co. v. HIAR Holding, L.L.C. (Mo. 2013) (*en banc*).

New York: Sportsfield Specialties, Inc. v. Twin City Fire Insurance Co., 116 A.D.3d 1270, 984 N.Y.S.2d 447 (N.Y. App. Dept. 2014); Bonded Concrete, Inc. v. Transcontinental Insurance Co., 12 A.D.3d 761, 784 N.Y.S.2d 212 (N.Y. App. Div. 2004).

Ohio: Schuetz v. State Farm Fire and Casualty Co., 147 Ohio Misc.2d 22, 890 N.E.2d 374 (Ohio C.P. Franklin Cnty. 2007).

Texas: TIG Insurance Co. v. Dallas Basketball, Ltd., 129 S.W.3d 232 (Tex. App. 2004).

Utah: Nova Casualty Co. v. Able Construction, Inc., 983 P.2d 575 (Utah 1999).

West Virginia: Bowyer v. Hi-Lad, Inc., 216 W. Va. 634, 609 S.E.2d 895 (W. Va. 2004).

Wisconsin: Sawyer v. West Bend Mutual Insurance Co., 343 Wis.2d 714, 821 N.W.2d 250 (Wis. App. 2012).

See also, Goodwin and Mazour, "Insuring Corporate Competitive Practices" 661 PLI/Comm 69, 72–76 (1993).

62 See ISO Forms CG 00 01 10 01 and CG 00 01 12 07. See also:

Second Circuit: Bridge Metal Industries, L.L.C. v. Travelers Indemnity Co., 559 Fed. Appx. 15 (2d Cir. 2014); Elite Brands, Inc. v. Pennsylvania General Insurance Co., 164 Fed. Appx. 60 (2d Cir. 2006); U.S. Fidelity and Guaranty Co. v. Ashley Reed Trading, Inc., 43 F. Supp.3d 271 (S.D.N.Y. 2014).

Third Circuit: NorFab Corp. v. Travelers Indemnity Co., 555 F. Supp.2d 505 (E.D. Pa. 2008).

Fourth Circuit: Teletronics International, Inc. v. CNA Insurance Co./Transportation Insurance Co., 120 Fed. Appx. 440 (4th Cir. 2005).

Fifth Circuit: Test Masters Educational Services, Inc. v. State Farm Lloyds, 791 F.3d 561 (5th Cir. 2015); Mid-Continent Casualty Co. v. Kipp Flores Architects, L.L.C., 602 Fed. Appx. 985 (5th Cir. 2015); America's Recommended Mailers, Inc. v. Maryland Casualty Co., 579 F. Supp.2d 791 (E.D. Tex. 2008).

Sixth Circuit: Pizza Magia International, LLC v. Assurance Company of America, 447 F. Supp.2d 766 (W.D. Ky. 2006).

Seventh Circuit: Skylink Technologies, Inc. v. Assurance Company of America, 400 F.3d 982 (7th Cir. 2006); Design Basics L.L.C. v. Campbellsport Building Supply, Inc., 99 F. Supp.3d 899 (E.D. Wis. 2015); Kreuger International, Inc. v. Federal Insurance Co., 637 F. Supp.2d 604 (E.D. Wis. 2008); Capitol Indemnity Corp. v. Elston Self Service Wholesale Groceries, Inc., 551 F. Supp.2d 711 (N.D. Ill. 2008).

Eighth Circuit: Interstate Bakeries Corp. v. OneBeacon Insurance Co., 686 F.3d 539 (8th Cir. 2012).

Ninth Circuit: Street Surfing, L.L.C. v. Great American E & S Insurance Co., 776 F.3d 603 (9th Cir. 2014); Ohio Casualty Insurance Co. v. Cloud Nine LLC, 464 F. Supp.2d 1161 (D. Utah 2006); Peterson Tractor Co. v. Travelers Indemnity Company of Illinois, 156 Fed. Appx. 21 (9th Cir. 2005).

Tenth Circuit: Dish Network Corp. v. Arrowood Indemnity Co., 772 F.3d 856 (10th Cir. 2014); Triple M Financing Co. v. Universal Underwriters Insurance Co., 164 Fed. Appx. 702 (10th Cir. 2006).

Eleventh Circuit: State Farm Fire & Casualty Co. v. Steinberg, 393 F.3d 1226 (11th Cir. 2004).

State Courts:

California: Peerless Lighting Corp. v. American Motorists Insurance Co., 82 Cal. App.4th 995, 98 Cal. Rptr.2d 753 (Cal. App. 2000).

Idaho: Construction Management Systems, Inc. v. Assurance Company of America, 135 Idaho 680, 23 P.3d 142 (Idaho 2001).

Illinois: Erie Insurance Exchange v. Compeve Corp., 2015 IL App (1st) 142508, 32 N.E.3d 160, 392 Ill. Dec. 160 (2015); Konami (America), Inc. v. Hartford Insurance Company of Illinois, 326 Ill. App.3d 874, 260 Ill. Dec. 721, 761 N.E.2d 1277 (Ill. App.), *appeal denied* 770 N.E.2d 219 (Ill. 2002).

Minnesota: Fallon McElligott, Inc. v. Seaboard Surety Co., 607 N.W.2d 801 (Minn. App. 2000).

Mississippi: Farmland Mutual Insurance Co. v. Scruggs, 886 So.2d 714 (Miss. 2004).

New Jersey: Information Spectrum, Inc. v. The Hartford, 182 N.J. 34, 860 A.2d 926 (N.J. 2004).

New York: Cosser v. One Beacon Insurance Group, 15 A.D.3d 871, 789 N.Y.S.2d 586 (N.Y. App. Div. 2005).

Ohio: Westfield Insurance Co. v. Factfinder Marketing Research, Inc., 168 Ohio App.3d 391, 860 N.E.2d 145 (Ohio App. 2006).

Tennessee: Ralph v. Pipkin, 183 S.W.3d 362 (Tenn. App. 2005).

Texas: KLN Steel Products Co. v. CNA Insurance Companies, 278 S.W.3d 429, (Tex. App. 2008); Cigna Lloyds Insurance Co. v. Bradleys' Electric, Inc., 33 S.W.3d 102 (Tex. App. 2000).

Washington: Australia Unlimited, Inc. v. Hartford Casualty Insurance Co., 147 Wash. App. 758, 198 P.3d 514 (Wash. App. 2008); Auto Sox USA, Inc. v. Zurich North America, 121 Wash. App. 422, 88 P.3d 1008 (Wash. App. 2004), *review denied* 103 P.3d 1248 (Wash. 2005).

Wisconsin: Acuity v. Bagadia, 310 Wis.2d 197, 750 N.W.2d 817 (Wis. 2008); Fireman's Fund Insurance Company of Wisconsin v. Bradley Corp., 261 Wis.2d 4, 660 N.W.2d 666 (Wis. 2003); Acuity v. Ross Glove Co., 344 Wis.2d 29, 817 N.W.2d 455 (Wis. App. 2012).

See also, Goodwin and Mazour, "Insuring Corporate Competitive Practices" 661 PLI/Comm 69, 72–76 (1993).

[63] See ISO Forms CG 00 01 10 01 and CG 00 01 12 07. See also:

Third Circuit: Atlantic Mutual Insurance Co. v. Brotech Corp., 857 F. Supp. 423 (E.D. Pa. 1994), *aff'd* 60 F.3d 813 (3d Cir. 1995).

Sixth Circuit: Weiss v. St. Paul Fire & Marine Insurance Co., 283 F.3d 790 (6th Cir.), *cert. denied* 537 U.S. 883 (2002); Heritage Mutual Insurance Co. v. Advanced Polymer Technology, Inc., 97 F. Supp.2d 913 (S.D. Ind. 2000).

Seventh Circuit: Heil Co. v. Hartford Accident & Indemnity Co., 937 F. Supp. 1355 (E.D. Wis. 1996).

Ninth Circuit: Time Warner Entertainment Co. v. Continental Casualty Co., 72 Fed. Appx. 586 (9th Cir. 2003); Iolab Corp. v. Seaboard Surety Co., 15 F.3d 1500 (9th Cir. 1994); Alliance Insurance Co. v. Colella, 995 F.2d 944 (9th Cir. 1993); United States Fidelity & Guaranty Co. v. Star Technologies, Inc., 935 F. Supp. 1110 (D. Or. 1996); Owens-Brockway Glass Container, Inc. v. International Insurance Co., 884 F. Supp. 363 (E.D. Cal. 1995), *aff'd* 94 F.3d 652 (9th Cir. 1996); New Hampshire Insurance Co. v. R.L. Chaides Construction Co., 847 F. Supp. 1452 (N.D. Cal. 1994).

Eleventh Circuit: Gencor Industries, Inc. v. Wausau Underwriters Insurance Co., 857 F. Supp. 1560 (M.D. Fla. 1994).

State Courts:

Illinois: Konami (America), Inc. v. Hartford Insurance Company of Illinois, 326 Ill. App.3d 874, 260 Ill. Dec. 721, 761 N.E.2d 1277 (Ill. App.), *appeal denied* 770 N.E.2d 219 (Ill. 2002).

Minnesota: Fluroware, Inc. v. Chubb Group of Insurance Companies, 545 N.W.2d 678 (Minn. App. 1996).

Nebraska: Union Insurance Co. v. Land & Sky, Inc., 247 Neb. 696, 529 N.W.2d 773 (Neb. 1995).

New Jersey: Filenet Corp. v. Chubb Insurance Corp., 324 N.J. Super. 419, 735 A.2d 1170 (N.J. Super. App. Div. 1999).

See also, Goodwin and Mazour, "Insuring Corporate Competitive Practices" 661 PLI/Comm 69, 72–76 (1993).

64 See ISO Forms CG 00 01 10 01 and CG 00 01 12 07. See also:

First Circuit: Open Software Foundation, Inc. v. United States Fidelity and Guaranty Co., 307 F.3d 11 (1st Cir. 2002).

Third Circuit: I.C.D. Industries, Inc. v. Federal Insurance Co., 879 F. Supp. 480 (E.D. Pa. 1995); Atlantic Mutual Insurance Co. v. Brotech Corp., 857 F. Supp. 423 (E.D. Pa. 1994), *aff'd* 60 F.3d 813 (3d Cir. 1995).

Sixth Circuit: Weiss v. St. Paul Fire & Marine Insurance Co., 283 F.3d 790 (6th Cir. 2002); Heritage Mutual Insurance Co. v. Advanced Polymer Technology, Inc., 97 F. Supp.2d 913 (S.D. Ind. 2000).

Seventh Circuit: Curtis-Universal, Inc. v. Sheboygan Emergency Medical Services, Inc., 43 F.3d 1119 (7th Cir. 1994) ("unfair competition" includes tortious interference with contract); Knoll Pharmaceutical Co. v. Automobile Insurance Company of Hartford, 152 F. Supp.2d 1026 (N.D. Ill. 2001); Attorneys' Title Guaranty Fund, Inc. v. Maryland Casualty Co., 1991 WL 171339 (N.D. Ill. Aug. 23, 1991) ("unfair competition" included tortious interference with contract between competitor and third parties).

Ninth Circuit: Mutual of Enumclaw Insurance Co. v. Jonas, 35 Fed. Appx. 556 (9th Cir. 2002); Owens-Brockway Glass Container, Inc. v. International Insurance Co., 884 F. Supp. 363 (E.D. Cal. 1995), *aff'd* 94 F.3d 652 (9th Cir. 1996); Simply Fresh Fruit, Inc. v. Continental Insurance Co., 94 F.3d 1219 (9th Cir.), *cert. denied* 519 U.S. 965 (1996); Dogloo, Inc. v. Northern Insurance Company of New York, 907 F. Supp. 1383 (C.D. Cal. 1995).

Eleventh Circuit: Gencor Industries, Inc. v. Wausau Underwriters Insurance Co., 857 F. Supp. 1560 (M.D. Fla. 1994).

State Courts:

California: Rombe Corp. v. Allied Insurance Co., 128 Cal. App.4th 482, 27 Cal. Rptr.3d 99 (Cal. App. 2005).

Connecticut: QSP, Inc. v. Aetna Casualty and Surety Co., 256 Conn. 343, 773 A.2d 906 (Conn. 2001).

Florida: Tire Kingdom, Inc. v. First Southern Insurance Co., 573 So.2d 885 (Fla. App. 1990), *review denied* 589 So.2d 290 (Fla. 1991) (duty to defend antitrust claim because advertising injury offenses included "unfair competition" and "defamation").

New Jersey: Filenet Corp. v. Chubb Corp., 324 N.J. Super. 419, 735 A.2d 1170 (N.J. Super. App. Div. 1999).

New York: Allou Health & Beauty Care, Inc. v. Aetna Casualty & Surety Co., 269 A.D.2d 478, 703 N.Y.S.2d 253 (N.Y. App. Div. 2000).

See also, Goodwin and Mazour, "Insuring Corporate Competitive Practices" 661 PLI/Comm 69, 72–76 (1993).

65 See ISO Forms CG 00 01 10 01 and CG 00 01 12 07. See also:

First Circuit: Ekco Group, Inc. v. Travelers Indemnity Company of Illinois, 273 F.3d 409 (1st Cir. 2001).

Second Circuit: Suwannee American Cement L.L.C. v. Zurich Insurance Co., 885 F. Supp.2d 611 (S.D.N.Y. 2012); United States Fidelity & Guaranty Co. v. Frosty Bites, Inc., 232 F. Supp.2d 101 (S.D.N.Y. 2002).

Third Circuit: Westport Reinsurance Management, LLC v. St. Paul Fire & Marine Insurance Co., 80 Fed. Appx. 277 (3d Cir. 2003); Cat Internet Services, Inc. v. Providence Washington Insurance Co., 333 F.3d 138 (3d Cir. 2003); Frog, Switch & Manufacturing Co. v. Travelers Insurance Co., 193 F.3d 742 (3d Cir. 1999); Charter Oak Insurance Co. v. Maglio Fresh Food, 979 F. Supp.2d 581 (E.D. Pa. 2013); Cincinnati Insurance Cos. v. Pestco, Inc., 374 F. Supp.2d 451 (W.D. Pa. 2004).

Fourth Circuit: State Automobile Property & Casualty Insurance Company v. Travelers Indemnity Company of America, 343 F.3d 249 (4th Cir. 2003).

Fifth Circuit: Nationwide Mutual Insurance Co. v. Gum Tree Property Management, L.L.C., 597 Fed. Appx. 241 (5th Cir. 2015); Sport Supply Group, Inc. v. Columbia Casualty Co., 335 F.3d 453 (5th Cir. 2003).

Sixth Circuit: Liberty Corporate Capital Ltd. v. Security Safe Outlet, 577 Fed. Appx. 399 (6th Cir. 2014); Pizza Magia International, LLC v. Assurance Company of America, 447 F. Supp.2d 766 (W.D. Ky. 2006).

Seventh Circuit: Skylink Technologies, Inc. v. Assurance Company of America, 400 F.3d 982 (7th Cir. 2006); AU Electronics, Inc. v. Harleysville Group, Inc., 82 F. Supp.3d 805 (N.D. Ill. 2015).

Eighth Circuit: American Simmental Association v. Coregis Insurance Co., 282 F.3d 582 (8th Cir. 2002).

Ninth Circuit: Peterson Tractor Co. v. Travelers Indemnity Company of Illinois, 156 Fed. Appx. 21 (9th Cir. 2005); Edwards Theatres, Inc. v. United National Insurance Co., 126 Fed. Appx. 831 (9th Cir. 2005); Cooper Engineering, Inc. v. Westchester Fire Insurance Co., 126 Fed. Appx. 808 (9th Cir. 2005); Time Warner Entertainment Co. v. Continental Casualty Co., 72 Fed. Appx. 586 (9th Cir. 2003); Dogloo, Inc. v. Northern Insurance Company of New York, 907 F. Supp. 1383 (C.D. Cal. 1995).

Tenth Circuit: DISH Network Corp. v. Arch Specialty Insurance Co., 659 F.3d 1010 (10th Cir. 2011); Wardcraft Homes, Inc. v. Employers Mutual Casualty Co., 70 F. Supp.3d 1198 (D. Colo. 2014).

Eleventh Circuit: Colony Insurance Co. v. Corrosion Control, Inc., 187 Fed. Appx. 918 (11th Cir. 2006); State Farm Fire & Casualty Co. v. Steinberg, 393 F.3d 1226 (11th Cir. 2004).

State Courts:

California: Hameid v. National Fire Insurance of Hartford, 71 P.3d 761 (Cal. 2003).

Illinois: Lexmark International, Inc. v. Transportation Insurance Co., 761 N.E.2d 1214 (Ill. App. 2001), *appeal denied* 770 N.E.2d 220 (Ill. 2002).

Indiana: Hoosier Insurance Co. v. Audiology Foundation of America, 745 N.E.2d 300 (Ind. App. 2001).

Kansas: Aselco, Inc. v. Hartford Insurance Group, 21 P.3d 1011 (Kan. App. 2001).

Mississippi: Farmland Mutual Insurance Co. v. Scruggs, 886 So.2d 714 (Miss. 2004).

New Jersey: Information Spectrum, Inc. v. The Hartford, 860 A.2d 926 (N.J. 2004).

Ohio: Westfield Insurance Co. v. Factfinder Marketing Research, Inc., 860 N.E.2d 145 (Ohio App. 2006).

Texas: Pennsylvania Pulp & Paper Co. v. Nationwide Mutual Insurance Co., 100 S.W.3d 566 (Tex. App. 2003).

Utah: Basic Research, L.L.C. v. Admiral Insurance Co., 297 P.3d 578 (Utah 2013).

Washington: Auto Sox USA, Inc. v. Zurich North America, 88 P.3d 1008 (Wash. App. 2004), *review denied* 103 P.3d 1248 (Wash. 2005); Amazon.com International, Inc. v. American Dynasty Surplus Lines Insurance Co., 85 P.3d 974 (Wash. App.), *review denied* 103 P.3d 200 (Wash. 2004).

Wisconsin: Fireman's Fund Insurance Company of Wisconsin v. Bradley Corp., 660 N.W.2d 666 (Wis. 2003).

See also, Goodwin and Mazour, "Insuring Corporate Competitive Practices" 661 PLI/ Comm 69, 72–76 (1993).

66 See ISO Forms CG 00 01 10 01 and CG 00 01 12 07. See also, Goodwin and Mazour, "Insuring Corporate Competitive Practices" 661 PLI/Comm 69, 72–76 (1993).

67 See, e.g.:

First Circuit: Cynosure, Inc. v. St. Paul Fire and Marine Insurance Co., 645 F.3d 1 (1st Cir. 2011).

Third Circuit: St. Paul Fire and Marine Insurance Co. v. Brother International Corp., 319 Fed. Appx. 121 (3d Cir. 2009); Melrose Hotel Co. v. St. Paul Fire and Marine Insurance Co., 432 F. Supp.2d 488 (E.D. Pa. 2006).

Fourth Circuit: Resource Bankshares Corp. v. St. Paul Mercury Insurance Co., 407 F.3d 631 (4th Cir. 2005); Prime TV, LLC. v. Travelers Insurance Co., 223 F. Supp.2d 744 (M.D.N.C. 2002).

Fifth Circuit: Registry Dallas Associates v. Wausau Business Insurance Co., 2004 WL 614836 (N.D. Tex. Feb. 26, 2004); Western Rim Investment Advisors, Inc. v. Gulf Insurance Co., 269 F. Supp.2d 836 (N.D. Tex. 2003), *affirmed* 96 Fed. Appx. 960, 2004 WL 1160165 (5th Cir. 2004); American Safety and Risk Services, Inc. v. Legion Indemnity Co., 153 F. Supp.2d 869 (E.D. La. 2001).

Sixth Circuit: National Union Fire Insurance Co. of Pittsburgh, Pa. v. Papa John's International, Inc., 29 F. Supp.3d 961 (W.D. Ky. 2014).

Seventh Circuit: Auto-Owners Insurance Co. v. Websolv Computing, Inc., 580 F.3d 543 (7th Cir. 2009); American States Insurance Co. v. Capital Associates of Jackson County, Inc., 392 F.3d 939 (7th Cir. 2004); Indiana Insurance Company v. CE Design Limited, 6 F. Supp.3d 858 (N.D. Ill. 2013); Maxum Indemnity Co. v. Eclipse Manufacturing Co., 848 F. Supp.2d 871 (N.D. Ill. 2012); Ace Rent-A-Car, Inc. v. Empire Fire & Marine Insurance Co., 580 F. Supp.2d 678 (N.D. Ill. 2008); American Home Assurance Co. v. McLeod USA, Inc., 475 F. Supp.2d 766 (N.D. Ill. 2007).

Eighth Circuit: State Farm Fire and Casualty Co. v. National Research Center for College and University Admissions, 445 F.3d 1100 (8th Cir. 2006); Universal Underwriters Insurance Co. v. Lou Fusz Automotive Network, Inc., 401 F.3d 876 (8th Cir. 2005); Owners Insurance Co. v. European Auto Works, Inc., 695 F.3d 814 (8th Cir. 2012); Nationwide Mutual Insurance Co. v. Harris Medical Associates, L.L.C., 973 F. Supp.2d 1045 (E.D. Mo. 2013).

Ninth Circuit: Big 5 Sporting Goods Corp. v. Zurich American Insurance Co., 957 F. Supp.2d 1135 (C.D. Cal. 2013).

Tenth Circuit: Park University Enterprises, Inc. v. American Casualty Company of Reading, PA., 442 F.3d 1239 (10th Cir. 2006).

Eleventh Circuit: Alea London Ltd. v. American Home Services, Inc., 638 F.3d 768 (11th Cir. 2011); Penzer v. Transportation Insurance Co., 605 F.3d 1112 (11th Cir. 2010); Hooters of Augusta, Inc. v. American Global Insurance Co., 157 Fed. Appx. 201 (11th Cir. 2005); Penzer v. Transportation Insurance Co., 509 F. Supp.2d 1278 (S.D. Fla. 2007).

State Courts:

California: State Farm General Insurance Co. v. JT's Frames, Inc., 181 Cal. App.4th 429, 104 Cal. Rptr.3d 573 (2010); ACS Systems, Inc. v. St. Paul Fire and Marine Insurance Co., 147 Cal. App.4th 137, 53 Cal. Rptr.3d 786 (Cal. App. 2007).

Florida: Penzer v. Transportation Insurance Co., 29 So.3d 1000 (Fla. 2010).

Illinois: Valley Forge Insurance Co. v. Swiderski Electronics, Inc., 223 Ill.2d 352, 860 N.E.2d 307, 307 Ill. Dec. 653 (2006); Standard Mutual Insurance Co. v. Lay, 2014 IL

App (4th) 110527-B, 2 N.E.3d 1253, 377 Ill. Dec. 972 (2014); Landmark American Insurance Co. v. NIP Group, Inc., 2011 IL App (1st) 101155, 962 N.E.2d 562, 356 Ill. Dec. 877 (2011); Pekin Insurance Co. v. Xdata Solutions, 2011 Ill. App. Lexis 1056, 958 N.E.2d 397, 354 Ill. Dec. 654 (2011).

Maryland: Walk v. Hartford Casualty Insurance Co., 852 A.2d 98 (Md. 2004).

Massachusetts: Terra Nova Insurance Co. v. Fray-Witzer, 449 Mass. 406, 869 N.E.2d 565 (Mass. 2007).

Missouri: Columbia Casualty Co. v. HIAR Holding, L.L.C., 411 S.W.3d 258 (Mo. 2013) (*en banc*).

Ohio: Motorists Mutual Insurance Co. v. Dandy-Jim, Inc., 182 Ohio App.3d 311, 912 N.E.2d 659 (2009); Schuetz v. State Farm Fire and Casualty Co., 147 Ohio Misc.2d 22, 890 N.E.2d 374 (Ohio C P. Franklin Cnty. 2007).

Pennsylvania: Telecommunications Network Design and Paradise Distributing, Inc. v. The Brethren Mutual Insurance co., 5 A.3d 331 (Pa. Super. 2010).

Texas: TIG Insurance Co. v. Dallas Basketball, Ltd., 129 S.W.3d 232 (Tex. App. 2004).

Wisconsin: Sawyer v. West Bend Mutual Insurance Co., 343 Wis.2d 714, 821 N.W.2d 250 (Wis. App. 2012).

[68] See, e.g.:

Seventh Circuit: Discover Financial Services L.L.C. v. National Union Fire Insurance Company of Pittsburgh, PA, 527 F. Supp.2d 806 (N.D. Ill. 2007).

Ninth Circuit: Hyundai Motor America v. National Union Fire Insurance Company of Pittsburgh, PA, 600 F.3d 1092 (9th Cir. 2010).

Tenth Circuit: DISH Network Corp. v. Arch Specialty Insurance Co., 659 F.3d 1010 (10th Cir. 2011).

State Courts:

Washington: Amazon.com International, Inc. v. American Dynasty Surplus Lines Insurance Co., 120 Wash. App. 610, 85 P.3d 974 (Wash. App. 2004).

[69] See:

Seventh Circuit: Skylink Technologies, Inc. v. Assurance Company of America, 400 F.3d 982 (7th Cir. 2006) (competitor's action against garage door opener manufacturer, alleging manufacturer falsely advertised its openers as compatible with competitor's "rolling code" technology, did not give rise to a suit for disparagement); Knoll Pharmaceutical Co. v. Automobile Insurance Co., 152 F. Supp.2d 1026 (N.D. Ill. 2001).

Ninth Circuit: Philips Oral Healthcare, Inc. v. Federal Insurance Co., 83 Fed. Appx. 963 (9th Cir. 2003) (competitor's allegations of false advertising stated claim for disparagement).

State Courts:

Illinois: Pekin Insurance Co. v. Phelan, 799 N.E.2d 523 (Ill. App. 2003), *appeal denied* 807 N.E.2d 976 (Ill. 2004) (competitor's claim against insured hair salon alleging false statements made to lure away competitor's customers involved allegations of disparagement).

New York: Bonded Concrete, Inc. v. Transcontinental Insurance Co., 784 N.Y.S.2d 212 (N.Y. App. Div. 2004) (deceptive business practices claim asserted against concrete supplier by general contractor was not "advertising injury" or "personal injury" because it was not a "publication" of material that libeled or slandered another or violated a person's right to privacy).

[70] See:

First Circuit: Town of Stoddard v. Northern Security Insurance Co., 718 F. Supp. 1062 (D.N.H. 1989).

Third Circuit: New Castle County v. National Union Fire Insurance Company of Pittsburgh, Pennsylvania, 243 F.3d 744 (3d Cir. 2001).

State Courts:

California: Sterling Builders, Inc. v. United National Insurance Co., 93 Cal. Rptr.2d 697 (Cal. App. 2000).

New Hampshire: Town of Goshen v. Grange Mutual Insurance Co., 424 A.2d 822 (N.H. 1980).

[71] See, e.g.:

First Circuit: Cynosure, Inc. v. St. Paul Fire and Marine Insurance Co., 645 F.3d 1 (1st Cir. 2011).

Third Circuit: St. Paul Fire and Marine Insurance Co. v. Brother International Corp., 319 Fed. Appx. 121 (3d Cir. 2009); Melrose Hotel Co. v. St. Paul Fire and Marine Insurance Co., 432 F. Supp.2d 488 (E.D. Pa. 2006).

Fourth Circuit: Resource Bankshares Corp. v. St. Paul Mercury Insurance Co., 407 F.3d 631 (4th Cir. 2005); Prime TV, LLC. v. Travelers Insurance Co., 223 F. Supp.2d 744 (M.D.N.C. 2002).

Fifth Circuit: Registry Dallas Associates v. Wausau Business Insurance Co., 2004 WL 614836 (N.D. Tex. Feb. 26, 2004); Western Rim Investment Advisors, Inc. v. Gulf Insurance Co., 269 F. Supp.2d 836 (N.D. Tex. 2003), *affirmed* 96 Fed. Appx. 960, 2004 WL 1160165 (5th Cir. 2004); American Safety and Risk Services, Inc. v. Legion Indemnity Co., 153 F. Supp.2d 869 (E.D. La. 2001).

Sixth Circuit: National Union Fire Insurance Co. of Pittsburgh, Pa. v. Papa John's International, Inc., 29 F. Supp.3d 961 (W.D. Ky. 2014).

Seventh Circuit: Auto-Owners Insurance Co. v. Websolv Computing, Inc., 580 F.3d 543 (7th Cir. 2009); American States Insurance Co. v. Capital Associates of Jackson County, Inc., 392 F.3d 939 (7th Cir. 2004); Indiana Insurance Co. v. CE Design Limited, 6 F. Supp.3d 858 (N.D. Ill. 2013); Maxum Indemnity Co. v. Eclipse Manufacturing Co., 848 F. Supp.2d 871 (N.D. Ill. 2012); Ace Rent-A-Car, Inc. v. Empire Fire & Marine Insurance Co., 580 F. Supp.2d 678 (N.D. Ill. 2008); American Home Assurance Co. v. McLeod USA, Inc., 475 F. Supp.2d 766 (N.D. Ill. 2007).

Eighth Circuit: State Farm Fire and Casualty Co. v. National Research Center for College and University Admissions, 445 F.3d 1100 (8th Cir. 2006); Universal Underwriters Insurance Co. v. Lou Fusz Automotive Network, Inc., 401 F.3d 876 (8th Cir. 2005); Owners Insurance Co. v. European Auto Works, Inc., 695 F.3d 814 (8th Cir. 2012); Nationwide Mutual Insurance Co. v. Harris Medical Associates, L.L.C., 973 F. Supp.2d 1045 (E.D. Mo. 2013).

Ninth Circuit: Big 5 Sporting Goods Corp. v. Zurich American Insurance Co., 957 F. Supp.2d 1135 (C.D. Cal. 2013).

Tenth Circuit: Park University Enterprises, Inc. v. American Casualty Company of Reading, PA., 314 F. Supp.2d 1094 (D. Kan. 2004).

Eleventh Circuit: Alea London Ltd. v. American Home Services, Inc., 638 F.3d 768 (11th Cir. 2011); Penzer v. Transportation Insurance Co., 545 F.3d 1303 (11th Cir. 2008); Hooters of Augusta, Inc. v. American Global Insurance Co., 157 Fed. Appx. 201 (11th Cir. 2005); Penzer v. Transportation Insurance Co., 509 F. Supp.2d 1278 (S.D. Fla. 2007).

State Courts:

California: State Farm General Insurance Co. v. JT's Frames, Inc., 181 Cal. App.4th 429, 104 Cal. Rptr.3d 573 (2010); ACS Systems, Inc. v. St. Paul Fire and Marine Insurance Co., 147 Cal. App.4th 137, 53 Cal. Rptr.3d 786 (Cal. App. 2007).

Florida: Penzer v. Transportation Insurance Co., 29 So.3d 1000 (Fla. 2010).

Illinois: Valley Forge Insurance Co. v. Swiderski Electronics, Inc., 223 Ill.2d 352, 307 Ill. Dec. 653, 860 N.E.2d 307 (Ill. 2006); Pekin Insurance Co. v. Xdata Solutions, 2011 Ill. App.

Lexis 1056, 958 N.E.2d 397, 354 Ill. Dec. 654 (2011); Standard Mutual Insurance Co. v. Lay, 2014 IL App (4th) 110527-B, 2 N.E.3d 1253, 377 Ill. Dec. 972 (2014); Landmark American Insurance Co. v. NIP Group, Inc., 2011 IL App (1st) 101155, 962 N.E.2d 562, 356 Ill. Dec. 877 (2011).

Maryland: Walk v. Hartford Casualty Insurance Co., 382 Md. 1, 852 A.2d 98 (Md. 2004).

Massachusetts: Terra Nova Insurance Co. v. Fray-Witzer, 449 Mass. 406, 869 N.E.2d 565 (Mass. 2007).

Missouri: Columbia Casualty Co. v. HIAR Holding, L.L.C., 411 S.W.3d 258 (Mo. 2013) (*en banc*).

Ohio: Motorists Mutual Insurance Co. v. Dandy-Jim, Inc., 182 Ohio App.3d 311, 912 N.E.2d 659 (2009); Schuetz v. State Farm Fire and Casualty Co., 147 Ohio Misc.2d 22, 890 N.E.2d 374 (Ohio C.P. Franklin Cnty. 2007).

Pennsylvania: Telecommunications Network Design and Paradise Distributing, Inc. v. The Brethren Mutual Insurance Co., 5 A.3d 331 (Pa. Super. 2010).

Texas: TIG Insurance Co. v. Dallas Basketball, Ltd., 129 S.W.3d 232 (Tex. App. 2004).

Wisconsin: Sawyer v. West Bend Mutual Insurance Co., 343 Wis.2d 714, 821 N.W.2d 250 (Wis. App. 2012).

72 See Butler v. Clarendon America Insurance Co., 494 F. Supp.2d 1112 (N.D. Cal. 2007) ("'to the extent the listed offenses [in personal injury coverage of liability policy] are framed in generic terms, they should be construed broadly to encompass all specific torts which reasonably could fall within the general category'"). But see Purdue Frederick Co. v. Steadfast Insurance Co., 40 A.D.3d 285, 836 N.Y.S.2d 28 (N.Y. App. Div. 2007) (claims against policyholder for antitrust violations were not enumerated personal injury offenses, even though claims referred to certain "sham litigation" allegedly brought by insureds to maintain their monopoly on the manufacture and sale of a drug).

73 See:

First Circuit: Great American Insurance Co. v. Riso, Inc., 479 F.3d 158 (1st Cir. 2007) (no coverage for antitrust claim involving potential commercial disparagement); Open Software Foundation, Inc. v. United States Fidelity and Guaranty Co., 307 F.3d 11 (1st Cir. 2002) (no coverage for antitrust claim on basis of disparagement allegation).

Third Circuit: Transportation Insurance Co. v. Pennsylvania Manufacturers' Association Insurance Co., 346 Fed. Appx. 862 (3d Cir. 2009) (commercial disparagement triggers defense obligation); Charter Oak Insurance Co. v. Maglio Fresh Food, 979 F. Supp.2d 581 (E.D. Pa. 2013).

Fifth Circuit: Nationwide Mutual Insurance Co. v. Gum Tree Property Management, L.L.C., 597 Fed. Appx. 241 (5th Cir. 2015); Uretek (USA), Inc. v. Continental Casualty Co., 92 F. Supp.3d 589 (S.D. Tex. 2015).

Seventh Circuit: Tews Funeral Home, Inc. v. Ohio Casualty Insurance Co., 832 F.2d 1037 (7th Cir. 1987); Skylink Technologies, Inc. v. Assurance Company of America, 400 F.3d 982 (7th Cir. 2006) (competitor's action against garage door opener manufacturer, alleging that manufacturer falsely advertised its openers as compatible with competitor's "rolling code" technology, did not give rise to a suit for disparagement); ProLink Holdings Corp. v. Federal Insurance Co., 688 F.3d 828 (7th Cir. 2012); JAR Laboratories, L.L.C. v. Great American E & S Insurance Co., 945 F. Supp.2d 937 (N.D. Ill. 2013).

Eighth Circuit: Sletten & Brettin Orthodontics, L.L.C. v. Continental Casualty Co., 782 F.3d 931 (8th Cir. 2015); Hartford Fire Insurance Co. v. Vita Craft Corp., 911 F. Supp.2d 1164 (D. Kan. 2012).

Ninth Circuit: Philips Oral Healthcare, Inc. v. Federal Insurance Co., 83 Fed. Appx. 963 (9th Cir. 2003) (competitor's claim for false advertising stated claim for disparagement).

Tenth Circuit: Yousuf v. Cohlmia. 741 F.3d 31 (10th Cir. 2014).

Eleventh Circuit: Finger v. State Farm Fire and Casualty Insurance Co., 459 Fed. Appx. 828 (11th Cir. 2012).

State Courts:

California: Hartford Casualty Insurance Co. v. Swift Distribution, Inc., 59 Cal.4th 277, 326 P.3d 253, 172 Cal. Rptr.3d 653 (2014); CNA Casualty of California v. Seaboard Surety Co., 222 Cal. Rptr. 276 (Cal. App. 1986).

Illinois: Pekin Insurance Co. v. Phelan, 799 N.E.2d 523 (Ill. App. 2003), *appeal denied* 807 N.E.2d 976 (Ill. 2004) (competitor's claim against insured hair salon alleging false statements made to lure away competitor's customers involved allegations of disparagement).

New York: Ruder & Finn, Inc. v. Seaboard Surety Co., 439 N.Y.S.2d 858 (N.Y. 1981); Natural Organics, Inc. v. OneBeacon America Insurance Co., 102 A.D.3d 756, 959 N.Y.S.2d 204, (N.Y. App. Div. 2013); Bonded Concrete, Inc. v. Transcontinental Insurance Co., 784 N.Y.S.2d 212 (N.Y. App. Div. 2004) (deceptive business practices claim asserted against concrete supplier by general contractor was not "advertising injury" or "personal injury" because it was not a "publication" of material that libeled or slandered another or violated a person's right to privacy).

Ohio: Motorists Mutual Insurance Co. v. National Dairy Herd Improvement Association, Inc., 750 N.E.2d 1169 (Ohio App. 2001) (no defense owed for antitrust claim based upon defamation or disparagement).

74 See:

Third Circuit: Charter Oak Insurance Co. v. Maglio Fresh Food, 979 F. Supp.2d 581 (E.D. Pa. 2013).

Fifth Circuit: Nationwide Mutual Insurance Co. v. Gum Tree Property Management, L.L.C., 597 Fed. Appx. 241 (5th Cir. 2015); Uretek (USA), Inc. v. Continental Casualty Co., 92 F. Supp.3d 589 (S.D. Tex. 2015).

Seventh Circuit: Acme United Corp. v. St. Paul Fire and Marine Insurance Co., 214 Fed. Appx. 596 (7th Cir. 2007) (duty to defend owed because complaint alleged claim of product superiority); Knoll Pharmaceutical Co. v. Automobile Insurance Company of Hartford, 152 F. Supp.2d 1026 (N.D. Ill. 2001) (disparagement of competitor's product included statements that "there is no substitute" for policyholder's thyroid drug, "no proven bioequivalent" product, and "product is more effective than or superior to other drugs available to treat hypothyroidism"); ProLink Holdings Corp. v. Federal Insurance Co., 688 F.3d 828 (7th Cir. 2012); JAR Laboratories, L.L.C. v. Great American E & S Insurance Co., 945 F. Supp.2d 937 (N.D. Ill. 2013).

Eighth Circuit: Sletten & Brettin Orthodontics, L.L.C. v. Continental Casualty Co., 782 F.3d 931 (8th Cir. 2015); Hartford Fire Insurance Co. v. Vita Craft Corp., 911 F. Supp.2d 1164 (D. Kan. 2012).

Ninth Circuit: Edwards Theatres, Inc. v. United National Insurance Co., 126 Fed. Appx. 831 (9th Cir. 2005) (competitor's claim against movie theatre owner for injuring its institutional reputation by advertisements using its trademark fell within provision of owner's commercial liability policy covering claims arising out of "use of another's advertising idea" in owner's advertisements); E.piphany, Inc. v. St. Paul Fire & Marine Insurance Co., 590 F. Supp.2d 1244 (N.D. Cal. 2008) (defense owed where underlying complaint alleged that insured made false claims about superiority of insured's own products that clearly and necessarily implied inferiority of competitor's products).

Tenth Circuit: Yousuf v. Cohlmia. 741 F.3d 31 (10th Cir. 2014).

Eleventh Circuit: Finger v. State Farm Fire and Casualty Insurance Co., 459 Fed. Appx. 828 (11th Cir. 2012).

State Courts:

California: Hartford Casualty Insurance Co. v. Swift Distribution, Inc., 59 Cal.4th 277, 326 P.3d 253, 172 Cal. Rptr.3d 653 (2014).

Connecticut: QSP, Inc. v. Aetna Casualty and Surety Co., 256 Conn. 343, 773 A.2d 906 (Conn. 2001) (commercial disparagement in antitrust).

New York: Natural Organics, Inc. v. OneBeacon America Insurance Co., 102 A.D.3d 756, 959 N.Y.S.2d 204, (N.Y. App. Div. 2013).

North Carolina: Harleysville Mutual Insurance Co. v. Buzz Off Insect Shield, L.L.C., 190 N.C. App. 28, 664 S.E.2d 317 (N.C. App. 2008) (allegations of false, negative comparative statements about manufacturer's goods in the course of advertising on websites and in materials stated personal and advertising injury claim).

75 See Ethicon, Inc. v. Aetna Casualty & Surety Co., 737 F. Supp. 1320 (S.D.N.Y. 1990) (duty to defend antitrust claim that included a pattern of conduct involving bad-faith litigation because such conduct could be deemed malicious prosecution). But see, QSP, Inc. v. Aetna Casualty & Surety Co., 773 A.2d 906 (Conn. Super. 2001) (antitrust claim including threatening and instituting bad-faith litigation did not implicate insurance company's duty to defend); Purdue Frederick Co. v. Steadfast Insurance Co., 40 A.D.3d 285, 836 N.Y.S.2d 28 (N.Y. App. Div. 2007) (claims against policyholder for antitrust violations were not enumerated personal injury offenses, even though claims referred to certain "sham litigation" allegedly brought by insureds to maintain their monopoly on the manufacture and sale of a drug).

76 See:

Seventh Circuit: Curtis-Universal, Inc. v. Sheboygan Emergency Medical Services, Inc., 43 F.3d 1119 (7th Cir. 1994) ("unfair competition" includes tortious interference with contract); Attorneys' Title Guaranty Fund, Inc. v. Maryland Casualty Co., 1991 WL 171339 (N.D. Ill. Aug. 23, 1991) ("unfair competition" included tortious interference with contract between competitor and third parties).

State Courts:

Florida: Tire Kingdom, Inc. v. First Southern Insurance Co., 573 So.2d 885 (Fla. App. 1990), *review denied* 589 So.2d 290 (Fla. 1991) (duty to defend antitrust claim because advertising injury offenses included "unfair competition" and "defamation").

See also, Goodwin and Mazour, "Insuring Corporate Competitive Practices" 661 PLI/Comm 69, 88 (1993), stating that the court in CNA Casualty of California v. Seaboard Surety Co., 222 Cal. Rptr. 276 (Cal. App. 1986), accepted CNA's argument that "there is no need 'to strain the construction of the term "unfair competition" in order to find coverage, since even an antitrust violation is commonly considered unfair competition.'"

But see, St. Paul Insurance Cos. v. Taladega Nursing Home, Inc., 606 F.2d 631 (5th Cir. 1979) (coverage for antitrust claims against public policy).

As previously in discussed in § 7.10[2][b] *supra,* a renewal insurance policy contains the same terms as the original policy if the insurance company does not affirmatively notify the policyholder of changes in coverage. If the policyholder renews coverage with the same insurance company over a number of years and there is no indication that the insurance company ever notified the policyholder of the change in coverage when it switched from the 1973 Form to the 1986 Form, Coverage B under the renewal policy could arguably contain the 1973 Form, including the additional "unfair competition" offense.

77 See:

First Circuit: Town of Stoddard v. Northern Security Insurance Co., 718 F. Supp. 1062 (D.N.H. 1989) (applying New Hampshire law) (amendment to zoning ordinance to prevent development of particular property was covered).

Third Circuit: New Castle County v. National Union Fire Insurance Company of Pittsburgh, Pennsylvania, 243 F.3d 744 (3d Cir. 2001) (claim against county for violations of due process in zoning and permitting process which interfered with developer's project was covered as an "invasion of the right of private occupancy").

Fifth Circuit: Lexington Insurance Co. v. St. Bernard Parish Government, 548 Fed. Appx. 176 (5th Cir. 2013).

Ninth Circuit: American International Surplus Lines Insurance Co. v. City of San Diego, 121 Fed. Appx. 692 (9th Cir. 2005).

Eleventh Circuit: Continental Casualty Co. v. City of Jacksonville, 654 F. Supp.2d 1338 (M.D. Fla. 2009).

State Courts:

California: County of Sacramento v. Scottsdale Insurance Co., 2003 WL 21246688 (Cal. App. May 30, 2003).

New Hampshire: Town of Goshen v. Grange Mutual Insurance Co., 424 A.2d 822 (N.H. 1980) (town entitled to insurance coverage for suit by developer for economic hardship created by zoning determination that prevented development of a project because such conduct created an "invasion of the right of private occupancy"; physical invasion is not required, only an interference with enjoyment of property).

Louisiana: Johnson v. Orleans Parish School Board, 975 So.2d 698 (La. App. 2008).

But see:

California: Sterling Builders, Inc. v. United National Insurance Co., 93 Cal. Rptr.2d 697 (Cal. App. 2000) (requiring physical invasion of property).

[78] See, e.g.:

First Circuit: Cynosure, Inc. v. St. Paul Fire and Marine Insurance Co., 645 F.3d 1 (1st Cir. 2011).

Third Circuit: St. Paul Fire and Marine Insurance Co. v. Brother International Corp., 319 Fed. Appx. 121 (3d Cir. 2009); Melrose Hotel Co. v. St. Paul Fire and Marine Insurance Co., 432 F. Supp.2d 488 (E.D. Pa. 2006).

Fourth Circuit: Resource Bankshares Corp. v. St. Paul Mercury Insurance Co., 407 F.3d 631 (4th Cir. 2005); Prime TV, LLC. v. Travelers Insurance Co., 223 F. Supp.2d 744 (M.D.N.C. 2002).

Fifth Circuit: Registry Dallas Associates v. Wausau Business Insurance Co., 2004 WL 614836 (N.D. Tex. Feb. 26, 2004); Western Rim Investment Advisors, Inc. v. Gulf Insurance Co., 269 F. Supp.2d 836 (N.D. Tex. 2003), *affirmed*, 96 Fed. Appx. 960, 2004 WL 1160165 (5th Cir. 2004); American Safety and Risk Services, Inc. v. Legion Indemnity Co., 153 F. Supp.2d 869 (E.D. La. 2001).

Sixth Circuit: National Union Fire Insurance Co. of Pittsburgh, Pa. v. Papa John's International, Inc., 29 F. Supp.3d 961 (W.D. Ky. 2014).

Seventh Circuit: Auto-Owners Insurance Co. v. Websolv Computing, Inc., 580 F.3d 543 (7th Cir. 2009); American States Insurance Co. v. Capital Associates of Jackson County, Inc., 392 F.3d 939 (7th Cir. 2004); Indiana Insurance Company v. CE Design Limited, 6 F. Supp.3d 858 (N.D. Ill. 2013); Maxum Indemnity Co. v. Eclipse Manufacturing Co., 848 F. Supp.2d 871 (N.D. Ill. 2012); Ace Rent-A-Car, Inc. v. Empire Fire & Marine Insurance Co., 580 F. Supp.2d 678 (N.D. Ill. 2008); American Home Assurance Co. v. McLeod USA, Inc., 475 F. Supp.2d 766 (N.D. Ill. 2007).

Eighth Circuit: State Farm Fire and Casualty Co. v. National Research Center for College and University Admissions, 445 F.3d 1100 (8th Cir. 2006); Universal Underwriters Insurance Co. v. Lou Fusz Automotive Network, Inc., 401 F.3d 876 (8th Cir. 2005); Owners Insurance Co. v. European Auto Works, Inc., 695 F.3d 814 (8th Cir. 2012); Nationwide Mutual Insurance Co. v. Harris Medical Associates, L.L.C., 973 F. Supp.2d 1045 (E.D. Mo. 2013).

Ninth Circuit: Big 5 Sporting Goods Corp. v. Zurich American Insurance Co., 957 F. Supp.2d 1135 (C.D. Cal. 2013).

Tenth Circuit: Park University Enterprises, Inc. v. American Casualty Company of Reading, PA., 314 F. Supp.2d 1094 (D. Kan. 2004).

Eleventh Circuit: Alea London Ltd. v. American Home Services, Inc., 638 F.3d 768 (11th Cir. 2011); Penzer v. Transportation Insurance Co., 545 F.3d 1303 (11th Cir. 2008); Hooters of Augusta, Inc. v. American Global Insurance Co., 157 Fed. Appx. 201 (11th Cir. 2005); Penzer v. Transportation Insurance Co., 509 F. Supp.2d 1278 (S.D. Fla. 2007).

State Courts:

California: State Farm General Insurance Co. v. JT's Frames, Inc., 181 Cal. App.4th 429, 104 Cal. Rptr.3d 573 (2010); ACS Systems, Inc. v. St. Paul Fire and Marine Insurance Co., 147 Cal. App.4th 137, 53 Cal. Rptr.3d 786 (Cal. App. 2007).

Florida: Penzer v. Transportation Insurance Co., 29 So.3d 1000 (Fla. 2010).

Illinois: Valley Forge Insurance Co. v. Swiderski Electronics, Inc., 223 Ill.2d 352, 860 N.E.2d 307, 307 Ill. Dec. 653 (2006); Standard Mutual Insurance Co. v. Lay, 2014 IL App (4th) 110527-B, 2 N.E.3d 1253, 377 Ill. Dec. 972 (2014); Landmark American Insurance Co. v. NIP Group, Inc., 2011 IL App (1st) 101155, 962 N.E.2d 562, 356 Ill. Dec. 877 (2011); Pekin Insurance Co. v. Xdata Solutions, 2011 Ill. App. Lexis 1056, 958 N.E.2d 397, 354 Ill. Dec. 654 (2011).

Maryland: Walk v. Hartford Casualty Insurance Co., 852 A.2d 98 (Md. 2004).

Massachusetts: Terra Nova Insurance Co. v. Fray-Witzer, 449 Mass. 406, 869 N.E.2d 565 (Mass. 2007).

Missouri: Columbia Casualty Co. v. HIAR Holding, L.L.C., 411 S.W.3d 258 (Mo. 2013) (*en banc*).

Ohio: Motorists Mutual Insurance Co. v. Dandy-Jim, Inc., 182 Ohio App.3d 311, 912 N.E.2d 659 (2009); Schuetz v. State Farm Fire and Casualty Co., 147 Ohio Misc.2d 22, 890 N.E.2d 374 (Ohio C.P. Franklin Cnty. 2007).

Pennsylvania: Telecommunications Network Design and Paradise Distributing, Inc. v. The Brethren Mutual Insurance Co., 5 A.3d 331 (Pa. Super. 2010).

Texas: TIG Insurance Co. v. Dallas Basketball, Ltd., 129 S.W.3d 232 (Tex. App. 2004).

Wisconsin: Sawyer v. West Bend Mutual Insurance Co., 343 Wis.2d 714, 821 N.W.2d 250 (Wis. App. 2012).

[79] See ISO Forms CG 00 01 10 01 and CG 00 01 12 07. See also, Goodwin and Mazour, "Insuring Corporate Competitive Practices" 661 PLI/Comm 69, 88 (1993). See §§ 9.03[a]-[b] *supra*.

[80] See:

Second Circuit: CGS Industries, Inc. v. Charter Oak Fire Insurance Co., 720 F.3d 71 (2d Cir. 2013); Transamerica Insurance Group v. Rubens, 1999 WL 673338 (S.D.N.Y. Aug. 27, 1999).

Third Circuit: Brotherhood Mutual Insurance Co. v. Salem Baptist Church of Jenkintown, 985 F. Supp.2d 624 (E.D. Pa. 2013); Regent Insurance Co. v. Strausser Enterprises, Inc., 902 F. Supp.2d 628 (E.D. Pa. 2012).

Fifth Circuit: Nationwide Mutual Insurance Co. v. Lake Caroline, Inc., 515 F.3d 414 (5th Cir. 2008); Manis v. St. Paul Fire and Marine Insurance Co., 2001 WL 1397318 (E.D. La. Nov. 8, 2001).

Sixth Circuit: North Bank v. Cincinnati Insurance Cos., 125 F.3d 983, 986 (6th Cir. 1997) (false arrest, false imprisonment, malicious prosecution, humiliation, libel, slander, defamation of character, invasion of privacy, and discrimination are intentional torts) (refusing to enforce expected or intended defense to claim for "personal injury" because "personal injury" offenses are inherently intentional in character and enforcing the "expected or intended" defense would defeat reasonable expectations of the policyholder); School District of the City of Royal Oak v. Continental Casualty Co., 912 F.2d 844, 847–848 (6th Cir. 1990) (intentional civil rights violations are insurable and not void on public policy grounds).

Seventh Circuit: Hurst-Roche Engineers v. Commercial Union Insurance Co., 51 F.3d 1336 (7th Cir. 1995).

Eighth Circuit: Chicago Insurance Co. v. City of Council Bluffs, 713 F.3d 963 (8th Cir. 2013); AMCO Insurance Co. v. Inspired Technologies, Inc., 648 F.3d 875 (8th Cir. 2011).

Ninth Circuit: Western Protectors Insurance Co. v. Shaffer, 2009 WL 86551 (W.D. Wash. Jan. 9, 2009).

Tenth Circuit: Harris v. Zurich Holding Company of America, Inc., 2006 WL 120258 (D. Utah Jan. 17, 2006).

Eleventh Circuit: Travelers Property Casualty Co. of America v. Kansas City Landsmen, L.L.C., 592 Fed. Appx. 876 (11th Cir. 2015); Lincoln National Health and Casualty Insurance Co. v. Brown, 782 F. Supp. 110 (M.D. Ga. 1992).

State Courts:

California: Aetna Casualty & Surety Co. v. Superior Court, 23 Cal. Rptr.2d 442 (Cal. App. 1993) (coverage for inducing infringement would be against public policy as coverage for loss caused by willful act); Stonelight Tile, Inc. v. California Insurance Guarantee Association, 150 Cal. App.4th 19, 58 Cal. Rptr.3d 74 (Cal. App. 2007).

Connecticut: Imperial Casualty and Indemnity Co. v. State, 246 Conn. 313, 714 A.2d 1230 (Conn. 1998); Allstate Insurance Co. v. Limone, 2009 Conn. Super. Lexis 3253 (Conn. Super. New Britain Cnty. Dec. 3, 2009).

Illinois: Illinois Farmers Insurance Co. v. Keyser, 2011 IL App (3d) 090484, 956 N.E.2d 575, 353 Ill. Dec. 713 (Ill. App. 2011); Cincinnati Insurance Co. v. American Hardware Manufacturers' Association, 387 Ill. App.3d 85, 325 Ill. Dec. 483, 898 N.E.2d 216 (Ill. App. 2008).

Indiana: Liberty Mutual Insurance Co. v. OSI Industries, Inc., 831 N.E.2d 192 (Ind. App. 2005) (advertising injury coverage was enforceable despite public policy against insurance coverage for intentional acts as insurance company sold a policy covering intentional acts of advertising).

Maryland: Bailer v. Erie Insurance Exchange, 344 Md. 515, 687 A.2d 1375 (Md. 1997).

Michigan: Bradley v. Mid-Century Insurance Co., 294 N.W.2d 141, 163 (Mich. 1980) ("When members of the public purchase policies of insurance they are entitled to the broad measure of protection necessary to fulfill their reasonable expectations. . . . Where particular provisions, if read literally, would largely nullify the insurance, they will be severely restricted so as to enable fair fulfillment of the stated policy objective.") (finding that an insurance company may not enforce its exclusion where application would frustrate the reasonable expectations of the policyholder).

Missouri: Missouri Property and Casualty Insurance Guaranty Association v. Petrolite Corp., 918 S.W.2d 869 (Mo. App. 1996).

New Hamphire: Northern Security Insurance Co. v. Connors, 20 A.3d 912 (N.H. 2011).

New York: Sportsfield Specialties, Inc. v. Twin City Fire Insurance Co., 116 A.D.3d 1270, 984 N.Y.S.2d 447 (N.Y. App. 2014).

Rhode Island: Town of Cumberland v. Rhode Island Interlocal Risk Management Trust, Inc., 860 A.2d 1210 (R.I. 2004).

Wisconsin: Air Engineering, Inc. v. Industrial Air Power, L.L.C., 346 Wis.2d 9, 828 N.W.2d 565 (Wis. App. 2013).

But see, State Auto Property & Casualty Insurance Co. v. LaGrotta, 529 Fed. Appx. 271 (3d Cir. 2013).

[81] See ISO Forms CG 00 01 10 01 and CG 00 01 12 07.

[82] See, e.g.:

Second Circuit: Bridge Metal Industries, L.L.C. v. Travelers Indemnity Co., 559 Fed. Appx. 15 (2d Cir. 2014).

Third Circuit: Houbigant, Inc. v. Federal Insurance Co., 374 F.3d 192 (3d Cir. 2004) (exclusion not applied).

Fourth Circuit: Danby of North America, Inc. v. Travelers Insurance Co., 25 Fed. Appx. 186 (4th Cir. 2002) (exclusion applied).

Fifth Circuit: Gemini Insurance Co. v. The Andy Boyd Company, LLC, 243 Fed. Appx. 814 (5th Cir. 2007) (exclusion applied).

Sixth Circuit: Capitol Specialty Insurance Co. v. Industrial Electronics, L.L.C., 407 Fed. Appx. 47 (6th Cir. 2011); Liberty Corporate Capital, Ltd. v. Security Safe Outlet, Inc., 937 F. Supp.2d 891 (E.D. Ky. 2013).

Seventh Circuit: Supreme Laundry Service, L.L.C. v. Hartford Casualty Insurance Co., 521 F.3d 743 (7th Cir. 2008) (exclusion not applied).

Eighth Circuit: Callas Enterprises, Inc. v. Travelers Indemnity Company of America, 193 F.3d 952 (8th Cir. 1999) (exclusion applied).

Ninth Circuit: Paper Recovery of Northern California v. Travelers Casualty and Surety Company of Illinois, 92 Fed. Appx. 478 (9th Cir. 2004) (exclusion applied).

Eleventh Circuit: Penzer v. Transportation Insurance Co., 545 F.3d 1303 (11th Cir. 2008) (exclusion not applied).

State Courts:

Georgia: City of College Park v. Georgia Interlocal Risk Management Agency, 313 Ga. App. 239, 721 S.E.2d 97 (2011).

Illinois: American Family Mutual Insurance Co. v. Roth, 381 Ill. App.3d 760, 320 Ill. Dec. 80, 886 N.E.2d 1149 (Ill. App. 2008) (exclusion applied).

Montana: Town of Geraldine v. Montana Municipal Insurance Authority, 347 Mont. 267, 198 P.3d 796 (2008).

New Jersey: Glenmark Pharmaceuticals, Inc., USA v. Franklin Mutual Insurance Co., 2008 WL 5194305 (N.J. Super. App. Div. Dec. 12, 2008) (exclusion applied); Tradesoft Technologies, Inc. v. Franklin Mutual Insurance Co., 329 N.J. Super. 137, 746 A.2d 1078 (N.J. Super. App. Div. 2000) (exclusion applied).

New York: Natural Organics, Inc. v. OneBeacon America Insurance Co., 102 A.D.3d 756, 959 N.Y.S.2d 204 (N.Y. App. Div. 2013).

Ohio: Meyers Lake Sportsman's Club, Inc. v. Auto-Owners Mutual Insurance Co., 2013-Ohio-3115, 2013 Ohio App. LEXIS 3164 (Ohio App. July 15, 2013); Westfield Insurance Co. v. Factfinder Marketing Research, Inc., 168 Ohio App.3d 391, 860 N.E.2d 145 (Ohio App. 2006) (exclusion applied).

Texas: Gilbert Texas Construction, L.P. v. Underwriters at Lloyd's London, 327 S.W.3d 118 (Tex. 2010); Yates Carpet, Inc. v. Travelers Lloyds Insurance Co., 2008 WL 2467881 (Tex. App. June 19, 2008) (exclusion applied); Southstar Corp. v. St. Paul Surplus Lines Insurance Co., 42 S.W.3d 187 (Tex. App. 2001) (exclusion applied).

Wisconsin: Dairy Source, Inc. v. Biery Cheese Co., 269 Wis.2d 542, 674 N.W.2d 680 (Wis. App. 2003).

[83] See ISO Form CG 00 01 10 01.

[84] See § 5.03[6] *supra*.

[85] See § 9.03[3][c] *supra*.

[86] See, e.g.:

Third Circuit: OneBeacon America Insurance Co. v. Urban Outfitters, Inc., 21 F. Supp.3d 426 (E.D. Pa. 2014).

Sixth Circuit: National Union Fire Insurance Co. of Pittsburgh, Pa. v. Papa John's International, Inc., 29 F. Supp.3d 961 (W.D. Ky. 2014).

Eighth Circuit: Nationwide Mutual Insurance Co. v. Harris Medical Associates, L.L.C., 973 F. Supp.2d 1045 (E.D. Mo. 2013).

Ninth Circuit: National Union Fire Insurance Co. of Pittsburgh, Pa. v. Coinstar, Inc., 39 F. Supp.3d 1149 (W.D. Wash. 2014); Big 5 Sporting Goods Corp. v. Zurich American Insurance Co., 957 F. Supp.2d 1135 (C.D. Cal. 2013).

Tenth Circuit: Emasco Insurance Co. v. C.E. Design, Ltd., 784 F.3d 1371 (10th Cir. 2015). *Cf.* Carolina Casualty Insurance Co. v. Nanodetex Corp., 733 F.3d 1018 (10th Cir. 2013) (malicious prosecution akin to statutory claim regardless of label attached to claim).

Eleventh Circuit: Interline Brands, Inc. v. Chartis Specialty Insurance Co., 749 F.3d 962 (11th Cir. 2014); James River Insurance Co. v. Medical Waste Management, L.L.C., 46 F. Supp.3d 1350 (S.D. Fla. 2014); American Casualty Co. of Reading, PA v. Superior Pharmacy, L.L.C., 86 F. Supp.3d 1307 (M.D. Fla. 2015).

CHAPTER 10

Directors and Officers Liability and Professional Liability Insurance

Chapter Contents

❖

§ 10.01 Overview

In addition to CGL insurance, there are some other types of third-party insurance policies[1] that may be relevant for real estate-related businesses including, among other things:

1. directors and officers ("D&O") liability insurance; and
2. errors and omissions ("E&O") or professional liability insurance.

D&O and E&O liability policies are extremely different in scope, as they provide insurance coverage for incomparable risks. D&O liability insurance is important for real estate-related entities that are either publicly traded entities or have directors, officers, or other key employees answerable to investors or other third parties, because D&O insurance provides protection for liabilities that amount to principally economic losses suffered by these third parties as a result of the director's, officer's, or other key employee's negligence or other breaches of duties committed in their capacities running or employed by the entity.[2]

In contrast, E&O liability insurance is important for all real estate-related entities, including engineers, architects, designers, builders, and developers, because it provides an additional layer of protection for economic losses suffered by a third party should a professional commit an act of negligence or other breach of duty in his or her professional capacity.[3]

Although D&O and E&O liability insurance differ markedly, they share many of the same coverage issues. The similarity of issues stems from the fact that D&O and E&O liability insurance policies use similar language in their insuring agreements, exclusions, conditions, and limitations. As a result of the commonality of the D&O and E&O form policies' language, they are combined as the subject of this chapter.

This chapter first sets forth the insuring agreements of the E&O[4] and D&O[5] policies and then covers their common elements.[6] This is followed by a discussion of the significant coverage issues emanating from the common elements of the insuring agreements, including the identity of the policyholder,[7] the scope of "loss,"[8] "wrongful act" in the correct capacity,[9] and the myriad of claim-made issues.[10] Finally, the chapter discusses and analyzes some of the exclusions used in these types of policies.[11]

§ 10.02 Insuring Agreements

[1]—E&O Insuring Agreement

A commonly used form of E&O insuring agreement provides:

> "The Company will pay for all *loss* that the *policyholder* becomes legally obligated to pay as a result of *claims first made* against the policyholder and reported to the insurance company during the policy period and arising out of any actual or alleged *Wrongful Act* in the policyholder's *performance of professional services*." (emphasis added to highlight the coverage issues that emanate from the language of the agreement)[12]

[2]—D&O Insuring Agreement

Coverage under a regularly utilized form of D&O insurance provides:

> "The Company will pay for all *loss* that the *policyholder* becomes legally obligated to pay as a result of *claims first made* against the policyholder and reported to the insurance company during the policy period and arising out of any actual or alleged *Wrongful Act* in the policyholder's *capacity as a director or officer*." (emphasis added to highlight the coverage issues that arise from the language of the agreement)[13]

[3]—Common Elements

E&O and D&O insurance policies both provide third-party liability insurance for principally economic harms,[14] as opposed to liabilities for "bodily injury" or "property damage" suffered by third parties, which is covered under CGL insurance policies.[15]

D&O and E&O insurance policies share a number of other common issues and concepts including:

1. Identity of the policyholder;[16]
2. "Loss";[17]
3. Claims-Made;[18]
4. "Wrongful Act";[19]
5. Capacity;[20] and
6. Exclusions.[21]

§ 10.03 Coverage Issues

[1]—Identity of the Policyholder

Generally, the word "policyholder" includes all professionals and/or all directors/officers employed by the entity as well as the entity itself that employs those individual professionals or managerial employees.[22] In fact, in D&O and E&O insurance, the employer may be entitled to entity coverage for both indemnification of the individual professional or director/officer, and separate coverage for entity liability for certain claims (i.e., employment and securities or professional liability).[23]

However, the broad interpretation of "policyholder" (i.e., covering many individuals in the same organization) and the existence of entity coverage may have some coverage consequences. First, if there is a single aggregate indemnity or overall limit, the expansive definition actually may operate to reduce the limits available to protect each such "policyholder"—each employed individual professional, officer, and/or director and the employing entity itself.[24] As will be discussed, this presents a shrinking limits problem, the coverage-limiting effects of which can be minimized by adequate advance planning and use of skilled insurance professionals, such as brokers, consultants, and attorneys.[25] Moreover, expansive interpretations of "policyholder" and entity coverage present serious conflicts of interest issues that might require separate defense counsel and separate coverage counsel for each "policyholder."[26]

[2]—"Loss"

E&O and D&O insurance policies generally define "loss" to include all damages and judgments rendered against, or settlements entered into by, the policyholder.[27]

[a]—Punitive Damages

[i]—Policy Language

Coverage for punitive damages presents an interesting "loss" issue. With respect to whether punitive damages are covered, the first place one would need to consult is the insurance policy itself, because an insurance policy is an ordinary, albeit specialized, contract whose language generally controls its construction and interpretation.[28] Within the insurance policy itself, one would first read the definition of "loss." If the question remains unresolved, one would then need to review the exclusions. For example, some policies exclude fines, penalties, and punitive damages from the definition of "loss."[29] Many courts hold that these exclusions are unambiguous and exclude punitive damages from the scope of coverage.[30] An interesting issue arises as to whether treble or multiple damages, such as those awardable under various state and federal statutes, would be excluded by a "punitive damages" exclusion.[31]

[ii]—Implicit Exclusion

If the damages at issue (punitive, statutory, or otherwise) are not expressly excluded in the "loss" definition or in a specific "punitive damages" or similarly applicable exclusion, the next place one would consider would be other exclusions or other portions of the policy. The question would be whether the punitive damages would be excluded by implication. For instance, an "intentional act" exclusion might exclude such punitive or exemplary damages that are assessed for intentional misconduct.[32]

Likewise, in a CGL policy, "occurrence" is defined as conduct resulting in unintentional and accidental losses. If punitive or similar damages are assessed based upon intentional conduct (as opposed to negligent, reckless, or other non-intentional conduct), the damages may be implicitly excluded as not resulting from an "occurrence."[33] With respect to E&O and D&O liability policies, which are usually written on a "claims-made" basis,[34] the "occurrence" analysis will have no impact on the coverage determination. Nonetheless, one should consult the definition of "wrongful act" because such definition might explicitly or implicitly exclude penalties resulting from intentional conduct in ways similar to the ways the definition of "occurrence" does in CGL occurrence-based policies.[35] In both of these instances of implicit exclusion, there is a distinction between intentional conduct and reckless or grossly negligent conduct, and usually damages resulting from only the former would be implicitly excluded.[36]

[iii]—Common Law/Public Policy

Where punitive damages are not excluded expressly or by implication, the common law would control. In some jurisdictions, punitive damages are uninsurable as a matter of public policy.[37] In other jurisdictions, directly assessed punitive damages are not insurable, but vicariously assessed punitive damages are insurable.[38] Some jurisdictions have no public policy against insuring for punitive damages, regardless of whether they are vicariously or directly assessed.[39]

[b]—Defense Costs

With respect to defense costs, E&O and D&O policies can be written in either of two ways. First, they can be written like a standard CGL insurance policy as "duty-to-defend" policies, which contain promises by the insurance companies to defend their policyholders in potentially covered actions. These duty-to-defend policies provide defense obligations that extend until establishment that the claims can no longer potentially be covered or until exhaustion of the indemnity limits.[40]

On the other hand, the majority of E&O and D&O policies are "defense-cost reimbursement" policies, which contain promises to pay or indemnify the policyholder for losses incurred in connection with covered claims.[41] In the defense-cost reimbursement insurance policies, "loss" includes, in addition to judgments, settlements, and other monetary reparations paid to third parties, all costs of the policyholder's defense, i.e., costs to investigate a claim and to pay for lawyers to defend the policyholder in a lawsuit.[42] Accordingly, in the majority of cases, the "loss" element is satisfied as soon as a claim results in a defense cost expenditure.[43]

Under both types of insurance policies, the obligation to defend is triggered by the existence of any claims or allegations in an underlying complaint that creates even a possibility of coverage.[44] However, defense-cost reimbursement policies have some differences with duty-to-defend policies, as will be highlighted below.

[i]—Defense Costs within Limits

For example, the extent of the defense provided is different. To wit, because defense costs are included within the definition of "loss" and therefore are reimbursed under the defense-cost reimbursement type of liability policy's indemnity limits, the amount of defense costs are usually limited in reimbursement policies. On the other hand, because defense costs are not included in the indemnity limits in the duty-to-defend type of liability policies, defense cost accounts are normally unlimited in duty-to-defend policies.[45]

[ii]—Consent Prior to Incurring Defense Costs

A second difference concerns control and selection of defense counsel. In defense-cost reimbursement policies, the policyholder retains the right to select and control defense counsel, whereas, as long as the insurance company actually undertakes the policyholder's defense in the underlying action and/or the insurance company's interests do not interfere with independent representation by defense counsel, such rights belong to the insurance company in duty-to-defend policies.[46] However, with the benefits of having the right to selection and control over the defense comes the obligation to consult with the insurance company. For instance, D&O and E&O policies often have "voluntary payment" provisions, which require the policyholder to obtain the consent of the insurance company before incurring any defense costs, in addition to obtaining consent before admitting liability or before settling any claim. A fiduciary duty often accompanies an insurance company that controls the defense.[47]

In some instances, although selection and control of defense counsel remain with the policyholder, the policyholder may be limited to a designated set of panel counsel—a list of pre-approved firms.[48] Requirements regarding the use of panel counsel somewhat undercut the policyholder's right to selection and control of defense counsel.[49] Therefore, it may be important to review the designated list of panel counsel before purchasing the policy, to ensure that the list includes counsel the policyholder feels is at least acceptable. It also is important to check the particular policy at issue for such requirements and to obtain the necessary written approvals before incurring significant defense costs.[50] Such consent should not be unreasonably withheld, even if the policy does not explicitly so state.[51]

The reasonableness of the amount of defense costs might also be at issue.[52] For instance, insurance companies may argue that too many lawyers worked on the case, the hourly rate was excessive, or that a particular motion should have been made.[53] Policyholders can anticipate these arguments in a number of ways. Initially, insurance companies generally have defense cost guidelines, which are ordinarily given to policyholders when the policy is issued. Policyholders should read these guidelines before deciding to purchase a policy from a particular insurance company and negotiate any necessary modifications. Policyholders must also make sure that defense counsel complies with those guidelines.

The policyholder also should regularly provide its insurance company with defense counsel's billing statements, and otherwise inform, and seek the participation of, the insurance company in defense of the claim. Whether or not the insurance company actually assists in the defense is irrelevant. The goal is to give the insurance company the opportunity to object at the earliest possible date and to ask for changes in defense practices if the insurance company deems it necessary. To the extent that the insurance company is silent, it arguably has waived the right to object at a later date.

[iii]—Timing of Reimbursement

In defense-cost reimbursement liability insurance policies, the timing of reimbursement can be significant. In fact, the question becomes whether defense costs need to be advanced as they are incurred on an ongoing basis or whether they may be reimbursed after the policyholder pays for them.

Some decisions involve clear and explicit policy language directing or negating the right to ongoing reimbursement.[54] Where the policy does not address the issue, many courts have found that policy language is ambiguous on the question of when defense costs must be paid.[55] If the language is ambiguous, the policyholder should prevail.[56] Even if the insurance policy does not expressly require the insurance company to fund the officer's, director's, or professional's defense on an ongoing basis, some insurance companies will do so if asked or pressed.[57] A few courts have required insurance companies to advance directors' and officers' or professionals' defense costs, notwithstanding insurance policy provisions to the contrary.[58] Other courts interpret the policy differently and will not require reimbursement on an ongoing basis.[59]

Unless the policy specifically states that reimbursement for defense costs is not owed until resolution of the underlying claim, the insurance company should be obligated to pay for the defense of the claim on an ongoing basis, although this is an area of dispute.[60]

There are good reasons for a rule requiring reimbursement of defense costs on an ongoing basis. A defense that does not timely operate does nothing to assist in the defense of claims. The insurance company's "duty to defend the insured is one of the main benefits of the insurance [policy]."[61] The promise of a defense means that an insurance company will act promptly; otherwise, the policyholder is robbed of the principal value of this promise.[62] Some courts have described an insurance company's duty to provide a timely defense as "litigation insurance."[63]

The duty to defend on a current basis involves more than an obligation by the insurance company to pay someday those amounts expressly ordered to be paid by the court. By paying for defense currently, an insurance company protects the policyholder's right to peace of mind and security.[64]

The purpose of obligating an insurance company to assume defense costs timely is so that "policyholders thus are assured they need not expend their own funds in order to receive protection for liability."[65] The courts have emphasized the unique importance of the time element of the duty to defend in awarding specific performance of the obligation and rejecting the claim that a later damage award is equivalent.[66] For the defense to be effective, costs must be paid "as they were and are incurred."[67]

Besides denying the policyholder's bargained-for "peace of mind,"[68] an insurance company's failure to provide a current defense narrows the policyholder's options for defending its interests.[69] In one case, the court held that an insurance company's failure to assume its policyholder's defense as promised in a settlement agreement harmed the policyholder's ability to settle the claim against it.[70] In sum, policyholders purchase liability insurance policies so that their insurance companies will bear the defense of alleged claims.[71]

Even in defense-cost reimbursement policies, reimbursement should be made on an ongoing and current basis based upon the express language of the coverage grant. E&O and D&O policies require the insurance company to pay all "loss," which expressly includes defense expenditures, "that the policyholder becomes legally obligated to pay" for certain covered claims within the claims-made period and including wrongful acts committed by the policyholder in his or her professional or director or officer capacities.[72] The policyholder becomes legally obligated to pay for defense expenditures when the defense expenditures are incurred, and, therefore, indemnity for defense costs differs from indemnity for judgments or settlements.

[iv]—Shrinking Limits

Because most D&O and E&O policies generally include defense costs within the definition of "loss,"[73] defense costs expended will actually reduce the coverage "limits" available.[74] Policyholders should pay close attention to this distinction. In an era of heightened accountability, losses arising out of errors or other "wrongful acts" may continue to expand and result in corresponding increases in the sizes of judgments and settlements. As settlements and judgments rise, professionals, directors, and officers and/or their insurance companies will have more economic incentive to litigate. The likely consequence is that real estate businesses and the professionals, directors, and officers they employ will use up more of their insurance limits on defense costs, leaving less for settlements and judgments.[75]

A policyholder can minimize the consequences of the shrinking limits problem by obtaining a D&O or E&O policy with a separate duty to defend.[76] Alternatively, it can address the problem by purchasing additional limits, either in the form of a primary policy with greater limits or umbrella and excess liability insurance policies.[77]

[c]—Consent to Settlement

Although "loss" typically includes settlements, D&O and E&O policies often contain prohibitions against "voluntary payments," and such provisions require the insurance company's prior consent to settlements that are entered into by the policyholder.[78] Under such a provision, an insurance company cannot unreasonably withhold its consent.[79] One court held that a policyholder may enter into a reasonable settlement without insurance company consent if: (1) a conflict of interest arises entitling the policyholder to control the defense or (2) the insurance company breaches its duty to defend the policyholder.[80] Some courts apply a prejudice standard to any breach; others refuse.[81]

[d]—Hammer Clause

D&O and E&O policies usually contain a so-called "hammer clause," which purports to protect a professional's reputation rights by allowing the policyholder veto rights over any contemplated settlement, but also attempts to limit the insurance company's response in the event such veto rights are exercised.[82]

Unlike other liability insurance policies, under which an insurance company completely controls the defense and can settle cases in its own discretion, a policyholder who is a professional generally has veto rights regarding settlements, in part, to protect his or her own professional reputation.[83] Usually, these provisions also state that in exercise of its veto rights, the policyholder must act reasonably.[84]

The hammer clause provides that the insurance company has the right to settle a claim with the policyholder's consent but if the policyholder does not consent, the insurance company's liability is capped by the amount for which the insurance company could have settled the claim, plus defense costs incurred as of that date. A typical clause provides:

> "The insurance company shall not settle any claim without the written consent of the insured. If however, the insured shall refuse to consent to any settlement recommended by the insurance company and shall elect to contest the claim or continue any legal proceeding in connection with such claim, then the insurance company's liability for the claim shall not exceed the amount for which the claim would have been settled, plus the cost and expenses incurred, with its consent, up to the date of such refusal."[85]

Insurance companies may attempt to limit their liability when they know that the professional will invoke the hammer clause. For example, the insurance company may propose that a low settlement offer be made. If the policyholder asserts veto rights, the insurance company may later argue that its liability is limited to the amount of its initial proposed settlement offer. A policyholder can counter this by demonstrating that it withheld consent reasonably. To further protect themselves, policyholders should document the initial offer, their reasons for withholding consent, and/or evidence that plaintiff would never settle for the initial offer.[86]

[3]—"Wrongful Act" in Correct Capacity

D&O and E&O policies provide coverage when there is a "wrongful act" committed by the policyholder during the policy period, or after a retroactive date under a policy with "prior acts" coverage.[87] The "wrongful act" must also have been committed in the performance of a correct capacity, i.e., in performance of "professional services" for E&O insurance or in the "capacity of a director or officer" for D&O insurance.[88]

[a]—Timing

It will normally be evident from the face of the underlying action pleading or the facts discovered whether the "wrongful act" was allegedly committed during the requisite time period, i.e., during the policy period or after the retroactive date in policies providing "prior acts" coverage. If the complaint is unclear as to timing, the policyholder should be entitled to a defense under the universal principle that coverage is afforded until the claim can be confined definitively to one entirely not covered by the policy.[89]

[b]—"Wrongful Act"

Whether a "wrongful act" is alleged should be fairly straightforward. "Wrongful act" is variously defined to include such things as negligence, errors, omissions, misstatements, and other breaches of duties.[90] It should be readily discernible from the facts or allegations in the underlying lawsuit whether and which particular "wrongful act" the policyholder allegedly committed during the relevant time period. If the underlying complaint is unclear as to the existence of "wrongful acts," the professional or director/officer is entitled to coverage under the universally accepted principle that unless the claim can be confined to claims that are clearly not covered, coverage must be afforded.[91]

One interesting issue is whether a breach of contract and other intentional breaches of duty are considered "wrongful acts" covered by D&O or E&O policies. Ultimately, the policy language controls in each case.[92] However, when the policy is unclear, case law is split on the issue.[93]

[c]—Capacity

The most difficult subissue under the "wrongful act" issue is determining whether the "wrongful act" occurred in the correct capacity, i.e., the policyholder's rendition of "professional services" or the policyholder's "capacity as a director or officer." One way the issue can arise is when a director or officer acts in a dual capacity. In labor strikes, for example, a person may assume dual roles of officer or director and as a non-managerial employee. Another context in which the situation can arise is when a director or officer of a corporation is also an in-house practicing professional (i.e., attorney or accountant). Professionals can also act in dual capacities. For instance, a real estate lawyer may also perform title insurance brokerage or notary services.

[i]—"Professional Services"

For E&O policies, resolution of the capacity issue depends upon the particular policy language. The "wrongful act" generally must be committed by the policyholder in performance or rendition of "professional services."[94]

The term "professional services" is usually defined in either the declarations page of the policy or in the original application submitted for coverage.[95] It is important to check the definition of "professional services" to determine if the coverage matches a professional firm's activities and/or delineates clearly and broadly the services, including clerical services, the professional firm performs.

A common error that should be cautioned against is when a firm purchases incomplete coverage. Professional liability policies for securities firms, for example, may provide coverage for broker/dealer activities or investment banker activities, but not both. Similarly, professional liability policies for insurance salespersons should include coverage for activities as a "managing general insurance agent, general insurance agent, insurance agent, or insurance broker."[96] Developers, property owners, and real estate sales professionals should ensure their policies include all of their activities, lest any claim for an activity not listed could be denied. For instance, a developer or real estate salesperson can be denied coverage for a faulty design or construction claim if design and construction activities are not listed as professional services.[97]

If "professional services" is not sufficiently defined in a policy, the courts will attempt to define it by applying their own determinations. A few courts have taken the position that "professional services" requires "[s]omething more than . . . employment or vocation."[98]

> "Something more than an act flowing from mere employment or vocation is essential. The act or service must be such as exacts the use or application of special learning or attainments of some kind. The term 'professional' in the context used in the policy provision means something more than mere proficiency in the performance of a task and implies intellectual skill as contrasted with that used in an occupation for production or sale of commodities. A 'professional' act or service is one arising out of a vocation, calling, occupation, or employment involving specialized knowledge, labor, or skill, and the labor or skill involved is predominantly mental or intellectual, rather than physical or manual. . . . In determining whether a particular act is of a professional nature or a 'professional service' we must look not to the title or character of the party performing the act, but to the act itself."[99]

[ii]—Director or Officer

Like E&O policies, D&O policies also have capacity issues. For D&O policies, the "wrongful act" must be committed in the policyholder's "capacity as a director or officer," rather than his or her professional capacity.[100] Definitions of "director" and "officer" are generally not provided in the policy.

Frequently, insurance companies reserve their right to deny coverage on the grounds that the "wrongful acts" were not committed in the defined capacity. They may argue that the individual was acting to advance his or her own particular interest,[101] was acting in the capacity of a lesser employee or of a professional employee,[102] or was acting outside the scope of his or her authority.[103] Resolution depends on whether the action complained of was committed in the correct capacity and with adequate authority.[104]

[4]—Claims-Made Trigger

[a]—Contrast with "Occurrence" Policies

Most D&O and E&O policies are written on a "claims-made," as opposed to an "occurrence," basis.[105] Coverage under an "occurrence" policy is provided for "wrongful acts" that result in harm and/or take place, arise, or are committed during the policy period, even though the claim may be made after the policy period has expired.[106] In contrast, under the typical D&O and E&O "claims-made" policy forms, coverage is triggered by a "claim" being first made against the policyholder during the policy period, irrespective of when the harm arose or the "wrongful act" took place.[107] One court differentiated between "claims-made" and "occurrence" policies by saying:

> "An 'occurrence' policy also covers a different spectrum of claims than a 'claims made' policy. A 'claims made' policy covers claims which are 'asserted' against the insured by a third party during the policy period regardless of when the underlying damage occurred. . . . An 'occurrence' policy, on the other hand, does not restrict the period during which a claim may be made. This type of policy covers losses for which the insured is liable so long as the damage 'occurs' during the policy period."[108]

[b]—Claims-Made and Reported Variety

In addition to the claim being made during the policy period, some forms of D&O and E&O policies also require that the claim be reported to the insurance company during the policy period.[109]

[c]—"Claim"

The central inquiry for the "claims-made" issue is whether a claim has been made or whether a claim has been made and reported. A "claim" is typically defined to include a complaint filed in a lawsuit or alternative dispute resolution.[110] A "claim" can also be defined more broadly to include any demand for money or services, sometimes even including oral demands.[111]

Case law is unanimous in defining "claim" to be a demand for something as a right, including the filing of a lawsuit.[112] Sometimes, the definition of "claim" could include initiation of a formal civil or criminal investigation.[113] Some courts hold that a formal judicial proceeding is not required to establish a "claim."[114] Other courts require the institution of a formal judicial proceeding.[115]

Policyholders cannot rely on the definition, however, to determine when it is necessary to provide notice to their insurance companies, as many policies contain provisions that require that the policyholder give notice not only of "claims," but also of circumstances and events that are likely to give rise to "claims" in the future.[116]

However, whatever form the claim takes, the relevant date for the claims-made issue is not the date that the wrongful act is alleged to have taken place but the date that the claim is made or the date the claim is made and the date the claim is reported to the insurance company.[117]

[d]—Late Notice

Courts are fairly strict in requiring the triggering event to take place during the policy period, refusing to find coverage when the claim or notice occurs outside of the policy period.[118] A federal district court in California held that notice given eight hours after the policy had expired was a violation of the policy's strict notice provisions.[119] Other courts applying California law have been more lenient in interpreting notice provisions, requiring that the insurance company show it was prejudiced by the late notice.[120] One court held that late notice in a claims-made policy may be equitably excused to prevent forfeiture.[121] Nevertheless, it should be kept in mind that strict construction of notice provisions may also bar coverage for subsequent litigation related to a claim that was actually first made prior to inception of the claims-made policy.[122]

[e]—Interrelated Claims

A related issue is whether multiple claims are treated as a single claim for purposes of coverage. D&O and E&O policies typically provide that when claims arise out of the same wrongful act or interrelated wrongful acts, they are treated as one claim and deemed to have been made at the time of the first such claim.[123]

The result of treating several or multiple claims as one claim assigned to a single policy is to: (1) limit coverage to the aggregate indemnity limit of the single policy to which the claim is assigned; and (2) apply a single deductible or self-insured retention to that claim. If, on the other hand, the claims were treated as separate claims assigned to several policies, more limits of indemnity may be available, but multiple deductibles or self-insured retentions may also have to be satisfied.[124] Considering what is at stake, disputes can arise as to whether the wrongful acts involved in multiple claims are identical or interrelated. In most of the cases that have addressed this issue, the courts have refused to aggregate claims.[125]

[f]—Dispute Preceding Claim

Regardless of the extent of prior acts coverage afforded, most, if not all, E&O and D&O policies exclude coverage for prior acts if, as of the time of inception of the policy, the policyholder knew or should have known of circumstances that might lead to a claim.[126]

An interesting illustration of the claims-made issue presents itself when a dispute arises in one policy period but the claim does not arise until the next policy period. The insurance company in the first period will take the position that no coverage is afforded during its policy period because a claim did not arise until the second period. The insurance company in the second period will argue either that the claim arose in the first period when the dispute arose, or that there were circumstances that the policyholder knew would result in a claim prior to the inception of its policy period but which were not disclosed on the application.

Faced with this scenario, the policyholder should notify the first insurance company when the dispute arises. The policyholder should notify the second insurer both (1) when the claim arises and (2) when it fills out the application, to avoid being accused of misrepresentation. In this way, the policyholder is more likely to recover from at least one of the insurance companies. Resolution of which one will depend upon the court's resolution of when a claim arose, because notice was provided in both periods.[127]

[g]—Change of Employment

In the E&O context, when a professional changes employers or sells a business, a potential gap in coverage could arise. This could occur if the covered professional commits a negligent act, error, or omission while employed by a prior employer, and the claim is not made against the employee until he or she is under new employment. The current employer's insurance company will deny coverage claiming that the negligent act, error, or omission took place while the policyholder was employed elsewhere. This argument has support in some case law, and there is no countervailing authority.[128] Coverage under the prior employer's E&O insurance policy will depend on the extent of the prior employer's coverage under its optional extended reporting period, something often outside the control of the professional.[129]

§ 10.04 Exclusions

[1]—General Construction

The seeming breadth of coverage granted under D&O and E&O insurance is contrasted with the myriad of exclusions that are tacked onto policies, which have the potential to take away much of what appears to be given by the coverage grant. In fact, it is not uncommon for D&O or E&O policies to have more than twenty standard exclusions, plus others added by endorsement.

Insurance policy exclusions should be construed narrowly in favor of coverage.[130] As many courts have noted, the doctrine of *contra proferentem*—pursuant to which policy language is construed against the insurance company drafter and in favor of coverage—is afforded a "heightened application," where ambiguities exist in an exclusionary provision.[131]

[2]—Common Exclusions

[a]—Bodily Injury, Property Damage, or Personal Injuries

D&O and E&O policies may have exclusions for "bodily injury"[132] or "property damage,"[133] or "personal injuries,"[134] to eliminate coverage afforded by CGL policies. In similar vein, a D&O policy might contain an exclusion for professional errors and omissions, and vice versa.[135]

[b]—Fraud, Dishonesty, and Intentional Misconduct

A common exclusion in D&O and/or E&O policies is for fraud, dishonesty, and other intentional misconduct.[136] An issue arises where a claimant sues the policyholder for a number of tortious acts, ranging from negligence to recklessness to intentional misconduct.[137] Most cases hold that the claim is covered.[138]

The issue becomes to what extent is coverage afforded. There is a split as to how much is covered. The majority view is that if any claims are potentially covered, a policyholder is entitled to reimbursement of defense costs for the entire action.[139] A minority of courts holds that the policyholder is only entitled to reimbursement of those defense costs associated with potentially covered claims.[140]

Another issue is whether mere allegations of excluded misconduct trigger the exclusion. Usually, the exclusion states that it only applies when the misconduct has been finally adjudged in a court of competent jurisdiction.[141] It is important to ascertain what "final adjudication" means because the term could merely require the entry of a judgment by a trial court or, alternatively, require exhaustion of all appellate rights.[142] Further, there may be an issue as to whether "final adjudication" can be avoided by settlement before any adjudication reaches the stage of "final."[143] Arguably, claims of criminal or fraudulent acts that are never proven through "final adjudication," through settlement or otherwise, would require the insurance company to indemnify.[144]

[c]—Negligence or Mishandling of Funds

Some E&O policies contain an exclusion for errors, omissions, and negligence in connection with claims for mishandling of funds, which could be relevant to realtors real estate-related entities that regularly handle funds of other people, such as title companies.[145]

[d]—Asbestos/Pollution

Virtually all D&O and E&O policies attempt to limit the insurance company's liability through exclusions regarding pollution[146] or asbestos. Pollution exclusions typically state that insurance does not apply to liability "arising out of the actual, alleged, or threatened discharge, dispersal, seepage, migration, release or escape of pollutants at any time."[147] Asbestos exclusions similarly attempt to limit or eliminate coverage for liability concerning asbestos.[148]

[e]—Insured vs. Insured

D&O and E&O policies often might also contain an "insured v. insured" exclusion, purporting to exclude coverage for claims made by one policyholder against another policyholder. Insurance companies argue that the exclusion applies to claims made against directors or officers by either the insured corporation or other directors or officers.[149]

[f]—Known Prior Acts

Circumstances known by the policyholder prior to inception of the policy period as likely to lead to a claim are usually the subject of an exclusion.[150] Some policies may expand the scope of this exclusion to include, in addition to known claims, claims the policyholder reasonably should have expected or foreseen, and cases generally test the policyholder's foreseeability objectively rather than subjectively.[151] Most policies contain a provision deeming the claim to have been made when the notice of circumstances is given. As previously noted, a policyholder should provide notice of any circumstance it believes might lead to a claim.[152]

A prior acts exclusion may purport to bar coverage for claims arising out of an insured's wrongful acts prior to a specified date. The date may coincide with the termination of coverage under a previous policy or with a change in corporate status. One court upheld the validity of the prior acts exclusion against the policyholder's argument that the exclusion was against public policy because it narrowed coverage so substantially that the policy unfairly provided little effective protection.[153] The court reasoned that the policy was negotiated between two sophisticated corporations that must have understood the import of the agreement's terms.[154]

[g]—Remuneration or Amounts Due under Contract

D&O and E&O policies often have an "amounts owing under contract" exclusion, which purports to exclude claims for losses that are for amounts due under a written contract or agreement. A standard exclusion provides:

> "The Underwriter shall not be liable for that part of Loss, other than Defense Costs, which constitutes:
>
> 1. amounts owing under or assumed by the Insured pursuant to any express written contract or agreement with the Insured; provided, however, this exclusion shall not apply to the extent the Insured would be liable for such Loss in the absence of such contract or agreement."[155]

E&O and D&O policies might also have a "remuneration exclusion," which similarly purports to exclude that portion of a loss that constitutes earned but unpaid compensation, including bonuses and severance:

> "The Underwriter shall not be liable for that part of Loss, other than Defense Costs, which constitutes:

▼

3. compensation earned by the claimant in the course of employment but not paid by the Company, including any unpaid salary, bonus, wages, severance pay, retirement benefits, vacation days or sick days; provided, however, this exclusion shall not apply to any back pay or front pay."[156]

Courts construing similarly worded exclusions have come to diametrically opposite results. Some cases hold that they apply to exclude coverage for settlements that include payments for these purportedly excluded items.[157] On the other hand, there are cases holding that similarly worded exclusions do not apply in these situations.[158]

[h]—Inadequate Consideration for Shares

With the recent revelation of changed strike prices in options and similar misconduct, insurers have added an exclusion for claims arising out of or related to the payment of inadequate consideration for shares. This exclusion has been sparsely litigated.[159]

[3]—Severability

Do exclusions operate to eliminate D&O and E&O insurance for all directors, officers, or professionals even if the conduct of a single one of them activates an exclusion? Innocence or lack of knowledge has been acknowledged by some courts as providing the basis for finding coverage under some circumstances. "Severability" of conduct determines whether the exclusion applies to the innocent or ignorant policyholder.[160]

An interesting issue, where courts come to different conclusions, involves whether an exclusion that applies to an act of "any insured" trumps a severability-of-interests clause or vice versa.[161]

Severability usually applies only when the exclusion is triggered by intentional or knowingly wrongful conduct.[162] The concept may be applicable to exclusions for fraud, dishonesty or criminal conduct, known prior wrongful acts, or misrepresentation in the policy application.[163] Severability would likely be of no assistance for asbestos or pollution exclusions.[164]

Under common law, an insurance policy might be voidable if the policyholder either affirmatively made material misrepresentations or omitted material facts in his application for insurance, but innocent directors, officers, or professionals would not be denied coverage solely due to the actions of the other bad actors.[165] Given a severability clause, the policy should only be rescinded as to those individuals who had knowledge of the misrepresentations being made in the application.[166] An explicit severability clause will be enforced in favor of the innocent directors, officers, or professionals.[167] However, an express antiseverability clause may have the opposite effect.[168]

If there is no severability clause or the contract is not specific in its handling of the question of severability, courts rely on the intent of the parties to determine if there should be severability.[169] For example, the severability of a contract may be considered a question of the parties' intent, "to be determined from the language employed by the parties, viewed in the light of the circumstances surrounding them at the time they contracted."[170] As a general rule, "the contract is considered severable and divisible when by its terms, nature, and purpose, it is susceptible of division and apportionment."[171] The absence of a clear-cut rule in the D&O and E&O insurance area suggests that the policies should be interpreted consistent with their purpose, which is to insure. If severability enhances the insurance, it should be applied.

Notes

1 As a discussed previously, third-party insurance, also known as "litigation insurance," deals with situations where a third party (which is defined as a person or entity other than the policyholder or the insurance company) has suffered a loss and is seeking compensation from the policyholder by way of a civil action or suit, and the policyholder seeks insurance for such third-party liability and litigation. See Chapter 2 *supra.* See also, e.g., White v. Insurance Company of State of Pennsylvania, 282 F. Supp.2d 618, 625 (N.D. Ohio 2003), *vacated on other grounds* 405 F.3d 455 (6th Cir. 2005).

> "'Liability' insurance constitutes 'an agreement to cover a loss resulting from one's liability to a third party, such as a loss incurred by a driver who injures a pedestrian.' The claim under the policy 'arises once the insured's liability to a third party has been asserted.' In contrast to this 'third-party insurance,' there is also 'indemnity' insurance which is characterized as 'first-party insurance' and defined as '[a] policy that applies to oneself or one's own property, such as life insurance, health insurance, disability insurance, and fire insurance.'" (citations omitted).

2 See, e.g.:

Third Circuit: G-I Holdings v. Hartford Fire Insurance Co., 2007 WL 842009 (D.N.J. Mar. 16, 2007).

Ninth Circuit: Sierra Foothills Public Utility District v. Clarendon America Insurance Co., 2006 WL 1350345 (E.D. Cal. May 17, 2006).

State Courts:

Delaware: AT&T Corp. v. Clarendon America Insurance Co., 2006 WL 2685081 (Del. Super. Sept. 18, 2006).

Pennsylvania: Anglo-American Insurance Co. v. Molin, 547 Pa. 504, 691 A.2d 929 (Pa. 1997).

3 See, e.g., HCC Employer Services, Inc. v. Westchester County Surplus Lines Insurance Co., 2006 WL 1663343 (S.D. Tex. June 5, 2006).

4 See § 10.02[1] *infra.*

5 See § 10.02[2] *infra.*

6 See § 10.02[3] *infra.*

7 See § 10.03[1] *infra.*

8 See § 10.03[2] *infra.*

9 See § 10.03[3] *infra.*

10 See § 10.03[4] *infra.*

11 See § 10.04 *infra.*

12 HCC Employer Services, Inc. v. Westchester County Surplus Lines Insurance Co., 2006 WL 1663343 (S.D. Tex. June 5, 2006).

13 See, e.g.:

Third Circuit: G-I Holdings v. Hartford Fire Insurance Co., 2007 WL 842009 (D.N.J. Mar. 16, 2007).

Ninth Circuit: Sierra Foothills Public Utility District v. Clarendon America Insurance Co., 2006 WL 1350345 (E.D. Cal. May 17, 2006).

State Courts:

Delaware: AT&T Corp. v. Clarendon America Insurance Co., 2006 WL 2685081 (Del. Super. Sept. 18, 2006).

Pennsylvania: Anglo-American Insurance Co. v. Molin, 547 Pa. 504, 691 A.2d 929 (Pa. 1997).

[14] See, e.g.:

Third Circuit: American Guarantee & Liability Insurance Co. v. Fojanini, 90 F. Supp.2d 615 (E.D. Pa. 2000).

Fourth Circuit: Tankovtis v. Del Suppo, Inc., 129 Fed. Appx. 829 (4th Cir. 2005).

Eighth Circuit: McAninch v. Wintermute, 478 F.3d 882 (8th Cir. 2007).

State Courts:

Connecticut: Employers Reinsurance Corp. v. Muro, 86 Conn. App. 551, 861 A.2d 1216 (2004), *cert. denied* 273 Conn. 907, 868 A.2d 747 (2005).

Indiana: Stevenson v. Hamilton Mutual Insurance Co., 672 N.E.2d 467 (Ind. App. 1996).

Minnesota: Foster v. Summit Medical Systems, Inc., 610 N.W.2d 350 (Minn. App. 2000).

New Jersey: Hebela v. Healthcare Insurance Co., 370 N.J. Super. 260, 851 A.2d 75 (N.J. Super. App. Div. 2004).

New York: Watkins Glen Central School District v. National Union Fire Insurance Company of Pittsburgh, Pennsylvania, 286 A.D.2d 48, 732 N.Y.S.2d 70 (N.Y. App. Div. 2001).

Ohio: American Chemical Society v. Leadscope, Inc., 2005 WL 1220746 (Ohio App. May 24, 2005), *appeal denied* 107 Ohio St.3d 1412, 836 N.E.2d 1231 (2005).

Texas: Venture Encoding Service, Inc. v. Atlantic Mutual Insurance Co., 107 S.W.3d 729 (Tex. App. 2003).

Wisconsin: 1325 North Van Buren, LLC v. T-3 Group, Ltd., 293 Wis.2d 410, 716 N.W.2d 822 (2006).

Medical care providers usually also have bodily injury coverage under their E&O policies and building professionals should have property damage coverage under their E&O policies.

[15] For a discussion of the bodily injury or property damage covered by CGL insurance, see Chapter 5 *supra*.

[16] See § 10.03[1] *infra*.

[17] See § 10.03[2] *infra*.

[18] See § 10.03[4] *infra*.

[19] See § 10.03[3][b] *infra*.

[20] See § 10.03[3][c] *infra*.

[21] See § 10.04 *infra*.

[22] See, e.g.:

First Circuit: Medical Mutual Insurance Company of Maine v. Indian Harbor Insurance Co., 583 F.3d 57 (1st Cir. 2009); Bank of Rhode Island v. Progressive Casualty Insurance Co., 19 F. Supp.3d 378 (D.R.I. 2014).

Second Circuit: MBIA Inc. v. Certain Underwriters at Lloyd's, London, 33 F. Supp.3d 344 (S.D.N.Y. 2014); Jewish Community Center of Staten Island v. Trumbull Insurance Co., 957 F. Supp.2d 215 (E.D.N.Y. 2013); Julio & Sons Co. v. Travelers Casualty and Surety Company of America, 591 F. Supp.2d 651 (S.D.N.Y. 2008); *In re* Adelphia Communications Corp., 298 B.R. 49 (Bankr. S.D.N.Y. 2003); *In re* First Central Financial Corp., 238 B.R. 9 (Bankr. E.D.N.Y. 1999); *In re* Ambassador Group, Inc. Litigation, 738 F. Supp. 57 (E.D.N.Y. 1990).

Third Circuit: Verticalnet, Inc. v. U.S. Specialty Insurance Co., 492 F. Supp.2d 452 (E.D. Pa. 2007); American Guarantee & Liability Insurance Co. v. Fojanini, 90 F. Supp.2d 615 (E.D. Pa. 2000); Clark v. General Accident Insurance Company PR. Ltd., 951 F. Supp. 559 (D.V.I. 1997).

Fourth Circuit: In re Beach First National Bancshares, Inc., 451 B.R. 406 (Bankr. D.S.C. 2011); ACE American Insurance Co. v. Ascend One Corp., 570 F. Supp.2d 789 (D. Md. 2008).

Fifth Circuit: Mary Kay Holding Corp. v. Federal Insurance Co., 309 Fed. Appx. 843, 2009 WL 290485 (5th Cir. 2009).

Sixth Circuit: Alvord Investments, L.L.C. v. The Hartford Financial Services Group, Inc., 660 F. Supp.2d 850 (W.D. Tenn. 2009); Florists' Mutual Insurance Co. v. Ludy Greenhouse Manufacturing Corp., 521 F. Supp.2d 661 (S.D. Ohio. 2007).

Seventh Circuit: Sigma Chi Corp. v. Westchester Fire Insurance Co., 587 F. Supp.2d 891 (N.D. Ill. 2008).

Eighth Circuit: Wintermute v. Kansas Bankers Surety Co., 630 F.3d 1053 (8th Cir. 2011); St. Paul Fire and Marine Insurance Co. v. Compaq Computer Corp., 539 F.3d 809 (8th Cir. 2008).

Ninth Circuit: Goerner v. Axis Reinsurance Co., 400 Fed. Appx. 226 (9th Cir. 2010); Pan Pacific Retail Properties, Inc. v. Gulf Insurance Co., 471 F.3d 961 (9th Cir. 2006); *In re* Mila, Inc., 423 B.R. 537 (Bankr. App. 9th Cir. 2010); Raychem Corp. v. Federal Insurance Co., 853 F. Supp. 1170 (N.D. Cal. 1994).

Tenth Circuit: Kite Family Investment Co. v. Levings, 188 Fed. Appx. 714 (10th Cir. 2006).

Eleventh Circuit: Office Depot, Inc. v. National Union Fire Insurance Co. of Pittsburgh, Pa., 453 Fed. Appx. 871 (11th Cir. 2011); Langdale Co. v. National Union Fire Insurance Co. of Pittsburgh, Pa., 2014 U.S. Dist. LEXIS 184163 (N.D. Ga. June 4, 2014); MedAssets, Inc. v. Federal Insurance Co., 705 F. Supp.2d 1368 (N.D. Ga. 2010); Assurance Company of America v. Lucas Waterproofing Co., 581 F. Supp.2d 1201 (S.D. Fla. 2008).

State Courts:

Illinois: Illinois Insurance Guaranty Fund v. Santucci, 384 Ill. App.3d 927, 323 Ill. Dec. 775, 894 N.E.2d 801 (2008).

Kansas: Miller v. Westport Insurance Corp., 288 Kan. 27, 200 P.3d 419 (2009).

Minnesota: Benilde-St. Margaret's High School v. St. Paul Mercury Insurance Co., 575 N.W.2d 127 (Minn. App. 1998).

Mississippi: Noxubee County School District v. United National Insurance Co., 883 So.2d 1159 (Miss. 2004).

New York: Westpoint International, Inc. v. American International South Insurance Co., 71. A.D.3d 561, 899 N.Y.S.2d 8 (N.Y. App. Div. 2010); Watkins Glen Central School District v. National Union Fire Insurance Company of Pittsburgh, Pennsylvania, 286 A.D.2d 48, 732 N.Y.S.2d 70 (N.Y. App. Div. 2001).

Wisconsin: 1325 North Van Buren, LLC v. T-3 Group, Ltd., 293 Wis.2d 410, 716 N.W.2d 822 (2006).

[23] See, e.g.:

First Circuit: Medical Mutual Insurance Company of Maine v. Indian Harbor Insurance Co., 583 F.3d 57 (1st Cir. 2009); Bank of Rhode Island v. Progressive Casualty Insurance Co., 19 F. Supp.3d 378 (D.R.I. 2014).

Second Circuit: MBIA Inc. v. Certain Underwriters at Lloyd's, London, 33 F. Supp.3d 344 (S.D.N.Y. 2014); Jewish Community Center of Staten Island v. Trumbull Insurance Co., 957 F. Supp.2d 215 (E.D.N.Y. 2013); Julio & Sons Co. v. Travelers Casualty and Surety Company of America, 591 F. Supp.2d 651 (S.D.N.Y. 2008); *In re* Adelphia Communications Corp., 298 B.R. 49 (Bankr. S.D.N.Y. 2003); *In re* First Central Financial Corp., 238 B.R. 9 (Bankr. E.D.N.Y. 1999).

Third Circuit: Verticalnet, Inc. v. U.S. Specialty Insurance Co., 492 F. Supp.2d 452 (E.D. Pa. 2007); American Guarantee & Liability Insurance Co. v. Fojanini, 90 F. Supp.2d 615 (E.D. Pa. 2000); Clark v. General Accident Insurance Company PR. Ltd., 951 F. Supp. 559 (D.V.I. 1997).

Fourth Circuit: In re Beach First National Bancshares, Inc., 451 B.R. 406 (Bankr. D.S.C. 2011); ACE American Insurance Co. v. Ascend One Corp., 570 F. Supp.2d 789 (D. Md. 2008).

Fifth Circuit: Mary Kay Holding Corp. v. Federal Insurance Co., 309 Fed. Appx. 843, 2009 WL 290485 (5th Cir. 2009).

Sixth Circuit: Alvord Investments, L.L.C. v. The Hartford Financial Services Group, Inc., 660 F. Supp.2d 850 (W.D. Tenn. 2009); Florists' Mutual Insurance Co. v. Ludy Greenhouse Manufacturing Corp., 521 F. Supp.2d 661 (S.D. Ohio 2007).

Seventh Circuit: Sigma Chi Corp. v. Westchester Fire Insurance Co., 587 F. Supp.2d 891 (N.D. Ill. 2008).

Eighth Circuit: Wintermute v. Kansas Bankers Surety Co., 630 F.3d 1053 (8th Cir. 2011); St. Paul Fire and Marine Insurance Co. v. Compaq Computer Corp., 539 F.3d 809 (8th Cir. 2008).

Ninth Circuit: Goerner v. Axis Reinsurance Co., 400 Fed. Appx. 226 (9th Cir. 2010); Pan Pacific Retail Properties, Inc. v. Gulf Insurance Co., 471 F.3d 961 (9th Cir. 2006); *In re* Mila, Inc., 423 B.R. 537 (Bankr. App. 9th Cir. 2010); Raychem Corp. v. Federal Insurance Co., 853 F. Supp. 1170 (N.D. Cal. 1994).

Tenth Circuit: Kite Family Investment Co. v. Levings, 188 Fed. Appx. 714 (10th Cir. 2006).

Eleventh Circuit: Office Depot, Inc. v. National Union Fire Insurance Co. of Pittsburgh, Pa., 453 Fed. Appx. 871 (11th Cir. 2011); Langdale Co. v. National Union Fire Insurance Co. of Pittsburgh, Pa., 2014 U.S. Dist. LEXIS 184163 (N.D. Ga. June 4, 2014); MedAssets, Inc. v. Federal Insurance Co., 705 F. Supp.2d 1368 (N.D. Ga. 2010); Assurance Company of America v. Lucas Waterproofing Co., 581 F. Supp.2d 1201 (S.D. Fla. 2008).

State Courts:

Illinois: Illinois Insurance Guaranty Fund v. Santucci, 384 Ill. App.3d 927, 323 Ill. Dec. 775, 894 N.E.2d 801 (2008).

Kansas: Miller v. Westport Insurance Corp., 288 Kan. 27, 200 P.3d 419 (2009).

Minnesota: Benilde-St. Margaret's High School v. St. Paul Mercury Insurance Co., 575 N.W.2d 127 (Minn. App. 1998).

Mississippi: Noxubee County School District v. United National Insurance Co., 883 So.2d 1159 (Miss. 2004).

New York: Westpoint International, Inc. v. American International South Insurance Co., 71. A.D.3d 561, 899 N.Y.S.2d 8 (N.Y. App. Div. 2010); Watkins Glen Central School District v. National Union Fire Insurance Company of Pittsburgh, Pennsylvania, 286 A.D.2d 48, 732 N.Y.S.2d 70 (N.Y. App. Div. 2001).

Wisconsin: 1325 North Van Buren, LLC v. T-3 Group, Ltd., 293 Wis.2d 410, 716 N.W.2d 822 (2006).

[24] See:

Second Circuit: In re Adelphia Communications Corp., 298 B.R. 49 (Bankr. S.D.N.Y. 2003).

State Courts:

California: Helfand v. National Union Fire Insurance Co., 10 Cal. App.4th 869, 13 Cal. Rptr.2d 295 (1992), *cert. denied* 510 U.S. 824 (1993).

[25] See § 10.03[2][b][iv] *infra*.

[26] See § 6.02[3] *supra*. See also, *In re* Adelphia Communications Corp., 298 B.R. 49 (Bankr. S.D.N.Y. 2003).

[27] See, e.g.:

First Circuit: TranSched Systems Ltd. v. Federal Insurance Co., 67 F. Supp.3d 523 (D.R.I. 2014); Bank of Rhode Island v. Progressive Casualty Insurance Co., 19 F. Supp.3d 378 (D.R.I. 2014).

Third Circuit: Peerless Insurance Co. v. Pennsylvania Cyber Charter School, 19 F. Supp.3d 635 (W.D. Pa. 2014); G-I Holdings v. Hartford Fire Insurance Co., 2007 U.S. Dist. LEXIS 19069 (D.N.J. Mar. 16, 2007).

Fifth Circuit: In re Trans Texas Gas Corp., 597 F.3d 298 (5th Cir. 2010); HCC Employer Services, Inc. v. Westchester County Surplus Lines Insurance Co., 2006 WL 1663343 (S.D. Tex. June 5, 2006).

Seventh Circuit: Ryerson, Inc. v. Federal Insurance Co., 676 F.3d 610 (7th Cir. 2012); Sigma Chi Corp. v. Westchester Fire Insurance Co., 587 F. Supp.2d 891 (N.D. Ill. 2008).

Eighth Circuit: St. Paul Fire and Marine Insurance Co. v. Compaq Computer Corp., 539 F.3d 809 (8th Cir. 2008); Zayed v. Arch Insurance Co., 932 F. Supp.2d 956 (D. Minn. 2013).

Ninth Circuit: Bayley Construction v. Great American E & S Insurance Co., 980 F. Supp.2d 1281 (W.D. Wash. 2013); Sierra Foothills Public Utility District v. Clarendon America Insurance Co., 2006 WL 1350345 (E.D. Cal. May 17, 2006).

Eleventh Circuit: Culbreath Isles Property Owners Ass'n v. Travelers Casualty and Surety Co. of America, 601 Fed. Appx. 876 (11th Cir. 2015); Office Depot, Inc. v. National Union Fire Insurance Company of Pittsburgh, Pa, 734 F. Supp.2d 1304 (S.D. Fla. 2010); MedAssets, Inc. v. Federal Insurance Co., 705 F. Supp.2d 1368 (N.D. Ga. 2010).

State Courts:

Arizona: Cohen v. Lovitt & Touche, Inc., 233 Ariz. 45, 308 P.3d 1196 (Ariz. App. 2013).

California: Executive Risk Indemnity, Inc. v. Jones, 171 Cal. App.4th 319, 89 Cal. Rptr.3d 747 (2009).

Delaware: AT&T Corp. v. Clarendon America Insurance Co., 2006 WL 2685081 (Del. Super. Sept. 18, 2006).

Florida: First Specialty Insurance Co. v. Caliber One Indemnity Co., 988 So.2d 708 (Fla. App. 2008).

Illinois: City of Collinsville v. Illinois Municipal League Risk Management Association, 385 Ill. App.3d 224, 328 Ill. Dec. 308, 904 N.E.2d 70 (2008).

Kansas: Kansas Health Care Stabilization Fund v. St. Francis Hospital, 41 Kan. App.2d 488, 203 P.3d 33 (2009).

New York: XL Specialty Insurance Co. v. Loral Space & Communications, Inc., 82 A.D.3d 108, 918 N.Y.S.2d 57 (N.Y. App. Div. 2011).

Pennsylvania: Anglo-American Insurance Co. v. Molin, 547 Pa. 504, 691 A.2d 929 (Pa. 1997).

Washington: St. Paul Fire and Marine Insurance Co. v. Onvia, Inc., 165 Wash.2d 122, 196 P.3d 664 (2008).

Wisconsin: Liebovich v. Minnesota Insurance Co., 310 Wis.2d 751, 751 N.W.2d 764 (2008).

[28] See § 3.02 *supra*.

[29] See, e.g.:

Third Circuit: Legion Indemnity Co. v. Carestate Ambulance Co., 152 F. Supp.2d 707, 719–720 (E.D. Pa. 2001).

Seventh Circuit: United States v. Thorson, 300 F. Supp.2d 828, 834 (W.D. Wis. 2003).

State Courts:

Florida: First Specialty Insurance Co. v. Caliber One Indemnity Co., 988 So.2d 708 (Fla. App. 2008).

Georgia: Southern v. Sphere-Drake Insurance Co., 486 S.E.2d 674, 676 (Ga. App. 1997).

Louisiana: McDaniel v. DeJean, 556 So.2d 1336, 1339 (La. App. 1990).

Massachusetts: Terra Nova Insurance Co. v. Fray-Witzer, 449 Mass. 406, 869 N.E.2d 565 (Mass. 2007).

Missouri: Naucke v. Missouri Public Entity Risk Management Fund, 95 S.W.3d 166, 170–171 (Mo. App. 2003).

New Hampshire: American Home Assurance Co. v. Fish, 451 A.2d 358 (N.H. 1982).

West Virginia: West Virginia Fire & Casualty Co. v. Stanley, 602 S.E.2d 483, 491 (W. Va. 2004).

30 See, e.g.:

Third Circuit: Legion Indemnity Co. v. Carestate Ambulance Co., 152 F. Supp.2d 707, 719–720 (E.D. Pa. 2001).

Fourth Circuit: USF Insurance Co. v. Orion Development RA XXX, L.L.C., 756 F. Supp.2d 749 (N.D. W. Va. 2010); Zurich American Insurance Co. v. Public Storage, 743 F. Supp.2d 525 (E.D. Va. 2010).

Fifth Circuit: American International Specialty Lines Insurance Co. v. Res-Care, Inc., 529 F.3d 649 (5th Cir. 2008).

Seventh Circuit: United States v. Thorson, 300 F. Supp.2d 828, 834 (W.D. Wis. 2003).

State Courts:

Florida: First Specialty Insurance Co. v. Caliber One Indemnity Co., 988 So.2d 708 (Fla. App. 2008).

Georgia: Southern v. Sphere-Drake Insurance Co., 486 S.E.2d 674, 676 (Ga. App. 1997).

Kentucky: Certain Underwriters at Lloyd's, London v. Abundance Coal, Inc., 2011 WL 2496203 (Ky. App. June 24, 2011).

Louisiana: McDaniel v. DeJean, 556 So.2d 1336, 1339 (La. App. 1990).

Massachusetts: Terra Nova Insurance Co. v. Fray-Witzer, 449 Mass. 406, 869 N.E.2d 565 (Mass. 2007).

Missouri: Naucke v. Missouri Public Entity Risk Management Fund, 95 S.W.3d 166, 170–171 (Mo. App. 2003).

New Hampshire: American Home Assurance Co. v. Fish, 451 A.2d 358 (N.H. 1982).

Ohio: Neal-Pettit v. Lahman, 125 Ohio St.3d 327, 928 N.E.2d 421 (2010); Ward v. United Foundries, Inc., 2010 WL 692 3354 (Ohio App. May 3, 2010).

Texas: Laine v. Farmers Insurance Exchange, 325 S.W.3d 661 (Tex. App. 2010).

West Virginia: West Virginia Fire & Casualty Co. v. Stanley, 602 S.E.2d 483, 491 (W. Va. 2004).

31 See, e.g.:

Third Circuit: Whole Enchilada, Inc. v. Travelers Property Casualty Company of America, 581 F. Supp.2d 677 (W.D. Pa. 2008) (Under Pennsylvania law, public policy prevents payment for willful non-compliance under the Fair and Accurate Credit Transactions Act (FACTA) in regard to either statutory or punitive damages alleged by the FACTA complaint.).

Fourth Circuit: USF Insurance Co. v. Orion Development RA XXX, L.L.C., 756 F. Supp.2d 749 (N.D. W. Va. 2010); Zurich American Insurance Co. v. Public Storage, 743 F. Supp.2d 525 (E.D. Va. 2010).

Eleventh Circuit: Alea London Ltd. v. American Home Services, Inc., 638 F.3d 768 (11th Cir. 2011); Penzer v. Transportation Insurance Co., 545 F.3d 1303 (11th Cir. 2008) (Telephone Consumer Protection Act (TCPA) trebled damages not "punitive" damages excluded by public policy of Florida); Creative Hospitality Ventures, Inc. v. U.S. Liability Insurance Co., 655 F. Supp.2d 1316 (S.D. Fla. 2010); Creative Hospitality Ventures, Inc. v. United States Liability Insurance Co., 655 F. Supp.2d 1316 (S.D. Fla. 2009) (same).

State Courts:

Florida: First Specialty Insurance Co. v. Caliber One Indemnity Co., 988 So.2d 708 (Fla. App. 2008).

Illinois: Central Mutual Insurance Co. v. Tracy's Treasures, Inc., 2014 IL App (1st) 123339, 19 N.E.3d 1100, 385 Ill. Dec. 904 (2014).

Massachusetts: Terra Nova Insurance Co. v. Fray-Witzer, 449 Mass. 406, 869 N.E.2d 565 (2007) (Under New Jersey law, statutory damages under the Telephone Consumer Protection Act (TCPA) are not "punitive damages" within the meaning of the commercial general liability (CGL) insurance policy exclusion for punitive or exemplary damages.).

New York: McCabe v. St. Paul Fire & Marine Insurance Co., 79 A.D.3d 1612, 914 N.Y.S.2d 814 (N.Y. App. Div. 2010).

Ohio: Neal-Pettit v. Lahman, 125 Ohio St.3d 327, 928 N.E.2d 421 (2010); Motorists Mutual Insurance Co. v. Dandy-Jim, Inc., 182 Ohio App. 311, 912 N.E.2d 659 (2009) (TCPA trebled damages not "punitive" damages excluded by public policy of Ohio).

Texas: Fairfield Insurance Co. v. Stephens Martin Paving, LP, 51 Tex. 491, 246 S.W.3d 653 (2008) (public policy did not prohibit coverage under employer's liability policy for exemplary damages for employer's gross negligence causing employee's death).

[32] See, e.g., Indiana Farmers Mutual Insurance Co. v. North Vernon Drop Forge, Inc., 917 N.E.2d 1258 (Ind. App. 2009).

[33] See § 5.03[6] *supra*.

[34] See § 10.03[4] *infra*.

[35] See § 10.03[3] *infra*.

[36] See §§ 5.03[6] *supra* and 10.03[3] *infra*. See also:

Ninth Circuit: Regence Group v. TIG Specialty Insurance Co., 903 F. Supp.2d 1152 (D. Or. 2012).

Eleventh Circuit: Geovera Specialty Insurance Co. v. Kruse, 860 F. Supp.2d 1310 (S.D. Ala. 2012); Creative Hospitality Ventures, Inc. v. United States Liability Insurance Co., 655 F. Supp.2d 1316 (S.D. Fla. 2009) (reckless conduct leading to imposition of exemplary damages not excluded).

State Courts:

Arizona: Irvin v. Lexington Insurance Co., 2010 WL 3450986 (Ariz. App. Sept. 2, 2010).

Ohio: Chiquita Brands International, Inc. v. National Union Insurance Co., 2013-Ohio-759, 988 N.E.2d 897 (Ohio App. 2013).

Texas: Fairfield Insurance Co. v. Stephens Martin Paving, LP, 51 Tex. 491, 246 S.W.3d 653 (Tex. 2008) (exemplary damages based upon employer's gross negligence covered by employers liability policy).

[37] See, e.g.:

Second Circuit: Industrial Risk Insurers v. Port Authority of New York & New Jersey, 387 F. Supp.2d 299, 311–312 (S.D.N.Y. 2005); *In re* September 11th Litigation, 494 F. Supp.2d 232 (S.D.N.Y. 2007).

Third Circuit: Wolfe v. Allstate Property and Casualty Insurance Co., 790 F.3d 487 (3d Cir. 2015); Regent Insurance Co. v. Strausser Enterprises, Inc., 902 F. Supp.2d 628 (E.D. Pa. 2012); Whole Enchilada, Inc. v. Travelers Property Casualty Company of America, 581 F. Supp.2d 677 (W.D. Pa. 2008).

Fifth Circuit: Minter v. Great American Insurance Company of New York, 394 Fed. Appx. 47 (5th Cir. 2010); American International Specialty Lines Insurance Co. v. Res-Care Inc., 529 F.3d 649 (5th Cir. 2008).

Eighth Circuit: Carlson Marketing Group, Inc. v. Royal Indemnity Co., 517 F. Supp.2d 1089 (D. Minn. 2007).

Eleventh Circuit: Penzer v. Transportation Insurance Co., 545 F.3d 1303 (11th Cir. 2008).

State Courts:

California: Carter v. Entercom Sacramento, L.L.C., 219 Cal. App.4th 337, 161 Cal. Rptr.3d 782 (Cal. App. 2013).

Illinois: Beaver v. County Mutual Insurance Co., 95 Ill. App.3d 1122, 51 Ill. Dec. 500, 420 N.E.2d 1058 (1981).

Kansas: Pugh v. Munguia, 36 Kan. App.2d 879, 146 P.3d 1108 (2006).

Missouri: Brand v. Kansas City Gastroenterology and Hepatology, L.L.C., 414 S.W.3d 546 (Mo. App. 2013).

New Jersey: Johnson and Johnson v. Aetna Casualty and Surety Co., 285 N.J. Super. 575, 667 A.2d 1089 (N.J. Super. App. Div. 1995).

New York: J.P. Morgan Securities, Inc. v. Vigilant Insurance Co., 21 N.Y.3d 324, 992 N.E.2d 1076, 970 N.Y.S.2d 733 (2013); McCabe v. St. Paul Fire & Marine Insurance Co., 79 A.D.3d 1612, 914 N.Y.S.2d 814 (N.Y. App. Div. 2010); Home Insurance Co. v. American Home Products Corp., 75 N.Y.2d 196, 551 N.Y.S.2d 481, 550 N.E.2d 930, 933 (1990).

Ohio: Neal-Pettit v. Lahman, 125 Ohio St.3d 327, 928 N.E.2d 421 (2010); Motorists Mutual Insurance Co. v. Dandy-Jim, Inc., 182 Ohio App. 311, 912 N.E.2d 659 (2009); Casey v. Calhoun, 40 Ohio App. 83, 531 N.E.2d 1348 (1987).

Pennsylvania: Aetna Casualty and Surety Co. v. Roe, 437 Pa. Super. 414, 650 A.2d 94 (1994).

South Dakota: American Family Mutual Insurance Group v. Kostaneski, 688 N.W.2d 410, 415 (S.D. 2004); City of Fort Pierre v. United Fire & Casualty Co., 463 N.W.2d 845, 848 (S.D. 1990).

Washington: Dailey v. North Coast Life Insurance Co., 129 Wash.2d 572, 919 P.2d 589 (1996).

[38] See:

Fourth Circuit: Rossman v. State Farm Mutual Automobile Insurance Co., 832 F.2d 282 (4th Cir. 1987).

Fifth Circuit: Northwestern National Casualty Co. v. McNulty, 307 F.2d 432 (5th Cir. 1962).

Seventh Circuit: Utica Mutual Insurance Co. v. David Agency Insurance, Inc., 327 F. Supp.2d 922, 928–929 (N.D. Ill. 2004).

Eighth Circuit: Union Limited Partnership Gas Syndicate, Inc. v. International Surplus Lines Insurance Co., 869 F.2d 1109 (8th Cir. 1989).

Ninth Circuit: Continental Casualty Corp. v. Fibreboard Corp., 762 F. Supp. 1368 (N.D. Cal. 1991), *aff'd* 953 F.2d 1386 (9th Cir.), *judgment vacated on other grounds* 506 U.S. 948 (1992).

State Courts:

California: Peterson v. Superior Court, 31 Cal.3d 147, 181 Cal. Rptr. 784, 642 P.2d 1305 (1982); City Products Corp. v. Globe Indemnity Co., 88 Cal. App.3d 31,151 Cal. Rptr. 494 (1979).

Connecticut: Avis Rent A Car System, Inc. v. Liberty Mutual Insurance Co., 203 Conn. 667, 526 A.2d 522 (1987).

Delaware: Whalen v. On-Deck, Inc., 514 A.2d 1072 (Del. 1986).

Florida: United States Concrete Pipe Co. v. Bould, 437 So.2d 1061 (Fla. 1983).

Illinois: Beaver v. Country Mutual Insurance Co., 95 Ill. App.3d 1122, 51 Ill. Dec. 508, 420 N.E.2d 1058 (1981).

Missouri: Crull v. Gleb, 382 S.W.2d 17 (Mo. App. 1964).

New Jersey: LoRocco v. New Jersey Manufacturers Indemnity Insurance Co., 82 N.J. Super. 323, 197 A.2d 591 (N.J. Super. App. Div.), *cert. denied* 42 N.J. 144, 199 A.2d 655 (1964).

New York: Hartford Accident & Indemnity Co. v. Village of Hempstead, 48 N.Y.2d 218, 422 N.Y.S.2d 47, 397 N.E.2d 737 (1979).

Ohio: Neal-Pettit v. Lahman, 125 Ohio St.3d 327, 928 N.E.2d 421 (2010); GNFH, Inc. v. West American Insurance Co., 172 Ohio App.3d 127, 873 N.E.2d 345 (2007); Casey v. Calhoun, 40 Ohio App.3d 83, 531 N.E.2d 1348 (1987).

Oklahoma: Dayton Hudson Corp. v. American Mutual Liability Insurance Co., 621 P.2d 1155 (Okla.1980).

Pennsylvania: Butterfield v. Giuntoli, 448 Pa. Super. 1, 670 A.2d 646 (1995), *alloc. denied* 546 Pa. 635, 683 A.2d 875 (1996); Esmond v. Liscio, 209 Pa. Super. 210, 224 A.2d 793 (1966); Creed v. Allstate Insurance Co., 365 Pa. Super. 136, 529 A.2d 10 (1987), *alloc. denied* 517 Pa. 616, 538 A.2d 499 (1988).

Virginia: United Services Automobile Association v. Webb, 235 Va. 655, 369 S.E.2d 196 (1988); United States Fire Insurance Co. v. Aspen Building Corp., 235 Va. 263, 367 S.E.2d 478 (1988).

See also, Couch, 15A *Couch on Insurance* § 56.9.

39 See:

Arizona: Irvin v. Lexington Insurance Co., 2010 WL 3450986 (Ariz. App. Sept. 2, 2010).

Georgia: Nationwide Mutual Fire Insurance Co. v. Kim, 294 Ga. App. 548, 669 S.E.2d 517 (2008).

Iowa: Skyline Harvestore Systems, Inc. v. Centennial Insurance Co., 331 N.W.2d 106 (Iowa 1983).

Louisiana: Creech v. Aetna Casualty & Surety Co., 516 So.2d 1168 (La. App. 1987), *writ denied* 519 So.2d 128 (La. 1988).

Montana: First Bank (NA)-Billings v. TransAmerica Insurance Co., 209 Mont. 93, 679 P.2d 1217 (1984).

North Carolina: Mazza v. Medical Mutual Insurance Company of North Carolina, 311 N.C. 621, 319 S.E.2d 217 (1984).

Oregon: Harrell v. Travelers Indemnity Co., 279 Or. 199, 567 P.2d 1013 (1977).

Texas: Fairfield Insurance Co. v. Stephens Martin Paving, LP, 246 S.W.3d 653 (Tex. 2008); American Home Assurance Co. v. Safeway Steel Products Co., Division of Figgie International, Inc., 743 S.W.2d 693 (Tex. App. 1987).

Virginia: United Service Automobile Association v. Webb, 238 Va. 655, 369 S.E.2d 196 (1988).

Wyoming: Sinclair Oil Corp. v. Columbia Casualty Co., 682 P.2d 975 (Wyo. 1984).

40 See, e.g.:

Ninth Circuit: Goerner v. Axis Reinsurance Co., 400 Fed. Appx. 226 (9th Cir. 2010).

Eleventh Circuit: MedAssets, Inc. v. Federal Insurance Co., 705 F. Supp.2d 1368 (N.D. Ga. 2010).

See also Chapter 6 *supra*.

41 See, e.g., Wintermute v. Kansas Bankers Surety Co, 630 F.3d 1063 (8th Cir. 2011).

42 *Second Circuit:* Julio & Sons Co. v. Travelers Casualty and Surety Company of America, 591 F. Supp.2d 651 (S.D.N.Y. 2008); *In re* Adelphia Communications Corp., 298 B.R. 49

(Bankr. S.D.N.Y. 2003); *In re* Ambassador Group, Inc. Litigation, 738 F. Supp. 57 (E.D.N.Y. 1990).

Fifth Circuit: Chicago Property Interests, L.L.C. v. Broussard, 8 So.3d 42 (5th Cir. 2009); TIG Insurance Co. v. Eagle Inc., 294 Fed. Appx. 920 (5th Cir. 2008).

Eighth Circuit: Wintermute v. Kansas Bankers Surety Co, 630 F.3d 1063 (8th Cir. 2011); Liberty Mutual Insurance Co. v. Pella Corp., 650 F.3d 1161 (8th Cir. 2011).

Ninth Circuit: Pan Pacific Retail Properties, Inc. v. Gulf Insurance Co., 471 F.3d 961 (9th Cir. 2006).

Eleventh Circuit: Douglas County Chamber of Commerce, Inc. v. Philadelphia Indemnity Insurance Co., 237 Fed. Appx. 410 (11th Cir. 2007); MedAssets, Inc. v. Federal Insurance Co., 705 F. Supp.2d 1368 (N.D. Ga. 2010).

State Courts:

California: Helfand v. National Union Fire Insurance Co., 10 Cal. App.4th 869, 13 Cal. Rptr.2d 295 (1992), *cert. denied* 510 U.S. 824 (1993); Executive Risk Indemnity, Inc. v. Jones, 171 Cal. App.4th 319, 89 Cal. Rptr.3d 747 (2009).

Delaware: AT & T Corp. v. Clarendon American Insurance Co., 931 A.2d 409 (Del. 2007).

Indiana: Cinergy Corp. v. Associated Electric & Gas Insurance Services, Ltd., 865 N.E.2d 571 (Ind. 2007).

New York: XL Specialty Insurance Co. v. Loral Space & Communications, Inc., 82 A.D.3d 108, 918 N.Y.S.2d 57 (N.Y. App. Div. 2011); Federal Insurance Co. v. Tyco International Ltd., 57 A.D.3d 335, 871 N.Y.S.2d 9 (N.Y. App. Div. 2008).

Some E&O policies do not include defense costs within the definition of "loss" but instead contain a duty to defend, which is the duty to pay such defense costs directly regardless of the merits of the action. As stated previously, the duty to defend is unlimited in terms of maximum defense expenditures, is paid for in addition to limits available to pay for judgments and settlements, and is triggered when the claim alleged is arguably or potentially within the scope of coverage. See Chapter 6 *supra*.

[43] See, e.g., Helfand v. National Union Fire Insurance Co., 10 Cal. App.4th 869, 13 Cal. Rptr.2d 295 (1992) *cert. denied* 510 U.S. 824 (1993).

[44] Many of the normal duty-to-defend rules discussed in the chapter on CGL insurance also apply in reimbursement policies. See Chapter 6 *supra*. See also:

Second Circuit: Julio & Sons Co. v. Travelers Casualty & Surety Company of America, 591 F. Supp.2d 651 (S.D.N.Y. 2008); Lowy v. Travelers Property & Casualty Co., 2000 WL 526702 (S.D.N.Y. 2000); PepsiCo, Inc. v. Continental Casualty Co., 640 F. Supp. 656 (S.D.N.Y. 1986).

Fifth Circuit: Basic Energy Services, Inc. v. Liberty Mutual Insurance Co., 655 F. Supp.2d 666 (W.D.Tex. 2009).

Sixth Circuit: Pattison v. Employers Reinsurance Corp., 900 F.2d 986 (6th Cir. 1990); United States Fidelity & Guaranty Co. v. Fireman's Fund Insurance Co., 896 F.2d 200 (6th Cir. 1990).

Ninth Circuit: Westport Insurance Corp. v. Northern California Relief, 76 F. Supp.3d 869 (N.D. Cal. 2014).

Eleventh Circuit: Worthington Federal Bank v. Everest National Insurance Co., 2015 U.S. Dist. LEXIS 85888 (N.D. Ala. June 4, 2015); MapleWood Partners Limited Partnership v. Indian Harbor Insurance Co., 295 F.R.D. 550 (S.D. Fla. 2013).

State Courts:

Alabama: St. Paul Fire & Marine Insurance Co. v. Molton, Allen & Williams Corp., 592 So.2d 199 (Ala. 1991).

Ohio: American Chemical Society v. Leadscope, Inc., 2005 WL 1220746 (Ohio App. May 24, 2005), *appeal denied* 836 N.E.2d 1231 (Ohio 2005).

But see:

Second Circuit: Petroterminal de Panama, S.A. v. Houston Casualty Co., 2015 U.S. Dist. LEXIS 92653 (S.D.N.Y. July 16, 2015) (defense cost reimbursement only available after claims are established by judgment or settlement to be covered); Julio & Sons Co. v. Travelers Casualty and Surety Company of America, 591 F. Supp.2d 651 (S.D.N.Y. 2008) (actual facts determine duty to reimburse defense costs).

State Courts:

New Jersey: Polarome International, Inc. v. Greenwich Insurance Co., 404 N.J. Super. 241, 961 A.2d 29 (N.J. Super. App. Div. 2008) (duty to reimburse defense costs does not apply to uncovered claims).

45 See Chapter 6 *supra,* and § 10.03[2][b][iv] *infra.* See also:

Third Circuit: CAMICO Mutual Insurance Co. v. Heffler, Radetich & Saitta, L.L.P., 587 Fed. Appx. 726 (3d Cir. 2014).

Fifth Circuit: Gabarick v. Laurin Maritime (America), Inc., 650 F.3d 545 (5th Cir. 2011).

Sixth Circuit: Medpace, Inc. v. Darwin Select Insurance Co., 13 F. Supp.3d 839 (S.D. Ohio 2014).

Ninth Circuit: In re Mila, Inc., 423 B.R. 537 (Bankr. App. 9th Cir. 2010); Pan Pacific Retail Properties, Inc. v. Gulf Insurance Co., 471 F.3d 961 (9th Cir. 2006).

Tenth Circuit: D.R. Horton, Inc. v. Mountain States Mutual Casualty Co., 69 F. Supp.3d 1179 (D. Colo. 2014).

Eleventh Circuit: Scottsdale Insurance Co. v. GFM Operations, Inc., 789 F. Supp.2d 1278 (S.D. Fla. 2011).

State Courts:

California: Executive Risk Indemnity, Inc. v. Jones, 171 Cal. App.4th 319, 89 Cal. Rptr.3d 747 (2009); Helfand v. National Union Fire Insurance Co., 10 Cal. App.4th 869, 13 Cal. Rptr.2d 295 (1992), *cert. denied* 510 U.S. 824 (1993).

Florida: Mid-Continent Casualty Co. v. Royal Crane, L.L.C., 169 So.3d 174 (Fla. App. 2015).

Massachusetts: Omega Flex, Inc. v. Pacific Employers Insurance Co, 78 Mass. App. Ct. 262, 937 N.E.2d 52 (2010).

Ohio: American Chemical Society v. Leadscope, Inc., 2005 WL 1220746 (Ohio App. May 24, 2005), *appeal denied* 836 N.E.2d 1231 (Ohio 2005).

Utah: Summerhaze Co., v. FDIC, 332 P.3d 908 (Utah 2014).

Washington: Grange Insurance Ass'n v. Roberts, 179 Wash. App. 739, 320 P.3d 77 (2013).

46 *Compare* ISO Form CG 00 01 10 01 *with* § 10.02 *supra.*

See also:

Second Circuit: MBIA Inc. v. Federal Insurance Co., 652 F.3d 152 (2d Cir. 2011).

Third Circuit: Charter Oak Insurance Co. v. Maglio Fresh Food, 979 F. Supp.2d 581 (E.D. Pa. 2013).

Fourth Circuit: Episcopal Church in South Carolina v. Church Insurance Co. of Vermont, 53 F. Supp.3d 816 (D.S.C. 2014).

Fifth Circuit: Graper v. Mid-Continent Casualty Co., 756 F.3d 388 (5th Cir. 2014); Yowell v. Seneca Specialty Insurance Co., 2015 U.S. Dist. LEXIS 98719 (E.D. Tex. July 28, 2015).

Seventh Circuit: R.C. Wegman Construction Co. v. Admiral Insurance Co., 629 F.3d 724 (7th Cir. 2011); National Casualty Co. v. Forge Industry Staffing Inc., 567 F.3d 871 (7th Cir. 2009); National Union Fire Insurance Co. of Pittsburgh, Pa. v. Mead Johnson & Co., 735 F.3d

539 (7th Cir. 2013); AU Electronics, Inc. v. Harleysville Group, Inc., 82 F. Supp.3d 805 (N.D. Ill. 2015).

Eighth Circuit: Heubel Materials Handling Co. v. Universal Underwriters Insurance Co., 704 F.3d 558 (8th Cir. 2013); Purscell v. TICO Insurance Co., 959 F. Supp.2d 1195 (W.D. Mo. 2013).

Ninth Circuit: Haskins v. Employers Insurance of Wausau, 2015 U.S. Dist. LEXIS 114059 (N.D. Cal. Aug. 26, 2015); Nucor Corp. v. Employers Insurance Company of Wausau, 975 F. Supp.2d 1048 (D. Ariz. 2013).

Eleventh Circuit: Mid-Continent Casualty Co. v. American Pride Bldg. Co., 601 F.3d 1143 (11th Cir. 2010); Maronda Homes of Florida v. Progressive Express Insurance Co., 2015 U.S. Dist. LEXIS 103893 (M.D. Fla. Aug. 7, 2015); Petro v. Travelers Casualty and Surety Co. of America, 54 F. Supp.3d 1295 (N.D. Fla. 2014).

State Courts:

California: Centex Homes v. St. Paul Fire and Marine Insurance Co., 237 Cal. App.4th 23, 187 Cal. Rptr.3d 542 (2015); Janopaul + Block Companies, L.L.C. v. Superior Court, 200 Cal. App.4th 1239, 133 Cal. Rptr.3d 380 (2011); Gray v. Begley, 182 Cal. App.4th 1509, 106 Cal. Rptr.3d 729 (2010); Executive Risk Indemnity, Inc. v. Jones, 171 Cal. App.4th 319, 89 Cal. Rptr.3d 747 (Cal. App. 2009).

Illinois: Standard Mutual Insurance Co. v. Lay, 2014 IL App (4th) 110527-B, 2 N.E.3d 1253, 377 Ill. Dec. 972 (2014).

New York: Forcelli v. Gelco Corp., 109 A.D.3d 244, 972 N.Y.S.2d 570 (N.Y. App. Div. 2013).

Ohio: Bruce v. Junghun, 182 Ohio App.3d 341, 912 N.E.2d 1144 (2009).

Pennsylvania: Penn-America Insurance Co. v. Peccadillos, Inc., 27 A.3d 259 (Pa. Super. 2011).

Texas: Taylor v. Allstate Insurance Co., 2011 WL 1233331 (Tex. App. March 31, 2011).

[47] See § 5.04[3] *supra*.

[48] See:

Second Circuit: Pronti v. CNA Financial Corp., 353 F. Supp.2d 320 (N.D.N.Y. 2005).

Fifth Circuit: Partain v. Mid-Continent Specialty Insurance Services, Inc., 838 F. Supp.2d 547 (S.D. Tex. 2012).

Ninth Circuit: Sierra Pacific Industries v. American States Insurance Co., 883 F. Supp.2d 967 (E.D. Cal. 2012); Bosch v. First Financial Insurance Co., 2006 U.S. Dist. LEXIS 41803 (N.D. Cal. June 7, 2006); IBP, Inc. v. National Union Fire Insurance Company of Pittsburgh, Pennsylvania, 299 F. Supp.2d 1024 (D.S.D. 2003); Glenn K. Jackson, Inc. v. Roe, 273 F.3d 1192 (9th Cir. 2001).

Eleventh Circuit: Sphinx International, Inc. v. National Union Fire Insurance Company of Pittsburgh, Pennsylvania, 2002 WL 33804169 (M.D. Fla. Nov. 25, 2002).

State Courts:

California: Hartford Casualty Insurance Co. v. J.R. Marketing, L.L.C., 61 Cal.4th 988, 353 P.3d 319, 190 Cal. Rptr.3d 599 (2015); Centex Homes v. St. Paul Fire and Marine Insurance Company, 237 Cal. App.4th 231, 87 Cal. Rptr.3d 542 (2015); Swanson v. State Farm General Insurance Co., 219 Cal. App.4th 1153, 162 Cal. Rptr.3d 477 (2013); E.O.C. Ord, Inc. v. Unique Investment Corp., 2005 Cal. App. Unpub. LEXIS 8793 (Cal. App. Sept. 28, 2005); Gafcon, Inc. v. Ponsor & Associates, 98 Cal. App.4th 1388, 120 Cal. Rptr.2d 392 (2002).

Pennsylvania: ACE American Insurance Co. v. Columbia Casualty Co., 2002 WL 31898365 (Pa. C.P. 2002).

Texas: McVicker v. Johnson County, 616 S.W.2d 430 (Tex. App. 1981).

[49] *Id.*

[50] *Id.* See also, Fireman's Fund Insurance Cos. v. Ex-Cell-O Corp., 790 F. Supp. 1318 (E.D. Mich. 1992).

[51] See:

Third Circuit: Fisher v. USAA Casualty Insurance Co., 973 F.2d 1103, 1106–1107 (3d Cir. 1992) (applying Pennsylvania law); Coregis Insurance Co. v. Carol F. Kafrissen, P.C., 140 F. Supp.2d 461, 463 (E.D. Pa. 2001) (applying Pennsylvania law).

State Courts:

Missouri: Kearns v. Interlex Insurance Co., 231 S.W.3d 325 (Mo. App. 2007).

Pennsylvania: Boyle v. Erie Insurance Co., 441 Pa. Super. 103, 656 A.2d 941, 944, *alloc. denied* 542 Pa. 656, 668 A.2d 1120 (1995); Archer v. State Farm Automobile Insurance Co., 419 Pa. Super. 558, 615 A.2d 779 (1992), *alloc. denied* 535 Pa. 612, 629 A.2d 1375 (1993); Resource America, Inc. v. Certain Underwriters, 2004 WL 2580554, at *4 (Pa. C.P. Nov. 12, 2004); Hockenberry v. Horace Mann Insurance Co., 19 Pa. D. & C.4th 567, 571 (Pa. C.P. Cumberland Cnty. 1993).

[52] See:

Eleventh Circuit: Bankers Security Life Insurance Society v. Kane, 692 F. Supp. 1326 (S.D. Fla. 1988), *aff'd* 885 F.2d 820 (11th Cir. 1989).

State Courts:

California: Long v. Century Indemnity Co., 163 Cal. App.4th 1460, 78 Cal. Rptr.3d 483 (2008); Compulink Management Center, Inc. v. St. Paul Fire and Marine Insurance Co., 169 Cal. App.4th 289, 87 Cal. Rptr.3d 72 (2008).

Massachusetts: Northern Security Insurance Co. v. R.H. Realty Trust, 78 Mass. App. Ct. 691, 941 N.E.2d 688 (2011).

[53] See Bankers Security Life Insurance Society v. Kane, 692 F. Supp. 1326 (S.D. Fla. 1988), *aff'd* 885 F.2d 820 (11th Cir. 1989).

[54] See, e.g.:

Second Circuit: MBIA Inc. v. Certain Underwriters at Lloyd's, London, 33 F. Supp.3d 344 (S.D.N.Y. 2014) (ongoing reimbursement not required).

State Courts:

Texas: Burks v. XL Specialty Insurance Co., 2015 Tex. App. LEXIS 9638 (Tex. App. Sept. 15, 2015) (ongoing reimbursement required).

[55] See:

Second Circuit: MBIA Inc. v. Federal Insurance Co., 652 F.3d 152 (2d Cir. 2011); Pepsico, Inc. v. Continental Casualty Co., 640 F. Supp. 656 (S.D.N.Y. 1986).

Third Circuit: Little v. MGIC Indemnity Corp., 836 F.2d 789, 793 (3d Cir. 1987).

Fifth Circuit: Gabarick v. Laurin Maritime (America), Inc., 650 F.3d 545 (5th Cir. 2011).

Sixth Circuit: Lafayette Life Insurance Co. v. Arch Insurance Co., 784 F. Supp.2d 1034 (N.D. Ind. 2011).

Eighth Circuit: McCuen v. American Casualty Company of Reading, Pennsylvania, 946 F.2d 1401 (8th Cir. 1991).

Ninth Circuit: In re Mila, Inc., 423 B.R. 537 (Bankr. App. 9th Cir. 2010); Okada v. MGIC Indemnity Corp., 823 F.2d 276 (9th Cir. 1986).

But see:

Second Circuit: Board of Education, Yonkers City School District v. CNA Insurance Co., 647 F. Supp. 1495 (S.D.N.Y. 1986), *aff'd* 839 F.2d 14 (2d Cir. 1988).

Seventh Circuit: Zaborac v. American Casualty Company of Reading, Pennsylvania, 663 F. Supp. 330, 334 (C.D. Ill. 1987).

[56] See Little v. MGIC Indemnity Corp., 836 F.2d 789, 793 (3d Cir. 1987).

[57] See Wayne County Neighborhood Legal Services v. National Union Fire Insurance Co., 971 F.2d 1 (6th Cir. 1992).

[58] See, e.g.:

Second Circuit: Petroterminal de Panama, S.A. v. Houston Casualty Co., 2015 U.S. Dist. LEXIS 92653 (S.D.N.Y. July 16, 2015) (defense cost reimbursement only available after claims are established by judgment or settlement to be covered); Julio & Sons Co. v. Travelers Casualty and Surety Company of America, 591 F. Supp.2d 651 (S.D.N.Y. 2008).

Fifth Circuit: In re Enron Corporation Securities, Derivative and ERISA Litigation, 391 F. Supp.2d 541 (S.D. Tex. 2005) (applying Texas law).

Ninth Circuit: Commercial Capital Bankcorp., Inc. v. St. Paul Mercury Insurance Co., 419 F. Supp.2d 1173 (C.D. Cal. 2006).

Eleventh Circuit: MapleWood Partners Limited Partnership v. Indian Harbor insurance Co., 295 F.R.D. 550 (S.D. Fla. 2013); National Union Fire Insurance Company of Pittsburgh, Pennsylvania v. Brown, 787 F. Supp 1424 (S.D. Fla. 1991), *aff'd* 963 F.2d 385 (11th Cir. 1992).

State Courts:

California: Executive Risk Indemnity, Inc. v. Jones, 171 Cal. App.4th 319, 89 Cal. Rptr.3d 747 (Cal. App. 2009).

Indiana: Cinergy Corp. v. Associated Electric & Gas Insurance Services, Ltd., 865 N.E.2d 571 (Ind. 2007).

Ohio: American Chemical Society v. Leadscope, Inc., 2005 WL 1220746 (Ohio App. May 24, 2005).

[59] See:

Fifth Circuit: TIG Insurance Co. v. Eagle, Inc., 294 Fed. Appx. 920 (5th Cir. 2008) (applying Louisiana law).

Ninth Circuit: Pan Pacific Retail Properties, Inc. v. Gulf Insurance Co., 471 F.3d 961 (9th Cir. 2006).

Eleventh Circuit: Northland Casualty Co. v. HBE Corp., 160 F. Supp.2d 1348, 1364 (M.D. Fla. 2001); Matter of Celotex Corp., 152 B.R. 661, 666 (Bankr. M.D. Fla. 1993) (Florida decisions hold that an insurance company is not required to make contemporaneous payments of defense costs; the duty to indemnify for legal expenses arises at the same time as the duty to indemnify for judgments and settlements.).

State Courts:

Florida: National Union Fire Insurance Co. v. Goldman, 548 So.2d 790, 792 (Fla. App. 1989).

[60] See *In re* Ambassador Group, Inc. Litigation, 738 F. Supp. 57 (E.D.N.Y. 1990) (parties can contract around advancement of costs).

[61] Safeco Insurance Company of America v. Butler, 823 P.2d 499, 504 (Wash. 1992).

[62] Olympic Steamship Co. v. Centennial Insurance Co., 811 P.2d 673, 681 (Wash. 1991).

> "When an insured purchases a contract of insurance, it seeks protection from expenses arising from litigation, not 'vexatious, time-consuming, expensive litigation, with [its] insurer.' . . . Whether the insured must defend a suit filed by third parties, appear in a declaratory action, or . . . file a suit for damages to obtain the benefit of its insurance contract is irrelevant. In every case, the conduct of the insurer imposes upon the insured the cost of compelling the insurer to honor its commitment and, thus, is equally burdensome to the insured."

See also, Appleman, 7C *Insurance Law & Practice,* § 4684, at 83 (1979 & Supp. 1989).

[63] See, e.g., City of Johnstown v. Bankers Standard Insurance Co., 877 F.2d 1146, 1148 (2d Cir. 1989).

[64] Montrose Chemical Corp. v. American Motorists Insurance Co., 16 Cal. Rptr.2d 516, 530 (Cal. App. 1993) (upholding order requiring immediate payment of policyholder's defense costs in underlying action and reimbursement for past defense costs with interest).

> "By requiring the prompt resolution of a carrier's duty to defend prior to the resolution of the underlying liability actions, the courts protect the insured's right to peace of mind and security, a right which 'would ring resoundingly hollow were the holder compelled to simultaneously enforce rights under the policy and defend a costly and potentially devastating claim. . . .'"

See also Kalama Chemical, Inc. v. Allianz Insurance Co., No. 90-2-05011-4, Findings and Conclusions in Support of Order of Immediate Payment and Denial of Stay of Enforcement, at 4 (Wash. Super. Dec. 14, 1993) ("[The policyholder] is continuing to defend itself and to incur defense cost at the subject sites, and [the insurer] is continuing to breach its obligation to provide a defense in those cases, with the attendant loss of security and peace of mind for which the [policyholder] bargained.").

[65] Okada v. MGIC Indemnity Corp., 823 F.2d 276, 280 (9th Cir. 1986).

[66] Avondale Industries, Inc. v. Travelers Indemnity Co., 123 F.R.D. 80 (S.D.N.Y. 1988), *aff'd* 887 F.2d 1200 (2d Cir 1989).

> "[T]his Court does not see any reason why [the policyholder] should have to wait until some indefinite future date to receive the defense to which it is entitled. . . . To suggest that the passage of time matters not to the plaintiffs in such circumstances, and that enforcement of the duty to defend can await another day, denigrates the professional obligation here found to have been undertaken." 123 F.R.D. at 83.

See also:

Second Circuit: McGinnis v. Employers Reinsurance Corp., 648 F. Supp. 1263, 1271 (S.D.N.Y. 1986) ("Without contemporaneous payment of defense costs, the insurance 'would not truly protect the insureds from financial harm caused by the suits against them.'").

Eleventh Circuit: National Union Fire Insurance Co. v. Brown, 787 F. Supp. 1424, 1429–1434 (S.D. Fla. 1991), *aff'd* 963 F.2d 385 (11th Cir. 1992) ("a plain reading of the 'loss' provision in the 1987 D&O Policy leads to the conclusion that [the insurance company] is obligated to pay the Insureds' defense costs as they are incurred, not at some future time when the underlying action giving rise to a claim is adjudicated or settled").

[67] Village Management, Inc. v. Hartford Accident & Indemnity Co., 662 F. Supp. 1366, 1374 n.13 (N.D. Ill. 1987) (ordering immediate payment of defense costs and rejecting the holding in Burd v. Sussex Mutual Insurance Co., 56 N.J. 383, 267 A.2d 7 (1970) suggesting that an insurance company could delay payment until the conclusion of coverage disputes; "that notion is hard to reconcile with the concept that the duty to defend is not at all coextensive with policy coverage").

[68] Montrose Chemical Corp. v. American Motorists Insurance Co., 16 Cal. Rptr.2d 516, 530 (Cal. App. 1993).

[69] Emons Industries, Inc. v. Liberty Mutual Insurance Co., 749 F. Supp. 1289 (S.D.N.Y. 1990).

[70] *Id.,* 749 F. Supp. at 1293.

> "The value of these lost opportunities mutually to resolve the [underlying] cases cannot be readily determined with sufficient accuracy, as the costs and uncertainties of litigation are multifarious. Consequently, the injury to [the policyholder] is effectively irreparable, as 'interim damages cannot be calculated with sufficient accuracy to make damages an adequate substitute.'"

71 *Ninth Circuit:* Constandi v. AAMCO Automatic Transmissions, Inc., 356 F.2d 941 (9th Cir. 1972).

State Courts:

Washington: Boeing Co. v. Sierracin Corp., 108 Wash.2d 38, 738 P.2d 665, 682 (1987).

72 See §§ 10.02[1] and [2] *supra,* for the contractual language.

73 See, e.g.,

Fifth Circuit: Gabarick v. Laurin Maritime (America), Inc., 650 F.3d 545 (5th Cir. 2011).

Ninth Circuit: In re Mila, Inc., 423 B.R. 537 (Bankr. App. 9th Cir. 2010).

State Courts:

California: Helfand v. National Union Fire Insurance Co., 10 Cal. App.4th 869, 13 Cal. Rptr.2d 295 (1992), *cert. denied* 510 U.S. 824 (1993).

Delaware: AT&T Corp. v. Clarendon American Insurance Co., 931 A.2d 409 (Del. 2007).

Massachusetts: Omega Flex, Inc. v. Pacific Employers Insurance Co, 78 Mass. App. Ct. 262, 937 N.E.2d 52 (2010).

74 *Id.*

75 *Id.*

76 See Chapter 6 *supra.*

77 See § 6.02[6] *supra.*

78 See §§ 5.04[3], 10.03[2][b][ii] *supra.* See also:

First Circuit: Colony Insurance Co. v. Danly, Inc., 755 F. Supp.2d 219 (D. Me. 2010).

Second Circuit: MBIA Inc. v. Federal Insurance Co., 652 F.3d 152 (2d Cir. 2011); General Star National Insurance Co. v. Universal Fabricators, Inc., 427 Fed. Appx. 32 (2d Cir. 2011); SI Venture Holdings, L.L.C. v. Catlin Specialty Insurance Co., 2015 U.S. Dist. LEXIS 89925 (S.D.N.Y. July 10, 2015); Sunham Home Fashions, L.L.C. v. Diamond State Insurance Co., 813 F. Supp.2d 411 (S.D.N.Y. 2011).

Third Circuit: McMahon v. Medical Protective Co., 92 F. Supp.3d 367 (W.D. Pa. 2015).

Fourth Circuit: Putnam v. Alea London Ltd., 2011 WL 489968 (D.S.C. Feb. 4, 2011).

Sixth Circuit: Demolition Contractors, Inc. v. Westchester Surplus Lines Insurance Co., 381 Fed. Appx. 526 (6th Cir. 2010); American Towers, L.L.C. v. BPI, Inc., 2015 U.S. Dist. LEXIS 121921 (W.D. Ky. Sept. 14, 2015).

Seventh Circuit: Kmart Corp. v. Footstar, Inc., 2010 WL 1541296 (N.D. Ill. April 14, 2010).

Ninth Circuit: Trishan Air, Inc. v. Federal Insurance Co., 635 F.3d 422 (9th Cir. 2011); Haskins v. Employers Insurance of Wausau, 2015 U.S. Dist. LEXIS 114059 (N.D. Cal. Aug. 26, 2015); Dietz International Public Adjusters of California, Inc. v. Evanston Insurance Co., 796 F. Supp.2d 1197 (C.D. Cal. 2011); Columbia Casualty Co. v. Gordon Trucking, Inc., 758 F. Supp.2d 909 (N.D. Cal. 2010).

Eleventh Circuit: Rolyn Cos. v. R & J Sales of Texas, Inc., 412 Fed. Appx. 252 (11th Cir. 2011).

State Courts:

Georgia: Piedmont Office Realty Trust, Inc. v. XL Specialty Insurance Co., 297 Ga. 38, 771 S.E.2d 864 (2015).

Illinois: Pekin Insurance Co. v. Xdata Sollutions, Inc., 958 N.E.2d 397, 354 Ill. Dec. 654 (Ill. App. 2011).

Indiana: Travelers Insurance Cos. v. Maplehurst Farms, Inc., 18 N.E.3d 311 (2014).

Mississippi: Minnesota Life Insurance Co. v. Columbia Casualty Co., 164 So.3d 954 (Miss. 2014).

Nebraska: Rent-A-Roofer, Inc. v. Farm Bureau Property and Casualty Insurance Co., 291 Neb. 786, 869 N.W.2d 99 (2015).

79 See, e.g., Stryker Corp. v. XL Insurance Co., 57 F. Supp.3d 823 (W.D. Mich. 2014).

80 See, e.g.:

Eleventh Circuit: Petro v. Travelers Casualty and Surety Co. of America, 54 F. Supp.3d 1295 (N.D. Fla. 2014).

State Courts:

Illinois: Central Mutual Insurance Co. v. Tracy's Treasures, Inc., 2014 IL App (1st) 123339, 19 N.E.3d 1100, 385 Ill. Dec. 904 (2014).

81 See, e.g.:

Fourth Circuit: Perini/Tompkins Joint Venture v. Ace American Insurance. Co., 738 F.3d 95 (4th Cir. 2013) (prejudice rule inapplicable).

State Courts:

Colorado: Stresscon Corp. v. Travelers Property Casualty Co. of America, 2013 Colo. App. LEXIS 1451 (Colo. App. Sept. 12, 2013) (prejudice presumed but rebuttable).

Maryland: Morse v. Eris Insurance Exchange, 217 Md. App. 1, 90 A.3d 512 (2014) (prejudice rule inapplicable).

Texas: Lennar Corp. v. Markel American Insurance Co., 413 S.W.3d 750 (Tex. 2013) (prejudice rule applies).

82 See Pope, "Hammered by the Hammer Clause: Does It Mean What It Says," *Defense Counsel Journal* (April 2001). See also:

First Circuit: Clauson v. New England Insurance Co., 254 F.3d 331 (1st Cir. 2001) (applying Rhode Island law).

Fifth Circuit: Scottsdale Insurance Co. v. Alabama Municipal Insurance Corp., 2013 U.S. Dist. LEXIS 131779 (M.D. Ala. Sept. 16, 2013).

Seventh Circuit: Security Insurance Company of Hartford v. Schipporeit, Inc., 69 F.3d 1377 (7th Cir. 1995); Sutton v. Bernard, 2002 WL 1794048 (N.D. Ill. Aug. 5, 2002).

Eighth Circuit: McCollough v. Minnesota Lawyers Mutual Insurance Co., 2013 U.S. Dist. LEXIS 30995 (D. Mont. March 6, 2013).

Ninth Circuit: Freedman v. United National Insurance Co., 2011 WL 781919 (C.D. Cal. March 1, 2011).

Tenth Circuit: Larson v. One Beacon Insurance Co., 2013 U.S. Dist. LEXIS 81181 (D. Colo. June 10, 2013).

State Courts:

California: Commercial Union Cos. v. Safeway Stores, Inc., 26 Cal.3d 912, 164 Cal. Rptr. 709, 610 P.2d 1038 (1980); Transit Casualty Co. v. Spink Corp., 94 Cal. App.3d 124, 156 Cal. Rptr. 360 (1979).

Colorado: Bankruptcy Estate of Morris v. COPIC Insurance Co., 192 P.3d 519 (Colo. App. 2008).

Illinois: Illinois State Bar Ass'n Mutual Insurance Co. v. Burkart, 2015 IL App (4th) 140936-U (Ill. App. Sept. 24, 2015).

New Jersey: Webb v. Witt, 379 N.J. Super. 18, 876 A.2d 858 (N.J. Super. App. Div. 2005).

Ohio: Bartulica v. American Physicians Capital, Inc., 2002 WL 31386666 (Ohio. App. Oct. 23, 2002).

83 See Pope, "Hammered by the Hammer Clause: Does It Mean What It Says," *Defense Counsel Journal* (April 2001).

84 See:

First Circuit: Clauson v. New England Insurance Co., 254 F.3d 331 (1st Cir. 2001) (applying Rhode Island law).

Seventh Circuit: Security Insurance Company of Hartford v. Schipporeit, Inc., 69 F.3d 1377 (7th Cir. 1995); Sutton v. Bernard, 2002 WL 1794048 (N.D. Ill. Aug. 5, 2002).

State Courts:

California: Commercial Union Assurance Cos. v. Safeway Stores, Inc., 26 Cal.3d 912, 164 Cal. Rptr. 709, 610 P.2d 1038 (1980); Transit Casualty Co. v. Spink Corp., 94 Cal. App.3d 124, 156 Cal. Rptr. 360 (1979).

Colorado: Bankruptcy Estate of Morris v. COPIC Insurance Co., 192 P.3d 519 (Colo. App. 2008).

New Jersey: Webb v. Witt, 379 N.J. Super. 18, 876 A.2d 858 (N.J. Super. App. Div. 2005).

Ohio: Bartulica v. American Physicians Capital, Inc., 2002 WL 31386666 (Ohio. App. Oct. 23, 2002).

85 Windt, *Insurance Claims And Disputes: Representation of Insurance Companies and Insureds* § 5.03 n.22 (2d ed. 1982).

See also:

Fifth Circuit: Scottsdale Insurance Co. v. Alabama Municipal Insurance Corp., 2013 U.S. Dist. LEXIS 131779 (M.D. Ala. Sept. 16, 2013).

Eighth Circuit: McCollough v. Minnesota Lawyers Mutual Insurance Co., 2013 U.S. Dist. LEXIS 30995 (D. Mont. Mar. 6, 2013).

Tenth Circuit: Larson v. One Beacon Insurance Co., 2013 U.S. Dist. LEXIS 81181 (D. Colo. June 10, 2013).

State Courts:

Illinois: Illinois State Bar Ass'n Mutual Insurance Co. v. Burkart, 2015 IL App (4th) 140936-U, 2015 Ill. App. Unpub. LEXIS 2146 (Ill. App. Sept. 24, 2015).

86 In Clauson v. New England Insurance Co., 254 F.3d 331 (1st Cir. 2001) (applying Rhode Island law), a client sued his attorney for malpractice in connection with representation during a divorce and received a $97,000 judgment. Before judgment, the client had offered to settle the case for $29,000, but the attorney rejected the settlement against his malpractice insurance company's recommendation. The client brought a claim against the malpractice insurance company for the full amount of the judgment. The insurance company argued that the hammer clause limited recovery to $29,000. The clause provided:

> "The Company shall have the right to make any investigation it deems necessary and with the written consent of the insured, said consent not to be unreasonably withheld, any settlement of any claim covered by the terms of this policy.
>
> "If the Insured shall refuse to consent to any settlement or compromise recommended by the Company and acceptable to the claimant, and elects to contest the claim, suit or proceeding, then the Company's liability shall not exceed the amount for which the Company would have been liable for damages if the claim or suit or proceeding had been so settled or compromised, when so recommended. The Company shall have no liability for claims expenses accruing thereafter and the Company shall have the right to withdraw from the further defense thereof by tendering control of said defense to the Insured." 254 F.3d at 336–337.

The insurer argued that the word "any" in the second paragraph meant that the company was not liable if the insured objected to "any" settlement. However, the court held that the hammer clause only applied when the policyholder "unreasonably" refuses to consent to a settlement because otherwise the provision requiring that withholding consent be reasonably exercised would be superfluous. The court concluded that the insurer's interpretation was unreasonable because it failed to give effect to every term in the policy. See also:

Seventh Circuit: Security Insurance Company of Hartford v. Schipporeit, Inc., 69 F.3d 1377 (7th Cir. 1995) (insurance company not justified in denying coverage on the basis of policyholder's refusal to consent to settlement because offer did not include release of entire claim).

Ninth Circuit: Freedman v. United National Insurance Co., 2011 WL 781919 (C.D. Cal. March 1, 2011) (hammer clause may be invoked only where the policyholder withholds consent to settlement unreasonably).

State Courts:

California: Commercial Union Assurance Cos. v. Safeway Stores, Inc., 26 Cal.3d 912, 164 Cal. Rptr. 709, 610 P.2d 1038 (1980) (dismissing case by excess insurance company against policyholder for failure to settle within the limits of the primary policy); Transit Casualty Co. v. Spink Corp., 94 Cal. App.3d 124, 156 Cal. Rptr. 360 (1979) (hammer clause did not eliminate policyholder's liability to excess carrier for refusing to settle because implied covenant of good faith requires that policyholder's exercise of its right to refuse to consent to settlement must be reasonable).

See also, Pope, "Hammered by the Hammer Clause: Does It Mean What It Says," *Defense Counsel Journal* (April 2001); See also, Jordan, "For 'Hammer Clause' in Professional Liability Insurance Policy to Apply, Insured's Refusal to Consent to Settlement Must Be Unreasonable," *Professional Liability Reporter*, Vol. 36, No. 4 (April 2011).

87 See § 10.02 *supra*. Some policies also provide "prior acts" coverage, meaning that the negligent act, error or omission may take place either (1) during the policy period, or (2) at some time before the inception of the policy but after a retroactive date stated on the declaration page. Not all policies have prior acts coverage. When prior acts coverage is provided, retroactive dates vary significantly. Typically, the retroactive period may range from between a few months to a few years before the policy period. A policy with an earlier retroactive date increases the insurance company's risk and will likely come at a higher premium.

88 See § 10.02 *supra*.

89 See, e.g., Lime Tree Village Community Club Ass'n v. State Farm General Insurance Co., 980 F.2d 1402, 1405 (11th Cir. 1993). See § 6.02[2] *supra*.

90 See, e.g.:

First Circuit: TransSched Systems Limited v. Federal Insurance Co., 67 F. Supp.3d 523 (D.R.I. 2014); Bank of Rhode Island v. Progressive Casualty Insurance Co., 19 F. Supp.3d 378 (D.R.I. 2014).

Second Circuit: Euchner-USA, Inc. v. Hartford Casualty Insurance Co., 754 F.3d 136 (2d Cir. 2014); Jewish Community Center of Staten Island v. Trumbull Insurance Co., 957 F. Supp.2d 215 (E.D.N.Y. 2013); U.S. Underwriters Insurance Co. v. Tauber, 604 F. Supp.2d 521 (E.D.N.Y. 2009).

Third Circuit: Peerless Insurance Co. v. Pennsylvania Cyber Charter School, 19 F. Supp.3d 635 (W.D. Pa. 2014); G-I Holdings v. Hartford Fire Insurance Co., 2007 U.S. Dist. LEXIS 19069 (D.N.J. March 16, 2007) (D&O policy; "wrongful act" defined as "error, misstatement, misleading statement, act, omission, neglect or breach of duty").

Fifth Circuit: Elliott Appraisers, L.L.C. v. J.M. Insurance Services, L.L.C., 2011 WL 722186 (S.D. Tex. Feb. 22, 2011); HCC Employer Services, Inc. v. Westchester County Surplus Lines Insurance Co., 2006 WL 1663343 (S.D. Tex. June 5, 2006) (E&O policy defining "wrongful act" as "any error, misstatement, misleading statement, act, omission, neglect or breach of duty").

Sixth Circuit: Matthew T. Szura and Co. v. General Insurance Co. of America, 543 Fed. Appx. 538 (6th Cir. 2013); Florists' Mutual Insurance Co. v. Ludy Greenhouse Manufacturing Corp., 521 F. Supp.2d 661 (S.D. Ohio. 2007).

Seventh Circuit: Ryerson, Inc. v. Federal Insurance Co., 676 F.3d 610 (7th Cir. 2012); Sigma Chi Corp. v. Westchester Fire Insurance Co., 587 F. Supp.2d 891 (N.D. Ill. 2008).

Eighth Circuit: Wintermute v. Kansas Bankers Surety Co., 630 F.3d 1063 (8th Cir. 2011); St. Paul Fire and Marine Insurance Co. v. Compaq Computer Corp., 539 F.3d 809 (8th Cir. 2008); Metropolitan Property and Casualty Insurance Co. v. Westport Insurance Corp., 2015 U.S. Dist. LEXIS 125049 (D. Neb. Sept. 18, 2015).

Ninth Circuit: Goerner v. Axis Reinsurance Co., 400 Fed. Appx. 226 (9th Cir. 2010); S.J. Amoroso Construction Co. v. Executive Risk Indemnity, Inc., 325 Fed. Appx. 548 (9th Cir. 2009); Millennium Laboratories, Inc. v. Allied World Insurance Co., 2015 U.S. Dist. LEXIS 133534 (C.D. Cal. Sept. 30, 2015); Isaacs v. Chartis Specialty Insurance Co., 12 F. Supp.3d 1256 (S.D. Cal 2014); Bayley Construction Co. v. Great American E & S Insurance Co., 980 F. Supp.2d 1281 (W.D. Wash. 2013) *In re* Payrollamerica, Inc., 459 B.R. 94 (Bankr. D. Idaho 2011); Sierra Foothills Public Utility District v. Clarendon America Insurance Co., 2006 WL 1350345 (E.D. Cal. May 17, 2006) (E&O policy defining "wrongful act" as "any actual or alleged error or misstatement or act or omission or neglect or breach of duty including misfeasance, malfeasance, and nonfeasance").

Tenth Circuit: Travelers Property Casualty Co. of America v. Federal Recovery Services, Inc., 103 F. Supp.3d 1297 (D. Utah 2015).

Eleventh Circuit: Culbreath Isles Property Owners Ass'n v. Travelers Casualty and Surety Co. of America, 601 Fed. Appx. 876 (11th Cir. 2015); Langdale Co. v. National Union Fire Insurance Co. of Pittsburgh, Pa., 2014 U.S. Dist. LEXIS 184163 (N.D. Ga. June 4, 2014).

State Courts:

California: Health Net, Inc. v. RLI Insurance Co., 206 Cal. App.4th 232, 141 Cal. Rptr.3d 649 (2012).

Delaware: AT&T Corp. v. Clarendon America Insurance Co., 931 A.2d 409 (Del. Super. 2007) (D&O policy; "wrongful act" defined as "any actual or alleged act, omission, misstatement, misleading statement, neglect, error or breach of duty").

Illinois: Margulis v. BCS Insurance Co., 2014 IL App (1st) 140286, 23 N.E.3d 472, 387 Ill. Dec. 780 (2014).

Indiana: Tri-Etch, Inc. v. Cincinnati Insurance Co., 909 N.E.2d 997 (Ind. 2009).

Kansas: Miller v. Westport Insurance Corp., 288 Kan. 27, 200 P.3d 419 (2009).

Louisiana: Sova v. Cove Homeowner's Ass'n, 102 So.3d 863 (La. App. 2012).

Massachusetts: Allmerica Financial Corp. v. Certain Underwriters at Lloyd's, London, 81 Mass. App. Ct. 674, 966 N.E.2d 854 (2012).

Missouri: Todd v. Missouri United School Insurance Council, 223 S.W.3d 156 (Mo. 2007).

New York: Gladstein & Isaac v. Philadelphia Indemnity Insurance Co., 82 A.D.3d 468, 918 N.Y.S.2d 92 (N.Y. App. Div. 2011); Federal Insurance Co. v. International Business Machines Corp., 78 A.D.3d 763, 911 N.Y.S.2d 148 (N.Y. App. Div. 2010).

Washington: Sauter *ex rel.* Sauter v. Houston Casualty Co., 168 Wash. App. 348, 276 P.3d 358 (2012).

Wisconsin: 1325 North Van Buren, LLC v. T-3 Group, Ltd., 293 Wis.2d 410, 716 N.W.2d 822 (2006).

Cf., Anglo-American Insurance Co. v. Molin, 547 Pa. 504, 691 A.2d 929 (1997) (a D&O case defining "wrongful act" to "include: self-dealing, falsifying assets; and improper investing").

[91] See, e.g., Lime Tree Village Community Club Association v. State Farm General Insurance Co., 980 F.2d 1402, 1405 (11th Cir. 1993). See § 6.02[2] *supra*.

[92] See, e.g., Catucci v. Greenwich Insurance Co., 830 N.Y.S.2d 281 (N.Y. App. Div. 2007). See § 3.02[2] *supra*.

[93] See, e.g.:

First Circuit: TransSched Systems Limited v. Federal Insurance Co., 67 F. Supp.3d 523 (D.R.I. 2014) (intentional breaches covered); Financial Resources Network, Inc. v. Brown and Brown, Inc., 754 F. Supp.2d 128 (D. Mass. 2010) (breach of contract covered).

Second Circuit: Jewish Community Center of Staten Island v. Trumbull Insurance Co., 957 F. Supp.2d 215 (E.D.N.Y. 2013) (intentional breach covered).

Third Circuit: Peerless Insurance Co. v. Pennsylvania Cyber Charter School, 19 F. Supp.3d 635 (W.D. Pa. 2014) (intentional breach covered).

Fourth Circuit: Republic Franklin Insurance Co. v. Albemarle County School Board, 670 F.3d 563 (4th Cir. 2012) (intentional breach covered).

Sixth Circuit: Matthew T. Szura and Co. v. General Insurance Co. of America, 543 Fed. Appx. 538 (6th Cir. 2013) (intentional act not covered); United States Fidelity & Guaranty Co. v. Fireman's Fund Insurance Co., 896 F.2d 200 (6th Cir. 1990) (insurance agency's mailing of defamatory telegram constituted malicious and intentional act; only careless and negligent, acts are covered under E&O policy); Medpace, Inc. v. Darwin Select Insurance Co., 13 F. Supp.3d 839 (S.D. Ohio 2014) (breach of contract covered).

Eighth Circuit: Wintermute v. Kansas Bankers Surety Co., 630 F.3d 1063 (8th Cir. 2011) (intentional breach allegations covered); St. Paul Fire and Marine Insurance Co. v. Compaq Computer Corp., 539 F.3d 809 (8th Cir. 2008).

Ninth Circuit: Bayley Construction Co. v. Great American E & S Insurance Co., 980 F. Supp.2d 1281 (W.D. Wash. 2013) (breach of contract covered); Screen Actors Guild, Inc. v. Federal Insurance Co., 957 F. Supp.2d 1157 (C.D. Cal. 2013) (breach of contract not covered); Catlin Specialty Insurance Co. v. CAMICO Mutual Insurance Co., 896 F. Supp.2d 808 (N.D. Cal.) (breach of contract not covered).

Tenth Circuit: Travelers Property Casualty Co. of America v. Federal Recovery Services, Inc., 103 F. Supp.3d 1297 (D. Utah 2015) (intentional breaches not covered); Golf Course Superintendents Association of America v. Underwriters at Lloyd's, London, 761 F. Supp. 1485 (D. Kan. 1991) ("wrongful acts" does not include intentional conduct such as retaliation against employee for filing suit under 42 U.S.C. § 1981).

Eleventh Circuit: Langdale Co. v. National Union Fire Insurance Company of Pittsburgh, PA, 2014 U.S. Dist. LEXIS 184163 (N.D. Ga. June 4, 2014) (intentional breach allegations covered); National Union Fire Insurance Company of Pittsburgh, Pennsylvania v. Brown, 787 F. Supp. 1424 (S.D. Fla. 1991), *aff'd* 963 F.2d 385 (11th Cir. 1992) (criminal and civil actions brought against former officers and directors of corporation fell within definition of "wrongful acts" when conduct involved alleged scheme to defraud home buyers and investors).

State Courts:

California: Health Net, Inc. v. RLI Insurance Co., 206 Cal. App.4th 232, 141 Cal. Rptr.3d 649 (2012) (breach of contract not covered); August Entertainment, Inc. v. Philadelphia Indemnity Insurance Co., 146 Cal. App.4th 565, 52 Cal. Rptr.3d 908 (2007) (breach of contract claim against corporate officer for signing contract without indicating corporate capacity was not covered).

Maryland: Faulkner v. American Casualty Company of Reading, Pennsylvania, 85 Md. App. 595, 584 A.2d 734, *cert. denied* 323 Md. 1, 590 A.2d 158 (1991) (reckless participation in preparation and issuance of public statements and reports that were misleading would be within definition of "wrongful act," but knowing participation would be within exclusion from coverage of claims brought about or contributed to by dishonesty).

Minnesota: Independent School District No. 697, Eveleth v. St. Paul Fire & Marine Insurance Co., 515 N.W.2d 576 (Minn. 1994) (construction of school administration policy as providing coverage for alleged intentional age discrimination was not contrary to public policy); St. Paul Fire & Marine Insurance Co. v. Briggs, 464 N.W.2d 535 (Minn. App. 1990) (public policy prohibits coverage for liability of employer's president and executive vice-president for failure to pay certain taxes); Foster v. Summit Medical Systems, Inc., 610 N.W.2d 350 (Minn. App. 2000) (improper recognition of revenue from letters of intent and sham transactions were alleged "wrongful acts").

Missouri: Brand v. Kansas City Gastroenterology and Hepatology, L.L.C., 414 S.W.3d 546 (Mo. App. 2013) (intentional torts not covered).

Nevada: American Casualty Company of Reading, Pennsylvania v. Hotel & Restaurant Employees & Bartenders International Union Welfare Fund, 113 Nev. 764, 942 P.2d 172 (1997) (trustees required to pay for breach of contract for failing to defend trustees of local union was not loss that arose from a "wrongful act" because the wrongful act of refusal to pay was not cause of obligation, which arose from contract, such that "loss" would have occurred without any wrongful act).

New York: Soho Plaza Corp. v. Nationwide Mutual Insurance Co., 244 A.D.2d 184, 664 N.Y.S.2d 23 (N.Y. App. Div. 1997) (tortious interference with contract by refusing to allow corporation to close on option in belief it was invalid asserted "wrongful acts" by policyholders in carrying out their duties as officers and directors); Volney Residence, Inc. v. Atlantic Mutual Insurance Co., 195 A.D.2d 434, 600 N.Y.S.2d 707 (N.Y. App. Div. 1993) (RICO claim covered by D&O policy as breaches of duty constituting "wrongful acts" are not limited to negligent breaches).

Wisconsin: 1325 North Van Buren, LLC v. T-3 Group, Ltd., 293 Wis.2d 410, 716 N.W.2d 822 (Wis. 2006) (condominium project owner's claim against general contractor for breach of contract was "wrongful act" in contractor's E&O policy because the claim was based on its failure to adhere to professional standards, and the policy did not define "wrongful act" by a tort claim or preclude coverage for contract claim).

94 See § 10.02[1] *supra*. See also:

First Circuit: Saint Consulting Group, Inc. v. Endurance American Specialty Insurance Co., 699 F.3d 544 (1st Cir. 2012).

Second Circuit: Westport Insurance Corp. v. Hamilton Wharton Group, Inc., 483 Fed. Appx. 599 (2d Cir. 2012); MBIA Inc. v. Certain Underwriters at Lloyd's, London, 33 F. Supp.3d 344 (S.D.N.Y. 2014).

Sixth Circuit: Medpace, Inc. v. Darwin Select Insurance Co., 13 F. Supp.3d 839 (S.D. Ohio 2014).

Eighth Circuit: Metropolitan Property and Casualty Insurance Co. v. Westport Insurance Corp., 2015 U.S. Dist. LEXIS 125049 (D. Neb. Sept. 18, 2015).

Ninth Circuit: DeMarco v. Everest Indemnity Insurance Co., 370 Fed. Appx. 795 (9th Cir. 2010); *In re* C.M. Meiers Co., 527 B.R. 388 (Bankr. C.D. Cal. 2015); Isaacs v. Chartis Specialty Insurance Co., 12 F. Supp.3d 1256 (S.D. Cal 2014); Bayley Construction Co. v. Great American E & S Insurance Co., 980 F. Supp.2d 1281 (W.D. Wash. 2013).

Eleventh Circuit: Culbreath Isles Property Owners Ass'n v. Travelers Casualty and Surety Co. of America, 601 Fed. Appx. 876 (11th Cir. 2015); General Star National Insurance Co. v. Higginbotham, 877 F. Supp.2d 1181 (N.D. Ala. 2012).

State Courts:

California: Health Net, Inc. v. RLI Insurance Co., 206 Cal. App.4th 232, 141 Cal. Rptr.3d 649 (2012).

Georgia: Garland, Samuel & Loeb, P.C. v. American Safety Casualty Insurance Co., 287 Ga. App. 254, 651 S.E.2d 177 (2007).

Illinois: Hilco Trading, L.L.C. v. Liberty Surplus Insurance Corp., 2014 IL App (1st) 123503, 8 N.E.3d 166, 380 Ill. Dec. 235 (2014).

Indiana: Stevenson v. Hamilton Mutual Insurance Co., 672 N.E.2d 467 (Ind. App. 1996).

New York: Georgetown Capital Group, Inc. v. Everest National Insurance Co., 104 A.D.3d 1150, 961 N.Y.S.2d 622 (N.Y. App. Div. 2013); Executive Risk Indemnity, Inc. v. Starwood Hotels & Resorts Worldwide, Inc., 98 A.D.3d 878, 951 N.Y.S.2d 13 (N.Y. App. Div. 2012); Watkins Glen Central School District v. National Union Fire Insurance Company of Pittsburgh, Pennsylvania, 286 A.D.2d 48, 732 N.Y.S.2d 70 (N.Y. App. Div. 2001).

[95] Some policy definitions can be very specific and are tailored to a particular business. See, e.g., Biborosch v. Transamerica Insurance Co., 412 Pa. Super. 505, 603 A.2d 1050, 1052 (Pa. Super.), *alloc. denied* 615 A.2d 1310 (Pa. 1992), which provided insurance for someone in the insurance business.

"'PROFESSIONAL SERVICES' shall mean those services necessary or incidental in the conduct of the insurance business of the NAMED INSURED including:

1. the sale and/or servicing of life insurance, disability income insurance, annuities, accident and health insurance plans (including Blue Cross/Blue Shield Organizations);
2. the sale and/or servicing of variable annuities. . . .
3. the sale and/or servicing of employee benefit plans. . . .
4. advice, consultation, administration and services in conjunction with all of the above, whether or not a separate fee is charged."

See also:

Third Circuit: Smith v. Continental Casualty Co., 2008 WL 4462120 (M.D. Pa. Sept. 30, 2008).

[96] See, e.g., Metropolitan Property and Casualty Insurance Co. v. Westport Insurance Corp., 2015 U.S. Dist. LEXIS 125049 (D. Neb. Sept. 18, 2015).

[97] See, e.g.:

Eleventh Circuit: General Star National Insurance Co. v. Higginbotham, 877 F. Supp.2d 1181 (N.D. Ala. 2012).

State Courts:

New York: Executive Risk Indemnity, Inc. v. Starwood Hotels & Resorts Worldwide, Inc., 98 A.D.3d 878, 951 N.Y.S.2d 13 (N.Y. App. Div. 2012).

[98] Marx v. Hartford Accident & Indemnity Co., 183 Neb. 12, 157 N.W.2d 870 (1968).

[99] *Id.,* 157 N.W.2d at, 871–872. See also:

First Circuit: Saint Consulting Group, Inc. v. Endurance American Specialty Insurance Co., 699 F.3d 544 (1st Cir. 2012); Massamont Insurance Agency, Inc. v. Utica Mutual Life Insurance Co., 448 F. Supp.2d 329 (D. Mass. 2006), *aff'd* 489 F.3d 71 (1st Cir. 2007).

Second Circuit: Specialty National Insurance Co. v. English Brothers Funeral Home, 606 F. Supp.2d 466 (S.D.N.Y. Mar. 30, 2009); U.S. Underwriters Insurance Co. v. Tauber, 604 F.Supp.2d 521 (E.D.N.Y. Mar. 27, 2009).

Third Circuit: Mallalieu-Golder Insurance Agency, Inc. v. Executive Risk Indemnity, Inc., 255 Fed. Appx. 673 (3d Cir. 2007).

Fifth Circuit: Essex Ins. Co. v. Greenville Convalescent Home Inc., 236 Fed. Appx. 49 (5th Cir. 2007); Gregg & Valby, L.L.P. v. Great American Insurance Co., 316 F. Supp.2d 505 (S.D. Tex. 2004).

Eighth Circuit: Firepond Liquidating Trust v. Vigilant Insurance Co., 288 Fed. Appx. 306 (8th Cir. 2008).

Ninth Circuit: Clear Logic, Inc. v. Federal Insurance Co., 244 Fed. Appx. 164 (9th Cir. 2007); *In re* C.M. Meiers Co., 527 B.R. 388 (Bankr. C.D. Cal. 2015).

State Courts:

Georgia: Garland, Samuel & Loeb, P.C. v. American Safety Casualty Insurance Co., 287 Ga. App. 254, 651 S.E.2d 177 (2007).

Illinois: Westport Insurance Corp. v. Jackson National Life Insurance Co., 387 Ill. App.3d 408, 326 Ill. Dec. 741, 900 N.E.2d 377 (2008).

Kansas: Miller v. Westport Insurance Corp., 288 Kan. 27, 200 P.3d 419 (2009).

Louisiana: Specialized Commercial Lending, Inc. v. Murphy-Blossman Appraisal Services, L.L.C., 978 So.2d 927 (La. App. 2007).

Massachusetts: Roe v. Federal Insurance Co., 412 Mass. 43, 587 N.E.2d 214 (1992).

In one case in which the policy provided no definition of "professional services," the court was forced to turn to the dictionary. See Lincoln County Ambulance District v. Pacific Employers Insurance Co., 15 S.W.3d 739, 744 (Mo. App. 1998).

"Since 'professional services' are not defined in the policy, we look to *Webster's Collegiate Dictionary*, Tenth Edition, 930 (1995), which defines 'professional' as 'of, relating to, or characteristic of a profession or calling' and 'service' as 'an act done for the benefit or command of another.' 'Profession' is defined as 'a calling requiring specialized knowledge and often long and intensive academic preparation' or as 'a principal calling, vocation or employment'."

Nebraska: R.W. v. Schrein, 264 Neb. 818, 652 N.W.2d 574 (2002).

Wisconsin: 1325 North Van Buren, LLC v. T-3 Group, Ltd., 293 Wis.2d 410, 716 N.W.2d 822 (Wis. 2006).

Wyoming: T.M. *ex rel.* Cox v. Executive Risk Indemnity, Inc., 59 P.3d 721 (Wyo. 2002).

100 See § 10.02[2] *supra*.

101 See:

Sixth Circuit: Salvati Insurance Group, Inc. v. Utica Mutual Insurance Co., 45 F. Supp.3d 637 (E.D. Mich. 2014) (professional liability policy).

Eighth Circuit: Meadows v. Century Healthcare, Inc., 445 F. Supp.2d 1297 (N.D. Okla. 2006) (private practice of physician who was employed as the medical director for a psychiatric treatment center was not within scope of his duties as medical director); Farr v. Farm Bureau Insurance Company of Nebraska, 61 F.3d 677 (8th Cir. 1995) (no coverage for claim against directors and officers based on injuries arising from their breach of duty owed to corporation).

State Courts:

Ohio: American Chemical Society v. Leadscope, Inc., 2005 WL 1220746 (Ohio App. May 24, 2005), *appeal denied* 107 Ohio St. 3d 1412, 836 N.E.2d 1231 (2005) (conversion claim covered and not excluded as outside capacity).

Washington: Sauter *ex rel.* Sauter v. Houston Casualty Co., 168 Wash. App. 348, 276 P.3d 358 (2012) (personal guaranty of CEO not covered even if it guaranteed corporate debt).

102 For instance, during a labor strike, senior management frequently performs tasks usually handled by lower-level employees. Officers and directors who have advanced degrees, such as CPA or attorney licenses, often perform "professional services" and services as directors/officers on behalf of the company.

See:

Eighth Circuit: Yocum v. St. Paul Mercury Insurance Co., 2010 U.S. Dist. LEXIS 52814 (E.D. Ark. May 27, 2010) (dual capacity).

Tenth Circuit: ClearOne Communications, Inc. v. National Union Fire Insurance Company of Pittsburgh, PA, 494 F.3d 1238 (10th Cir. 2007)

State Courts:

Illinois: Illinois Insurance Guarantee Fund v. Santucci, 384 Ill. App.3d 927, 323 Ill. Dec. 775, 894 N.E.2d 801 (2008).

Insurance companies may contest coverage under professional services exclusions. For example, a suit brought against an officer of a brokerage company by a customer may result in the insurance company denying coverage on the ground that the "wrongful act" was committed while rendering professional services, rather than in the capacity as an officer or director. Indeed, any suit brought by a customer or client against a director or officer is likely to trigger this defense to coverage. This defense may arise from a policy exclusion for professional services, as well as under the "capacity" concept. In Chapman v. Mutual Service Casualty Insurance Co., 35 F. Supp.2d 693 (E.D. Wis. 1999), a real estate broker sought coverage under its business owner's liability insurance policy against a suit brought by home purchasers who alleged that the broker was liable for a faulty inspection and negligent repainting of their newly purchased home, leading to their child's lead-paint poisoning. The broker's alleged wrongdoing included negligent hiring of a home inspector and paint contractor, failure to warn, and failure to inspect. The insurance company denied coverage, relying on a professional services exclusion similar to the exclusion found in D&O policies. 35 F. Supp.2d at 696. The court rejected assertion of the professional services exclusion and found the "the effect of the exclusion on these facts is ambiguous, in which case it should be narrowly construed against the insurer. . . . More likely, the exclusion does not apply, and the policy provides coverage." This was because the actions of which the broker was accused did not require "'specialized knowledge, labor or skill' of an intellectual nature" and because "[t]he realtor's duty of care here simply did not involve the exercise of advanced knowledge or training." 35 F. Supp.2d at 698.

See also, Neighborhood Housing Services of America, Inc. v. Turner-Ridley, 742 F. Supp.2d 964 (N.D. Ind. 2010) (professional services exclusion in D&O policy does not renew coverage illusory).

103 See:

Eighth Circuit: Gulf Insurance Co. v. Skyline Displays, Inc., 361 F. Supp.2d 986 (D. Minn. 2005) (breach of fiduciary duty claim based upon frustrated former director's expectations of continued employment and participation in insured's management was not covered).

State Courts:

California: August Entertainment, Inc. v. Philadelphia Indemnity Insurance Co., 146 Cal. App.4th 565, 52 Cal. Rptr.3d 908 (2007) (breach of contract claim against corporate officer for signing contract without indicating corporate capacity was not covered); Kronemyer v. Philadelphia Indemnity Insurance Co., 2003 WL 21213243 (Cal. App. May 27, 2003) (former president was not entitled to coverage for company's trade libel claim against president because statements at issue were made after president's employment had been terminated); Olson v. Federal Insurance Co., 268 Cal. Rptr. 90 (Cal. App. 1990) (director's alleged interference with corporation's supplier, which was managed by corporation and partly owned by director, was outside coverage because director was not discharging duties to corporation when engaged in allegedly actionable conduct and was not sued solely because he was director).

Massachusetts: Royal Surplus Lines Insurance Co. v. Cotton States Mutual Insurance Co., 67 Mass. App. 1104, 852 N.E.2d 1143 (2006) (fraternity member acted intentionally outside the scope of his duties as an officer of the local fraternity in connection with hazing incident).

New York: Federal Insurance Co. v. International Business Machines Corp., 78 A.D.3d 763, 911 N.Y.S.2d 148 (N.Y. App. Div. 2010) (ERISA claim against plan trustee not covered because ERISA imposes liability on settlors not fiduciaries).

Ohio: Cincinnati Insurance Co. v. Irwin Co., 2000 WL 1867297, at *3 (Ohio App. Dec. 22, 2000) (suit by shareholders who had sold shares to the company below book value, where claim was based upon lack of prior corporate approval, was not covered because the acts for which the directors and officers sought coverage were not made "in their respective capacities as directors and officers of the company").

[104] See:

Second Circuit: Jewish Community Center of Staten Island v. Trumbull Insurance Co., 957 F. Supp.2d 215 (E.D.N.Y. 2013).

Eighth Circuit: Yocum v. St. Paul Mercury Insurance Co., 2010 WL 2179137 (E.D. Ark. May 27, 2010); Carlson v. Twin City Fire Insurance Co., 2009 WL 1793887 (D. Minn. June 23, 2009).

Ninth Circuit: S.J. Amoroso Construction Co. v. Executive Risk Indemnity, Inc., 325 Fed. Appx. 548 (9th Cir. 2009); Wolfes v. Burlington Insurance Co., 2010 WL 842327 (N.D. Cal. Mar. 10, 2010); Mt. Hood, L.L.C. v. Travelers Casualty and Surety Company of America, 2009 WL 536848 (D. Or. March 3, 2009).

State Courts:

New York: Federal Insurance Co. v. International Business Machines Corp., 78 A.D.3d 763, 911 N.Y.S.2d 148 (N.Y. App. Div. 2010); Soho Plaza Corp. v. Nationwide Mutual Insurance Co., 244 A.D.2d 184, 664 N.Y.S.2d 23 (N.Y. App. Div. 1997) (tortious interference with contract claim against directors and officers for refusing to allow corporation to close on option in belief it was invalid asserted wrongful acts by policyholders in carrying out their duties as officers and directors).

[105] See Gulf Insurance Co. v. Dolan, Fertig & Curtis, 433 So.2d 512, 514 (Fla. 1983). See also, Long, *The Law of Liability Insurance,* Vol. 3, § 12E.03[1] (1996).

[106] See § 5.03[6] *supra*. See also, Kvaerner Metals Division of Kvaerner U.S., Inc. v. Commercial Union Insurance Co., 589 Pa. 317, 908 A.2d 888, 892 n.1 (Pa. 2006) ("'An "occurrence" policy protects the policyholder from liability for any act done while the policy is in effect, whereas a "claims-made" policy protects the holder only against claims made during the life of the policy.'").

First Circuit: New England Environmental Technologies v. American Safety Risk Retention Group, Inc., 738 F. Supp.2d 249 (D. Mass. 2010).

Second Circuit: Hanover Insurance Co. v. Vermont Mutual Insurance Co., 69 F. Supp.3d 302 (N.D.N.Y. 2014); Boys v. Continental Casualty Co., 808 F. Supp.2d 410 (D. Conn. 2011).

Third Circuit: American Automobile Insurance Co. v. Murray, 658 F.3d 311 (3d Cir. 2011); McMillen Engineering, Inc. v. Travelers Indemnity Co., 744 F. Supp.2d 416 (W.D. Pa. 2010).

Fourth Circuit: Minnesota Lawyers Mutual Insurance Co. v. Batzli, 442 Fed. Appx. 40 (4th Cir. 2011); Bryan Brothers, Inc. v. Continental Casualty Co., 660 F.3d 827 (4th Cir. 2011).

Fifth Circuit: Byrd and Associates, P.L.L.C. v. Evanston Insurance Co., 378 Fed. Appx. 391 (5th Cir. 2010).

Sixth Circuit: Lafayette Life Insurance Co. v. Arch Insurance Co., 784 F. Supp.2d 1034 (N.D. Ind. 2011); Michigan Millers Mutual Insurance Co. v. Fidelity and Deposit Company of Maryland, 809 F. Supp.2d 702 (W.D. Mich. 2011).

Seventh Circuit: James River Insurance Co. v. Kemper Casualty Insurance Co., 585 F.3d 382 (7th Cir. 2009); Community Bank v. Progressive Casualty Insurance Co., 2010 WL 2985932 (S.D. Ind. July 27, 2010).

Eighth Circuit: Owatonna Clinic-Mayo Health System v. Medical Protective Company of Fort Wayne, Ind., 639 F.3d 806 (8th Cir. 2011).

Ninth Circuit: Westport Insurance Corp. v. Markham Group, Inc., 403 Fed. Appx. 264 (9th Cir. 2010); Eastwood Insurance Services, Inc. v. U.S. Specialty Insurance Co., 391 Fed. Appx. 611 (9th Cir. 2010); Moody v. American Guarantee and Liability Insurance Co., 804 F. Supp.2d 1123 (W.D. Wash. 2011).

Tenth Circuit: Cohen-Esrey Real Estate Services, Inc. v. Twin City Fire Insurance Co., 636 F.3d 1300 (10th Cir. 2011).

Eleventh Circuit: Eddy v. Continental Casualty Co., 784 F. Supp.2d 1331 (M.D. Fla. 2011); Jennings Construction Services Corp. v. Ace American Insurance Co., 783 F. Supp.2d 1209 (M.D. Fla. 2011); Simpson & Creasy, P.C. v. Continental Casualty Co., 770 F. Supp.2d 1351 (S.D. Ga. 2011); Office Depot, Inc. v. National Union Fire Insurance Company of Pittsburgh, Pa., 734 F. Supp.2d 1304 (S.D. Fla. 2010).

District of Columbia Circuit: Capitol Specialty Insurance Corp. v. Sanford Wittels & Heisler, L.L.P., 793 F. Supp.2d 399 (D.D.C. 2011).

State Courts:

California: Feldman v. Illinois Union Insurance Co., 198 Cal. App.4th 1495, 130 Cal. Rptr.3d 770 (2011); Century Indemnity Co. v. Hearrean, 98 Cal. App.4th 734, 120 Cal. Rptr.2d 66 (2002); Homestead Insurance Co. v. American Empire Surplus Lines Insurance Co., 44 Cal. App.4th 1297, 52 Cal. Rptr.2d 268, 272 (1996).

Delaware: Axis Reinsurance Co. v. HLTH Corp., 993 A.2d 1057 (Del. 2010).

Florida: Gulf Insurance Co. v. Dolan, Fertig & Curtis, 433 So.2d 512, 514 (Fla. 1983); Acosta, Inc. v. National Union Fire Insurance Co., 39 So.3d 565 (Fla. App. 2010).

Illinois: Illinois Insurance Guaranty Fund v. Chicago Insurance Co., 2014 IL App (5th) 140033-U (2015).

Indiana: Ashby v. Bar Plan Mutual Insurance Co., 949 N.E.2d 307 (Ind. 2011).

Louisiana: Wright v. Willis-Knighton Medical Center, 57 So.3d 382 (La. App. 2011); Bell v. Parry, 61 So.3d 1 (La. App. 2010).

Maryland: Sherwood Brands, Inc. v. Great American Insurance Co., 13 A.3d 1268 (Md. 2011).

Nebraska: Countryside Co-op. v. Harry A. Koch Co., 790 N.W.2d 873 (Neb. 2010).

New Jersey: Hodge v. Garrett, 263 N.J. Super. 278, 622 A.2d 930 (N.J. Super. App. Div. 1993).

New York: CPA Mutual Insurance Company of America Risk Retention Group v. Weiss & Co., 915 N.Y.S.2d 57 (N.Y. App. Div. 2011); McCabe v. St. Paul Fire & Marine Insurance Co., 79 A.D.3d 1612 (N.Y. App. Div. 2010).

Pennsylvania: Fletcher v. Pennsylvania Property & Casualty Insurance Guarantee Association, 27 A.3d 299 (Pa. Commw. 2011); West Penn Allegheny Health System v. Medical Care Availability and Reduction of Error Fund, 11 A.3d 598 (Pa. Commw. 2010).

Texas: Reeves County v. Houston Casualty Co., 356 S.W.3d 664 (Tex. App. 2011).

[107] See § 5.03[6] *supra*. See also, Kvaerner Metals Division of Kvaerner U.S., Inc. v. Commercial Union Insurance Co., 589 Pa. 317, 908 A.2d 888, 892 n.1 (Pa. 2006) ("'An "occurrence" policy protects the policyholder from liability for any act done while the policy is in effect, whereas a "claims made" policy protects the holder only against claims made during the life of the policy.'").

First Circuit: New England Environmental Technologies v. American Safety Risk Retention Group, Inc., 738 F. Supp.2d 249 (D. Mass. 2010).

Second Circuit: Hanover Insurance Co. v. Vermont Mutual Insurance Co., 69 F. Supp.3d 302 (N.D.N.Y. 2014); Boys v. Continental Casualty Co., 808 F. Supp.2d 410 (D. Conn. 2011).

Third Circuit: American Automobile Insurance Co. v. Murray, 658 F.3d 311 (3d Cir. 2011); McMillen Engineering, Inc. v. Travelers Indemnity Co., 744 F. Supp.2d 416 (W.D. Pa. 2010).

Fourth Circuit: Minnesota Lawyers Mutual Insurance Co. v. Batzli, 442 Fed. Appx. 40 (4th Cir. 2011); Bryan Brothers, Inc. v. Continental Casualty Co., 660 F.3d 827 (4th Cir. 2011).

Fifth Circuit: Byrd and Associates, P.L.L.C. v. Evanston Insurance Co., 378 Fed. Appx. 391 (5th Cir. 2010).

Sixth Circuit: Lafayette Life Insurance Co. v. Arch Insurance Co., 784 F. Supp.2d 1034 (N.D. Ind. 2011); Michigan Millers Mutual Insurance Co. v. Fidelity and Deposit Company of Maryland, 809 F. Supp.2d 702 (W.D. Mich. 2011).

Seventh Circuit: James River Insurance Co. v. Kemper Casualty Insurance Co., 585 F.3d 382 (7th Cir. 2009); Community Bank v. Progressive Casualty Insurance Co., 2010 WL 2985932 (S.D. Ind. July 27, 2010).

Eighth Circuit: Owatonna Clinic-Mayo Health System v. Medical Protective Company of Fort Wayne, Ind., 639 F.3d 806 (8th Cir. 2011).

Ninth Circuit: Westport Insurance Corp. v. Markham Group, Inc., 403 Fed. Appx. 264 (9th Cir. 2010); Eastwood Insurance Services, Inc. v. U.S. Specialty Insurance Co., 391 Fed. Appx. 611 (9th Cir. 2010); Moody v. American Guarantee and Liability Insurance Co., 804 F. Supp.2d 1123 (W.D. Wash. 2011).

Tenth Circuit: Cohen-Esrey Real Estate Services, Inc. v. Twin City Fire Insurance Co., 636 F.3d 1300 (10th Cir. 2011).

Eleventh Circuit: Eddy v. Continental Casualty Co., 784 F. Supp.2d 1331 (M.D. Fla. 2011); Jennings Construction Services Corp. v. Ace American Insurance Co., 783 F. Supp.2d 1209 (M.D. Fla. 2011); Simpson & Creasy, P.C. v. Continental Casualty Co., 770 F. Supp.2d 1351 (S.D. Ga. 2011); Office Depot, Inc. v. National Union Fire Insurance Company of Pittsburgh, Pa., 734 F. Supp.2d 1304 (S.D. Fla. 2010).

District of Columbia Circuit: Capitol Specialty Insurance Corp. v. Sanford Wittels & Heisler, L.L.P., 793 F. Supp.2d 399 (D.D.C. 2011).

State Courts:

California: Feldman v. Illinois Union Insurance Co., 198 Cal. App.4th 1495, 130 Cal. Rptr.3d 770 (2011); Century Indemnity Co. v. Hearrean, 98 Cal. App.4th 734, 120 Cal. Rptr.2d 66 (2002); Homestead Insurance Co. v. American Empire Surplus Lines Insurance Co., 44 Cal. App.4th 1297, 52 Cal. Rptr.2d 268, 272 (1996).

Delaware: Axis Reinsurance Co. v. HLTH Corp., 993 A.2d 1057 (Del. 2010).

Florida: Gulf Insurance Co. v. Dolan, Fertig & Curtis, 433 So.2d 512, 514 (Fla. 1983); Acosta, Inc. v. National Union Fire Insurance Co., 39 So.3d 565 (Fla. App. 2010).

Illinois: Illinois Insurance Guaranty Fund v. Chicago Insurance Co., 2014 IL App (5th) 140033-U (2015).

Indiana: Ashby v. Bar Plan Mutual Insurance Co., 949 N.E.2d 307 (Ind. 2011).

Louisiana: Wright v. Willis-Knighton Medical Center, 57 So.3d 382 (La. App. 2011); Bell v. Parry, 61 So.3d 1 (La. App. 2010).

Maryland: Sherwood Brands, Inc. v. Great American Insurance Co., 13 A.3d 1268 (Md. 2011).

Nebraska: Countryside Co-op. v. Harry A. Koch Co., 790 N.W.2d 873 (Neb. 2010).

New Jersey: Hodge v. Garrett, 263 N.J. Super. 278, 622 A.2d 930 (N.J. Super. App. Div. 1993).

New York: CPA Mutual Insurance Company of America Risk Retention Group v. Weiss & Co., 915 N.Y.S.2d 57 (N.Y. App. Div. 2011); McCabe v. St. Paul Fire & Marine Insurance Co., 79 A.D.3d 1612 (N.Y. App. Div. 2010).

Pennsylvania: Fletcher v. Pennsylvania Property & Casualty Insurance Guarantee Association, 27 A.3d 299 (Pa. Commw. 2011); West Penn Allegheny Health System v. Medical Care Availability and Reduction of Error Fund, 11 A.3d 598 (Pa. Commw. 2010).

Texas: Reeves County v. Houston Casualty Co., 356 S.W.3d 664 (Tex. App. 2011).

108 Century Indemnity Co. v. Hearrean, 98 Cal. App.4th 734, 120 Cal. Rptr.2d 66, 69 (Cal. App. 2002). See also:

California: Homestead Insurance Co. v. American Empire Surplus Lines Insurance Co., 44 Cal. App.4th 1297, 52 Cal. Rptr.2d 268, 272 (1996).

Florida: Gulf Insurance Co. v. Dolan, Fertig & Curtis, 433 So.2d 512, 514 (Fla. 1983).

New Jersey: Hodge v. Garrett, 263 N.J. Super. 278, 622 A.2d 930 (N.J. Super. App. Div. 1993).

Pennsylvania: Kvaerner Metals v. Commercial Union Insurance Co., 589 Pa. 317, 908 A.2d 888, at n.1 (Pa. 2006) ("'An "occurrence" policy protects the policyholder from liability for any act done while the policy is in effect, whereas a "claims made" policy protects the holder only against claims made during the life of the policy.'").

109 See, e.g.:

First Circuit: New England Environmental Technologies v. American Safety Risk Retention Group, Inc., 738 F. Supp.2d 249 (D. Mass. 2010).

Second Circuit: Boys v. Continental Casualty Co., 808 F. Supp.2d 410 (D. Conn. 2011); American Home Assurance Co. v. Abrams, 69 F. Supp.2d 339 (D. Conn. 1999).

Third Circuit: American Automobile Insurance Co. v. Murray, 658 F.3d 311 (3d Cir. 2011).

Fourth Circuit: Minnesota Lawyers Mutual Insurance Co. v. Batzli, 442 Fed. Appx. 40 (4th Cir. 2011).

Fifth Circuit: Brumfield v. Shelton, 831 F. Supp. 562 (E.D. La. 1993).

Eighth Circuit: Ritrama, Inc. v. HDI-Gerling America Insurance Co., 796 F.3d 962 (8th Cir. 2015); Owatonna Clinic-Mayo Health System v. Medical Protective Company of Fort Wayne, Ind., 639 F.3d 806 (8th Cir. 2011).

Ninth Circuit: Burns v. International Insurance Co., 929 F.2d 1422 (9th Cir. 1991); Moody v. American Guarantee and Liability Insurance Co., 804 F. Supp.2d 1123 (W.D. Wash. 2011).

Eleventh Circuit: Eddy v. Continental Casualty Co., 784 F. Supp.2d 1331 (M.D. Fla. 2011); Jennings Construction Services Corp. v. Ace American Insurance Co., 783 F. Supp.2d 1209 (M.D. Fla. 2011); Simpson & Creasy, P.C. v. Continental Casualty Co., 770 F. Supp.2d 1351 (S.D. Ga. 2011); Office Depot, Inc. v. National Union Fire Insurance Company of Pittsburgh, Pa., 734 F. Supp.2d 1304 (S.D. Fla. 2010).

District of Columbia Circuit: Capitol Specialty Insurance Corp. v. Sanford Wittels & Heisler, L.L.P., 793 F. Supp.2d 399 (D.D.C. 2011).

State Courts:

California: Slater v. Lawyers' Mutual Insurance Co., 227 Cal. App.3d 1415, 278 Cal. Rptr. 479, 481–483 (1991).

Connecticut: ITC Investments, Inc. v. Employers Reinsurance Corp., 2000 WL 1996233 (Conn. Super. Dec. 11, 2000).

Delaware: Homsey Architects, Inc. v. Harry David Zutz Insurance, Inc., 2000 WL 973285, at *12 (Del. Super. May 25, 2000).

Indiana: Ashby v. Bar Plan Mutual Insurance Co., 949 N.E.2d 307 (Ind. 2011); Bar Plan Mutual Insurance Co. v. Likes Law Office, L.L.C., 2015 Ind. App. LEXIS 680 (Ind. App. Oct. 15, 2015).

Louisiana: Wright v. Willis-Knighton Medical Center, 57 So.3d 382 (La. App. 2011).

Nebraska: Countryside Co-op. v. Harry A. Koch Co., 280 Neb. 795, 790 N.W.2d 873 (2010).

New Jersey: Zuckerman v. National Union Fire Insurance Co., 100 N.J. 304, 495 A.2d 395, 406 (N.J. 1985).

New York: McCabe v. St. Paul Fire & Marine Insurance Co., 79 A.D.3d 1612, 914 N.Y.S.2d 814 (N.Y. App. Div. 2010).

Insurance companies may also provide for an automatic extended reporting period, which, in the event of cancellation for anything other than nonpayment of premiums, provides additional insurance for claims first made and reported to the insurance company during the extended reporting period, typically thirty to sixty days after the end of the policy period, provided the negligent act, error, or omission took place during the policy period or after the retroactive date stated in the declarations. Some insurance companies also sell optional extended reporting periods, which, for an additional premium, provide coverage for cancelled or non-renewed policyholders for claims first made and reported during the extended reporting period, provided the negligent act took place during the initial policy period or after the retroactive date stated in the declarations.

[110] See, e.g., AT&T Corp. v. Faraday Capital Limited, 918 A.2d 1104 (Del. 2007).

[111] See, e.g.:

Third Circuit: G-I Holdings v. Hartford Fire Insurance Co., 2007 WL 842009 (D.N.J. March 16, 2007).

Fifth Circuit: HCC Employer Services, Inc. v. Westchester County Surplus Lines Insurance Co., 2006 WL 1663343 (S.D. Tex. June 5, 2006).

Ninth Circuit: Prime Insurance Syndicate, Inc. v. Damaso, 471 F. Supp.2d 1087 (D. Nev. 2007); Oakland-Alameda County Coliseum, Inc. v. National Union Fire Insurance Company of Pittsburgh, Pennsylvania, 480 F. Supp.2d 1182 (N.D. Cal. 2007); Sierra Foothills Public Utility District v. Clarendon America Insurance Co., 2006 WL 1350345 (E.D. Cal. May 17, 2006).

State Courts:

Delaware: AT&T Corp. v. Faraday Capital Limited, 918 A.2d 1104 (Del. 2007); AT&T Corp. v. Clarendon America Insurance Co., 2006 WL 2685081 (Del. Super. Sept. 18, 2006).

Pennsylvania: Anglo-American Insurance Co. v. Molin, 547 Pa. 504, 691 A.2d 929 (Pa. 1997).

[112] See, e.g.:

California: Safeco Surplus Lines Co. v. Employer's Reinsurance Corp., 11 Cal. App.4th 1403, 15 Cal. Rptr.2d 58 (1992).

Wyoming: Doctors' Company v. Insurance Corporation of America, 864 P.2d 1018 (Wyo. 1993).

[113] See, e.g., Millennium Laboratories, Inc. v. Allied World Insurance Co., 2015 U.S. Dist. LEXIS 133534 (C.D. Cal. Sept. 30, 2015).

[114] See:

Third Circuit: John Hancock Healthplan of Pennsylvania, Inc. v. Lexington Insurance Co., 1989 WL 106992, at *4 (E.D. Pa. Sept. 11, 1989) ("a lawsuit need not be commenced in order to trigger the claim requirement under [a D&O insurance] policy"; a threat of a lawsuit is sufficient to trigger coverage).

Eighth Circuit: Polychron v. Crum & Forster Insurance Cos., 916 F.2d 461, 463 (8th Cir. 1990) (because definition of a "claim" is broader than "cause of action," grand jury subpoena directed to a bank regarding documents relating to the bank president's conduct constituted a "claim" under the policy); Berry v. St. Paul Fire & Marine Insurance Co., 70 F.3d 981, 983 (8th Cir. 1995) (letter asking attorney to forward information to insurance company qualified as "claim" because it was "sufficiently demanding in tone and substance" despite absence of specific request for money damages).

Ninth Circuit: Charles Dunn Co. v. Tudor Insurance Co., 308 Fed. Appx. 149 (9th Cir. 2009).

Tenth Circuit: City of Shawnee, Kansas v. Argonaut Insurance Co., 546 F. Supp.2d 1163 (D. Kan. 2008).

State Courts:

California: Westrec Marina Management, Inc. v. Arrowood Indemnity Co., 163 Cal. App.4th 1387, 78 Cal. Rptr.3d 264 (2008).

Colorado: National Casualty Co. v. Great Southwest Fire Insurance Co., 833 P.2d 741, 745 (Colo. 1992) (letter from terminated employee asserting wrongful termination and requesting reinstatement "was a demand made to enforce a right and, as such, was a claim").

Michigan: Pinckney Community Schools v. Continental Casualty Co., 213 Mich. App. 521, 540 N.W.2d 748, *appeal denied* 453 Mich. 882, 554 N.W.2d 10 (1995) (sex discrimination charge filed with state agency or EEOC constitutes a "claim").

Montana: Herron v. Schutz-Foss Architects, 282 Mont. 94, 935 P.2d 1104, 1108 (1997) (letter from claimant's attorney requesting contact with alleged tortfeasor's insurance carrier constituted a "claim" under professional liability insurance policy; holding otherwise "would encourage litigation as opposed to negotiation and settlement").

New York: In re Ancillary Receivership of Reliance Insurance Co., 55 A.D.3d 43, 863 N.Y.S.2d 415 (N.Y. App. Div. 2008).

115 See:

Fourth Circuit: ACE American Insurance Co. v. Ascend One Corp., 570 F. Supp.2d 789 (D. Md. 2008); Hyde v. Fidelity & Deposit Company of Maryland, 23 F. Supp.2d 630 (D. Md. 1998) (Resolution Trust Corporation's ("RTC's") notice of intent to hold directors liable and RTC's investigation did not constitute "claim" for which defense costs were due under D&O policy, even though D&O insurer indemnified the settlement paid to the RTC).

Fifth Circuit: FDIC v. Booth, 82 F.3d 670, 676 (5th Cir. 1996) (correspondence from a governmental agency threatening action is not a "claim").

Tenth Circuit: North American Specialty Insurance Co. v. Correctional Medical Services, Inc., 527 F.3d 1033 (10th Cir. 2008).

District of Columbia Circuit: American Center for International Labor Solidarity v. Federal Insurance Co., 548 F.3d 1103 (D.C. Cir. 2008).

State Courts:

California: Abifadel v. Cigna Insurance Co., 8 Cal. App.4th 145, 9 Cal. Rptr.2d 910 (1992) (demands and threats to sue a director were not "claims," but were "potential claims").

116 See § 10.04[2][f] *infra*.

117 See:

First Circuit: New England Environmental Technologies v. American Safety Risk Retention Group, Inc., 738 F. Supp.2d 249 (D. Mass. 2010).

Second Circuit: Hanover Insurance Co. v. Vermont Mutual Insurance Co., 69 F. Supp.3d 302 (N.D.N.Y. 2014); Boys v. Continental Casualty Co., 808 F. Supp.2d 410 (D. Conn. 2011).

Third Circuit: American Automobile Insurance Co. v. Murray, 658 F.3d 311 (3d Cir. 2011); McMillen Engineering, Inc. v. Travelers Indemnity Co., 744 F. Supp.2d 416 (W.D. Pa. 2010).

Fourth Circuit: Minnesota Lawyers Mutual Insurance Co. v. Batzli, 442 Fed. Appx. 40 (4th Cir. 2011); Bryan Brothers, Inc. v. Continental Casualty Co., 660 F.3d 827 (4th Cir. 2011).

Fifth Circuit: Byrd and Associates, P.L.L.C. v. Evanston Insurance Co., 378 Fed. Appx. 391 (5th Cir. 2010); Jones v. Lexington Manor Nursing Center, L.L.C., 480 F. Supp.2d 865 (S.D. Miss. 2006).

Sixth Circuit: Lafayette Life Insurance Co. v. Arch Insurance Co., 784 F. Supp.2d 1034 (N.D. Ind. 2011); Michigan Millers Mutual Insurance Co. v. Fidelity and Deposit Company of Maryland, 809 F. Supp.2d 702 (W.D. Mich. Aug. 15, 2011).

Seventh Circuit: James River Insurance Co. v. Kemper Casualty Insurance Co., 585 F.3d 382 (7th Cir. 2009); Community Bank v. Progressive Casualty Insurance Co., 2010 WL 2985932 (S.D. Ind. July 27, 2010).

Eighth Circuit: Ritrama, Inc. v. HDI-Gerling America Insurance Co., 796 F.3d 962 (8th Cir. 2015); Owatonna Clinic-Mayo Health System v. Medical Protective Company of Fort Wayne, Ind., 639 F.3d 806 (8th Cir. 2011).

Ninth Circuit: Westport Insurance Corp. v. Markham Group, Inc., 403 Fed. Appx. 264 (9th Cir. 2010); Eastwood Insurance Services, Inc. v. U.S. Specialty Insurance Co., 391 Fed. Appx. 611 (9th Cir. 2010); Moody v. American Guarantee and Liability Insurance Co., 804 F. Supp.2d 1123 (W.D. Wash. 2011); Prime Insurance Syndicate, Inc. v. Damaso, 471 F. Supp.2d 1087 (D. Nev. 2007).

Tenth Circuit: Cohen-Esrey Real Estate Services, Inc. v. Twin City Fire Insurance Co., 636 F.3d 1300 (10th Cir. 2011).

Eleventh Circuit: Eddy v. Continental Casualty Co., 784 F. Supp.2d 1331 (M.D. Fla. 2011); Jennings Construction Services Corp. v. Ace American Insurance Co., 783 F. Supp.2d 1209 (M.D. Fla. 2011); Simpson & Creasy, P.C. v. Continental Casualty Co., 770 F. Supp.2d 1351 (S.D. Ga. 2011); Office Depot, Inc. v. National Union Fire Insurance Company of Pittsburgh, Pa., 734 F. Supp.2d 1304 (S.D. Fla. 2010).

District of Columbia Circuit: Capitol Specialty Insurance Corp. v. Sanford Wittels & Heisler, L.L.P., 793 F. Supp.2d 399 (D.D.C. 2011).

State Courts:

California: Feldman v. Illinois Union Insurance Co., 198 Cal. App.4th 1495, 130 Cal. Rptr.3d 770 (2011).

Delaware: Axis Reinsurance Co. v. HLTH Corp., 993 A.2d 1057 (Del. 2010).

Florida: Acosta, Inc. v. National Union Fire Insurance Co., 39 So.3d 565 (Fla. App. 2010).

Illinois: Illinois Insurance Guaranty Fund v. Chicago Insurance Co., 2014 IL App (5th) 140033-U (2015).

Indiana: Ashby v. Bar Plan Mutual Insurance Co., 949 N.E.2d 307 (Ind. 2011); Bar Plan Mutual Insurance Co. v. Likes Law Office, L.L.C., 2015 Ind. App. LEXIS 680 (Ind. App. Oct. 15, 2015).

Louisiana: Wright v. Willis-Knighton Medical Center, 57 So.3d 382 (La. App. 2011); Bell v. Parry, 61 So.3d 1 (La. App. 2010).

Maryland: Sherwood Brands, Inc. v. Great American Insurance Co., 418 Md. 300, 13 A.3d 1268 (2011).

Missouri: Todd v. Missouri United School Insurance Council, 2007 WL 1532741 (Mo. May 29, 2007).

Nebraska: Countryside Co-op. v. Harry A. Koch Co., 280 Neb. 795, 790 N.W.2d 873 (2010).

New York: CPA Mutual Insurance Company of America Risk Retention Group v. Weiss & Co., 80 A.D.3d 431, 915 N.Y.S.2d 57 (N.Y. App. Div. 2011); McCabe v. St. Paul Fire & Marine Insurance Co., 79 A.D.3d 1612, 914 N.Y.S.2d 814 (N.Y. App. Div. 2010).

Pennsylvania: Fletcher v. Pennsylvania Property & Casualty Insurance Guarantee Association, 27 A.3d 299 (Pa. Commw. 2011); West Penn Allegheny Health System v. Medical Care Availability and Reduction of Error Fund, 11 A.3d 598 (Pa. Commw. 2010).

Texas: Reeves County v. Houston Casualty Co., 356 S.W.2d 664 (Tex. App. 2011).

118 See, e.g.:

First Circuit: Bauz-Gonzalez v. Presbyterian Community Hospital, 60 F. Supp.3d 324 (D.P.R. 2014); Gargano v. Liberty International Underwriters, Inc., 575 F. Supp.2d 300 (D. Mass. 2008).

Second Circuit: United National Insurance Co. v. Granoff, Walker & Forlenza, P.C., 598 F. Supp.2d 540 (S.D.N.Y. 2009); American Home Assurance Co. v. Abrams, 69 F. Supp.2d 339 (D. Conn. 1999).

Third Circuit: American Automobile Insurance Co. v. Murray, 658 F.3d 311 (3d Cir. 2011); McMillen Engineering, Inc. v. Travelers Indemnity Co., 744 F. Supp.2d 416 (W.D. Pa. 2010).

Fourth Circuit: Humane Society of the United States v. National Union Fire Insurance Co. of Pittsburgh, Pa., 2015 U.S. Dist. LEXIS 100003 (D. Md. July 30, 2015).

Fifth Circuit: Brumfield v. Shelton, 831 F. Supp. 562 (E.D. La. 1993).

Sixth Circuit: State Farm Fire and Casualty Co. v. Estes, 2015 U.S. Dist. LEXIS 126235 (W.D. Ky. Sept. 22, 2015); Michigan Millers Mutual Insurance Co. v. Fidelity and Deposit Company of Maryland, 809 F. Supp.2d 702 (W.D. Mich. 2011).

Eighth Circuit: Ritrama, Inc. v. HDI-Gerling America Insurance Co., 796 F.3d 962 (8th Cir. 2015); Philadelphia Consolidated Holding Corp. v. LSI-Lowery Systems, Inc., 775 F.3d 1072 (8th Cir. 2015); Metropolitan Property and Casualty Insurance Co. v. Westport Insurance Corp., 2015 U.S. Dist. LEXIS 125049 (D. Neb. Sept. 18, 2015).

Ninth Circuit: Oregon Schools Activities Association v. National Union Fire Insurance Company of Pittsburgh, 279 Fed. Appx. 494 (9th Cir. 2008); Burns v. International Insurance Co., 929 F.2d 1422 (9th Cir. 1991); Moody v. American Guarantee and Liability Insurance Co., 804 F. Supp.2d 1123 (W.D. Wash. 2011).

Tenth Circuit: Axis Surplus Insurance Co. v. Johnson, 2008 WL 4525409 (N.D. Okla. Oct. 3, 2008); Schleusner v. Continental Casualty Co., 102 F. Supp.3d 1148 (D. Mont. 2015).

Eleventh Circuit: Direct General Insurance Co. v. Houston Casualty Co., 2015 U.S. Dist. LEXIS 143847 (S.D. Fla. Sept. 30, 2015); Jennings Construction Services Corp. v. Ace American Insurance Co., 783 F. Supp.2d 1209 (M.D. Fla. 2011); Simpson & Creasy, P.C. v. Continental Casualty Co., 770 F. Supp.2d 1351 (S.D. Ga. 2011).

State Courts:

California: Slater v. Lawyers' Mutual Insurance Co., 227 Cal. App.3d 1415, 278 Cal. Rptr. 479, 481–483 (1991).

Colorado: Craft v. Philadelphia Indemnity Co., 343 P.3d 951 (Colo. 2015).

Connecticut: ITC Investments, Inc. v. Employers Reinsurance Corp., 2000 WL 1996233 (Conn. Super. Dec. 11, 2000).

Delaware: Homsey Architects, Inc. v. Harry David Zutz Insurance, Inc., 2000 WL 973285, at *12 (Del. Super. May 25, 2000).

Indiana: Bar Plan Mutual Insurance Co. v. Likes Law Office, L.L.C., 2015 Ind. App. LEXIS 680 (Ind. App. Oct. 15, 2015).

Kansas: American Special Risk Management Corp. v. Cahow, 286 Kan. 1134, 192 P.3d 614 (Kan. 2008).

Louisiana: Hood v. Cotter, 5 So.3d 819 (La. 2008); Lalonde v. Vallot, 168 So.3d 457 (La. App. 2014).

Nebraska: Countryside Co-op. v. Harry A. Koch Co., 280 Neb. 795, 790 N.W.2d 873 (2010).

New Jersey: Zuckerman v. National Union Fire Insurance Co., 100 N.J. 304, 495 A.2d 395, 406 (N.J. 1985).

North Carolina: Eagle Engineering, Inc. v. Continental Casualty Co., 191 N.C. App. 593, 664 S.E.2d 62 (2008).

Oklahoma: Chandler v. Valentine, 330 P.3d 1209 (Okla. 2014).

Pennsylvania: Warrantech Consumer Products Services, Inc. v. Reliance Insurance Company in Liquidation, 626 Pa. 218, 96 A.3d 346 (2014); Gingerlowski v. Commonwealth of Pennsylvania, Insurance Department, 961 A.2d 237 (Pa. 2008); Ace American Insurance Co. v. Underwriters at Lloyds and Companies, 939 A.2d 935 (Pa. Super. 2007).

Texas: Prodigy Communications Corp. v. Agricultural Excess & Surplus Insurance Co., 288 S.W.3d 374 (Tex. 2009).

West Virginia: West Virginia Mutual Insurance Co. v. Adkins, 234 W. Va. 226, 764 S.E.2d 757 (2014).

Wisconsin: Anderson v. Aul, 361 Wis.2d 63, 862 N.W.2d 304 (2015).

But see, Northwestern Title Security Co. v. Flack, 6 Cal. App.3d 134, 85 Cal. Rptr. 693, 698 (1970).

119 Brumfield v. Shelton, 831 F. Supp. 562 (E.D. La. 1993). See also, Sapp v. Greif, 141 F.3d 1185 (10th Cir. 1998) (finding inadequate notice because notice letter was too general and vague and failed to mention the specific loans that gave rise to claims).

One commentator has opined that the result in *Brumfield, supra,* may have been brought about by the insurance industry's stacking the deck in getting a number of previous decisions favorable to policyholders de-published or abandoned: See Works, "Excusing Non-occurrence of Insurance Policy Conditions in Order to Avoid Disproportionate Forfeiture: Claims-Made Formats as a Test Case," 5 Conn. Ins. L.J. 505, 538–543 (1999).

120 Northwestern Title Security Co. v. Flack, 6 Cal. App.3d 134, 85 Cal. Rptr. 693, 698 (Cal. App. 1970). See also:

Ninth Circuit: Mt. Hawley Insurance Co. v. Federal Savings & Loan Insurance Corp., 695 F. Supp. 469 (C.D. Cal. 1987) (applying California law).

State Courts:

California: Village Escrow Co. v. National Union Fire Insurance Co., 248 Cal. Rptr. 687, 691 (Cal. App. 1988).

Maryland: Sherwood Brands, Inc. v. Great American Insurance Co., 418 Md. 300, 13 A.3d 1268 (2011).

New York: McCabe v. St. Paul Fire & Marine Insurance Co., 79 A.D.3d 1612, 914 N.Y.S.2d 814 (N.Y. App. Div. 2010).

121 See:

Eleventh Circuit: Direct General Insurance Co. v. Houston Casualty Co., 2015 U.S. Dist. LEXIS 143847 (S.D. Fla. Sept. 30, 2015).

State Courts:

California: Root v. American Equity Specialty Insurance Co., 130 Cal. App.4th 926, 30 Cal. Rptr.3d 631 (2005).

122 For instance, in Ameriwood Industries International Corp. v. American Casualty Co., 840 F. Supp. 1143, 1152 (W.D. Mich. 1993), insurance coverage was denied even though a subsequent amended complaint was filed that included different claims against different individuals and notice was promptly given on the amended complaint.

Whenever a claim is filed, whatever kind of claim it might be, one of the immediate and necessary responses must be: Is there insurance coverage? It is also important to recognize that a claim or lawsuit can potentially trigger coverage under many separate lines of coverage: general liability policies; D&O insurance; E&O insurance; as well as a number of other specialized business policies. Notice must be given promptly and to all possible insurance companies under all possible lines of coverage.

See also:

Fifth Circuit: Westport Insurance Corp. v. Cotten Schmidt, LLP, 605 F. Supp.2d 796, (N.D. Tex. 2009).

[123] See:

Second Circuit: Zunenshine v. Executive Risk Indemnity, Inc., 1998 WL 483475 (S.D.N.Y. Aug. 17, 1998), *aff'd* 182 F.3d 902 (2d Cir. 1999); Nomura Holding America, Inc. v. Federal Insurance Co., 45 F. Supp.3d 354 (S.D.N.Y. 2014).

Third Circuit: Borough of Moosic v. Darwin National Assurance Co., 556 Fed. Appx. 92 (3d Cir. 2014).

Fourth Circuit: Atlantic Permanent Federal Savings & Loan v. American Casualty Company of Reading, Pennsylvania, 839 F.2d 212, 219–220 (4th Cir.), *cert. denied* 486 U.S. 1056 (1988); Darwin National Assurance Co. v. Matthews & Megna L.L.C., 36 F. Supp.3d 636 (D.S.C. 2014); ACE American Insurance Co. v. Ascend One Corp., 570 F. Supp.2d 789 (D. Md. 2008).

Fifth Circuit: John M. O'Quinn P.C. v. National Union Fire Insurance Co. of Pittsburgh, PA, 33 F. Supp.3d 756 (S.D. Tex. 2014).

Sixth Circuit: Lafayette Life Insurance Co. v. Arch Insurance Co., 784 F. Supp.2d 1034 (N.D. Ind. 2011).

Seventh Circuit: Community Bank v. Progressive Casualty Insurance Co., 2010 WL 2985932 (S.D. Ind. July 27, 2010).

Eighth Circuit: McCuen v. American Casualty Company of Reading, Pennsylvania, 946 F.2d 1401, 1407–1408 (8th Cir. 1991).

Ninth Circuit: Eastwood Insurance Services, Inc. v. U.S. Specialty Insurance Co., 391 Fed. Appx. 611 (9th Cir. 2010).

Tenth Circuit: Templeton v. Catlin Specialty Insurance Co., 612 Fed. Appx. 940 (10th Cir. 2015).

Eleventh Circuit: Zodiac Group, Inc. v. Axis Surplus Insurance Co., 542 Fed. Appx. 844 (11th Cir. 2013); Direct General Insurance Co. v. Houston Casualty Co., 2015 U.S. Dist. LEXIS 143847 (S.D. Fla. Sept. 30, 2015); Worthington Federal Bank v. Everest National Insurance Co., 2015 U.S. Dist. LEXIS 85888 (N.D. Ala. June 4, 2015); Langdale Co. v. National Union Fire Insurance Company of Pittsburgh, PA, 2014 U.S. Dist. LEXIS 184163 (N.D. Ga. June 4, 2014).

State Courts:

California: Feldman v. Illinois Union Insurance Co., 198 Cal. App.4th 1495, 130 Cal. Rptr.3d 770 (2011).

Connecticut: Southridge Capital Management, LLC v. Twin City Fire Insurance Co., 2006 WL 2730312 (Conn. Super. Sept. 8, 2006).

Florida: Gidney v. Axis Surplus Insurance Co., 140 So.3d 609 (Fla. App. 2014).

Louisiana: Wright v. Willis-Knighton Medical Center, 57 So.3d 382 (La. App. 2011).

New York: CPA Mutual Insurance Company of America Risk Retention Group v. Weiss & Co., 80 A.D.3d 431, 915 N.Y.S.2d 57 (N.Y. App. Div. 2011).

Oregon: Oregon State Bar Professional Liability Fund v. Benfit, 225 Or. App. 409, 201 P.3d 936 (Or. App. 2009).

Texas: Burks v. XL Specialty Insurance Co., 2015 Tex. App. LEXIS 9638 (Tex. App. Sept. 15, 2015); Reeves County v. Houston Casualty Co., 356 S.W.2d 664 (Tex. App. 2011).

[124] See:

Second Circuit: Nomura Holding America, Inc. v. Federal Insurance Co., 45 F. Supp.3d 354 (S.D.N.Y. 2014).

Third Circuit: Borough of Moosic v. Darwin National Assurance Co., 556 Fed. Appx. 92 (3d Cir. 2014); Lehigh Valley Health Network v. Executive Risk Indemnity, Inc., 2001 WL 21505, at *8 (E.D. Pa. Jan. 10, 2001).

Fourth Circuit: Atlantic Permanent Federal Savings & Loan v. American Casualty Company of Reading, Pennsylvania, 839 F.2d 212, 219–220 (4th Cir.), *cert. denied* 486 U.S. 1056 (1988); Darwin National Assurance Co. v. Matthews & Megna L.L.C., 36 F. Supp.3d 636 (D.S.C. 2014).

Fifth Circuit: John M. O'Quinn P.C. v. National Union Fire Insurance Co. of Pittsburgh, PA, 33 F. Supp.3d 756 (S.D. Tex. 2014).

Eighth Circuit: Polychron v. Crum & Forster Insurance Co., 916 F.2d 461 (8th Cir. 1990); McCuen v. American Casualty Company of Reading, Pennsylvania, 946 F.2d 1401, 1407–1408 (8th Cir. 1991).

Eleventh Circuit: Zodiac Group, Inc. v. Axis Surplus Insurance Co., 542 Fed. Appx. 844 (11th Cir. 2013); Direct General Insurance Co. v. Houston Casualty Co., 2015 U.S. Dist. LEXIS 143847 (S.D. Fla. Sept. 30, 2015); Worthington Federal Bank v. Everest National Insurance Co., 2015 U.S. Dist. LEXIS 85888 (N.D. Ala. June 4, 2015); Langdale Co. v. National Union Fire Insurance Company of Pittsburgh, PA, 2014 U.S. Dist. LEXIS 184163 (N.D. Ga. June 4, 2014).

State Courts:

Florida: Gidney v. Axis Surplus Insurance Co., 140 So.3d 609 (Fla. App. 2014).

Oregon: Oregon State Bar Professional Liability Fund v. Benfit, 225 Or. App. 409, 201 P.3d 936 (2009).

Texas: Burks v. XL Specialty Insurance Co., 2015 Tex. App. LEXIS 9638 (Tex. App. Sept. 15, 2015).

125 In Lehigh Valley Health Network v. Executive Risk Indemnity, Inc., 2001 WL 21505, (E.D. Pa. Jan. 10, 2001), a doctor sued a hospital for failing to consider a candidate to whom the doctor proposed granting medical staff privileges at the hospital. The hospital's insurance company defended and indemnified the hospital for this litigation. Approximately two years later, the proposed candidate also sued the hospital based on the same application and consideration process. The insurance company that insured the hospital at the time of the second lawsuit denied coverage for this second lawsuit based on a "Related Claims" provision linking it back to the first "claim." The court disagreed, holding that the hospital was entitled to coverage:

> "[T]here must be some reasonable limitation to the succession of claims which could be excluded under [an insurance policy]. Courts have already noted the word 'related' does not encompass every conceivable logical relationship. 'A relationship between two claims might be so attenuated or unusual that an objectively reasonable insured could not have expected that they would be treated as a single claim under the policy.'" *Id.*, at *8.

In reaching this conclusion, the court reasoned that, "[a]lthough there is a modicum of overlap between the two suits, their connection is too attenuated to constitute a single claim." *Id.*, at *9. Governing the court's decision were the facts that each of the two suits was filed by a different plaintiff and that the second of the suits (filed by the candidate) alleged "distinctive," "specific," and "direct" injuries on behalf of the candidate. Significantly, the court also cited the fact that the first lawsuit did not even mention the candidate, but rather, that the candidate's name was only raised in a subsequent petition to enforce the settlement agreement reached in the first lawsuit. The court held that with respect to the "Related Claims" provision, "what governs is the initial claim brought by [the first lawsuit] and not later developments in the lawsuit." See also:

Fourth Circuit: Atlantic Permanent Federal Savings & Loan v. American Casualty Company of Reading, Pennsylvania, 839 F.2d 212, 219–220 (4th Cir.), *cert. denied* 486 U.S. 1056 (1988) (claims arising from nine loan transactions comprised a single loss because they arose from a series of interrelated acts—"the planning and carrying out of [the S&L's]

home improvement loan program"); ACE American Insurance Co. v. Ascend One Corp., 570 F. Supp.2d 789 (D. Md. 2008).

Eighth Circuit: Polychron v. Crum & Forster Insurance Co., 916 F.2d 461 (8th Cir. 1990) (grand jury investigation constituted a claim during the policy period and the subsequent indictment, which occurred after the policy expired, was part of the same claim as the investigation, and thus covered by the policy); McCuen v. American Casualty Company of Reading, Pennsylvania, 946 F.2d 1401, 1407–1408 (8th Cir. 1991) (directors and officers of savings and loan were sued in underlying action for breach of fiduciary duty and negligent management; in the coverage action, insurer argued there were three claims because there were three borrowers; policyholder argued there were seventeen separate loans and therefore seventeen separate claims; policy held ambiguous with the ambiguity resolved in favor of covering seventeen separate claims).

State Courts:

Connecticut: Southridge Capital Management, LLC v. Twin City Fire Insurance Co., 2006 WL 2730312 (Conn. Super. Sept. 8, 2006).

But see:

Oregon: Oregon State Bar Professional Liability Fund v. Benfit, 225 Or. App. 409, 201 P.3d 936 (2009) (investor claims against attorney arising from sale of membership interests in limited liability company were interrelated to claims against another attorney for merger of limited liability company and exchange of membership interests for stock shares).

126 See, e.g.:

First Circuit: Clark School for Creative Learning, Inc. v. Philadelphia Indemnity Insurance Co., 734 F.3d 51 (1st Cir. 2013); Gandor v. Torus National Insurance Co., 2015 U.S. Dist. LEXIS 140542 (D. Mass. Oct. 15, 2015).

Second Circuit: Nomura Holding America, Inc. v. Federal Insurance Co., 45 F. Supp.3d 354 (S.D.N.Y. 2014).

Third Circuit: Ettinger & Associates, L.L.C. v. Hartford/Twin City Fire Insurance Co., 22 F. Supp.3d 447 (E.D. Pa. 2014); Fishman v. The Hartford, 980 F. Supp.2d 672 (E.D. Pa. 2013); McMillen Engineering, Inc. v. Travelers Indemnity Co., 744 F. Supp.2d 416 (W.D. Pa. 2010).

Fourth Circuit: Bryan Brothers, Inc. v. Continental Casualty Co., 660 F.3d 827 (4th Cir. 2011); Humane Society of the United States v. National Union Fire Insurance Co. of Pittsburgh, Pa., 2015 U.S. Dist. LEXIS 100003 (D. Md. July 30, 2015).

Fifth Circuit: Regency Title Co. v. Westchester Fire Insurance Co., 5 F. Supp.3d 836 (E.D. Tex. 2013).

Sixth Circuit: Realcomp II, Ltd. v. Ace American Insurance Co., 46 F. Supp.3d 736 (E.D. Mich. 2014).

Seventh Circuit: James River Insurance Co. v. Kemper Casualty Insurance Co., 585 F.3d 382 (7th Cir. 2009).

Eighth Circuit: Ritrama, Inc. v. HDI-Gerling America Insurance Co., 796 F.3d 962 (8th Cir. 2015); LSI-Lowery Systems, Inc., 775 F.3d 1072 (8th Cir. 2015); George K. Baum & Co. v. Twin City Fire Insurance Co., 760 F.3d 795 (8th Cir. 2014).

Ninth Circuit: Westport Insurance Corp. v. Markham Group, Inc., 403 Fed. Appx. 264 (9th Cir. 2010); Millennium Laboratories, Inc. v. Allied World Insurance Co., 2015 U.S. Dist. LEXIS 133534 (C.D. Cal. Sept. 30, 2015); HB Development, L.L.C. v. Western Pacific Mutual Insurance Co., 86 F. Supp.3d 1164 (E.D. Wash. 2015).

Tenth Circuit: Cohen-Esrey Real Estate Services, Inc. v. Twin City Fire Insurance Co., 636 F.3d 1300 (10th Cir. 2011).

Eleventh Circuit: Worthington Federal Bank v. Everest National Insurance Co., 2015 U.S. Dist. LEXIS 85888 (N.D. Ala. June 4, 2015).

District of Columbia Circuit: Capitol Specialty Insurance Corp. v. Sanford Wittels & Heisler, L.L.P., 793 F. Supp.2d 399 (D.D.C. 2011).

State Courts:

California: Crown Capital Securities, L.P. v. Endurance American Specialty Insurance Co., 235 Cal. App.4th 1122, 186 Cal. Rptr.3d 115 (2015).

Delaware: Axis Reinsurance Co. v. HLTH Corp., 993 A.2d 1057 (Del. 2010).

Florida: Acosta, Inc. v. National Union Fire Insurance Co., 39 So.3d 565 (Fla. App. 2010).

Indiana: Bar Plan Mutual Insurance Co. v. Likes Law Office, L.L.C., 2015 Ind. App. LEXIS 680 (Ind. App. Oct. 15, 2015).

Missouri: Fremont Indemnity Co. v. Lawton-Byrne-Bruner Insurance Agency Co., 701 S.W.2d 737 (Mo. App. 1985).

New York: Sirius XM Radio, Inc. v. XL Speciality Insurance Co., 117 A.D.3d 652, 987 N.Y.S.2d 324 (N.Y. App. Div. 2014); CPA Mutual Insurance Company of America Risk Retention Group v. Weiss & Co., 80 A.D.3d 431, 915 N.Y.S.2d 57 (N.Y. App. Div. 2011).

See also, Long, *The Law of Liability Insurance* Vol. 3, § 12E.03[1].

[127] An example of how this situation might arise occurred in Fremont Indemnity Co. v. Lawton-Byrne-Bruner Insurance Agency Co., 701 S.W.2d 737 (Mo. App. 1985), in which Illinois Union sold an E&O policy to an insurance broker covering claims made between September 1, 1981 and September 1, 1982, and Fremont Indemnity sold an E&O policy to the same broker covering claims made between September 1, 1982 and September 1, 1983. For years, the broker had been selling insurance to a hospital. However, as a result of competitive bidding, the hospital discovered that the broker may have been failing to obtain cost-effective insurance. Consequently, in April 1982, during Illinois Union's policy period, the hospital wrote a complaint to the state insurance commissioner, which forwarded a copy to the broker for a response. In May 1982, the broker responded, and the insurance commissioner dismissed the matter. Later, in September 1982, during Fremont's policy period, the hospital initiated a lawsuit against the broker for failure to obtain cost-efficient insurance. Both insurance companies contested coverage. Illinois Union successfully argued that the letter to the insurance commissioner did not constitute a "claim." Fremont Indemnity argued that prior to its policy period's inception, the broker had knowledge or reasonably should have foreseen of circumstances that might lead to a claim, due to the same insurance commissioner letter. Fortunately, for the policyholder, Fremont Indemnity was unsuccessful in its argument.

See also, Evanston Insurance Co. v. GAB Business Services, Inc., 132 A.D.2d 180, 521 N.Y.S.2d 692 (N.Y. App. Div. 1987).

[128] See:

Texas: Yancey v. Floyd West & Co., 755 S.W.2d 914 (Tex. App. 1988).

Washington: Swift v. American Home Assurance Co., 22 Wash. App. 777, 591 P.2d 1216 (1979).

[129] In Yancey v. Floyd West & Co., 755 S.W.2d 914 (Tex. App. 1988), an insurance agent owning his own agency was insured by E&O policies covering claims made between July 14, 1980 and July 14, 1982. On April 1, 1982, the agent sold his agency to a competitor and became an employee of the competitor. The competitor's insurance policy provided coverage for claims made between January 29, 1982 and January 29, 1983. On September 10, 1982, the business was sold, a former client of the agent sued the agent for failure to submit an application for flood insurance as requested in October 1981 when the agent worked for his own agency. The agent sought coverage under his own agency's prior E&O policy and his competitor's E&O policy. The court found no coverage existed for the claim. The agent's own policy provided no coverage because the claims occurred after the expiration of that policy period. The competitor's policy provided no coverage because the retroactive date for the agent's becoming a named insured under that policy was April 23, 1982.

Similarly, in Swift v. American Home Assurance Co., 22 Wash. App. 777, 591 P.2d 1216 (1979), an insurance broker mistakenly failed to include a parsonage on the property insured under a client's property insurance policy. After the broker changed employers, the parsonage, which was inadvertently omitted from coverage, was destroyed by fire. The client sued the broker for losses arising from the error. The broker tendered the matter to his current employer's E&O carrier. The court held that no coverage existed for the claim because the broker's prior acts were committed while working for someone other than the policyholder.

130 See, e.g.: Jefferson Insurance Company of New York v. Travelers Indemnity Co., 92 N.Y.2d 363, 681 N.Y.S.2d 208, 212, 703 N.E.2d 1221 (1998); Continental Casualty Co. v. Rapid-American Corp., 80 N.Y.2d 640, 593 N.Y.S.2d 966, 972, 609 N.E.2d 506 (1993).

131 See, e.g., §3.02[2], *supra*. See also:

First Circuit: U.S. Liability Insurance Co. v. Benchmark Construction Services, Inc., 797 F.3d 116 (1st Cir. 2015); Pfeiffer v. American Alternative Insurance Corp., 2015 U.S. Dist. LEXIS 153299 (D.R.I. Nov. 12, 2015).

Second Circuit: Sea Insurance Co. v. Westchester Fire Insurance Co., 51 F.3d 22, 25 n.4 (2d Cir. 1995).

Third Circuit: American Automobile Insurance Co. v. Murray, 658 F.3d 311 (3d Cir. 2011); Heebner v. Nationwide Insurance Enterprise, 818 F. Supp.2d 853 (E.D. Pa. 2011).

Fourth Circuit: Westfield Insurance Co. v. Pinnacle Group, L.L.C., 2015 U.S. Dist. LEXIS 136669 (S.D. W. Va. Oct. 7, 2015).

Fifth Circuit: American Home Assurance Co. v. Cat Tech L.L.C., 660 F.3d 216 (5th Cir. 2011).

Sixth Circuit: Park-Ohio Holdings Corp. v. Liberty Mutual Fire Insurance Co., 2015 U.S. Dist. LEXIS 147602 (N.D. Ohio Oct. 30, 2015).

Seventh Circuit: Little Lady Foods, Inc. v. Houston Casualty Co., 879 F. Supp.2d 759 (N.D. Ill. 2011).

Eighth Circuit: Tactical Stop-Loss, L.L.C. v. Travelers Casualty and Surety Company of America, 657 F.3d 757 (8th Cir. 2011).

Ninth Circuit: Probuilders Specialty Insurance Co. v. Coaker, 2015 U.S. Dist. LEXIS 152789 (W.D. Wash. Nov. 10, 2015).

Tenth Circuit: BancInsure, Inc. v. FDIC, 796 F.3d 1226 (10th Cir. 2015).

Eleventh Circuit: E.S.Y., Inc. v. Scottsdale Insurance Co., 2015 U.S. Dist. LEXIS 143848 (S.D. Fla. Oct. 14, 2015).

State Courts:

California: Wallman v. Suddock, 200 Cal. App.4th 1288, 134 Cal. Rptr.3d 566 (2011); Palp, Inc. v. Williamsburg National Insurance Co., 200 Cal. App.4th 282, 132 Cal. Rptr.3d 592 (2011).

Florida: State Farm Mutual Automobile Insurance Co. v. Menendez, 70 So.2d 566 (Fla. 2011).

Georgia: Laun v. AXA Equitable Life Insurance Co., 311 Ga. App. 646, 716 S.E.2d 760 (2011).

Indiana: Dodd v. American Family Mutual Insurance Co., 956 N.E.2d 769 (Ind. App. 2011).

Minnesota: Latterell v. Progressive Northern Insurance Co., 801 N.W.2d 917 (Minn. 2011).

New York: Breed v. Insurance Company of North America, 46 N.Y.2d 351, 413 N.Y.S.2d 352, 357, 385 N.E.2d 1280 (1978); Farm Family Casualty Insurance Co. v. Nason, 89 A.D.3d 1401, 932 N.Y.S.2d 275 (N.Y. App. Div. 2011).

Wisconsin: Progressive Northern Insurance Co. v. Jacobson, 337 Wis.2d 533, 804 N.W.2d 838 (2011).

[132] See:

Fourth Circuit: Federal Insurance Co. v. Evian Horizontal Property Regime, 126 Fed. Appx. 589 (4th Cir. 2005); Resource Bank v. Progressive Casualty Insurance Co., 503 F. Supp.2d 789 (E.D. Va. 2007).

Sixth Circuit: Reed v. Netherlands Insurance, Co., 860 F. Supp.2d 407 (E.D. Mich. 2012); Lifeline Health Group, Inc. v. National Union Fire Insurance Company of Pittsburgh, PA, 665 F. Supp.2d 770 (W.D. Ky. 2009).

Eleventh Circuit: Maryland Casualty Co. v. Florida Atlantic Orthopedics, P.L., 469 Fed. Appx. 722 (11th Cir. 2012); James River Insurance Co. v. Maier, 795 F. Supp.2d 1378 (S.D. Ga. 2011).

State Courts:

Illinois: Rosalind Franklin University of Medicine and Science v. Lexington Insurance Co., 2014 IL App (1st) 113755, 8 N.E.3d 20, 380 Ill. Dec. 89 (2014).

Louisiana: Haun v. Cusimano, Inc., 86 So.3d 84 (La. App. 2012).

Maryland: Philadelphia Indemnity Insurance Co. v. Maryland Yacht Club, Inc., 129 Md. App. 455, 742 A.2d 79 (1999).

New Jersey: Somerset Medical Center v. Executive Risk Indemnity, Inc., 2010 N.J. Super. Unpub. LEXIS 605 (App. Div. 2010).

South Carolina: Pulliam v. Travelers Indemnity Co., 403 S.C. 332, 743 S.E.2d 117 (S.C. App. 2013).

[133] See:

First Circuit: Cytosol Laboratories, Inc. v. Federal Insurance Co., 536 F. Supp.2d 80 (D. Mass. 2008).

Second Circuit: Employers Insurance of Wausau v. Duplan Corp., 899 F. Supp. 1112 (S.D.N.Y. 1995).

Third Circuit: Covington Township v. Pacific Employers Insurance Co., 639 F. Supp. 793 (M.D. Pa. 1986).

Fourth Circuit: Resource Bank v. Progressive Casualty Insurance Co., 503 F. Supp.2d 789 (E.D. Va. 2007).

Fifth Circuit: Evanston Insurance Co. v. Forest Oil Corp., 2015 U.S. Dist. LEXIS 105827 (W.D. La. Aug. 10, 2015); Carolina Casualty Insurance Co. v. Sowell, 603 F. Supp.2d 914 (N.D. Tex. 2009).

Sixth Circuit: Reed v. Netherlands Insurance, Co., 860 F. Supp.2d 407 (E.D. Mich. 2012).

Eleventh Circuit: Eastpointe Condominium I Association, Inc. v. Travelers Casualty and Surety Company of America, 379 Fed. Appx. 906 (11th Cir. 2010).

State Courts:

New York: Scharf v. Federal Insurance Co., 261 A.D.2d 257, 690 N.Y.S.2d 265 (N.Y. App. Div. 1999); Board of Managers of Yardarm Condominium II v. Federal Insurance Co., 260 A.D.2d 6, 669 N.Y.S.2d 332 (N.Y. App. Div. 1998).

[134] See:

First Circuit: Welch Foods, Inc. v. National Union Fire Insurance Company of Pittsburgh, PA, 659 F.3d 191 (1st Cir. 2011).

Sixth Circuit: Reed v. Netherlands Insurance Co., 860 F. Supp.2d 407 (E.D. Mich. 2012).

Seventh Circuit: Lemko Corp. v. Federal Insurance Co., 70 F. Supp.3d 905 (N.D. Ill. 2014).

Eleventh Circuit: MedAssets, Inc. v. Federal Insurance Co., 705 F. Supp.2d 1368 (N.D. Ga. 2010).

State Courts:

California: Feldman v. Illinois Union Insurance Co., 198 Cal. App.4th 1495, 130 Cal. Rptr.3d 770 (2011).

135 See, e.g.:

Second Circuit: Hollis Park Manor Nursing Home v. Landmark American Insurance Co., 803 F. Supp.2d 205 (E.D.N.Y. 2011) (professional services exclusion included in D&O policy).

Ninth Circuit: Corky McMillin Construction Services, Inc. v. U.S. Specialty Insurance Co., 597 Fed. Appx. 925 (9th Cir. 2015) (E&O policy not applied in D&O policy).

Tenth Circuit: Western Heritage Bank v. Federal Insurance Co., 557 Fed. Appx. 807 (10th Cir. 2014) (professional services exclusion included in D&O policy).

State Courts:

Hawaii: Keown v. Tudor Insurance Co., 129 Haw. 64, 293 P.3d 137 (Haw. App. 2012) (D&O exclusion in professional liability policy).

Wisconsin: Marks v. Houston Casualty Co., 363 Wis.2d 505, 866 N.W.2d 393 (Wis. App. 2015) (D&O exclusion in professional liability policy).

136 See, e.g.:

First Circuit: New Fed Mortgage Corp. v. National Union Fire Insurance Company of Pittsburgh, PA, 543 F.3d 7 (1st Cir. 2008); Lifespan Corp. v. National Union Fire Insurance Co. of Pittsburgh, PA, 59 F. Supp.3d 427 (D.R.I. 2014) (unfair profit or advantage or fraud exclusion not applied).

Second Circuit: In re Donald Sheldon & Co., 186 B.R. 364 (Bankr. S.D.N.Y. 1995), *aff'd* 182 F.3d 899 (2d Cir. 1999) (illegal personal gain exclusion did not apply to judgment of Chapter 7 trustee of debtor corporation for damages awarded against officers of debtor for breaches of their fiduciary duty for violations of net capital rule and illegal hypothecation of securities).

Third Circuit: Alstrin v. St. Paul Mercury Insurance Co., 179 F. Supp.2d 376 (D. Del. 2002) (D&O policy's "illegal profit or advantage" exclusion required profit or gain that was itself illegal, not an illegal act that produced profit or gain as by-product).

Fourth Circuit: Protection Strategies, Inc. v. Starr Indemnity and Liability Co., 611 Fed. Appx. 775 (4th Cir. 2015) (profit and fraud exclusion applied); Graham v. National Union Fire Insurance Company of Pittsburgh, PA, 474 Fed. Appx. 956 (4th Cir. 2012) (fraud exclusion inapplicable); Farkas v. National Union Fire Insurance Co. of Pittsburgh, PA, 861 F. Supp.2d 716 (E.D. Va. 2012) (fraud or criminal act exclusion applied); Gulf Underwriters Insurance Co. v. KSI Services, Inc., 416 F. Supp.2d 417 (E.D. Va. 2006), *aff'd* 233 Fed. Appx. 239 (4th Cir. 2007) (bookkeeper's embezzlement of funds from customer's escrow account was within scope of her employment with escrow services firm and claim was excluded from coverage for insured's dishonest or criminal acts).

Fifth Circuit: Pendergest-Holt v. Certain Underwriters at Lloyd's of London, 600 F.3d 562 (5th Cir. 2010); Federal Savings & Loan Insurance Corp. v. Mmahat, 97 B.R. 293 (Bankr. E.D. La. 1988), *aff'd in part* 907 F.2d 546 (5th Cir. 1990), *cert. denied* 499 U.S. 936 (1991) (lawyer and director of financial institution, who breached his fiduciary duty as lawyer by using his position as director in furtherance of his legal business, was not covered under either his lawyer's E&O policy or institution's D&O policy based on exclusions for dishonest conduct); National Surety Corp. v. Musgrove, 310 F.2d 256 (5th Cir. 1962) (E&O policy covered claim for negligent failure to provide pilot's coverage; jury verdict that fraud exclusion did not apply was upheld because of factual issues regarding the agent's state of mind);

TIG Specialty Insurance Co. v. Pinkmonkey.com, Inc., 375 F.3d 365 (5th Cir. 2004) (personal profit exclusion, precluding coverage for any claim against insured, based on insured's gain of any personal profit, remuneration, or advantage, to which he was not legally entitled, barred coverage for judgment obtained by investors, against corporation's chief operating officer and majority shareholder in state court action for stock fraud).

Sixth Circuit: United States Fidelity & Guaranty Co. v. Fireman's Fund Insurance Co., 896 F.2d 200 (6th Cir. 1990) (E&O policy does not cover claims for intentional interference with prospective contractual relations, defamation, and violations of the consumer protection statute).

Seventh Circuit: General Star National Insurance Co. v. Adams Valuation Corp., 69 F. Supp.3d 742 (N.D. Ill. 2014) (fraud exlusion applied).

Eighth Circuit: Continental Casualty Co. v. Reed, 306 F. Supp. 1072 (D. Minn. 1969) (E&O policy covered claim by insurance company against agent for violating underwriting authority in issuing a performance bond; fraud exclusion did not apply because although agent knew or should have known he lacked authority to issue bond, there was no evidence that he intended to harm the insurance company or personally profit from the transaction); Kansas Bankers Surety Co. v. First Premier Bank, N.A., 242 F.3d 375 (8th Cir. 2000) (claims asserted against bank's chief executive officer came within personal profit exclusion from coverage under bank's directors and officers insurance policy).

Ninth Circuit: National Bank of California v. Progressive Casualty Insurance Co., 938 F. Supp.2d 919 (C.D. Cal. 2013) (fraud exclusion applied); *In re* C.M. Meiers Co., 527 B.R. 388 (Bankr. C.D. Cal. 2015) (fraud exclusion inapplicable).

Tenth Circuit: Nicholls v. Zurich American Insurance Group, 244 F. Supp.2d 1144 (D. Colo. 2003) ("personal profit" exclusion in policy applied to prevent trustee from recovering based on sham stock transaction in which parent company's officers and directors engaged, where these officers and directors received all of the proceeds directly from putative private placement of parent company's stock, and none of the funds remained with corporations).

Eleventh Circuit: First National Bank Holding Co. v. Fidelity & Deposit Company of Maryland, 885 F. Supp. 1533 (N.D. Fla. 1995) (dishonesty exclusion in D&O policy, requiring that loss be contributed to by dishonest acts of officer or director, precluded coverage for losses resulting from bank holding company's principal's crimes); International Insurance Co. v. Johns, 685 F. Supp. 1230 (S.D. Fla. 1988), *aff'd* 874 F.2d 1447 (11th Cir. 1989) (exclusion in D&O policy for illegal remuneration did not apply to exclude payments pursuant to settlement of shareholder's derivative action against insureds to recover corporate funds disbursed under management compensation plan and consulting agreement; plan was properly adopted by corporation's board of directors without shareholder approval, and consulting agreement was ratified by shareholders, and thus neither plan nor agreement constituted illegal remuneration).

State Courts:

Alabama: Graham v. Preferred Abstainers Insurance Co., 689 So.2d 188 (Ala. App. 1997) (exclusion barring coverage for acts as to which judgment or final adjudication established deliberate or intentional dishonesty did not apply to claim against minister seeking damages for conversion, fraud, and undue influence based on allegations that minister improperly obtained monies belonging to claimant conservator's deceased mother, where claim alleged reckless as well as intentional misrepresentation and no judgment had yet been entered on the claim); Gardner v. Cumis Insurance Society, Inc., 582 So.2d 1094 (Ala. 1991) (credit union officer who was tried and acquitted of criminal charges involving conspiracy and defrauding a federal credit union was not entitled to recovery of attorney fees from D&O policy because of personal profit exclusion).

Iowa: Employers Reinsurance Corp. v. Mutual Medical Plans, Inc., 504 N.W.2d 885 (Iowa 1993) (E&O policy does not cover claims for intentional interference with present or prospective economic advantage).

New York: Federal Insurance Co. v. Kozlowski, 18 A.D.2d 33, 792 N.Y.S.2d 397 (N.Y. App. Div. 2005) (personal profit exclusion did not apply to relieve insurance company of its obligation to pay all of insured's defense costs as incurred in underlying criminal proceeding and civil securities action, which contained personal profit claims; underlying actions also contained claims that did not involve personal profit, duty to defend was broader than duty to indemnify, and allocation and recoupment for cost of defense of non-covered claims would have to wait until insured's liabilities, if any, were determined).

Ohio: American Chemical Society v. Leadscope, Inc., 2005 WL 1220746 (Ohio App. May 24, 2005), appeal denied 107 Ohio St.3d 1412, 836 N.E.2d 1231 (2005) (clause in D&O policy that precluded coverage for claims attributable to the gaining "in fact" of any profit or advantage to which an insured was not legally entitled did not preclude coverage for conversion claim against policyholders brought by former employer; the phrase "in fact" as used in the clause required that a final determination that an act of conversion had taken place that resulted in the gaining of a profit or advantage before its applicability could be determined, and the mere allegation of conversion was insufficient).

137 See, e.g., Graham v. Preferred Abstainers Insurance Co., 689 So.2d 188 (Ala. App. 1997).

138 *Id.*

139 *Fifth Circuit:* National Casualty Co. v. Franklin County, Mississippi, 718 F. Supp.2d 785 (S.D. Miss. 2010).

Eleventh Circuit: Lime Tree Village Community Club Association v. State Farm General Insurance Co., 980 F.2d 1402, 1405 (11th Cir. 1993); Trizec Properties, Inc. v. Biltmore Construction Co., 767 F.2d 810, 811 (11th Cir. 1985).

State Courts:

Colorado: TerraMatrix, Inc. v. United States Fire Insurance Co., 939 P.2d 483 (Colo. App. 1997); City of Englewood v. Commercial Union Assurance Co., 940 P.2d 948 (Colo. App. 1996).

Ohio: Sanborn Plastics Corp. v. St. Paul Fire & Marine Insurance Co., 84 Ohio App.3d 302, 616 N.E.2d 988, 996 (1993).

Pennsylvania: General Accident Insurance Company of America v. Allen, 547 Pa. 693, 692 A.2d 1089, 1095 (Pa. 1997); Erie Insurance Exchange v. Transamerica Insurance Co., 516 Pa. 574, 533 A.2d 1363, 1368 (Pa. 1987).

140 *Iowa:* First Newton National Bank v. General Casualty Company of Wisconsin, 426 N.W.2d 618, 630 (Iowa 1988) (noting that partial defense is minority rule).

Oregon: Mutual of Enumclaw Insurance Co. v. Gutman, 172 Or. App. 528, 21 P.3d 101 (2001).

Washington: Waite v. Aetna Casualty & Surety Co., 77 Wash.2d 850, 467 P.2d 847, 851 (Wash. 1970).

141 *Fourth Circuit:* Atlantic Permanent Federal Savings & Loan Ass'n v. American Casualty Company of Reading, Pennsylvania, 839 F.2d 212 (4th Cir.), *cert. denied* 486 U.S. 1056 (1988) (dishonesty exclusion in officers' liability policy did not apply where there had been no final adjudication of deliberate dishonest conduct in underlying action against officer).

Fifth Circuit: Pendergest-Holt v. Certain Underwriters at Lloyd's of London, 600 F.3d 562 (5th Cir. 2010).

State Courts:

Alabama: Graham v. Preferred Abstainers Insurance Co., 689 So.2d 188 (Ala. App. 1997) (exclusion barring coverage for acts as to which judgment or final adjudication established deliberate or intentional dishonesty did not apply to claim against minister seeking damages for conversion, fraud, and undue influence based on allegations that minister improperly obtained monies belonging to claimant conservator's deceased mother, where claim alleged reckless as well as intentional misrepresentation and no judgment had yet been entered on the claim).

142 *Id.*

143 See, e.g.:

Fourth Circuit: Atlantic Permanent Federal Savings & Loan Association v. American Casualty Company of Reading, Pennsylvania., 670 F. Supp. 168, 171–172 (E.D. Va. 1986), *aff'd* 839 F.2d 212 (4th Cir. 1988) (settlement of underlying claim means that insurance company is not permitted to rely on fraud and dishonest exclusion requiring judgment or final adjudication).

Fifth Circuit: Pendergest-Holt v. Certain Underwriters at Lloyd's of London, 600 F.3d 562 (5th Cir. 2010) (similar).

144 *Id.* There is also a question of whether there is coverage when policyholder who does not commit or does not know about a fraudulent or criminal act is deprived of coverage on account of a colleague who did. This issue is discussed in connection with severability in § 10.04[3] *infra.*

145 See, e.g.:

First Circuit: Utica Mutual Insurance Co. v. Impallaria, 892 F.2d 1107 (1st Cir. 1989) (exclusion not applied to insurance company's claim for damages resulting from improperly binding insurance company to policy that resulted in significantly inadequate premiums charged because claim was not a claim for premiums).

Third Circuit: Westport Insurance Corp. v. Black, Davis & Shue Agency, Inc., 513 F. Supp.2d 157 (M.D. Pa. 2007).

Fourth Circuit: First Tennessee Bank National Ass'n v. St. Paul Fire and Marine Insurance Co., 501 Fed. Appx. 255 (4th Cir. 2012); Global Title, L.L.C. v. St. Paul Fire and Marine Insurance Co., 788 F. Supp.2d 453 (E.D. Va. 2011).

Sixth Circuit: Pattison v. Employers Reinsurance Corp., 900 F.2d 986 (6th Cir. 1990) (exclusion not applied; because claim did not seek the return of premiums, as insurance professional never received premiums that were allegedly stolen by its subagent).

Eighth Circuit: Bethel v. Darwin Select Insurance Co., 735 F.3d 1035 (8th Cir. 2013); Lexington Insurance Co. v. Integrity Land Title Co., 721 F.3d 958 (8th Cir. 2013); Murray v. Greenwich Insurance Co., 533 F.3d 644 (8th Cir. 2008); McAninch v. Wintermute, 491 F.3d 759 (8th Cir. 2007).

Ninth Circuit: Evanston Insurance Co. v. Fred A. Tucker & Co., 872 F.2d 278 (9th Cir. 1989) (exclusion applied to claim for return of premiums for insurance paid for but not bought).

State Courts:

California: GGIS Insurance Services, Inc. v. Superior Court, 168 Cal. App.4th 1493, 86 Cal. Rptr.3d 515 (2008).

Florida: St. Paul Fire & Marine Insurance Co. v. Llorente, 156 So.3d 511 (Fla. App. 2014); Chicago Title Insurance Co. v. Northland Insurance Co., 31 So.3d 214 (Fla. App. 2010).

Michigan: Five Star Real Estate, LLC v. Kemper Casualty Insurance Co., 2006 WL 1294238 (Mich. App. May 11, 2006).

Missouri: Fremont Indemnity Co. v. Lawton-Byrne-Bruner Insurance Agency Co., 701 S.W.2d 737 (Mo. App. 1985) (exclusion inapplicable to claim for procurement of cost-inefficient insurance, which was not a claim for return of premiums).

New York: Associated Community Bancorp, Inc. v. St. Paul Mercury Insurance Co., 118 A.D.3d 608, 989 N.Y.S.2d 15 (N.Y. App. Div. 2014).

Pennsylvania: Southcentral Employment Corp. v. Birmingham Fire Insurance Company of Pennsylvania, 926 A.2d 977 (Pa. Super. 2007).

146 See Chapter 8 *supra*.

147 See ISO Form CG 00 01 10 01. See also Chapter 8.

148 See ISO Form CG 00 01 10 01. In Owens Corning v. National Union Fire Insurance Co., 1998 WL 774109 (6th Cir. Oct. 13, 1998), court held that an asbestos claims exclusion in a D&O policy did not bar coverage for a shareholders' securities fraud claim based on the company's alleged misrepresentation of future financial exposure to asbestos claims. The court found the exclusion inapplicable because "the use of asbestos is not causally related to the harm alleged in the [shareholders'] complaint." *Id.*, at *5.

> "The complaint alleges that the named directors and officers were responsible for filing misleading financial-disclosure statements, resulting in an artificially inflated stock price. Only the alleged misrepresentations can be considered the cause of the artificially inflated prices. This is unchanged by the possibility that the motive behind the alleged misrepresentations was to hide the fact that the company was suffering financially from asbestos. Thus, any negligence or wrongful act by the directors and officers with regard to the use of asbestos is irrelevant here." *Id.*

Noting that the policyholder's business "largely concerns the sale of asbestos and asbestos-containing products," the court found that the insurance companies' broad reading of the asbestos claims exclusion "would swallow up all of the coverages." *Id.,* at *6.

See also, "Court Denies Federal Insurance Summary Judgment Motion in D&O Policy Case," Andrews Breast Implant Litigation Reporter, Dec. 8, 1998, p. 13, reporting that federal district court in Michigan denied a D&O insurance company's motion for summary judgment in a corporation's suit for coverage of shareholder suits brought against it for failure to disclose the company's exposure to breast implant liability litigation. The court rejected the insurer's overbroad reliance on a so-called "absolute" bodily injury exclusion.

149 See Township of Center, Butler County, Pennsylvania v. First Mercury Syndicate, Inc., 117 F.3d 115, 119 (3d Cir. 1997).

> "The primary focus of the [insured v. insured] exclusion is to prevent collusive suits in which an insured company might seek to force its insurer to pay for the poor business decisions of its officers or managers. The exclusion arose from a wave of litigation in the mid-1980's when corporations attempted to use their director and officer policies to recoup operational losses. . . . Where, however, it is clear that the underlying action is not collusive, the exclusion has not precluded coverage."

See also:

First Circuit: W. Holding Co. v. AIG Insurance Co., 748 F.3d 377 (1st Cir. 2014); Financial Resources Network, Inc. v. Brown and Brown, Inc., 754 F. Supp.2d 128 (D. Mass. 2010); Strange v. Genesis Insurance Co., 536 F. Supp.2d 71 (D. Mass. 2008).

Second Circuit: Macey v. Carolina Casualty Insurance Co., 674 F.3d 125 (2d Cir. 2012); Burke v. Ulico Casualty Co., 165 Fed. Appx. 125 (2d Cir. 2006) ("insured v. insured" exclusion in fiduciary liability insurance policy did not unambiguously exclude coverage of pension fund trustees for pension participants' breach of fiduciary duty claims against them, on ground that one of the participants originally named as a plaintiff was also an insured trustee, where claims of remaining plaintiffs did not originate from, and were not causally connected to, participant/trustee's withdrawn claim); Levy v. National Union Fire Insurance Company of Pittsburgh, Pennsylvania, 889 F.2d 433 (2d Cir. 1989) (action by corporation against former directors was excluded from coverage under D&O policy based on insured v. insured exclusion); Paraco Gas Corp. v. Travelers Casualty and Surety Co. of America, 51 F. Supp.3d 379 (S.D.N.Y. 2014); Intelligent Digital Systems, L.L.C. v. Beazley Insurance Co., 906 F. Supp.2d 80 (E.D.N.Y. 2012); Julio & Sons Co. v. Travelers Casualty & Surety Company of America, 684 F. Supp.2d 330 (S.D.N.Y.2010); *In re* County Seat Stores, Inc., 280

B.R. 319 (Bankr. S.D.N.Y. 2002) ("insured v. insured" exclusion inapplicable to prevent a trustee in bankruptcy from asserting a claim on behalf of the bankruptcy estate, which was formerly the policyholder, against the former policyholder's directors and officers); Macey v. Carolina Casualty Insurance Co., 585 F. Supp.2d 277 (D. Conn. 2008) (exclusion applied to claim by former officers against current officers).

Third Circuit: Redmond v. ACE American Insurance Co., 614 Fed. Appx. 77 (3d Cir. 2015); Foodtown, Inc. v. National Union Fire Insurance Company of Pittsburgh, PA., 412 Fed. Appx. 502 (3d Cir. 2011); Alstrin v. St. Paul Mercury Insurance Co., 179 F. Supp.2d 376 (D. Del. 2002) ("insured v. insured" exclusion in D&O policy did not apply to claims brought by bankruptcy estate representative on behalf of creditors against former executives of debtor-insured).

Fourth Circuit: Miller v. St. Paul Mercury Insurance Co., 709 F. Supp.2d 397 (D. Md. 2009); *In re* R.J. Reynolds, 315 B.R. 674 (Bankr. W.D. Va. 2003).

Fifth Circuit: In re Central Louisiana Grain Co-op., Inc., 467 B.R. 390 (Bankr. W.D. La. 2012); Medford v. Lavergne, 2010 WL 1285406 (W.D. La. March 31, 2010); Carolina Casualty Insurance Co. v. Sowell, 603 F. Supp.2d 914 (N.D. Tex. 2009) (exclusion applied to shareholder derivative suit against former officers and directors).

Sixth Circuit: Anderson-Tully Co. v. Federal Insurance Co., 347 Fed. Appx. 171 (6th Cir. 2009); Foster v. Kentucky Housing Corp., 850 F. Supp. 558 (E.D. Ky. 1994) ("insured v. insured" exclusion in D&O policy, which defined officers and directors as those persons employed as officers and directors and excluded them from coverage when sued by another policyholder, was unambiguous in excluding coverage for employee's wrongful discharge and breach of contract suit).

Seventh Circuit: Miller v. St. Paul Mercury Insurance Co., 683 F.3d 871 (7th Cir. 2012); Level 3 Communications, Inc. v. Federal Insurance Co., 168 F.3d 956 (7th Cir. 1999), rev'd on other grounds 272 F.3d 908 (7th Cir. 2001) ("insured v. insured" exclusion simply required allocation of covered and uncovered losses, with the policyholder "entitled to insurance proceeds equal to the amount of the settlement in the fraud case minus the amount that went to the [insured claimant]"); Strategic Capital Bancorp Inc. v. St. Paul Mercury Insurance Co., 723 F. Supp.2d 1053 (C.D. Ill. 2010); Link Snacks, Inc. v. Federal Insurance Co., 664 F. Supp.2d 944 (W.D. Wis. 2009).

Eighth Circuit: Westchester Fire Insurance Co. v. Wallerich, 563 F.3d 707 (8th Cir. 2009); Jerry's Enterprises, Inc. v. U.S. Specialty Insurance Co., 2015 U.S. Dist. LEXIS 126241 (D. Minn. Sept. 22, 2015); Progressive Casualty Insurance Co. v. Federal Deposit Insurance Co., 80 F. Supp.3d 923 (N.D. Iowa 2015); Thomas Engineering Co. v. Twin City Fire Insurance Co., 2010 U.S. Dist. LEXIS 127481 (D. Minn. 2010); Miller v. ACE USA, d/b/a American Insurance Co., 261 F. Supp.2d 1130 (D. Minn. 2003) ("insured v. insured" exclusion of D&O policy applied to former employee's sex discrimination action against insured executive); St. Paul Fire & Marine Insurance Co. v. FDIC, 765 F. Supp. 538 (D. Minn. 1991), *aff'd* 968 F.2d 695 (8th Cir. 1992) ("insured v. insured" exclusion in D&O policy, which provided that insurer would not be liable for any payment for loss in connection with claim made against insured by any other insured, was susceptible to more than one reasonable interpretation as to whether it applied to FDIC).

Ninth Circuit: Biltmore Associates, L.L.C. v. Twin City Fire Insurance Co., 572 F.3d 663 (9th Cir. 2009); VierraMoore, Inc. v. Continental Casualty Co., 940 F. Supp.2d 1270 (E.D. Cal. 2013); Chartrand v. Illinois Union Insurance Co., 2009 WL 2776484 (N.D. Cal. Aug. 28, 2009); Megavail v. Illinois Union Insurance Co., 2006 WL 2045862 (D. Or. July 19, 2006) (lawsuit in which shareholders of corporation sued its directors was not collusive action and was outside of the scope of the "insured v. insured" exclusion); Harris v. Gulf Insurance Co., 297 F. Supp.2d 1220 (N.D. Cal. 2003) ("insured v. insured" exclusion in D&O policy precluding coverage for any claim brought or maintained by any security holder unless security holder was acting totally independently of, and totally without assistance of any director or officer, bars coverage for securities fraud claims against insured directors only if other directors or officers actively and voluntarily provided substantial aid or help to securities fraud plaintiff with intent to aid prosecution of lawsuit in order to obtain economic benefit); American Casualty Company of Reading, Pennsylvania v. Baker, 758 F. Supp. 1340 (C.D. Cal. 1991), *aff'd* 22 F.3d 880 (9th Cir. 1994) (exclusion for suits between insureds did not bar coverage for claims against officers and directors brought by bank's receiver when receiver represented depositors, creditors, and shareholders, in addition to representing bank).

Tenth Circuit: BancInsure, Inc. v. FDIC, 796 F.3d 1226 (10th Cir. 2015); Powell v. American Casualty Company of Reading, Pennsylvania, 772 F. Supp. 1188 (W.D. Okla. 1991) (D&O policy excluding actions brought by officers and directors of bank against each other did not violate public policy).

Eleventh Circuit: St. Paul Mercury Insurance Co. v. FDIC, 774 F.3d 702 (11th Cir. 2014); Vulcan Engineering Co. v. XL Insurance America, Inc., 201 Fed. Appx. 678 (11th Cir. 2006) (underlying suit of former minority stockholder in his own name was direct, rather than security holder derivative action, to which "insured v. insured" exclusion applied); Sphinx International, Inc. v. National Union Fire Insurance Company of Pittsburgh, Pennsylvania, 412 F.3d 1224 (11th Cir. 2005) (D&O policy "insured v. insured" exclusion applied to former director and officer's securities class action against insured); United States Liability Insurance Co. v. Kelley Ventures, L.L.C., 2015 U.S. Dist. LEXIS 135619 (S.D. Fla. 2015); Cox Communications, Inc. v. National Union Fire Insurance Company of Pittsburgh, PA., 708 F. Supp.2d 1322 (N.D. Ga. 2010); PowerSports, Inc. v. Royal & Sunalliance Insurance Co., 307 F. Supp.2d 1355 (S.D. Fla. 2004) ("insured v. insured" exclusion in D&O policy barring coverage for claims made against corporation by or on behalf of any insured person, precluded coverage for underlying suit by former directors and their company against corporation alleging breach of contract and related tort causes of actions, notwithstanding fact that company was not an insured under the policy).

State Courts:

Colorado: FDIC v. Bowen, 865 P.2d 868 (Colo. App. 1993) ("insured v. insured" exclusion in bank's policy was ambiguous with respect to claims brought by receiver for bank against insurance company).

Illinois: Yessenow v. Executive Risk Indemnity, Inc., 953 N.E.2d 433, 352 Ill. Dec. 194 (Ill. App. 2011).

Florida: Rigby v. Underwriters at Lloyd's, London, 907 So.2d 1187 (Fla. App. 2005) ("insured v. insured" exclusion in bankrupt corporation's D&O policy did not preclude coverage for lawsuit against former director of corporation by bankruptcy trustee because trustee sued in his capacity as trustee and not as corporate director or officer).

Maryland: Finci v. American Casualty Company of Reading, Pennsylvania, 323 Md. 358, 593 A.2d 1069 (1991) ("insured v. insured" exclusion in D&O policy issued to S&L was not ambiguous and did not exclude claims made by receiver of S&L against directors and officers).

Missouri: Maritz Holdings, Inc. v. Federal Insurance Co., 298 S.W.3d 92 (Mo. App. 2009).

New York: American Casualty Co. of Reading, PA v. Gelb, 132 A.D.3d 476, 18 N.Y.S.3d 30 (N.Y. App. Div. 2015); Franklin Holding Corp. (Delaware) v. National Union Fire Insurance Company of Pittsburgh, Pennsylvania, 261 A.D.2d 146, 689 N.Y.S.2d 492 (N.Y. App. Div. 1999) ("insured v. insured" exclusion in D&O policy applied to bar coverage for derivative and class action claims against insured corporation by its former director who was an insured).

South Carolina: Pulliam v. Travelers Indemnity Co., 403 S.C. 332, 743 S.E.2d 117 (S.C. App. 2013).

Texas: Primo v. Great American Insurance Co., 455 S.W.3d 714 (Tex. App. 2014).

Utah: Equine Assisted Growth and Learning Association v. Carolina Casualty Insurance Co., 266 P.3d 733 (Utah 2011).

[150] RHI Holdings, Inc. v. National Union Fire Insurance Company of Pittsburgh, Pennsylvania, 1994 WL 167946 (E.D. Pa. May 4, 1994), aff'd 47 F.3d 1161 (3d Cir. 1995).

[151] See:

First Circuit: Clark School for Creative Learning, Inc. v. Philadelphia Indemnity Insurance Co., 734 F.3d 51 (1st Cir. 2013); Gandor v. Torus National Insurance Co., 2015 U.S. Dist. LEXIS 140542 (D. Mass. Oct. 15, 2015).

Second Circuit: Nomura Holding America, Inc. v. Federal Insurance Co., 45 F. Supp.3d 354 (S.D.N.Y. 2014); United National Insurance Co. v. Granoff, Walker & Forlenza, P.C., 598 F. Supp.2d 540 (S.D.N.Y. 2009).

Third Circuit: Ettinger & Associates, L.L.C. v. Hartford/Twin City Fire Insurance Co., 22 F. Supp.3d 447 (E.D. Pa. 2014); Fishman v. The Hartford, 980 F. Supp.2d 672 (E.D. Pa. 2013).

Fourth Circuit: Humane Society of the United States v. National Union Fire Insurance Co. of Pittsburgh, Pa., 2015 U.S. Dist. LEXIS 100003 (D. Md. July 30, 2015).

Fifth Circuit: Westport Insurance Corp. v. Cotten Schmidt, LLP, 605 F. Supp.2d 796 (N.D. Tex. 2009).

Sixth Circuit: Realcomp II, Ltd. v. Ace American Insurance Co., 46 F. Supp.3d 736 (E.D. Mich. 2014).

Eighth Circuit: Ritrama, Inc. v. HDI-Gerling America Insurance Co., 796 F.3d 962 (8th Cir. 2015); Philadelphia Consolidated Holding Corp. v. LSI-Lowery Systems, Inc., 775 F.3d 1072 (8th Cir. 2015); George K. Baum & Co. v. Twin City Fire Insurance Co., 760 F.3d 795 (8th Cir. 2014); H & R Block, Inc. v. American International Specialty Lines Insurance Co., 546 F.3d 937 (8th Cir. 2008).

Ninth Circuit: Millennium Laboratories, Inc. v. Allied World Insurance Co., 2015 U.S. Dist. LEXIS 133534 (C.D. Cal. Sept. 30, 2015); HB Development, L.L.C. v. Western Pacific Mutual Insurance Co., 86 F. Supp.3d 1164 (E.D. Wash. 2015).

Eleventh Circuit: United States Liability Insurance Co. v. Kelley Ventures, L.L.C., 2015 U.S. Dist. LEXIS 135619 (S.D. Fla. 2015).

State Courts:

California: Crown Capital Securities, L.P. v. Endurance American Specialty Insurance Co., 235 Cal. App.4th 1122, 186 Cal. Rptr.3d 115 (2015).

Florida: National Union Fire Insurance Company of Pittsburgh, PA v. Underwriters at Lloyd's, London, 971 So.2d 885 (Fla. App. 2007).

Indiana: Bar Plan Mutual Insurance Co. v. Likes Law Office, L.L.C., 2015 Ind. App. LEXIS 680 (Ind. App. Oct. 15, 2015).

Kansas: American Special Risk Management Corp. v. Cahow, 286 Kan. 1134, 192 P.3d 614 (2008).

New York: Sirius XM Radio, Inc. v. XL Speciality Insurance Co., 117 A.D.3d 652, 987 N.Y.S.2d 324 (N.Y. App. Div. 2014); Executive Risk Indemnity Inc. v. Pepper Hamilton LLP, 56 A.D.3d 196, 865 N.Y.S.2d 25 (N.Y. App. Div. 2008).

Oklahoma: Chandler v. Valentine, 330 P.3d 1209 (Okla. 2014).

Pennsylvania: Ace American Insurance Co. v. Underwriters at Lloyds and Companies, 939 A.2d 935 (Pa. Super. 2007).

[152] See § 10.03[4][f] *supra*.

[153] RHI Holdings, Inc. v. National Union Fire Insurance Company of Pittsburgh, Pennsylvania, 1994 WL 167946 (E.D. Pa. May 4, 1994), *aff'd* 47 F.3d 1161 (3d Cir. 1995).

[154] *Id.*, at *6. See also, Mathias, Burns, Neumeier & Burgdoerfer, *Directors and Officers Liability: Prevention, Insurance and Indemnification* (Law Journal Press, 2000).

[155] See, e.g.:

First Circuit: Andover Newton Theological School, Inc. v. Continental Casualty Co., 930 F.2d 89, 93–95 (1st Cir. 1990).

Eighth Circuit: Convent of Visitation School v. Continental Casualty Co., 707 F. Supp. 412, 414–415 (D. Minn. 1989).

Ninth Circuit: Big 5 Corp. v. Gulf Underwriters Insurance Co., 2003 WL 22127029 (C.D. Cal. May 19, 2003); TVN Entertainment Corp. v. General Star Indemnity Co., 59 Fed. Appx. 211 (9th Cir. 2003); CIM Insurance Co. v. Midpac Auto Center, Inc., 108 F. Supp.2d 1092, 1104 (D. Haw. 2000).

State Courts:

New Hampshire: Contoocook Valley School District v. Graphic Arts Mutual Insurance Co., 147 N.H. 302, 788 A.2d 259 (2001).

[156] See, e.g.:

First Circuit: Andover Newton Theological School, Inc. v. Continental Casualty Co., 930 F.2d 89, 93–95 (1st Cir. 1990).

Eighth Circuit: Convent of Visitation School v. Continental Casualty Co., 707 F. Supp. 412, 414–415 (D. Minn. 1989).

Ninth Circuit: Big 5 Corp. v. Gulf Underwriters Insurance Co., 2003 WL 22127029 (C.D. Cal. July 14, 2003); TVN Entertainment Corp. v. General Star Indemnity Co., 59 Fed. Appx. 211 (9th Cir. 2003); CIM Insurance Corp. v. Midpac Auto Center, Inc., 108 F. Supp.2d 1092, 1104 (D. Haw. 2000).

State Courts:

New Hampshire: Contoocook Valley School District v. Graphic Arts Mutual Insurance Co., 147 N.H. 302, 788 A.2d 259 (2001).

[157] See, e.g.:

Ninth Circuit: Big TVN Entertainment Corp. v. General Star Indemnity Co., 59 Fed. Appx. 211 (9th Cir. 2003) (exclusion for losses determined to be owing under any express contract and exclusion for losses in the form of bonus, commissions, salary, pursuant to an employment contract applied to arbitrator's award of terminated employee based upon the value of stock options); 5 Corp. v. Gulf Underwriters Insurance Co., 2003 WL 22127029 (C.D. Cal. July 14, 2003) (exclusion for wage payments bars coverage for an underlying wage payment collection settlement for unpaid overtime); CIM Insurance Corp. v. Midpac Auto Center, Inc., 108 F. Supp.2d 1092, 1104 (D. Haw. 2000) (no coverage for wrongful termination claim because policy had an exclusion for losses arising from employment agreement and claim was for breach of an employment agreement).

State Courts:

New York: Associated Community Bancorp, Inc. v. St. Paul Mercury Insurance. Co., 118 A.D.3d 608, 989 N.Y.S.2d 15 (N.Y. App. Div. 2014).

[158] See:

First Circuit: Andover Newton Theological School, Inc. v. Continental Casualty Co., 930 F.2d 89, 93–95 (1st Cir. 1990) (clause excluding coverage "[f]or any amounts due, under the terms of any contractual obligation" is ambiguous; implies that only claims invoking terms of contract itself are excluded and not that statutory discrimination claims for contract-type damages are excluded).

Seventh Circuit: OneBeacon America Insurance Co. v. City of Zion, 2015 U.S. Dist. LEXIS 99438 (N.D. Ill. July 29, 2015).

Eighth Circuit: Convent of Visitation School v. Continental Casualty Co., 707 F. Supp. 412, 414–415 (D. Minn. 1989) (exclusion for any amounts due under terms of any contractual obligation does not apply to settlement of a statutory claim).

State Courts:

New Hampshire: Contoocook Valley School District v. Graphic Arts Mutual Insurance Co., 147 N.H. 302, 788 A.2d 259 (2001) (exclusions for remuneration were ambiguous and did not apply to settlement of discrimination claim even though settlement included damages for wages and other benefits).

[159] See:

First Circuit: Genzyme Corp. v. Federal Insurance Co., 622 F.3d 62 (1st Cir. 2010).

Third Circuit: In re Delta Financial Corp., 378 Fed. Appx. 241 (3d Cir. 2010).

[160] See:

First Circuit: Miles v. Great Northern Insurance Co., 656 F. Supp.2d 218 (D. Mass. 2009); Shapiro v. American Home Assurance Co., 616 F. Supp. 900 (D. Mass. 1984) (former officers and directors of a corporation could not be barred from coverage under Securities Act liability policies solely on the basis of fraudulent acts of other policyholders in procurement of the policy).

Second Circuit: Axis Reinsurance Co. v. Bennett, 2008 WL 2485388 (S.D.N.Y. June 19, 2008); Wedtech Corp. v. Federal Insurance Co., 740 F. Supp. 214, 218 (S.D.N.Y. 1990) (when an insurance policy contains a severability provision, some officers and directors still may be entitled to insurance coverage).

Sixth Circuit: Great American Insurance Co. v. Geostar Corp., 2010 WL 845953 (E.D. Mich. Mar. 5, 2010).

Seventh Circuit: St. Katherine Insurance Co. v. Insurance Company of North America, 11 F.3d 707 (7th Cir.1993); Archer Daniels Midland Co. v. Burlington Insurance Co., 785 F. Supp.2d 722 (N.D. Ill. 2011).

Eighth Circuit: Bethel v. Darwin Select Insurance Co., 735 F.3d 1035 (8th Cir. 2013).

Ninth Circuit: Minkler v. Safeco Insurance Co., 399 Fed. Appx. 230 (9th Cir. 2010); United Guarantee Mortgage Indemnity Co. v. Countrywide Financial Corp., 660 F. Supp.2d 1163 (C.D. Cal. 2009).

State Courts:

California: Minkler v. Safeco Insurance Company of America, 49 Cal.4th 315, 232 P.3d 612, 110 Cal. Rptr.3d 612 (2010).

Illinois: Yessenow v. Executive Risk Indemnity, Inc., 953 N.E.2d 433, 352 Ill. Dec. 194 (Ill. App. 2011).

Massachusetts: Society for Christian Activities, Inc. v. Markel Insurance Co., 440 Mass. 1006, 795 N.E.2d 545 (2003).

Minnesota: SECURA Supreme Insurance Company v. M.S.M., 755 N.W.2d 320 (Minn. App. 2008).

New York: DRK, L.L.C. v. Burlington Insurance Co., 74 A.D.3d 693, 905 N.Y.S.2d 58 (N.Y. App. Div. 2010).

[161] See:

First Circuit: Miles v. Great Northern Insurance Co., 656 F. Supp.2d 218 (D. Mass. 2009).

Second Circuit: Axis Reinsurance Co. v. Bennett, 2008 WL 2485388 (S.D.N.Y. June 19, 2008); XL Specialty Insurance Co. v. Agoglia, 2009 WL 1227485 (S.D.N.Y. Apr. 30, 2009); Murphy v. Allied World Assurance Co., 2009 WL 1528527 (S.D.N.Y. May 29, 2009).

Sixth Circuit: Great American Insurance Co. v. Geostar Corp., 2010 WL 845953 (E.D. Mich. Mar. 5, 2010).

Seventh Circuit: Archer Daniels Midland Co. v. Burlington Insurance Co., 785 F. Supp.2d 722 (N.D. Ill. 2011).

Eighth Circuit: Bethel v. Darwin Select Insurance Co., 735 F.3d 1035 (8th Cir. 2013).

Ninth Circuit: Minkler v. Safeco Insurance Co., 399 Fed. Appx. 230 (9th Cir. 2010); Minkler v. Safeco Insurance Co., 561 F.3d 1033 (9th Cir. 2009); United Guarantee Mortgage Indemnity Co. v. Countrywide Financial Corp., 660 F. Supp.2d 1163 (C.D. Cal. 2009).

Tenth Circuit: West American Insurance Co. v. AV&S, 145 F.3d 1224 (10th Cir. 1998).

State Courts:

California: Minkler v. Safeco Insurance Company of America, 49 Cal.4th 315, 232 P.3d 612, 110 Cal. Rptr.3d 612 (2010).

Massachusetts: Worcester Mutual Insurance Co. v. Marnell, 398 Mass. 240, 496 N.E.2d 158 (1986).

Michigan: Home Owners Insurance Co. v. Selfridge, 2008 WL 5273418 (Mich. App. Dec. 18, 2008); Gorzon v. Westfield Insurance Co., v. Westfield Insurance Co., 526 N.W.2d 43 (Mich. App. 1994).

Minnesota: SECURA Supreme Insurance Co. v. M.S.M., 755 N.W.2d 320 (Minn. App. 2008).

New Jersey: C.B. v. Evdokimoff, 2008 WL 5025018 (N.J. Super App. Div. Nov. 28, 2008).

New York: DRK, L.L.C. v. Burlington Insurance Co., 74 A.D.3d 693 (N.Y. App. Div. 2010).

Wisconsin: Taryn E.F. by Grunewald v. Joshua M.C., 178 Wis.2d 719, 505 N.W.2d 418 (1993).

[162] See:

First Circuit: Shapiro v. American Home Assurance Co., 616 F. Supp. 900 (D. Mass. 1984) (former officers and directors of a corporation could not be barred from coverage under Securities Act liability policies solely on the basis of fraudulent acts of other policyholders in procurement of the policy).

Second Circuit: Wedtech Corp. v. Federal Insurance Co., 740 F. Supp. 214, 218 (S.D.N.Y. 1990) (when an insurance policy contains a severability provision, some officers and directors still may be entitled to insurance coverage).

[163] The above-enumerated exclusions are the relevant exclusions dealing with knowing or intentional misconduct. See § 10.04[2] *supra*.

[164] The asbestos and environmental exclusions apply irrespective of fault, meaning there can be no innocent insured excuse.

[165] See:

First Circuit: Shapiro v. American Home Assurance Co., 616 F. Supp. 900 (D. Mass. 1984) (former officers and directors could not be barred from coverage solely on the basis of fraudulent acts of other policyholders in procurement of the policy).

Second Circuit: Wedtech Corp. v. Federal Insurance Co., 740 F. Supp. 214, 218 (S.D.N.Y. 1990) (when an insurance policy contains a severability provision, some officers and directors still may be entitled to insurance coverage).

Fourth Circuit: Atlantic Permanent Federal Savings & Loan Ass'n v. American Casualty Company of Reading, Pennsylvania, 839 F.2d 212 (4th Cir. 1987), *cert. denied* 486 U.S. 1056 (1988).

[166] See Federal Savings & Loan Insurance Corp. v. Burdette, 718 F. Supp. 649 (E.D. Tenn. 1989).

[167] See:

First Circuit: Shapiro v. American Home Assurance Co., 616 F. Supp. 900 (D. Mass. 1984) (innocent policyholders remain covered even if another policyholder made affirmative misrepresentations to the insurance company).

Fifth Circuit: Mazur v. Gaudet, 826 F. Supp. 188, 194 (E.D. La. 1992) (innocent policyholders remain covered even if another policyholder made affirmative misrepresentations).

[168] See Shapiro v. American Home Assurance Co., 584 F. Supp. 1245 (D. Mass. 1984).

[169] See:

Second Circuit: Atlantic Mutual Insurance Co. v. Balfour MacLaine International Ltd., 85 F.3d 68, 80 (2d Cir. 1996).

State Courts:

New York: Christian v. Christian, 42 N.Y.2d 63, 396 N.Y.S.2d 817, 365 N.E.2d 849, 856 (1977).

[170] Christian v. Christian, 42 N.Y.2d 63, 396 N.Y.S.2d 817, 365 N.E.2d 849, 856 (1977).

[171] See First Savings & Loan Association of Jersey City, New Jersey v. American Home Assurance Co., 29 N.Y.2d 297, 327 N.Y.S.2d 609, 277 N.E.2d 638, 639 (1971).

CHAPTER 11

Surety Bonds

Chapter Contents

§ 11.01 Overview

The real estate and construction industries face substantial risks of contractual defaults. Costs of projects can skyrocket when there are such defaults. The surety plays a significant role in minimizing these risks of default for lenders and various real estate-related entities.

This chapter discusses the types of surety bonds and the risks underwritten by them;[1] the nature of the relationship between a surety and its principal;[2] the mechanics involved in creation of the relationship;[3] the nature and extent of liability under a surety bond;[4] the commencement and duration of the risk underwritten by the surety bond;[5] the right to indemnity under the bond;[6] and bad-faith claims handling and damages available to an obligee.[7]

§ 11.02 Types of Bonds

Surety bonds are often purchased by a party to a contract to provide a financial guaranty to the other party to the contract, or a third party beneficiary, that effectively insures that the first party (party purchasing the bond) will perform its obligations thereunder.[8] In particular, all surety bonds are underwritten by a third party, usually a financial institution, and their purpose is to ensure the performance of obligations promised in a contract to an obligee or promisee. The person or entity that needs the third party to underwrite the risk of non-performance is known as a principal, who is the obligor or promisor under the contract. The risk underwritten by the bond is the risk of unjustified default by the principal or obligor. The beneficiary of this surety bond is the obligee or promisee, who obtains beneficial interest in the bond as assurance that the promisor or principal actually performs its contractual obligations, the risk of default of which is underwritten by the bond itself.

There are three principal types of surety bonds:

1. Bid bonds ensure that a contractor or subcontractor will not wrongfully refuse to honor its bid when such bids are relied on by the owner or general contractor in accepting or submitting a bid.[9]
2. Performance bonds ensure that a contractor or subcontractor will not inexcusably fail to perform a contract in accordance with its terms but instead will complete the work.[10]
3. Payment bonds ensure against the risk that a contractor or owner will unjustifiably fail to pay a subcontractor or general contractor for labor or materials placed or used in a job.[11]

§ 11.03 Nature of the Surety Relationship

A surety contract involves a tripartite relationship between the surety, the principal, and the obligee. A surety is a person or entity who undertakes, underwrites, or bears the risk of non-performance of the obligation of another (the principal), which is owed under a contract to an obligee. The surety is jointly and severally (with the principal) answerable to the obligee for the principal's performance or non-performance under the specific contract, the default of which is underwritten by the bond. Stated differently, a surety is liable for the payment of its principal's debt or the performance of its principal's obligation under the specific contract, the default of which is underwritten by the bond.[12]

The surety contract is akin to a guaranty contract, because it provides an economic bond to ensure performance under the contract at issue. However, unlike the surety relationship, the guaranty context does not involve secondary liability, but instead involves solely a joint and several primary obligation.[13]

A surety contract is also distinct from an insurance policy in which there is a relationship between the two contracting parties—the policyholder and the insurance company. Even in the liability or "litigation" insurance context, the duties under the contract are owed to the policyholder, not the third-party claimant.[14] On the other hand, in the surety context, the surety obligation runs primarily to a third-party beneficiary of the surety contract—namely, the obligee under a contract between the principal and the obligee, not to the other contracting party that had purchased the bond in the first place—the principal.[15]

§ 11.04 Creation of Suretyship and the Nature and Extent of Surety's Liability

There are two requirements for the creation of the suretyship relationship:

1. a valid and binding contract between the principal and the obligee; and
2. a valid and binding suretyship contract or bond between the principal, surety, and obligee.[16]

Just as with insurance-policy construction,[17] the nature and extent of a surety's liability is determined by the precise terms of the surety bond or contract.[18] Although limited by and subject to the terms of the bond,[19] the liability of the surety is generally measured by the principal's liability to the obligee under the separate agreement, the risk of non-performance of which is being underwritten by the surety bond. For instance, the liability of the surety to the obligee under the bond mirrors the principal's liability to the obligee because the surety is deemed to stand in the shoes of the principal.[20]

Unless otherwise provided under a surety bond, the surety's maximum liability will generally be co-extensive with that of the principal.[21] This means that the rights and liabilities of the surety are no greater than those of the principal and may be less if the bond limits the liabilities of the surety.[22] In fact, the surety will not be liable to the obligee unless the principal is liable.[23]

§ 11.05 Commencement and Duration of the Risk

The commencement and duration of the risk are determined by the bond itself.[24] The bond may have a commencement and/or expiration date.[25] Alternatively, the bond might have an implicit commencement or termination date. For example, the commencement and expiration date might be triggered by a specific event, such as architect's execution of a certificate of completion.[26] In addition, the surety's obligation is usually undertaken at the same time as, concurrently with, and jointly with the principal.[27]

Payment and performance bonds may differ on the duration of the risk covered. A surety's liability under a payment bond usually terminates on payment by the principal to the obligee, even if there is a warranty period for the work performed by the obligee. This is because the nature of a payment bond is to ensure the payment for labor and materials, not the performance of the work.[28] On the other hand, a surety's liability under a performance bond will usually run into any express or implied warranty period.[29]

[1]—Pre-Existing Defaults

Unless otherwise provided in the bond, a surety bond generally does not cover pre-existing defaults, although it may cover work that has already started.[30]

[2]—Breaches by Principal

An uncured breach by the principal ordinarily requires the surety to complete the principal's performance or pay the obligee the reasonable costs of completion.[31] However, not all breaches will entitle the obligee to terminate a contract and call on the surety to perform the principal's unfulfilled obligations. The breaches permitting termination are material breaches.[32]

[3]—Conditions of Liability

Depending on the terms of the bond, a surety's liability only attaches on a default by the principal,[33] and an obligee's default may be an absolute defense to payment or performance of the surety.[34] Case law and commentators interpreting the standard-form A312 Bond, widely used in the industry,[35] have determined that lack of "owner default" is a condition precedent to the surety's obligations thereunder.[36]

Similarly, a bond may contain more expansive liabilities than the underlying contract, the performance of which is secured by the surety bond. For example, where the bond does not have a "paid when paid" provision, conditioning payment to a subcontractor when the contractor/principal is paid by the owner, a surety's obligation under a payment bond is triggered on completion of the work of the subcontractor, even if the underlying subcontract has a "paid when paid" provision.[37]

In order to trigger a surety's liability under the bond, the obligee must follow all conditions; failure to do so prevents the surety's liability from accruing.[38] An obligee is not required to utilize the surety bond if he can complete the performance at a cheaper price than the remaining contract price.[39]

[4]—Discharge of Surety

The surety's obligation under the surety bond can be discharged under a variety of circumstances. First, the surety's obligations are discharged when the principal's obligation is released or extinguished.[40] The surety's obligation can also be discharged by operation of law. For example, if the obligee commits a material breach justifying rescission or fails to disclose something material to the transaction, the surety cannot be required to complete performance.[41] Additionally, a material increase in the risk by the principal may have the effect of discharging the surety's obligation. Changing the nature or increasing the scope of the obligation secured or changing the identity of the principal are circumstances that will excuse performance by the surety.[42]

[5]—Right to Indemnity

After paying under the bond, the surety generally retains the right to indemnity against the defaulting principal whose obligation is secured by the bond.[43]

§ 11.06 Liabilities, Damages, and Bad Faith

Additional remedies may be available beyond payment or performance under a surety bond. These potentially additional remedies include bad-faith and/or punitive damages[44] and consequential and/or liquidated damages.[45]

[1]—Bad-Faith and Punitive Damages

Punitive damages may be awarded for egregious tortious conduct or through a statutory grant.[46] Here, the question is whether a bad-faith statute[47] or the common law recognizes a claim for bad faith by an obligee against a surety.[48]

The majority of jurisdictions addressing the issue have held that a surety owes the duty of good faith to the owner.[49] A minority holds that the duty of good faith and fair dealing is not owed by the surety to the principal.[50] Some jurisdictions are split on the issue.[51]

[2]—Consequential and Liquidated Damages and Attorneys' Fees

An obligee's ability to recover consequential and liquidated damages and attorneys' fees from the surety depends on the posture of the case. Under general contract law, a party aggrieved by a breach of contract can recover consequential damages if those damages are such that ordinarily flow from the breach and such damages were at the time of contract formation either within the contemplation of the parties or reasonably foreseeable.[52] In the surety context, however, consequential damages, liquidated damages, and attorneys' fees are only recoverable if the terms of the bond expressly permit it.[53]

The commonly used A312 Bond[54] provides the surety with several options in the event of "contractor default" and owner's exercise of its rights under the bond:

1. arrange completion through completion by contractor with the owner's consent;
2. completion of the contract itself;
3. tender substitute contractor to owner under terms and bonds acceptable to owner and payment of excess costs up to amount of bond;
4. waive rights to use options (1) through (3) and instead "buy back" the bond by investigating and tendering the amount for which it may be liable to owner; and
5. deny liability in whole or in part and notify the owner of its rationale.[55]

If the surety exercises options (1), (2), or (3), the surety's obligation is no greater than the contractor's under the construction contract.[56] The bond provides for liquidated or actual damages for delay and additional construction, legal costs, or design costs.[57] However, in all events, the surety's liability is limited by the amount of the bond and is subject to the owner's commitment to use the unpaid portion of the contract to mitigate damages.[58] Thus, the A312 Bond permits liquidated, delay, and consequential damages and attorneys' fees subject to the limits available.[59]

Notes

[1] See § 11.02 *infra*.

[2] See § 11.03 *infra*.

[3] See § 11.04 *infra*.

[4] See § 11.04 *infra*.

[5] See § 11.05 *infra.*

[6] See § 11.05[5] *infra.*

[7] See § 11.06 *infra.*

[8] See:

Third Circuit: In re Holler, 463 B.R. 733 (Bankr. E.D. Pa. 2011).

Sixth Circuit: Commercial Money Center, Inc. v. Illinois Union Insurance Co., 508 F.3d 327 (6th Cir. 2007).

Seventh Circuit: BMD Contractors, Inc. v. Fidelity and Deposit Company of Maryland, 2011 WL 6065104 (S.D. Ind. Jan. 13, 2011).

Eighth Circuit: Ensco Environmental Services, Inc. v. United States, 650 F. Supp. 583 (W.D. Mo. 1986).

Ninth Circuit: In re Flamingo 55, Inc., 378 B.R. 893 (Bankr. D. Nev. 2007).

State Courts:

Alabama: Town & Country Property, L.L.C. v. Amerisure Insurance Co., 2011 WL 5009777 (Ala. Oct. 21, 2011).

California: Fort Bragg Unified School District v. Solano County Roofing, Inc., 194 Cal. App.4th 891, 124 Cal. Rptr.3d 144 (2011); Cates Construction, Inc. v. Talbot Partners, 21 Cal.4th 28, 86 Cal. Rptr.2d 855, 980 P.2d 407 (1999); Arrowhead Financial Group, Inc. v. Welty, 2002 WL 31661269 (Cal. App. Nov. 26, 2002).

Indiana: Town of Plainfield v. Paden Engineering Co., 943 N.E.2d 904 (Ind. App. 2011).

Louisiana: Veterans Commercial Properties, L.L.C. v. Barry's Flooring, Inc., 67 So.3d 627 (La. App. 2011).

New Jersey: Feigenbaum v. Guaracini, 402 N.J. Super. 7, 952 A.2d 511 (N.J. Super. App. Div. 2008).

Oregon: Man-Data, Inc. v. B & A Automotive, Inc., 247 Or. App. 429, 270 P.3d 318 (2011).

Pennsylvania: County of Dauphin v. City of Harrisburg, 24 A.3d 1083 (Pa. Commw. 2011).

See also, Philip Bruner and Patrick O'Connor, *Bruner & O'Connor on Construction Law,* § 12:1 (2006).

[9] Bruner and O'Connor, *Bruner & O'Conner on Construction Law,* § 12:1 (2006).

[10] *Id.*, at 12:13. See also:

First Circuit: Belanger v. North American Specialty Insurance Co., 504 F.3d 147 (1st Cir. 2007).

Eighth Circuit: Angelo Iafrate Construction LLC v. Potashnick Construction, Inc., 370 F.3d 715 (8th Cir. 2004); Pennsylvania National Mutual Casualty Insurance Co. v. City of Pine Bluff, 354 F.3d 945 (8th Cir. 2004).

State Courts:

Alabama: Town & Country Property, L.L.C. v. Amerisure Insurance Co., 2011 WL 5009777 (Ala. Oct. 21, 2011).

California: Rossa v. D.L. Falk Construction, Inc., 53 Cal.4th 387, 266 P.3d 1022, 135 Cal. Rptr.3d 329 (2012).

Florida: U.S. Fire Insurance Co. v. J.S.U.B., Inc., 979 So.2d 871 (Fla. 2007); Z.P. No. 54 Limited Partnership v. Fidelity & Deposit Company of Maryland, 917 So.2d 368 (Fla. App. 2005).

Nebraska: State *ex rel.* Wagner v. Gilbane Building Co., 276 Neb. 686, 757 N.W.2d 194 (Neb. 2008).

New York: WBP Central Associates, L.L.C. v. DeCola, 91 A.D.3d 861, 937 N.Y.S.2d 306 (N.Y. App. Div. 2012).

Pennsylvania: Kiski Area School District v. Mid-State Surety Corp., 600 Pa. 444, 967 A.2d 368 (2008).

[11] See Bruner and O'Connor, *Bruner & O'Conner on Construction Law*, § 12:1 (2006). See also:

Eighth Circuit: Angelo Iafrate Construction LLC v. Potashnick Construction, Inc., 370 F.3d 715 (8th Cir. 2004).

State Courts:

California: Rossa v. D.L. Falk Construction, Inc., 53 Cal.4th 387, 266 P.3d 1022, 135 Cal. Rptr.3d 329 (Cal. 2012).

Pennsylvania: Diener Brick Co. v. Mastro Masonry Contractor, 885 A.2d 1034 (Pa. Super. 2005).

[12] See Bruner and O'Connor, *Bruner & O'Conner on Construction Law*, §§ 12:1–12:2 (2006). See also:

Tenth Circuit: In re Hopkins, 328 B.R. 575 (Bankr. D. Utah 2005).

State Courts:

Alabama: Town & Country Property, L.L.C. v. Amerisure Insurance Co., 2011 WL 5009777 (Ala. Oct. 21, 2011).

California: Rossa v. D.L. Falk Construction, Inc., 53 Cal.4th 387, 266 P.3d 1022, 135 Cal. Rptr.3d 329 (2012).

Connecticut: Rosado v. Bridgeport Roman Catholic Diocesan Corp., 276 Conn. 168, 884 A.2d 981 (2005).

Maryland: National Union Fire Insurance Company of Pittsburgh, Pennsylvania v. David A. Bramble, Inc., 388 Md. 195, 879 A.2d 101 (2005).

Mississippi: Fidelity and Guaranty Insurance Co. v. Blount, 63 So.3d 453 (Miss. 2011).

New York: RM 14 FK Corp. v. Bank One Trust Co., 11 Misc.3d 283, 811 N.Y.S.2d 860 (N.Y. Sup. 2005), *rev'd on other grounds* 37 A.D.3d 272, 831 N.Y.S.2d 120 (N.Y. App. Div. 2007).

Ohio: Smith v. Leis, 106 Ohio St.3d 309, 835 N.E.2d 5 (2005).

Pennsylvania: J.F. Walker Co. v. Excalibur Oil Group, Inc., 792 A.2d 1269 (Pa. Super. 2002).

Texas: Nova Casualty Co. v. Turner Construction Co., 335 S.W.3d 698 (Tex. App. 2011); Kendziorski v. Saunders, 191 S.W.3d 395 (Tex. App. 2006).

[13] See:

Second Circuit: Valley National Bank v. Greenwich Insurance Co., 254 F. Supp.2d 448 (S.D.N.Y. 2003).

State Courts:

Georgia: Marett v. Brice Building Co., 268 Ga. App. 778, 603 S.E.2d 40 (2004).

Louisiana: Fleet Fuel, Inc. v. Mynex, Inc., 924 So.2d 480 (La. App.), *writ denied* 930 So.2d 977 (La. 2006).

Maryland: Middlebrook Technology, LLC v. Moore, 157 Md. App. 40, 849 A.2d 63 (2004); ULICO Casualty Co. v. Atlantic Contracting & Material Co., 150 Md. App. 40, 822 A.2d 1257 (2003), *aff'd* 380 Md. 285, 844 A.2d 460 (2004); Mercy Medical Center, Inc. v. United Healthcare of Mid-Atlantic, Inc., 149 Md. App. 336, 815 A.2d 886 (Md. App.), *cert. denied* 874 Md. 583, 824 A.2d 59 (2003).

North Carolina: United Leasing Corp. v. Plumides, 138 N.C. App. 696, 531 S.E.2d 891 (2000).

Pennsylvania: McIntyre Square Associates v. Evans, 827 A.2d 446 (Pa. Super. 2003).

[14] See Chapter 2 *supra*. See also:

First Circuit: Liberty Mutual Insurance Co. v. Black & Decker Corp., 383 F. Supp.2d 200, 219 (D. Mass. 2004); American Employers' Insurance Co. v. DeLorme Publishing Co., 39 F. Supp.2d 64 (D. Me. 1999); Ryan v. Royal Insurance Company of America, 916 F.2d 731 (1st Cir. 1990); City of West Haven v. Liberty Mutual Insurance Co., 639 F. Supp. 1012 (D. Conn. 1986).

Second Circuit: Allianz Insurance Co. v. Lerner, 416 F.3d 109, 116 (2d Cir. 2005).

Third Circuit: NL Industries, Inc. v. Commercial Union Insurance Co., 926 F. Supp. 446 (D.N.J. 1996); Harristown Development Corp. v. International Insurance Co., 1988 WL 123149, at *12 (M.D. Pa. Nov. 15, 1988); *In re* Asousa Partnership, 2004 WL 1043149, at *8 (Bankr. E.D. Pa. Apr. 26, 2004).

Fourth Circuit: Perdue Farms, Inc. v. Travelers Casualty & Surety Co., 448 F.3d 252, (4th Cir. 2006); Provident Bank of Maryland v. Travelers Property Casualty Corp., 236 F.3d 138 (4th Cir. 2000).

Sixth Circuit: White v. Insurance Company of State of Pennsylvania, 282 F. Supp.2d 618, 625 (N.D. Ohio 2003), *vacated on other grounds* 405 F.3d 455 (6th Cir. 2005); Ndabishuriye v. Albert Schweitzer Society, USA, Inc., 136 Fed. Appx. 795, 796 (6th Cir. 2005); Taylor v. Temple & Cutler, 192 F.R.D. 552, 558 (E.D. Mich. 1999).

Ninth Circuit: Kla-Tencor Corp. v. National Union Fire Insurance Company of Pittsburgh, Pennsylvania, 2006 WL 2479106 (N.D. Cal. Aug. 28, 2006).

Tenth Circuit: Allstate Insurance Co. v. Johnston, 339 F. Supp.2d 1191, 1195 (D. Kan. 2004); American States Insurance Co. v. Ridco, Inc., 1996 WL 33401184, at *3 (D. Wyo. Feb. 8, 1996); Weitzman v. Blazing Pedals, Inc., 151 F.R.D. 125 (D. Colo. 1993).

Eleventh Circuit: Colonial Oil Industries, Inc. v. Underwriters Subscribing to Policy Nos. T031504670, 1995 WL 692691, at *10–11 (S.D. Ga. Nov. 6, 1995), *rev'd on other grounds* 133 F.3d 1404 (11th Cir. 1998).

District of Columbia Circuit: Pierce Associates, Inc. v. St. Paul Mercury Insurance Co., 421 F. Supp.2d 11, 17 (D.D.C.), *vacated on other grounds* 437 F. Supp.2d 16 (D.D.C. 2006).

State Courts:

Alaska: United States *ex. rel.* North Star Terminal & Stevedore Co. v. Nuggett Insurance Construction Co., 2006 WL 2251122, at *2 n.3 (D. Alaska July 28, 2006); Langdon v. Champion, 752 P.2d 999 (Alaska 1988).

California: Montrose Chemical Co. v. Admiral Insurance Co., 10 Cal.4th 645, 42 Cal. Rptr.2d 324, 332, 913 P.2d 878 (1995); Garvey v. State Farm Fire & Casualty Co., 48 Cal.3d 395, 770 P.2d 704 (1989); Black Diamond Asphalt Co. v. Superior Court, 114 Cal. App.4th 109, 7 Cal. Rptr.3d 466, 470 n.2 (2003); Century Indemnity Co. v. Hearrean, 98 Cal. App.4th 734, 120 Cal. Rptr.2d 66, 69 (2002).

Delaware: Liggett Group, Inc. v. Ace Property & Casualty Insurance Co., 798 A.2d 1024, 1031 (Del. 2002).

Hawaii: Sentinel Insurance Co. v. First Insurance Company of Hawaii, Ltd., 76 Haw. 277, 875 P.2d 894, 906 (1994); Ferrer v. Ngo, 102 Haw. 119, 73 P.3d 73, 81 (Haw. App. 2003).

Illinois: Emerson Electric Co. v. Aetna Casualty & Surety Co., 852 Ill. App.3d 399, 287 Ill. Dec, 280, 815 N.E.2d 924, 950 (2004).

Indiana: Sanyo Laser Products, Inc. v. Royal Insurance Company of America, 2003 WL 23101793, at *3 n.2 (S.D. Ind. Nov. 7, 2003).

Kentucky: Aetna Casualty & Surety Co. v. Kentucky, 179 S.W.3d 830, 845 (Ky. 2005).

Louisiana: Felham Enterprises, Ltd. v. Certain Underwriters at Lloyds, London, 2004 WL 2984296, at *4 (E.D. La. Dec. 6, 2004).

Maryland: BGE Home Products & Services, Inc. v. Owens, 377 Md. 236, 833 A.2d 8, 14 (Md. 2003); Sherwood Brands, Inc. v. Hartford Accident & Indemnity Co., 347 Md. 32, 698 A.2d 1078, 1083 (Md. 1997); Brohawn v. Transamerica Insurance Co., 276 Md. 396, 347 A.2d 842, 851 (Md. 1975).

Massachusetts: Hanover Insurance Co. v. Golden, 436 Mass. 584, 766 N.E.2d 838, 841 (2002).

Michigan: Allstate Insurance Co. v. Freeman, 432 Mich. 656, 443 N.W.2d 734 (1989).

Mississippi: Watson Quality Ford, Inc. v. Great River Insurance Co., 909 So.2d 1196, 1199 (Miss. App. 2005).

New York: BP Air Conditioning Corp. v. One Beacon Insurance Group, 33 A.D.3d 116, 821 N.Y.S.2d 1, 4–5 (2006); Automobile Insurance Co. v. Cook, 7 N.Y.3d 131, 850 N.E.2d 1152, 1155 (2006); City of New York v. Certain Underwriters at Lloyd's, London, 15 A.D.3d 228, 790 N.Y.S.2d 82, 83–84 (2005).

North Carolina: Brown v. Lumbermens Mutual Casualty Co., 90 N.C. App. 464, 369 S.E.2d 367 (N.C. App.), *review denied* 323 N.C. 363, 373 S.E.2d 541 (1988).

Virginia: Veney v. Duke, 2005 WL 3476760, at *2 (Va. Cir. Ct. Oct. 26, 2005).

Washington: State Farm Fire & Casualty Co. v. English Cove Association, Inc., 121 Wash. App. 358, 88 P.3d 986, 992 (2004).

Wyoming: Shoshone First Bank v. Pacific Employers Insurance Co., 2 P.3d 510, 516 (Wyo. 2000); First Wyoming Bank, N.A. v. Continental Insurance Co., 860 P.2d 1064 (Wyo.), *vacated in part* 860 P.2d 1094 (Wyo. 1993).

15 See:

Third Circuit: Norwood Co. v. RLI Insurance Co., 2002 WL 485694 (E.D. Pa. Apr. 1, 2002); Superior Precast, Inc. v. Safeco Insurance Co., 71 F. Supp.2d 438 (E.D. Pa. 1999).

Eleventh Circuit: American Manufacturing Mutual Insurance Co. v. Tison Hog Market, Inc., 182 F.3d 1284 (11th Cir. 1999), *cert. denied* 531 U.S. 819 (2000).

State Courts:

Alabama: Town & Country Property, L.L.C. v. Amerisure Insurance Co., 2011 WL 5009777 (Ala. Oct. 21, 2011).

California: Department of Industrial Relations v. Fidelity Roof Co., 60 Cal. App.4th, 70 Cal. Rptr.2d 465 (1997); Conservatorship of Estate of O'Connor, 48 Cal. App.4th 1076, 56 Cal. Rptr.2d 386 (1996); Arntz Construction Co. v. St. Paul Fire & Marine Insurance Co., 47 Cal. App.4th 464, 54 Cal. Rptr.2d 888 (1996).

North Carolina: Beachcrete, Inc. v. Water Street Center Associates, LLC, 172 N.C. App. 156, 615 S.E.2d 719 (2005).

Pennsylvania: Ferrick Construction Co. v. One Beacon Insurance Co., 2004 WL 3051443 (Pa. C.P. 2004); M.A. Bruder & Sons, Inc. v. Williams, 47 Pa. D. & C.4th 243 (Pa. C.P. 2000).

Texas: Nova Casualty Co. v. Turner Construction Co., 335 S.W.3d 698 (Tex. App. 2011).

16 See:

Second Circuit: In re Chemtura Corp., 448 B.R. 635 (Bankr. S.D.N.Y 2011).

Third Circuit: First Indemnity of America Insurance Co. v. Tiedeken, 139 Fed. Appx. 375 (3d Cir. 2000).

Fifth Circuit: International Fidelity Insurance Co. v. Sweet Little Mexico Corp., 665 F.3d 671 (5th Cir. 2011); Shell Oil Co. v. S.S. Orient Coral, 548 F. Supp. 1385 (E.D. La. 1982).

Sixth Circuit: Commercial Money Center, Inc. v. Illinois Union Insurance Co., 508 F.3d 327 (6th Cir. 2007); *In re* Campbell, 207 B.R. 861 (Bankr. W.D. Mich. 1997).

Seventh Circuit: In re Kreisler, 407 B.R. 321 (Bankr. N.D. Ill. 2009).

Ninth Circuit: In re Flamingo 55, Inc., 378 B.R. 893 (Bankr. D. Nev. 2007).

Eleventh Circuit: Westchester Fire Insurance Co. v. City of Brooksville, 731 F. Supp.2d 1298 (M.D. Fla. 2010).

Federal Circuit: United States Surety Co. v. United States, 83 Fed. Cl. 306 (Fed. Cl. 2008).

State Courts:

Arkansas: Harrison v. Benton State Bank, 6 Ark. App. 355, 642 S.W.2d 331 (1982).

California: Rossa v. D.L. Falk Construction, Inc., 53 Cal.4th 387, 266 P.3d 1022, 135 Cal. Rptr.3d 329 (2012); First National Insurance Co. v. Cam Painting, Inc., 173 Cal. App.4th 1355, 93 Cal. Rptr.3d 808 (2009).

Connecticut: Martin Printing, Inc. v. Sone, 89 Conn. App. 336, 873 A.2d 232 (Conn. App. 2005).

District of Columbia: Purcell v. Thomas, 28 A.3d 1138 (D.C. App. 2011).

Georgia: Ameris Bancorp v. Ackerman, 296 Ga. App. 295, 674 S.E.2d 358 (2009).

Illinois: Rosewood Care Center, Inc. v. Caterpillar, Inc., 226 Ill.2d 559, 315 Ill. Dec. 762, 877 N.E.2d 1091 (2007).

Indiana: Town of Plainfield v. Paden Engineering Co., 943 N.E.2d 904 (Ind. App. 2011).

Louisiana: Regions Bank v. Louisiana Pipe and Steel Fabricators, L.L.C., 80 So.3d 1209 (La App. 2011); Fleet Fuel, Inc. v. Mynex, Inc., 924 So.2d 480 (La. App.), *writ denied* 930 So.2d 977 (La. 2006); Wright v. Mark C. Smith & Sons Partnership, 264 So.2d 304 (La. App. 1972), *aff'd* 283 So.2d 85 (La. 1973).

Nebraska: State v. Gilbane Building Co., 276 Neb. 686, 757 N.W.2d 194 (Neb. 2008).

Nevada: Great American Insurance Co. v. General Builders, Inc., 113 Nev. 346, 934 P.2d 257 (1997).

New Jersey: Feigenbaum v. Guaracini, 402 N.J. Super. 7, 952 A.2d 511 (N.J. Super. App. Div. 2008).

New York: Hall & Company v. Continental Casualty Co., 34 A.D.2d 1028, 310 N.Y.S.2d 950 (N.Y. App. Div. 1970), *aff'd* 262 A.D. 312, 30 N.Y.S.2d 517 (N.Y. 1972).

Oregon: Man-Data, Inc. v. B & A Automotive, Inc., 247 Or. App. 429, 270 P.3d 318 (2011).

[17] See Chapter 3 *supra*.

[18] See:

Second Circuit: Arch Insurance Co. v. Precision Stone, Inc., 584 F.3d 33 (2d Cir. 2009); Elm Haven Construction Limited Partnership v. Neri Construction LLC, 376 F.3d 96 (2d Cir. 2004).

Third Circuit: R.W. Sidley, Inc. v. United States Fidelity & Guaranty Co., 319 F. Supp.2d 554 (W.D. Pa. 2004); Wise Investments, Inc. v. Bracy Contracting, Inc., 232 F. Supp.2d 390 (E.D. Pa. 2002).

Fourth Circuit: Mid-State Surety Corp. v. Thrasher Engineering, Inc., 575 F. Supp.2d 731 (S.D. W. Va. 2008).

Sixth Circuit: Commercial Money Center, Inc. v. Illinois Union Insurance Co., 508 F.3d 327 (6th Cir. 2007).

Ninth Circuit: Contractors Equipment Maintenance Co. v. Bechtel Hanford, Inc., 514 F.3d 899 (9th Cir. 2008).

Eleventh Circuit: Westchester Fire Insurance Co. v. City of Brooksville, 731 F. Supp.2d 1298 (M.D. Fla. 2010)

District of Columbia Circuit: Hunt Construction Group, Inc. v. National Wrecking Corp., 542 F. Supp.2d 87 (D.D.C. 2008).

State Courts:

California: First National Insurance Co. v. Cam Painting, Inc., 173 Cal. App.4th 1355, 93 Cal. Rptr.3d 808 (2009); Amwest Surety Insurance Co. v. Patriot Homes, Inc., 135 Cal. App.4th 601, 37 Cal. Rptr.3d 195 (2005); Electrical Electronic Control, Inc. v. Los Angeles Unified School District, 126 Cal. App.4th 601, 24 Cal. Rptr.3d 316 (2005).

Connecticut: Goldberg v. Hartford Fire Insurance Co., 269 Conn. 550, 849 A.2d 368 (2004).

District of Columbia: Purcell v. Thomas, 28 A.3d 1138 (D.C. App. 2011).

Georgia: Fielbon Development Co. v. Colony Bank of Houston County, 290 Ga. App. 847, 660 S.E.2d 801 (2008).

Idaho: State v. Castro, 145 Idaho 993, 188 P.3d 935 (Idaho App. 2008).

Indiana: In re Kemper Insurance Co., 819 N.E.2d 485 (Ind. App. 2004).

Kansas: Tradesmen International, Inc. v. Wal-Mart Real Estate Business Trust, 35 Kan. App.3d 146, 129 P.3d 102 (2006).

Louisiana: Regions Bank v. Louisiana Pipe and Steel Fabricators, L.L.C., 80 So.3d 1209 (La App. 2011); Wooley v. Lucksinger, 7 So.3d 660 (La. App. 2008).

Maryland: Williamson v. National Grange Mutual Insurance Co., 166 Md. App. 150, 887 A.2d 665 (2005); National Union Fire Insurance Company of Pittsburgh, Pennsylvania v. Wadsworth Golf Construction Co., 160 Md. App. 257, 863 A.2d 347 (2004), *aff'd sub nom.* National Union Fire Insurance Co. of Pittsburgh v. David A. Bramble, Inc., 388 Md. 195, 879 A.2d 101 (2005).

Massachusetts: C & I Steel, LLC v. Travelers Casualty and Surety Co. of America, 70 Mass. App. Ct. 653, 876 N.E.2d 442 (2007).

Mississippi: Fidelity and Guaranty Insurance Co. v. Blount, 63 So.3d 453 (Miss. 2011).

Missouri: Jerry Bennett Masonry, Inc. v. Crossland Construction Co., 171 S.W.3d 81 (Mo. App. 2005).

New York: WBP Central Associates, L.L.C. v. DeCola, 91 A.D.3d 861, 937 N.Y.S.2d 306 (N.Y. App. Div. 2012); Gillies v. National Fire Insurance Company of Hartford, 56 A.D.3d 1236, 867 N.Y.S.2d 295 (N.Y. App. Div. 2008).

Pennsylvania: Fessenden Hall of Pennsylvania, Inc. v. Mountainview Specialties, Inc., 863 A.2d 578 (Pa. Super. 2004), *alloc. denied* 822 A.2d 479 (Pa. 2005); Downingtown Area School District v. International Fidelity Insurance Co., 671 A.2d 782 (Pa. Commw. 1996); Reliance Universal of Ohio, Inc. v. Ernest Renda Contracting Co., 454 A.2d 39 (Pa. Super. 1982); Peter J. Mascaro Co. v. Milonas, 166 A.2d 15 (Pa. 1960).

Texas: Kendziorski v. Saunders, 191 S.W.3d 395 (Tex. App. 2006); Pavecon, Inc. v. R-Com, Inc., 159 S.W.3d 219 (Tex. App. 2005).

Wisconsin: All Cities Privacy Class v. Hartford Fire Insurance Co., 333 Wis.2d 483, 798 N.W.2d 909 (Wis. App. 2011).

[19] See:

Second Circuit: Arch Insurance Co. v. Precision Stone, Inc., 584 F.3d 33 (2d Cir. 2009); Elm Haven Construction Limited Partnership v. Neri Construction LLC, 376 F.3d 96 (2d Cir. 2004).

Third Circuit: R.W. Sidley, Inc. v. United States Fidelity & Guaranty Co., 319 F. Supp.2d 554 (W.D. Pa. 2004); Wise Investments, Inc. v. Bracy Contracting, Inc., 232 F. Supp.2d 390 (E.D. Pa. 2002).

Fourth Circuit: Mid-State Surety Corp. v. Thrasher Engineering, Inc., 575 F. Supp.2d 731 (S.D. W. Va. 2008).

Sixth Circuit: Commercial Money Center, Inc. v. Illinois Union Insurance Co., 508 F.3d 327 (6th Cir. 2007).

Ninth Circuit: Contractors Equipment Maintenance Co. v. Bechtel Hanford, Inc., 514 F.3d 899 (9th Cir. 2008).

Eleventh Circuit: Westchester Fire Insurance Co. v. City of Brooksville, 731 F. Supp.2d 1298 (M.D. Fla. 2010)

District of Columbia Circuit: Hunt Construction Group, Inc. v. National Wrecking Corp., 542 F. Supp.2d 87 (D.D.C. 2008).

State Courts:

California: First National Insurance Co. v. Cam Painting, Inc., 173 Cal. App.4th 1355, 93 Cal. Rptr.3d 808 (2009); Amwest Surety Insurance Co. v. Patriot Homes, Inc., 135 Cal. App.4th 601, 37 Cal. Rptr.3d 195 (2005); Electrical Electronic Control, Inc. v. Los Angeles Unified School District, 126 Cal. App.4th 601, 24 Cal. Rptr.3d 316 (2005).

Connecticut: Goldberg v. Hartford Fire Insurance Co., 269 Conn. 550, 849 A.2d 368 (2004).

District of Columbia: Purcell v. Thomas, 28 A.3d 1138 (D.C. App. 2011).

Georgia: Fielbon Development Co. v. Colony Bank of Houston County, 290 Ga. App. 847, 660 S.E.2d 801 (2008).

Idaho: State v. Castro, 145 Idaho 993, 188 P.3d 935 (Idaho App. 2008).

Indiana: In re Kemper Insurance Co., 819 N.E.2d 485 (Ind. App. 2004).

Kansas: Tradesmen International, Inc. v. Wal-Mart Real Estate Business Trust, 35 Kan. App.3d 146, 129 P.3d 102 (2006).

Louisiana: Regions Bank v. Louisiana Pipe and Steel Fabricators, L.L.C., 80 So.3d 1209 (La App. 2011); Wooley v. Lucksinger, 7 So.3d 660 (La. App. 2008).

Maryland: Williamson v. National Grange Mutual Insurance Co., 166 Md. App. 150, 887 A.2d 665 (2005); National Union Fire Insurance Company of Pittsburgh, Pennsylvania v. Wadsworth Golf Construction Co., 160 Md. App. 257, 863 A.2d 347 (2004), *aff'd sub nom.* National Union Fire Insurance Co. of Pittsburgh v. David A. Bramble, Inc., 388 Md. 195, 879 A.2d 101 (2005).

Massachusetts: C & I Steel, LLC v. Travelers Casualty and Surety Co. of America, 70 Mass. App. Ct. 653, 876 N.E.2d 442 (2007).

Mississippi: Fidelity and Guaranty Insurance Co. v. Blount, 63 So.3d 453 (Miss. 2011).

Missouri: Jerry Bennett Masonry, Inc. v. Crossland Construction Co., 171 S.W.3d 81 (Mo. App. 2005).

New York: WBP Central Associates, L.L.C. v. DeCola, 91 A.D.3d 861, 937 N.Y.S.2d 306 (N.Y. App. Div. 2012); Gillies v. National Fire Insurance Company of Hartford, 56 A.D.3d 1236, 867 N.Y.S.2d 295 (N.Y. App. Div. 2008).

Pennsylvania: Fessenden Hall of Pennsylvania, Inc. v. Mountainview Specialties, Inc., 863 A.2d 578 (Pa. Super. 2004), *alloc. denied* 822 A.2d 479 (Pa. 2005); Downingtown Area School District v. International Fidelity Insurance Co., 671 A.2d 782 (Pa. Commw. 1996); Reliance Universal of Ohio, Inc. v. Ernest Renda Contracting Co., 454 A.2d 39 (Pa. Super. 1982); Peter J. Mascaro Co. v. Milonas, 166 A.2d 15 (Pa. 1960).

Texas: Kendziorski v. Saunders, 191 S.W.3d 395 (Tex. App. 2006); Pavecon, Inc. v. R-Com, Inc., 159 S.W.3d 219 (Tex. App. 2005).

Wisconsin: All Cities Privacy Class v. Hartford Fire Insurance Co., 333 Wis.2d 483, 798 N.W.2d 909 (Wis. App. 2011).

[20] See:

Second Circuit: Morin v. Empiyah & Co., 389 F. Supp.2d 506 (S.D.N.Y. 2005).

Third Circuit: County of Hudson v. Janiszewski, 520 F. Supp.2d 631 (D.N.J. 2007).

Fifth Circuit: International Fidelity Insurance Co. v. Sweet Little Mexico Corp., 665 F.3d 671 (5th Cir. 2011).

Seventh Circuit: In re Kreisler, 407 B.R. 321 (Bankr. N.D. Ill. 2009).

Eleventh Circuit: Westchester Fire Insurance Co. v. City of Brooksville, 731 F. Supp.2d 1298 (M.D. Fla. 2010).

Federal Circuit: United States Surety Co. v. United States, 83 Fed. Cl. 306 (Fed. Cl. 2008).

State Courts:

California: Rossa v. D.L. Falk Construction, Inc., 53 Cal.4th 387, 266 P.3d 1022, 135 Cal. Rptr.3d 129 (2012).

District of Columbia: Purcell v. Thomas, 28 A.3d 1138 (D.C. App. 2011).

Florida: First Sealord Surety, Inc. v. Suffolk Construction Co., 995 So.2d 609 (Fla. App. 2008).

Indiana: Town of Plainfield v. Paden Engineering Co., 943 N.E.2d 904 (Ind. App. 2011).

Michigan: City of Ferndale v. Florence Cement Co., 269 Mich. App. 452, 712 N.W.2d 522 (2006).

Missouri: Jerry Bennett Masonry, Inc. v. Crossland Construction Co., 171 S.W.3d 81 (Mo. App. 2005).

Oregon: Man-Data, Inc. v. B and A Automotive, Inc., 247 Or. App. 429, 270 P.3d 318 (2011).

Pennsylvania: Kiski Area School District v. Mid-State Surety Corp., 600 Pa. 444, 967 A.2d 368 (2008).

[21] See Bruner and O'Connor, *Bruner & O'Conner on Construction Law,* § 12:10 (2006).

[22] See Jerry Bennett Masonry, Inc. v. Crossland Construction Co., 171 S.W.3d 81 (Mo. App. 2005).

[23] *Third Circuit:* Wise Investments, Inc. v. Bracy Contracting, Inc., 232 F. Supp. 390 (E.D. Pa. 2002); North American Specialty Insurance Co. v. Chichester School District, 158 F. Supp.2d 468 (E.D. Pa. 2001).

Eleventh Circuit: National Union Fire Insurance Company of Hartford v. Fortune Construction Co., 320 P.3d 1260 (11th Cir.), *cert. denied* 540 U.S. 873 (2003).

State Courts:

Arkansas: Travelers Casualty & Surety Company of America v. Arkansas State Highway Commission, 120 S.W.3d 50 (Ark. 2003).

Florida: Team Land Development, Inc. v. Anzac Contractors, Inc., 811 So.2d 698 (Fla. App. 2002).

Michigan: Will H. Hall & Son, Inc. v. Ace Masonry Construction, Inc., 677 N.W.2d 51 (Mich. App. 2003), *appeal denied* 682 N.W.2d 97 (Mich. 2004).

West Virginia: Wellington Power Corp. v. CNA Surety Corp., 614 S.E.2d 680 (W. Va. 2005).

[24] See *In re* Estate of Camarda, 103 Misc.2d 362, 425 N.Y.S.2d 1012 (N.Y. Sur. 1980). See also, *Nebraska:* Wagner v. Amwest Surety Insurance Co., 274 Neb. 110, 738 N.W.2d 805 (2007); § 10.04 *supra*.

[25] See Insurance Company of North America v. DEC International, Inc., 220 Wis.2d 840, 586 N.W.2d 691 (Wis. App.), *review denied* 221 Wis.2d 634, 588 N.W.2d 631 (1998).

[26] See, e.g.:

Fourth Circuit: MCI Constructors, Inc. v. City of Greensboro, 125 Fed. Appx. 471 (4th Cir. 2005).

Fifth Circuit: Hartford Fire Insurance Co. v. City of Mont Belvieu, Texas, 611 F.3d 289 (5th Cir. 2010).

State Courts:

Georgia: Georgia State Financing & Investment Commission v. XL Specialty Insurance Co., 303 Ga. App. 540, 694 S.E.2d 193 (2010).

[27] See Crestar Mortgage Corp. v. Peoples Mortgage Corp., 818 F. Supp. 816 (E.D. Pa. 1993). See also, Milwaukee Board of School Directors v. BITEC, Inc., 321 Wis.2d 616, 775 N.W.2d 127 (Wis. App. 2009).

[28] See T & A Painting, Inc. v. United States, 673 F. Supp. 994 (N.D. Cal. 1987).

[29] See:

Fourth Circuit: MCI Contractors, Inc. v. City of Greensboro, 125 Fed. Appx. 471 (4th Cir. 2005) (where bond is valid for one year after substantial completion, it ensures work for one year after completion).

State Courts:

Georgia: McDevitt & Street Co. v. K-C Air Conditioning Service, Inc., 203 Ga. App. 640, 418 S.E.2d 87 (1992) (surety liable beyond one year warranty period where construction contract provided warranty for a period prescribed by law and the law extended the warranty period six years after completion).

Michigan: Hunters Pointe Partners Limited v. United States Fidelity & Guaranty Co., 194 Mich. App. 294, 486 N.W.2d 136 (1992) (latent defects within one year of completion were covered by surety bond where bond stated liability attached upon principal's failure to perform under the construction contract and construction contract provided express warranty for defects appearing within one year of completion).

[30] *Eighth Circuit:* Larson v. Granite Re, Inc., 532 F.3d 724 (8th Cir. 2008).

State Courts:

California: Electrical Electronic Control, Inc. v. Los Angeles Unified School District, 126 Cal. App.4th 601, 24 Cal. Rptr.3d 316 (2005).

Minnesota: Ima Concrete Breaking Corp. v. Jewat Trucking, Inc., 444 N.W.2d 865 (Minn. App. 1989).

Missouri: King v. Jones, 971 S.W.2d 916 (Mo. App. 1998).

New York: Crisafulli Brothers, Inc. v. Clanton, 128 A.D.2d 963, 512 N.Y.S.2d 927 (N.Y. App. Div. 1987).

But see:

Second Circuit: Greenblatt v. Delta Plumbing & Heating Corp., 834 F. Supp. 86 (S.D.N.Y. 1993), *vacated on other grounds* 68 F.3d 561 (2d Cir. 1995) (where words of bond do not limit surety's liability to future transactions, surety may be liable for breaches in existence before becoming a surety).

[31] See:

Second Circuit: United States Fidelity and Guaranty Co. v. Braspetro Oil Services Co., 369 F.3d 34 (2d Cir. 2004); Stonington Water Street Associates, L.L.C. v. Hodess Building Co., 792 F. Supp.2d 253 (D. Conn. 2011).

Third Circuit: Turner Construction Co. v. First Indemnity of America Insurance Co., 829 F. Supp. 752 (E.D. Pa. 1993), *aff'd* 22 F.3d 303 (3d Cir. 1994).

Fourth Circuit: Mid-State Surety Corp. v. Thrasher Engineering, Inc., 575 F. Supp.2d 731 (S.D. W. Va. 2008).

Sixth Circuit: Frontier Insurance Company in Rehabilitation v. M.C. Management, 2009 WL 1374544 (W.D. Ky. 2009).

State Courts:

Florida: Current Builders of Florida, Inc. v. First Sealord Surety, Inc., 984 So.2d 526 (Fla. App. 2008); Z.P. No. 54 Limited Partnership v. Fidelity & Deposit Company of Maryland, 917 So.2d 368 (Fla. App. 2005).

Nebraska: Wagner v. Amwest Surety Insurance Co., 274 Neb. 110, 738 N.W.2d 805 (2007).

Pennsylvania: Trumbull Corp. v. Boss Construction, Inc., 801 A.2d 1289 (Pa. Commw. 2002).

32 See Colorado Structures, Inc. v. Insurance Company of the West, 106 P.3d 815 (Wash. App. 2005).

33 See Cates Construction, Inc. v. Talbot Partners, 980 P.2d 407 (Cal. 1999).

34 See Bruner and O'Connor, *Bruner & O'Conner on Construction Law,* § 12:43 (2006). See also:

Second Circuit: Stonington Water Street Associates, L.L.C. v. Hodess Building Co., 792 F. Supp.2d 253 (D. Conn. 2011).

State Courts:

Texas: Gulf Liquids New River Project, L.L.C. v. Gulsby Engineering, Inc., 356 S.W.3d 54 (Tex. App. 2011).

35 See Bruner and O'Connor, *Bruner & O'Connor on Construction Law,* § 12:43 (2006).

36 See, e.g., Wise Investments, Inc. v. Bracy Contracting, Inc., 232 F. Supp.2d 390 (E.D. Pa. 2002) (motion for summary judgment on surety bond denied because there were genuine issues of material fact as to who defaulted under the construction contract first—the contractor or the owner). See also, Bruner and O'Connor, *Bruner and O'Connor on Construction Law,* § 12:16 (2006).

37 See:

Fourth Circuit: Moore Brothers Co. v. Brown & Root, Inc., 207 F.3d 717 (4th Cir. 2000).

State Courts:

Alabama: Hartford Accident & Indemnity Co. v. Cochran Plastering Co., 935 So.2d 462 (Ala. App. 2006).

38 *Second Circuit:* United States Fidelity & Guaranty Co. v. Braspatro Oil Services Co., 369 F.3d 34 (2d Cir. 2004) (obligee must follow termination provisions in bond to trigger surety's obligations under the bond); Stonington Water Street Associates, L.L.C. v. Hodess Building Co., 792 F. Supp.2d 253 (D. Conn. 2011); Millgard Corp. v. E.E. Cruz/Nab/Frontier-Kemper, E.E. Cruz & Co., 2002 WL 31812710 (S.D.N.Y. Dec. 12, 2002) (notice of default is condition precedent to liability under a surety bond only where there is an express contract provision making such notice a condition precedent).

Tenth Circuit: AgGrow Oils, L.L.C. v. National Union Fire Insurance Company of Pittsburgh, Pennsylvania, 276 F. Supp.2d 999 (D.N.D. 2003), *aff'd* 420 F.3d 751 (8th Cir. 2005) (owner's failure to comply with conditions precedent to payment under bond because after notice of default, owner failed to terminate and offer to pay balance of contract to surety).

State Courts:

Florida: Current Builders of Florida, Inc. v. First Sealord Surety, Inc., 984 So.2d 526 (Fla. App. 2008).

39 See National Union Fire Insurance Company of Hartford v. Fortune Construction Co., 320 F.3d 1260 (11th Cir.), *cert. denied* 540 U.S. 873 (2003) (suit by surety for balance under contract fails).

40 See:

Second Circuit: In re Chemtura Corp., 448 B.R. 635 (Bankr. S.D.N.Y 2011).

Fourth Circuit: First American Title Insurance Co. v. First Alliance Title, Inc., 718 F. Supp.2d 669 (E.D. Va. 2010).

Fifth Circuit: In re Davis Petroleum Corp., 420 B.R. 399 (Bankr. S.D. Tex. 2009).

Ninth Circuit: Blackfeet Tribe of Blackfeet Indian Reservation v. Blaze Construction, Inc., 108 F. Supp.2d 1122 (D. Mont. 2000).

State Courts:

Mississippi: McClatchy v. Anthony Farms, 936 So.2d 456 (Miss. App. 2006).

Ohio: O'Brien v. Ravenswood Apartments, Ltd., 169 Ohio App.3d 233, 862 N.E.2d 549 (2006).

Pennsylvania: Kiski Area School District v. Mid-State Surety Corp., 600 Pa. 444, 967 A.2d 368 (2008).

[41] See:

First Circuit: Augusta Fuel Co. v. Bond Safeguard Insurance Co., 502 F. Supp.2d 124 (D. Me. 2007).

Second Circuit: Stonington Water Street Associates, L.L.C. v. Hodess Building Co., 792 F. Supp.2d 253 (D. Conn. 2011).

State Courts:

Texas: Gulf Liquids New River Project, L.L.C. v. Gulsby Engineering, Inc., 356 S.W.3d 54 (Tex. App. 2011).

Washington: Peoples National Bank of Washington v. Taylor, 42 Wash. App. 518, 711 P.2d 1021 (1985).

[42] *Second Circuit:* Stonington Water Street Associates, L.L.C. v. Hodess Building Co., 792 F. Supp.2d 253 (D. Conn. 2011); Federal Insurance Co. v. Turner Construction Co., 779 F. Supp.2d 345 (S.D.N.Y. 2011); Israel v. Surinder Chabra, 418 F. Supp.2d 509 (S.D.N.Y. 2006).

Third Circuit: R.L.I. Insurance Co. v. Indian River School District, 556 F. Supp.2d 356 (D. Del. 2008); Travelers Indemnity Co. v. Ballantine, 436 F. Supp.2d 707 (M.D. Pa. 2006).

Fourth Circuit: Spencer v. Frontier Insurance Co., 290 Fed. Appx. 571 (4th Cir. 2008).

Fifth Circuit: In re Davis Petroleum Corp., 420 B.R. 399 (Bankr. S.D. Tex. 2009).

State Courts:

California: State Bar of California v. Statile, 168 Cal. App.4th 650, 86 Cal. Rptr.3d 72 (2008); Central Contra Costa Sanitary District v. National Surety Corp., 112 Cal. App.2d 61, 246 P.2d 150 (1952).

Georgia: West Cash & Carry Building Materials of Savannah, Inc. v. Liberty Mortgage Corp., 160 Ga. App. 323, 287 S.E.2d 320 (1981); SuperValu, Inc. v. K.R. Douglasville, L.L.C., 272 Ga. App. 710, 613 S.E.2d 154 (2005).

Indiana: Keesling v. T.E.K. Partners, L.L.C., 861 N.E.2d 1246 (Ind. App. 2007).

Michigan: Howard v. Lud, 119 Mich. App. 55, 325 N.W.2d 623 (1982).

New Mexico: State v. Davis, 67 N.M. 6 350 P.2d 748 (1960).

New York: Better Engineered Systems Technology, Inc. v. Sound Electric Corp., 289 A.D.2d 174, 736 N.Y.S.2d 316 (N.Y. App. 2001).

Pennsylvania: Kiski Area School District v. Mid-State Surety Corp., 600 Pa. 444, 967 A.2d 368 (2008); Moon Motel, Inc. v. Sun Insurance Company of New York, 36 Pa. D. & C.2d 491 (Pa. C.P. 1964).

Texas: Gulf Liquids New River Project, L.L.C. v. Gulsby Engineering, Inc., 356 S.W.3d 54 (Tex. App. 2011).

[43] See Bruner and O'Connor, *Bruner & O'Conner on Construction Law,* § 12:2 (2006). See also:

Second Circuit: U.S. Fidelity and Guaranty Co. v. Challenge Construction Corp., 704 F. Supp.2d 73 (D.P.R. 2009).

Sixth Circuit: In re TML, Inc., 291 B.R. 400 (Bankr. W.D. Mich. 2003).

District of Columbia Circuit: In re M & T Electric Contractors, Inc., 267 B.R. 434 (Bankr. D.D.C. 2001).

State Courts:

Mississippi: Fidelity and Guaranty Insurance Co. v. Blount, 63 So.3d 453 (Miss. 2011).

New York: WBP Central Associates, L.L.C. v. DeCola, 937 N.Y.S.2d 306 (N.Y. App. Div. 2012).

Oklahoma: Bank of Wichitas v. Ledford, 151 P.3d 103 (Okla. 2006).

South Carolina: Masterclean, Inc. v. Star Insurance Co., 556 S.E.2d 371 (S.C. 2001).

Virginia: XL Specialty Insurance Co. v. Commonwealth, Department of Transportation, 269 Va. 362, 611 S.E.2d 356 (2005).

[44] See § 10.06[1] *infra.*

[45] See § 10.06[2] *infra.*

[46] See generally, Bruner and O'Connor, *Bruner & O'Conner on Construction Law,* § 12:7 (2006).

[47] See, e.g., 42 Pa. Cons. Stat. Ann. § 8371.

[48] See generally, Bruner and O'Connor, *Bruner & O'Conner on Construction Law,* § 12:7 (2006).

[49] See:

Third Circuit: United States v. Atul Construction Co., 85 F. Supp.2d 414 (D.N.J. 2000).

Eighth Circuit: Old St. Paul Missionary Baptist Churst v. First Nation Insurance Group, 707 F. Supp.2d 811 (E.D. Ark. 2010).

State Courts:

Alaska: Loyal Order of Moose, Lodge 1392 v. International Fidelity Insurance Co., 797 P.2d 622 (Alaska 1990).

Arizona: Dodge v. Fidelity & Deposit Co., 161 Ariz. 344, 778 P.2d 1240 (1989).

Colorado: City of Westminster v. Cedric-Jones Constructors, 100 P.3d 472 (Colo. App. 2003); Cary v. United of Omaha Life Insurance Co., 68 P.3d 462 (Colo. 2003); Transamerica Premier Insurance Co. v. Brighton School District, 940 P.2d 348 (Colo. 1997).

Connecticut: PSE Consulting, Inc. v. Frank Mercede & Sons, Inc., 267 Conn. 279, 838 A.2d 135 (2004).

Illinois: Fischer v. Fidelity & Deposit Company of Maryland, 125 Ill. App.3d 632, 80 Ill. Dec. 880, 466 N.E.2d 332 (Ill. App. 1984).

Oklahoma: Worldlogics Corp. v. Chatham Reinsurance Corp., 108 P.3d 5 (Okla. App. 2004).

But see:

Third Circuit: U.S. *ex rel.* SimplexGrinnell, L.P. v. Aegis Insurance Co., 2009 WL 90233 (M.D. Pa. Jan. 14, 2009).

Fourth Circuit: Boldt Co. v. Thomason Electric and American Contractors Indemnity Co., 820 F. Supp.2d 703 (D.S.C. 2007).

[50] See:

Fourth Circuit: Cincinnati Insurance Co. v. Centech Buildings Corp., 286 F. Supp.2d 669 (M.D.N.C. 2003); Bell BCI Co. v. HRGM Corp., 276 F. Supp.2d 462 (D. Md. 2003).

State Courts:

California: Cates Construction, Inc. v. Talbot Partners, 21 Cal.4th 28, 980 P.2d 407 (1999).

Texas: Great American Insurance Co. v. North Austin Municipal Utility District, 908 S.W.2d 415 (Tex. 1995).

[51] For example, despite a statute governing the issue, 42 Pa. Cons. Stat. Ann. § 8371, courts in Pennsylvania are split on the issue, although the rationale supporting its application is

neither strong nor convincing. The courts rejecting the bad-faith statute's application in surety cases base their holding on the fact that the statute refers to claims under an "insurance policy" and contrast the bipartate relationship between an insurance company and its policyholder with the tripartite relationship between an owner, surety, and contractor. See:

Third Circuit: U.S. *ex rel.* SimplexGrinnell, L.P. v. Aegis Insurance Co., 2009 WL 90233 (M.D. Pa. Jan. 14, 2009); Norwood Co. v. RLI Insurance Co., No. 01-CV-6153, 2002 WL 485694 (E.D. Pa. Apr. 1, 2002); Tudor Development Group, Inc. v. United States Fidelity & Guaranty Co., 692 F. Supp. 461 (M.D. Pa. 1988); Superior Precast, Inc. v. Safeco Insurance Co., 71 F. Supp.2d 438 (E.D. Pa. 1999).

State Courts:

Pennsylvania: Ferrick Construction Co. v. One Beacon Insurance Co., 2004 WL 3051443 (Pa. C.P. 2004); M.A. Bruder & Sons, Inc. v. Williams, 47 Pa. D. & C.4th 243 (Pa. C.P. 2000).

On the other hand, the cases adopting the bad-faith statute's applicability in the surety context are older and contain little or no reasoning. See: Turner Construction Co. v. First Indemnity of America Insurance Co., 829 F. Supp. 752 (E.D. Pa. 1993) (assuming cause of action existed but finding no evidence of bad faith); Reading Tube Corp. v. Employers Insurance of Wausau, 944 F. Supp. 398 (E.D. Pa. 1996) (relying on Turner Construction for existence of bad-faith cause of action).

The better-reasoned and later decisions reject application of the bad-faith statute in the surety context. It is noteworthy, however, that Pennsylvania recognizes bad faith as a defense to indemnification brought by a surety against its principal. Mountbatten Surety Co. v. Jenkins, 2004 WL 2297405 (E.D. Pa. Oct. 13, 2004). Accordingly, the duty of good faith and fair dealing at least has some relevance to the surety context, even if a claim for bad faith is not recognized

[52] See:

Third Circuit: National Controls Corp. v. National Semiconductor Corp., 833 F.2d 491 (3d Cir. 1987); McDermott v. Party City Corp., 11 F. Supp.2d 612 (E.D. Pa. 1998).

State Courts:

Pennsylvania: R.I. Lampus Co. v. Neville Cement Products Corp., 474 Pa. 199, 378 A.2d 288 (1977).

[53] See:

Third Circuit: Titan Stone, Tile & Masonry, Inc. v. Hunt Construction Group, Inc., 394 Fed. Appx. 862 (3d Cir. 2010); North American Specialty Insurance Co. v. Chichester School District, 158 F. Supp.2d 468 (E.D. Pa. 2001) (bond included delay and liquidated damages and attorneys' fees provisions); Wise Investments, Inc. v. Bracy Contracting, Inc., 232 F. Supp.2d 390 (E.D. Pa. 2002) (only recovery for costs of performance, but not liquidated damages or attorneys' fees, permitted); Ragan v. Tri-County Excavating, Inc., 62 F.3d 501 (3d Cir. 1995) (similar).

State Courts:

California: Cates Construction, Inc. v. Talbot Partners, 21 Cal.4th 28, 980 P.2d 407 (1999) (consequential damages recoverable); Mepco Services, Inc. v. Saddleback Valley Unified School District, 189 Cal. App.4th 1027, 117 Cal. Rptr.3d 494 (2010).

Mississippi: Fidelity and Guaranty Insurance Co. v. Blount, 63 So.3d 453 (Miss. 2011).

Pennsylvania: Downingtown Area School District v. International Fidelity Insurance Co., 769 A.2d 560 (Pa. Commw.), *alloc. denied* 567 Pa. 731, 786 A.2d 991 (2001) (bond's failure to mention consequential or liquidated damages or attorney's fees limited owner's recovery to costs of completion minus balance of contact price).

See also Dweier, Landen, & Glover, "Preserving Consequential Damages Through Waivers and Insurance Coverage," *Construction Lawyer* (Summer 2002); *Bruner and O'Connor on Construction Law*, § 12:34 (2006).

[54] See Bruner and O'Connor, *Bruner and O'Connor on Construction Law* (2006).

[55] Form A312 Bond § 4.

[56] Form A312 Bond § 6.

[57] Form A312 Bond § 6.

[58] Form A312 Bond.

[59] Form A312 Bond.

CHAPTER 12

Title Insurance

Chapter Contents

§ 12.01 Overview

Title insurance is merely a subset of real property law because it involves title issues rather than insurance issues. Nonetheless, title insurance has become the financial instrument that allows lenders to lend on real property without the necessity of knowing the particular jurisdiction or locality at issue.

Entities that purchase real property or lend on the purchase of such property want to ensure that at the time of purchase the real property acquired is free of any unknown defects to title. In some states, real estate lawyers perform title searches. In others, title insurance is used to insure against these defects.

§ 12.02 Coverage

[1] Purpose

Unlike other forms of insurance, title insurance does not guarantee against future events. Rather it guarantees against events existing at the time of issuance of the insurance policy.[1] Title insurance protects against the existence of liens, encumbrances, or other items that interfere with free and clear title on real property but are not found on the title search or disclosed in the title report.[2] The insurance company does not guarantee perfect title but merely agrees to pay damages for or clear title to defects in title that were not disclosed or did not appear at the time of closing.[3]

[2] Duration of Coverage

The insurance coverage lasts for as long as the policyholder owns an interest in the property or, in some jurisdictions under some contract clauses, longer if the policyholder has given a warranty of title to a buyer.[4]

[3] Covered Defects in Title

Title insurance protects against a number of encumbrances to title, including liens (such as tax liens, judgment liens, and mechanics' or contractors' liens),[5] mortgages,[6] claims to real propery known as *lis pendens*,[7] recorded easements,[8] unmarketability of title,[9] which is distinct from economic unmarketability,[10] and encroachments.[11]

[4] Common Exceptions

Usually excepted from coverage by title insurance are unrecorded encumbrances, such as claims based upon adverse possession or unrecorded options to purchase,[12] zoning, land use, or other governmental restrictions,[13] and defects created by or known to the policyholder.[14]

Notes

[1] See, e.g.:

California: Hovannisian v. First American Title Insurance Co., 14 Cal. App.5th 420, 221 Cal. Rptr.3d 883 (Cal. App. 2017).

Florida: Village Carver Phase 1, LLC v. Fidelity National Title Insurance Co., 128 So.3d 107 (Fla. App. 2013).

Maryland: Back Creek Partners, LLC v. First American Title Insurance Co., 75 A.3d 394 (Md. App. 2013).

Massachusetts: Deutsche Bank, N.A. v. First American Title Insurance Co., 991 N.E.2d 638 (Masss. 2013).

New Jersey: Princeton South Investors LLC v. First American Title Insurance Co., 97 A.3d 1190 (NJ. Super., App. Div. 2014).

[2] See, e.g.:

Eighth Circuit: Associated Bank, N.A. v. Stewart Title Guaranty Co., 881 F. Supp.2d 1058 (D. Minn. 2012).

Eleventh Circuit: Regions Bank v. Commonwealth Land Title Insurance Co., 977 F. Supp.2d 1237 (S.D. Fla. 2013).

State Courts:

Arizona: First American Title Insurance Co. v. Johnson Bank, 372 P.3d 292 (Ariz. 2016).

California: Hovannisian v. First American Title Insurance Co., 14 Cal. App.5th 420, 221 Cal. Rptr.3d 883 (Cal. App. 2017).

Illinois: Wade v. Stewart Title Guaranty Co., 82 N.E.3d 763 (Ill. App. 2017).

Minnesota: Twin Cities Metro-Certified Development Co. v. Stewart Title Guaranty Co., 868 N.W.3d 713 (Minn. App. 2015).

Maryland: Back Creek Partners, LLC v. First American Title Insurance Co., 75 A.3d 394 (Md. App. 2013).

Massachusetts: Deutsch Bank, N.A. v. First American Title Insurance Co., 991 N.E.2d 638 (Masss. 2013).

New York: A. Gugliotta Development, Inc. v. First American Title Insurance Co., 976 N.Y.S.2d 172 (N.Y. Sup. Ct., App. Div. 2013).

Texas: McGonagle v. Stewart Title Guaranty Co., 432 S.W.3d 535 (Tex. App. 2014).

[3] See, e.g.:

Eighth Circuit: Associated Bank, N.A. v. Stewart Title Guaranty Co., 881 F. Supp.2d 1058 (D. Minn. 2012).

State Courts:

Arizona: First American Title Insurance Co. v. Johnson Bank, 372 P.3d 292 (Ariz. 2016).

California: Hovannisian v. First American Title Insurance Co., 14 Cal. App.5th 420, 221 Cal. Rptr.3d 883 (Cal. App. 2017).

Idaho: Cummings v. Stephens, 336 P.3d 281 (Idaho 2014).

Illinois: Wade v. Stewart Title Guaranty Co., 82 N.E.3d 763 (Ill. App. 2017).

Minnesota: Twin Cities Metro-Certified Development Co. v. Stewart Title Guaranty Co., 868 N.W.3d 713 (Minn. App. 2015).

Massachusetts: Deutsch Bank, N.A. v. First American Title Insurance Co., 991 N.E.2d 638 (Masss. 2013).

New York: A. Gugliotta Development, Inc. v. First American Title Insurance Co., 976 N.Y.S.2d 172 (N.Y. Sup. Ct., App. Div. 2013).

Texas: McGonagle v. Stewart Title Guaranty Co., 432 S.W.3d 535 (Tex. App. 2014).

[4] See:

Ninth Circuit: Londen Land Co. v. Title Resources Guaranty Co., 467 Fed. Appx. 706 (9th Cir. 2012).

State Courts:

California: Hovannisian v. First American Title Insurance Co., 14 Cal. App.5th 420, 221 Cal. Rptr.3d 883 (Cal. App. 2017); RNT Holdings, LLC v. United General Title Insurance Co., 179 Cal. Rptr.3d 175 (Cal. App. 2014).

Idaho: Bank of Idaho v. First American Title Insurance Co., 329 P.3d 1066 (Idaho 2014).

Maryland: Back Creek Partners, LLC v. First American Title Insurance Co., 75 A.3d 394 (Md. App. 2013).

New York: Soldiers', Sailors', Marines' and Airmen's Club, Inc. v. Carlton Regency Corp., 911 N.Y.S.2d 774 (N.Y. Sup. Ct. N.Y. Cnty. 2010).

New Jersey: Shotmeyer v. New Jersey Realty Title Insurance Co., 948 A.2d 600 (N.J. 2008).

South Carolina: Preservation Capital Consulatnts, LLC v. First American Title Insurance Co., 751 S.E.2d 256 (S.C. 2013).

[5] See:

Seventh Circuit: First Tennessee Bank, N.A. v. Lawyers Title Insurance Corp., 282 F.R.D. 423 (N.D. Ill. 2012) (applying Illinois law).

Eighth Circuit: Captiva Lake Investments, LLC v. Fidelity National Title Insurance Co., 883 F.3d 1038 (8th Cir. 2018) (applying Missouri law).

Tenth Circuit: BV Jordanelle, LLC v. Old Republic National Title Insurance Co., 830 F.3d 1195 (10th Cir. 2016) (applying Utah law).

State Courts:

California: Stockton Mortgage, Inc. v. Tope, 183 Cal. Rptr.3d 186 (Cal. App. 2014).

Illinois: Rhone v. First American Title Insurance Co., 928 N.E.2d 1185 (Ill. App. 2010).

Indiana: House v. First American Title Co., 883 N.E.2d 197 (Ind. App. 2008).

Louisiana: Degueyter v. First American Title Insurance Co., 230 So.3d 652 (La. App. 2017).

Minnesota: Twin Cities Metro-Certified Development Co. v. Stewart Title Guaranty Co., 868 N.W.3d 713 (Minn. App. 2015).

New Jersey: Princeton South Investors LLC v. First American Title Insurance Co., 97 A.3d 1190 (NJ. Super. App. Div. 2014).

New York: Nastasi v. County of Suffolk, 966 N.Y.S.2d 172 (N.Y. App. Div. 2013).

Oklahoma: Choate v. Lawyers Title Insurance Corp., 385 P.3d 670 (Okla. App. 2015).

Pennsylvania: Brogan v. Rosenn, Jenkins & Greenwald, LLP, 35 Pa. D.&C.5th 500 (Pa. Lackawanna Cnty. Jan. 31, 2014).

South Carolina: Preservation Capital Consulatnts, LLC v. First American Title Insurance Co., 751 S.E.2d 256 (S.C. 2013).

Texas: McGonagle v. Stewart Title Guaranty Co., 432 S.W.3d 535 (Tex. App. 2014).

[6] See:

Eleventh Circuit: Regions Bank v. Commonwealth Land Title Insurance Co., 977 F. Supp.2d 1237 (S.D. Fla. 2013).

State Courts:

Louisiana: Degueyter v. First American Title Insurance Co., 230 So.3d 652 (La. App. 2017).

New York: E.C.I. Financial Corp v. First American Title Insurance Co., 995 N.Y.S.2d 100 (N.Y. App. Div. 2014).

[7] See:

Third Circuit: Gresko v. Stewart Title Guaranty Co., 2009 WL 1010964 (D.N.J. Apr. 15, 2009) (applying New Jersey law)

Eleventh Circuit: Ticor Title Insurance Co. v. University Creek, Inc., 767 F. Supp. 1127 (M.D. Fla. 1991) (applying Florida law).

State Courts:

California: Safeco Title Insurance Co. v. Moscopoulos, 172 Cal. Rptr. 248 (Cal. App. 1981).

[8] See:

Fifth Circuit: Lawyers Title Insurance Corp. v. Doubletree Partners, L.P., 739 F.3d 848 (5th Cir. 2014) (applying Texas law).

State Courts:

Illinois: Perry v. Fidelity National Title Insurance Co., 48 N.E.3d 1168 (Ill. App. 2015).

Montana: James v. Chicago Title Insurance Co., 339 P.3d 420 (Mont. 2014).

Pennsylvania: Brogan v. Rosenn, Jenkins & Greenwald, LLP, 35 Pa. D.&C.5th 500 (Pa. Lackawanna Cnty. Jan. 31, 2014).

[9] See:

First Circuit: CH Properties, Inc. v. First American Title Insurance Co., 43 F. Supp.3d 83 (D.P.R. 2014).

State Courts:

Alabama: M&F Bank v. First American Title Insurance Co., 144 So.3d 222 (Ala. 2013).

California: Dollinger DeAnza Associates v. Chicago Title Insurance Co., 131 Cal. Rptr.3d 596 (Cal. App. 2011).

Connecticut: Trinder v. Connecticut Attorneys Title Insurance Co., 22 A.3d 493 (Conn. 2011).

Illinois: Perry v. Fidelity National Title Insurance Co., 48 N.E.3d 1168 (Ill. App. 2015).

Louisiana: Degueyter v. First American Title Insurance Co., 230 So.3d 652 (La. App. 2017).

Maryland: Back Creek Partners, LLC v. First American Title Insurance Co., 75 A.3d 394 (Md. App. 2013).

Minnesota: Mattson Ridge, LLC v. Clear Rock Title, LLP, 824 N.W.3d 622 (Minn. 2012).

Oklahoma: Choate v. Lawyers Title Insurance Corp., 385 P.3d 670 (Okla. App. 2015).

*Washington:*Dave Robbins Construction, LLC v. First American Title Insurance Co., 158 Wash. App.2d 895 (Wash. App. 2010).

Wyoming: Sonnett v. First American Title Insurance Co., 309 P.3d 799 (Wyo. 2013).

[10] See:

Fifth Circuit: MGD Partners LLC v. First American Title Insurance Co., 440 Fed. Appx. 368 (5th Cir. 2011).

State Courts:

Connecticut: Trinder v. Connecticut Attorneys Title Insurance Co., 22 A.3d 493 (Conn. 2011).

Washington: Dave Robbins Construction, LLC v. First American Title Insurance Co., 158 Wash. App.2d 895 (Wash. App. 2010).

Wyoming: Sonnett v. First American Title Insurance Co., 309 P.3d 799 (Wyo. 2013).

[11] See

Eighth Circuit: Chicago Title Insurance Co. v. Arkansas Riverview Development, LLC, 573 F. Supp.2d 1152 (E.D. Ark. 2008) (applying Arkansas law).

State Courts:

New York: Ben-Avraham v. Lawyers Title Insurance Corp., 786 N.Y.S.2d 272 (N.Y. Sup. Ct. N.Y. Cnty. 2004).

Wisconsin: First American Title Insurance Co. v. Dahlmann, 715 N.W.2d 609 (Wis. App. 2006).

[12] See:

Missouri: Fischer v. First American Title Insurance Co., 388 S.W.3d 181 (Mo. App. 2012).

New York: 236 West 40th Street Corp. v. Chicago Title Insurance Co., 864 N.Y.S.2d 416 (N.Y. App. Div. 2008).

Texas: Koenig v. First American Title Insurance Co., 209 S.W.3d 870 (Tex. App. 2006).

[13] See:

Washington: Dave Robbins Construction, LLC v. First American Title Insurance Co., 158 Wash. App.2d 895 (Wash. App. 2010).

Wyoming: Sonnett v. First American Title Insurance Co., 309 P.3d 799 (Wyo. 2013).

[14] See:

First Circuit: First American Title Insurance Co. v. Lane Powell P.C., 764 F.3d 114 (1st Cir. 2014) (applying Massachussets law).

Third Circuit: Beneficial Mutual Savings Bank v. Stewart Title Guaranty Co., 36 F. Supp.3d 537 (E.D. Pa. 2014) (applying New Jersey law).

Seventh Circuit: BB Syndication Services, Inc. v. First American Title Ins. Co., 780 F.3d 825 (7th Cir. 2015) (applying Wisconsin law).

Eighth Circuit: Captiva Lake Investments, LLC v. Fidelity National Title Insurance Co., 883 F.3d 1038 (8th Cir. 2018) (applying Missouri law).

State Courts:

California: RNT Holdings, LLC v. United General Title Insurance Co., 179 Cal. Rptr.3d 175 (Cal. App. 2014).

Louisiana: Degueyter v. First American Title Insurance Co., 230 So.3d 652 (La. App. 2017).

CHAPTER 13

Other Persons' Insurance

Chapter Contents

❖

§ 13.01 Overview

One of the most important, yet often overlooked, sources of insurance to pay for any liability (both defense and indemnity obligations) is other persons' insurance, which is simply insurance purchased and maintained by other people. There are two essential ways to access other persons' insurance: (1) directly and (2) indirectly.

This chapter initially discusses indirect access to other persons' insurance, which occurs when the other person(s) remains(remain) able to use its(their) own insurance but access thereto is given to the real estate-related entity. Indirect access to other persons' insurance is generally afforded pursuant to a contract between the other person(s) (to whose insurance access is sought) and the person(s) seeking to access such the other persons' insurance. Here, with a focus on real estate-related entities, indirect access to other persons' insurance occurs when the real estate-related entity requires the other person(s) to name the real estate-related entity as an additional insured under the other person's(persons') insurance. The indirect access topics include additional named insured status[1] and certificates of insurance.[2]

The chapter then examines the direct means of access to another's coverage, through the transfer of insurance from the other person(s) or entity(ies) to the real estate-related entity.[3] These assignments usually, but not always, occur through the purchase and sale of a business. The transfer of coverage encompasses a discussion on anti-assignment provisions in policies,[4] contractual assignments,[5] and transfers by operation of law.[6]

§ 13.02 Indirect Access to Other Persons' Policies

One way to obtain and use another person's insurance is indirectly. Indirect access to another person's insurance occurs when another person retains rights under his or her own policies but also grants access to those policies to the real estate-related entity.[7] As stated above, indirect access to other persons' insurance is generally afforded pursuant to a contract between the other person (to whose insurance access is sought) and the person seeking to access such other persons' insurance. Here, we focus on real estate-related entities. Indirect access to other persons' insurance occurs when the real estate-related entity requires the other person to name the real estate-related entity as an additional insured under the other person's insurance.

[1]—Named Insured Status

One way to have access to other persons' insurance is to be named and/or to qualify otherwise on the other persons' policies as an "insured." If the other entity is under the control of the first person or entity, such as a corporate subsidiary, access to the insurance is rather easy to accomplish.

If, as is most often the case, the other persons are not under the subject's control, the subject will want to request or require, to the extent it can be accomplished through contractual negotiation, that it be named on the other persons' insurance policies as a "named insured." This happens in a builders risk policy when the realty owner requires a contractor to name the owner a policyholder.[8] Likewise, banks and other lenders often have themselves named as a policyholder or loss payee under first-party policies covering property on which they have a mortgage or other security interest.[9] Additionally, landlords may require tenants to purchase fire insurance to protect the landlord's interest in the estate.[10] Similarly, general contractors and subcontractors often work into their contracts that they be named as a policyholder under another contractor's or subcontractor's CGL insurance policies.[11]

Great care should be taken to ensure that the subject who is claiming rights to coverage under another's insurance policy actually has those rights. Specifically, there may be a difference between being an "additional insured" and an "additional named insured." Rights of a "named insured," whether original or additional, generally are better and more extensive than those of an "additional insured."[12]

[a]—Effectuation of Status

To be named as an additional insured or additional named insured under another's insurance policy can be accomplished in two ways. First, the entity seeking such status can be specifically enumerated in a policy endorsement or in the declarations page. Alternatively, many policies have additional definitions and provisions that provide coverage to other persons or entities by virtue of their relationship to the policyholder (such as a family member, employee, affiliate), and there is a broad-form additional insured endorsement that may include certain additional parties that the policyholder has contracted with and/or agreed to indemnify.[13]

[b]—Extent of Coverage Afforded by Status

Irrespective of how an entity obtains additional insured status, an issue arises as to the extent of coverage afforded. For example, is the additional insured entitled to coverage for its own negligence or only for the policyholder's negligence, which is attributed vicariously to the additional insured. Courts have come to mixed results with this question.[14]

[2]—Certificates of Insurance

One of the ways to ensure that the subject is getting the rights it requested or required under other persons' insurance policies is through receipt of certificates of insurance, which evidence the coverage. Brokers and agents generally issue these one-page documents, which are similar to a declarations page of a policy. Certificates of insurance are not contracts between the insurance company and the certificate holder.[15] Rather, they are merely evidence that an insurance policy has been sold and issued.[16]

Certificates of insurance do not amplify, extend, or modify the coverage afforded under the insurance policy.[17] However, if an insurance company or its agent issues the certificate of insurance, the doctrine of estoppel may bind the insurance company to reasonable and justifiable reliance on statements contained therein.[18] Nonetheless, some courts have denied estoppel when reliance is unjustified because of a disclaimer in the certificate.[19]

Certificates of insurance, albeit helpful, are far from foolproof and should not be the only thing relied upon in ensuring accessibility to other persons' insurance. Two specific problems arise when certificates of insurance are the sole source of proof that insurance has been obtained by the other person(s) to whose insurance someone wants accessibility. First, certificates of insurance do not spell out all the terms of the coverage purchased, which is often necessary to ensure that the other person(s) has(have) adequately protected the entity seeking to use such other persons' insurance. Second, and equally as significant, certificates of insurance do not demonstrate that premiums have been or will be paid going forward. Obtaining a copy of the policy would resolve the question of who is covered, but the only solution to making sure that premiums are paid is, if possible or feasible, to earmark funds in the contract for payment of premiums directly from the real estate-related entity to the insurance company, perhaps out of funds owed by the real estate-related entity to the other party.

§ 13.03 Transfer of Coverage

Direct access to another person's insurance may be achieved either by obtaining control over the other person or entity or acquiring the other entity. A corporation acquiring other companies needs to structure its deals or otherwise make arrangements to make sure there is insurance coverage under the predecessor's policies in case it is sued as a successor to the companies it acquires. The transfer of property does not automatically also transfer the insurance coverage on that property.[20] Rights under insurance policies may be assigned by:

1. contract or gift;[21] or
2. operation of law.[22]

[1]—Anti-Assignment Provisions

Insurance policies typically contain provisions restricting assignments without the insurance company's consent.[23] In the vast majority of jurisdictions, these anti-assignment provisions have been enforced only as to assignments that are made *before* the loss has occurred.[24] The rational most often advanced in favor of this majority rule involves the risk underwritten by the insurance company at the time of the sale of the insurance policy. If that risk is changed, as by an assignment to a policyholder before a loss transpires, it would be unfair to the insurance company to underwrite the changed risk because it never had the opportunity to perform adequate underwriting due diligence. As for circumstances after a loss has transpired, the rule is different because the risk cannot thereafter be changed. Once the loss occurred, the risk becomes fixed.[25] When the assignment is made *after* the occurrence of an event that creates the liability of the insurance company, assignment clauses do not operate to invalidate the assignments, whether made by agreement or through operation of law.[26]

California, among other states, including Texas and Louisiana,[27] is at odds with the majority with respect to anti-assignment provisions. The California Supreme Court held that an anti-transfer provision in an insurance policy is enforceable unless the claim has been "reduced to a sum of money due or to become due under the policy."[28] As the dissent pointed out, this holding ignores the rule that "an insured can assign policy benefits once the loss insured against has occurred."[29] In other words, it is the date a chose in action arises, not the date the claim has been "reduced to a sum of money" that should be controlling.[30]

Of less controversy, the court also held that a corporation that contracts to take on the assets and liabilities of its predecessor does so voluntarily and not by operation of law.[31] Consequently, if the predecessor's insurance policy had an anti-transfer clause, the insurance will not follow the liabilities without the insurer's consent.[32] In addition, the court held that assignment without the insurer's consent is permissible "when at the time of the assignment the insurer has breached a duty to the insured, and the assignment is of a cause of action to recover damages for that breach."[33]

The court's decision presents an anomaly that breaks with the law in the vast majority of jurisdictions.[34] Acquiring entities will need to be aware of this California decision and cases that have likewise adopted the minority approach and to develop strategies to avoid the seemingly harsh consequences of having it applied to any transactions in which they are involved. Otherwise, insurance coverage might not follow the acquired liabilities. Some strategies to deal with the minority view are discussed immediately hereafter.[35]

[a]—Corporate History and Insurance Review

The first strategy a corporation would want to consider entails a thorough search of the corporate history and insurance of the entity it wishes to acquire. In particular, the acquirer should ensure that the business it is buying actually owns the liability insurance policies that cover its operations. By performing such due diligence, an acquiring entity can discern coverage issues at a time when it still possesses an ability to try to alleviate the situation, rather than when it is too late, after the acquisition takes place.

[b]—Structure of Transaction

[i]—Merger or Stock Purchase

If a review of the corporate history and insurance of the proposed acquisition presents no problems, an acquiring company should consider structuring the transaction as a stock purchase, merger, or consolidation, because under those circumstances, the majority of jurisdictions hold that all of the liabilities and assets of the acquired entity pass to the acquiring entity by operation of law.[36] For example, a stock purchase or merger of a company that owns its own liability insurance policies should operate to permit the acquiring entity to utilize the acquired entity's insurance coverage for liabilities resulting from the acquired company's operations.[37]

[ii]—Asset Purchase

If the corporate history and insurance of the proposed acquired company present problems, the acquirer may want to consider structuring the transaction in the form of an asset purchase agreement, because if the insurance will be difficult to obtain, the acquirer will certainly want to avoid assuming pre-acquisition liabilities associated with the business. However, the acquiring entity has to be extremely careful if it takes this path, because events can occur that will transfer the pre-acquisition liabilities to it. For example, the acquiring company will face liability if it can be proved that:

1. the acquirer is a mere continuation of the acquired entity's business, or
2. the acquirer continued the acquired entity's product line, or
3. the acquisition effectively destroyed any claimant's remedy against the original manufacturer, or
4. the transfer of assets was accomplished to escape liability to creditors.[38]

[c]—Assignment of Policies

An acquiring entity should consider obtaining an assignment of the insurance policies that cover the acquired entity. Typically, liability insurance policies contain provisions preventing assignment without the insurance company's consent.[39] The vast majority of jurisdictions that have addressed the issue hold that after the occurrence giving rise to the loss has taken place, a policyholder is free to assign rights under the policy related to that loss, irrespective of the insurance company's consent.[40]

However, as previously discussed,[41] California is one of a handful of states the laws from which differ from the majority. In California and these other minority jurisdictions, the only circumstances under which an assignment without the insurer's consent has been upheld is: "(1) when at the time of the assignment the benefit has been reduced to a claim for money due or to become due[;] or (2) when at the time of the assignment the insurer has breached a duty to the insured, and the assignment is of a cause of action to recover damages for that breach."[42]

In situations where an acquirer is confident that California law will not apply (i.e., there are no California contacts), the acquirer is free to obtain assignments of policies without the insurance companies' consent, and such assignments of "expired" policies should satisfy the rule that the losses already have occurred. However, if there are California contacts, the acquirer would be required to seek consent of the insurance company to the assignment, an eventuality that may prove unlikely or unfeasible.

[2]—Contractual Assignment

To effectuate a valid contractual assignment of rights under an insurance policy, there must be a manifestation of intent to assign the rights.[43] A contractual assignment must be supported by consideration,[44] and the policy itself, or a written assignment of it, must be delivered to the assignee.[45] There must also be the absence of a legal justification or excuse to non-performance of the assignment contract, such as, among other things, fraud, misrepresentation, duress, and waiver.[46] To the extent there is an anti-assignment provision, the insurance company will need to agree to the assignment, unless, in the vast majority of jurisdictions, the assignment occurs after the loss.[47]

[3]—Transfer by Operation of Law

Insurance coverage may be transferred by operation of law.[48] These "legal" transfers occur when the transaction amounts to either a merger or a product-line successorship.[49] However, a corporation that contracts to take on the assets and liabilities of its predecessor does so voluntarily and not by operation of law.[50] Consequently, if the predecessor's insurance policy had an anti-transfer clause, the insurance will not follow the liabilities without the insurer's consent.[51]

[a]—Mergers and the *De Facto* Merger Doctrine

Under a merger, a successor acquires the policies of its predecessor by operation of law.[52] Similarly, some jurisdictions recognize the *de facto* merger doctrine, which states that when the transaction essentially amounts to a merger even though it technically does not comply with the state merger statute, the successor acquires, by operation of law, all liabilities and assets, including insurance coverage, of the predecessor.[53]

Jurisdictions recognizing the doctrine apply it when the following factors are satisfied:

1. There is a continuation of the enterprise of the seller corporation, so that there is a continuity of management, personnel, physical location, assets, and general business operations.

2. There is a continuity of shareholders that results from the purchasing corporation paying for the acquired assets with shares of its own stock, this stock ultimately coming to be held by the shareholders of the seller corporation so that they become a constituent part of the purchasing corporation.
3. The seller corporation ceases its ordinary business operations, liquidates, and dissolves as soon as legally and practically possible.
4. The purchasing corporation assumes those liabilities and obligations of the seller ordinarily necessary for the uninterrupted continuation of normal business operations of the seller corporation.[54]

[b]—Product-Line Successorship

Some jurisdictions recognize the product-line successorship doctrine, which provides:

> "[W]here one corporation acquires all or substantially all the manufacturing assets of another corporation, even if exclusively for cash, and undertakes essentially the same manufacturing operation as the selling corporation, the purchasing corporation is strictly liable for injuries caused by defects in units of the same product line, even if previously manufactured and distributed by the selling corporation or its predecessor."[55]

The successor's assumption of the obligations for product liability claims arising from the predecessor's pre-sale activities results in the successor's acquisition, by operation of law, of the insurance coverage for such transferred obligations.[56] The relevant factors are:

1. the virtual destruction of the plaintiff's remedy against the original manufacturer—the predecessor—as a result of the successor's acquisition of the predecessor's business;
2. the successor's ability to assume the liabilities of the predecessor;
3. the fairness of requiring the successor to assume a responsibility for defective products as a *quid pro quo* for enjoying the predecessor's good will;
4. the successor's advertising itself as an ongoing enterprise;
5. the successor's maintaining the same product, name, personnel, property, and clients of the predecessor;
6. the successor's acquiring the predecessor's name and good will; and
7. the requirement that the predecessor dissolve.[57]

Only the first factor is mandatory for application of the doctrine.[58]

Notes

[1] See § 13.02[1] *infra*.

[2] See § 13.02[2] *infra*.

[3] See § 13.03 *infra*.

[4] See § 13.03[1] *infra*.

[5] See § 13.03[2] *infra*.

[6] See § 13.03[3] *infra*.

[7] See, e.g.:

Third Circuit: Landmark American Insurance Co. v. Rider University, 2009 WL 1905107 (D.N.J. June 30, 2009).

Fourth Circuit: Admiral Insurance Co. v. G4S Youth Services, 634 F. Supp.2d 605 (E.D. Va. 2009).

Fifth Circuit: Barden Mississippi Gaming L.L.C. v. Great Northern Insurance Co., 576 F.3d 235 (5th Cir. 2009).

Seventh Circuit: Prisco Serena Sturm Architects, Ltd. v. Liberty Mutual Insurance Co., 126 F.3d 886, 892 (7th Cir. 1997).

Eighth Circuit: SFH, Inc. v. Millard Refrigerated Services, Inc., 339 F.3d 738, 744 (8th Cir. 2003); Lexington Insurance Co. v. Integrity Land Title Co., 2012 WL 458791 (E.D. Mo. Feb. 13, 2012).

Tenth Circuit: Marathon Ashland Pipe Line LLC v. Maryland Casualty Co., 243 F.3d 1232 (10th Cir. 2001).

Eleventh Circuit: Dehres L.L.C. v. Underwriters at Interest at Lloyds London, 826 F. Supp.2d 1338 (S.D. Fla. 2011).

State Courts:

Connecticut: Reyes v. Nautilus Insurance Co., 2012 WL 1004302 (Conn. Super. Mar. 6, 2012).

Florida: Sommerville v. Allstate Insurance Co., 65 So.3d 558 (Fla. App. 2011).

Massachusetts: Massachusetts Turnpike Authority v. Perini Corp., 349 Mass. 448, 208 N.E.2d 807, 812 (1965).

New Jersey: Cassilli v. Soussou, 408 N.J. Super. 147, 973 A.2d 986 (2009).

New York: Balyszak v. Siena College, 63 A.D.3d 1409, 882 N.Y.S.2d 335 (N.Y. App. Div. 2009).

Pennsylvania: Line Lexington Lumber & Millwork Co. v. Pennsylvania Publishing Corp., 451 Pa. 154, 301 A.2d 684, 687–688 (1973); General Electric Credit Corp. v. Aetna Casualty & Surety Co., 437 Pa. 463, 263 A.2d 448, 455 (1970); Overholt v. Reliance Insurance Co., 319 Pa. 340, 179 A. 554, 556–557 (1935).

Virginia: K & W Builders, Inc. v. Merchants & Business Men's Mutual Insurance Co., 255 Va. 5, 495 S.E.2d 473, 476 (1998).

See also, Philip Bruner and Patrick O'Connor, *Bruner & O'Connor on Construction Law*, § 11:63 (2006).

[8] See Bruner and O'Connor, *Bruner & O'Connor on Construction Law*, § 11:63 (2006). See also:

First Circuit: Tocci Building Corp. v. Zurich American Insurance Co., 659 F. Supp.2d 251 (D. Mass. 2009).

Second Circuit: Indian Harbor Insurance Co. v. Assurance Company of America, 2010 WL 2365571 (D.R.I. May 21, 2010).

Third Circuit: Zurich American Insurance Co. v. Keating Building Corp., 513 F. Supp.2d 55 (D.N.J. 2007).

Eighth Circuit: Fireman's Fund v. Structural Systems Technology, Inc., 426 F. Supp.2d 1009 (D. Neb. 2006).

Ninth Circuit: Oceanside Pier View, L.P. v. Travelers Property Casualty Company of America, 2008 WL 7822214 (S.D. Cal. May 6, 2008).

Eleventh Circuit: Ajax Building Corp. v. Hartford Fire Insurance Co., 358 F.3d 795 (11th Cir. 2004).

State Courts:

Iowa: Hendricks v. Great Plains Supply Co., 609 N.W.2d 486 (Iowa 2000).

Missouri: Black & Veatch Corp. v. Wellington Syndicate, 302 S.W.3d 114 (Mo. App. 2009).

North Carolina: Gore v. Assurance Company of America, 704 S.E.2d 6 (N.C. App. 2010).

Washington: Frank Coluccio Construction Co. v. King County, 150 P.3d 1147 (Wash. App. 2007).

[9] See, e.g.:

Fifth Circuit: Graphia v. Balboa Insurance Co., 517 F. Supp.2d 854 (E.D. La. 2007).

State Courts:

California: Home Savings of America, F.S.B. v. Continental Insurance Co., 87 Cal. App.4th 835, 104 Cal. Rptr.2d 790 (2001).

Minnesota: Border State Bank of Greenbush v. Farmers Home Group, 620 N.W.2d 721 (Minn. App. 2000).

Pennsylvania: General Electric Credit Corp. v. Aetna Casualty & Surety Co., 437 Pa. 463, 263 A.2d 448, 455 (1970); Overholt v. Reliance Insurance Co., 319 Pa. 340, 179 A. 554, 556–557 (1935).

[10] See, e.g.: *Fifth Circuit:* Milchem, Inc. v. M. A. Smith Well Service, Inc., 351 F. Supp. 1307 (E.D. La. 1972).

State Courts:

New York: SUS, Inc. v. St. Paul Travelers Group, 87 Cal. App.4th 835, 905 N.Y.S.2d 321 (N.Y. App. Div. 2010).

Pennsylvania: Line Lexington Lumber & Millwork Co. v. Pennsylvania Publishing Corp., 451 Pa. 154, 301 A.2d 684, 687–688 (1973).

[11] See Bruner and O'Connor, *Brunner & O'Connor Construction Law*, § 11:63 (2006). See also:

Seventh Circuit: Prisco Serena Sturm Architects, Ltd. v. Liberty Mutual Insurance Co., 126 F.3d 886, 892 (7th Cir. 1997).

Eighth Circuit: SFH, Inc. v. Millard Refrigerated Services, Inc., 339 F.3d 738, 744 (8th Cir. 2003).

Tenth Circuit: Marathon Ashland Pipe Line LLC v. Maryland Casualty Co., 243 F.3d 1232 (10th Cir. 2001).

State Courts:

Massachusetts: Massachusetts Turnpike Authority v. Perini Corp., 349 Mass. 448, 208 N.E.2d 807, 812 (1965).

Virginia: K & W Builders, Inc. v. Merchants & Business Men's Mutual Insurance Co., 255 Va. 5. 495 S.E.2d 473, 476 (1998).

[12] See § 5.03[3] *supra*.

[13] See:

First Circuit: Wright-Ryan Construction, Inc. v. AIG Insurance Company of Canada, 647 F.3d 411 (1st Cir. 2011); Pro Con, Inc. v. Interstate Fire and Casualty Co., 794 F. Supp.2d 242 (D. Me. 2011).

Third Circuit: Interstate Aerials, L.L.C. v. Great American Insurance Company of New York, 352 Fed. Appx. 637 (3d Cir. 2009); Dale Corp. v. Cumberland Mutual Fire Insurance Co., 2010 WL 4909600 (E.D. Pa. Nov. 30, 2010).

Fourth Circuit: Parts Inc. v. Utica Mutual Insurance Co., 602 F. Supp.2d 617 (D. Md. 2009).

Fifth Circuit: Gilbane Building Co. v. Admiral Insurance Co., 664 F.3d 589 (5th Cir. 2011); Town Center Mall v. Zurich American Insurance Co., 797 F. Supp.2d 786 (S.D. Tex. 2011).

Ninth Circuit: Tri-Star Theme Builders, Inc. v. OneBeacon Insurance Co., 426 Fed. Appx. 506 (9th Cir. 2011); Certain Underwriters at Lloyd's of London v. American Safety Insurance Services, Inc., 702 F. Supp.2d 1169 (C.D. Cal. 2010).

Tenth Circuit: Behar v. Certain Underwriters at Lloyds, London, 554 F. Supp.2d 1262 (W.D. Okla. 2008).

State Courts:

California: Oliver Machinery Co. v. United States Fidelity and Guaranty Co., 187 Cal. App.3d 1510, 232 Cal. Rptr. 691 (1986).

Florida: Continental Casualty Co. v. Ryan Inc. Eastern, 974 So.2d 368 (Fla. 2008).

Illinois: United Stationers Supply Co. v. Zurich American Insurance Co., 386 Ill. App.3d 88, 896 N.E.2d 425, 324 Ill. Dec. 639 (2008).

Nevada: Federal Insurance Co. v. American Hardware Mutual Insurance Co., 124 Nev. 319, 184 P.3d 390 (2008).

New Jersey: Cassilli v. Soussou, 408 N.J. Super. 147, 973 A.2d 986 (N.J. Super. App. Div. 2009).

New York: Stillwater Central School District v. Great American E & S Insurance Co., 66 A.D.3d 1260, 887 N.Y.S.2d 719 (N.Y. App. Div. 2009).

Tennessee: Lancaster v. Ferrell Paving, Inc., 2011 WL 4357308 (Tenn. App. Sep. 20, 2011), *appeal denied* (Feb. 15, 2012).

Texas: Certain Underwriters at Lloyd's, London v. LM Ericsson Telefon, AB, 272 S.W.3d 691 (Tex. App. 2008).

[14] See:

Third Circuit: Landmark American Insurance Co. v. Rider University, 2009 WL 1905107 (D.N.J. June 30, 2009).

Fourth Circuit: Admiral Insurance Co. v. G4S Youth Services, 634 F. Supp.2d 605 (E.D. Va. 2009).

Fifth Circuit: Barden Mississippi Gaming L.L.C. Doing Business As Fitzgerald's Casino v. Great Northern Insurance Co., 576 F.3d 235 (5th Cir. 2009).

Sixth Circuit: Bondex International, Inc. v. Hartford Accident and Indemnity Co., 667 F.3d 669 (6th Cir. 2011).

Eighth Circuit: UnitedHealth Group, Inc. v. Columbia Casualty Co., 2011 WL 56781007 (D. Minn. Dec. 27, 2011).

Ninth Circuit: Teck Metals, Ltd. v. Certain Underwriters at Lloyd's, London, 735 F. Supp.2d 1260 (E.D. Wash. 2010).

Eleventh Circuit: United Rentals, Inc. v. Mid-Continent Casualty Co., 2012 WL 539362 (S.D. Fla. Feb. 16, 2012).

State Courts:

Florida: Garcia v. Federal Insurance Co., 969 So.2d 288 (Fla. 2007).

Illinois: Hartford Fire Insurance Co. v. Everest Indemnity Insurance Co., 369 Ill. App.3d 757, 861 N.E.2d 306 (2006).

Nevada: Federal Insurance Co. v. American Hardware Mutual Insurance Co., 184 P.3d 390 (Nev. 2008).

New Jersey: East Coast Residential Associates, L.L.C. v. Builders Firstsource-Northeast Group, L.L.C., 2012 N.J. Super. Unpub. LEXIS 64 (N.J. Super. App. Div. Jan. 11, 2012).

New York: Balyszak v. Siena College, 63 A.D.3d 1409, 882 N.Y.S.2d 335 (N.Y. App. Div. 2009); Cohen v. Medical Malpractice Insurance Pool of New York State, 56 A.D.3d

296, 868 N.Y.S.2d 14 (N.Y. App. Div. 2008); Chunn v. New York City Housing Authority, 55 A.D.3d 437, 866 N.Y.S.2d 145 (N.Y. App. Div. 2008).

Ohio: Efficient Lighting Sales Co. v. Neverman, 2009 WL 348828 (Ohio App. Feb. 12, 2009).

Washington: International Marine Underwriters v. ABCD Marine, L.L.C., 165 Wash. App. 223, 267 P.3d 479 (2011).

15 *Fifth Circuit:* United States Pipe & Foundry Co. v. United States Fidelity & Guaranty Co., 505 F.2d 88, 89 (5th Cir. 1974); National Marine, Inc. v. Glencore, Ltd., 1998 WL 204734, at *3 (E.D. La. Apr. 23, 1998).

Ninth Circuit: Atlas Assurance Co. v. Harper, Robinson Shipping Co., 508 F.2d 1381, 1386 (9th Cir. 1975); Riverport Insurance Co. v. Oakland Community Housing, Inc., 2009 WL 3733332 (N.D. Cal. Nov. 6, 2009).

Eleventh Circuit: Becks v. Emery-Richardson, Inc., 1990 WL 303548, at *26 (S.D. Fla. Dec. 21, 1990).

State Courts:

California: Empire Fire & Marine Insurance Co. v. Bell, 55 Cal. App.4th 1410, 64 Cal. Rptr.2d 749, 757 n.25 (1997).

Colorado: Broderick Investment Co. v. Strand Nordstrom Stailey Parker, Inc., 794 P.2d 264, 266 (Colo. App. 1990).

Illinois: Lezak & Levy Wholesale Meats, Inc. v. Illinois Employers Insurance Company of Wausau, 121 Ill. App.3d 954, 77 Ill. Dec. 419, 460 N.E.2d 475, 477 (1984).

New York: Hunt v. Ciminelli-Cowper Co., 93 A.D.3d 1152, 939 N.Y.S.2d 781 (N.Y. App. Div. 2012).

Washington: Postlewait Construction Co. v. Great American Insurance Cos., 106 Wash.2d 96, 720 P.2d 805, 807 n.7 (1986).

16 See:

Fifth Circuit: United States Pipe & Foundry Co. v. United States Fidelity & Guaranty Co., 505 F.2d 88, 89 (5th Cir. 1974).

Ninth Circuit: Riverport Insurance Co. v. Oakland Community Housing, Inc., 2009 WL 3733332 (N.D. Cal. Nov. 6, 2009).

State Courts:

California: Empire Fire & Marine Insurance Co. v. Bell, 55 Cal. App.4th 1410, 64 Cal. Rptr.2d 749, 757 n.25 (Cal. App. 1997).

New York: Hunt v. Ciminelli-Cowper Co., 93 A.D.3d 1152, 939 N.Y.S.2d 781 (N.Y. App. Div. 2012).

17 See Citgo Petroleum Corp. v. Yeargin, Inc., 690 So.2d 154, 164 (La. App.), *writ denied* 701 So.2d 169 (La. 1997).

18 See:

Florida: Criterion Leasing Group v. Gulf Coast Plastering & Drywall, 582 So.2d 799, 800 (Fla. App. 1991) (issuance of certificate by insurance company allowed application of equitable estoppel).

Illinois: Dumenric v. Union Oil Company of California, 238 Ill. App.3d 208, 179 Ill. Dec. 398, 606 N.E.2d 230 (1992), *appeal denied* 148 Ill.2d 639, 183 Ill. Dec. 15, 610 N.E.2d 1259 (1993) (agent's actions bound insurance company).

Massachusetts: O'Connell v. Reliance Insurance Co., 50 Mass. App. Ct. 334, 737 N.E.2d 13 (2000).

Rhode Island: General Accident Insurance Company of America v. American National Fireproofing, Inc., 716 A.2d 751, 755 (R.I. 1998) (issuance of certificate by insurance company allowed application of equitable estoppel).

[19] See:

Fifth Circuit: National Marine, Inc. v. Glencore, Ltd., 1998 WL 204734, at *3-4 (E.D. La. Apr. 23, 1998) (estoppel not available because reliance was unjustifiable given disclaimer in certificate of insurance).

State Courts:

Colorado: Broderick Investment Co. v. Strand Nordstrom Stailey Parker, Inc., 794 P.2d 264, 266 (Colo. App. 1990) (promissory estoppel unavailable because of disclaimer and terms of certificate of insurance made reliance unjustified).

[20] See:

Third Circuit: Newark Fire Insurance Company of Hartford, Connecticut v. Turk, 6 F.2d 533, 534–535 (3d Cir. 1925); Semple v. State Farm Mutual Automobile Insurance Co., 215 F. Supp. 645, 647 (E.D. Pa. 1963).

Fifth Circuit: Ford, Bacon and Davis, L.L.C. v. Travelers Insurance Co., 635 F.3d 734 (5th Cir. 2011).

Sixth Circuit: Pilkington North America, Inc. v. Travelers Casualty and Surety Co., 2009 WL 2243590 (N.D. Ohio July 27, 2009).

Seventh Circuit: Athena Restaurant, Inc. v. Sheffield Insurance Co., 681 F. Supp. 561 (N.D. Ill. 1988).

Ninth Circuit: In re Courson, 409 B.R. 516 (Bankr. E.D. Wash. 2009).

State Courts:

Arkansas: Fireman's Fund Insurance Co. v. Rogers, 18 Ark. App. 142, 712 S.W.2d 311 (1986).

California: General Accident Insurance Co. v. Superior Court, 55 Cal. App.4th 1444, 64 Cal. Rptr.2d 781 (1997); Quemetco Inc. v. Pacific Automobile Insurance Co., 24 Cal. App.4th 494, 29 Cal. Rptr.2d 627 (Cal. App. 1994).

Hawaii: Del Monte Fresh Produce (Hawaii), Inc. v. Fireman's Fund Insurance Co., 117 Haw. 357, 183 P.3d 734 (2007).

Maine: Waltman & Co. v. Leavitt, 722 A.2d 862 (Me. 1999).

Pennsylvania: Spector v. Grossman, 115 Pa. Super. 372, 175 A. 890, 891 (1934).

Washington: CLS Mortgage, Inc. v. Bruno, 86 Wash. 390, 937 P.2d 1106 (Wash. 1997).

Wisconsin: Red Arrow Products Co. v. Employers Insurance of Wausau, 233 Wis.2d 114, 607 N.W.2d 294 (Wis. App.), *review denied* 234 Wis.2d 177, 612 N.W.2d 733 (2000)

[21] See:

Third Circuit: Newark Fire Insurance Company of Hartford, Connecticut v. Turk, 6 F.2d 533, 535 (3d Cir. 1925); Phoenix Mutual Life Insurance Co. v. Reich, 75 F. Supp. 886, 895 (W.D Pa. 1948); Federal Insurance Company By and Through Associated Aviation Underwriters v. Purex Industries, Inc., 972 F. Supp. 872 (D.N.J. 1997).

Fifth Circuit: Ford, Bacon and Davis, L.L.C. v. Travelers Insurance Co., 635 F.3d 734 (5th Cir. 2011).

Sixth Circuit: Pilkington North America, Inc. v. Travelers Casualty and Surety Co., 2009 WL 2243590 (N.D. Ohio July 27, 2009); Elliott Co. v. Liberty Mutual Insurance Co., 434 F. Supp.2d 483 (N.D. Ohio 2006).

Ninth Circuit: In re Courson, 409 B.R. 516 (Bankr. E.D. Wash. 2009).

State Courts:

Hawaii: Del Monte Fresh Produce (Hawaii), Inc. v. Fireman's Fund Insurance Co., 117 Haw. 357, 183 P.3d 734 (2007).

Missouri: Smith v. Smith, 313 S.W.2d 753 (Mo. App. 1958).

Ohio: Pilkington North America, Inc. v. Travelers Casualty & Surety Co., 112 Ohio St.3d 482, 861 N.E.2d 121 (2006).

Pennsylvania: Riley v. Wirth, 313 Pa. 362, 169 A. 139, 140–141 (1933); National Memorial Services, Inc. v. Metropolitan Life Insurance Co., 159 Pa. Super. 292, 48 A.2d 143, 144–145 (Pa. Super.), *aff'd* 355 Pa. 155, 49 A.2d 382 (1946); Spector v. Grossman, 115 Pa. Super. 372, 175 A. 890, 891 (1934).

See also §§ 13.03[1][c], [2] *infra*.

22 See:

First Circuit: Total Waste Management Corp. v. Commercial Union Insurance Co., 857 F. Supp. 140 (D.N.H. 1994).

Third Circuit: Brunswick Corp. v. St. Paul Fire & Marine Insurance Co., 509 F. Supp. 750, 752–753 (E.D. Pa. 1981); Federal Insurance Company By and Through Associated Aviation Underwriters v. Purex Industries, Inc., 972 F. Supp. 872 (D.N.J. 1997).

Fifth Circuit: Ford, Bacon and Davis, L.L.C. v. Travelers Insurance Co., 635 F.3d 734 (5th Cir. 2011).

Ninth Circuit: Northern Insurance Company of New York v. Allied Mutual Insurance Co., 955 F.2d 1353, 1357 (9th Cir.), *cert. denied* 505 U.S. 1221 (1992); *In re* Courson, 409 B.R. 516 (Bankr. E.D. Wash. 2009); B.S.B. Diversified Co. v. American Motorist Insurance Co., 947 F. Supp. 1476 (W.D. Wash. 1996).

State Courts:

California: General Accident Insurance Co. v. Superior Court, 55 Cal. App.4th 1444, 64 Cal. Rptr.2d 781 (1997); Quemetco Inc. v. Pacific Automobile Insurance Co., 24 Cal. App.4th 494, 29 Cal. Rptr.2d 627 (Cal. App. 1994).

Hawaii: Del Monte Fresh Produce (Hawaii), Inc. v. Fireman's Fund Insurance Co., 117 Haw. 357, 183 P.3d 734 (2007).

Wisconsin: Red Arrow Products Co. v. Employers Insurance of Wausau, 233 Wis.2d 114, 607 N.W.2d 294 (Wis. App.), *review denied* 234 Wis.2d 177, 612 N.W.2d 733 (2000).

See also § 13.03[3] *infra*.

23 See ISO Form CG 00 01 10 01.

24 See:

Second Circuit: Globecon Group, LLC v. Hartford Fire Insurance Co., 434 F.3d 165 (2d Cir. 2006); Peck v. Public Service Mutual Insurance Co., 114 F. Supp.2d 51, 56 (D. Conn. 2000); Texaco A/S S.A. v. Commercial Insurance Company of Newark, New Jersey, 1995 WL 628997, at *6–7 (S.D.N.Y. Oct. 26, 1995), *opinion amended* 1996 WL 603915 (S.D.N.Y. Oct. 21, 1996).

Third Circuit: In re Federal-Mogul Global, 402 B.R. 625 (Bankr. D. Del. 2009); Viola v. Fireman's Fund Insurance Co., 965 F. Supp. 654 (E.D. Pa. 1997); Continental Casualty Co. v. Diversified Industries, Inc., 884 F. Supp. 937 (E.D. Pa. 1995); Brunswick Corp. v. St. Paul Fire & Marine Insurance Co., 509 F. Supp. 750, 753 (E.D. Pa. 1981); Federal Insurance Company By and Through Associated Aviation Underwriters v. Purex Industries, Inc., 972 F. Supp. 872 (D.N.J. 1997); International Rediscount Corp. v. Hartford Accident & Indemnity Co., 425 F. Supp. 669, 672–673 (D. Del. 1977).

Fourth Circuit: National Union Fire Insurance Co. of Pittsburgh, PA v. Porter Hayden Co., 408 B.R. 66 (D. Md. 2009).

Fifth Circuit: National Union Fire Insurance Co. of Pittsburgh, PA v. Puget Plastics Corp., 649 F. Supp.2d 613 (S.D. Tex. 2009); *In re* Katrina Canal Breaches Consolidated Litigation, 2009 WL 1046016 (E.D. La. Apr. 16, 2009); ARM Properties Management Group v. RSUI Indemnity Co., 642 F. Supp.2d 592 (W.D. Tex. 2009); Pontchartrain Gardens, Inc. v. State Farm General Insurance Co., 2009 WL 86671 (E.D. La. Jan. 13 2009).

Sixth Circuit: Elliott Co. v. Liberty Mutual Insurance Co., 434 F. Supp.2d 483 (N.D. Ohio 2006).

Seventh Circuit: Edgewood Manor Apartment Homes L.L.C. v. RSUI Indemnity Co., 782 F. Supp.2d 716 (E.D. Wis. 2011).

Ninth Circuit: Alexander Manufacturing, Inc. Employee Stock Ownership Plan and Trust v. Illinois Union Insurance Co., 560 F.3d 984 (9th Cir. 2009); Insurance Company of North America v. Snyder Moving & Storage, Inc., 52 Fed. Appx. 899, 903–904 (9th Cir. 2002).

Tenth Circuit: In re Baird, 567 F.3d 1207 (10th Cir. 2009).

State Courts:

California: Executive Risk Indemnity, Inc. v. Jones, 171 Cal. App.4th 319, 89 Cal. Rptr.3d 747 (2009).

Delaware: Viking Pump, Inc. v. Century Indemnity Co., 2 A.3d 76 (Del. Chancery Ct. 2009).

Colorado: Lincoln General Insurance Co. v. Bailey, 2009 WL 1331094 (Colo. App. May 14, 2009).

Florida: Progressive Express Insurance Co. v. Hartley, 21 So.3d 119 (Fla. App. 2009; Continental Casualty Co. v. Ryan Inc. Eastern, 974 So.2d 368 (Fla. 2008).

Georgia: Santiago v. Safeway Insurance Co., 196 Ga. App. 480, 396 S.E.2d 506 (1990).

Illinois: Illinois Tool Works, Inc. v. Commerce and Industry Insurance Co., 962 N.E.2d 1042, 357 Ill. Dec. 141 (Ill. App. 2011); Cincinnati Insurance Co. v. American Hardware Manufacturers Association, 387 Ill. App.3d 85, 325 Ill. Dec. 483, 898 N.E.2d 216 (2008).

Indiana: Travelers Casualty and Surety Co. v. United States Filter Corp., 895 N.E.2d 1172 (Ind. 2008).

Iowa: Conrad Brothers v. John Deere Insurance Co., 640 N.W.2d 231, 237 (Iowa 2001).

Minnesota: Star Windshield Repair, Inc. v. Western National Insurance Co., 768 N.W.2d 346 (Minn. 2009); Gopher Oil Co. v. American Hardware Mutual Insurance Co., 588 N.W.2d 756 (Minn. App. 1999).

New York: Greenhomes America, L.L.C. v. Farm Family Casualty Insurance Co., 91 A.D.3d 1352, 936 N.Y.S.2d 829 (N.Y. App. Div. 2012); Home Depot U.S.A., Inc. v. National Fire & Marine Insurance Co., 55 A.D.3d 671, 866 N.Y.S.2d 255 (N.Y. App. Div. 2008).

Ohio: Pilkington North America, Inc. v. Travelers Casualty & Surety Co., 112 Ohio St.3d 482, 861 N.E.2d 121 (2006); Fiorentino v. Lightning Rod Mutual Insurance Co., 114 Ohio App.3d 188, 682 N.E.2d 1099, 1101–1103 (1996).

Pennsylvania: National Memorial Services, Inc. v. Metropolitan Life Insurance. Co., 159 Pa. Super 292, 48 A.2d 143, 144–145 (Pa. Super.), *aff'd* 355 Pa. 155, 49 A.2d 382 (1946).

Accord, Couch on Insurance, § 35:7 (3d ed. 2003).

But see:

Fifth Circuit: Keller Foundations, Inc. v. Wausau Underwriters Insurance Co., 626 F.3d 871 (5th Cir. 2010); Nautilus Insurance Co. v. Concierge Care Nursing Centers, Inc., 804 F. Supp.2d 557 (S.D. Tex. 2011).

State Courts:

California: Henkel Corp. v. Hartford Accident & Indemnity Co., 29 Cal.4th 934, 129 Cal. Rptr.2d 828, 62 P.3d 69, 75–76 (2003).

Louisiana: In re Katrina Canal Breaches Litigation, 63 So.3d 955 (La. 2011).

[25] As stated by the United States Supreme Court in Century Tablet Manufacturing Company v. United States, 417 U.S. 673, 685, 94 S.Ct. 2516, 41 L.Ed.2d 398 (1974):

"With a fire loss, the obligation to pay arises upon the fire. Unlike an executory contract to sell, the casualty contract cannot be rescinded. Details, including even the basic question of liability, may be contested, but the fundamental contractual obligation that precipitates the transformation from a chose in action consisting of a claim for insurance proceeds is fixed by the fire."

The New York intermediate appellate court likewise explained the rationale as follows:

"As a general matter, New York follows the majority rule that [a no-transfer clause] is valid with respect to transfers that were made prior to, but not after, the loss has occurred. . . . The idea behind the majority rule is that, once the insured-against loss has occurred, the policy-holder essentially . . . is transferring a cause of action [or its liability] rather than a particular risk profile."

Greenhomes America, L.L.C. v. Farm Family Casualty Insurance Co., 91 A.D.3d 1352, 936 N.Y.S.2d 829 (N.Y. App. Div. 2012) (quotations and citations omitted).

26 *Id.*

27 *Second Circuit:* Globecon Group, LLC v. Hartford Fire Insurance Co., 434 F.3d 165 (2d Cir. 2006); Peck v. Public Service Mutual Insurance Co., 114 F. Supp.2d 51, 56 (D. Conn. 2000); Texaco A/S S.A. v. Commercial Insurance Company of Newark, New Jersey, 1995 WL 628997, at *6–7 (S.D.N.Y. Oct. 26, 1995), *opinion amended* 1996 WL 603915 (S.D.N.Y. Oct. 21, 1996).

Third Circuit: In re Federal-Mogul Global, 402 B.R. 625 (Bankr. D. Del. 2009); Viola v. Fireman's Fund Insurance Co., 965 F. Supp. 654 (E.D. Pa. 1997); Continental Casualty Co. v. Diversified Industries, Inc., 884 F. Supp. 937 (E.D. Pa. 1995); Brunswick Corp. v. St. Paul Fire & Marine Insurance Co., 509 F. Supp. 750, 753 (E.D. Pa. 1981); Federal Insurance Company By and Through Associated Aviation Underwriters v. Purex Industries, Inc., 972 F. Supp. 872 (D.N.J. 1997); International Rediscount Corp. v. Hartford Accident & Indemnity Co., 425 F. Supp. 669, 672–673 (D. Del. 1977).

Fourth Circuit: National Union Fire Insurance Co. of Pittsburgh, PA v. Porter Hayden Co., 408 B.R. 66 (D. Md. 2009).

Fifth Circuit: National Union Fire Insurance Co. of Pittsburgh, PA v. Puget Plastics Corp., 649 F. Supp.2d 613 (S.D. Tex. 2009); *In re* Katrina Canal Breaches Consolidated Litigation, 2009 WL 1046016 (E.D. La. Apr. 16, 2009); ARM Properties Management Group v. RSUI Indemnity Co., 642 F. Supp.2d 592 (W.D. Tex. 2009); Pontchartrain Gardens, Inc. v. State Farm General Insurance Co., 2009 WL 86671 (E.D. La. Jan. 13, 2009).

Sixth Circuit: Elliott Co. v. Liberty Mutual Insurance Co., 434 F. Supp.2d 483 (N.D. Ohio 2006).

Seventh Circuit: Edgewood Manor Apartment Homes L.L.C. v. RSUI Indemnity Co., 782 F. Supp.2d 716 (E.D. Wis. 2011).

Ninth Circuit: Alexander Manufacturing, Inc. Employee Stock Ownership Plan and Trust v. Illinois Union Insurance Co., 560 F.3d 984 (9th Cir. 2009); Insurance Company of North America v. Snyder Moving & Storage, Inc., 52 Fed. Appx. 899, 903–904 (9th Cir. 2002).

Tenth Circuit: In re Baird, 567 F.3d 1207 (10th Cir. 2009).

State Courts:

California: Executive Risk Indemnity, Inc. v. Jones, 171 Cal. App.4th 319, 89 Cal. Rptr.3d 747 (2009).

Delaware: Viking Pump, Inc. v. Century Indemnity Co., 2 A.3d 76 (Del. Chancery Ct. 2009).

Colorado: Lincoln General Insurance Co. v. Bailey, 2009 WL 1331094 (Colo. App. May 14, 2009).

Florida: Progressive Express Insurance Co. v. Hartley, 21 So.3d 119 (Fla. App. 2009; Continental Casualty Co. v. Ryan Inc. Eastern, 974 So.2d 368 (Fla. 2008).

Georgia: Santiago v. Safeway Insurance Co., 196 Ga. App. 480, 396 S.E.2d 506 (1990).

Illinois: Illinois Tool Works, Inc. v. Commerce and Industry Insurance Co., 962 N.E.2d 1042, 357 Ill. Dec. 141 (Ill. App. 2011); Cincinnati Insurance Co. v. American Hardware Manufacturers Association, 387 Ill. App.3d 85, 325 Ill. Dec. 483, 898 N.E.2d 216 (2008).

Indiana: Travelers Casualty and Surety Co. v. United States Filter Corp., 895 N.E.2d 1172 (Ind. 2008).

Iowa: Conrad Brothers v. John Deere Insurance Co., 640 N.W.2d 231, 237 (Iowa 2001).

Minnesota: Star Windshield Repair, Inc. v. Western National Insurance Co., 768 N.W.2d 346 (Minn. 2009); Gopher Oil Co. v. American Hardware Mutual Insurance Co., 588 N.W.2d 756 (Minn. App. 1999).

New York: Greenhomes America, L.L.C. v. Farm Family Casualty Insurance Co., 91 A.D.3d 1352, 936 N.Y.S.2d 829 (N.Y. App. Div. 2012); Home Depot U.S.A., Inc. v. National Fire & Marine Insurance Co., 55 A.D.3d 671, 866 N.Y.S.2d 255 (N.Y. App. Div. 2008).

Ohio: Pilkington North America, Inc. v. Travelers Casualty & Surety Co., 112 Ohio St.3d 482, 861 N.E.2d 121 (2006); Fiorentino v. Lightning Rod Mutual Insurance Co., 114 Ohio App.3d 188, 682 N.E.2d 1099, 1101–1103 (1996).

Pennsylvania: National Memorial Services, Inc. v. Metropolitan Life Insurance. Co., 159 Pa. Super 292, 48 A.2d 143, 144–145 (Pa. Super.), *aff'd* 355 Pa. 155, 49 A.2d 382 (1946).

Accord, Couch on Insurance, § 35:7 (3d ed. 2003).

But see:

Fifth Circuit: Keller Foundations, Inc. v. Wausau Underwriters Insurance Co., 626 F.3d 871 (5th Cir. 2010); Nautilus Insurance Co. v. Concierge Care Nursing Centers, Inc., 804 F. Supp.2d 557 (S.D. Tex. 2011).

State Courts:

California: Henkel Corp. v. Hartford Accident & Indemnity Co., 29 Cal.4th 934, 129 Cal. Rptr.2d 828, 62 P.3d 69, 75–76 (2003).

Louisiana: In re Katrina Canal Breaches Litigation, 63 So.3d 955 (La. 2011).

[28] See Henkel Corp. v. Hartford Accident & Indemnity Co., 29 Cal.4th 934, 129 Cal. Rptr.2d 828, 62 P.3d 69, 75 (2003). Other courts, albeit very few, are in accord with California law. See, e.g.:

Fifth Circuit: Keller Foundations, Inc. v. Wausau Underwriters Insurance Co., 626 F.3d 871 (5th Cir. 2010); Nautilus Insurance Co. v. Concierge Care Nursing Centers, Inc., 804 F. Supp.2d 557 (S.D. Tex. 2011).

State Courts:

Indiana: Travelers Casualty and Surety Co. v. United States Filter Corp., 895 N.E.2d 1172 (Ind. 2008).

Louisiana: In re Katrina Canal Breaches Litigation, 63 So.3d 955 (La. 2011).

[29] See Henkel Corp. v. Hartford Accident & Indemnity Co., 29 Cal.4th 934, 129 Cal. Rptr.2d 828, 62 P.3d 69, 77 (2003).

[30] *Id.*

[31] *Id.*, 62 P.3d at 73–74.

[32] *Id.*, 62 P.3d at 73–74.

[33] *Id.*, 62 P.3d at 76.

[34] See:

Second Circuit: Globecon Group, LLC v. Hartford Fire Insurance Co., 434 F.3d 165 (2d Cir. 2006); Peck v. Public Service Mutual Insurance Co., 114 F. Supp.2d 51, 56 (D. Conn. 2000); Texaco A/S S.A. v. Commercial Insurance Company of Newark, New Jersey, 1995 WL 628997, at *6–7 (S.D.N.Y. Oct. 26, 1995), *opinion amended* 1996 WL 603915 (S.D.N.Y. Oct. 21, 1996).

Third Circuit: In re Federal-Mogul Global, 402 B.R. 625 (Bankr. D. Del. 2009); Viola v. Fireman's Fund Insurance Co., 965 F. Supp. 654 (E.D. Pa. 1997); Continental Casualty Co. v. Diversified Industries, Inc., 884 F. Supp. 937 (E.D. Pa. 1995); Brunswick Corp. v. St. Paul Fire & Marine Insurance Co., 509 F. Supp. 750, 753 (E.D. Pa. 1981); Federal Insurance Company By and Through Associated Aviation Underwriters v. Purex Industries, Inc., 972 F. Supp. 872 (D.N.J. 1997); International Rediscount Corp. v. Hartford Accident & Indemnity Co., 425 F. Supp. 669, 672–673 (D. Del. 1977).

Fourth Circuit: National Union Fire Insurance Company of Pittsburgh, PA v. Porter Hayden Co., 408 B.R. 66 (D. Md. 2009).

Fifth Circuit: National Union Fire Insurance Company of Pittsburgh, PA v. Puget Plastics Corp., 649 F. Supp.2d 613 (S.D. Tex. 2009); *In re* Katrina Canal Breaches Consolidated Litigation, 2009 WL 1046016 (E.D. La. Apr. 16, 2009); ARM Properties Management Group v. RSUI Indemnity Co., 642 F. Supp.2d 592 (W.D. Tex. 2009); Pontchartrain Gardens, Inc. v. State Farm General Insurance Co., 2009 WL 86671 (E.D. La. Jan. 13, 2009).

Sixth Circuit: Elliott Co. v. Liberty Mutual Insurance Co., 434 F. Supp.2d 483 (N.D. Ohio 2006).

Seventh Circuit: Edgewood Manor Apartment Homes L.L.C. v. RSUI Indemnity Co., 782 F. Supp.2d 716 (E.D. Wis. 2011).

Ninth Circuit: Alexander Manufacturing, Inc. Employee Stock Ownership Plan and Trust v. Illinois Union Insurance Co., 560 F.3d 984 (9th Cir. 2009); Insurance Company of North America v. Snyder Moving & Storage, Inc., 52 Fed. Appx. 899, 903–904 (9th Cir. 2002).

Tenth Circuit: In re Baird, 567 F.3d 1207 (10th Cir. 2009).

State Courts:

California: Executive Risk Indemnity, Inc. v. Jones, 171 Cal. App.4th 319, 89 Cal. Rptr.3d 747 (2009).

Colorado: Lincoln General Insurance Co. v. Bailey, 2009 WL 1331094 (Colo. App. May 14, 2009).

Delaware: Viking Pump, Inc. v. Century Indemnity Co., 2009 WL 3297559 (Del. Ch. Oct. 14, 2009).

Florida: Progressive Express Insurance Co. v. Hartley, 21 So.3d 119 (Fla. App. 2009); Continental Casulaty Co. v. Ryan Inc. Eastern, 974 So.2d 368 (Fla. 2008).

Georgia: Santiago v. Safeway Insurance Co., 196 Ga. App. 480, 396 S.E.2d 506 (1990).

Illinois: Illinois Tool Works, Inc. v. Commerce and Industry Insurance Co., 962 N.E.2d 1042, 357 Ill. Dec. 141 (Ill. App. 2011); Cincinnati Insurance Co. v. American Hardware Manufacturers Association, 387 Ill. App.3d 85, 325 Ill. Dec. 483, 898 N.E.2d 216 (2008).

Indiana: Travelers Casualty and Surety Co. v. United States Filter Corp., 895 N.E.2d 1172 (Ind. 2008).

Iowa: Conrad Brothers v. John Deere Insurance Co., 640 N.W.2d 231, 237 (Iowa 2001).

Minnesota: Star Windshield Repair, Inc. v. Western National Insurance Co., 768 N.W.2d 346 (Minn. 2009); Gopher Oil Co. v. American Hardware Mutual Insurance Co., 588 N.W.2d 756 (Minn. App. 1999).

New York: Greenhomes America, L.L.C. v. Farm Family Casualty Insurance Co., 91 A.D.3d 1352, 936 N.Y.S.2d 829 (N.Y. App. Div. 2012); Home Depot U.S.A., Inc. v. National Fire & Marine Insurance Co., 55 A.D.3d 671, 866 N.Y.S.2d 255 (N.Y. App. Div. 2008).

Ohio: Pilkington North America, Inc. v. Travelers Casualty & Surety Co., 861 N.E.2d 121 (Ohio 2006); Fiorentino v. Lightning Rod Mutual Insurance Co., 682 N.E.2d 1099, 1101–1103 (Ohio App. 1996).

Pennsylvania: National Memorial Services, Inc. v. Metropolitan Life Insurance. Co., 48 A.2d 143, 144–145 (Pa. Super.), *aff'd* 49 A.2d 382 (Pa. 1946).

Vermont: In re Ambassador Insurance Co., 965 A.2d 486 (Vt. 2008).

Accord, Couch on Insurance, § 35:7 (3d ed. 2003).

But see:

California: Henkel Corp. v. Hartford Accident & Indemnity Co., 29 Cal.4th 934, 129 Cal. Rptr.2d 828, 62 P.3d 69, 75–76 (2003).

Indiana: Travelers Casualty and Surety Co. v. United States Filter Corp., 895 N.E.2d 1172 (Ind. Oct 15, 2008).

[35] See §§13.03[1][a] through 13.03[1][c] *infra.*

[36] See:

First Circuit: Total Waste Management Corp. v. Commercial Union Insurance Co., 857 F. Supp. 140 (D.N.H. 1994).

Third Circuit: Federal Insurance Company By and Through Associated Aviation Underwriters v. Purex Industries, Inc., 972 F. Supp. 872 (D.N.J. 1997) (under merger, successor acquires insurance policies of predecessor); Brunswick Corp. v. St. Paul Fire & Marine Insurance Co., 509 F. Supp. 750 (E.D. Pa. 1981) (as a result of a merger or stock acquisition, rights under liability insurance policies of an acquired entity pass on to the purchaser by operation of law).

Fifth Circuit: Imperial Enterprises, Inc. v. Fireman's Fund Insurance Co., 535 F.2d 287 (5th Cir. 1976) (on completion of merger, assets, including liability insurance policies, are transferred by operation of law).

Sixth Circuit: Elliott Co. v. Liberty Mutual Insurance Co., 434 F. Supp.2d 483 (N.D. Ohio 2006).

Seventh Circuit: Knoll Pharmaceutical Co. v. Automobile Insurance Co., 167 F. Supp.2d 1004 (N.D. Ill. 2001) (merger results in successor's assumption of liabilities and acquisition of assets, including insurance coverage rights, of the acquired company).

Eighth Circuit: Paxton & Vierling Steel Co. v. Great American Insurance Co., 497 F. Supp. 573 (D. Neb. 1980) (under Nebraska merger statute, insurance policy transfers to surviving corporation by operation of law).

State Courts:

California: Henkel Corporation v. Hartford Accident & Indemnity Co., 29 Cal.4th 934, 129 Cal. Rptr.2d 828, 62 P.3d 69, 73–74 (2003).

Indiana: Travelers Casualty and Surety Co. v. United States Filter Corp., 895 N.E.2d 1172 (Ind. 2008).

[37] See:

First Circuit: Total Waste Management Corp. v. Commercial Union Insurance Co., 857 F. Supp. 140 (D.N.H. 1994).

Third Circuit: Federal Insurance Company By and Through Associated Aviation Underwriters v. Purex Industries, Inc., 972 F. Supp. 872 (D.N.J. 1997) (under merger, successor acquires insurance policies of predecessor); Brunswick Corp. v. St. Paul Fire & Marine Insurance Co., 509 F. Supp. 750 (E.D. Pa. 1981) (as a result of a merger or stock acquisition, rights under liability insurance policies of an acquired entity pass on to the purchaser by operation of law).

Fifth Circuit: Imperial Enterprises, Inc. v. Fireman's Fund Insurance Co., 535 F.2d 287 (5th Cir. 1976) (on completion of merger, assets, including liability insurance policies, are transferred by operation of law).

Sixth Circuit: Elliott Co. v. Liberty Mutual Insurance Co., 434 F. Supp.2d 483 (N.D. Ohio 2006).

Seventh Circuit: Knoll Pharmaceutical Co. v. Automobile Insurance Co., 167 F. Supp.2d 1004 (N.D. Ill. 2001) (merger results in successor's assumption of liabilities and acquisition of assets, including insurance coverage rights, of the acquired company).

Eighth Circuit: Paxton & Vierling Steel Co. v. Great American Insurance Co., 497 F. Supp. 573 (D. Neb. 1980) (under Nebraska merger statute, insurance policy transfers to surviving corporation by operation of law).

State Courts:

California: Henkel Corporation v. Hartford Accident & Indemnity Co., 29 Cal.4th 934, 129 Cal. Rptr.2d 828, 62 P.3d 69, 73–74 (2003).

Indiana: Travelers Casualty and Surety Co. v. United States Filter Corp., 895 N.E.2d 1172 (Ind. 2008).

See also § 13.03[3][a] *supra.*

[38] See:

Fifth Circuit: Ford, Bacon, and Davis, L.L.C. v. Travelers Insurance Co., 635 F.3d 734 (5th Cir. 2011).

Sixth Circuit: Century Indemnity Co. v. Aero-Motive Co., 318 F. Supp.2d 530 (W.D. Mich. 2003).

State Courts:

California: Henkel Corp. v. Hartford Accident & Indemnity Co., 29 Cal.4th 934, 129 Cal. Rptr.2d 828, 62 P.3d 69, 73–74 (2003).

Illinois: Illinois Tool Works, Inc. v. Commerce and Industry Insurance Co., 962 N.E.2d 1042, 357 Ill. Dec. 141 (Ill. App. 2011).

[39] See § 13.03[1] *supra.*

[40] See:

Second Circuit: Globecon Group, LLC v. Hartford Fire Insurance Co., 434 F.3d 165 (2d Cir. 2006); Peck v. Public Service Mutual Insurance Co., 114 F. Supp.2d 51, 56 (D. Conn. 2000); Texaco A/S S.A. v. Commercial Insurance Company of Newark, New Jersey, 1995 WL 628997, at *6–7 (S.D.N.Y. Oct. 26, 1995), *op. amended* 1996 WL 603915 (S.D.N.Y. Oct. 21, 1996).

Third Circuit: In re Federal-Mogul Global, 402 B.R. 625 (Bankr. D. Del. 2009); Viola v. Fireman's Fund Insurance Co., 965 F. Supp. 654 (E.D. Pa. 1997); Continental Casualty Co. v. Diversified Industries, Inc., 884 F. Supp. 937 (E.D. Pa. 1995); Brunswick Corp. v. St. Paul Fire & Marine Insurance Co., 509 F. Supp. 750, 753 (E.D. Pa. 1981); Federal Insurance Company By and Through Associated Aviation Underwriters v. Purex Industries, Inc., 972 F. Supp. 872 (D.N.J. 1997); International Rediscount Corp. v. Hartford Accident & Indemnity Co., 425 F. Supp. 669, 672–673 (D. Del. 1977).

Fourth Circuit: National Union Fire Insurance Company of Pittsburgh, PA v. Porter Hayden Co., 408 B.R. 66 (D. Md. 2009).

Fifth Circuit: National Union Fire Insurance Company of Pittsburgh, PA v. Puget Plastics Corp., 649 F. Supp.2d 613 (S.D. Tex. 2009); *In re* Katrina Canal Breaches Consolidated Litigation, 2009 WL 1046016 (E.D. La. Apr. 16, 2009); ARM Properties Management Group

v. RSUI Indemnity Co., 642 F. Supp.2d 592 (W.D. Tex. 2009); Pontchartrain Gardens, Inc. v. State Farm General Insurance Co., 2009 WL 86671 (E.D. La. Jan. 13 2009).

Sixth Circuit: Elliott Co. v. Liberty Mutual Insurance Co., 434 F. Supp.2d 483 (N.D. Ohio 2006).

Seventh Circuit: Edgewood Manor Apartment Homes L.L.C. v. RSUI Indemnity Co., 782 F. Supp.2d 716 (E.D. Wis. 2011).

Ninth Circuit: Alexander Manufacturing, Inc. Employee Stock Ownership Plan and Trust v. Illinois Union Insurance Co., 560 F.3d 984 (9th Cir. 2009); Insurance Company of North America v. Snyder Moving & Storage, Inc., 52 Fed. Appx. 899, 903–904 (9th Cir. 2002).

Tenth Circuit: In re Baird, 567 F.3d 1207 (10th Cir. 2009).

State Courts:

California: Executive Risk Indemnity, Inc. v. Jones, 171 Cal. App.4th 319, 89 Cal. Rptr.3d 747 (2009).

Colorado: Lincoln General Insurance Co. v. Bailey, 2009 WL 1331094 (Colo. App. May 14, 2009).

Delaware: Viking Pump, Inc. v. Century Indemnity Co., 2 A.2d 76 (Del. Ch. 2009).

Florida: Progressive Express Insurance Co. v. Hartley, 21 So.3d 119 (Fla. App. 2009); Continental Casulaty Co. v. Ryan Inc. Eastern, 974 So.2d 368 (Fla. 2008).

Georgia: Santiago v. Safeway Insurance Co., 196 Ga. App. 480, 396 S.E.2d 506 (1990).

Illinois: Illinois Tool Works, Inc. v. Commerce and Industry Insurance Co., 962 N.E.2d 1042, 357 Ill. Dec. 141 (Ill. App. 2011); Cincinnati Insurance Co. v. American Hardware Manufacturers Association, 387 Ill. App.3d 85, 325 Ill. Dec. 483, 898 N.E.2d 216 (2008).

Indiana: Travelers Casualty and Surety Co. v. United States Filter Corp., 895 N.E.2d 1172 (Ind. 2008).

Iowa: Conrad Brothers v. John Deere Insurance Co., 640 N.W.2d 231, 237 (Iowa 2001).

Minnesota: Star Windshield Repair, Inc. v. Western National Insurance Co., 768 N.W.2d 346 (Minn. 2009); Gopher Oil Co. v. American Hardware Mutual Insurance Co., 588 N.W.2d 756 (Minn. App. 1999).

New York: Greenhomes America, L.L.C. v. Farm Family Casualty Insurance Co., 91 A.D.3d 1352, 936 N.Y.S.2d 829 (N.Y. App. Div. 2012); Home Depot U.S.A., Inc. v. National Fire & Marine Insurance Co., 55 A.D.3d 671, 866 N.Y.S.2d 255 (N.Y. App. Div. 2008).

Ohio: Pilkington North America, Inc. v. Travelers Casualty & Surety Co., 112 Ohio St.3d 482, 861 N.E.2d 121 (2006); Fiorentino v. Lightning Rod Mutual Insurance Co., 114 Ohio App.3d 188, 682 N.E.2d 1099, 1101–1103 (1996).

Pennsylvania: National Memorial Services, Inc. v. Metropolitan Life Insurance Co., 159 Pa. Super. 292, 48 A.2d 143, 144–145, *aff'd* 355 Pa. 155, 49 A.2d 382 (1946).

See also, *Couch on Insurance*, § 35:7 (3d ed. 2003).

> "[T]he great majority of courts adhere to the rule that general stipulations in policies prohibiting assignments thereof except with the consent of the insurer apply only to assignments before loss, and do not prevent an assignment after loss, for the obvious reason that the clause by its own terms ordinarily prohibits merely the assignment of the policy, as distinguished from a claim arising thereunder, and the assignment before loss involves a transfer of a contractual relationship while the assignment after loss is the transfer of a right to a money claim. The purpose of a no assignment clause is to protect the insurer from increased liability, and after events giving rise to the insurer's liability have occurred, the insurer's risk cannot be increased by a change in the insured's identity."

Vermont: In re Ambassador Insurance Co., 184 Vt. 408, 965 A.2d 486 (2008).

But see: *Fifth Circuit:* Keller Foundations, Inc. v. Wausau Underwriters Insurance Co., 626 F.3d 871 (5th Cir. 2010); Nautilus Insurance Co. v. Concierge Care Nursing Centers, Inc., 804 F. Supp.2d 557 (S.D. Tex. 2011).

State Courts:

California: Henkel Corp. v. Hartford Accident & Indemnity Co., 9 Cal.4th 934, 129 Cal. Rptr.2d 828, 62 P.3d 69, 75–76 (2003).

Louisiana: In re Katrina Canal Breaches Litigation, 63 So.3d 955 (La. 2011).

41 See § 13.03[1] *supra*.

42 See:

Henkel Corp. v. Hartford Accident & Indemnity Co., 9 Cal.4th 934, 129 Cal. Rptr.2d 828, 62 P.3d 69, 76 (Cal. 2003). Other courts, albeit very few, are in accord with California law. See e.g.:

Fifth Circuit: Keller Foundations, Inc. v. Wausau Underwriters Insurance Co., 626 F.3d 871 (5th Cir. 2010); Nautilus Insurance Co. v. Concierge Care Nursing Centers, Inc., 804 F. Supp.2d 557 (S.D. Tex. 2011).

State Courts:

Indiana: Travelers Casualty and Surety Co. v. United States Filter Corp. 895 N.E.2d 1172 (Ind. 2008).

Louisiana: In re Katrina Canal Breaches Litigation, 63 So.3d 955 (La. 2011).

43 *First Circuit:* Colasanto v. Life Insurance Company of North America, 100 F.3d 203 (1st Cir. 1996).

Third Circuit: Edner v. Mathews, 76 F. Supp. 3, 4–5 (W.D. Pa. 1948); Phoenix Mutual Life Insurance Company of Hartford, Connecticut v. Reich, 75 F. Supp. 886, 895 (W.D. Pa. 1948).

Fifth Circuit: Estate of O'Daniel v. United States, 6 F.3d 321 (5th Cir. 1993).

Sixth Circuit: Elliott Co. v. Liberty Mutual Insurance Co., 434 F. Supp.2d 483 (N.D. Ohio 2006).

Seventh Circuit: Stilwell v. American General Life Insurance Co., 555 F.3d 572 (7th Cir. 2009).

Eighth Circuit: Ocean Accident & Guaranty Corp. v. Southwestern Bell Telephone Co., 100 F.2d 441, 443, 447 (8th Cir.), *cert. denied* 306 U.S. 658 (1939); Matter of Redfeather Fast Freight, Inc., 1 B.R. 446 (Bankr. D. Neb 1979).

Ninth Circuit: In re Courson, 409 B.R. 516 (Bankr. E.D. Wash. 2009).

State Courts:

Illinois Tool Works, Inc. v. Commerce and Industry Insurance Co., 962 N.E.2d 1042, 357 Ill. Dec. 141 (Ill. App. 2011);

Nebraska: Albracht v. Prudential Insurance Company of America, 201 Neb. 249, 267 N.W.2d 511 (1978).

Oklahoma: Prudential Insurance Company of America v. Glass, 959 P.2d 586 (Okla. 1998).

Pennsylvania: Riley v. Wirth, 313 Pa. 362, 169 A. 139, 140–141 (1933); Fulforth v. Prudential Insurance Company of America, 147 Pa. Super. 516, 24 A.2d 749, 753 (1942).

44 See:

First Circuit: In re Charles River Press Lithography, Inc., 338 B.R. 148 (Bankr. D. Mass. 2006).

Third Circuit: Edner v. Mathews, 76 F. Supp. 3, 4 (W.D. Pa. 1948).

Fifth Circuit: Estate of O'Daniel v. United States, 6 F.3d 321 (5th Cir. 1993); Moody National Bank of Galveston v. General Electric Life and Annuity Assurance Co., 270 F. Supp.2d 875 (S.D. Tex. 2003).

Sixth Circuit: Elliott Co. v. Liberty Mutual Insurance Co., 434 F. Supp.2d 483 (N.D. Ohio 2006).

Seventh Circuit: Stilwell v. American General Life Insurance Co., 555 F.3d 572 (7th Cir. 2009).

Eighth Circuit: Ocean Accident & Guaranty Corp. v. Southwestern Bell Telephone Co., 100 F.2d 441, 443, 447 (8th Cir.), *cert. denied* 306 U.S. 658 (1939); Redfeather Fast Freight, Inc., 1 B.R. 446 (Bankr. D. Neb 1979).

Ninth Circuit: In re Courson, 409 B.R. 516 (Bankr. E.D. Wash. 2009).

State Courts:

Alabama: Rogers v. First National Bank of Birmingham, 282 Ala. 379, 211 So.2d 796 (1968).

Illinois: In re Estate of Maslowski, 204 Ill. App.3d 379, 149 Ill. Dec. 487, 561 N.E.2d 1183 (1990).

Missouri: Smith v. Smith, 313 S.W.2d 753 (Mo. App. 1958).

Nebraska: Albracht v. Prudential Insurance Company of America, 201 Neb. 249, 267 N.W.2d 511 (1978).

Oklahoma: Prudential Insurance Company of America v. Glass, 959 P.2d 586 (Okla. 1998).

Pennsylvania: Riley v. Wirth, 313 Pa. 362, 169 A. 139, 140–141 (1933); Fulforth v. Prudential Insurance Company of America, 147 Pa. Super. 516, 24 A.2d 749, 753 (1942).

Tennessee: Hamilton National Bank of Knoxville v. Graning Paint Co., 59 Tenn. App. 37, 436 S.W.2d 883 (1968).

Texas: Seymour v. American Engine & Grinding Co., 956 S.W.2d 49 (Tex. App. 1996).

[45] See:

Third Circuit: In re Tyson Metal Products, Inc., 117 B.R. 181, 185 (Bankr. W.D. Pa. 1990) (actual delivery of policy to assignee is unnecessary to effectuate assignment, when written documents manifest a clear intent to assign); Phoenix Mutual Life Insurance Company of Hartford, Connecticut v. Reich, 75 F. Supp. 886, 895 (W.D. Pa. 1948) (written assignment is legally effective without actual delivery of the policy).

Fourth Circuit: Metropolitan Life Insurance Co. v. Petersen, 156 F. Supp. 765 (D. Md. 1957).

Fifth Circuit: Morgan v. E. J. Evans Co., 266 F.2d 423 (5th Cir. 1959); Massachusetts Mutual Life Insurance Co. v. Sanders, 787 F. Supp.2d 628 (S.D. Tex. 2011).

Sixth Circuit: In re Swartwout, 123 B.R. 794 (Bankr. S.D. Ohio 1991).

Eighth Circuit: Matter of Redfeather Fast Freight, Inc., 1 B.R. 446 (Bankr. D. Neb 1979).

State Courts:

Nebraska: Albracht v. Prudential Insurance Company of America, 201 Neb. 249, 267 N.W.2d 511 (1978).

New York: Katzman v. Aetna Life Insurance Co., 309 N.Y. 197, 128 N.E.2d 307 (1955).

Washington: Occidental Life Insurance Company of California v. Gannon, 57 Wash.2d 868, 360 P.2d 350 (Wash. 1961).

[46] See, e.g., *In re* Charles River Press Lithography, Inc., 338 B.R. 148 (Bankr. D. Mass. 2006).

[47] See ISO Form CG 00 01 10 01. See § 13.03[1] *supra*.

[48] See:

First Circuit: Total Waste Management Corp. v. Commercial Union Insurance Co., 857 F. Supp. 140 (D.N.H. 1994).

Third Circuit: Koppers Industries, Inc. v. North River Insurance Co., 1996 WL 33577709 (W.D. Pa. Mar. 5, 1996); Brunswick Corp. v. St. Paul Fire & Marine Insurance Co., 509 F. Supp. 750, 752–753 (E.D. Pa. 1981).

Sixth Circuit: Century Indemnity Co. v. Aero-Motive Co., 318 F. Supp.2d 530 (W.D. Mich. 2003); Trinity Homes LLC v. Ohio Casualty Insurance Co., 2007 WL 1021825 (S.D. Ind. March 30, 2007).

Eighth Circuit: Ocean Accident & Guaranty Corp. v. Southwestern Bell Telephone Co., 100 F.2d 441, 443, 447 (8th Cir.), *cert. denied* 306 U.S. 658 (1939).

Ninth Circuit: Northern Insurance Co. v. Allied Mutual Insurance Co., 955 F.2d 1353, 1357 (9th Cir.), *cert. denied* 505 U.S. 1221 (1992); *In re* Courson, 409 B.R. 516 (Bankr. E.D. Wash. 2009); B.S.B. Diversified Co. v. American Motorist Insurance Co., 947 F. Supp. 1476 (W.D. Wash. 1996); Insurance Company of North America v. Snyder Moving and Storage, Inc., 52 Fed. Appx. 899 (9th Cir. 2002); Concept Enterprises, Inc. v. Hartford Insurance Company of the Midwest, 2001 WL 34050685, at *4 (C.D. Cal. May 22, 2001).

State Courts:

California: General Accident Insurance Co. v. Superior Court, 55 Cal. App.4th 1444, 64 Cal. Rptr.2d 781 (1997); Quemetco Inc. v. Pacific Automobile Insurance Co., 24 Cal. App.4th 494, 29 Cal. Rptr.2d 627 (1994).

Hawaii: DelMonte Fresh Produce (Hawaii), Inc. v. Fireman's Fund Insurance Co., 183 P.3d 734 (Haw. 2007).

Minnesota: Gopher Oil Co. v. American Hardware Mutual Insurance Co., 588 N.W.2d 756 (Minn. App. 1999).

Ohio: Pilkington North America, Inc. v. Travelers Casualty & Surety Co., 112 Ohio St.3d 482, 861 N.E.2d 121 (2006); Fiorentino v. Lightning Rod Mutual Insurance Co., 114 Ohio App.3d 188, 682 N.E.2d 1099, 1101–1103 (1996).

Washington: Unigard Insurance Co. v. Leven, 97 Wash App. 417, 983 P.2d 1155 (1999), *review denied* 140 Wash.2d 1009, 999 P.2d 1263 (2000); Griffin v. Allstate Insurance Co., 29 P.3d 777 (Wash. App.), *modified* 36 P.3d 552 (Wash. App. 2001), *review denied* 45 P.3d 551 (Wash. 2002).

Wisconsin: Red Arrow Products Co. v. Employers Insurance of Wausau, 233 Wis.2d 114, 607 N.W.2d 294 (Wis. App.), *review denied* 239 Wis.2d 177, 612 N.W.2d 733 (Wis. 2000).

[49] See:

Third Circuit: Brunswick Corp. v. St. Paul Fire & Marine Insurance Co., 509 F. Supp. 750, 752–753 (E.D. Pa. 1981).

Ninth Circuit: Northern Insurance Company of New York v. Allied Mutual Insurance Co., 955 F.2d 1353, 1357 (9th Cir.), *cert. denied* 505 U.S. 1221 (1992).

[50] See, e.g., Henkel Corp. v. Hartford Accident & Indemnity Co., 62 P.3d 69 (Cal. 2003).

[51] *Id.*

[52] See:

First Circuit: Total Waste Management Corp. v. Commercial Union Insurance Co., 857 F. Supp. 140 (D.N.H. 1994).

Third Circuit: Brunswick Corp. v. St. Paul Fire & Marine Insurance Co., 509 F. Supp. 750, 752–753 (E.D. Pa. 1981); Federal Insurance Company By and Through Associated Aviation Underwriters v. Purex Industries, Inc., 972 F. Supp. 872 (D.N.J. 1997).

Fifth Circuit: Imperial Enterprises, Inc. v. Fireman's Fund Insurance Co., 535 F.2d 287 (5th Cir. 1976).

Sixth Circuit: Trinity Homes LLC v. Ohio Casualty Insurance Co., 2007 WL 1021825 (S.D. Ind. Mar. 30, 2007).

Seventh Circuit: See Knoll Pharmaceutical Co. v. Automobile Insurance Co., 167 F. Supp.2d 1004 (N.D. Ill. 2001).

Eighth Circuit: Paxton & Vierling Steel Co. v. Great American Insurance Co., 497 F. Supp. 573 (D. Neb. 1980).

[53] See:

Third Circuit: Koppers Industries, Inc. v. North River Insurance Co., 1996 WL 33577709 (W.D. Pa. Mar. 5, 1996); General Refractories Co. v. Travelers Insurance Co., 1995 WL 634451 (E.D. Pa. Oct. 27, 1995), *rev'd on other grounds* 107 F.3d 7 (3d Cir. 1996); Knapp v. North American Rockwell Corp., 506 F.2d 361 (3d Cir. 1974), *cert. denied* 421 U.S. 965 (1975) (applying Pennsylvania law).

Sixth Circuit: Trinity Homes LLC v. Ohio Casualty Insurance Co., 2007 WL 1021825 (S.D. Ind. Mar. 30, 2007).

Seventh Circuit: Binder v. Bristol-Myers Squibb Co., 184 F. Supp.2d 762 (N.D. Ill. 2001).

State Courts:

California: Henkel Corporation v. Hartford Accident & Indemnity Co., 9 Cal.4th 934, 129 Cal. Rptr.2d 828, 62 P.3d 69 (2003); Baxter Healthcare Corp. v. California Insurance Guarantee Association, 85 Cal. App.4th 306, 102 Cal. Rptr.2d 87 (2000); Westoil Terminals Co. v. Harbor Insurance Co. 73 Cal. App.4th 634, 86 Cal. Rptr.2d 636 (1999); General Accident Insurance Co. v. Superior Court, 55 Cal. App.4th 1444, 64 Cal. Rptr.2d 781 (1997); Quemetco Inc. v. Pacific Automobile Insurance Co., 24 Cal. App.4th 494, 29 Cal. Rptr.2d 627 (1994).

Indiana: P.R. Mallory & Co. v. American States Insurance Co., 2004 WL 1737489 (Ind. App. July 29, 2004).

Minnesota: Gopher Oil Co. v. American Hardware Mutual Insurance Co., 588 N.W.2d 756 (Minn. App. 1999).

[54] See Suarez v. Sherman Gin Co., 697 S.W.2d 17 (Tex. App. 1985). See also:

Sixth Circuit: Shannon v. Samuel Langston Co., 379 F. Supp. 797 (W.D. Mich. 1974).

State Courts:

Pennsylvania: In Pennsylvania, the *de facto* merger doctrine was abolished by statute on December 21, 1988, effective October 1, 1989. See 15 Pa. Cons. Stat. Ann. § 1904 (West Supp. 1995).

Texas: Western Resources Life Insurance Co. v. Gerhardt, 553 S.W.2d 783 (Tex. App. 1977).

See Knapp v. North American Rockwell Corp., 506 F.2d 361 (3d Cir. 1974), *cert. denied* 421 U.S. 965 (1975) (applying Pennsylvania law), which is illustrative of the *de facto* merger doctrine. In *Knapp,* the predecessor corporation closed on an asset purchase agreement with the successor corporation in 1968 under which the successor acquired substantially all of the assets of the predecessor in exchange for stock in the successor. Pursuant to the agreement, the predecessor was required to change its name at the closing, distribute the successor's stock to its shareholders, and as soon as practicable thereafter, dissolve itself.

In 1969, the plaintiff was injured when his hand was caught in a machine manufactured by the predecessor corporation and sold to plaintiff's employer. Plaintiff sued the successor for negligence in design and manufacture. The successor argued that because the transaction with its predecessor was an asset sale, it had neither merged nor consolidated with the predecessor, and was not responsible for its predecessor's tort obligations.

The Third Circuit held that the effect of the transaction was a *de facto* merger because: (1) plaintiff would be deprived of a remedy against the predecessor due to the contractual requirement that it dissolve; (2) as a shell corporation prior to dissolution, the predecessor disposed of substantially all its assets, was deprived of the ability to engage in active operations, could not divest itself of the stock of the successor, and was required to dissolve; and (3) the successor acquired and assumed substantially all of the assets and liabilities of the predecessor.

Subsequently, the Pennsylvania *de facto* merger doctrine was abolished by statute, effective October 1, 1989. See 15 Pa. Cons. Stat. Ann. § 1904.

[55] Ramirez v. Amsted Industries, 86 N.J. 332, 431 A.2d 811, 825 (1981). See also:

Third Circuit: Conway v. White Trucks, Division of White Motor Corp., 885 F.2d 90, 94 (3d Cir. 1989); Koppers Industries, Inc. v. North River Insurance Co., 1996 WL 33577709 (W.D. Pa. March 5, 1996); General Refractories Co. v. Travelers Insurance Co., 1995 WL 634451 (E.D. Pa. Oct. 27, 1995), *rev'd on other grounds* 107 F.3d 7 (3d Cir. 1996); Federal Insurance Company By and Through Associated Aviation Underwriters v. Purex Industries, Inc., 972 F. Supp. 872 (D.N.J. 1997).

Ninth Circuit: Northern Insurance Co. v. Allied Mutual Insurance Co., 955 F.2d 1353, 1357 (9th Cir.), *cert. denied* 505 U.S. 1221 (1992).

State Courts:

Indiana: P.R. Mallory & Co. v. American States Insurance Co., 2004 WL 1737489 (Ind. App. July 29, 2004).

Pennsylvania: Dawejko v. Jorgensen Steel Co., 290 Pa. Super. 15, 434 A.2d 106 (1981).

[56] See:

Third Circuit: Conway v. White Trucks, Division of White Motor Corp., 885 F.2d 90, 94 (3d Cir. 1989); Koppers Industries, Inc. v. North River Insurance Co., 1996 WL 33577709 (W.D. Pa. Mar. 5, 1996); General Refractories Co. v. Travelers Insurance Co., 1995 WL 634451 (E.D. Pa. Oct. 27, 1995), *rev'd on other grounds* 107 F.3d 7 (3d Cir. 1996).

Ninth Circuit: Northern Insurance Co. v. Allied Mutual Insurance Co., 955 F.2d 1353, 1357 (9th Cir.), *cert. denied* 505 U.S. 1221 (1992).

State Courts:

Indiana: P.R. Mallory & Co. v. American States Insurance Co., 2004 WL 1737489 (Ind. App. July 29, 2004).

Pennsylvania: Dawejko v. Jorgensen Steel Co., 290 Pa. Super. 15, 434 A.2d 106, 110 (1981).

But see:

Ninth Circuit: B.S.B. Diversified Co. v. American Motorist Insurance Co., 947 F. Supp. 1476 (W.D. Wash. 1996).

State Courts:

California: Henkel Corp. v. Hartford Accident & Indemnity Co., 9 Cal.4th 934, 129 Cal. Rptr.2d 828, 62 P.3d 69 (2003); General Accident Insurance Co. v. Superior Court, 55 Cal. App.4th 1444, 64 Cal. Rptr.2d 781 (1997).

Ohio: Pilkington North America, Inc. v. Travelers Casualty & Surety Co., 112 Ohio St.3d 482, 861 N.E.2d 121 (Ohio 2006).

Wisconsin: Red Arrow Products Co. v. Employers Insurance of Wausau, 233 Wis.2d 114, 607 N.W.2d 294 (Wis. App.), *review denied* 234 Wis.2d 177, 612 N.W.2d 733 (2000).

[57] See:

Third Circuit: Conway v. White Trucks, Division of White Motor Corp., 885 F.2d 90, 93 (3d Cir. 1989).

State Courts:

Pennsylvania: Dawejko v. Jorgensen Steel Co., 290 Pa. Super.15, 434 A.2d 106, 111 (1981).

[58] See:

Third Circuit: Conway v. White Trucks, Division of White Motor Corp., 885 F.2d 90, 93 (3d Cir. 1989).

State Courts:

Pennsylvania: Dawejko v. Jorgensen Steel Co., 290 Pa. Super.15, 434 A.2d 106, 111 (1981).

CHAPTER 14

Loss Control Services

Chapter Contents

❖

§ 14.01 Overview

Insurance companies routinely perform loss control services in conjunction with the sale and service of commercial insurance policies.[1] Often, the companies attempt to limit the use of these services solely to themselves, to help assess the risk and accurately price the subject they are contemplating to insure.[2] Other times, the services are provided for a fee or as an inducement to policyholders who purchase the insurance being offered.[3]

Loss control services might be very important for real estate-related businesses, as they can help them assess risks involved in their businesses. Irrespective of the circumstances surrounding the provision of the services, policyholders have used and should continue to consider using the information gathered from these services creatively in litigation. This chapter discusses current issues in the litigation of loss control services. In particular, policyholders or their employees, customers, or invitees may initiate litigation for negligent provision of loss control services to recover for losses not ordinarily covered by insurance.[4] Additionally, to the extent insurance companies attempt to deny coverage based on the policyholder's knowledge, such as with regard to construction liabilities, loss control information becomes relevant as a defense.[5]

§ 14.02 Offensive Use of Loss Control: Assertion of Claim

As stated above, loss control services help an insurance company and its policyholder understand and evaluate risks, and they can be used to limit or eliminate such risks through recommendations and loss mitigations activites.[6] When a loss occurs that is either incompletely or not covered by insurance, a policyholder may institute a suit against its insurance company/loss control service provider for the negligent provision of loss control services. In this vein, insurance companies face suits asserted by their policyholders and suits asserted by third parties.

[1]—*Restatement (Second) of Torts* and the "Good Samaritan" Rule

The *Restatement (Second) of Torts ("Restatement")* sets forth the general "good Samaritan" rule,[7] which courts recognize as applicable to both policyholder and third-party claims for negligent provision of loss control services.[8] The *Restatement* provision applicable to policyholder claims provides:

> "One who undertakes, gratuitously or for consideration, to render services to another which he should recognize as necessary for the protection of the other's person or things, is subject to liability to the other for physical harm resulting from his failure to exercise reasonable care to perform his undertaking, if:
>
> (a) his failure to exercise reasonable care increases the risk of such harm, or
>
> (b) the harm is suffered because of the other's reliance upon the undertaking."[9]

A similarly worded *Restatement* provision sets forth the general rule that applies to claims by third parties:

> "One who undertakes, gratuitously or for consideration, to render services to another which he should recognize as necessary for the protection of a third person or his things, is subject to liability to the third person for physical harm resulting from his failure to exercise reasonable care to protect his undertaking, if:
>
> (a) his failure to exercise reasonable care increases the risk of such harm, or
>
> (b) he has undertaken to perform a duty owed by the other to the third person, or

(c) the harm is suffered because of reliance of the other or the third person upon the undertaking."[10]

Thus, the elements that a plaintiff needs to prove to prevail on a claim for negligent provision of loss control services are:

1. a legal duty owed by defendant to plaintiff;[11]
2. a breach of that duty;[12]
3. damages suffered by the plaintiff that are proximately caused by defendant's breach of duty;[13] and
4. special circumstances under the "good Samaritan" rule.[14]

In addition, a policyholder will need to be aware of any statutory immunity in the particular jurisdictions.[15]

[2]—Duty

[a]—Existence: Contract or Conduct

The first issue is whether the insurance company/loss control provider owes the policyholder a duty of care with respect to the provision of loss control services. The case law uniformly holds that the duty exists if:

(a) there is a contract that specifically requires the insurance company to undertake loss control services; or

(b) the insurance company actually performs loss control services.[16]

[b]—Effect of Disclaimer

Insurance policies or loss control service agreements often contain disclaimers stating that the insurance company has the right, but not the obligation, to perform inspections and other loss control services, and that such inspections and other loss control services, to the extent they are performed, are done for the sole benefit of the insurance company. For example, in one case, the insurance policy contained the following disclaimer:

> "The [insurance] company shall be permitted but is not obligated to inspect the named insured's property and operations at anytime. Neither the company's right to make inspections nor the making thereof nor any report thereon shall constitute any undertaking on behalf of, or for this benefit of, the named insured or others, to determine or warrant that such property or operations are safe or healthful or are in compliance with any law, rule or regulation."[17]

The interesting issue is whether such disclaimers eliminate the duty of care with respect to loss control services. Although courts have split on the issue, the majority has held that although the disclaimer is effective to eliminate a duty that arises by contract, it does not eliminate the duty created by conduct.[18] One court aptly noted that with such a disclaimer, evidence "is insufficient to create a duty to inspect . . . [, but] a contractual waiver is ineffective to negate a duty to inspect which has arisen through an insurer's conduct."[19] A few courts have held that the disclaimer effectively eliminates any duty, even one arising by conduct.[20]

[3]—Breach of Duty

If a duty of care exists, the issue arises as to whether the duty has been breached by the insurance company/loss control provider. This issue can be divided into two sub-issues:

(a) the level of proof necessary to prove breach;[21] and

(b) whether the failure to inspect amounts to a breach.[22]

[a]—Proof

Whether a breach has occurred requires proof that the actor did something erroneously or failed to do something that he or she should have done. The *Restatement (Second) of Torts* provides that "[o]ne who undertakes . . . to render services to another . . . is subject to liability to the other for physical harm resulting from his failure to exercise reasonable care to perform his undertaking."[23] Usually, the resolution of whether the duty of care was breached—i.e., whether the loss control provider failed "to exercise reasonable care" in the performance of "his undertaking"—is fact intensive, and no hard and fast rules can be discerned from the case law.[24]

[b]—Misfeasance/Malfeasance vs. Nonfeasance

The more interesting issue is whether the failure to inspect can amount to a breach of duty of care. In determining if the duty of care was breached the question arises as to whether "misfeasance," "malfeasance," or "nonfeasance" may be used to prove negligence. "Misfeasance," "malfeasance," and "nonfeasance" are ancient terms of art in the law. "Misfeasance" means "the improper performance of some act which a man may lawfully do."[25] "Malfeasance" means "the doing of an act which a person ought not to do at all."[26] "Nonfeasance" means "the omission of an act which a person ought to do."[27] Thus, "misfeasance" and "malfeasance" refer to negligence through affirmative acts, such as the alteration of a boiler that later explodes because of the actor's negligent alterations.[28] "Nonfeasance," on the other hand, is negligence by omission or failure to act, such as failing to discover a problem that reasonably should have been discovered in a boiler that later explodes.[29]

The significance of the dichotomy between negligent acts and negligent omissions arises in loss control cases because the issue is whether a mere promise to perform loss control services or a representation that loss control services will be performed, without more, amounts to an "undertaking" leading to liability. If the mere promise or representation to perform loss control services is an undertaking, then nonfeasance or failure to fulfill that promise or representation can amount to a breach. On the other hand, if a mere promise or representation does not trigger the duty of care, a breach cannot occur until and unless the services are actually performed.[30]

Case law is split on the issue of whether the mere promise or representation constitutes an "undertaking" under the *Restatement*.[31] The modern view is that if the duty is based in contract, a loss control provider can be liable for failure to undertake the inspections, but if the duty depends on conduct, the undertaking that creates the duty is the actual performance of services, and the insurance company cannot be liable for negligently failing to inspect.[32]

[4]—Damages and Proximate Causation

Once a breach of a duty of care has been established, the next determination is whether the injury was proximately caused by the breach of duty, i.e., whether there was a loss suffered by the policyholder, whether the loss would have occurred but for the loss control provider's negligence, and whether the loss could have been avoided in the absence of negligence. As with cases determining whether there was a breach of the duty of care,[33] the determination of proximate causation and damages is fact intensive.[34]

An important damages consideration concerns the appropriate theory of recovery namely, whether it resonates in contract or in tort? For example, if the policyholder or third party suffers a loss as a result of non-performance or poor performance of an insurance company in connection with its loss control activities, can the injured party sue in contract (as a contracting party or third-party beneficiary) or in tort? The answer to that question will impact the type of damages that are recoverable, because the measure of damages differs in contract and in tort. Courts have come to different conclusions on this issue with: (1) some courts holding that the economic-loss and/or gist-of-the-action doctrines apply to limit recovery in contract; and (2) other courts allowing for the assertion of a tort claim.[35]

[5]—Enumerated Exceptions

In addition to proof of duty, breach, causation, and damages, a plaintiff will need to satisfy one of the "special circumstances" enumerated in the *Restatement (Second) of Torts:*

Prong (a): failure to exercise care increases the risk of harm;

Prong (b): undertaking to perform a duty owed by the policyholder to a third person; and

Prong (c): the harm is suffered because of reliance of the policyholder or a third person on the undertaking.[36]

Prong (b) applies only when there is a claim by a third party.[37] The other two can apply to either first-party or third-party claims.[38]

[a]—Increased Risk of Harm

Prong (a) of the *Restatement,* requiring "failure to exercise reasonable care increases the risk of such harm," deals with situations in which the loss inspector does something to increase the risk of harm, such as alteration of a machine he is inspecting.[39] In the words of one court, prong (a) "requires some change in conditions that increases the risk of harm to the plaintiff over the level of risk that existed before the defendant became involved. . . . A failure to detect a hazardous condition does not by itself implicate [prong (a)]."[40]

[b]—Delegation of Duty

Prong (b) of the *Restatement* requires an "undertak[ing] to perform a duty owed by the [policyholder] to the third person." This prong deals with situations in which the policyholder has contracted with the loss control provider for loss control services.[41]

In these situations, the case law is split on the amount of delegation of responsibility that must take place for prong (b) to be satisfied. Some courts read prong (b) as requiring that a defendant undertake "'not merely to *supplement* the employers' own safety inspections, but rather to *supplant* those inspections."[42] Under this reading of prong (b), a defendant would have to "'perform tasks on *behalf* of another and *in lieu* of that other' in order to be liable."[43] Other courts take a broader approach to prong (b), holding that the requirements have been met when "'the party who owes the plaintiff a duty of care has delegated to the defendant any particular part of that duty.'"[44] There is also an intermediate third view:

> "The correct approach to this issue seems to lie between these two positions. The touchstone of § 324A is that the defendant has undertaken some service for another party which is of a nature to give rise to a duty on the part of the actor to use reasonable care. . . . In order for such a duty to arise, one does not have to assume the entire responsibility of another party. Employers have the duty to provide safe workplaces for their employees. This duty includes providing light, air, and heat for their workers. It also includes providing a workplace that is not dangerous and the provision of safe tools. This duty could never, in reality, be fully delegated and assumed by another party; the duty is too broad. To accept the interpretation of subsection (b) urged by [the loss control company] would be tantamount to holding that liability for an on-the-job injury could never be imposed on a non-employer based on § 324A.
>
> "I do not imply, however, that any type of contractual relationship could form the basis of liability under § 324A. In order for subsection (b) to apply to any given situation, the relationship involved must be one that has given rise to a duty to use reasonable care. In the instant case, [the employer] retained [the loss control company] to perform safety evaluations and to advise it on safety-related matters. In performing its functions, [the loss control company] inspected the plant and its machinery in light of various applicable safety standards. It then recommended certain changes in the plant and its operation. [The employer] apparently implemented at least some of those changes. It would be difficult to interpret the relationship between [the employer] and [the loss control company] as not giving rise to a duty on [the loss control company's] part to exercise reasonable care. [The employer] did, in fact, delegate some portion of their concern for safety to [the loss control company]; to conclude otherwise would force the conclusion that [the employer] paid for services for which it had no need and which it did not use. I refuse to reach this conclusion. Based on the available record, I cannot say that plaintiff cannot prove that [the loss control company] is liable under subsection (b) as a matter of law."[45]

Under this intermediate approach to the "Good Samaritan" rule, loss control services provided by contract would almost always constitute special circumstances under prong (b).

[c]—Reliance on Undertaking

Prong (c) of the *Restatement,* which requires that "the harm is suffered because of the other's reliance upon the undertaking,"[46] is a more common issue. This special circumstance is present when the policyholder can demonstrate that it relied on the loss control services in its operations. This prong, like prong (a), only applies to a duty owed to the policyholder not third parties.

Case law is split on the degree of reliance necessary. Older cases require complete reliance, i.e., complete delegation of loss control services.[47] The more modern approach requires only partial delegation. For example, a policyholder's decreasing its own loss control activities in some way is evidence of reliance.[48] As one court explained: "The reliance element . . . is satisfied if, in relying on the defendant's undertaking, the employer 'neglect[s] or reduce[s]' its own safety program."[49]

[6]—Statutory Immunity

An issue unique to third-party claims is whether statutory immunity has been granted to an insurance company that performs loss control services. Some states similarly have passed "Good Samaritan" laws that may grant volunteers who render aid gratuitously immunity from tort liability, and absence bad faith, this immunity will be upheld.[50]

Similarly, most if not all, states have statutes that make workers' compensation the employees' exclusive remedy against their employers for work-related injuries.[51] Absent employers' reckless or intentional misconduct, employees are generally entitled to workers' compensation benefits, and are barred from suing their employers for negligence.[52] A number of states have statutes that explicitly or implicitly grant immunity to a workers' compensation insurance company that performs loss-control services.[53] Some states do so by expressly or implicitly including a workers' compensation insurance company within the definition of "statutory employer."[54]

Other states grant immunity to the workers compensation insurance company separately.[55] In Connecticut, for example, an employee injured as a result of third-party negligence can normally sue the third party, despite receipt of workers' compensation benefits.[56] However, the statute grants immunity to a workers' compensation insurance company that performs loss control services, but also provides that "immunity from liability . . . shall not be extended to any insurer or self-insurance service organization other than where the immunity is incident to the provision of workers' compensation insurance or workers' compensation related services."[57] Similarly, in Kansas, workers compensation insurance companies are required to provide loss control services and are granted statutory immunity for negligent provision of loss control services.[58]

Basic requirements for immunity under these statutes include the identity of the entity that is entitled to immunity[59] and whether the insurance company is providing services as a workers' compensation insurance company.[60]

[a]—Identity of Loss Control Provider

To be eligible for statutory immunity, the loss control provider claiming immunity must be the actual supplier of workers' compensation insurance. One court held that a loss control provider that was a wholly-owned subsidiary of the workers' compensation insurance company was not eligible for statutory immunity.[61] Although statutory immunity extends to a workers' compensation insurer, it does not extend to other insurers, such as property or liability insurers,[62] and it does not extend to a worker's compensation insurer acting in the dual role of a liability insurer.[63]

[b]—Functionality Approach

To be eligible for immunity, the insurance company must provide loss control services as a workers' compensation insurance company. Some courts have held that loss control services are beyond the normal functions of a workers' compensation insurance company and denied immunity to workers' compensation insurers against claims by employees for negligent provision of loss control services.[64] Other courts have taken a different view and held that loss control services may be integral to a workers' compensation insurer's activities.[65] South Carolina has taken an intermediate approach:

> "Carriers may perform safety inspections to assess risk and reduce on-the-job injuries in order to minimize benefit payments and premium increases. In such a case, safety inspections would be integral to the function of a worker's compensation carrier. On the other hand, a carrier may contract with an employer as an independent provider of safety inspections undertaking the employer's legal duty to provide a reasonably safe work place. In this situation, the carrier would be performing as a third party and would not be immune from liability. Evidence of such an agreement could include specific contractual language or payment of additional fees for these services."[66]

§ 14.03 Defensive Use of Loss Control: Estoppel

As previously discussed, insurance companies may expressly exclude from coverage losses that are "expected or intended"[67] or those that are known to the insured but not to the insurer.[68] Establishing that the insurance company has similar or superior knowledge or information about the loss as the policyholder can be an effective way to attempt to negate the fortuity defense. In fact, policyholders have used insurance company loss-control reports to estop the insurance companies from relying on the "expected-" or "intended-" or known-loss defenses.[69] In these cases, insurance companies have urged application of the known-loss rule that states that "an insurer need not cover a loss known to the insured at the time the parties enter into an insurance contract, unless the loss was also known to the insurer at the time of the formation of an insurance contract."[70] Policyholders argue that both they and the insurance company had the same knowledge concerning the likelihood of the loss, but the company, nevertheless, chose to grant insurance and accept premiums without taking any steps to eliminate coverage for such losses or to discontinue the insurance without a reduction in coverage to exclude the foreseeable loss.[71]

Notes

[1] See, e.g.:

Second Circuit: Zurich American Insurance Co. v. ABM Industries, Inc., 397 F.3d 158 (2d Cir. 2005).

Third Circuit: Continental Casualty Co. v. Diversified Industries, Inc., 884 F. Supp. 937, 954 (E.D. Pa. 1995); Santillo v. Chambersburg Engineering. Co., 603 F. Supp. 211 (E.D. Pa. 1985), *aff'd* 802 F.2d 447 (3d Cir. 1986).

Fifth Circuit: Facility Insurance Corp. v. Employers Insurance of Wausau, 357 F.3d 508 (5th Cir. 2004).

Sixth Circuit: Chubb Custom Insurance Co. v. Mutual Grange Casualty Co., 2011 WL 4543896 (S.D. Ohio Sept. 29, 2011).

Seventh Circuit: Hartford Steam Boiler Inspection & Insurance Co. v. Pabst Brewing Co., 201 F. 617 (7th Cir. 1912).

Eighth Circuit: Calico Trailer Manufacturing Co. v. Insurance Company of North America, 155 F.3d 976 (8th Cir. 1998); Travelers Property Casualty Company of America v. National Union Insurance Company of Pittsburgh, PA, 557 F. Supp.2d 1040 (W.D. Mo.2008); Kaapa Ethanol, L.L.C. v. Affiliated FM Insurance Co., 2008 WL 2783142 (D. Neb. July 17, 2008).

Eleventh Circuit: Uniforce Temporary Personnel, Inc. v. National Council on Compensation Insurance, Inc., 87 F.3d 1296 (11th Cir. 1996).

State Courts:

Alabama: Fireman's Fund Insurance Co. v. Coleman, 394 So.2d 334 (Ala. 1980).

Arkansas: Wilson v. Rebsamen Insurance, Inc., 330 Ark. 687, 957 S.W.2d 678 (1997).

Colorado: Compton v. Safeway, Inc., 169 P.3d 135 (Colo. 2007).

Georgia: Sims v. American Casualty Co., 131 Ga. App. 461, 206 S.E.2d 121 (Ga. App.), *aff'd* 232 Ga. 787, 209 S.E.2d 61 (1974); Pennsylvania Millers Mutual Insurance Co. v. Thomas Milling Co., 137 Ga. App. 430, 224 S.E.2d 55 (1976).

Pennsylvania: Wisniski v. Brown & Brown Insurance Co. of Pennsylvania, 906 A.2d 571 (Pa. Super. 2006).

Vermont: Derosia v. Liberty Mutual Insurance Co., 155 Vt. 178, 583 A.2d 881 (1990).

Washington: Stouffer & Knight v. Continental Casualty Co., 96 Wash. App. 741, 982 P.2d 105 (1999), *review denied* 139 Wash.2d 1018, 994 P.2d 849 (Wash. 2000).

Wisconsin: American Mutual Liability Insurance Co. v. St. Paul Fire & Marine Insurance Co., 48 Wis.2d 305, 179 N.W.2d 864 (1970).

[2] See, e.g.:

Second Circuit: Zurich American Insurance Co. v. ABM Industries, Inc., 397 F.3d 158 (2d Cir. 2005).

Third Circuit: Continental Casualty Co. v. Diversified Industries, Inc., 884 F. Supp. 937, 954 (E.D. Pa. 1995); Santillo v. Chambersburg Engineering. Co., 603 F. Supp. 211 (E.D. Pa. 1985), *aff'd* 802 F.2d 447 (3d Cir. 1986).

Fifth Circuit: Facility Insurance Corp. v. Employers Insurance of Wausau, 357 F.3d 508 (5th Cir. 2004).

Sixth Circuit: Chubb Custom Insurance Co. v. Mutual Grange Casualty Co., 2011 WL 4543896 (S.D. Ohio Sept. 29, 2011).

Seventh Circuit: Hartford Steam Boiler Inspection & Insurance Co. v. Pabst Brewing Co., 201 F. 617 (7th Cir. 1912).

Eighth Circuit: Calico Trailer Manufacturing Co. v. Insurance Company of North America, 155 F.3d 976 (8th Cir. 1998); Travelers Property Casualty Company of America v. National Union Insurance Company of Pittsburgh, PA, 557 F. Supp.2d 1040 (W.D. Mo.2008); Kaapa Ethanol, L.L.C. v. Affiliated FM Insurance Co., 2008 WL 2783142 (D. Neb. July 17, 2008).

Eleventh Circuit: Uniforce Temporary Personnel, Inc. v. National Council on Compensation Insurance, Inc., 87 F.3d 1296 (11th Cir. 1996).

State Courts:

Alabama: Fireman's Fund Insurance Co. v. Coleman, 394 So.2d 334 (Ala. 1980).

Arkansas: Wilson v. Rebsamen Insurance, Inc., 330 Ark. 687, 957 S.W.2d 678 (1997).

Colorado: Compton v. Safeway, Inc., 169 P.3d 135 (Colo. 2007).

Georgia: Sims v. American Casualty Co., 131 Ga. App. 461, 206 S.E.2d 121 (Ga. App.), *aff'd* 232 Ga. 787, 209 S.E.2d 61 (1974); Pennsylvania Millers Mutual Insurance Co. v. Thomas Milling Co., 137 Ga. App. 430, 224 S.E.2d 55 (1976).

Pennsylvania: Wisniski v. Brown & Brown Insurance Co. of Pennsylvania, 906 A.2d 571 (Pa. Super. 2006).

Vermont: Derosia v. Liberty Mutual Insurance Co., 155 Vt. 178, 583 A.2d 881 (1990).

Washington: Stouffer & Knight v. Continental Casualty Co., 96 Wash. App. 741, 982 P.2d 105 (1999), *review denied* 139 Wash.2d 1018, 994 P.2d 849 (Wash. 2000).

Wisconsin: American Mutual Liability Insurance Co. v. St. Paul Fire & Marine Insurance Co., 48 Wis.2d 305, 179 N.W.2d 864 (1970).

3 See, e.g.:

Second Circuit: Zurich American Insurance Co. v. ABM Industries, Inc., 397 F.3d 158 (2d Cir. 2005).

Third Circuit: Continental Casualty Co. v. Diversified Industries, Inc., 884 F. Supp. 937, 954 (E.D. Pa. 1995); Santillo v. Chambersburg Engineering. Co., 603 F. Supp. 211 (E.D. Pa. 1985), *aff'd* 802 F.2d 447 (3d Cir. 1986).

Fifth Circuit: Facility Insurance Corp. v. Employers Insurance of Wausau, 357 F.3d 508 (5th Cir. 2004).

Sixth Circuit: Chubb Custom Insurance Co. v. Mutual Grange Casualty Co., 2011 WL 4543896 (S.D. Ohio Sept. 29, 2011).

Seventh Circuit: Hartford Steam Boiler Inspection & Insurance Co. v. Pabst Brewing Co., 201 F. 617 (7th Cir. 1912).

Eighth Circuit: Calico Trailer Manufacturing Co. v. Insurance Company of North America, 155 F.3d 976 (8th Cir. 1998); Travelers Property Casualty Company of America v. National Union Insurance Company of Pittsburgh, PA, 557 F. Supp.2d 1040 (W.D. Mo.2008); Kaapa Ethanol, L.L.C. v. Affiliated FM Insurance Co., 2008 WL 2783142 (D. Neb. July 17, 2008).

Eleventh Circuit: Uniforce Temporary Personnel, Inc. v. National Council on Compensation Insurance, Inc., 87 F.3d 1296 (11th Cir. 1996).

State Courts:

Alabama: Fireman's Fund Insurance Co. v. Coleman, 394 So.2d 334 (Ala. 1980).

Arkansas: Wilson v. Rebsamen Insurance, Inc., 330 Ark. 687, 957 S.W.2d 678 (1997).

Colorado: Compton v. Safeway, Inc., 169 P.3d 135 (Colo. 2007).

Georgia: Sims v. American Casualty Co., 131 Ga. App. 461, 206 S.E.2d 121 (Ga. App.), *aff'd* 232 Ga. 787, 209 S.E.2d 61 (1974); Pennsylvania Millers Mutual Insurance Co. v. Thomas Milling Co., 137 Ga. App. 430, 224 S.E.2d 55 (1976).

Pennsylvania: Wisniski v. Brown & Brown Insurance Co. of Pennsylvania, 906 A.2d 571 (Pa. Super. 2006).

Vermont: Derosia v. Liberty Mutual Insurance Co., 155 Vt. 178, 583 A.2d 881 (1990).

Washington: Stouffer & Knight v. Continental Casualty Co., 96 Wash. App. 741, 982 P.2d 105 (1999), *review denied* 139 Wash.2d 1018, 994 P.2d 849 (Wash. 2000).

Wisconsin: American Mutual Liability Insurance Co. v. St. Paul Fire & Marine Insurance Co., 48 Wis.2d 305, 179 N.W.2d 864 (1970).

[4] See § 14.02 *infra.*

[5] See § 14.03 *infra.*

[6] See § 14.01 *supra.*

[7] *Restatement (Second) of Torts*, §§ 323, 324A.

[8] See, e.g:

Second Circuit: J.D. Cousins & Sons, Inc. v. Hartford Steam Boiler Inspection and Insurance Co., 341 F.3d 149 (2d Cir. 2002).

Third Circuit: Continental Casualty Co. v. Diversified Industries, Inc., 884 F. Supp. 937 (E.D. Pa. 1995); Santillo v. Chambersburg Engineering Co., 603 F. Supp. 211 (E.D. Pa. 1985), *aff'd* 802 F.2d 447 (3d Cir. 1986).

Fifth Circuit: Canipe v. National Loss Control Service Corp., 736 F.2d 1055, 1061 (5th Cir. 1984), *cert. denied* 469 U.S. 1191 (1985); Northern King Shipping Co. v. MAPCO Petroleum Co., 96 F. Supp.2d 542 (E.D. La. 2000).

Seventh Circuit: Hartford Steam Boiler Inspection & Insurance Co. v. Pabst Brewing Co., 201 F. 617 (7th Cir. 1912); A. O. Smith Corp. v. Viking Corp., 79 F.R.D 91 (E.D. Wis. 1978).

State Courts:

Alabama: Ramsey v. General Accident Fire and Life Assurance Corp., 545 So.2d 20 (Ala. 1989); Price v. Management Safety, Inc., 485 So.2d 1093 (Ala. 1986); Fireman's Fund Insurance Co. v. Coleman, 394 So.2d 334 (Ala. 1980).

Arkansas: Wilson v. Rebsamen Insurance, Inc., 330 Ark. 687, 957 S.W.2d 678 (1997).

Georgia: Pennsylvania Millers Mutual Insurance Co. v. Thomas Milling Co., 137 Ga. App. 430, 224 S.E.2d 55, 58 (1976); Sims v. American Casualty Co., 131 Ga. App. 461, 206 S.E.2d 121, 130 (Ga. App.), *aff'd* 232 Ga. 787, 209 S.E.2d 61 (1974).

Missouri: Wurst v. National Oil & Supply Co., 780 S.W.2d 97 (Mo. App. 1989).

New Jersey: Rutkowski v. Liberty Mutual Insurance Co., 209 N.J. Super. 140, 506 A.2d 1302 (N.J. Super. App. Div. 1986).

Pennsylvania: Wisniski v. Brown & Brown Insurance Company of Pennsylvania, 906 A.2d 571 (Pa. Super. 2006).

Texas: Chickasha Cotton Oil Co. v. Houston General Insurance Co., 2002 WL 1792467 (Tex. App. Aug. 6, 2002).

Vermont: Derosia v. Liberty Mutual Insurance Co., 155 Vt. 178, 583 A.2d 881 (1990).

Washington: Stouffer & Knight v. Continental Casualty Co., 96 Wash. App. 741, 982 P.2d 105, 113 n.5 (1999), *review denied* 139 Wash.2d 1018, 994 P.2d 849 (2000).

Wisconsin: American Mutual Liability Insurance Co. v. St. Paul Fire & Marine Insurance Co., 48 Wis.2d 305, 179 N.W.2d 864, 868 (1970); Samuels Recycling Co. v. CNA Insurance Cos., 223 Wis.2d 233, 588 N.W.2d 385 (Wis. App. 1998).

[9] *Restatement (Second) of Torts*, § 323.

[10] *Restatement (Second) of Torts*, § 324A.

[11] See § 14.02[2] *infra.*

[12] See § 14.02[3] *infra.*

[13] See § 14.02[4] *infra.*

[14] See § 14.02[5] *infra.*

[15] See § 14.02[6] *infra.*

[16] See, e.g:

Second Circuit: Gray v. Derderian, 448 F. Supp.2d 351 (D.R.I. 2005); Mountain Pride Farms, Inc. v. Dow Chemical Co., 95 F.R.D. 400 (S.D.N.Y. 1982).

Third Circuit: Moyer Packing Co. v. United States, 567 F. Supp.2d 737 (E.D. Pa. 2008); Stern Family Real Estate Partnership v. Pharmacists Mutual Insurance Co., 2007 WL 951603 (W.D. Pa. Mar. 27, 2007); Continental Casualty Co. v. Diversified Industries, Inc., 884 F. Supp. 937, 954 (E.D. Pa. 1995) (even if duty of care did not arise out of contract, it could have arisen out of the performance of loss control services; duty of care may arise "as a result of the insurer's conduct"); Santillo v. Chambersburg Engineering Co., 603 F. Supp. 211 (E.D. Pa. 1985), *aff'd* 802 F.2d 447 (3d Cir. 1986).

Fifth Circuit: Canipe v. National Loss Control Service Corp., 736 F.2d 1055 (5th Cir. 1984) (duty of loss control service provider recognized).

Seventh Circuit: Hartford Steam Boiler Inspection & Insurance Co. v. Pabst Brewing Co., 201 F. 617 (7th Cir. 1912); A. O. Smith Corp. v. Viking Corp., 79 F.R.D 91 (E.D. Wis. 1978).

State Courts:

Alabama: Fireman's Fund Insurance Co. v. Coleman, 394 So.2d 334 (Ala. 1980) (duty of care may arise by contract or by conduct).

Arkansas: Wilson v. Rebsamen Insurance, Inc., 330 Ark. 687, 957 S.W.2d 678 (1997) (loss control company that performed inspection services owed duty of care to policyholder and its employees).

Georgia: Pennsylvania Millers Mutual Insurance Co. v. Thomas Milling Co., 137 Ga. App. 430, 224 S.E.2d 55, 58 (1976) (even if a duty of care is not founded on a contract, it can arise if the insurance company performs loss control services and makes reports to its policyholder; "insurer's duty may arise from contract or from undertaking actual inspections without contract"); Sims v. American Casualty Co., 181 Ga. App. 461, 206 S.E.2d 121, 130 (Ga. App.), *aff'd* 232 Ga. 787, 209 S.E.2d 61 (1974) ("duty may arise from contract or from undertaking actual inspections without contract").

Missouri: Wurst v. National Oil & Supply Co., 780 S.W.2d 97 (Mo. App. 1989).

Ohio: Schrolucke v. Auglaize Farmers Cooperative, Inc., 2006 WL 319147 (Ohio App. Feb. 13, 2006).

Texas: Chickasha Cotton Oil Co. v. Houston General Insurance Co., 2002 WL 1792467 (Tex. App. Aug. 6, 2002).

*Vermont***:** Derosia v. Liberty Mutual Insurance Co., 156 Vt. 178, 583 A.2d 881 (1990) (duty of care to insured's employee arose from the insurance company's conduct in performing loss control services gratuitously).

Washington: Stouffer & Knight v. Continental Casualty Co., 96 Wash. App. 741, 982 P.2d 105, 113 n.5 (1999), *review denied* 189 Wash.2d 1018, 994 P.2d 849 (2000) (theft by employee not covered due to employee-dishonesty exclusion in policy and finding that insurer had no duty to perform loss control services or inform company of steps it could have taken to prevent thefts).

Wisconsin: American Mutual Liability Insurance Co. v. St. Paul Fire & Marine Insurance Co., 418 Wis.2d 308, 179 N.W.2d 864, 868 (1970) ("[I]t is immaterial in a negligence action whether or not the defendant contractually obligated itself to inspect the boilers. It is enough that it undertook to inspect the boilers and that it did so negligently."); Samuels Recycling Co. v. CNA Insurance Cos., 588 N.W.2d 385 (Wis. App. 1998) (active negligence exception inapplicable to immunity statute).

[17] Continental Casualty Co. v. Diversified Industries, Inc., 884 F. Supp. 937, 953 (E.D. Pa. 1995).

[18] See:

Second Circuit: Riverbay Corp. v. Allendale Mutual Insurance Co., 1988 WL 52783 (S.D.N.Y. May 18, 1988).

Third Circuit: Continental Casualty Co. v. Diversified Industries, Inc., 884 F. Supp. 937, 956 (E.D. Pa. 1995).

Fifth Circuit: Weaver v. Flintkote Co., 1988 WL 110598 (E.D. La. Oct. 18, 1988).

Seventh Circuit: Hartford Steam Boiler Inspection & Insurance Co. v. Pabst Brewing Co., 201 F. 617, 629 (7th Cir. 1912); A. O. Smith Corp. v. Viking Corp., 79 F.R.D 91 (E.D. Wis. 1978).

Eighth Circuit: Leroy v. Hartford Steam Boiler Inspection and Insurance Co., 695 F. Supp. 1120 (D. Kan 1988).

Ninth Circuit: Industrial Insurance Company of Hawaii v. Matsco Financial Corp., 1994 WL 238291 (N.D. Cal. May 19, 1994).

Eleventh Circuit: Clarendon America Insurance Co. v. Bayside Restaurant, LLC, 567 F. Supp.2d 1379 (M.D. Fla. 2008).

State Courts:

Alabama: Commercial Union Insurance Co. v. DeShazo, 845 So.2d 766 (Ala. 2002).

Connecticut: Oberdick v. Allendale Mutual Insurance Co., 1993 WL 338717 (Conn. Super. 1993).

Louisiana: Heath v. B.J. Hughes, Inc., 431 So.2d 68 (La. App. 1983).

Michigan: Smith v. Allendale Mutual Insurance Co., 410 Mich. 685, 303 N.W.2d 702 (1981).

Mississippi: Goodwin v. Jackson, 484 So.2d 1041 (Miss. 1986).

Missouri: Wurst v. National Oil & Supply Co., 780 S.W.2d 97 (Mo. App. 1989).

Montana: Riefflin v. Hartford Steam Boiler Inspection & Insurance Co., 164 Mont. 287, 521 P.2d 675, 679 (1974).

New Hampshire: Corson v. Liberty Mutual Insurance Co., 110 N.H. 210, 265 A.2d 315 (1970).

New York: James v. State, 90 A.D.2d 342, 457 N.Y.S.2d 148 (N.Y. App. Div. 1982), *aff'd* 60 N.Y.2d 737, 469 N.Y.S.2d 695, 457 N.E.2d 802 (1983).

Vermont: O'Brien v. Island Corp., 157 Vt. 135, 596 A.2d 1295 (1991); Derosia v. Liberty Mutual Insurance Co., 155 Vt. 178, 583 A.2d 881, 885 (1990).

Wisconsin: American Mutual Liability Insurance Co. v. St. Paul Fire & Marine Insurance Co., 48 Wis.2d 365, 179 N.W.2d 864, 868 (1970).

In other contexts, one cannot unilaterally create a duty. See:

First Circuit: Clarkeies Market, L.L.C. v. Associated Grocers of New England, Inc., 322 B.R. 487 (Bankr. D.N.H. 2005).

State Courts:

Arizona: Lipps v. Scottsdale Healthcare Corp., 224 Ariz. 266, 229 P.3d 1008 (Ariz. 2010).

In similar light, although a duty of care may be limited or eliminated by contract, it may not be abolished unilaterally. See Kirshenbaum v. General Outdoor Advertising, 258 N.Y. 489, 180 N.E. 245 (1932); Cohen v. City of New York, 190 Misc. 901, 75 N.Y.S.2d 846 (N.Y. Queens Cty. 1947).

[19] Continental Casualty Co. v. Diversified Industries, Inc., 884 F. Supp. 937, 956 (E.D. Pa. 1995).

[20] See:

Fifth Circuit: Philadelphia Manufacturers Mutual Insurance Co. v. Gulf Forge Co., 555 F. Supp. 519, 526 (S.D. Tex. 1982).

State Courts:

Alabama: Commercial Union Insurance Co. v. DeShazo, 845 So.2d 766 (Ala. 2002); Ranger Insurance Co. v. Hartford Steam Boiler Inspection & Insurance Co., 410 So.2d 40, 41–42 (Ala. 1982).

[21] See § 14.02[3][a] *infra.*

[22] See § 14.02[3][b] *infra.*

[23] *Restatement (Second) of Torts,* § 323. See also, § 324A from the *Restatement,* stating, "One who undertakes . . . to render services to another . . . is subject to liability to the third person for physical harm resulting from his failure to exercise reasonable care to protect his undertaking."

[24] See:

Third Circuit: Santillo v. Chambersburg Engineering Co., 603 F. Supp. 211, 214 (E.D. Pa. 1985), *aff'd* 802 F.2d 447 (3d Cir. 1986) (denying motion for summary judgment on negligent provision of loss control services claim because there were genuine issues of material fact with respect to breach and proximate cause).

Fifth Circuit: Canipe v. National Loss Control Service Corp., 736 F.2d 1055, 1061 (5th Cir. 1984), *cert. denied* 469 U.S. 1191 (1985) (reversing grant of summary judgment because "[t]here was . . . at least a genuine issue as to whether the defendant negligently performed its contractual undertaking and whether this negligence proximately caused the plaintiff's injury").

State Courts:

Alabama: Fireman's Fund Insurance Co. v. Coleman, 394 So.2d 334, 339 (Ala. 1980) (reviewing trial court's finding of breach of duty under a deferential standard for factual conclusions, rather than a de novo standard for legal conclusions).

Arkansas: Wilson v. Rebsamen Insurance, Inc., 330 Ark. 687, 957 S.W.2d 678, 682 (1997) (finding genuine issue of material fact on claim for negligent provision of loss control services because defendants owed plaintiff a duty of care and there was "'sufficient evidence to make [a] jury question regarding breach of duty and proximate cause'").

Georgia: Pennsylvania Millers Mutual Insurance Co. v. Thomas Milling Co., 137 Ga. App 430, 224 S.E.2d 55, 58 (1976) ("This is not to say that we find evidence of the underlying cause of the injury; whether or not inspections were made gratuitously or pursuant to agreement; whether these inspections were made for the insurer's internal rating purposes, or for safety or for other purposes; whether the inspections were relied upon by the insured; whether the inspections were actually negligent—all of these points may influence the result in the trial court, and we address none of them [on a dispositive motion].")

Vermont: Derosia v. Liberty Mutual Insurance Co., 155 Vt. 178, 583 A.2d 881, 886 (1990) (affirming verdict for plaintiff because "[o]nce the jury decided that defendant had undertaken that duty, it was free to conclude that defendant had not performed the duty with reasonable care, resulting in physical harm to plaintiff.").

[25] *Black's Law Dictionary,* 902 (West 1979).

[26] *Id.,* at 862, 902.

[27] *Id.,* at 902, 950.

[28] *Id.,* at 862, 902, 950.

[29] *Id.,* at 862, 902, 950.

[30] Of course, once the services are performed, a breach may potentially be found if the actor commits "misfeasance," "malfeasance," or "nonfeasance."

[31] See *Restatement (Second) of Torts,* § 323, cmt. D.

[32] See:

Third Circuit: International Association of Bridge, Structural, Ornamental and Reinforcing Iron Workers Local 45 AFL-CIO v. Kearney, 2011 WL 3329272 (D.N.J. Aug. 2, 2011);

Ozanne v. State Farm Mutual Automobile Insurance Co., 2011 WL 1743683 (W.D. Pa. May 5, 2011); Continental Casualty Co. v. Diversified Industries, Inc., 884 F. Supp. 937, 955 n.21 (E.D. Pa. 1995) ("[C]ounterclaim defendants could not be liable for negligently providing loss control services by merely failing to inspect the Site. Because counterclaim defendants were not under a contractual obligation to inspect, they could be liable only for negligent conduct during inspections actually performed.").

Fourth Circuit: Lucarelli v. Renal Advantage, Inc., 2009 WL 2730275 (D. Md. Aug. 25, 2009).

Fifth Circuit: Boatner v. ABC Insurance Co., 2012 WL 1143833 (M.D. La. Apr. 3, 2012).

Sixth Circuit: Hagen v. U-Haul Company of Tennessee, 613 F. Supp.2d 986 (W.D. Tenn. 2009).

Seventh Circuit: O'Neill v. Ford Motor Co., 2009 WL 4757268 (N.D. Ill. Dec. 9, 2009).

State Courts:

California: Polanco v. Truck Insurance Exchange, 2010 WL 2179722 (Cal. App. June 2, 2010).

Colorado: Montoya v. Connolly's Towing, Inc., 216 P.3d 98 (Colo. App. 2008).

Delaware: Price v. E.I. DuPont de Nemours & Co., 26 A.3d 162 (Del. 2011).

Georgia: Rasnick v. Krishna Hospitality, Inc., 302 Ga. App. 260, 690 S.E.2d 670 (2010).

Washington: Stouffer & Knight v. Continental Casualty Co., 96 Wash. App. 741, 982 P.2d 105, 113 n.15 (1999), *review denied* 139 Wash.2d 1018, 994 P.2d 849 (2000) ("[The] 'good Samaritan' section of the restatement [sic] requires that the defendant actually have undertaken the action alleged to have led to the loss. If an insurer does not inspect, it incurs no responsibility to either the insured or an injured third party.").

33 See § 14.02[3][a] *supra*.

34 See:

Third Circuit: Santillo v. Chambersburg Engineering Co., 603 F. Supp. 211, 214 (E.D. Pa. 1985), *aff'd* 802 F.2d 447 (3d Cir. 1986) (denying motion for summary judgment on negligent provision of loss control services claim because there were genuine issues of material fact with respect to breach and proximate cause).

Fifth Circuit: Canipe v. National Loss Control Service Corp., 736 F.2d 1055, 1061 (5th Cir. 1984), *cert. denied* 469 U.S. 1191 (1985) (reversing grant of summary judgment because "[t]here was . . . a genuine issue as to whether the defendant negligently performed its contractual undertaking and whether this negligence proximately caused the plaintiff's injury").

State Courts:

Arkansas: Wilson v. Rebsamen Insurance, Inc., 957 S.W.2d 678, 682 (Ark. 1997) (genuine issue of material fact on claim for negligent provision of loss control services because defendants owed plaintiff a duty of care and there was "'sufficient evidence to make [a] jury question regarding breach of duty and proximate cause'").

Georgia: Pennsylvania Millers Mutual Insurance Co. v. Thomas Milling Co., 224 S.E.2d 55, 58 (Ga. App. 1976) ("This is not to say that we find evidence of the underlying cause of the injury; whether or not inspections were made gratuitously or pursuant to agreement; whether these inspections were made for the insurer's internal rating purposes, or for safety or for other purposes; whether the inspections were relied upon by the insured; whether the inspections were actually negligent—all of these points may influence the result in the trial court, and we address none of them [on a dispositive motion].").

Not surprisingly, cases involving the negligent provision of loss control services are similar to negligence cases in other contexts. Causation and damages are generally factual questions for a jury unless reasonable minds could not differ in which case they become legal questions. See, e.g.:

Eighth Circuit: Nemmers v. Ford Motor Co., 686 F.3d 486 (8th Cir. 2012).

State Courts:

Minnesota: Johnson v. Paynesville Farmers Union Cooperative Oil Co., 2012 WL 3101667 (Minn. Aug. 1, 2012).

Missouri: Shifflette v. Missouri Department of Natural Resources, 308 S.W.3d 331 (Mo. App. 2010).

Ohio: Mann v. Northgate Investors, L.L.C., 2012 WL 2393945 (Ohio App. June 26, 2012).

[35] See, e.g.:

First Circuit: In re WellNx Marketing and Sales Practices Litigation, 673 F. Supp.2d 43 (D. Mass. 2009).

Second Circuit: Icebox-Scoops, Inc. v. Finanz St. Honore, B.V., 676 F. Supp.2d 100 (E.D.N.Y. 2009); *In re* Adelphia Communications Corp., 2008 WL 3919198 (S.D.N.Y. Aug 22, 2208).

Third Circuit: Partners Coffee Co. v. Oceana Services and Products Co., 2009 WL 4572911 (W.D. Pa. Dec. 4, 2009); Addie v. Kjaer, 2009 WL 1140006 (D.V.I. Apr. 28, 2009); Sunquest Information Systems v. Dean Witter Reynolds, Inc., 40 F. Supp.2d 644 (W.D. Pa. 1999); Factory Market, Inc. v. Schuller International, Inc. 987 F. Supp. 387 (E.D. Pa. 1998).

Sixth Circuit: Flex Homes, Inc. v. Ritz-Craft Corporation of Michigan, Inc., 2008 WL 746669 (N.D. Ohio Mar. 18, 2008).

Eighth Circuit: In re Genetically Modified Rice Litigation, 2009 WL 4801399 (E.D. Mo. Dec. 9, 2009).

Ninth Circuit: Khan v. Shamrock Partners, 2009 WL 481660 (C.D. Cal. Feb. 23, 2009).

Tenth Circuit: First Franklin Financial Corp. v. United Title Co., 2009 WL 3698526 (D. Colo. Nov. 5, 2009).

Eleventh Circuit: Taylor, Bean & Whitaker Mortgage Corp. v. GMAC Mortgage Corp., 2008 WL 3200286 (M.D. Fla. Aug. 6, 2008).

District of Columbia Circuit: Mobile Satellite Communications, Inc. v. Intelsat USA Sales Corp., 646 F. Supp.2d 124 (D.D.C. 2009).

State Courts:

Colorado: Makoto USA, Inc. v. Russell, 250 P.3d 625 (Colo. App. 2009), *cert. denied* 2010 Colo. LEXIS 648 (Colo., Aug. 30, 2010).

Delaware: Palma, Inc. v. Claymont Fire Co., No. 1, 2009 WL 3865395 (Del. Super. Nov. 18, 2009).

Florida: Agrofollajes, S.A. v. E.I. Du Pont De Nemours & Co., 48 So.3d 976 (Fla. App. 2010).

Illinois: Village of Deerfield v. Commonwealth Edison Co., 2009 WL 4829005 (Ill. App. Dec. 15, 2009).

Massachusetts: Cumis Insurance Society, Inc. v. BJ's Wholesale Club, Inc., 455 Mass. 458, 918 N.E.2d 36 (2009).

Minnesota: Glorvigen v. Cirrus Design Corp., 816 N.W.2d 572 (Minn. 2012).

New York: Petito v. City of New York, 95 A.D.3d 1095, 944 N.Y.S.2d 300 (2012).

North Carolina: Hardin v. York Memorial Park, 2012 WL 2304364 (N.C. App. June 19, 2012).

Oregon: Murphy v. Allstate Insurance Co., 2012 WL 3055565 (Or. App. July 25, 2012).

Pennsylvania: Erie Insurance Exchange v. Abbott Furnace Co., 927 A.2d 1232 (Pa. Super. 2009); Redevelopment Authority of Cambira v. International Insurance Co., 454 Pa. Super. 374, 685 A.2d 581 (1996); Phico Insurance Co. v. Presbyterian Medical Services Corp., 444 Pa. Super. 221, 663 A.2d 753 (1995); Brickman Group Ltd. v. CGU Insurance Company, 2001 WL 1736482 (Pa. C.P. Philadelphia Cnty. Aug. 3, 2001).

Wisconsin: Wallskog v. East West Development, LLC, 2009 WL 4800099 (Wis. App. Dec. 15, 2009).

[36] *Restatement (Second) of Torts,* § 324A. See also, *Restatement (Second) of Torts,* § 323.

[37] *Compare Restatement (Second) of Torts,* § 324A *with Restatement (Second) of Torts,* § 323. See §§ 2.01–2.02 *supra,* for a more distilled discussion on the differences between first-party and third-party insurance.

[38] *Id.*

[39] See *Restatement (Second) of Torts,* § 324A. See also, Philadelphia Manufacturers Mutual Insurance Co. v. Gulf Forge Co., 555 F. Supp. 519, 527 (S.D. Tex. 1982).

[40] Canipe v. National Loss Control Service Corp., 736 F.2d 1055, 1062 (5th Cir. 1984), *cert. denied* 469 U.S. 1191 (1985). See also, § 14.02[3][b] *supra,* and the following cases:

Third Circuit: International Association of Bridge, Structural, Ornamental and Reinforcing Iron Workers Local 45 AFL-CIO v. Kearney, 2011 WL 3329272 (D.N.J. Aug. 2, 2011); Ozanne v. State Farm Mutual Automobile Insurance Co., 2011 WL 1743683 (W.D. Pa. May 5, 2011); Continental Casualty Co. v. Diversified Industries, Inc., 884 F. Supp. 937 (E.D. Pa. 1995); Santillo v. Chambersburg Engineering Co., 603 F. Supp. 211, 214 (E.D. Pa. 1985), *aff'd* 802 F.2d 447 (3d Cir. 1986) ("the activities of the defendant must have somehow increased the risk of harm to the plaintiff. It is well-settled that under § 324A negligent inspection does not meet the requirements of § 324A(a).").

Fourth Circuit: Lucarelli v. Renal Advantage, Inc., 2009 WL 2730275 (D. Md. Aug. 25, 2009).

Fifth Circuit: Boatner v. ABC Insurance Co., 2012 WL 1143833 (M.D. La. Apr. 3, 2012); Coachmen Industries, Inc. v. Willis of Illinois, Inc., 565 F. Supp.2d 755 (S.D. Tex 2008).

Sixth Circuit: Hagen v. U-Haul Company of Tennessee, 613 F. Supp.2d 986 (W.D. Tenn. 2009).

Seventh Circuit: O'Neill v. Ford Motor Co., 2009 WL 4757268 (N.D. Ill. Dec. 9, 2009); Dowling v. American District Telegraph Co., 1988 WL 93939 (N.D. Ill. Sept. 2, 1988).

Eleventh Circuit: Zinn v. United States, 835 F. Supp.2d 1280 (S.D. Fla. 2011).

State Courts:

Alabama: Ramsey v. General Accident Fire and Life Assurance Corp., 545 So.2d 20 (Ala. 1989); Price v. Management Safety, Inc., 485 So.2d 1093 (Ala. 1986).

California: Polanco v. Truck Insurance Exchange, 2010 WL 2179722 (Cal. App. June 2, 2010).

Colorado: Montoya v. Connolly's Towing, Inc., 216 P.3d 98 (Colo. App. 2008); Western Innovations, Inc. v. Sonitrol Corp., 187 P.3d 1155 (Colo. App. 2008).

Delaware: Price v. E.I. DuPont de Nemours & Co., 26 A.3d 162 (Del. 2011).

Georgia: Yearwood v. Club Miami, Inc., 316 Ga. App. 155, 728 S.E.2d 790 (2012); Rasnick v. Krishna Hospitality, Inc., 302 Ga. App. 260, 690 S.E.2d 670 (2010).

Kansas: Superior Boiler Works, Inc. v. Kimball, 292 Kan. 885, 259 P.3d 676 (2011).

New York: Arab v. Rouse Company of New York, L.L.C., 90 A.D.3d 680, 935 N.Y.S.2d 41 (2011).

North Carolina: Lampkin *ex rel.* Lampkin v. Housing Management Resources, Inc., 725 S.E.2d 432 (N.C. App. 2012).

Texas: Seay v. Travelers Indemnity Co., 730 S.W.2d 774 (Tex. App. 1987).

Vermont: Derosia v. Liberty Mutual Insurance Co., 155 Vt. 178, 583 A.2d 881, 886 (1990) ("Reading § 324A(a) as a section intended to describe negligent conduct that directly increases risk of harm, we agree that there is no evidence, for example, that defendant caused or sanctioned the removal of the saw guard.").

Virginia: Burns v. Gagnon, 283 Va. 657, 727 S.E.2d 634 (2012).

Washington: Stouffer & Knight v. Continental Casualty Co., 96 Wash. App. 741, 982 P.2d 105 (1999).

Wisconsin: Samuels Recycling Co. v. CNA Insurance Cos., 223 Wis.2d 233, 588 N.W.2d 385, (Wis. App. 1998).

41 *Restatement (Second) of Torts,* § 324A. See also, *Restatement (Second) of Torts,* § 323.

42 Santillo v. Chambersburg Engineering Co., 603 F. Supp. 211, 214 (E.D. Pa. 1985), *aff'd* 802 F.2d 447 (3d Cir. 1986) (emphasis in original). See also: Davis v. Liberty Mutual Insurance Co., 525 F.2d 1204 (5th Cir. 1976); Tillman v. Travelers Indemnity Co., 506 F.2d 917 (5th Cir. 1975).

43 Santillo v. Chambersburg Engineering Co., 603 F. Supp. 211, 214 (E.D. Pa. 1985), *aff'd* 802 F.2d 447 (3d Cir. 1986) (emphasis in original). See also: Davis v. Liberty Mutual Insurance Co., 525 F.2d 1204 (5th Cir. 1976); Tillman v. Travelers Indemnity Co., 506 F.2d 917 (5th Cir. 1975).

44 Santillo v. Chambersburg Engineering Co., 603 F. Supp. 211, 214 (E.D. Pa. 1985), *aff'd* 802 F.2d 447 (3d Cir. 1986). See also, Canipe v. National Loss Control Service Corp., 736 F.2d 1055, 1063 (5th Cir. 1984), *cert. denied* 469 U.S. 1191 (1985) (citations omitted) (prong (b) "'comes into play as long as the party who owes the plaintiff a duty of care has delegated to the defendant any particular part of that duty.'").

45 Santillo v. Chambersburg Engineering Co., 603 F. Supp. 211, 215 (E.D. Pa. 1985), *aff'd* 802 F.2d 447 (3d Cir. 1986).

46 *Restatement (Second) of Torts,* § 324A. See also, *Restatement (Second) of Torts,* § 323.

47 See, e.g., Davis v. Liberty Mutual Insurance Co., 525 F.2d 1204, 1208 (5th Cir. 1976).

48 See Pennsylvania Millers Mutual Insurance Co. v. Thomas Milling Co., 137 Ga. App. 430, 224 S.E.2d 55, 58 (Ga. App. 1976).

49 Canipe v. National Loss Control Service Corp., 736 F.2d 1055, 1063 (5th Cir. 1984), *cert. denied* 469 U.S. 1191 (1985). See also, Bussey v. Travelers Insurance Co., 643 F.2d 1075, 1078 (5th Cir. 1981) (per curiam) ("'The carrier may also be liable if the employer so relied on the insurers undertaking that it neglected its own safety inspection program to his (the employees) detriment.'").

50 See:

Ninth Circuit: Maynard v. Ferno-Washington, Inc., 22 F. Supp.2d 1171 (E.D. Wash. 1998).

State Courts:

Minnesota: Swenson v. Waseca Mutual Insurance Co., 653 N.W.2d 794 (Minn. 2002).

New Jersey: N.J.S.A. 2A:62A-1 (immunity to emergency medical care providers).

New York: McDaniel v. Keck, 53 A.D.3d 869, 861 N.Y.S.2d 516 (2008) (discussing various "Good Samaritan" statutory immunities).

Texas: McIntyre v. Ramirez, 109 S.W.3d 741 (Tex. 2003) (discussing Texas statute).

Wisconsin: Mueller v. McMillian Warner Insurance Co., 290 Wis.2d 571, 714 N.W.2d 183 (2006) (discussing emergency care immunity).

51 See, e.g.:

Connecticut: Conn. Gen. Stat. Ann. § 31–293(d).

Kansas: Kan. Gen. Stat. Ann. § 44–5,104(a), (g).

52 *Id.*

53 *Id.*

54 See, e.g., Sims v. American Casualty Co., 131 Ga. App. 461, 206 S.E.2d 121, 131 (Ga. App.), *aff'd* 232 Ga. 787, 209 S.E.2d 61 (1974) ("insurers other than the compensation carrier are third parties in the absence of a statute clearly identifying them with the employer"). See

also, Wetzel v. Employers Service Corporation of West Virginia, 221 W.Va. 610, 656 S.E.2d 55 (2007).

[55] See, e.g.:

Connecticut: Conn. Gen. Stat. Ann. § 31–293(d).

Kansas: Kan. Gen. Stat. Ann. § 44–5,104(a), (g).

Montana: Sherner v. National Loss Control Services Corp., 329 Mont. 247, 124 P.3d 150 (2005).

[56] Conn. Gen. Stat. Ann. § 31–293(d).

[57] *Id.*

[58] Kan. Gen. Stat. Ann. § 44–5,104(a), (g):

> "(a) Each insurance company or group-funded self-insurance plan providing workers compensation insurance coverage in Kansas shall maintain and shall provide accident prevention programs upon request of the covered employer as a prerequisite for authority to provide such insurance or coverage. The accident prevention programs shall be adequate to furnish accident prevention services required by the nature of the operations of the policyholders or other covered entities and the accident prevention services shall include surveys, recommendations, training programs, consultations, analyses of accident causes, industrial hygiene and industrial health services to implement the program of accident prevention services.
>
> ▼
>
> "(g) The insurance company or group-funded self-insurance plan, and any agent, servant, or employee thereof, shall have no liability with respect to any accident based on the allegation that such accident was caused or could have been prevented by a program, inspection or other activity or by a service undertaken or not undertaken by the insurance company or group-funded self-insurance plan for the prevention of accidents in connection with operations of the employer. This immunity shall not affect the liability of the insurance company or group-funded self-insurance plan for compensation or as otherwise provided in this act."

[59] See § 14.02[6][a] *infra.*

[60] See § 14.02[6][b] *infra.*

[61] Wilson v. Rebsamen Insurance, Inc., 330 Ark. 687, 957 S.W.2d 678, 681 (1997).

[62] See, e.g., Sims v. American Casualty Co., 131 Ga. App. 461, 206 S.E.2d 121, 131 (Ga. App.), *aff'd* 232 Ga. 787, 209 S.E.2d 61 (1974) ("insurers other than the compensation carrier are third parties in the absence of a statute clearly identifying them with the employer").

[63] See, e.g., Latour v. Commercial Union Insurance Co., 528 F. Supp. 231 (D.R.I. 1981) (immunity did not apply to workers' compensation carrier that acted in dual roles of general liability insurer and risk management consultant).

[64] See, e.g.: Bayley v. Liberty Mutual Insurance Co., 728 F. Supp. 56, 59–60 (D. Me. 1990) (providing loss control services is beyond the role of a compensation insurer); Sims v. American Casualty Co., 131 Ga. App. 461, 206 S.E.2d 121, 132 (Ga. App.), *aff'd* 232 Ga. 787, 209 S.E.2d 61 (1974) ("the compensation carrier itself [is subject] to common law tort liability for functions it performs—including safety inspections—other than actual payment of compensation").

[65] Brown v. Travelers Insurance Co., 434 Pa. 507, 254 A.2d 27, 30 (1969).

> "[W]e do not think that the legislature intended to place insurance carriers in such a position that they would be forced to abandon these safety programs. Today many insurance carriers undertake such safety programs in the factories and business places of employers whom they insure. Admittedly, these programs are not moti-

vated by an altruistic feeling toward workers, since it is to the financial advantage of the insurance carrier to reduce accidents and safety programs reduce accidents. Nevertheless, although the insurance carriers are attempting to save money, the safety programs they institute directly benefit the workers."

See also, Mills v. Travelers Insurance Co., 567 A.2d 446, 448 (Me. 1989).

66 Ancrum v. United States Fidelity & Guaranty Co., 301 S.C. 32, 389 S.E.2d 645, 646 (1989). See also, Hinojo v. New Jersey Manufacturers Insurance Co., 353 N.J. Super. 261, 802 A.2d 551, 556–557 (N.J. App. Div.), *certif. denied* 175 N.J. 76, 812 A.2d 1109 (2002), in which the loss control provider actually designed a guard for the machine that ultimately injured the worker, and the court determined such actions went beyond the normal functions of a workers' compensation insurance company, holding that, "if an insurer undertakes to perform services that go beyond simply providing workers' compensation coverage to an employer, it becomes subject to the same tort liability as any other party who performs such services."

67 See, e.g., Nestle Foods Corp. v. Aetna Casualty & Surety Co., 842 F. Supp. 125 (D.N.J. 1993). See also, §§ 7.02[1] and [4] *supra*.

68 See, e.g., Missouri Pacific Railroad Co. v. American Home Assurance Co., 286 Ill. App.3d 305, 221 Ill. Dec. 648, 675 N.E.2d 1378 (Ill. App.), *appeal denied* 173 Ill.2d 527, 226 Ill. Dec. 133, 684 N.E.2d 1336 (1997). See also, §§ 7.02[1] and [4] *supra*.

69 See, e.g., Affiliated FM Insurance Co. v. Board of Education of City of Chicago, 1992 WL 409442, at *16 (N.D. Ill. Oct. 6, 1992), *rev'd on other grounds* 1993 WL 189808 (N.D. Ill. June 3, 1993), *aff'd* 23 F.3d 1261 (7th Cir.), *cert. denied* 513 U.S. 963 (1994).

70 Anderson v. Cooperative Insurance Cos., 179 Vt. 288, 895 A.2d 155 (2006).

71 See:

Third Circuit: Nestle Foods Corp. v. Aetna Casualty & Surety Co., 842 F. Supp. 125, 128 (D.N.J. 1993) ("'If facts are shown as to a particular site from which it is concluded that the insured "intended or expected" the particular harm in question . . . an insurer may be estopped from asserting such as a basis for non-coverage if the insured can establish that the insurer in question had knowledge of essentially the same facts possessed by the insured and continued to renew coverage and collect premiums.'"); J.T. Baker, Inc. v. Aetna Casualty & Surety Co., No. 86-4794, slip op. at 42–43 (D.N.J. Sept. 23, 1993), reprinted in 7 Mealey's Litigation Reports (Insurance) No. 48, at A-21–A-22 (Oct. 28, 1993) ("insurers may be estopped from asserting [the insured's knowledge] as a basis for non-coverage if [the insured] can establish that the insurer in question had knowledge of essentially the same facts possessed by the insured and continued to renew coverage and collect premiums").

Seventh Circuit: Affiliated FM Insurance Co. v. Board of Education of City of Chicago, 1992 WL 409442, at *16 (N.D. Ill. Oct. 6, 1992), *rev'd on other grounds* 1993 WL 189808 (N.D. Ill. June 3, 1993), *aff'd* 23 F.3d 1261 (7th Cir.), *cert. denied* 513 U.S. 963 (1994) (when both insured and insurer knew of asbestos danger, coverage imposed without a specific exclusion).

Eleventh Circuit: Waters v. Miller, 564 F.3d 1355 (11th Cir. 2009).

District of Columbia Circuit: Thorpe v. Banner Life Insurance Co., 632 F. Supp.2d 8 (D.D.C. 2009).

State Courts:

Illinois: Lumbermen's Mutual Casualty Co. v. Sykes, 384 Ill. App.3d 207, 322 Ill. Dec. 167, 890 N.E.2d 1086 (2008); Missouri Pacific Railroad Co. v. American Home Assurance Co., 286 Ill. App.3d 305, 221 Ill. Dec. 648, 675 N.E.2d 1378 (Ill. App.), *appeal denied* 173 Ill.2d 527, 226 Ill. Dec. 133, 684 N.E.2d 1336 (1997) ("an insurer does not have the duty to defend or indemnify a known loss unless the parties intended the known loss to be covered").

Indiana: Crawfordsville Square, LLC. v. Monroe Guaranty Insurance Co., 906 N.E.2d 934 (Ind. App. 2009) (known-loss doctrine inapplicable if insurance company also knew of loss); General Housewares Corp. v. National Surety Co., 741 N.E.2d 408 (Ind. App. 2000) (known-loss doctrine inapplicable if, at the time the policyholder knew of the loss, insurance company all knew of the same circumstances on which it is basing its known-loss defense).

Kansas: Atchison, Topeka and Santa Fe Railway Co. v. Stonewall Insurance Co., 1995 WL 854763 at *4 (Kan. Dist. Sept. 18, 1995), *rev'd on other grounds,* 1997 WL 1048134 (Kan. Jan. 31, 1997).

New Jersey: Layton v. Alkhatib, 2009 WL 1108243 (N.J. Super. App. Div. Apr. 27, 2009).

Washington: Joseph Simon & Sons, Inc. v. Aetna Fire Underwriters Insurance Co., No. 90-2-14568-9, slip op. 2–3 (Wash. Super. Ct. King Cty. May 14, 1991), reprinted in 5 Mealey's Litigation Reports (Insurance), No. 28, at D-1–D-2 (May 28, 1991) ("Among the issues of fact still in dispute are . . . [w]hether, in the course of collecting data for underwriting purposes, the insurers independently acquired information as to plaintiff's risks substantially the same as the plaintiff's own information as to those risks.").

Index

D

E

F

R

S

T

U

V

W

Y